g pages of each unit, chapter, and section assist the teacher in establishing purpose
g the new material to students' experiences and prior knowledge.

p the teacher identify the ma-
struction and establish a clear
ose.

the major themes covered in
the unit.

stions help teachers use stu-
nces and prior knowledge as a
earning.

① **UNIT OBJECTIVES**
Upon completing Unit 1, students will be able to:
1. Describe the three discoveries of America and evaluate the impact of each.
2. Compare Spanish, French, English, Dutch, and Swedish colonies in the Americas.
3. Trace the development of democracy in the English colonies.
4. Explain how geography influenced patterns of settlement in the Americas.
5. Evaluate the different patterns of life that evolved in the northern, southern, and western sections of the English colonies.
6. Describe the tensions that developed between Great Britain and the colonies from 1763 to 1772.

New York Historical Association, Cooperstown
The prosperous Van Bergen farm at the foot of the Catskill Mountains was painted by a traveling artist in about 1735.

② **OVERVIEW**
Migrating hunters from Asia, Vikings, and Europeans all discovered the Americas at different times. The Europeans arrived last and established colonies throughout the Americas. These European settlers adapted to their new environment in a variety of ways and established new forms of government. The English colonists, for example, made the first steps toward democratic government as tensions between England and the colonies grew.

③ **CONNECTING WITH PAST LEARNING**
Ask students to tell who Christopher Columbus was and why he is important. Point out that although we celebrate Columbus' "discovery" of America each October, at least three groups—migrants from Asia, the Vikings, and Europeans—discovered America at different times. Tell students that in this unit they will be learning about all three discoveries and the impact that Europeans had on the Americas.

THE AMERICAN COLONIES UNIT 1

I n Unit 1 of THE STORY OF AMERICA you will learn about the many peoples who contributed to the foundation of the United States and other nations of the Americas. Here are some main points to keep in mind as you read the unit.

• America was "discovered" at least three times: by Asian hunters—the ancestors of native Americans; by Vikings from Norway; and by Christopher Columbus.

• Native Americans, strongly influenced by their environment, developed many unique ways of life.

• Europeans came to America for many reasons. Among the most important were economic opportunity, religious freedom, and adventure. In contrast, most Africans were brought to the New World as enslaved people.

• Despite difficult beginnings, European colonies in the Americas prospered.

• In the 1760s, the British Parliament passed a series of taxes on the colonists, enraging many of them.

1

1

Annotated Teacher's Edition

More than another textbook . . .

A Story That Brings Over 500 Years to Life

In *The Story of America*, Dr. John Garraty tells the story
of our country—using the words, thoughts, and viewpoints
of the people who lived our past.

With the resource materials that accompany the program,
your students will be able to see, hear, and experience
the story, bringing their history to life.

COMPONENTS

PUPIL'S EDITION
ANNOTATED TEACHER'S EDITIONS
TEACHER'S RESOURCE BINDERS:

Graphic Organizers
Directed Reading and Comprehension Worksheets
Reteaching Worksheets
Geography Worksheets
Test Masters, Forms A and B
Unit Syntheses
Answer Keys
The Constitution: Past, Present, and Future
Writing About American History
Alternative Assessment Forms

OTHER PROGRAM MATERIALS

- Creative Strategies for Teaching American History
- Map Transparencies with Teacher's Discussion Guide
- Art History Transparencies with Teacher's Discussion
- Eyewitnesses and Others, Volumes 1 and 2 with Teach
- The Constitution: Foundation of Our Freedom, PE a
- Voices of America, Audiocassettes and Teacher's N
- Audio Program and Teacher's Notes (English and S
- Video Library
- The Historian: Investigative Software (Apple® II
- Test Generator (IBM® PC and Compatibles and

RESOURCES
■ You may wish to have students complete the Chapter 1 Graphic Organizer as they work through this chapter.

CHAPTER OBJECTIVES
Upon completing this chapter, students will be able to:

1. Analyze how the governments of early American cultures were basically democratic.
2. Explain how environment affected the development of early American cultures.
3. Describe the three discoveries of America.
4. Discuss the cause-and-effect relationship between the Crusades, the Commercial Revolution, and the Age of Discovery.

OVERVIEW
Indians, Vikings, and Europeans all discovered America at different times. Of the three, the Indians and the Europeans had the most impact on the Americas.

FOCUS/MOTIVATION: MAKING CONNECTIONS
Student Experiences.
Ask students if they have ever moved across town or across the country. Discuss with them how they adapted to their new homes. Next, point out that the first Americans crossed a land bridge from Asia to the Americas. Then ask students how they think the problems people face when they move today compare with those faced by the Indians who migrated to the Americas.

SECTION 1

PREVIEW & REVIEW RESPONSES
Understanding Issues, Events, & Ideas.
Comparisons should demonstrate an understanding of the terms used.
1. It caused the animals that people hunted to move, and people followed the animals.
2. Because of a series of ice ages
3. The Hopi built dwellings in cliffs; the Ute wandered the Great Basin in search of food; the Kwakiutl fished the rivers and bays of the Northwest.

Thinking Critically.
1. Farmers were more peaceful and had a more secure and comfortable life. The two groups were similar in

CHAPTER 1
Three Discoveries of America

■ America was discovered at least three times. The first time was between 20,000 and 60,000 years ago, when people from northern Asia touched foot on American soil in what is now Alaska. A second discovery of America occurred about the year 1000, but we know little about the Viking sailors who reached Newfoundland. The last discovery, 500 years ago, was made by a persistent Italian who sailed under the colors of Spain and claimed what he believed to be the Indies for King Ferdinand and Queen Isabella. Thus began the age of exploration and conquest of the Americas by Spain. Would Spain come to dominate the New World?

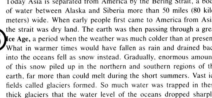

Preview & Review

Use these questions to guide your reading. Answer the questions after completing Section 1.
Understanding Issues, Events, & Ideas. Use the following words to compare early American Indians: Ice Age, historical imagination, society, culture, Stone Age, clan, generalization, environment, adobe, pueblo, Mound Builders, Five Nations, confederation, artifact, archaeologist, carbon-14 dating, anthropologist, folk tale.
1. How did the Ice Age lead Asian people to discover America?
2. Why did the first immigrants to America come in waves?
3. Give three examples of how environment influenced the customs of early American Indian societies.
Thinking Critically. 1. Compare the way of life of farmers with that of hunters and wanderers. **2.** You know that the peoples of North and South America spoke many different languages. Other than speaking, how could people from two different tribes communicate?

1. THE FIRST AMERICANS

The Ice Age

Today Asia is separated from America by the Bering Strait, a body of water between Alaska and Siberia more than 50 miles (80 kilometers) wide. When early people first came to America from Asia, the strait was dry land. The earth was then passing through a great Ice Age, a period when the weather was much colder than at present. What in warmer times would have fallen as rain and drained back into the oceans fell as snow instead. Gradually, enormous amounts of this snow piled up in the northern and southern regions of the earth, far more than could melt during the short summers. Vast ice fields called glaciers formed. So much water was trapped in these thick glaciers that the water level of the oceans dropped sharply, exposing a land bridge between Asia and North America.

Plants froze, but their seeds and spores lay dormant until warmer weather came. With each period of warmth the plants that grew from the seeds and spores spread to new areas. Eventually they spread across the land bridge into North America. The animals that fed on them followed. The bones of ancient Asian elephants, called mammoths, and of saber-toothed tigers have been found in dozens of places in the United States. Following the animals came people, the first Americans.

2

2   THREE DISCOVERIES OF AMERICA

Annotated Teacher's Edition

④
The **Resources** label identifies material from the ancillary components that may be useful in the lesson. Matching symbols on the pupil's page indicate the suggested point of use.

⑤
The **Preview & Review** questions alert students *before* reading that certain information is critical. These questions focus students' attention on essential vocabulary and content so that they may concentrate on reading for meaning. **Thinking Critically** questions encourage students to use their imagination in order to understand and evaluate the past.

At the end of each section a hand symbol refers students back to these preview questions for summary and discussion.

Suggested **Responses** are provided in the side column.

⑥
Each vocabulary term identified in the **Preview & Review** is boldfaced in the student's text. Each of these words is defined in the **Glossary** and phonetically respelled when helpful.

A narrative enriched with authentic voices from the past

The art and abundant historical records that document our history bring the past to life. *The Story of America* **uses these voices and artifacts from the past to give students a strong visual sense of the times and to help them recognize the personal nature of history.**

Superb visuals, most drawn from the time being studied, show the faces and moments that characterized an historical period. The extensive captions provide background information and often a question to stimulate class discussion.

Points of View are succinct primary sources that provide students with vivid commentary.

Primary Sources identified by bold quotation marks, are interspersed throughout the narrative, giving students the opportunity to read the actual words of the participants. A footnote identifies the source from which each quotation was taken. Any editorial changes are explained in the *Annotated Teacher's Edition*.

America's Hispanic Heritage

The Prado, Madrid; Courtesy Art Resource

Courtesy Christie's N.Y.

The "Maids of Honor" shows Princess Margarita surrounded by her friends. Velázquez himself stands to the left, holding a brush. The mirror at the back reflects the smiling king and queen. How do you think the artist was able to paint himself into the picture?

"Princess Margarita after Velázquez" was painted by Fernando Botero of Colombia in 1978. His figures with large heads recall the sculptures made by early Indian artisans.

More than 300 years pass before our eyes when we see these two paintings of the same little Spanish princess. The first is by Diego Rodríguez de Silva y Velázquez. In 1656 he painted *Las Meñinas* ("Maids of Honor") in the court of Philip IV of Spain. The second portrait of Princess Margarita was painted in 1978 by Fernando Botero of Colombia. His painting, like the others on these pages, shows our Hispanic heritage. Botero is modern and at the same time pays homage to the American Indians whose art and architecture flourished long before the painted sails of Columbus' ships hove into view.

America's Hispanic Heritage

Special **Portfolios,** four-page illustrated essays, depict the ethnic diversity of American society. Each **Portfolio** includes portraits and art representative of one ethnic group, showing its contributions to America's culture.

Chief Joseph

■ The search for gold also drew miners to Indian lands in the mountains of western Idaho. The whites called the Indians of this region the **Nez Perce,** or "pierced nose," because they wore nose ornaments made of shell. They were a peace-loving people. They claimed that no member of their tribe had ever killed a white. When Lewis and Clark traveled through Nez Perce lands on their expedition to the Pacific Coast, the explorers had been treated as honored guests.

The Nez Perce chief was a man the whites called Joseph. His real name was Hinmaton-Yalaktit, which means "Thunder coming out of the water and over the land." Like Tecumseh, the great Shawnee leader, Joseph believed that Indians had no right to sell the land they lived on. Joseph had promised his father that he would not surrender the lands to white settlers. It was his father's dying wish. Joseph was one of the greatest Indian spokesmen. Oratory was a fine art among the Nez Perce. Much of the power and prestige of the chiefs depended on their ability to speak. Perhaps when you read his words you can understand why he fought so hard.

❝My father sent for me. I saw he was dying. I took his hand in mine. He said: 'My son, my body is returning to my mother earth, and my spirit is going very soon to see the Great Spirit Chief. When I am gone, think of your country. You are the chief of these people. They look to you to guide them. Always remember that your father never sold his country. You must stop your ears whenever you are asked to sign a treaty selling your home. A few years more, and white men will be all around you. They have eyes on this land. My son, never forget my dying words. This country holds your father's body. Never sell the bones of your father and your mother.' I pressed my father's hand and told him I would protect his grave with my life. My father smiled and passed away to the spirit-land.

I buried him in that beautiful valley of winding waters. I love that land more than all the rest of the world. A man who would not love his father's grave is worse than a wild animal.❞[1]

Now the government insisted that Joseph make way for the whites and move his band to the Lapwai Reservation in Idaho. Joseph had only 55 men of fighting age. He decided to yield. He selected land on the reservation in May 1877. Then the government gave him only one month to move his people and their possessions to the reservation.

While on the march to Idaho, a few angry Nez Perce killed some white settlers. Troops were sent to capture them. Chief Joseph

Chief Joseph was the subject for Cyrenius Hall in 1878, just after his flight for Canada. Although there is no evidence of his pierced nose—hence the tribal name in French, Nez Perce—can you find other decorations in this portrait?

National Portrait Gallery

Point of View

Plains Indians were divided and conquered by disease as well as by soldiers.

❝How many Indians from the Missouri tribes died of smallpox within the next few years can hardly be estimated. Possibly one hundred thousand. Some who recovered from the plague committed suicide after seeing their faces in a mirror. Vacant lodges stood on every hilltop. Starving people wandered aimlessly back and forth. 'No sound but the raven's croak or the wolf's howl breaks the solemn stillness. . . .'❞
From Son of the Morning Star,
Evan S. Connell, 1984

634 **THE LAST FRONTIER**

[1]From *Touch the Earth: A Self-Portrait of Indian Existence* by T.C. McLuhan

HEROES OF THE REVOLUTION

In the flush of victory Americans celebrated their first national heroes. Benjamin Franklin had been widely known for his experiments with electricity and for *Poor Richard's Almanack*. Now he was admired everywhere for his staunch support of the Revolution.

Thomas Jefferson had also become a national hero by the 1780s. American pride in the Declaration of Independence swelled when the Revolution succeeded and the courage of the document's signers could be fully appreciated.

The greatest hero of all was Washington. "The Father of His Country" was, by all accounts, a stern man who stood alone and said little. Yet all Americans admired his personal sacrifice and his careful use of power. One admirer called him "no harum

"John Paul Jones" by Charles Willson Peale.

Starum ranting Swearing fellow but Sober, steady, and calm."

A Scot, John Paul Jones, was revered as the founder of the strong United States naval tradition. In his little ship *Bon*

Homme Richard ("Poor Richard," named in admiration of Franklin), Jones came upon a British convoy led by the powerful *Serapis*. He lashed his ship to the *Serapis* and fought from sunset into moonlight until both ships were seriously damaged. Still Jones refused to surrender. "I have not yet begun to fight," he proclaimed. Finally the British vessel surrendered and was boarded by Jones as the *Bon Homme Richard* sank in a storm of fire.

All men and women who had been brave enough to take up arms against the British were now heroes. One, Andrew Jackson, was only a boy of nine when war broke out. For refusing to black the boots of a British officer, he was struck sharply in the face with the flat of a sword. He carried the scar to his grave.

The **Features** highlight particularly interesting personalities and events.

INTERPRETING HISTORY: The American Revolution

Historians study the past much like detectives solve crimes. Like a detective, an historian gathers evidence, such as letters, diaries, newspaper articles, and eyewitness accounts, interprets it, and reaches a conclusion. But different historians may interpret that evidence differently.

For example, historians have debated for nearly 200 years the reasons behind the American Revolution. Many historians, such as James Franklin Jameson, support the theory that the Revolution was an economic and social struggle. In his book *The American Revolution Considered as a Social Movement* he stresses that democratic ideals were growing among the colonists and the Revolution brought about significant economic and social changes. Historian Mary Beth Norton agrees in her

book *Liberty's Daughters: The Revolutionary Experience of American Women 1750–1800*. She points out that even the status of women in America improved after the Revolution.

Historian Gordon Wood in *The Creation of the American Republic 1776–1787* takes a contrasting view. He maintains that the colonists were motivated by patriotism. Historian Edmund S. Morgan supports this, arguing that the colonists were united by the principles expressed by Patrick Henry's "Give me liberty or give me death!"

Whether the Revolution was prompted by economic reasons or patriotic ones will always remain open to debate. Historians will continue to pursue the answers. This detective work makes history exciting.

132 **GOVERNING THE AMERICAN COLONIES**

Students explore the dynamic aspects of history through **Interpreting History.** Citations from a variety of historians prove that there is no single point of view on major issues, a fact which encourages students to examine their own understanding of events.

A strong link between our land and our history

Throughout *The Story of America*, the vital influence of geography on the growth and history of the United States is a dominant theme.

Maps are large, colorful, and clearly labeled. More than 82 maps illustrate the resources and physical features of America, while detailing the growth of the nation and population shifts.

In addition to the text maps, the **Atlas** provides physical, political, and resource maps that may be used for reference throughout the year.

Each map includes a **Learning from Maps** caption that pinpoints the purpose of the map and helps students understand the crucial interrelationship between history and geography. **Relating History to Geography** strategies in the *Teacher's Edition* provide additional activities that reinforce geographic skills and themes.

Every unit includes a two-page essay that explores with students the impact of geography. The topics chosen for **Linking History and Geography** integrate the five basic themes: location, place, relationships within places, movement, and regions.

This proclamation stated that after January 1, 1863, "all persons held as slaves within any States . . . in rebellion against the United States shall be . . . forever free."

Notice that the Proclamation did not liberate a single slave that the government could control. It applied only to areas ruled by the Confederates. Slaves in Maryland, Kentucky, Missouri, and even in those parts of the Confederacy that had been captured by Union armies, remained in bondage.

Yet when the armies of the United States advanced into new territory after January 1, 1863, the slaves there were freed. At last the war was being fought for freedom, not only to save the Union. Lincoln also ordered that freed slaves should be encouraged to enlist in the army. In August 1863 Lincoln wrote to Grant that enlisting them "works doubly, weakening the enemy and strengthening us." In December 1863, upon hearing of the bravery of these segregated units, Lincoln said, "It is difficult to say they are not as good soldiers as any." All told, about 180,000 African American soldiers fought for the United States during the Civil War. More than 38,000 lost their

THE WAR IN THE EAST, 1861–63

→ Union forces
★ Union victory
☗ No victor
— Confederate forces
☗ Confederate victory

0   25   50 Mi.
0   25   50 Km.
Albers Equal-Area Projection

LEARNING FROM MAPS. *Most of the early battles were fought in the East. Why do you think so many battles took place in eastern and northern Virginia?*

570   THE CIVIL WAR

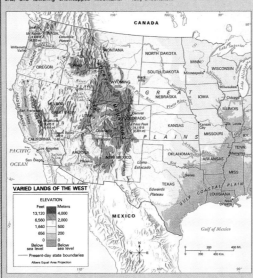

LINKING HISTORY & GEOGRAPHY

THE NATION MOVES WEST

During the mid-1800s hardy pioneers, looking ever westward, ventured beyond the Mississippi into an entirely new frontier. The West was an enormous land of many physical regions—grass-covered but treeless plains, parched deserts, and towering snowcapped mountains.

Each region was different in landforms, climate, soil, and vegetation from anything the pioneers had seen east of the Mississippi. These were lands whose mysteries had to be probed and tested before permanent settlements could be fully undertaken.

VARIED LANDS OF THE WEST

ELEVATION

Feet	Meters
13,120	4,000
6,560	2,000
1,640	500
656	200
0	0
Below sea level	Below sea level

— Present-day state boundaries
Albers Equal Area Projection

0   200   400 Mi.
0   200   400 Km.

The Great Plains
1. How did the pioneers view the Plains? Why?

The first geographic region the pioneers encountered was a grassy region that became known as the Great Plains. The Plains feature level to rolling land with few trees. The dry region receives too little rain to support forests, but enough for a carpet of low-growing grasses to flourish.

Travelers who crossed the Great Plains reacted in many different ways to the vast empty space. Pioneers raised in the eastern United States were struck by the lack of trees and apparent worthlessness of its dry landscape. Familiar with abundant rainfall and thick forests, they agreed with Major Stephen H. Long, who labeled the region the Great American Desert. Days and weeks of dry weather greeted travelers. Because many sought farmland, few stayed to farm the seemingly too-dry plains. In fact, the Great Plains would be the last area of the United States to be fully settled—awaiting farming advances such as the steel plow and the windmill that would help make the dry land of the plains productive.

A Geographic Explanation
2. What natural forces created the Plains?

The geographic explanation for this broad, dry grassland lies in the nature of the western landscape. In the United States the prevailing wind blows from west to east. This wind crosses the Pacific Ocean, picking up moisture. As the rain-bearing air blows onto North America, it runs headlong into the towering Cascade and Sierra Nevada mountain ranges. The mountains force the air to rise and cool. Because cool air cannot hold as much moisture as warm air, the now-cool air drops its moisture as rain or snow. Thus, rain or snow falls frequently on the western slopes of the Cascades and Sierra Nevadas.

The drier and lighter air crosses the peaks and slides down the eastern slopes. With its downward rush, the air warms, snatching whatever moisture it can from the land between the Pacific Ranges and the Rocky Mountains. The warming air thus dries the landscape as far as the western slopes of the Rockies. Then the air is once again forced to rise, cool, and lose its moisture. The air slides down the eastern slopes of the Rockies, becoming the warm dry winds that cross the western Great Plains.

The Rocky Mountains
3. Why did the trails west follow irregular routes rather than straight lines?

Looming in the path of the pioneers who crossed the plains rose the great masses of the Rocky Mountains. This mountain range extends from Alaska into Texas and southward. Rain and snow, available from the air that was forced to rise over the mountain peaks, support the dense forests of pine, fir, and spruce covering the mountainsides. Most of the precipitation, however, occurs as snow during the late winter and early spring. Depths of 25 feet (7.6 meters) or more are common. Pioneers trapped in such snows faced death from cold and starvation, so journeys were planned to cross the Rockies before winter. To the early pioneers, the Rocky Mountains seemed more suited to trappers and miners than farmers, so they pushed on.

The Intermountain Region
4. Why did most of the pioneers find the Intermountain landscape forbidding?

Travelers now crossed the vast desert area that fills the entire country between the Rockies and the Pacific ranges. Jagged rocks and dry sands characterize this Intermountain Region. It is hardly a landscape that the early pioneers found attractive, especially the farmers used to the lush green of the lands east of the Mississippi. Hardy prospectors, however, soon uncovered the region's valuable treasury of minerals.

The Pacific Coast
5. What attracted settlers to the Pacific Coast?

Near the western edge of the continent the pioneers discovered many fertile valleys. In the northwest, sheltered by the Cascades from winter blasts, lie valleys watered by broad rivers and streams. To the south in California, between the Sierra Nevada and the Coastal Ranges, stretch great valleys of rich soil and water for irrigation. The pioneers, their descendants, and other newcomers turned this westernmost edge of the United States into a land of great abundance.

Applying Your Knowledge
You will work in groups to plan a trip by wagon train across the West. Your group should prepare a list of items you will need on the journey. Create a class list by combining the items on individual group lists.

444   MANIFEST DESTINY

Linking History & Geography   445

Applying Your Knowledge provides opportunities for students to make creative use of the information in cooperative projects.

Developing essential skills

Skill development in *The Story of America* is an integrated part of each chapter. The **Strategies for Success** lessons teach skills within the framework of the chapter's historical content.

The **Strategies for Success** present a variety of skills, including map and globe, study, and critical-thinking skills. In the *Annotated Teacher's Edition,* alternative activities to practice the skill being taught are provided under the heading **Integrating Strategies for Success**.

Each lesson opens with an introduction that describes the purpose of the skill and its usefulness in studying history as well as in understanding contemporary issues.

The lesson presents step-by-step guidance for identifying when and how the skill may be used.

STRATEGIES FOR SUCCESS

READING GRAPHS

The successful student is able to gather information from a variety of sources, including graphs. *The Story of America* contains many graphs. Graphs present information visually. There are several types of graphs, each used to present a certain type of data. A *pie*, or *circle*, graph is used to show proportions. A *line* graph shows changes in two factors. It most often shows changes over time. A *bar* graph shows comparisons, making highs and lows stand out. A *picture* graph, or *pictograph*, uses pictures to illustrate amounts.

Because graphs can contain so much information and are so common in histories, it is important to know how to read them.

How to Read a Graph
Follow these steps to read a graph.
1. **Read the title.** The title will tell you the subject and purpose of the graph. It may also contain other information, such as dates.
2. **Study the labels.** Line and bar graphs show two sets of data, one set displayed on the horizontal axis and the other on the vertical axis. The *horizontal* axis is the line at the bottom of the graph that runs across the page. The *vertical* axis is at the left side of the graph and runs up and down. Labels on these axes identify the type of data and the unit of measurement, when appropriate.

3. **Analyze the data.** Note all trends, relationships, and changes among the data. Note increases and decreases in quantities.
4. **Put the data to use.** Use the information to form generalizations and hypotheses and to draw conclusions.

Applying the Strategy
You may have heard the expression, "A picture is worth a thousand words." The picture graph may also be worth a thousand words. Study the picture graph below. Note that small figures are used to make a simple comparison of the population of the American colonies in 1730. Each symbol stands for 10,000 persons. A partial figure represents a fraction of 10,000. For example, the population of Delaware in 1730 was 9,170 persons, so it is represented by part of a figure. What is the population of Virginia? New York? If you said 1,014,000 for Virginia and 48,000 for New York, you have read the graph correctly!

There also are examples of other types of graphs in this unit. The pie graph on page 89 shows the ethnic makeup of the colonial population. (For an example of a bar graph, turn to page 139 in the next chapter.)

For independent practice, see Practicing the Strategy on page 107.

COLONIAL POPULATIONS, 1730*	
New Hampshire	Maryland
Massachusetts	Virginia
Connecticut	North Carolina
Rhode Island	South Carolina
New York	= 10,000 persons
New Jersey	= 8,000 persons
Pennsylvania	= 6,000 persons
Delaware	= 4,000 persons
	= 2,000 persons *Georgia not yet

Source: Historical Statistics of the United States

78　LIFE IN COLONIAL AMERICA

STRATEGIES FOR SUCCESS

SYNTHESIZING INFORMATION

To synthesize information you must combine ideas from several sources. *The Story of America* is a synthesis. The author studied many historical sources and used that information to create this textbook. You, too, are asked to synthesize information in this and other courses. Each time you are directed to read information *and* study a map to gain a new understanding, you are synthesizing information.

How to Synthesize Information
To effectively synthesize information, follow these guidelines.
1. **Select sources carefully.** Make sure that the sources you are studying cover the same information and complement, or add to, each other.
2. **Read for understanding.** Identify main ideas and important supporting evidence in each source.
3. **Compare and contrast.** Note where sources agree or build on each other. More importantly, note where they differ.
4. **Interpret all the information.** Use what you have found to interpret the information. This is the key step in synthesizing.

Applying the Strategy
You know that after the end of the Revolutionary War, settlers moved into the lands beyond the Appalachian Mountains. Here troubles erupted. Study the map on this page and then reread "War in the Northwest" on pages 295–99.

By studying these two sources, you should be able to answer some key questions about these events. Why were so many settlers attracted to these lands? What would most of the settlers do with the land? The map shows the area beyond the Appalachians as gently rolling, with abundant streams and rivers. Could this be what many of the settlers were looking for? As you know, many of these pioneers were farmers. They were looking for fertile soil on which to start farms. Do you think they found what they were searching for?

This surge of land-hungry settlers across the mountains caused trouble with the Indians already there. Why? Synthesize the information by using your prior knowledge about how the Indians and settlers differed on their view of land

ownership and the information from your reading and the map to answer this question.

LANDS WEST OF THE APPALACHIANS

ELEVATION	
Feet	Meters
13,120	4,000
6,560	2,000
1,640	500
656	200
0	0
Below sea level	Below sea level

Present-day state boundaries
Albers Equal-Area Projection

For independent practice, see Practicing the Strategy on page 326.

296　WAR AND PEACE, 1812–1823

STRATEGIES FOR SUCCESS

LEARNING FROM ART

Many books you study, as *The Story of America* does, contain reproductions of famous paintings and other artwork. Gathering information from these sources is a key strategy to understanding history. An engraving such as Currier & Ives' "Westward the Course of Empire Takes Its Way," shown below, can provide a great deal of historical information. This engraving, made by Fanny Palmer and James M. Ives in 1868, gives the artists' view of manifest destiny. More importantly, such a work of art can help shape the ideas of a nation. This Currier & Ives print has appeared in more history books than any other and greatly influenced the way Americans in the 1870s and 1880s viewed westward expansion.

How to Gather Information from Art
To effectively gather information from art, follow these steps.
1. **Determine the subject of the work.** Check its title or caption. Study the people, objects, and actions it depicts.
2. **Examine the details.** If it is a painting or drawing, study the background. Remember that *all* the visual evidence is important to understanding the historical event or period.

3. **Note the artist's point of view** to determine whether the events are portrayed favorably or unfavorably. Ask what impact the work might have on other viewers.
4. **Use the information carefully.** Remember that a work of art may be an artist's *interpretation* of an event. Try to determine how accurately it depicts the event before deciding how to use the information.

Applying the Strategy
James M. Ives and Nathaniel Currier were America's most popular makers of hand-colored prints (pictures from engravings). Carefully study their print below. The main title is "Across the Continent." Close study discloses a picture full of clues to the artists' optimistic view of the westward movement. Note the locomotive puffing on its endless tracks, hardworking men and women building their community, covered wagons heading for further frontiers, and the vast open spaces of yet-to-be-settled America. See if you can spot other historical details.

For independent practice, see Practicing the Strategy on page 446.

Museum of the City of New York

Westward Movement　415

Applying the Strategy helps students use the skill to identify relationships and draw new meaning from the history unfolding within the chapter. **Practicing the Strategy** in the Chapter Review provides students with additional reinforcement.

Reviews that stress application

Chapter and **Unit Reviews** engage students in a variety of activities that stretch across disciplines and require active, imaginative responses.

CHAPTER REVIEWS

Chapter Reviews begin with colorful **Time Lines** and **Chapter Summaries**. This material is useful in working with **Reviewing Chronological Order** and **Understanding Main Ideas**, sections that help students to place events in perspective and recall major trends.

The next two sections of the Chapter Review, **Thinking Critically** and **Writing About History**, promote the use of historical imagination and speculative thinking as students put themselves into the center of historical events and attempt to predict their own attitudes and actions.

The ability to use skills in understanding and probing the causes of historical movements is tested in the next three activities: **Practicing the Strategy**, **Using Primary Sources**, and **Linking History and Geography**. Each of these activities provides opportunities for evaluative thinking.

The concluding activity, **Enriching Your Study of History**, encourages both individual initiative and cooperative learning. The options include research, role playing, creative dramatics, expository and narrative writing, and the creation of graphic organizers.

UNIT REVIEWS

Unit Reviews also provide a variety of summary activities which allow for either individual or group participation. **Connecting Ideas** provides opportunities to synthesize information from several chapters. **Practicing Critical Thinking** provides questions that encourage students to develop higher-order thinking skills. In addition, the **Unit Reviews** include a bibliography of both fiction and nonfiction works.

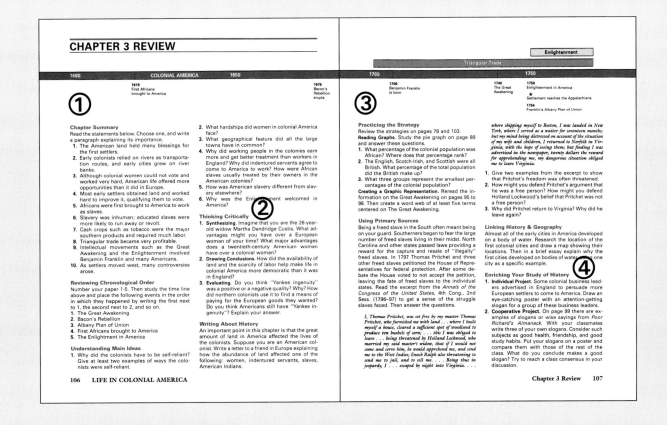

A plan for success

The **Chapter Planning Guide** and the **teaching plans** establish objectives, provide a variety of teaching strategies for every section, and correlate components.

CHAPTER 3

Life in Colonial America

PLANNING THE CHAPTER

TEXTBOOK	RESOURCES
1. An American Civilization	*Unit 1 Worksheets and Tests:* Chapter 3 Graphic Organizer; Directed Reading 3:1, Reteaching 3:1 *Eyewitnesses and Others, Volume 1:* Reading 11: The Secret Diary of William Byrd II (1709); Reading 9: Tapping the Sugar Tree (1600s); Reading 10: Madam Knight Travels by Horseback (1704); Reading 14: A Collection of Runaways (1740s) *American History Map Transparencies:* Transparency 2: Geographical Influences on the Colonial Economy
2. Slavery and the Economy	*Unit 1 Worksheets and Tests:* Directed Reading 3:2, Reteaching 3:2, Geography 3A and 3B *Creative Strategies for Teaching American History:* Page 17 *Eyewitnesses and Others, Volume 1:* Reading 16: A Slave's Story (ca. 1750); Reading 12: Slavery in Virginia (1720s)
3. Americans Share New Ideas	*Unit 1 Worksheets and Tests:* Directed Reading 3:3, Reteaching 3:3 *Creative Strategies for Teaching American History:* Page 21 *Eyewitnesses and Others, Volume 1:* Reading 15: Jonathan Edwards Describes the Peace of Christ (1741)
4. East-West Disputes	*Unit 1 Worksheets and Tests:* Directed Reading 3:4, Reteaching 3:4
Chapter Review	*Audio Program:* Chapter 3 *Unit 1 Worksheets and Tests:* Chapter 3 Tests, Forms A and B (see also *Alternative Assessment Forms*) *Test Generator*

STRATEGIES FOR STUDENTS WITH SPECIAL NEEDS

Gifted Students.
Organize interested students into three groups. Have each group represent colonists from one of the three sections of the British colonies. Tell students that the year is 1760. Have the groups do research in the school or public library to find more information on life in their section of the colonies. Then have each group write a script for a play in which the scenes portray a day in the life of a typical family in the region. Have students memorize their lines and prepare costumes and scenery for their skits. Then have each group videotape its presentation and show it to the rest of the class and possibly the school. Retain the videotapes to use them as references when students study the rapid changes that transformed America in the 1800s and early 1900s.

Students Having Difficulty with the Chapter.
You may wish to have students listen to Chapter 3 in *The Story of America Audio Program.* Then have them study the illustration on pages 72–73. Ask students to imagine that they are the figures in the illustration. Ask them to describe who they are and what they are doing at this very moment. What are they feeling? Do they enjoy their lives? What are they looking forward to as far as what life might bring them in the weeks or months ahead? Why did they come to America? Then ask students to study the illustration on page 88, and have them answer the same series of questions. Ask: How are your feelings different in the second illustration? Why? *(Answers will vary, but students should point out that the first illustration shows a prosperous family enjoying their home in the country. Although they must work very hard to survive, they are probably optimistic about the future. The second illustration shows slaves being transported to America. They are probably bewildered and fearful of the future.)*

BOOKS FOR TEACHERS
Bernard Bailyn, *The Peopling of British North America: An Introduction.* New York: Knopf, 1986.
Daniel J. Boorstin, *The Americans: The Colonial Experience.* New York: Random House, 1958.
Carl Bridenbaugh, *Cities in the Wilderness: The First Century of Urban Life in America, 1625–1742.* New York: Ronald Press, 1938.
Edmund S. Morgan, *American Slavery, American Freedom: The Ordeal of Colonial Virginia.* New York: W.W. Norton, 1975.

Gary Nash, *Red, White, and Black: The Peoples of Early America.* Englewood Cliffs, N.J.: Prentice-Hall, 1974.
Louis B. Wright, *Cultural Life of the American Colonies, 1607–1763.* New York: Harper, 1957.

BOOKS FOR STUDENTS
Robert Carse, *Early American Boats.* Illus. by Hans Zander. Albuquerque: World, 1968.
Charles Paul May, *The Uprooted.* Philadelphia: Westminster, 1976.
Cornelia Neigs, *Master Simon's Garden.* New York: Macmillan, 1916.
Edwin Tunis, *Colonial Craftsmen and the Beginnings of American Industry.* Menasha, WI: Crowell, 1965.
Betty Wilson Story, *Gospel Trailblazer: The Exciting Story of Francis Asbury.* Nashville: Abington, 1984.

MULTIMEDIA MATERIALS
African Heritage (filmstrip), Pitman. Parts 1 and 2. Explores the African background of African Americans.
The Atlantic Slave Trade (film, 17 min.) JSCA. West Africa: An Introduction to the Peoples and Cultures series. Dan Schafer and Tom O'Toole/University of Minnesota. 1973. Filmed in Ghana.
Benjamin Franklin (film, 15 min.) EBEC. Offers highlights of Benjamin Franklin's life.
Colonial America—A Series (filmstrip), EBEC. Peter Zenger: Struggle for a Free Press; William Bradford: Leader of Plymouth Colony; Massachusetts Bay: Life in Puritan New England; Charles Town: Life in the Southern Colonies; The French and Indian Wars; The Salem Witchcraft Trials.
Colonial Life Series (filmstrip), Ed. Projections. Six filmstrips: How Our Democracy Developed; Life in a New England Town; Life in a Southern Town; Life in New Netherland; Life in Plymouth; Life on a Southern Plantation.
The Look of America, 1750–1800 (film, 26 min.) JSCA. Charles and Ray Eames/Pyramid Films. 1977. Brilliant photographic essay on the diversity of life in colonial America.
The Middle Colonies (filmstrip). EBEC. Portrays early colonial life.
The New England Colonies (filmstrip). EBEC. Portrays early colonial life.
The Southern Colonies (filmstrip). EBEC. Portrays early colonial life.

71A

71B

CHAPTER PLANNING GUIDES

At the beginning of each chapter, interleafed pages provide a quick planning chart that previews strategies and materials.

- **Resources** provides a list of all components that may be used to reinforce or extend instruction.
- The **Strategies for Students with Special Needs** provides varied instruction to meet the needs of LEP, gifted, or special education students.
- A **Bibliography** provided for both the teacher and the student suggests additional readings, both fiction and nonfiction, that may be used for research, extension, or enjoyment.
- Specific **Audiovisual** and **Computer** programs are recommended to enhance instruction.

TEACHING PLAN

A seven-step lesson plan for each section guides teachers in preparing an instructional program that is active and focused. (For a more complete explanation of the teaching plans, please see p. Tvii.)

- **Focus/Motivation** suggests opening activities that relate the content to students' experiences or that draw on their prior knowledge.
- **Guided Instruction** provides one or more discussion suggestions or activities that help students to clarify their understanding and to develop their citizenship skills and attitudes.
- **Checking Understanding** is an informal assessment activity that allows the teacher to verify students' comprehension and grasp of essential skills.
- The **Reteaching** activity always follows Checking Understanding and is a cooperative learning strategy that engages students in working teams to complete tasks that reexamine the major point of the lesson.
- **Independent Practice** reminds the teacher to have students complete the **Preview & Review** activity.
- **Closure** provides teachers with a suggestion for summarizing the lesson.

- **Homework** suggests ways for students to review and synthesize the lesson. Often, students are asked to construct charts, do creative writing, or engage in additional research.

In addition to the basic teaching plan, the *Annotated Teacher's Edition* is rich in opportunities to extend instruction beyond the lesson and beyond the classroom.

- **Art in History** uses the abundant art program in the text as a source for discussion and instruction.
- **Extension** activities promote **Home Involvement** and **Community Involvement** by suggesting ways in which parents and the resources of the community may be utilized to support instruction.
- **Using Historical Imagination** and **Multicultural Perspectives** help students place themselves in other times, to see the world as it was then and to understand the attitudes and values of various people.
- **Historical Sidelights** provides interesting anecdotes and personal details concerning people and events.

THE STORY OF
America

John A. Garraty

Gouverneur Morris Professor Emeritus of History
Columbia University

HOLT, RINEHART AND WINSTON

Austin • *New York • Orlando • Chicago • Atlanta • San Francisco • Boston • Dallas • Toronto • London*

An Annotated Teacher's Edition is not automatically included with each shipment of a classroom set of textbooks. However, an Annotated Teacher's Edition will be forwarded when requested by a teacher, an administrator, or a representative of Holt, Rinehart and Winston.

The Annotated Teacher's Edition of *THE STORY OF AMERICA* is complemented by the Teacher's Resource Binders and other program materials. When used with the Pupil's Edition, they provide a complete American history program.

Printed in the United States of America
ISBN 0-03-097636-7

1 2 3 4 5 6 7 036 97 96 95 94 93

Contents

Introduction

THE STORY OF AMERICA by John A. Garraty is a highly readable, straightforward chronological history of the United States from prehistory to the present. The book's narrative is filled with anecdotes that engage the attention of students. Average students readily comprehend the lively text. Below-average students are encouraged by strong reading aids built into the text itself, while above-average students are challenged to engage in research and other extension activities.

In short, THE STORY OF AMERICA provides a comprehensive course in American history. Yet this book is most distinguished by its author, John A. Garraty. His unique gift for generating student enthusiasm may be seen on every page. His college text, The American Nation, has been used by more than 5 million students. Now John Garraty has turned his considerable writing talents to the teaching of history to young people, using anecdote, humor, and historical imagination to bring the past alive.

GOALS OF THE PROGRAM

THE STORY OF AMERICA helps students meet three special curriculum goals. The textbook and the supplementary and reference materials all systematically address these major goals.

The first goal is to help students develop knowledge and cultural understanding. In meeting this goal, students will be able to incorporate what they have learned in history with the other humanities, geography, and the social sciences. A key part of this goal is the development of empathy for people of the past. Students are often asked to use their historical imaginations and place themselves in the roles of the many people they are studying. By doing so, students can more fully appreciate the motives of the people and the forces that have molded our nation. Another part of this goal is to understand the diverse cultures that have helped shape American

society and to respect the many different groups in America today.

The second goal is to help students develop democratic understanding and civic values. In meeting this goal, students will be able to understand both the national identity of our country and their individual identities as Americans. Key to mastering this goal is an understanding of our constitutional and democratic heritage. By emphasizing the continuing evolution of our democratic society, THE STORY OF AMERICA fosters this understanding.

The third goal is to help students develop basic study skills, critical thinking skills, and social participation skills. In meeting this goal, students will be able to complete learning activities that help them master basic study skills and critical thinking skills. Students will also take part in group activities that help them master skills for successful social participation. The comprehensive skills program as well as the assessment program and the emphasis placed on cooperative learning in THE STORY OF AMERICA help students meet this important goal.

ORGANIZATION OF THE TEXTBOOK

THE STORY OF AMERICA is divided into 10 units and 30 chapters. Each chapter is divided into short titled sections. The inclusion of 143 sections in the textbook makes it possible to cover the material in this textbook in the school year with ample time for review and testing.

The Declaration of Independence and the Constitution are placed where they occurred chronologically in America's history, highlighting their historical context. Reading aids and additional information appear in their margins.

The Reference Section at the back of the text includes an atlas, a statistical profile of the United States in charts and graphs, a glossary, a list of sources for the Points of View that appear throughout the text, and a comprehensive index.

Strategies for Success

Each of the 32 Strategies for Success in THE STORY OF AMERICA teaches a social studies skill at the point in the text where it may be most appropriately applied. Thus, "Reading a Time Line" near the beginning of the book prepares students to use the time lines at the end of each chapter; "Tracing Movements on a Map" helps students interpret battle maps for the Revolutionary War; and "Interpreting a Physical Map" allows students to hone their map-reading skills and stresses the interplay of history and geography as Americans cross the Appalachians into new lands of the frontier.

The Strategies for Success teach students to interpret and practice using maps, graphs, charts, and several types of primary and secondary sources, including legal documents, photographs, and editorial cartoons.

The format for the Strategies for Success consists of a brief explanation, a step-by-step process for using the skill, and an opportunity for students to apply what they have learned. Other opportunities for application of each skill are given throughout the text. In addition, students are asked to demonstrate mastery of the skill in each Chapter Review under the heading Practicing the Strategy.

The Vocabulary Program

The strong vocabulary program in THE STORY OF AMERICA has two main parts:
1. Key words are introduced in **boldface** type and defined in context in the text itself. These words are always related immediately to the subject at hand.
2. All words appearing in boldface are included in the Glossary in the Reference Section. In the Glossary, pronunciations are given for more difficult words. Remind students to refer to the pronunciation guide at the beginning of the Glossary to help them use the phonetic respellings. A page reference is given for each entry. Thus students may refer back to the narrative to find the new word used in context and better understand its

use. The vocabulary word will always appear in boldface type on the page for which the reference is given and is therefore easily found.

The Illustration Program

The superb illustration program in *THE STORY OF AMERICA* consists of works of fine art or other important primary sources, carefully reproduced. The illustrations are entirely functional. Each work of art comments upon and extends the written information on the page.

Each illustration is captioned with general information, such as an identification of the artist, medium, and period and with background information, some of it amusing. A question appears at the end of many captions. Thus each piece of art is a ready-made discussion starter. The illustrations are especially important to students who are having difficulty comprehending the text. The answer to each caption question is found in the text itself or in each student's historical imagination. For your convenience, in this Annotated Teacher's Edition the answers are printed at the top of the page. For each chapter in the Annotated Teacher's Edition at least one of the Teaching Strategies in the **Sidetext**, entitled *Art in History*, suggests ways to use the art program to motivate students and to focus their reading.

The Map, Graph, and Chart Program

The maps in *THE STORY OF AMERICA* were designed especially for this book and are appropriate for the needs and abilities of a broad variety of students. The design is deliberately uncluttered so that students can practice their map-reading skills. Colors are distinctive and labels are easy to read. Each map appears in the text at the point where it is most useful. Many of the maps contain relief shading, highlighting the interactions of history and geography. Several of the maps are part of the Strategies for Success, wherein students learn to read and practice using maps. Other special maps are placed in an atlas in the Reference Section at the back of the textbook.

All maps have scales, which give both English and metric measures, as does the text itself. Students should be encouraged to practice using both of these scales of measurement.

Charts, tables, diagrams, and graphs have been designed for simplicity and clear presentation of new information. Types of graphs include line graphs, bar graphs, picture graphs, double bar graphs, and bell curves. Charts include flow charts as well as diagrams.

Study Helps

Reviews are provided in the text for each section, chapter, and unit. The **Preview & Review** activities for each section include reading comprehension questions and critical thinking questions. These activities serve two important functions. First, they provide students with key words and concepts to guide their study of the section before they begin reading. Second, the Preview & Review activities provide students with questions to assess their understanding of the section after they have finished reading. Chapter Reviews test reading comprehension, help students develop critical thinking skills and writing skills, interpret primary sources, relate history and geography, and provide suggestions for individual and cooperative projects. They give students ample opportunity to demonstrate their mastery of content and skills and to undertake classroom projects for further exploration.

Each **Chapter Review** is organized in the following manner:

Time Line: Presents a two-page time line that highlights the major events of the chapter.

Chapter Summary: Provides a list of key concepts discussed in the chapter. Students are instructed to choose one of the concepts and write a paragraph explaining its importance.

Reviewing Chronological Order: Contains an activity stressing the importance of chronology. Students are instructed to use the time line to place the five items listed in correct chronological order.

Understanding Main Ideas: Includes reading comprehension questions designed to test students' understanding of key concepts of the chapter.

Thinking Critically: Provides questions that call for students to develop critical thinking skills, such as how to analyze, evaluate, and synthesize ideas.

Writing About History: Gives students a detailed writing assignment.

Practicing the Strategy: Gives students the opportunity to practice the skill that they

learned in the Strategies for Success lesson in the chapter.

Using Primary Sources: Provides a primary source and asks a series of interpretative questions.

Linking History & Geography: Allows students to see the vital relationship between history and geography and fully incorporates the five themes of geography—*location, place, movement, relationships within places,* and *region*—into the study of American history.

Enriching Your Study of History: Includes suggestions for an individual project and a cooperative learning project.

Each **Unit Review** is organized in the following manner:

Summing Up and Predicting: Consists of a list of key concepts discussed in the unit. Students are instructed to choose one of the concepts and write a paragraph explaining its importance and possible future effects and consequences.

Connecting Ideas: Provides several reading comprehension questions designed to help students synthesize various concepts presented in chapters throughout the book.

Practicing Critical Thinking: Contains several questions that call for students to practice critical thinking skills such as synthesizing and analyzing.

Cooperative Learning: Provides suggestions for cooperative learning projects that are designed to allow students to work together.

Reading in Depth: Contains an annotated bibliography. For your convenience the Annotated Teacher's Edition includes notes describing which of these readings are suitable for students having reading difficulties.

The **Sidetext** of the Annotated Teacher's Edition includes suggested responses for the questions in the Preview & Review activities as well as in the Chapter and Unit Reviews.

ORGANIZATION OF THE ANNOTATED TEACHER'S EDITION

The Annotated Teacher's Edition (ATE) of *THE STORY OF AMERICA* includes all the Pupil's Edition pages, slightly reduced in size to create top and side margins. Each chapter of this Annotated Teacher's Edition includes a variety of resources and teaching suggestions. The Annotated Teacher's Edition is organized into three parts—an **Interleaf,** a **Sidetext,** and **Annotations.** The **Interleaf** is inserted at the beginning of each chapter and contains information to help the teacher develop effective lesson plans. The **Sidetext** is printed in the side-margins of the ATE next to the corresponding material in the Pupil's Edition. The point-of-use location will help the teacher develop effective presentation of chapter information. The **Annotations** appear in the top margins and provide a wealth of supplementary information for teachers.

Interleaf

The **Interleaf** provides teachers with several teaching resources:

Planning the Chapter: Each Chapter **Interleaf** begins with a convenient chart that identifies all of the sections of the chapter and lists the many additional resources of THE STORY OF AMERICA program that teachers may use to plan their lessons for the section and chapter.

Strategies for Students with Special Needs: Each **Interleaf** includes a strategy for teaching gifted students and a strategy for teaching students who are having difficulty with the chapter. These strategies are designed to be used throughout the entire chapter. The **Sidetext** includes other such strategies designed to be used with specific sections.

Books for Teachers: Each **Interleaf** contains a bibliography of appropriate reference materials.

Books for Students: The **Interleaf** also includes a bibliography of books appropriate for students.

Multimedia Materials: The **Interleaf** also provides a list of resource materials to accompany the chapter. Many of the materials listed in this Annotated Teacher's Edition may be obtained through local or regional sources. Although some of the materials may no longer be available from the publisher, information concerning them may be obtained from the following sources. (The names or abbreviations in italics are the shortened forms in which the sources are listed in the **Interleaf.**)

ADL, Anti-Defamation League of B'nai B'rith, 315 Lexington Ave., New York, NY 10016

American Educational Computer, 7506 North Broadway Extension, Suite 505, Oklahoma City, OK 73116

BBC/Time-Life: See Life

Benchmark Films Inc., 145 Scarborough Road, Briarcliff Manor, NY 10510

BFA Educational Media, 2211 Michigan Ave., Santa Monica, CA 90404

Caedmon Films, 409 West 32nd St., New York, NY 10550

Churchill Film, 662 North Robertson Blvd., Los Angeles, CA 90069

Clearvue, Inc., 6666 N. Oliphant Ave., Chicago, IL 60631

Coronet Instructional Films, 65 East South Water St., Chicago, IL 60601

CORF: See Coronet

EAV, Educational Audio Visual, Inc., 29 Marble Ave., Pleasantville, NY 10570

EBEC, EBE, or *EBF* Encyclopedia Britannica Educational Corp., 425 North Michigan Ave., Chicago, IL 60611

Ed. Projections, Inc., 242 Broadway, Yonkers, NY 10706

Educational Audio-Visual, Inc. 17 Marble Ave., Pleasantville, NY 10570

Educational Enrichment Materials, *New York Times,* Catalog Dept. BK, 357 Adams Street, Bedford Hills, NY 10507

EGH, Eye Gate House Inc., 146-01 Archer Ave., Jamaica, NY 11435

Films, Inc., 1144 Wilmette Ave., Wilmette, IL 60091

Filmstrip House, 1052 Briarcliff, Chicago, IL 60613

Focus Media, 839 Stuart Ave., Garden City, NJ 11530

Folkways-Scholastic Records, 50 W. 44th St., New York, NY 10036

Graphic Curriculum, P.O. Box 565, Lenox Hill Station, New York, NY 10021

Guidance Associates, Box 3000, Communication Park Video, Mt. Kisco, NY 10549

Handel, 322 West Pompano Avenue, Orlando, FL 32812

Heritage Filmstrips Inc., 89-11 63rd Drive, Rego Park, NY 11374

HRW, Holt, Rinehart and Winston, 1627 Woodland Ave., Austin, TX 78741

Intellectual Software, 338 Commerce Drive, Fairfield, CT 06430

International Film Bureau, 332 South Michigan Ave., Chicago, IL 60604

IPG, International Picture Guidance, 4412 West 42nd St. New York, NY 10012

JSCA, Junior Scholastic Catalog Address, 223 Glen Echo Heights Road, Glen Echo Heights, MD 22213

LCOA, Learning Corporation of America, 108 Wilmot Rd., Deerfield, IL 60015

Life, Time-Life Broadcast, Inc., 9 Rockefeller Plaza, New York, NY 10020

Listening Library, Inc., 1 Park Ave., Old Greenwich, CT 06870

McGraw-Hill Films, 1221 Avenue of the Americans, New York, NY 10020

MGHT: See McGraw-Hill

Mindscape, 3444 Dundee Road, Northbrook, IL 60062.

Multimedia Productions, Inc., P.O. Box 5097, Stanford, CA 94305

NBCTV, National Broadcasting Co. Educational Enterprises, 30 Rockefeller Plaza, New York, NY 10020

New York Times, Office of Educational Activities, 229 W. 43rd St., New York, NY 10036

Pitman Publishing Corp., 6 E. 43rd St., New York, NY 10017

Prentice-Hall Media, 150 White Plains Rd., Tarrytown, NY 10591

SSSS, Social Studies School Service, 10,000 Culver Blvd., Culver City, CA 90230

SVE, Society for Visual Education Inc., 1345 Diversey Pkwy., Chicago, IL 60614

Time-Life Multimedia, 1271 Avenue of the Americas, New York, NY 10020

TV Ontario, 12 King's Row, Ontario Canada

U. of California, PO Box 11134, Berkeley, CA 91243

Yale University Audio-Visual Center, 30 Wall St., New Haven, CT 06511

Young American Films, distributed by McGraw-Hill

Sidetext

The **Sidetext** provides teachers with point-of-use teaching resources. Material on the opening page of each unit includes:

Unit Objectives: States the major objectives that students should master after they have studied the unit.

Overview: Gives a brief overview stressing key concepts.

Connecting with Past Learning: Provides an introductory activity designed to introduce the unit to the students.

The **Sidetext** for each chapter includes:

Chapter Objectives: States the major objectives that students should master after they have studied the chapter.

Overview: Presents a brief overview stressing key concepts.

Focus/Motivation: Making Connections: Contains an introductory activity designed to spark student interest in the topic about to be studied. These activities have two formats. In one format, students are asked to relate what they have already learned in the course to what they will be studying in the chapter. In the other format, students are asked to relate their own experiences to what they will be learning.

The **Sidetext** for each section of a chapter contains the following:

Preview & Review Responses. Provides model, or suggested, responses to the Preview & Review activity.

Focus/Motivation: Making Connections: Contains an introductory activity designed to spark student interest in the topic about to be studied. These activities have two formats. In one format, students are asked to relate what they have already learned in the course to what they will be studying in the chapter. In the other format, students are asked to relate their own experiences to what they will be learning.

Guided Instruction: Provides a suggested strategy or strategies suitable to use with the entire class while students are studying the section.

Checking Understanding: Presents a suggestion for assessing student understanding of key concepts.

Reteaching Strategy: Suggests how teachers can help students who are having difficulty mastering the chapter content. These strategies are part of the program's emphasis on helping teachers reach students with different learning styles, special education students, and limited English proficient students.

Independent Practice: Refers students back to the Preview & Review.

Closure: Provides teachers with suggestions for bringing the lesson to a close.

Homework: Provides suggestions for assignments that may be given after students have completed the section.

The **Sidetext** for *THE STORY OF AMERICA* includes a wide variety of other teaching suggestions where appropriate to chapter content:

Extension: Home Involvement: Provides suggestions for getting family members of students involved in the lessons.

Extension: Community Involvement: Includes suggestions for getting students involved in their own community.

Relating History to Geography: Contains suggestions for integrating the five basic themes of geography into the study of American history.

Art in History: Provides suggestions for integrating the study of art with that of history. These cross-curricular strategies stress the goals that the humanities and history share.

Music in History: Presents suggestions for using the music of a specific time to fully understand the culture of the time.

Integrating Strategies for Success: Contains strategies to reinforce the Strategy for Success in each chapter.

Using Historical Imagination: Offers students opportunities to imagine that they live in a particular period and to take part in the events of the time.

Multicultural Perspectives: Encourages students to become acquainted with customs and ideas of people who may be different from themselves. An important goal of these exercises is to help students build an understanding and tolerance of others.

Primary Source: Provides teachers with a brief description of the primary sources included in the narrative and a brief rationale for their inclusion.

In addition to the strategies included in the **Sidetext** for each chapter narrative, the **Sidetext** for the Chapter and Unit Review pages includes model, or suggested, answers to the questions in the reviews.

Annotations

The Annotated Teacher's Edition contains **Annotations** printed in the top margins. These annotations are grouped into three categories:

Historical Sidelights: Contain background information for the teacher.

Suggested Caption Responses: Provide model, or suggested, answers to the questions contained in captions.

Resources: Include references to the other components of the program that promote student comprehension of the chapter.

A system of coding helps teachers match specific **Annotations** to the content. Whenever a symbol appears in front of an **Annotation,** a similar symbol is placed next to the appropriate line on the Pupil's Edition page.

In addition to the Annotated Teacher's Edition, the following is a list of resources designed to enhance instruction.

Reading Supplements

EYEWITNESSES AND OTHERS: Readings in American History, Volume I Pupil's Edition: Provides a collection of primary and secondary source readings from the beginnings of North American settlement through the Civil War. A teacher's manual is available.

EYEWITNESSES AND OTHERS: Readings in American History, Volume II Pupil's Edition: Includes a collection of primary and secondary source readings from Reconstruction to the present. A teacher's manual is available.

THE CONSTITUTION: Past, Present, and Future: Contains the Constitution, selected Federalist Papers, and landmark Supreme Court cases as well as worksheets for the Constitution and questions for the other readings. An answer key is available.

THE CONSTITUTION: Foundation of Our Freedom: Presents readings developed by former Chief Justice Warren Burger on events surrounding the writing and ratification of the Constitution. A teacher's edition is available.

Teacher Resource Materials

Creative Strategies for Teaching American History: Provides a variety of detailed teaching strategies and suggestions as well as resource materials and student worksheets.

Transparency Packages

American History Map Transparencies With Thematic Overlays and Teacher's Discussion Guide: Contains map transparencies with teaching strategies and worksheets.

ART IN AMERICAN HISTORY: Transparencies and Teacher's Discussion Guide with Worksheets: Includes transparencies, student worksheets, and a teacher's discussion guide.

Software

THE HISTORIAN: Investigative Software: Contains program disks on six different themes in American history. These themes include: The Spaniards and California, Anasazi Civilization, Boom Towns, Lincoln and Fort Sumter, The Labor Movement Before 1915, and The United States in Vietnam. A teacher's guide is included.

Audio Programs

The Story of America Audio Program, English and Spanish Editions: Contains audiocassettes that retell the story of American history. This component may be particularly useful for students with limited English proficiency or those with reading or comprehension difficulties. A teacher's guide is included.

VOICES OF AMERICA: Speeches and Documents: Provides a 90-minute audiocassette of famous American speeches and documents. A teacher's guide with a brief historical background on each speech is included.

Video Program

The Story of America Video Library: Contains three videocassettes: *The American Constitution: A Blueprint for Freedom; Golden Dreams: The California Gold Rush;* and *Wheels of Change: The American Auto.* A teacher's discussion guide with activity worksheets and answer key are included.

Worksheets

The Story of America Section and Chapter Worksheets: Provide a comprehensive worksheet program with Blackline Masters for each chapter. The Blackline Masters include Graphic Organizers, Geography Worksheets, and for each section within a chapter, Directed Reading and Comprehension Worksheets and Reteaching Worksheets. Included with the worksheets are Unit Syntheses and Answer Keys.

Writing Booklet

Writing About American History: Explains the writing process and offers guidelines for writing and revising reports and research papers. Worksheets and an answer key are included.

Assessment

The Story of America Unit and Chapter Tests, Forms A and B with Answer Key: Give teachers tests and answer keys for all chapters and units in the textbook as well as mid-book and end-of-book tests.

Test Generator: Enables teachers to create tests for each chapter of the textbook using questions stored on the Question Disks. A test may be viewed on the screen and changed, if necessary, before printing. Questions may be edited and new questions may be written. The Test Generator is available for the Macintosh Series as well as IBM PC and Compatibles computers.

Alternative Assessment Forms: An Assessment Program for Courses in United States History: Provides forms for informal assessment that offer suggestions for students to evaluate their own progress as well as that of their peers. Forms with which teachers may assess student progress are also included.

HELPING STUDENTS WITH SPECIAL NEEDS

Your classroom undoubtedly includes students from a variety of cultural backgrounds who have different learning styles. THE STORY OF AMERICA program can be used to meet the needs of all types of students.

Strategies for Limited English Proficient Students

As a teacher, you make a variety of instructional decisions in addressing the needs of children with different learning abilities. This task becomes more complex when teaching the limited English proficient child who often faces the stress and anxiety of not being able to understand instructions or communicate in the classroom.

These instructional strategies will help you meet the needs of limited English proficient students. You can use **The Story of America Audio Program** for each of these strategies.

Plan Frequent/Quality Exposure to English: Use intense language activities that incorporate a variety of methods and materials. Devote a high percentage of time to direct teacher instruction.

Include small group activities: Plan small group activities that include students who are proficient in English with those who have limited English proficiency.

Vary the Context of Language Learning: Through simulations, field trips, role-playing, or dramatization have students practice using language for a variety of purposes.

Bridge Cultural/Conceptual Gaps: Plan activities that expand a child's knowledge of American culture.

Build a Positive Self-Concept: Reduce stress and anxiety by accepting simple responses like nodding and *yes/no* answers. Make learning fun by using games and listening centers. Another way to build self-concept is to introduce group activities that involve the students in problem solving and decision making. Such activities allow students to perform on a variety of levels and to always achieve a certain degree of success. Many of the teaching strategies included in this ATE provide suggestions for such strategies.

Make Learning Comprehensible: Use visuals, props, and demonstrations to convey meaning. Stress important points of the lesson by repeating, labeling, and using voice inflection.

Strategies for Teaching Students with Different Learning Styles

It is likely that you have auditory, visual, and kinesthetic learners in your classroom. THE STORY OF AMERICA provides ample opportunities to meet each of these needs.

Auditory Learners: Auditory learners benefit from discussions and any oral activities. THE STORY OF AMERICA Audio Program is ideally suited for such learners.

Visual Learners: Visual learners benefit from such activities as studying pictures, analyzing charts, and interpreting other visuals. All of the components of THE STORY OF AMERICA program contain materials to use with visual learners.

Kinesthetic Learners: Kinesthetic learners benefit from hands-on activities. The Annotated Teacher's Editions include many strategies that have students complete maps, draw pictures, or construct time lines. These activities meet the needs of students who learn best by manipulating and organizing materials. For example, many Guided Instruction strategies have students draw maps or pictures.

Strategies for Teaching Gifted Students

Teaching gifted students can be a very rewarding experience for the classroom teacher. At the same time it presents the teacher with a variety of challenges and goals. Gifted and talented students, like other students, are a diversified group. You should keep in mind the individual learning styles of each of these students, while motivating and directing them to develop their natural abilities to the fullest.

If you are teaching a class of gifted students, these guidelines may help you meet the learning needs of gifted students.

Allow Gifted Students to Choose Their Own Topics for Assignments or Activities: Activities that allow gifted students to research topics of special interest tend to keep them motivated and promote independent thinking.

Utilize Group Activities: You may wish to have students take part in panel discussions, informal discussions, debates, and interviews, all of which allow gifted students to exchange ideas. When practiced enough, these activities can help students to arrive at logical solutions to problems.

Utilize Activities Involving Real Problems Requiring Real Solutions: By having your gifted students research problems facing the world today and propose possible solutions, you are helping them to broaden their perspectives and increase their ability to solve challenging problems. Some examples of these problems to be researched are: How can the president reduce the federal deficit? How can science deal with the problem of the "greenhouse effect"? What are some of the ways in which the government can help the homeless?

Strategies for Teaching Less Prepared Students

Less prepared students are those who are not able to learn at an average rate from the available materials, such as textbooks or other written instructional materials. It is usually easy for teachers to spot less prepared students because some of the noticeable characteristics are short attention spans, deficiency in basic language and math skills, and an inability to grasp abstract ideas and concepts.

Teaching less prepared students is especially challenging. These instructional strategies may help you meet the needs of less prepared students.

Plan Lessons Around the Interests and Experiences of Less Prepared Students: Less prepared students need to feel a part of the instruction. This raises their interest level and increases their attention spans.

Make Frequent Use of Audio and Visual Materials: Often less prepared students are audio or visual learners. By utilizing audio and video materials, you are adapting the learning situation to accommodate their learning strengths. This can produce a positive learning experience for both students and teacher.

Provide Reteaching and Review Activities: Because less prepared students need constant reinforcement, reteaching activities or worksheets at the end of a lesson and review activities or worksheets before a quiz or test are essential for students' success.

Cooperative Learning Strategies

Many of the teaching strategies in *THE STORY OF AMERICA* program involve cooperative learning. In cooperative learning, small groups of students of different ability levels work together to solve problems and complete assigned tasks. The major goal of this instructional strategy is to create an environment in which students work toward a common goal. Simply putting students in groups and asking them to do the cooperative assignments, however, will not guarantee successful learning. The following aspects should be taken into consideration when asking students to tackle cooperative learning assignments in *THE STORY OF AMERICA* program.

Positive Interdependence: Students must feel they need each other to complete the assignment. Establish positive interdependence by requiring the group to turn in one assignment that they have worked on together. Also, tell students that answers must reflect ideas from *every* member.

Individual Accountability: Stress to students that they will be held personally responsible for learning and helping their group. Circulate around the room while the groups are working and quiz individuals to see if they can explain the answers their group has finished so far. If they cannot, ask group members to review until each student can. Reward groups when everyone shows that they can explain answers. Also, give each group member a job to do such as reader, recorder, or quizzer.

Face-to-Face Interaction: Maximize learning by making sure all students in each group orally exchange ideas, information, and explanations.

Cooperative Skill Teaching: To get students to take responsibility for interacting with their group, insist on standards of group behavior. Discuss with students the behaviors you expect to see, display those behaviors prominently, remind students to use them while in groups, and use a checklist to document their use. Behaviors might include: *Everyone contribute, Listen carefully, Ask others to explain, Praise good ideas,* and *Disagree with ideas, not people.*

Processing Group Effectiveness: Groups will improve only if students take time to evaluate their group's progress and formulate a plan for improvement. At the end of each cooperative learning assignment, have groups list what they are doing well and how they can improve. Also, have students tell other group members something *positive* they do that helps the group. Such statements will help all students feel valuable to the group and will help build self-esteem.

THE STORY OF
America

GEOGRAPHY CONSULTANT

Phillip Bacon
Professor Emeritus of Geography and Anthropology
University of Houston

Grateful acknowledgment is made to the scholars who read portions of *The Story of America* in manuscript.

Willard Bill
University of Washington

Ray A. Billington
Late of the Huntington Library

John Morton Blum
Yale University

John Bracey, Jr.
University of Massachusetts,
Amherst

Gloria Contreras
University of North Texas

Frank De Varona
Dade County Public Schools
Florida

Robert Farrell
Indiana University

Eric Foner
Columbia University

Thomas R. Frazier
Baruch College
City University of New York

William H. Harbaugh
University of Virginia

Asa G. Hilliard, III
Georgia State University

Michael Holt
University of Virginia

Ari Hoogenboom
Brooklyn College, CUNY

Arthur S. Link
Princeton University

Robert Middlekauff
University of California, Berkeley

Edmund Morgan
Yale University

Robert V. Remini
University of Illinois, Chicago

Timothy L. Smith
Johns Hopkins University

George C. Wright
University of Texas

In preparing *The Story of America* extensive discussions also were held with district administrators, faculty leaders, and teachers in California, Texas, Michigan, Illinois, Ohio, and Virginia

THE STORY OF
America

John A. Garraty

Gouverneur Morris Professor Emeritus of History
Columbia University

HOLT, RINEHART AND WINSTON
Austin • *New York • Orlando • Chicago • Atlanta • San Francisco • Boston • Dallas • Toronto • London*

JOHN A. GARRATY is a distinguished historian and writer and the Gouverneur Morris Professor Emeritus of History at Columbia University. His books include the widely adopted college textbook *The American Nation*, biographies of Henry Cabot Lodge and Woodrow Wilson, *The Great Depression*, and the popular *1,0001 Things Everyone Should Know About American History*. He has held Guggenheim, Ford, and Social Science Research Council Fellowships. Professor Garraty is a former president of the Society of American Historians, editor of the *Dictionary of American Biography*, and coeditor of the *Encyclopedia of American Biography*.

PHILLIP BACON is Professor Emeritus of Geography and Anthropology at the University of Houston. He served on the faculties of Columbia University and the University of Washington and is former Dean of the Graduate School of Peabody College for Teachers at Vanderbilt University.

Cover photograph: © B. Gelberg, Sharpshooters.

Maps: R.R. Donnelley Company Cartographic Services

Printed in the United States of America

ISBN 0-03-097559-X

1234567   041   97 96 95 94 93 92

Parts I and II of the Annotated Teacher's Edition of *The Story of America* both include a complete Table of Contents and other front matter, and a complete Reference Section, including Glossary and Index. Part I contains Units 1–5. Part II contains Units 6–10.

Contents

Unit One
THE AMERICAN COLONIES
Beginnings to 1770

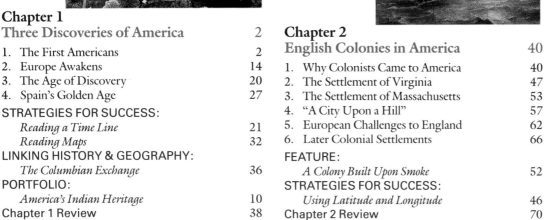

v

Unit Two
THE AMERICAN NATION
1770-1798

Unit Three
A GROWING AMERICA
1790-1840

Unit Four
A WESTERING AMERICA
1816-1860

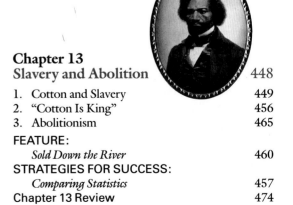

Unit Five
A DIVIDED AMERICA
1850-1877

Unit Nine
A GLOBAL AMERICA
1940–1963

Unit Ten
MODERN AMERICA
1964 to the Present

REFERENCE SECTION

STRATEGIES FOR SUCCESS

FEATURES

CHARTS, GRAPHS, TABLES, & DIAGRAMS

HOW TO USE *The Story of America*

The Story of America contains a vast amount of information. It has many useful features to help you understand and use this information. Some features help you preview what you are about to read. Others help you read for that information or find additional information. Still other features help you review what you have read. Using the features of *The Story of America* wisely will help you become a better student of history.

Using the Textbook's Features

To get the most from *The Story of America,* here are some guidelines.

1. **Use the Table of Contents.** Make yourself familiar with the **Table of Contents** (pages v–xvii). A quick skimming shows you how the book is organized and helps you anticipate what you will be reading. It shows that *The Story of America* is organized into ten units, and the units are further divided into 30 chapters. As its name implies, the Table of Contents shows the content of each chapter, the special features the textbook contains, and the page on which each unit, chapter, and feature can be found. To the right is a sample.

2. **Study the unit opening pages.** Each unit gives a preview of its content with a unit title, an illustration, an introduction, and a list of chapters that are included. Take time to study the unit opening page. It contains clues to what you are about to read. For example, after studying the opening page of Unit One on page 1, what can you tell about the people and times covered in this unit?

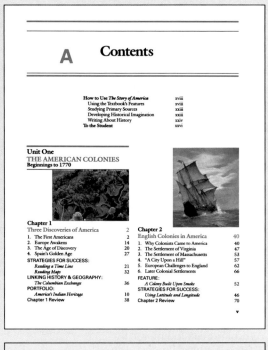

A Contents

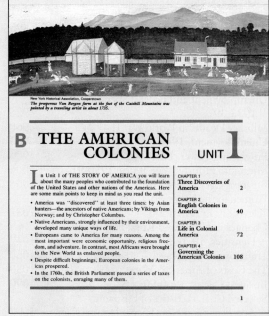

New York Historical Association, Cooperstown
The prosperous Van Bergen farm at the foot of the Catskill Mountains was painted by a traveling artist in about 1735.

B THE AMERICAN COLONIES UNIT **1**

In Unit 1 of THE STORY OF AMERICA you will learn about the many peoples who contributed to the foundation of the United States and other nations of the Americas. Here are some main points to keep in mind as you read the unit.

• America was "discovered" at least three times: by Asian hunters—the ancestors of native Americans; by Vikings from Norway; and by Christopher Columbus.
• Native Americans, strongly influenced by their environment, developed many unique ways of life.
• Europeans came to America for many reasons. Among the most important were economic opportunity, religious freedom, and adventure. In contrast, most Africans were brought to the New World as enslaved people.
• Despite difficult beginnings, European colonies in the Americas prospered.
• In the 1760s, the British Parliament passed a series of taxes on the colonists, enraging many of them.

1

CHAPTER 2

English Colonies in America

The wealth and splendor of Spain's American empire attracted other Europeans the way flowers in springtime attract honeybees. The English in particular were envious of Spain. They longed to build an empire in the Americas. They hoped for a share of the gold and silver that almost everyone believed was so plentiful in the new land, and they wanted American products such as sugar and rice, which could not be grown in their cold climate. The English colonists came to America to trade and sell, to practice their religions, and to find work. Would they find a better life in a New World?

Preview & Review

Use these questions to guide your reading. Answer the questions after completing Section 1.
Understanding Issues, Events, & Ideas. Explain the English rise to power and its first journeys to America, using the following words: sea dog, Spanish Armada, charter, Roanoke, enclosure movement, northwest passage, joint-stock company.
1. How did Queen Elizabeth try to weaken Spain?
2. Why did the first settlers on Roanoke Island want to return to England?
3. Why were each of the following interested in colonizing America: the queen? landowners? merchants? explorers?
Thinking Critically. Imagine that you find a lost diary explaining what happened to the colonists of Roanoke Island. What does it say?

At right is Nicholas Hilliard's 1572 miniature portrait of Elizabeth I.

1. WHY COLONISTS CAME TO AMERICA

England Challenges Spain

In 1497, not very long after the news of Columbus' discovery reached England, its king, Henry VII, sent John Cabot on a voyage of exploration. Cabot sailed along the coast of Newfoundland, giving England a claim to the northern regions of America. But in the 1550s, after Elizabeth I inherited the throne, the English became seriously interested in America.

Elizabeth, ruling England alone in a world dominated by men, was a person of the strongest will and ambition. She was a shrewd ruler and a clever diplomat who paid little attention to right and wrong. Elizabeth never married, perhaps because no man could be her equal. She had a temper to match her fiery red hair and a tongue to match her sharp features. She was well aware of England's limited strength compared to Spain's. She proceeded with caution.

National Portrait Gallery, London

40   ENGLISH COLONIES IN AMERICA

4. "A CITY UPON A HILL"

The Puritans

While the London Company was making plans to settle Virginia, another joint-stock company, the Virginia Company of Plymouth, or the Plymouth Company, tried to establish a settlement far to the north near the mouth of the Kennebec River in what is now Maine. The settlers arrived in 1607 but remained only one winter. However, fishermen and traders continued to set up temporary camps in the area. In 1614 the Plymouth Company sent John Smith to explore the region further. It was Smith who first called the area **New England.**

In the early 1620s the Plymouth Company, now called the Council of New England, gave away several tracts of land in the northern regions, including much of what are now Maine and New Hampshire.

Preview & Review

Use these questions to guide your reading. Answer the questions after completing Section 4.
Understanding Issues, Events, & Ideas. Use the following words to compare Puritan settlements with Jamestown: New England, Puritans, Massachusetts Bay Company, freemen, commonwealth, Fundamental Orders, proprietary colony, Toleration Act.
1. Who were the Puritans? How did the Puritans differ from the Pilgrims? Why did they leave England?
2. Why did Puritan leaders expel Roger Williams? Anne Hutchinson?
3. What kind of powers did the king's grant give Lord Baltimore? Why were these powers never used?
Thinking Critically. You are a Puritan living in Massachusetts in 1634. Write a letter to your cousins in England, convincing them to come to America.

Metropolitan Museum of Art

The great 19th-century American sculptor, Augustus Saint-Gaudens, made this bronze, "The Puritan." What does this sculpture show you about Puritan life?

"A City upon a Hill"   57

---

3. **Read the chapter introduction.** Every chapter of *The Story of America* begins with an introduction that provides an overview and states the main ideas of the chapter. When you read the introduction, begin forming questions you may have about the chapter's content.

4. **Use the section Preview & Review to guide your reading.** Every section of *The Story of America* begins with a **Preview & Review**. These contain key words and questions that can help guide your reading of the section. The questions are *the same ones* you use to review your mastery of the information in the section. The symbol 📖 shows you when you have reached the end of the section. A note in the margin tells you to return to the Preview & Review to begin your review of the section. By carefully reading the Preview & Review *before* beginning the section, you can identify important words or terms and major questions or ideas discussed in the section.

5. **Read the chapters and sections.** *The Story of America* has many features that make reading it easier. First, the headings and subheadings provide a kind of outline of the main ideas and important details.

Second, pay special attention to words printed in bold black type. These **boldfaced terms** call your attention to important history words. A definition follows most, right in that sentence or the next. You can also check a word's meaning in the glossary.

Third, study the illustrations and read the captions. Relate what you see to what you read. All of the pictures are chosen carefully to help you better understand what you are reading. One picture can be worth a thousand words.

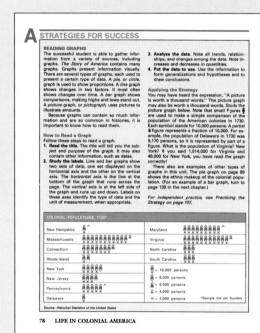

Study the special features. *The Story of America* has many features that enrich history and help you develop the tools of the historian. These features appear on tinted backgrounds.

On blue pages are **Strategies for Success**. These features appear in each chapter. They present additional information related to the specific chapter content and provide an opportunity for you to develop or sharpen your study skills.

Most chapters also contain one or more brief features that highlight an important person, event, or idea. These features are easily identified by their three-column format and special heading. They are meant to give the reader a chance to pause and to consider their significance in our history.

A third feature, **Interpreting History,** teaches the historian's craft by discussing interpretations of events or ideas that have created historical controversy. Examples include the causes of the American Revolution, the motives of the writers of the Constitution, and the importance of the frontier in the development of the American character.

Every chapter of *The Story of America* uses the words of historical figures whenever possible. Besides lengthy primary source quotations, marked with large red quotation marks, you will often find a *Point of View* in the margin. This feature presents a brief statement about a key event, person, or situation. Sometimes opposing opinions are presented as *Points of View.*

Another key feature is the map program. The maps illustrate physical, cultural, and historical information clearly and accurately. Almost every map contains relief shading showing major physical features, so you are constantly aware of the interplay of history and geography. Several Strategies for Success will help you hone your map-reading skills.

The Story of America highlights the ethnic and cultural contributions of different groups to American culture. To help you visualize some of the many contributions, you will find four pictorial essays, or portfolios, that contain the art and artifacts of some of the groups that have come to America. These four portfolios are titled: America's Indian Heritage, America's

The Grange Collection, New York

seen far more of the world than any of the other settlers. He had fought in a number of wars in eastern Europe against the Turks. In one war he was captured, taken to Constantinople, and sold into slavery. However, he managed to kill his master and escape. After many other remarkable adventures Smith found himself in the colony of Virginia.

In 1608 Smith was elected president of the Virginia council. Once in charge, he bargained with the Indians for food. He stopped the foolish searching for gold. Instead he put people to work building shelters and planting food crops. Hard work and strict discipline became the order of the day.

Reforms for Virginia

Virginia's difficulties finally convinced the merchant adventurers in England that the London Company needed to be reorganized. In 1609 Sir Edwin Sandys, a councilor who was also a member of Parliament, England's legislative body, obtained a new charter from King James. This charter called for the appointment of a governor who would rule the colony in Jamestown rather than from London.

The London Company then raised a good deal more money and outfitted a fleet of nine ships to carry about 600 new settlers across the Atlantic. Those who paid their own fare received one share of stock in the company. Those who could not pay agreed to work as servants of the company for seven years in return for their passage. Until 1616 everything the colonists produced was to be put into a common storehouse or fund. On that date the servants would have worked off their debt to the company. Then the profits of the enterprise were to be divided among the shareholders—both the investors back in England and the settlers. Every shareholder would also receive a grant of Virginia land.

These were fine plans but hard to put into effect. Conditions in Virginia got worse and worse. The first governor, Lord De La Warr, put off coming to Jamestown. Smith returned to England for supplies and colonists, and to convince company managers to invest more money in the colony. Without his firm hand, the organization and rules he had begun quickly fell apart. The years from 1609 to 1610 were a **starving time.** As Smith described it:

John Smith was 27 years old when he took command of the Jamestown settlement. This engraving portrays him at the age of 33.

Point of View

An Algonquin leader asked John Smith why the colonists used force with the Indians.

❝Why will you take by force what you may have quietly by love? Why will you destroy us who supply you with food? What can you get by war? We can hide our provisions and run into the woods; then you will starve for wronging your friends. Why are you jealous of us? We are unarmed, and willing to give you what you ask, if you come in a friendly manner.❞

Powhatan, 1607

❝ By their [the Indians'] cruelty, our Governours indiscretion [poor judgment] and losse of our ships, of five hundred [colonists] within six months after Captaine Smith's departure, there remained not past sixtie men, women and children, most miserable and poore creatures; and those were preserved for the most part, by roots, herbes, acornes, walnuts, berries, now and then a little fish . . . yea, even the very skinnes of our horses. . . . This was that time,

D

48 ENGLISH COLONIES IN AMERICA

And how was the new, larger empire in America to be governed? The old system of 13 separate colonies, each controlled from London, worked well enough when the colonies were separated from one another by thick forests. Now the wilderness was shrinking. Four colonies—Virginia, Pennsylvania, Connecticut, and Massachusetts—each claimed parts of the Ohio Valley just won from France. Each based its case on a royal charter drafted before anyone knew much about American geography. Who would untangle these conflicting claims?

There were also the Indians in the Ohio Valley. Everyone expected them to stop fighting when the French surrendered. Instead they organized behind Pontiac, a chief of the Ottawa, and tried to drive the settlers back across the Appalachians. How could an area claimed by so many different colonies be defended? Who would pay the cost if British troops were used?

These last questions were the most pressing in 1763. The answers were that the British put down **Pontiac's Rebellion** and paid the cost of doing so. To keep the peace the British stationed 6,000 soldiers in the land won from the French and closed the entire region beyond the Appalachian Mountains to settlers. This decision was announced in the **Proclamation of 1763.** Only licensed fur traders might enter the Ohio region. No one could purchase Indian lands.

Most American colonists did not like the Proclamation of 1763. It seemed to put the great West as far out of reach as it had been when the forts built by Governor Duquesne had first barred the way ten years earlier.

LEARNING FROM MAPS. *The French and Indian War significantly changed the face of North America. Study these maps. What changes can you discover?*

Return to the Preview & Review on page 116.

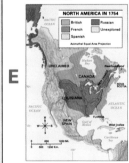

E

America's Indian Heritage

MAJOR CULTURAL REGIONS AND INDIAN TRIBES OF NORTH AMERICA, c. 1500

Albers Equal-Area Projection

F

This map shows the geographic location of the major cultural groups into which American Indian tribes have been divided. It also shows some of the hundreds of tribes in each group. Of course many tribes moved about a great deal, so the locations shown are approximate.

St. Louis Science Center

This stone pipe found in Oklahoma shows a man playing chunky, a game popular everywhere in the region of the Mound Builders. Games lasted all day. Chunky was a bit like bowling, a bit like the javelin toss.

Peabody Museum of Archaeology and Ethnology, Harvard University

The Hopewell mounds yielded this mica serpent. Mica is a mineral silvery in color and so fine it is translucent—diffused light passes through.

10 THREE DISCOVERIES OF AMERICA

America's Pacific Heritage

Since ships first sailed or land caravans carried off its treasure, westerners have been fascinated by the East. Marco Polo was bedazzled even though he came from Venice, a western jewel. The art of the Orient is the oldest in the world, but it was hidden behind the walls of Forbidden Cities. Emigrants from Asia were too poor to own eastern treasures such as we see on these pages, but traders like John Ellerton Lodge filled the holds of the *Kremlin* and *Magnet* with china, silk, ivory, even fireworks that bloomed like chrysanthemums to bring Pacific culture to America.

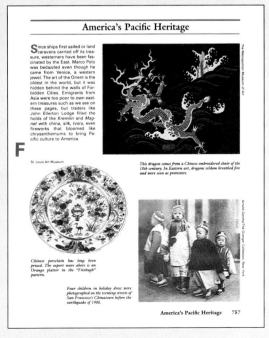

The Metropolitan Museum of Art

This dragon comes from a Chinese embroidered chair of the 18th century. In Eastern art, dragons seldom breathed fire and were seen as protectors.

St. Louis Art Museum

Chinese porcelain has long been prized. The export ware above is an Orange platter in the "Fitzhugh" pattern.

Arnold Genthe/The Grange Collection, New York

Four children in holiday dress were photographed on the teeming streets of San Francisco's Chinatown before the earthquake of 1906.

America's Pacific Heritage 757

F

LINKING HISTORY & GEOGRAPHY

A

CROSSING THE ATLANTIC

By the 15th century Europe had two groups of sea powers. One, the Italian city states, located on the relatively calm and sheltered waters of the Mediterranean Sea, traded with China, the Indies, and India. The second group, the Hanse Towns, which later became the Hanseatic League, sailed the North and Baltic seas, carrying goods from Russia and Siberia to the towns of northern Europe. Both groups developed from unique geographic environments—the linking of great overland trade routes from the east with the indented coastlines of tideless seas. Captains and crews sailed in comparative security, knowing land lay not too far away.

Looking to the Atlantic

1. Why did the other nations of Europe begin to look for their own trade routes?

The merchants in Italy and the Hanse Towns charged other Europeans very high prices for the goods they traded. Because these merchants held monopolies, other nations had difficulty establishing their own trade routes. Slowly the leaders of the other European nations began to realize that their only realistic alternative was to look westward—to the Atlantic Ocean. But that meant facing a landless horizon and the vastness of an uncharted watery wilderness.

It is interesting to note that only those nations that actually faced the Atlantic—Spain, Portugal, England, France, and the Netherlands—actually met the challenge of the Atlantic (as Norway had centuries earlier). They, and they alone, took the knowledge of navigation, map making, and shipbuilding and applied it to a much sterner test of seamanship in the open Atlantic Ocean.

Geography of the Ocean Frontier

2. What manner of watery frontier did these early sailors find as they ventured westward?

We can get some sense of what lay ahead by looking at a map or globe. As you can see, the Atlantic covers one fifth of the earth's surface. And you can see it occupies a unique space on Planet Earth, separating Europe and Africa from the Americas and creating a barrier—or, for some, a highway—between those continents.

A map or globe shows you, too, that the Atlantic is a long body of water that resembles an hourglass. The widest part of the ocean, spanning some 4,150 miles (6,640 kilometers), stretches between Spain and Florida. It was precisely this expanse crossed by Columbus in 1492! The narrowest part lies between Norway and Greenland in the north. Here the distance is a mere 930 miles. Across this narrowest section, with islands scattered like stepping stones, the Vikings sailed around the year 1000.

Mixing the Waters of the Atlantic

3. How else is the Atlantic's geography unique?

Perhaps the most amazing aspect of the Atlantic's geography is its huge *drainage basin,* the area of land whose rivers flow into an ocean. Most of the world's great rivers empty their waters into the Atlantic.

In North American the Atlantic basin stretches all the way to the Rocky Mountains. There, in western North America, the many tributaries of the mighty Mississippi begin. At mid-continent they join to form the river that drains two thirds of the continent toward the Gulf of Mexico, an arm of the Atlantic.

In South America the Atlantic's drainage area extends across the continent to the soaring Andes Mountains. Among those towering peaks the world's greatest flow of water begins its journey to the Atlantic. So great is this rush of water—carried by the Amazon River—that the volume of water is greater than that of the Mississippi, Nile, and Yangzte rivers *combined.*

The Atlantic also gathers much of the water from Africa. Waters of the Nile, Congo, and Niger rivers eventually reach the Atlantic. The Atlantic also claims the Rhine and the other great rivers of Western Europe as well as many of those of Eastern Europe and central Russia.

The immense size of the drainage basin opened the way to yet-to-be-explored lands. In North America, the Gulf of St. Lawrence, Hudson Bay, and Gulf of Mexico carried sailing vessels from Europe to the continent's edge. Rivers carried explorers to its very heart.

Sailing West

4. What propelled the early sailing ships from Europe to the Americas?

One other aspect of the Atlantic's geography

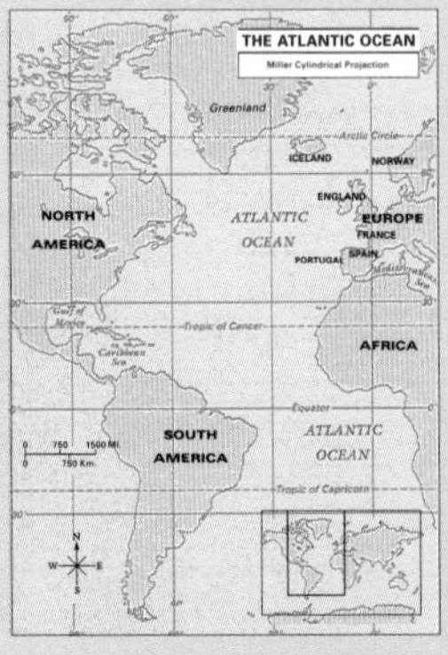

played a vital role in the discovery and exploration of the New World. Winds and ocean currents helped transport people and cargoes from Europe to the Americas and back.

As you can see from the map on page 24, Columbus first headed south to the Canary Islands before turning westward. This was no accident. Early explorers voyaging southward along Africa's west coast found strong and steady winds from the northeast between 30° and 5° north of the equator. These winds carried the sleek sailing ships ever westward.

What causes these winds? Air always flows from centers of high atmospheric pressure to areas of lower pressure. The winds along the African coast result from air flowing from zones of high pressure near 30°N to a low-pressure zone always found near the equator.

Of course, if the world did not turn on its axis, the air would simply flow from north to south in the Northern Hemisphere and south to north in the Southern Hemisphere. The earth's rotation causes the winds to deflect, or bend.

These wonderful winds, among the steadiest and most reliable on earth, soon became invaluable for ships sailing westward. Within a remarkably short period of time they were known to sailors everywhere as the *trade winds.*

The Return Trip

5. Once in the Americas, how did people return to Europe?

Just as the trade winds carried ships westward, the Gulf Stream helped propel them back to Europe. The Gulf Stream begins in the eastern portions of the Gulf of Mexico. It flows northward along the eastern seaboard of the United States. At about 40°N the current swings eastward across the Atlantic toward the British Isles. It is one of the strongest and most consistent ocean currents. Coupled with the northeast trade winds, it provided knowledgeable navigators with the means to complete roundtrip voyages between Europe and the New World.

The geography of the Atlantic made it ideal as a pathway of discovery. Winds and currents moved the sailing ships on just the right paths. Plentiful bays and gulfs, fed by huge rivers, provided entrances into continents. Soon the forbiddingly vast waters of the Atlantic became one of the most heavily traveled routes in the world.

APPLYING YOUR KNOWLEDGE

Your class will work in three groups to create a profile map of the Atlantic Ocean. One group should map the major ocean currents. Another should identify and label on a map the major rivers eventually draining into the Atlantic. The third group should measure distances across the ocean from various spots (such as Virginia) in North America to Norway, Spain, and England. You will then combine the groups' findings to create your profile map of the Atlantic.

176 THE REVOLUTIONARY WAR

Linking History & Geography 177

CHAPTER 3 REVIEW

B

Enlightenment

Triangular Trade

1600 | COLONIAL AMERICA | 1650 | 1700 | 1750

1619 First Africans brought to America

1676 Bacon's Rebellion erupts

1706 Benjamin Franklin is born

1740 The Great Awakening

1750 Enlightenment in America

★ Settlement reaches the Appalachians

1754 Franklin's Albany Plan of Union

Chapter Summary

Read the statements below. Choose one, and write a paragraph explaining its importance.

1. The American land held many blessings for the first settlers.
2. Early colonists relied on rivers as transportation routes, and early cities grew on river banks.
3. Although colonial women could not vote and worked very hard, American life offered more opportunities than it did in Europe.
4. Most early settlers obtained land and worked hard to improve it, qualifying them to vote.
5. Africans were first brought to America to work as slaves.
6. Slavery was inhuman; educated slaves were more likely to run away or revolt.
7. Cash crops such as tobacco were the major southern products and required much labor.
8. Triangular trade became very profitable.
9. Intellectual movements such as the Great Awakening and the Enlightenment involved Benjamin Franklin and many Americans.
10. As settlers moved west, many controversies arose.

Reviewing Chronological Order

Number your paper 1-5. Then study the time line above and place the following events in the order in which they happened by writing the first next to 1, the second next to 2, and so on.

1. The Great Awakening
2. Bacon's Rebellion
3. Albany Plan of Union
4. First Africans brought to America
5. The Enlightment in America

Understanding Main Ideas

1. Why did the colonists have to be self-reliant? Give at least two examples of ways the colonists were self-reliant.
2. What hardships did women in colonial America face?
3. What geographical feature did all the large towns have in common?
4. Why did working people in the colonies earn more and get better treatment than workers in England? Why did indentured servants agree to come to America to work? How were African slaves usually treated by their owners in the American colonies?
5. How was American slavery different from slavery elsewhere?
6. Why was the Enlightenment welcomed in America?

Thinking Critically

1. **Synthesizing.** Imagine that you are the 26-year-old widow Martha Dandridge Custis. What advantages might you have over a European woman of your time? What major advantages does a twentieth-century American woman have over a colonial woman?
2. **Drawing Conclusions.** How did the availability of land and the scarcity of labor help make life in colonial America more democratic than it was in England?
3. **Evaluating.** Do you think "Yankee ingenuity" was a positive or a negative quality? Why? How did northern colonists use it to find a means of paying for the European goods they wanted? Do you think Americans still have "Yankee ingenuity"? Explain your answer.

Writing About History

An important point in this chapter is that the great amount of land in America affected the lives of the colonists. Suppose you are an American colonist. Write a letter to a friend in Europe explaining how the abundance of land affected one of the following: women, indentured servants, slaves, American Indians.

Practicing the Strategy

Review the strategies on pages 78 and 103.

Reading Graphs. Study the pie graph on page 89 and answer these questions.

1. What percentage of the colonial population was African? Where does that percentage rank?
2. The English, Scotch-Irish, and Scottish were all British. What percentage of the total population did the British make up?
3. What three groups represent the smallest percentages of the colonial population?

Creating a Graphic Representation. Reread the information on the Great Awakening on pages 95 to 98. Then create a word web of at least five terms centered on The Great Awakening.

Using Primary Sources

Being a freed slave in the South often meant being on your guard. Southerners began to fear the large number of freed slaves living in their midst. North Carolina and other states passed laws providing a reward for the capture and resale of "illegally" freed slaves. In 1797 Thomas Pritchet and three other freed slaves petitioned the House of Representatives for federal protection. After some debate the House voted to not accept the petition, leaving the fate of freed slaves to the individual states. Read the excerpt from the *Annals of the Congress of the United States,* 4th Cong., 2nd Sess. (1796–97) to get a sense of the struggle slaves faced. Then answer the questions.

> *I, Thomas Pritchet, was set free by my master Thomas Pritchet, who furnished me with land . . . where I built myself a house, cleared a sufficient spot of woodland to produce ten bushels of corn; . . . this I was obliged to leave . . . being threatened by Holland Lockwood, who married my said master's widow, that if I would not come and serve him, he would apprehend me, and send me to the West Indies; Enoch Ralph also threatening to send me to jail, and to sell me. . . . Being thus in jeopardy, I . . . escaped by night into Virginia. . . . where shipping myself to Boston, I was landed in New York, where I served as a waiter for seventeen months; but my mind being distressed on account of the situation of my wife and children, I returned to Norfolk in Virginia, with the hope of seeing them; but finding I was advertised in the newspaper, twenty dollars the reward for apprehending me, my dangerous situation obliged me to leave Virginia.*

1. Give two examples from the excerpt to show that Pritchet's freedom was often threatened.
2. How might you defend Pritchet's argument that he was a free person? How might you defend Holland Lockwood's belief that Pritchet was not a free person?
3. Why did Pritchet return to Virginia? Why did he leave again?

Linking History & Geography

Almost all of the early cities in America developed on a body of water. Research the location of the first colonial cities and draw a map showing their locations. Then in a brief essay explain why the first cities developed on bodies of water, using one city as a specific example.

Enriching Your Study of History

1. **Individual Project.** Some colonial business leaders advertised in England to persuade more European settlers to come to America. Draw an eye-catching poster with an attention-getting slogan for a group of these business leaders.
2. **Cooperative Project.** On page 99 there are examples of slogans or wise sayings from *Poor Richard's Almanack.* With your classmates write three of your own slogans. Consider such subjects as good health, friendship, and good study habits. Put your slogans on a poster and compare them with those of the rest of the class. What do you conclude makes a good slogan? Try to reach a class consensus in your discussion.

106 LIFE IN COLONIAL AMERICA

Chapter 3 Review 107

West African Heritage, America's Hispanic Heritage, and America's Pacific Heritage. The first contains unique works by American Indian artisans. The last three present beautiful and representative works of art from the native lands of their group's members.

A   **Linking History & Geography** features appear on beige pages. These two-page features are part of the narrative and appear in each unit. They highlight the importance of geography in the unfolding of America's history. Most contain beautifully detailed maps.

7. **Reviewing your study.** To check your understanding and to help you remember what you have learned, always take time to review.

B   When you finish a section, return to the Preview & Review and answer the questions. Complete the **Chapter Review** when you finish your study of the chapter. Do the same for the **Unit Review.**

8. **Use the Reference Section.** *The Story of America* provides a **Reference Section.** When you want to know the meaning of a boldfaced term, turn to the **Glossary,** which begins on page 1149. Entries are listed alphabetically, with page references for pages in the text where the word appears in boldface type. When you need to know on which page something is mentioned, turn to the **Index,** which begins on page 1181. Index entries are always in alphabetical order. Become familiar with the rest of the **Reference Section,** which contains an atlas and charts and graphs full of data about the story of America.

Studying Primary Sources

There are many sources of historical information. They include diaries, journals, and letters; memoirs and autobiographies; paintings and photographs; editorials and editorial cartoons. All of these are *primary sources.* They give firsthand eyewitness accounts of history.

Primary sources appear frequently in *The Story of America,* for they are the historian's most important tool. You should use primary sources, usually bracketed by large quotation marks, to gain an understanding of events that only eyewitness accounts can provide.

How to Study Primary Sources

To study primary sources, follow these guidelines.

1. **Read the material carefully.** Look for main ideas and supporting details. Note what the writer or speaker has to say about the atmosphere or the mood of the people.
2. **Ask yourself questions.** Ask *who* or *what* is described. If sources conflict, and they often might, *who* is speaking and *what special insights do they have?* You may also want to ask *why* an action took place.
3. **Check for bias.** Be alert for words, phrases, or information that present a one-sided view of a person or situation when it seems evident that more than one point of view is possible.
4. **When possible, compare sources.** Study more than one primary source on a topic if available. By comparing what they have to say, you can get a much more complete picture than by using only one source.

Also, remember that historians use *secondary sources* as well as primary sources. These are descriptions or interpretations of events written after the events have occurred. History books such as *The Story of America,* biographies, encyclopedias, and other reference works are examples of secondary sources.

Developing Historical Imagination

When we read history, we tend to form opinions about events in the past. Sometimes these opinions can keep us from fully understanding history. To judge people and events of the past using today's standards can lead to a false picture of history. We need instead to develop our historical imagination.

To develop historical imagination, we need to put ourselves in the place of those who lived in the past. In that way we can better see why they thought and acted as they did. Remember that science, education, and all other fields of endeavor have advanced greatly in a relatively short time. So it is important to keep in mind what people in the past knew and *what they did not know.* Throughout

The Story of America you will have the opportunity to use your historical imagination, to take yourself back to another time.

Writing About History

Writing is an important intellectual process. It helps us clarify our thoughts, learn information, and discover new ideas. *The Story of America* contains numerous writing opportunities. Although you may not always have time to use them all, the guidelines that follow can help you improve your writing. This is especially true of longer writing assignments.

How to Write More Effectively

To write more effectively, follow these guidelines.

1. **Prewrite.** Prewriting includes all the thinking and planning that you do before you write. Before you write, ask yourself these questions: Why am I writing? Who will read my writing? What will I write about? What will I say about the topic? How will I organize my ideas?
2. **Collect information.** Do research if necessary. You can write more effectively if you have many details to choose from.
3. **Write a first draft and evaluate it.** In your first draft, remember to use your prewriting plan as a guide. Write freely, but consider your purpose and audience.

   As you review and evaluate your first draft, note places where you need to add or clarify. It may help to read your draft aloud or to exchange it with a partner.
4. **Revise and proofread your draft.** Add, cut, replace, and reorganize your draft as needed to say what you want to say. Then check for proper spelling, punctuation, and grammar.
5. **Write your final version.** Prepare a neat and clean final version. Remember that appearance is important. Although it does not affect the quality of your writing itself, it can affect the way your writing is perceived and understood.

Many writing opportunities in *The Story of America* ask you to create a specific type of writing—a diary entry, a letter, an advertisement, a poem, or a newspaper editorial. Most of these opportunities ask you to use your historical imagination—to write from the point of view of a person living then rather than now.

A diary is a personal log of your experiences. Each entry is dated and is a brief statement of what has happened and your reactions. Your diary entries should be the personal recollections of a person *at a particular time in history.*

You are probably familiar with writing letters. When you write a letter, be sure to indicate to whom you are writing and include in your letter the specific details called for in the assignment.

You also are probably familiar with advertisements. An effective advertisement captures the attention and highlights an important feature of the "product." When you develop an advertisement, make it memorable and to the point.

Writing a poem often can seem difficult. Remember, however, that poems do not have to rhyme. An example of such free verse is Carl Sandburg's "Chicago" on pages 789-90. Notice that although the lines do not rhyme, they are organized in a specific way. That is what makes it poetry. When you write a poem, let the words flow but keep them focused.

A newspaper editorial is a statement of opinion or point of view. It states a stand about an issue and provides the reasons for that stand. You might wish to read the editorial page of your local paper to see how the editorials are written there.

Using the guidelines listed in this section together with those developed in the *Strategies for Success* should help you write with confidence as you study *The Story of America.* Remember to have a plan and to use historical imagination when it is called for. Now, enjoy *The Story of America.*

THE STORY OF
America

To the Student

The Story of America tells our story because it is important in itself. It is a great epic and the unique tale of how hundreds of millions of people came to live on this vast continent, while the original inhabitants lost their lands. There are other reasons for telling our story. It may be read as a grand lesson that permits us to understand how past affects present. Our story is composed of many pasts that allow us to explain how our present experiment in democracy has gone on for more than 200 years. Thus we read history knowing full well that those who study the past can come to understand who we are and how far we've come and are sometimes able to caution us about our present course toward the future. But we also realize that historians have never been any better at telling the future than politicians, economists, or fortune tellers.

The Story of America was written especially for you, young Americans born in the last half of the 20th century. It provides the background to help you know about the people and values that make America great. It also presents the many controversies and challenges that have faced Americans from time to time throughout history. You can learn from their successes—and failures.

The author of *The Story of America* is ever mindful that chronology is the spine of history. Events are presented in the order in which they occurred. Time lines at the end of each chapter help you see and remember the chronology of important events.

The Story of America contains many original documents and lengthy excerpts from primary and secondary sources. These include eyewitness accounts, poems, song lyrics, diary entries, and excerpts from a variety of other sources. These materials can give you special insight into the thinking and attitudes of Americans. *The Story of America* also is filled with striking and memorable illustrations. These paintings, photographs, and other illustrations may indeed be worth a thousand words. Each captures a bit of the history of its time. The illustrations in *The Story of America* also show changing aspects of American life such as dress, art, and architecture.

An integral part of the story of America is the relationship of people to the land. The beautifully detailed maps and special geography features in *The Story of America* illustrate this relationship and show its importance in the unfolding of our nation's story. The textbook also introduces you to the five themes of geography: location, place, relationships within places, movement, and regions. Charts, graphs, tables, and diagrams highlight the economic and sociological trends. Together, they portray a nation that has grown dramatically from such small beginnings.

When you have finished *The Story of America* you should understand the democratic values and ethical ideas that guide the American people and appreciate the civic responsibilities of all Americans to participate in American democracy. *The Story of America* will help you recognize the multicultural character of the American society and have empathy for the struggles of people to secure a place in society. With this information you will be able to take your place in society as an informed voter, more appreciative of the legacy that is the story of America.

UNIT OBJECTIVES
Upon Completing Unit 6, students will be able to:
1. Analyze the factors that led to the end of Indian independence.
2. Recognize the geographic and economic impact of settlement of the Great Plains.
3. Describe the impact of the growth of industry following the Civil War.
4. Trace the origins of immigration and the patterns of settlement after 1880.
5. Evaluate the benefits and drawbacks of big-city political machines.
6. Identify the major political issues in the years after the Civil War.

Parts I and II of the Annotated Teacher's Edition of *The Story of America* both include a complete Table of Contents and other front matter, and a complete Reference Section, including Glossary and Index. Part I contains Units 1–5. Part II contains Units 6–10.

The Fine Arts Museum of San Francisco

The arrival of the daily train to Sacramento, California, is the subject of "Sacramento Railway Station."

OVERVIEW
The government policy of concentration, the slaughter of the buffalo, and the building of the transcontinental railroad all led to the end of Indian independence. New farming techniques and inventions made it possible to turn the Great Plains into the breadbasket of America. America was in transition between 1860 and 1900 with industrial growth, the growth of labor unions, increased immigration, and the growth of cities. National politics between 1867 and 1896 revolved around three major issues: the tariff, the money question, and civil service reform. The Populist party grew out of farmers' attempts to increase their political power. American culture changed with the times as the realism of the Industrial Age replaced the romanticism of earlier times.

A CHANGING AMERICA — UNIT 6

CONNECTING WITH PAST LEARNING
Ask students to define the term *progress*. Then point out that in this unit they will be studying about an era in American history that was full of progress and change. Settlers pushed west, the Industrial Revolution transformed life in the United States, and new political alliances emerged. Tell students to keep this in mind as they study the unit.

I n Unit 6 you will learn why Native Americans of the Plains lost their lands to white settlers and how the United States became one of the world's great industrial nations. Here are some main points to keep in mind as you read the unit.

- After the Civil War, thousands of Americans from the East moved westward to the Great Plains and other regions of the West.
- Andrew Carnegie, John D. Rockefeller, and others built huge industrial empires.
- Immigrants from Northwestern European lands such as Germany and Scandinavia poured into the United States.
- Mark Twain wrote *Tom Sawyer*, and James McNeill Whistler painted *Mrs. George Washington Whistler*, now known as "Whistler's Mother."
- The populist movement championed the interest of farmers and labor.

The Last Frontier

PLANNING THE CHAPTER	
TEXTBOOK	**RESOURCES**
1. The Battle for the Plains	**Unit 6 Worksheets and Tests:** Chapter 18 Graphic Organizer, Directed Reading 18:1, Reteaching 18:1, Geography 18A and 18B **Creative Strategies for Teaching American History:** Pages 271, 319 **Eyewitnesses and Others, Volume 1:** Reading 67: The Blackfoot Genesis (1800s) **Eyewitnesses and Others, Volume 2:** Reading 5: Chinese Railroad Workers on the Frontier (1865–1890) **Art in American History:** Transparency 15: Navajo Eye Dazzler Blanket
2. Indian Wars	**Unit 6 Worksheets and Tests:** Directed Reading 18:2, Reteaching 18:2, Geography 18C **Creative Strategies for Teaching American History:** Page 281 **Eyewitnesses and Others, Volume 2:** Reading 1: Speeches of Seattle and Ten Bears (1854, 1867), Reading 7: Annie Bidwell Attends a Mechoopda Dance (1870s) **Voices of America: Speeches and Documents:** Chief Joseph's ''I Shall Fight No More Forever''
3. Mining the West	**Unit 6 Worksheets and Tests:** Directed Reading 18:3, Reteaching 18:3 **Eyewitnesses and Others, Volume 2:** Reading 15: A Teacher's Life in the Common Schools (1888), Reading 17: Lesson One from McGuffey's *Eclectic Fourth Reader* (1880s)
4. The End of the Open Range	**Unit 6 Worksheets and Tests:** Directed Reading 18:4, Reteaching 18:4 **American History Map Transparencies:** Transparency 6: Cattle Trails, Railroads, and Mining Centers **Art in American History:** Transparency 17: Prospecting for Cattle Range **Eyewitnesses and Others, Volume 2:** Reading 8: The Vaquero (1870s), Reading 10: Cowpunching on the Texas Trail (1883), Special Feature: Two Cowboy Songs (with music), Reading 9: Wolves and Grasshoppers Plague the Kansas Frontier (1870s), Reading 2: A Norwegian Pioneer Woman Describes Her New Home in Iowa (1863–1865)

Chapter Review	*Audio Program:* Chapter 18 *Unit 6 Worksheets and Tests:* Chapter 18 Tests, Forms A and B (See also *Alternative Assessment Forms*) *Test Generator*

STRATEGIES FOR STUDENTS WITH SPECIAL NEEDS

Gifted Students.
Have students research and prepare a statistical chart showing the population of the states of the Great Plains in 10-year intervals from 1870 to 1900. The list of states should include the following: North Dakota, South Dakota, Nebraska, Kansas, Oklahoma, Texas, Montana, Wyoming, Colorado, and New Mexico. Based on the statistics they have gathered for their charts, have students draw conclusions about why some states grew more rapidly than others and why population growth declined after 1890.

Students Having Difficulty with the Chapter.
You may wish to have students listen to Chapter 18 in *The Story of America Audio Program.* Then organize the class into eight cooperative learning groups. Assign each group one of the following Indian tribes: Arapaho, Arikara, Cheyenne, Comanche, Crow, Mandan, Pawnee, Sioux. Have each group research their tribe and prepare a pictorial essay to be presented to the class. Essays may include newspaper and magazine clippings, drawings, and photographs. Each group member should be prepared to demonstrate his or her contribution by describing their drawing or picture to the class.

BOOKS FOR TEACHERS
Ray A. Billington and James B. Hedges, *Westward Expansion: A History of the American Frontier.* New York: Macmillan, 1974.

Joe B. Frantz and Julian E. Choate, *The American Cowboy: The Myth and the Reality.* Norman: University of Oklahoma Press, 1955.

William T. Hagan, *American Indians.* Chicago: University of Chicago Press, 1961.

P. N. Limerick, *The Legacy of Conquest: The Unbroken Past of the American West.* New York: Norton, 1987.

Rodman W. Paul, *Mining Frontiers of the Far West, 1848–1880.* Austin: Holt, Rinehart and Winston, 1963.

BOOKS FOR STUDENTS
Bess Streeter Aldrich, *A Lantern in Her Hand.* Mattituck, NY: Amereon, 1928.

Stephen Vincent Benét, *The Ballad of William Sycamore.* Boston: Little, Brown, 1972.

Dee Brown (adapted by Linda Proctor), *Lonesome Whistle: The Story of the First Transcontinental Railroad.* Austin: Holt, Rinehart and Winston, 1980.

Willa Cather, *My Ántonia.* Boston: Houghton Mifflin, 1962.

Pamela Conrad, *Prairie Song.* New York: Harper & Row, 1985.

Russell Davis, *Chief Joseph: War Chief of the Nez Perce.* New York: McGraw-Hill, 1962.

Louis L'Amour, *How the West Was Won.* Thorndike, ME: Thorndike Press, 1988.

Eloise McGraw, *Moccasin Trail.* New York: Coward, 1952.

Liza Ketchum Murrow, *West Against the Wind.* New York: Holiday, 1987.

Theodore Taylor, *Walking up a Rainbow.* New York: Delacorte, 1986.

Ann Turner, *Third Girl From the Left.* New York: Macmillan, 1986.

MULTIMEDIA MATERIALS
Andrew J. Russell—A Visual Historian (film, 29 min.), EBEC. Focuses on the man who used his camera to capture pivotal events of the 1800s.

The Big Push West—American Episode 1865–1886 (film, 24 min.), Graphic Curriculum. Deals with Indians, buffalo, cattle, and range wars.

The Closing Frontier (filmstrip), EBEC. Details the last days of the open range.

Donner Pass: The Road to Survival (videocassette, 98 min.), SSSS. Dramatizes the Donner party.

The Oregon Trail (software), SSSS. Students assume roles of various Americans on their journey West.

Settling the West (filmstrip), SSSS. Series of six filmstrips that detail settling the West.

SUGGESTED CAPTION RESPONSE
No, they killed only what they needed for food and used all parts of the animal, including its bones.

RESOURCES
■ You may wish to have students complete the Chapter 18 Graphic Organizer as they work through this chapter.

CHAPTER OBJECTIVES
Upon completing this chapter, students will be able to:
1. Explain why the buffalo and horse were important to the Plains Indians.
2. Analyze the factors that led to the end of Indian independence.

OVERVIEW
The demand for land by settlers led to a series of conflicts with the Plains Indians. The government policy of concentration helped to end Indian independence. New farming techniques and inventions made it possible to farm on the plains.

**FOCUS/MOTIVATION:
MAKING CONNECTIONS
Prior Knowledge.**
Write the name of each of the following groups as a heading on the chalkboard or an overhead projector: *Plains Indians, Mexican American settlers, miners, cowhands,* and *farmers.* Then ask students to give words and phrases they associate with the Plains Indians. Write down all suggestions. *(Responses should include bows and arrows, horses, buffalo, teepees.)* Follow this procedure for Mexican American settlers, miners, cowhands, and farmers. To see how the five groups relate to one another, go back through the list to see whether any words or phrases appear under more than one group. Have students discuss the relationships of these groups to each other.

CHAPTER 18

The Last Frontier

■ The history of the Plains Indians shows that truth is often stranger and more interesting than fiction. A favorite subject of American books and movies is the "Winning of the West," or the plunder of the prairie and the end of the American Indian way of life, depending on your point of view. For about a hundred years, from around 1780 to 1880, the Plains Indians lived in the midst of an immense grassland, feeding upon the numberless buffalo and moving freely on their fleet ponies. Yet much of their culture was a direct result of the Indians' adopting such elements of European civilization as horses, guns, and metal tools. And in the end the European lust for land, the diseases spread by the conquerors and settlers, and the deadly efficiency of America's mechanical genius ended the Plains civilization. With the discovery of vast gold, silver, and copper deposits on the Indian lands—and the buffalo's grazing lands taken by the ranchers of the cattle kingdom—could there be much hope for the first Americans and their independent way of life?

The Great Plains is strewn with skulls in Albert Bierstadt's 1889 oil painting, "The Last of the Buffalo." But would Plains Indians have been such wasteful killers?

In the collection of The Corcoran Gallery of Art, Gift of Mrs. Albert Bierstadt, 1909

OBJECTIVES *(Continued)*

3. Discuss the role of the railroads in the settlement of the West.
4. Describe life in a mining town.
5. Describe the life of a cowhand.
6. Describe the place characteristics of the Great Plains.
7. Identify new inventions and farming techniques that turned the Great Plains into the breadbasket of America.
8. Demonstrate the ability to form hypotheses and draw conclusions about economic and social activities of various regions by reading a climate map.

1. THE BATTLE FOR THE PLAINS

The Great Plains

The vast region we call the **Great Plains** extends from western Texas north to the Dakotas and on into Canada. Endless acres of grassland roll westward from the Mississippi, gradually rising until they reach the towering ranges of the Rocky Mountains. Explorers and hunters once described this region and the mountains beyond as the **"Great American Desert,"** although it was *no* desert. Before the 1850s the Spanish Americans in the Southwest and the Mormons in Utah had made the only permanent settlements in this huge area with its few lonely travelers.

The land of the Great Plains is mostly level. There are few trees. Winter blizzards roar unchecked out of the Arctic. Temperatures fall far below freezing. In summer the thermometer can soar halfway to the boiling point when hot winds sweep north from Mexico.

Until well after the Civil War, farming on the plains seemed impossible. There was too little rain to raise crops and no wood to build houses or fences. Most people thought the desert was home only for the donkey-eared jackrabbit, the prairie dog, the antelope, the wolflike coyote, and the great, shaggy buffalo. The buffalo in particular seemed the lords of the Great Plains, by their numbers alone. About 12 million of them grazed on the seemingly arid prairie there at the time the Civil War ended.

The Plains Indians

Long before the European settlement of America, many people lived on the Great Plains. They knew it was not really a desert. These were the Plains Indians. They had survived and prospered there for thousands of years.

There were 31 Plains tribes. The **Apache** and **Comanche** lived in Texas and eastern New Mexico. The **Pawnee** occupied western Nebraska, the **Sioux** the Dakotas. The **Cheyenne** and **Arapaho** were the principal tribes of the central plains. In 1850 these tribes contained about 175,000 people. Although they spoke many different languages, all could communicate with one another. They had developed a complex and efficient sign language.

The Plains Indians differed from tribe to tribe. Some were divided into several groups, or bands, of about 500 people each. The Cheyenne, for example, consisted of ten bands with names like the Aorta Band, the Hairy Band, the Scabby Band, and the Dogmen Band. Although each band was a separate community, bands joined together for religious ceremonies and to fight other tribes or the European invaders. Their chiefs and councils of elders acted mostly as judges. Their decisions were enforced by small groups of warriors

Preview & Review

Use these questions to guide your reading. Answer the questions after completing Section 1.
Understanding Issues, Events, & Ideas. Using the following words, trace the history of the Plains Indians: Great Plains; "Great American Desert"; Apache; Comanche; Pawnee; Sioux; Cheyenne; Arapaho; concentration; divide and conquer; Pacific Railway Act; right of way; Promontory, Utah; transcontinental railroad; Mexican American.
1. Why did farming on the Great Plains seem impossible?
2. What was the purpose of the system of concentration?
3. How did Congress encourage the building of a transcontinental railroad?
4. Why were settlers in the Southwest able to gain much of the land held for many years by Mexican Americans?
Thinking Critically. 1. Imagine that you are a member of the Dogmen Band. Describe a typical day in your life. 2. It is 1865. You are a Chinese worker on the Central Pacific railroad line. Write a letter to your family in China, describing your job.

PREVIEW & REVIEW RESPONSES
Understanding Issues, Events, & Ideas.
Paragraphs should demonstrate an understanding of the terms used.
1. There was too little rain and no wood for building houses or fences.
2. The purpose was to divide the Indians so they could be conquered separately.
3. Congress passed the Pacific Railway Act which granted a charter to the Union Pacific Railroad to build a line west-ward from Nebraska, and the Central Pacific Railway to build a line east-ward from the Pacific.
4. The land-hungry settlers took advantage of the fact that most of the land was not registered.

Thinking Critically.
1. Students should use historical imagination when describing their lives as members of the Dogmen Band.
2. Student letters should demonstrate an understanding of work on the Central Pacific railroad from the Chinese immigrant's point of view.

① Some of the Plains Indian tribes had a practice called "counting coup." This involved having an Indian brave touch an enemy warrior or capture his weapon and escape without bloodshed.

Little rainfall; innovative farming techniques and inventions

RESOURCES
■ You may wish to have students view Transparency 15: "Navajo Eye Dazzler" and complete the accompanying worksheet in *Art in American History*.

FOCUS/MOTIVATION: MAKING CONNECTIONS
Student Experiences.
To reinforce the geographic theme of *location,* have students look at a classroom map and locate and identify the states that are part of the Great Plains. *(North Dakota, South Dakota, Nebraska, Kansas, Oklahoma, western Texas, eastern Montana, eastern Wyoming, eastern Colorado, eastern New Mexico.)* To provide students the opportunity to consider *place* characteristics of the Plains states, ask students if any of them have ever lived or traveled through these states. If they have, ask them to describe the physical appearance of this region. If they have not, ask them what they think this region is like. *(They should mention that it is flat, with few trees, and contains many farms.)* Tell them to keep this in mind as they read this section.

RELATING HISTORY TO GEOGRAPHY
After reading the description of the Great Plains in their textbook under the title "The Great Plains," have students research and write a report on the ways that people have adapted to the geography of this region. Their report should include a description of the earliest inhabitants as well as the later Indian and white settlers.

called soldier bands. The soldier bands settled disputes between band members, punished those who broke tribal laws, and protected the group against surprise attacks.

Within the circle of their band, warriors tried to prove their courage and daring on the battlefield. To touch an enemy or capture ① his weapon was proof of highest bravery, called counting coup.

The Plains Indians, as we have seen, had always depended heavily on the buffalo. After the European invasion of America they also captured and tamed wild horses. Spanish explorers had brought the first horses with them to America. Some of these animals escaped and ran wild. Eventually, large herds roamed the West.

■ The Indians quickly became expert riders. On horseback they were better hunters and fighters. They could cover large distances swiftly and run down buffalo and other game. Horses became so

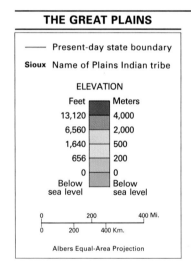

THE GREAT PLAINS

—— Present-day state boundary

Sioux Name of Plains Indian tribe

ELEVATION

Feet	Meters
13,120	4,000
6,560	2,000
1,640	500
656	200
0	0
Below sea level	Below sea level

0   200   400 Mi.
0 200 400 Km.

Albers Equal-Area Projection

LEARNING FROM MAPS. *Many of the first European explorers of the Great Plains considered it a desert. Today, however, it is a region of rich agricultural production. Why did some of the first explorers consider it a desert? What has made it productive today?*

Courtesy Colorado Historical Society

important to the Plains Indians that many tribes went to war against their neighbors for them. Many counted their wealth in horses. Some paid their debts with horses. Some men swapped horses for wives.

Indians wore many kinds of clothing. In some tribes the men 1 wore breechcloths and long leggings which went from hip to ankle. During the winter they wore buffalo robes. Women might wear sleeveless dresses made of deerskin. In desert regions Indians wore moccasins with double leather soles for protection against the heat or the hard ground.

The typical Plains warrior carried a bow about three feet long ■ (nearly one meter). It was usually made of bone or ash wood. His arrows had points made of bone, flint, or metal. Some warriors were armed with long, stone-tipped lances and carried round shields made of buffalo hide. These buffalo-hide shields were smoked and hardened with glue made from buffalo hooves. They were so tough that bullets striking them at an angle would not go through.

In battle an Indian warrior could fire off half a dozen arrows from his stubby, powerful bow while an enemy was cramming a single bullet into his muzzle-loading rifle. Galloping on horseback at full speed, a warrior could shoot arrows so fast that the next would be in the air before the first found its target. These arrows struck with great force. At short range an Indian could sink the entire shaft of an arrow into the body of a buffalo.

The simplicity of the lives of Plains Indians is depicted in S.C. Stobie's "Indian Camp." From your other reading and observations, how much 1 *can you find in this camp that is already familiar to you—in lodging, family roles, child care, food preparation, and so on?*

The Battle for the Plains 625

① Many of the supplies the U.S. government sent the Indians were inadequate. The food was often spoiled and the blankets filled with bugs.

SUGGESTED CAPTION RESPONSE
Students may mention that Indians often traveled in large groups that included their families.

RESOURCES
■ You may wish to have students complete Essay 34: "Indians vs. Settlers: The View from Both Sides" in *From Plymouth Rock to the Cincinnati Reds.*

RELATING HISTORY TO GEOGRAPHY
Have students look at the map titled "Western Railroads and Cattle Trails" in Section 4. Using the scale of miles on the map, ask them the following questions: Approximately how long is the Great Northern Railroad between Seattle and Duluth? *(approximately 1,450 miles—2,320 kilometers)* Approximately how long is the Kansas Pacific between Kansas City and Denver? *(approximately 550 miles—880 kilometers)* Approximately how long is the Southern Pacific between Los Angeles and New Orleans? *(approximately 1,720 miles—2,752 kilometers)*
Have students discuss how the building of the railroads permanently changed the Old West.

MULTICULTURAL PERSPECTIVES: USING HISTORICAL IMAGINATION
Have students imagine that they are Mexican Americans who live in the southwestern United States following the Treaty of Guadalupe Hidalgo. They watch as settlers come pouring into the area from other parts of the United States. Many of the original settlers have already lost their land titles to the newcomers. They are to attempt to stop this injustice by first writing a warning to other Mexican Americans stating how they feel about this situation. Then have them write an appeal to the federal government pleading the cause of the Mexican Americans. You may wish to have some of the students present their warnings and pleas to the class.

Mabel Brady Garvan Collection, Yale University Art Gallery

Fort Laramie, shown in this water-color sketch by Alfred Jacob Miller, was a fur-trading post built in 1834. The army bought it in 1849 to protect travelers on the Oregon Trail. How does this picture add to the description of Indian life begun on page 623?

Removing the Plains Indians

■ The Plains Indians rarely came into conflict with settlers before the 1850s. They usually traded in peace with hunters. The pioneers who crossed the plains on their way to Oregon avoided the Indians.

In the early 1850s settlers began moving into Kansas and Nebraska. After the Mexican War, promoters planned to build railroads to the Pacific through the newly won territory. They demanded that the government remove the Plains Indians from this territory.

In 1851 agents of the United States called a meeting of the principal Plains tribes at Fort Laramie, in what is now Wyoming. The agents persuaded the Indians to sign the Fort Laramie Treaty. The Indians agreed to stay within limited areas. In exchange the
① government would give them food, money, and presents.

This new system was called **concentration**. It was a way of dividing the Indians so that they could be conquered separately. **Divide and conquer** is a very old military strategy. Once a tribe had agreed to live in a particular region, it could be forced to give up its holdings without arousing the others. Neither side fully realized that this would mean the end of the Plains culture.

As soon as Senator Stephen A. Douglas pushed the Kansas-Nebraska Act through Congress, settlers and storekeepers came pouring into lands that had been reserved for the Indians. The Indians were pushed into even smaller areas. By 1860 there were very few native Americans left in Kansas and Nebraska.

Railroads in the West

In 1862 Congress passed the **Pacific Railway Act.** This law granted a charter to the Union Pacific Railroad Company to build a line westward from Nebraska. Another company, the Central Pacific Railway ① of California, was authorized to build a connecting line eastward from the Pacific.

The government granted each company the **right of way**—the thin strip of land on which the tracks were actually laid. In addition it gave them large amounts of land for every mile of track built. This land could be sold and the money used for construction. Or it could be held in reserve and sold later when the land became more valuable. The government also lent the companies large amounts of money at low interest. Private fortunes were to be had here.

The Central Pacific employed thousands of Chinese immigrants to lay its tracks. Most of the Union Pacific workers came from Ireland. All were underpaid. Construction got under way in 1865. ②

Building the railroad was tremendously difficult. The Central Pacific had to cross the snow-capped Sierra Nevada range. Omaha, Nebraska, where the Union Pacific began, had not yet been connected to eastern railroads. Thousands of tons of rails, crossties, and

While Chinese railroad workers watch, the Central Pacific train enters a snow shed in the Sierra Nevada. Snow sheds kept tracks clear and gave some protection to the wooden cars in the event of an avalanche. Why is it so appropriate that the workers pictured are Chinese Americans?

Thomas Gilcrease Institute

The Battle for the Plains 627

SUGGESTED CAPTION RESPONSE
Because the east and west coasts of the U.S. were now connected.

(1865-1890)" in Volume II of *Eyewitnesses and Others*.

RESOURCES
■ You may wish to have students complete Reading 5: "Chinese Railroad Workers on the Frontier

CHECKING UNDERSTANDING
Have students discuss the factors that led to the loss of independence of the Plains Indians. *(Students should mention the following: The government policy of concentration, which was a way of dividing the Indians so that they could be conquered; the wanton slaughter of the buffalo by white hunters; the building of the transcontinental railroad, which brought additional settlers to the Plains.)*

RETEACHING STRATEGY:
Students with Special Needs.
Pair students who are having difficulty with students who are performing well. Have the more proficient students ask the others the following questions:
1. What were some of the Indian tribes that lived on the Great Plains? *(Apache, Comanche, Pawnee, Cheyenne, Arapaho)*
2. Why was the loss of the buffalo harmful to the Plains Indians? *(The buffalo provided them with food, shelter, and clothing.)*
3. Why was the federal government's policy of concentration harmful to the Plains Indians? *(It forced them to live on lands unlike their traditional homes, totally disrupting their culture, and in particular regions where they couldn't unite to fight unfair encroachment on their land.)*
4. Why was the building of the railroads in the West harmful to the Plains Indians? *(Railroads, built across Indian lands, brought more white settlers to the Plains.)*

other supplies had to be shipped up the Missouri River by boat or hauled across Iowa by wagon.

■ The two companies competed with each other in order to get the lion's share of the land and money authorized by the Pacific Railway Act. Charles Crocker, manager of the Central Pacific's construction crews, drove his men mercilessly. During one winter they dug tunnels through 40-foot (12-meter) snowdrifts high in the Sierras in order to lay tracks on the frozen ground.

The two lines met on May 10, 1869, at **Promontory,** Utah. The Union Pacific had built 1,086 miles of track (1,738 kilometers), the Central Pacific 689 miles (1,102 kilometers). There was a great celebration. Leland Stanford of the Central Pacific was given the honor of hammering home the last spike connecting the two rails. The spike was of gold, the hammer of silver.

Soon other **transcontinental railroads** were built. These included the Atchison, Topeka & Santa Fe and the Southern Pacific in the Southwest and the Northern Pacific, which ran south of the Canadian border. The transcontinentals connected with the eastern railroads at Chicago, St. Louis, and New Orleans. Once they were completed, a traveler could go from the Atlantic Coast to San Francisco and other Pacific Coast cities in a week's time. The swiftest clipper ship had taken three months to make the journey from New York to San Francisco.

This painting shows "East and West Shaking Hands" in the 1869 meeting of the Union Pacific and Central Pacific at Promontory, Utah. Why was this a day to celebrate?

Union Pacific Railroad

Larry Sheerin

Theodore Gentilz, whose paintings capture much of our Spanish heritage, called this scene "Selling of the Cardinals on the Plaza." Research the layout of a typical Spanish settlement with its plaza, church, and workshops.

INDEPENDENT PRACTICE
Have students complete the Preview & Review activity at the beginning of the section.

CLOSURE
Point out to students that both Native Americans and Mexican Americans lost their land when land-hungry settlers began pouring into the Great Plains, the West, and the Southwest.

HOMEWORK
Have students prepare reports on the settlement of the Southwest. Their reports should include a description of life on one of the major western routes and a map showing the following: the Santa Fe Trail, the Old Spanish Trail, the Overland Mail Route, Los Angeles, San Diego, Santa Fe, Albuquerque, El Paso, St. Joseph, Independence, St. Louis should accompany their reports. They should discuss the impact of the geographic theme of *place* on the life they describe. For information students should check the map of the routes to the west in Chapter 12 and an historical atlas in their school or local library.

Settling the Southwest

During these same years settlers poured into the Southwest—western Texas, New Mexico, Arizona, and southern California—to look for gold, raise cattle, and claim land. When they arrived, they found the land occupied by Mexican Americans. These people were the descendants of the Mexicans who found themselves in United States territory after the Treaty of Guadalupe Hidalgo. Rather than learn Spanish, most settlers looked down on the Mexican Americans. The newcomers treated the old settlers like foreigners.

This was unjust. Many Mexican Americans had lived on their land long before it became United States territory. The land-hungry settlers discovered that most of the land was not registered. Often they simply claimed the already occupied land or bought it from the territorial government. By the 1880s Mexican Americans owned but one fourth of the land they had owned in 1848. 🖳

Return to the Preview & Review on page 623.

HISTORICAL SIDELIGHTS

1 The Chivington Massacre is also known as the Sand Creek Massacre.

SUGGESTED CAPTION RESPONSE

Student answers will vary, but should be based on historical fact.

PREVIEW & REVIEW RESPONSES

Understanding Issues, Events, & Ideas.

Explanations should demonstrate an understanding of the terms used.

1. It cut through the rolling foothills of the Big Horn Mountains, which were the hunting grounds of the western Sioux.

2. They were near starvation and could no longer hold out.

3. Helen Jackson attempted to show the public how poorly Indians were treated in her two books, *A Century of Dishonor* and *Ramona*. Sarah Winnemucca wrote a book and gave lectures on the unjust treatment of Indians and demanded that the U.S. return much of the land it had taken from the Indians.

4. It was written from the white point of view, ignoring Indian culture and tradition. It was an attempt to turn them into farmers, which would destroy their tribal traditions.

Thinking Critically.

1. Student obituaries should show an understanding of and sensitivity toward the great loss suffered by the Nez Perce upon the death of Chief Joseph.

2. Students should use historical imagination and show an understanding of the point of view from which they are writing.

Preview & Review

Use these questions to guide your reading. Answer the questions after you complete Section 2.

Understanding Issues, Events, & Ideas. Use the following words to explain the tragedies of the Indian Wars: Fifty-Niners, Chivington Massacre, Washita, Bozeman Trail, ambush, Battle of the Little Bighorn, Nez Perce, Wounded Knee, Dawes Severalty Act.

1. Why did the Sioux try to stop prospectors from using the Bozeman Trail?
2. What finally forced the Sioux to surrender?
3. How did Helen Hunt Jackson and Sarah Winnemucca help Indians?
4. How did the Dawes Act show lack of understanding of Indian ways of life?

Thinking Critically. 1. Write a newspaper obituary for Chief Joseph. 2. Write a diary entry about Wounded Knee from the point of view of either an Indian or a member of the 7th Cavalry.

Red Cloud, the Oglala Sioux chief, and his grandaughter Burning Heart were painted by Henry Cross. From your reading or a cooperative research project, what statements can you make to describe the family life of the Plains Indians?

The Thomas Gilcrease Institute of American History and Art, Tulsa, Oklahoma

2. INDIAN WARS

"Pikes Peak or Bust"

The transcontinental railroads brought many more settlers into the West. Wherever they went, fighting with the Indians followed. Even before the Civil War there was trouble in the Pikes Peak area of Colorado, where gold was discovered. By 1859 a seemingly endless stream of wagons was rolling across the plains. Many had the slogan "Pikes Peak or Bust!" lettered on their canvas covers. The attraction of the West remained the same: a new start for discontented Americans, mostly easterners.

About 100,000 of these **Fifty-Niners** elbowed their way onto Cheyenne and Arapaho land. The Indians fiercely resisted this invasion. Between 1861 and 1864 they rode several times into battle against army units. Then, in November 1864, Colonel John M. Chivington attacked a peaceful Cheyenne encampment at Sand Creek without warning. The Cheyenne, under Chief Black Kettle, tried to surrender by first raising an American flag and then a white flag of truce.

Chivington ignored these flags. "Kill and scalp all, big and little," he ordered. His soldiers scalped the men, ripped open the bodies of the women, and clubbed the little children to death with their gun butts.

1 During this **Chivington Massacre** about 450 Cheyenne were killed. The Cheyenne answered with equally bloody attacks on undefended white settlements. In 1868 the Cheyenne and Arapaho were defeated at **Washita,** in present-day Oklahoma. They were forced to settle on reservations, one in the Black Hills of Dakota, the other in Oklahoma.

Meanwhile, the Pikes Peak boom had become a bust. Little gold was found. About half the miners returned to their homes. This time the signs on their wagons read "Busted, By Gosh!"

Yet if Colorado had proved a bust, many prospectors still believed that gold could be found elsewhere. New prospectors crossed the Great Plains and spread through the mountains in the 1860s. Many followed a route pioneered by John M. Bozeman, a prospector from Georgia. This **Bozeman Trail** ran from Fort Laramie in Wyoming north to Montana. It cut through the rolling foothills of the Big Horn Mountains, the hunting grounds of the western Sioux.

The Sioux pitched their teepees beneath the sheltering mountains. There they hunted the plentiful game—deer, buffalo, elk, antelope, and bear. The Sioux chief, Red Cloud, protested strongly when prospectors and settlers began to use the new Bozeman Trail. He warned that the Sioux would fight to save their hunting grounds.

In 1865 Red Cloud's warriors made repeated attacks on white parties. The United States army responded by building forts along

630

SUGGESTED CAPTION RESPONSE
Estimates will vary, but students should indicate that the encampment was large.

Courtesy of The Library of Congress

the trail. In December 1866 an army supply caravan approaching one of the forts was attacked. When a small troop of soldiers commanded by Captain W. J. Fetterman appeared, Red Cloud's warriors quickly dashed off into the wilderness. Captain Fetterman foolishly followed them. He blundered into a trap, or **ambush.** Fetterman and all 82 of his soldiers were killed. A few months later John Bozeman himself ① was killed crossing the Yellowstone River on the very trail he had marked.

At this point prospectors stopped crossing the Sioux country. A new treaty was signed in 1868. The Sioux agreed to live on a reservation in the Dakota Territory west of the Missouri River.

Custer's Last Stand

Still the fighting went on. Between 1869 and 1875 over 200 clashes between Indians and army units took place. In 1876 the territory of the Sioux was again invaded, this time by the construction crews of the Northern Pacific Railroad and by prospectors looking for gold in the Black Hills. War broke out.

This historic photograph of a Sioux camp was taken in 1891 near Pine Ridge, South Dakota. Make an estimate of the size of the encampment.

FOCUS/MOTIVATION: MULTICULTURAL PERSPECTIVES
Student Experiences.
Ask students to describe how they might feel if a group of Native Americans on horseback came into their town and, at gunpoint, demanded that the inhabitants leave their homes and all but a few of their belongings and move to another place. Tell them that this other place is not as nice as their home and that they will be forced to live in tents, hunt for their food, and cook it over open fires. They will not be allowed to leave this new place to attend school or church and must participate in rituals which they often know nothing about. *(Most students will respond that they are angry or in some way very displeased with this situation.)* Point out to them that this is what Native Americans had to endure in the latter part of the 1800s in the United States. Not only were they moved from their homes, but an attempt was made to force them to adopt American culture. In some cases attempts were even made to destroy their culture.

HISTORICAL SIDELIGHTS

① Custer had cut his long yellow (and graying) hair before the battle.

SUGGESTED CAPTION RESPONSES

(Top) It is an accurate portrayal.

(Bottom) Opinions will vary, but students might find his long flowing hair and neat mustache a sign of vanity.

Courtesy of The Library of Congress

Above is "Custer's Last Stand," the situation already hopeless for his cavalry troops. How is the artist's view similar to the real battle described on these pages?

The Thomas Gilcrease Institute of American History and Art, Tulsa, Oklahoma

This is one of many portraits we have of George Armstrong Custer, with his flowing yellow hair and moustache. Do you agree with critics who found him a vain man searching for glory?

At this time Lieutenant Colonel George Armstrong Custer made his famous last stand in the **Battle of the Little Bighorn** in southern Montana. George Custer looked more like an actor than a soldier. ① He had long, flowing yellow hair. He wore buckskin trousers, red-topped boots, and a broad-brimmed hat. He was a good soldier, a graduate of the United States Military Academy at West Point. During the Civil War he fought at Bull Run and Gettysburg, and he accepted a Confederate flag of truce on the battlefield near Appomattox. But he sometimes deliberately led his men into dangerous situations in hopes of winning what he called "glory."

On June 25, 1876, Custer led a cavalry troop of 264 men toward what he believed to be a small Sioux camp. Instead, at the Little Bighorn River, his tiny force stumbled upon between 2,500 and 4,000 Sioux, commanded by chiefs Sitting Bull, Crazy Horse, and Rain-in-the-Face.

Sitting Bull helped prepare for battle. He had become chief of his band nine years earlier. He was a solid, muscular man, 42 years old in 1876. He had a slightly hooked nose and piercing black eyes. Deep lines marked his weather-beaten brow. His dark hair hung in two heavy braids in front of his shoulders.

The Sioux left Custer's naked body unmutilated and unscalped out of respect for his ability as a military leader.

INTERPRETING HISTORY: The American Frontier

During the late 19th century millions of Americans headed westward into vast frontier lands. As each area along the frontier became "settled," the next wave of pioneers pushed the frontier farther west. What role did the frontier play in the development of America and the American character? Was it merely a safety valve for an ever-increasing population? Or did Greeley write "Go west, young man!" because America was a land of unlimited opportunity?

Frederick Jackson Turner is the historian most closely linked to theories about the American frontier. In 1893 Turner published his theories in "The Significance of the Frontier on American History." In it he claimed that the seemingly inexhaustible frontier, more than the country's European heritage, shaped America. He wrote that frontier life spurred the development of independence and rugged individualism. He even suggested that the growth of democracy in America could be directly traced to the frontier experience. Simply put, he felt that the most important values and characteristics of the American spirit—courage, determination, democracy, independence, and others—grew out of people's trials on the frontier. Many generations of Americans experienced frontier life as they moved westward, and they drew on their experiences as they continually refined American values. This national experience officially came to an end, according to Turner, with the 1890 census. Maps in that census no longer carried a frontier line showing where population was less than two persons per square mile. "Now four centuries from the discovery of America, at the end of a hundred years of life under the Constitution, the frontier is gone, and with its going, has closed the first period of American history," wrote Turner.

Historians have since debated the validity of Turner's "frontier thesis." Professor Robert E. Riegal accused Turner of placing too much emphasis on the impact of the physical environment on the American people. He and many other historians attacked Turner's idea that the frontier was the "seedbed of democracy." He carefully traced America's democratic ideals to their roots in European life. He added, "Turner's feeling that each new frontiersman shed his old customs, started anew and became a real American appears to have been more a hope than a fact. Several historians have demonstrated very clearly the extent to which national characteristics were retained in western settlement."

The noted historian Ray Allen Billington disagreed with many of Turner's conclusions. But he agreed that the frontier indeed endowed its inhabitants with "characteristics and institutions that distinguished them from other nations." In other words, the frontier made Americans uniquely American.

Historians studying American society continue to argue to what degree the frontier shaped American life.

Sitting Bull was a fiercely proud and independent man. He resisted all efforts to get his people to give up their ancient customs. He would never sign a treaty with the whites, no matter how favorable the terms might seem. More than most Indians, he believed that no compromise with the whites was possible.

Now Sitting Bull faced Custer. Swiftly the Sioux warriors surrounded Custer's little force. Racing round and round on their ponies, they poured a deadly fire upon the troops. Desperately the soldiers dismounted and tried to use their horses as shields. Their situation was hopeless. A hail of bullets and arrows poured upon them from every direction. One bullet struck Custer in the temple, another in the chest. Within half an hour the entire company was wiped out.

This great victory at the Little Bighorn only delayed the final defeat of Sitting Bull and the rest of the Sioux. The chief held out until 1881. Then, his people near starvation, he surrendered to army units. In 1883 he was placed on the Standing Rock reservation in the Dakotas.

The Thomas Gilcrease Institute of American History and Art, Tulsa, Oklahoma

This portrait of Sitting Bull is by Henry Cross.

RESOURCES
■ You may wish to have students complete Reading 1: "Speeches of Seattle and Ten Bears (1854, 1867)" in Volume II of *Eyewitnesses and Others.*

Chief Joseph

National Portrait Gallery, Smithsonian Institution

Chief Joseph was the subject for Cyrenius Hall in 1878, just after the chief's flight for Canada. Although there is no evidence of his pierced nose—hence the tribal name in French, Nez Perce—can you find other decorations in this portrait?

Point of View

Plains Indians were divided and conquered by disease as well as by soldiers.

"How many Indians from the Missouri tribes died of smallpox within the next few years can hardly be estimated. Possibly one hundred thousand. Some who recovered from the plague committed suicide after seeing their faces in a mirror. Vacant lodges stood on every hilltop. Starving people wandered aimlessly back and forth. 'No sound but the raven's croak or the wolf's howl breaks the solemn stillness. . . ."

From *Son of the Morning Star*,
Evan S. Connell, 1984

■ The search for gold also drew miners to Indian lands in the mountains of western Idaho. The whites called the Indians of this region the **Nez Perce,** or "pierced nose," because they wore nose ornaments made of shell. They were a peace-loving people. They claimed that no member of their tribe had ever killed a white. When Lewis and Clark traveled through Nez Perce lands on their expedition to the Pacific Coast, the explorers had been treated as honored guests.

The Nez Perce chief was a man the whites called Joseph. His real name was Hinmaton-Yalaktit, which means "Thunder coming out of the water and over the land." Like Tecumseh, the great Shawnee leader, Joseph believed that Indians had no right to sell the land they lived on. Joseph had promised his father that he would not surrender the lands to white settlers. It was his father's dying wish. Joseph was one of the greatest Indian spokesmen. Oratory was a fine art among the Nez Perce. Much of the power and prestige of the chiefs depended on their ability to speak. Perhaps when you read his words you can understand why he fought so hard.

"My father sent for me. I saw he was dying. I took his hand in mine. He said: 'My son, my body is returning to my mother earth, and my spirit is going very soon to see the Great Spirit Chief. When I am gone, think of your country. You are the chief of these people. They look to you to guide them. Always remember that your father never sold his country. You must stop your ears whenever you are asked to sign a treaty selling your home. A few years more, and white men will be all around you. They have eyes on this land. My son, never forget my dying words. This country holds your father's body. Never sell the bones of your father and your mother.' I pressed my father's hand and told him I would protect his grave with my life. My father smiled and passed away to the spirit-land.

I buried him in that beautiful valley of winding waters. I love that land more than all the rest of the world. A man who would not love his father's grave is worse than a wild animal.[1]"

Now the government insisted that Joseph make way for the whites and move his band to the Lapwai Reservation in Idaho. Joseph had only 55 men of fighting age. He decided to yield. He selected land on the reservation in May 1877. Then the government gave him only one month to move his people to the reservation.

While on the march to Idaho, a few angry Nez Perce killed some white settlers. Troops were sent to capture them. Chief Joseph and the other chiefs decided to take their people to Montana and

[1]From *Touch the Earth: A Self-Portrait of Indian Existence* by T.C. McLuhan

PRIMARY SOURCES
Description of change: excerpted.
Rationale: excerpted to focus on why Chief Joseph fought white encroachment.
(Point of View) Description of change: excerpted.
Rationale: excerpted to focus on the toll that disease took on Plains Indians.

THE BUFFALO VANISHES

Courtesy of The Library of Congress

The Granger Collection, New York

William Cody

What finally put an end to Indian independence was the killing off of the buffalo. Thousands had been slaughtered to feed the gangs of laborers who built the western railroads. In one 18-month period the scout William Cody shot some 4,000 buffalo for the Kansas Pacific Railroad construction camps. This won him the nickname Buffalo Bill.

Once the railroads were built, shooting buffalo became a popular sport for tourists and hunters from the East. Bored rail passengers sometimes opened their windows to blast away at the grazing buffalo.

In 1871 a Pennsylvania tanner discovered that buffalo hides could be made into useful leather. Hides that were once worthless now brought $1 to $3 each. Buffalo hunting then became a profitable business. Between 1872 and 1874, 9 million buffalo were killed. By 1900 there were fewer than 50 buffalo left in the entire United States! The buffalo had been nearly sacred to many Indian tribes. It gave them food, clothing, and shelter. Without it, the Indians were powerless to resist the advance of the whites.

Wyoming and later into Canada instead of Idaho. For months the band slipped away from thousands of pursuing troops in the rugged country along the border between Oregon and Montana. In September 1877 they reached the Bear Paw Mountains, only 30 miles (48 kilometers) from Canada.

Joseph thought they were safe at last. He stopped to rest. Many of his people were starving. Children were dying. This is when army cavalry units suddenly attacked. Joseph and his warriors held out for four days. Finally they surrendered.

SUGGESTED CAPTION RESPONSE
Montana Territory, Dakota Territory, Colorado, Indian
Territory (Oklahoma); wide open spaces of most un-
wanted land

RESOURCES
■ You may wish to have students complete Reading
7: "Annie Bidwell Attends a Mechoopda Dance
(1870s)" in Volume II of *Eyewitnesses and Others*.

CHECKING UNDERSTANDING
Have students discuss the events that led up to the end of Indian independence. *(Students should mention the following: The wars that erupted between federal troops and the Cheyenne and Arapaho, ending in the Chivington Massacre and the defeat of the Cheyenne and Arapaho at Washita; wars between federal troops and the Sioux, which led to the Battle of the Little Big Horn and the final defeat of Sitting Bull; the defeat of Chief Joseph and the resettlement of the Nez Perce on reservations in Oklahoma; the massacre of the Sioux at Wounded Knee; the "Ghost Dance" revival; the Dawes Act which aimed at destroying tribal organization.)*

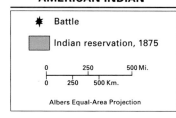

CONCENTRATION OF THE
AMERICAN INDIAN

★ Battle

▨ Indian reservation, 1875

0   250   500 Mi.

0   250   500 Km.

Albers Equal-Area Projection

LEARNING FROM MAPS. *As settlers moved westward they pushed the Indians off much of the land they once held. In what states and territories were the largest reservations in 1875? Why do you think they were located in those places?*

Joseph's speech upon surrender is one of the most famous and admired of all such speeches. He hoped his words would carry a message to the warriors who were still fighting. He told his captors:

❝ I am tired of fighting. Our chiefs are killed. Looking Glass is dead. It is the young men who say yes or no. He who led the young men is dead. It is cold and we have no blankets. The little chidren are freezing to death. My people, some of them have run away to the hills and have no blankets, no food; no one knows where they are—perhaps freezing to death. I want to have time to look for my children and see how many I can find. Maybe I shall find them among the dead. Hear me my chiefs. I am tired; my heart is sick and sad. From where the sun now stands, I will fight no more forever.[1] ❞

■ Wetatonmi, widow of Ollokot, Joseph's brother, spoke of leaving the tribe's lands the night of Joseph's surrender. Compare her words and Joseph's to those of the Choctaw chiefs on pages 397 and 398. Imagine the sadness of being torn from your home as the Indians were. Wetatonmi said:

❝ It was lonesome, the leaving. Husband dead, friends buried or held prisoners. I felt that I was leaving all that I had but

[1]From *Touch the Earth: A Self-Portrait of Indian Existence* by T.C. McLuhan

PRIMARY SOURCE
Description of change: excerpted.
Rationale: excerpted to focus on why Chief Joseph surrendered.

did not cry. You know how you feel when you lose kindred [family] and friends through sickness—death. You do not care if you die. With us it was worse. Strong men, well women and little children killed and buried. They had not done wrong to be so killed. We had only asked to be left in our own homes, the homes of our ancestors. Our going was with heavy hearts, broken spirits. . . . All lost, we walked silently into the wintry night.[1] "

The Nez Perce were settled on a barren reservation in Oklahoma. Far from the mountains of Idaho, this land was "the malarial bottom of the Indian Territory." Joseph, however, was sent to a reservation in Washington state. There he lived in exile, separated from his people and removed from the land he loved. When he died in 1904, the official cause of his death was listed as a broken heart.

The Ghost Dance

The final bloody battle in this chapter of the story of America was fought on the northern plains. In 1889 a religious revival swept ① through the Indian tribes. Chiefs and medicine men called their people to what whites called the "Ghost Dance." The celebration was based on the vision that an Indian leader would come to drive the whites from Indian lands and the buffalo would again roam the plains.

The Ghost Dance was not a call to war but a celebration of treasured Indian ways of life. Settlers and miners were alarmed at the energy and the mystery of the celebration. They demanded the army put an end to it.

The end came at **Wounded Knee** in South Dakota in December 1890. The 7th Calvary arrested a band of Sioux men, women, and children who were traveling in search of food and shelter as winter came. Suddenly a shot rang out. Without warning the troops opened fire with rifles and Hotchkiss guns, a type of small cannon. They poured a deadly hail of lead into the Indian band, killing 90 men and 200 women and children. The massacre ended armed Indian resistance to white demands.

The End of Indian Independence

All of the wars between the Indians and the army were hard fought. Yet many of the soldiers sympathized with their enemies. They understood why the Indians were fighting. Even Colonel John Gibbon, who discovered the bodies of Custer's men after the Battle of the Little Bighorn, blamed the wars on the settlers. Another officer said, "If I had been a red man . . . I should have fought as bitterly." The way the government treated Indians shocked a great many

[1]From *Touch the Earth: A Self-Portrait of Indian Existence* by T.C. McLuhan

---

Point of View

An Oglala Sioux holy man told John G. Neihardt, a poet of the Middle West, of the coming of a new world.

"They saw the Wanekia ["One Who Makes Live"], who was the son of the Great Spirit, and they talked to him. . . . He told them that there was another world coming, just like a cloud. It would come in a whirlwind out of the west and would crush everything on this world, which was old and dying. In that other world there was plenty of meat, just like the old times; and in that world all the dead Indians were alive, and all the bison that had ever been killed were roaming around again."

Black Elk, 1930

RETEACHING STRATEGY: COOPERATIVE LEARNING Students with Special Needs. Organize the class into cooperative learning groups. Then have the more proficient students reread Section 2 to the others. Put the following questions on the chalkboard or an overhead projector, and then have students help each other answer them.
1. How did the Cheyenne and Arapaho lose their independence? *(After fighting federal troops several times, they were finally defeated at Washita in Oklahoma.)*
2. How did the Sioux lose their independence? *(After the Battle of the Little Bighorn and later the defeat of their chief, Sitting Bull, they were finally defeated at Wounded Knee.)*
3. How did the Nez Perce lose their independence? *(They tried to escape to Canada under Chief Joseph but finally surrendered to federal troops and were resettled in Oklahoma.)*

PRIMARY SOURCES
Description of change: excerpted and bracketed.
Rationale: excerpted to focus on Wetatonmi's sadness at leaving the tribe's lands; bracketed words added to clarify meaning.
(Point of View) Description of change: excerpted and bracketed.
Rationale: excerpted to focus on the Sioux holy man's description of the coming of the Indian Messiah; bracketed words added to clarify meaning.

① Senator Henry L. Dawes of Massachusetts sponsored this act.

SUGGESTED CAPTION RESPONSES
(Top) He looks like a defeated captive, as a soldier appears in the background.
(Bottom) They were upset and shocked.

INDEPENDENT PRACTICE
Have students complete the Preview & Review activity at the beginning of the section.

CLOSURE
Remind students that the bitter wars fought between the Indians and settlers resulted in mistrust and resentment which has been felt by many Native Americans to the present day.

HOMEWORK
In recent years some Indian tribes have sued in the courts for the return of their ancestral lands. Many have won huge monetary awards. Have students prepare an argument taking either the federal government's side or the Indians' side on the issue of returning Indian land to the tribes or paying them for it. They may find information on this subject in either their school or public library.

Courtesy of The Library of Congress

Head held in his hand, the Hunkpapa Sioux Sitting Bull squints at the camera in this 1882 photograph. Here at Standing Rock reservation in the Dakota Territory the chief is living in exile. What clues in the photograph tell you that Sitting Bull's wars have all been waged?

Culver Pictures

Helen Hunt Jackson's novel Ramona *told the plight of the Indian people when the frontier closed. How did many Americans react to the government's treatment of the Indians?*

Return to the Preview & Review on page 630.

Americans. They were particularly upset when the government broke treaties it had made with the tribes. In *A Century of Dishonor*, published in 1881, Helen Hunt Jackson showed how the government broke promises to Indians. In her novel *Ramona* she tried to do for the Indians what Harriet Beecher Stowe's *Uncle Tom's Cabin* had done for the slaves.

Another fighter for Indian rights was Sarah Winnemucca, the daughter of a Paiute chief. Winnemucca wrote a book and gave lectures describing how unjustly the Indians had been treated. She demanded that the United States return much of the land it had taken from her people.

① Congress finally responded by passing the **Dawes Severalty Act** of 1887. This law broke up reservation lands into individual family units. Each family got 160 acres (64 hectares). To protect the owners against speculators, they were not allowed to sell the property for 25 years. Only then did they have full rights to the land. And only then were they allowed to become citizens of the United States.

The Dawes Act was supposed to protect and help the Indians. However, it was written entirely from a white point of view. It ignored the Indians' culture and traditions. Its aim was to turn them into farmers, which would destroy their tribal organizations. It was well meant, but it simply showed once again that most white Americans had little understanding of or sympathy for the plight of the Indians. In this sense it was typical of most of the laws that Congress passed affecting the lives of the original Americans. ▣

HISTORICAL SIDELIGHTS
❶ Between 1890 and 1915 the greatest strikes occurred in Alaska, the Klondike region of the Yukon
in Canada, and South Africa.
❷ There was a gold rush in the Black Hills of South
Dakota in 1874-75. The Homestake mine at Lead,
South Dakota, is still the richest gold mine in the
U.S.

3. MINING THE WEST

The Comstock Lode

The Dawes Act spoke of encouraging the Indians to adopt "the habits of civilized life." The lawmakers apparently wanted them to copy the life styles of their white neighbors. How "civilized" those life styles were is another question!

The miners of the West offered one model. They carried their "civilization" into the mountains of Colorado, Nevada, Arizona, Idaho, Montana, and Wyoming. In each case they struck the region like a tornado.

The first important strikes after the California discovery of gold in 1848 came in Nevada in 1859. The center of this activity was Gold ❶ Canyon, a sagebrush-covered ravine on the southern slope of Mt. Davidson. At first the miners panned for gold in the gravel beds of streams. When their yields began to decline, the prospectors moved farther up the mountainside. Among these miners was Henry Comstock, known to his friends as "Old Pancake." His partner, James Fennimore, was called "Old Virginia." They began digging at the head of Gold Canyon on a small rise called Gold Hill. Another pair, Peter O'Riley and Patrick McLaughlin, started digging at Six Mile Canyon, a ravine on the northern slope of Mt. Davidson.

O'Riley and McLaughlin soon came upon a dark, heavy soil sprinkled with gold. Just as they were shouting news of their discovery, Henry Comstock came riding by. Jumping from his horse, he made a quick examination of the find. "You have struck it, boys!" he announced.

Then the old prospector bluffed his way into a partnership. "Look here," he said, "this spring was Old Man Caldwell's. You know that. . . . Well, Manny Penrod and I bought this claim last winter, and we sold a tenth interest to Old Virginia the other day. You two fellows must let us in on equal shares."

At first O'Riley and McLaughlin said no. Then they were afraid they might lose everything, so they said yes.

The partners went to work at once. They found very little gold. Instead they struck large deposits of heavy, bluish sand and blue-gray quartz. Not knowing what that "blasted blue stuff" was, they simply piled it beside the mine. Another miner, however, gathered up a sack of the blue quartz and had it tested, or **assayed**. The assayers' reports went beyond anyone's wildest dreams. The "blue stuff" was rich in silver and gold. The partners had hit upon what was known as a **bonanza**—a large find of extremely rich ore.

News of the discovery caused 15,000 people to swarm into the region in the next few months. Henry Comstock gained everlasting fame by giving the find his name. The enormous **Comstock Lode** ran ❷ along the eastern face of Mt. Davidson. It crossed the heads of Gold

Preview & Review

Use these questions to guide your reading. Answer the questions after completing Section 3.
Understanding Issues, Events, & Ideas. Describe mining discoveries in the West, using the following words: assayed, bonanza, Comstock Lode, Virginia City, boom town, vigilance committee, vigilante.
1. Where was the Comstock Lode struck?
2. What was life in a mining camp like? How was life in these camps similar to life in California mining camps in 1849?
3. How did vigilantes keep the law?

Thinking Critically. The author says that the Dawes Act encouraged the Indians to "adopt 'the habits of civilized life.' . . . How 'civilized' those life styles were is another question!" Suppose you are a native American who has been displaced under the Dawes Act. What is your opinion of your neighbors, the miners? Explain your answer.

Culver Pictures

"Old Pancake"

Mining the West   639

SECTION 3

PREVIEW & REVIEW RESPONSES
Understanding Issues, Events, & Ideas.
Descriptions should demonstrate an understanding of the terms used.
1. In Nevada, along the eastern face of Mt. Davidson, at the heads of Gold and Six Mile Canyons
2. Usually lawless, full of gunslingers, gamblers, claim jumpers, and other questionable types; both attracted undesirable types of people.
3. They hunted down the worst criminals, gave them speedy trials, and usually hanged them.

Thinking Critically.
Student opinions should show an understanding of the Indian point of view.

FOCUS/MOTIVATION: MAKING CONNECTIONS
Prior Knowledge.
Remind students that the California Gold Rush of 1849 had a large impact on western settlement. Have them discuss what happened at this time. *(Students should mention that people came from all over to mine gold, traveling by very long water or land routes. They set up temporary mining camps or towns that were often lawless and very dangerous places to live.)* Have students discuss the importance of the geographic themes of *location, place,* and *movement* on the Gold Rush. *(For example, location: the Gold Rush brought swarms of prospectors and settlers clear to the other side of the continent.)*

HISTORICAL SIDELIGHTS

1 Gold is mined primarily in three ways: *placer mining* (in stream beds or glacial deposits); *lode mining* (mine tunnels deep underground); *as a byproduct of mining other metals* (particularly copper).

GUIDED INSTRUCTION: COOPERATIVE LEARNING

Divide the class into several small groups. Have each group imagine that they are prospectors who have just discovered a valuable mineral where they have been digging. Have them describe the *place* characteristics of their claim. Then they are to draw up a plan for dealing with their situation. Their plans should include decisions on whether or not to form partnerships, how to divide their wealth, and how to protect their claim against claim jumpers or other swindlers. Have each group present their plan to the class.

RELATING HISTORY TO GEOGRAPHY

Refer students to the maps in Sections 1, 2, and 4 of this chapter. To reinforce the geographic theme of *location,* have students list the names of the western towns and settlements that appear on the maps, as well as other features such as the names of rivers, railroads, and trails. Have students prepare an oral report on one of these towns. The report should include the following topics: reasons why the town was founded; the geographic features of the town such as climate, rainfall, seasons, and type of soil; how these geographic features played a role in the development of the town; any major events that took place in the town.

Montana Historical Society

THE RICHEST HILL IN THE WORLD

"Main Street will run north and south in a direct line through that cow," said the planners of Anaconda in 1887.

In Montana and Arizona the mining riches were in copper, not gold and silver. In the late 1870s Marcus Daly bought a small silver mine in Butte, Montana, for $30,000. For some reason this silver mine was named Anaconda. An anaconda is a large snake like a boa constrictor. Perhaps the silver ore ran in a curved, snakelike vein.

To finance the Anaconda, Daly turned to George Hearst, a millionaire California developer who had already invested in many western mines. Daly began operations in 1880.

The silver of Anaconda soon gave out. Beneath it, however, Daly found a rich vein of copper.

Hearst supplied the huge sums needed to mine and smelt this copper. By the late 1880s the Anaconda Copper Corporation had become the greatest producer of copper in the world. Eventually, Daly and his associates took over $2 billion worth of copper out of the "richest hill in the world."

and Six Mile Canyons and dipped underneath the crowded mining camps.

1 Most of the gold and silver the prospectors sought was buried deep in veins of hard quartz rock. Heavy machinery was needed to dig it out. Huge steam-powered drills, tested in California, chiseled away massive chunks of earth. Newly developed steam shovels moved the chunks to waiting wagons, which carried them to smelters. The smelters, some like giant blast furnaces and some like huge rock crushers, separated the ore from the rock. By 1872 a railway wound through the mining communities, bringing coal to the smelters. But mine owners soon realized that large smelters, located in Golden or Denver, were more efficient. So the railroad hauled raw ore—rich with silver, copper, lead, and gold—to these plants. Tunneling operations called for experienced mining engineers. Powerful pumps were needed to remove groundwater that seeped in as the shafts grew deeper. Prospectors like Comstock, O'Riley, and McLaughlin did not have the skill or the money such operations required. Comstock eventually sold his share of the mine for a mere $10,000.

Nevada Historical Society

"Old Virginia"

The real "bonanza kings" were John W. Mackay, James G. Fair, James C. Flood, and William S. O'Brien. All were of Irish ancestry. All had been born poor. All had come to California during the Gold Rush. In 1868-69 these four men formed a partnership. They used the profits of one strike to buy up other mines. Eventually they took precious metals worth over $150 million from the rich Nevada lode.

Mining Camp Life

Whenever a strike was made, mining camps seemed to sprout out of the surrounding hillsides like flowers after a desert rain. The camps were ramshackle towns of tents and noisy saloons. The most famous was **Virginia City,** Nevada. It was given its name by Henry Comstock's partner, "Old Virginia." While on a spree, "Old Virginia" tripped and fell, smashing his bottle of whiskey. Rising to his knees he shouted drunkenly, "I baptize this town Virginia Town."

Virginia City was a typical **boom town,** so crowded that a horse ① and wagon could take half an hour to cross the main street. The life of miners, shopkeepers, and others in these mining towns was sometimes as difficult as life on the open range. In these towns it was difficult to keep the peace. Smooth-talking gamblers, gunslingers, and other outlaws sidled alongside claim jumpers, shifty types who specialized in seizing ore deposits that had been staked out by others. Some camps were taken over by these outlaws, who ruled the terror-filled citizens at gunpoint. Such communities provided rich material for American writers. Mark Twain in *Roughing It* and Bret Harte in "The Luck of Roaring Camp" told of life in California mining camps. Charles Farrar Browne wrote this somewhat fictionalized account of a Nevada silver-mining town:

> 66 Shooting isn't as popular in Nevada as it once was. A few years since [ago] they used to have a dead man for breakfast every morning. A reformed desperado [bandit] told me that he supposed he had killed enough to stock a grave-yard. 'A feeling of remorse,' he said, 'sometimes comes over me! But I'm an altered man now. I hain't killed a man for over two weeks! What'll you poison yourself with?' he added, dealing a resonant [noisy] blow to the bar.[1] 99

Compare Browne's description to the following remembrances of some Virginia City residents. Which seems to be closer to the image of the "Old West" you have?

> 66 The men who worked in the mines . . . were [a] happy-go-lucky set of fellows, fond of good living, and not particularly interested in religious affairs. . . .
>
> As regarded deportment [behavior], everyone was a law unto himself. . . . Most of the men employed in the

[1]From *Artemus Ward: His Travels* by Charles Farrar Browne

CHECKING UNDERSTANDING
Have students discuss how gold and silver were mined in the West. *(Heavy machinery was used to dig out the ore buried in the vein of the quartz rock. Steam-powered drills were used to get at the ore. The chunks of earth containing the ore were moved to waiting wagons by steam shovels. The wagons carried them to smelters, which were like huge blast furnaces that separated the ore from the rock by heat. As the mining shafts grew deeper, powerful pumps were used to remove groundwater that seeped in.)*

RETEACHING STRATEGY: Students with Special Needs.
Pair students who are having difficulty with students who are performing well. Have the more proficient students ask the others the following questions:
1. How was the ore dug out of the quartz rock? *(steam-powered drills)*
2. How were the chunks of earth containing the ore moved to waiting wagons? *(steam shovels)*
3. How was the ore separated from the rock? *(smelters)*
4. How was groundwater removed from the mining shafts? *(powerful pumps)*
5. Why couldn't individuals do this type of mining? *(It was very expensive.)*

PRIMARY SOURCE
Description of change: excerpted and bracketed.
Rationale: excerpted to focus on Charles Farrar Browne's account of a mining town; bracketed words added to clarify meaning.

Mining the West   641

RESOURCES
■ You may wish to have students complete reading 15: "A Teacher's Life in the Common Schools (1888)" in Volume II of *Eyewitnesses and Others.*
◄ You may wish to have students complete Reading 17: "Lesson One from McGuffey's *Eclectic Fourth Reader* (1880s)" in Volume II of *Eyewitnesses and Others.*

INDEPENDENT PRACTICE
Have students complete the Preview & Review activity at the beginning of the section.

CLOSURE
Point out to students that although many people attempted to find wealth in the mines of the West, very few were successful.

HOMEWORK
Have students research and then write a biographical sketch of one of the prominent miners mentioned in this section such as Henry Comstock, James Fennimore, Peter O'Riley, or Patrick McLaughlin.

PRIMARY SOURCE
Description of change: excerpted and bracketed.
Rationale: excerpted to focus on some Virginia City residents' remembrances of the miners; bracketed words added to clarify meaning.

mines were unmarried and enjoyed none of the refining, humanizing influences of home life. They boarded at a restaurant, slept in a lodging-house, and, as a general rule, spent their leisure time on the street or at the gambling-tables.

During the flush times [when there was plenty of money] as many as twenty-five faro games [a gambling game in which players bet on cards drawn from a box] were in full blast night and day. When sporting men . . . sat down of an evening to a friendly game of poker it was no uncommon occurrence for five or six thousand dollars to change hands in a single sitting. Some idea of the amount of money in circulation may be inferred from the fact that every working-man's wages amounted to at least 120 dollars per month.

From what has already been written there is no desire to convey the impression that a low standard of morality was the rule in the Comstock mining district. Men quarreled at times and firearms were discharged [fired] with but slight provocation [cause]. Nevertheless they all had an acute instinct of right and wrong, a high sense of honor, and a chivalrous feeling of respect for the gentler sex. . . .

One of the most prominent traits of character as regarded the miners was their generous response to any worthy object. If a man of family lost his life in the mines thousands of dollars would be contributed to those dependent on him. Each miner contributed regularly one or two days' wages for benevolent causes [those for the public good]. . . .[1]**99**

[1]From *The Mining Frontier: Contemporary Accounts from the American West in the Nineteenth Century,* edited by Marvin Lewis

When conditions in a mining camp got too bad, the respectable residents took action. They formed **vigilance committees** to watch over their towns. Sometimes they even drew up formal constitutions, pledging their members, called **vigilantes,** to restore order.

As soon as enough vigilantes had been signed up, the worst troublemakers were hunted down. These villains were given speedy trials before judges and juries made up of the same vigilantes who had run them down. The trials, of course, were not legal. The usual punishment for the guilty was death by hanging. In one six-week period Montana vigilantes hanged 22 outlaws.

Once a town was properly governed, more and more settlers moved in. Some opened stores. Others turned to farming. Lawyers, ministers, teachers, and doctors moved in. The people built schools and churches, started newspapers and opened hospitals. They built roads to other communities. They put down solid roots.

Return to the Preview & Review on page 639.

HISTORICAL SIDELIGHTS
① Although their price was high, longhorns did not produce a high quality of beef.

RESOURCES
■ You may wish to have students view Transparency 6: "Cattle Trails, Railroads, and Mining Centers"

and complete the accompanying worksheet in *American History Map Transparencies*.

4. THE END OF THE OPEN RANGE

The Cattle Kingdom

While the miners were searching the mountains for gold and silver, other pioneers were seeking their own fortunes on the grasslands of the High Plains. The land that formed the **cattle kingdom** stretched from Texas into Canada and from the Rockies to eastern Kansas. This area made up nearly one quarter of the entire United States.

Spanish explorers had brought the first European cattle into Mexico in the early 1500s. Over the years their cattle had grown to enormous herds. Many ran wild. New breeds developed. These great herds spread northward as far as Texas.

By 1860 about 5 million wild cattle were grazing in Texas. These were the famous **Texas longhorns,** so named because their horns had a spread of as much as seven feet (over two meters). After the Civil War, cattle that were worth from $3 to $5 a head in Texas could be sold for $30 to $50 a head in the cities of the eastern United States. ① The problem was how to get them there. Joseph G. McCoy, an Illinois meat dealer, thought he knew the answer. He could make a fortune, he believed, if he could establish a convenient meeting place for eastern buyers and Texas cattle ranchers.

McCoy chose **Abilene,** Kansas, as this meeting place. There he put up a hotel for the cowhands and dealers and built barns, pens, and loading chutes for the cattle. He persuaded officials of the Kansas Pacific Railroad to ship cattle to **Chicago,** the meat packing center of the United States, at special low rates.

To get Texas longhorns to Abilene and other **cattle towns** meant herding them slowly northward over the empty plains. This **long drive** was a two-month journey. On the first drive Texans herded 35,000 longhorns over the **Chisholm Trail** to Abilene. During the next 20 years about 6 million head of cattle were driven north over the grasslands crossed by trails such as the Goodnight-Loving, Western, and Shawnee.

Open-Range Ranching

The key to the success of the long drive was the grass and water ■ along the trail northward from Texas. Cattle ranchers discovered that prairie grass made an excellent food for their cattle. Then they discovered that the tough, rangy longhorns got along very well in the harsh winters of the northern plains. Soon millions of cattle were grazing on land belonging to the government. Ranchers could fatten their herds on this **open range** of lush grass without paying a cent for it. The cattle roamed freely across the unfenced plains.

Of course the cattle also needed water. It was a very dry region, almost a desert. Water rights, or **range rights,** along a stream meant

Use these questions to guide your reading. Answer the questions after completing Section 4.
Understanding Issues, Events, & Ideas. Describe the work on a cattle drive, using the following words: cattle kingdom, Texas longhorns, Abilene, Chicago, cattle towns, long drive, Chisholm Trail, open range, range rights, cattle baron, round up, brand, *vaquero*, Dodge City, boot hill, range war, sod house, drought, dry farming, bread basket of America.
1. How did Joseph G. McCoy plan to ship Texas longhorns to eastern cities?
2. Why was the open range so important to cattle ranchers?
3. What caused range wars?
4. What was the importance of the windmill, barbed wire, the steel plow, and the twine binder?
Thinking Critically. 1. You are a magazine reporter in 1875. Compose an article titled "A Day in the Life of a Cowhand." **2.** It is the late 1800s. You can be a rancher, a cowhand, or a farmer. Which occupation will you choose? Why?

PREVIEW & REVIEW RESPONSES
Understanding Issues, Events, & Ideas.
Descriptions should demonstrate an understanding of the terms used.
1. McCoy found a meeting place for eastern buyers and Texas ranchers in Abilene, Kansas. He built hotels for the cowhands and dealers, and barns, pens and loading chutes for the cattle. He persuaded officials of the Kansas Pacific Railroad to ship cattle to Chicago at low rates.
2. Cattle ranchers could allow their herds to fatten on the lush grass of the open range without paying a cent for it because it belonged to the U.S. government.
3. Overstocking; both cattle ranchers and sheep ranchers wanted control of the grasslands, and sheep and cattle could not graze the same land.
4. The windmill powered the pumps that got the water from deep in the ground; barbed wire kept cattle and farm animals out of the crops; the steel plow was able to slice through the heavy sod of the plains; the twine binder could harvest an acre of wheat in 3 hours, making large-scale farming possible.

Thinking Critically.
1. Students should use historical imagination when composing their article on the cowhand.
2. Students should show ingenuity and imagination in answering the questions.

HISTORICAL SIDELIGHTS
● Most of the open range was controlled by large companies owned by investors from the East and England, as well as the cattle barons.

SUGGESTED CAPTION RESPONSE
Approximately 850 miles; approximately 700 miles

FOCUS/MOTIVATION: MAKING CONNECTIONS Student Experiences.
Have students look over the paintings and photographs in this section. Judging from what they see, ask them to speculate on what they think this section is about. *(cattle raising and Great Plains farming)* Ask them to relate any stories or tales they know regarding cowhands. Ask them if they think these are exaggerated. Tell them to keep these stories in mind as they read this section.

ART IN HISTORY
Have students look at the painting titled "Jerked Down" by Charles Marion Russell in this section. Begin a class discussion by asking individual students to describe some of the details in the painting. Ask: Judging from what you see in the painting, do you think you would like to have been a cowhand? Why or why not?

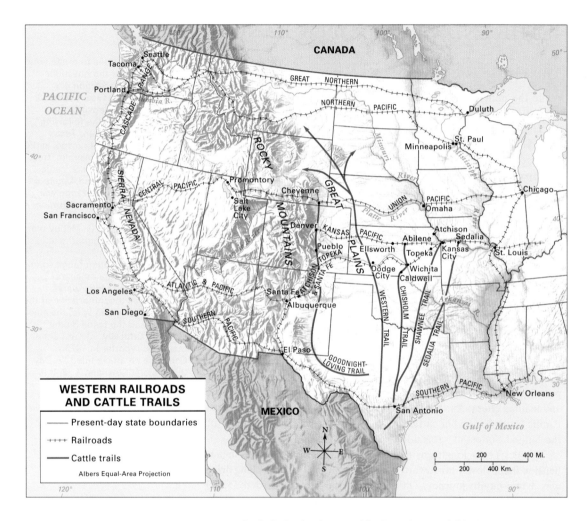

WESTERN RAILROADS AND CATTLE TRAILS
—— Present-day state boundaries
++++ Railroads
—— Cattle trails
Albers Equal-Area Projection

LEARNING FROM MAPS. *Extension of the railroads across the nation meant many economic changes. One of the most important was the development of the cattle industry in Texas. Cattle were driven along established trails to railroad depots. How far was a long drive from the southern end of the Sedalia Trail to Sedalia? How long was the Chisholm Trail?*

control of all the land around it. Ranchers quickly bought up all the land around their water supply. By owning a few acres along a small river, a rancher could control thousands of acres of surrounding grasslands without actually owning it.

One Colorado **cattle baron,** John F. Iliff, had the use of an area the size of Connecticut and Rhode Island. Yet he owned only about 15,500 acres (6,200 hectares). His land consisted of 105 small parcels on which there was running water.

To secure adequate range rights, a number of ranchers would band together into an association. They would buy up all the land along the banks of a stream or claim it under the Homestead Act. Only *their* cattle would be allowed on this private property. Only *their* cattle could drink from the stream. Although the rest of the range was public property, no other rancher for miles around could graze cattle without water.

◀ You may wish to have students complete Reading 8: "The Vaquero (1870s)" in Volume II of *Eyewitnesses and Others.*

The Thomas Gilcrease Institute of American History and Art, Tulsa, Oklahoma

Under this system the cattle belonging to the ranchers who ■ owned the banks of the stream became thoroughly mixed. Each spring and fall, cowhands would **round up** all the animals to a central place. The cowhands would fan out across the range, each riding up a canyon or hill. Each would return driving all the cattle in the area before him.

Charles Marion Russell painted "Jerked Down." These cowhands rope a steer while scrambling to get free of its sharp hooves and horns. How does a great painter like Russell tell an entire story with his brushes and oil paints?

Next the cowhands sorted each rancher's cattle from the rest by checking every animal's marking, called a **brand.** The brand mark was a scar made by pressing a red-hot branding iron onto the animal's hide. Each rancher's brand had a distinct shape, so it was easy to determine who owned which cattle. Those that were ready for market were penned up and shipped off by rail. The rest were turned loose, free to roam the range again until the next roundup.

Of course, newborn calves had not been branded. But calves always trailed close beside their mothers, so it was easy to tell whose property they were. They were branded and sent bawling back to their mothers.

The Cowhand

That colorful western figure, the cowhand, was the master of the ◀ long drive and the roundup. Mexican Americans were the first cowhands. These *vaqueros* invented almost all the tools of the cowhand's trade, from his broad-brimmed felt hat, his cotton bandana, and his

The End of the Open Range   645

SUGGESTED CAPTION RESPONSE
Mexican Americans introduced most of the cowhands to new clothes and equipment.

**USING HISTORICAL
IMAGINATION**
Remind students that sheep
and cattle cannot share the
same range because sheep eat
the grass down to the ground,
leaving too little for the cattle
to eat. Divide the class into two
groups. Have one group imagine that they are cattle ranchers and the other that they are
sheep ranchers. They are at
war because the other side refuses to understand their point
of view in the range wars. Have
students prepare an argument
justifying why their side is right
in these wars. Have students
choose a spokesperson to argue their side's case before the
class. Have the class act as ar-
bitrator and suggest solutions.

MUSIC IN HISTORY
You may wish to have students
experience the atmosphere of
the West by playing albums
that contain cowboy ballads
and other western songs. Have
students discuss how the lyrics
related to the lives of the people.

The Anschutz Collection

*Above are "California Vaqueros" by
James Walker. How did Mexican
Americans influence the life of every
cowhand?*

rope lariat to his special western saddle. The word *rodeo* is the
Spanish word for "roundup."

A cowhand's life was a hard one. The men worked sunup to
sundown and received lower wages than most factory workers. Their
legs became bowed from long days in the saddle. They developed
permanent squints from peering into the glaring sunlight of the treeless plains. Their faces were lined and leathery, their hands calloused
from constantly handling coarse ropes.

Not all cowhands were the strong, silent types portrayed in the
movies by white actors. Many came from poor families or from
groups outside the mainstream. About one third of the men who
worked cattle on the open range were either Mexican Americans or
African Americans.

Every item of the cowhand's clothes and equipment served a
necessary function. The wide brim of his "ten-gallon hat" could be
turned down to shade his eyes or drain off rainfall. His bandana could
be tied over his nose and mouth to keep out the dust raised by the
pounding hooves of countless cattle. The bandana also served as a
towel, a napkin, a bandage, and a handkerchief. Cowhands sometimes wore leather trousers, called chaps, over regular overalls.
Chaps were fastened to a broad belt buckled at the back. They

protected a rider's legs from injury if he fell from his horse or when ■ he had to ride through cactus, sagebrush, or other thorny plants.

The cowhand's western saddle had a sturdy horn, or pommel, for help in roping powerful steers and horses. These western saddles were heavy but comfortable. A weary cowhand could doze in the saddle while he rode. At night his saddle became a pillow and his saddlecloth a blanket when he stretched out beside the campfire and settled down to sleep. Around the campfire cowboys sang—to relax themselves and the herd. Their songs, such as "Home on the Range," have become a rich part of American music.

To the riders, the trail cook was the most important member of the team! Cowhands drank potfuls of thick, strong coffee to stay awake on the trail. They ate mostly stews, kidney beans, biscuits, and corn bread.

It was a lonely life. This explains why cowhands were famous for letting off steam when they reached cattle towns such as **Dodge City,** Kansas, the "Cowboy's Capital." Many cowhands were big drinkers and heavy gamblers when they came to town. Sometimes there were brawls and gunfights, but the violence and disorder have been exaggerated. Life in the West was much calmer and more orderly than it is usually pictured in the movies. Nevertheless, many cattle towns did have **boot hills**—cemeteries for those who "died with their boots on," either from overwork or on a spree.

The End of the Open Range

The cowhand rode tall on the open range. In the 1880s, however, the days of the open range were ending. By 1884 there were more than 4.5 million head of cattle roaming free on the Great Plains. The range was becoming overstocked. Good grazing land was scarce. In the foothills of the Rockies sheepherders squared off against local cattle

Montana Historical Society, Helena

Cowboy F.H. Corbin prepares to mount a "bronc" in a Montana corral.

647

1 Farmers began to use barbed wire after its invention in 1873, and this greatly reduced the area for cattle to range.

2 Approximately four fifths (80 percent) of the cattle died on the Great Plains during those winters.

Point of View

A cattleman gave this testimony on pasturing his livestock on the open range.

> **I have two miles of running water. That accounts for my ranch being where it is. The next water from me in one direction is 23 miles; now no man can have a ranch between these two places. I have control of the grass, the same as though I owned it.**
> Testimony Before Public Laws Commision, c. 1880s

ranchers. Cattle ranchers believed that sheep cropped the grass right down to the roots so that cattle could no longer find it. Many **range wars** broke out between cattle ranchers and sheep ranchers for control of the grasslands.

Farmers also competed with ranchers for land. Longhorns trampled their crops. The farmers feared the free-roaming herds would **1** infect their cattle with a dread disease called "Texas fever."

Then came two terrible winters. In 1885-86 and in 1886-87 blizzards howled across the plains. Theodore Roosevelt, then a "gentleman rancher" in Dakota Territory, wrote:

> Furious gales blow down from the north, driving before them the clouds of blinding snow-dust, wrapping the mantle of death around every unsheltered being. . . .

2 When the spring came in 1887, ranchers discovered that the storms had all but wiped out their herds.

The boom times were over. Cattle ranchers could no longer count on the free grass of the plains. They had to fence in their herds and feed them hay and fodder in the winter. Cattle ranchers became cattle feeders, their work, like mining, less risky but also less adventurous. This change was important, especially to farmers on the Great Plains. Demand for corn, grains, and hay soared, as did the prices paid for them. Now economics urged Americans to find ways to farm the hard, dry soil of the plains.

Farming on the Great Plains

The soil of the Great Plains was fertile, but farming there proved to be very difficult. Still, settlers came by the thousands to claim their 160 acres under the Homestead Act or to buy land from the railroads. Some were the sons and daughters of farmers in states like Illinois and Iowa and Arkansas. Others were emigrants from Norway, Sweden, and a dozen other lands. O. E. Rölvaag wrote of several Norwegian families and the land they settled. Imagine the plains they saw as he describes them:

> Bright, clear sky over a plain so wide that the rim of the heavens cut down on it around the horizon. . . . Bright, clear sky, to-day, to-morrow, and for all time to come.
>
> . . . And sun! And still more sun! It sets the heavens afire every morning; it grew with the day to a quivering golden light—then softened into all the shades of red and purple as evening fell. . . . Pure colour everywhere. A gust of wind, sweeping across the plain, threw into life waves of yellow and blue and green. Now and then a dead black wave would race across the scene . . . a cloud's gliding shadow . . . now and then. . . .

STRATEGIES FOR SUCCESS

INTEGRATING STRATEGIES
FOR SUCCESS
By looking at the climate map
on this page, have students determine the climate region in
which they live and draw conclusions about the social and
economic patterns of the region based on this climate.

READING A CLIMATE MAP

Like election maps, climate maps are special-
purpose maps. They show the climate of an
area. *Climate* is the average daily weather conditions over a long period of time. Climate often
influences human activity and decision making.

There are 13 major climate types. *Tropical wet*
areas are hot and rainy all year. *Tropical wet-
and-dry* areas are hot, with most rain falling in
the summer. *Desert* regions receive little or no
rain, while *semiarid* areas receive between 10
and 20 inches (25 and 50 centimeters) of rain a
year. *Mediterranean* areas are mild and dry in
the winter and hot and dry in the summer. *West
coast marine* climates have cool summers and
abundant rain all year. *Humid subtropical* areas
have mild winters, hot and rainy summers. Regions with *continental* climates vary. All have
severely cold winters, but some have cool summers while others have scorching ones. *Polar*
climates—boreal, subarctic, and ice cap—are
very cold. *Mountain* climates vary depending on
elevation.

How to Read a Climate Map

To read a climate map, follow these guidelines.
1. **Study the key.** The key explains what the
   colors and special symbols on the map mean.
   Generally different colors will indicate different climatic regions.
2. **Note the map's patterns.** Climatic regions often follow a predictable pattern.
3. **Use the information.** The information on the
   climate map can help you form hypotheses
   and draw conclusions about economic activities and life styles in each climate area.

Applying the Strategy

Study the climate map of the United States below. Note that there are nine major climate regions in the United States. What generalization
can you make about climate and human activity
after studying the map?

*For independent practice, see Practicing the
Strategy on page 657.*

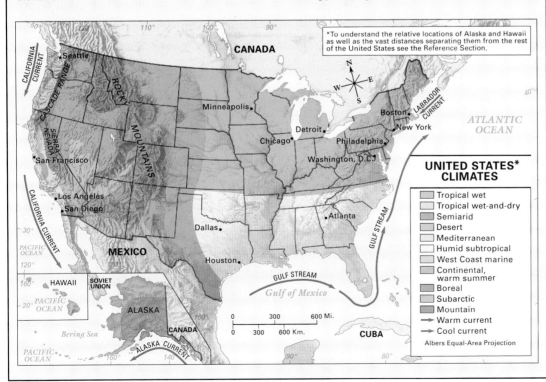

*To understand the relative locations of Alaska and Hawaii
as well as the vast distances separating them from the rest
of the United States see the Reference Section.

UNITED STATES* CLIMATES

- Tropical wet
- Tropical wet-and-dry
- Semiarid
- Desert
- Mediterranean
- Humid subtropical
- West Coast marine
- Continental, warm summer
- Boreal
- Subarctic
- Mountain
- → Warm current
- → Cool current

Albers Equal-Area Projection

RELATING HISTORY TO GEOGRAPHY
Remind students that climate and soil conditions have important influences on human activity. Have students list various aspects of the climate and soil of the Plains. Have them use their lists to discuss the influence of those conditions of life on the Plains.

It was late afternoon. A small caravan was pushing its way through the tall grass. The track that it left behind was like the wake of a boat—except that instead of widening out astern it closed in again.

'Tish-ah!' said the grass. . . . 'Tish-ah, tish-ah!' . . . Never had it said anything else—never would it say anything else. It bent resiliently under the trampling feet; it did not break, but it complained aloud every time—for nothing like this had ever happened to it before. . . . 'Tish-ah, tish-ah!' it cried, and rose up in surprise to look at this rough, hard thing that had crushed it to the ground so rudely, and then moved on. . . .

This was the caravan of Pers Hansa, who with his family and all his earthly possessions was moving west from Fillmore County, Minnesota, to Dakota Territory. There he intended to take up land and build himself a home; he was going to do something remarkable out there, which should become known far and wide. No lack of opportunity in that country, he had been told![1]"

On the treeless plains the pioneers built their first homes out of the earth itself. The thick roots of the wild grasses made it possible  to cut sod into bricklike chunks. Only the roofs of these **sod houses** were made of wood. Sod houses were smoky and damp, but they provided shelter until the railroads reached the frontier. Then lumber could be brought in at reasonable rates.

This sod house is typical of those built in the land where few trees grew. Use historical imagination to ask what the boy will do next.

[1]From *Giants in the Earth* by O.E. Rölvaag

PRIMARY SOURCE
Description of change: excerpted.
Rationale: excerpted to focus on the description of Norwegian settlers by O. E. Rölvaag.

RESOURCES

■ You may wish to have students complete Reading 9: "Wolves and Grasshoppers Plague the Kansas Frontier (1870s)" in Volume II of *Eyewitnesses and Others*.

Fencing was a more difficult problem. Farmers had to protect ■ their crops. But nothing they used stood up to the pounding of the cattle and other farm animals. The problem was solved by Joseph Glidden, who invented barbed wire in 1873. Barbed-wire fences soon crisscrossed the open range.

In the East farmers got water from bubbling springs or from wells. They hauled ground water to the surface in buckets or pumped it up easily by hand. But on the Great Plains water flowed deep beneath the surface. Farmers needed powerful pumps to get it. Fortunately, the winds of the plains blew steadily enough to turn windmills. These powered the pumps that drew up the water.

The biggest problem facing the farmers of frontier Nebraska, Kansas, and the Dakotas was the lack of rainfall. In some years there was plenty of rain to grow wheat and other grain crops. But often there were dry years, even **droughts,** when almost no rain fell. Well water could be used to irrigate a small plot or a vegetable garden, but it was not enough for any large-scale farming.

Hardy W. Campbell, a Nebraska farmer, developed a technique called **dry farming** that made it possible to raise certain crops when as little as 15 or 20 inches (37 to 50 centimeters) of rain fell a year. Campbell plowed the land deeply and repeatedly until the soil was almost as absorbent as blotting paper. The idea was to make sure that all the rain that did fall was absorbed directly into the soil where the roots of the plants could use it. Campbell also planted special varieties of wheat that did not need as much water as other types. Using dry-farming methods, farmers could raise crops in drought years.

Despite such advances farming the plains remained tremendously hard work. Willa Cather captured this in her widely read *My Ántonia*. In this excerpt Jim Burden, the narrator, tells of a visit with his friend Ántonia Shimerda, the only daughter of immigrant parents from Czechoslovakia. Remember as you read that Ántonia's day is fairly typical.

The windmill above might have pumped water for the thirsty pony.

“ The Shimerdas were in their new log house by then. The neighbors had helped them to build it in March. It stood directly in front of their old cave, which they used as a cellar. The family were now fairly equipped to begin their struggle with the soil. They had four comfortable rooms to live in, a new windmill—bought on credit—a chicken-house and poultry. Mrs. Shimerda had paid grandfather ten dollars for a milk cow, and was to give him fifteen more as soon as they harvested their first crop. . . .

When the sun was dropping low, Ántonia came up the big south draw with her team. How much older she had grown in eight months! She had come to us a child, and now she was a tall, strong young girl, although her fifteenth

CHECKING UNDERSTANDING
Have students discuss the physical features of the plains that caused hardships for farmers and some of the ways they were able to overcome these difficulties. *(Students should mention that there were almost no trees on the plains, forcing the first farmers to build their homes of sod. They had no way of protecting their crops from cattle and other farm animals until Joseph Glidden invented barbed wire in 1873. Water flowed deep beneath the surface on the plains, so farmers used windmills to power the pumps that brought up the water. There was very little rainfall on the plains, so Hardy W. Campbell developed a technique called dry farming, which made it possible to grow certain crops with little rainfall. The sod was tough on the plains, so James Oliver manufactured a cast iron plow that could cut through it. John Appleby invented the twine binder, which gathered up bundles of wheat and bound them with twine or string automatically.)*

RESOURCES
■ You may wish to have students complete Reading 2: "A Norwegian Pioneer Woman Describes Her New Home in Iowa (1863-1865)" in Volume II of *Eyewitnesses and Others.*
◄ You may wish to have students review Transparency 22: "Chama Running Red" in *Art in American History.*

RETEACHING STRATEGY
Students with Special Needs. Pair students who are having difficulty with students who are performing well. To reinforce the impact of the physical setting on plains farmers, write the following questions on the chalkboard or an overhead projector and have the more proficient students ask the questions.

1. What did the first farmers on the plains use to build their homes and why? *(sod, because there were almost no trees on the plains)*

2. How were farmers on the plains eventually able to protect their crops from cattle and other farm animals? *(with barbed wire invented in 1874)*

3. How were farmers able to bring up water that flowed deep beneath the surface of the plains? *(with windmills that powered pumps which brought up the water)*

4. How did farmers deal with a lack of sufficient rainfall on the plains? *(with a technique called dry farming, which made it possible to grow certain crops with little rainfall)*

5. How did farmers plow the tough sod of the plains? *(with a steel plow that could cut through it)*

6. How were farmers able to gather wheat on the plains? *(with the twine binder, which gathered up bundles of wheat and bound them with twine or string automatically)*

Brown Brothers

Willa Cather, a Nebraskan, wrote her novels set in the Midwest after she herself moved to New York City. Her novels include O Pioneers!, One of Ours, A Lost Lady, *and* Death Comes for the Archbishop—*her masterpiece, set in colonial New Mexico.*

■ birthday had just slipped by. I ran out and met her as she brought her horses up to the windmill to water them. She wore the boots her father had so thoughtfully taken off before he shot himself, and his old fur cap. Her outgrown cotton dress switched about her calves, over the boot-tops. She kept her sleeves rolled up all day, and her arms and throat were burned as brown as a sailor's. Her neck came up strongly out of her shoulders, like the bole [trunk] of a tree out of the turf. One sees that draught-horse neck among the peasant women in all old countries.

She greeted me gaily, and began at once to tell me how much ploughing she had done that day. Ambrosch, she said, was on the north quarter, breaking sod with the oxen.

'Jim, you ask Jake how much he ploughed to-day. I don't want that Jake get more done in one day than me. I want we have very much corn this fall.'

While the horses drew in the water, and nosed each
◄ other, and then drank again, Ántonia sat down on the windmill and rested her head on her hand.

'You see the big prairie fire from your place last night? I hope your grandpa ain't lose no [hay] stacks?'

'No, we didn't. I came to ask you something, Tony. Grandmother wants to know if you can't go to the term of school that begins next week over at the sod school-house. She says there's a good teacher, and you'd learn a lot.'

Ántonia stood up, lifting and dropping her shoulders as if they were stiff. 'I ain't got time to learn. I can work like mans now. My mother can't say no more how Ambrosch do all and nobody to help him. I can work as much as him. School is all right for little boys. I help make this land one good farm.'

She clucked to her team and started for the barn. I walked beside her, feeling vexed. Was she going to grow up boastful like her mother, I wondered? Before we reached the stable, I felt something tense in her silence, and glancing up I saw that she was crying. She turned her face from me and looked off at the red streak of dying light, over the dark prairie.

I climbed up into the loft and threw down the hay for her, while she unharnessed her team. We walked slowly back toward the house. Ambrosch had come in from the north quarter, and was watering his oxen at the tank.

Ántonia took my hand. 'Sometime you will tell me all those nice things you learn at the school, won't you, Jimmy?' she asked with a sudden rush of feeling in her voice. 'My father, he went much to school. He know a great deal; how to make the fine cloth like what you not got here.

National Archives

He play horn and violin, and he read so many books that the priests in Bohemie [Bohemia, a district now in southern Germany] come to talk to him. You won't forget my father, Jim?'

'No,' I said, 'I will never forget him.' . . .'"

¹From *My Ántonia* by Willa Cather.

This farmer was photographed while turning the soil of the prairie. The picture is titled "Mares of Percheron," which is the type of work horse pulling the plow. What time of year do you suppose this photograph was taken? Explain your answer.

The gigantic "bonanza farms" of the Red River Valley of North Dakota and Minnesota were the most spectacular farms on the plains. These farms spread over thousands of acres. One big wheat farm in Dakota Territory was managed by Oliver Dalrymple. He ran the farm like a factory. Everything possible was mechanized. When the wheat was ripe, he used 155 binders and 26 steam threshers to harvest it. In 1877 Dalrymple's workers harvested 75,000 bushels of wheat.

Farms of this type were unusual. Still, by the 1880s the average plains farmer was using a great deal of machinery. In 1868 James Oliver of Indiana began manufacturing a cast iron plow. This plow could easily slice through the tough sod of the plains. In the 1870s John Appleby invented a twine binder. This machine gathered up bundles of wheat and bound them with twine or string automatically. Soon an acre of wheat that had taken 60 hours to harvest by hand could be harvested in only 3 hours by machine.

By the 1890s the land west of the Mississippi Valley was no longer thought of as a desert. It had become the **breadbasket of America** and the greatest wheat-producing region in the world. By 1 1890 about 5 million people were living on the Great Plains. There was still unsettled land, but there was no longer a frontier separating settlement from wilderness. The march westward that had begun in Virginia in 1607 had overrun the continent. ▣

Return to the Preview & Review on ■ page 643.

The End of the Open Range   653

Have students report on the
impact of the railroads on life
in the West. Their report should
focus on the geographic theme
of *movement.* Or have students choose one of the mining
areas that appear on the map
in this activity, and prepare an
oral report on the history of
mining in this region. You may
wish to invite a geologist to
speak to students and explain
why particular ores are found
in some regions of the country
and not others.

LINKING HISTORY & GEOGRAPHY

GOLD! GOLD! GOLD!

Prospectors differed from typical pioneers. They dreamed not of fertile valleys and rich farmlands. They sought steep mountainsides where roaring streams covered beds of ore, deserts where shifting sand hid precious metal, or highlands where jagged rock outcroppings protected great veins of mineral wealth.

Prospecting in California

1. What were the chief methods of mining used by prospectors and miners?

Gold! The word was magic. Like a magnet it attracted hopeful prospectors from all over the world to California in 1849. These Forty-Niners used simple devices—usually a pan or sluice box—to wash the ore to separate the particles of gold.

Once the easily obtained surface gold was gone, however, more sophisticated mining methods were necessary. Gold still remained but it was often locked in hard rock called quartz and was typically found deep beneath the earth's surface. To extract this gold, shafts had to be dug to reach the beds of ore. Crushing mills then separated the unyielding ore from the quartz. But shafts and crushing mills were too expensive for most miners. As a result, eastern bankers furnished the money to develop California's mining industry. Individual prospectors had to look elsewhere if they were to realize their dream of striking it rich on their own.

Searching the West

2. What attracted miners to Colorado?

Throughout the late 1850s and 1860s prospectors scoured the West, ranging from the Pacific to the Rockies. Every likely stream was panned and every promising outcropping of rock was examined in their quest to find pay dirt. Whenever a strike was made, a horde of hopeful miners swarmed in. A handful quickly became rich. Most were lucky if they found enough gold to pay their expenses.

Then in 1858 a number of important discoveries were made, all the way from British Columbia to Colorado. The Colorado strike was the most exciting. Rumors of gold in the region had persisted for years. These rumors were kept alive by the tales of an occasional trapper who would emerge from the mountains with a leather pouch filled with gold nuggets and of Indians who were said to fire bullets made of yellow metal. Add these rumors to the very real presence of water available from the many mountain streams and Colorado had all of the makings of a prospector's paradise.

The site of the original Colorado discovery was on the Cherry Creek near its junction with the Platte River—the very site of Denver, a dozen miles east of the Rockies. A number of small strikes were made during the summer of 1858 and news of each discovery was carried in newspapers throughout the country. By the spring of 1859 more than 100,000 hopeful prospectors flocked to what was known as Pikes Peak Country.

Most of Colorado's gold seekers came from California rather than from the settled lands of the Mississippi Valley. They had learned the basic elements of mining in California, and they attacked the Colorado gold fields with the same techniques. But by 1865 the day of the lone prospector in Colorado had ended, as it had 10 years earlier in California.

The Colorado Mining Industry

3. How did mining develop in Colorado?

Although Pikes Peak gold turned out to be a disappointment to most individual miners, mining continued to grow in Colorado. Large mining companies soon arrived, sinking deep mine shafts and feeding hungry milling machinery. Boom towns such as Central City and Blackhawk were squeezed into narrow ravines. Buildings appeared to be glued to steep slopes and jammed into gulch bottoms. Diggings and test pits were as thick as anthills.

As the miners burrowed deeper and deeper in their search for gold, new mining, milling, and smelting techniques were developed. A railroad wound its way to the communities by 1872, bringing coal to fuel the smelters. But people soon realized smelting was done more efficiently in Golden or Denver, nearer both coal and labor. So the railroad carried heavy machinery into the mining communities and the raw ore—rich with silver, copper, and lead as well as precious gold—out. By 1880 the population of the Central City-Blackhawk area had soared to 10,000. The area became known around the

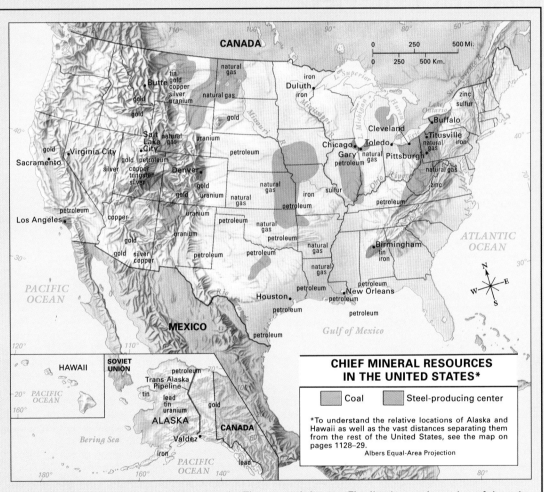

CHIEF MINERAL RESOURCES IN THE UNITED STATES*

Coal   Steel-producing center

*To understand the relative locations of Alaska and Hawaii as well as the vast distances separating them from the rest of the United States, see the map on pages 1128–29.

Albers Equal-Area Projection

world as the richest square mile on earth. The future of Colorado gold mining seemed assured.

The Decline of Mining

4. Why did the large-scale mining industry in Colorado decline?

The ultimate decline of the mining industry would have been difficult to foresee during its heyday of the 1870s and 1880s. But decline did come. Mining costs continued to rise as shafts got deeper. The quality of the ore lessened. Problems with ground water became very real. It seeped into the mines as miners penetrated below the water table. Costs of pumping were enormous. Ventilation also became increasingly complex and costly as the shafts angled deeper

and deeper. Finally, the market value of the minerals, with the exception of gold, began a downward slide. In time, copper, lead, and silver could be mined far more inexpensively in other parts of the country.

Applying Your Knowledge

Your class will create an exhibition of America's mineral wealth. Each group will select or be assigned a mineral to display in the exhibition. The display should include a description (or sketch) of the mineral (and a sample if available), a list of its uses, and a map of the locations of major deposits. Your class may wish to set up the exhibition in an appropriate place in the school or community.

Linking History & Geography   655

CHAPTER 18 REVIEW

				1860		
1845						

1848 Treaty of Guadalupe Hildago

1849 California Gold Rush

1851 Treaty of Fort Laramie

1859 Fifty-Niners surge to Colorado

1860 Cattle kingdom established on Plains

1862 Pacific Railway Act

1864 Chivington Massacre

Chapter Summary
Read the statements below. Choose one, and write a paragraph explaining its importance.

1. Before the 1850s only Indians, Spanish Americans, and Mormons lived on the Great Plains. Until then it was considered a desert.
2. Plains Indians developed unique ways of life, even adapting European items such as the horse and metal tools to their life-styles.
3. As settlers and railroads sought land on the Plains the Indians were removed to reservations. This process led to brief but bitter battles between the Indians and government troops. Settlers also seized land from Mexican Americans living in the Southwest.
4. Rich ore deposits west of the Plains brought a flurry of prospectors who built ramshackle mining camps.
5. The grasslands of the High Plains soon became the cattle kingdom. Thousands of cattle grazed on the open range and were then shipped to Chicago.
6. The open range closed as technical improvements made it possible to farm the Great Plains. Chief among these was dry farming, barbed wire, the steel plow, and the twine binder.

Reviewing Chronological Order
Number your paper 1–5. Then study the time line above and place the following events in the order in which they happened by writing the first next to 1, the second next to 2, and so on.
1. Treaty of Fort Laramie
2. Dawes Act
3. Wounded Knee
4. Transcontinental Railroad completed
5. Cattle kingdom established

Understanding Main Ideas
1. How was the system called concentration used to remove the Plains Indians?

2. How did the government encourage the building of transcontinental railroads?
3. Describe life in a typical mining town.
4. Describe the life of a cowhand. What were some inventions of the *vaqueros* used by cowhands?
5. What ended the open range? Why?
6. Describe the inventions and farming techniques that helped turn the Great American Desert into the breadbasket of America.

Thinking Critically
1. **Analyzing.** Putting yourself in the place of a Plains Indian of the early 1800s, make a list of the animals that are important to your tribe. Alongside the name of each animal, list the uses you make of it.
2. **Synthesizing.** Imagine that you are Leland Stanford writing your autobiography in June 1869. Describe your company's part in building America's first transcontinental railroad. Then tell of the important role other such railroads will play in the nation's future.
3. **Problem Solving.** You are a member of a vigilance committee in a rowdy boom town. You have called a meeting with other vigilantes to make plans for bringing law and order to your town. To prepare for your opening remarks at the meeting, outline the problems facing you. Then outline two or three ideas for how to solve these problems.

Writing About History
Use historical imagination to place yourself in one of the mining boom towns of the 1860s or as a cowhand on a long drive. Write a letter home to your family in the East telling about your life in the West. Describe your life as a miner and the town where you trade or a typical day on the drive as a cowhand. Use the information in Chapter 18 and in reference books to prepare your letter.

imagination and an understanding of what boom towns were like. The best answers will include sound ideas for solving problems.

Era of the Long Drive			
	1875	**SETTLING THE GREAT PLAINS**	**1890**

1868
cast iron plow developed

1869
Transcontinental railroad completed

1874
Barbed wire patented

1876
Battle of the Little Bighorn

1877
Chief Joseph surrenders

1881
Sitting Bull surrenders

★
A Century of Dishonor

1887
Dawes Act

★
Blizzards end open range

1890
Wounded Knee

Practicing the Strategy

Review the strategy on page 649.

Reading a Settlement Map. Study the settlement map in the Reference Section and answer the following questions.

1. Into what three states of the Ohio Valley had settlement spread by 1790?
2. Large parts of Wyoming, Montana, western Texas, and several other states were not fully settled until after 1880. Why?
3. Oklahoma was not considered settled until much later than most of its neighbors. What fact in Oklahoma's history explains this?
4. Compare the settlement map to the population distribution map below it. How are the patterns similar? How would you explain this similarity?

Using Primary Sources

The winter of 1884–85 was one of the most disastrous in America's cattle-ranching history. As you read the following excerpt from J. Frank Dobie's *The Longhorns,* think about how people and animals struggled to survive on the Great Plains. Then answer the questions that follow.

When a terrible blizzard struck in late December, cattle from southwestern Kansas and No Man's Land [a geographic area in northern Oklahoma] went with it. The grass lay under a pavement of sleet and ice. The plains afforded no harbor or shelter. As endless strings of cattle going with the wind crowded up to the first drift fence, the leaders stopped, stiffened and went down, to be trampled on by followers until piles of dead made overpasses. In places the posts were shoved over and cattle struggling through cut themselves to pieces on the barbed wire. . . . After the storm the fence lines were marked by tens of thousands of frozen bodies. In the spring cattle from the upper ranges were found five hundred miles south in Texas.

1. How do you think cowboys might have described "No Man's Land?"

2. Although the drift fences presented problems for trail drivers during a blizzard, what purpose does the reading suggest the fences served?
3. How do you think the harsh winters during the mid-1880s affected the cattle industry economically? Use evidence from the excerpt to support your opinion.

Linking History & Geography

As you read in this chapter, water is an especially valuable resource on the Great Plains. In 1820 Major Stephen Long led an army expedition through the region. Noting the dry, treeless plain, he labeled it the "Great American Desert." Except for reservoirs, there are no lakes on the Great Plains. Rivers are generally fewer and shallower than back east. On the eastern plains, precipitation—rain and snow together—averages 25 inches (64 centimeters) or more; on the western plains it is as little as 10 inches (25 centimeters). How did this lack of water affect the settlement of the Great Plains?

Enriching Your Study of History

1. **Individual Project.** A *diorama* is an exhibit of lifelike figures in natural settings in the foreground with a painting in the background. Make a diorama of an Indian camp on the Great American Desert, of a mining boom town, or of a farm on the Great Plains in the 1880s.
2. **Cooperative Project.** Your class will prepare a special section for a newspaper. Each group will use historical imagination to be newspaper reporters assigned to cover the Battle of Little Bighorn. Some of you will write biographical sketches of the key figures. Others will create illustrations, and still others will prepare a relief map of the battle site, showing the topography.

Chapter 18 Review   657

RESPONSES *(Continued)*
their letters on their lives as either miners or cowhands in the West.

Practicing the Strategy
1. Kentucky, Ohio, Tennessee
2. Lack of transportation, large numbers of Indians
3. It was Indian territory.
4. Concentration of settlement on east coast, sparser settlement further west; the frontier had not yet been completely settled.

Using Primary Sources
1. Answers will vary, but students may suggest that cowboys would describe "No Man's Land" as a desolate place where distances were endless.
2. The reading indicates that the drift fences kept cattle within certain boundaries.
3. Because so many cattle died, cattlemen must have suffered great economic losses. The excerpt suggests that many cattle died because the grass was covered by sleet and ice; surviving cattle would lose weight, thereby decreasing their market value.

Linking History & Geography
Settlement of the Great Plains was sparse until new farming inventions and techniques made it possible to farm this region, even though it lacked sufficient rainfall.

PRIMARY SOURCE
Description of change: excerpted and bracketed.
Rationale: excerpted to focus on J. Frank Dobie's description of the destruction from the blizzard of 1884-85; bracketed words added to clarify meaning.

The Rise of Industrial America

PLANNING THE CHAPTER	
TEXTBOOK	**RESOURCES**
1. The Power of the Rails	***Unit 6 Worksheets and Tests:*** Chapter 19 Graphic Organizer, Directed Reading 19:1, Reteaching 19:1 ***Eyewitnesses and Others, Volume 2:*** Reading 6: Andrew Carnegie Becomes a Businessman (1868)
2. The Communications Revolution	***Unit 6 Worksheets and Tests:*** Directed Reading 19:2, Reteaching 19:2 ***Eyewitnesses and Others, Volume 2:*** Reading 12: Thomas Edison Observed (1885); Reading 11: Football Without Helmets (1884)
3. Regulation of Big Business	***Unit 6 Worksheets and Tests:*** Directed Reading 19:3, Reteaching 19:3 ***Creative Strategies for Teaching American History:*** Page 287
4. Workers and Work	***Unit 6 Worksheets and Tests:*** Directed Reading 19:4, Reteaching 19:4, Geography 19A ***The Historian (Investigative Software):*** The Labor Movement Before 1915
5. The Growth of Cities	***Unit 6 Worksheets and Tests:*** Directed Reading 19:5, Reteaching 19:5, Geography 19B and 19C ***Creative Strategies for Teaching American History:*** Page 267 ***Eyewitnesses and Others, Volume 2:*** Reading 16: An Immigrant Family Goes to School (1880s); Reading 31: Poems of the Chinese Immigrants (ca. 1910); Reading 22: A Farm Girl Arrives in the Big City (1895); Reading 18: Jacob Riis Describes a New York City Gang (1880s)
Chapter Review	***Audio Program:*** Chapter 19 ***Unit 6 Worksheets and Tests:*** Chapter 19 Tests, Forms A and B (See also *Alternative Assessment Forms*) ***Test Generator***

STRATEGIES FOR STUDENTS WITH SPECIAL NEEDS

Gifted Students.
Have interested students write a play about an individual or family who immigrated to the United States after 1880. The play should be an enactment of one of the following: events in the native country that led to the decision to come to America; the reaction upon arrival in a strange land; how the immigrant or immigrants went about finding housing and employment in America. Encourage students to be imaginative but remind them to use historical fact as a basis for their play.

Students Having Difficulty with the Chapter.
You may wish to have students listen to Chapter 20 in *The Story of America Audio Program.* Then pair students who are having difficulty with students who are performing well. Have students in one class make a list of some of the important inventions of the late 1800s and a separate list of the inventors. In another class have students make a list of the railroad barons and business tycoons from the late 1800s and another list of the corporations that they headed. Have the first class exchange their lists with the other class and attempt to match the lists. Return the lists to the students who originally wrote them for corrections. You may wish to monitor to make sure that student corrections are accurate. Then give the lists back to the students who did the matching so that they may correct their mistakes.

BOOKS FOR TEACHERS
Leonard Dinnerstein and David Reimers, *Ethnic Americans: A History of Immigration and Assimilation.* New York: Harper & Row, 1975.

John A. Garraty, *The New Commonwealth, 1877–1890.* New York: Harper & Row, 1968.

Oscar Handlin, *The Uprooted: The Epic Story of the Great Migrations That Made the American People.* Boston: Little, Brown, 1951.

Matthew Josephson, *The Robber Barons: The Great American Capitalists, 1861–1901.* Orlando: Harcourt Brace Jovanovich, 1934.

Page Smith, *The Rise of Industrial America: A People's History of the Post-Reconstruction Era.* New York: McGraw-Hill, 1984.

BOOKS FOR STUDENTS
Horatio Alger, *Jed, the Poorhouse Boy.* Mattituck, NY: Amereon House, reprint of 1889 edition.

Leonard Everett Fisher, *The Unions.* New York: Holiday House, 1982.

Sidney Lens, *Strikemakers and Strikebreakers.* New York: Lodestar, 1985.

John J. Loeper, *Going to School in 1876.* New York: Macmillan, 1984.

N. A. Perez, *Breaker.* Boston: Houghton Mifflin, 1988.

Jacob Riis, *Children of the Tenements.* Salem, NH: Ayer Co., reprint of 1903 edition.

O. E. Rolvaag, *Giants of the Earth.* New York: Harper & Row, 1965.

Gloria Skurzynski, *The Tempering.* Boston: Clarion, 1983.

MULTIMEDIA MATERIALS
America Becomes an Industrial Nation (film, 25 min.), McGraw-Hill. Shows how industrialization helped bring great wealth and power as well as social, economic, and political problems.

Industrial America (filmstrip), SSSS. Depicts growth of American industry.

Industrializing America (software), SSSS. Students invest money in any of eight industries as America industrializes.

The Lions of Capitalism: Great American Millionaires (videocassette, 55 min.), SSSS. Chronicles the industrialists who shaped the American economy.

Labor Movement, the Beginnings and Growth in America (film, 14 min.), CORF. Key events from the end of the Civil War to World War I.

Money on the Land (film, 52 min.), U. of California. Part of the *America* series narrated by Alistair Cooke. Discusses the development of industrial America as the nation became urbanized at the end of the 1800s.

SUGGESTED CAPTION RESPONSE
They show the impact of the Industrial Revolution;
they would note the absence of pollution controls.

RESOURCES
■ You may wish to have students complete the
Chapter 19 Graphic Organizer as they work
through this chapter.

CHAPTER OBJECTIVES
Upon completing this chapter, students will be able
to:
1. Describe the rise of industrial America between
1860 and 1900.
2. Demonstrate how the railroad industry stimulated
growth in other industries.

OVERVIEW
In the years between 1860 and
1900, the United States saw
dramatic change associated
with the growth of industry,
trusts, labor unions, immigration, and cities.

FOCUS/MOTIVATION:
MAKING CONNECTIONS
Prior Knowledge.
Before students read the chapter, tell them that it covers a
period of dramatic changes.
Ask students what the economy of the United States was
like before 1860. *(primarily rural, with most people living on
farms and in small towns,
some early factories in the
Northeast)* Then ask them what
kind of changes had to occur
for the United States to have
the kind of economy that exists
today. *(industrial growth, development of large corporations, population moving from
farms to cities or suburbs)* Tell
students that between 1860
and 1900 the United States
changed from a primarily rural
economy to a primarily industrial economy and that many
other important developments
accompanied industrialization.

CHAPTER 19

The Rise of Industrial America

■ B etween 1860 and 1900 the United States went through one of the
most dramatic periods of change in its entire history. In 1860
about 80 percent of the nation's 31 million inhabitants lived on farms.
About 1.5 million, less than 5 percent, worked in factories. By the
1890s about 5 million Americans worked in factories. America's
manufactured products were worth almost as much as the manufactured goods of Great Britain, France, and Germany combined. By
the end of the century the new industrial growth was visible nearly
everywhere. Railroads crossed and recrossed the continent. Small
towns had been changed as if by magic into great cities. In 1900
about 40 percent of America's 76 million people lived in towns and
cities. The steel, oil, and electrical industries, tiny in 1865, had
become giants. Imagine how the United States would have seemed
in 1900 to a person who had been out of the country since the Civil
War!

*An appropriate symbol for America in
the 19th century is the ironworks at
Pittsburgh. What can you say about
the forms of transportation in this engraving? How would environmentalists today appraise this scene?*

The Granger Collection, New York

3. Identify inventions that were part of the communications revolution and explain how they influenced the growth of business.
4. Explain why people feared trusts.
5. Evaluate government attempts to regulate and control industry.
6. Describe the changing role of workers in America's industrial economy.

7. Comment on the attitudes of native-born Americans toward the immigration of the 1880s and 1890s.
8. Analyze the problems created by the rapid growth of cities and list some attempts to solve them.
9. Read a statistical table.

1. THE POWER OF THE RAILS

The Railroad Network

Americans were fascinated by railroads. Poets celebrated the "pant and roar" of the locomotives, so powerful as to shake the ground, and the elaborate decorations painted on their sides. They even praised the "dense and murky" clouds that belched from the locomotives' smokestacks. To all sorts of people railroads symbolized the boundless energy of the nation. In 1879 the great American poet Walt Whitman traveled by rail west from Philadelphia to the Rocky Mountains and back. He then wrote this prose poem in tribute to railroads:

66 What a fierce weird pleasure to lie in my berth at night in the luxurious palace-car, drawn by the mighty Baldwin [a make of locomotive]—embodying, and filling me, too, full of the swiftest motion, and most resistless strength! It is late, perhaps midnight or after—distances join'd like magic—as we speed through Harrisburg, Columbus, Indianapolis. The element of danger adds zest to it all. On we go, rumbling and flashing, with our loud whinnies thrown out from time to time, or trumpetblasts, into the darkness. Passing the homes of men, the farms, barns, cattle—the silent villages. And the car itself, the sleeper, with curtains drawn and lights turn'd down—in the berths the slumberers, many of the women and children—as on, on, on, we fly like lightning through the night—how strangely sound and sweet we sleep! . . .¹ 99

When the Civil War began, there were only 30,000 miles (48,000 kilometers) of railroad track in the United States. Most railroads were very short, averaging only about 100 miles (160 kilometers). They had been built to serve local needs. Few direct lines connected distant cities. Passengers and freight traveling between New York and Chicago, for example, had to be transferred from one line to another 17 times! The trip took at least 50 hours.

The main task of the postwar generation was to connect these lines into one network. "Commodore" Cornelius Vanderbilt was a pioneer in this work. Vanderbilt could barely read and write, but he was aggressive and hard-nosed. He had made a fortune in shipping, but when river traffic fell during the Civil War, he invested in railroads. By 1869 he had control of the New York Central Railroad, which ran between Buffalo and Albany, and two other lines that connected the Central with New York City.

¹From *The Collected Prose* (1891–1892) by Walt Whitman

Preview & Review

Use these questions to guide your reading. Answer the questions after completing Section 1.

Understanding Issues, Events, & Ideas. Using the following words, describe the economic changes in the United States after 1870: railroad baron, corporation, stock certificate, stockholder, board of directors, limited liability, partnership, Bessemer converter, Mesabi Range, smelt, division of labor, mass production, oil refining, "Drake's Folly," wildcatter, "black gold."

1. How did railroads stimulate the national economy?
2. Why did the railroad boom lead business leaders to set up corporations?
3. What effect on the production of steel did the Bessemer converter have?
4. What created the demand for kerosene? How did the discovery of oil lead to a boom?

Thinking Critically. 1. The year is 1870. You have just seen a passing locomotive for the first time. Write a brief description of your impressions. 2. Which do you think was the most important scientific achievement in the 1800s: mass production of steel or the process of oil refining? Why?

PREVIEW & REVIEW RESPONSES
Understanding Issues, Events, & Ideas.
Descriptions should demonstrate an understanding of the terms used.

1. The railroad companies had to buy raw materials to build and operate the lines; they made it possible to ship goods relatively quickly and cheaply over long distances—goods that had once been luxuries could now be purchased at reasonable prices; new towns sprang up along the railroad lines, and older towns grew into cities.
2. To build and operate a railroad required more money that one person or family could command. Developers raised money from many investors and therefore needed to organize their businesses as corporations.
3. It made it possible to make steel easily and cheaply.
4. Samuel M. Kier refined petroleum into kerosene which could be used in lamps. It was much cheaper than whale oil. When E. L. Drake successfully drilled for oil, wildcatters, hoping to duplicate his success, rushed to western Pennsylvania.

PRIMARY SOURCE
Description of change: excerpted and bracketed.
Rationale: excerpted to focus on the fascination with railroads; bracketed words added to clarify meaning.

The Granger Collection, New York

Travelers to ancient Greece saw the bronze Colossus of Rhodes, over 100 feet (30.5 meters) high. It was one of the seven wonders of the ancient world. Ships were said to have sailed between its legs, but in truth the Colossus stood on a hillside. "The Colossus of Roads" by Joseph Keppler makes Cornelius Vanderbilt a modern colossus with his empire of railroads. Explain how a man barely able to read and write amassed a fortune of 100 million dollars.

① In 1870 Vanderbilt bought the Lake Shore and Michigan Southern Railroads. His growing New York Central system then extended 965 miles (1,544 kilometers) from New York to Chicago by way of Cleveland and Toledo. Passengers could travel between New York and Chicago in less than 24 hours without leaving their seats. When Vanderbilt died in 1877, he left a railroad system of over 4,500 miles (7,200 kilometers) serving a vast region. He left a personal fortune of $100 million.

In much the same way J. Edgar Thomson, head of the Pennsylvania Railroad, built up direct routes from Philadelphia to St. Louis and Chicago by way of Pittsburgh. In 1871 the Pennsylvania Railroad extended its tracks to New York City. Other lines were extended by wealthy developers such as Jay Gould, Jim Fisk, and James J. Hill.

② Besides combining railroads to make through connections, the **railroad barons,** as the men who financed and profited from railroads were called, built many new lines. By 1900 the United States had about 200,000 miles (320,000 kilometers) of railroad track. This was more than were in all the nations of Europe combined.

In addition to speeding the movement of goods and passengers, the railroads supplied thousands of jobs for laborers, train crews, repair workers, and clerks. By 1891 the Pennsylvania Railroad alone employed over 110,000 workers. The largest United States government employer, the post office, had only 95,000 on its payroll in 1891.

Railroads stimulated the national economy in countless ways. ③They were great users of wood, copper, and steel. They made it possible to move bulky products like coal and iron ore cheaply over long distances. This made such products available at reasonable prices in regions where they had formerly been very expensive. Railroads enabled farmers in California to sell their fruits and vegetables in New York. Flour milled in Minneapolis could be purchased in Boston. Wherever railroads went, new towns sprang up almost overnight, and older towns grew to be big cities.

LEARNING FROM TABLES. *This table illustrates the growth of railroads between 1870 and 1900. Why was the extension of the railroad network essential to the development of the American economy?*

RAILROADS, 1870-1900			
Year	Miles of Track	Capital Invested (Millions)	Total Income (Millions)
1870	52,922	$ 2,476	NA
1880	93,262	$ 5,402	$ 503
1890	166,703	$10,122	$1,092
1900	193,346	$12,814	$2,013
NA= Not Available			

Source: *Historical Statistics of the United States*

The Corporation

Railroads were very expensive to build and operate. The sums needed to build even a small one were far larger than the amount John C. Calhoun had to raise to buy his South Carolina plantation, more than John Ellerton Lodge had invested in his fleet of merchant ships, greater than Francis Cabot Lowell and the Boston Associates needed when they built their first textile mill.

One person or family or even a group of partners rarely had enough money to construct and operate a railroad. Railroad developers had to raise money from other investors. To do this, they set up their businesses as **corporations.**

When a corporation is formed, the organizers sell shares called **stock certificates.** People who buy shares are called **stockholders.** These stockholders own the corporation, which is usually run by a **board of directors.** Stockholders can sell their shares to anyone for whatever price they can get. If the business is doing poorly, the value of the shares will fall.

For the organizers of big businesses the chief advantage of the corporation is that it brings together the money of many investors. For the investors the chief advantage is **limited liability.** This means that the individual investors risk only the money they have paid for their stocks. In a **partnership,** on the other hand, all the partners are responsible for the debts of the firm. For example, a partner who had invested only $100 could be held responsible for a $5,000 debt of a partnership. The same person investing $100 in the stock of a corporation could lose only that $100, no matter how much money the corporation owed.

Changing Iron into Steel

The railroad industry could not have grown as large as it did without steel. The first rails were made of iron. But iron rails were not strong enough to support heavy trains running at high speeds. Railroad executives wanted to replace them with steel rails because steel was 10 or 15 times stronger and lasted 20 times longer. Before the 1870s, however, steel was too expensive to be widely used. It was made by a slow and expensive process of heating, stirring, and reheating iron ore.

Then an English inventor, Henry Bessemer, discovered that directing a blast of air at melted iron in a furnace would burn out the impurities that made the iron brittle. As the air shot through the furnace, the bubbling metal would erupt in showers of sparks. When the fire cooled, the metal had been changed, or *converted,* to steel. The **Bessemer converter** made possible the mass production of steel. Now three to five tons of iron could be changed into steel in a matter of minutes.

ART IN HISTORY
Ask students to skim the chapter, looking only at the illustrations. These portray many of the changes that took place from 1860 to 1900. Explain the changes suggested by one illustration and ask students to find other "portraits of change" in the chapter. Discuss each student response and refer the entire class to the illustration under discussion. This activity will help remind students that illustrations are important tools to use in studying history and will also establish readiness to begin the chapter.

SUGGESTED CAPTION RESPONSE
Reward imaginative, creative descriptions.

RESOURCES
■ You may wish to have students complete Reading 6: ''Andrew Carnegie Becomes a Businessman (1868)'' in Volume II of *Eyewitnesses and Others.*

GUIDED INSTRUCTION: COOPERATIVE LEARNING

Organize students into cooperative learning groups and assign each group one of the captains of industry—e.g., Andrew Carnegie, Cornelius Vanderbilt, J. P. Morgan, Jay Gould, John D. Rockefeller—as a subject for a report. Have students consult encyclopedias or biographies on the subject in their school or local libraries. Then each group should prepare a class presentation on their assigned subject. The group should present both their subject's point of view of his contributions and motives and the point of view of his critics. Encourage students to bring copies of pictures or newspaper cartoons about their subject to show the class. Use the presentations as the basis for a class discussion on whether the influence of these men was good or bad for the United States.

Metropolitan Museum of Art

"Forging the Shaft: A Welding Heat" was painted in 1877 by John F. Weir. It captures the glow of molten metal that filled American steel mills in the 19th century. Use your historical imagination to describe the sensations you would have felt working in front of a blast furnace.

Just when the demand for more and more steel developed, prospectors discovered huge new deposits of iron ore in the **Mesabi Range,** a 120-mile-long region (192 kilometers) in Minnesota near Lake Superior. The Mesabi deposits were so near the surface that they could be mined with steam shovels.

Barges and steamers carried the iron ore through Lake Superior to depots on the southern shores of Lake Michigan and Lake Erie. With dizzying speed Gary, Indiana, and Toledo, Youngstown, and Cleveland, Ohio, became major steel-manufacturing centers. Pittsburgh was the greatest steel city of all. The large coal fields near Pittsburgh supplied cheap fuel to **smelt** the ore—that is, to melt it down to remove impurities.

Steel was the basic building material of the industrial age. After steel rails came steel bridges. Next came steel skeletons for tall buildings. Nails, wire, and other everyday objects were also made of steel. Production skyrocketed from 77,000 tons in 1870 to over 11 million tons in 1900.

■ Andrew Carnegie was by far the most important producer of steel. Born in 1835 in Scotland, he came to the United States at age 12 and settled with his parents in Allegheny, now a part of Pittsburgh. At 14 he was working 12 hours a day as a bobbin boy in a cotton mill for $1.20 a week. He studied hard and at 16 had progressed to a telegraph clerk earning $4.00 a week—a fair salary in those days. At 17 Carnegie became the private secretary to the president of the Pennsylvania Railroad.

SUGGESTED CAPTION RESPONSES
(Top) Steel was necessary for building railroad tracks, bridges, steel-framed buildings, heavy machinery, large factories and mills. Iron was needed to produce steel.
(Bottom) Through the hard work, shrewd investments, and excellent timing, Carnegie was able to build a large up-to-date steel mill at a bargain price. He was also a successful promoter and salesperson.

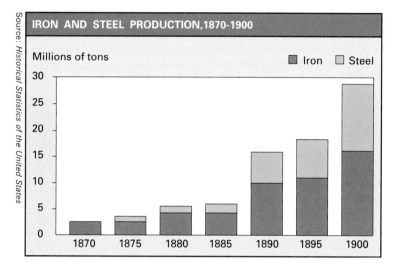

Source: *Historical Statistics of the United States*

IRON AND STEEL PRODUCTION, 1870-1900

Millions of tons

◼ Iron ◻ Steel

LEARNING FROM GRAPHS.
Note the rapid increase in the production of iron and steel shown on this graph. Iron and steel, like railroad and communication networks, were necessary for modern industrial growth. Why?

Carnegie then invested in an oil well and began to make money in the new oil industry. But he soon turned to the steel industry. He frankly admitted he knew nothing about making steel when he started. Early in his career as an ironmaster, he visited a plant in England where the Bessemer process was being used. This new process made large quantities of steel cheaply. Now Carnegie became convinced that the day of cheap steel had arrived. He rushed home and built the largest Bessemer plant in America. He did so in the midst of the worst depression in the history of the United States. Labor and materials were cheap. Thus Carnegie got a large, up-to-date steel mill at a bargain price.

But Carnegie's true success was as a promoter and seller. He captured the largest share of the railroad business—the nation's largest steel users—with several shrewd deals. He also knew how to gather specialists and manage them. He was a relentless boss. By 1900 Andrew Carnegie, who came to America as a poor immigrant boy, was the second richest man in the world. In 1901 he sold his steel property for nearly $500 million!

Brown Brothers

Andrew Carnegie came to America from Scotland and began work in the factories as a bobbin boy. How did this hard-working immigrant make his fortune?

Mass Production

The rapidly growing production of steel formed the foundations of an industrial system that would eventually make the United States the most productive country in the world. Besides rails, bridges, and steel-framed buildings, steel went into heavy machines, factories, and mills. Businesses expanded and factories grew larger. Owners and managers developed more efficient production methods.

You have read about Eli Whitney's development of interchangeable parts. This led to a **division of labor.** A shoemaker no longer made an entire shoe. Instead, in large shoe factories one worker

HISTORICAL SIDELIGHTS
SUGGESTED CAPTION RESPONSE

HISTORICAL SIDELIGHTS
● The American whaling fleet lost ships during the Civil War and in 1871 lost 34 more when they became trapped in Arctic ice. However, other developments in processing and hunting had made whalers more efficient, and it was the petroleum industry that effectively curtailed whaling.

SUGGESTED CAPTION RESPONSE
Refined into kerosene for use in lamps; also refined into waxes, lubricating oils, gasoline, and heating oil

INDEPENDENT PRACTICE
Have students complete the Preview & Review activity at the beginning of the section.

CLOSURE
Tell students that the development of a cheap way to mass produce steel and the development of corporations helped to make large railroad systems possible. The beginnings of the oil refining industry, which had the immediate advantage of providing cheaper fuel for lighting, would become important to future developments in transportation.

HOMEWORK
Give students outline maps of the United States. To help students visualize the geographic extent of the railroad network, ask them to use the library resources to make maps of the railroads in place at the end of the 19th century. Use these maps as a basis for a class discussion of how the extension of railroad lines might have influenced the lives of ordinary people. *(Possible responses are: made a wider range of goods available to consumers and at cheaper prices; made it more feasible for western settlers to visit family and friends left behind.)*

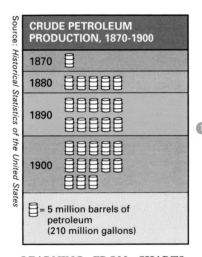

Source: Historical Statistics of the United States

CRUDE PETROLEUM PRODUCTION, 1870-1900

1870

1880

1890

1900

= 5 million barrels of petroleum (210 million gallons)

LEARNING FROM CHARTS. *Petroleum production boomed during the second half of the 19th century, as you can see from this chart. What were its main uses in American industry?*

Return to the Preview & Review on page 659.

might run a machine that cut only heels. Another might run a machine that cut out the soles, and so forth. All the parts were then brought together at a central place and assembled by still other workers into a shoe. Vast quantities of shoes could be made quickly in this way. Most American industries soon adopted division of labor. It made possible the **mass production** of large quantities of products of every kind.

"Black Gold"

An important new industry, **oil refining,** grew after the Civil War. Crude oil, or petroleum—a dark, thick ooze from the earth—had been known for hundreds of years. But little use had ever been made of it. In the 1850s Samuel M. Kier, a manufacturer in western Pennsylvania, began collecting the oil from local seepages and refining it into kerosene. Refining, like smelting, is a process of removing impurities from a raw material.

● Kerosene was used to light lamps. It was a cheap substitute for whale oil, which was becoming harder to get and therefore more expensive. Soon there was a large demand for kerosene. People began to search for new supplies of petroleum.

The first oil well was drilled by E. L. Drake, a retired railroad conductor. In 1859 he began drilling in Titusville, Pennsylvania. The whole venture seemed so impractical and foolish that onlookers called it **"Drake's Folly."** But when he had drilled down about 70 feet (21 meters), Drake struck oil. His well began to yield 20 barrels of crude oil a day.

News of Drake's success brought oil prospectors to the scene. By the early 1860s these **wildcatters** were drilling for **"black gold"** all over western Pennsylvania. The boom rivaled the California gold rush of 1848 in its excitement and Wild West atmosphere. And it brought far more wealth to the prospectors than any gold rush.

At first oil was shipped to refineries in barrels. The barrel was replaced first by railroad tank cars and then by oil pipelines. Crude oil could be refined into many products. For some years kerosene continued to be the principal one. It was sold in grocery stores and door-to-door. In the 1880s refiners learned how to make other petroleum products such as waxes and lubricating oils for new industrial machines. The discovery of these oils and the invention by Elijah McCoy, the son of runaway slaves, of a lubricating cup that fed the oil to parts of a machine while it was operating were important industrial breakthroughs.

Not until the 1890s was petroleum used to make gasoline or heating oil. The development then of the internal combustion engine, which burned gasoline or diesel fuel, finally turned oil into one of the nation's major sources of power. By the turn of the century modern factories were turning to oil as their source of energy.

2. THE COMMUNICATIONS REVOLUTION

The Telegraph and Telephone

Rapid, cheap communication over long distances is an essential part of modern industrial society. The **communications revolution** began in 1837 when Samuel F. B. Morse invented the **telegraph** to send electronic signals over wire. By 1861 telegraph lines connected all parts of the country. One line stretched all the way across the still-unsettled Great Plains to the Pacific Coast.

The telegraph made it possible for people to communicate over great distances in seconds. It took much of the guesswork out of business. Managers could know when supplies would arrive, where demand was greatest for their products, and what prices were being charged across the country.

In 1866 the Western Union Telegraph Company obtained control of the national telegraph network. The same year Cyrus W. Field succeeded in laying the first successful telegraph cable across the Atlantic Ocean to Europe. Not long after that, a telegraph network gave the United States almost instant communication with countries all over the world.

Next came the **telephone.** The telephone was invented in 1876 by Alexander Graham Bell, a teacher of the deaf in Boston. Work

Preview & Review

Use these questions to guide your reading. Answer the questions after completing Section 2.
Understanding Issues, Events, & Ideas. Using the following words, summarize how inventions in the late 1800s changed the nation: communications revolution, telegraph, telephone, quadruplex telegraph, phonograph, electric light, suspension bridge, skyscraper, department store, chain store.

1. How did the communications revolution affect business?
2. How did Samuel F. B. Morse contribute to the communications revolution? How did Alexander Graham Bell contribute?
3. What did Thomas Edison say was the secret of his success as the great inventor of the era?
4. How did new marketing techniques help business grow?

Thinking Critically. It is 1880. Write and send a telegram to your family, telling them what you think is the most important invention of the late 1800s.

Cyrus Field, above, made the world a little smaller with his Atlantic cable. Mathew Brady was his photographer. Left is Alexander Graham Bell demonstrating a long-distance call from New York to Chicago for a group of businessmen in 1892.

Brown Brothers

Chicago Historical Society

SECTION 2

PREVIEW & REVIEW RESPONSES
Understanding Issues, Events, Ideas.
Summaries should demonstrate an understanding of the terms used.
1. Because the telegraph made instant communication across great distances possible, it took much of the guess work out of business. Managers now knew when orders would arrive, where demand for their products was greatest, and what prices were all over the country.
2. Morse invented the telegraph. Bell invented the telephone.
3. Edison believed that hard work and sticking to a goal were the secrets of his success.
4. New kinds of stores, such as chain stores, could buy large quantities of goods at lower prices and, therefore, sell their goods at lower prices. Mail order businesses, such as Montgomery Ward and Sears, Roebuck expanded the retail market to isolated, rural areas. In the 1880s the beginnings of a professional advertising industry helped create and sustain national demand for products.

Thinking Critically.
Student opinions will vary. Students should use the following format: MOST IMPORTANT INVENTION (STOP) . . . TELEPHONE (STOP) . . .

**FOCUS/MOTIVATION:
MAKING CONNECTIONS
Student Experiences.**
To help students recognize the geographic impact of the telegraph, tell them that the Battle of New Orleans in 1815 might have been avoided if the telegraph and transatlantic cable had existed. Ask them why. (*The Treaty of Ghent ending the War of 1812 had been signed before the battle, but the news took weeks to cross the Atlantic.*) Discuss with them the idea that the telegraph seemed to "make the world smaller." Ask students what other inventions or innovations have done the same. (*telephone, radio, television, automobile, airplane, jet engine, communications satellites*)

GUIDED INSTRUCTION
On the chalkboard compose a four-column chart that lists the inventions of the communications revolution. Head the columns: *INVENTION, HOW DONE BEFORE, EFFECTS ON PERSONAL LIFE,* and *ECONOMIC EFFECTS.* Have students suggest an invention and other information, such as (1) the way things had been done before, (2) the effect each invention had on people's lives, and (3) the economic effects. (*Examples of economic effects of all the inventions: new businesses were created, and business managers knew instantly where their raw materials or products were, what prices were in other parts of the country, and where the demand was greatest, etc.*) Fill in the chart with their suggestions. They should copy the chart in their notebooks and add later information about inventions to it *(Continued)*

with the deaf had led to the study of *acoustics*, the science of sound. His telephone turned sound waves into an electrical current. The current passed through a long wire and was then changed back into sound in a distant receiver.

Bell first demonstrated the telephone in 1876. When he offered Western Union the right to use his invention, the telegraph company turned him down. President William Orton of Western Union called the telephone an "electrical toy."

Fortunately, other people realized the telephone's usefulness. By 1880, 85 towns and cities had telephone systems. Five years later, more than 100 telephone companies were combined to create the American Telephone and Telegraph Company. Telephone wires soon wove spidery webs across the skies of America.

A web of wires—electric and telephone—crisscrosses Broadway in New York City. Perhaps no scene better illustrates the coming of the electrical age than this 1880s lithograph. But the wires came tumbling down when the wet snows fell during the Blizzard of 1888. Where are most electric and telephone lines in cities today?

Courtesy of The New York Historical Society

HISTORICAL SIDELIGHTS
① Edison gave the address of his laboratory at Menlo Park (about halfway between New York and Philadelphia) as follows: "Menlo Park, Western Div., Globe, Planet Earth, Middlesex County, four miles from Rahway, the prettiest spot in New Jersey, on the Penna. Railway, on a High Hill, Will show you around, go strawberrying."

RESOURCES
■ You may wish to have students complete Reading 12: "Thomas Edison Observed (1885)" in Volume II of *Eyewitnesses and Others.*

SUGGESTED CAPTION RESPONSE
"Sticking to it"

Edison National Historic Site, National Park Service, Department of the Interior

The Wizard of Menlo Park

In the same year that Bell invented the telephone, Thomas Alva ① Edison established the nation's first industrial research laboratory, at Menlo Park, New Jersey. Edison was the greatest inventor of the age. He was an inspired tinkerer and a hard worker, not a great thinker. "Sticking to it is the genius," he once said. He had only four years of off-and-on schooling.

Edison's first major invention, the **quadruplex telegraph,** was a machine that could send four messages over one wire at the same time. At Menlo Park he made several improvements on Bell's telephone. He invented the **phonograph** in 1877. But the **electric light** was his most important invention.

Using electricity to make light was not a new idea. In 1867 the boulevards of Paris were illuminated with arc lights. Arc lights, in which an electric discharge passed continuously between electrodes, were noisy and smoky. They could only be used outdoors. Edison was able to design a small light for indoors. His basic idea was to pass electricity through a fine wire inside an airless glass globe. The electricity heated the wire white hot, causing it to glow brightly. The wire could not burn up because there was no oxygen in the globe.

Edison spent two years experimenting with different filaments,

At five o'clock in the morning of June 16, 1888, Thomas Edison first heard his recorded voice reciting "Mary Had a Little Lamb." He perfected his "talking machine," while going without sleep for 72 hours. What did Edison say made him successful?

as they continue reading the text. Use the chart as the basis of a class discussion on which of the great inventions of the 1800s are now less important or have been replaced by new inventions or innovations.

GUIDED INSTRUCTION
Tell students that one historian predicts that future generations may decide that the technological achievements made in the United States during the 100 years from 1870 to 1970 may be America's most impressive achievement, "an era comparable to the Renaissance in Italian history, the era of Louis XIV in France, or the Victorian period in British history." Ask students what they think about this statement. Do they think that these technological achievements outweigh the political legacy of the American Revolutionary and Constitutional period? Do they think political innovations or technological ones have the greatest impact on their lives? *(Student opinions will vary.)* Tell students that during this period Americans created a modern technological nation. The number of patents doubled annually between 1866 and 1896. The period from 1876, beginning with Alexander Graham Bell and Thomas A. Edison, to about 1900 was the great age of independent inventors. After World War I industrial scientists, working in industrial research laboratories, replaced the independent inventors. After World War II most research was done in large government-supported laboratories. Despite changes over the years, the independent inventors began a tradition of creativity that is still found in Silicon Valley in California and along Route 128 outside Boston.

1 Edison organized a number of manufacturing companies that became Edison General Electric. Another inventor, Elihu Thomson, organized Thomson-Houston Electric Company. J.P. Morgan, the financier, merged the two to form the General Electric Company. It was common practice to form a company to protect the rights to an invention and to manufacture it.

Ask students to name the subject of each of the following descriptions:
1. "I invented the quadruplex telegraph, the phonograph, and the electric light." (Thomas Alva Edison)
2. "I invented the air brake and was called 'the greatest electrician in the world.'" (Granville T. Woods)
3. "I taught the deaf and invented the telephone." (Alexander Graham Bell)
4. "I invented the telegraph." (Samuel F. B. Morse)
5. "I laid the first telegraph cable across the Atlantic Ocean." (Cyrus W. Field)
6. "I opened the first rural mail order business." (Aaron Montgomery Ward)
7. "I opened the first department store." (John C. Wanamaker)

RETEACHING STRATEGY
Students with Special Needs.
Organize students into cooperative learning groups each of which includes students who are having difficulty and those who are performing well. Give each group a list of the people mentioned in the section. Then have the group list the accomplishments of each person. Have the groups exchange lists and check them for accuracy.

PRIMARY SOURCES
Description of change: excerpted and bracketed.
Rationale: excerpted to focus on co-workers' opinion of Latimer; bracketed words added to clarify meaning.
(Point of View) Description of change: excerpted.
Rationale: excerpted to focus on the expectations the public had for Thomas Edison.

Point of View

A biographer of Thomas Edison writes about what great expectations the public had for the inventor.

"On April 1 the *New York Daily Graphic* bannered: "Edison Invents a Machine that will Feed the Human Race—manufacturing Biscuits, Meat, Vegetables, and Wine out of Air, Water, and Common Earth." It was, of course, an April Fool's story, but other newspapers around the country picked it up and ran it straight. Nothing seemed impossible for a man who could make a machine that talked. . . ."
From *A Streak of Luck*,
Robert Conot, 1979

or wires, that would glow for long periods without breaking. In December 1879 he found one. Soon "the Wizard of Menlo Park" was setting up city lighting companies and power stations to generate electricity and selling light bulbs by the millions. In 1900 only about 2 percent of America's manufacturing plants were powered by electricity. But soon it would join oil as the most important sources of energy for industry.

More American Inventiveness

The telegraph, the underwater cable, the telephone, and the discoveries of Thomas Edison were landmarks in the history of communications. But other important inventions and developments also reshaped American life. Engineers and architects tackled the most difficult problems. **Suspension bridges,** their roadways held by heavy cables, crossed broad bays and rivers. **Skyscrapers** poked their steel fingers into the sky. New machines for making cheap paper from wood pulp for printing newspapers, books, and magazines contributed to more effective communications. The typewriter, developed in the 1860s, and adding machine, invented in the 1870s, both soon became essential tools of American business. George Eastman's roll film and "Kodak" camera provided new forms of recreation as well as new techniques for industry and research.

Inventors of all races were caught up in the creative spirit. An African American inventor, Granville T. Woods, developed the automatic air brake for trains and was called "the greatest electrician in the world." Lewis Howard Latimer, who worked with both Bell and Edison, was the only African American member of the famous Edison Pioneers. That famous group of inventors issued a statement of their high regard upon his death in 1928.

" It was Mr. Latimer who executed the drawings and assisted in the preparing the application for the telephone patents of Alexander Graham Bell. In 1880 he entered the employ of Hiram S. Maxim, Electrician of the United States Electric Lighting Co., then located at Bridgeport, Connecticut. It was while working in this employ that Mr. Latimer successfully produced a method of making carbon filaments for the Maxim electric incandescent lamp, which he patented. His keen perception of the possibilities of the electric light and kindred [related] industries resulted in his being the author of several other inventions. . . . Broadmindedness, versatility in the accomplishment of things intellectual and cultural, a linguist, a devoted husband and father, all were characteristic of him, and his genial presence will be missed from our gatherings.[1] **"**

[1]From "Statement of the Edison Pioneers," December 11, 1928

RESOURCES
■ You may wish to have students complete Reading
11: "Football Without Helmets (1884)" in Volume
II of *Eyewitnesses and Others.*

Courtesy of The Woolworth Corporation

Surely most Americans have shopped in the five- and ten-cent stores that spread across the country at the turn of the century. Pictured at left is the first Woolworth store, opened in 1879.

New Ways of Selling Products

Businesses came up with creative new ways to market their products. Just as factories and businesses grew bigger, so did stores. The small general store became less important. New types of stores arose to handle the ever-growing number of products.

The specialty store carried a single line of goods—hardware, clothing, groceries, shoes, and so forth. The **department store** combined many specialty stores under one roof. John C. Wanamaker opened the first department store in the United States in Philadelphia. Marshall Field opened another in Chicago in 1881. Soon others opened in larger cities.

Chain stores—stores with branches in many cities—also began to appear. The Great Atlantic and Pacific Tea Company (A & P) stores and Woolworth's were the first chain stores. Like department stores, they bought large quantities of goods at lower prices and passed the savings on to shoppers. And since women were both the major customers and commonly were paid less than men, managers gladly hired women as clerks.

Specialty stores, department stores, and chain stores were part of cities. In 1872, Aaron Montgomery Ward started a mail-order business aimed at the rural market. A few years later the Sears, Roebuck mail-order company started business. Customers received catalogs picturing goods for sale. They placed orders and paid for goods by mail; their goods were shipped to them by mail or railway express. Catalogs from the two companies became prized possessions in rural areas, helping bring the outside world to isolated parts of America.

Professional advertising also began to appear in the 1880s. It■ introduced new products and helped create large national markets for the streams of new manufactured products becoming available almost weekly. ▣

Return to the Preview & Review on page 665.

INDEPENDENT PRACTICE
Have students complete the Preview & Review activity at the beginning of the section.

CLOSURE
Tell students that the communications revolution and other inventions of the era, such as electric lights and skyscrapers, along with new ways of selling the great variety of products that were now available to a national market all contributed to transforming a rural society into the industrial society we know.

HOMEWORK
Have students imagine that they are one of the inventors discussed in this section. Tell them to use their historical imagination to write a journal entry in which they discuss why they pursued their particular invention and how they felt once they achieved success. Or they may wish to imagine they are inventors today. Have them describe their latest invention and explain why it is needed. Make a bulletin board display of some of the most interesting ones.

Preview & Review

Use these questions to guide your reading. Answer the questions after completing Section 3.
Understanding Issues, Events, & Ideas. Defend government regulation of big business, using the following words: entrepreneur, fixed cost, overhead, rebate, monopoly, pool, Standard Oil Company, trust, Interstate Commerce Act, regulatory agency, antitrust movement, interstate commerce, Sherman Antitrust Act, free enterprise.
1. In what ways were new American business leaders pioneers?
2. What practice did railroads use to reduce competition?
3. How did Rockefeller accomplish his objective of combining the country's oil refineries?
4. Why were the Interstate Commerce Act and Sherman Antitrust Act ineffective?

Thinking Critically. You are a farmer in a small "one-railroad town" in 1887. Write a letter to the Interstate Commerce Commission, complaining of the problems you are having.

3. REGULATION OF BIG BUSINESS

American Business Pioneers

The people who presided over new worlds of throbbing machines, noisy factories, and crowded cities were business leaders and financiers called **entrepreneurs.** They invested their money in new businesses. Although they varied greatly in personalities, abilities, and business methods, they were all pioneers. Some were rough, some were refined. All were eager to seize the seemingly unlimited opportunities of the new industrial world emerging around them. Some were fabulously successful. Others, the small business owners, never gained a huge fortune or power. But all of them—big-business leaders and small-business owners alike—shared the American ideal of self-reliant individualism. The men as well as the women of this group such as Nettie Fowler McCormick in farm machinery, Lydia Pinkham in patent medicine, and Kate Gleason in machine tools became the most influential people in America.

What motivated these people to take the risks of investing their money in business? See if you can feel his excitement as Andrew Carnegie describes receiving his first dividend:

> Adams Express stock then paid monthly dividends of one per cent, and the first check for five dollars arrived. I can see it now, and I well remember the signature of 'J.C. Babcock, Cashier'. . . .
>
> The next day being Sunday, we boys—myself and my ever-constant companions took our usual Sunday afternoon stroll in the country, and sitting down in the woods, I showed them this check, saying, 'Eureka! We have found it.'
>
> Here was something new to all of us, for none of us had ever received anything except from toil. A return from capital was something strange and new.
>
> How money could make money, how, without any attention from me, this mysterious golden visitor should come, led to much speculation upon the art of the young fellows, and I was for the first time called a 'capitalist.'
>
> You see, I was beginning to serve my apprenticeship as a business man in a very satisfactory manner.[1]

Many of America's business leaders—Vanderbilt, Rockefeller, and others—told the same story: poor boy works hard and gets rich. Horatio Alger, Jr. made this "rags to riches" theme the most popular reading of the day. Alger, the son of a Massachusetts minister, had been the chaplain of a shelter for orphaned youth in New York City.

[1] From *The American Society* by Kenneth S. Lynn

He wrote over 130 books for boys, each preaching the rewards of hard work and good fortune. In his most famous, *Ragged Dick and Mark, the Match Boy*, he wrote:

66 'I hope, my lad [said Mr. Whitney], you will prosper and rise in the world. You know in this free country poverty in early life is no bar to a man's advancement. I haven't risen very high myself,' he added, with a smile, 'but have met with moderate success in life; yet there was a time when I was as poor as you.'

'Were you, sir?' asked Dick, eagerly.

'Yes, my boy, I have known the time when I have been obliged to go without my dinner because I didn't have enough money to pay for it.'

'How did you get up in the world?' asked Dick, anxiously. . . .

'A taste for reading and study. During my leisure hours I improved myself by study, and acquired a large part of the knowledge which I now possess. Indeed, it was one of my books that first put me on the track of the invention, which I afterwards made. So you see, my lad, that my studious habits paid me in money, as well as in another way.

'I'm awful ignorant,' said Dick, soberly [seriously].

'But you are young, and, I judge, a smart boy. If you try to learn, you can, and if you ever expect to do anything in the world, you must know something of books.'

'I will,' said Dick, resolutely [determined]. 'I ain't always goin' to black boots for a livin'.'

'All labor is respectable, my lad, and you have no cause to be ashamed of any honest business; yet when you can get something to do that promises better for your future prospects, I advise you to do so. Till then earn your living in the way you are accustomed to, avoid extravagance, and save up a little money if you can.'[1] 99

The new American hero was the successful entrepreneur. One minister even crossed the country telling people that "acres of diamonds" lay at their feet. He said, "It is your duty to get rich" and assured Americans that "Money is power, and you ought to be reasonably ambitious to have it." He preached his "gospel of wealth" over 6,000 times. The people heard his message.

The American economy began to shift into high gear. Fine transportation and communication networks had been completed. New sources of energy were developed and used to run the new machines of industry. Business leaders and investors created bigger businesses,

[1]From *Ragged Dick and Mark, the Match Boy* by Horatio Alger, Jr.

**FOCUS/MOTIVATION:
MAKING CONNECTIONS
Student Experiences.**
Write the word *philanthropy* on the chalkboard. Ask students what they think it means. Then ask if they have heard of the Ford Foundation or the Rockefeller Foundation. Tell students that many of the self-made millionaires of the Industrial Revolution in America returned a portion of the money they accumulated through philanthropy, or acts that promote human welfare. Ask students why they think these "robber barons" gave their money away. (*Answers will vary. Some may have felt guilty about accumulating such unheard-of riches; others did so for religious or patriotic reasons.*) Tell students that most of the early philanthropists came from relatively poor Yankee Protestant backgrounds. Frugality and thrift were necessities as well as virtues. For example, Rockefeller was a pious Baptist. These men were deluged with requests for money—John D. Rockefeller got 50,000 letters a month from people asking for money for various causes. To escape this, most philanthropists established *foundations* to screen applications and to donate the money to causes they deemed worthy. Rockefeller gave away $531 million. His son, John D. Rockefeller, Jr., gave away $473 million, and Andrew Carnegie, $351 million.

PRIMARY SOURCE
Description of change: excerpted and bracketed.
Rationale: excerpted to focus on the philosophy promoted by the Horatio Alger books; bracketed words added to clarify meaning.

ROOT, HOG, OR DIE

The Granger Collection, New York

This political cartoon is titled "A Tournament of Today—A Set To Between Labor and Monopoly." Which side represents monopoly? Which labor?

One observer of Industrial America called the period the "Great Barbecue." Everyone seemed to be rushing to get a share of the national inheritance. People were like hungry picnickers crowding around the roasting pit at one of the popular political outings of the time.

Yet one should not take too dark a view of Industrial America. At this time, perhaps more than any other, the American people showed their greatest vigor, imagination, and confidence in themselves and in the future of their country.

For some, especially the new arrivals from Eastern Europe and those crowded into teeming cities, this was an age of "survival of the fittest." This notion is sometimes called Social Darwinism, the argument that if left to themselves without government regulations or other restrictions, the most efficient would survive in every field—farming, commerce, industry. When a Yale student asked his professor, "Don't you believe in any government aid to industries?," the response was, "No! It's root, hog, or die."

A sugar baron added to the barnyard metaphor. "Let the buyer beware; that covers the whole business. You cannot wetnurse people from the time they are born until the time they die. They have to wade in and get stuck, and that is the way men are educated."

Fortunately few practical people held such extreme views. Yet the notion of Social Darwinism was sometimes used to excuse child labor, unregulated working conditions, and hands-off policies of government toward big business.

and developed new methods of producing, distributing, and selling their products and services. Everywhere it seemed that creative Americans were improving ways of doing things. Businesses, both agricultural and industrial, sprang up throughout the land, each playing its part in the ever-expanding, interlocking economic system.

Competition Among the Railroads

The railroad industry had extremely heavy **fixed costs.** Track and stations had to be maintained. Cars had to be cleaned and painted. It cost almost as much to run an empty train as one crowded with passengers or freight. These fixed costs, or **overhead,** were the same whether business was good or bad.

To attract more business, railroads often used what was called "cutthroat competition"—using any means to shoulder aside rival companies. Railroads often reduced rates. Between February and July 1869 the cost of sending 100 pounds (45 kilograms) of wheat from Chicago to New York fell from $1.80 to 25 cents.

Railroads also gave large shippers illegal kickbacks called **rebates.** In return for their business they would give these shippers lower rates than those charged their smaller competitors. In this way railroad competition was a force leading to **monopoly** in other fields. Monopoly is the total control of a product, service, or trade in a region.

Sometimes railroads tried to make up for low, competitive rates by charging high rates for shipping goods from places where no other railroad existed. It often cost more to ship a product from a small "one-railroad town" a short distance from the market than from a large city much farther away. This "long haul" versus "short haul" pricing also led to monopoly because it favored producers in large cities where railroads competed for traffic.

Railroads tried to reduce competition by making agreements called **pools.** Those who joined the pool agreed to divide up available business and charge a common price for shipments. Pools rarely worked very long. Whenever business fell off, the railroads could not resist the temptation to cut rates. There was no way to enforce pooling agreements when individual companies broke them.

John D. Rockefeller

Most industries were eager to keep business steady and to avoid costly struggles for customers. A new way of doing this was developed in the oil industry by John D. Rockefeller. The method helped Rockefeller become the richest man in the United States, possibly in the entire world.

Rockefeller was born in Richford, New York, in 1839. After

GUIDED INSTRUCTION

Have students read the subsection, "The Antitrust Movement." Ask them to identify the following terms from the textbook and write them in their notebooks: **cutthroat competition** *(using any means to push aside rival companies)*; **rebates** *(illegal kickbacks or lower rates to larger shippers)*; **monopoly** *(domination of an industry by a small number of firms)*; **pools** *(dividing up available business and charging a common price in order to reduce competition)*; **Interstate Commerce Act of 1887** *(legislation that set up Interstate Commerce Commission to regulate unfair competition, pools, and rebates)*; **trust** *(business arrangement in which separate companies turn over shares to a supercompany whose trustees, or directors, control the industry)*; **regulatory agency** *(government agency such as the ICC which controls a particular industry to prevent abuses and unlawful practices)*; **antitrust movement** *(breakup of large businesses that tended to monopolize an industry into smaller, competitive businesses)*; **Sherman Antitrust Act of 1890** *(legislation that banned combinations or trusts that restricted interstate trade)*. Ask students to name other regulatory agencies (Environmental Protection Agency, Securities and Exchange Commission, etc.). Ask students if they think these agencies are successful or relatively powerless in the face of big business interests. Do they think such agencies are necessary?

Culver Pictures

This photograph of John D. Rockefeller brings to mind the lines of Edward Arlington Robinson: "He was a gentleman from sole to crown, / Clean-favored, and imperially slim." Do you think a man can be deeply religious and at the same time a deadly competitor, as Rockefeller was said to be?

making a modest fortune in the wholesale food business in Cleveland, he decided to go into the oil business. He bought his first refinery in 1865. In 1870 he organized the **Standard Oil Company.** Soon he expanded from refining into drilling for oil and selling kerosene and other oil-based products to consumers. By the late 1870s Rockefeller controlled 90 percent of the oil business in the United States.

Rockefeller was a deeply religious person. Even before he became wealthy, he made large contributions to charity. But he was a deadly competitor. He forced railroads to give him rebates on his huge oil shipments. He sold below cost in particular communities to steal business from local refiners. Then he gave the refiners a choice: sell out to Standard Oil or face bankruptcy. He hired spies and paid bribes to informers to tell secrets about other refiners' activities.

Rockefeller was also an excellent businessman. His plants were so efficient that he could undersell competitors and still make sizable profits. He detested waste. He kept close track of every detail of Standard Oil's complicated affairs.

Rockefeller wanted to buy all the refineries in the country and combine them. Then the industry could develop without petty business squabbles. He always gave competitors a chance to join Standard Oil. Only if they refused did he destroy them.

The man who designed Rockefeller's supercompany was Samuel C. T. Dodd. Dodd's creation was called a **trust**—a legal agreement under which several companies group together to regulate production and eliminate competition. To do this, stockholders of the separate oil companies turned their stock over to a group of directors called trustees. By controlling the stock of all the companies in the supercompany, the trustees could control the industry.

The Antitrust Movement

The trust idea soon spread to other businesses. By 1900 almost every branch of manufacturing was dominated by a small number of large producers. The size and power of these trusts alarmed many Americans. They were afraid that the trusts would destroy small companies and cheat consumers by charging high prices once competition had been eliminated. In the following excerpt from his article, one journalist warned Americans of what he called "the dangers of the age of combination:"

❤ On the theory of 'too much of everything' our industries, from railroads to workingmen, are being organized to prevent milk, nails, lumber, freights, labor, soothing syrup, and all these other things from becoming too cheap. The majority have never yet been able to buy enough of anything. The minority have too much of everything to sell. Seeds of social trouble germinate fast in such conditions. Society is letting these combinations become institutions without compelling them to adjust their charges to the cost of production, which used to be the universal rule of price. . . . The change from competition to combination is nothing less than one of those revolutions which march through history with giant strides. . . .[1]"

Rockefeller, the leader most responsible for business combinations, often defended the practice. His defense was simple. He was in business to make money, and combinations were more profitable. He told a government commission:

" *Question*. What are . . . the chief advantages [of] industrial combinations?

Answer. It is too late to argue about the advantages of industrial combinations. They are a necessity. And if Americans are to have the privilege of extending their business in all the states of the Union, and into foreign countries as well, they are a necessity on a large scale, and require the agency of more than one corporation. Their chief advantages are:

(1) Command of necessary capital.
(2) Extension of limits of business.
(3) Increase in the number of people interested in business.
(4) Economy in business.
(5) Improvements and economies which are derived from knowledge of many interested persons of wide experience.
(6) Power to give the public improved products at less prices and still make a profit for stockholders.
(7) Permanent work and good wages for laborers. . . .

I speak from experience. . . . Our first combination was a partnership and afterwards a corporation in Ohio. That was sufficient for a local refining business. But dependent solely upon local business we should have failed years ago. We were forced to extend our markets and to seek for export trade.

We soon discovered as the business grew that the primary method of transporting oil in barrels could not last. . . . Hence we . . . adopted the pipe-line system, and found capital for pipe-line construction. . . . To perfect the pipe-line system required fifty millions in capital. This could not be obtained or maintained without industrial combination.
. . .

[1]From "Lords of Industry," by Henry D. Lloyd in *North American Review*, CXXXVIII (June 1884)

Organize students into cooperative learning groups. Have each group imagine that they are a farmer, small shipper, or other small business owner who has been financially hurt by one of the business combinations. Have each group prepare a statement to the government commission on why the government should regulate business. Have several students act as commissioners and have each group present their testimony and answer the commissioners' questions.

PRIMARY SOURCE
Description of change: excerpted.
Rationale: excerpted to focus on arguments against combinations.

Ask students to define the following terms and names:
1. Entrepreneur *(invested
   money in new businesses)*
2. Horatio Alger *(wrote books
   around the theme of "rags
   to riches" or "poor boy
   makes good")*
3. Social Darwinism *(belief
   that if kept free from any restraint or aid, the most efficient businesses and people
   in every field would be the
   ones to survive)*
4. Overhead *(fixed costs)*
5. Monopoly *(total control of a
   product, service, or trade in
   a particular area)*
6. Trust *(legal agreement combining several companies
   under one supercompany
   and its directors)*
7. Interstate Commerce Act
   *(law that regulated railroads
   by prohibiting pools, rebates, and other unfair practices, by mandating "reasonable and just" rates, and
   by establishing the Interstate Commerce Commis-
   sion)*
8. Sherman Antitrust Act *(law
   that banned trust and combinations that restricted interstate trade and commerce)*

RETEACHING STRATEGY
Students with Special Needs.
Pair students who are having
difficulty with students who are
performing well. Ask each pair
to make a list of the ways entrepreneurs tried to ensure
their success and another list
(Continued)

PRIMARY SOURCE
Description of change: excerpted and bracketed.
Rationale: excerpted to focus
on Rockefeller's defense of
combinations; bracketed word
added to clarify meaning.

Every step taken was necessary in the business if it was to be properly developed, and only through successive steps and by such an industrial combination is America to-day enabled to utilize the bounty which its land pours forth, and to furnish the world with the best and cheapest light ever known.[1] **99**

The demand for government regulation of the economy increased steadily. The first target was the railroad industry. In 1887 Congress passed the **Interstate Commerce Act.** This law stated that railroad rates must be "reasonable and just." Rates must be made public and could not be changed without public notice. Pools, rebates, and other unfair practices were declared unlawful. To oversee the affairs of railroads and to hear complaints from shippers, the law created the Interstate Commerce Commission (ICC), a board of experts. This was the first of the many **regulatory agencies**—government commissions charged with protecting the public interest—that came to control so many aspects of American life.

The ICC had to overcome many difficulties. The Interstate Commerce Act was vague. How was it possible to decide what a "reasonable and just" freight rate was? The Commission did not have a large enough staff to handle the more than 1,000 complaints it received in its first few months of operation. Nor did the Commission have the power to enforce its decisions. It could only sue violating railroads in court. Of the 16 cases it brought to trial between 1887 and 1905, it won only 1.

The Interstate Commerce Act was supposed to *regulate* competition—that is, to make certain that railroads did not cheat the public. It did not attempt to *control* the size of any railroad company. The way of dealing with the monopoly problem was to break up large businesses into smaller businesses which would compete with one another. This approach was called the **antitrust movement.**

In the late 1880s several states tried to restore competition by passing laws prohibiting trusts. These laws were difficult to enforce because industrial combinations usually did business in more than one state. Under the Constitution only the federal government could regulate such **interstate commerce.**

Then, in 1890, Congress passed the **Sherman Antitrust Act.** This law banned combinations "in the form of trust or otherwise" that restricted interstate trade or commerce. Anyone "who shall monopolize, or attempt to monopolize" such commerce could be fined or sent to jail for up to a year. This law was also difficult to enforce. It did not define "restraint of trade" or monopoly. Every attempt the government made to break up a trust resulted in a lawsuit.

[1]From "Report of the United States Industrial Commission, I," December 30, 1899 in *Government and the American Economy, 1870-Present* by Thomas G. Manning and David M. Potter

The Granger Collection, New York

The courts usually sided with the business combinations. The first important Supreme Court case involving the Sherman Act was *U.S. v. E. C. Knight Co.* (1895). It involved an attempt to break up the American Sugar Refining Company. This trust had obtained control of about 90 percent of the sugar refining of the country by buying up four competing companies. The Court ruled that this combination was not illegal because it did not restrain trade. Since the trust refined its sugar in one state, interstate commerce was not involved. How it could dispose of all its sugar without selling it in many different states, the Court did not say.

The Interstate Commerce Act and the Sherman Antitrust Act had little effect on big business at this time. Most judges still put great stress on the right of individuals to run their affairs more or less as they pleased. Nevertheless, these two laws were extremely important. Both are still in effect and have been greatly strengthened over time. They established the practice of the federal government attempting to control the way American companies do business. After 1890 totally **free enterprise** was diminished in the United States. Free enterprise is the private operation of business with no government interference. The Industrial Revolution had made the power of business so great that some public control over business practices came to be increasingly accepted. 📁

When Congress began to debate the Sherman Antitrust Act, Joseph Keppler drew this cartoon for Puck, *a popular humor magazine. Titled "Bosses of the Senate," the cartoon shows bloated trusts symbolized by bulging money bags entering the Senate through a door marked "Monopolists." The "People's Entrance" at the left is padlocked shut. With what opinion of the Senate does this artist leave us?*

Return to the Preview & Review on page 670.

of the ways the antitrust movement tried to protect the rights of the public. *(Entrepreneurs wanted to reduce competition. Companies tried to establish monopolies so that they could control the market. Railroads felt this was necessary because they were expensive to operate, and it cost almost as much to run an empty train as a full one. Some railroads tried to form pools to limit competition. Rockefeller used a trust agreement to combine refineries into one company. The individuals concerned about the power of large corporations tried to limit their power through legislation. The Interstate Commerce Act and the Sherman Antitrust Act were vague and difficult to enforce.)*

INDEPENDENT PRACTICE
Have students complete the Preview & Review activity at the beginning of the section.

CLOSURE
Tell students that the business pioneers successfully established railroads, steel, oil, and other industries and helped to create a dynamic economic system. However, the big corporations threatened to destroy small companies and then, once competition had been eliminated, to charge consumers excessive prices. In an effort to control the corporations' size and power, Congress passed the Interstate Commerce Act and the Sherman Antitrust Act.

HOMEWORK
Ask students to imagine that they own a small oil refinery. Have them write a letter to their Representative detailing the problems that they are having with large competitors.

SUGGESTED CAPTION RESPONSE
It more than doubled in size, and the proportion of
females and those under 16 in the work force increased.

**PREVIEW & REVIEW
RESPONSES
Understanding Issues, Events,
Ideas.**
Explanations should demonstrate an understanding of the
terms used.
1. It was one response to the
power corporations had
over their workers. Uriah
Stephens founded it as a secret organization of skilled
workers, but later it began
openly to organize workers
into a brotherhood. Under
Powderly the Knights ad-
mitted all workers.
2. Skilled workers organized
by craft, such as printers,
bricklayers, and plumbers.
3. Carnegie's steel plant reduced wages in response to
a slump in its business;
locked out workers, hired
strikebreakers and Pinkertons; after a violent confrontation, the strikers eventually returned to work on
Frick's terms.

Thinking Critically.
1. Students should mention
regimentation, long hours,
repetitive work. Encourage
students to use their historical imagination.

Preview & Review

Use these questions to guide your
reading. Answer the questions
after completing Section 4.
**Understanding Issues, Events, &
Ideas.** Explain how industrial
growth affected American workers
in the 1800s. Use the following
words: specialization, Knights of
Labor, strike, Haymarket bombing,
American Federation of Labor,
bread and butter issue, collective
bargaining, Homestead Strike,
lockout, yellow-dog contract,
blacklist.
1. Why was the Knights of Labor
organized? How was it changed
under the leadership of Terence
Powderly?
2. Who were the members of the
American Federation of Labor?
3. What caused the Homestead
Strike? How did Henry Frick respond? What was the outcome?
Thinking Critically. Imagine that
you are a worker in a large factory
in 1900. Describe your typical day
at work, and explain how the
increased use of machines has
affected your job.

4. WORKERS AND WORK

Specialization

Post-Civil War industrial changes also greatly affected the men and
women who worked in the factories of the United States. Division
of labor changed the way things were made. Factory jobs became
steadily more specialized. More and more workers tended machines.
Usually they performed one task over and over, hundreds of times
each day. In a steel plant, for example, some laborers shoveled coke
and ore. Others loaded furnaces. Still others moved the finished steel.
No single worker could make steel alone. This division of labor was
called **specialization.**

Machines greatly increased the amount a worker could produce.
This tended to raise wages and lower prices. Machines brought more
goods within the reach of the average family. But they made work
less interesting because it took little skill to operate most machines.

Manufacturing corporations grew larger and larger. In 1850 Cyrus McCormick's reaper manufacturing plant in Chicago employed
150 workers. By 1900 it had 4,000.

Such large factories had to be run like armies. The boards of
directors were the generals. They set policy and appointed the people
who carried it out. Next in the chain of command were the plant
superintendents. Like the colonels of regiments, they were responsible for actually running the operation. They issued instructions to
the foremen of the various departments, who were like army ser-
geants. The foremen in turn issued orders to the men and women
who did the actual work.

LEARNING FROM TABLES.
*One of the most important needs of
American business and industry was
a large labor force. This chart contains data about those workers. In
what ways did the labor force change
between 1870 and 1900?*

LABOR FORCE BY SEX AND AGE*, 1870-1900					
	TOTAL LABOR FORCE	**SEX**		**AGE**	
YEAR		**Male**	**Female**	**10-15 Years**	**16 and Older**
1870	12,925	11,008	1,917	765	12,160
1880	17,392	14,745	2,647	1,118	16,274
1890	23,318	19,313	4,006	1,504	21,814
1900	27,640	22,641	4,999	4,064**	23,576†

* in thousands of workers
** 16 to 19 Years
† 20 and Older

Source: Historical Statistics of the United States

Bettmann Archives

Factory workers by the hundreds use lathes and presses to create their product. What do you suppose the wires are for? What hazards do you see in this workplace?

These workers were expected to follow orders as obediently as army privates. In a Rochester, New York, carriage factory each worker had a number. To get a drink of water, a worker had to get the foreman's permission. To make sure that the rule was followed, the water faucets were locked up. In a Massachusetts tannery, guards patrolled the shop and reported any worker who talked during the workday. These were extreme examples. Workers hated all such rules. Many did not meekly submit to them. Instead, they sought ways to get around overly strict regulations.

Conditions in the clothing industries often were among the worst. In cities like New York and Chicago much of the work was done in "sweatshops," with the labor done mostly by women and children. Imagine the lives of those who toiled in the shop described in this excerpt.

“ The *sweat-shop* is a place where, separate from the tailor-shop or clothing-warehouse, a "sweater" (middleman) assembles journeymen tailors and needle-women to work under his supervision. He takes a cheap room outside the dear [expensive] and crowded business center, and within the neighborhood where the work-people live. Thus is rent saved to the employer, and time and travel to the employed. The men can do work more hours than was possible under the centralized system [in a factory], and their wives and children can help. . . . For this service, at the prices paid, they cannot earn more than twenty-five to forty cents a day, and the work is largely done by Italian, Polish, and Bohemian women and girls. . . .

**FOCUS/MOTIVATION:
MAKING CONNECTIONS
Student Experiences.**
Ask students if they are familiar with labor unions. *(Most will be.)* Then tell them that the labor union movement began in the United States after the Civil War. Ask students why they think that workers began to organize during this period. *(more people working in factories; factory work regimented and working conditions dangerous; low pay)* You may wish to tell students that the history of American labor is one of the industrial world's more violent. Employer violence had the cover of law. At the beginning of the 20th century, no employer had to recognize the union. The law gave the employer the right to defend his or her property and to have free access to labor, raw materials, and commodity markets. The community might be sympathetic to the needs of the employees, but when violence took place, the public shifted its emphasis to stopping it.

Workers and Work   679

Girls, hand-sewers, earn nothing for the first month, then as unskilled workers they get $1 to $1.50 a week, $3 a week, and (as skilled workers) $6 a week. . . .

The 'sweat-shop' day is ten hours; but many take work home to get in overtime; and occasionally the shops themselves are kept open for extra work, from which the hardest and ablest workers sometimes make $14 to $16 a week. . . . The average weekly living expenses of a man and wife, with two children . . . are as follows: Rent (three or four small rooms), $2; food, fuel, and light, $4; clothing, $2; and beer and spirits, $1. . . .

A city ordinance enacts that rooms provided for workmen shall contain space equal to five hundred cubic feet of air for each person employed; but in the average 'sweat-shop' only about a tenth of that quantity is found. In one such place there were fifteen men and women in one room, which contained also a pile of mattresses on which some of the men sleep at night. The closets [toilets] are disgraceful. In an adjoining room were piles of clothing, made and unmade, on the same table with the food of the family. Two dirty children were playing about the floor. . . .[1] **99**

Unionization

■ In part because large corporations had so much power over their labor force, more workers began to join unions after the Civil War. This was especially true of skilled workers. In 1869 the **Knights of Labor** was founded in Philadelphia by Uriah Stephens, a tailor. At first it was a secret organization, with an elaborate ritual. Soon it expanded and began to work openly to organize workers into a "great brotherhood." By 1879 the Knights claimed to have 9,000 members. In that year Terence V. Powderly, a Pennsylvania machinist and one-time mayor of Scranton, Pennsylvania, became its head.

Under Powderly the Knights admitted women, African Americans, immigrants, and unskilled workers. This was a radical step. Most unions would not accept these workers. But Isaac Myers, the leading African American labor leader of the time, told the group: "American citizenship for the black man is a complete failure if he is proscribed [barred] from the workshops of the country." After his speech a majority of the delegates voted to admit all workers to the union. The Knights advocated the eight-hour workday and strict regulation of trusts. They hoped to avoid **strikes,** the refusal of laborers to work until their demands are met. Cooperation between

[1]From "Among the Poor of Chicago" by Joseph Kirkland in *The Poor in the Great Cities*

① Governor Oglesby decided that if a substantial number of Chicago business leaders favored clemency for the Haymarket defendants, he would commute the sentences to life imprisonment. Many agreed until Marshall Field, the richest man in Chicago, announced his opposition. The business leaders feared opposing the powerful Field for business and social reasons. Four of the seven defendants were hanged on November 11, 1887. In 1893 a new governor pardoned those whose sentences were commuted.

SUGGESTED CAPTION RESPONSE
Ask students to make a list of adjectives and phrases that describe the picture.

Collection, Lee Baxandall, Laurie Platt Winfrey, Inc.

owners, workers, and consumers should be possible, Powderly insisted.

Powderly was a good speechmaker but a very poor administrator. He had little patience with anyone who disagreed with him. He tried to supervise every detail of the union's business.

In the 1880s local leaders of the Knights organized and won several important strikes against railroads. Membership soared. By 1886, 700,000 workers belonged to the organization. This was more than the central leadership could manage. Local units called strikes, which failed. Workers became discouraged and dropped out of the union.

Then the Knights were blamed, quite unfairly, for a terrible bombing incident in Haymarket Square in Chicago in 1886. When the police tried to break up a meeting called by radicals during a strike, someone threw a bomb that killed seven policemen. Public ① opinion turned against unions after the **Haymarket bombing.** Thousands of workers dropped out of the Knights of Labor as a result.

In 1881, long before the Knights of Labor began to decline, representatives of a number of craft unions founded the Federation of Organized Trades and Labor Unions of the United States and Canada. In 1886 this group changed its name to the **American Federation of Labor** (AFL).

The AFL was led by Samuel Gompers, a cigar maker. Unlike the Knights, the AFL was made up exclusively of skilled workers, organized by particular crafts such as printers, bricklayers, and plumbers. The AFL concentrated on **bread and butter issues**—higher

Angry workers bring their grievances to the top-hatted factory owner in "The Strike" by Robert Koehler. Use historical imagination to tell what argument is making tempers flare.

He may look like a sheriff sent to break up a strike, but this is Samuel Gompers, head of the AFL. The photograph was taken during a drive to organize West Virginia coal miners. Report on any accounts of strikes you may find in today's newspapers.

The George Meany Archives, AFL-CIO

GUIDED INSTRUCTION
Organize the class into two groups. Have one group represent the workers in a factory with dangerous and unsanitary conditions and the other group, the factory owners. Arrange the groups so that they are facing each other from opposite sides of the room. Then tell the workers to ask the factory owners to improve their working conditions and wages. Ask: Who has the advantage in this situation? What can the workers do? Do the students representing the workers feel that they would be more successful if they organized into a union? How else might they achieve their goals?

CHECKING UNDERSTANDING
Ask students to identify:
1. The Knights of Labor *(began as a secret organization; first union to admit all workers)*
2. Strike *(to refuse to work until demands are met.)*
3. Haymarket bombing *(Police tried to break up a meeting that had been called by radicals; seven policemen died when someone threw a bomb; turned public opinion against unions.)*
4. American Federation of Labor *(Samuel Gompers founded; federation of craft unions; concentrated on bread-and-butter issues)*
5. Collective bargaining *(union officials represent workers; negotiate with management for better working conditions and wages)*
6. Homestead Strike *(Violent strike; Frick, who was in charge of the plant, resisted striking workers by hiring strikebreakers and Pinkertons; violent confrontation (Continued)*

① During his interrogation, Berkman told the only striker in prison, Jack Tinford, that he had tried to assassinate Frick for Tinford and the strikers. Tinford told him, "You better not talk that way in court, they'll hang you." Tinford added that the steelworkers "don't believe in killing; they respect the law. . ." and want nothing to do with anarchists. Berkman was sentenced to 22 years in prison and released after 14.

left seven Pinkertons and nine strikers dead; union lost the struggle; public opinion turned against Frick until Berkman attacked him.)

wages, shorter hours, better working conditions. The way to obtain these benefits, Gompers and other leaders of the AFL insisted, was **collective bargaining** with employers. In collective bargaining union officials, representing the workers, negotiate with management about wages, working conditions, and other aspects of employment. If negotiation fails, workers may strike to support union demands.

The Homestead Strike

One of the most violent strikes in American history involved an AFL union, the Amalgamated Association of Iron and Steel Workers. In the early 1890s the Amalgamated was the most powerful union in the country. It had 24,000 dues-paying members. Some worked at the Carnegie steel plant in Homestead, Pennsylvania. In 1892, when the company reduced wages because of a slump in its business, the union called a strike.

Carnegie was in Scotland when the **Homestead Strike** began. The company was being run by one of his partners, Henry Clay Frick. Frick was a tough executive and a bitter opponent of unions. He decided to resist the strike and to try to destroy the Amalgamated with a **lockout**. With Carnegie's approval he closed the mill. He then announced that he would hire strikebreakers—nonunion workers— and reopen the Homestead mill. To protect the new workers, he hired private police from the Pinkerton Detective Agency, a company known to specialize in strikebreaking.

The Pinkerton Agency sent 300 armed men—Pinkertons—to Homestead. They approached the plant on barges on the Monongahela River in the dead of night. The strikers had been warned of their coming. They met them at the docks with gunfire and dynamite. A small-scale war broke out. When it ended, seven Pinkertons and nine strikers were dead. The governor of Pennsylvania then sent 8,000 National Guard troops to Homestead to keep the peace. The strike went on for more than four months. Finally the union gave up the struggle. The workers went back to the plant on Frick's terms.

Frick won the contest, but public opinion turned against him. Then a Russian immigrant, Alexander Berkman, attacked Frick in his Homestead office. To protest the use of Pinkertons, Berkman shot Frick three times in the neck and shoulder. He then stabbed him once in the leg and after that tried to chew a percussion capsule, ① an explosive device, which guards pried from his mouth. Frick survived, Berkman went to prison, and the public's attitude softened.

Employers looked for ways to keep their workers from forming or joining unions. Some used **yellow-dog contracts,** a written agreement not to join a union. An employee who broke the contract was fired. Others used **blacklists.** These were lists of workers who were members of unions and therefore undesirable employees. Blacklisted workers often found it impossible to get jobs. 🖘

Return to the Preview & Review on page 678.

① Immigration very often was heaviest when economic conditions were worst in Europe. Some Germans, however, came not only to take advantage of the Homestead Act giving them free land but also to escape the draft in Bismarck's Germany. Swedes emigrated when a famine occurred from 1865 to 1868.

② Beginning with Michigan in 1845, state and territorial governments set up recruitment agencies and sent agents with guidebooks and brochures to Europe. Kansas exempted Mennonites from service in the state militia. Private companies such as the railroads and steamship companies also encouraged immigration.

5. THE GROWTH OF CITIES

The New Immigration

About three quarters of the workers in the Carnegie steel mills had been born in Europe. Like most immigrants, including Carnegie himself, they had come to America to find work. To millions of poor people in other parts of the world, industrial expansion had made the United States seem like the pot of gold at the end of the rainbow. Mark Twain used a similar metaphor when he called this era the **Gilded Age.** The surface was dazzling, but only base metal lay below.

It was as though the country were an enormous magnet drawing people into it from every direction. Between 1860 and 1900 about 14 million immigrants arrived. Most settled in large cities. In 1880, 87 percent of the residents of Chicago were either immigrants or the children of immigrants. The situation was similar in New York, San Francisco, Milwaukee, Cleveland, Boston, and most other cities.

Before the 1880s most immigrants had come from western and northern Europe, especially from England, Ireland, Germany, and the Scandinavian countries. We have already noted that established Americans frequently resented the newcomers of this "Old Immigration." However, people from western Europe had certain advantages that helped them to adjust in their new homeland. British and Irish immigrants spoke English. Many German immigrants were well educated and skilled in one or another useful trade. Scandinavians were experienced farmers and often came with enough money to buy land in the West. Except for the Irish, most of these immigrants were Protestants, as were most Americans.

In the 1880s the trend of immigration changed. Thousands of Italians, Poles, Hungarians, Greeks, and Russians flocked in. People believed in the golden dream of opportunity. America was the "golden door." One Jewish girl living in Russia, 13 years old at the time, waited for her father already in America to send for the family. When the letter arrived, she wrote:

    ❝ So at last I was going to America! Really, really going, at last! The boundaries burst. The arch of heaven soared. A million suns shone out for every star. The winds rushed in from outer space, roaring in my ears, 'America! America!'❞[1]

The trip to America was still a trial. But all were buoyed by hopes of a better life. Anzia Yezierska, a sixteen-year-old Jewish girl from Poland, remembered:

    ❝ [We traveled in] steerage [the cheapest section of the ship] dirty bundles—foul odors—seasick humanity—but I saw and

[1]From *The Promised Land* by Mary Antin

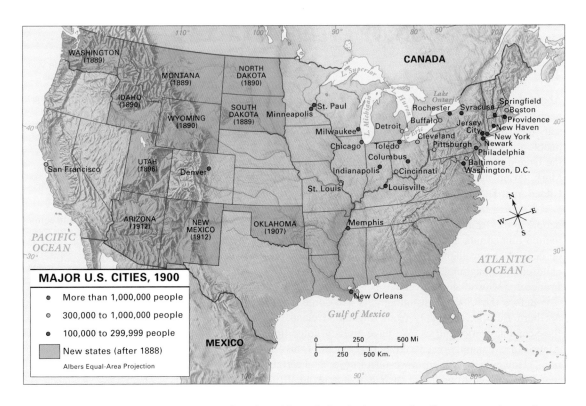

MAJOR U.S. CITIES, 1900

- More than 1,000,000 people
- 300,000 to 1,000,000 people
- 100,000 to 299,999 people
- New states (after 1888)

Albers Equal-Area Projection

LEARNING FROM MAPS. *The second half of the 19th century saw the growth of many of America's largest cities. Still, even by 1900 few of the largest cities are west of the Mississippi River. Why do you think this is true?*

heard nothing of the foulness and ugliness around me. I floated in showers of sunshine; visions upon visions of the new world opened before me.

From lips to lips flowed the golden legend of the golden country:

'In America you can say what you feel—you can join your friends in open streets without fear. . . .'

'In America is a home for everybody. The land is your land. . . .'

'Everybody is with everybody alike in America. . . .'

'Everybody can do what he wants with his life in America. . . .'

'Plenty for all. Learning flows free like milk and honey.'[1] 🔊

After 1886 the immigrants' first sight of America was often the **Statue of Liberty.** At the base of the statue were the words written by the poet Emma Lazarus:

❝ Give me your tired, your poor,
Your huddled masses yearning to breathe free,

[1]From *Hungry Hearts* by Anzia Yezierska

EXTENSION:
HOME INVOLVEMENT
Multicultural Perspectives.
Ask students to interview family members about when their families came to the United States, where they came from, and why they left their previous homes. Ask student volunteers to tell the class about their family's immigration experience. Students might tell the class about a family member's initial impressions and how they compared to expectations, where the family initially settled and how they were received, and the kind of work they did. If any students are immigrants, they may want to tell the class about their own experiences.

Museum of the City of New York

The colossal Statue of Liberty raises the torch of freedom in New York Harbor. It was first known as "Liberty Enlightening the World." Here we see the dedication of the magnificent gift from France. The sculptor, F. A. Bartholdi, wished to pay tribute to the alliance of France with the American colonies during the Revolution. What does the statue symbolize today?

The wretched refuse of your teeming shore,
Send these the homeless, tempest-tossed, to me:
I lift my lamp beside the golden door. . . . 99

But although America was a vast improvement in most cases, it had a hard time living up to the dreams of most immigrants. Their ■ first experiences were not what they had expected. Anzia Yezierska wrote:

66 Between the buildings that loomed like mountains, we
struggled with our bundles. . . . Up Broadway, under the
bridge, and through the swarming streets of the ghetto [a
segregated neighborhood], we followed Gedalyeh Mindel
[a friend].
I looked about the narrow streets of squeezed-in stores
and houses, ragged clothes, dirty bedding oozing out of the
windows, ashcans and garbage cans cluttering the sidewalks. A vague sadness pressed down on my heart—the
first doubt of America.[1] 99

[1]From *Hungry Hearts* by Anzia Yezierska

PRIMARY SOURCES
(Top) *Description of change:* excerpted.
Rationale: excerpted to focus on Emma Lazarus' invitation to immigrants to come to the United States.
(Bottom) *Description of change:* excerpted and bracketed.
Rationale: excerpted to focus on the first impressions of immigrants; bracketed words added to clarify meaning.

The Growth of Cities 685

① Geographic location of the *new* immigrants: Eighty percent settled in the region from the Atlantic Ocean as far south as Washington, D.C., west to St. Louis, up the Mississippi River to Canada, and back to the Atlantic Ocean. Two thirds lived in New York, New England, Pennsylvania, and New Jersey.

② None of the new immigrants escaped the contempt of older generations of Americans. Even northern Italians, who had come earlier, resented immigrants from southern Italy. (They regarded them as "barbarians.")

RELATING HISTORY TO GEOGRAPHY

To reinforce the importance of *movement* as a geographic theme, point out to students that the movement of people to North America since the beginning of the 17th century is one of the great migrations of history. Have students mark on an outline map of the world their families' places of origin. Remind students that their families may have come from more than one place. Then have students prepare a statistical table showing the percentage of the class that originally came from each area.

PRIMARY SOURCES

Description of change: excerpted and bracketed.
Rationale: excerpted to focus on the difficulties that immigrants faced; bracketed words added to clarify meaning.
(Point of View) Description of change: excerpted.
Rationale: excerpted to focus on one person's view of Irish emigration.

Point of View

For many immigrants it was sail the crowded ships to America or starve. The author of *The Fitzgeralds and the Kennedys* explains the Irish exodus

66 As anybody who knows the history of Ireland knows, the potato failed. . . . The failure of four successive crops sentenced one out of every six peasants to death by starvation and forced more than a quarter of the Irish population to emigrate. . . . Before the Great Famine, as it came to be called, the Irish had regarded the idea of leaving their country as the most appalling of fates. But now, terrified and desperate in the wake of starvation and fever, they made their way out of Ireland by the tens of thousands. . . . burrowing their way onto the great "coffin ships," so named because of the great numbers who died on board. . . . 99

Doris Kearns Goodwin, 1987

Most immigrants were indeed poor. They had little or no education and no special skills. They knew no English. Their habits and cultures were very different from those of native-born Americans. The majority were Roman or Greek Orthodox Catholics or Jews.

Many of these immigrants came from areas where money was seldom used. People there exchanged food for cloth, a cow for a wagon, and so on. It was difficult for such people to adjust to life in a large industrial city. Most took the lowest-paid jobs. Whole families toiled to earn enough to survive. As Yezierska recalled:

66 I felt a strangling in my throat as I neared the sweatshop prison; all my nerves screwed together into iron hardness to endure the day's torture.

For an instant I hesitated as I faced the grated window of the old dilapidated building—dirt and decay cried out from every crumbling brick.

In the maw of the shop, raging around me the roar and the clatter, the clatter and the roar, the merciless grind of the pounding machines. Half maddened [crazy], half deadened, I struggled to think, to feel, to remember—what I am—who am I—why was I here?

I struggled in vain—bewildered and lost in a whirlpool of noise.

'America—America—where was America?' it cried in my heart.[1] 99

① The immigrants from each country or district tended to cluster together in the same city neighborhood. In 1890 a New York reporter wrote that a map of the city showing where different nationalities lived would have "more stripes than the skin of a zebra, and more colors than any rainbow." These **ethnic neighborhoods** were like cities within cities. They offered people newly arrived in the strange new world of America a chance to hold on to a few fragments of the world they had left. There the immigrants could find familiar foods, people who spoke their language, churches and clubs based on old-country models.

② Many native-born Americans resented this **New Immigration.** They insisted that the newcomers were harder to assimilate, or "Americanize" than earlier generations. Workers were disturbed by the new immigrants' willingness to work long hours for low wages. American Protestants believed the mass immigration would weaken their political and social clout. A new nativist organization, the American Protective Association, blamed the hard times of the 1890s on immigration. Nativists charged that the new immigrants were physically and mentally inferior. They were dangerous radicals, the nativists said, who wanted to destroy American democratic institutions.

[1]From *Hungry Hearts* by Anzia Yezierska

Museum of the City of New York

"The Battery, New York" was painted about 1855 by Samuel B. Waugh. This detail shows a shipful of immigrants arriving in New York. Immigrants were processed at Castle Garden, at the left in the background. Why did some Americans resent the new immigration?

One poet expressed these fears in this excerpt.

     Wide open and unguarded stand our gates,
       And through them presses a wild motley throng—
       Men from the Volga and the Tartar steppes [Russia],
       Featureless figures from the Hwang Ho [China],
       Malayan, Scythian [Greek], Teuton [German], Celt [Irish],
         and Slav,
       Flying the Old World's poverty and scorn;
       These bringing with them unknown gods and rites,
       Those, tiger passions, here to stretch their claws,
       In street and alley what strange tongues are loud. . . .[1]

In the 1890s the Immigration Restriction League called for a law preventing anyone who could not read and write some language from entering the country. The League knew that such a **literacy test** would keep out many immigrants from southern and eastern Europe. In ■ that part of the world many regions did not have public school systems.

     Congress passed a literacy test bill in 1897, but President Grover Cleveland vetoed it. He insisted that America should continue to be a place of refuge for the world's poor and persecuted. Many

[1]From "Unguarded Gates" by Thomas Bailey Aldrich in *The Works of Thomas Bailey Aldrich, Poems, vol. II*

STRATEGIES FOR SUCCESS

READING A TABLE

Tables, like charts, are ways visually to organize statistics. (Review the strategy on page 558.) Tables are most often used to show the changes in numbers over time. In a table, statistics are usually listed side-by-side in columns for easy reference. Effectively using a statistical table can tell you a great deal about a particular topic.

How to Read a Statistical Table

To read a statistical table, follow these guidelines.

1. **Note the title.** As in all graphics, the title of a table will tell you the subject for which statistics are given. Remember that all the numbers are related in some way to the subject of the table. Part of the skill of reading a table is understanding how all its parts are related. (As with charts, be sure to read any footnotes or other special notes.)
2. **Read the headings.** Quickly skimming the headings will show you how the data is organized and into what categories it has been divided.
3. **Study the information.** Read across each row. Note the statistical trends.
4. **Apply critical thinking skills.** Compare the numbers. Ask questions about the trends. Form hypotheses, make inferences, and draw conclusions.

Applying the Strategy

Study the statistical table above. It provides population statistics for major United States cities for three years—1860, 1880, and 1900. Note that these are at 20-year intervals. Why do you think that is so? The equal intervals give you a clearer picture of the rate of growth than random years

GROWTH OF MAJOR U.S. CITIES, 1860–1900

City	1860	1880	1900
New York City	1,174,800	1,912,000	3,437,000
Philadelphia	565,500	847,000	1,294,000
Boston	177,800	363,000	561,000
Baltimore	212,400	332,000	509,000
Cincinnati	161,000	255,000	326,000
St. Louis	160,800	350,000	575,000
Chicago	109,300	503,000	1,698,000

might. As you read across each row you can see how the population of a given city changed. New York City grew from 1,174,800 to 3,437,000 during that time period. Reading down the columns allows you to compare the statistics among the cities. In 1880 847,000 people lived in Philadelphia while 255,000 lived in Cincinnati. Based on what you have read in *The Story of America,* what is one reason why Philadelphia was larger than Cincinnati in 1880? Can you think of other reasons? Studying the chart as a whole gives you the opportunity to note trends and ask questions. What generalizations can you state about the growth of United States cities in the second half of the 19th century based on the seven cities in this table? Note that all the cities more than doubled in population between 1860 and 1900. Which ones grew the fastest? Note that Chicago grew much faster than Baltimore. Why do you think that happened? What other trends do you notice? Which ones can you explain from your reading of *The Story of America* and other books on American history?

For independent practice, see Practicing the Strategy on page 694.

RESOURCES
■ You may wish to have students complete Reading 31: "Poems of the Chinese Immigrants (ca. 1910)" in Volume II of *Eyewitnesses and Others.*

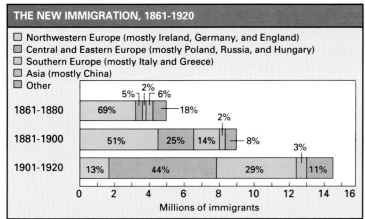

THE NEW IMMIGRATION, 1861-1920

☐ Northwestern Europe (mostly Ireland, Germany, and England)
☐ Central and Eastern Europe (mostly Poland, Russia, and Hungary)
☐ Southern Europe (mostly Italy and Greece)
☐ Asia (mostly China)
☐ Other

1861-1880: 69%, 5%, 2%, 6%, 18%

1881-1900: 51%, 25%, 14%, 2%, 8%

1901-1920: 13%, 44%, 29%, 3%, 11%

Millions of immigrants

Source: *Historical Statistics of the United States*

LEARNING FROM GRAPHS. *Before 1900, most immigrants to the United States came from Northwestern Europe, particularly England, Ireland, and Germany. In the last decades of the 1800s, the proportion of immigrants from this region began to decline. By the early part of the 20th century, Northwestern Europe accounted for only a small share of newcomers to America. According to the graph, from which regions did most immigrants come after 1900?*

GUIDED INSTRUCTION
Organize students into small groups. Tell each group to imagine that they have been hired by their state's legislature or territorial government to make a poster supporting the New Immigration. Then have each group design and make a poster. Make a classroom display of their completed work.

employers opposed any check on immigration for less humane reasons. They knew that unlimited immigration would assure them a steady force of low-paid but hard-working laborers.

Congress *did* exclude one type of immigrant during this period—the Chinese. By 1880 there were about 75,000 Chinese immigrants in ■ California. They were extremely hard-working people. Most were Buddhists, a religion little understood in America. Because of language and cultural differences, the Chinese tended even more than most immigrants to stick together. They seemed unwilling to try American ways. Older residents feared and resented them. When a depression swept the country, California workers worried that Chinese workers would steal their jobs at lower wages. In 1882 Congress responded to the demands of Californians by passing the **Chinese Exclusion Act.** It prohibited Chinese workers from entering the United States for a period of ten years. Later the ban was extended. It was not lifted until 1965.

By 1900 about 80,000 Mexicans had emigrated to the United States. Increasingly they provided the labor force that developed the southwestern part of the nation. Unlike most other immigrants, these newcomers seldom settled in large cities. Many had to move continually from place to place. They encountered many social, economic, and political handicaps. Yet Mexican American communities survived and even thrived, strengthened by their cultural traditions and community life. Some Mexican Americans found jobs as laborers building the Southern Pacific and Santa Fe Railroads. When the lines were completed, they became section hands—men whose job it was to maintain the railroad right-of-way and repair damaged tracks and ties. Many families had to live in railroad boxcars. Other Mexican immigrants worked as cowhands on cattle ranches. Still others became farm laborers. Like so many immigrants, most were poorly paid and oftentimes badly treated.

The "dumbbell tenements" of eastern cities were named for their shape. An area 20 feet by 90 feet held four apartments. An indentation only 2.5 feet wide and from 5 feet to 50 feet long created an airshaft 5 feet wide. Three of the apartment's rooms faced on this shaft; only one room faced on the street or the rear yard or alley. The dumb-bell tenement buildings were from 6 to 8 stories high. They held from 24 to 32 families.

RESOURCES

■ You may wish to have students complete Reading 22: "A Farm Girl Arrives in the Big City (1895)" in Volume II of *Eyewitnesses and Others.*

GUIDED INSTRUCTION

Before beginning this subsection, have students select any aspect of 19th-century urban life—working conditions, housing, transportation, public health, schools, social work—and prepare a short report to read to the class. Use these reports as a basis for a class discussion on urban problems. Encourage artistically inclined students to draw pictures to accompany their reports. Make a bulletin board display of the drawings.

PRIMARY SOURCE

Description of change: excerpted.
Rationale: excerpted to focus on conditions in tenements.

Point of View

In a major study of Jewish immigration to America in the late 1800s, the author found this account.

“Not everyone was equally poor. When an immigrant family could occupy a two- or three-room apartment without several boarders, they were considered lucky. Boarders were a natural institution, particularly in the early years when most immigrants came without their families. But even the privilege of being a boarder was not enjoyed by every greenhorn. There were various categories of boarders. A star boarder slept on a folding bed. But I knew a printer who every night unscrewed a door, put it on two chairs; he couldn't pay as much as the one who had the bed.”

From *The World of Our Fathers,*
Irving Howe, 1976

Problems of City Life

American agriculture was expanding with American industry. But machinery was reducing the need for human labor on farms. Cyrus McCormick's reapers and other new farm machines were displacing thousands of farmhands who had previously plowed, planted, hoed, and harvested the nation's crops. For every city dweller who took up the plow between 1860 and 1900, 20 farmers moved to the city.

The growth of cities after the Civil War was both rapid and widespread. In 1860 places like Denver, Memphis, and Seattle were no more than small towns. By 1900 they were major urban centers. In that same year there were 50 cities of over 100,000 people.

The largest cities were centers of both manufacturing and commerce, and they did not depend on any one activity for their prosperity. Some smaller cities specialized in making a particular product. Dayton, Ohio, manufactured cash registers. Minneapolis, Minnesota, became a flour-milling center.

People moved to cities far more rapidly than housing and other facilities could be built to care for their needs. City land values soared. A New York City lot selling for $80 in the early 1840s sold for $8,000 in 1880. Because of the high cost of property, builders put up tenement apartments on plots only 25 feet (about 8 meters) wide. They were crowded so closely together that light and moving air were blocked out.

A five- or six-story tenement usually had four apartments on each floor. Front apartments contained four rooms, rear apartments three. Many of the rooms had no windows. In most cases two families had to share a single toilet located in a dark and narrow hallway. Dark, musty, garbage-cluttered "air shafts" separated one tenement building from the next. One resident described the air shaft of his tenement to the New York State Tenement House Commission in 1900:

“ **The Secretary:** How long have you lived in tenement houses?
Mr. Moscowitz: Seventeen years. . . .
The Secretary: What have you to say about the air shaft; do you think it is a good thing?
Mr. Moscowitz: I think it is decidedly a bad thing. I must confirm the statements made by other witnesses that the air shaft is a breeder of disease, and especially that there can be no fresh air in any building with an air shaft, from my experience, because of the refuse [garbage] thrown down the air shaft, the stench is so vile and the air is so foul that the occupants do not employ the windows as a means of getting air. . . .

The Secretary: Are there any other objections to the air
shaft?

Mr. Moscowitz: It destroys privacy.

The Secretary: How does it do that?

Mr. Moscowitz: I know where I lived in a house where there
was a family opposite, the windows which are usually
diagonal, I heard everything, especially loud noises, and
when the windows are not covered one sees into the
house. . . .[1]

Police and fire protection remained inadequate in most cities.
Garbage collection was haphazard at best. City water was often
impure. Sewers were smelly and often clogged. Disease could spread
quickly under these conditions. In one crowded Chicago neighborhood three out of every five babies born in 1900 died before they
were three years old. Jacob Riis, who wrote *How the Other Half* ■
Lives, the most famous book on the tenements, described similar
conditions in New York City:

> There are tenements everywhere. Suppose we look into one
> on Cherry Street. Be a little careful, please! The hall is dark
> and you might fall over the children pitching pennies back
> there. Not that it would hurt them. Kicks and punches are
> their daily diet. They have little else. . . .
>
> Here is a door. Listen! that short hacking cough, that
> tiny helpless cry—what do they mean? They mean that the
> soiled bow of white you saw on the door downstairs [when
> someone died, a bow was hung on the door—black for an
> adult, white for a child] will have another story to tell—oh,
> a sadly familiar story—before the day ends. The child is
> dying of measles. With half a chance it might have lived.
> But it had none. That dark bedroom killed it. . . .[2]

Of course, many people worked hard trying to solve the cities'
problems and improve urban living conditions. Boards of health made
studies and established standards for sewage and garbage disposal.
Elaborate systems of pipes and reservoirs brought pure water from
distant lakes and rivers. Social workers established community centers called **settlement houses** in poor neighborhoods. Settlement
houses had something for everyone—day nurseries for little children,
gymnasiums and social activities for young and old, English classes
for immigrants.

The most famous of the settlement houses was **Hull House** in
Chicago, founded in 1889 by Jane Addams. Many of the settlement

[1]From "Testimony of a Tenant" by Dr. Henry Moscowitz in *The Tenement House
Problem*, edited by Robert W. DeForest and Lawrence Veiller
[2]From *How the Other Half Lives* by Jacob Riis

Jane Addams Memorial Collection, The University
Library, The University of Illinois at Chicago

*This photograph of Jane Addams as a
young woman was taken in about
1890. She founded Hull House in
Chicago with Ellen Gates Starr. In
1931, Addams was awarded the Nobel
Peace Prize. In your own words, describe life for a poor person before and
after settlement houses.*

The Growth of Cities 691

workers were young women who had graduated from college. They lived in the settlement houses and tried to become part of the community. They believed that they could grow personally by involving themselves in local political and social affairs. At the same time they were helping local people.

As cities grew larger, transportation became a problem. In 1865 most large cities had streetcars drawn by horses. Horses were slow and needed a great deal of care. In 1873 Andrew S. Hallidie installed **cable cars** on the steep hills of San Francisco, which horses could not climb. Hallidie used a long wire cable attached to a stationary steam engine to pull the cars.

Then, in the late 1880s, Frank J. Sprague designed the first electrified street railway in America. In 1887 he opened a 12-mile line (about 19 kilometers) in Richmond, Virginia. By 1890, 51 American cities had **electric trolley** systems.

As time passed, hundreds of bridges, paved roads, parks, and grand public buildings improved the appearance of cities and the

The Brooklyn Bridge is a fitting symbol of the rise of industrial America. The bridge opened in 1883 with fireworks and a water parade.

Metropolitan Museum of Art

quality of city life. The most famous symbol of the modern city was the **Brooklyn Bridge** in New York City. The Brooklyn Bridge took 13 years to build. It was designed by John A. Roebling and built by his son Washington. Washington Roebling was disabled during the construction and unable to walk about. He supervised the project from a nearby apartment, keeping track of progress with binoculars and a telescope. The bridge is now more than 100 years old and heavily

Culver Pictures

Watching from his window is the son of the designer of the Brooklyn Bridge, Washington Roebling, who was disabled for life by working in the compressed air caissons—watertight chambers used in construction work under water.

traveled by commuters moving between Brooklyn and Manhattan. New Yorkers remain fiercely proud of their bridge.

Thus arose industrial America. In 1865 most people lived much the same way as their parents and grandparents had. The lives of the people of 1900 were far different—closer to what we know today. 🖼

INDEPENDENT PRACTICE
Have students complete the Preview & Review activity at the beginning of the section.

CLOSURE
Tell students that the massive industrialization that occurred after the Civil War affected many aspects of American life. It brought about changes in business organization; it affected how and where people worked; it encouraged urbanization as workers settled near factories; its excesses brought about the birth of the labor union movement and calls for government regulation of business; it encouraged immigration because of the demand for cheap labor.

HOMEWORK
Ask students to imagine that they are considering immigrating to the United States. Have them write a letter to a relative in which they discuss the pros and cons of such a move. Read some of the best ones to the class.

■ Return to the Preview & Review on page 683.

1. Responses will vary. Students should support their choice with sound reasoning.
2. Responses will vary. In 1895 most judges ruled in favor of corporations. The Sherman Antitrust Act vaguely banned restrictions of interstate trade or commerce. The government would have to prove that the salt trust restrained trade—a difficult task.

3. Responses will vary. Students should use their historical imagination and support their position with facts and sound reasoning.

REVIEW RESPONSES

Chapter Summary
Paragraphs will vary but should be evaluated on the logic of student arguments.

Reviewing Chronological Order
4, 5, 1, 2, 3

Understanding Main Ideas
1. Railroad networks established; development of powerful steel, oil, and electrical industries; development of mass production; development of business monopolies and trusts; communications revolution; development of department stores; mail order businesses; beginnings of efforts to regulate big business; new efforts to unionize workers; increased immigration from eastern, central, and southern Europe; and the rapid growth of cities and the problems this caused
2. Railroads needed cheap steel for tracks if they were to be economically viable; steel companies benefited through increased demand and by the availability of cheap transportation, which allowed them to expand their markets even more.
3. Total control of a product, service, or trade in a region; railroads, in an effort to establish their own monopolies, gave lower rates to large shippers—giving these shippers an advantage over their smaller competitors.
4. Inadequate sanitation, housing, police and fire protection; establishment of standards for sewage and

CHAPTER 19 REVIEW

Gilded Age

1860		THE RISE OF INDUSTRIAL AMERICA	

1861	1865	1869	1876
Telegraph wires span nation	Civil War ends	Knights of Labor founded	Bell demonstrates telephone
	1866	★	
	Field lays transatlantic cable	Vanderbilt begins railroad empire	
	1870		
	Standard Oil Company		

Chapter Summary
Read the statements below. Choose one, and write a paragraph explaining its importance.
1. Soon after the Civil War railroads and a communications network linked the nation.
2. The expense of developing railroads led to the new business arrangement of the corporation.
3. The growth of the steel industry paralleled the growth of railroads. At the same time, the oil industry began to develop.
4. Eventually the government banned business practices that harmed the public.
5. Workers fought to improve their conditions, eventually turning to unionization.
6. Immigrants from new regions—southern and eastern Europe, China, and Mexico—provided many of the workers for the industrial surge.
7. Most of the new immigrants crowded into ethnic neighborhoods in the growing cities.

Reviewing Chronological Order
Number your paper 1–5. Then study the time line above and place the following events in the order in which they happened by writing the first next to 1, the second next to 2, and so on.
1. Chinese Exclusion Act
2. Sherman Antitrust Act
3. Homestead Strike
4. Knights of Labor founded
5. Standard Oil Company

Understanding Main Ideas
1. What were some of the major changes in the United States in the years between the Civil War and 1900?
2. How did the railroads and the steel industry help each other grow?
3. What is a monopoly? How did railroad competition lead to monopoly in other fields?
4. What were some problems faced by growing cities between 1860 and 1900? What were some attempts to improve city life?

Thinking Critically
1. **Analyzing.** Suppose you have $500 to invest. Your choices are: a corporation with shares whose value has risen slowly but steadily for six years, or a partnership that stands a 50-percent chance of doubling your money in two years. In which business would you invest? Why?
2. **Judging.** You are a Supreme Court judge in 1895. The case before you involves a salt manufacturing trust in Louisiana. It has purchased five competing companies in its own state and three competing companies in the adjacent state of Texas. Would you rule that this trust violated the law? If so, which law or laws, and how? If not, why not?
3. **Evaluating.** If you were a member of Congress in the late 1800s, would you have voted for the literacy test bill? The Chinese Exclusion Act? Why or why not?

Writing About History
Write a story on the following idea: An ordinary citizen who lived in 1800 returns for a look at America in 1900. What are the reactions of this traveler from the time of Jefferson's "nation of farmers" to the sprawling cities and industries of 1900? Which changes impress your time traveler, and which might be upsetting? Use the information in Chapter 15 and in other reference books to prepare your story.

Practicing the Strategy
Review the strategy on page 688.
Reading a Table. Study the table on page 678, then answer the following questions.
1. What is the interval between the years in this table? What information is contained in the headings?

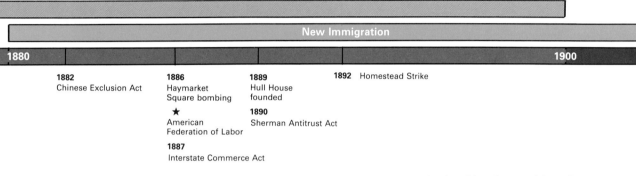

New Immigration

| 1880 | | | | | 1900 |

1882
Chinese Exclusion Act

1886
Haymarket
Square bombing

★
American
Federation of Labor

1887
Interstate Commerce Act

1889
Hull House
founded

1890
Sherman Antitrust Act

1892 Homestead Strike

2. Between 1870 and 1900, what was the rate of increase of the male workers as compared to the female workers?
3. Which 10-year interval saw the greatest increase in the total number of workers?
4. In 1900, the table shows a new age group: 16–19. What changes may have resulted in this new age group for workers?

Using Primary Sources
In the late 1800s people began arriving in America from eastern Europe. The following excerpt is from an essay that was submitted in a competition organized by the Committee for Immigrants in America. The essay appeared in a journal called *Immigrants in America Review*. As you read the excerpt from "What America Means to a Russian Jewess," think about an immigrant's point of view of "Americanization."

America means for an Immigrant a fairy promised land that came out true, a land that gives all they need for their work, a land which gives them human rights, a land that gives morality through her churches and education through her free schools and libraries. The longer I live in America the more I think of the question of Americanising the immigrants. At first I thought that there is not such a question as that, for the children of immigrants naturally are Americans and good Americans. America is a land made up of foreigners and the virtues of American life is the best Americaniser. The first generation of American immigrants can't be Americanized much for they were raised in different ways the mode of living is different. And yet how much it is when they love America and are such patriots.

1. According to the excerpt, what has America given the new immigrants?

2. The author thinks that "the virtues of American life is the best Americaniser." What do you think the author means by this statement?
3. What might the use of grammar and spelling tell you about the author of the article?
4. Think about recent immigrants to the United States. Do you think that "Americanization" is necessary? Why or why not?

Linking History & Geography
Immigration has been an important aspect of the development of the United States. To understand immigration, reread "The New Immigration" on pages 683–89 and on an outline map of the world, color the countries from which most of these new immigrants came. Then review "Immigration from Europe" on page 343. Mark the countries from which these earlier immigrants came in a different color.

Enriching Your Study of History
1. **Individual Project**. Complete one of the following projects. Use historical imagination to place yourself in a telegraph office in Homestead, Pennsylvania, in 1892. Prepare a telegraph message that reports on the clash of strikers and Pinkertons. Include the views of both sides in the Homestead strike. Or using historical imagination, place yourself in the year 1890. A few months ago, on your twenty-first birthday, you moved from your parents' farm to find work in the city. Write a letter to the folks at home telling them about city life.
2. **Cooperative Project**. Your class will prepare a multimedia presentation on the railroad network that was built after the Civil War. Various groups will use pictures, stories, and songs to show the development and effects of railroads.

RESPONSES *(Continued)*
garbage disposal, drinking water, establishment of settlement houses to aid poor immigrants, improvements in local transportation

Writing About History
Stories will vary; reward creative uses of historical imagination.

Practicing the Strategy
1. 10 years; the sex and age of workers
2. The number of women workers increased 161% compared to an increase of 106% for male workers.
3. 1880-1890
4. Restrictions on child labor

Using Primary Sources
1. Opportunity to work, human rights, freedom of religion, education
2. Students may suggest that the author means that people must be raised with the benefits of American life to be completely Americanized.
3. English is not her native language.
4. Opinions will vary; students should support their opinions with sound reasoning.

PRIMARY SOURCE
Description of change: excerpted.
Rationale: excerpted to focus on what America means to a particular immigrant.

National Politics and Culture, 1867–1896

PLANNING THE CHAPTER	
TEXTBOOK	**RESOURCES**
1. Politics After the War	*Unit 6 Worksheets and Tests:* Chapter 20 Graphic Organizer, Directed Reading 20:1, Reteaching 20:1 *Eyewitnesses and Others, Volume 2:* Reading 29: A View of the Political Machine (ca. 1905) *Art in American History:* Transparency 14: The Centennial Quilt
2. The Age of Realism	*Unit 6 Worksheets and Tests:* Directed Reading 20:2, Reteaching 20:2 *Eyewitnesses and Others, Volume 1:* Reading 77: Mark Twain Describes the Pony Express (1860) *Eyewitnesses and Others, Volume 2:* Reading 24: A Farmer in the Grip of the "Octopus" (1890s), Reading 27: The Squid and the Lobster, from Dreiser's *The Financier* (ca. 1900) *Art in American History:* Transparency 16: The Pathetic Song, Transparency 19: Summertime: Woman and Child in a Rowboat
3. Populism	*Unit 6 Worksheets and Tests:* Directed Reading 20:3, Reteaching 20:3, Geography 20
4. Unemployment and Unrest	*Unit 6 Worksheets and Tests:* Directed Reading 20:4, Reteaching 20:4 *Eyewitnesses and Others, Volume 2:* Reading 20: The Sweatshops of Chicago (1891) *The Constitution: Past, Present, and Future:* Case 5: *Lochner v. New York*, Case 9: *Youngstown Sheet & Tube Co. v. Sawyer*
5. Gold Versus Silver	*Unit 6 Worksheets and Tests:* Directed Reading 20:5, Reteaching 20:5

Chapter Review	**Audio Program:** Chapter 20 **Unit 6 Worksheets and Tests:** Chapter 20 Tests, Forms A and B (See also *Alternative Assessment Forms*) **Test Generator**
Unit Review	**Unit 6 Worksheets and Tests:** Unit 6 Tests, Forms A and B (see also *Alternative Assessment Forms*), Unit 6 Synthesis **Test Generator**

STRATEGIES FOR STUDENTS WITH SPECIAL NEEDS

Gifted Students.

Have interested students prepare a report on one of the following: the railroad strike of 1877, the Homestead strike of 1892, or the Pullman strike of 1894. Student reports should include the reasons for the strike, the goals of both management and labor, events that occurred during the strike, government involvement, and the outcome of the strike.

Students Having Difficulty with the Chapter.

You may wish to have students listen to Chapter 20 in *The Story of America Audio Program.* Then organize students into cooperative learning groups. Have each group draw a map of the United States and identify the various agricultural regions of the country by drawing a symbol on the map representing the chief product grown there (for example, a corn stalk for the corngrowing region). Students may find information on this subject by checking in an atlas in their school library. You may wish to display the maps in the classroom or in the hallways of the school.

BOOKS FOR TEACHERS

Paul W. Glad, *The Trumpet Soundeth: William Jennings Bryan and his Democracy.* Westport, CT: Greenwood, 1986.

Lawrence Goodwyn, *Democratic Promise: The Populist Movement in America.* New York: Oxford University Press, 1976.

L. Gould, *The Presidency of William McKinley.* Lawrence: University Press of Kansas, 1981.

Morton Keller, *Affairs of State: Public Life in Late Nineteenth Century America.* Cambridge: Harvard University Press, 1979.

G. McFarland, *Mugwumps, Morals and Politics, 1884–1920.* Amherst: University of Massachusetts Press, 1975.

BOOKS FOR STUDENTS

Harold Dunn, *Our Political Heritage: The American Presidential Election Process, Out of the Mouths of Babes.* Owings Mills, MD: Stemmer House, 1980.

Karnet T. Kane, *Young Mark Twain and the Mississippi.* New York: Random House, "Landmark Series," 1966.

Mark Twain, *Adventures of Huckleberry Finn.* Various editions.

MULTIMEDIA MATERIALS

American Industrial Ballads (record), Folkways. Workers' and farmers' protest songs.

Cross of Gold Speech by William J. Bryan (record), SSSS. Explains Bryan's position and presents quotations from the speech.

The Dynamics of Change: The Emerging Giant: The U.S. in 1900 (filmstrip), MultiMedia. Problems of industrialization in a rural-oriented society; reform movements; labor unions.

Farmer in a Changing America (filmstrip), EBF. Explores the history of farming in the U.S.

Women's Work: America 1720–1920 (filmstrip), Clearvue. Part 2: How the beginnings of mechanized industry liberated some women from the home.

RESOURCES
■ You may wish to have students complete the Chapter 20 Graphic Organizer as they work through this chapter.

CHAPTER OBJECTIVES
Upon completing this chapter, students will be able to:
1. Explain what was meant by "waving the bloody shirt."
2. Describe the importance of the close states in the presidential elections following the Civil War.

OVERVIEW
Three major issues—the tariff, the money question, and civil service reform—dominated politics between 1867 and 1896. At the same time, farmers attempted to increase their political power through the Populist party.

FOCUS/MOTIVATION:
MAKING CONNECTIONS
Prior Knowledge.
Point out that in 1876 the nation celebrated its one hundredth birthday with an exposition in Philadelphia. Ask students to compose a chart on the chalkboard or an overhead projector. The chart should show some of the changes that the signers of the Declaration of Independence in 1776 would have observed in the United States during those 100 years. *(United States less rural and more industrialized, more and bigger cities, immigration of many peoples of non-English background, slaves freed, women able to vote in territorial elections in Wyoming, transcontinental railroads linking the coasts, the nation had fought a civil war and the Union was preserved, great territorial expansion, etc.)* Ask: How many states were there? *(38, Colorado admitted in 1876)* Have students make copies of the charts. They should add to this material for their study of all the changes the country underwent between 1876 and its two hundredth anniversary in 1976.

CHAPTER 20
National Politics and Culture, 1867–1896

■ The Civil War and the rapid expansion of the economy that followed it had important effects on American government and politics. So did the great social changes, especially the flood of new immigrants and the shift of population from the farms to the cities. New issues arose as conditions changed. Older political questions had to be reconsidered too. The Democratic and Republican parties had to deal with difficult and confusing social, economic, and human rights issues. By and large, they failed to find clear solutions. Their efforts are worth studying closely if we are to understand how industrialization, the rise of cities, and the new immigration affected American politics and culture.

The Democratic donkey and the Republican elephant were the creation of the great political cartoonist Thomas Nast, who also gave us the plump bearded image of Santa Claus. Do you think the elephant and donkey are good symbols of the parties they represent?

Culver Pictures

The Granger Collection, New York

3. Criticize and defend big-city political machines.

4. Identify the major political issues in the years following the Civil War.

5. Explain the reasons that led farmers to form the Populist party.

6. Describe the groups that supported the Republi-

can and Democratic candidates for president in 1896.

7. Recognize the impact of geographic factors such as regional voting patterns and the rural-urban split on election results.

8. Interpret election results by studying a pie graph and a map of electoral and popular votes.

1. POLITICS AFTER THE WAR

Republican North and Democratic South

From a political point of view the Civil War did not end in 1865. Nor did it end in 1877 when the North gave up trying to control the South by force. Indeed, the war affected American politics for more than a century.

In the 1850s the controversy over slavery in the territories led most white southerners to become Democrats. When the war ended, most stayed Democrats. After southern whites regained control of their local governments in the 1870s, they voted Democratic in national elections almost to a man. With southern blacks not permitted to vote, the Republican party had no chance at all in any southern state. People spoke of the **Solid South.** Every state that had seceded from the Union cast its electoral votes for the Democratic candidate in every presidential election from 1880 until 1928.

The Republican party had become the leading party in the North and West by 1860. It remained so throughout the decades after the Civil War. Memories of the war stirred up strong emotions and had a great influence on how people voted. Tens of thousands saw the Republicans as the saviors of the Union, the Democrats as the disloyal dividers of the United States. These views held long after slavery had been done away with and the idea of secession abandoned by even its most extreme southern supporters.

After the war Congress had dozens of important issues to decide. Few of these issues had any connection with the geographical division that separated Democrats from Republicans. Yet Republican politicians constantly made emotional appeals to voters by reminding them that the Democrats were "ex-rebels."

This tactic was called "waving the bloody shirt." It got the name in 1866. During a speech in Congress, Benjamin Franklin Butler of Massachusetts displayed the blood-stained shirt of a carpetbagger official who had been beaten by a mob in Mississippi. The incident, according to Butler, proved that the South was still disloyal and must not be trusted.

Here is a famous example of the bloody shirt oratory of the period:

66 Every man that tried to destroy this nation was a Democrat.
. . . Soldiers, every scar you have on your heroic bodies
was given you by a Democrat.**99**

Waving the bloody shirt helped keep northerners voting Republican. Yet Republicans never dominated the northern states as completely as the Democrats controlled the South. New England and most states west of the Mississippi River were Republican strongholds. So were Pennsylvania, Wisconsin, and Michigan. But New

Preview & Review

Use these questions to guide your reading. Answer the questions after completing Section 1.
Understanding Issues, Events, & Ideas. **1.** Create a word web about politics after the Civil War, using these words: Solid South, close state, native son, political machine, Tammany Hall, boss, franchise, kickback, sitting on the fence. **2.** Briefly describe the domestic issues such as the tariff, money crisis, and government jobs, using these words: monetary policy, greenback, hard money, deflation, inflation, civil service reform, merit system, patronage, Pendleton Act, Civil Service Commission.
1. What was "waving the bloody shirt"? How did it influence elections?
2. How did the political machines in northern cities attract the votes of recent immigrants?
3. Why were political parties afraid to take a stand on controversial issues?
4. How were farmers hurt by deflation after the Civil War?
Thinking Critically. **1.** If you were a member of Congress in 1875, would you have voted for or against protective tariffs? Why?
2. The year is 1882. Write a newspaper editorial explaining the need for civil service reform.

PREVIEW & REVIEW RESPONSES
Understanding Issues, Events & Ideas.
1. Word webs will vary but should show an understanding of the terms used.
2. Descriptions will vary but should define the terms used in context.
1. Republicans made emotional appeals to voters by reminding them that the Democrats were "ex-rebels." The tactic helped keep northerners voting Republican.
2. They helped immigrants find jobs, fed the unemployed, ran community picnics on holidays, and helped youngsters who were in trouble with the law.
3. Each was afraid it would cost votes.
4. During the war farmers had borrowed money to buy more land and machinery. They had paid high prices because of the wartime inflation. As prices fell, they had to produce more to pay off the debt.

Thinking Critically.
1. Answers will vary. Students who believe that industry should be protected would vote yes. Students who believe that prices should be kept low would vote no.
2. Editorials will vary but should point out the need to end corruption.

PRIMARY SOURCE
Description of change: excerpted.
Rationale: excerpted to focus on bloody shirt oratory.

HISTORICAL SIDELIGHTS
① Every elected president between 1868 and 1904 except Grover Cleveland had served in the Union army during the Civil War.

RESOURCES
■ You may wish to have students view Transparency 14: "The Centennial Quilt" and complete the accompanying worksheet in *Art in American History.*

FOCUS/MOTIVATION: MAKING CONNECTIONS
Prior Knowledge.

Ask students to state the major agreements included in the Compromise of 1877. *(President Hayes would withdraw troops from the South, appoint a southerner to his Cabinet, and support a proposed railroad between Texas and California.)* Point out that the election of 1876 was only one in a long string of very close elections after the Civil War. Mention to students that they will be studying political developments between 1867 and 1896 in this section and that the section will include many new terms. Then have everyone skim the section and make a list of any words they cannot define. Organize the class into teams of five students. Set up a rotation by which each team takes a turn asking other teams for the meanings of a word on its list. The responding team scores a point for a correct meaning. When you have finished the game, collect the lists and look through them. If there are any words that several students have listed, you may want to review them the next day.

PRIMARY SOURCE

Description of change: excerpted and bracketed.
Rationale: excerpted to focus on Goodwin's description of Matthew Keany; bracketed words added to clarify meaning.

Point of View

Doris Kearns Goodwin has written this description of Matthew Keany—the North End boss in Boston. John Fitzgerald goes to Keany for help after his father's death.

“Fitzgerald found the bluff and genial Keany in his usual position, behind his desk in the back room of the red brick grocery store. . . . Into this low-ceilinged room which served as his headquarters, thousands of men and women had entered over the years in search of assistance. By Keany's word, a man's son could be liberated from prison, a widow provided with food, an aspiring peddler issued a permit and a destitute father given a coffin to bury his infant child. . . . [There] Fitzgerald reported all summer long in order to help the boss dispense the hundred and one favors regularly awarded in the course of a day, favors which spread the boss's influence, like a huge spider, over the entire district. . . .”
From *The Fitzgeralds and the Kennedys,* 1987

York, New Jersey, and Connecticut were a cluster of states where Democrats could sometimes win. Ohio, Indiana, and Illinois made another group where elections were usually very close.

In nearly every presidential election after the Civil War, the party that won the majority of the electoral votes of the "close" northern states won the presidency. For this reason both parties usually chose presidential and vice presidential candidates from these **close states.** These candidates were called **native sons.** Their names on the ballot could increase the chances of carrying the candidates' home states and perhaps winning the election.

■ Every president from Rutherford B. Hayes, elected in 1876, to William Howard Taft, elected in 1908, came from either Ohio, Indiana, or New York. Of the 27 men who were nominated for president or vice president by the Democrats and Republicans between 1876 ① and 1908, 19 came from these three states. Not a single southerner was nominated by the major parties for either office during the period. This shows how the Civil War continued to affect politics.

Ordinary people paid a great deal of attention to politics. A much larger proportion of eligible voters actually voted than has been true in recent times. Did they do so because the campaigns were so intense and colorful? Or were the campaigns intense and colorful because the people were so interested in politics? Unfortunately, these are questions almost impossible for historians to answer!

The Poor and Political Machines

One reason why elections were close in northern industrial states like New York and Ohio was that large numbers of recent immigrants lived in them. These immigrants, as we have noted, tended to settle in the cities. They were "outsiders," poor and without much influence. Most people with wealth and social position looked down upon them. And in the northern states the wealthy and socially prominent were nearly all Republicans.

This explains why most immigrants in the cities joined the Democratic party. Their position was somewhat like that of blacks in the southern states. Each group supported the minority party of its part of the country. Northern immigrants voted Democratic, southern blacks Republican. Northern blacks, on the other hand, while definitely not part of the majority, supported the Republican party. They were mindful that it was the Republican party that had abolished slavery.

In most northern cities local politicians took advantage of the immigrants' preference for the Democratic party to build up **political machines.** These organizations nominated candidates for local office and turned out large numbers of loyal voters on election day. One such machine was **Tammany Hall,** which was run by New York City Democrats.

SUGGESTED CAPTION RESPONSE
The figures show corrupt politicians.

RESOURCES
■ You may wish to have students complete Reading
29: "A View of the Political Machine (ca. 1905)" in
Volume II of *Eyewitnesses and Others*.

Culver Pictures

The leaders of the machines, called **bosses,** provided many ben-■
efits to poor city dwellers. Well-to-do residents and most political
reformers disliked the machines. The bosses used shady and even
clearly illegal methods to win votes. But they certainly helped new
people, especially immigrants, to make the adjustment to city life.
They helped immigrants find jobs. When neighborhood workers were
ill or out of work, the bosses would supply their families with food
and small sums of money. The machines ran community picnics on
holidays. They helped local youngsters who got in trouble with the
law.

In return for their help the bosses expected the people to vote
for the machine's candidates. By controlling elections, the bosses
could reward their friends or line their own pockets. For example,
companies that wanted to operate streetcar lines or sell gas or electricity for lighting homes or businesses needed city permits called
franchises. Bosses often demanded bribes before they would have
these franchises issued by the local officials they controlled. They
also made deals with contractors who put up public buildings or did
other work for the city. The bosses agreed to pay needlessly high
prices for the work in return for large **kickbacks,** the illegal return to
them of part of the payment made to contractors.

Politics for profit seemed to be the method of operation. This
made politics and politicians the target of many reformers. Lincoln

*"New York's New Solar System" was
drawn by Joseph Keppler in 1898.
Here Richard Croker, the head of
the Tammany machine, is the sun.
Around him revolve lesser corrupt politicians. Why are these figures definitely not heavenly bodies?*

GUIDED INSTRUCTION
Organize the class into two
groups: Republicans and Democrats. Have each group meet
separately to nominate a presidential and vice presidential
candidate from among the candidates who actually ran for the
offices anytime between 1876
and 1896. Students should try
to select a candidate from a
state that will help the party
win the election. (Point out that
19 of the 27 candidates for
president and vice president
came from Ohio, Indiana, or
New York.) Students should
also develop a political platform based on actual issues
between 1876 and 1896. Have
some students represent
bosses of political machines in
large states. They should consider which city and people
they will represent and whose
votes they will control. Then
hold a mock election. Assign
an arbitrary number of voters
to these machine politicians.
(Remind these students that
they *must* vote as the boss
commands.) Use the mock
election as the basis for a class
discussion of the several presidential elections that took
place after 1876. How did they
differ from presidential elections in the 1970s and 1980s?
(*Sometimes the winner of the
popular vote did not win the
electoral vote.*)

Politics After the War   699

The Granger Collection, New York

*Thomas Nast first drew a Tammany
tiger in 1871. When this cartoon appeared in* Harper's *magazine, the
city bosses threatened to cancel all orders of Harper Brothers' textbooks.
"The Tammany Tiger" upset Boss
Tweed, who controlled Tammany
Hall and who had said, "As long as I
count the votes, what are you going to
do about it?" Nast asked the same
question in the cartoon's subtitle,
"What Are You Going to Do About
It?" On what ancient Roman practice
is this cartoon based?*

Steffens, the leading reformer of political corruption, wrote:

❝ There is hardly a government office from United States
Senator down to alderman in any part of the country to
which some business leader has not been elected. Yet politics remains corrupt and government pretty bad. Business
leaders have failed in politics as they have in good citizenship. Why?

Because politics is business. . . . The commercial spirit
is the spirit of profit, not patriotism; of credit, not honor;
of individual gain, not national prosperity; of trade, not
principle. . . .

We cheat our government and we let our leaders rob it.
We let them persuade and bribe our power away from us.
True, they pass strict laws for us, but we let them pass bad
laws too, giving away public property in exchange. Our
good, and often impossible, laws we allow to be used for
oppression and blackmail. And what can we say? We break
our own laws and rob our own government—the woman at
the tax office, the lyncher with his rope, and the captain of
industry with his bribe and his rebate. The spirit of graft
and of lawlessness is the American spirit.

We Americans have failed. We may be selfish and influenced by gain. . . . [But] there is pride in the character of
American citizenship. This pride may be a power in the
land. So this record of shame and yet of self-respect, disgraceful confession, yet a declaration of honor, is dedicated,

in all good faith, to the accused—to all the citizens of all the cities in the United States.[1] **"**

The machines did both good and harm in their day. Not all of them were associated with the Democratic party. The powerful Philadelphia machine, for example, was a Republican organization. So were many of the machines in middle-sized cities. But most of the big-city machines were run by the Democrats. They were very useful to the national Democratic party in presidential elections in close states like New York.

Sitting on the Fence

Extremely important social and economic problems were being discussed and settled after the Civil War. There were problems caused by industrial expansion and technological change. Other problems resulted from the growth of cities. Still other problems related to racial questions and to immigration. Logically, the parties should have fought their campaigns on these issues.

They rarely did so. Each was afraid that a strong stand on any controversial question would cost votes. It seemed politically safer to make vague statements that everyone could accept, even if no one entirely agreed with them. This was called **sitting on the fence.**

Still, the issues remained, and politicians had to deal with them in one way or another. For example, the need to regulate railroads and other big businesses resulted in the Interstate Commerce Act and the Sherman Antitrust Act. The Indian lands of the West were seized and divided up. During these years Congress and the presidents struggled with high protective tariffs on imported manufactured goods. They tried to solve what was known as "the money question." And they attempted to reform the way government employees were hired and fired.

The Tariff Issue

When the United States first began to develop manufacturing about the time of the War of 1812, a strong case could be made for tariffs that heavily taxed foreign manufactured goods. American "infant industries" needed protection in order to compete with larger, more efficient producers in Europe.

After the Civil War the need for protection was much less clear. America was rapidly becoming the greatest manufacturing nation in the world. Its factories were efficient. The costs of doing business were lower than in many foreign countries. Manufacturers did not, however, want to give up the extra profits that the protective tariffs made possible.

[1]From the *The Shame of the Cities* by Lincoln Steffens

GUIDED INSTRUCTION
Organize the class into two groups: those favoring a protective tariff and those opposed to it. Have students review the history of tariffs in the United States. You may wish to refer them to the graph of tariff rates in the Reference Section. Then have students debate the tariff issue and give solid reasons for their positions.

PRIMARY SOURCE
Description of change: excerpted and bracketed.
Rationale: excerpted to focus on Steffens' major views on government corruption in the United States; bracketed words added to clarify meaning.

HBJ Photo

This cartoon captured the plight of the American farmer. Its title tells all: "The Tariff Cow—the Farmer Feeds Her—the Monopolist Gets the Milk." Hasn't the artist made the farmer a hayseed and the rich man a gentleman? But whose side is he on?

High tariffs raised the prices that farmers and other consumers had to pay for manufactured goods. Many, therefore, were opposed to the policy of protection. A number of tariff laws were passed by Congress between 1865 and 1900. Democrats and Republicans devoted much time to arguing about tariff policy. Neither party took a clear stand on the question. The rates of various imported products were raised and lowered, then lowered and raised, then raised again. No firm decision was ever made about whether protective tariffs were good for the nation as a whole.

The Democrats tended to be for lowering the tariff, the Republicans for keeping it high. But so many members of Congress from each party voted the other way that it is impossible to say that the tariff was a clear-cut party issue.

The Money Question

From the days of Andrew Jackson to the Civil War, the United States had followed a **monetary policy** that was conservative and cautious. All paper money in circulation could be exchanged for gold or silver coins at a bank. Yet during the Civil War, as we have seen, the government could not raise enough money by taxing and borrowing to pay all its expenses. It had to print $431 million in paper money called **greenbacks,** which could not be exchanged for coin. The back sides of these bills were printed in green ink. Paper money printed in yellow ink, popularly called **hard money,** could be exchanged for gold.

The question after the war was what should be done about the greenbacks? Most people believed either that they should be able to

HISTORICAL SIDELIGHTS
1. Greenbacker interests later joined with silver interests to form a powerful political group. People who opposed the unlimited printing of paper money also had many objections to the unlimited coining of silver.

SUGGESTED CAPTION RESPONSE
Inflation occurs when the prices for goods and services rise because people have more money to spend. Deflation occurs when the prices for goods and services fall because people have less money to spend.

exchange greenbacks for gold or silver or that greenbacks should be withdrawn from circulation entirely.

People who had bought government bonds during the war had paid for them with greenback dollars, which were worth much less than gold or silver coins of the same face value. If these purchasers were paid back in gold when the bonds fell due, they would make very large profits. If the greenbacks were withdrawn by the government, the amount of money in circulation would decline. This would cause **deflation.** Prices of all goods would fall. Every dollar would buy more. Once again, those with money on hand would make large gains. But those people who had borrowed greenbacks would have to repay their loans with more valuable money. They would lose.

Farmers in particular tended to be hurt by deflation after the Civil War. During the war they had borrowed money to buy more land and machinery. They had paid high prices because of the war-time inflation. If the price level fell, the money they paid out to cancel their debts would be more valuable than the money they had borrowed. If wheat sold for $1.50 a bushel when the money was borrowed and for only 50 cents a bushel when it had to be repaid, the farmer would have to produce three times as much wheat to pay off the debt.

Beginning in 1866, the government gradually withdrew greenbacks from circulation. This was called "retiring the greenbacks." The fewer greenbacks in public hands, the less people would fear that the government would print more and cause **inflation.** As the secretary of the treasury explained, the purpose of retiring the greenbacks was to end uncertainty about the money supply and encourage people to be "industrious, economical [and] honest."

However, reducing the money supply alarmed many business leaders. Early in 1878 Congress decided not to allow any further retirement of greenbacks. The argument continued until 1879 when the remaining greenbacks were made convertible into gold. Thereafter, greenbacks were the same as other American bank notes.

Cooper-Hewitt Museum

Peter Cooper was the candidate of the National Greenback party in 1876. He received 81,000 votes for president. He was the builder of the Tom Thumb *(page 355) and Cooper Union, where working folks could get an education. His party supported currency inflation. Explain the difference between inflation and deflation.*

EXTENSION:
COMMUNITY INVOLVEMENT
Ask students to read the subsection "Civil Service Reform." Have them make a list (the telephone book is a good source) of federal, state, and local agencies in their community. Then assign small groups of students to each of the agencies on the list. Then ask each group to learn which positions in their agency are civil service positions and which are appointed through political patronage. They should also find out the requirements for both types of positions. They will probably have to call the agency to get answers to their questions. When students have assembled their information, have spokespersons present their findings to the class. Use the findings as the basis for a class discussion comparing civil service requirements with patronage requirements. Students may wish to invite contact from their agencies to speak to the class on civil service.

Civil Service Reform

As the United States grew larger, the number of people who worked for the government increased rapidly. There were about 27,000 postmasters in 1869 and over 75,000 in 1900. In the same period the treasury department payroll grew from about 4,000 persons to over 24,000. In the 1830s the entire government had employed fewer than 24,000 people.

Much of the work done by the government became increasingly technical. This meant that federal workers needed more skills and experience to perform their jobs efficiently. The new department of agriculture, created in the 1860s, employed chemists and biologists in large numbers. Even so-called routine jobs required people with

Politics After the War   703

CHECKING UNDERSTANDING

Write the following headings on the chalkboard or an overhead projector: *Republicans* and *Democrats.* Then read the following generalizations to the class and ask students to place each generalization under its proper heading. (Remind students that these are generalizations and that, as with all generalizations, exceptions can be found.)

1. Solid South *(Democrats)*
2. Waved the "bloody shirt" *(Republicans)*
3. Ran political machines in northern cities *(Democrats)*
4. Tended to favor lower tariffs *(Democrats)*
5. Supported by African Americans in the North *(Republicans)*

RETEACHING STRATEGY
Students with Special Needs.

Pair students who are having difficulty with students who are performing well. Ask the more proficient students to help the others list generalizations about the groups that supported the Republicans and the Democrats after Reconstruction. To emphasize the geographic pattern of that support, have them identify the geographic areas where each party was the strongest. *(Republicans: opposed lowering tariffs, strongest in the North; Democrats: favored lower tariffs, strongest in the Solid South, ran political machines in the North)*

The Granger Collection, New York

The good ship Democracy *tosses in stormy seas while its captain, Grover Cleveland, cuts away at mutineers who promote a silver purchase bill. On deck is the Tammany tiger gorging itself. The message of this cartoon from an 1894* Harper's Weekly *is that reforms in civil service and tariffs are about to be "deep sixed," or tossed overboard to drown. Explain how the cartoonist shows this.*

specialized skills. The introduction of the typewriter in the 1880s, for example, affected the training needed to become a government secretary or clerk.

These developments made the spoils system and the Jacksonians' idea of rotation in office badly out-of-date. The dismissal of large numbers of government workers each time a new president took office caused much confusion and waste. The president and other officials had to spend weeks deciding who of the tens of thousands of employees was to be kept, who fired, and who hired.

At the same time it became difficult to recruit properly trained people for government service. Men and women of ability did not want to give up good jobs to work for a government department. They knew that they might be fired after the next election no matter how well they had done their work.

After the Civil War many thoughtful people began to urge **civil service reform.** Most government jobs below the level of policy makers like cabinet members and their assistants should be taken out of politics, the reformers said. Applicants should have to take tests, and those with the best scores should be selected without regard for which political party they supported. Once appointed, civil service workers should be discharged only if they failed to perform their duties properly. This was known as the **merit system.**

President Rutherford B. Hayes was a leading advocate of reform. In his inaugural address in 1877 he stated his support:

❝ I ask the attention of the public to the paramount [most important] necessity of reform in our civil service—a reform not merely as to certain abuses and practices of so-called official patronage which have come to have the sanction of usage in several Departments of Government, but a change in the system of appointment itself; a reform that shall be thorough, radical, and complete; a return to the principles and practices of the founders of the Government. They neither expected nor desired from public officers any partisan [favoring one political party] service. They meant that the officer should owe their whole service to the Government and the people. They meant that the officer should be secure in his tenure as long as his personal character remained untarnished and the performance of his duties satisfactory. They held that appointments for office were not to be made nor expected as rewards for partisan services. . . .[1]"

[1]From *Inaugural Addresses of the Presidents of the United States*

The problem with civil service reform was that the political parties depended upon the spoils system for rewarding the organizers who ran political campaigns. Presidents and state governors used their powers of appointment, called **patronage,** to persuade legislators to support their programs. They would promise to give government jobs to friends and supporters of the legislators in exchange for the legislators' votes on key issues.

Civil service reform was not an issue that a particular party favored. When the Republicans were in office, the Democrats called for reform. When the Democrats won elections, the Republicans became civil service reformers. The party that controlled the government tended to resist reform. Its leaders needed the jobs to reward their supporters. Nevertheless, the need for government efficiency could not be ignored much longer.

Then came the tragic assassination of President James A. Garfield. Shortly after he took office in 1881, Garfield was shot in a Washington railroad station by Charles Guiteau, a Republican who had been trying without success to get a job in the state department. Chester A. Arthur succeeded to the presidency. A great public cry went up for taking government jobs out of politics. Finally, in 1883, Congress passed the **Pendleton Act,** which created a **Civil Service Commission.** Its charge was to make up and administer examinations for applicants seeking certain government jobs. Those with the best scores on the tests were to get the appointments. The Pendleton Act also outlawed the practice of making government employees contribute to political campaign funds.

At first only 15,000 jobs were classified, or placed under civil service rules, by the 1883 law. But the number of posts covered was steadily increased over the years. By 1900 about half of all federal employees were under the civil service system. 🖅

James Garfield, above, was assassinated in 1881 and Chester A. Arthur, below, succeeded him.

Both, Copyright by the White House Historical Association; photographs by the National Geographic Society

Return to the Preview & Review on page 697.

Have students complete the Preview & Review activity at the beginning of the section.

CLOSURE
To reinforce the influence of the geographic theme of *region* in national politics, point out that in the decades after the Civil War, the North and West became solidly Republican, while the South became solidly Democratic. Tariffs, greenbacks, and civil service reform became important issues during these decades.

HOMEWORK
Have students write a newspaper editorial favoring or opposing lowering tariffs. Use completed editorials to create an editorial page for the bulletin board.

PRIMARY SOURCE
Description of change: excerpted and bracketed.
Rationale: excerpted to focus on President Hayes' emphasis on reform; bracketed words added to clarify meaning.

① Mark Twain's premature birth in 1835 occurred at the same time that Halley's comet appeared. Twain said that the comet and he were nature's "unaccountable freaks."

It would have provided him the opportunity to witness many events firsthand and given him the experience to write about these events realistically.

SECTION 2

PREVIEW & REVIEW RESPONSES
Understanding Issues, Events & Ideas.
Explanations should point out that the Age of Realism helped capture the true spirit of the times.
1. Slum life, labor unrest, and political corruption
2. The experience would allow the reporter to see life as it really was.
3. The artists gloried in presenting ordinary subjects.

Thinking Critically.
Realistic character descriptions should emphasize the ordinary.

Preview & Review

Use these questions to guide your reading. Answer the questions after completing Section 2.
Understanding Issues, Events & Ideas. In your own words, explain the historical importance of the Age of Realism.
1. What was the source of inspiration for American realists?
2. How would working as a newspaper reporter serve as good training for a realist?
3. What subjects did realistic painters illustrate?
Thinking Critically. Write a character description of a boss of a political machine, a cowhand, or a factory worker as if you were a realist writer.

2. THE AGE OF REALISM

Changes in American Literature

American literature was still dominated by the romantics after the Civil War. Poe, Hawthorne, Melville, and the New England poets Longfellow, Whittier, and Holmes still held sway. As today, many of the most popular offerings were by women. Susan Warner's *The Wide, Wide World* (1850) was the sad tale of a meek and pious little girl who cried "more readily and steadily than any other tormented child." "Tears on almost every page" could have been her advertising slogan.

But the great changes of industrial America—the cities teeming, the family farmland no longer worked by its children—brought about a new style of writing, known as Realism. Novelists treated such problems as slum life, labor unrest, and political corruption. They created three-dimensional characters and wrote about persons of every walk of life. The period came to be known as the **Age of Realism.** Dialect and slang helped capture the flavor of local types. A good example is Joel Chandler Harris, whose "Uncle Remus" stories reproduced the dialect of the black people of Georgia so faithfully that some critics today think the stories make fun of the southern traditions they relate.

Mark Twain

The outstanding figure of western literature, the first great American realist, was Samuel Clemens, who wrote under the name Mark ① Twain. Clemens was born in 1835 and grew up in Hannibal, Missouri, on the banks of the Mississippi. He worked for a time as a riverboat pilot and in 1861 went west to Nevada to look for gold. Soon he began publishing humorous stories about the local life. In 1865, while working in California, Twain wrote "The Celebrated Jumping Frog of Calaveras County," a story that made him famous. He then toured Europe and the Holy Land and published *Innocents Abroad*.

In Mark Twain we find all the zest and enthusiasm of the Gilded Age—and its materialism, as well. Twain pursued the almighty dollar with his pen and lost a fortune in foolish business ventures. He wrote tirelessly about America and Europe and created some of America's most famous characters. From *The Gilded Age* there was eyewash salesman Colonel Beriah Sellers and his "Infallible Imperial Oriental Optic Liniment." From the classic *Huckleberry Finn* (1884), came the slave Jim, loyal, patient, yet above all a man. When Huck takes advantage of Jim, the slave turns from him coldly and says: "Dat trick duh is *trash;* and trash is what people is dat puts dirt on de head er ey fren's en makes 'em ashamed." And, of course, there is

Mark Twain papers, The Bancroft Library

Here we see Samuel Clemens as a printer's apprentice. How might the newspaper office have provided a good training for the future Mark Twain?

RESOURCES
- ■ You may wish to have students review Reading 54: "Mark Twain Describes a 'Lightning Pilot' (ca. 1840)" in Volume I of *Eyewitnesses and Others*."
- ◀ You may wish to have students complete Reading 77: "Mark Twain Describes the Pony Express (1860)" in Volume I of *Eyewitnesses and Others*.

Huck Finn himself on a raft with Jim floating down the Mississippi ■ River. Through Huck's voice, Twain criticizes a corrupt society overrun with violence and brutality. It contrasts with the tranquility of the river. ◀

“ It was kind of solemn, drifting down the big, still river, laying on our backs looking up at the stars, and we didn't ever feel like talking loud, and it warn't often that we laughed—only a little kind of a low chuckle. We had mighty good weather as a general thing, and nothing ever happened to us at all—that night, nor the next, nor the next.

From *The Adventures of Tom Sawyer*, 1876.

This is the frontispiece of the original 1876 edition of Tom Sawyer. *From your reading could you produce a similar illustration for the front of* Huckleberry Finn?

FOCUS/MOTIVATION: MAKING CONNECTIONS Prior Knowledge.
Work with students to compose a chart on "Romanticism in the Arts" on the chalkboard or an overhead projector. Have students give examples from art and literature showing how the romantic authors and artists attempted to show ideals. Head column 1 *Artist/Writer,* column 2 *Works,* and column 3 *How Works Show Ideals.* (You may wish to have students review Chapter 14 to fill in information on the chart.) Then point out that after the Civil War, realism replaced romanticism. Ask: How do you think realism was different from romanticism? *(Students might suggest that realism portrayed the world as it was, while romanticism portrayed the world as the individual artists thought it should be.)* Add a fourth column titled *Realism* to the charts. After students have completed this section, return to the chart. Have them suggest ways realists would have portrayed each work on your list differently. Ask students to keep their suggestions in mind as they study the section. Then ask: What events in America that you read about in Chapter 19 and the first section of this chapter might have prompted the change from romanticism to realism *(problems in cities, poor working conditions, corrupt politicians, etc.)*

🔵 Stephen Crane was a reform journalist in the ranks with Lincoln Steffens and Jacob Riis. His interest in the lives of city prostitutes led to *Maggie: A Girl of the Streets* (1892), which Crane published under a pseudonym at the age of 21. *The Red Badge of Courage* (1895) is a great war classic although at that time Crane had not experienced fighting. He would fight later in the Greek-Turkish wars and serve as a war correspondent in Cuba. The hardships he endured led to his early death from tuberculosis in 1900.

Every night we passed towns, some of them away up on black hillsides, nothing but just a shiny bed of lights; not a house could you see. The fifth night we passed St. Louis, and it was like the whole world lit up. In St. Petersburg they used to say there was twenty or thirty thousand people in St. Louis, but I never believed it till I see that wonderful spread of lights at two o'clock that still night. There warn't a sound there; everybody was asleep.🙤

Twain's other works include *Tom Sawyer* (1876), *Life on the Mississippi* (1883), and *A Connecticut Yankee in King Arthur's Court* (1889). "The truth is," he once wrote, "my books are mainly autobiographies." A story, he said, "must be written with the blood out of a man's heart." His works catch the spirit of the Age of Realism more than those of any other writer.

William Dean Howells

Mark Twain's long-time friend William Dean Howells of Ohio, born in 1837, was self-educated. He learned the printer's trade, then became a newspaper reporter. In 1860 he wrote a campaign biography of Abraham Lincoln. After the Civil War he became editor of the *Atlantic Monthly* and then, in 1886, of *Harper's*. Both these magazines are still published today.

Howells wrote many novels, one of which, *The Rise of Silas Lapham* (1885) dealt with the ethics of business in a competitive society. But Howells' greatest impact on American literature was as a critic. He encouraged important young novelists such as Stephen 🔵 Crane, Frank Norris, and Theodore Dreiser. Like Twain and Howells, many novelists of the Age of Realism began as reporters, a job that provided an excellent training for any realist. They wrote about the most primitive emotions—fear, lust, hate, and greed. Crane's best-known work is *The Red Badge of Courage* (1895), which captures the pains and horrors of a young soldier in the Civil War. You can almost feel the youth's fear as those around him flee the battle:

🙥 He slowly lifted his rifle and catching a glimpse of the thick-spread field he blazed at a cantering cluster [trotting group of enemy]. He stopped then and began to peer as best he could through the smoke. He caught changing views of the ground covered with men who were all running like pursued imps and yelling.

To the youth it was an onslaught of redoubtable [fearful] dragons. He became like a man who had lost his legs at the approach of the red and green monster. He waited in a sort

¹From *The Adventures of Huckleberry Finn* by Mark Twain

24: "A Farmer in the Grip of 'the Octopus' (1890s)" in Volume II of *Eyewitnesses and Others*.
◄ You may wish to have students complete Reading 27: "The Squid and the Lobster, from Dreiser's *The Financier* (ca. 1900)" in Volume II of *Eyewitnesses and Others*.

Brown Brothers

Brown Brothers

Stephen Crane Collection, Syracuse University, Manuscript Division

Brown Brothers

of horrified, listening attitude. He seemed to shut his eyes and wait to be gobbled.

A man near him who up to this time was working feverishly at his rifle suddenly stopped and ran with howls. A lad whose face had borne an expression of exalted courage, the majesty of he who dares to give his life, at an instant, smitten abject [struck down with degrading fear]. He blanched [turned white] like one who has come to the edge of a cliff at midnight and is suddenly made aware. There was a revelation. He, too, threw down his gun and fled. There was no shame in his face. He ran like a rabbit.[1]**"**

Norris' *McTeague*, published in 1899, is the story of a brutal, ■ dull-witted dentist and his miserable wife Trina, the winner of $5,000 in a lottery. Dreiser's *An American Tragedy* (1925) is the account of ◄ a young man's seduction by the apparent wealth and beauty of a social circle to which he does not belong.

Clockwise from top left are Frank Norris, Theodore Dreiser, Stephen Crane, and William Dean Howells. How did these "realists" portray America?

Realism in Art

American painters after the Civil War also treated more "realistic" subjects. The most prominent realist was Thomas Eakins. He mastered human anatomy and painted graphic illustrations of surgical operations. He experimented with early motion pictures to capture the attitudes of humans and animals in motion. Like his friend Walt Whitman, whose portrait is one of his greatest achievements, Eakins gloried in the ordinary.

Realism was also characteristic of the work of Winslow Homer, a Boston-born painter best known for his watercolors. He worked during the Civil War as a reporter for *Harper's Weekly*, and he

[1]From *The Red Badge of Courage* by Stephen Crane

RESOURCES
■ You may wish to have students view Transparency 16: *"The Pathetic Song"* and complete the accompanying worksheet in *Art in American History*.

CHECKING UNDERSTANDING
Work with the class to prepare a chart showing the major writers and artists of the realistic school. Write the names of the writers and artists in the left column of the chart and ask students to state something significant about the person's works or style in the right column. *(Completed charts should include the following: Mark Twain—wrote humorous stories about life, created some of America's most famous characters; William Dean Howells—greatest impact was as a critic; Stephen Crane—wrote of the pains and horrors of the Civil War; Frank Norris—wrote of brutality; Theodore Dreiser—wrote of a man being seduced by the wealth and beauty of a social circle to which he did not belong; Thomas Eakins—painted graphic illustrations of surgical operations; Winslow Homer—best known for watercolors of homey subjects; James A. McNeill Whistler—best known for* Arrangement in Gray and Black; *Mary Cassatt—painted mothers and daughters.)*

RETEACHING STRATEGY
Students with Special Needs. Pair students who are having difficulty with students who are performing well. Distribute copies of the following list to each group. Ask the more proficient students to read each item to the others who should answer "Who Am I?". Encourage the more proficient students to add information to that included on the list. Allow students who have difficulty verbalizing to point out the picture of the writer or an illustration by the artist, all of which are included in this section.
(Continued)

Metropolitan Museum of Art

■ *Thomas Eakins, "Max Schmitt in a Single Scull," 1871.*

Winslow Homer, "The Croquet Game."

Art Institute of Chicago

HISTORICAL SIDELIGHTS

 Impressionists sought to create art based on immediacy of expression. Moral, political, and literary associations held little interest for them. They sought to capture optical realism, an instantaneous vision, a sensation rather than a perception. A new method of visual representation emerged that did not show, but rather implied, space and form through varying intensities of light and color.

RESOURCES

■ You may wish to have students view Transparency 19: *"Summertime: Woman and Child in a Rowboat"* and complete the accompanying worksheet in *Art in American History*.

Musee d'Orsay

Art Institute of Chicago

James McNeill Whistler, "Arrangement in Gray and Black."

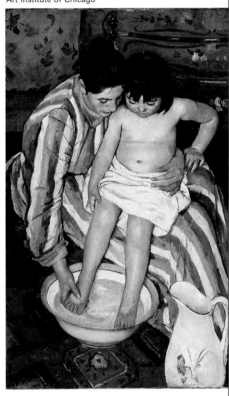

Mary Cassatt, "The Bath."

1. "I wrote humorous stories about life and created some of America's most famous characters." *(Mark Twain)*
2. "Although I was a writer, my greatest impact on American literature was as a critic." *(William Dean Howells)*
3. "I wrote of the pains and horrors of the Civil War in *The Red Badge of Courage*." *(Stephen Crane)*
4. "I wrote about a brutal, dull-witted dentist and his miserable wife in *McTeague*." *(Frank Norris)*
5. "One of my most famous works was *An American Tragedy*, which told of a social misfit." *(Theodore Dreiser)*
6. "We were both famous expatriates who lived in France." *(James A. McNeill Whistler and Mary Cassatt)*
7. "I was the most prominent realist who painted graphic illustrations of surgical operations." *(Thomas Eakins)*
8. "I was best known for my watercolors of everyday life." *(Winslow Homer)*

INDEPENDENT PRACTICE
Have students complete the Preview & Review activity at the beginning of the section.

CLOSURE
Point out that during the late 1800s the Age of Realism replaced the Romantic Age in American literature and art. Remind students that this change grew out of the changes in American society as it became industrialized and urbanized.

HOMEWORK
Ask students to use resources in their public or school library to prepare a brief biography of one of the writers or artists discussed in this section.

continued to create illustrations for some years thereafter. He roamed America, painting scenes of southern life, Adirondack camps, and magnificent seascapes.

At least two of America's great painters of the era abandoned their country for Paris. James A. McNeill Whistler left the United States when he was 21. His best-known painting, *Arrangement in Gray and Black* ("Whistler's Mother"), is probably the most famous canvas ever painted by an American. It hangs in the Orsay Museum in Paris.

A second expatriate artist was Mary Cassatt. (An expatriate is ■ one who rejects and leaves the country of his—or her—birth.) The daughter of a wealthy Pittsburgh banker, she went to Paris as a tourist and remained, caught up in the Impressionist movement. Her studies of women, particularly mothers and daughters, hang in the finest museums in the world, including the Art Institute in Chicago.

Return to the Preview & Review on page 706.

**PREVIEW & REVIEW
RESPONSES
Understanding Issues. Events
& Ideas.**
Descriptions should demonstrate an understanding of the
terms used.
1. They were elected by such
   narrow margins. Turnover
   among representatives in
   Congress was extremely
   rapid. As a result, without
   experienced membership
   Congress was inefficient.
2. The Granger laws set the
   rates that railroads and
   grain warehouses could collect so farmers would not be
   overcharged.
3. The best way to push up
   prices seemed to be by
   causing inflation. Putting
   more money in circulation
   would do this. One way was
   by coining silver money. It
   meant there would be 16
   times as much silver in the
   silver dollar as gold in the
   gold dollar.
4. The Populists took clear
   stands on controversial issues.
5. Cultural traditions—particularly the spirit of community—strengthened their
   communities.

Thinking Critically.
1. Articles will vary but should
   point out that it will put
   more money in circulation
   and cause prices to rise.
2. Notes should reflect logical
   reasoning, positions should
   be supported by rational
   reasons.

**FOCUS/MOTIVATION:
MAKING CONNECTIONS
Prior Knowledge.**
Ask students to describe why
(Continued)

Preview & Review

Use these questions to guide your
reading. Answer the questions
after completing Section 3.
**Understanding Issues, Events, &
Ideas.** Describe the issues faced by
farmers in the late 1800s, using the
following words: third party,
mandate, National Grange,
Crime of 1873, Bland-Allison Act,
Sherman Silver Purchase Act, free
coinage, Farmers Alliance, co-op,
People's party, Populist party.
1. Why did the presidents elected
   after the Civil War have little
   influence? Why was Congress
   inefficient?
2. How were Granger Laws supposed to help farmers?
3. Why did farmers favor coining
   silver money? What did the ratio of 16 to 1 mean in coinage?
4. How did the Populists differ
   from Republicans and Democrats in the election of 1892?
5. Why were Hispanic communities often able to thrive despite
   economic troubles and discrimination?
Thinking Critically. 1. Write an article for the business section of an
1890 newspaper, explaining how
the coinage of silver will change
the economy. 2. Compose a note
to a friend, explaining why you will
or will not vote for the Populist
candidate in the 1892 election.

---

3. POPULISM

Political "Musical Chairs"

Since neither Democrats nor Republicans took firm stands on the
real issues, there were few real differences between them. This helps
explain why elections were usually close.

In 1880 James A. Garfield got 48.3 percent of the popular vote
for president. He defeated the Democrat, Winfield Scott Hancock,
by only 7,000 votes out of nearly 9.2 million cast. Four years later,
Grover Cleveland, a Democrat, won with 48.5 percent of the popular
vote. His margin over Republican James G. Blaine was 4.87 million
to 4.85 million.

In 1888 Cleveland was defeated by Benjamin Harrison. Although
President Cleveland got more popular votes, Harrison had a majority
of the electoral vote, 233 to 168. In the next presidential election
Cleveland defeated Harrison and returned to the White House. Yet
he got only 46 percent of the popular vote to Harrison's 43 percent.

In all of these elections no one got a majority of the popular
vote because third-party candidates were in the field. A **third party**
is a political party competing with the two major parties. Third-party
candidates *did* stand for "real issues." There were Greenback party
candidates running in 1880 and 1884, for example. They demanded
that more rather than fewer greenbacks be put in circulation. Other
candidates ran on platforms calling for prohibition of liquor.

The presidents were elected by such narrow margins that they
had relatively little influence while in office. They could not claim to
have a **mandate**—the backing of a solid majority of the people—when
they presented their programs to Congress.

Ewing Galloway   National Portrait Gallery

*Presidents Grover Cleveland, left,
and Benjamin Harrison played political leapfrog with the White House.
Explain how. Harrison's portrait is by
the distinguished photographer Eastman Johnson, c. 1889.*

The Granger Collection, New York

*"His grandfather's hat was too big for
his head," sang the opponents of Benjamin Harrison when he became president. A bust of President William
Henry Harrison, his grandfather, is
above the door. Joseph Keppler drew
this caricature. What seems to be his
opinion of the man who was elected
president in 1888? Can you identify
the poem to which Keppler refers?*

the presidential election of
1876 was unusual. *(Although
Hayes did not receive a majority of the popular vote, he became president.)* Then ask:
What in the American electoral
process makes this situation
possible? *(The winner is determined by the electoral vote
rather than by the popular
vote.)* Point out that after the
Civil War the positions that the
major political parties took on
important issues of the day
were so close that candidates
who did not get a majority of
the popular vote sometimes
became president. Ask: Do you
think that a person who gets
the second highest total of
popular votes should be allowed to become president?
Then tell students that many
Americans think that the electoral process should be
changed and that the popular
vote alone should determine
who becomes president.

GUIDED INSTRUCTION
Tell students that with the end
of Reconstruction, the Radical
Republicans were called *Stal-
warts.* Reform-minded Republicans were called *Mugwumps.*
Many Mugwumps such as Carl
Schurz came out against Blaine
in the election of 1884. The final blow to his chances of becoming president may have
occurred during an interview
with clergymen. One of them
called the Democratic party the
party of "Rum, Romanism, and
Rebellion." Blaine did not re-
pudiate the remark. By 1884
President Arthur had offended
too many of his former Stal-
wart colleagues, so he was not
renominated. Remind students
that under Arthur's administration, the Pendleton Act for civil
service reform was passed.

In Congress the Democrats had a majority of the House of
Representatives from 1874 to 1880 and from 1882 to 1888. But they
had a majority of the Senate for only two years during this entire
period. Turnover among representatives was extremely rapid. Often
more than half the members of the House were in their first terms.
Without experienced members, Congress was inefficient. With narrow, shifting majorities, controversial measures seldom were passed.

Hard Times for the Farmer

The times were particularly frustrating for farmers. Falling agricultural prices hurt them badly. So did the protective tariffs which raised the prices of the manufactured goods they purchased. But neither party was willing to work for laws that would bring much relief. The farmers found themselves left behind in American society's pursuit of wealth and status. Between 1860 and 1891 the number of farms rose from 2 million to 4.5 million. But farmers lacked the political clout of industry. So some farmers turned elsewhere in their agonizing search for help.

"I Pay for All" says the legend below this sturdy Granger. Rural scenes in this 1873 poster include the biblical Ruth and Boaz, lower right; a harvest dance, lower left; and the Grange in session, upper right. Study the picture to find other scenes of agrarian life.

Courtesy of The Library of Congress

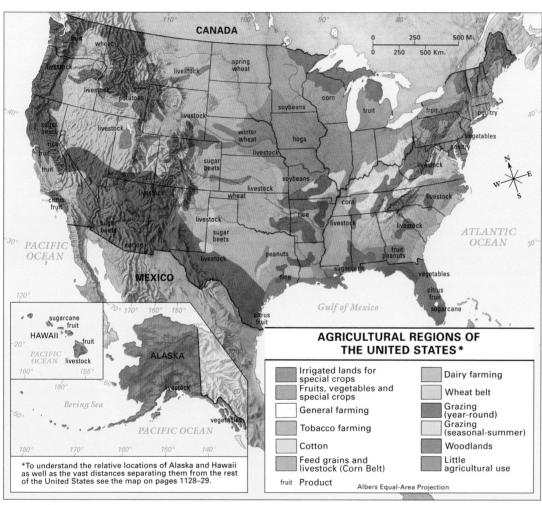

AGRICULTURAL REGIONS OF
THE UNITED STATES *

Irrigated lands for
special crops

Fruits, vegetables and
special crops

General farming

Tobacco farming

Cotton

Feed grains and
livestock (Corn Belt)

Dairy farming

Wheat belt

Grazing
(year-round)

Grazing
(seasonal-summer)

Woodlands

Little
agricultural use

fruit   Product

Albers Equal-Area Projection

*To understand the relative locations of Alaska and Hawaii
as well as the vast distances separating them from the rest
of the United States see the map on pages 1128–29.

In the 1870s many farmers joined the **National Grange.** The
Grange was originally a kind of social club. It soon became a political
organization as well. Many branches sprang up, especially in New
York, Pennsylvania, Ohio, and the Middle West.

Granger leaders believed that railroad freight charges were too
high. Because railroads had a monopoly on moving bulky goods to
distant markets, Granger leaders demanded government regulation
of rates. Their efforts led to the passage of Granger laws in many
states. These measures set the rates that railroads and grain warehouses could collect so farmers would not be overcharged.

This raised the question of whether businesses like railroads
could be regulated "in the public interest." Yes, ruled the Supreme
Court in the case of *Munn v. Illinois* (1877). Granger laws were
constitutional. Businesses like railroads that provided broad public
services could not be considered completely private.

LEARNING FROM MAPS. *The
United States has long been noted for
its agricultural abundance. Note the
wide variety and the productiveness of
such a large percentage of the land.
Compare this map to the one on page
649 and state a generalization about
agriculture and climate in the
United States.*

Populism   715

**INTEGRATING STRATEGIES
FOR SUCCESS**
Pair students who having difficulty with students who are
performing well. To reinforce
the geographic themes of *location* and *region,* distribute to
each pair an outline map of the
United States and the following election results from the
presidential election of 1988.
*States Casting Electoral Votes
for George Bush:*
Alabama (9); Alaska (3); Arizona (7); Arkansas (6); California (47); Colorado (8); Connecticut (8); Delaware (3);
Florida (21); Georgia (12);
Idaho (4); Illinois (24); Indiana
(12); Kansas (7); Kentucky (9);
Louisiana (10); Maine (4);
Maryland (10); Michigan (20);
Mississippi (7); Missouri (11);
Montana (4); Nebraska (5); Nevada (4); New Hampshire (4);
New Jersey (16); New Mexico
(5); North Carolina (13); North
Dakota (3); Ohio (23); Oklahoma (8); Pennsylvania (25);
South Carolina (8); South Dakota (3); Tennessee (11); Texas
(29); Utah (5); Vermont (3); Virginia (12); Wyoming (3)
*States Casting Electoral Votes
for Michael Dukakis:*
District of Columbia (3); Hawaii
(4); Iowa (8); Massachusetts
(13); Minnesota (10); New York
(36); Oregon (7); Rhode Island
(4); Washington (10); West Virginia (6); Wisconsin (11)
Have the more proficient students help the others fill in the
map and answer the following
questions.
1. How has the allegiance of
   the Solid South changed
   since 1888? *(It is no longer
   solidly Democratic.)*
(Continued)

STRATEGIES FOR SUCCESS

INTERPRETING ELECTION RESULTS

Every four years the people of the United States
elect a president. Or more correctly they elect
electors who choose the president. This group
of electors is called the *electoral college.* Election results are given for both *popular votes*—
votes by the people—and *electoral votes*—votes
by the electoral college. It is the electoral votes
that determine which of the candidates becomes
president.

The members of the electoral college are faceless and, in two thirds of the states, nameless
on the ballot. They never assemble as a national
group but meet instead in their respective states
after each general election to cast their votes.

Every state has one electoral vote for each
senator and representative. Thus, the more populous states have more electoral votes. What
state today has the most? The states with the
least population have three votes. In addition,
the District of Columbia now has three votes.
Today there are a total of 538 electoral votes. In
order to be elected, a candidate must receive a
simple majority, or 270, of those 538 votes.

The electoral system has often been criticized
for its *unit rule.* That is, in each state the winner
takes all. A candidate who receives one more
vote than the closest rival gets all the state's
electoral votes. Why do you think such a result
would be controversial?

How to Interpret Election Results

To interpret election results, follow these steps.
1. **Check the figures.** Note both popular and
   electoral vote totals. In some elections the
   result of the popular vote is extremely close
   but the electoral vote is not.
2. **Note the trends.** See which states and regions voted for which candidate. Candidates
   have learned to effectively use the electoral
   system to their benefit. They spend a majority
   of their campaign time and money in the
   states with the largest populations—and electoral votes.
3. **Study the results.** Consider what factors influenced the election's outcome and resulted
   in the voting figures.

Applying the Strategy

Study the map and pie graphs below. They show
the electoral and popular vote totals for the election of 1888. The map shows the electoral votes
held by each state. Which three states had the
largest totals? The close states have always
played an important part in deciding elections.
Which candidate won the close states of New
York and Indiana in 1888?

*For independent practice, see Practicing the
Strategy on page 732.*

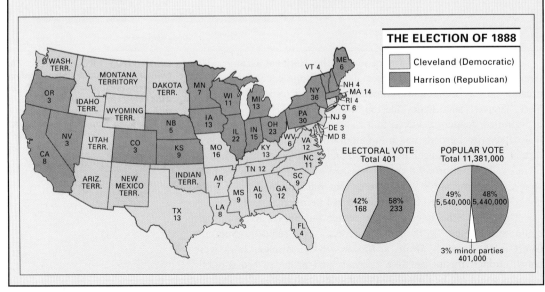

THE ELECTION OF 1888
Cleveland (Democratic)
Harrison (Republican)

ELECTORAL VOTE
Total 401
42% 168
58% 233

POPULAR VOTE
Total 11,381,000
49% 5,540,000
48% 5,440,000
3% minor parties 401,000

Other farmers, especially Hispanics, African Americans, and new immigrants, had nowhere to turn. As in other occupations, they faced prejudice and discrimination. They were not welcomed in many of the local granges and they had even less political clout than established white farmers.

Yet though life was shockingly hard for these people, in many places their communities thriyed. In the West and Southwest Mexican American communities grew, strengthened by cultural traditions. As you have read, one of the most important of those traditions was the spirit of community—everyone pitching in to help. See if you can get a feeling for life in the Southwest through the following excerpt, written by Jovita Gonzalez about her life in Texas:

66 In August, down towards the Rio Grande, the rays of the sun beat vertically upon the sandy stretches of land, from which all tender vegetation has been scorched, and the white, naked land glares back at the sun; the only palpitating [moving] things discoverable between the two poles of heat are heat devils. The rattlesnakes are as deeply holed up and as quiet as in midwinter. In the thickets of brush the roadrunners, rusty lizards, mockingbirds, and all other living things pant. Whirlwinds dance across the stretches of prairie interspersed between the thickets of thorn. At six o'clock it is hotter than at midday. Seven o'clock, and then the sun, a ball of orange-pink, descends below the horizon at one stride. The change is magical. A soft cooling breeze, the pulmotor [breathing apparatus] of the Border lands, springs up from the south.

Down in the *cañada* [brook between mountains], which runs by the ranch, doves coo. Out beyond, cattle are grazing and calves are frisking. In the cottonwood tree growing beside the dirt "tank" near the ranch house the redbird sings. Children shout and play. From the corrals come the voices of vaqueros [cowboys] singing and jesting. Blended with the bleatings of goats and sheep are the whistles and hisses of the *pastor* (shepherd). The locusts complete the chorus of evening noises. Darkness subdues them; then, as the moon rises, an uncounted mob of mongrel curs [mixed-breed dogs] set up a howling and barking at it that coyotes out beyond mock.

It was on a night like this that the ranch folk gathered at the Big House to shell corn. All came: Tío Julianito, the *pastor,* with his brood of sunburned half-starved children ever eager for food; Alejo the fiddler, Juanito the idiot, called the Innocent, because the Lord was keeping his mind in heaven; Pedro the hunter, who had seen the world and spoke English; the vaqueros; and, on rare occasions, Tío

2. What generalization can you make about the West in the election of 1988? *(Except for Washington and Oregon, it voted Republican.)*

EXTENSION:
HOME INVOLVEMENT
Most students have either parents, grandparents, or other relatives who are or were farmers. Ask these students to discuss with family members the role that farming has played in the history of their particular family. If they are currently farmers, ask them to discuss current conditions and concerns facing farmers in the United States. If family members used to engage in farming, ask students to find out what made these relatives leave the occupation and seek jobs elsewhere. Use what students have learned about their own families as the basis for a class discussion about the status of farming in the United States today. Point out that American farmers are the most productive in the world; yet they have seen difficult times in recent years because of falling land prices and crop prices coupled with rising costs for labor, seed, fertilizer, and other necessities. In addition, many farmers have been unable to repay loans and have lost their land. Have interested students do further research on the crisis that American farmers are facing today and report their findings to the class. Use this information as the basis for a class discussion comparing problems facing farmers in the late 1800s with problems facing farmers today.

PRIMARY SOURCE
Description of change: excerpted and bracketed.
Rationale: excerpted to focus on the spirit of community; bracketed words added to clarify meaning.

Esteban, the mail carrier. Even the women came, for on such occasions supper was served.

A big canvas was spread outside, in front of the kitchen. In the center of this canvas, ears of corn were piled in pyramids for the shellers, who sat about in a circle and with their bare hands shelled the grains off the cobs.

It was then, under the moonlit sky, that we heard stories of witches, buried treasures, and ghosts. . . . Then the *pastor* told of how he had seen spirits in the shape of balls of fire floating through the air. They were souls doing penance for their past sins. As a relief to our fright, Don [a title of respect] Francisco suggested the Tío Julianito do one of his original dances to the tune of Alejo's fiddle. A place was cleared on the canvas, and that started the evening's merriment. . . .[1]**"**

The Silver Issue

Lower freight and storage charges did not help farmers as much as the Grangers had hoped. Costs were not reduced much. So farmers tried instead to raise the prices of their produce. The best way to push up prices seemed to be by causing inflation. Farmers looked for a way to put more money in circulation so their prices would rise. One way was by coining silver money.

Throughout the period before the Civil War both gold and silver had been minted into coins and used to back bank notes. But in 1873 Congress had voted to stop coining silver. That seemed a terrible mistake to those who favored inflation.

Many new silver mines had been discovered. If miners could bring their silver to the United States mint for coining, more money would be created. With more money in circulation, prices would rise. Yet silver was a relatively scarce metal. The amount that could be mined would place a limit on the amount of new money that could be put into circulation. This would prevent "runaway" inflation, which might result if there was no limit on how much paper money could be printed.

Farmers and silver miners joined to make a powerful political force. People began to refer to the law that had discontinued the coining of silver as the **Crime of 1873.** They demanded that the government once again coin all the silver brought to the mint.

The result of their pressure was a political compromise. In 1878 Congress passed a bill sponsored by Representative Richard Bland of Missouri and Senator William B. Allison of Iowa. Bland was a Democrat who believed sincerely in coining both gold and silver.

[1]From *Among My People* by Jovita Gonzalez

The Granger Collection, New York

A silverite runs away with the Democratic donkey pursued by a sound money Democrat. Which side of the pursuit does this 1896 cartoon seem to favor? The sign can help you answer.

Allison, a Republican, was a shrewd political manipulator. (It was said of Allison that he would make no more noise walking across the Senate floor in wooden shoes than a fly made walking on the ceiling.)

The **Bland-Allison Act** ordered the secretary of the treasury to purchase and coin between $2 and $4 million in silver each month. In 1890 another coinage law, the **Sherman Silver Purchase Act,** increased the amount of silver bought to 4.5 million ounces a month. This came to about the total being mined at that time.

The price of silver was usually expressed by comparing it to the price of gold. In 1873, when the mint had stopped coining silver, an ounce of gold was worth about 16 times as much as an ounce of silver. By 1890, when the Sherman Silver Purchase Act was passed, an ounce of gold was worth 20 times as much. This was because the

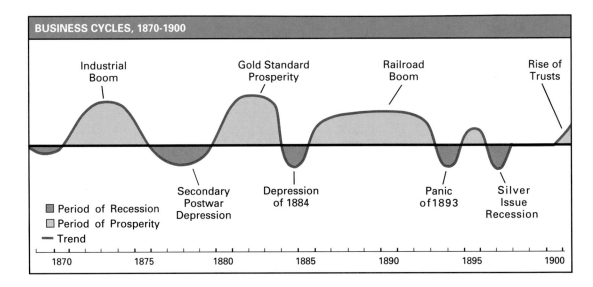

BUSINESS CYCLES, 1870-1900

Industrial Boom — Gold Standard Prosperity — Railroad Boom — Rise of Trusts

Secondary Postwar Depression — Depression of 1884 — Panic of 1893 — Silver Issue Recession

■ Period of Recession
□ Period of Prosperity
— Trend

1870   1875   1880   1885   1890   1895   1900

LEARNING FROM GRAPHS. *As you can see, the United States economy had extended ups and downs between 1870 and 1900. Why might there have been little change in the economy between 1898 and 1900?*

price of silver was falling steeply at the same time as the supply was increasing from new mines in the West.

Farmers and others who favored inflation wanted as much silver coined as possible in order to increase the money supply. If the United States would coin all the world's silver, the price of other products would rise because more money would be in circulation. Those who favored inflation therefore urged **free coinage**—that is, a law requiring the mint to turn all the silver offered it into silver dollars.

The silver miners were more interested in driving up the price of their silver than in what was done with it. They wanted the United States to exchange an ounce of gold for 16 ounces of silver. Thus, farmers and silver miners combined their interests. They demanded free coinage of silver at a ratio of 16 to 1 with gold.

The Populist Party

While the demand for free silver was developing, farmers were looking for other ways out of their hard times. First in Texas, and then elsewhere in the South, a new movement was spreading. It was the **Farmers Alliance.**

Like the earlier National Grange, the Alliance began as a social organization. In many areas local Alliance clubs formed cooperatives, or **co-ops,** to sell their crops at better prices. These co-ops set a single price for produce and purchased goods wholesale to save money for their members. By 1890 the Alliance movement had spread northward into Kansas, Nebraska, and the Dakotas.

Like the Grange, the Alliance became an important political

① The Populist party was formally organized at a meeting in Cincinnati, Ohio, in 1891 by a group made up chiefly of leaders of the Farmers' Alliance from the West and the Middle West.

force. Its leaders campaigned against high railroad freight rates and high interest rates charged by banks for mortgages and other loans. Alliance members began to run for local offices, promising if elected to help farmers.

An angry rural editor wrote in 1890:

" There are three great crops raised in Nebraska. One is a crop of corn, one is a crop of freight rates, and one is a crop of interest. One is produced by farmers who by sweat and toil farm the land. The other two are produced by men who sit in their offices and behind their bank counters and farm the farmers. "

In 1890 several southern states elected governors backed by the Alliance. More than 45 "Alliancemen" were elected to Congress. Alliance officials were encouraged by these results. They decided to establish a new political party and run a candidate for president in 1892. To broaden their appeal, they persuaded representatives of labor unions to join with them. They named their new organization the **People's party,** but it is usually referred to as the **Populist party.** ①

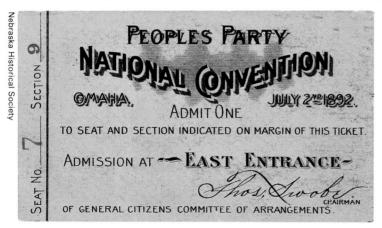

In July 1892 the first Populist nominating convention met in Omaha, Nebraska. The delegates adopted a platform that called for a long list of specific reforms. One was government ownership of railroads and of the telegraph and telephone network. Another was a federal income tax. Still another was a program of government loans to farmers who would store their crops in government warehouses as security for the loans.

To win the support of industrial workers, the Populist platform called for the eight-hour workday and for restrictions on immigration. It also demanded the "free and unlimited coinage of silver and gold at . . . 16 to 1."

The Populists chose James Baird Weaver of Iowa as their candidate for president in 1892. He had fought bravely for the Union in

SUGGESTED CAPTION RESPONSES
(Top) In 1888 there were only two political parties. In 1892 there were three. In both elections the popular vote was very close.
(Bottom) They chose James G. Field of Virginia, a former general in the Confederate army.

INDEPENDENT PRACTICE

Have students complete the Preview & Review activity at the beginning of the section.

CLOSURE

Point out that the Republicans and Democrats took such similar positions on issues after the Civil War that their candidates often seemed indistinguishable. Both ignored the plight of farmers, who formed the Grange, the Farmers' Alliance, and the Populist party to further their own goals.

HOMEWORK

Have students imagine that they have just attended a campaign rally for one of the candidates in the presidential election of 1892. Ask them to write a letter to a friend detailing the candidate's position on key issues.

PRIMARY SOURCE

Description of change: excerpted.
Rationale: excerpted to focus on the farmers' view of the cause of their troubles.

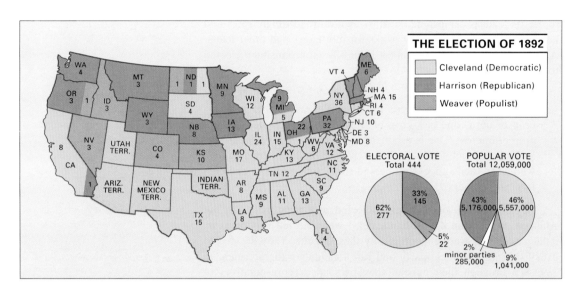

THE ELECTION OF 1892

- Cleveland (Democratic)
- Harrison (Republican)
- Weaver (Populist)

ELECTORAL VOTE
Total 444

POPULAR VOTE
Total 12,059,000

LEARNING FROM MAPS. *Compare the results of the election of 1892 shown on this map with the results of the 1888 election shown on the map on page 716. What major differences do you see? What major similarities?*

HBJ Collection

James B. Weaver was the nominee of the People's party at its convention in Omaha in 1892. How did the party balance its ticket?

Return to the Preview & Review on page 712.

the Civil War, rising from lieutenant to brigadier general. Their candidate for vice president was James G. Field of Virginia, a former general in the Confederate army.

The Populists created "a multi-sectional institution of reform," according to historian Lawrence Goodwyn. But they were not revolutionaries. They felt betrayed by what we today call "the establishment." They did not share the national passion for free enterprise, and they felt their problems were created by clever and selfish interests who used the American system to their advantage. As one Populist writer stated it:

66 The farmer has been the victim of a gigantic scheme of plunder. Never has such a vast combination of brains and money forced people into labor for the benefit of a few. . . .¹ 99

¹From *The Farmer's Side: His Troubles and Their Remedy* by William A. Peffer

The Populists took clear stands on controversial issues, seeking voters who agreed with their ideas. Democratic and Republican leaders continued to duck controversial questions. In the South the Populists tried to unite black and white farmers. There were many blacks in the Alliance movement in the southern states, although their groups were segregated from the whites.

The 1892 presidential election was an exciting one. General Weaver got over a million votes, a large number for a third-party candidate. The Populist party won many local contests. On balance, however, the results disappointed the Populists. They lost many votes in the South because large numbers of their white supporters refused to vote for candidates who appealed openly for black support.

HISTORICAL SIDELIGHTS
① Kansas Governor Lorenzo Lewelling wrote a "Tramp Circular" to the police in his state urging them to treat the wandering unemployed leniently.

SUGGESTED CAPTION RESPONSE
He was arrested, and the police disbanded his army.

4. UNEMPLOYMENT AND UNREST

The Depression of 1893

Shortly after the presidential election, which Grover Cleveland won, the country entered into the worst period of hard times in its history. Business activity slowed down. Unemployment increased. By the end of 1893 more than a hundred railroads had gone bankrupt. People hoarded money, withdrawing their savings in gold from the banks.

As usual the depression hurt African Americans, Hispanics, and recent immigrants worst of all. Many held the lowest-paying jobs and were therefore the first to be laid off. Others barely scraping out a living as farmers now could not sell their produce. One historian wrote of "the absolute destitute condition of the colored people of the South." It was as bad if not worse elsewhere.

The long period of deflation that began in the 1870s was an important cause of this depression. Farmers and wage earners blamed the depression on "tight money." They felt the Sherman Silver Purchase Act had not gone far enough. They demanded that the government coin even more money.

President Cleveland believed the business decline was caused by the uncertainty people had about the safety of their money. The government should stop coining silver, he insisted, and go back to the single **gold standard.** This meant that only gold would be used to back the currency. In October 1893 he persuaded Congress to repeal the Sherman Silver Purchase Act.

This action angered those who favored coining silver as well as gold. It split the Democratic party. And it did not end the depression. During 1894–1895, economic conditions got worse rather than better.

Other people blamed the depression on the government's failure to regulate business. Unsafe working conditions, child labor, low wages, and unfair pricing policies had gone on for most of the century. Government on all levels had ignored these and other effects of industrialization. Even more, they seemed to support business leaders in their pursuit of profit. These people claimed the depression of 1893 was another result of the lack of government regulation of American business.

Coxey's Army

As the depression dragged on, large numbers of unemployed men took to wandering about the countryside. These people were called tramps. Some thought them dangerous troublemakers, perhaps even revolutionaries who wanted to overthrow the government. In truth, they only wanted work.

Small groups of unemployed workers began making protest marches to seek government relief. This increased fear of the "tramp ①

Preview & Review

Use these questions to guide your reading. Answer the questions after completing Section 4.
Understanding Issues, Events, & Ideas. Using the following words, describe the key instances of labor unrest during the Depression of 1893: gold standard, Coxey's Army, Pullman Strike.
1. Why did President Cleveland want the nation to return to the gold standard?
2. How would Coxey's plan have put people to work and caused prices to rise?
3. Why did many people turn against President Cleveland after the Pullman Strike? Why was the president hurt by Governor Altgeld's criticism?
Thinking Critically. Which amendment in the Bill of Rights might Jacob Coxey have used to protest his arrest in March 1894? Why?

The Granger Collection, New York

Jacob Coxey seems to be a timid, mild sort of man in this 1894 photograph. But appearances can be deceiving. You know him as the leader of Coxey's Army. How successful was he?

SECTION 4

PREVIEW & REVIEW RESPONSES
Understanding Issues. Events & Ideas.
Descriptions should demonstrate an understanding of the terms used.
1. He believed that the Depression of 1893 was caused by the uncertainty people had about the safety of their own money.
2. The government would spend $500 million to employ people to improve rural roads and to lend local governments money for public works. The money would be printed by the treasury and would not be backed by gold or silver. This would inflate the money supply and cause prices to rise.
3. Cleveland's use of the army to break a strike alarmed union members.

Thinking Critically.
The First Amendment guarantees people the right to petition the government.

FOCUS/MOTIVATION:
MAKING CONNECTIONS
Student Experiences.
Have students review the "Strategies for Success" feature on business cycles in Chapter 17. Then ask them what the business climate in the United States is like today. Ask: Have you seen newspaper articles or news programs about the current state of the economy? What do forecasters predict for the near future? Point out that the American free enterprise system is subject to fluctuations in the business cycle. Then have students
(Continued)

RESORCES

■ You may wish to have students complete Reading 20: "The Sweatshops of Chicago (1891)" in Volume II of *Eyewitnesses and Others*.

◀ You may wish to have students complete Case 5: "*Lochner v. New York*" in *THE CONSTITUTION: Past, Present, and Future.*

study the graph of business cycles in Section 3. Ask: What do you think economic conditions were like in 1893? *(They were depressed.)* On what do you base your conclusion? *(The graph shows that the economy was in a period of recession.)* Point out that in this section students will be learning about the effects this economic downturn had on the American economy.

GUIDED INSTRUCTION: COOPERATIVE LEARNING

Organize the class into two groups, one representing Congressional leaders in 1894 and the other representing members of Coxey's Army. Have the members of Coxey's Army prepare arguments for why their demands should be met, while the members of Congress prepare arguments for why Coxey's demands cannot be met. Have spokespersons from each group present their cases. Then have both groups meet to work out a compromise acceptable to both sides.

CHECKING UNDERSTANDING

Ask: How did the Depression of 1893 lead to social unrest in the United States? *(Many people were out of work. Some, like the members of Coxey's Army, tried to get relief measures passed. Others, like the workers at Pullman's factory, went on strike.)*

problem." The most important of these marches was headed by Jacob Coxey, who was himself a prosperous business leader.

Coxey's Army marched from Massillon, Ohio, to Washington, attracting an enormous amount of attention. One observer claimed that for every two marchers there was at least one newspaper reporter tagging along to describe the happenings.

Coxey's Army set out in March 1894 and reached Washington in May. There were only a few hundred marchers, most of them obviously harmless people. But when Coxey tried to present a petition to Congress, he was arrested for trespassing on the grounds of the Capitol. The police then broke up Coxey's followers and sent the marchers straggling home. Their march came to nothing.

What makes Coxey's Army important historically is the plan that Coxey worked out for dealing with the depression. The federal government should spend $500 million improving rural roads, he said. It should also lend money to state and local governments for other public works projects. The work itself should be done by the unemployed. Anyone without a job should be put to work.

Coxey further proposed that both the $500 million spent by the federal government and the money lent to local governments should simply be printed by the treasury. Like the Civil War greenbacks, this money would not be backed by gold or silver. This inflation of the money supply would cause prices to rise. That would help farmers and debtors of all sorts. Coxey's program seemed radical and impractical in 1894. Forty years later it appeared a perfectly reasonable way to deal with deflation and unemployment in a depression.

The Pullman Strike

Since he was president when the depression struck, Cleveland was blamed for the hard times. Emergency soup kitchens were set up to feed the long lines of hungry people who could not find work. Critics unfairly called them "Cleveland Cafes." But Cleveland did little to help the jobless or to stimulate the lagging economy.

More people turned against Cleveland when a great strike broke out in May 1894, shortly after the arrest of Jacob Coxey. The strike
■ had begun in the factory of the Pullman Palace Car Company in Illinois, which manufactured and operated sleeping and dining cars for the railroads. After the strike had gone on for several weeks, engineers, conductors, and other workers of the American Railway Union, in sympathy with the strikers, voted not to handle trains to which Pullman cars were attached. This paralyzed the railroads in and around Chicago. It threatened to disrupt the nation's already depressed economy.

A federal judge ordered the railroad workers back to work. When they refused, President Cleveland sent troops into Chicago to make
◀ sure that the United States mail was not held up. The union was

SUGGESTED CAPTION RESPONSE
The guardsmen would say that they were doing their duty to keep American railroads functioning. The strikers would say that the army was interfering with their right to try to better their working conditions by striking.

RESOURCES

■ You may wish to have students complete Case 9: "*Youngstown Sheet & Tube Co. v. Sawyer*" in *THE CONSTITUTION: Past, Present, and Future.*

The Granger Collection, New York

willing to operate mail trains. However, railroad officials insisted on attaching Pullman cars to these trains. The **Pullman Strike** continued.

Rioting broke out when blue-coated soldiers entered the Chicago ■ rail yards. The violence turned public opinion against the union. Its president, Eugene Victor Debs, was arrested and thrown in jail. The strike collapsed.

Conservatives praised Cleveland's defense of "law and order." But thousands of union members were alarmed by his use of the army to break a strike. The governor of Illinois, John Peter Altgeld, had bitterly objected to the use of federal troops in his state. Altgeld claimed that Chicago police and state militia units could preserve order. He accused Cleveland of being a strikebreaker. Altgeld's opposition weakened Cleveland politically since Altgeld, like Cleveland, was a Democrat. 🖳

Illinois national guardsmen are firing on striking Pullman Company workers in this artist's sketch. Their fortress is the equipment brought in to get the train back on track. Describe this scene from both points of view—that of the guardsmen and that of the strikers.

Return to the Preview & Review on page 723.

RETEACHING STRATEGY: COOPERATIVE LEARNING
Students with Special Needs. Organize the class into cooperative learning groups. Have each group make a list of the problems caused by the Depression of 1893. *(unemployment; Coxey's Army marching on Washington, only to be rebuffed; violent strike at Pullman's factory that was squelched by federal troops)*

INDEPENDENT PRACTICE
Have students complete the Preview & Review activity at the beginning of the section.

CLOSURE
Point out that the Depression of 1893 caused hardships for many Americans and led to widespread social unrest.

HOMEWORK
Have students locate more information on the Pullman Strike or a more recent strike nearer to their community or one of interest to them. They should bring to class newspaper or periodical clippings that describe the attitudes of striking union members, employers, and the rest of the community. Each student should summarize for the class the events leading up to the strike, the strike itself, and its resolution. After each class presentation, have other students make comments or ask questions of the presenter.

Unemployment and Unrest 725

PREVIEW & REVIEW RESPONSES
Understanding Issues. Events & Ideas.
Accounts should focus on Bryan's emotional appeal to the people.
1. They backed the gold standard.
2. The Republicans had a large amount of money and hired orators to tour the country, while McKinley stayed home and greeted specific groups in carefully planned interviews. The Democrats had little money and relied upon Bryan's eloquence to help them.
3. Within a few years, new gold discoveries and improved methods of refining gold ore ended the issue of free silver. The changes in voting patterns caused by the Depression of 1893 and the free-silver fight continued for many years. The election marked the birth of the modern industrial age.

Thinking Critically.
Republican pamphlets should support the gold standard. Democratic pamphlets should support the free coinage of silver.

Preview & Review

Use these questions to guide your reading. Answer the questions after completing Section 5.
Understanding Issues, Events & Ideas. Give a brief eyewitness account of William Jennings Bryan's Cross of Gold speech.
1. What stand did the Republicans take on the money issue in their platform of 1896?
2. How did the Republican campaign of 1896 differ from the Democratic campaign?
3. How did McKinley's victory in 1896 mark the end of the post-Civil War era?
Thinking Critically. From the point of view of either a Republican or a free-silver Democrat, write a brief campaign pamphlet about the money issue for the election of 1896.

The Bettmann Archive

In a wicker rocker on his front porch William McKinley waits for visitors during his presidential campaign in 1896.

5. GOLD VERSUS SILVER

The Democrats Choose Silver

As the election of 1896 drew near, the Democrats had to make a difficult decision. President Cleveland was extremely unpopular. Rightly or wrongly, he was being blamed for the continuing depression. Furthermore, the public knew he was totally opposed to measures that would stimulate the economy by raising prices, especially the coining of silver.

In the southern states where the Democrats were in control, the Populist party was making large gains by calling for the free coinage of silver. Southern farmers were hard hit by the depression. If the Democrats again chose Cleveland, who defended the gold standard, they seemed sure to be defeated in the national election. They might even lose the South to the Populists.

The 1896 election was one which gave the Democrats a chance to hold the presidency and to take Republican seats in Congress. This was because the Republican party convention in June 1896 had nominated Congressman William McKinley of Ohio as its candidate for president. McKinley would be running on a platform that declared squarely for the gold standard. "We are . . . opposed to the free coinage of silver," the platform stated.

Many normally Republican farmers in the Middle West and nearly all the miners in the Rocky Mountain states were in favor of free silver. The Republican platform made them furious. States like Nebraska and Colorado, traditionally Republican, might go Democratic if that party would come out for free silver.

The Democratic convention met in St. Louis in July. Before picking a candidate, the delegates had to adopt a platform. The key issue to be decided was the money question. A formal debate took place. Three speakers defended the gold standard. Three others spoke in favor of the free coinage of silver.

The final debater was William Jennings Bryan, a young ex-congressman from Nebraska. Bryan was not a particularly thoughtful person, but he had a deep faith in democracy. He believed that legislators should represent the ideas of the people who elected them. As early as 1892 he said, "The people of Nebraska are for free silver, and [therefore] I am for free silver. I will look up the arguments later."

Bryan had served two terms in Congress. But few people outside Nebraska had ever heard of him. He was only 36, barely a year older than the minimum age set by the Constitution for becoming president. Nevertheless, he decided that he had a good chance of getting the 1896 presidential nomination.

Bryan's speech on the silver question was his great opportunity to attract attention. He succeeded brilliantly. Bryan was one of the

HISTORICAL SIDELIGHTS

① Bryan's oratorical skills did not come easily. He had to take lessons and learned to speak with pebbles in his mouth. He was practicing in the woods one time and frightened away some picknickers who thought he might have escaped from a nearby mental institution.

SUGGESTED CAPTION RESPONSE

He is carrying a cross and a crown of thorns. He has quotations from the Bible in his pocket. One of his supporters is waving a banner of anarchy in the background.

The Granger Collection, New York

William Jennings Bryan's "Cross of Gold" speech inspired this caricature. He is seen here as one who abuses the Bible, but Bryan was actually a very religious person who based courtroom arguments on the Bible. In what other ways does this cartoonist criticize Bryan?

greatest political orators in American history. He did not make any ① new economic arguments for free silver. Instead, like a skillful musician, he played upon the emotions of the delegates. His voice rang through the hall like a mighty organ in a great cathedral. As he approached the climax of his appeal, almost every sentence brought forth a burst of applause.

He likened those who favored coining silver to the Crusaders who had freed Jerusalem from the Moslems. He praised western farmers as "hardy pioneers who have braved the dangers of the wilderness" and "made the desert bloom." The country could exist without the cities, Bryan said, but without the nation's farms, "grass will grow in the streets of every city in the country." He concluded by likening the silver forces to Jesus Christ, saying to the defenders of the gold standard:

❝ You shall not press down upon the brow of labor this crown of thorns, you shall not crucify mankind upon a cross of gold. ❞

FOCUS/MOTIVATION: MAKING CONNECTIONS
Student Experiences.

Show students a pre-1965 quarter and a more recently minted quarter. Ask them to describe the differences between the two. *(The more recent coin has a bronze glint.)* Point out that before 1965, dimes and quarters contained 90 percent silver. Since 1965, however, the coins have been made of nickel and copper. Then ask students to describe the free silver issue that dominated politics in the late 1800s. *(Many people wanted the government to mint silver coins at the ratio of 16:1 with gold coins.)* Tell students that the free coinage of silver dominated politics through 1896. At that time, the United States was on the gold standard. Ask students to define the gold standard. *(It is a system of coinage whereby all money can be exchanged for gold.)* Ask students whether they can still redeem their money for gold. *(no)* Then point out that our currency today is based on faith in our economic system and our government rather than by gold. Tell students that such money is called *fiat money.* It has value simply because the government says that it is legal tender that can be used to pay all debts.

PRIMARY SOURCE

Description of change: excerpted.
Rationale: excerpted to focus on Bryan's opposition to maintaining the gold standard.

① William Jennings Bryan became one of the best known Americans. He was the Democratic party's candidate for president three times—1896, 1900, and 1908. Each time he lost. He served two years as Woodrow Wilson's secretary of state.
② With its advertising campaign and corporate contributions, the McKinley election campaign set the standards for the twentieth century. The Republicans also used millions of American flags to symbolize the struggle to save the gold standard.

SUGGESTED CAPTION RESPONSE
They have repudiated the gold standard even though it means that the economy will be out of control.

GUIDED INSTRUCTION
Organize the class into two groups, one representing Republicans in the election of 1896 and one representing Democrats in the same election. Have each group meet to formulate a specific platform for their candidate and party. Then have spokespersons for each group debate the merits of their particular points of view. Conclude the activity by holding a mock election in which students use secret ballots to vote for president. You may wish to use this activity as the basis for a class discussion focusing on the workings of the voting process in modern America, emphasizing voter registration and the use of the secret ballot.

① After cheering this **Cross of Gold speech,** the Democratic convention adopted a platform calling for "the free and unlimited coinage of both silver and gold at the . . . ratio of 16 to 1." The next day the delegates nominated the "Nebraska Cyclone," William Jennings Bryan, for president.

The Election of 1896

The presidential campaign of 1896 roused people throughout the nation. When it was over, many Republicans and Democrats had changed sides.

Nearly all business people and manufacturers supported Mc-
② Kinley. Like most other wealthy citizens, these people felt that the issue of silver inflation versus the gold standard and "sound money" was more important than party loyalty. They believed that if Bryan were elected, their businesses would collapse and their wealth would vanish.

Beyond question these people were wrong. There was nothing magical about the gold standard, and Bryan was no threat to their wealth. But they misunderstood the situation. They saw the campaign as a crusade. They thought that McKinley was a great patriotic hero, almost a Washington or a Lincoln, who would save the nation in an hour of terrible danger.

Free silverites have unhitched their wagon from the Democratic donkey as they roll out of control. This is the view of C. J. Taylor, who made this lithograph in 1896. Bryan has his arms stubbornly crossed while Governor Altgeld of Illinois waves a firebrand. Explain why the red banner says "Repudiation."

The Granger Collection, New York

THE FRONT-PORCH CAMPAIGN

McKinley ran what was called a front-porch campaign for the presidency. He stayed home in Canton, Ohio, partly to be near his wife, Ida, who had epilepsy. Groups from all over the country came to hear his views.

These visits were carefully planned. Each delegation was greeted at the railroad station by the "Canton Home Guards" mounted on horses. The visitors then marched to McKinley's modest house. The town took on the appearance of one long Fourth of July celebration. The streets were lined with flags and banners. Pictures of McKinley were everywhere. Stands along the route sold hot dogs, lemonade, and souvenirs.

When a delegation reached McKinley's house, the candidate came out to meet them, usually with his wife and mother at his

Ida McKinley

side. He called their leaders by name and seemed to show keen interest in their problems. A member of the delegation would make a speech while McKinley listened to him "like a child looking at Santa Claus."

McKinley's responses showed how well he knew his audience. To a group of Civil War veterans he might speak about pensions. To manufacturers or factory workers he might stress the importance of the protective tariff. Always he pictured himself as a patriot defending America and the gold standard against the dangerous free-silver Democrats. "Patriotism," he would say, "is above party and National honor is dearer than party name. The currency and credit of the government are good, and must be kept good forever."

Newspaper reporters covered each of these visits. They wrote articles describing the crowds. They quoted the remarks of the candidate in detail. In this way McKinley reached voters all over the country without stepping off the front porch of his house.

Actually, McKinley was a rather ordinary person. He was hard working, forward looking, and politically shrewd. But he was not especially intelligent, imaginative, or creative. His greatest advantage in the election was the solid support of his business backers.

The Republican campaign was organized by Marcus Alonzo Hanna, an Ohio industrialist. Mark Hanna and his assistants raised enormous amounts of money for the contest. Some of the contributions came from wealthy individuals, many of whom were normally Democrats. But most of the money came from large corporations. As one bank president explained, "We have never before contributed a cent to politics, but the present crisis we believe to be as important as the [Civil] war." It was not then illegal for corporations to give money to political candidates.

Hanna used this money very cleverly. Republican speakers spread across the country. At one point 250 Republican orators were campaigning in 27 states. Pamphlets explaining the Republican program were printed and 250 million distributed. Over 15 million pamphlets on the money question were handed out in two weeks.

Committees were set up to win the support of all kinds of special groups. One committee tried to influence German American voters,

① Bryan traveled more than 18,000 miles and made over 600 speeches to almost 5 million people. His campaign marked a clear break with tradition. In former campaigns, the presidential candidate tried to appear as though he did not seek the office overtly.

② Almost every social group shifted toward the Republicans in the election of 1896. In the North and West, they gave the Republicans a *national* majority that they did not lose until the 1930s. The Democrats maintained control of the South.

③ The industrial workers abandoned William Jennings Bryan because they feared that free silver meant higher food prices and a continuation of the depression.

GUIDED INSTRUCTION: COOPERATIVE LEARNING

Place the labels *McKinley* and *Bryan* on the bulletin board. Then organize the class into nine groups. Distribute to each group a 4 x 6 card labeled with one of the following names: business leaders, factory workers, silver miners, gold miners, farmers, city dwellers, factory owners, newspaper editors-in-chief, wealthy people. Tell students that it is 1896 and that they are voters who fit the category written on their card. Have them work together to determine which candidate they will support in the election and write on the card why they have chosen to support that candidate. When the groups have finished filling in their cards, have them place the card in the appropriate column on the bulletin board. Use the completed chart as the basis for a class discussion focusing on the major issues of the election.

another those of African descent, and so on. There was even a committee assigned to campaign among bicycle riders, for bicycling was an especially popular sport in the 1890s.

The Democrats had very little campaign money, in part because so many wealthy Democrats were supporting the Republican candidate. The party organization was also weak. In many of the industrial states Democratic politicians would not support free silver. These "Gold Democrats" formed a National Democratic party and nominated Senator John M. Palmer of Illinois for president.

① The Democrats did have one very valuable asset—Bryan himself. His magnetic personality and his brilliance as a speaker made him a great campaigner. He traveled constantly, speaking all over the nation. Sometimes he addressed huge crowds in city auditoriums. Sometimes he spoke to only a handful of listeners at rural railroad stations from the back platform of his train. All told, he made over 600 speeches between August and election day in November.

Most important newspapers supported McKinley. Their reporters frequently misquoted Bryan in order to make him appear foolish or radical. *The New York Times* even suggested that he might well be insane. But the papers did report Bryan's speeches in detail. In this election voters could readily learn where both candidates stood on all the issues of the day.

② The election caused major shifts in voting patterns. After much debate the Populists nominated Bryan instead of running a candidate of their own. The effect was to end the Populist movement. Yet if the Populist party had run someone else, the free-silver vote would have been split. Then McKinley would have been certain to win the election.

Populist strongholds in the South and West went solidly for Bryan in November. So did the mountain states, where silver mining was important. But thousands of formerly Democratic industrial

③ workers voted Republican. City people did not find Bryan as attractive as did farmers and residents of small towns. McKinley was popular with workers, despite his close connections with big business. He convinced workers that free silver would be bad for the economy. And he argued that a high tariff would protect their jobs by keeping out goods made by low-paid foreign laborers.

Boston, New York City, Baltimore, Chicago, and many other cities that had gone Democratic in the presidential election of 1892 voted Republican in 1896. Chicago, for example, had given Grover Cleveland a majority of over 35,000 in 1892. In 1896 McKinley carried the city by more than 56,000 votes.

The Election Ends an Era

The election was a solid Republican triumph. The electoral vote was 271 for McKinley, 176 for Bryan. Looked at one way, McKinley won

Courtesy Museum of Fine Arts, Boston, Gift of Miss Maude E. Appleton

simply because his party spent more money and was better organized than the Democrats. He carried all the crucial close states of the ① Northeast by relatively small margins. If Bryan had won in New York, Ohio, Indiana, and Illinois, he would have been president.

In a larger sense, however, McKinley's victory marked the end of the post-Civil War era. Within a year or two, new gold discoveries and improved methods of refining gold ore ended the money shortage. Free silver was no longer an issue. But the changes in voting patterns caused by the Depression of 1893 and the free-silver fight continued long after those problems were settled.

The farm states voted for Bryan, the industrial states for McKinley. But the election was not a victory for industry nor a defeat for American farmers. Agriculture remained important. As Bryan had said in his Cross of Gold speech, the cities and their industries could not prosper unless farmers were prosperous too.

The election marked the birth of the modern industrial age. To most people of that day, Bryan seemed to be pressing for change, McKinley defending the old, established order. In fact, McKinley was far more forward looking than Bryan. His view of the future was much closer to what the reality of the 20th century would be. 🖾 ■

The century ends with the glow of lamplight on Boston Common. Childe Hassam painted this twilight scene in the early 1900s. But what lies ahead in the story of America? How do you imagine this scene will appear in 1920? 1960? 2000?

Return to the Preview & Review on page 726.

Gold Versus Silver   731

1. Pamphlets will vary. Many students will point out that the machine has tricked immigrants into believing that the machine politicians are sincerely working to make conditions better for them.
2. Answers will vary. Students should back up their choice with sound reasoning.
3. Students who choose (a) should focus on what farmers can do to improve economic conditions (b) should focus on the need to end corruption in government.

REVIEW RESPONSES

Chapter Summary
Paragraphs will vary but should be evaluated on the logic of student arguments.

Reviewing Chronological Order
3, 5, 1, 4, 2

Understanding Main Ideas
1. The name of a native son from one of these states could increase the chances of carrying the candidate's home state and perhaps of winning the election.
2. The Civil Service Commission made up and administered examinations. The practice of making government employees contribute to political campaign funds was outlawed.
3. During the Civil War, the government had issued paper money that could not be exchanged for gold or silver. The money question concerned whether the government should now exchange these greenbacks for gold or silver.
4. Labor unions and farmers supported the Populists. The platform of 1892 called for government ownership of railroads and of the telegraph and telephone network, a federal income tax, a program of government loans to farmers, an eight-hour workday, restrictions on immigration, and free coinage of silver.
5. Business people, manufacturers, and city dwellers supported the Republicans. Farmers, miners, and residents of small towns supported the Democrats. The Republicans won because

CHAPTER 20 REVIEW

| 1865 | A CHANGING AMERICA | | | 1875 | |

1866
Tammany Hall

1870
National Grange movement

1872
Eakin's *The Agnew Clinic*

1873
Coining of silver discontinued

1876
Tom Sawyer

1877
Hayes elected president

★
Reconstruction ends

★
Munn v. Illinois

1878
Bland-Allison Act

Chapter Summary
Read the statements below. Choose one, and write a paragraph explaining its importance.
1. The United States remained politically divided after the Civil War into the Republican North and Democratic South.
2. Political machines controlled many local elections. These machines helped the poor and immigrants, and then counted on their votes.
3. Tariffs, the money question, and civil service reform posed important issues for Americans after the Civil War.
4. American writers and artists turned to a movement called Realism after the Civil War.
5. Presidential elections during the last half of the 19th century were very close. This happened because few candidates took a real stand on the issues.
6. After the war, times were hard for American farmers. They created the Grange and the Farmers Alliance to help them deal with their problems.
7. Farmers and consumers wanted free coinage of silver. Many wealthy people wanted to remain on the gold standard.
8. The Depression of 1893 led to severe unemployment and unrest such as Coxey's Army and the Pullman Strike.
9. McKinley's defeat of Bryan in 1896 ended the post-Civil War era.

Reviewing Chronological Order
Number your paper 1–5. Then study the time line above and place the following events in the order in which they happened by writing the first next to 1, the second next to 2, and so on.
1. Pendleton Act
2. Cross of Gold speech
3. National Grange formed
4. Coxey's Army marches to Washington
5. Garfield assassinated

Understanding Main Ideas
1. Why did the Democrats and Republicans nominate so many national candidates from close states after the Civil War?
2. What reforms were made in civil service after Congress acted in 1883?
3. What was the money question? How were greenbacks a part of it?
4. Which groups supported the Populist party? What was its platform in 1892?
5. Which groups supported the Republicans in 1896? Which supported the Democrats? Why did the Republicans win?

Thinking Critically
1. **Evaluating.** Suppose you are a political reformer in 1898. You will publish a pamphlet exposing the corruption of your local political machine. Write the introduction to the pamphlet, explaining various wrongs that the machine has committed in your community.
2. **Analyzing.** Although the Populist party lost the election of 1892, several reforms listed in the party's platform were later put into effect. Of these reforms, which do you think was the most important? Why?
3. **Synthesizing.** It is 1896. Write a letter to a friend, giving your eyewitness account of either (a) a meeting of the local Grange discussing farmers' concerns or (b) a Congressional debate on the pros and cons of civil service reform.

Writing About History
Use historical imagination to write a letter to a friend describing what you saw and heard at the Democratic convention in July 1896 when Bryan delivered his "Cross of Gold" speech. Or describe a visit to McKinley during his front-porch campaign. Use the information in Chapter 20 and in reference books to prepare your letter.

Practicing the Strategy
Review the strategy on page 716.

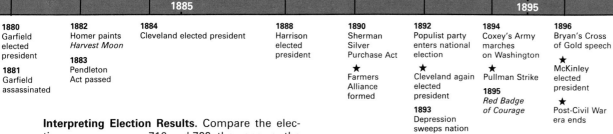

1880
Garfield
elected
president

1881
Garfield
assassinated

1882
Homer paints
Harvest Moon

1883
Pendleton
Act passed

1884
Cleveland elected president

1888
Harrison
elected
president

1890
Sherman
Silver
Purchase Act

★
Farmers
Alliance
formed

1892
Populist party
enters national
election

★
Cleveland again
elected
president

1893
Depression
sweeps nation
and world

1894
Coxey's Army
marches
on Washington

★
Pullman Strike

1895
*Red Badge
of Courage*

1896
Bryan's Cross
of Gold speech

★
McKinley
elected
president

★
Post-Civil War
era ends

Interpreting Election Results. Compare the election maps on pages 716 and 722, then answer the following questions.

1. In which part of the country were the Democrats strongest in 1888? In 1892?
2. In which part were the Republicans strongest in 1888? In 1892?
3. In which part of the country were the Populists strongest?
4. How would you explain the geographic location of each party's strength?
5. How can you tell that the unit rule was in effect in 1888 but not in 1892?

Using Primary Sources

The following excerpt from Richard Hofstadter's book *The Age of Reform* examines the controversy that arose from the Populist movement. As you read the excerpt, note differences in the two points of view presented. Then answer the questions that follow.

On the one hand the failure of the revolt has been described . . . as the final defeat of the American farmer. John Hicks, in his history of the movement, speaks of the Populists as having begun "the last phase of a long and perhaps a losing struggle—the struggle to save agricultural America from the devouring jaws of industrial America," while another historian calls Populism "the last united stand of the country's agricultural interest . . . the final attempt made by the farmers of the land to beat back an industrial civilization whose forces had all but vanquished them already."

1. According to the excerpt, how did the perspectives of the two historians differ?
2. Which of the views presented by the two historians reveals bias against industrial America? Quote from the reading to support your answer.
3. How might American farmers today agree or disagree with the views of Populism presented in the excerpt? Support your answer with specific examples.

Linking History & Geography

Agricultural land use is in part determined by a number of natural factors. Topography, rainfall, length of growing season, and other variables influence what is produced in an area. Study the maps on pages 624, 649, and 715 and answer these questions.

1. Why is the Great Plains topography well suited to growing grain?
2. What factors limit the agricultural use of land in Alaska? Wyoming?
3. What natural features help make the Central Valley of California so productive?

Enriching Your Study of History

1. **Individual Project** In your library and other American history books find examples of the cartoons of Thomas Nast. It was Nast who created the symbols of the Tammany Hall tiger, the Republican elephant, and the Democratic donkey. Study a copy of a Nast cartoon from this era and explain his use of one of these symbols. You also may wish to draw your own cartoon to express your view of a key point in the chapter.
2. **Cooperative Project** Presidential campaigns after the Civil War were hard fought and much discussed. Yet time seems to drop a veil over the occupants of the White House during this period, to say nothing of the candidates they defeated. Various members of your group will research and report on each of the following campaigns:
   1868 Grant v. Seymour
   1872 Grant v. Greeley
   1876 Hayes v. Tilden
   1880 Garfield v. Hancock
   1884 Cleveland v. Blaine, Butler
   1888 Harrison v. Cleveland
   1892 Cleveland v. Harrison, Weaver

Practicing Critical Thinking

1. For Indians, it meant more settlers to take their land. For railroad barons, it meant more passengers traveling west and an increase in demand for shipping. For farmers, it meant a chance to own land. For cattle barons, it meant a chance to claim land near water and thus control the countryside.

2. Symbols will vary, but students should use sound reasoning in explaining their choices.
3. Answers will vary. Many students will choose Edison because electricity so revolutionized our way of life. Others might choose Bell for the same reason.

REVIEW RESPONSES
Summing Up and Predicting
Paragraphs will vary but should be evaluated on the logic of student arguments.

Connecting Ideas
1. Advantages include a sense of community derived from living among those with a similar cultural heritage. Disadvantages include a sense of isolation from what is going on in the rest of the country and possible discrimination.
2. Some Americans might fear that the immigrants will take their jobs or be prejudiced against the immigrants because of their different cultural background that the Americans do not understand. The problems are very similar to those faced by earlier immigrants. They are different in that most of the new immigrants come from completely different cultural backgrounds.
3. Answers will vary, but many students will suggest that the author is more sympathetic to the Indians' point of view.

*These sources are suitable for students reading below grade level.

734

UNIT SIX REVIEW

Summing Up and Predicting
Read the summary of the main ideas in Unit Six below. Choose one statement, then write a paragraph predicting its outcome or future effect.
1. The tremendous growth of America brought it to the last frontier—the Great Plains. Settlers eventually displaced the Plains Indians who, after several bloody battles, were placed on reservations.
2. A cattle kingdom thrived on the open range of the southern plains.
3. Discoveries of great mineral resources brought increased mining to the West. Many of the resources bolstered American industry.
4. Completion of railroad and communications networks prepared the nation for the rise of industry.
5. American industry became so large that new business organizations, such as corporations and trusts, were developed.
6. Workers turned to unionization to make their demands for improved conditions heard.
7. The "New Immigration" brought people from southern and eastern Europe to American cities and factories.
8. After the Civil War political machines controlled many of the nation's cities.
9. Farmers, workers, and the poor formed organizations to represent them.

Connecting Ideas
1. Ethnic neighborhoods developed in cities in the late 1800s and still exist in many cities. List some advantages and disadvantages of living in an ethnic neighborhood today.
2. What problems might immigrants to the United States today face? How are these problems like those faced by immigrants in the late 1800s? How are they different?
3. Does the author's description of what happened to the Indians in the late 1800s differ from what you have seen in movies and on television? Why or why not?

Practicing Critical Thinking
1. **Drawing Conclusions.** It is the late 1800s. How has the Homestead Act changed your life if you are a Plains Indian? A railroad baron? A farmer? A cattle baron?
2. **Synthesizing.** You know that cartoonist Thomas Nast created the elephant to represent the Re-

publican party and the donkey to represent the Democratic party. Create two new symbols for these political parties and explain why you chose these symbols.
3. **Evaluating.** Of Thomas Edison, Alexander Graham Bell, Henry Bessemer, Jane Addams, John D. Rockefeller, and Cornelius Vanderbilt, who do you think made the greatest contribution to the world? Why?

Cooperative Learning
1. Have your group use the library or other American histories to report on the life of each of the following figures in industrial America:

Cornelius Vanderbilt   Samuel F. B. Morse
Andrew Carnegie   Alexander Graham Bell
John D. Rockefeller   Thomas A. Edison
Cyrus W. Field   Samuel Gompers
Terence V. Powderly   Jane Addams

2. The two great artists of the West were Frederic Remington and Charles Marion Russell. Members of your group will report on these popular artists and show reproductions of their works. Then make one or more poster-size drawings of the cowhands of the Old West.
3. Your group will make a scale model of an Indian village or a sod house that might have stood on the Great Plains. Design a roof that will lift off so you can show how the inside of the house might have been furnished.

Reading in Depth
Durham, Philip and Everett L. Jones. *The Adventures of the Negro Cowboys.* New York: Dodd Mead. Contains stories about the most famous African American cowboys.
* Harvey, Brett. *Cassie's Journey: Going West in the 1860s.* New York: Holiday House. Describes the dangers and struggles of Cassie and her family as they migrate westward to California.
Hoexter, Corinne. *From Canton to California: The Epic of Chinese Immigration.* New York: Four Winds Press. Portrays the immigration of Chinese to California and their reception there.
* Josephy, Alvin. *The Patriot Chiefs.* New York: Viking. Contains biographies of great Indian leaders such as Chief Joseph and Crazy Horse.
Wolfson, Evelyn. *From Abenaki to Zuñi: A Dictionary of Native American Tribes.* Includes discussions of tribal customs, foods, clothing, and means of travel.

UNIT OBJECTIVES
Upon completing Unit 7, students will be able to:
1. Explain the causes and results of the U.S. involvement in Latin America.
2. Describe the progressives' spirit, and the problems that they hoped to solve.
3. Explain the causes and results of World War I.
4. Analyze the social and economic changes that occurred in the U.S. between the two world wars.
5. Explain the reasons for and results of changes in U.S. foreign policy in the 20th century.
6. Trace the course of U.S. history from World War II to the present.

U.S. Naval Academy

Ships of the U.S. Fleet, a symbol of what a mighty power America had become by the turn of the century, enter San Francisco's Golden Gate.

AN EXPANDING AMERICA UNIT 7

I n Unit 7 you will learn how the United States acquired an overseas empire and how the Progressive movement fought to improve the lives of the American people. Here are some main points to keep in mind as you read the unit.

- American expansionism led the United States to win control of Alaska and Hawaii.
- As a result of the Spanish-American War of 1898, Cuba was freed from Spanish rule and the United States annexed Puerto Rico, Guam, and the Philippines.
- The Panama Canal was built by the United States and opened in 1914. The Canal drastically cut travel time between the Atlantic and Pacific oceans.
- Journalists called muckrakers attacked corruption and the terrible conditions in cities and industry.
- As president, Theodore Roosevelt led the charge for reform, earning the nickname *trustbuster*.

OVERVIEW
The manifest destiny felt in the United States during the pre-Civil War era was translated into expansionism in the Western Hemisphere and Pacific in the late 1800s. The acquisition of overseas territory, which was a result of the victory in the Spanish-American War, thrust America into a new role as an imperial power. Within the nation a new mood developed called the progressive spirit. This led many Americans to seek solutions to the problems brought about by rapid industrialization.

America's involvement in world affairs and attempts to improve its own society have continued throughout the 20th century.

CONNECTING WITH PAST LEARNING
Ask students to list some of the major problems that the United States confronted following the Civil War. (*Students should mention the following: Indian Wars, immigration, labor strikes, the growth of powerful trusts and political machines, farmers' problems, silver issue, economic depression.*) Ask them if these problems were domestic or international, and why. (*domestic, because they focused on internal issues*) Point out that as the United States approached the new century and began to focus on countries and territories beyond its borders, its problems became more international in scope.

America in World Affairs, 1865–1912

PLANNING THE CHAPTER

TEXTBOOK	RESOURCES
1. Extending America's Influence	*Unit 7 Worksheets and Tests:* Chapter 21 Graphic Organizer, Directed Reading 21:1, Reteaching 21:1
2. America and Its Southern Neighbors	*Unit 7 Worksheets and Tests:* Directed Reading 21:2, Reteaching 21:2
3. The Spanish-American War	*Unit 7 Worksheets and Tests:* Directed Reading 21:3, Reteaching 21:3 *Creative Strategies for Teaching American History:* Page 295 *Eyewitnesses and Others, Volume 2:* Reading 23: The Rough Riders Charge San Juan Hill (1898)
4. America Expands Further	*Unit 7 Worksheets and Tests:* Directed Reading 21:4, Reteaching 21:4 *Creative Strategies for Teaching American History:* Page 313 *Eyewitnesses and Others, Volume 2:* Reading 13: Clergyman and Critics: A Debate over Imperialism (1885–1899)
5. Roosevelt and His Canal	*Unit 7 Worksheets and Tests:* Directed Reading 21:5, Reteaching 21:5, Geography 21 *Creative Strategies for Teaching American History:* Page 311
Chapter Review	*Audio Program:* Chapter 21 *Unit 7 Worksheets and Tests:* Chapter 21 Tests, Forms A and B (See also *Alternative Assessment Forms*) *Test Generator*

STRATEGIES FOR STUDENTS WITH SPECIAL NEEDS

Gifted Students.

Have interested students research and prepare a panel discussion on the effects of American imperialism in the Philippines. The following are some points which students may wish to include in their discussion: both the positive and negative aspects of imperialism; a comparison of American imperialism and the imperialism of other powers such as Great Britain or France; the role the United States plays in the Philippines today.

Students Having Difficulty with the Chapter.

You may wish to have students listen to Chapter 21 in *The Story of America Audio Program.* Pair students who are having difficulty with students who are performing well. Have students skim through Chapter 21 and write down the names of important people, places, and events mentioned in the chapter. Then have them draw a time line and place the events and appropriate dates on which they occurred in chronological order. You may wish to display the time lines in the classroom.

BOOKS FOR TEACHERS

C. S. Campbell, *The Transformation of American Foreign Relations, 1865–1900.* New York: Harper & Row, 1976.

P. S. Foner, *The Spanish-Cuban-American War and the Birth of American Imperialism, 1895–1902.* New York: Monthly Review Press, 1972.

Alfred Thayer Mahan, *The Influence of Sea Power upon History.* New York: Hill & Wang, 1957.

S. C. Miller, *Benevolent Assimilation: American Conquest of the Philippines.* New Haven, CT: Yale University Press, 1982.

T. J. Osborne, *Empire Can Wait: American Opposition to Hawaiian Annexation, 1893–1898.* Kent, OH: Kent State University Press, 1981.

M. B. Young, *American Expansionism: The Critical Issues.* Boston: Little, Brown & Co., 1973.

BOOKS FOR STUDENTS

Noel B. Gerson, *Sad Swashbuckler: The Life of William Walker.* Nashville: Thomas Nelson, 1976.

Don Lawson, *The United States in the Spanish-American War.* New York: Abelard-Schuman Books, 1976.

John Nance, *The Land and People of the Philippines.* Philadelphia: J. B. Lippincott Co., 1977.

MULTIMEDIA MATERIALS

The Building of the Panama Canal: "The Land Divided, the World United" (3 color filmstrips and 3 cassettes), SSSS. Deals with the history of the canal project from the 1860s to 1920.

The Panama Canal: Turning Point in History (color filmstrip and cassette), SSSS. Deals with the decision to build the canal, the actual building of the canal, and the canal's influence on American foreign policy.

The Philippine-American War (filmstrip and cassette), SSSS. Deals with American fight against Filipino insurgents at the end of the Spanish-American War. Touches on the underside of American colonialism.

The Sinking of the Maine (filmstrip and cassette), SSSS. Deals with the causes and effects of American involvement in the Spanish-American War. Makes use of period newspapers and artworks.

The Spanish-American War (filmstrip and cassette), SSSS. Uses period photographs. Deals with the causes, the costs, and the effects of the war.

RESOURCES
■ You may wish to have students complete the Chapter 21 Graphic Organizer as they work through this chapter.

CHAPTER OBJECTIVES
Upon completing this chapter, students will be able to:

1. Describe the acquisition of Alaska and Hawaii by the U.S.
2. Define *isolationism* and *expansionism.*
3. Discuss the effects of the Pan-American Conference and the Chilean Crisis on Latin American attitudes toward the U.S.
4. Explain the causes, events, and results of the Spanish-American War.

OVERVIEW
Following the Civil War, the United States began to grow as a world power. It acquired new territory, some as a result of the Spanish-American War.

FOCUS/MOTIVATION:
MAKING CONNECTIONS
Student Experiences.
To reinforce the geographic theme of *location*, have students look at the map of U.S. possessions on page 767 or the World Map in the Reference Section. Discuss both the locations and distances from the contiguous U.S. of both Alaska and Hawaii. To provide students the opportunity to consider the *place* characteristics of Alaska and Hawaii, ask students who have been to either of these states to describe what they are like.

SECTION 1

PREVIEW & REVIEW RESPONSES
Understanding Issues, Events, & Ideas.
Descriptions should demonstrate an understanding of the terms used.
1. American policy of keeping out of European affairs and of not permitting Europeans to meddle in American affairs
2. They may have been frightened by American technology and naval power.
3. For about two cents an acre the U.S. bought land that contained immense resources of lumber, gold, copper, and other metals.
4. New England whalers and traders; Christian missionaries

CHAPTER 21

America in World Affairs, 1865–1912

■ Even those who thought manifest destiny a bold American notion might have been surprised by what happened after the Civil War. The parade of settlers marching "from sea to shining sea" stopped only to catch its breath before pressing on. Americans seemed to forget George Washington's warning to avoid foreign involvements. The country began to expand its influence in Latin America. Alaska and Hawaii were acquired. After the war with Spain, fought to free Cuba, the Philippines and Puerto Rico were taken by the United States. By the time Theodore Roosevelt became president at the turn of the century, America's influence in the Western Hemisphere was great. But how far could America stretch itself in world affairs?

Preview & Review

Use these questions to guide your reading. Answer the questions after completing Section 1.
Understanding Issues, Events, & Ideas. Describe American expansion overseas, using the following words: isolationism, American expansionism, Midway Islands, Alaskan Purchase, Seward's Folly, Hawaiian Islands, archipelago, McKinley Tariff, absolute monarch.
1. What was isolationism?
2. Why did the Japanese agree to open trade with the U.S.?
3. How did "Seward's Folly" turn out to be an immense bargain?
4. Who were the first Americans to reach Hawaii? Who followed?
Thinking Critically. 1. You are with Perry in Tokyo harbor. Describe your reactions. 2. You are a member of Congress. Would you vote for or against the purchase of Alaska? For or against the acquisition of Hawaii? Why?

1. EXTENDING AMERICA'S INFLUENCE

Isolationism

For many Americans longtime suspicions of Europe had increased during the Civil War. Great Britain and France had sympathized with the Confederate government. British companies had built ships for the southerners. This had enabled the Confederacy to get around the United States blockade of southern ports. The *Alabama*, a British-built warship flying the Confederate flag, destroyed many American merchant ships during the rebellion. For a time Great Britain even considered entering the war on the side of the Confederacy.

While the United States was fighting its desperate struggle, France boldly sent an army into Mexico. The French then named a European prince, Maximilian of Austria, as Emperor of Mexico. This was a direct challenge to the Monroe Doctrine, which had stated that no European colonies were to be established in the Americas.

Once the Civil War ended, the United States sent 50,000 soldiers to the Mexican border to aid the Mexican patriots who were fighting Maximilian and demand that France withdraw its army. The French pulled out. In June 1867 Mexican patriots led by Benito Juárez entered Mexico City. Maximilian was captured and put to death.

5. Contrast the views of imperialists and anti-imperialists.

6. Discuss the steps taken by the U.S. to build and control the Panama Canal.

7. Demonstrate the ability to analyze political information by interpreting editorial cartoons.

8. Recognize the geographic and political impact of American expansion overseas.

SUGGESTED CAPTION RESPONSE
The 19th

These events demonstrated that European powers were eager to take advantage of any weakness of the United States. Americans wanted nothing from Europe except the right to buy and sell goods. They considered European governments undemocratic. They also believed that European diplomats were tricky and untrustworthy. To get involved with a European diplomat meant the risk of becoming involved in the wars and rivalries of Europe. Better, believed the average American, to have as little as possible to do with Europe.

This was the popular view. American political leaders never took such an extreme position. But the policy of American relations with the European powers was **isolationism.** The United States should keep pretty much to itself, as Washington had cautioned in his Farewell Address. It should not meddle in European affairs. And it should not permit Europeans to meddle in American affairs. This latter point had been most strongly stated in the Monroe Doctrine.

Americans who were isolationists were taking no serious risks. As the nation grew in wealth and numbers, the possibility that any European country might attack it rapidly disappeared.

The Closing of the Frontier

Manifest destiny had carried the American people more than three thousand miles across the North American continent. They had conquered all obstacles as they spread from "sea to shining sea," from the Atlantic to the Pacific. But by the late 19th century the frontiers of the continent had virtually disappeared. The lands of the Great Plains and the Southwest were filling with people and within two decades—by 1912—all would become states. Only Alaska in the frigid north still represented an American frontier.

What did the closing of the frontier mean to America? To what would that boundless energy that had fueled manifest destiny be

Benito Juárez was the high-minded leader of the Mexican people when France attempted to make Mexico its colony.

RESPONSES *(Continued)*
Thinking Critically.

1. Answers will vary, but students may mention how exciting it was to be present at the historic moment when East met West.

2. Answers will vary, but student responses should be based on facts and sound logic.

FOCUS/MOTIVATION:
MAKING CONNECTIONS
Prior Knowledge.
Have students define manifest destiny. *(the belief that it was the obvious future role of the people of the United States to control the continent)* Ask them if they think manifest destiny went beyond having the U.S. spread from coast to coast. *(yes)* To reinforce the geographic theme of *location,* ask students to locate places on the map where the U.S. extended this original definition of manifest destiny. *(Alaska, Hawaii, Puerto Rico, American Samoa, Guam)* Point out to students that as they read this section, they will begin to see just how the U.S. began acquiring this new territory.

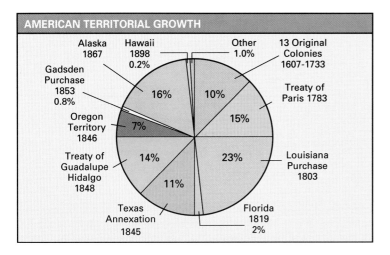

AMERICAN TERRITORIAL GROWTH

Alaska 1867 — Hawaii 1898 0.2% — Other 1.0% — 13 Original Colonies 1607-1733
Gadsden Purchase 1853 0.8%
16% — 10% — Treaty of Paris 1783
Oregon Territory 1846 — 7% — 15%
Treaty of Guadalupe Hidalgo 1848 — 14% — 23% — Louisiana Purchase 1803
11%
Texas Annexation 1845 — Florida 1819 2%

LEARNING FROM GRAPHS.
This chart shows how the United States has added to its territory throughout its history. During which century did the country add the most territory?

① The U.S. was not the only nation to take up the policy of expansionism in the latter part of the 1800s. Belgium, Germany, Italy, Japan, and Russia also sought overseas colonies.

② Another reason for America's interest in expansionism was that it needed to find new markets overseas for its agricultural and industrial products.

GUIDED INSTRUCTION
Divide the class into two groups. One group is to be Americans sailors in Perry's fleet arriving in Tokyo Harbor. The second group is Japanese people watching as the American fleet approaches. Both groups are to make lists of questions to ask the other group such as where they live, what they eat, what kind of clothes they wear, and what religion they practice. Pair students from each group with one another so that they can ask and answer the questions. You may want to have students switch roles after they have gone through their first set of questions and answers.

turned? Certainly there were problems and challenges to be solved within the United States. Yet manifest destiny was something else, a part of the adventurous restlessness that was so much a part of the American character. Had the first period of American history ended with the closing of the frontier, as Frederick Jackson Turner claimed? Or would Americans turn their restless spirits elsewhere and continue to expand the nation's boundaries?

Expansionism

Americans never adopted an isolationist attitude toward the rest of the world. Many people believed that the same manifest destiny that had brought the Great West into the Union would eventually bring all of North and South America under the control of the Stars and Stripes—and the islands of the Pacific Ocean as well. This attitude ① was known as **American expansionism.**

Remember that the Monroe Doctrine had stated that no more *European* colonies should be established in the Americas. It said nothing about the United States extending its control in the Western Hemisphere.

In the years after the Civil War Americans began to extend their influence in Latin America and in the Pacific Ocean. In August 1867 the United States navy occupied the **Midway Islands,** located about 1,000 miles (1,600 kilometers) northwest of Hawaii. Most Americans then gave not another thought to these uninhabited flyspecks on the map of the vast Pacific until a great American-Japanese naval battle was fought there in World War II.

② What convinced Americans to look beyond their boundaries? Writers such as Josiah Strong, a Congregational minister, claimed America had an "Anglo-Saxon" mission to expand overseas. These writers based their views on two ideas. The first was the concept of an Anglo-Saxon "race," which to Americans meant the people of Great Britain and their descendants. This concept of race is scientifically inaccurate. Although Anglo Saxons share certain physical characteristics, they are actually part of the Caucasoid race. The other idea, called Social Darwinism, applied the theories of scientist Charles Darwin—especially the theory of the "survival of the fittest"—to people and nations. According to Social Darwinism, the energetic, strong, and fit should rule everyone else. As you have read, people had used Social Darwinism to justify unsafe and unsanitary working conditions, child labor, and the exploitation of workers by American business leaders. Now the same argument claimed that the American people—the energetic, strong, and fit—should rule the other peoples of the earth, or at least teach them what was "right." As Strong stated it:

    ❝ The Anglo-Saxon is the representative of two great ideas, which are closely related. One of them is that of civil liberty.

① Japan had joined the imperialist nations in 1894 when it went to war with China, taking the island of Formosa.

SUGGESTED CAPTION RESPONSE
Students may mention the enormous size of the ship compared to the sampan and the fact that the ship was powered by steam rather than oars or sails.

Nearly all the civil liberty in the world is enjoyed by Anglo-Saxons. . . . The other great idea represented by the Anglo-Saxon is that of pure, spiritual Christianity. It follows, then, that Anglo-Saxons, as the great representatives of these two ideas, have a special relationship to the world's future. They are divinely commissioned to be, in a sense, their brother's keeper. . . .[1] 》

The Opening of Japan

The first example of this mood of global expansion took place in Japan. For centuries Japan had kept itself isolated from the rest of the world. Except for Chinese and Dutch traders, Japan did not permit any foreigners to enter the country. Then, quite suddenly, their peaceful harbor was invaded.

On July 8, 1853, a crowd of astonished Japanese watched a fleet ① of ships move into Tokyo harbor. These ships had no sails or oars and belched black smoke from their funnels. The "black dragons," as the Japanese called them, were the coal-powered steamships of the American fleet.

[1]From *Our Country: Its Possible Future and Its Present Crisis* by Josiah Strong

Point of View

In the opening lyric for *Pacific Overtures,* a musical based on the opening of Japan, a reciter sings:

《In the middle of the
  world we float
In the middle of the sea.
The realities remain
  remote
In the middle of the sea.
Kings are burning
  somewhere.
Wheels are turning
  somewhere,
Trains are being run,
Wars are being won,
Things are being done
Somewhere out there, not
  here.
Here we paint
  screens. . . .》
from *Pacific Overtures,*
Music and lyrics by
Stephen Sondheim, 1975

RELATING HISTORY TO GEOGRAPHY
To reinforce the geographic themes of *location* and *physical regions,* have students find physical maps of Alaska and Hawaii in an atlas. Have them trace the maps and then locate the following places on each: Nome, Fairbanks, Anchorage, Seward, Juneau, Ketchikan, Kodiak, Mt. McKinley, Aleutian Islands, Yukon River, Bering Strait, Arctic Ocean, Gulf of Alaska, Kauai, Oahu, Honolulu, Maui, Hawaii, Mauna Kea, Hilo, and Pacific Ocean. In order to enhance their study of these states, have them place features of the regions such as climate, soil, and vegetation on their maps.

The British Library

This detail from a Japanese painted scroll shows one of Commodore Perry's four ships in Edo (Tokyo) Bay. His arrival by steamship in July 1853 was described by the Japanese as "four black dragons" entering their tranquil harbor. Imagine you are aboard one of the small Japanese boats, or sampans, in the foreground. What would be your impression of Perry's steamship?

PRIMARY SOURCES
Description of change: excerpted.
Rationale: excerpted to focus on Strong's argument defending Anglo-Saxon superiority.
(Point of View) Description of change: excerpted.
Rationale: excerpted to focus on a modern lyricist's depiction of one Japanese person's attitudes toward life in Japan.

SUGGESTED CAPTION RESPONSE
Students may mention that Alaska is roughly about
one-fourth the size of the continental U.S.

Commodore Matthew Perry commanded the American fleet.
President Millard Fillmore had sent him to ask the Japanese emperor
to open several Japanese ports to American trade. Perhaps frightened
by American technology and naval power, the Japanese signed a
treaty of friendship with the United States.

The Purchase of Alaska

Americans also knew little to nothing about Alaska, then called
Russian America, until William H. Seward, secretary of state, purchased it from Russia in March 1867. Russian explorers, fur trappers,
and merchants had been in the area since the 1790s. But Alaska had
never brought them the riches they sought. The Russian government
decided to sell the vast land. The United States seemed the logical
customer. Seward jumped at the opportunity to add more territory
to the United States. He agreed to a purchase price of $7.2 million.

News of this **Alaskan Purchase** surprised everyone in America.
Congress knew little about the negotiations until the treaty was presented to it, along with the bill for $7.2 million.

To win support, Seward launched a nationwide campaign.
Alaska was worth far more than $7.2 million, he claimed. Its fish,
furs, and lumber were very valuable. By controlling it, America
would increase its influence in the North Pacific. These arguments
convinced the senators to accept the treaty by a vote of 37 to 2.

The House of Representatives, however, hesitated to provide
the $7.2 million. Seward again ran through his arguments about the
virtues of this land in the frozen North. The Russian minister to the

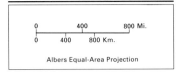

ALASKA AND
THE UNITED STATES

0   400   800 Mi.
0   400   800 Km.

Albers Equal-Area Projection

LEARNING FROM MAPS. *Alas-
ka's size is truly amazing. It is by far
the largest state. This map compares
the size of Alaska to that of the continental United States. In your own
words, state how they compare in size.*

United States, Baron Edouard de Stoeckl, wined, dined, and probably bribed a number of House members. Stoeckl later claimed that he had spent almost $200,000 getting the House to appropriate the money.

Many Americans thought buying Alaska was a mistake. They called the territory **"Seward's Folly,"** "Frigidia," and "President Andrew Johnson's Polar Bear Garden." One joke said that in Alaska a cow would give ice cream instead of milk. But most people were pleased. What a bargain Seward made! For about two cents an acre he obtained nearly 600,000 square miles (1,560,000 square kilometers) of land, a region twice the size of the state of Texas. The land contained immense resources of lumber, gold, copper, and other metals. A gold rush in the 1890s brought thousands of eager Americans to Alaska and led to the development of Seattle as a major Pacific port. More recently, rich deposits of oil and natural gas have been discovered there.

Hawaii

After the Civil War Americans also became interested in the **Hawaiian Islands.** This **archipelago,** or island group, is located in the Pacific about 2,000 miles (3,200 kilometers) southwest of San Francisco.

The first Americans to reach these beautiful, sunny islands were New England whalers and traders. Beginning in the late 1700s, they stopped there for rest and fresh supplies on their lonely voyages. These sailors were followed by missionaries who came to Hawaii hoping to convert the inhabitants to Christianity.

The foreign missionary movement, long important to both Catholics and Protestants, offered many Americans their first glimpse of the world beyond American shores. These Americans felt that the spread of Christianity around the world must precede the spread of democracy and social justice. The Hawaiian missionaries, besides spreading the gospel, settled down, built houses, and raised crops. In the 1840s and 1850s their children and grandchildren were beginning to cultivate sugar.

By the time of the American Civil War, the missionary families dominated the Islands' economy and government. Sugar was the Hawaiians' most important export. They sold most of it in the United States.

The Hawaiians were ruled by a king who made all the decisions and owned all the land. But in 1840 King Kamehameha III issued a constitution modeled after the United States Constitution. This was not surprising since many of Kamehameha's advisers were Americans. In 1875 the two countries signed a treaty which allowed Hawaiian sugar to enter the United States without payment of a tariff. In exchange the Hawaiian government agreed not to give territory or special privileges in the islands to any other nation.

CHECKING UNDERSTANDING
Ask students to summarize the reasons on which many Americans based their belief that the U.S. should extend its boundaries overseas. *(Many Americans, such as the Congregational minister Josiah Strong, believed that it was America's "Anglo-Saxon" mission to extend its boundaries overseas. By "Anglo-Saxon" they meant the people of British ancestry. They also believed in the theory of Social Darwinism, which incorporated the idea of survival of the fittest. They applied this theory to people and nations, saying that Americans were energetic, strong, and fit and should therefore rule other peoples of the earth.)*

**RETEACHING STRATEGY:
Students with Special Needs.**
Pair students who are having difficulty with students who are performing well. Write the following questions on the chalkboard or an overhead projector. Have students reread the section titled "Expansionism," and then have the more proficient students ask the others the following questions:

1. What convinced many Americans to look beyond their boundaries to expand? *(the belief by many that America had an "Anglo-Saxon" mission to expand)*

2. What was meant by the "Anglo-Saxon" mission? *(This meant that America, whose culture was based on Britain's, and which many believed to be a superior culture, had almost a duty to expand overseas so that this culture could be spread to other parts of the world.)*

3. What was Social Darwinism? *(This was an idea that took the scientific theories of Darwin, especially the one concerning the survival of the fittest, and applied them to people and nations.)*

4. How was this theory applied by Americans to justify expansion? *(They claimed that Americans were energetic, strong, and fit and should therefore rule other peoples of the earth.)*

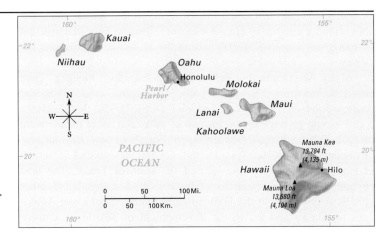

HAWAII

Refer to map on pages 1128–29 for relative location to the United States.

Albers Equal-Area Projection

LEARNING FROM MAPS. *The Hawaiian Islands lie like a string of pearls in the Pacific Ocean. What are the three largest islands?*

The Bishop Museum

Queen Liliuokalani took the throne in 1891. She wrote the popular song "Aloha Oe" or "Farewell to Thee." Read these pages and Queen Liliuokalani's letter on page 779 to decide whom she might wish to bid farewell.

The 1875 treaty greatly encouraged sugar production. The missionary families formed corporations and imported thousands of low-paid Chinese and Japanese immigrants to work on the plantations. Most of these laborers signed long-term contracts similar to the ones that indentured servants had signed with Virginia tobacco planters 250 years earlier.

Between 1875 and 1890 the amount of Hawaiian sugar shipped to the United States jumped from 18 million to 160 million pounds (about 8 million to 72 million kilograms). But the Hawaiian sugar boom came to a sudden end when Congress passed the **McKinley Tariff** of 1890, a law that took away the special advantage of the Hawaiians. Their sugar now had to compete with sugar grown in the United States and also with sugar produced in Cuba and other countries. Prices fell, and the economy of the Hawaiian Islands suffered a serious depression.

Along with Hawaii's economic crisis came a political crisis. In 1891 the government changed hands. The new ruler was Queen Liliuokalani. She was intelligent and fiercely patriotic. She resented the influence of American planters and merchants in her country. Her attitude was expressed in the slogan "Hawaii for the Hawaiians."

Queen Liliuokalani was determined to break the power of the foreign-dominated Hawaiian legislature. In January 1893 she proclaimed a new constitution making her an **absolute monarch**—a ruler who holds all power.

The Americans responded by organizing a revolution. John L. Stevens, the American minister to Hawaii, supported the rebels. He ordered 150 marines ashore from an American warship in Honolulu harbor. They did not have to fire a shot to persuade Liliuokalani and the Hawaiians not to resist. The revolutionaries promptly raised the American flag.

Stevens announced that Hawaii was now under the protection of the United States. A delegation hurried off to Washington to

HISTORICAL SIDELIGHTS
① Congress voted to annex Hawaii in 1898, and it became a U.S. territory in 1900.

SUGGESTED CAPTION RESPONSES
(Top) That the Hawaiian culture will change forever
(Bottom) Where it says, "whose pineapples would soon be well-known in the United States"

Peabody Museum of Salem

The Hawaiian Island of Oahu seems a paradise in this 1821 watercolor. The ship lying at anchor in the foreground flies the U.S. flag. What do you predict the U. S. presence will mean to Oahu and the rest of the Hawaiian Islands?

INDEPENDENT PRACTICE
Have students complete the Preview & Review activity at the beginning of the section.

CLOSURE
To reinforce the geographic theme of *movement,* point out to students that as the American frontier disappeared in the West, many Americans began looking beyond the borders of the continental U.S. to fulfill that adventurous restlessness fueled by the spirit of manifest destiny.

HOMEWORK
To reinforce the geographic themes of *location, place,* and *movement,* have students prepare a multimedia report for the class on either the state of Alaska or the state of Hawaii. Their report should trace the history of the state from territory to statehood and describe the present-day concerns of each state, including ecology, economy, and social well-being. They may use maps, drawings, pictures, paintings, or slides in their presentation.

negotiate a treaty of annexation to bring Hawaii under American control. In February 1893 President Benjamin Harrison sent this treaty to the Senate for approval. But Harrison's term was about to end. President-elect Cleveland asked the Senate not to vote on the treaty until he had a chance to consider it. The Senate therefore postponed action.

After taking office, Cleveland withdrew the treaty. He sent a special commission headed by James H. Blount of Georgia to investigate conditions in the islands. Blount reported that the Hawaiian people did not want to be annexed to the United States.

After reading Blount's report, Cleveland decided to scrap the treaty. He called Stevens back to Washington and sent a new representative to the islands. This new United States minister met with the president of the revolutionary government, Sanford B. Dole, and urged him to resign. Cleveland wanted to return control of the islands to Queen Liliuokalani, who by this time was popularly known in America as "Queen Lil."

Dole (whose pineapples would soon be well-known in the United States) refused to resign. If the United States did not want Hawaii, the revolutionaries would remain independent. On July 4, 1894, they proclaimed Hawaii a republic. 🖼

Brown Brothers

Sanford B. Dole was born in Hawaii to American missionaries. He was president of the government that overthrew the queen. He later became first governor of the Territory of Hawaii. What hint can you find in the last paragraph on this page that pineapples as well as politics may have been behind Dole's motives?

Return to the Preview & Review on
① page 736.

PREVIEW & REVIEW RESPONSES

Understanding Issues, Events, & Ideas.

Explanations should demonstrate an understanding of the terms used.

1. So they would see themselves as belonging to a group with common interests, under U.S. domination
2. He was afraid that if the British took any more territory in the Western Hemisphere, other European powers might follow, injuring U.S. interests in Latin America.
3. That the U.S. was the supreme power in the Western Hemisphere, and would intervene to enforce the Monroe Doctrine

Thinking Critically.

Students may mention that countries who feel powerless may do this to wield a measure of control over a more powerful nation.

FOCUS/MOTIVATION: MAKING CONNECTIONS
Prior Knowledge.

Have students recall what important events were going on in Latin America in the 1820s. *(Many Latin American countries were fighting for their independence from Spain.)* How did the U.S. respond? *(with the Monroe Doctrine)* Do you think this put the U.S. in the role of protector of the Western Hemisphere? Why? *(yes, because by issuing the Monroe Doctrine the U.S. was taking this role upon itself)*

Preview & Review

Use these questions to guide your reading. Answer the questions after completing Section 2.
Understanding Issues, Events, & Ideas. Use the following words to explain American attempts to police the Western Hemisphere: Pan-American Conference, Chilean Crisis, arbitration, Venezuela Boundary Dispute.
1. Why did Secretary of State Blaine want to bring the nations of the Western Hemisphere together?
2. Why did President Cleveland want to arbitrate the Venezuela Boundary Dispute?
3. What was the United States' notice to Europe and Latin America in the Venezuela Boundary Dispute?
Thinking Critically. Americans in the 1800s enjoyed "twisting the British lion's tail." Name a country or foreign group that recently has done the same thing to the United States. Why do you think they did it?

2. AMERICA AND ITS SOUTHERN NEIGHBORS

Pan-Americanism

American interest in the nations of Latin America also increased after the Civil War. Again American missionaries led the way. These countries sold large quantities of coffee, bananas, fertilizer, and many other products to the United States. But they bought most of their manufactured goods in Europe. In the 1890s James G. Blaine, who was secretary of state under Presidents Garfield and Harrison, set out to develop closer trade ties with Latin America. His strategy was simple but one-sided.

Blaine wanted all the nations of the Western Hemisphere to see themselves as belonging to a group with common interests. In his opinion the United States would obviously dominate such a group. This was one reason why many Latin American nations hesitated to cooperate with Blaine. In 1889 Blaine invited the Latin American countries to send representatives to Washington for a meeting. After a whirlwind tour of 41 cities, these representatives assembled for the first **Pan-American Conference.**

The conference did not accomplish much. The delegates rejected Blaine's suggestion that they lower their tariffs on American goods. Still, it was the first time the nations of North and South America had come together. They began to sense that the common interests of the Western Hemisphere were in many ways different from those of other nations.

The Chilean Crisis

Any goodwill that the Pan-American Conference generated suffered a setback in the **Chilean Crisis** of 1891-92. During a civil war in Chile between a faction supporting its president and one backing its congress, the United States supported the presidential side. Unfortunately for the United States, the other side won the war. The Chileans called people from the United States *Yanquis.* Anti-*Yanqui* feeling was now high.

In this heated atmosphere some sailors from the U.S.S. *Baltimore,* on shore leave in the city of Valparaiso, got in a fight outside the True Blue Saloon. Apparently the fight started when a local civilian spat in the face of one of the sailors. A mob attacked the sailors, and the Valparaiso police did nothing to stop the fighting. Two sailors were killed and 16 injured.

President Harrison threatened to break diplomatic relations unless the Chilean government apologized. A war scare resulted. Fortunately, the Chilean government did apologize. It also paid $75,000 in damages to the injured sailors and to the families of the dead.

HISTORICAL SIDELIGHTS

① As the United States industrialized, its trade with other nations increased. As a result, many Americans began to urge the building of a more modern navy. The old wooden fleet was then replaced with a new one made of steel. Construction began in the 1890s on what became known as the "great white fleet."

The Venezuela Boundary Dispute

In 1895 the United States again flexed its muscles in South America. ① For decades Great Britain and Venezuela had haggled over the boundary line separating Venezuela and British Guiana, a small British colony on the north coast of South America. Venezuela had tried to settle the dispute in the past, but Great Britain had always refused to permit an outside judge to draw the boundary. Tensions increased in the 1880s when one of the largest gold nuggets ever found—509 ounces (14,252 grams)—was discovered in the territory both countries claimed.

President Grover Cleveland was afraid that if the British took any more territory in the Western Hemisphere, other European powers might follow. Then the economic and political interests of the United States in Latin America would be injured. He was determined to make Great Britain agree to settle the argument of who owned the territory by **arbitration**—that is, to allow a neutral judge to decide. President Cleveland ordered Richard Olney, his secretary of state, to send a stern message to the British government.

Olney's note of July 20, 1895, was extremely strong and quite insulting in tone. Cleveland described it as a "20-inch gun." The United States, said Olney, was the supreme power in the hemisphere. The Monroe Doctrine prohibited further European expansion in the Western Hemisphere. The United States would intervene in disputes between European and Latin American nations to make certain that the Monroe Doctrine was not violated.

Despite the harsh tone of Olney's message, the British prime minister, Lord Salisbury, dismissed it as a bluff. He thought Cleveland was playing the political game called "twisting the British lion's tail." The game's goal was to try to anger Great Britain. Any statement threatening Great Britain was sure to be popular with Americans of Irish origin. Most Irish Americans hated the British because they refused to give Ireland its independence. Instead of answering the note promptly, Salisbury delayed nearly four months.

When he did reply, Salisbury rejected Olney's argument that the Monroe Doctrine applied to the boundary dispute. Britain's dispute with Venezuela, he said politely but firmly, was no business of the United States.

This response made Cleveland "mad clean through." The Monroe Doctrine *did* apply to the situation. The United States would "resist by every means in its power" any British seizure of Venezuelan territory. The president asked Congress for money to finance a United States commission that would investigate the dispute. If the British refused to accept its findings, the United States would use force.

Nearly all people seemed to approve of Cleveland's tough stand. Venezuelans were delighted. When the news reached the capital of

America and Its Southern Neighbors   745

**RETEACHING STRATEGY:
Students with Special Needs.**
Pair students who are having
difficulty with students who are
performing well. Have the
more proficient students ask
the others the following:
1. What was the Pan American
   Conference? *(A meeting of
   the countries of the Western
   Hemisphere called by the
   U.S. so that the countries
   could see themselves as a
   group with a common interest under U.S. domination)*
2. What was the Chilean Crisis? *(A mob of Chileans attacked a group of American
   sailors, killing 2 and injuring
   16. The Chilean government
   apologized.)*
3. What was the Venezuelan
   boundary dispute? *(The
   U.S. stepped in when a dispute arose between Venezuela and Britain over the
   boundary between Vene-
   zuela and British Guiana.)*

INDEPENDENT PRACTICE
Have students complete the
Preview & Review activity at
the beginning of the section.

CLOSURE
Remind students that as the
U.S. expanded its sphere of influence, or areas that it either
directly or indirectly controlled,
in the Western Hemisphere
many Latin American nations
began to resent the U.S.

HOMEWORK
Have students prepare a written report on relations between
the U.S. and the countries of
Latin America from 1889 to
1914.

The Granger Collection, New York

*President Grover Cleveland twists the
tail of an outraged British lion while
his supporters cheer him on. Judging
from the president's supporters, had
the old feelings against England
cooled over a hundred years?*

Return to the Preview & Review on
page 744.

Venezuela, Caracas, a cheering crowd of at least 200,000 people
gathered at the home of the United States representative.

For a brief time war between the United States and Great Britain
seemed possible. But neither government wanted war. Cleveland was
mainly interested in reminding the world of the Monroe Doctrine.
Great Britain had too many other diplomatic problems to be willing
to fight over what they considered a relatively unimportant piece of
land in South America.

As soon as he realized that the situation had become dangerous,
Lord Salisbury agreed to let an impartial commission decide where
to place the boundary. In 1899 this commission gave Britain nearly
all the land in question.

On the surface the United States seemed to be defending a small
Latin American nation against a great European power in what came
to be known as the **Venezuela Boundary Dispute.** In fact, it was putting
both Europe and Latin America on notice that the United States was
the most important nation in the Western Hemisphere. Throughout
the crisis Cleveland ignored Venezuela. Its minister in Washington
was never once consulted. 🗒

3. THE SPANISH-AMERICAN WAR

Cuba and Spain

Early in 1895, shortly before Secretary Olney fired his "20-inch gun" over the Venezuela boundary, real gunfire broke out in Cuba. The Spanish had called their colony in Cuba the "Ever-Faithful Isle." Cuba was one of Spain's few colonies in America that had not revolted in the early 1800s. It was Spain's last important possession in the Americas.

In 1868 there had been a revolution in Cuba which lasted for ten years. It had failed, but now, in 1895, Cuban patriots again took up arms. Independence was their objective. The rebels engaged in the surprise attacks of **guerrilla warfare.** They burned sugar cane fields, blocked railroads, and ambushed small parties of Spanish soldiers. By the end of 1896 they controlled most of rural Cuba.

The Cuban patriots were led by José Martí, a poet, statesman, ① and essayist. Martí was a tireless critic of Spanish rule in Cuba. His poems, articles, and speeches were carried in many American newspapers. They helped focus America's attention on the brutality taking place in Cuba. When fighting broke out, Martí returned to Cuba. He was killed in the fighting a few days after his arrival. Martí became a national hero. Although he died three years before Cuban independence, he is often credited with doing more than any other individual to win his Cuba's freedom. An excerpt from one of Martí's patriotic poems is followed by the English translation.

" **Dos patrias**

Dos patrias tengo yo: Cuba y la noche.
¿O son una las dos? No bein retira
su majestad el Sol, con largos velos
un clavel en la mano, silenciosa
Cuba cual viuda triste me aparece.
¡Yo sé cuál es ese clavel sangriento
que en la mano le tiembla! Esté vació
mi pecho, destrozado está y vació
en donde estaba el corazón. Ya es hora
de empezar a morir. La noche es buena
para decir adiós. La luz estorba
y la palabra humana. El universo
habla mejor que el hombre.
            Cual bandera
que invita a batallar, la llama roja
de la vela flamea. Las ventanas
abro, ya estrecho en mí. Muda, rompiendo
las hojas del clavel, como una nube
que enturbia el cielo, Cuba, viuda, pasa. . . . "

Preview & Review

Use these questions to guide your reading. Answer the questions after completing Section 3.
Understanding Issues, Events, & Ideas. Discuss the Spanish-American War, using the following words: guerrilla warfare, *reconcentrado, junta,* yellow journalism, Teller Amendment, ultimatum, Spanish-American War, Manila Bay, Rough Riders, expeditionary force, Santiago, El Caney, San Juan Hill, Puerto Rico.
1. Why had the Spanish called Cuba their "Ever-Faithful Isle"?
2. Why did General Weyler place farm people in concentration camps?
3. Why was the *Maine* sent to Cuba? How did the explosion of the *Maine* bring the United States and Spain to the brink of war?
4. How did President McKinley try to prevent war with Spain? In general, what was the attitude of Congress?
Thinking Critically. **1.** If you were an ambassador to Cuba in the 1890s, would you have urged the United States to go to war? Explain your reasoning. **2.** Yellow journalists wrote very persuasive articles that influenced many people. Imagine that you are a journalist. Select a current issue about which you feel strongly and write a persuasive article about it.

The Granger Collection, New York

José Martí

SECTION 3

PREVIEW & REVIEW RESPONSES
Understanding Issues, Events, & Ideas.
Descriptions should demonstrate an understanding of the terms used.
1. Cuba had been one of Spain's few colonies in America that had not revolted in the early 1800s.
2. First, Cubans in the camps could not supply the rebels with food. Second, anyone outside the camps could be considered an enemy and arrested or shot.
3. There had been riots in Havana, and President McKinley sent the *Maine* there to protect American citizens against possible attacks. An American investigation concluded that the *Maine* was destroyed by an outside explosion, which was quickly blamed on Spain. The Spanish government claimed the explosion came from inside the ship, implying that an internal problem was the cause.
4. He did not let the sinking of the *Maine* cause a break with Spain, and he proposed that the Spanish do away with the concentration camps in Cuba, negotiate a truce with the Cubans, and that the Cubans be given more self-government. Congress favored war.

Thinking Critically.
1. Answers will vary, but should be based on sound reasoning and logic.
2. Student articles should demonstrate an understanding of the issue about which they are writing.

The Granger Collection, New York

The inspiration for this 1898 cartoon is the old saying, "Out of the frying pan and into the fire." The young woman who represents Cuba must decide between "Spanish Misrule" (the pan) and the flame of "Anarchy" burning on the isle of Cuba. Explain the artist's caption: "The Duty of the Hour—To Save Her Not Only from Spain, but from a Worse Fate."

66   **Two Motherlands**

I have two homelands: Cuba and the night.
Or are they both one? No sooner has the sun
withdrawn its grandeur than Cuba appears
beside me in silence, a mournful widow
who clasps a carnation to funeral robes.
I know the bloody carnation
that trembles in her hand. My breast
is now hollow, the niche that once held my heart
is empty and shattered. Now is the hour
to start dying. Night is a good time
for bidding farewell. Human words and the light
only stand in our way. The universe
speaks more clearly than man.
                              Like a banner
that calls us to battle, the flame of the candle
is burning red. My body no longer contains me,
I open the window. In silence, as she crushes
the carnation's petals, like a cloud
that darkens the sky, Cuba, the widow, passes. . . .[1] 99

[1]Both versions from "Two Motherlands" by José Martí in *The Canary Whose Eye Is So Black*, edited and translated by Cheli Duran

PRIMARY SOURCE
Description of change: excerpted.
Rationale: excerpted to focus on José Martí's feelings of patriotism.

① Emotions were inflamed by another incident which occurred prior to the explosion of the *Maine.* In December 1897 the Spanish minister to the United States, Dupuy de Lome, wrote a letter to a friend in Cuba calling McKinley a "crowd pleaser." Someone stole the letter and sold it to the New York *Journal,* a newspaper known for its yellow journalism. The American public became inflamed when they read the insult to their president.

In an effort to regain control of the countryside, the Spanish Governor-General, Valeriano Weyler, began herding farm people into what were called *reconcentrados*—concentration camps. He penned up about 500,000 Cubans in these camps. Weyler did this for two reasons. First, Cubans in the camps could not supply the rebels with food. Second, anyone outside the camps could be considered an enemy of Spain and arrested or shot on the spot.

Conditions inside the concentration camps were unspeakably bad. About 200,000 Cubans died in the camps, victims of disease and malnutrition.

Most people in the United States sympathized with the Cubans' wish to be independent. They were horrified by the stories of Spanish cruelty. Cuban revolutionaries fanned these fires. They established committees called *juntas* in the United States to raise money, spread propaganda, and recruit volunteers.

Explosion in Havana

Both President Cleveland and President McKinley had tried to persuade Spain to give the Cuban people more say about their government. They failed to make much impression. Tension increased. Then, in January 1898, President McKinley sent a battleship, the U.S.S. *Maine,* to Cuba. There had been riots in Havana, the capital city. McKinley sent the *Maine* to protect American citizens there against possible attack.

On February 15, while the *Maine* lay at anchor in Havana Harbor, a tremendous explosion rocked the ship. Of the 350 men aboard, 266 were killed. The *Maine* quickly sank.

To this day no one knows for sure what happened. Many Americans jumped to the conclusion that the Spanish had sunk the ship with a mine, a kind of underwater bomb. The navy conducted an investigation. It concluded that the *Maine* had indeed been destroyed by a mine. Another American investigation in 1911 also judged that an explosion from outside destroyed the ship.

The Spanish government claimed the disaster was caused by an explosion inside the *Maine*. This is certainly possible. A short circuit in the ship's wiring might have caused the *Maine*'s ammunition to explode, for example. It is difficult to imagine that the Spanish would have blown up the ship. The last thing Spain wanted was a war with the United States.

Emotions were inflamed on all sides. The Spanish government, ① or some individual officer, may indeed have been responsible. Or it is possible that the Cuban rebels did the job, knowing that Spain would be blamed.

In any case, a demand for war against Spain swept the United States. In New York City a man in a Broadway bar raised his glass and proclaimed, "Remember the *Maine!*" This became a battle cry

---

Point of View

A selected list of speeches delivered in 1898 by graduating high school seniors in Black River Falls, Wisconsin.

"Girls:
   A Woman's Sphere
   Home Training
   Our Duty to Unfortunates
   A Modern Reformer
Boys:
   Individual Independence
   Is the Cuban Capable of Self-Government?
   The Stars and Stripes
   Spain's Colonial System
   Should the United States Extend Its Territory?
   War and Its Effects on the Nation."
From *Wisconsin Death Trip,*
Michael Lesy, 1973

SUGGESTED CAPTION RESPONSE
If the explosion was external, it suggests that either the Spanish or Cuban rebels set it off; if it was internal, it may have been an accident caused by a short circuit.

GUIDED INSTRUCTION: COOPERATIVE LEARNING
Organize the class into two groups. The first group is to represent American citizens who oppose war with Spain, while the other group represents American citizens who favor war. Both groups are to assign different members the tasks of writing newspaper headlines, newspaper articles, and letters to the editor, or drawing editorial cartoons designed to persuade the American public to agree with their point of view. Have each group select representatives to present their group's newspaper campaign to the class.

PRIMARY SOURCE
Description of change: excerpted.
Rationale: excerpted to focus on McKinley's strong antiwar feelings.

The Granger Collection, New York

In strong detail this 1898 lithograph shows the explosion of the Maine *in Havana Harbor. What are two theories that might explain such a terrible explosion?*

similar to "Remember the Alamo!" during the Texas Revolution of the 1830s.

As tension mounted, the publisher of the New York *Journal*, William Randolph Hearst, had sent the artist Frederic Remington to Cuba to draw pictures of the Cuban Revolution. When Remington complained that there was no revolution and asked to come home, Hearst telegraphed:

❝ PLEASE REMAIN. YOU FURNISH THE PICTURES AND I'LL FURNISH THE WAR. ❞

War Is Declared

President McKinley wanted to avoid war. He told a friend:

❝ I have been through one war. I have seen the dead piled up, and I do not want to see another. ❞

McKinley did not let the sinking of the *Maine* cause a break with Spain. But he also wanted to stop the bloodletting in Cuba. He believed the Spanish must do away with the concentration camps and negotiate a truce with the Cubans. He also felt that more self-government should be granted Cuba.

Spain was willing to do this. However, the rebels demanded total independence. The Spanish government did not dare to give in completely. The Spanish people were proud and patriotic. Any government that "gave away" Cuba would surely be overthrown. Perhaps the king himself would be deposed. These unsettling thoughts made Spain stand firmly against Cuban independence.

Still, some peaceful solution might have been found if all sides had been patient. McKinley knew that Spain was earnestly exploring several possible compromises. He had also been promised that in time all his demands would be met. But he finally made up his mind that Spain would never give up Cuba voluntarily.

On April 11, 1898, the president told Congress that he had "exhausted every effort" to end the "intolerable" situation in Cuba. He asked Congress to give him the power to secure in Cuba "a stable government, capable of . . . insuring peace."

Congress had been thundering for war for weeks. By huge majorities it passed a joint resolution stating that the people of Cuba "are, and of right ought to be, free and independent." If the Spanish did not withdraw "at once" from the island, the president should use "the entire land and naval forces of the United States" to drive them out. Then Congress protected itself against being accused of going to war for selfish reasons. Its members approved a resolution

This elaborate 1898 cartoon shows President McKinley in a plumed hat, like Shakespeare's Hamlet, who also was unable to make up his mind. McKinley has several choices: heed the pleas of Uncle Sam to protect Cuba and close down the concentration camps, or revenge the watery ghosts who have risen from the Maine by going to war or compensating the victims' families. How did he decide? What had Congress already decided?

EXTENSION: COMMUNITY INVOLVEMENT

Have students present an oral report on the role their community played during the Spanish-American War. Their report may include copies of the local newspaper from that time with articles written about the war or stories of people from the community that served in the war. They may find this information at their local historical society or at the public library.

Culver Pictures

GUIDED INSTRUCTION
Have students draw a time line
showing the major events that
led up to and occurred during
the Spanish-American War.
Point out to students the cause-
and-effect relationships such
as the effect the explosion of
the *Maine* had on the American
public, the Spanish officials,
and the Cuban revolutionaries.

proposed by Senator Henry M. Teller of Colorado. This **Teller Amendment** stated that the United States had no intention of taking Cuba for itself or trying to control its government.

McKinley gave the Spanish government three days to accept his terms or face war. Unwilling to yield to McKinley's **ultimatum**—do this or face the consequences—the Spanish broke relations with the United States.

The Battle of Manila Bay

The first important battle of the **Spanish-American War** was fought not in Cuba but rather in the Far East on the Spanish-held Philippine Islands. The United States had a naval squadron stationed in Hong Kong, China, under the command of Commodore George Dewey. When war was declared, Dewey's ships sailed for instant action. He had been ordered weeks earlier to prepare for battle by Theodore Roosevelt, the assistant secretary of the navy.

Dewey steamed swiftly from Hong Kong across the China Sea to Manila, capital of the Philippines. His fleet entered **Manila Bay** on the night of April 30. Early the next morning, he gave the captain of his flagship, the cruiser *Olympia,* the famous command "You may fire when ready, Gridley." The American fleet far outgunned the

A great cheer rises from the crowds who have come to see the 10th Pennsylvania Volunteers set sail for Manila. What signs of patriotism are apparent in this lithograph?

The Granger Collection, New York

YELLOW JOURNALISM

The Granger Collection, New York

In the 1890s two popular New York newspapers, the *Journal,* owned by William Randolph Hearst, and the *World,* owned by Joseph Pulitzer, were competing bitterly for readers. Both played up crime and scandals to increase sales. This type of writing was called yellow journalism because the *World* printed a comic strip called "The Yellow Kid."

Both the *World* and the *Journal* supported the Cuban revolution. General Weyler's policy of *reconcentrado* provided the raw material for many of their stories about Spanish brutality. The actual conditions in Cuba were bad enough. But Hearst and Pulitzer made the camps seem even more shocking. Their exaggerated and untrue stories were topped by screaming headlines and accompanied by spine-chilling drawings and ugly cartoons.

This one-sided picture of the revolution no doubt influenced the United States' decision to go to war with Spain. How much influence the newspapers had is not an easy question to answer. It had some effect on many people. What is more clear is that Hearst and Pulitzer favored war partly for selfish reasons. They knew it would produce exciting news that would help them sell more papers.

ART IN HISTORY
Have students examine the painting titled "Charge of the Rough Riders Up San Juan Hill" by Frederic Remington in this section. Help them get a sense of place and time by telling them to imagine that they are one of the Rough Riders at the very moment of the charge. They are to put themselves behind Teddy Roosevelt, charging up San Juan Hill. Ask them to describe what they are thinking, what they see, smell, and hear, and how they feel at that moment.

Spanish warships guarding Manila. By noon the Spanish fleet had been smashed. Not one American sailor was killed. It was a marvelous triumph.

Dewey's victory made him an instant hero in the United States. Many people named babies after him. A chewing gum manufacturer came out with a gum named "Dewey's Chewies." However, until troops arrived from America, Dewey did not have enough men to occupy Manila or conquer any other part of the Philippine archipelago. So he set up a blockade of Manila harbor. When reinforcements reached him in August, he captured the city.

Moving an Army to Cuba

The war in Cuba did not begin so quickly. McKinley called for volunteers and received an enthusiastic response. In two months 200,000 recruits enlisted. Theodore Roosevelt, for example, promptly resigned as assistant secretary of the navy. Although he was nearly 40, he announced that he would organize a regiment and go off to fight in Cuba. He was commissioned a lieutenant colonel in the First Volunteer Cavalry.

Roosevelt led people as easily as the fabled Pied Piper of Hamelin. He came from a wealthy New York family of Dutch origin. He had been a sickly child with poor eyesight, but he had enormous determination. He built up his scrawny body and became a skillful boxer. He loved hunting, hiking, and horseback riding. He also loved

Have students recount the events that led up to the Spanish-American War. *(Cuban patriots took up arms against Spain in 1895 and by 1896 controlled most of the Cuban countryside. In order to regain control of the countryside, Spanish officials herded people into concentration camps. The conditions in the camps were horrible, causing disease, malnutrition, and death. Americans were outraged when they learned of these atrocities. Both Presidents Cleveland and McKinley attempted to get Spain to give the Cubans more freedom but failed. In 1898 McKinley sent the battleship* Maine *to Cuba to protect American citizens who were caught there in riots in Havana. No one is sure what happened, but the* Maine *blew up, killing 266 men. Many Americans believed that the Spanish had sunk the ship with a mine. The Spanish were angry, saying that the explosion came from inside the ship. Tension mounted as the yellow journalism of the* Journal *and the* World, *two New York newspapers, reported sensationalized accounts of the incident. Although McKinley tried to prevent war, Spain was unwilling to listen to his plea to give the Cubans more self-government. McKinley then gave Spain three days to accept his ultimatum; when they refused, war was declared.)*

Remington Art Museum

Frederic Remington painted this masterful "Charge of the Rough Riders Up San Juan Hill" in 1898. The scene is as Remington saw it, for he was a war correspondent in Cuba. Roosevelt leads the charge on horseback. You and your classmates might take turns describing Roosevelt's Rough Riders, about whom you have just read.

politics and scholarship. While still in college, he wrote an excellent history of the naval side of the War of 1812.

Roosevelt had served in the New York state legislature. He had been police commissioner of New York City. And he had run a cattle ranch on the open range of the Dakota Territory until the terrible winter of 1885-86 wiped out his herds.

Roosevelt's call for volunteers brought forth no fewer than 23,000 applicants. The colorful colonel chose a remarkable collection of soldiers from this mass. He enlisted several hundred cowboys, many of whom he had known in his ranching days, and 20 American Indians. Several well-known athletes and some police who had worked for him in New York City also joined up. The chaplain of the regiment was a former football player. The outfit became known to the public as the **Rough Riders.**

With men like Roosevelt recruiting, the army soon had more volunteers than it could efficiently organize in so short a time. Dozens of new units were shipped off to Tampa, Florida, where the invasion force was to be trained and supplied. That city became a near madhouse.

All the railroad lines around Tampa were clogged by long lines of unopened freight cars jammed with guns and ammunition, uniforms, and food. The trainees sweated in heavy blue woolen uniforms while the temperature climbed into the humid 90s. Lightweight summer uniforms for the **expeditionary force** did not arrive at Tampa until after the soldiers had sailed off for Cuba. Tropical fevers and other diseases raged through camp. Spoiled foods caused outbreaks of

SUGGESTED CAPTION RESPONSE
Students may mention that Remington portrayed the Rough Riders accurately in appearance, as the soldiers' uniforms appear the same, both in the painting and in the photograph. They may also mention that although Remington was at the scene, he had to have painted most of the picture from memory. However, the photograph shows the subjects as they really were the moment the shutter snapped. Students may also mention that the subject matter differs. Remington chose to portray the actual charge and shows casualties. The photographer chose to photograph a posed group in a moment of glory and does not allude to the costs of victory.

diarrhea and more serious illnesses. The longer the army remained at Tampa, the worse conditions became. Roosevelt raged:

> No words could describe . . . the confusion and lack of system and the general mismanagement of the situation here.

The Capture of Santiago

The slow-moving transport ships that would carry the army to Cuba could not put to sea until the Spanish fleet in the Atlantic had been located. That fleet could not stand up against American warships, but it could raise havoc with the transports.

The Spanish commander, Admiral Pascual Cervera, had tried to avoid the American navy by putting into the harbor of **Santiago,** a city on the southern coast of Cuba. In late May an American squadron discovered his fleet there and blockaded the entrance to the harbor. It was then safe for the army transports to set out.

In mid-June 17,000 men boarded ship in Tampa. There was incredible confusion. Many lost contact with their units. Fearful of being left behind, dozens simply climbed aboard whatever ship they could find. At last the expedition managed to set sail.

Courtesy of the Library of Congress

Colonel Roosevelt and some of his Rough Riders posed for this picture atop San Juan Hill shortly after taking the strategic point. Compare and contrast this photograph with the painting on the opposite page.

755

**RETEACHING STRATEGY:
COOPERATIVE LEARNING
Students with Special Needs.**
Organize students into cooperative learning groups. Have students reread the sections titled "Cuba and Spain," "Explosion in Havana," and "War is Declared." Have the more proficients students ask the others the following questions.
1. What started the problems that led to the Spanish-American War? *(Cuban patriots took up arms against Spain and by 1896 controlled most of the Cuban countryside.)*
2. How did the Spanish react to this? *(Spanish officials herded people into concentration camps.)*
3. What were the camps like? *(They were horrible, causing disease, malnutrition, and death.)*
4. How did Americans react to these conditions? *(They were outraged.)*
5. What was the incident which really stirred up anti-Spanish feelings in the U.S.? *(McKinley sent the battleship* Maine *to Cuba to protect American citizens who were caught there in riots. No one is sure what happened, but the* Maine *blew up, killing 266 Americans.)*
6. Why did this incident anger the Americans? *(Many Americans believed that the Spanish had sunk the ship with a mine.)*

PRIMARY SOURCE
Description of change: excerpted.
Rationale: excerpted to focus on Roosevelt's dissatisfaction.

755

HISTORICAL SIDELIGHTS
1 The Spanish-American War lasted only 100 days.

SUGGESTED CAPTION RESPONSES
(Top) El Caney, San Juan Hill
(Bottom) For its strategic military location, which provided U.S. protection of the Panama Canal

RESOURCES
■ You may wish to have students complete Reading 23: "The Rough Riders Charge San Juan Hill (1898)" in Volume II of *Eyewitnesses and Others.*

INDEPENDENT PRACTICE
Have students complete the Preview & Review activity at the beginning of the section.

CLOSURE
Remind students that presidents have often had military backgrounds. Ask them who the popular military leader of the Spanish-American War was who later became president. *(Theodore Roosevelt)* Ask them to name a Civil War hero who had later become president. *(U. S. Grant)*

HOMEWORK: MULTICULTURAL PERSPECTIVES
Have students write an account of the Spanish-American War from the Spanish perspective. They should write as though they are Spanish officials in Cuba, defending the actions taken by their government. Their account should show an understanding and sensitivity toward the Spanish point of view.

PRIMARY SOURCE
Description of change: excerpted and bracketed.
Rationale: excerpted to focus on the description of the battle; bracketed words added to clarify meaning.

LEARNING FROM MAPS. *Most of the Spanish-American War in the Caribbean was fought on Cuba. Where were the important battles?*

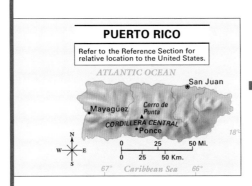

LEARNING FROM MAPS. *Puerto Rico, the only American commonwealth, lies in the Caribbean. Mountains slope from the center to sandy beaches along the sea. Puerto Ricans are American citizens. Why did the United States value control of Puerto Rico in the early 1900s?*

Return to the Preview & Review on page 747.

American strategy called for an attack on Santiago. The army, commanded by General William R. Shafter, landed at Daiquiri, a town to the east of Santiago. Once ashore, it began its advance. The Spanish put up a stiff resistance.

Major battles were fought at **El Caney** and **San Juan Hill.** At El Caney a member of the Second Massachusetts regiment complained:

❝ [The Spaniards] are hidden behind rocks, in weeds and in underbrush, and we just simply can't locate them. They are shooting our men all to pieces. ❞

The Rough Riders and African American soldiers of the Ninth Cavalry took San Juan Hill by storm on July 1. In this battle Colonel Roosevelt seemed to have no care for his own safety. He galloped back and forth along the line, urging his men forward. Luckily, Roosevelt was not hit. Many of his men were not so fortunate. Most were firing bullets charged with black powder. Each time they fired, a puff of black smoke marked their location for Spanish gunners on top of the hill.

After the capture of San Juan Hill the American artillery could be moved within range of Santiago harbor. Admiral Cervera's fleet had to put to sea. When it did, the powerful American fleet swiftly blasted it. Every one of the Spanish vessels was lost. Only one American sailor was killed in this one-sided fight.

On July 16 the Spanish army commander surrendered Santiago. A few days later another American force completed the occupation of the Spanish island of **Puerto Rico,** about 500 miles (800 kilometers) east of Cuba. The Spanish-American War was over.

America's Pacific Heritage

Since ships first sailed or land caravans carried off its treasure, westerners have been fascinated by the East. Marco Polo was bedazzled even though he came from Venice, a western jewel. The art of the Orient is the oldest in the world, but it was hidden behind the walls of Forbidden Cities. Emigrants from Asia were too poor to own eastern treasures such as we see on these pages, but traders like John Ellerton Lodge filled the holds of the *Kremlin* and *Magnet* with china, silk, ivory, even fireworks that bloomed like chrysanthemums to bring Pacific culture to America.

This dragon comes from a Chinese embroidered chair of the 18th century. In Eastern art, dragons seldom breathed fire and were seen as protectors.

Chinese porcelain has long been prized. The export ware above is an Orange platter in the "Fitzhugh" pattern.

Four children in holiday dress were photographed on the teeming streets of San Francisco's Chinatown before the earthquake of 1906.

A gilded bronze Buddha from 10th-century Thailand reminds us that Buddhism has nearly 245 million followers in the East.

"Four black dragons spitting fire" is how Japanese artists described Commodore Perry's ships landing at Yokohama, above.

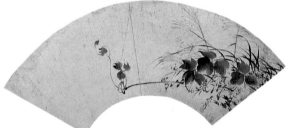

Autumn leaves and grasses were painted c. 1850 for this Japanese fan by Shibata Zeshiu.

A Filipino woman shows her considerable skill at weaving from Manila hemp fibers, right.

758   **AMERICA IN WORLD AFFAIRS, 1865–1912**

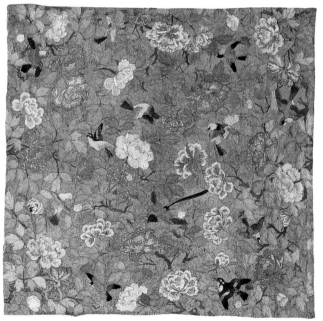

The Metropolitan Museum of Art

Birds and flowers are the subjects of this 18th-century silk embroidery from Korea (right).

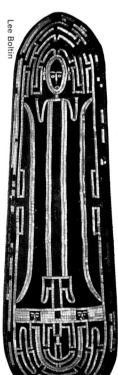

Lee Boltin

Little known before World War II, the Solomon Islands were home to artisans who produced the prized mother-of-pearl inlay for this mid-19th-century ceremonial shield (left).

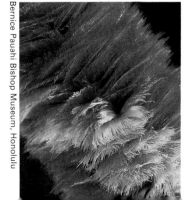

Bernice Pauahi Bishop Museum, Honolulu

Hawaiians have a tradition of creating and wearing leis, garland necklaces usually made of flowers. Leis made from the feathers of birds have adorned the nobility of Hawaii even before the rule of Kamehameha III or his successor.

America's Pacific Heritage 759

Isamu Noguchi, one of the greatest sculptors of the 20th century, was born in Los Angeles but taken to Japan when he was two. He called the sleek sculpture environment at right "California Scenario." It was completed in 1982 and covers 1.6 acres in Costa Mesa, California.

In the shadow of the Capitol is the east building of the National Gallery of Art. I.M. Pei, a Chinese American, designed this streamlined structure. Other works by Pei and his partners include the John F. Kennedy Library in Boston and the glass pyramid that is now part of the Louvre museum in Paris.

HISTORICAL SIDELIGHTS

① In 1917 Puerto Rico became a U.S. territory, which gave its people U.S. citizenship. In 1949 Puerto Ricans elected their own governor, and on July 25, 1952, Puerto Rico became a commonwealth under its own constitution.

4. AMERICA EXPANDS FURTHER

The Treaty of Paris

On July 30 President McKinley sent the Spanish government his peace terms. Spain must leave Cuba. It must give Puerto Rico and an island in the Pacific midway between Hawaii and the Philippines to the United States. American troops would continue to hold the city of Manila until the future of the Philippine Islands could be settled at a peace conference.

These demands were far greater than the original aim of winning independence for Cuba. The excitement of military victory caused McKinley and many other Americans to forget why they had first gone to war.

There was little the Spaniards could do. They accepted McKinley's preliminary terms. Representatives of the two nations then met in Paris in the autumn of 1898. There they framed a formal treaty of peace.

McKinley appointed five American peace commissioners. Three of these were United States senators. The president put the senators on the commission because he expected them to influence their fellow senators. Under the Constitution the treaty would be submitted to the Senate for its approval.

The Spanish commissioners agreed to give up Cuba and to turn Puerto Rico and the island of **Guam** in the Pacific over to the United ① States. The Americans, acting on McKinley's order, also demanded possession of the Philippines. The Spaniards objected strongly. The United States had not conquered the islands, they argued. Even Manila had not been captured until after the preliminary terms of peace had been agreed to. McKinley said this of his decision to annex the Philippines:

> ❝ I walked the floor of the White House night after night until midnight, and I am not ashamed to tell you . . . that I went down on my knees and prayed Almighty God for light and guidance more than one night. And one night late it came to me this way—I don't know what it was, but it came . . . that there was nothing left for us to do but to take them all, and to educate the Filipinos, and uplift them and civilize and Christianize them, and by God's grace do the very best we could by them, as our fellow-men for whom Christ died. And then I went to bed, and went to sleep, and slept soundly. . . .¹ ❞

The Spaniards had to give in. To make it easier for them, the Americans agreed to pay $20 million for the islands. This Treaty of

¹From *In the Days of McKinley* by Margaret Leech

Preview & Review

Use these questions to guide your reading. Answer the questions after completing Section 4.

Understanding Issues, Events, & Ideas. Use the following words to first explain America's expansion and then the opposition to it: Guam, imperialism, anti-imperialist, anarchist, sphere of influence, Open Door Note, Boxer Rebellion, Second Open Door Note.

1. What peace terms did President McKinley demand of the Spanish? Why had he increased his demands?
2. What did the U.S. gain by its victory in the war?
3. How would ruling the Philippines make the United States an imperialist nation? What position did anti-imperialists take on annexing the Philippines?
4. What two principles were stated by the Open Door Notes?

Thinking Critically. 1. Often public sentiment can influence political decisions. The Filipinos and the Boxers opposed American involvement in their countries. Why did America get involved anyway? Do you agree with the American decision? Explain. 2. Imagine that you are William Jennings Bryan in 1901, and you are writing your memoirs. Explain your reasons for supporting the Treaty of Paris of 1898.

SECTION 4

PREVIEW & REVIEW RESPONSES

Understanding Issues, Events, & Ideas.
Explanations should demonstrate an understanding of the terms used.
1. That Spain leave Cuba, give up Puerto Rico and the island of Guam, and that U.S. troops hold the city of Manila until the future of the Philippines could be determined; military victory caused McKinley to forget why the U.S. had first gone to war.
2. Puerto Rico, Guam, and the Philippines
3. It was done without the Filipinos' consent. They opposed it and attempted to defeat the peace treaty in the Senate.
4. Equal trade rights for all in China and a guarantee of China's independence

Thinking Critically.
1. Answers will vary, but students may mention for political and economic reasons. Student opinions will vary.
2. Student explanations should show an understanding of Bryan's position on the treaty.

PRIMARY SOURCE
Description of change: excerpted.
Rationale: excerpted to focus on McKinley's description of how he came to the decision to annex the Philippines.

HISTORICAL SIDELIGHTS

1 Shortly after the Spanish-American War the U.S. acquired Wake Island and American Samoa. Naval bases were built on these Pacific islands.

Paris was signed on December 10, 1898, only eight months after the war was declared.

At relatively little cost in money and lives, the United States had accomplished its objective of freeing Cuba. It had also won itself an empire. No wonder that McKinley's secretary of state, John Hay, called the conflict "a splendid little war." Of course, it was splendid only if one put aside the fact that the United States had defeated a country that was much smaller and poorer than itself. Nor was it splendid for the brave soldiers who died or were injured or for their families.

The Fight Against the Treaty

Many people in the United States opposed the treaty with Spain. They insisted that owning colonies, or **imperialism,** was un-American. Taking Puerto Rico was bad enough, but it was one small island. It might be needed for national defense in case of another war. However, ruling the Philippine Islands without the consent of the Filipinos would make the United States an imperialist nation like Britain, France, Germany, and other European countries that owned colonies in Africa and Asia.

The Filipinos certainly would not consent to American rule. They wanted their independence. After his victory at Manila Bay, Commodore Dewey had returned the exiled leader of the Filipino patriots, Emilio Aguinaldo, on an American warship. Dewey encouraged Aguinaldo to resume his fight against the Spanish. Aguinaldo did so. He assumed that the United States was there to help liberate his country from Spanish rule, just as it had promised to free Cuba.

The **anti-imperialists,** as they were called, included many important Americans. Among the best-known were Andrew Carnegie, the steel manufacturer; Samuel Gompers, the labor leader; Jane Addams, the social worker; and Mark Twain, the author of *Tom Sawyer, Huckleberry Finn,* and many other novels. The anti-imperialists in the Senate were led by George F. Hoar of Massachusetts. Hoar argued:

66 [The United States was] trampling . . . on our own great Charter, which recognizes alike the liberty and the dignity of individual manhood. 99

Brown Brothers

Emilio Aguinaldo was the popular Filipino patriot whom the United States returned from exile to fight the Spanish. Later he opposed the U.S. occupation of his country and fought for Filipino freedom.

Many anti-imperialists were not opposed to expansion. Senator Hoar, for example, voted for the annexation of Hawaii, which was finally approved during the Spanish-American War. Andrew Carnegie always favored adding Canada to the United States. But they all believed that it was morally wrong to annex the Filipinos without their consent.

PRIMARY SOURCE
Description of change: excerpted and bracketed.
Rationale: excerpted to focus on Hoar's anti-imperialism; bracketed words added to clarify meaning.

RESOURCES
■ You may wish to have students complete Reading 13: "Clergyman and Critics: A Debate over Imperialism (1885-1899)" in Volume II of *Eyewitnesses and Others.*

Few issues have erupted into such a national debate as the fate ■ of the Philippines. The issue bitterly divided the American people. Like slavery, most of the arguments, pro and con, centered on right and wrong. Still, the success of the United States in the Spanish-American War led some Americans to dream of a colonial empire. One enthusiastic supporter stated his position in a Senate campaign speech in 1898. Note how close his argument is to that of Josiah Strong on pages 738–39.

❝ It is a noble land God has given us—a land that can feed and clothe the world; a land set like a guard between the two oceans of the globe. It is a mighty people that God has planted on this soil. It is a people descended from the most masterful blood of history and constantly strengthened by the strong working folk of all the earth. It is a people imperial by virtue of their power, by right of their institutions, by authority of their heaven-directed purposes. . . .

Shall the American people continue their restless march toward the commercial supremacy of the world? Shall free institutions extend their blessed reign until the empire of our principles is established over the hearts of all humanity?

We have no mission to perform, no duty to discharge to our fellow humans? Has the Almighty Father given us gifts and marked us with His favor, only to rot in our own selfishness? . . .

We cannot escape our world duties. We must carry out the purpose of a fate that has driven us to be greater than our small intentions. We cannot retreat from any soil where Providence has placed our flag. It is up to us to save that soil for liberty and civilization. For liberty and civilization and God's purpose fulfilled, the flag must from now on be the symbol of all mankind.[1] ❞

In 1899 Rudyard Kipling, a British writer, penned a poem called "The White Man's Burden." On quick reading, the poem seems to state the expansionist attitude well. It immediately became a popular defense of American expansion. But Kipling meant the poem to be a satire and is actually critical of America's determination to civilize childlike and untamed captive people. Can you see the satire in this first stanza of Kipling's seven-stanza poem?

> ❝ Take up the White Man's burden—
> Send forth the best ye breed—
> Go bind your sons to exile
> To serve your captives' need;

[1]From *Modern Eloquence*, vol. 10, by Albert J. Beveridge, edited by Ashley H. Thorndike

---

Point of View

To the American peace commissioners looking into freedom for Filipinos, one prominent American wrote.

> ❝ You seem to have about finished your work of civilizing the Filipinos. About 8,000 of them have been civilized and sent to Heaven. I hope you like it. ❞
> Andrew Carnegie, 1899

FOCUS/MOTIVATION: MAKING CONNECTIONS Prior Knowledge.
To reinforce the geographic theme of *location,* have students locate the Philippines on a classroom map. Ask them if they know why the Philippines has been in the news in recent years. *(The government of the dictator Ferdinand Marcos was overthrown and replaced by a democratically elected government under Corazon Aquino. Also the military has made repeated attempts to overthrow the civilian government.)* Ask if they know what connections the U.S. presently has to the Philippines. *(The U.S. maintains military bases there.)* Point out that the U.S. ties to the Philippines began with the Spanish-American War.

PRIMARY SOURCE
Description of change: excerpted.
Rationale: excerpted to focus on a supporter's view that America ought to have a colonial empire.
(Point of View) Description of change: excerpted.
Rationale: excerpted to focus on Carnegie's satirical remark about civilizing the Filipinos.

Divide the class into two groups. They are all U.S. senators, with one group representing those opposed to annexing the Philippines and the other group in favor of annexing the Philippines. Each group is to meet and come up with a statement defending its side's stand on the issue. Have each group choose a spokesperson to present their side's argument to the class. Then take a vote on whether to ratify the treaty.

PRIMARY SOURCES

(Top) Description of change: excerpted.
Rationale: excerpted to focus on the satire in Kipling's poem, "The White Man's Burden."
(Bottom) Description of change: excerpted and bracketed.
Rationale: excerpted to focus on Carl Schurz's anti-imperialist views; bracketed words added to clarify meaning.

> To wait in heavy harness,
>   On fluttered folk and wild—
> Your new-caught sullen peoples,
>   Half-devil and half-child.[1] 99

The anti-imperialists even started a national organization, the American Anti-Imperialist League in 1899. Carl Schurz, a former senator from Missouri and secretary of the interior in President Hayes' cabinet, was its spokesman. Schurz stated the league's view:

66 We hold that the policy known as imperialism is hostile to liberty and tends toward militarism, an evil from which it has been our glory to be free. We regret that it has become necessary in the land of Washington and Lincoln to reaffirm that all men, of whatever race or color, are entitled to life, liberty, and the pursuit of happiness. We maintain that governments derive their just powers from the consent of the governed. We insist that the subjugation of any people is 'criminal aggression' and open disloyalty to the distinctive principles of our government. . . .

We earnestly condemn the policy of the present national administration [McKinley's presidency] in the Philippines. It seeks to extinguish the spirit of 1776 in those islands. We deplore [hate] the sacrifice of our soldiers and sailors, whose bravery deserves admiration even in an unjust war. We denounce the slaughter of Filipinos as a needless horror. . . .

We hold with Abraham Lincoln, that 'no man is good enough to govern another man without the other's consent. When the white man governs himself, that is self-government, but when he governs himself and also governs another man, that is more than self-government—that is despotism [rule by an absolute authority].' 'Our reliance is in the love of liberty which God has planted in us. Our defense is in the spirit which prizes liberty as the heritage of all men in all lands. Those who deny freedom to others deserve it not for themselves, and under a just God cannot long retain it.'[2] 99

Albert J. Beveridge, now a senator, led the imperialists in Congress. He responded to the Anti-Imperialist League statement:

66 The opposition tells us that we ought not to govern a people without their consent. I answer, the rule of liberty that all just government derives its authority from the consent of the governed, applies only to those who are capable of self-

[1] From "The White Man's Burden" by Rudyard Kipling
[2] From "The Policy of Imperialism" by Carl Schurz in *A History of the American People*, vol. 2, by Stephan Thernstrom

SUGGESTED CAPTION RESPONSE
American flag, Liberty Bell, Statue of Liberty, American shield, American eagle

The Granger Collection, New York

Smithsonian Institution

government. We govern the Indians without their consent; we govern our Territories without their consent; we govern our children without their consent. I answer, would not the natives of the Philippines prefer the just, humane, civilizing government of the Republic to the savage, bloody rule of pillage [ruthless plunder] and extortion [forcible theft] from which we have rescued them? Do not the blazing fires of joy and the ringing bells of gladness in Puerto Rico prove the welcome of our flag? And . . . do we owe no duty to the world? Shall we turn these peoples back to the reeking hands from which we have taken them? . . .[1]"

Campaign posters for the 1900 presidential election show the Republican "ticket" of McKinley and Roosevelt on the left and William Jennings Bryan, the Democratic nominee, above. Which patriotic symbols can you find in these posters?

The anti-imperialists needed the votes of only one more than one third of the Senate to defeat the treaty. They seemed likely to succeed. Many Democratic senators would vote against the treaty to embarrass President McKinley and the Republican party.

But the McKinley administration received unexpected help from William Jennings Bryan. Although Bryan was against taking the Philippines, he believed that the Senate should consent to the treaty in order to bring an official end to the war.

Bryan planned to run for president again in 1900. He would make imperialism an issue in the campaign. He was convinced that a majority of the people were opposed to annexing the Philippines. After winning the election, he intended to grant the Filipinos their independence.

Bryan persuaded enough Democratic senators to vote for the

[1]From "The March of the Flag" by Albert J. Beveridge in *A History of the American People*, vol. 2, by Stephan Thernstrom

To reinforce the geographic themes of *location* and *movement,* refer students to a classroom map of China about 1900. Point out to students the location of the various ports that were under the sphere of influence of different Western countries. (for example: Hong Kong — British; Zhanjiang — French; Macao — Portuguese) Have students suggest reasons why the Chinese nationalists wanted to throw all foreigners out of China. *(The Chinese feared that the Western nations would not be satisfied to stay within their spheres of influence. They rightly suspected that these nations would continue to encroach on Chinese territory and trade.)* Ask students if they agree with the position taken by the Boxers. *(Student opinions will vary, but students who agree with the Boxers may mention that the Western nations had no right to impose their will on another nation. Students who disagree may mention that by closing their doors to Western influence, China was closing itself off from social, economic, and political growth.)*

PRIMARY SOURCE
Description of change: excerpted and bracketed.
Rationale: excerpted to focus on Lodge's summary of the Senate's debate over the treaty with Spain; bracketed words added to clarify meaning.

treaty to get it through. The vote was 57 to 27, only one vote more than the two thirds necessary. Senator Henry Cabot Lodge of Massachusetts, a leading supporter of the treaty, described the Senate debate this way:

> 66 [It was] the closest, most bitter, and most exciting struggle I have ever known. 99

Fighting in the Philippines

William Jennings Bryan's strategy backfired. He was nominated again for president in 1900, and he did make the Philippines a prominent issue in the campaign. But McKinley, running for reelection, defeated him easily. The electoral vote was 292 to 155.

The Republican ticket had been strengthened by the nomination of the popular Rough Rider Theodore Roosevelt for vice president. After returning from Cuba in triumph, Roosevelt had been elected governor of New York. He had intended to run for reelection as

By wagon these U.S. soldiers move to Malabon in the Philippines. This photograph shows how ammunition was carried to the front during the Filipino uprising of 1898.

Courtesy of the Library of Congress

① The U.S. established a colonial government in the Philippines until 1916 when the Filipinos first began electing their own legislators. The Philippines became a commonwealth with its own elected president in 1935. It also adopted a constitution based on that of the U.S. On July 4, 1946, the Philippines was given its independence.

SUGGESTED CAPTION RESPONSE
9,750 miles (15,600 km); 6,640 miles (10,624 km); it would have been difficult to be well-informed about local issues or to defend these territories in 1903.

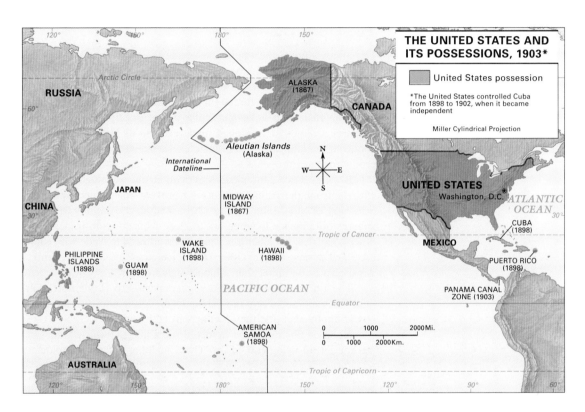

THE UNITED STATES AND ITS POSSESSIONS, 1903*

United States possession

*The United States controlled Cuba from 1898 to 1902, when it became independent

Miller Cylindrical Projection

CHECKING UNDERSTANDING
Have students summarize the terms of the Treaty of Paris and discuss the results in the Philippines. *(Cuba was given its independence from Spain; the islands of Puerto Rico and Guam were given to the United States; the Philippines was also turned over to the United States after it agreed to pay $20 million to Spain. Taking possession of the Philippines stirred up a great debate in the United States. Many Americans opposed taking the Philippines against the will of the Filipino people. After a long and bitter struggle in the Senate, the treaty was narrowly approved. Even before the treaty was approved, however, a revolution against American rule broke out in the Philippines. It took four years before this violent revolution was put down.)*

governor in 1900. However, in November 1899 McKinley's vice president, Garret A. Hobart, had died. Roosevelt was persuaded to accept the Republican vice presidential nomination.

Then, less than a year after the election, President McKinley was shot and killed by an anarchist named Leon Czolgosz. An **anarchist** is one who believes that all government should be done away with. Theodore Roosevelt had been a mere assistant secretary of the navy two and one-half years earlier. Now he was president of the United States! This was the third time in the young nation's history that an assassin's bullet thrust the vice president to the seat of power in the White House.

There was still another unforeseen result of the Treaty of Paris. Even before the Senate voted for the treaty, the Filipino leader Emilio Aguinaldo had organized a revolution against American rule. Bloody jungle fighting broke out.

Peace was not restored until 1902. By that time more than 4,000 Americans and tens of thousands of Filipinos had been killed, a great many more wounded. ①

The United States continued to have great influence in many regions. Often it acted in ways that the local people resented. But opposition to imperialism was growing. Most Americans quickly lost their taste for owning colonies in distant parts of the world.

LEARNING FROM MAPS. *This map shows the extent of United States territory in 1903. How far is it from Washington, D.C., to the Philippines? To American Samoa? How could this distance create problems?*

HISTORICAL SIDELIGHTS

① Unlike many of the nations in the West, China had not industrialized in the 1800s. At the time of the Open Door Notes, China was an undeveloped nation ruled by a weak government and defended by a weak army.

RETEACHING STRATEGY: COOPERATIVE LEARNING
Students with Special Needs.
Organize the class into cooperative learning groups. Have students reread the sections titled "The Treaty of Paris" and "The Fight Against the Treaty." Have the more proficient students ask the others the following questions:

1. What happened to Cuba as a result of the treaty? *(Cuba was given its independence from Spain.)*
2. What territories did the U.S. receive as a result of the treaty? *(the islands of Puerto Rico, Guam, and the Philippines)*
3. How much did the U.S. pay for the Philippines? *($20 million)*
4. How did taking possession of the Philippines stir up great debate in the U.S.? *(America was taking possession of the Philippines against the will of the Filipino people.)*
5. What happened in the Philippines as a result of the U.S. taking possession? *(A revolution against American rule broke out.)*
6. How did the treaty change the status of the U.S.? *(It made the U.S. an imperialist nation.)*

The Open Door Notes

The annexation of the Philippines made the United States a power in the Far East. For many years Great Britain, France, Germany, and other European nations had been seizing **spheres of influence** in
① China. This meant they forced the weak Chinese government to grant them the right to develop particular areas, mostly around Chinese seaports. China's undeveloped resources and its huge population of about 400 million made such spheres seem likely to bring in large profits for the Europeans.

If the practice continued, American businesses might be cut off entirely from the China market. To prevent that from happening, Secretary of State John Hay in 1899 asked all the nations with such spheres of influence to agree not to close their doors to traders from other countries. All businesses should be allowed to trade with China on equal terms. Hay's **Open Door Note** was intended to protect America's trade rather than China's rights.

The European powers sent vague answers to Hay's note. Certainly they did not accept the "Open Door" principle. However, Hay boldly announced that they *had* agreed with him.

None of this exchange involved the Chinese, whose trade and territory were being carved up. Then, members of a secret society

Fogg Art Museum

Tz'u-Hsi was the dowager empress of China who encouraged the Boxer Rebellion. This detail comes from her portrait.

HISTORICAL SIDELIGHTS

1 The Chinese name for this society literally means "righteous harmonious band," which Westerners wrongly translated to "righteous harmonious *fists*" and hence called the society "the Boxers."

Courtesy of the Library of Congress

An international army of Americans, British, French, Germans, Russians, and Japanese storm into Peking to free their diplomats trapped inside by the Boxer Rebellion in China.

INDEPENDENT PRACTICE
Have students complete the Preview & Review activity at the beginning of the section.

CLOSURE
Point out to students that the United States emerged from the Spanish-American War as an imperialist power, controlling territory in the Caribbean and the Pacific, and dictating terms of trade in China to European nations.

HOMEWORK
Have students make a series of drawings or cartoons displaying the theme of imperialism. You may wish to give them the following as ideas for their drawings: Uncle Sam stepping on the Philippines and Puerto Rico; Great Britain, France, and Germany carving up China. Display student drawings around the classroom.

of Chinese nationalists known as the "Righteous, Harmonious Fists," or Boxers, launched an attack on foreigners in Peking, the 1 capital, and in other parts of China.

Armed with swords and spears, the Boxers destroyed foreign property and killed missionaries and business people. Frightened foreigners fled for protection to the buildings which housed their governments' representatives in Peking (Beijing). They remained there for weeks, virtual prisoners cut off from the outside world.

The western nations quickly organized an international army to put down this **Boxer Rebellion** of 1900. A force of 20,000, including 2,500 Americans, was rushed to the area. They rescued the trapped foreign civilians and crushed the Boxers.

Meanwhile, Hay feared that the European powers would use the Boxer Rebellion as an excuse to expand their spheres of influence. He sent off a **Second Open Door Note.** This one stated that the United States opposed any further carving up of China by foreign nations. The Open Door thus included two principles: equal trade rights for all in China and a guarantee of independence for China.

None of the European nations officially accepted these principles. In practice, however, Hay got what he wanted. American business interests were able to trade freely in the spheres and throughout the sprawling Chinese Empire. 🖎

Return to the Preview & Review on page 761.

**PREVIEW & REVIEW
RESPONSES**
**Understanding Issues, Events,
& Ideas.**
Descriptions should demonstrate an understanding of the terms used.
1. The Spanish-American War and the expansion of the U.S. into the Pacific made it obvious that a canal was needed to link the Atlantic and Pacific Oceans.
2. A canal through Panama would be shorter but would have to pass through mountainous country covered by dense jungle. A canal through Nicaragua would pass through more level land and make use of Lake Nicaragua. The total distance was longer, but Nicaragua was closer to the U.S.
3. The rebels had the support of the U.S.
4. Many Americans protested the use of force, so it was easier to win popular support with dollar diplomacy than with gunboat diplomacy.

Thinking Critically.
1. Student articles should show that they researched the life and work of Dr. Walter Reed.
2. Students should mention that they lost their independence to large U.S. owned companies. Students should answer negatively because they no longer have control of the economic aspects of their lives or their future.

Preview & Review

Use these questions to guide your reading. Answer the questions after completing Section 5.
Understanding Issues, Events, & Ideas. Describe American efforts to build the Panama Canal, using the following words: Clayton-Bulwer Treaty, Hay-Pauncefote Treaty, isthmus, canal zone, Republic of Panama, Hay-Bunau-Varilla Treaty, lock, Roosevelt Corollary, dollar diplomacy, gunboat diplomacy.
1. Why did the U.S. feel a canal was needed?
2. What were the arguments for and against building a canal across Panama? Across Nicaragua?
3. Why did Bunau-Varilla's "revolution" in Panama succeed?
4. Why did dollar diplomacy replace gunboat diplomacy?
Thinking Critically. 1. Imagine that you are Dr. Walter Reed, just returned from Cuba. Explain how you wiped out yellow fever in Cuba and the influence of your work on Major Gorgas. 2. If you had been a Cuban tobacco farmer in 1910, how would Taft's dollar diplomacy change your way of life? How would you view this change? Why?

5. ROOSEVELT AND HIS CANAL

The Panama Canal

The United States needed to link the Atlantic and Pacific Oceans. The Spanish-American War and the expansion of the United States into the Pacific made it obvious that a canal across Central America would be extremely valuable.

During the war the new American battleship *Oregon* had to steam 12,000 miles (19,200 kilometers) from the West Coast around South America in order to help destroy Admiral Cervera's fleet at Santiago. It took the *Oregon* 68 days, traveling at top speed. A canal would have reduced the *Oregon*'s voyage to 4,000 miles (6,400 kilometers) or one third the distance.

The United States government was eager to build a canal. The first step was to get rid of the **Clayton-Bulwer Treaty** of 1850 with Great Britain. That agreement stated that any such canal would be controlled by *both* nations.

The treaty had made sense in 1850 when the United States had barely reached the Pacific. It did not make sense in 1900. Therefore, in 1901, Secretary Hay negotiated a new agreement with the British. This **Hay-Pauncefote Treaty** gave the United States the right to build and control a canal by itself. In return the United States promised that all nations would be allowed to use the canal on equal terms.

There were two possible canal routes across Central America. One roughly followed the path the explorer Balboa had taken across the Isthmus of Panama when he discovered the Pacific in 1513. An **isthmus** is a narrow neck of land connecting two landmasses. This route was short, but it passed through mountainous country covered by dense tropical jungles. The other was in the Republic of Nicaragua. There the land was more level, and part of the route could make use of Lake Nicaragua, which was 50 miles (80 kilometers) wide. The total distance was much longer, but Nicaragua was closer to the United States.

A private French company had obtained the right to build a canal across Panama, which was then part of the Republic of Colombia. This company had spent a fortune but made little progress. Thousands of its laborers had died of yellow fever and malaria. The company was now bankrupt. There was no chance that it would ever be able to complete a canal. In an effort to regain some of its losses, the company offered to sell its right to build a canal to the United States for $40 million.

A representative of the bankrupt company, Philippe Bunau-Varilla, worked to persuade Congress to take over the canal project. His campaign succeeded. By 1903 President Roosevelt had made up his mind to build the canal in Panama. Congress went along with this decision.

THE ONE-CENTAVO STAMP

To persuade Congress to choose Panama over Nicaragua for the new canal, Philippe Bunau-Varilla depended heavily on 90 one-centavo stamps. Bunau-Varilla was the representative of the bankrupt French company that had begun the canal.

Bunau-Varilla had mailed out 13,000 copies of a pamphlet, *Panama or Nicaragua?* One of his arguments against a Nicaraguan canal was that there were volcanoes there. No matter that nearly all had long been inactive. He wrote, "What have the Nicaraguans chosen to characterize their country . . . on their postage stamps? Volcanoes!"

The Senate was about to begin debate on the canal site. Far from Washington (and from Nicaragua) rumblings began coming from Mount Pele, a long-dormant volcano on the island of Martinique. On May 8, 1902, the entire mountain exploded,

killing nearly 30,000 people in two minutes. "What an unexpected turn of the wheel of fortune," wrote Bunau-Varilla. He thought again of the Nicaraguan stamp.

Bunau-Varilla went to every stamp dealer in Washington until he had 90 of the one-centavo Nicaraguan stamps. Each one showed a puffing locomotive in the foreground and an erupting volcano in the background. Bunau-Varilla pasted the stamps on sheets of paper. He mailed one to each of the 90 United States senators with the neatly typed caption: "An official witness of the volcanic activity on the isthmus of Nicaragua."

The Panama "Revolution"

Next, Secretary of State Hay and the Colombian representative in Washington negotiated a treaty in which Colombia leased a **canal zone** across Panama to the United States. Colombia was to receive $10 million and a rent of $250,000 a year. The United States Senate promptly consented to this treaty.

But the Colombian senate rejected it. The reason was simple. The Colombians wanted more money. The bankrupt French company was being offered four times as much for its rights in Colombia. And Colombia had granted those rights in the first place.

When Colombia rejected the treaty, Bunau-Varilla organized a revolution in Panama. There had been many such uprisings against Colombia there in the past. All had been easily put down. But this time the rebels had the support of the United States. Their "revolution" therefore succeeded.

The small rebel army was made up of railroad workers and members of the Panama City fire department. But when Colombian troops, sent by sea, landed at the port of Colón, they were met by the powerful U.S.S. *Nashville*. The Colombians were forced to return to their home port.

Thus was born the **Republic of Panama.** Only three days later, on November 6, 1903, the United States government officially recognized Panama. On November 18, in Washington, Secretary Hay signed a canal treaty with a representative of the new nation. This

Point of View

Just how massive a project was the Panama Canal is revealed in this study.

> **"To build the Great Pyramid or the Wall of China or the cathedrals of France, blocks of stone were set one on top of the other in the age-old fashion. But the walls of the Panama locks were poured from overhead, bucket by bucket, into gigantic forms. . . ."**
> From *The Path Between the Seas,*
> David McCullough, 1977

FOCUS/MOTIVATION:
MAKING CONNECTIONS
Prior Knowledge.
Ask students if they know why the country of Panama has recently been in the news. *(U.S. troops were sent to Panama to capture the dictator Manuel Noriega and return him to the U.S. to stand trial on drug charges.)* Ask why they think the U.S. became involved in Panamanian affairs. *(The U.S. controls the Panama Canal, and an unstable or anti-American government in Panama might jeopardize this control.)* Ask: Why is the Panama Canal important to the U.S.? *(It is important because much of U.S. commercial shipping passes through the canal.)* Point out to students that the U.S. and Panama negotiated a treaty in 1977 which will give control of the Panama Canal to Panama by the year 2000.

PRIMARY SOURCE
Description of change: excerpted.
Rationale: excerpted to focus on the massive scope of building the Panama Canal.

Divide the class into three groups. The first group represents officials from Panama attempting to persuade the U.S. government to build the canal across their country. The second group is officials from Nicaragua attempting to persuade the U.S. government to build the canal across their country. The third group is officials from the U.S. The groups are to meet and come up with a list of advantages which their country has to offer. Have a spokesperson from the Panamanian and Nicaraguan groups present their list to the U.S. officials. After hearing both sides, the U.S. officials should decide on where they intend to build the canal. Have them give reasons for their choice.

Death took a holiday (right) in the fever-ridden swamps of Panama when William Gorgas, top, drained the swamps to eliminate yellow fever. Below him is Colonel George Goethals of the Army Engineers who led the canal builders.

representative was none other than Philippe Bunau-Varilla. The **Hay-Bunau-Varilla Treaty** granted the United States a ten-mile-wide Canal Zone (16 kilometers). The financial arrangements were the same ones that Colombia had turned down.

Building the Canal

Before work on the Panama Canal could begin, malaria and yellow fever had to be stamped out. Carlos Juan Finlay, a Cuban doctor trained in Philadelphia, had first suggested that yellow fever was spread by a certain kind of mosquito. The United States sent a delegation headed by Doctor Walter Reed to Cuba to find a way to wipe out the disease. Reed studied Finlay's experiments and agreed with his findings. The United States army under the direction of Major William Gorgas then proceeded to eliminate yellow fever in Cuba. Gorgas was now sent to Panama to rid the area of the mosquitoes which carried the disease. He drained the swamps and ponds where the mosquitoes laid their eggs.

Now the actual construction could begin. Colonel George Goethals of the Army Engineers had charge of the project. The level of the canal had to be raised as high as 85 feet (over 25 meters) above the sea. Water-filled chambers called **locks** would raise and lower ships from one level to another.

● For ten years, from 1904 to 1914, a small army of workers drilled and blasted, dug and dredged. They had to cut a 9-mile-long channel (over 14 kilometers) through mountains of solid rock. In this

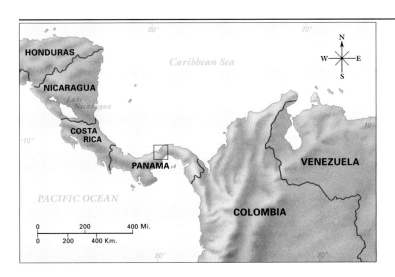

PANAMA AND THE CANAL ZONE

RELATING HISTORY TO GEOGRAPHY
To reinforce the geographic themes of *location* and *regions*, have students do research at their school or local library on the country of Panama. Ask them to trace a map, drawing in physical features such as elevation, and labeling the cities and important bodies of water bordering the country. They should also write a report on the cultural features of Panama such as language and economic and political systems.

excerpt a writer captured the problems of cutting through a particularly stubborn spot near the middle of the canal.

> Culebra Cut! Here the barrier of the continental divide resisted to the utmost the attacks of the canal army; here disturbed and outraged Nature conspired with gross mountain mass to make the defense stronger and stronger; here the mountain must be moved. . . .
>
> Grim, now, but still confident, the attackers fought on. The mountain was defeated.
>
> Now stretches a man-made canyon across the backbone of the continent; now lies a channel for ships through the barrier; now is found what Columbus sought in vain—the gate through the West to the East. Men call it the Culebra Cut.
>
> Nine miles long, it has an average depth of 120 feet (37 meters). At places its sides tower nearly 500 feet (152 meters) above the channel bottom, which is nowhere narrower than 300 feet (91 meters).
>
> It is the greatest single trophy of the triumph of man over the terrestrial arrangement of the world. . . . It is majestic. It is awful. It is the Canal. . . .
>
> No one had the remotest idea of the actual difficulties that would beset the canal builders; no one dreamed of the avalanches of material that would slide into the cut. . . . No less than 26 slides and breaks were encountered in the construction of the Culebra cut.
>
> To remove the 105,000,000 cubic yards of earth from the backbone of America required about 6,000,000 pounds of high-grade dynamite each year to break up the material, so

LEARNING FROM MAPS. *Completion of the Panama Canal meant a new route to the West Coast. How had ships traveled before the canal? American control of the canal also involved the United States more deeply in Latin American affairs. What are the advantages for the United States of that involvement? What are the disadvantages?*

Roosevelt and His Canal   773

USING HISTORICAL IMAGINATION
Ask students to imagine that
the United States chose Nicaragua as the place to build the
canal. Have them research
U.S.-Nicaraguan relations from
1979 to the present. Tell them
to use historical imagination
and write a report describing
the situation with the "Nicaraguan Canal" today. Their report should include an account
of who presently controls the
canal, what the U.S. has done
as an alternative if they are not
in control of the canal, and
what effect this has had on
both countries politically and
economically.

Culver Pictures

*The Cut of Las Cascadas, shown
above, and the Gaillard Cut were two
of the engineering wonders that made
it possible to complete the Panama
Canal in just ten years. Do you think
such a project could be completed so
quickly today? Why or why not?*

that it might be successfully attacked by the steam shovel.
. . . So carefully was the dynamite handled that during a
period of three years, in which time some 19,000,000 pounds
were exploded in Culebra Cut, only eight men were
killed. . . .

Today Culebra Mountain bows its lofty head to the genius
of the American engineer and to the courage of the canal
army. . . . Through it now extends a ribbon of water broad
enough to permit the largest vessels afloat to pass one another under their own power and deep enough to carry a
ship with a draft [depth in the water] beyond anything in
the minds of naval constructors today. . . . It is the might-
iest deed the hand of man has done.[1] "

The channel was named the Gaillard Cut after Colonel David Gaillard, the engineer in charge of this part of the project.

The canal was finally finished in 1914. It was a truly magnificent

[1] From "The Culebra Cut" by Frederic Haskin

PRIMARY SOURCE
Description of change: excerpted and bracketed.
Rationale: excerpted to focus
on the writer's description of
the difficulties of the task and
the sense of accomplishment
in building the Panama Canal;
bracketed words added to clarify meaning.

STRATEGIES FOR SUCCESS

INTERPRETING EDITORIAL CARTOONS
Editorial cartoons are drawings that present points of view on particular issues. They are usually found in the editorial sections of newspapers and magazines and have been used throughout history to influence public opinion. Although some cartoons present a positive point of view, most are critical of a policy, situation, or person.

The two most important techniques cartoonists use to express their message are caricature and symbolism. A caricature is a drawing that exaggerates physical features. Symbolism is the use of one thing to represent another idea, feeling, or object. Common symbols for the United States, for example, are the bald eagle and Uncle Sam. Cartoons also use titles, labels, and captions to get their message across.

How to Interpret Editorial Cartoons
To interpret editorial cartoons, follow these steps.
1. **Identify the caricatures.** Note the people or objects being characterized and note what is exaggerated.
2. **Identify the symbols.** Determine the meaning of each of the symbols used.
3. **Read the title, labels, and caption.** Check the title, labels, and caption to help you understand the artist's message.
4. **Analyze the information.** Decide if the cartoonist's point of view is positive or negative. Determine what events or situation led to the cartoon.

Applying the Strategy
President Theodore Roosevelt was a favorite of editorial cartoonists. Study the cartoon of him at the top of the next column. Does the cartoonist use caricature? If so, what features are exaggerated? Is there symbolism? If so what symbols are used and what do they stand for? Does the cartoonist present a positive or negative point of view? How can you tell? In your own words, state the cartoonist's message. Now answer the same questions for the cartoon at the lower right.

For independent practice, see Practicing the Strategy on page 778.

NO MOLLY-CODDLING HERE

Both, The Granger Collection, New York

HISTORICAL SIDELIGHTS

① Roosevelt often used the saying, "Speak softly, and carry a big stick; you will go far." It appeared that Roosevelt was applying this statement when he sent U.S. marines into the Dominican Republic.

macy, dollar diplomacy required a more indirect method. The U.S. would invest money in Latin American countries, hoping that their governments and economies would stabilize. The end result of both policies was the same. They disrupted the lives of the people, resulting in very bitter anti-American feelings.)

RETEACHING STRATEGY: Students with Special Needs.

Pair students who are having difficulty with students who are performing well. Have students reread the section titled "The Roosevelt Corollary," and have the more proficient students ask the others the following questions:

1. What did the Roosevelt Corollary say? *(It extended the Monroe Doctrine and said that the U.S. would make Western Hemisphere nations pay their debts.)*
2. What is an example of the Roosevelt Corollary being enforced? *(In 1905 the U.S. sent marines into the Dominican Republic.)*
3. What was the name given to this method of handling Latin American countries? *(This became known as gunboat diplomacy.)*
4. Why did Taft change this approach? *(Many Americans were not in favor of this heavy-handed approach to dealing with the nations of Latin America.)*
5. What was Taft's method of diplomacy called? *(dollar diplomacy)*
6. How were gunboat diplomacy and dollar diplomacy alike? *(The purpose of both was for the U.S. to control the nations of Latin America.)*

(Continued)

achievement. President Roosevelt took full credit for the project and for its swift completion:

> ❝ I am interested in the Panama Canal because I started it. If I had followed traditional conservative methods . . . debate would have been going on yet. But I took the Canal Zone and let Congress debate, and while the debate goes on the canal does also. ❞

Roosevelt blamed Colombia for the revolution in Panama. He once told a friend that trying to make a deal with that country was like trying to nail jelly to a wall. Yet many Americans at that time and many more in later years felt that Roosevelt's behavior had been entirely wrong. In 1921, after Roosevelt was dead, Congress gave Colombia $25 million to make up for the loss of Panama. And in 1978 a new treaty provided that at the end of this century the Canal Zone itself would be turned back to Panama.

White House Historical Association

This portrait of Theodore Roosevelt was painted by John Singer Sargent. Portraits of all former presidents and first ladies hang in the White House and are worth a tour of the president's house. Your representative in Congress can get you tickets in advance.

The Roosevelt Corollary

President Roosevelt was eager to prevent any European country from interfering in the affairs of the small nations of the Caribbean. These countries were all poor, and most of them were badly governed. Their governments frequently borrowed money from European banks and investors and did not repay them when the loans fell due. Sometimes, European governments sent in warships and marines to force them to pay their debts.

Before he became president, Roosevelt did not object. "If any South American state misbehaves toward any European country," he wrote, "let the European country spank it." After Roosevelt became president, he had second thoughts. Any European interference in the affairs of Latin American nations violated the Monroe Doctrine, he decided.

Debts, however, must be paid. If a nation in the Western Hemisphere did not pay its debts, the United States must make it do so. That way justice could be done to the lenders, but there would be no European interference in the hemisphere. This policy became known as the **Roosevelt Corollary** to the Monroe Doctrine. *Corollary* means "what naturally follows from."

① Roosevelt always said that he applied the Corollary with the greatest reluctance. When he sent marines into the Dominican Republic in 1905, he insisted that he had no more desire to make that nation a colony of the United States than a snake would have to swallow a porcupine backwards. Many Americans always protested the use of force in such situations.

After William Howard Taft became president in 1909, it seemed shrewder to try to control the nations of the region indirectly. By

The Granger Collection, New York

The American eagle stretches all the way to the Philippines in this 1904 cartoon by Joseph Keppler. He called it "His 126th Birthday—'Gee, But this Is an Awful Stretch.'" Do you agree, particularly when you use historical imagination to put yourself back to the beginning of this century?

investing money in countries like Cuba, Nicaragua, and the Dominican Republic, more stable economies would result. Then the governments of these countries would also be more stable. This policy came to be known as **dollar diplomacy** to distinguish it from the **gunboat diplomacy** of the Roosevelt Corollary.

The difficulty with dollar diplomacy was that, without meaning to, it often injured the people of the countries involved. An American company might purchase a number of small tobacco farms in Cuba. Then it might convert the land into a vast sugar plantation. The plantation would be more efficient. Its crops could be sold for larger amounts of money. But the Cubans who had been independent tobacco farmers now became hired plantation laborers. They were forced to change their entire way of life.

At this time people were just beginning to realize how heavy-handed the United States had become in the Western Hemisphere. Most people still assumed that the Latin American nations shared the values of the United States. Later they would understand that they were seriously mistaken. ⬛

■ Return to the Preview & Review on page 770.

Roosevelt and His Canal 777

Thinking Critically
1. Answers will vary, but should demonstrate an understanding of the economic situation in the U.S. in the 1890s.
2. Answers will vary, but students should support their answers with sound reasoning and judgement.

3. Student views should be based on an understanding of Roosevelt's foreign policy.

REVIEW RESPONSES

Chapter Summary
Paragraphs will vary but should be evaluated on the logic of student arguments.

Reviewing Chronological Order
3, 5, 2, 1, 4

Understanding Main Ideas
1. Great Britain and France had sympathized with the Confederate government. The British even considered for a time entering the war on the side of the Confederacy.
2. To bring together all the countries of the Western Hemisphere so they could see themselves as a group; a civil war broke out in Chile and the U.S. supported the losing side, causing anti-American feeling there.
3. Equal trade rights in China and a guarantee of China's independence
4. First, the U.S. sent Major William Gorgas to Panama to rid that country of malaria. Next, a small army of workers drilled, blasted, dug, and dredged a 9-mile long channel through the mountains. The U.S. gained control of the canal zone in a treaty with the Republic of Panama, which won its independence in a U.S.-backed revolution.
5. A statement which said that the U.S. would step in if a nation of the Western Hemisphere did not pay its debts and that there would be no European interference; he wanted the U.S. to be the protector of the Western Hemisphere.

CHAPTER 21 REVIEW

1865		1875 THE AGE OF AMERICAN EXPANSION 1885

1867
U.S. occupies the Midway Islands

Alaskan Purchase

1875
U.S. and Hawaii sign sugar treaty

Chapter Summary
Read the statements below. Choose one, and write a paragraph explaining its importance.
1. Manifest destiny led many Americans to look beyond the nation's borders, especially across the Pacific and into the Caribbean.
2. Spanish rule in Cuba had become increasingly harsh. When the fight for Cuban independence finally erupted, the United States backed the rebels, leading to the Spanish-American War.
3. Spanish and American forces fought in the Philippines and in the Caribbean.
4. As a result of the U.S. victory in the Spanish-American War, the country gained Puerto Rico, Guam, and the Philippines.
5. Despite strong anti-imperialist opposition, the U.S. continued to expand. The Open Door Notes secured American trading rights in China and the Panama "Revolution" cleared the way for the American-controlled Panama Canal.
6. The Roosevelt Corollary to the Monroe Doctrine further warned against foreign interference in the Western Hemisphere. Dollar diplomacy soon replaced the gunboat diplomacy of the Corollary as America sought to help its neighbors pay their foreign debts.

Reviewing Chronological Order
Number your paper 1–5. Then study the time line above and place the following events in the order in which they happened by writing the first next to 1, the second next to 2, and so on.
1. Open Door Notes
2. U.S.S. *Maine* explodes
3. Alaskan Purchase
4. Panama Canal completed
5. Chilean Crisis erupts

Understanding Main Ideas
1. What events during the Civil War caused Americans to be suspicious of Europe?
2. What was the purpose of the Pan-American Conference? How was its goodwill set back by the Chilean Crisis?

3. What did John Hay call for in the Open Door Notes?
4. Explain the steps the U.S. took to build and control the Panama Canal?
5. What was the Roosevelt Corollary? Why did the president issue this policy?

Thinking Critically
1. **Synthesizing.** Suppose you are an American farmer or business owner in the 1890s. Would you have favored an American policy of isolation or expansion? Why?
2. **Evaluating.** Was the United States justified in going to war against Spain in 1898? Explain your reasoning. Would the same circumstances cause the United States to go to war today? Why or why not?
3. **Analyzing.** Some people criticized Theodore Roosevelt for extending American influence and for his aggressive foreign policy. State and support your view of his actions.

Writing About History
Imagine you are in Alaska in 1890, Manila Bay with Dewey, San Juan Hill with Roosevelt, or in Panama during the building of the Panama Canal. Use your historical imagination to write a letter describing what is happening. Use the information in Chapter 21 to help you develop your letter.

Practicing the Strategy
Review the strategy on page 775.
Interpreting Editorial Cartoons. Study the cartoon at the bottom of page 797 and answer the following questions.
1. What symbols are used by the cartoonist? What caricatures?
2. Why do you think the cartoonist chose those symbols? Why did the cartoonist caricature those particular features?
3. What is the message of the cartoon?

1889
Pan-American Conference

1890
McKinley Tariff

1891
Chilean Crisis erupts

1893
American revolt in Hawaii

1894
Republic of Hawaii declared

1895
Cuban Revolution begins

★

Venezuela Boundary Dispute

1898
U.S.S. *Maine* explodes in Havana

★

U.S. declares war on Spain

★

Treaty of Paris ends war

1899
Open Door Notes

1900
Boxer Rebellion

★

McKinley reelected president

1901
McKinley assassinated

★

Roosevelt becomes president

★

Fighting in the Philippines

1903
Republic of Panama

1904
Roosevelt Corollary proclaimed

★

Building of Panama Canal begins

1909
Dollar diplomacy begins

★

Taft becomes president

1914
Panama Canal completed

Using Primary Sources

One of the most eloquent voices raised in opposition to American expansion was that of Queen Liliuokalani of Hawaii. Read the following excerpt from *Hawaii's History By Hawaii's Queen* to understand her argument. Then answer the questions below.

Perhaps there is a kind of right, depending on the precedents of all ages, and known as the "Right of Conquest," under which robbers and marauders may establish themselves in possession of whatsoever they are strong enough to ravish for their fellows. I will not pretend to decide how far civilization and Christian enlightenment have outlawed it. But we have known for many years that our Island monarchy has relied upon the protection always extended to us by the policy and the assured friendship of the great American republic.

Oh, honest Americans, . . . hear me for my downtrodden people! Their form of government is as dear to them as yours is precious to you. Quite as warmly as you love your country, so they love theirs. With all your goodly possessions, covering territory so immense that there yet remain parts unexplored . . . do not covet the little vineyard of Naboth's [Hawaii], so far from your shores.

1. According to Queen Liliuokalani, what is the "Right of Conquest"? Do you think a country should be allowed to take what it is strong enough to control? Why or why not?
2. In the second paragraph of the excerpt, the Hawaiian queen appeals directly to "honest Americans." What argument does she use? Do you agree or disagree with her? Why?

Linking History & Geography

Building the Panama Canal was a great engineering feat. Panama is a land of rugged mountains and dense jungles. To help understand the difficulty of building the canal and how the canal works, make a model of the Isthmus of Panama, using clay or plaster of paris. Show the route of the Panama Canal and label the locks. Use the model to explain the stages by which a ship passes through the canal.

Enriching Your Study of History

1. **Individual Project**. Choose one of the nations of Latin America and present a short report in class on its historical and present-day relationships with the U.S. Choose from among these countries:

Argentina	Guatemala
Bolivia	Haiti
Brazil	Honduras
Chile	Mexico
Colombia	Nicaragua
Costa Rica	Panama
Cuba	Paraguay
Dominican Republic	Peru
Ecuador	Uruguay
El Salvador	Venezuela

2. **Cooperative Project**. Less than 20 years after the Spanish-American War the American flag flew over many new lands. To illustrate the extent of the expansion, different groups in your class will research the following information: the lands that came into U.S. possession between 1865 and 1918, how America gained control of these lands, and the present political status of each. Then your class will create a three-column chart illustrating this information.

Chapter 21 Review   779

779

Reformers and the Progressive Movement

PLANNING THE CHAPTER

TEXTBOOK	RESOURCES
1. The Progressive Idea	***Unit 7 Worksheets and Tests:*** Chapter 22 Graphic Organizer, Directed Reading 22:1, Reteaching 22:1 ***Art in American History:*** Transparency 20: Thompson and Bleeker Streets
2. Reformers	***Unit 7 Worksheets and Tests:*** Directed Reading 22:2, Reteaching 22:2, Geography 22A ***Creative Strategies for Teaching American History:*** Pages 315, 321, 325 ***Eyewitnesses and Others, Volume 2:*** Reading 25: New York in the Golden Nineties (1890), Reading 30: Jack London Reports on the San Francisco Earthquake (1906), Reading 14: Susan B. Anthony and Senator Joseph Brown Debate a Woman's Suffrage Amendment (1884, 1887), Reading 26: Carry Nation Attacks "Dens of Vice" (1900)
3. Government Versus Big Business	***Unit 7 Worksheets and Tests:*** Directed Reading 22:3, Reteaching 22:3, Geography 22B ***Eyewitnesses and Others, Volume 2:*** Reading 28: Lincoln Steffens Tells How Theodore Roosevelt Began the Square Deal (1901)
4. A Progressive Victory	***Unit 7 Worksheets and Tests:*** Directed Reading 22:4, Reteaching 22:4
5. Limits of Progressivism	***Unit 7 Worksheets and Tests:*** Directed Reading 22:5, Reteaching 22:5 ***Creative Strategies for Teaching American History:*** Page 307
Chapter Review	***Audio Program:*** Chapter 22 ***Unit 7 Worksheets and Tests:*** Chapter 22 Tests, Forms A and B (See also *Alternative Assessment Forms*) ***Test Generator***
Unit Review	***Unit 7 Worksheets and Tests:*** Unit 7 Tests, Forms A and B (See also *Alternative Assessment Forms*); Unit 7 Synthesis ***Test Generator***

STRATEGIES FOR STUDENTS WITH SPECIAL NEEDS

Gifted Students.

Have interested students prepare reports on either the Supreme Court Case of *Muller v. Oregon* or the Northern Securities Case. Reports should include a detailed profile of the people and issues involved in the case and conclude with the students' evaluation of the Supreme Court's ruling in the case based on its long-range social and economic effects.

Students Having Difficulty with the Chapter.

You may wish to have students listen to Chapter 22 in *The Story of America Audio Program.* So that students may get an idea of what a political party is really like, organize the class into three cooperative learning groups. Tell students to imagine that it is 1912, and the presidential election is about to take place. The first group supports Theodore Roosevelt for president, the second group supports William Howard Taft for president, and the third group supports Woodrow Wilson for president. Each group is to prepare a campaign rally for their candidate. The campaign should include posters, campaign buttons, campaign slogans, campaign songs, and a short speech given by the candidate. Each group should hold a campaign rally in which a member of their group acts as the candidate and gives the prepared speech to the class. In an effort to raise support for their candidate, the remaining members of the group may wave their posters, wear their buttons, and chant the slogans and songs before and after their candidate speaks.

BOOKS FOR TEACHERS

J. W. Chambers, *The Tyranny of Change: America in the Progressive Era, 1900–1917.* New York: St. Martin's Press, 1980.

R. L. McCormick, *From Realignment to Reform.* Ithaca: Cornell University Press, 1981.

D. McCullough, *Mornings on Horseback.* New York: Touchstone Books, 1982.

T. K. McCraw, *Prophets of Regulation.* Cambridge: Harvard University Press, 1984.

James T. Patterson, *America's Struggle Against Poverty.* Cambridge: Harvard University Press, 1981.

Robert H. Wiebe, *The Search for Order, 1880–1920.* New York: Hill and Wang, 1967.

BOOKS FOR STUDENTS

Eden Force Eskin, *Theodore Roosevelt.* New York: Watts, 1987.

Trudy Hanmer, *The Growth of Cities.* New York: Watts, 1985.

William Loren Katz and Jacqueline Hunt Katz, *Making Our Way: America at the Turn of the Century in the Words of the Poor and Powerless.* New York: Dial, 1978.

MULTIMEDIA MATERIALS

The Age of Theodore Roosevelt (filmstrip), GA. Shows American life at the turn of the century, focuses on Roosevelt's foreign policy, and examines Roosevelt, the man.

The American Woman: A Social Chronicle (filmstrip), Educational Enrichment. Explores the roles women have played in American history and some of the problems they have faced in trying to achieve economic, social, and political equality.

The Indomitable Teddy Roosevelt (videocassette, 94 min.). Portrays life of Roosevelt.

Innocent Years, Part 1 (film, 28. min.). McGraw-Hill. Discusses the years 1908–1914 and the topics of prosperity, woman suffrage, and aspects of the Taft and Wilson administrations.

The Progressives (film, 25 min.), McGraw-Hill. Traces the progressive movement from its beginnings in 1890 through World War I. Emphasizes that the movement was a revolt of the American conscience against corruption, prejudice, poverty, and other social evils.

Social Reform Movements (filmstrip), EAV. Reform efforts as seen through the eyes of contemporary observers.

CHAPTER 22

Reformers and the Progressive Movement

Hopeful and expectant at the turn of the century, these strollers in New York's Central Park were painted in about 1905 by William Glackens. His art is impressionistic. Rather than try to paint a photographic likeness, impressionists seized upon a detail of light or shadow that played on their subjects. What parts of this scene would you say are more impressionistic than realistic?

■ Around the turn of the century a new mood spread through the nation. People seemed to be full of hope about the future. This mood lasted for about 15 years in the early 1900s and was known as the Progressive Era. It was a time when large numbers of people were working to improve society. These reformers were called progressives. They were trying to make progress. They hoped to make a better world. This belief in progress was part of the American character. Thomas Jefferson and nearly every westward-moving pioneer had shared it. During the Progressive Era the feeling was especially strong. People consciously spoke of themselves and the times as "progressive." Some progressives belonged to the Republican party, some to the Democratic. Theodore Roosevelt, one of the two great presidents of the era, was a Republican. The other, Woodrow Wilson, was a Democrat. Progressivism was a point of view about society and politics, not a political organization.

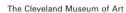

The Cleveland Museum of Art

780

3. Explain how the progressives hoped to make local and state governments more responsive.
4. Explain why Theodore Roosevelt worked to strengthen the presidency.
5. Give the reasons for the formation of the Progressive party.

6. Compare and contrast Roosevelt's New Nationalism with Wilson's New Freedom.
7. Evaluate the results of the 1912 election.
8. Criticize the progressives' views of immigrants and African Americans.
9. Identify geographic regions using various criteria.

1. THE PROGRESSIVE IDEA

The Turn of the Century

What causes shifts of public feeling such as the **Progressive Movement** is a mystery. There were several reasons, but no one can say exactly how they were related to one another.

People looked forward because they were beginning the 20th century. They sensed they were at the beginning of new and probably better times. The return of prosperity after the long depression of the 1890s changed their mood. The easy victory in the Spanish-American War increased their self-confidence. They seemed likely to accomplish whatever they set out to do. These **progressives** felt stronger and more important because the war had added new territory to the nation in many parts of the world. When Senator Albert J. Beveridge of Indiana made a speech describing "the march of the flag" in the Caribbean and Pacific, he was cheered to the rafters.

Many Americans looked back on the time after the Civil War as good years. Tremendous technological changes had advanced life. The telephone, the camera, and other scientific breakthroughs had a positive effect on people's lives. So did changes in the educational system. Individual schools had been consolidated into district systems. A manager, usually the superintendent, oversaw its operations and consulted with professional educators. Curriculum changed with the times. Less attention was paid to "the classics," to Latin and Greek. More was spent on mathematics, science, and the mechanical arts. High school enrollments soared. No longer was high school the reserve of the wealthy few. More and more families were making enough money to allow their children to attend.

Problems of Growth

Yet the same Americans who were so confident and hopeful were aware that conditions in the country were far from perfect. Many serious problems remained unsolved. Speaking broadly, these problems were produced by the Industrial Revolution.

In the great cities of the United States lived both the richest and poorest people in the country. The mansions of millionaire manufacturers stood only a few blocks from ugly, unhealthy districts that housed the poor families who labored in their factories. Few Americans objected to the Carnegies and Rockefellers and Morgans being so wealthy. But sometimes the rich seemed too powerful, the poor too weak. What power the poor did have was in the control of the big-city political machines, which used their votes to steal from the rich and the middle class.

The continued growth of great corporations and trusts was

Preview & Review

Use these questions to guide your reading. Answer the questions after completing Section 1.
Understanding Issues, Events, & Ideas. Explain the goals of the reforms in the late 1800s and early 1900s, using the following words: Progressive Movement, progressives.
1. What changes were there in the national mood at the turn of the century?
2. How did the world's first billion-dollar corporation come into being?
3. How did the progressives differ from reformers of the past?
4. What was the role of the government as progressives saw it?
Thinking Critically. Why do you think the national mood of America changed around 1900? What might cause a change today?

AVERAGE RETAIL PRICE OF SELECTED ITEMS, 1905*	
Item	**Price**
Beef (per pound)	$0.10
Butter (per pound)	$0.19
Bacon (per pound)	$0.11
Eggs (per dozen)	$0.13
Oranges (per dozen)	$0.20
Ice cream cone	$0.10
Men's suit	$9.50
Ladies' shoes (per pair)	$1.65
*in Omaha, Nebraska	

LEARNING FROM TABLES. *Compare the 1905 prices for the listed items with their prices today. How would you explain the differences?*

PREVIEW & REVIEW RESPONSES
Understanding Issues. Events & Ideas.
Explanations should show an understanding of the terms used.
1. Increased national self-confidence, optimistic view of the future, anticipation of better times
2. Banker J. P. Morgan bought Carnegie Steel and combined it with other corporations to create the United States Steel Corporation.
3. Their mood differed—they believed that people were basically decent and that, once informed, the public would do what needed to be done to improve society.
4. Government should take action to control special interests and to improve the condition of the weaker members of society.

Thinking Critically.
Students should mention the optimism associated with beginning a new century; renewed self-confidence that came with easy success in the Spanish-American War; and the sense of progress that accompanied the tremendous technological changes that had occurred since the Civil War. We are also approaching a new century, and positive worldwide changes are occurring.

■ *John Sloan, who painted "Women's Work" in 1911, is another American impressionist. He and his contemporaries painted common scenes from everyday life rather than fancy formal pictures. Critics called their group the "Ashcan School," but today these paintings give us valuable views of life at the turn of the century. Compare this painting with the one on page 780. In what ways is this painting impressionistic?*

Oil on canvas, The Cleveland Museum of Art. Gift of Amelia Elizabeth White, 64.160

another cause of concern. The revival of the economy increased business profits. This encouraged businesses to expand their operations. Big companies bought out small ones. In the year 1899 alone, over 1,000 firms were swallowed up.

The largest corporations were merging with each other to form giant monopolies. In 1901 the banker J. P. Morgan bought Andrew Carnegie's huge steel company. He then combined it with corporations that made finished steel products like pipe and wire and rails. He called the result the United States Steel Corporation.

U.S. Steel became the world's first billion-dollar corporation. Because it was so large and powerful, many people considered such

① Social Darwinism drew upon the long-standing American ideal of individualism. Americans had long distrusted any kind of establishment and any intrusion of government into their lives. Earlier, de Tocqueville had observed that Americans "acquire the habit of always considering themselves as standing alone, and they are apt to imagine that their whole destiny is in their own hands." Intellectual trends in other areas of life also emphasized individualism. For example, religious revivalism emphasized the power of the individual to save himself or herself; classical economics stressed the existence of a natural economic order which worked best when left alone.

a supercompany dangerous no matter what the policies of its owners and managers.

Many people asked how, in America, these problems could have grown so large. Working conditions in factories and living conditions in parts of most cities were unsafe and unsanitary. The nation's wealth seemed to belong to a few very rich people. Why didn't governments—national, state, and local—do something? Why did they seem to pass laws that favored what was called "big business."

As you have read, Social Darwinism was the excuse most often given for the hands-off approach of governments. Charles Darwin had used certain theories to explain the development of animals. One, survival of the fittest, became a theory of social change as well. The most energetic and aggressive people would rise to the top of ① society and take control. And that is just what was happening. Business leaders were transforming America into an economic and industrial power. Government should do everything it could to help. Often that meant looking the other way!

It was just that attitude the progressive set out to combat. Social Darwinism was based on incorrect assumptions, they said. Perhaps survival of the fittest did apply to animals and plants in the wild. But Americans lived in a society, not the wilderness. And further, the United States was a democracy. And a democracy, as Theodore Parker had written and Abraham Lincoln had paraphrased in his *Gettysburg Address,* "is government of all the people, by all the people, for all the people." American government should work for *all* Americans, not just the fit. Many progressive reformers realized that changing American attitudes toward industrial growth and progress would be as hard as tackling the problems caused by it.

The Progressive Mood

The concerns of the reformers did not suddenly come in with the 20th century. The problems of the Industrial Revolution existed long before 1900. Reformers had been fighting political bosses and machine politics for years. Efforts had been made to improve conditions in the slums. Many state laws had been passed to protect workers. The federal government had tried to check the growth of monopolies by the Sherman Antitrust Act. It had regulated the great railroad corporations through the Interstate Commerce Act. In the 1890s the Populists had vigorously attacked the evils they saw in the industrial age.

What was different about progressives was their new mood. They were happy, cheerful reformers. Most Populists had seen themselves as underdogs being taken advantage of by powerful bankers and railroad tycoons. Progressives attacked bankers and tycoons of all sorts. But they did so more to protect others than to help themselves. Good times made it possible for people to be more generous.

Point of View

A fictional family feels the sting of society in this brief excerpt from the novel *Ragtime.*

"One Sunday, in a wild impractical mood, they spent twelve cents for three fares on the streetcar and rode uptown. They walked on Madison Avenue and Fifth Avenue and looked at the mansions. Their owners called them palaces. They had all been designed by Stanford White. Tateh [the father] was a socialist. He looked at the palaces and his heart was outraged. The family walked quickly. The police in their tall helmets looked at them. On these empty sidewalks in this part of the city the police did not like to see immigrants. Tateh explained that this was because an immigrant some years before had shot the steel millionaire Henry Frick in Pittsburgh...."

E. L. Doctorow, 1975

CHECKING UNDERSTANDING
Ask students to explain the theory of Social Darwinism and the progressive response to it. *(It was an attempt to apply Charles Darwin's theories of species evolution to human society. Social Darwinists said that the most energetic and aggressive people would gain control of society; they cited business leaders and their giant corporations and trusts as evidence of Social Darwinism at work. The progressives said that Darwin's ideas did not apply to society. They said that the United States was a democracy in which the government should work for the welfare of all its citizens, not just the fit.)*

RETEACHING STRATEGY
Students with Special Needs.
Pair students who are having difficulty with students who are performing well. Have the more proficient students help the less proficient ones write a definition of Social Darwinism. Then have the pairs write an explanation of how Social Darwinists would react to J. P. Morgan's formation of the United States Steel Corporation.

PRIMARY SOURCE
Description of change: excerpted and bracketed.
Rationale: excerpted to focus on Doctorow's account of an immigrant family seeing a wealthy neighborhood; bracketed words added to clarify meaning.

INDEPENDENT PRACTICE
Have students complete the Preview & Review activity at the beginning of the section.

CLOSURE
Point out that at the beginning of the 20th century reformers brought a new attitude to their efforts. They confidently attacked business interests and tried to aid the less fortunate. They believed that if Americans were informed of social evils, they would demand that the government act to right them.

HOMEWORK
Ask students to write editorials about current social problems. When they have completed the assignment, organize students into small groups. Have each group read the editorials of its members and decide whether they exemplify a progressive or populist approach to the problems they address.

PRIMARY SOURCE
Description of change: excerpted and bracketed.
Rationale: excerpted to focus on one progressive's opinion; bracketed words added to clarify meaning.

The Granger Collection, New York

On a paper horse, William Jennings Bryan rides to rouse his longtime Populist followers. "The Populist Paul Revere" was made in 1904. The horse is made of The Commoner, *a newspaper read by Populists. What does the age of Bryan's followers suggest was the status of the Populists in the early 1900s?*

Return to the Preview & Review on page 781.

Progressives wanted to share their prosperity with people less fortunate than themselves.

Like Thomas Jefferson, the progressives believed that if the people knew the truth, they would do what was right. Like Alexander Hamilton, they believed that the government should act forcefully to increase the national wealth and to improve the standard of living for all.

This is how the typical progressive reasoned. First of all, most ordinary people are basically decent and public spirited. When they realize what needs to be done to improve society, they will do it. Informing the people is the first step toward reform.

Next, the political system must be thoroughly democratic. If the wishes of the people are to be carried out, the government must respond to public opinion. Government officials must be both honest and efficient. It must be easy to remove dishonest or lazy officials and replace them with good public servants.

Then, with the will of the people behind it, the government should take action. It should check and control greedy special interests seeking selfish benefits at the expense of the people. It should try to improve the condition of weaker members of society—children, old people, the poor. And as one progressive put it:

❝ That would change all of us—not alone our neighbors, not alone the grafters [dishonest people], but you and me. ❞

2. REFORMERS

The Muckrakers

Progressives depended heavily on newspapers and magazines to get their messages to the people. They placed more stress on describing what was wrong with society than on offering specific plans for reform. They assumed that once the people knew what was wrong, they would do something to correct the problem.

A small army of writers and researchers was soon engaged in what later came to be called investigative journalism. These writers dug into public records. They talked to politicians and business people, to city clerks and police officers, to factory workers and recent immigrants. Then they published their results in hard-hitting articles and books. They were specific. They named names. They demanded that "something be done." Improvements in printing and better ways of reproducing photographs added greatly to the effectiveness of their writing.

Theodore Roosevelt, not intending to praise the authors who exposed the evils of the time, called them **muckrakers.** They were raking up muck, or dirt, in order to make people aware of it. Muckrakers exposed the corrupt activities of political bosses. They described the terrible living conditions of the slums. They showed children laboring in factories and sweatshops. They wrote about the sale of impure foods and drugs. There were even articles describing secret payments of money to college football players and other evils resulting from an "overemphasis" on college sports.

Among the best-known of the muckrakers were Lincoln Steffens, Ida Tarbell, and Upton Sinclair. Steffens specialized in exposing

Use these questions to guide your reading. Answer the questions after completing Section 2.
Understanding Issues, Events, & Ideas. Evaluate the success of some of the reformers, using the following words: muckrakers, Golden Rule, Wisconsin Idea, direct primary, primary election, lobbyist, initiative, referendum, recall, Seventeenth Amendment, municipal socialism, socialist, free enterprise, Triangle Fire, minimum wage, Brandeis brief.
1. How did the Wisconsin Idea give voters more voice in selecting their candidates for public office?
2. Why did reformers believe states should make laws to protect workers?
3. What is the importance of the decision in *Muller v. Oregon?*

Thinking Critically. Imagine that you are a muckraker. What problem would you publicize? Why? How would you propose solving the problem or at least improving conditions?

PREVIEW & REVIEW RESPONSES
Understanding Issues. Events & Ideas.
Evaluations should show an understanding of the terms used.
1. The direct primary law established primary elections. Candidates now had to campaign for party nominations and be selected by the voters rather than by party officials.
2. Reformers argued that states could regulate working hours and conditions not only to protect workers but to protect their families and society in general.
3. It was the first case in which the Supreme Court took into account social and economic evidence and changed the way future such cases were argued and decided. Louis Brandeis presented a brief prepared by Florence Kelley and Josephine Goldmark showing that long hours of work injured women's health and thus the public health.

Thinking Critically.
Students' choices and the reasons for their choices will vary. Reward thoughtful, creative proposals.

Both, Brown Brothers

Lincoln Steffens and Ida Tarbell were two of the leading muckrakers of the early 1900s. Steffens examined city governments. Tarbell wrote a landmark study of Standard Oil.

HISTORY OF STANDARD OIL BY Ida M. Tarbell

Mc CLURE'S MAGAZINE

NOVEMBER

PUBLISHED MONTHLY BY THE S. S. McCLURE CO., 141-155 E. 25th ST., NEW YORK CITY

Culver Pictures

*The November 1902 issue of Mc-
Clure's magazine contains stronger
stuff than its cover would indicate.
Inside is an installment of Ida Tarbell's History of Standard Oil.*

corrupt city governments. In *McClure's* magazine, which was the
most important muckraking periodical, he reported on conditions in
St. Louis, Minneapolis, Cincinnati, and other "boss-ridden" cities.
In 1904 Steffens published these articles in a book, *The Shame of
the Cities.* He also wrote about corruption in state governments. But
Steffens was not a mere scandal seeker. When he discovered well-
run cities and honest officials, he praised them highly.

Ida Tarbell was one of the leading journalists of her day. She
was also an important historian. Before she turned to muckraking,
she wrote biographies of the French Emperor Napoleon as well as

HISTORICAL SIDELIGHTS

① Tarbell's study of Standard Oil is still considered to be one of the best studies ever written of a business monopoly. One research technique that she used was interviewing former employees of Standard Oil. Later she wrote her autobiography, *All in the Day's Work* (1939).

Abraham Lincoln. But she specialized in business investigations. Her detailed study of the methods used by John D. Rockefeller's Standard ① Oil Company was published in 19 installments in *McClure's*. She claimed Rockefeller "employed force and fraud to obtain his end."

Sinclair, along with Frank Norris and Jack London, were primarily novelists. Sinclair's sensational novel *The Jungle* exposed the disgustingly unsanitary conditions in meat-packing plants. Norris' *The Octopus* described the railroads' control over the economic life of farmers. London's stories, such as *The War of the Class*, *The Iron Heel*, and *Revolution*, warned of a workers' uprising that could wipe out private capitalism.

Few muckrakers called attention to the plight of black Americans. The most important work was *Following the Color Line* by Ray Stannard Baker. In this series of magazine articles Baker reported on segregation and racial discrimination in America.

Some reformers used the camera to tell their story. As you have read, Jacob Riis made a study of life in the tenements of New York City. His photographs and essays captured the terrible conditions of the slums and tenements. Scenes of cramped conditions, dilapidated buildings, and filth shocked middle-class Americans who had never seen the slums. In *How the Other Half Lives*, Riis wrote:

Ray Stannard Baker, above, was one of the few muckrakers concerned with the plight of African Americans.

Culver Pictures

EXTENSION:
COMMUNITY INVOLVEMENT
Invite an investigative reporter from your local newspaper to talk to the class about the role of journalists in social reform today. Organize students into groups to write questions they might ask the speaker. For example, one question they might ask is whether the role of journalism in promoting social reform has changed since the beginning of the century.

❝ Go into any of the 'respectable' tenement neighborhoods . . . where live the great body of hard-working Irish and German immigrants and their descendants, who accept naturally the conditions of tenement life, because for them there is nothing else in New York. . . .

With the first hot nights in June police dispatches, that record the killing of men and women by rolling off roofs and windows-sills while asleep, announce that the time of greatest suffering among the poor is at hand. It is the hot weather, when life indoors is well-nigh [nearly] unbearable with cooking, sleeping, and working, all crowded into the small rooms together, that the tenement expands, reckless of all restraint. . . . In the stifling July nights, when the big barracks [buildings] are like fiery furnaces, their very walls giving out absorbed heat, men and women lie in restless, sweltering rows, panting for air and sleep. Then every truck on the street, every crowded fire-escape, becomes a bedroom, infinitely preferable to any the house affords. A cooling shower [rain] on such a night is hailed as a heaven-sent blessing in a hundred thousand homes.

Life in the tenements in July and August spells death to an army of little ones whom the doctor's skill is powerless to save. When the white badge of mourning [a white ribbon] flutters from every second door, sleepless mothers walk the streets in the gray of the early dawn, trying to stir a cooling

ART IN HISTORY

ART IN HISTORY

Ask students to select one of the photographs on this page. Then ask them to write down everything that they see in the picture. Next ask them to pretend that they are one of the people in the photograph. Tell them to write down everything that the person with whom they are identifying would hear, would smell, would touch, and finally how they would be feeling. When students have completed writing about each of the senses, have them write an imaginary diary entry that the person with whom they are identifying might have written or an end-of-the-day conversation he or she might have had with a friend. Make a bulletin board display of the diary entries and conversations.

Both, Museum of the City of New York

Jacob Riis documented the slums of the cities with his camera as well as his pen. Two of his most famous scenes are "Baxter Street Alley—Rag Picker's Row" (left) and "Street Arabs in Night Quarters, Mulberry Street" (right). Describe in your own words what you think is happening in each photograph.

breeze to fan the brow of the sick baby. There is no sadder sight than this patient devotion striving against fearfully hopeless odds. Fifty 'summer doctors,' especially trained to this work, are sent into the tenements by the Board of Health, with free advice and medicine for the poor. Devoted women follow their track with care and nursing for the sick. . . . but despite all efforts the grave-diggers in Calvary [a city cemetery] work over-time, and little coffins are stacked moutains high in the deck of the Charity Commissioners' boat that makes its semi-weekly trips to the city cemetery. . . .[1]"

Riis also documented crowded and dangerous working conditions in sweatshops. Because of his active interest in helping the poor and the immigrants in the slums, Riis was called by many "the most useful citizen of New York."

[1]From *How the Other Half Lives* by Jacab Riis

PRIMARY SOURCE

Description of Change: excerpted and bracketed.
Rationale: excerpted to focus on conditions in the slums; bracketed words added to clarify meaning.

RESOURCES
■ You may wish to have students complete Reading 25: "New York in the Golden Nineties (1890s)" in Volume II of *Eyewitnesses and Others*.
◀ You may wish to have students complete Reading 30: "Jack London Reports on the San Francisco Earthquake (1906)" in Volume II of *Eyewitnesses and Others*.

Reforming City Governments

The struggle to rid cities of corrupt political bosses and their powerful machines was almost endless because more large cities were developing as the nation grew larger and more industrialized. By 1910 there were 50 American cities with populations of more than 100,000.

Among the notable reformer mayors of the Progressive Era was Samuel M. Jones. Jones was a poor farm boy who made a fortune drilling for oil. Then he sold out to Standard Oil and became a manufacturer of oil-drilling equipment in Toledo, Ohio.

During the depression of the 1890s Jones was shocked by the condition of the unemployed men who came to his plant looking for jobs. He set out to apply the **Golden Rule** in his factory: "Do unto others as you would have them do unto you." He raised wages. He reduced the workday to eight hours. He sold lunches to workers at cost. He created a park, gave picnics for his employees, and invited them to his home.

In 1897 "Golden Rule" Jones was elected mayor of Toledo. He held this office until his death in 1904. His election was a victory for honest government. He stressed political independence rather than party loyalty. He established the eight-hour day for many city workers. He built playgrounds and a city golf course. He provided kindergartens for young children.

Another progressive mayor, also from Ohio, was Tom L. Johnson of Cleveland. Johnson was less idealistic than Jones, but he got even more done. He forced the local streetcar company to lower its fares. He reduced taxes by cutting out wasteful city agencies and running others more efficiently. He improved the Cleveland parks. And he reformed the city prisons. After his investigation of Cleveland, Lincoln Steffens called Johnson "the best mayor of the best-governed city in the United States."

Other cities where important reform movements were organized by progressives included Philadelphia, Chicago, and Los Angeles. In San Francisco the corrupt machine of Boss Abraham Ruef was defeated by reformers led by Fremont Older, editor of the San Francisco *Bulletin,* and Rudolph Spreckles, a wealthy sugar manufacturer. In St. Louis a lawyer, Joseph W. Folk, headed the reformers.

And despite their problems, America's cities were a wonder. ■ They were places of energy, industry, of progress. Most Americans ◀ were proud of their cities. Carl Sandburg's poem is an example.

" **Chicago**

Hog Butcher for the World,
Tool Maker, Stacker of Wheat,
Player with Railroads and the Nation's Freight Handler;
Stormy, husky, brawling,
City of the Big Shoulders:

Point of View

Compare this fictional account, also from *Ragtime,* with Riis' description.

"This was early in the month of June and by the end of the month a serious heat wave had begun to kill infants all over the slums. The tenements glowed like furnaces and the tenants had no water to drink. . . . Families slept on stoops and in doorways. Horses collapsed and died in the streets. The Department of Sanitation sent drays around the city to drag away horses that had died. But it was not an efficient service. Horses exploded in the heat."
E. L. Doctorow, 1975

EXTENSION:
COMMUNITY INVOLVEMENT
Invite someone from your local government to talk to the class about your community's government. The speaker could tell the class about the way local government is organized and how it came to be organized in that fashion. Students could ask the speaker whether the progressive reformers were active in their community and, if so, what kind of an effect they had. Students might also ask if there are any current efforts to reform local government and the reasons for these efforts.

PRIMARY SOURCE
Description of change: excerpted.
Rationale: excerpted to focus on Doctorow's account of summer in the tenements.

① La Follette was a Republican who wanted to aid small farmers and businesspeople by returning to the kind of free competition that had existed before the emergence of the large corporations. He was also concerned about the power that the large corporations had wrested from state and local government.

They tell me you are wicked and I believe them, for I
    have seen your painted women under the gas lamps
    luring the farm boys.
And they tell me you are crooked and I answer: Yes, it is
    true I have seen the gunman kill and go free to kill
    again.
And they tell me you are brutal and my reply is: On the
    faces of the women and children I have seen the marks
    of wanton hunger.
And having answered so I turn once more to those who
    sneer at this my city, and I give them back the sneer
    and say to them:
Come and show me another city with lifted head singing
    so proud to be alive and coarse and strong and cunning.
Flinging magnetic curses amid the toil of piling job on job,
    here is a tall bold slugger set vivid against the little soft
    cities;
Fierce as a dog with tongue lapping for action, cunning as
    a savage pitted against the wilderness,
        Bareheaded,
        Shoveling,
        Wrecking,
        Planning,
        Building, breaking, rebuilding.
Under the smoke, dust all over his mouth, laughing with
    white teeth,
Under the terrible burden of destiny laughing as a young
    man laughs,
Laughing even as an ignorant fighter laughs who has
    never lost a battle,
Bragging and laughing that under his wrist is a pulse, and
    under his ribs the heart of the people,
        Laughing!
Laughing the stormy, husky, brawling laughter of Youth,
    half-naked, sweating, proud to be Hog Butcher, Tool
    Maker, Stacker of Wheat, Player with Railroads and
    Freight Handler of the Nation.[1] 99

Reforming State Governments

Progressives also tried to make state governments more responsive to the wishes of the people. The most "progressive" state by far was ① Wisconsin. The leading Wisconsin progressive was Robert M. La Follette, who was elected governor of the state in 1900.

La Follette's program was known as the **Wisconsin Idea.** To give

Brown Brothers

Robert M. La Follette was the progressive governor and later senator from Wisconsin. His strongest adviser was his wife, Belle Case La Follette, who studied law and worked for women's suffrage.

[1] "Chicago" by Carl Sandburg

voters more control over who ran for public office, he persuaded the legislature to pass a **direct primary** law. Instead of being chosen by politicians, candidates had to campaign for party nominations in **primary elections.** The people, not the politicians, could then select the candidates who would compete in the final election.

While La Follette was governor, the Wisconsin legislature also passed a law limiting the amount of money candidates for office could spend. Another law restricted the activities of **lobbyists**—those who urge legislatures to pass laws favorable to special interests.

La Follette had great faith in the good judgment of the people. If they were "thoroughly informed," he said, they would always do what was right. La Follette also realized that state government had to perform many tasks which called for special technical knowledge that ordinary citizens did not have.

La Follette believed that complicated matters such as the regulating of railroads and banks and the setting of tax rates should *not* be decided by popular vote. Appointed commissions of experts ought to handle these tasks. This idea was not original with La Follette. There were state boards of education and railroad commissions in nearly every state long before 1900. But the spread of such organizations in the Progressive Era was rapid.

The Wisconsin Idea was copied in other states. Many passed direct primary laws. Some allowed ordinary citizens to sign petitions which would force the legislature to vote on particular bills. Others authorized the initiative, the referendum, and the recall. The **initiative** enables voters to initiate, or propose, laws when the state legislatures have not done so. Under the **referendum** a particular proposal could be placed on the ballot to be decided by the yes or no votes of the people at a regular election. The **recall** allowed voters to remove an elected official before the official's term expired.

Many states responded to the demands of women that they be allowed to vote. By 1915 two thirds of the states permitted women to vote in certain elections, such as for members of school boards. About a dozen states had given women full voting rights by that date.

The National American Women's Suffrage Association led this fight. The president of the association from 1900 to 1904 was Carrie Lane Chapman Catt. She was an intelligent person and certainly better informed about public issues than the average man. But she could not vote. She had become active in the fight for women's rights in her home state of Iowa in the 1880s and later in the national suffrage movement.

One further progressive effort to give the people more control over elected officials was the **Seventeenth Amendment** to the Constitution, which was ratified in 1913. Article I of the Constitution had provided that United States senators should be elected by members of the state legislatures. Sometimes, such as in the contest in Illinois between Abraham Lincoln and Stephen A. Douglas in 1858, the

Point of View

In *Richard Milhous Nixon,* his biographer sees a darker side of reform.

> **"Intended as tools of popular participation in government, the new and exploitable levers of petition politics allowed well-financed special interest groups and other disciplined factions—those with the price of a public relations firm, the quarter-a-signature for petitions, the budget for advertising—to seize the legislative agenda or punish a foe."**
> **Roger Morris, 1990**

National Portrait Gallery, detail

Carrie Lane Chapman Catt was painted in 1927 by Mary Foote. Remembered as the founder of the League of Women Voters, Carrie Lane was once the superintendent of schools in Mason City, Iowa (the model for River City in The Music Man, *a musical comedy).*

Remind students that criticism of business practices did not end with the progressives. People have continued to criticize corporations and their products. Ask students to bring in articles from newspapers or magazines that criticize corporate practices or products. Have the students summarize their material for the class. Then discuss the information with the class. Ask them how critics today compare with the muckrakers.

Culver Pictures

To call attention to their cause, these women hiked from New York City to Washington, D.C. in 1913.

voters were able to make their wishes clear before the legislators acted. Often they were not. The Seventeenth Amendment changed the system. Thereafter, senators were to be "elected by the people" of the state.

Social and Economic Reforms

Progressives were making state and local governments more democratic. At the same time they were insisting that these governments do something about the social and economic problems of the times. Many city governments responded by taking over waterworks that had been privately owned. Some extended this policy, sometimes called **municipal socialism,** to the public ownership of streetcar lines and to gas and electric companies.

Not many progressives were **socialists.** Socialists favored government ownership of all the means of production. Most progressives believed in the **free enterprise** system—that is, the right of a business to take its own course without government controls. Its success or failure lay in how fit it was to survive, argued the Social Darwinists, whom we discussed earlier. But many progressives made an exception for local public utilities. To have more than one privately owned gas company or to set up competing streetcar lines would have been inefficient. Believers in municipal socialism thought the best way to protect the public against being overcharged was to have the people, through their local governments, own all public utilities.

The progressives continued the efforts to improve the health and housing of poor city dwellers begun by earlier reformers. In New York City, for example, an improved tenement house law was passed in 1901. Better plumbing and ventilation had to be installed in all new tenements. Older buildings had to be remodeled to meet the new standards. During the Progressive Era more than 40 other cities passed similar tenement house laws.

Conditions in factories also attracted much attention, especially after the terrible tragedy known as the **Triangle Fire.** In 1911 a fire in the Triangle Shirtwaist Company factory on the upper floors of a building in New York City caused the deaths of over 140 women. Some were burned to death. Others were overcome by smoke. Many died jumping from the windows in a desperate effort to escape the flames. After this disaster New York state passed 35 new factory

A policeman guards the broken bodies of some of the 140 women who died at their workplace in the Triangle Shirtwaist fire. These women died when they leaped from windows to escape the flames. Others were burned or overcome by smoke. What do you think of the camera when it becomes an eyewitness: do you want to turn away or do you look more closely at the picture?

Brown Brothers

CHECKING UNDERSTANDING
Ask students to name the principal political reforms of the Progressive Movement. *(Direct primaries, restricting lobbyists' activities, initiatives, recall, direct election of senators)*

RETEACHING STRATEGY
Students with Special Needs.
Pair students who are having difficulty with students who are performing well. Ask the more proficient students to help the others make a chart of the political reforms, the social/economic reforms, and the legal reforms of the Progressive Era. *(Political reforms: direct primaries, restrictions on lobbyists' activities, initiative, recall, direct election of senators; social/economic reforms: public ownership of public utilities, laws mandating improved plumbing and ventilation in tenement housing, factory inspection laws, laws forbidding employment of young children, restrictions on the hours women, older children, and miners could work; legal reforms:* Muller v. Oregon *was the first successful use of economic and social evidence and influenced future cases.)*

George Eastman House

Children who worked at home were safer than those who worked in factories, but the work was repetitive and tedious. And after such long days at the sewing machines, what could they know of the world beyond their tenement dwellings?

inspection laws. Other states also passed stronger laws to improve the safety of factories. Many began to require manufacturers to insure their workers against accidents.

Urged on by progressives, most states outlawed the employment of young children in factories. Many also limited the hours that women and older children could work. Most people agreed that states had the power to regulate child labor. But many employers and large numbers of workers claimed that laws regulating where or how long adults could work took away the right of individuals to decide such matters for themselves.

The Fourteenth Amendment, these people argued, says a state may not "deprive any person of life, liberty, or property." Laws that say women cannot work more than ten hours a day, or that coal miners cannot work more than eight hours a day, violate this amendment, they claimed. These employers and workers ignored the fact that the Fourteenth Amendment had been added to the Constitution to protect the civil rights of blacks in the southern states after the Civil War.

794

RESOURCES
■ You may wish to have students complete Reading 26: "Carry Nation Attacks 'Dens of Vice' (1900)" in Volume II of *Eyewitnesses and Others.*

Those favoring reforms argued back by stressing the power of the state to protect the public. Despite the Fourteenth Amendment, criminals can be jailed or fined. Such actions must deprive them of liberty and property in order to protect the public against crime. By the same reasoning, laws that prevent people from working long hours or under unhealthy conditions protect their families and society in general, not only the workers themselves. Reformers even insisted that the state had the right to make laws setting a **minimum wage.** They argued that if workers did not earn a certain minimum wage, their families would suffer. Crime and disease and a general loss of ■ energy would result. This would injure the entire society.

Reformers in the Courts

Both state and federal courts tried to resolve the conflict between the Fourteenth Amendment and the need for state governments to look after the common good. In the case of *Lochner v. New York* (1905) the Supreme Court decided that a New York law limiting bakers to a ten-hour workday was unconstitutional. Such laws were "meddlesome interference with the rights of the individual," the Court ruled. Bakers could work as long as they liked.

Three years later, however, the Supreme Court took the opposite position. This time the case involved an Oregon law that limited women laundry workers to a ten-hour workday. The Court decided that this law was a proper use of a state's power. Many women laundry workers are also mothers, the Court noted. If working too long injured their health, the health of any children they might have would suffer. Therefore, said the Court, "the well-being of the race" would be threatened.

This case, known as *Muller v. Oregon* (1908), is particularly important. For the first time the Supreme Court paid attention to economic and social evidence, not only to legal arguments. A lawyer for Oregon, Louis D. Brandeis, presented a detailed brief, or argument, showing that long hours of work in fact injured the health of women and thus the public health.

The research on which this **Brandeis brief** was based was done by two remarkable women, Florence Kelley and Josephine Goldmark. Kelley and Goldmark were officials of the National Consumers' League. They were deeply interested in many progressive reforms. The material they collected for Brandeis had a direct influence on the justices. More important, it changed the way future cases of this type were argued and decided.

Muller v. Oregon did not end the controversy about the power of a state to protect its weaker members. But by the end of the Progressive Era, many state laws had been passed to help workers and poor people. 🗒

Culver Pictures

Louis D. Brandeis was called "the people's attorney" after he persuaded the Supreme Court that limited work hours for women was reasonable. In 1916 he himself became a member of the Court.

Return to the Preview & Review on page 785.

INDEPENDENT PRACTICE
Have students complete the Preview & Review activity at the beginning of the section.

CLOSURE
Tell students that the Progressive Movement was responsible for many modern reforms in government, in working conditions, and in urban housing. The reforms they instituted are still an important part of American life.

HOMEWORK: USING HISTORICAL IMAGINATION
Have students imagine that they are writing a letter to a friend. Have them describe how their life has been changed by progressive reforms. Tell students to write about the reform that they think was most important. Read some of the best letters to the class, and add them to the bulletin board display.

The Reformers   795

PREVIEW & REVIEW RESPONSES
Understanding Issues. Events & Ideas.
Descriptions should show an understanding of the terms used.

1. Progressives agreed that supercompanies had too much power. Some wanted to break up supercompanies because they exerted too much power over important industries and took advantage of consumers. However, some believed that large corporations were more efficient and should be allowed to exist under government regulation and supervision.

2. He took action to expand government regulation of industry; expanded the powers of the president; was the first president to involve himself in a national strike; used executive orders to place forest land in federal reserves; focused public attention on the need to conserve natural resources.

3. Roosevelt used his influence to get Taft the Republican nomination for president.

Thinking Critically.
1. Students' opinions will vary, but they should support their opinion with sound reasoning.
2. Students should mention that Roosevelt made the charge that the Northern Securities Company restrained trade and that the Supreme Court ordered the combination dissolved.

Preview & Review

Use these questions to guide your reading. Answer the questions after completing Section 3.
Understanding Issues, Events, & Ideas. Use the following words to describe Theodore Roosevelt's actions as a progressive: trust buster, restraint of trade, Northern Securities Case, Hepburn Act, Pure Food and Drug Act, conservation.

1. Why did some progressives want to break up supercompanies? Why did others believe corporations should be allowed to combine?
2. Why is Roosevelt described as an activist president?
3. Why was President Taft expected to carry on Roosevelt's policies?

Thinking Critically. 1. Do you think large corporations today are becoming too powerful? Why or why not? 2. You are J.P. Morgan. Write a memo to your employees at the Northern Securities Company, explaining why your company is being broken up and giving your view of Roosevelt.

3. GOVERNMENT VERSUS BIG BUSINESS

Progressives and Big Business

The "trust problem" of the 1880s and 1890s continued to be a matter of great concern in the early 1900s. All progressives looked with some alarm at large corporations—the supercompanies. They argued that supercompanies like U.S. Steel had too much power over important industries. Some sort of government check or control on these large corporations was necessary. But progressives did not agree as to how these giants should be regulated.

Some progressives favored using the Sherman Antitrust Act to break up large combinations into smaller competing businesses. Others argued that big businesses were more efficient than small ones. Competition between them would be dangerous and wasteful. Corporations in the same field should be allowed to combine or to cooperate with one another, these progressives believed. But the government should supervise and regulate their activities. They should not be allowed to use their great size and power to hold down small producers or take advantage of the consuming public.

Roosevelt and the Trusts

During Theodore Roosevelt's first term as president, he developed a reputation for being a **trust buster.** He charged a railroad combination, the Northern Securities Company, with violating the Sherman Antitrust Act.

The Northern Securities Company controlled three railroads—the Great Northern Railroad, which ran from St. Paul, Minnesota, to the West Coast; the Northern Pacific Railroad, another transcontinental line; and the Chicago, Burlington, and Quincy Railroad. These three lines carried most of the rail traffic between Chicago and the Pacific Northwest.

The Northern Securities Company was owned by J. P. Morgan and two railroad tycoons, E. H. Harriman and James J. Hill. Harriman also controlled the Union Pacific and Southern Pacific lines. Roosevelt charged that the Northern Securities Company was so powerful a combination that it caused **restraint of trade** and that it should be broken up.

The **Northern Securities Case** was decided by the Supreme Court in 1904. The Court agreed with Roosevelt. It ordered the combination dissolved. Roosevelt then brought antitrust suits against the meatpackers trust, the tobacco trust, and the Standard Oil trust.

But President Roosevelt did not want to break up all large combinations. There were, he insisted, "good" trusts and "bad" trusts.

RESOURCES

■ You may wish to have students complete Reading 28: "Lincoln Steffens Tells How Theodore Roosevelt Began the Square Deal (1901)" in Volume II of *Eyewitnesses and Others.*

Culver Pictures   Brown Brothers   Riehle Studios

(He tended to see things as all bad or all good.) Only the bad ones must be destroyed. Good trusts should be allowed to exist. But they must operate under rules laid down by the government.

In 1903 Roosevelt established a Bureau of Corporations. The bureau was to conduct investigations and issue reports indicating whether or not large corporations were being run properly. When "wrongdoing" was discovered, the bureau should call the evil to the attention of a corporation's executives. If they did not correct their errors voluntarily, their corporations could be broken up under the Sherman Act.

During his second term President Roosevelt became completely convinced that federal regulation was the only practical solution to the problems caused by the growth of big business combinations. In 1906 he persuaded Congress to increase the powers of the Interstate Commerce Commission. Under this law, the **Hepburn Act,** the Commission could inspect the business records of railroad companies to see how much money they were making. It also could fix the maximum rates the railroad lines could charge for moving freight and passengers.

At Roosevelt's urging, Congress also passed the **Pure Food and Drug Act** of 1906 as well as a meat inspection law. Roosevelt had read Sinclair's *The Jungle* and was revolted by its revelations. The Pure Food and Drug Act provided for federal control of the quality of most foods and drugs and for the supervision of slaughterhouses.

Roosevelt and the Presidency

In addition to expanding the government's regulation of businesses, ■ Roosevelt strengthened the powers of the office of the president. His own personality had much to do with this. He was an activist by nature. He had to grit his powerful teeth to control himself whenever

These three giants of industry were owners of the Northern Securities Company. They are, from left to right, J. Pierpont Morgan, Edward Henry Harriman, and James Jerome Hill. The photographer of J. P. Morgan was Edward Steichen, who became an artist of the camera lens.

"Uncle Sam Unmasked" perfectly captures the popularity of President Teddy Roosevelt.

FOCUS/MOTIVATION:
MAKING CONNECTIONS
Student Experiences.
Ask students if they expect the government to inspect the meat and other food they buy. *(Most will respond that they do.)* Then tell them that laws regulating the quality of meat, food, and drugs are part of the progressive legacy. After reading *The Jungle,* President Theodore Roosevelt urged Congress to pass the Pure Food and Drug Act and a meat inspection law.

798

GUIDED INSTRUCTION

Organize a class discussion on centralization of power. Ask students if they agree with Roosevelt's view that since life in an industrialized country had become more complicated, decision making should become more centralized. What arguments might be used in favor of this position? *(more efficient; need expertise to make decisions)* What arguments might be used against this position? *(can't be sensitive to local differences, problems)*

CHECKING UNDERSTANDING

Ask students why Theodore Roosevelt is considered a progressive president. *(He established a Bureau of Corporations to make sure large corporations did not unfairly take advantage of the public. Those that did not correct their errors were to be broken up under the Sherman Act. He became involved in settling strikes. He took action after reading* The Jungle *to get the Pure Food and Drug Act and a meat inspection law passed. He informed the public of the importance of protecting the environment, assuming that once they were aware of the facts they would take the necessary action.)*

PRIMARY SOURCE

Description of change: excerpted.
Rationale: excerpted to focus on Morris's opinion of Roosevelt's peaceful presidency.

"TR"

Culver Pictures

Theodore Roosevelt was an extremely popular president. People responded eagerly to his colorful personality. They admired his tremendous energy and his vivid imagination. There was a youthful, almost childlike quality to him. An English friend said of him: "You must always remember that the president is about six." Yet no one could doubt that he was also tough, brave, and public spirited.

"TR" was the first president to be affectionately referred to by his initials. He loved to make visitors go on long hikes with him in the woods around Washington, especially those who were overweight and unused to exercise. He invited the heavyweight champion of the world to the White House so that he could box with him.

Ordinary citizens read about events like these with glee. Newspaper reporters could count on Roosevelt to say something interesting or do something that was newsworthy almost every day. He made their work easy. They liked him and tended to write favorable stories about him.

Another Englishman said of Theodore Roosevelt: "Do you know the two most wonderful things I have seen in your country? Niagara Falls and the President of the United States, both great wonders of nature!" Some observers came to agree with the cartoon on page 797, "Uncle Sam Unmasked."

Point of View

Theodore Roosevelt's biographer explains what a peaceful presidency the Rough Rider had.

> **"Yet the extraordinary truth about this most pugnacious of Presidents is that his two terms in that office have been completely tranquil. . . . At the same time he has managed, without so much as firing one American pistol, to elevate his country to the giddy heights of world power."**
>
> From *The Rise of Theodore Roosevelt,* Edmund Morris, 1979

Congress or the courts or some state governor was dealing with an important problem.

Life in a large industrial country like the United States had become so complicated that Roosevelt believed decision making had to be centralized. The president was the logical person to make the decisions. Large elected legislatures like Congress were inefficient, he claimed. They could not "meet the new and complex needs of the times."

As early as 1902 Roosevelt involved himself in a national coal strike by forcing mine owners and miners into arbitration. Today presidents routinely bring pressure to bear on employers and workers when strikes threaten to disrupt the economy. But it had never been dealt with as Roosevelt did. Roosevelt threatened to take over the mines unless the owners agreed to a settlement. Then he appointed a special commission to work out the terms to end the dispute.

Because he was a great nature lover, Roosevelt was particularly interested in **conservation** of the nation's natural resources. He used his power as president very effectively in this area. He did not object to allowing lumber companies to cut down trees on government lands. But he believed in scientific forestry. Bypassing Congress, he placed large forest areas in federal reserves by executive order. Reserved land could not be claimed or purchased by special interests. But it could be leased to lumber companies. Their cutting, however, was strictly controlled by government experts.

Roosevelt applied the same principle to resources such as coal, waterpower, and grazing lands. He did a great deal to focus public attention on the importance of conserving natural resources and protecting the natural environment. In this respect he was a typical progressive. He assumed that when the people were informed, they would bring pressure on their representatives to do the right thing.

William Howard Taft

Roosevelt's views about federal regulation of business and about presidential power eventually caused a split in the Republican party. They also divided the Progressive Movement.

When he completed his second term as president, Roosevelt did not run again. Instead he used his influence to get the Republican nomination for his close friend William Howard Taft. Taft was easily elected, defeating William Jennings Bryan, who was running for president for the third and last time.

Taft was from Cincinnati, where he had been a federal judge. After the Spanish-American War he had moved from the court of appeals to the post of governor general of the Philippine Islands. In 1904 Roosevelt had appointed him secretary of war.

By the time he became president, Taft weighed over 300 pounds. He was good natured. He had an excellent sense of humor. When he laughed, his belly shook like the well-known bowlful of jelly. But Taft was not a success as president, and his great weight was partly to blame.

Taft found it hard to get all his work done. Because he was so overweight, he needed much rest and relaxation. Further, he was a poor politician. Theodore Roosevelt had often been able to keep both sides happy by taking a middle position on controversial questions. When Taft took a middle position, he usually made both sides angry with him.

Taft tried to continue the policies of the Roosevelt administration. He supported a new law to further increase the powers of the Interstate Commerce Commission. He added more forest lands to the national reserves. He also continued Roosevelt's policy of attacking "bad" trusts under the Sherman Act.

Taft allowed conservative Republicans to influence his policies in many ways. He bungled a well-meant attempt to get Congress to lower the tariffs on manufactured goods. There was a nasty fight within his administration over conservation policy between Secretary of the Interior Richard A. Ballinger and Gifford Pinchot, the chief forester of the department. The controversy was over Alaskan coal lands. Taft sided with Ballinger and dismissed Pinchot. He was probably correct in doing so. But Pinchot then persuaded ex-president Roosevelt that Ballinger and the president were not true friends of conservation.

Copyright by the White House Historical Association; photograph by the National Geographic Society

William Howard Taft, like the other presidents of the United States, had his portrait painted while he was in the White House.

Return to the Preview & Review on page 796.

Government Versus Big Business   799

❶ J. P. Morgan reportedly voiced his hope that "some lion will do its duty."

❷ As early as 1910 Roosevelt began outlining the New Nationalism. In his speeches he made proposals that were more radical than any he had espoused as president. For example, he affirmed the government's duty to protect private property, but he said that when there was a conflict between property and human welfare, the latter should prevail. In 1912 the Progressive party platform supported women's suffrage, limitations on campaign contributions, occupational health and safety standards, prohibition of child labor, minimum wage standards, and many other elements of the progressive agenda.

Preview & Review

Use these questions to guide your reading. Answer the questions after completing Section 4.

Understanding Issues, Events, & Ideas. Explain how President Wilson's program continued the spirit of reform, using the following words: Progressive party, Bull Moose party, New Nationalism, welfare state, New Freedom, Underwood Tariff, income tax, Sixteenth Amendment, Federal Reserve Act, Federal Reserve Board, Clayton Antitrust Act, Federal Trade Commission.

1. Why did ex-president Roosevelt form the Progressive party? What did Roosevelt mean by the New Nationalism?

2. How did Woodrow Wilson's New Freedom differ from Roosevelt's New Nationalism?

3. Why did Wilson win the presidency so easily?

Thinking Critically. Of the legislative acts passed under Wilson's New Freedom, which do you think is the most important? Why?

4. A PROGRESSIVE VICTORY

The Progressive Party

Roosevelt did not want to interfere with Taft's handling of the presidency. Nor did he want to second-guess him. As soon as Taft was ❶ inaugurated, Roosevelt went off to hunt big game in Africa. But when he returned to the United States in 1910, he quickly came into conflict with Taft. He soon decided that Taft was not really a progressive. Taft was not using the powers of his office forcefully, the way Roosevelt had. Roosevelt decided that Taft was a weak leader.

In particular Roosevelt objected to the president's antitrust policy. When Taft ordered an antitrust suit against the U.S. Steel Corporation, Roosevelt was furious. In his opinion U.S. Steel was a "good" trust. Its officers had cooperated faithfully with the Bureau of Corporations.

By 1911 all sorts of Republican leaders, conservatives as well as progressives, were telling Roosevelt that Taft was so unpopular that he could not be reelected in 1912. They urged Roosevelt to seek the nomination. Roosevelt finally agreed. He entered and won nearly all the Republican primaries.

However, there were far fewer presidential primaries in 1912 than there are today. In most states party professionals chose the convention delegates, and Taft got nearly all of them. When the Republican convention met in June, the Taft delegates were in the majority. The president was renominated on the first ballot.

Roosevelt was now ready for a fight. Large numbers of Republican progressives urged him to make the run for president. He agreed to form a new **Progressive party** and seek the presidency under its banner.

In his enthusiasm for the coming battle for the White House, Roosevelt announced that he felt "as strong as a bull moose." Cartoonists promptly began to use a moose as the symbol for the Progressive party to go along with the Republican elephant and the Democratic donkey. Soon people were referring to the party as the **Bull Moose party.**

❷ Roosevelt's 1912 platform was ahead of its time. Corporations should be brought "under complete federal control," he said. Presidential candidates should be chosen by the people in primary elections, not by machine politicians at conventions. He also came out for a law to insure workers who were injured on the job, to assure a minimum wage for women, and to do away with child labor. He supported a Constitutional amendment giving women the right to vote.

Roosevelt called his program the **New Nationalism.** By nationalism he meant a stronger and more active national government. He

SUGGESTED CAPTION RESPONSE
Both parties wanted to attract Roosevelt's supporters
so that they would win the election.

New York Public Library

was thinking of something similar to what we today call the **welfare
state.** The government should be prepared to do "whatever . . . the
public welfare may require," he said.

*"Come Moosie," shows the Bull Moose
of Roosevelt's third party. Why are
both the Democrats and the Republicans eager that the bull moose eat
their oats?*

The Election of 1912

Roosevelt hoped to attract Democratic as well as Republican voters
to the Progressive party. But since he had been a lifelong Republican,
the new party was sure to draw most of its support from Republicans.
This presented Democrats with a golden opportunity. With Republican voters split between Taft and Roosevelt, the Democrats' chances
of winning the election were excellent. All they needed to nail down
the victory was an attractive presidential candidate.

National Portrait Gallery, detail

Woodrow Wilson was a relative newcomer to politics. He had served as president of Princeton and governor of New Jersey. His slate was clean and therefore he had great appeal for progressives. Do you think teaching is good preparation for the presidency?

The struggle for the nomination at the Democratic convention was hard fought. The person who won it was Woodrow Wilson, the governor of New Jersey.

Wilson was a newcomer to politics. He had been born in Virginia in 1856. After graduating from Princeton College and studying law, he studied political science and became a professor. Most of his teaching was done at Princeton, where he was very popular. In 1902 he had been elected president of Princeton. As president he introduced several important reforms in education. He hired more teachers and encouraged closer contacts between professors and students. He also added a large number of courses to the curriculum.

In 1910, however, Wilson resigned as president of Princeton to run for governor of New Jersey on the Democratic ticket. He was elected. He immediately proposed a number of progressive reforms. More important, he displayed remarkable political skill in getting the state legislature to enact his proposals into law. This success explains how he defeated the other Democratic presidential hopefuls in 1912.

The Democratic program was in the progressive tradition. Wilson called it the **New Freedom.** The *objectives* of the New Freedom were quite similar to those of the New Nationalism. The *methods* proposed were quite different.

Wilson did not believe in close government regulation of big business. Instead he wished to rely on antitrust laws to break up monopolies. Unlike Roosevelt, who thought that competition was wasteful, Wilson thought competition made business more efficient. The federal government should pass laws defining fair competition, Wilson believed. Any company or individuals who broke those laws should be severely punished.

Wilson also disliked Roosevelt's New Nationalism because he thought it would make government too big and let it interfere too much in the affairs of citizens. He opposed federal laws that told large corporations how to manage their affairs. He also opposed laws that gave special privileges to labor unions or farmers or women or any other group.

In a way, Wilson wanted the federal government to act like the referee in a football game. The government should enforce the rules of the game strictly but evenhandedly. It should keep a sharp eye on the players and penalize any team that broke the rules. But it should not try to call the plays or choose sides.

A Victory for Reform

Wilson easily won the election of 1912. He received 435 electoral votes to Roosevelt's 88 and Taft's 8. However, he got less than 42 percent of the popular vote. Slightly over half the voters cast their ballots for either Roosevelt or Taft. In other words, Wilson was elected because of the breakup of the Republican party.

A candidate had only to win a state by one vote to get all that state's electoral votes. Wilson had less than 42% of the popular vote but 82% of the electoral vote.

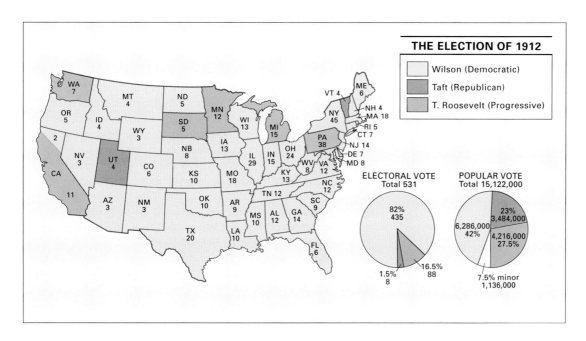

THE ELECTION OF 1912

- Wilson (Democratic)
- Taft (Republican)
- T. Roosevelt (Progressive)

ELECTORAL VOTE
Total 531

82%
435

1.5%
8

16.5%
88

POPULAR VOTE
Total 15,122,000

23%
3,484,000

4,216,000
27.5%

6,286,000
42%

7.5% minor
1,136,000

Nevertheless, the election was an overwhelming victory for progressivism and reform. Together, Wilson and Roosevelt received almost 70 percent of the popular vote. In addition almost 900,000 voters, about 6 percent of the total, cast their ballots for the Socialist party. The Socialists were demanding government ownership of railroads, banks, and "all large-scale industries."

The Socialist presidential candidate was Eugene V. Debs, the leader of the railroad workers who had been jailed for his role in the Pullman strike in 1894. While in prison, Debs had done a good deal of reading about government and politics. He became a socialist. He had run for president on the Socialist ticket in 1904 and in 1908, each time receiving about 400,000 votes. In 1912 his vote more than doubled. Clearly the American people were in a reform-minded mood.

Was the election a victory for Wilson's New Freedom philosophy? The answer to this question is unclear. The argument between Wilson and Roosevelt was the same one that Jefferson had with Hamilton in the 1790s about the role of the federal government. On the one hand, the large Socialist vote suggests increased support for the Hamilton (and Roosevelt) "big government" position. On the other hand, both Taft and Wilson believed, as Jefferson had, in competition rather than government regulations. Both promised to enforce the antitrust law strictly. When the Taft and Wilson votes are combined, they come to about 65 percent of the total.

Probably most citizens did not have a firm opinion about how reform should be accomplished. Most were voting for "a reformer" but not for a particular program.

LEARNING FROM MAPS. *Roosevelt's nomination by the Progressive party may have cost the Republicans the election of 1912. Roosevelt captured several states outright. How did the unit rule of the electoral college make the split of the Republican party that much more damaging?*

Wilson's New Freedom

As soon as he took office, President Wilson set out to put his ideas into practice. The Democrats had majorities in both houses of Congress, so he confidently expected to see his proposals passed.

He first urged Congress to lower the high protective tariff. The resulting **Underwood Tariff** of 1913 allowed food products, iron and steel, agricultural machinery—things that could be produced more cheaply in the United States than abroad—to enter the country without any tariff at all. For goods that needed some protection, the duties were lowered but not done away with. In addition, the Underwood Act provided for an **income tax.** This was possible because another progressive reform, the **Sixteenth Amendment** authorizing federal income taxes, had just been added to the Constitution.

Congress also passed the **Federal Reserve Act** in 1913. This law created 12 Federal Reserve Districts, each with a Federal Reserve Bank. These were banks for banks, not for businesses or individuals. The Federal Reserve Banks were supervised by the **Federal Reserve Board** in Washington. The board was not controlled by the federal government. It was an independent regulator of the money supply.

All national banks were members of the Federal Reserve system. All state banks that met certain requirements could also join. In times of depression when weak banks were on the brink of failing, Federal Reserve Banks could transfer money to prevent losses. The Federal Reserve system also made it possible to put more money into circulation to stimulate the economy or take some out to slow it down.

In practice the Federal Reserve system did not work quite so smoothly. It was not always easy to know whether to stimulate the economy or slow it down. Still, the Federal Reserve was a great improvement over the old national banking system established during the Civil War. It is still in operation today.

Then, in 1914, Congress passed the **Clayton Antitrust Act.** This law made it illegal for directors of one corporation to be directors of other corporations in the same field. It provided that the officers and managers of a company that violated the antitrust laws could be held personally responsible for the violations. It also stated that labor unions were *not* to be considered "combinations . . . in restraint of trade under the antitrust laws."

In 1914 Congress also created the **Federal Trade Commission.** This Commission conducted investigations of large corporations. If it found them acting unfairly toward competitors or the public, it issued "cease and desist orders," making them stop.

The Federal Trade Commission was closer in spirit to Theodore Roosevelt's New Nationalism than to the New Freedom. So was the Federal Reserve system. Wilson was not a rigid believer in old-style competition. Like Roosevelt, he was willing to use more than one technique in order to check the power of big business. 🖼

Return to the Preview & Review on page 800.

1 In return for votes, the urban political machines provided much-needed services to recent immigrants: speedy naturalization, jobs, access to authority, and other social services.

5. LIMITS OF PROGRESSIVISM

Restrictions on Immigration

By the end of 1914 the Progressive Movement had accomplished many political, social, and economic reforms. But the progressives had prejudices and blind spots that limited their achievements. Most were not very sympathetic to immigrants during a time of heavy immigration. Some years at the height of the progressive period, more than 1 million newcomers settled in the United States. In 1907 Americans demanded that the government stem the tide of Japanese immigration. In 1907 the United States and Japan reached what is known as the **Gentlemen's Agreement.** Japan promised not to allow unskilled workers to come to the United States.

Progressives who were alarmed about corruption in politics blamed the recent immigrants. These people cast a large proportion of the votes that kept corrupt bosses in power. Social workers and many others who were trying to help the poor thought that too many immigrants were crowding into the slums. They argued that the famous American **melting pot** could not absorb so many people so quickly. They were afraid that the character of American life would be undermined unless immigration was somehow limited.

Even Uncle Sam seems disturbed by the horde of new arrivals—"Anarchists in Chicago" and "Socialists in New York." What reveals the artist's prejudice?

The Granger Collection, New York

Preview & Review

Use these questions to guide your reading. Answer the questions after completing Section 5.
Understanding Issues, Events, & Ideas. Explain the limits of progressivism, using these words: Gentlemen's Agreement, melting pot, Niagara Movement, National Association for the Advancement of Colored People, Great War.

1. Why were progressives not sympathetic to immigrants? What was the attitude of most progressives toward blacks? Why?
2. How did Booker T. Washington continue to work for black people? How did William E. B. Du Bois work for blacks?
3. What event slowed the pace of progressive reform?

Thinking Critically. Suppose you are a speaker at the Niagara Falls meeting of 1905. What demands would you make? How would you expect the government to meet those demands?

PREVIEW & REVIEW RESPONSES
Understanding Issues. Events & Ideas.
Explanations will vary but should show an understanding of the terms used.

1. Progressives thought that the votes of recent immigrants helped to keep corrupt political bosses in power. They also thought that immigrants were arriving too quickly for them to be assimilated and that the character of American society would be changed if immigration were not limited. Progressives varied in their attitudes toward African Americans. However, most considered African Americans second-class citizens.
2. Washington raised money for African American schools, worked behind the scenes to get political jobs for African Americans, and fought discrimination in court. Du Bois urged African Americans to be proud of their heritage and to demand their rights. To further these aims, he helped to form the Niagara Movement and the National Association for the Advancement of Colored People (NAACP).
3. The War in Europe focused Americans' attention on international problems.

Thinking Critically.
Responses will vary but should be evaluated on the logic of student arguments.

COOPERATIVE LEARNING:
INTEGRATING STRATEGIES
FOR SUCCESS
Ask students to write down the topic sentence for all the paragraphs in this section of the chapter. Then organize the students into cooperative learning groups. Tell students to check each other's work to make sure they have all correctly identified the topic sentences. When students have completed this part of the exercise, have them work together to write a paragraph that summarizes the material in the section.

STRATEGIES FOR SUCCESS

COMPOSING PARAGRAPHS

You will often be asked to write a description or explanation. To do so effectively, you must organize your thoughts into paragraphs. A paragraph consists of several sentences that state a main idea and add an explanation or supporting details. For the paragraph to communicate your message, these sentences should be presented in a logical sequence.

How to Write a Paragraph

To write a paragraph, follow these guidelines.

1. **State a main idea.** Develop a clear statement of the main point you want your readers to understand.
2. **Support your main idea.** Include sentences that add detail or interest. These sentences should explain, support, or expand the main idea of the paragraph.
3. **Explain key terms.** Define or explain any special words you use in the paragraph. This can be done best in a separate sentence within the paragraph.
4. **Connect the sentences.** Make sure that your paragraph has a beginning and an end. Also make sure that all the information is tied logically together.

Applying the Strategy

Read the paragraph in the next column. The main idea is stated in the first sentence: *Progressives who were alarmed about corruption in politics blamed the recent immigrants.* This main idea is supported by the sentence: *These people cast a large proportion of the votes that kept corrupt bosses in power.* The other sentences in the paragraph expand on the situation faced by immigrants: *Social workers and many others who were trying to help the poor thought that too many immigrants were crowding into the slums. They argued that the famous American melting pot could not absorb so many people so quickly. They were afraid that the character of American life would be undermined unless immigration was somehow limited. How would you restate the main idea of the paragraph?*

Progressives who were alarmed about corruption in politics blamed the recent immigrants. These people cast a large proportion of the votes that kept corrupt bosses in power. Social workers and many others who were trying to help the poor thought that too many immigrants were crowding into the slums. They argued that the famous American melting pot could not absorb so many people so quickly. They were afraid that the character of American life would be undermined unless immigration was somehow limited.

Culver Pictures

For independent practice, see Practicing the Strategy on page 812.

① Du Bois studied in Germany and received his Ph.D. from Harvard. At first he held views typical of the progressives: if informed about African Americans' accomplishments along with the injustices they faced, European Americans would change their behavior. Later, however, he became convinced that only by demanding their rights, particularly their right to education, would African Americans be able to achieve equality.

② Du Bois was particularly critical of Washington's emphasis on vocational education.

Equality in the Progressive Era

The most glaring weakness of the progressive reformers was their attitude toward racial problems. The Progressive Era was probably the low point in the history of racial relations after the Civil War.

There was no one progressive point of view on the racial question. A few progressives were strong believers in racial equality. Northern progressives tended to be less prejudiced against black people than southerners. But most progressives believed that blacks were entitled at best to second-class citizenship. The most common attitude was that of the Alabama progressive who said that blacks were meant "to be protected by Government, rather than to be the directors of Government."

Most progressives claimed not to be prejudiced and to want to help blacks. But being white and comfortably well off in most cases, they had little understanding of the effects of racial discrimination on black people. Theodore Roosevelt once invited Booker T. Washington to have a meal with him at the White House. When newspapers reported that the president had eaten with a black man, Roosevelt was flooded with complaints, many from progressives. Instead of defending his invitation, Roosevelt practically apologized for it. It had been a spur-of-the-moment act, he explained. Washington had just happened to be there on public business at mealtime. Roosevelt never invited another black person to dine at the White House.

Still, the early 20th century marked a turning point in the history of racial relations. Booker T. Washington remained an important figure. He raised a great deal of money for black schools. He worked cleverly behind the scenes to get political jobs for blacks and to fight racial discrimination cases in the courts. However, he was no longer the only significant black public figure. Younger leaders were beginning to reject his whole approach to the racial problem.

William E. B. Du Bois was the most important of the new black ① leaders. Du Bois was a historian and sociologist. Although he had very light skin, he was proud of being black. "Beauty is black," he said. He urged people to be proud of their African origins and culture. He set out to make other blacks realize that they must speak out for their rights. If they did not, they would actually be inferior, he warned. The trouble with Booker T. Washington is that he "apolo- ② gizes for injustice," Du Bois wrote in 1903. Blacks will never get their "reasonable rights" unless they stop "voluntarily throwing them away," Du Bois said. He continued:

> While it is a great truth to say that the Negro must strive and strive mightily to help himself, it is equally true that unless his striving be not simply seconded, but rather aroused and encouraged, by the initiative action of the richer and wiser environing group [whites and wealthy African Americans], he cannot hope for success.

Culver Pictures

Booker T. Washington remained a powerful leader of African Americans as a younger generation joined the struggle for equality.

SUGGESTED CAPTION RESPONSE
He meant that African Americans should take pride
in being black.

CHECKING UNDERSTANDING
Ask students how W. E. B. Du Bois' approach differed from that of Booker T. Washington. *(He believed that it was not just the responsibility of African Americans but everyone's responsibility to help end discrimination. He felt that Washington placed too much responsibility on African Americans.)*

RETEACHING STRATEGY
Students with Special Needs.
Pair students who are having difficulty with students who are performing well. Ask the more proficient students to help the others make a list of the ways Washington worked to eliminate racism and the ways Du Bois worked. When students have completed the assignment, have the groups exchange lists and check them for accuracy. *(Washington: raised money for schools, helped others get political jobs, fought discrimination through court cases; Du Bois: urged African Americans to take pride in their heritage and to demand their rights, helped to found the Niagara Movement and the NAACP)*

PRIMARY SOURCES
(Top) Description of change: excerpted and bracketed.
Rationale: excerpted to focus on Du Bois' strategy for combating racism; bracketed words added to clarify meaning.
(Bottom) Description of change: excerpted and bracketed.
Rationale: excerpted to focus on what the Niagara Movement's statement of what African Americans' responsibilities are; bracketed words added to clarify meaning.

National Portrait Gallery

This portrait of Du Bois was made in 1925. What did Du Bois mean by "beauty is black?"

In his failure to realize and impress this last point, Mr. Washington is especially to be criticized. His doctrine has tended to make the whites, North and South, shift the burden of the problem to the Negro's shoulders and stand aside as critical and rather pessimistic spectators; when in fact the burden belongs to the nation, and the hands of none of us are clean if we bend not our energies to righting these great wrongs.[1] **"**

In 1905, at a meeting at Niagara Falls, Canada, Du Bois and a few other black leaders began the **Niagara Movement.** They demanded equality of economic and educational opportunities for blacks, an end to racial segregation, and protection of the right to vote. And they closed with this:

" *Duties:* And while we are demanding, and ought to demand, and will continue to demand the rights enumerated [listed] above, God forbid that we should ever forget to urge corresponding duties upon our people:

The duty to vote.
The duty to respect the rights of others.
The duty to work.
The duty to obey the laws.
The duty to be clean and orderly.
The duty to send our children to school.
The duty to respect ourselves, even as we respect others.

This statement, complaint, and prayer we submit to the American people, and Almighty God.[2] **"**

Then in 1909, Du Bois joined with seven white liberals to form the **National Association for the Advancement of Colored People** (NAACP). Du Bois became editor of the NAACP journal, *The Crisis*.

The NAACP's chief purpose in its early years was to try to put an end to lynching. Lynching was a terrible American problem. Ku Klux Klan mobs had killed many blacks during the Reconstruction period, and western vigilantes had hanged large numbers of gunslingers, horse thieves, and outlaws.

During the 1880s and 1890s about 150 to 200 persons a year were lynched. Many were white. Of 638 persons lynched between 1882 and 1886, 411 were whites. Throughout the Progressive Era about 100 persons were lynched each year in the United States. More than 90 percent of the victims were black. The NAACP crusade to end lynching followed the effort of African American journalist Ida B. Wells, who started her campaign against lynchings in 1901. She studied the records of hundreds of lynchings and found that most of the

[1]From *The Souls of Black Folk* by W.E.B. Du Bois
[2]From *The Niagara Movement Declaration of Principles* in *Afro-American History: Primary Sources*, edited by Thomas R. Frazier

RESOURCES
■ You may wish to have students complete one or
more of the Chapter 22 Tests.

Johnson Publications

*Leaders of the Niagara Movement
posed for this photograph in front of a
studio backdrop after their meeting in
1905. W.E.B. Du Bois is second from
right in the second row.*

victims were killed for "no offense, unknown offense, offenses not
criminal, misdemeanors, and crimes not capital."

The NAACP did not succeed in reducing the number of black
lynchings, which remained high until well into the 1920s. Yet the
organization grew rapidly both in members and in influence. By the
end of the Progressive Era more and more blacks were speaking out
strongly for their rights.

The Great War

After 1914 the pace of progressive reform slowed. President Wilson
announced that the major goals of the New Freedom had been
reached. Former president Roosevelt turned his attention to other
matters.

This does not mean that the national mood that we call progressivism came to an end. Such movements rarely stop suddenly. Indeed, the basic beliefs of the progressives still influence American
life. But in 1914 what was soon to be called the **Great War** broke out
in Europe. After 1914 that war turned the thoughts of Americans
from local problems to international ones.

Return to the Preview & Review on
page 805.

INDEPENDENT PRACTICE
Have students complete the
Preview & Review activity at
the beginning of the section.

CLOSURE
Point out that progressive
achievements were limited by
prejudice. Most progressives
believed that immigration
would have to be limited if the
character of American society
was to be preserved. They also
failed to appreciate the effects
of racial discrimination. However, a new generation of African American leaders did not
ignore discrimination and
urged African Americans to demand their rights.

**HOMEWORK: MULTICULTURAL
PERSPECTIVES**
Ask students to imagine that
they are working for their community's newspaper in 1910
and then write an editorial supporting the NAACP's campaign
against lynching. Remind students to take into account the
attitudes of their hypothetical
readers. Read some of the best
ones to the class and make an
editorial page bulletin board
display.

LINKING HISTORY & GEOGRAPHY

IDENTIFYING GEOGRAPHIC REGIONS

In the vocabulary of geographers the word *region* is very important. It is used to describe parts of the earth that share certain specific features. These features may be physical, such as climate, soil, or vegetation. They may be cultural, such as language, economic activity, or cultural heritage. Or, the region may represent a combination of both. Whatever the qualities used to identify the region, it is the commonality of features that make an area a region. Understanding how regions are identified is an important geographic skill.

The American West

1. What are some of the common images of the American West?

One of the regions of the United States that Americans today are most familiar with is the one that is labeled "The West." The very word *west* conjures up an entire collection of images in the minds of Americans. These images usually include both physical features—mountains, deserts, bright blue skies, buffalo, cattle, and cactuses—and cultural features—Indians, hearty cowboys, villainous outlaws, long barbed-wire fences, waving fields of wheat, and gold mines.

You should note, however, that all these images of the geographic region we call the West are comparatively recent. Most are scarcely more than a century old. What, then, was "the West" to the first explorers and settlers who arrived on the shores of North America in the 1500s and 1600s?

The Importance of Point of View

2. Why has the geographic label "West" referred to so many different regions during America's history?

As the brave European explorers and settlers first turned their eyes toward the New World, even the Atlantic Ocean was the West to them. When they stepped off their ships on the eastern seaboard, the West must have been just a short distance inland or the not-so-distant horizon.

The West, then, like all regions, is really a mental function. A region is what and where we *think* it is, and its boundaries are the boundaries we place upon it. What makes up a region depends greatly on our point of view. As a result, through the centuries there have been many "Wests" in the minds of the American people.

The First American West

3. Where was the first area of America labeled "the West"?

The first of the Wests that colonists spoke about and labeled on maps was the territory just beyond the Appalachian Mountains. Settlers quickly filled the lands between the Atlantic and the Appalachians, looking across the mountainous spine to the frontier—the West. Rugged terrain, hostile Indians and French colonists, and British laws kept many from crossing the mountains until after the Revolutionary War. As soon as the war was over, settlers began pouring across the Appalachians, and Congress set about organizing these "western territories." In 1785 and 1787 laws established what they called the Northwest Territory (see pages 189-90).

A New "West"

4. What new area became the West?

As the westward movement of American people continued, the concept of the West moved with them. People pushed beyond the Northwest Territory and in time this first American west became known as "The Old Northwest." And for good reason. By the late 1830s and early 1840s another Northwest—the Oregon Territory—was being settled. This "new" Northwest, named for its geographic location, was soon labeled "The Pacific Northwest."

Actually the term "Old Northwest" never really did occupy a prominent place in the minds of its inhabitants or other Americans. More frequently another regional label was used—"The Middle West," or more simply stated, "The Midwest." As pioneers settled the lands west of the Mississippi, the "Old West" just beyond the Appalachians was now between the East and the frontier. Such labels demonstrate an important geographic concept: it is people, not the compass or the map, that create regional labels.

This concept is illustrated quite simply. What if the United States had been settled by explorers landing along the West Coast. What regional titles would have been applied to the land between the coasts? Would the region that we now call the Middle West have been called the Middle East? (If so, that would make the Rocky Mountain states the Near East!) All this shows that regional labels reflect a particular point of view.

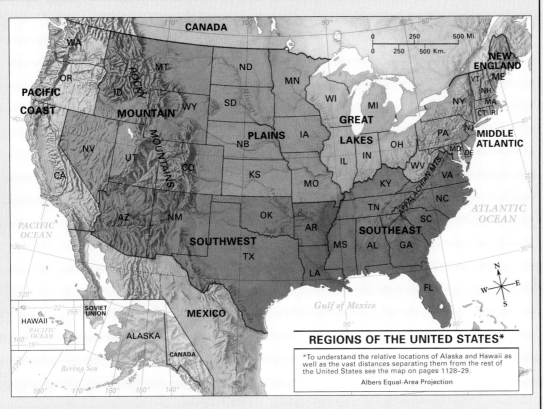

REGIONS OF THE UNITED STATES*

*To understand the relative locations of Alaska and Hawaii as well as the vast distances separating them from the rest of the United States see the map on pages 1128–29.

Albers Equal-Area Projection

The Concept of Regions

5. Why do regional labels depend on your point of view?

In the late 1840s and 1850s prospectors and entrepreneurs flocked to California, Colorado, and Nevada, adding still another "West" to the map of the United States! How could the same geographic term be applied to so many different areas? Because, like all regions, labeling depends on point of view. What was the West to colonists arriving along the East Coast was now *back East* to California miners!

So the term "the West"—confusing in its many uses—was applied to different areas as Americans settled the land. "The West" was a point just beyond the frontier. Americans soon learned that compass direction alone did not determine the limits and labels of regions. Instead, point of view, changing as the nation grew, became the most important element in labeling regions in America.

Regions of the United States Today

6. Into what regions do geographers divide the United States today?

Geographers use a variety of criteria to divide the United States into regions today. For that reason, not all regional divisions are identical. The map illustrates one of the most common regional divisions of the nation. What common features do you think were the basis for each of these regions?

Applying Your Knowledge

Your class will create a regional map of the United States that differs from the one on this page. After a class discussion identifies the new criteria for grouping the states, groups will recommend regional groupings. A volunteer from each group should then explain the group's reasoning. The class will then reach a consensus and create a map illustrating the new regional groupings.

Thinking Critically
1. Responses will vary. Students should back up their choices with sound reasoning.
2. Students should mention that they would want to increase elected officials' accountability to the people they are supposed to serve. Progressives supported direct primaries so that the people could select the candidates that would run for of-

fice; they wanted to restrict the activities of lobbyists; they supported the initiative so that people could propose legislation, the referendum so that particular proposals could be placed on the ballot, and the recall so that poorly performing elected officials could be removed before their term of office expired; and they supported the Seventeenth Amendment to the Constitution which pro-

REVIEW RESPONSES

Chapter Summary
Paragraphs will vary but should be evaluated on the logic of student arguments.

Reviewing Chronological Order
2, 1, 3, 5, 4

Understanding Main Ideas
1. It was a movement whose members hoped to make political and social reforms.
2. The problems caused by the Industrial Revolution; they attacked bankers, tycoons, and corrupt government officials in order to help the less fortunate.
3. He believed that decision making had to be centralized because the Congress was too large and inefficient to handle complex issues. Roosevelt threatened to take over the mines if owners did not agree to a settlement, and he appointed a commission to work out the terms of the settlement. He used his executive powers to establish federal reserves of forest land.
4. Together Wilson and Roosevelt, both reformers, got almost 70% of the popular vote; the Socialists got another 6%.
5. Unsympathetic; most progressives felt immigrants were arriving too quickly to be absorbed and feared that they would change the character of American society. They did not understand the effects of racism and at best seem to believe that African Americans were entitled to second class citizenship.

CHAPTER 22 REVIEW

1890		1895	THE PROGRESSIVE ERA	1900	

1890
Sherman Antitrust Act

1900
La Follette elected in Wisconsin

1901
Morgan forms U.S. Steel

Chapter Summary
Read the statements below. Choose one, and write a paragraph explaining its importance.
1. Around the turn of the century a new progressive mood swept the country. Reformers hoped to make a better world.
2. Many of the problems attacked by progressives stemmed from rapid industrial and urban growth.
3. Investigative journalists called muckrakers helped publicize political, industrial, and social conditions that called for reforms.
4. Political reforms focused on city and state governments. Social reforms sought to improve the welfare of the people, particularly the poor and workers.
5. Reformers in government tackled the problem of big business. Many supercompanies had formed trusts and had eliminated competition. Led by Theodore Roosevelt, the government began to break the trusts.
6. Although Taft continued many of Roosevelt's reform programs, he was not as effective. With the Republican party split between Taft and Roosevelt, the Democrats won the election of 1912.
7. President Wilson's New Freedom continued the progressive direction in government.
8. Although the progressive spirit continued in America, the Great War in Europe ended the Progressive Era.

Reviewing Chronological Order
Number your paper 1–5. Then study the time line above and place the following events in the order in which they happened by writing the first next to 1, the second next to 2, and so on.
1. Morgan forms U.S. Steel
2. La Follette elected In Wisconsin
3. *The Shame of the Cities*
4. Progressive, Bull Moose, party formed
5. Pure Food and Drug Act

Understanding Main Ideas
1. What was the Progressive Movement?
2. What national problems did the progressives hope to solve?
3. How and why did Roosevelt strengthen the powers of the presidency?
4. How was the result of the election of 1912 a victory for reform?
5. What were the views of most progressives toward immigrants and blacks?

Thinking Critically
1. **Relating Past to Present.** If the muckrakers were investigating problems in American society today, what do you think would be the top five problems on their list?
2. **Synthesizing.** You are a progressive in the early 1900s. How do you propose to make local and state governments more responsive to society's needs?
3. **Evaluating.** Review the cases of *Lochner v. New York* and *Muller v. Oregon*. Do you think a feminist in 1908 would have supported the Court's decision regarding working women? Why or why not?

Writing About History
The progressive spirit continues in America. Newspapers and news magazines often carry articles about problems similar to those tackled by the progressives at the turn of the century. Choose a current issue that calls for reform. Write a letter to your representative in Congress stating your views and ask what stand he or she takes.

Practicing the Strategy
Review the strategy on page 806.
Composing Paragraphs. Reread Section 1 of this chapter on pages 780–84. Then write a paragraph of at least six sentences restating the main idea and supporting it.

vided for the direct election of all United States senators.

3. Yes; women's relatively powerless position in society led most feminists to support legislation to prevent their exploitation.

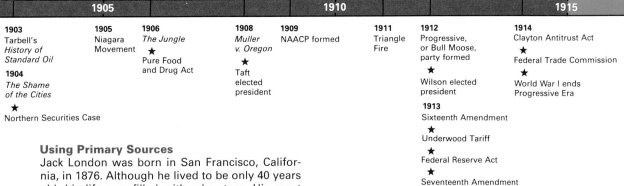

1903	1905	1906	1908	1909	1911	1912	1914
Tarbell's *History of Standard Oil*	Niagara Movement	*The Jungle* ★ Pure Food and Drug Act	*Muller v. Oregon* ★ Taft elected president	NAACP formed	Triangle Fire	Progressive, or Bull Moose, party formed ★ Wilson elected president	Clayton Antitrust Act ★ Federal Trade Commission ★ World War I ends Progressive Era
1904 *The Shame of the Cities* ★ Northern Securities Case						1913 Sixteenth Amendment ★ Underwood Tariff ★ Federal Reserve Act ★ Seventeenth Amendment	

Using Primary Sources

Jack London was born in San Francisco, California, in 1876. Although he lived to be only 40 years old, his life was filled with adventure. His most popular novels, *The Call of the Wild* and *White Fang,* were set in the Klondike, which is part of Yukon Territory in northwestern Canada. There London spent time as a gold prospector. But on April 17, 1906, Jack London was in San Francisco. The following excerpt is from an article he wrote for a local newspaper. As you read, think about the effects of natural disasters on the people they strike.

On Wednesday morning at a quarter past five came the earthquake. A minute later the flames were leaping upward. In a dozen different quarters south of Market Street, in the working-class ghetto, and in the factories, fires started. There was no opposing the flames. There was no organization, no communication. All the cunning adjustments of a twentieth-century city had been smashed by the earthquake. The streets were humped into ridges and depressions and piled with debris of fallen walls. The steel rails were twisted into perpendicular and horizontal angles. The telephone and telegraph systems were disrupted. And the great water mains had burst. All the shrewd contrivances and safeguards of man had been thrown out of gear by thirty seconds' twitching of the earth crust.

1. From London's account, what seems to be the biggest problem faced by the city?
2. What effect will the damage caused by the earthquake have on the people who live in San Francisco?
3. What does the last sentence suggest about people and nature?

Linking History & Geography

Many people were horrified at the abuse the natural environment had taken. They became deter-

mined to conserve natural resources and protect the environment. To understand the situation the progressives found so shocking, answer these questions.

1. What effect had the booming Industrial Revolution on America's natural resources?
2. How was urbanization affecting the natural landscape of America?
3. Many business owners and builders claimed that resources were a God-given gift to the people who owned the land. The government countered by saying such gifts belonged to all Americans—especially future generations. To use them up or to destroy the natural setting was not fair to others. Which argument do you support? Explain your reasoning.

Enriching Your Study of History

1. **Individual Project.** Read further in your library and other American history books into the life of Theodore Roosevelt. Report on one of the following topics, or on a topic of your own:
   Roosevelt the Young Naturalist
   Roosevelt the Rancher
   Roosevelt the Rough Rider
   Roosevelt the Trust Buster
   Roosevelt the Conservationist
   Roosevelt the Family Man
2. **Cooperative Project.** Groups in your class will collect examples of contemporary journalism and classify them as objective or biased reporting. Your group will find stories in magazines and newspapers, then exchange them with the collections of another group. Compare your classifications, and reach a consensus.

Practicing Critical Thinking

1. Some possible risks students may mention are: political instability leading to the close or mismanagement of the canal and the emergence of a government hostile to the United States. Opinions will vary; students should support their opinions with sound reasoning.

2. Responses will vary. Students might suggest building low-cost housing, increasing the minimum wage, and offering job training programs.

3. Answers will vary, but students should present evidence to support their answer.

REVIEW RESPONSES

Summing Up and Predicting
Paragraphs will vary but should be evaluated on the logic of student arguments.

Connecting Ideas

1. Answers will vary. Students might suggest that it is human nature for people to want independence. Some benefits from American rule include the possibility of economic aid and support for the development of democratic institutions.

2. Some of the progressive reforms that are still in effect are primary elections, restrictions on lobbyists, the referendum, direct election of senators, minimum wage laws, Pure Food and Drug Act, meat inspection laws, the Federal Reserve system, antitrust laws, Federal Trade Commission.

3. Responses will vary. Students should support their opinions with sound reasoning.

*These sources are suitable for students who are reading below grade level.

UNIT SEVEN REVIEW

Summing Up and Predicting

Read the summary of the main ideas in Unit Seven. Choose one statement, then write a paragraph predicting its outcome or future effect.

1. In the late 1800s the United States began to acquire territories overseas.
2. For partly humanitarian and partly imperialistic reasons, the United States became involved in the Spanish-American War.
3. The United States secured trading rights in Japan and China, and built the Panama Canal, and issued the Roosevelt Corollary to the Monroe Doctrine.
4. As the progressive mood swept America around 1900, reformers attacked problems in industry, cities, politics, and society.
5. Muckrakers were journalists who called attention to areas needing reform.
6. Theodore Roosevelt was an active reformer, leading the way as a trustbuster.
7. Taft and Wilson followed in Roosevelt's footsteps as reformers.

Connecting Ideas

1. As you have learned, Filipinos and others who came under American control in the late 1800s protested that control. Why do you think they did not want the United States to take control? What were some benefits for those areas controlled by the U.S.?
2. What reforms begun by the progressives at the turn of the century are continuing today?
3. Scandals and corruption in government have been widely publicized in recent years, as they were in the early 1900s. Do you think there will always be corruption in government? Why or why not?

Practicing Critical Thinking

1. **Evaluating.** In 1977 the United States and Panama signed a treaty returning control of the canal zone to Panama in the year 2000. What are the risks of turning the canal zone over to Panama? Do you agree with this action? Explain your reasoning.
2. **Synthesizing.** You are a turn-of-the-century progressive who has been transported by a time machine into the 1990s. How would you solve the problem of homelessness in America?

3. **Drawing Conclusions.** Do you agree with Roosevelt, who thought competition in business was wasteful, or with Wilson, who thought it made business more efficient? Why?

Cooperative Learning

1. Working in groups, your class will assemble a notebook on the key people who helped build the Panama Canal. Include brief biographies of Theodore Roosevelt, Philippe Bunau-Varilla, Carlos Juan Finlay, Walter Reed, William Gorgas, George Goethals, David Galliard, and William Howard Taft. Donate your notebook to the school library.
2. You know that a spirit of reform swept the United States at the turn of the 20th century. Now another century approaches. Imagine you are filled with the spirit of the progressive movement. Write a letter to a classmate, telling why you are so optimistic, or pessimistic, about the events at the turn of the 21st century. Have your classmate respond, agreeing or disagreeing with you. Your teacher may post all pairs of letters in the classroom so that you can compare yours with others.

Reading in Depth

*Antin, Mary. *The Promised Land.* Boston: Houghton Mifflin. Tells the story of a young immigrant's experiences.

Brau, M.M. *Island in the Crossroads: The History of Puerto Rico.* New York: Doubleday. Describes the importance of Puerto Rico's location.

*Castor, Henry. *Teddy Roosevelt and the Rough Riders.* New York: Random House. Presents the exciting story of Americans in combat.

Cook, Fred J. *The Muckrakers: Crusading Journalists Who Changed America.* New York: Doubleday. Provides an inside look at investigative reporting in the progressive era.

Gluck, Sherna, ed. *From Parlor to Prison: Five American Suffragists Talk About Their Lives.* New York: Random House. Contains vignettes on the crusade for women's right to vote.

Reynolds, Robert L. and Douglas MacArthur, 2nd. *Commodore Perry in Japan.* New York: American Heritage. Describes Perry's landing and the events surrounding the opening of Japan.

Upon completing Unit 8, students will be able to:
1. Explain Wilson's view of America's role in world affairs.
2. Describe how America organized its economy to produce supplies for the war effort.
3. Show how the Washington Disarmament Conference was an example of both isolationism and internationalism.
4. Analyze the postwar reaction of the 1920s.
5. Explain the workings of the "normal" business cycle and the economic and psychological effects of the Great Depression.
6. Assess the significance of the New Deal in American History.

J.S. Curry, *Tornado Over Kansas*, Hackley Picture Fund, Collection of The Muskegon Museum of Art. (Detail).

John Steuart Curry painted "Tornado over Kansas" in 1929.

A TROUBLED AMERICA

UNIT 8

In Unit 8 you will learn about World War I, the economic boom of the 1920s, and the Great Depression that followed in the 1930s. Here are some main points to keep in mind as you read the unit.

- Quarrels among the nations of Europe led to the outbreak of World War I in 1914.
- The United States was drawn into the conflict in 1917.
- At the peace conference following the war, President Wilson promoted the idea of peace without victory. But Britain and France wanted to punish Germany.
- A period of prosperity, the 1920s was a golden age for movies, radio, and the automobile.
- President Roosevelt's New Deal helped relieve the suffering of many, but it did not end the Depression.

OVERVIEW

The United States tried to follow a policy of isolation toward Europe, while intervening in Latin America. But the United States was drawn into Europe's Great World War, fighting to "make the world safe for democracy." After Germany's surrender, the Allies rejected Wilson's plea for "peace without victory," and the U.S. Senate rejected the Versailles treaty because it included the League of Nations.

The following decade saw the reappearance of isolationism, a resurgence of intolerance, and the advent of the Roaring Twenties. The prosperity of the Twenties, however, evaporated with the stock market crash of 1929 and the Great Depression.

Roosevelt's New Deal relieved the suffering of millions, but it was World War II that led to full economic recovery.

CONNECTING WITH PAST LEARNING

Ask students how the Spanish-American War influenced United States' conduct of foreign affairs. *(Students should mention that the United States had become an imperial power and did not hesitate to become involved in the affairs of Latin American nations. However, the country still mistrusted Europe and avoided involvement in European affairs.)* Tell students that the U.S. under Wilson continued to intervene in Latin America. He tried to avoid European entanglements, but his insistence on exercising the traditional rights of neutral nations drew the United States into World War I.

The Great World War

PLANNING THE CHAPTER

TEXTBOOK	RESOURCES
1. The Spark Is Lit	*Unit 8 Worksheets and Tests:* Chapter 23 Graphic Organizer, Directed Reading 23:1, Reteaching 23:1 *Creative Strategies for Teaching American History:* Page 329
2. War on Land and Sea	*Unit 8 Worksheets and Tests:* Directed Reading 23:2, Reteaching 23:2
3. America Enters the War	*Unit 8 Worksheets and Tests:* Directed Reading 23:3, Reteaching 23:3
4. The War at Home and Abroad	*Unit 8 Worksheets and Tests:* Directed Reading 23:4, Reteaching 23:4, Geography 23 *Creative Strategies for Teaching American History:* Page 291 *Eyewitnesses and Others, Volume 2:* Reading 32: General Pershing Arrives in France (1917), Reading 33: Two Doughboys in the Great War (1918), Reading 35: An Ambulance Driver's Story (1919)
5. The Search for Peace	*Unit 8 Worksheets and Tests:* Directed Reading 23:5, Reteaching 23:5 *Art in American History:* Transparency 21: Flags on the Waldorf *Eyewitnesses and Others, Volume 2:* Reading 34: Senator Henry Cabot Lodge Demands Harsh Peace Terms (1918)
Chapter Review	*Audio Program:* Chapter 23 *Unit 8 Worksheets and Tests:* Chapter 23 Tests, Forms A and B (See also *Alternative Assessment Forms*) *Test Generator*

STRATEGIES FOR STUDENTS WITH SPECIAL NEEDS

Gifted Students.
Organize interested students into two teams. Present the groups with the following debate topic:

RESOLVED: The Versailles Peace Treaty was a just settlement because Germany deserved to be punished.

Have one group prepare a debate in favor of the resolution. The other group should argue against it. Remind students to follow the standard procedure for preparing and conducting a debate that they learned earlier in the course. Have the students present their debate for the rest of the class.

Students Having Difficulty with the Chapter.
Your may wish to have students listen to Chapter 23 in *The Story of America Audio Program.* Then organize the class into several cooperative learning groups. Instruct each group to prepare a political cartoon intended to elicit support for the American cause in World War I. When the groups have completed their cartoons, have spokespersons present them to the rest of the class. Use the completed cartoons as a bulletin board display.

BOOKS FOR TEACHERS
Thomas A. Bailey, *The* Lusitania *Disaster: An Episode in Modern Warfare and Diplomacy.* New York: Free Press, 1975.

John W. Chambers, *To Raise an Army: The Draft Comes to America.* New York: Free Press, 1987.

Robert H. Ferrell, *Woodrow Wilson and World War I, 1917–1921.* New York: Harper & Row, 1985.

D. M. Kennedy, *Over Here: The First World War and American Society.* New York: Oxford University Press, 1980.

Arthur Walworth, *Wilson and His Peacemakers: The Paris Peace Conference, 1919.* New York: W. W. Norton, 1986.

BOOKS FOR STUDENTS
Felice Holman, *The Wild Children.* New York: Viking, 1985.

Pierre Miguel, *World War I.* Englewood Cliffs, NJ: Silver-Burdett, 1986.

Martin Windrow, *World War I Tommy.* New York: Franklin Watts, 1986.

Robert I. Vexler, *Woodrow Wilson, 1856–1924.* Dobbs Ferry, NY, 1969.

MULTIMEDIA MATERIALS
America's 20th-Century Wars: The International Challenge, Part 1, *World War I* (filmstrip), Educational Enrichment. Describes the conflict in a telescoped time span, covering facts and figures, military tactics, peace, and effects.

Armistice and the Versailles Treaty (filmstrip), Coronet. Discusses the outstanding events and leading figures in the treaty negotiations.

The Causes of World War I (filmstrip), Listening Library. Explains why the war started and how it developed using photographs, maps, cartoons, and newspaper headlines for 1914–1918.

Goodbye Billy—America Goes to War—1917–1918 (film, 25 min.), CF. Highlights Americans' feelings about World War I.

World War I—Background Tensions (film, 14 min.), CORF. Examines the basic causes of the war.

CHAPTER 23

The Great World War

■ The Great War that began in Europe in 1914 had been simmering since the late 19th century. Germany, France, Great Britain, Russia, and Austria-Hungary continually quarreled. Holding colonies in Africa and spheres of influence in China caused frequent disputes. While some European countries were expanding their influence abroad, others like Austria-Hungary and Germany had become unified nations, forged together in war by "blood and steel." The Slavic people—including Poles, Czechs, Slovaks, Serbs, and Croatians—resented being ruled by German-speaking Austria-Hungary. Complicated alliances prevented outright war for a time, but in 1914 the Allies (Great Britain, France, Russia, Serbia, and Belgium) began fighting against the Central Powers (Germany and Austria). How long could the United States resist entering what was becoming the largest war yet fought on the planet?

UPI/Bettmann Newsphotos

Guards drag Gavrilo Princip, assassin of the Archduke of Austria-Hungary and his wife, through the streets of Sarajevo. Explain why this assassination had such wide consequences.

4. Explain how both the British and Germans violated neutral trade rights.
5. Give three reasons why the United States declared war on Germany.
6. Describe how the United States organized the war effort at home.
7. Assess the war's effects on African American,

Mexican American, and women workers.
8. Identify major battles in which American troops fought.
9. Evaluate the Fourteen Points and the Versailles Treaty.
10. Analyze boundary changes contained in the Versailles Treaty.

1. THE SPARK IS LIT

War in Europe

The **Great War,** which Americans came to call World War I, began in Europe during the summer of 1914. It broke out following the assassination of an Austro-Hungarian prince, Archduke Ferdinand, and his wife in the city of Sarajevo in what later became Yugoslavia. The killer was a member of the Black Hand, a terrorist organization in the part of Yugoslavia that was then the nation of Serbia. Serbians wanted the southern Austro-Hungarian territories populated by Serbs. Austria declared war on Serbia. What had led to this explosive situation?

At first there seemed no reason why these murders would lead to a long and terrible war. However, several pressures were at work in Europe under the surface. The most important was **nationalism,** the feeling of pride and loyalty that people have for their country or for a shared language or customs. Nationalism helped unite Germany and brought many Slavic people closer together. However, some national groups such as the Serbians were ruled by other nations. Increasingly these people called for independence.

Another powerful force was **imperialism.** Some European nations had built great colonial empires in Asia and Africa. Others, such as Germany and Italy, envied these empires and wanted to build their own. Their attempts to do this brought them into conflict with the established imperialist nations. Empires brought power and prestige. So did military might. By 1900 the kaiser—the king of Germany—had built Germany's army into Europe's largest and best equipped. The other nations of Europe also began to strengthen their forces. Before long a dangerous arms race was underway.

To further increase their power, European nations had signed a complicated network of treaties. Two powerful groups called **alliances** had been created. European leaders claimed these alliances maintained a **balance of power.** That is, they kept the two groups of nations at nearly equal strength. These leaders hoped that a balance of power would preserve the fragile peace.

But alliances proved to be a grave danger. When a member of one alliance was threatened, the other members were pledged to support it. Austria and Serbia belonged to rival alliances. Austria held Serbia responsible for the assassinations. Quickly allies on both sides became involved, and their conflict resulted in a war that spread throughout Europe.

Germany and Austria were the principal members of one alliance. They were known as the **Central Powers** because they dominated the middle of Europe. Later they were joined in the war by Bulgaria and Turkey. Opposing them were a number of nations known as the **Allies.** Great Britain, France, and Russia were the

Preview & Review

Use these questions to guide your reading. Answer the questions after completing Section 1.
Understanding Issues, Events, & Ideas Using the following words, describe the events that led to war in Europe: Great War, nationalism, imperialism, alliance, balance of power, Central Powers, Allies.

Use the following words to explain how most Americans felt about going to war: arbitration treaty, peace movement, neutrality.

Describe Wilson's foreign policy in Mexico, using the following words: Mexican Revolution, military dictatorship, ABC Powers, mediate.
1. What did signers of arbitration treaties agree to do?
2. What did President Wilson believe should be the role of the United States in foreign affairs?
3. Why did the United States become involved in the Mexican Revolution?
Thinking Critically. Imagine that it is 1910, and you are a Mexican refugee who has crossed the Mexican border into New Mexico. Write a diary entry explaining why you have left Mexico and your hopes for the future.

SECTION 1

PREVIEW & REVIEW RESPONSES
Understanding Issues, Events, & Ideas.
Descriptions and explanations will vary but should define the terms used in context.
1. They agreed to discuss their differences during a year-long "cooling off" period. They would consider war only if they failed to find a solution.
2. It should be to promote democracy, help other nations, and try to make life better for their people.
3. The United States became involved in the Mexican Revolution because Wilson believed American investments were threatened and because Mexican refugees were entering Texas, New Mexico, Arizona, and California against U.S. wishes.

Thinking Critically.
Reward imaginative, sympathetic diary entries.

FOCUS/MOTIVATION:
MAKING CONNECTIONS
Student Experiences.
Ask students how they respond to a conflict between friends or family members. *(Students might offer several responses. Some might join the conflict, some might try to stop it, or others might try to ignore it.)* Then ask them if the nature of the conflict determines how they react. *(Most will probably say that it does; they will try to ignore it if they feel it does not concern them, or they may become involved in some way if they care about the outcome.)* Explain to students that Wilson's response to conflict in Mexico was very different from his response to war in Europe.

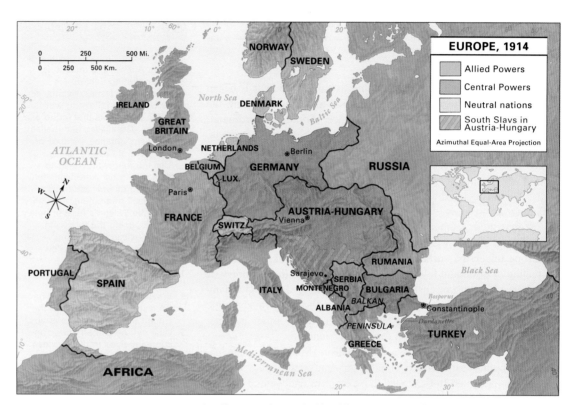

LEARNING FROM MAPS. *By 1914 Austria-Hungary had been unified into a huge country occupying central Europe. Many ethnic groups had been brought under its control. The struggles of these groups, seeking independence and the chance to form a nation of their own, helped cause the Great War. What countries made up the Central Powers? Why were they called that?*

leading members of this alliance. The United States was most concerned by the fighting between Great Britain and Germany.

American Neutrality

News of the outbreak of war caught Americans by surprise. There had not been a major war in Europe since the defeat of Napoleon at the battle of Waterloo in 1815. Prosperity and progress had encouraged people to hope that the nations of the world had become too "civilized" to resort to warfare to settle their disagreements.

Under Presidents Taft and Wilson the United States had negotiated **arbitration treaties** with a number of nations. The signers agreed in advance to discuss any differences during a "cooling off" period to last about a year. Only if a solution could not be found would they consider going to war.

In America the search for worldwide peace went even further. Both religious and secular groups became deeply involved in a **peace movement**. The Carnegie Endowment for International Peace, drawing upon funds provided by Andrew Carnegie's millions, mounted a campaign to promote peaceful solutions to international problems. William Jennings Bryan, Wilson's secretary of state, used both rational and religious arguments to further the quest for peace.

This American attitude helps explain why President McKinley

hesitated to ask Congress to declare war on Spain in 1898. Wars were to be fought only for a noble purpose and only after every reasonable effort had been made to negotiate a settlement.

Nearly all Americans felt the United States should not become involved in the war in Europe. Many persons of German or Austrian origin hoped that the Central Powers would win. So did large numbers of Irish Americans, who were anti-British because Great Britain still refused to grant Ireland its independence. People whose ancestors had come from the Allied nations tended to favor that side in the war. But for the vast majority of Americans the obvious policy for the United States was **neutrality.** Europe was far away. Its rivalries had always been viewed by Americans with distrust.

President Wilson expressed the general attitude clearly on August 18, 1914. Every American ought to "act and speak in the true spirit of neutrality," he said. This meant behaving with "impartiality and fairness and friendliness" to all the nations at war.

Wilson's Foreign Policy

As president of the United States, Woodrow Wilson had the chief responsibility for deciding the country's foreign policy. He had run for president, however, on the domestic issues of the Progressive Era. Foreign questions had not played much part in the 1912 campaign. Before 1912 Wilson had never been especially concerned with foreign affairs. Nevertheless, he had very strong opinions about what was morally correct in foreign affairs.

This is how Wilson reasoned: The United States did not need any more territory. It had no enemies. It did not want to injure any foreign country. Indeed, Wilson thought, being rich and powerful, the United States had a duty to help less fortunate nations, particularly its neighbors in Central and South America. America's destiny was not to control other countries but to encourage the spread of democratic ideas. After all, he felt no other country knew as much about democracy as the United States. The brief period of American imperialism had been a bad mistake, the president insisted.

Wilson thought the United States should help other nations and try to make life better for their people. His trouble was that he was convinced that he knew what was best for the rest of the world. He often tried to impose his ideas on people who did not agree with him.

Wilson did not seem to understand that nations with different cultures and traditions often saw things differently than he did. Even nations which sought the same goals as Wilson sometimes resented his efforts to assist them. Perhaps because he had been a teacher for so many years, the president had a tendency to lecture to the officials of other nations. His manner, rather than his actual words, created the impression that Wilson thought he knew better than foreign leaders what was best for their countries.

GUIDED INSTRUCTION: COOPERATIVE LEARNING
Organize the class into two groups. One group is to represent Americans who oppose intervening in Mexican affairs during the Mexican Revolution. The other group is to represent Americans who favor intervention in Mexico during the Mexican Revolution. Have the groups meet separately to develop arguments supporting their positions on intervention. After the groups have developed their arguments, have spokespersons explain them to the class.

RELATING HISTORY TO GEOGRAPHY
To highlight the importance of *relative location* in foreign policy decisions, have students study a world map. Have them locate Mexico and Germany. Ask them why the United States would be more likely to intervene in events in Mexico than in Germany. *(Students should note that Mexico is much closer to the United States than Germany is and shares a long border with the United States.)*

HISTORICAL SIDELIGHTS
① Wilson also intervened militarily in Nicaragua, the Dominican Republic, and Haiti.

SUGGESTED CAPTION RESPONSE
Responses will vary; most will probably suggest that Huerta sought to impress those who saw him.

CHECKING UNDERSTANDING
Ask students to explain why the United States became involved in the Mexican Revolution. *(Two motives led Wilson to interfere. First he believed that the United States should promote the spread of democracy. Also, American companies that had property in Mexico urged Wilson to take action. Wilson then used an incident in which some American soldiers on shore leave in Tampico, Mexico, were arrested as an excuse to use the U.S. military to try to overthrow Huerta.)*

RETEACHING STRATEGY
Students with Special Needs. Pair students who are having difficulty with students who are performing well. Ask the more proficient students to help the others prepare a chart detailing American involvement in Mexican affairs in the early 1900s. Tell students to make two columns; on the left-hand side they should write the American actions and reactions and in the right-hand column the Mexican actions and reactions. After students have completed their charts, ask them to summarize step-by-step how America became involved in the Mexican Revolution.

Victoriano Huerta became military dictator of Mexico in 1913. President Wilson said he headed a "government of butchers." Do you suppose such a display of medals was worn in the memory of fallen comrades or to impress those who opposed Huerta's heavy-handed rule?

Revolution in Mexico

Even before the war in Europe began, Wilson had to deal with an important foreign problem. This was the **Mexican Revolution.** This upheaval, which began in 1910, was against the dictator Porfirio Díaz who had ruled Mexico for many years and allowed foreign companies ① to exploit his country's resources. It was of concern to Wilson because United States investments in Mexico were threatened by the troubles. Also, many Mexican refugees from the fighting were crossing the border into Texas, New Mexico, Arizona, and California against U.S. wishes.

Before Wilson became president, the revolution had been led by Francisco Madero, a progressive-type reformer who had forced Díaz to resign and leave Mexico. Madero became president but early in 1913 was murdered by General Victoriano Huerta. Huerta set up a **military dictatorship** with all powers of government held by the generals. Wilson called this "a government of butchers." He refused to recognize Huerta as the legitimate leader of the Mexicans.

Many Mexicans agreed with Wilson. A new revolt broke out, led by Venustiano Carranza. Wilson was urged on by United States companies whose Mexican properties were in danger. He asked Huerta to order free elections and promise not to be a candidate himself. If he agreed, the United States would try to persuade the Carranza forces to stop fighting.

Wilson meant well. But even supporters of Carranza resented Wilson's interference. Mexico's problems were none of his business, insisted both sides. If we agreed to United States interference, said an official of the Huerta government, "all the future elections for president [of Mexico] would be submitted to the veto of any president of the United States."

Then, in April 1914, some American sailors on shore leave in Tampico, Mexico, were arrested. They were soon released, but by this time Wilson was so angry at Huerta that he used the incident to try to overthrow him. He sent a naval force to occupy the city of Veracruz.

Wilson did not intend to start a war. He expected his "show of force" would cause the downfall of Huerta. But 19 United States sailors and 126 Mexicans were killed before Veracruz was captured. Again, Carranza joined with his enemy Huerta in speaking out against the interference of the United States in Mexican affairs.

Fortunately, the ambassadors of the **ABC Powers**—Argentina, Brazil, and Chile—offered to **mediate** the dispute—that is, to act as neutral go-betweens to find a peaceful settlement. Wilson eagerly accepted their offer. The crisis ended. By summer Carranza had forced Huerta from power. The United States then withdrew its naval force from Veracruz.

Yet Wilson's troubles in Mexico were far from over. No sooner

Culver Pictures

To some Mexicans Pancho Villa and Emiliano Zapata were Robin Hood and Little John. To others they were bandits. In this photograph of the only meeting of the two leaders, they have taken over the presidential palace in Mexico City in 1914. Villa is seated at the center, and Zapata is to his left. Do these men seem at ease in the palace of the president?

1931, Fresco, 7'9 ¾" × 6'2", Collection, The Museum of Modern Art, New York. Abby Aldrich Rockefeller Fund.

"¡Viva Zapata!" shouted supporters of Mexico's great fighter for land reform. The muralist Diego Rivera called his fresco of Zapata and his white horse "Agrarian Leader Zapata." With the slogan on his lips, "land and liberty," Zapata led an army of Indians in seizing plantations and villages. His movement called zapatismo had as its single purpose the breaking up of the large estates of the rich into small farms for the poor. How does this mural show that Rivera saw Zapata as a man of the people?

had Carranza defeated Huerta than one of his own generals, Francisco "Pancho" Villa, rebelled against him. Wilson supported Villa. He had resented Carranza's independence and refusal to follow United States advice. Villa seemed to be sincerely interested in improving the lives of poor Mexicans. Wilson also thought Villa could be more easily influenced by the United States.

Supporting Pancho Villa was probably the president's worst mistake. Villa was little better than a bandit, while Carranza was genuinely interested in improving the condition of the people of Mexico. From a practical point of view, Carranza had the stronger forces. His troops soon drove the Villistas, Villa's followers, into the mountains of northern Mexico.

At last, in October 1915, Wilson realized that the best policy for the United States was to keep hands off Mexico and let the people of that nation decide for themselves how they were to be governed. He then officially recognized the Carranza government.

This decision angered Pancho Villa. In January 1916 the Villistas stopped a train in northern Mexico and killed 17 citizens of the United States on board in cold blood. Then in March Villa and his men crossed the border and attacked the town of Columbus, New Mexico. They killed 17 more United States citizens and set the town on fire.

Wilson ordered troops under General John J. Pershing to capture Villa. This meant invading Mexico. Pershing was an experienced soldier. He had served during the Indian fighting of the 1880s, in Cuba during the Spanish-American War, and in the Philippine Islands. He earned the nickname "Black Jack" while commanding the l0th Cavalry regiment, which was made up entirely of black enlisted men. One of his first decisions when he was ordered to hunt down Villa was to include part of the l0th Cavalry in his expedition.

Pershing's men pursued Villa vigorously, but they could not ① catch him on his home ground. As had happened when Veracruz was occupied in 1914, United States interference angered Carranza. Wilson called off the invasion, which accomplished nothing. �’

Return to the Preview & Review on page 817.

The Spark Is Lit 821

822

SECTION 2

PREVIEW & REVIEW RESPONSES
Understanding Issues, Events, & Ideas.
Descriptions will vary but should define the terms used in context.
1. It was unlike any other war in history. The soldiers were confined to trenches, with a no man's land separating the two sides. The war settled into a stalemate that dragged on for years.
2. They refused to follow the rules for stopping merchant ships in wartime because it was very dangerous for U-boats to follow the rules. Instead of inspecting the cargo for contraband and letting the crew and passengers evacuate, they attacked from below the surface and without warning.
3. The profitable trade with the Allies was too important to the United States.

Thinking Critically.
Responses will vary; students should support their position with sound reasoning.

Preview & Review

Use these questions to guide your reading. Answer the questions after completing Section 2.
Understanding Issues, Events, & Ideas Describe the Great War, using the following terms: Eastern Front, Western Front, Battle of the Marne, no man's land, trench warfare, stalemate, U-boat, *Lusitania,* Sussex pledge.
1. What was the war on the Western Front like?
2. How did the U-boats break the rules of the high seas?
3. Why was Wilson unwilling to cut off trade with Great Britain?
Thinking Critically. Imagine that you are an American who has just learned about the torpedoing of the *Lusitania.* Write a letter to the editor of your local newspaper, describing your reaction and explaining what you think President Wilson should do about it.

---

2. WAR ON LAND AND SEA

The War on the Western Front

As early as 1915 the Great World War had become the bloodiest conflict ever fought. On the **Eastern Front** Russian troops clashed with Austrian and German armies in a series of seesaw battles. There was also fighting in Turkey and Serbia. In Africa and on the islands of the Pacific, Allied troops clashed with German colonial forces. In May 1915 Italy entered the war on the side of the Allies and attacked Austria-Hungary from the south.

The greatest interest of the United States at this time was in the fighting on the so-called **Western Front** in Europe—Belgium and France—and on the high seas. When the war began, the Germans marched into Belgium on their way to invade France. No matter that they had promised by treaty in 1870 to respect the neutrality of tiny Belgium in the event of war with France.

The Belgians resisted bravely, but they could not stop the invaders. By September 1914 the German armies had swept across Belgium and were within 20 miles (32 kilometers) of Paris. There, in the **Battle of the Marne,** they were checked by French and British troops.

The two armies then dug trenches to protect themselves from bullets and artillery shells. They put up mazes of barbed wire in front of their positions. Lines of these trenches ran all the way across

---

THE EASTERN FRONT

— Farthest German-Austrian advance, Nov. 1918

— Extent of Russian drive, Dec. 1914

0   200   400 Mi.
0 200 400 Km.

Azimuthal Equal-Area Projection

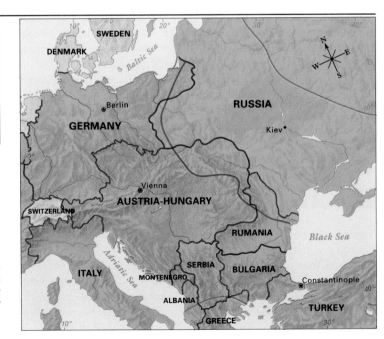

LEARNING FROM MAPS. *Russia invaded the Central Powers in 1914 in keeping with its alliance with Serbia. However, the Central Powers had soon pushed far into Russia. What ended the Russian war effort?*

SUGGESTED CAPTION RESPONSE
In both cases the attackers hoped to penetrate earth-works so that they could use their bayonets, and the defenders could successfully repel an attack as long as their ammunition and supplies lasted. However, millions of soldiers were fighting in World War I as opposed to only hundreds in the battle at Breed's Hill, and the guns and artillery used in the Great World War were much more deadly.

Culver Pictures

FOCUS/MOTIVATION:
MAKING CONNECTIONS
Prior Knowledge.
Ask students why the American Civil War was different from previous wars. *(It was the first modern war. Students should mention total war, the use of huge armies, and the reliance on artillery. They might also mention the 9-month siege of Petersburg.)* Explain to students that while World War I was indeed a modern war, it too was unlike any previous war. The armies were far larger, their fighting more widespread, and their weapons more deadly than ever before. On the Western Front the armies reached a stalemate that continued for years in spite of the terrible casualties and destruction.

northern France from the sea to Switzerland. Between the opposing trenches lay a narrow **no man's land.**

This was **trench warfare.** Soldiers ate and slept in the gravelike damp. First one side, then the other would try to break through at some point along the line. The artillery would begin the attack by firing exploding shells at the enemy trenches for hours. Soldiers would then climb from their trenches and rush "over the top" with fixed bayonets at the enemy line. The defender's artillery would rain shells upon them while sharpshooters and machine gunners from the trenches riddled the attackers with a hail of bullets. These attacks resembled the British attack at Breed's Hill in the first weeks of the American Revolution. But millions, not hundreds, of soldiers were involved. And their weapons were far more deadly.

The armies had reached a **stalemate**—neither side could win a decisive victory despite repeated attacks and counterattacks which cost hundreds of thousands of lives. No man's land came to look like the surface of the moon. No tree or house stood there. Scarcely a blade of grass could be found, so heavy was the bombardment. The surface, like the moon, was pockmarked by tens of thousands of craters where artillery shells had exploded.

The war on the Western Front was unlike any other war in

In the words of historian Barbara Tuchman, the soldiers who fought in these miserable trenches could do little more than "exchange one wet-bottomed trench for another." How was this kind of warfare like the early British attacks at Breed's Hill in the American Revolution? How was it far different?

War on Land and Sea   823

Point of View

Barbara Tuchman wrote of the visions of a better world after the Great War.

> "Men could not sustain a war of such magnitude and pain without hope— . . . Like the shimmering vision of Paris that kept Kluck's° soldiers on their feet, the image of a better world glimmered beyond the shell-pitted wastes and leafless stumps that had once been green fields and waving poplars. Nothing less could give dignity or sense to the monstrous offensives in which thousands and hundreds of thousands were killed to gain ten yards and exchange one wet-bottomed trench for another. When every autumn people said it could not last through the winter, and when every spring there was still no end in sight, only the hope that out of it all some good would accrue to mankind kept men and nations fighting."
>
> From *The Guns of August,* 1962

°Kluck was a German general.

history. The battle between the Union and Confederate armies around the city of Petersburg, Virginia, in the last stages of the Civil War comes closest to it. That battle lasted only a few months. The terrible struggle on the Western Front went on for years.

The War on the Atlantic

On the Atlantic Ocean a new kind of struggle developed in 1914-15. The British navy was far stronger than Germany's. It attempted to blockade all northern European ports in order to keep Germany from obtaining supplies from the United States and other neutral nations. The Germans, in turn, tried to keep supplies from the British by using swift submarines, which they called ''Undersea ships'' or **U-boats.**

All the major navies had submarines by 1914. Both Great Britain and the United States had more in operation at that time than Germany. Submarines were small, relatively slow vessels. Most naval authorities did not consider them important weapons. However, the German navy did not have enough surface ships to operate in the Atlantic against the Allied fleets. U-boats were the only naval weapon the Germans could use.

Like privateers during the American Revolution and the War of 1812, U-boats roamed the seas looking for unarmed merchant vessels to attack. When they sighted powerful enemy warships, they slipped away beneath the surface. These tactics worked so well that the Germans ordered that more U-boats be constructed as quickly as possible.

Both the British blockade and the German submarine campaign hurt American business interests. Both of these activities on the high seas also violated the rights of neutral nations according to international law. British warships stopped American ships and forced them to put into Allied ports for inspection. Goods headed for Germany were seized. The British even tried to limit the amount of goods shipped to neutral countries like Norway and Sweden. Otherwise, they claimed, those nations could import more American products than they needed for themselves and ship the surplus to the Central Powers.

The Germans refused to follow the international rules for stopping merchant ships in wartime. These rules provided that ships could be stopped and their cargoes examined. Enemy vessels and neutrals carrying war materials to enemy ports could be taken as prizes or sunk. Before destroying a merchant ship, the attacker was supposed to take the crew prisoner or give it time to get clear of the vessel in lifeboats.

It was extremely dangerous for submarines to obey these rules. If a submarine surfaced and ordered a merchant ship to stop, the merchant ship might turn suddenly and ram the submarine before it

Culver Pictures

With their hearts skipping a beat, the passengers on this Spanish steamer see the sleek German submarine surface from its prowls of the North Sea and ask to inspect their ship. Imagine such a close encounter at sea and describe it in your own words.

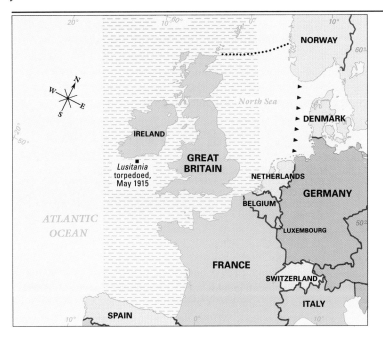

THE GREAT WAR IN THE ATLANTIC

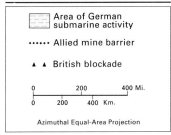

Area of German submarine activity

•••••• Allied mine barrier

▲ ▲ British blockade

| 0 | 200 | 400 Mi. |
| 0 | 200 | 400 Km. |

Azimuthal Equal-Area Projection

LEARNING FROM MAPS. *What was the purpose of each of the war strategies shown on this map?*

War On Land and Sea   825

❶ Wilson's idea of strict accountability included the right of Americans to travel unharmed on the ships of warring nations. Wilson's secretary of state, Bryan, resigned over Wilson's position. Bryan felt that Wilson should warn Americans against traveling on ships of nations involved in the war, especially because some of them, such as the *Lusitania,* secretly carried arms. Bryan protested that it was evidence of bias "in favor of the Allies to insist that ammunition intended for one of the belligerents should be safe-guarded in transit by the lives of American citizens."

CHECKING UNDERSTANDING
Ask students to explain why the war on the Atlantic was of particular concern to the United States. *(Students should mention that it had a direct impact on American citizens. Both the British blockade and the German submarine campaign affected American business interests. And more significantly, German U-boat attacks led to the loss of American lives. Americans also began to see the Atlantic as a highway that could bring the war closer to them.)*

RETEACHING STRATEGY
Students with Special Needs.
Pair students who are having difficulty with students who are performing well. Ask each pair to write a paragraph about the war on the Atlantic and a second paragraph about the war on the Western Front. Display some of the best paragraphs on the bulletin board. Students who do not write well or who are artistically talented may wish to create a detailed drawing, painting, or diorama of a typical scene during the war on the Atlantic or on the Western Front.

could react. Some merchant ships carried concealed cannon. A single cannon shell could send a submarine to the bottom in seconds. If an enemy warship should appear on the horizon while part of a U-boat's crew was examining the cargo of a merchant ship, the U-boat would almost certainly be blown out of the water before it could call back its men and submerge.

Therefore the U-boats attacked their targets from below the surface, firing torpedoes packed with TNT—a powerful explosive—without warning. Many sailors and passengers lost their lives when their ships went down.

Wilson on Neutral Rights

President Wilson protested strongly against both British and German violations of the international rules. If he had threatened to cut off trade with Great Britain as Jefferson had done in 1807, the British would undoubtedly have obeyed the rules. They could not fight the war without supplies from America. But Wilson was unwilling to go that far, in large part because the profitable trade with the Allies was extremely important to the United States.

Wilson took a much stronger stand against Germany. When U-boats began to sink ships without warning, he announced in February 1915 that Germany would be held to strict accountability for any American property destroyed or lives lost. In the language of diplomacy the phrase "strict accountability" was a polite way of saying, "If you don't do what we ask, we will probably declare war."

The danger of war over submarine attacks became suddenly critical on May 7, 1915, when the German *U-20* torpedoed the British liner ***Lusitania*** without warning. Technically this sinking could be defended. The *Lusitania* had deck guns. It was carrying a cargo of guns and ammunition. Its captain was guilty at least of carelessness, for a slow-moving submarine should never have been able to get close enough to a swift ocean liner to hit it with a torpedo.

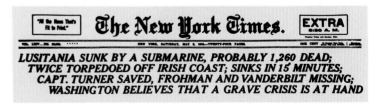

LUSITANIA SUNK BY A SUBMARINE, PROBABLY 1,260 DEAD; TWICE TORPEDOED OFF IRISH COAST; SINKS IN 15 MINUTES; CAPT. TURNER SAVED, FROHMAN AND VANDERBILT MISSING; WASHINGTON BELIEVES THAT A GRAVE CRISIS IS AT HAND

Brown Brothers

The *Lusitania* was crowded with civilian passengers. About 1,200 of them, including 128 American citizens, lost their lives in the sinking. The American public was shocked and furious. If Wilson had called for a declaration of war, Congress would probably have ❶ acted promptly. Instead, Wilson demanded only that the Germans

TORPEDO WARFARE

Brown Brothers

Aiming a torpedo accurately from a German U-boat was very difficult. Torpedoes were launched from tubes in the bow of the submarine. The submarine captain's vision was limited because he had to view the target through a periscope. He had to point the entire submarine in the direction he wanted to aim the torpedo.

The captain aimed ahead of his target the way a hunter "leads" a flying duck. He had to estimate the speed of the target and compare it to the speed of the torpedo, which traveled at about 30 miles (48 kilometers) an hour. Nowadays such calculations can be made accurately by computers. In 1915 such equipment was not available. Once fired, the torpedo traveled a fairly straight line. Its direction could not be changed by the captain, although waves and currents might cause it to veer off course.

The *Lusitania* had a top speed of about 25 miles (40 kilometers) per hour. If it had simply changed direction every few minutes, traveling in a zigzag course, it would have been prac-

tically impossible for the slow-moving *U-20* to get close enough to aim a torpedo. If by great luck he did get within range, the captain, Lieutenant Walter Schwieger, would not have known where to aim a torpedo if the *Lusitania* were zigzagging. Between the time the torpedo was fired and the time its course intersected with the *Lusitania's,* the liner would have changed direction. Obviously, Captain William T. Turner assumed the *Lusitania* was in no danger and took no evasive action.

apologize, pay damages, and promise not to attack passenger ships in the future. Long negotiations followed. In March 1916, after another passenger vessel, the *Sussex,* was torpedoed with the loss of 80 lives, Germany finally gave in. It promised not to sink any more passenger or merchant ships without warning. This promise is known as the **Sussex pledge.** 🖻

Return to the Preview & Review on page 822.

INDEPENDENT PRACTICE
Have students complete the Preview & Review activity at the beginning of the section.

CLOSURE
Tell students that the Great World War was unlike any other. Yet in spite of the terrible destruction and loss of life, the huge armies had reached a stalemate in Europe. Meanwhile the war on the Atlantic threatened to draw the United States into the conflict. Both British and German actions affected American shipping interests, and German U-boat attacks led to the loss of American lives.

HOMEWORK
Have students write a newspaper editorial favoring or opposing U. S. entry into the war in Europe after the sinking of the *Lusitania.* Use completed editorials to create an editorial page for the bulletin board.

SUGGESTED CAPTION RESPONSE
Broke the money trusts; supported the 8-hour workday; extended parcel post; gave farmers credit

Preview & Review

Use these questions to guide your
reading. Answer the questions
after completing Section 3.
**Understanding Issues, Events, &
Ideas** Describe the importance of
the following words: peace
without victory, Zimmermann Note.
1. Which groups of people opposed Woodrow Wilson's reelection? Why did each group
oppose his reelection?
2. Why did the Zimmermann Note
alarm many Americans?
3. What did President Wilson
mean by his statement, "The
world must be made safe for
democracy"?
Thinking Critically. If you had been
able to vote in the presidential
election of 1916, would you have
voted for the reelection of Woodrow Wilson or not? Why?

3. AMERICA ENTERS THE WAR

The Election of 1916

By late 1916 some Americans, including ex-president Theodore Roosevelt, were arguing that the United States should enter the war on
the side of the Allies. A larger number believed that the United States
should at least prepare for war by building up the armed forces. Still,
a majority of the people wanted to remain neutral. They appreciated
Wilson's patient attempts to avoid involvement and his efforts to
persuade the warring nations to make peace.

The depth of their feelings came out during the 1916 presidential
campaign. One Democratic slogan, "He kept us out of war," proved
to have enormous appeal. Wilson was not particularly popular in
1916. Many progressives who had voted for him in 1912 felt that he
had not done enough for reform. African Americans considered him
a racist, for he had actually increased the amount of segregation in
government offices in Washington. Women found him reluctant to
support their drive to obtain the right to vote. Yet the Progressive
party, led by Theodore Roosevelt, had decided not to run a separate
candidate in 1916. Instead the Progressives nominated the Republican
candidate, Charles Evans Hughes, a justice of the Supreme Court.

Wilson tried to hold his progressive supporters in 1916 by backing a bill making child labor illegal and another making it easier for
farmers to obtain low-interest loans. He approved a strong work-
man's compensation law. He appointed the liberal lawyer, Louis D.

*This Wilson campaign van has at
least one version of his popular slogan,
"He kept us out of war." What else
did Wilson do for the American people, according to the posters?*

Brandeis, famous for the "Brandeis brief" in the *Muller v. Oregon* case, to a vacancy on the Supreme Court. Many liberals applauded the choice of Brandeis, who was Jewish. But large numbers of Americans were prejudiced against Jews and probably voted against Wilson because he appointed Brandeis.

The presidential election was very close. Wilson got 277 electoral votes to Hughes's 254. Nearly everyone agreed that the president's success in keeping out of the Great War saved him from defeat.

Wilson was too intelligent to take comfort from this fact. He knew that if the Germans ever decided to sink merchant ships again without warning, America could not stay neutral.

America Seeks Peace Without Victory

Wilson's fear of being forced into the war led him to make a strong effort to end it by negotiation. On January 22, 1917, he made a moving speech calling for **peace without victory.** If either side tried to profit from the war by taking land or money from the other, Wilson said, the only result would be hatred that would cause more wars. All the nations, including the United States, must try to make a peace based on "justice throughout the world."

Unfortunately, neither the Allies nor the Central Powers would settle for peace without victory. The cost in lives and money had been so great after two and one-half years of war that neither side could face the idea that all that expense had been wasted. At the very least each intended to make the other pay the entire monetary cost of the war. The German government already had secretly decided to resume submarine attacks on shipping without warning.

The Germans realized that unleashing their sharklike U-boats would probably cause the United States to declare war. Nevertheless, they expected that "ruthless submarine warfare" would keep food and munitions from reaching Great Britain. Then the British would have to surrender. The war would be over before the United States could raise and train an army and get its soldiers across the Atlantic to France.

Less than two weeks after Wilson's "peace without victory" speech, an American merchant ship was sunk by a U-boat. Wilson then broke diplomatic relations with Germany. He ordered the German ambassador out of the United States and recalled his own ambassador from Germany.

Late in February the president learned that German Foreign Relations Secretary Arthur Zimmermann was trying to make an alliance with Mexico. Zimmermann had sent a telegram to the German ambassador in Mexico with the following instructions:

    " We intend to begin unrestricted submarine warfare on the first of February. We shall endeavor in spite of this to keep the United States neutral. In the event of not succeeding,

GUIDED INSTRUCTION
Ask students what they think would have happened had the United States remained neutral throughout the war. *(Responses will vary.)* Would the United States have been better off to have remained neutral? Why or why not? *(Responses will vary.)*

CHECKING UNDERSTANDING
Ask students what Wilson meant by "peace without victory." *(Neither side should try to profit from the war; a peace that severely punished one side would only lead to more wars.)* Then ask why the Allies and the Central Powers rejected peace without victory. *(The war had been so costly for both sides that neither could face the idea that it had all been for nothing.)*

RETEACHING STRATEGY
Students with Special Needs.
Pair students who are having difficulty with students who are performing well. Ask the more proficient students to help the others write a short statement explaining the significance of the following:
1. Peace without victory *(Wilson's attempt to keep the United States out of the war by making an effort to negotiate an end to it; he meant that a peace would have to be based on justice for all parties.)*
2. Ruthless submarine warfare *(The Germans realized that it would bring the United States into the war, but it would force the British to surrender when they could not get food and munitions.)*
3. Zimmermann Note *(It revealed that the Germans were trying to establish an alliance with Mexico.)*
(Continued)

4. "The world must be made safe for democracy." *(Wilson gave this as part of his reason for asking Congress to declare war. He meant that the war must end before the losses and hatreds became so great that no democracy could survive.)*

INDEPENDENT PRACTICE
Have students complete the Preview & Review activity at the beginning of the section.

CLOSURE
Tell students that Wilson was reelected with the slogan, "He kept us out of war." He realized, though, that events would eventually force the United States into the war unless it was ended quickly and fairly.

HOMEWORK
Have students use library resources to write a short report on an aspect of World War I that interests them, such as the German U-boats, the war's effect on the European civilian population, or American political cartoons about the war.

PRIMARY SOURCE
Description of change: excerpted and bracketed.
Rationale: excerpted to focus on the German offer of alliance to Mexico; bracketed words added to clarify meaning.

Courtesy of the Library of Congress

All eyes are upon President Wilson as he asks Congress to declare war on Germany. "The world," he said, "must be made safe for democracy."

Return to the Preview & Review on page 828.

we make Mexico a proposal of alliance on the following basis: Make war together, make peace together, generous financial support, and an understanding on our part that Mexico is to reconquer the lost territory of Texas, New Mexico, and Arizona. . . .

Inform the President [of Mexico] of the above most secretly as soon as the outbreak of war with the United States is certain. . . .[1]

[1]From *The Zimmermann Telegram* by Barbara Tuchman

In the event of war with the United States, Germany wanted an alliance with Mexico. Americans would then send some troops to the Mexican border rather than sending them all to Europe. In return, Germany would help Mexico "reconquer" the "lost territory" of Texas, New Mexico, and Arizona. Nothing officially came from this **Zimmermann Note.** Yet when it was made public, it caused many Americans to call for war against Germany.

In February and March the number of merchant ships sunk by U-boats increased steadily. The *Housatonic,* the *Laconia,* the *Algonquin* were all torpedoed and sunk. Against this grim background the president took the oath of office for his second term. Almost a month later, on April 2, 1917, Wilson asked Congress to declare war. The reason, he said, was to make a just peace possible. "The world," he added in a famous sentence, "must be made safe for democracy."

Wilson did not mean by this that the purpose of the war was to make all nations democracies. Rather he meant that the world must be made a place where democracies could exist and flourish. He believed that if the United States did not help to bring the conflict to an early end, the losses and hatreds would be so great that no democratic government could survive.

4. THE WAR AT HOME AND ABROAD

Organizing Wartime America

Building an army and supplying it in a hurry was a huge task. Many changes had to be made in the way goods were manufactured and businesses run. The antitrust laws were suspended. In wartime Wilson agreed with Theodore Roosevelt's argument that large-scale organizations supervised by the government were more efficient than small competing firms. Because so many goods had to be moved, it became necessary to place all the nation's railroads under government management. Wilson appointed William G. McAdoo, the secretary of the treasury, to run the entire system.

The president also set up a **War Industries Board** to oversee the production and distribution of manufactured goods. The head of this board was Bernard Baruch, a millionaire stockbroker. Baruch was active in Democratic party politics at a time when most wealthy stockbrokers were Republicans. A friend and adviser of Wilson, he was a natural choice to head the War Industries Board. In this post he performed brilliantly.

Baruch's idea was to organize American industry as though it were one big factory. He decided what was to be made and where the raw materials were to come from. He controlled the distribution of scarce commodities and in some cases even set the price at which they were to be sold. His job was made easier because most producers were eager to cooperate with the War Industries Board. Profit and patriotism were pushing them in the same direction.

Both, Culver Pictures

Preparing to fight a war 3,000 miles away are William G. McAdoo, left, who managed the nation's railroads, and Bernard Baruch, right, who organized American industry as if it were one big factory.

Baruch's board had to supply both American needs and much of the war supplies, called **matériel**, and food for the Allied nations. Great Britain, in particular, depended on American wheat, meat, and other products for its survival. Wilson appointed Herbert Hoover as United States Food Administrator. It was Hoover's job to make sure

RESPONSES (Continued)
Thinking Critically.
1. Responses will vary; students should support their answers with sound reasoning.
2. Students should mention that fighting was more mechanized than it had ever been. World War I saw the first use of tanks, poison gas, and the increased use of airplanes. However, the most important weapons were still artillery and machine guns.

FOCUS/MOTIVATION:
MAKING CONNECTIONS
Student Experiences.
Ask students if they can imagine a situation in which the United States government would nationalize—or take over control of—industry and engage in central planning. *(Answers will vary. Students might mention that this could happen in the case of a national emergency such as a war or depression.)* Explain to students that once the United States entered the war, it was necessary to build and supply a huge army. To aid the war effort, the government nationalized the railroads, and the War Industries Board planned and controlled production and distribution of many items.

UPI/Bettmann Newsphotos

Herbert Hoover, another of Wilson's advisers for the war on the homefront, is shown at right inspecting a shipment of supplies to Europe. Hoover campaigned to persuade Americans to eat less. What slogans did he use?

that enough foodstuffs were produced and that they were distributed fairly.

Hoover had been head of the Commission for the Relief of Belgium early in the war. As Food Administrator he set out both to increase production and to reduce domestic consumption. At the same time it was important to keep prices from skyrocketing.

Hoover had little trouble increasing production. It was in the farmers' interest to grow more because the demand for their crops was increasing. For example, they raised 619 million bushels (218 million hectoliters) of wheat in 1917 and 904 million bushels (318 million hectoliters) in 1918.

Getting Americans to consume less was more difficult. Hoover organized a vast campaign to convince the public of the need for conservation. Catchy slogans carried his message. "Food will win the war" was the best known. Others included "When in doubt, eat potatoes," which was designed to save wheat, and "If you have a sweet tooth, pull it," to reduce sugar consumption.

Hoover also organized "Meatless Tuesdays" when no one was supposed to eat meat and "Wheatless Wednesdays" too. He even started a campaign to get every American family to raise a pig. Pigs could live on scraps and garbage and eventually be turned into bacon and pork chops. Hoover's rules could not be enforced. His technique was to depend on (and praise) voluntary cooperation. He made it clear that patriotic citizens were *expected* to obey the rules. The results were excellent.

National Archives

African American men could be drafted under the Selective Service System, but they could not fight side by side with their white colleagues. Blacks who were not drafted began a great migration to the North, where many found jobs in war plants.

Labor in Wartime

Organizing the human resources of the nation was also complicated. During the war the United States Employment Service directed almost 4 million people to new jobs. When war was declared, thousands of young men volunteered for military service. To raise the huge **American Expeditionary Force** (AEF) that was to fight in Europe, however, it was necessary to pass a draft law, the **Selective Service Act** of 1917.

For those men who were not drafted, and for women workers, the war brought many benefits. Wages rose. Unskilled workers got opportunities to move to better jobs. Union membership rose from about 3 million to over 4 million in a year.

It was important to prevent strikes from slowing down the production of vital goods. In December 1917 a National War Labor Conference Board was set up to try to settle disputes between workers and their employers. This board also tried to make sure that workers were not fired for trying to organize unions.

The American Federation of Labor grew to about 3 million members in 1918. AFL unions cooperated with the Conference Board in most cases. Samuel Gompers, president of the AFL, served as a presidential adviser. Gompers never promised that union members would not strike during the war. But he went along with the government's request that workers agree to arbitrate conflicts with their employers whenever possible.

The need for laborers especially helped African Americans, women, and other groups that had been discriminated against in the job market in the past. Thousands of descendents of slaves had already migrated from the South to northern cities before the war began. Half a million more followed between 1914 and 1919. Most of these newcomers earned far more in war plants than they could make raising cotton or tobacco in the South.

The Selective Service System drafted people of all races although soldiers were still segregated in the armed forces. African

The Granger Collection, New York

THE NAVY NEEDS YOU! DON'T READ AMERICAN HISTORY — MAKE IT!

U·S·NAVY RECRUITING STATION
34 EAST 23rd ST., NEW YORK

What message for readers of **The Story of America** *is found in the navy's recruiting poster?*

The War at Home and Abroad 833

Organize the class into cooperative learning groups. Have each group use library and community resources to find out how World War I changed women's job opportunities. Have each group select two of its members to participate in a National Women's Trade Union League panel discussion on the future of women in the United States.

Americans soldiers were better treated and were given more opportunities than 20 years earlier during the Spanish-American War. About a thousand became officers. Emmett J. Scott of Tuskegee Institute was appointed an assistant to the secretary of war.

Of course, this did not amount to equal treatment. Yet while some African Americans protested, the strong-minded William E. B. Du Bois did not. "Fight for your rights but . . . have sense enough to know when you are getting what you are fighting for," Du Bois urged.

Women were not drafted under the Selective Service Act, although many served as army nurses and as volunteer workers overseas. Many others did volunteer work in hospitals and for such organizations as the Red Cross. Women from all walks of life, the wealthy of New York's Fifth Avenue and the poor immigrants from Grand Street, worked side by side preparing bandages for hospitals and first-aid stations. Most knew that it was only the war that threw such different people together. One American poet described her wartime experience.

> " I sat beside her, rolling bandages.
> I peeped. "Fifth Avenue" her clothes were saying.
> It's "Grand Street," I know well, my shirtwaist° says,
> And shoes, and hat, but then, she did not hear,
> Or she pretended not, for we were laying
> Our coats aside, as we were so near,
> She saw my pin like hers.
> And when girls are
> Wearing a pin these days that has a star°°,
> They smile out at each other. We did that,
> And then she didn't seem to see my hat.
>
> I sat beside her, handling gauze and lint,
> And thought of Jim. She thought of someone too;
> Under the smile there was a little glint
> In her eyelashes, that was how I knew.
> I wasn't crying—but I haven't any
> Pride in it; we've a better chance than they
> To take blows standing, for we've had so many.
> We two sat, fingers busy, all that day. . . .
>
> We're sisters while the danger lasts, it's true;
> But rich and poor's equality must cease
> (For women especially), of course, in peace.[1] "

Thousands of women also found jobs in factories and offices they could not have hoped to get before the war. "This is a woman's age!" the leader of the National Women's Trade Union League

PRIMARY SOURCE
Description of change: excerpted.
Rationale: excerpted to focus on how the war brought women of different classes together.

°a type of dress
°°Women wore star-shaped pins to show they had loved ones in the war.
[1]From "Fifth Avenue and Grand Street" by Mary Carolyn Davies

Culver Pictures

The Salvation Army brought its good works to France, where kitchens were set up to feed the hungry soldiers.

announced in 1917. "Women are coming into the labor [movement] on equal terms with men." This was an exaggeration. Yet women workers did make important gains. Recognizing how necessary women were to the war effort, the Wilson administration established a Women's Bureau in the department of labor.

Mexican Americans also benefited from the labor shortage in the United States. Beginning in 1911, thousands had crossed the border

National Archives

Women would have been thought incapable of rolling these steel cables until the shortage of men during the Great War made it necessary for them to do so. Of course they had been capable of factory work all along, and many did very well. What chance had these women for employment when the soldiers returned from the war?

835

Organize the class into cooperative learning groups. Have half of the groups use library resources to find examples of the Committee on Public Information's war propaganda. Have the rest of the groups use library and community resources to find out how German Americans were treated as a result of war propaganda and hysteria. Then have each group tell the class what they discovered and show examples of what they found. Then discuss with the class the propaganda techniques that the government used.

Courtesy of the Museum of New Mexico

Octaviano Larrazola was one of the thousands of Mexican Americans who came north for wartime jobs. Larrazola became the first Hispanic American governor of New Mexico and later represented New Mexico in the U.S. Senate.

to escape the disorder resulting from the Mexican Revolution. Even more came after the Great World War began. Most settled in the Southwest. Mexican American leaders worked hard to involve the new immigrants in American life. When New Mexico and Arizona became states in 1912, many Mexican Americans voted in their first United States election. In 1916 Octaviano Larrazolo was elected governor of New Mexico, the first Hispanic American governor. In 1928 he became the first Hispanic American in the United States Senate.

Besides working in the cotton fields of Texas and Arizona and on farms in Colorado and California, the Mexican Americans became railroad laborers, construction workers, and miners. Some settled in the northern cities, attracted by jobs in war plants. The jobs were mostly low paid and unskilled. Nevertheless, these workers could earn much more than they could by farming. By the end of the war there were communities of Mexican-born families in St. Louis, Chicago, Detroit, and several other northern cities. Many Mexican Americans served in the armed forces.

Propaganda and the Great War

From the beginning most Americans enthusiastically supported America's involvement in the war. But Wilson realized that other Americans opposed that involvement. So the government attempted to gain the cooperation of all Americans in the war effort. A week after war was declared, Wilson created the Committee on Public Information, headed by George Creel. The CPI used **propaganda** to influence people's opinions about the war. For example, it circulated millions of leaflets praising America's official war aims and criticizing the German government.

These releases portrayed the Germans as bloodthirsty Huns, willing to do anything to conquer the world. They even hinted that there were German spies in every office, factory, labor union, and university. And perhaps more importantly, they implied that any disagreement with the American war effort was unpatriotic.

Using propaganda also sold war bonds to raise money to pay for the war, convinced young men to join the armed forces, and even helped convert some doubters. Churches and religious groups, colleges, women's organizations, and civic groups joined in the government's efforts to "sell the war to the American people."

The Treatment of Protesters

The government's propaganda campaign failed to convince everyone of the rightness of United States actions. Despite the urgings of union leaders like Samuel Gompers, some workers were unwilling to go along with the government's labor policies. Radicals in the labor

HISTORICAL SIDELIGHTS

① Wilson's Committee on Public Information contributed to the mood of intolerance. Unaccepting of dissent, Wilson stated: "Woe be to the man or group of men that seeks to stand in our way . . . when every principle we hold dearest is to be vindicated and made secure."

② The Espionage Act and the Sedition Act led to the prosecution of more than 2,100 people. Conscientious objectors were sent to jail, and over 200 aliens were deported.

SUGGESTED CAPTION RESPONSE
The government believed that they were trying to interfere with war production.

movement had founded a new organization, the **Industrial Workers of the World** (IWW), in 1905. According to the IWW, "the working class and the employing class have nothing in common." Workers should organize, "take possession of the earth and the machinery of production, and abolish the wage system."

One of the founders of the IWW was William D. Haywood. "Big Bill" Haywood had gone to work as a miner in Colorado at the age of 15. In 1896 he joined the Western Federation of Miners. A few years later he became a socialist. In 1904 he led a violent strike of miners in Cripple Creek, Colorado. The next year he was accused of planning the assassination of the governor of Idaho. He was successfully defended by the famous attorney Clarence Darrow. When the Great War broke out, Haywood was secretary-treasurer of the IWW, whose members were known as **Wobblies,** probably because of the way some mispronounced its initials.

Workers should stick together, Haywood said in 1915. They could

> ❝ stop every wheel in the United States . . . and sweep off your capitalists and state legislatures and politicians into the sea. ❞

In 1917 the IWW staged strikes in the lumber and copper-mining industries. The reaction of the government was swift. Federal agents raided IWW headquarters looking for evidence that the Wobblies were trying to slow war production. Over a hundred members, including Haywood, were arrested.

The Wobblies were revolutionaries. Their arrest when they deliberately interfered with the war effort was perfectly proper. But the ① times made people fearful and uncertain. This led the government to violate the civil rights of many radicals who did nothing but speak or write unpopular words. In 1917 Congress passed the **Espionage Act.** This law made it a crime to aid enemy nations or to interfere with the recruiting of soldiers. It also allowed the Postmaster General to censor mail. The next year a much stronger law, the **Sedition Act,** was passed. This law even cracked down on expressions of opinion. ② Heavy fines and prison sentences of up to 20 years could be imposed on persons who spoke or wrote anything critical of the government, the army or navy, or even the uniforms worn by soldiers and sailors.

One national political party—the Socialist party of America— also opposed the war, the only political party to do so. Surprisingly, the Socialists' stance helped them at the polls. Many non-Socialists voted for Socialist candidates as a way to express their disagreement with America's involvement in the war.

The government moved quickly to end this antiwar movement. In New York seven Socialists were expelled from the state legislature simply because they opposed the war. Victor Berger, a Socialist representative from Wisconsin, was denied his seat in the House.

Culver Pictures

Big Bill Haywood was a radical founder of the IWW. He headed a violent strike of miners in Cripple Creek, Colorado. When war came, Federal agents raided IWW meeting places and sometimes arrested IWW members, known as Wobblies. Why did the government think it was proper to make such raids and arrests?

PRIMARY SOURCE
Description of change: excerpted.
Rationale: excerpted to focus on Haywood's views on the power of workers.

Culver Pictures

Oliver Wendell Holmes was known as the Great Dissenter for his carefully reasoned minority opinions as a justice of the Supreme Court. What did he say about the right of free speech?

Even more notable was the arrest of Eugene V. Debs, leader of the Socialist party. Debs was jailed following a speech opposing the draft. At his trial in 1918 Debs spoke forcefully against the government's suppression of opinions it disagreed with. But Wilson and other government officials made it clear they would not tolerate opposition on the war issue.

1 An unreasoning hatred of anything German swept the country. Persons with German names were likely to be insulted by strangers. Schools stopped teaching the German language. Libraries took books by long-dead German authors off the shelves. German-born immigrants who had not become United States citizens were forced to register so that they could be watched closely.

The nation seemed to be in constant fear that radicals and spies would cause the country to lose the war. This was especially true after November 1917, when the **Communist Revolution** occurred in Russia. Americans were suspicious of the communists, and feared they would try to spread their revolution. The Russian communist government quickly made peace with Germany. That enabled the Germans to transfer troops from the Eastern Front to France just when large numbers of American soldiers were going into battle and convinced Americans that the communists were against them.

A sensible limit on freedom of speech in wartime was finally set by the Supreme Court in *Schenck v. United States* (1919), a case that questioned the constitutionality of the Espionage Act. The decision, written by Justice Oliver Wendell Holmes, Jr., one of the greatest of American legal thinkers, upheld the law.

The right of free speech is not an unlimited right, Holmes declared. No one has the right, for example, of "falsely shouting *'Fire!'* in a theater and causing a panic." If there is "a clear and present danger" that something said or written might hurt the war effort, the government may take action. The Supreme Court did not hand down this decision until after the war was over. Before it did so, local, state, and national officials frequently punished persons whose words had no effect on the war effort at all.

Weapons of the Great War

After nearly four years of war, many new weapons had been developed. The fighting in Europe became more and more mechanized. The British and French were the first to use **tanks**—armored, truck-like vehicles that ran on treads rather than wheels. The first tanks were slow, clumsy, and unreliable. They were used to protect advancing troops rather than to attack enemy forces directly.

Another new weapon was **poison gas.** The Germans used gas first, but the Allies soon copied them. Gas was a horrible weapon, choking and blinding its victims. It was not very effective, however. If the wind shifted, it might blow back on those who released it.

Culver Pictures

Culver Pictures

Above, a British tank rolls through a devastated French village, where a horse lies dead near the road. The Great War was one of the last to use cavalry units but the first to use poison gas (left). This weapon choked and blinded its victims. Do you think chemical warfare should be banned? Explain.

GUIDED INSTRUCTION
Tell students to study one of the pictures on page 839. Then ask them to make four columns labeled *Sight, Smell, Touch,* and *Emotion* on their paper. Next ask them to imagine that they are one of the people in the picture. Have them write down, under the appropriate column, everything that that person would see, smell, touch, and feel. Then have them write a letter from that person to a friend back home. Tell students to include observations based on what they have written in their charts. Use the letters to make a bulletin board display.

The War at Home and Abroad 839

Captain Edward V. Rickenbacker was America's most famous flying ace. Below, Norman Rockwell, a popular artist of several decades, pictures soldiers around the campfire for the songsheet of George M. Cohan's "Over There." The tune inspired all kinds of people to sing, "The Yanks are coming, the Yanks are coming."

Airplanes were used increasingly as time passed. There were some bombing planes but none powerful enough to carry heavy loads of bombs for great distances. Mostly planes were used to locate enemy positions and signal artillery units where their shells were hitting so they could aim more effectively.

Yet control of the air was important. There were many exciting air battles called **dogfights** between Allied and German pilots. In this huge war of faceless fighters, pilots were individual heroes. Those who shot down five or more enemy planes were known as **aces.** Rene Fonck, a French ace, shot down 75 enemy planes. Edward Mannock, an Englishman, bagged 73. The most famous German ace, Baron Manfred von Richthofen, claimed 80 kills, but this was probably an exaggeration. Captain "Eddie" Rickenbacker was the leading American ace. He shot down 26 German planes.

But the deadliest weapons remained the artillery and **machine guns.** By 1917 each side had tens of thousands of cannon ranged behind the lines. To prepare for one offensive, the French fired 6 million shells into an area only 20 miles long (32 kilometers). The number of machine guns increased even more rapidly. Before the war American regiments were equipped with four machine guns. By the end of the war each regiment had 336.

Yet all these death-dealing weapons did not give either side enough advantage to end the long struggle quickly. Throughout the summer of 1918 the fighting continued with few movements in either direction. Day by day the number of Americans in the trenches increased from about 27,000 in early June to 500,000 by the end of August.

"Over There"

■ President Wilson put General Pershing in command of the American Expeditionary Force. The first units of the AEF reached Paris on Independence Day 1917 and took up positions on the front near ◀ **Verdun** in October. The AEF went into action in France just in the nick of time. In March 1918 the Germans launched a tremendous attack at the section of the Western Front nearest Paris. With the help of thousands of veterans transferred to France after the Russians left the war, the Germans advanced as far as **Château-Thierry,** a town on the Marne River northeast of Paris. There, in late May, American units were thrown into battle to reinforce French troops. The German advance was stopped.

The Americans who arrived at the front were shocked at the conditions. Soldiers spent weeks in muddy, rat-filled trenches. They faced steady artillery bombardment and the threat of poison gas attacks. One American soldier wrote home describing what it was like in an American artillery unit.

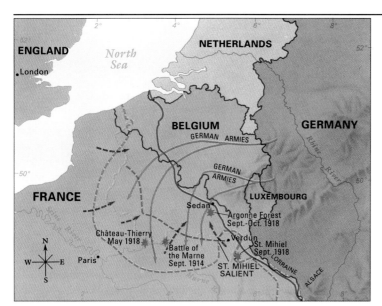

THE WESTERN FRONT

- - - - - Farthest German advance, Sept. 1914
- - - - German advance, Summer 1918
- - - - - Hindenburg Line
- ➤ - - Allied advance, Fall 1918
——— Armistice Line, Nov. 11, 1918
✸ Allied Victories

0   50   100 Mi.
0   50   100 Km.

Lambert Conformal Conic Projection

Source: *Encyclopedia Britannica*

LEARNING FROM MAPS. *After marching through Belgium and deep into France, the German advance on the Western Front ground to a halt. When American troops arrived in late 1917 the tide of war turned in favor of the Allies. How close to Paris did the German armies push?*

CASUALTIES IN THE GREAT WAR		
Country	**Number of Casualties**	
	Dead*	Wounded
Allies		
Russia	1,700,000	4,950,000
France	1,357,800	4,266,000
Britain	908,371	2,090,212
Italy	650,000	947,000
United States	126,000	234,300
Rumania	335,706	120,000
Serbia	45,000	133,148
Belgium	13,716	44,686
Others	15,522	45,658
Total	**5,152,115**	**12,831,004**
Central Powers		
Germany	1,773,700	4,216,058
Austria-Hungary	1,200,000	3,620,000
Turkey	325,000	400,000
Bulgaria	87,500	152,390
Total	**3,386,200**	**8,388,448**
Total	**8,538,315**	**21,219,452**
*Estimated deaths from all causes		

LEARNING FROM TABLES. *As this table of casualties in the Great War shows, the war had tremendous effects on the European population. Although American troops did not engage in combat until the last year, American casualty totals are quite high. Why do you think this is so?*

The War at Home and Abroad   841

GUIDED INSTRUCTION

GUIDED INSTRUCTION
Before students read Canright's letter that is reproduced in the textbook, have them describe what they imagine it was like to be in the midst of the fighting. After students have read the letter, have them compare their descriptions to Canright's. Then ask them to compare his vision of the war with that of Remarque in *All Quiet on the Western Front*. Discuss with students why the two men have such different perspectives.

Somewhere in France
July 8, 1918

My Dear Folks:

I believe I told you in another letter that because of the fine record we have made since we have been at the front, we have been chosen as "shock troops." Well, we sure are being shocked!

Try and picture the very worst thunderstorm you have ever heard. Then multiply it by about 10,000 and you will get some idea of the battle that has been and still is raging along this front and in which we are taking a very active part!

The battle started shortly after midnight a few days ago and had been raging ever since. It started with a very heavy bombardment all along the front, as the country here is very flat, you can see for a long way. I can tell you that it is some sight at night to see the blinding flashes of the guns all along the line. Even far off on the horizon you can see the pink glow flare up and die down and flare up and die down again—very much like a city burning in the distance. The roar and crash of the guns just seems to tear the air to pieces, and explosions shake the ground. To add to the confusion you have the whine and shriek of the shells, some coming and some going! . . .

Allied troops enter a devastated French village near Verdun, site of one of the major battles on the Western Front. At Verdun there were nearly 750,000 casualties. By the end of the war many villages and towns in northwestern France had been virtually destroyed.

National Archives

The Granger Collection, New York

Of course every so often the Germans send over poison gas. We have to be constantly on the alert for it and wear our gas clothes most of the time, and carry our gas masks all the time!

We all have cotton in our ears. Still, the noise of the guns has made us temporarily deaf. We have not taken off our clothes or gone to bed since the battle started. When it slows up a little we just lie down on the ground, right by the guns, and get what little rest and sleep we can. Our meals are brought to us, as we may not leave the position long enough to go and get them! . . .

This kind of warfare means a great many killed and wounded. But I prefer it, as it is the only way to end the war—just kill off all the Germans!

I have given you details and described disagreeable things, but I just wanted you to know what war is and what it means for us and for everyone!

But I think it's great sport and certainly am glad I'm here and taking part in this—one of the greatest battles the world has ever known.

> Love,
> E.J. Canright
> Medical Artillery
> 149th Field Artillery
> A.E.F.
> A.P.O. No. 715[1]

[1]From "Some War-Time Letters" by Eldon J. Canright in the *Wisconsin Magazine of History*, V: 192—195 (1921—1922)

The Rock of the Marne, by Mal Thompson, illustrates warfare along the Marne River on the Western Front. Here soldiers from the 30th and 38th U.S. Infantry Regiments line a trench near Mezy, France, in July 1918 as German shells explode around them. U.S. troops such as these reinforced Allied defenses and then led the surge that turned the tide of war against the Central Powers.

INDEPENDENT PRACTICE
Have students complete the Preview & Review activity at the beginning of the section.

CLOSURE
Tell students that once the United States decided to enter the war, the country efficiently organized its resources. By the time American troops arrived in Europe the war was stalemated and had become increasingly mechanized. The American forces arrived in time to help halt a tremendous German attack and turn the tide of war in favor of the Allies.

HOMEWORK
Have students use library resources to research and report on one of these European leaders in 1914–19: Kaiser William of Germany; Czar Nicholas of Russia; Emperor Franz Josef of Austria-Hungary; David Lloyd George of England; Georges Clemenceau of France; or Vittorio Orlando of Italy

PRIMARY SOURCE
Description of change: excerpted.
Rationale: excerpted to focus on how people reacted to the end of World War I.

These men wear masks in an attempt to protect themselves from the world-wide influenza epidemic that killed 20 million people, more than twice the number who died in the Great War.

Culver Pictures

Point of View

In his autobiography Charles Lindbergh recalls the end of the Great War.

❝I was attending a farm auction sale when the first announcement was made, on November 11, 1918. Word came by telephone. The auctioneer broke off his chant to tell us. Time was allowed for celebration before the sale continued. Men cheered, slapped each other on the back, and then, with nothing else to do, they simply stood about.❞
Charles A. Lindbergh, 1976

Return to the Preview & Review on page 831.

Finally the long stalemate began to break. In mid-September American and French forces pushed the Germans back from a wedge-shaped section of the front known as the **Saint-Mihiel salient.** Next came the long, desperate **Battle of the Argonne Forest.** The Argonne lay northwest of Saint-Mihiel. It was a rocky, hilly region crisscrossed by streams and blasted by constant shelling. Between September 26 and mid-October the Americans struggled through this hellish wilderness. German artillery rained high explosives upon them from the hills on their right flank.

Beyond the Argonne the Allies advanced against the **Hindenburg Line.** The line was actually three rows of trenches several miles apart. It bristled with machine gun nests and was guarded by mile after mile of rusty tangles of barbed wire. By this time over a million Americans were in combat. Another million had landed in France and more were arriving steadily.

On November 7 American units finally broke through the Hindenburg Line. They then advanced more swiftly toward Sedan, a city near the Belgian border. All along the front, French and British armies were also driving the Germans back, rapidly gaining ground. On November 11, 1918, the Germans gave up the hopeless fight. They signed an **armistice,** or truce, that was actually a surrender.

Some 126,000 Americans died during the Great War. Another 230,000 were wounded. About half the deaths were caused by disease, many by Spanish influenza. This world-wide epidemic killed 20 million people. America's war losses were much smaller than those of any of the other major nations. Still, during the last few months Americans bore their full share of the fighting and suffered their full share of the casualties.

5. THE SEARCH FOR PEACE

Wilson's Plans for Peace

President Wilson had been preparing for making peace even before the United States entered the war. As we have seen, he wanted a peace without victory. Wilson believed the terms must not be so hard on the Central Powers as to cause them to begin planning another war to regain what was taken from them.

In January 1918, even before the end of the war, Wilson made a speech to Congress describing his plans for peace. "The world must be made safe for every peace-loving nation," he said. Unless all the nations are treated fairly, none can count on being treated fairly. In this respect "all the peoples of the world are in effect partners." The president then listed **Fourteen Points** that he said made up "the only possible program" for peace.

The first of Wilson's points promised that the peace treaty would

Preview & Review

Use these questions to guide your reading. Answer the questions after completing Section 5.
Understanding Issues, Events, & Ideas Use the following words to describe the end of the Great War: Fourteen Points, self-determination, League of Nations, Big Four, reparations, Versailles Peace Treaty, sanction, mandate.
1. How did President Wilson describe to Congress his plans for peace?
2. What was to be the purpose of the League of Nations?
3. What were some outcomes of the Treaty of Versailles? Of what was President Wilson most proud?

Thinking Critically. Wilson felt that the 14th of his 14 Points was the most important. Of the points described in the textbook, which do you think is the most important? Why?

The National Gallery of Art

The flags of Great Britain, France, and the United States fly on Fifth Avenue. "Allies Day, May 1917" was painted by Childe Hassam in celebration of the alliance of these three nations.

SECTION 5

PREVIEW & REVIEW RESPONSES
Understanding Issues, Events, & Ideas.
Descriptions will vary but should show an understanding of the terms used.
1. Wilson told Congress that the goal of his peace proposal was a world that was safe for every peace-loving nation and that everyone had a stake in seeing that all nations were treated fairly.
2. Its purpose was to settle disputes between nations.
3. Poland and Czechoslovakia were new nations based on the idea of self-determination, and self-determination was more in evidence in the new map of Europe than it had ever been before; the League of Nations.

Thinking Critically.
Responses will vary; students should support their choices with sound reasoning.

RESOURCES
■ You may wish to have students view Transparency
21: *"Flags on the Waldorf"* and complete the accompanying worksheet in *Art in American History.*

FOCUS/MOTIVATION:
MAKING CONNECTIONS
Student Experiences.
Tell students to look at the
chart of World War I casualties
in the previous section. Then
write this summary of the costs
of the war on the chalkboard or
an overhead projector.

WORLD WAR I EXPENDITURES
Allies

U. S.	$22,000,000,000
Gt. Br.	38,000,000,000
France	26,000,000,000
Italy	13,000,000,000
Russia	18,000,000,000
Total:	$117,000,000,000

Central Powers

Germany	39,000,000,000
Austria-	
Hungary	21,000,000,000
Total:	$60,000,000,000

Ask students to imagine
trying to end a conflict of such
magnitude. Ask them what influences they think these horrifying expenditures of men
and money had on the peace
negotiations. *(Students will
probably respond that each
side wanted to feel that it got
something after spending so
much.)*

not contain secret clauses. "Diplomacy shall proceed . . . in the
public view." Another point called for freedom of the seas "in peace
and in war." Restrictions like the ones the Germans and the Allies
had imposed on neutral shipping must not be permitted. But this
point, like urging disarmament and calling for the lowering of protective tariffs "so far as possible," was more hopeful than practical.

A more important point dealt with the future of colonies. In
settling "all colonial claims," the interests of those who lived in the
colonies must be taken into account, not merely the interests of the
ruling powers.

Most of Wilson's other points concerned redrawing the boundaries of European nations. Belgium should get back all the territory
occupied by Germany during the war. France should regain the province of Alsace-Lorraine on its eastern border. This region had been
lost to Germany in an earlier war.

Elsewhere the boundaries should follow "lines of allegiance and
nationality." Areas where the inhabitants thought of themselves as
Italians should be part of Italy, Poles part of Poland, and so on. This
became known as the right of **self-determination.** All peoples should
be able to determine for themselves what nation they belonged to.

The 14th point was to Wilson the most important. It called for
the creation of an "association of nations." The purpose of this
international organization would be to guarantee the independence
and the territory "of great and small nations alike." This **League of
Nations,** as it was soon named, was to be a kind of international
congress that would settle disputes between nations. When necessary, the League would use force against any nation that defied its
rulings.

The "just peace" that Wilson was proposing appealed power-
fully to millions of people all over the world. It helped to shorten the
Great War by encouraging the Germans to surrender when their
armies began to suffer defeats in the autumn of 1918.

■ After the signing of the armistice on November 11, 1918, Wilson
became a world hero. Millions of people believed that his idealism,
backed by the wealth and power of the United States, would bring
about basic changes in international relations. A new era of peace
and prosperity seemed about to begin.

The Versailles Peace Conference

In January 1919 representatives of the victorious Allies gathered at
the Palace of Versailles, outside Paris, to write a formal treaty of
peace. President Wilson headed the American delegation himself. No
earlier president had ever left the nation while in office or personally
negotiated a treaty. The chief British representative was Prime Minister David Lloyd George. The French premier, Georges Clemenceau, and the Italian prime minister, Vittorio Orlando, completed the

STRATEGIES FOR SUCCESS

ANALYZING BOUNDARY CHANGES

Some national boundaries seem to change with amazing regularity while others remain the same for centuries. Recognizing why boundary changes take place will help you understand important events in history.

Boundary changes are usually the outcome of war or purchase, and are usually contained in the terms of a treaty. For example, as you read in Chapter 12, the United States acquired vast western lands as a result of the Treaty of Guadalupe Hidalgo at the end of the Mexican War. Other treaties are agreements of sale.

How to Analyze Boundary Changes

Before learning the steps for analyzing boundary changes, review Comparing Maps on page 517. Then to analyze boundary changes, follow these steps.

1. **Compare maps illustrating the changes.** Note where the differences in the boundaries are.
2. **Determine why the boundary changed.** Check if the change resulted from a war or a land purchase. If the change was an outcome of war, find out who won and why the boundary change was part of the treaty terms.

3. **Analyze the change.** Draw conclusions and form hypotheses about the new boundaries. Determine if the new boundaries solve a previous problem or create a new one. Consider how people in the area of the change feel about the change.

Applying the Strategy

The Treaty of Versailles, drawn up in 1919, ended the Great War. That treaty contained sweeping boundary changes in Europe. Compare the map below to the one on page 818. Note that some nations no longer exist—Serbia and Montenegro. Why? Several new countries now appear on the map. What are they? The delegates to the peace conference used such considerations as nationalism and self-determination to guide their redrawing of the map of Europe. Do you foresee any problems with creating new countries as the treaty did? Give some examples.

For independent practice, see Practicing the Strategy on pages 850–51.

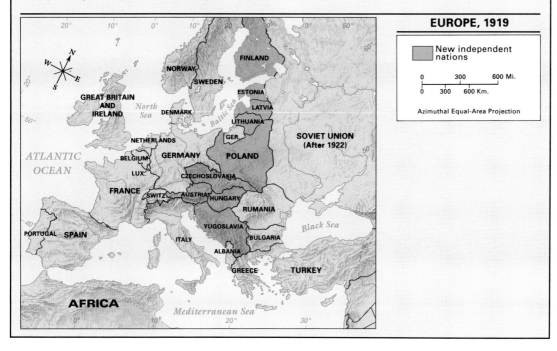

EUROPE, 1919

☐ New independent nations

0   300   600 Mi.
0 300 600 Km.

Azimuthal Equal-Area Projection

Applying the Strategy Responses

They have become parts of new nations. Finland, Estonia, Latvia, Lithuania, Poland, Czechoslovakia, Yugoslavia; Austria-Hungary is now two nations—Austria and Hungary. Answers will vary. Students might mention problems caused by incorporating groups that have been traditional rivals into one country, as in Yugoslavia.

INTEGRATING STRATEGIES FOR SUCCESS

Ask students to look at a map of Europe after World War I and compare it to a map of Europe after World War II. Ask students if they can tell who lost World War II by comparing these maps. *(Students should note that Germany was divided and also lost territory to Poland and that the Soviet Union gained territory.)* Ask students if these new boundaries solved previous problems or created new ones. *(It created problems. Estonia, Latvia, and Lithuania struggled to regain their independence from the Soviet Union; Germany is reunified; Poland wants guarantees that Germany will not try to regain the territory it lost to Poland; self-determination is still an issue—ethnic conflicts are emerging in several Eastern European countries and in the Soviet Union.)*

Council of Four, popularly called the **Big Four.** Working under them were many hundreds of lawyers, mapmakers, economists, historians, military leaders, and all sorts of other experts.

Wilson had a difficult time persuading the other leaders to accept his idea of peace without victory. Clemenceau wanted to make Germany pay the entire cost of the war. France especially had been bled white. Most of the fighting had taken place on French soil. The northern part of the country was a vast no man's land. And almost 1.4 million French soldiers had been killed out of the country's total population of only about 40 million, including women, children, and elderly people.

Lloyd George and Orlando also put the interests of their own nations first. Wilson was forced to agree to a clause in the treaty stating that Germany alone had caused the war. He even accepted a clause making Germany pay "for all damage done to the civilian population of the Allies and their property."

This sum, called **reparations,** was so enormous that the Allies were not able to decide an actual amount. They made the Germans sign "a blank check" agreeing to pay whatever the victors finally demanded. The amount eventually named was $33 billion. This was far more than the Germans could possibly pay, whether or not they

The "Big Four" of the Great War are, left to right: Vittorio Orlando of Italy, David Lloyd George of Great Britain, Georges Clemenceau of France, and Woodrow Wilson of the United States.

Culver Pictures

RESOURCES
■ You may wish to have students complete Reading 34: "Senator Henry Cabot Lodge Demands Harsh Peace Terms (1918)" in Volume II of *Eyewitnesses and Others.*
◄ You may wish to have students complete Chapter 23 Review Worksheet in the *Workbook.*

were entirely responsible for the war. This was certainly not the peace without victory Wilson had promised.

Even if the Big Four had wanted to do so, putting all the 14 Points into practice would have been impossible. Self-determination was an excellent idea, but in many parts of Europe people of different nationalities were mixed together. There were villages of Germans living in Polish areas, Slavs in the midst of Italians or Hungarians.

Many agreements already in existence conflicted with the idea of self-determination. The victorious nations had made promises in order to win the war that violated this and other of Wilson's points. Britain and France had promised Italy parts of Austria-Hungary. The British had agreed to back an Arab nation in the Middle East and also to support a homeland for the Jews in the same region.

Yet, on balance, the final **Versailles Peace Treaty** did come close to the goal Wilson had aimed at in his 14 Points speech. Poland and Czechoslovakia became new states based on the principle of self-determination. The new map of Europe probably came closer to putting all the people of that continent under the flag of their choice than had ever been done before.

The treaty included what Wilson considered his most important point of all. This was the Covenant, or constitution, of the League of Nations.

The League consisted of a General Assembly of representatives of 42 Allied and neutral nations and a Council controlled by the Big Four and Japan. All League members were required to protect one another's territories against attack. All disputes between members were to be submitted to arbitration. Nations which did not obey League decisions could be punished by **sanctions.** These could take the form of a ban on trade with the offending country or even military force.

Furthermore, the former German colonies in Africa and the Far East and the parts of the Middle East that were taken from Turkey were made **mandates,** or dependencies, of the League as a whole. They were to be managed by individual Allied nations. Great Britain, France, and Japan held most of them. The entire League was made responsible for seeing that the interests of the local inhabitants were properly protected.

The League of Nations was Woodrow Wilson's proudest accomplishment. He believed that its founding marked the beginning of an era of permanent world peace. He knew that the Versailles Treaty was not the true "peace without victory" he had sought. Yet he was absolutely certain that the League would be able to deal with the problems the treaty had created. He believed that the entire arrangement made at Versailles depended on the acceptance and support of the League by all the powers. This was the message he brought when he returned to the United States from France. In July 1919 he sub- ■ mitted the treaty to the Senate. 🖻

Return to the Preview & Review on
▶ page 845.

CHECKING UNDERSTANDING
Ask students how the Allies viewed Wilson's Fourteen Points. *(Clemenceau, George, and Orlando were primarily concerned with the interests of their respective nations and considered some of the points, such as self-determination, impossible to put into practice.)*

RETEACHING STRATEGY
Students with Special Needs.
Pair students who are having difficulty with students who are performing well. Ask the more proficient students to help the others make a chart showing in what ways the Treaty of Versailles promoted Wilson's idea of a just peace and in what ways it violated that idea.

INDEPENDENT PRACTICE
Have students complete the Preview & Review activity at the beginning of the section.

CLOSURE
Tell students that while the Versailles Treaty did establish the League of Nations and redraw boundary lines with more attention to self-determination than had ever before been the case, the demand that Germany pay enormous reparations prevented a lasting peace.

HOMEWORK: USING HISTORICAL IMAGINATION
Tell students that they are to use their historical imaginations to write a newspaper editorial for a Parisian newspaper favoring or opposing German reparations, which were finally assessed at $33 billion. Use completed editorials to create an editorial page for the bulletin board.

Thinking Critically
1. Responses will vary. Students should show understanding of Wilson's shortcomings in dealing with foreign leaders and offer sound advice for changing his behavior.
2. Answers should reflect the use of historical imagination and sound reasoning in support of students' opinions.

3. Answers will vary but might include: growing potatoes to eat instead of wheat, giving up candy and desserts, observing "meatless Tuesdays" and "wheatless Wednesdays," and raising pigs.
4. Whether or not students think Germany should have been held responsible for the total cost of World War I, they should support their opinions rationally.

CHAPTER 23

REVIEW RESPONSES
Chapter Summary
Paragraphs will vary but should be evaluated on the logic of student arguments.

Reviewing Chronological Order
2, 4, 5, 1, 3

Understanding Main Ideas
1. It threatened American investments in Mexico, and refugees were entering the United States. Mexicans all agreed that the United States had no right to interfere in Mexico's affairs.
2. Soldiers lived in the trenches, which provided a good defense against enemy fire. Between the trenches lay no man's land. Periodically, one side would try to break through the opposing line. First the artillery would begin the attack; then the soldiers would rush "over the top" into the fire from the defenders' artillery, sharpshooters, and machine gunners.
3. The Zimmermann note, the resumption of unrestricted submarine warfare, and the sinking of merchant ships
4. They consumed less; women worked as army nurses, volunteers, and in factories; labor agreed to arbitrate disputes.
5. It would ensure peace by treating all nations fairly; it established an international congress to settle disputes.

Writing About History
Students should use their historical imagination and include historical detail.

Practicing the Strategy
1. The Nueces; the Rio Grande

CHAPTER 23 REVIEW

1910

1910
Mexican Revolution

1914
American troops capture Veracruz
★
Great War starts
★
First Battle of the Marne

Chapter Summary
Read the statements below. Choose one, and write a paragraph explaining its importance.
1. A variety of factors caused Europe to erupt into war in 1914. The conflict grew into the largest war in history.
2. The United States peace movement tried to end war, and most Americans felt the country should remain neutral.
3. Wilson's foreign policy was unsuccessful in dealing with the Mexican Revolution.
4. After a swift advance into France, German troops were battled to a stalemate. Trench warfare across a no man's land yielded no winner.
5. German U-boats eventually led the U.S. to declare war on the Central Powers in 1917.
6. At home the war effort led to special industrial and food programs. Women and minorities found increased job opportunities.
7. Modern weapons made the Great War especially deadly.
8. The Treaty of Versailles that ended the war was not the peace without victory Wilson felt was so essential to future peace.

Reviewing Chronological Order
Number your paper 1-5. Then study the time line above and place the following events in the order in which they happened by writing the first next to 1, the second next to 2, and so on.
1. Wilson reelected president
2. Great War starts
3. Battle of the Argonne Forest
4. Battle of the Marne
5. *Lusitania* sunk

Understanding Main Ideas
1. Why was the Mexican Revolution of concern to the United States? Why was Wilson's interference resented?
2. Describe trench warfare on the Western Front.

3. Give at least three reasons why the U.S. declared war on Germany in 1917.
4. How did Americans at home contribute to the war effort?
5. What was Wilson's Fourteen-Points plan? Why did he consider the League of Nations his most important point?

Thinking Critically
1. **Problem Solving.** Suppose that you were a close friend of President Woodrow Wilson. What personal advice would you give to help him deal more effectively with leaders of foreign nations? Explain your answer.
2. **Evaluating.** Do you think that President Wilson was justified in asking Congress to declare war in order to make the world safe for democracy? Why or why not?
3. **Synthesizing.** If you had been a patriotic American in 1917, believing Hoover's slogan, "Food will win the war," what would you have done to conserve food supplies?
4. **Drawing Conclusions.** You are to help the Allies negotiate the Versailles Peace Treaty. Do you think Germany should be held totally responsible for the cost of the Great War? Explain.

Writing About History
Imagine you and your classmates are war reporters. Each of you will phone in a report on one of the following: an aerial dogfight, trench warfare, the spotting of a U-boat. The "general editor" who receives the calls will write reports from the descriptions given over the phone. Use the information in Chapter 23 to help you develop your report. Reporters should hand in their "notes" and the general editor should submit their groups' reports.

Practicing the Strategy
Review the strategy on page 847.

850

Wilson's Presidency

1915	THE GREAT WAR	1920

1915
Wilson announces "strict accountability"
★
Lusitania sunk

1916
American troops pursue Villa
★
Sussex pledge
★
Wilson reelected president

1917
Germans resume submarine warfare
★
U.S declares war
★
A.E.F. arrives in Europe

1918
Wilson issues 14 Points
★
Battle of Argonne Forest
★
Armistice ends fighting

1919
Versailles Peace Treaty
★
League of Nations established

Analyzing Boundary Changes. Study the maps on pages 422 and 442, and answer these questions.

1. Which river did Mexico insist was the southern boundary of the new state of Texas? Which river did the Americans claim was the boundary between the two countries?
2. How was that boundary dispute resolved?
3. What other large sections of land were acquired at about the same time? By what means did the United States gain possession of them?
4. How did the Texas boundary dispute with Mexico lead directly to the Mexican Cession?

Using Primary Sources

On April 2, 1917, only a month after his second inauguration, President Wilson knew that he had to make a formal request to Congress for a declaration of war. As you read the last paragraph of Wilson's message, note how Wilson appeals to the emotions of the American people.

. . . we shall fight for the things which we have always carried nearest our hearts—for democracy, for the right of those who submit to authority to have a voice in their own governments, for the rights and liberties of small nations, for a universal dominion of right by such a concert of free peoples as shall bring peace and safety to all nations and make the world itself at last free. To such a task we can dedicate our lives and our fortunes, everything that we are and everything that we have, with the pride of those who know that the day has come when America is privileged to spend her blood and her might for the principles that gave her birth and happiness and the peace which she has treasured. God helping her, she can do no other.

1. Why do you think President Wilson says that "America is privileged to spend her blood"?
2. After reading this excerpt, what inference can you make about what President Wilson thought was important for the world?

3. President Wilson was famous for his speaking ability. In your opinion, what is the most moving phrase or sentence in this excerpt? Why?

Linking History & Geography

New weapons and tactics used in the Great War changed the geography of warfare. Many geographic barriers no longer offered protection. Distances no longer seemed so great. To understand how advances in technology helped shape the Great War, answer the following questions.

1. What weapon enabled Germany to break through British naval defenses?
2. How did airplanes help overcome certain geographic barriers? How did tanks? How did new, more powerful guns lead to trench warfare and vast spaces of no man's land?
3. How have advances in the technology of war almost completely eliminated geography as a factor of war?

Enriching Your Study of History

1. **Individual Project**. Create a series of posters (at least 3) to promote the war on the home front. You might develop posters for recruiting, for the war effort in the U.S., or for the Food Administrator (such as "Food will win the war" or the campaign for "Meatless Tuesdays"). Display your posters for the class.
2. **Cooperative Project**. Your group will use its historical imagination to present to the class a White House meeting between President Wilson and his advisers. The president is considering U.S. involvement in the Great War. One of your group will portray Wilson, and others will speak for each of the following positions: (a) remaining neutral, (b) protesting strongly to Great Britain and Germany for violations of international shipping rules, (c) holding Germany "strictly accountable" for attacks on American ships, and (d) declaring war on Germany.

RESPONSES *(Continued)*
2. By the U.S. victory in the Mexican War
3. California and the Southwest; Treaty of Guadalupe Hidalgo.
4. It led to Mexico's defeat, permitting the United States to negotiate a favorable treaty.

Using Primary Sources
1. It is a privilege to fight to uphold the principles the country believes in and to which it owes its existence.
2. It should be a place where democracy can flourish.
3. Answers will vary; students should logically support their opinion.

Linking History & Geography
1. U-boat
2. Airplanes could quickly cross bodies of water and mountain ranges; tanks were not limited to roads and could cover rough terrain, knock down trees and walls; trenches protected against enemy fire, and the constant shelling created a no man's land between the trenches.
3. Distances, oceans, and mountains are no longer effective barriers against attack.

PRIMARY SOURCE
Description of change: excerpted.
Rationale: excerpted to focus on Wilson's emotional arguments for declaring war.

Chapter 23 Review 851

The Twenties

PLANNING THE CHAPTER

TEXTBOOK	RESOURCES
1. The Tragedy of Woodrow Wilson	*Unit 8 Worksheets and Tests:* Chapter 24 Graphic Organizer, Directed Reading 24:1, Reteaching 24:1 *American History Map Transparencies:* Transparency 7: Women's Suffrage
2. American Reaction to the War	*Unit 8 Worksheets and Tests:* Directed Reading 24:2, Reteaching 24:2 *The Constitution: Past, Present, and Future:* Case 6: *Schenck v. United States* *Eyewitnesses and Others, Volume 2:* Reading 43: A Black Texan's School Days (1920s), Reading 37: The NAACP Program of 1919 (1919), Reading 36: W.E.B. Du Bois Calls for Democracy After the War (1919), Reading 39: A Minister Calls for Christian Unity (1920)
3. The Roaring Twenties	*Unit 8 Worksheets and Tests:* Directed Reading 24:3, Reteaching 24:3 *Art in American History:* Transparency 28: Falling Water (Kaufmann House)
4. An Automobile Civilization	*Unit 8 Worksheets and Tests:* Directed Reading 24:4, Reteaching 24:4 *Eyewitnesses and Others, Volume 2:* Reading 38: A Novelist's Portrait of Henry Ford (ca. 1920) *The Story of America Video Library:* Wheels of Change: The American Automobile
5. America Heads for a Crash	*Unit 8 Worksheets and Tests:* Directed Reading 24:5, Reteaching 24:5, Geography 24 *Art in American History:* Transparency 23: Boomtown *Eyewitnesses and Others, Volume 2:* Reading 41: The Great Boom and the Big Crash (1928–1929)
Chapter Review	*Audio Program:* Chapter 24 *Unit 8 Worksheets and Tests:* Chapter 24 Tests, Forms A and B (See also *Alternative Assessment Forms*) *Test Generator*

STRATEGIES FOR STUDENTS WITH SPECIAL NEEDS

Gifted Students.

Point out to interested students that the Scopes trial created a great deal of public interest at the time and even later. In 1955, for example, Jerome Lawrence and Robert E. Lee wrote the play *Inherit the Wind,* which is based on the trial. Have students read the play and then produce a scene or selected scenes for the class. After the students have performed the play, ask students to explain what the scene means. Point out that the play is a fictionalized account of the trial.

Students Having Difficulty with the Chapter.

You may wish to have students listen to Chapter 24 in *The Story of America Audio Program.* Then organize the class into several cooperative learning groups. Play recordings of classical pianists such as Vladimir Horowitz and Van Cliburn and jazz pianists such as Oscar Peterson or David Benoit for the groups. Instruct each group to make a list of five differences between the two styles. Then have spokespersons for each group share their group's list with the rest of the class.

BOOKS FOR TEACHERS

W. E. Leuchtenburg, *Perils of Prosperity: Nineteen Fourteen to Nineteen Thirty Two.* Chicago: University of Chicago Press, 1972.

Robert K. Murray, *Harding Era: Warren G. Harding and His Administration.* Minneapolis: University of Minnesota Press, 1969.

Ralph A. Stone, *The Irreconcilables: The Fight Against the League of Nations.* New York: W. W. Norton, 1970.

W. C. Widenor, *Henry Cabot Lodge and the Search for an American Foreign Policy.* Berkeley: University of California Press, 1980.

BOOKS FOR STUDENTS

Naunerle Farr, *Roaring Twenties and the Great Depression, 1920–1940.* West Haven, CT: Pendulum Press, 1977.

Anita Gustafson, *Guilty or Innocent?* New York: Henry Holt, 1985.

Gerald Kurland, *Warren Harding: President Betrayed by Friends.* Charlotteville, NY: Sam Harris Press, 1972.

Margaret I. Rostkowski, *After the Dancing Days.* New York: Harper & Row, 1986.

MULTIMEDIA MATERIALS

Harlem Renaissance and Beyond (filmstrip), GA. Traces the advances in African American literature, concentrating on Harlem in the 1920s and 1930s.

Jazz Age (film, 52 min.), MGHT. Depicts American life in the 1920s.

1914–1929: American Letters (simulation), SSSS. Pairs of students pose as witnesses to historical events and write letters to one another describing how they view the events.

The Reckless Years 1919–1929 (filmstrip), GA. Pictures American isolationism following World War I and examines the dark side of the 1920s.

Will Rogers (film, 26 min.), Sterling. The personal life of one of America's great humorists.

RESOURCES
■ You may wish to have students complete the Chapter 24 Graphic Organizer as they work through this chapter.

CHAPTER OBJECTIVES
Upon completing this chapter, students will be able to:
1. Explain why the Versailles Treaty was rejected by the Senate.
2. Analyze America's postwar reaction to the Great War.

OVERVIEW

After the war many Americans favored a return to isolationism. Americans also became fearful of foreigners and minorities, which led to such events as the Big Red Scare. The Roaring Twenties, also called the Jazz Age, became a period of escape and rapid change.

FOCUS/MOTIVATION:
MAKING CONNECTIONS
Student Experiences.
Ask students what they think of when someone mentions the "Roaring Twenties." *(Answers will vary, but students may mention flappers, speakeasies, jazz, or the Charleston.)* Point out to students that these characteristics show that America was at a crossroads following World War I.

SECTION 1

PREVIEW & REVIEW RESPONSES
Understanding Issues, Events, & Ideas.
Explanations should demonstrate an understanding of the terms used.
1. In the Congressional election of 1918 the Republicans won a majority, making it impossible for Wilson to persuade Congress to ratify the peace treaty on his terms.
2. Wilson had a stroke in 1919. This seriously affected his judgment, and he refused to compromise on any issues of the treaty, particularly those regarding the League of Nations.
3. Voter turnout was large because women voted for the first time in a national election due to the ratification of the Nineteenth Amendment in 1920.

852

CHAPTER 24

The Twenties

■ When President Wilson returned to the United States with the Versailles Treaty, almost everyone believed the Senate would ratify it. Certainly everyone wanted the war to be officially over. And the idea of an organization like the League of Nations seemed a good one. A large majority of Americans probably favored the League, although few understood it entirely or were happy with its every detail. Now came the task of winning over the American Senate. But a difficult time lay ahead for the president.

Preview & Review

Use these questions to guide your reading. Answer the questions after completing Section 1.
Understanding Issues, Events, & Ideas. Explain Wilson's political troubles, using the following words: mild reservationists, strong reservationists, Lodge Reservations, Irreconcilables, Nineteenth Amendment.
1. What problem did the 1918 Congressional elections create for President Wilson?
2. How did Wilson's health influence the political situation in the United States?
3. Why was the voter turnout so large in 1920?
Thinking Critically. If you were a member of the Senate in 1919, would you have been a mild reservationist, a strong reservationist, or an Irreconcilable? Explain your answer.

1. THE TRAGEDY OF WOODROW WILSON

Republican Opponents

The Democrats had lost political power in the United States during the war. The Republicans gained in the Northeast by claiming that the heavy wartime income tax unfairly punished industrial areas. They gained in the Midwest and West, where farmers were angry over farm policies that seemed favorable to southern farmers. They also gained in urban areas, where laborers were unhappy with Democratic sponsorship of prohibition. As a result, in the 1918 Congressional elections the Republicans won majorities in both the House and the Senate. Wilson now needed the support of a large number of Republican senators to get the two-thirds majority necessary to ratify the Versailles Treaty.

Wilson had expected the Democrats would continue to control the Senate. He had campaigned for Democrats so that his peace policies would be carried out smoothly. After the election he made matters worse for himself by not including any Republican senators on the peace commission.

Why he did not is a mystery. Perhaps the president assumed the peace treaty would be so popular that senators would not dare vote against it. "The Senate must take its medicine," he said privately.

Wilson seemed to not realize that some parts of any complicated

OBJECTIVES *(Continued)*

3. Analyze the social and economic changes that occurred in the United States in the 1920s.
4. Evaluate the impact of the motion picture and radio on American life.
5. Describe the effects of the automobile on the American economy and on the life of the average American.

6. Identify the "sick" industries of the 1920s.
7. Analyze the effect 1920s prosperity had on the attitudes of most Americans.
8. Demonstrate the ability to compare points of view by reading and comparing two different points of view on ratification of the Versailles Treaty.

document like the Versailles Treaty were sure to displease many different people. When its details became known, various special interest groups demanded many changes in the treaty. But Wilson refused to agree to any changes whatsoever.

The most important criticism involved the League of Nations. The United States would be only one among many members. Suppose the League voted to use force against a nation. Was it not up to Congress to say when American troops were sent into battle? Old suspicions of tricky European diplomats now began to reappear. Senator William Borah, a leading foe of America's joining the League, stated the problem this way in a speech to the Senate:

> " What is the result of this Treaty of Versailles? We are in the middle of all of the affairs of Europe. We have entangled ourselves with all European concerns. We have joined in alliance with all the European nations which have thus far joined the League, and all nations which may be admitted to the League. We are sitting there dabbling in their affairs and meddling in their concerns. In other words—and this comes to the question which is fundamental to me—we have surrendered, once and for all, the great policy of 'no entangling alliances' upon which the strength of this Republic has been based for 150 years.[1] "

The Senate Debate

In the Senate debate nearly all the Democrats supported the League without question. Many Republican senators also favored joining the League. Some of these, known as **mild reservationists,** were willing to vote for the treaty if a few minor changes were made. They had reservations about the League, but their reservations would not block American membership.

Other Republicans were willing to vote for the treaty—and the League—only if more important changes were made. These **strong reservationists** were led by Senator Henry Cabot Lodge of Massachusetts. He introduced what were called the **Lodge Reservations** to the treaty. The most important of these stated that American armed forces could not be sent into action by the League of Nations until Congress gave its approval.

If Wilson had been willing to accept the Lodge Reservations, the Versailles Treaty would have been ratified easily. Only a small group of senators, known as the **Irreconcilables,** refused to vote for it on any terms. The president could probably have gotten the two-thirds vote by making some small concessions to the mild reservationists alone. Yet he refused to budge. It had to be all or nothing.

[1]From *American Problems: A Selection of Speeches and Prophecies by William E. Borah,* edited by Horace Green

National Portrait Gallery

Henry Cabot Lodge was the leading foe of President Wilson even before the fight over the Treaty of Versailles. Another of Lodge's Democratic enemies, Boston's legendary mayor John Fitzgerald (grandfather of President John Fitzgerald Kennedy), never forgot his first view of the Lodge wealth. A kindly cook for the Lodge family invited him to peek into the Beacon Street mansion where she worked. "That playroom was the most extraordinary sight," Fitzgerald later recalled, "filled with the most elaborate wooden toys you could ever imagine." Lodge's portrait is by John Singer Sargent.

RESPONSES *(Continued)*

Thinking Critically.
Student positions will vary, but their explanations should demonstrate sound judgment and reasoning.

FOCUS/MOTIVATION: MAKING CONNECTIONS
Prior Knowledge.
Ask students what the reaction of most Americans was at the time that Wilson asked Congress for a declaration of war in 1917. *(Students should mention that most Americans were enthusiastic about their country's participation in the war.)* Point out to students that this enthusiasm was prevalent because many Americans had a glorified and unrealistic picture of war. One reason for this was because the country had not been involved in a full-scale war since the American Civil War over 50 years before. Most of the people living in 1917 were not alive or old enough in 1865 to remember the horror and destruction brought on by that conflict. Tell them to keep this in mind as they read in this section about Americans' reactions following World War I.

PRIMARY SOURCE
Description of change: excerpted.
Rationale: excerpted to focus on the argument against America joining the League of Nations.

1 In one of his arguments for the League of Nations Wilson prophetically said, "Arrangements of the present peace cannot stand a generation unless they are guaranteed by the united forces of the civilized world."

GUIDED INSTRUCTION: COOPERATIVE LEARNING

Divide the class into four groups. Tell them that they are all members of the Senate in 1919 and are going to debate and vote on ratification of the Versailles Treaty. Assign each group one of the following roles: supporters of the treaty; mild reservationists—those willing to vote for the treaty if minor changes are made regarding the League of Nations; strong reservationists—those who are only willing to vote for the treaty if certain reservations are added, particularly one stating that the U.S. military can only be sent into action by the League of Nations if Congress approves; irreconcilables—those who refuse to vote for the treaty under any circumstances. Each group is to meet and prepare an argument for the group's position on the treaty. Have them choose a spokesperson to present the group's position to the class. After all of the presentations have been made, have the class vote on whether or not they would ratify the treaty.

Brown Brothers

Partially paralyzed by the stroke he suffered in 1919, Woodrow Wilson is helped by a servant as he leaves his home in 1923. He has just made an Armistice Day broadcast. Critics claimed his mind was impaired, but decide for yourself after reading Wilson's remarks on this page.

A White House Invalid

For Wilson the basic issue of the treaty ratification was the idea of a truly international government. He argued that the United States must join the League on the same terms as all the other nations. His position was *reasonable* but not *realistic*. America had too long seen itself as "different" from the countries of Europe.

Americans were being asked to enter into the kind of "entangling alliances" that Jefferson had warned against in his first inaugural address in 1801. It was true that the United States had become an international power. But people needed to adjust gradually to modern conditions. "All or nothing" was not the way to educate them.

If the president had been in good health, he would probably not have taken such a rigid stand. But he was in very poor health. While in Paris, he had suffered a mild stroke—the breaking of a blood vessel in his brain. It had not been recognized as a stroke at the time by his doctor. The attack seriously affected Wilson's judgment.

Still Wilson took the debate to the American people. He went on a whirlwind tour of the United States, making 37 speeches in 29 cities in early September. At the beginning of the tour he stated what he felt was at the heart of the matter:

❝ I wonder if some of the opponents of the League of Nations have forgotten the promises we made before we went to the peace table. We had taken men from every household, and we told mothers and fathers and sisters and wives and sweethearts that we were taking those men to fight a war to end all wars. If we do not end wars, we are unfaithful to the loving hearts who suffered in this war.

That is what the League of Nations is for—to end this war justly, and then to serve notice on other governments which might consider trying to do the same things that Germany attempted. The League of Nations is the only thing that can prevent another dreadful catastrophe and fulfill our promises. . . .

Now, look at what else is in the treaty. It is unique in the history of humankind, because the heart of it is the protection of weak nations. . . . If there is no League of Nations, the military point of view will win out in every instance, and peace will not last. . . .

If I were to state what seems to me to be the central idea of this treaty, it would be this: Nations do not consist of their governments but of their people. That is a simple idea. It seems to us in America to go without saying. But, my fellow citizens, it was never the leading idea in any other international congress made up of the representatives of governments. They were always thinking of national policy, of national advantage, of the rivalries of trade, of the

STRATEGIES FOR SUCCESS

COMPARING POINTS OF VIEW
Historical interpretations of an important event, person, or situation often vary widely. This is because people bring to their interpretations different points of view. One way you can better understand history is to compare historical points of view.

How to Compare Points of View
To compare points of view, follow these steps.
1. **Note the sources.** Find out about each author or speaker.
2. **Compare the main ideas expressed.** Note the similarities and differences. Some points will be quite similar. Others will be opposites.
3. **Compare supporting details.** Consider the amount of support and its logic as you make your comparison.
4. **Do research.** Find out as much as you can about the situation.
5. **Use your thinking skills.** Use your critical thinking skills to understand why people have different views of the event, person, or situation. Decide which point of view you think is most reliable, based on your study of the situation.

Applying the Strategy
As you have read, a lengthy debate over ratification of the Treaty of Versailles raged in the Senate in 1919. The main area of contention was the provision requiring the United States to join the League of Nations. President Woodrow Wilson fought long and hard in support of the United States joining the League. He thought that the League of Nations was "the only thing that can prevent another dreadful catastrophe" such as the Great World War. He also claimed that "the only country in the world that is trusted at this moment is the United States. The peoples of the world are waiting to see whether their trust is justified or not."

On the other hand, many Americans, including several influential members of Congress, opposed United States membership. Senator William E. Borah felt that joining the League would involve the United States in Europe's complex affairs and would mean "we have surrendered, once and for all, the great policy of 'no entangling alliances' upon which the strength of this Republic has been based for 150 years."

Now read and compare these other excerpts taken from the debate over American membership in the League.

Excerpt A
Our isolation ended twenty years ago. . . . There can be no question of our ceasing to be a world power. The only question is whether we refuse the leadership that is offered.
President Woodrow Wilson

Excerpt B
I object in the strongest possible way to having the United States agree, directly or indirectly, to be controlled by a League which may at any time . . . be drawn in to deal with internal conflicts in other countries. . . . It must be made perfectly clear that no American soldiers . . . can ever be engaged in war or ordered anywhere except by the constitutional authorities of the United States.
Senator Henry Cabot Lodge

Excerpt A is from a speech by President Woodrow Wilson urging the Senate to approve the treaty. Although he does not state it, Wilson's comments allude to the provision of the treaty which called for the United States to enter into the League of Nations.

What is Wilson's argument? He claims the United States is now a world power and must continue to assume that responsibility. What support did he use? He points out that the United States began overseas expansion, ending a period of isolation. It had annexed Hawaii, and had been involved in the Spanish-American War, events in Mexico, and the Great War. Why would Wilson hold the point of view he expresses—urging the Senate to ratify the treaty and join the League of Nations?

Excerpt B is taken from a speech against ratification by Senator Henry Cabot Lodge. As you have read, Lodge was a leading opponent of the treaty. His view is that the United States should not enter the League. What reasons does he give for his opposition?

As you know, the United States did not ratify the treaty or join the League of Nations. Why do you think Lodge's arguments were successful?

For independent practice, see Practicing the Strategy on page 893.

For independent practice, see Practicing the Strategy on page 893.

Applying the Skill Responses
Excerpt A: Wilson wanted the U.S. to take on a role of leadership in the League of Nations.
Excerpt B: Lodge believed the League might draw the U.S. into another world conflict; he only wanted American soldiers to be sent into war "by the constitutional authorities of the United States." Congress did not ratify the treaty.

INTEGRATING STRATEGIES FOR SUCCESS
Have students read the closing arguments of Clarence Darrow and William Jennings Bryan in the Scopes trial and compare the two points of view by applying the skill learned in the strategy. Students may need to look in their school or public library to find the trial's closing arguments.

PRIMARY SOURCES
(Top) Description of change: excerpted.
Rationale: excerpted to focus on Wilson's attitude toward the League of Nations.
(Bottom) Description of change: excerpted.
Rationale: excerpted to focus on Lodge's attitude toward the League of Nations.

SUGGESTED CAPTION RESPONSE
The Senate's defeat of the Versailles Treaty was a betrayal of humanity. It was the style of many artists and sculptors to portray government figures in the garb of the ancient Romans because it was considered a classic style. Editorial cartoonists often adapted this style to their work as well.

RESOURCES
■ You may wish to have students complete Reading 34: "Senator Henry Cabot Lodge Demands Harsh Peace Terms (1918)" in Volume II of *Eyewitnesses and Others.*

GUIDED INSTRUCTION:
COOPERATIVE LEARNING
Divide the class into cooperative learning groups. Ask students to imagine that they are American citizens living after World War I. The nation faces the problem of having a president who was recently incapacitated by a stroke that has impaired his judgment. They are concerned citizens who believe that the nation should not be left in the hands of an individual who is physically or mentally incapable of governing. Ask each group to recommend a solution to this problem. Then have each group choose a spokesperson who will present their group's decision to the class. Have the class vote on which recommendation they think will best solve the dilemma. Then have students read Amendment 25, Sections 3 and 4 to the Constitution to find out how this situation would be dealt with should it arise again.

After the U.S. Senate refused to ratify the Versailles Treaty, an American cartoonist in 1920 drew "The Accuser," showing the treaty stabbed by the Senate. What is this cartoonist's message? Why do you suppose editorial cartoonists of the time often portrayed their subjects as ancient Romans?

The Granger Collection, New York

advantages of territorial conquest. There is nothing of those things in this treaty.[1] 〟

Then, in September 1919, while he was trying to rally support for the League, he suffered another stroke. This time there was no mistake about it. His left side was partially paralyzed.

For weeks Wilson was an invalid in the White House. As he slowly recovered, his advisers pleaded with him to compromise with the moderate Republicans. Otherwise the treaty was sure to be defeated. Wilson refused. It was better "to go down fighting," he told his friends.

■ On November 19, 1919, the treaty, with the Lodge Reservations attached, came to a vote in the Senate. It was defeated by Democratic votes. Then it was voted on without reservations. This time the Republicans defeated it. The following March, after further debate, the Senate again voted on the treaty with reservations. This time some Democratic senators refused to follow Wilson's urging. They voted for ratification. Not enough of them did so, however, and for a third and final time the treaty was rejected.

The Election of 1920

Wilson had hoped that the presidential election of 1920 would prove that the people of the United States wanted to join the League. The

PRIMARY SOURCE
Description of change: excerpted.
Rationale: excerpted to focus on why Wilson felt the need for the League of Nations.

[1]From *War and Peace: The Public Papers of Woodrow Wilson,* Vol. 1

SUGGESTED CAPTION RESPONSE
Wyoming, Colorado, Utah, and Idaho; women had
traditionally had more rights in the West.

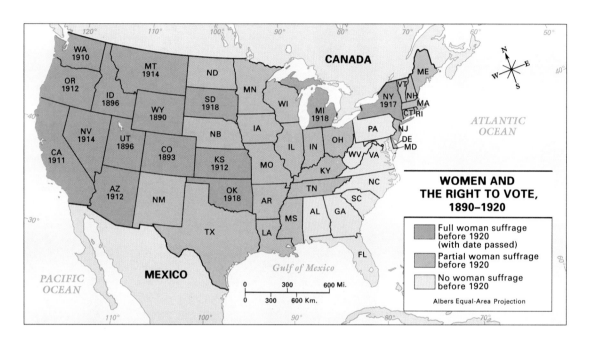

WOMEN AND
THE RIGHT TO VOTE,
1890–1920

■ Full woman suffrage
before 1920
(with date passed)

■ Partial woman suffrage
before 1920

□ No woman suffrage
before 1920

Albers Equal-Area Projection

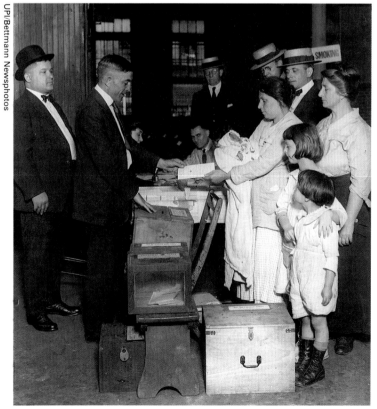

LEARNING FROM MAPS. *As you can see from this map, women's right to vote spread slowly between 1890 and the ratification of the 19th Amendment in 1920. What four states first granted women the right to vote? Why do you think this movement started in the West?*

The vote is theirs at last. After carrying the water, toting the firewood, ironing the clothes, and keeping the family together—these women have come to claim what is rightfully theirs as a result of the Nineteenth Amendment.

CHECKING UNDERSTANDING
Have students summarize the Senate debate that led to the defeat of the Versailles Treaty. *(Nearly all the Democrats in the Senate supported the treaty. Some of the Republican senators, known as mild reservationists, were willing to vote for the treaty if minor changes were made with regard to the League of Nations. Other Republicans, known as strong reservationists, were led by Senator Henry Cabot Lodge. Lodge introduced what were called the Lodge Reservations to the treaty. The most important stated that American armed forces could not be sent into action by the League of Nations unless Congress approved. A third group of Republicans, the irreconcilables, refused to vote for the treaty on any account. Wilson refused to compromise with the moderate Republicans. After being voted down on two previous occasions, the treaty was defeated for a final time when it was brought to a vote with reservations.)*

RETEACHING STRATEGY
Students with Special Needs.
Pair students who are having difficulty with students who are performing well. Have the more proficient students ask the others the following:
1. Who supported Wilson in the Senate? *(nearly all the Democrats)*
2. Who were the strong reservationists and what did they favor? *(other Republicans who wanted more important changes made to the treaty)*
3. Who led the strong reservationists and what did he introduce? *(Henry Cabot Lodge; he introduced what*
(Continued)

The Tragedy of Woodrow Wilson   857

were called the Lodge Reservations)

4. What did the most important of these reservations state? *(American armed forces could not be sent into action by the League of Nations unless Congress approved.)*

5. What happened when the treaty came to a vote the final time? *(It was defeated.)*

INDEPENDENT PRACTICE
Have students complete the Preview & Review activity at the beginning of the section.

CLOSURE
Point out to students that the rejection of the Versailles Treaty seemed to many Americans to be the right decision although American membership in the League of Nations might have helped prevent another major world war. At the time, however, Americans were understandably skeptical about getting involved in the affairs of other nations.

HOMEWORK
Have students prepare a report on the people and events in the women's suffrage movement beginning with the founding of the National American Women's Suffrage Association in 1890 and ending with the ratification of the Nineteenth Amendment in 1920. Students may include drawings, pictures, and newspaper clippings in their report.

Both, UPI/Bettmann Newsphotos

The 1920 presidential campaign was between Warren G. Harding and James M. Cox, both of Ohio. On the right Cox and his running mate Franklin D. Roosevelt (a year before he was crippled by polio). They lead a parade through Columbus, Ohio, after receiving official word of their nomination. Harding, below, campaigns from his front porch in Marion, Ohio. His wife, called Duchess, had great political aspirations for him, but his friends took advantage of his presidency with their shady schemes.

Return to the Preview & Review on page 852.

Democratic candidate, Governor James M. Cox of Ohio, campaigned on a platform which called for joining. The vice presidential candidate, Franklin D. Roosevelt, a distant cousin of Theodore Roosevelt, also supported the League strongly.

The Republican candidate, Senator Warren G. Harding, refused to take a clear position on the issue. Harding was an expert at avoiding controversial questions. During the presidential campaign he used a technique called "bloviating." This meant talking about a subject in a way that sounded intelligent but which actually made little or no sense. Citizens who favored the League could think that Harding favored it. Those who opposed it could interpret his statements the other way.

On Election Day, Harding won by a huge majority. The new ■ **Nineteenth Amendment,** which gave women the vote in national elections, caused a large voter turnout in 1920. The vote for president was nearly nine million more than it had been in 1916. Harding got 61 percent of the total, over 16 million votes to Cox's 9.1 million.

Once elected, Harding stopped bloviating about the League. He made it clear that he did not want the United States to join it. Since the League could not be separated from the Versailles Treaty, Congress simply passed a resolution in the summer of 1921 declaring that the war was over.

2. AMERICAN REACTION TO THE WAR

Foreign Policy in the 1920s

The American people were not ready to assume the kind of international responsibilities that Wilson called for, but they really had little choice. The United States had become the leading industrial and financial power in the world. After the huge foreign loans made by the United States during the war, the rest of the world owed the United States $13 billion. America could not retreat into an isolated cocoon.

In practice the presidents of the 1920s tried to follow a middle road between the narrow view of **isolationism** and the broader view of **internationalism.** They wanted to enjoy the benefits of America's commanding economic position in the world. Yet they did not want to make binding promises to other countries. This attitude was clearly revealed in the way President Harding approached the question of reducing the size of the navy.

After the huge cost of the Great War the public was eager to avoid building still more warships. In 1921 Harding invited nine European and Asian nations to Washington to discuss **disarmament—** limiting the manufacture of weapons of war. Far Eastern issues were also discussed at this Washington Disarmament Conference.

Several treaties were negotiated by the delegates. The most important was the **Five-Power Naval Treaty.** In this treaty the United States, Great Britain, Japan, France, and Italy agreed to a ten-year

Culver Pictures

PUTTING HIS FOOT DOWN.

Preview & Review

Use these questions to guide your reading. Answer the questions after completing Section 2.
Understanding Issues, Events, & Ideas. Describe the postwar reaction in America using the following words: isolationism, internationalism, disarmament, Five-Power Naval Treaty, Open Door, postwar reaction, anarchists, Big Red Scare, Palmer raid, Emergency Quota Act, National Origins Act. Explain the major changes in American society after the war using these words: prohibition, dry state, Eighteenth Amendment, Volstead Act, bootlegger, repeal, Twenty-first Amendment, fundamentalism.
1. Why did American presidents in the 1920s try to find a middle ground between isolationism and internationalism?
2. What effect did peacetime have on industry? Why?
3. Why was prohibition difficult to enforce?
4. How was the fundamentalist movement a part of the postwar reaction in America? How was the Sacco-Vanzetti case a part?
Thinking Critically. **1.** You have read that after the Great War, Americans "wanted peace without the responsibility of maintaining it." Do you think that Americans still have that attitude? Give reasons to support your answer. **2.** Write two editorials about the Scopes trial: one from the point of view of a person who favored the advances of science and technology being taught and the other from the point of view of a fundamentalist against teaching about them.

In this editorial cartoon, "Putting His Foot Down," Uncle Sam holds a copy of the "Trade Treaty with China" that began America's Open Door Policy. For a complete discussion of the Open Door Policy, see pages 768–69. What did the policy provide? Why did Americans consider such an agreement important in the 1920s?

RESOURCES
■ You may wish to have students complete Case 6: "Schenck v. United States" in THE CONSTITUTION: Past, Present, and Future.

RESPONSES (Continued)

Thinking Critically
1. Student opinions will vary but should be supported by sound reasoning.
2. Student editorials should demonstrate that they carefully researched the Scopes trial.

PRIMARY SOURCE
Description of change: excerpted.
Rationale: excerpted to focus on Barzini's opinions of American leaders and how they were chosen.

Point of View

Not all immigrants were as frightened of America as most Americans were of them. In *O America,* an Italian journalist wrote these lines.

> "Americans followed the leaders they chose, not those given to them by God or imposed by screaming and violent crowds. The leaders they freely chose, most of them anyway, who looked to me like Roman senators or Renaissance princes, were born on small farms, the sons of humble people. This free and easy flow of a whole nation toward the future seemed the enviable secret of America, a country where it was still possible to hope. But was that all there was, was it real or a creation of my imagination?"
>
> Luigi Barzini, 1977

"holiday" on the construction of battleships. They also agreed to maintain a fixed ratio, or balance, on all major warships. The United States and Great Britain were to have no more than 525,000 tons of such vessels. Japan's limit was 315,000 tons, France and Italy's 175,000 each. In another agreement all nine nations promised to uphold the principle of the **Open Door** in China. This was the policy which assured all nations equal trade rights with an independent China.

President Harding insisted that the Washington Conference treaties did not commit the United States "to any kind of alliance, entanglement, or involvement." This was true enough. The treaties were backed only by the good will of the nations that signed them. This satisfied most Americans. They wanted peace without the responsibility for maintaining it. They could accept the treaties and still believe that they could remain isolated in the old way from foreign "entanglements."

The Postwar Reaction

Isolation was an aspect of a larger **postwar reaction** in the United States. The Great War had been a Great Mistake, most people now thought. Millions of lives had been lost. Billions of dollars had been wasted. And for what purpose? The world had certainly not been made safe for democracy, as Wilson had promised.

■ In 1919 most Americans seemed more worried about making the United States safe for themselves. Many seriously believed that a communist revolution might break out in the United States at any moment. They were mindful that a tiny group of communists had taken over all of Russia in 1917. Now there were perhaps seventy thousand communists (called Reds) in the United States.

Communists wanted workers to raise the red flag of revolution, take up arms, and destroy the capitalist system. At the same time **anarchists,** who wanted all governments violently abolished, stirred up workers. But most workers were simply trying to keep their jobs. Going from war to peace had been difficult for American industry. Without contracts for war supplies, many plants shut down temporarily or slowed down their operations. Hundreds of thousands of wage earners were thrown out of work. Soldiers returning to civilian life found it almost impossible to get jobs. Many of the workers found their jobs had been filled by African Americans who had moved from the South during the war to work in factories. This added fuel to racial tensions that erupted in situations like the 1919 Chicago Race Riot.

As a result a wave of strikes spread over the land. At one time or another during 1919, 4 million workers were on strike. Seattle was paralyzed. In Boston even the police walked off their jobs. Strikes by police were unheard of at that time. With the streets of Boston

① African Americans were not the only targets of the Klan of the 1920s. They also harassed Catholics, Jews, foreigners, and anyone they considered un-American.

UPI/Bettmann Newsphotos

The Chicago Steel Strike of 1919 was one of the disturbing postwar walkouts. Even police went on strike in Boston. Most people blamed these strikes on "creeping Bolshevism"—a type of communism—as we see in the Red Scare cartoon below.

The Granger Collection, New York

unprotected, looters began breaking into stores. The governor of Massachusetts, Calvin Coolidge, finally called in troops to restore order in the city.

At the same time a series of bombings by terrorists took place. To this day no one knows who was responsible for most of the bombings. But the tendency was to blame "the Reds." A **Big Red Scare** swept over America.

President Wilson's attorney general, A. Mitchell Palmer, became convinced that a massive communist plot to overthrow the federal government was being organized. He ordered raids on the headquarters of suspected radical groups. These **Palmer raids** were often conducted without search warrants. Many suspected communists were held for weeks without formal charges. There was no evidence of a nationwide uprising. Yet in 1920 Palmer announced that such a revolution would take place on May 1, the communist Labor Day. When May 1 passed quietly, Americans realized that the danger of a revolution had been only in their minds. As quickly as it had begun, the Big Red Scare ended.

The nervous mood of the 1920s then took other forms. One was a revival of the Ku Klux Klan. Klan membership grew between 1920 ① and 1923 from about 5,000 members to several million. Unlike the Klan of Reconstruction days, this one spread into the northern states. It became a powerful but short-lived political and social force in the early 1920s and did much harm to many innocent people.

The postwar years brought despair for many African Americans. Aside from suffering at the hands of the Klan, they also faced hostility

FOCUS/MOTIVATION:
MAKING CONNECTIONS
Prior Knowledge.
Have students recall what they read about the Ku Klux Klan in Chapter 17 by asking the following questions: What was the main reason for the founding of the Ku Klux Klan? (The main reason for the founding of the Ku Klux Klan was to prevent African Americans from exercising their civil rights.) In what part of the country was this organization strongest? (the South) What caused the Ku Klux Klan to decline in membership and power after 1877? (Organizations such as the Ku Klux Klan were no longer needed because once the federal troops were withdrawn from the South white southerners began to regain their former power. They gradually began to pass laws depriving African American citizens of their civil rights.) Tell students to keep this in mind as they read about the resurgence of the Ku Klux Klan in this section.

HISTORICAL SIDELIGHTS

① Race riots broke out in 20 cities in both the North and South in 1919, causing hundreds of injuries and much property damage.

RESOURCES

■ You may wish to have students complete Reading 43: "A Black Texan's School Days (1920s)" in Volume II of *Eyewitnesses and Others*.

GUIDED INSTRUCTION: COOPERATIVE LEARNING

Divide the class into cooperative learning groups. Assign each group a topic involving a social problem of the 1920s. Have them research and then compile a report that includes a pictorial presentation. You may wish to assign some of the following topics: the status of African Americans in the 1920s; immigrants and immigration laws in the 1920s; and the status of women in the 1920s. Have each group present their report to the class.

Culver Pictures

The hooded figures are but a handful of the millions nationwide who joined the Ku Klux Klan in the 1920s. They burned crosses and lynched African Americans in the dead of night, some of their victims still wearing their uniforms from the Great War.

from middle-class Americans. They found it difficult to move up in the job market, where discrimination and segregation hindered their chances. At the same time, increasing numbers of southern blacks poured into northern cities. They were forced to live in ghettos, where life was vicious and degrading. Disease and crime rates soared.

■ Old prejudices resurfaced. Racial tensions sizzled. Mobs in the South lynched more than 60 African Americans, 10 of them Great
① War veterans still in uniform. Race riots erupted in Washington, D.C., and Chicago. To the surprise of many Americans, the NAACP now urged blacks to stand firm, to fight back. The violence increased throughout the country.

Some people blamed the communists for stirring up the racial trouble. Meanwhile black leaders and liberal whites pushed for anti-lynching laws. And many African Americans were attracted to the Universal Negro Improvement Association of Marcus Garvey. He appealed to the African American traditions and religious values. Garvey wanted African Americans to return to Africa where he hoped to create a kingdom with himself as the king. Although his plan failed, Garvey's movement boosted black pride and dignity and helped them deal with the frustrations of American society.

Garvey's ideas also had great influence in Central America, the Caribbean, and Africa. The leaders of independence crusades in countries such as Ghana and Kenya credited Garvey and his book, *Philosophy and Opinions,* for helping to fuel their fierce drive for freedom for their people. Even the African National Congress in southern Africa is a direct outgrowth of Garvey's movement.

At the same time the NAACP continued to battle for equal rights. Seeking to unify African Americans—in fact all Americans—the organization issued a national statement of its aims in 1919:

RESOURCES
■ You may wish to have students complete Reading 37: "The NAACP Program of 1919 (1919)" in Volume II of *Eyewitnesses and Others.*

" 1. A vote for every Negro man and woman on the same ■ terms as for white men and women.

2. An equal chance to acquire the kind of an education that will enable the Negro everywhere wisely to use this vote.

3. A fair trial in courts for all crimes of which he is accused, by judges in whose election he has participated without discrimination because of race.

4. A right to sit upon the jury which passes judgment upon him.

5. Defense against lynching and burning at the hands of mobs.

6. Equal service on railroad and other public carriers. This to mean sleeping car service, dining car service, Pullman service, at the same cost and upon the same terms as other passengers.

7. Equal right to use of public parks, libraries and other community services for which he is taxed.

8. An equal chance for a livelihood in public and private employment.

9. The abolition of color-hyphenation and the substitution of 'straight Americanism.'

If it were not a painful fact that more than four-fifths of the colored people of the country are denied the above

UPI/Bettmann Newsphotos

The flag passes by as a veteran of the 309th Colored Infantry pays his respects.

USING HISTORICAL IMAGINATION
Have students imagine that they are either John T. Scopes, Nicola Sacco, or Bartolomeo Vanzetti. Point out to them that all three of these people were tried in famous trials during the 1920s. They are to write entries in their diaries as their trial is taking place. They should include descriptions of the following: How they feel about being put on trial; the people who are participating in their trial; how the trial is proceeding; and what they think the outcome of the trial will be and why. You may wish to have some students read their diary entries to the class.

863

863

Cincinnati Art Museum, The Edwin and Virginia Irwin Memorial; © Estate of Grant Wood/VAGA New York 1990

Grant Wood was one of America's most popular 20th-century painters. Note that in this painting titled "Daughters of the Revolution" he posed the three subjects in front of a print of "Washington Crossing the Delaware."

■ named elementary rights, it would seem an absurdity that an organization is necessary to demand for American citizens the exercise of such rights. . . . Has not slavery been abolished? Are not all men equal before the law? Were not the Fourteenth and Fifteenth Amendments passed by the Congress of the United States and adopted by the states? Is not the Negro a man and a citizen?[1] 99

The NAACP also made a strong statement of principles and observations of the plight of blacks in America. In part it said:

66 When the fundamental rights of citizens are so wantonly denied and that denial justified and defended as it is by the lawmakers and dominant forces of so large a number of our states, it can be realized that the fight for the Negro's citizenship rights means a fundamental battle for real things, for life and liberty.

This fight is the Negro's fight. 'Who would be free, himself must strike the blow.' But, it is no less the white man's fight. The common citizenship rights of no group of people, to say nothing of nearly 12,000,000 of them, can be denied with impunity [freedom from harm] to the State and the social order which denies them. . . . Whoso loves America and cherishes its institutions, owes it to himself and his country to join hands with the members of the National Association for the Advancement of Colored People to 'Americanize' America and make the kind of democracy we Americans believe in to be the kind of democracy we shall have in *fact*, as well as in theory.[2] 99

[1] From "The Task for the Future—A Program for 1919" by the NAACP
[2] *Ibid.*

Despite these efforts, little progress was made in ending discrimination in America.

America's postwar mood was also reflected in new immigration laws. In 1921 Congress reacted to the isolationism of the times by taking steps to control the entry of foreigners into the United States. This made some sense at the time. The frontier had disappeared. In a machine age the nation no longer needed to import large numbers of unskilled laborers. The **Emergency Quota Act** limited the number of immigrants by nationality, reducing the number of newcomers from eastern and southern Europe. A still stiffer quota law, the **National** ① **Origins Act,** was passed in 1924. Beginning in 1929, a total of only 150,000 immigrants a year could enter the United States. In practice the number of actual immigrants fell below 100,000 every year from 1931 to 1946.

The Sacco-Vanzetti Case

Such xenophobia—the fear of foreigners—led to the Sacco-Vanzetti case. In April 1920 two men in Massachusetts killed a paymaster and a guard during a daring daylight robbery of a shoe factory. Shortly thereafter, Nicola Sacco and Bartolomeo Vanzetti were charged with the crime, and in 1921 they were convicted of murder. Sacco and Vanzetti were anarchists who believed that government was unnecessary and should be violently overthrown. They were also Italian immigrants. Their trial was a travesty of justice. There was little real evidence against them. Much of what was presented at the trial had been manufactured by the prosecution. In addition, the judge seemed prejudiced against the two, especially in his comments outside the courtroom.

Prominent people all over the world praised the dignity Sacco and Vanzetti showed throughout the trial. The noted lawyer Felix Frankfurter helped found the American Civil Liberties Union to fight for the two men. Other defenders of justice, including the novelist John Dos Passos and the poet Edna St. Vincent Millay, joined worldwide protests that for years kept Sacco and Vanzetti alive through efforts to obtain a new trial. Vanzetti's dignified words are still remembered:

“ You see me before you, not trembling. I never commit a crime in my life. . . . I am so convinced to be right that if you could execute me two times, and if I could be reborn two other times, I would live again and do what I have done already. ”

In August 1927 Sacco and Vanzetti were electrocuted. Historians now suspect that at least Sacco was guilty, but the truth and shame of the incident remain: at the time Sacco and Vanzetti paid with their lives for being radicals and foreigners as much as for any crime.

Whitney Museum of American Art

Were Nicola Sacco and Bartolomeo Vanzetti guilty of robbery and killing a paymaster? Or were they simply guilty of being foreigners at a time when xenophobia—fear of foreigners—swept America in the 1920s? Those who believed they were innocent may have hung Ben Shahn's lithograph, "The Passion of Sacco and Vanzetti," in their living rooms in protest against the death sentence.

Reynolda House, Museum of American Art, Winston Salem, N.C.

Thomas Hart Benton depicts the dark side of prohibition in "The Bootleggers," painted in 1927. Planes, trains, and fast cars bring the customers to buy illegal liquor.

Prohibition

During the Progressive Era there had been strong popular support for prohibiting the manufacture, transportation, and sale of alcoholic beverages. This temperance movement, like the one in the 1840s, was led by American religious groups who saw liquor as the devil's tool. By 1914 prohibition was in force in more than a quarter of the states, known as the dry states. Most of the dry states were in the South and rural areas, where many of the people were members of fundamentalist Protestant religious groups.

The outburst of moral and religious concern caused by the war gave energy to a national prohibition movement. Some saw it as an attack on the German custom of drinking beer; others as an attack on the drinking habits of European Catholics. What tipped the scales was a very effective campaign to protect young servicemen from the sale of alcohol on or near army bases. This fit closely with the prohibitionist charge that drinking was a cause of poverty and social disorder. As a result, in 1919 the **Eighteenth Amendment** was ratified. This amendment was enforced by the **Volstead Act,** which went into effect in January 1920, making the entire nation dry.

People who favored prohibition pointed to the sharp decline in arrests for drunkenness and to the lower number of deaths from alcoholism in the 1920s. Fewer workers spent their hard-earned dollars on drink. However, prohibition was impossible to enforce, even with the tough Volstead Act. Private individuals bought liquor smuggled by **bootleggers** or drank gin from teacups in "speakeasies"— secret bars or clubs.

Crime statistics soared in the 1920s. Most of the liquor was sold

SUGGESTED CAPTION RESPONSE
He has painted their faces with solemn, serious expressions.

RESOURCES
■ You may wish to have students complete Reading 39: "A Minister Calls for Christian Unity (1920)" in Volume II of *Eyewitnesses and Others.*

by gangsters such as "Scarface" Al Capone of Chicago. Hoodlums fought for territories with guns and bombs, killing innocent bystanders as well as their rivals. The scene was not much different from the one on some city streets today where drug deals are common. Dealers, like the bootleggers, fight over territory, often killing one another and innocent bystanders as well.

Still, in the 1920s powerful "dry" forces kept politicians in both parties from proposing that prohibition be lifted, or **repealed.** It remained in force until December 1933, when it was repealed by the **Twenty-first Amendment.**

The Fundamentalist Movement

America was rapidly changing in the postwar years. Over 19 million ■ people moved from the farm to the city in the 1920s. Problems such as crime, gambling, and corruption seemed to be all too common, especially in the cities. The progressive spirit had died in the disillusionment following the Great War. Many Americans searching for a system of values in this time of rapid change found it in the

In this farming community, Protestants gather to witness a group baptism. White dresses are worn by the women who will participate by being dipped in a water trough. How does the artist, John Steuart Curry, show the feelings of the onlookers?

Whitney Museum of Art

In a rare moment of relaxation during the Scopes Trial, Clarence Darrow, left, and William Jennings Bryan appear friendly. Notice the fan. The courtroom was sweltering. This was the last public appearance for Bryan, a man of long public prominence. He died a few days after the trial. How had Bryan electrified another audience in 1896? How did he fare in the Scopes trial?

Protestant religious movement called **fundamentalism.** It was strongest on the farms and in the small towns of America. Many people in these rural areas blamed society's economic and social problems on modern urban culture. Fundamentalists believed that the King James translation of the Bible was God's truth. They took its words literally.

Fundamentalists thought that the science and technology of the machine age were challenging the traditional values and beliefs they held dear. Every year new discoveries seemed to question ideas held for centuries. As an example they seized on Charles Darwin's theory of evolution described in *The Origin of Species*. They campaigned vigorously for laws banning all mention of Darwin's theory, especially in textbooks and classrooms. Darwin, a British naturalist, had theorized that modern species of plants and animals had evolved from a few earlier ones. From Darwin's theory came the idea that human beings had slowly evolved from ape-like creatures, which of course had gradually evolved from even lower life-forms. This idea directly opposed the fundamentalist's view of God having created the heavens and the earth in six days. Didn't the Bible describe how and when God created each of his creatures, including humans?

In their battle against evolution, the fundamentalists found a leader in William Jennings Bryan, the forceful orator who had been Wilson's secretary of state. Bryan went about the country charging that modern Americans had "taken the Lord away from the schools." He even offered $100 to anyone who would admit in public that he was descended from an ape as he claimed Darwin had said.

In 1925 the fundamentalists won a victory when Tennessee passed a law forbidding instructors in the state's schools and colleges to teach "any theory that denies the story of the Divine Creation of man taught in the Bible." Many people were shocked at the law, which they felt restricted academic freedom, maybe even the freedom of speech. The American Civil Liberties Union, a nonprofit group whose stated purpose was to protect the basic freedom of the people, offered to defend any Tennessee teacher who would challenge the constitutionality of the law. A young biology teacher in the Tennessee mountain town of Dayton, John T. Scopes, agreed to violate the law and teach Darwin's theory. He was taken to court by the state. Clarence Darrow, perhaps the greatest lawyer of the time, headed Scopes' defense. Darrow put the issue this way:

> 66 Scopes isn't on trial. Civilization is on trial. The prosecution is opening the doors of a reign of bigotry equal to anything in the Middle Ages. No man's belief will be safe if they win. 99

The prosecuting attorney was no less than William Jennings Bryan himself. Overnight the Dayton "Monkey Trial" attracted national attention. Sensing a story, big-city reporters like H. L. Mencken flocked to the trial.

The trial took place in a sweltering courtroom. The prosecution took every opportunity to state its view of creation. Bryan even testified as an expert witness on the Bible. On the stand he explained that he believed that the earth had been created in 4004 B.C., that a whale had swallowed Jonah, that Joshua had stopped the sun in its course, and that Eve had been created from Adam's rib, all as the Bible said. Under intense questioning by Darrow, Bryan showed an almost complete ignorance of modern scientific thought. And he doomed his own cause when he agreed that creation took hundreds of years, that a "day" in the Bible might actually be centuries.

This admission had no effect on the trial. The conviction of Scopes was a foregone conclusion. After rousing arguments from both sides, Scopes was found guilty and fined $100. That decision was soon overturned by the state supreme court. More important, Bryan had contradicted the fundamentalists' argument.

Still, the fundamentalism that prompted the trial had vigor throughout the country. Crusaders such as Billy Sunday found audiences over the airwaves.

And the vigor has not left the movement. Conservative church groups are the most rapidly growing segment of American Protestantism. Although their message and methods are different today, fundamentalists still seek to be heard by the American people. Through television they reach their widest audience ever. Many of the groups have become politically involved, taking active roles in a variety of movements.

The Scopes trial symbolized something larger than a controversy over Darwin's theory. It emphasized the divisions within American society—rural versus urban, traditional versus modern. The rising fortunes of the late 1920s made these divisions seem deeper. Business owners and urban laborers raked in the money. Yet prosperity seemed to pass by farmers and people in small towns, leaving many of them hostile to the new urban society. 🖃

Return to the Preview & Review on page 859.

INDEPENDENT PRACTICE
Have students complete the Preview & Review activity at the beginning of the section.

CLOSURE
Point out to students that following a dramatic upheaval such as a world war, people's attitudes are greatly affected because their lives have been drastically changed.

HOMEWORK
Have students research and write a report on one of the race riots that occurred in the United States in 1919. They should include the causes of the riot, where it occurred, and the effects on the blacks and whites in that community.

PRIMARY SOURCE
Description of change: excerpted.
Rationale: excerpted to focus on Darrow's view on the importance of the Scopes trial.

PREVIEW & REVIEW RESPONSES
Understanding Issues, Events, & Ideas.
Descriptions should demonstrate an understanding of the terms used.

1. Jazz was created in the South by African American musicians. It grew out of the "blues" that reflected the hard life and tough-minded humor of African Americans. Jazz reflected the 1920s in that it broke away from rigid, conventional rules and traditions.
2. Jack Dempsey—boxing; Red Grange—football; Babe Ruth—baseball; Helen Wills—tennis; Gertrude Ederle—swimming
3. People copied the hairstyles, dress, speech, and mannerisms of their favorite movie stars. Almost everyone could enjoy the radio because it was live entertainment that could be listened to at home without paying for a ticket. Large companies sprang up to manufacture radio sets and broadcasting equipment.
4. They were young expatriates who were disillusioned by the war. Many of them seemed to be searching for their lost innocence.

Thinking Critically
1. Student poems or songs should show creativity and imagination.
2. Answers will vary but should demonstrate an understanding of the postwar era of the 1920s.

Preview & Review

Use these questions to guide your reading. Answer the questions after completing Section 3.
Understanding Issues, Events, & Ideas. Describe the Roaring Twenties using the following words: jazz, Jazz Age, flappers, Harlem Renaissance, Golden Age of Sports, Harlem Globetrotters, expatriates.
1. What was the origin of jazz? How did jazz reflect the 1920s?
2. Name five heroes of the Golden Age of Sports and the sport for which each was famous.
3. How did movies influence people? What advantage did radio have over movies? Why did radio become a giant industry?
4. Who were the "lost generation?" Why does this name seem appropriate?
Thinking Critically. 1. Compose a poem or song about the changing values of women during the 1920s. 2. Why might someone want to become an expatriate? What reasons, if any, do you think are legitimate reasons to permanently leave America?

3. THE ROARING TWENTIES

The Jazz Age

Not all Americans were so troubled in the 1920s. Many were finding new ways to enjoy life. Industry continued to grow, producing new wealth and providing more leisure time for many millions of people. Change was in the air, and the speed of change was increasing. People everywhere were casting off old ways and seeking new ways to express themselves.

Consider the typical music of the period. The music that most Americans listened to and danced to during the 1920s was called **jazz.** Jazz was created by African American musicians in New Orleans in the late 1800s. It grew out of the "blues"—music that reflected the hard life of most blacks in America and the tough-minded humor that many displayed in trying to cope with it. W. C. Handy of Alabama was the "father of the blues." His most famous composition was "St. Louis Blues" (1914).

Most of the early African American jazz musicians had little or no formal training in music. Yet they were superb performers. Their music was often the only outlet for their emotions. Bessie Smith, a leading singer of the 1920s, sang movingly about her own sorrowful experiences. Louis "Satchmo" Armstrong was the most famous jazz musician of the day. He won international fame as a trumpeter, a singer, and as an ambassador of goodwill to other countries.

Jazz musicians *improvised* much of their music. Taking a theme or musical idea, they chased a tune up and down the scales as they played. This gave musicians and listeners alike a sense of freedom.

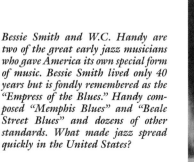

Bessie Smith and W.C. Handy are two of the great early jazz musicians who gave America its own special form of music. Bessie Smith lived only 40 years but is fondly remembered as the "Empress of the Blues." Handy composed "Memphis Blues" and "Beale Street Blues" and dozens of other standards. What made jazz spread quickly in the United States?

Both, Brown Brothers

SUGGESTED CAPTION RESPONSE
Like jazz it is innovative, or presented in a new and
different way.

RESOURCES
■ You may wish to have students view Transparency
28: "Falling Water" and complete the accompanying worksheet in Art in American History.

The New Britain Museum of American Art,
Friends Purchase Fund

*"Jazz" by Romare Bearden practi-
cally makes its own music with its rich
colors and rhythmic composition. Notice how the artist combines all kinds
of textures to make one unified image.
How is that like jazz itself?*

Jazz spread from New Orleans to Chicago and New York and
then throughout most of the world. White musicians as well as black
performed it. It became in its own way a powerful force for breaking
down racial barriers, both among the players and for those who
simply listened.

The decade of the 1920s is sometimes called the **Jazz Age.** In
part the popularity of its music is enough to explain this. But jazz
also symbolized the way many young people of the time felt about
life in general. They sought to break away from rigid, conventional
rules and traditions, just as jazz trumpeters and saxophonists de-
parted from written notes in order to express themselves.

This new spirit of freedom also influenced the other arts. Isadora
Duncan became world-famous for her beautiful and graceful free-
form dancing. Frank Lloyd Wright expressed the same spirit in his ■
architecture. Perhaps the most extreme expression of this break with
the conventional was dadaism, an outrageous art movement started
as a protest against all artistic and civilized standards.

Young women in particular seemed determined to free themselves from restricting "out-of-date" ideas and rules. They cast off
uncomfortable (and unhealthy) corsets and thick petticoats in favor
of short skirts and loose-fitting clothing. They cut their hair short.
They wore makeup. They drank and smoked in public.

The behavior of these "new women" shocked older people
deeply. They called them **flappers** and predicted they would come to
a bad end. Actually most of these young women were just trying to
liberate themselves. Not all of them were conscious feminists. Some
were merely trying to keep up with the latest fads and fashions. Still,
consciously or not, they were demanding the right to behave the
same way men behaved.

Point of View

Two stanzas from "Homage to
the Empress of the Blues," show
how much the poet admired
Bessie Smith.

❝She came out on the
stage in yards of pearls,
emerging like a favorite
scenic view, flashed her
golden smile and sang.
. . . .
She came out on stage in
ostrich feathers, beaded
satin, and shone that
smile on us and sang.❞
Robert Hayden, 1966

HISTORICAL SIDELIGHTS

1. Marcus Garvey, who was head of the Universal Negro Improvement Association, presented some extreme ideas. For example, he urged his followers to return to Africa and start a new empire.
2. The popularity of sports was due in part to the growing prosperity of the middle class who had the extra money to buy tickets, as well as more leisure time to spend attending events. Public relations firms fueled the sports boom by promoting extensive advertising campaigns that most people heard on the radio.

National Portrait Gallery

Langston Hughes, the most important poet of the Harlem Renaissance, also invented a character he called Jess B. Semple ("Simple" to his friends) who spoke out on life in Harlem in all its many aspects.

The Harlem Renaissance

The disappointments of the 1920s faced by African Americans produced the "New Negro," as they called themselves. These African Americans were determined to build pride and a better life for themselves and their children. Langston Hughes, one of the great poets of the era, expressed what life must have been like for African American children:

Merry-Go-Round

❝ *Colored child at carnival:*

Where is the Jim Crow section
On this merry-go-round,
Mister, cause I want to ride?
Down South where I come from
White and colored
Can't sit side by side.
Down South on the train
There's a Jim Crow car.
On the bus we're put in the back—
But there ain't no back
To a merry-go-round!
Where's the horse
For a kid that's black?[1] ❞

Leaders like W.E.B. Du Bois and Marcus Garvey preached black pride and self-confidence. The ghetto was home, a black world where black men and women could be themselves. Black writers, musicians, and artists such as Aaron Douglas, William H. Johnson, Palmer Hayden, and Meta Warwick Fuller found in the ghettos an audience that unleashed their creativity. Harlem, a part of Manhattan cut off by racial suspicion, was in fact the largest "black city" in the world. Here was the center of a cultural revitalization called the **Harlem Renaissance.** Poets and writers like Hughes, James Weldon Johnson, and Countee Cullen put the black experience into words. Newspapers and magazines along with theater troupes and libraries owned and operated by African Americans flourished. Hughes captured the spirit of the renaissance when he said, "Harlem! I . . . dropped my bags, took a deep breath, and felt happy again."

The Golden Age of Sports

The 1920s had its full share of gangsters, corrupt politicians, and other villains. It also had its heroes. Athletes were among the most popular. Spectator sports boomed. Public relations ballyhoo and the magic of radio created larger-than-life performers who attracted thousands to sporting events. The 1920s was truly the **Golden Age of Sports.**

[1]From "Merry-Go-Round" by Langston Hughes

THE LONE EAGLE

The most popular American hero of the 1920s was Charles A. Lindbergh. On May 20, 1927, Lindbergh took off from a muddy, rain-drenched airfield near New York City in a tiny, one-engine plane, the *Spirit of St. Louis.* He was headed for France. Alone, hour after hour, he guided his plane eastward across the Atlantic. He flew with a map in his lap and only some coffee and a few sandwiches to keep up his strength. Staying awake called for a tremendous feat of willpower. If he dozed off, even for a minute, the *Spirit of St. Louis* might crash into the sea. But Lindbergh did not doze off. About 33 and a half hours after takeoff he landed safely at Le Bourget airport on the outskirts of Paris. He was the first aviator to fly nonstop across the Atlantic—and he had done it alone.

Lindbergh's achievement captured the imagination of the entire world. Here is how *The New York Times* described his landing at Le Bourget:

> PARIS, May 21—Lindbergh did it. Twenty minutes after 10 o'clock tonight suddenly and softly there slipped out of the darkness a gray-white air-

Culver Pictures

plane as 25,000 pairs of eyes strained toward it. At 10:24 the *Spirit of St. Louis* landed and lines of soldiers, ranks of policemen and stout steel fences went down before a mad rush as irresistible as the tides of the ocean.

Lindbergh returned home a grinning, modest hero. The idol of millions, he was given a tremendous ticker tape parade through New York City. The newspapers named him "The Lone Eagle." He was also known as "Lucky Lindy," but his success was due far more to courage and skill than luck.

Now that dozens of giant jets fly across the Atlantic every day, Lindbergh's flight may not seem very important. But his flight marked the coming of age of the airplane. Lindbergh himself is the perfect symbol of the Air Age. He was two years old when Wilbur and Orville Wright made the first successful airplane flights at Kitty Hawk, North Carolina, in 1903. Those flights lasted only a few seconds and covered only a few hundred yards at most. Yet before Lindbergh died, American astronauts had landed on the moon.

Some 91,000 boxing fans paid a total of more than $1 million in July 1921 to watch the heavyweight champion, Jack Dempsey, knock out Georges Carpentier of France. Every fall weekend thousands of people jammed football stadiums to cheer for players like Harold "Red" Grange, the "Galloping Ghost" of the University of Illinois. One Saturday afternoon in 1924 Grange took the University of Michigan's opening kickoff 95 yards for a touchdown. He scored three more touchdowns in the first quarter and another before the game ended, Illinois winning 39-14. Grange carried the ball 21 times and gained an incredible 402 yards.

The most famous football coach of the 1920s was Knute Rockne of Notre Dame's "Fighting Irish." He began the decade with an

GUIDED INSTRUCTION
You may wish to obtain silent movies of the 1920s from your local library and turn the classroom into a silent movie theater for a day. Show one or two of the movies (accompanied by a recording or audiotape of 1920s music) to give students an idea of what it was like to see a silent movie in a theater. After viewing the films, discuss ways in which the actors used facial expressions and pantomime to convey emotions and meanings to the audience. Have students compare films of the silent era with films of today.

Culver Pictures

Culver Pictures

Culver Pictures

UPI/Bettmann Newsphotos

Four of the greatest sports heroes of the 1920s were, clockwise from the bottom, Red Grange, Jack Dempsey, Helen Wills, and Babe Ruth.

undefeated season. For many the 1920 highlight was Notre Dame's defeat of Army, 27-17, owing largely to the 357 yards gained by the team's captain, George Gipp. Years later, at halftime of an important game, Rockne implored his team to "win one for the Gipper," who had died of pneumonia. The locker room speech, recreated in a popular movie starring Ronald Reagan as Gipp, would later serve as a metaphor for Reagan's enormous popularity as president.

In 1927 one of the most famous barnstorming, or traveling, basketball teams in the world was formed by Abe Saperstein. He recruited most of his players from the slums of Chicago's South Side, but he called his team of black athletes the **Harlem Globetrotters.** They became magicians with the basketball and drew fans throughout the world, as they continue to do today.

Baseball was the national game. Its most famous hero at the time was Babe Ruth, the "Sultan of Swat." Ruth was originally a pitcher—and a very good one. He was also a tremendous hitter. The Boston Red Sox quickly made him an outfielder so he could play every day. Thereafter, year after year, he was baseball's home run leader. In 1927 he hit 60, a record that stood until Roger Maris hit 61 in 1961. By the end of his career he had knocked out 714 home runs, most of them for the New York Yankees.

Americans were good at nearly all sports. Tennis players William "Big Bill" Tilden and Helen Wills both won many national and international championships. Johnny Weismuller held a dozen world swimming records. Gertrude Ederle became the first woman to swim across the English Channel.

SUGGESTED CAPTION RESPONSE
People had more leisure time and money to spend on entertainment.

HISTORICAL SIDELIGHTS
① Live stage performances still remained a popular form of entertainment in the 1920s. Vaudeville shows and musical productions such as the Ziegfield Follies were popular among the American public.

Motion Pictures

Lindbergh's solo flight to Paris combined his own human abilities and the mechanical perfection of his plane. This combination was characteristic of the period. It explains the rapid growth of motion pictures, which, like the airplane, came of age in the 1920s.

Movies were popular even before the Great War. The early ① movie theaters were often installed in vacant stores. These "nickelodeons"—the usual admission charge was five cents—showed jerky, badly lit scenes. In the 1920s motion pictures became an important art form and one of the ten largest industries in the nation. In 1922, 40 million people a week went to the movies. By 1930 weekly attendance was averaging 100 million.

Every large city had its movie palaces—large, elaborate theaters seating several thousand people. Hollywood, California, became the motion picture capital of the world. The state's warm, sunny climate was ideal for outdoor movie making.

Americans in the 1920s flocked to every kind of film. There were historical pictures and the most durable of all movies—westerns. The leading actors and actresses were loved by millions. Movie fans followed the careers and personal lives of their favorites as though they were members of their families.

Movies influenced the way people dressed and talked. Women styled their hair like Greta Garbo or Mary Pickford. Men tried to copy Rudolph Valentino, the great lover of *The Sheik,* or Douglas Fairbanks, the sword-fighting hero of *The Three Musketeers.*

The greatest star of the 1920s was Charlie Chaplin. He wrote and directed his own films. In 1915 he created his world-famous character, the sad-looking "little tramp" who wore baggy pants and a battered derby hat and carried a springy bamboo cane. Chaplin

Millions of people flocked to the movies to see their favorite stars. Three of the most glittering were (below, left to right): swashbuckling Douglas Fairbanks, romantic idol Rudolph Valentino, and Charlie Chaplin, the most famous comic actor in the world. Why do you think sports and movies were popular in the 1920s?

All, Culver Pictures

CHECKING UNDERSTANDING
Have students discuss the social trends of the 1920s and compare them to social trends today. *(Jazz became the most popular form of music in the 1920s. Many young Americans identified with it because, like the jazz musicians had with their music, young people tried to break away from rigid, conventional rules and traditions in order to express themselves. Today many young people listen to rock and roll because they identify with it, and, like the musicians who perform it, this is their way of expressing themselves.*

Americans began to spend their leisure-time and money on spectator sports. As a result, athlete heroes who turned this era into a "Golden Age of Sports" emerged. Americans today continue to spend enormous amounts of time and money on sporting events and to raise their favorite athletes to hero status.

Movie attendance became another leisure-time activity that frequently occupied many Americans in the 1920s. People made heroes of their favorite movie stars and imitated their styles and mannerisms. This trend is also evident in American society today. People continue to flock to movie theaters and rent or buy enormous numbers of videocassettes. However, rock stars and sports figures have replaced movie stars as the heroes most Americans imitate.

Americans also began listening to the radio in the 1920s. Daily events, such as news, sports, and political speeches were now heard live in almost every home across the country. Families gathered around the radio to listen to situation com-
(Continued)

① It was not until 1927 that radios went from being battery operated to being powered by electricity.

edies, soap operas, stories, and commercials. Today the radio is used mainly to provide people with continuous music or live broadcasts of news and sports when they are unable to watch it on television.)

was a marvelous slapstick comedian and a gifted mimic. He was also a superb actor, who could literally make audiences laugh and cry at the same time.

For years the movies were silent. Usually a pianist in each theater played mood music to accompany the action on the screen. Then, in 1927, Warner Brothers, a major film company, released the first "talkie," a film that projected the actors' voices as well as their movements. This film was *The Jazz Singer,* starring Al Jolson. He sang three songs and then told the film audience, "You ain't heard nothin' yet, folks." The next year Walt Disney made the first sound cartoon, *Steamboat Willie,* which introduced Mickey Mouse to the world.

Radio

Radio had an even more powerful hold on the public in the 1920s than movies. Like the movies, it could not have been developed without the remarkable scientific and technological advances of the times.

Everyone could enjoy and profit from radio, even sick and bedridden people who could not get to the movies. Radio could be listened to without admission cost and in the privacy of one's home. It was also "live." What people heard was taking place at that very moment: a politician making a speech, the crack of the bat when Babe Ruth hit another home run, the roar of the crowd at a football game, the sound of a jazz band or a symphony orchestra. More people than ever before became interested in sports and music.

The first commercial radio station was KDKA in Pittsburgh. It was operated by the Westinghouse Electric Company. KDKA began broadcasting in 1920. Two years later there were more than 500 commercial stations. The National Broadcasting Company (NBC) began combining local stations into a nationwide radio network in 1926. A year later the Columbia Broadcasting System (CBS) created ① a competing network. Thereafter, people all over the country could hear the same program at the same time. Audiences grew to the millions.

Radio became still another giant industry. Large companies sprang up to manufacture radio sets and broadcasting equipment. Department stores devoted entire floors to radios. Repairing radios became an important craft. By 1922, 3 million families already had radios. In the single year 1929, 5 million sets were sold.

Radio brought an enormous variety of information and entertainment into American homes. News, music, plays, political speeches, and sports events filled the airwaves. Radio also influenced what Americans bought in stores. Audiences were bombarded with commercials by manufacturers of all sorts. These advertisers paid large sums to broadcast their "sales pitches."

Postwar American Writers

The Great World War had shocked and disillusioned people all over the world. This was especially true of Americans who had resisted the war at first, only to be drawn in by promises of a better future, one made safe for democracy. It was Gertrude Stein, an **expatriate** writer who had left America to live permanently in Europe, who gave these young people a name. She told a young American writer, Ernest Hemingway, about a mechanic who took a very long time to repair her Model T. The owner of the garage reprimanded him: "You are a génération perdue! (lost generation!)." "That's what you are," Stein told Hemingway, "That's what you all are. All of you young people who served in the war, you are a lost generation." To these people progressive ideals that had been so important before the war seemed less so now. Many writers expressed this loss of values in their works.

Culver Pictures

The Metropolitan Museum of Art, Bequest of Gertrude Stein, 1946.

Ernest Hemingway survived a wound while driving an ambulance in Italy; was nearly gored by bulls running in Pamplona, Spain; and later walked away from an airplane crash in Africa. For all his adventures, he paid close attention to Gertrude Stein at her home in Paris. There she critiqued his writing and urged him to use only the "perfect word." Of her portrait by Pablo Picasso, left, she complained that it didn't look like her. The confident Picasso is said to have replied, "It will."

RETEACHING STRATEGY
Students with Special Needs.
Pair students who are having difficulty with students who are performing well. Write the following list of popular trends on the chalkboard or an overhead projector. Have students copy the list into their notebooks. Under each heading, have them describe what the trend was like in the 1920s and what it is like today.

Spectator Sports—1920s
(One of the most common ways that Americans spent their leisure time in the 1920s was on spectator sports. People looked on the most famous athletes as heroes.)

Spectator Sports—Present
(Americans today continue to spend enormous amounts of time and money on sporting events and make heroes of their favorite athletes.)

Movie Attendance—1920s
(Movie attendance was another leisure-time activity that became very popular in the 1920s. People made heroes of their favorite movie stars and imitated their styles and mannerisms.)

Movie Attendance—Present
(Today people continue to flock to movie theaters and rent or buy enormous numbers of videocassettes. However, rock stars and sports figures have replaced movie stars as the heroes most Americans imitate.)

Radio Listening—1920s
*(Listening to the radio became extremely popular in the 1920s. People began listening to the radio daily to hear such events as news, sports, and political speeches as well as a variety of programs. By the end of the
(Continued)*

1 Hemingway spent a great deal of his spare time in gymnasiums, boxing and watching boxers. He was fascinated by this sport because boxers are tested by pain and danger. For similar reasons, he also developed an interest in bullfighting which he wrote about in a few of his novels.

1920s almost every home in the country had a radio.)

Radio Listening—Present
(Today the radio is used mainly to provide people with continuous music or live broadcasts of news and sports when they are unable to watch television.)

Culver Pictures

The Fitzgeralds, Zelda and Scott, pose with their daughter, Scottie. Fitzgerald wrote some of his best work in Paris, including his classic novel The Great Gatsby. *At the end of it, the narrator sees how America has changed: "And as soon as the moon rose higher the inessential began to melt away until gradually I became aware of the old island here [New York] that flowered once for Dutch sailor's eyes—a fresh, green breast of the new world."*

PRIMARY SOURCE
Description of change: excerpted.
Rationale: excerpted to focus on Hemingway's effort to write one true sentence.

Ernest Hemingway spent much of his youth hunting and fishing with his father in northern Michigan and had been wounded in the Great War while driving an ambulance for the Red Cross. These Michigan memories and his wartime experiences were the subjects of his early writing.

Hemingway's style is probably the most widely imitated of all American authors. He took considerable pains to choose exactly the right word and no other, writing prose the way poets write poetry. He wanted very badly, he said, to write "one true sentence." In one of his first major novels, *A Farewell to Arms,* we can see the result of Hemingway's painstaking effort:

&& In the late summer of that year we lived in a house in a village that looked across the river and the plain to the mountains. In the bed of the river there were pebbles and boulders, dry and white in the sun, and the water was clear and swiftly moving and blue in the channels. Troops went by the house and down the road and the dust they raised powdered the leaves of the trees. The trunks of the trees too were dusty and the leaves fell early that year and we saw troops marching along the road and the dust rising and leaves, stirred by the breeze, falling and the soldiers marching and afterward the road bare and white except for the leaves.

The plain was rich with crops; there were many orchards of fruit trees and beyond the plain the mountains were brown and bare. There was fighting in the mountains and at night we could see the flashes from the artillery. In the dark it was like summer lightning, but the nights were cool and there was not the feeling of a storm coming.[1] &&

Hemingway gave the writing of fiction a new rhythm of action and simple, straightforward dialogue. He also developed the image of life as a battlefield on which a new type of hero suffers with grace and dignity and accepts gratefully life's few moments of pleasure. In 1954 Hemingway received the Nobel prize for literature for such works as *The Sun Also Rises, For Whom the Bell Tolls,* and *The Old Man and the Sea.*

Francis Scott Key Fitzgerald, more than any other author, gave a voice to the "lost generation." His greatest work—for many *the* great American novel—was *The Great Gatsby.* In it the American dream of wealth and power goes terribly and tragically wrong. Throughout the novel Fitzgerald used the glitter of Gatsby's life to symbolize the purposeless lives of the rich and powerful. Nick Carraway, the narrator, notes after a spectacular party at Gatsby's:

[1]From *A Farewell to Arms* by Ernest Hemingway

“ The caterwauling [noisy crying] of horns had reached a crescendo and I turned away and cut across the lawn toward home. I glanced back once. A wafer of a moon was shining over Gatsby's house, making the night fine as before, and surviving the laughter and the sound of his still glowing garden. A sudden emptiness seemed to flow now from the windows and the great doors, endowing with complete isolation the figure of the host, who stood on the porch, his hand up in a formal gesture of farewell.[1] ”

[1] From *The Great Gatsby* by F. Scott Fitzgerald

Fitzgerald also wrote *Tender Is the Night*, an account of his own despair. He died in 1940 while writing *The Last Tycoon*.

While Fitzgerald and Hemingway wrote in Europe, William Faulkner in his native Mississippi invented a mythical county called Yoknapatawpha. He spent his life populating it with fallen southern aristocrats, new arrivals (all named Snopes), and the long-suffering blacks who tended what was left of the land. In this setting—the American South—he explored such universal themes as human suffering, the passions of the heart, and the destruction of the natural wilderness.

In Faulkner's novels the sudden shifts in time, frequent use of symbolism, and unusual syntax reveal the confused emotions of his characters and the disorder that surrounds them. His most noted works include *The Sound and the Fury, As I Lay Dying, Absalom, Absalom,* and *Light in August*.

Faulkner received a Nobel Prize for literature in 1950. In his acceptance speech at the ceremony in Stockholm, Sweden, he described his view of the writer:

“ . . . I decline to accept the end of man. It is easy enough to say that man is immortal simply because he will endure; that when the last ding-dong of doom has clanged and faded from the last worthless rock hanging tideless in the last red and dying evening, that even then there will still be one more sound: that of his puny inexhaustible voice, still talking. I refuse to accept this. I believe man will not merely endure: he will prevail. He is immortal, not because he alone among the creatures has an inexhaustible voice, but because he has a soul, a spirit capable of compassion and sacrifice and endurance. The poet's, the writer's, duty is to write about these things. It is his privilege to help man endure by lifting his heart, by reminding him of the courage and pity and sacrifice which have been the glory of his past. The poet's voice need not merely be the record of man, it can be one of the props, the pillars to help him endure and prevail. ”

Culver Pictures

William Faulkner was the inventor of a fictional world called Yoknapatawpha County. He emerged into the real world to surprise and delight listeners with his acceptance speech in Stockholm, where he was awarded the Nobel Prize for literature.

Return to the Preview & Review on page 870.

The Roaring Twenties 879

INDEPENDENT PRACTICE
Have students complete the Preview & Review activity at the beginning of the section.

CLOSURE
Point out to students that the 1920s marked the beginning of the modern era because for the first time the average American had access to the inventions of modern technology, such as the automobile and the media (movies and radio). These greatly changed their lives.

HOMEWORK
Have students choose a famous person from the 1920s (it may be a jazz musician, movie star, or sports figure) and prepare a pictorial essay showing the person at the height of his or her career. Students who cannot locate photographs should be encouraged to create their own pictures. You may wish to have students present their essays to the class and hang a few of the more interesting pictures around the classroom.

PRIMARY SOURCES
(Top) Description of change: excerpted and bracketed.
Rationale: excerpted to focus on the feeling of emptiness the narrator describes in F. Scott Fitzgerald's work; bracketed words added to clarify meaning.
(Bottom) Description of change: excerpted.
Rationale: excerpted to focus on Faulkner's inspiring words in his Nobel Prize acceptance speech.

879

Preview & Review

Use these questions to guide your reading. Answer the questions after completing Section 4.
Understanding Issues, Events, & Ideas. Explain how the automobile changed America, using the following words: Model T, mass production, moving assembly line, Model A, tourism, suburb, air pollution.
1. How did Henry Ford change the automobile industry? How did the growth of the automobile industry affect the entire economy?
2. How did the automobile bring freedom to ordinary people?
3. What effects, both good and bad, did the automobile have on family life?

Thinking Critically. Write an obituary for Henry Ford that might have appeared in a newspaper or magazine; or compose an advertisement for Henry Ford's Model T.

4. AN AUTOMOBILE CIVILIZATION

Henry Ford's Automobile

Of all the forces reshaping American life in the 1920s, the automobile probably had the most influence. The first gasoline-powered vehicles were built in the 1890s. By the time the United States entered the Great War, over 1 million cars a year were being produced. In the 1920s an average of more than 3 million a year were turned out.

Henry Ford was the key figure in this new industry. Ford had come to Detroit, Michigan, because he hated farm work. He had talent for all kinds of mechanical projects. While working in Detroit for the Edison Illuminating Company in the 1890s, Ford designed and built an automobile in his home workshop. A little later he built a famous racing car, "999," which he drove to several speed records himself. In 1903 he founded the Ford Motor Company.

The first American automobiles were very expensive. They were toys for the rich. Henry Ford dreamed of producing cars cheaply so that ordinary people could own them. (The name of the well-known German automobile, the Volkswagen, or "people's car," expresses his idea exactly.) In 1908 he achieved his goal with his **Model T** Ford. It sold for only $850. And by 1916 Ford had reduced the cost of the new Model T's to $360.

Ford's secret was **mass production** achieved through the use of the **moving assembly line.** His cars were put together, or assembled, while being moved past a line of workers. Each worker or team performed only one fairly simple task.

This method of production was highly efficient. Prices were also held down by Ford's policy of keeping his cars simple and making the same basic model year after year. The Model T was not changed in any important way until 1928, when the **Model A** replaced it. According to a joke of the day, you could have a Model T in any color you wanted as long as you chose black.

Other automobile manufacturers copied Ford's methods. But most made more expensive cars. In prosperous times many customers were willing to pay for larger and more comfortable cars than the Model T. By the end of the 1920s Ford was no longer the largest manufacturer. The General Motors Company had taken the lead.

New Wealth from the Automobile

The automobile fueled an economic boom. The 3 million or more cars produced each year were worth about $3.5 billion even before the car dealers added their expenses and profits. This was only part of the new wealth the automobile created. A huge rubber industry sprang up to produce tires, belts, and hoses for cars. Manufacturers

Henry Ford is as spare as his famous Model T in this photograph. How did the Model T resemble the more recent German Volkswagen?

Culver Pictures

of steel, glass, paint, and dozens of other products greatly increased ■ their output.

The automobile revolutionized the petroleum-refining industry. Before the war the most important petroleum product was kerosene. By 1919 ten times as much gasoline as kerosene was being refined. The total amount of petroleum refined in the United States soared from about 50 million barrels to 1 billion barrels a day.

Then there were the effects of the automobile on road building and on **tourism.** So long as people traveled no faster than a horse could pull a coach or wagon, the bumps and ruts of dirt and gravel roads did not matter much. By the 1920s, however, ordinary cars could speed along at 50 or 60 miles an hour or more. Such speeds were impossible on uneven surfaces. Hundreds of thousands of miles of smooth paved roads had to be built. Great amounts of asphalt and concrete were manufactured to surface them. New road-building machinery was designed and constructed. Thousands of new jobs were created in this road-building industry.

Better roads for cars meant more traveling, both for business and for pleasure. Gasoline stations appeared alongside each new highway. Roadside restaurants opened side by side with motor hotels—a new way of housing travelers, soon to be known as motels.

Point of View

Two of Henry Ford's biographers, Peter Collier and David Horowitz, tell of the first excursions in what Ford called the "baby carriage."

❝Seeing the strange little car coughing and wheezing along the narrow streets during the next few days, people would sometimes yell out the nickname his obsessive drive to build a horseless carriage had earned Ford—'Crazy Henry!' But whenever he stopped, crowds immediately surrounded his invention, examining it with such enthusiasm that he finally had to begin chaining it to lightposts for fear they would carry it off. 'Yes, crazy,' he sometimes said, tapping his temple with a forefinger. 'Crazy like a fox.'❞

From *The Fords: An American Epic,* 1987

An Automobile Civilization   881

SUGGESTED CAPTION RESPONSES
It gave them the freedom to travel and move out of the cities, but it also made them dependent on gasoline and other petroleum products.

RESOURCES
■ You may wish to have students view the videotape "Wheels of Change: The American Automobile" in *The Story of America Video Library.*

CHECKING UNDERSTANDING
Have students summarize the ways in which the automobile changed the American way of life. *(People could move to the suburbs and commute to their jobs in the cities. They could also take weekend trips or go on vacations thousands of miles away. Automobiles had both good and bad effects on family life. Families now took long distance trips together which brought them closer, but often these trips ended up in family squabbles. Family members fought over where to go, how to get there, and the driver's driving methods. Other negative side effects were: the increased number of road accidents; traffic jams; and pollution from exhaust.)*

RETEACHING STRATEGY
Students with Special Needs.
Pair students who are having difficulty with students who are performing well. Have the more proficient students ask the others the following questions:

1. How did the automobile change travel for average people? *(Ordinary people could now afford to buy cars and travel farther and more rapidly than ever before. They could now take weekend trips and vacations that covered thousands of miles.)*

2. How did the automobile affect where the average person chose to live? *(The average person could move to the suburbs and commute to his or her job in the city.)*

3. What were the good effects of the automobile on family life? *(Families now took long-distance trips together which brought them closer.)*

4. What were some bad effects *(Continued)*

Culver Pictures

Plans for a Sunday drive have gone awry in this early traffic jam outside St. Louis, Missouri. Notice the large number of Model T's. How did the automobile bring Americans both freedom and dependence?

Automobiles and American Life

■ For thousands of years the power to move about freely and easily was a sign that a person had social status. That is why in ancient times and throughout the Middle Ages ownership of a horse meant that a person belonged to the upper class. Now, because of Henry Ford and the other pioneers of the auto industry, nearly everyone in the United States could afford a car. A *new* Model T could cost as little as $300 in the early 1920s. A secondhand Ford still capable of good service could be bought for $25 to $50.

Automobiles freed ordinary people. Cars let them travel far more widely and rapidly than medieval knights had traveled. They could live in **suburbs** outside the cities, surrounded by trees and green fields, and drive daily to jobs in the cities. They could visit places hundreds of miles away on weekends or cover thousands of miles on a two-week summer vacation.

Little wonder that automobiles became status symbols—objects associated with the upper classes of society—for many people. Owners spent Saturday mornings washing and polishing their cars the way a trainer grooms a racehorse or a pedigreed dog before a show. Car owners decorated their autos with shiny hood ornaments and put flowers in small vases on the inside.

The personalities of many car owners seemed to be affected by their vehicles. Once behind the wheel, drivers were in command of half a ton or more of speeding metal. They often became "roadhogs" who turned into cursing bullies when another driver got in their way or tried to pass them on the road.

Automobiles had both good and bad effects on family life. Family picnics and sightseeing trips brought parents and children closer together. However, crowding five or six people into a small space on a hot summer afternoon hardly made for family harmony. Quarrels developed about where to go and how to get there. People complained about "backseat drivers"—those passengers who made a habit of criticizing the driver.

The automobile also tended to separate family members. Once children were old enough to drive, they generally preferred to be off by themselves or with friends their own age. Soon "two-car" and "three-car" families came into being. In extreme cases the home became little more than a motel or garage. Family members rested there before zooming off again in their Fords and Chevrolets or, if they were wealthy, in their Packards and Pierce-Arrows.

The new automobile civilization had other unfortunate side effects. Between 1915 and 1930 the number of road accidents soared. By 1930 automobile crashes caused more than half the accidental deaths in the nation.

As the number of cars on the roads increased, traffic tie-ups became common. The exhaust fumes of millions of cars caused serious **air pollution** in some areas.

Because of the automobile, the oil resources of the nation were being used up at a rapidly increasing rate. Anyone who thought about the question realized that there was only so much petroleum in the ground. It had taken millions of years to be formed and could never be replaced. Still, the supply was so large that most people assumed that it would last practically forever. During the 1920s huge new oil fields were discovered in Texas and Oklahoma. Only a tiny percentage of the petroleum used in America then came from foreign sources. That percentage was actually declining in those years.

The nation was becoming more and more dependent upon gasoline and other petroleum products. Giant industries could not exist without oil in one form or another. Neither could the new life style that was developing in the United States. Yet in the 1920s few people worried about these matters. Gasoline was cheap. There was plenty of it. Let us enjoy life while we can, most people reasoned. 🔲

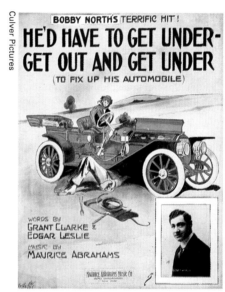

Culver Pictures

This song sheet cover takes a good-natured view of the plight of most car owners, who had to be their own mechanics. Scarcely a trip was made without at least patching a tire.

Return to the Preview & Review on page 880.

of the automobile? *(Some negative side effects were: the increased number of road accidents; traffic jams; and pollution from exhaust.)*

INDEPENDENT PRACTICE
Have students complete the Preview & Review activity at the beginning of the section.

CLOSURE
Remind students that the automobile had a tremendous impact on the American economy. Ask them to name some of the industries that were created or that expanded from the growth of the automobile industry. *(steel, glass, paint, rubber, petroleum refining, tourism, road building, asphalt and concrete manufacturing, gasoline stations, roadside restaurants, and motels)*

HOMEWORK
Have students prepare a report on one of the following major American car manufacturers: Chrysler, Ford, or General Motors. They should include a history and description of the firm and an account of its present-day status—particularly about how it is handling competition from the German and Japanese car manufacturers. You may wish to have students present their reports to the class.

① Harding had once admitted, "I am a man of limited talents from a small town." But he did have some bright moments. He made a speech in Alabama advocating expanded civil rights for African Americans, sponsored a successful disarmament conference, and pardoned Eugene V. Debs despite the opposition of his advisers and cabinet.

PREVIEW & REVIEW RESPONSES
Understanding Issues, Events, & Ideas.
Descriptions should demonstrate an understanding of the terms used.
1. The political mood of the 1920s was conservative. However, people's behavior was often the opposite as many became reckless in their attempt to break away from conventional rules and traditions.
2. Most businesses, with the encouragement of the federal government, expanded and prospered. Coal, textiles, and agriculture, however, were the sick industries. Coal had to compete with oil, natural gas, and electricity. Textiles had to compete with a synthetic product called rayon. Farmers had to compete with European farmers who regained their local markets after the war.
3. Under the Republican administrations, Americans were enjoying a greater period of prosperity than ever before, and so they came to see the Republican party as the symbol of economic progress and the guardian of good times.
4. Times were prosperous, which tended to make people ambitious and optimistic. A "get-rich-quick" attitude developed as people set out to make fortunes in the stock market.

Thinking Critically
1. Student articles should show creativity and imagination.
2. Letters should demonstrate

Preview & Review

Use these questions to guide your reading. Answer the questions after completing Section 5.
Understanding Issues, Events, & Ideas. Use the following words to describe American politics and the economy of the 1920s: Elk Hills, Teapot Dome, chain store, synthetic, sick industry, Farm Bloc, subsidy, Black Tuesday, Great Stock Market Crash.
1. How did the political mood of the 1920s differ from the way people behaved?
2. What changes took place in business in the 1920s? Which were the sick industries in the 1920s? Why were they sick?
3. Why did the Republicans win the election of 1928 so easily?
4. Why did people tend to adopt a "get-rich-quick" attitude in the 1920s?
Thinking Critically. 1. Imagine that you are a Wall Street reporter on October 29, 1929. Interview several people on the street and use their comments to write your newspaper article. 2. You are a farmer in the South in 1921. Write a letter to your congressman, a member of the Farm Bloc, explaining the troubles you are having.

5. AMERICA HEADS FOR A CRASH

Harding and Coolidge

The 1920s were a time when politics seemed to have little connection with how people lived and thought. While society was changing in dramatic and significant ways, most political leaders were conservative, slow moving, and lacking in imagination.

President Warren G. Harding looked like a statesman. He was friendly, good looking, firm jawed, and silver haired. He worked for conservative policies that favored big business. But he was not a ① creative leader. His programs included high protective tariffs on manufactured goods, lower taxes for the wealthy, and reducing the national debt, the same policies as earlier Republican presidents. Nor was he a strong leader. Harding was careless about the appointments he made to important public offices. Some people he appointed were incompetent. Others were plainly corrupt.

Harding died of a heart attack in 1923. Soon thereafter a series of government scandals was uncovered. Harding himself was not involved. It turned out that various members of his administration had stolen money intended for a veterans' hospital, mishandled government property, and accepted bribes.

The worst scandal involved Albert Fall, Harding's secretary of the interior. Fall leased government-owned land containing rich deposits of oil to private companies at very low rents. These included the **Elk Hills** reserve in California and the **Teapot Dome** reserve in Wyoming. In return the heads of the oil companies gave Fall bribes amounting to $400,000. When the facts were discovered by a government investigation in 1923, Fall was convicted and put in prison.

It was fortunate for the Republican party that Harding died before the scandals broke. His successor, Vice President Calvin Coolidge, had nothing to do with the corruption. Coolidge's personality was almost the exact opposite of Harding's. He was quiet and very reserved. He hated to spend money. Indeed, he was the only modern president who was able to save part of his salary while in office. He was thoroughly honest. His no-nonsense attitude made it difficult for the Democrats to take political advantage of the scandals.

In 1924 Coolidge easily received the Republican nomination for a full term. The Democratic nomination was decided only after a long and bitter struggle. The eastern wing of the party supported Governor Alfred E. Smith of New York. Most southern and western delegates favored William G. McAdoo, who had been President Wilson's secretary of the treasury.

Under the rules of the convention, a candidate needed a two-thirds majority to be nominated. Since neither Smith nor McAdoo could get two thirds, a deadlock developed. It lasted for days. Finally,

At left is a portrait of Warren G. Harding by Margaret Lindsay Williams. Right is Calvin Coolidge, nicknamed "Silent Cal" because he was a man of few words. Once, at a White House dinner, a lady bet Coolidge that she could coax at least three words from him. "You lose," he replied. Howard Chandler Christy painted Grace Goodhue Coolidge, the popular first lady, with her collie, Rob Roy.

on the 103rd ballot, the exhausted delegates nominated John W. Davis, a conservative lawyer from West Virginia.

The deadlock between Smith and McAdoo reflected the basic divisions within the Democratic party and within the nation itself. Smith was a Catholic. Many people were prejudiced against Catholics and would not vote for a Catholic for president. Some even feared that such a person would be a servant of the Pope rather than a servant of the American people.

Many rural people disliked Smith because he had been raised "on the sidewalks of New York." Yet the nation was becoming more and more urban. By the 1920s farmers no longer made up the majority of the population. Many farmers resented this fact. In Smith's candidacy they saw a symbol of the shift from a rural to an urban nation.

In addition to Coolidge and Davis, Senator Robert La Follette of Wisconsin ran for president in 1924. La Follette had been a leading progressive before the Great War. He found both the major parties too conservative for his taste after the war. He therefore formed a new Progressive party. La Follette campaigned on a platform calling for government ownership of railroads, protection of the right of workers to bargain collectively, aid for farmers, and other reforms. "The great issue before the American people," La Follette believed, was "the control of government and industry by private monopoly."

America Heads For a Crash   885

SUGGESTED CAPTION RESPONSE
It boomed; because as industrial output increased with the demand for weapons and war supplies, industry expanded and the number of jobs increased; it slumped; because as the demand for wartime supplies ceased, many plants were forced to close or temporarily slow down their operations, causing many to lose their jobs.

RESOURCES
■ You may wish to have students view Transparency 23: *"Boomtown"* and complete the accompanying worksheet in *Art in American History.*

GUIDED INSTRUCTION:
COOPERATIVE LEARNING
Divide the class into cooperative learning groups. Assign each group either a major appliance or a modern invention that became available to consumers in the 1920s (for example, refrigerator, vacuum cleaner, washing machine, or portable camera). Have each group prepare a classroom display showing how their invention changed American life. Student displays should include drawings, photographs, and clippings from old newspapers and magazines.

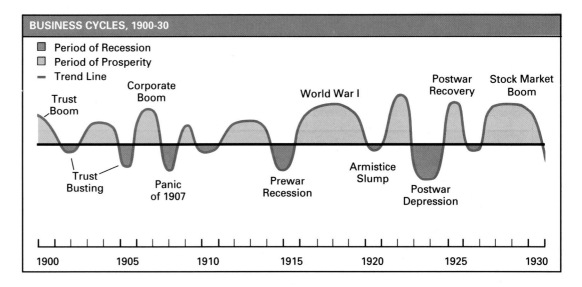

LEARNING FROM GRAPHS. *The graph above shows American business cycles between 1900 and 1930. What happened to the economy during the war? Why? What happened to the economy after the war ended? Why?*

Coolidge won the election easily. He received more than 15 million votes to Davis' 8.4 million and La Follette's 4.8 million. Clearly the national mood was politically conservative at a time when society was going through tremendous changes.

Business Growth in the 1920s

The policies of the federal government in the 1920s had large effects on the economy. These policies greatly influenced the lives of nearly everyone. President Coolidge believed that "the business of America is business." He also said, "The man who builds a factory builds a temple." His policies were designed to help business interests and other large investors.

Coolidge presided over one of the most business-minded administrations in American history. Its chief architect was Andrew Mellon, the secretary of the treasury. Mellon believed prosperity depended on the ability of Americans to invest and reinvest in business. He sponsored a tax cut that favored the wealthy and businesses by reducing the taxes for people making $60,000 a year or more. Within 3 years money was pouring into business investments.

To make up for the reduced revenues, the government raised tariffs and increased excise taxes slightly. The higher tariffs benefited businesses in two ways, allowing them to raise their prices while cutting down on their competition. The slight increases in excise taxes on consumer goods and a new tax on automobiles was paid primarily by the middle class.

■ The friendly attitude of the government encouraged businesses to make new investments. Once the switch back to peacetime production had been completed, the American economy certainly prospered. Many industries that had been established before the Great War expanded rapidly. Coolidge and his advisers expected this to create more jobs and a better standard of living for all.

Between 1915 and 1930 the number of telephone users in the United States doubled. Dial phones and improved switchboards speeded communication and cut costs. Electric light companies prospered. As more and more homes were hooked up for electricity, the electric appliance industry grew. Most families now had electric irons. Many had electric vacuum cleaners and washing machines and refrigerators as well. Electricity also became an important source of power for industry. By 1930 the United States was using more electricity than all the rest of the world *combined*.

Chain stores grew rapidly in the 1920s. The A&P grocery chain expanded from 400 outlets in 1912 to 15,000 in 1932. Woolworth "five and tens" were opened by the dozens in big cities and small towns. By the end of the decade Americans were buying more than 25 percent of their food and clothing in chain stores. With more and more people living in cities, sales of canned fruits and vegetables rose rapidly.

Even more impressive was the growth of entirely new industries. Chemical plants began turning out many **synthetics**—artificial substances such as rayon for clothing and Bakelite, a hard plastic, for radio cases. Other new mass-produced products included wristwatches, cigarette lighters, improved cameras, and Pyrex glass for cooking.

Some of the wonderful new labor-saving devices being advertised in the 1920s include the vacuum cleaner, refrigerator, and washing machine. Think how each made life a bit simpler.

All, The Granger Collection, New York

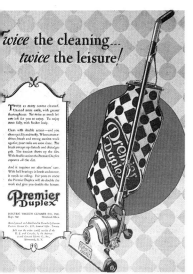

USING HISTORICAL IMAGINATION

Have students imagine that they are Herbert Hoover, president of the United States. They have just received word of the stock market crash and must address the American people on the radio regarding this matter. Tell them that while preparing their radio address they should bear in mind that they do not want to further panic the American people. Instead, they want to instill a feeling of confidence in the economy. They should also include a plan about how they intend to deal with the economic crisis. Have students present their addresses to the class.

"Sick" Industries

Despite the general economic expansion of the 1920s, there were several weak areas in the economy. **Sick industries** like coal and textiles did not prosper at all. Coal was meeting stiff competition from oil, natural gas, and electricity. Over 1,000 coal mines were shut down in the 1920s, and nearly 200,000 miners lost their jobs.

Manufacturers of cotton and woolen cloth did not prosper either. Partly because of competition from rayon, the new synthetic textile, these manufacturers were soon producing more cloth than the public was buying. Their profits therefore shrank, and the number of unemployed textile workers rose.

American agriculture also suffered. Once the Great War was over, European farmers quickly recaptured their local markets. The price of wheat and other farm products fell sharply. Farmers' incomes declined, but their expenses for mortgage interest, taxes, tractors, harvesters, and supplies did not.

In 1921 a group of congressmen from the South and West organized an informal **Farm Bloc.** (A bloc is a common interest group.) Their purpose was to unite congressmen from farm districts behind legislation favorable to agriculture. The Farm Bloc pushed through a bill providing for **subsidies** for farmers through government purchase of farm surpluses. President Coolidge was not sympathetic to proposals to subsidize farm prices. He vetoed the bill.

But the tremendous growth of the 1920s also had a down side. Business owners pushed their factories to produce more, faster. New and improved products continued to attract buyers, and old models wore out and had to be replaced. But by the late 1920s businesses were producing more than the public demanded. By the end of the decade warehouses were full of consumer goods waiting to be purchased.

LEARNING FROM GRAPHS. *Early America was a nation of farmers. Even as late as 1879 more than half of the value of the gross national product came from agriculture. But what trend does the graph illustrate? Why do you think this happened?*

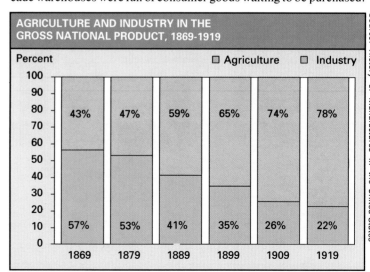

AGRICULTURE AND INDUSTRY IN THE GROSS NATIONAL PRODUCT, 1869-1919

| Percent | ☐ Agriculture | ☐ Industry |

Year	Industry	Agriculture
1869	43%	57%
1879	47%	53%
1889	59%	41%
1899	65%	35%
1909	74%	26%
1919	78%	22%

Source: *History of Manufactures in the United States*

UPI/Bettmann Newsphotos

The Election of 1928

President Coolidge played down the problems of farmers and workers in the "sick" industries. He believed the future was bright. In his 1928 State of the Union message he said:

" No Congress has met with a more pleasing prospect than that which appears at the present time. **"**

Herbert Hoover, candidate for president in 1928, says "hello" to Elizabeth, New Jersey, where a large and enthusiastic crowd greets him. What made him so popular at the time?

Most people agreed with Coolidge. Americans were enjoying the greatest period of prosperity in their history. Most were earning more money and working shorter hours than ever before. They had cars, radios, and household gadgets. Life was easy. It seemed likely to become easier still. The Republican party naturally took the credit for the good times.

In the 1928 presidential campaign, Herbert Hoover, the secretary of commerce, received the Republican nomination. The Democratic candidate was Alfred E. Smith. Smith had a record of solid accomplishment as governor of New York. He could not be denied the nomination. But his Catholic religion and his "big city" background hurt him in rural areas.   ①

Hoover won the election with 21 million votes to Smith's 15 million. The electoral vote was 444 to 87. Smith even lost his own state of New York as well as several Democratic states in the once Solid South. The main cause of Smith's defeat was the prosperity issue. A majority of the American people had come to believe that

America Heads For a Crash   889

RESOURCES
■ You may wish to have students complete Reading 41: "The Great Boom and the Big Crash (1928-1929)" in Volume II of *Eyewitnesses and Others.*

RETEACHING STRATEGY
Students with Special Needs.
Pair students who are having difficulty with students who are performing well. Have the more proficient students help the others match the following industries with the reason for their financial difficulties in the 1920s.
1. coal *(b)*
2. textiles *(c)*
3. agriculture *(a)*

a. This industry suffered because Europeans involved in it recaptured local markets after the war. As the price of products fell, the incomes of people in this field declined. However, their expenses remained the same.
b. Stiff competition from oil, natural gas, and electricity caused shutdowns and unemployment in this industry in the 1920s.
c. Manufacturers in this industry suffered because rayon was developed. More of these manufactured goods were produced than the public was buying, causing profits to shrink and unemployment to rise.

Culver Pictures

"Sold Out." These people could be two of thousands who lost their savings in the Stock Market Crash of 1929. What was the name given to the crash on October 29, 1929?

PRIMARY SOURCE
Description of change: excerpted.
Rationale: excerpted to focus on Adams' satirization of the stock market frenzy.

the Republican party was the symbol of economic progress and the guardian of good times.

The Great Crash

■ Prosperity tended to make people ambitious and optimistic. A "get-rich-quick" attitude developed in the United States as the decade advanced. More and more people set out to make fortunes in the stock market. They followed the prices of stocks in the newspapers as closely as they followed Babe Ruth's batting average. By mid-1929 stocks had been climbing steadily in price for several months. The profits of most corporations were on the rise. By 1929 the companies listed on the New York Stock Exchange, one market where stocks were bought and sold, were paying out three times as much money in dividends as they had in 1920. A newspaper writer of the day made fun of the stock buying frenzy.

❝ But nowadays the bores I find
Are of a single, standard kind:
For every person I may meet
At lunch, at clubs, upon the street,
Tells me, in endless wordy tales,
Of market purchases and sales;
Of how he bought a single share
Of California Prune and Pear;
Or how he sold at 33
A million shares of T. & T.
How McAvoy and Katzenstein°
Told him to sell at 99;
Of the thousands lost and millions made
In this or that egregious°° trade;
How bright he was to buy or sell
EP, GM, X or GL.
In herds, in schools, in droves, in flocks
The men and women talk of stocks.[1] ❞

This boom could not go on forever. Speculation—investing money in hopes of making a profit—ran on the false belief that no matter how much a person paid for stock, someone would buy it from them. But once stock prices reached a certain level, there would be no more buyers. The market reached that peak in September. Nervous speculators realized prices could only come down.

Quite suddenly, on October 24, 1929, thousands of investors wanted to sell stocks instead of buy them. Investors jammed tele-

°A Wall Street investment firm
°°Notable
[1]From *Christopher Columbus and Other Patriotic Verses* by Franklin P. Adams

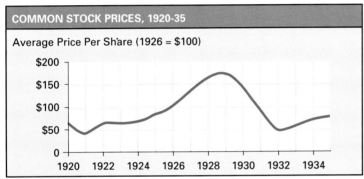

COMMON STOCK PRICES, 1920-35

Average Price Per Share (1926 = $100)

Source: *Historical Statistics of the United States.*

LEARNING FROM GRAPHS.
The graph shows the average price of a share of common stock for each year between 1920 and 1935. Because the graph shows the average price, remember that some stocks sold for much more and others for much less. What was the general trend in stock prices in the 1920s? What was the trend between 1930 and 1932? Why did the trend change?

phone lines and crowded into brokers' offices, desperate to turn their stocks into cash. With many sellers and few buyers, the prices of stocks plunged. People even began to sell at a loss in order to get something before prices fell still lower. General Electric Company shares dropped from $315 to $283 in that one day. U.S. Steel skidded from $205 to $193.

Then, on October 29, a day known as **Black Tuesday,** came an even steeper decline. The **Great Stock Market Crash** reached panic proportions. Day after day the drop continued. By the middle of November General Electric stock was down to $168, U.S. Steel to $150.

The Granger Collection, New York

The prosperity of the 1920s was over. Overproduction and overspeculation—investing too much money in hopes of making a profit—had caught up with the American people. The country was about to enter the Great Depression.

Return to the Preview & Review on
■ page 884.

Thinking Critically

1. Students may mention that Wilson should have attempted to compromise with the moderate Republicans in the Senate in order to ensure the U.S. joining the League of Nations.
2. Answers will vary but should demonstrate an understanding of the various fields in which American heroes and heroines were celebrated during the 1920s, and their choices should be supported by clear reasoning.
3. Possible answers are: advising Ford to offer his automobiles in colors other than black; offering optional luxury features or luxury models as well as the basic Model T.

REVIEW RESPONSES
Chapter Summary
Paragraphs will vary but should be evaluated on the logic of students' arguments.

Reviewing Chronological Order
3, 2, 5, 1, 4

Understanding Main Ideas
1. Wilson refused to compromise on the League of Nations so the treaty was rejected. Republican senators who would vote for the treaty with a few minor changes; Republican senators who supported the Lodge Reservations; senators who refused to vote for the treaty on any terms
2. It referred to the 1920s because jazz was popular during this period. Jazz, like young people in the 1920s, broke away from rigid rules.
3. Spectator sports boomed, helped by public relations and radio.
4. Utilized mass production techniques, kept cars simple, made the same basic model yearly
5. Coal, textile, agriculture; they did not prosper
6. More people wanted to sell rather than buy them.

Writing About History
Reports should demonstrate thorough research on Charles Lindbergh.

Practicing the Strategy
1. Wilson favors the League of Nations; Borah opposes it.
2. Answers will vary. Many students will suggest that Wilson was an expert because of his experience as president.

892

CHAPTER 24 REVIEW

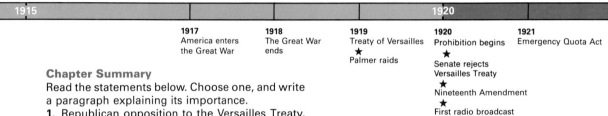

1915 — 1920
1917 America enters the Great War
1918 The Great War ends
1919 Treaty of Versailles ★ Palmer raids
1920 Prohibition begins ★ Senate rejects Versailles Treaty ★ Nineteenth Amendment ★ First radio broadcast
1921 Emergency Quota Act

Chapter Summary
Read the statements below. Choose one, and write a paragraph explaining its importance.
1. Republican opposition to the Versailles Treaty, especially to the League of Nations, caused Wilson political troubles.
2. Wilson's failing health added to the problems of getting the treaty ratified. It was eventually rejected.
3. The Nineteenth Amendment gave women the vote in national elections. The large voter turnout in 1920 elected Warren Harding.
4. The United States steered a middle course between isolationism and internationalism in the 1920s.
5. At home, Americans worried about anarchists and communists. This led to a series of actions aimed at limiting foreign influences in the United States. Other examples of the American reaction to the war included prohibition, the fundamentalist crusade, and the Sacco-Vanzetti Case.
6. Most Americans enjoyed life during the "Roaring Twenties." Music, sports, motion pictures, and the radio began their golden ages. Writers of the Lost Generation produced works that gave a voice to both the despair and the dazzle of the postwar period.
7. America also became an "automobile civilization" during the Twenties.
8. Despite the prevalent "get-rich-quick" attitude, problems of farmers and "sick" industries slowed the economy. The bubble of speculation burst in October 1929 when the stock market crashed, causing panic throughout the American economy.

Understanding Chronological Order
Number your paper 1–5. Then study the time line above and place the following events in the order in which they happened by writing the first next to 1, the second next to 2, and so on.
1. Sacco and Vanzetti executed
2. Teapot Dome
3. Senate rejects Versailles Treaty
4. Stock market crash
5. Lindbergh flies across the Atlantic

Understanding Main Ideas
1. Why was the Versailles Treaty rejected? Who were the mild reservationists? The strong reservationists? The irreconcilables?
2. What was meant by the term "the Jazz Age?" Why was jazz music a symbol for the times?
3. What were some reasons the 1920s was the Golden Age of Sports?
4. What methods did Henry Ford use to produce automobiles that ordinary people could afford?
5. Which were the "sick" industries of the 1920s? Why were they called "sick"?
6. What caused the price of stocks to plunge after October 24, 1929?

Thinking Critically
1. **Resolving Issues.** If you were President Wilson, how would you have acted differently in order to be sure that the Senate would approve the United States joining the League of Nations?
2. **Imagining.** If you could be a celebrity during the Twenties, would you rather be a jazz musician, a poet living in Harlem, an athlete, an airplane pilot, a movie star, a radio comedian, or a writer living in Paris? Why?
3. **Evaluating.** You know that Henry Ford's Model T dominated the automobile market until the end of the 1920s, when General Motors gained the lead. What changes would you have advised Ford to make in 1925 in order to maintain his advantage?

Writing About History
Write a report on the great hero of the 1920s, Charles A. Lindbergh. You might wish to focus on topics such as a) Lindbergh's barnstorming days, b) the planning and building of the *Spirit of St. Louis,* c) the day before the transatlantic flight, d) the May 1927 flight itself, e) the reception in Paris, and f) Lindbergh's welcome home. Conclude your report by explaining how Lindbergh's flight was a triumph for both man and machine.

automobiles in colors other than black; offering optional luxury features or luxury models as well as the basic Model T.

| 1925 THE TWENTIES | | 1930 |

1923
Harding dies suddenly
★
Coolidge succeeds Harding

1924
National Origins Act
★
Teapot Dome
★
Coolidge elected president

1925
Scopes "Monkey Trial"

1927
Harlem Globetrotters formed
★
Ruth hits 60 home runs
★
Lindbergh's solo flight
★
Sacco and Vanzetti executed

1928
Hoover elected president
★
Ford introduces Model A

1929
Stock market crash
★
Great Depression begins

Practicing the Strategy

Review the strategy on page 855.
Comparing Points of View. Reread the comments of Senator Borah and President Wilson on pages 853-54. Then answer the following questions.

1. How does Wilson's statement about the League of Nations differ from Borah's?
2. Would you consider Borah an expert on American foreign affairs? Why? Do you consider President Wilson an expert? Why?
3. Which view of the League of Nations do you agree with? Why?
4. Use your historical imagination to explain how Americans in 1919 might have had a different view of an international peace-keeping organization than people today.

Using Primary Sources

The 1920s were a time of drastic social change. Two social scientists, Robert S. Lynd and Helen M. Lynd, wrote a book called *Middletown,* which was a study of the way people lived in a mid-sized American town. The following quotations from the book indicate how people felt about the automobile. As you read the comments, think about how the automobile transformed America.

'We don't have no fancy clothes when we have the car to pay for,' said another. 'The car is the only pleasure we have.'

'I'll go without food before I'll see us give up the car,' said one woman.

'Our daughters [eighteen and fifteen] don't use our car much because they are always with somebody else in their car when we go out motoring,' lamented one business class mother.

1. Why do you think someone would go without food or clothing before they would give up their car?

2. What does the last quotation suggest about how the automobile changed family life?
3. Do you think cars are as important to people today as they were in the 1920s? Why or why not?

Linking History & Geography

Throughout the nation's history, improvements in transportation and communication have helped bring Americans closer together. The automobile, the airplane, and the radio came of age in the 1920s. To understand how these developments reshaped Americans' sense of geography, answer the following questions.

1. How did the automobile affect the number and quality of roads, the distances between where people lived and worked, and the amount of the country the average person visited?
2. What advantages did the airplane have over other types of transportation? What disadvantages did it have?
3. What advantages did the radio have over the telegraph and the telephone?
4. What generalization can you state about the effects of the automobile, the airplane, and the radio on regional differences in the U.S.?

Enriching Your Study of History

1. **Individual Project.** Prepare a classroom display to show how the automobile changed American life.
2. **Cooperative Project.** Have your group use its historical imagination to prepare and present on tape a radio broadcast from the 1920s. Each of you should select one of the following topics: news of the day, music, interviews with famous persons, comedy routines, and commercials. Then combine your parts into a radio program. Research the 1920s carefully so that your broadcast seems true to the times.

Chapter 24 Review   893

The Great Depression and the New Deal

PLANNING THE CHAPTER	
TEXTBOOK	**RESOURCES**
1. The Costs of Depression	***Unit 8 Worksheets and Tests:*** Chapter 25 Graphic Organizer, Directed Reading 25:1, Reteaching 25:1, Geography 25A ***Eyewitnesses and Others, Volume 2:*** Reading 47: The Impact of the Great Depression (1930s), Reading 42: Sketches from the Hispanic Southwest (1920s), Reading 44: Life in the Breadlines (1930)
2. Roosevelt Comes to Power	***Unit 8 Worksheets and Tests:*** Directed Reading 25:2, Reteaching 25:2, Geography 25B ***Eyewitnesses and Others, Volume 2:*** Reading 40: A Portrait of FDR, from *Sunrise at Campobello* (1924); Reading 49: From Steinbeck's *The Grapes of Wrath* (1930s) ***Art in American History:*** Transparency 31: Poster for *The Grapes of Wrath* ***Voices of America: Speeches and Documents:*** Franklin D. Roosevelt's First Inaugural Address (1933)
3. The New Deal	***Unit 8 Worksheets and Tests:*** Directed Reading 25:3, Reteaching 25:3 ***Creative Strategies for Teaching American History:*** Page 335 ***Art in American History:*** Transparency 29: The Sheridan Theater, Transparency 26: Classic Landscape, Transparency 27: Cow's Skull: Red, White, and Blue
4. Effects of the New Deal	***Unit 8 Worksheets and Tests:*** Directed Reading 25:4, Reteaching 25:4 ***Eyewitnesses and Others, Volume 2:*** Reading 46: Two Poems from Langston Hughes' *Don't You Want to Be Free?* (1937), Reading 48: James Agee Describes the Life of Tenant Farmers (1930s), Reading 45: Roosevelt Defends the New Deal (1937)
Chapter Review	***Audio Program:*** Chapter 25 ***Unit 8 Worksheets and Tests:*** Chapter 25 Tests, Forms A and B (See also *Alternative Assessment Forms*) ***Test Generator***

Unit Review	**Unit 8 Worksheets and Tests:** Unit 8 Tests, Forms A and B (see also *Alternative Assessment Forms*), Unit 8 Synthesis **Test Generator**

STRATEGIES FOR STUDENTS WITH SPECIAL NEEDS

Gifted Students.

Have interested students prepare questionnaires to use during an interview of a family member or a friend who lived through the Great Depression. Encourage students to include in their questionnaires items dealing with how the depression affected the interviewee and how the interviewee managed to cope with the difficult financial times. Instruct students to interview at least three people and then to prepare oral reports comparing the results of the three interviews. Have students present their reports to the rest of the class.

Students Having Difficulty with the Chapter.

You may wish to have students listen to Chapter 25 in *The Story of America Audio Program.* Then organize the class into several cooperative learning groups. Have each group prepare a 10-item objective test over material covered in the chapter. As the groups are preparing their tests, you may wish to circulate throughout the classroom to make certain that all group members are contributing items for the test. After the groups have completed their tests have them administer the tests to other groups.

BOOKS FOR TEACHERS

John M. Blum, *The Progressive Presidents: Theodore Roosevelt, Woodrow Wilson, Franklin D. Roosevelt, Lyndon B. Johnson.* New York: W. W. Norton, 1980.

Kenneth S. Davis, *FDR: The New York Years, 1928–1932.* Emmaus, PA: Rodale Press, 1985.

Mark H. Leff, *The Limits of Symbolic Reform: The New Deal and Taxation, 1933–1939.* New York: Cambridge University Press, 1984.

Richard H. Pells, *Radical Visions and American Dreams: Culture and Social Thought in the Depression Years.* Middletown, CT: Wesleyan University Press, 1973.

BOOKS FOR STUDENTS

Chester Aaron, *Lackawanna.* New York: Harper & Row, 1986.

Nathaniel Harris, *The Great Depression.* North Pomfret, VT: David & Charles, 1988.

Milton Meltzer, *Brother, Can You Spare a Dime? The Great Depression, 1929–1933.* New York: New American Library, 1977.

Milton Meltzer, *Langston Hughes: A Biography.* New York: Harper & Row, 1968.

Mary Stolz, *Ivy Larkin.* Orlando: Harcourt Brace Jovanovich, 1986.

MULTIMEDIA MATERIALS

The Black Community in the New Deal (film, 30 min.), CBSTV. Describes African Americans during the New Deal years including the demographic shifts that brought large numbers of African Americans to the North and into the Democratic party.

The Great Depression (filmstrip), GA. Reproduces the sights and sounds of the Depression from Jack Benny and Mae West to soup kitchens and shantytowns; includes the actual voices of Herbert Hoover and Franklin Delano Roosevelt.

Great Depression—A Human Diary (film, 52 min.), FILMEN. Portrays the lives of Americans during the 1930s.

To Lead a Nation (filmstrip), EMC. A four-part series about Franklin Delano Roosevelt, concentrating on his leadership qualities.

RESOURCES

■ You may wish to have students complete the Chapter 25 Graphic Organizer as they work through this chapter.

1. Describe the "normal" business cycle.
2. Explain how the Great Depression affected various groups of Americans.
3. Compare and contrast Hoover's and Roosevelt's strategies for ending the depression.
4. Understand how the depression was both economic and psychological.
5. Explain the aims of the New Deal.

OVERVIEW

Hoover and Roosevelt had very different philosophies as well as very different strategies for fighting the depression. Hoover did not think that the federal government should increase its power to deal with the crisis, and he opposed federal relief because it would destroy "real liberty." He felt the "rugged individualism" of Americans would see the depression through. He also felt relief was the job of local agencies and private charities. Roosevelt, on the other hand, was not concerned with theory. He felt the federal government must do something to help the people, regardless of "accepted" political theory. He took an activist approach, offering many programs to deal with the crisis. His New Deal had a major impact on American life.

FOCUS/MOTIVATION:
MAKING CONNECTIONS
Student Experiences.
Tell students to scan the art and photos in this chapter to get a sense of the chapter's scope and content. This will help students to see the human side of the Great Depression and to get an idea of its economic, social, and psychological effects, as well as the ways in which individuals and the government tried to combat the depression.

CHAPTER 25

The Great Depression and the New Deal

■ The stock market crash of 1929 was the first major event of what we call the Great Depression. There had been many earlier depressions in the United States, but the Great Depression lasted longer and was more severe than any before in the nation's history. Human suffering was widespread. Shopkeepers lost their businesses. Farmers lost their farms. Banks failed and investors lost their savings. Finally, in 1932, the nation turned to Franklin Delano Roosevelt, a man of wealth who understood suffering after his own struggle with the paralysis of polio he suffered in 1921. As president, could the popular FDR pull the nation from "the depths of depression"?

In this painting by Paul Starrett Sample titled "Unemployment," the city sidewalk and alley are crowded with people out of work. How do you think long-term mass unemployment might affect the nation? What would likely be some negative results?

6. Identify major New Deal measures.
7. Explain why the New Deal was so popular.
8. Analyze criticisms of the New Deal.
9. Contrast Roosevelt's strategies in the First and Second New Deals.
10. Discuss African Americans' attitudes toward the New Deal.

11. Write an essay assessing the effectiveness of the New Deal.

SUGGESTED CAPTION RESPONSE
The depth of the recession began to lessen during the New Deal, indicating that government spending was having a positive effect on the depression. The line indicating recession rises toward the trend line.

1. THE COSTS OF DEPRESSION

The "Normal" Business Cycle

People had come to accept depressions as a regular part of the **business cycle.** This is how business cycles worked:

In good times economic activity tended to expand. More goods were produced. Prices rose. More workers were hired. Eventually output increased faster than goods could be sold. Surpluses then piled up in company warehouses and in retail stores. Manufacturers had to slow down their production. They let go some of their workers. These unemployed people had less money to buy goods. More manufacturers then had to reduce output and lay off more workers. Prices fell. Producers who were losing money began to go out of business. The general economy was in a state of **depression.**

People believed that depressions were self correcting. When output became very low, the surpluses were gradually used up. Then the efficient producers who had not gone out of business increased output. They rehired workers. These workers, with wages in their pockets, increased their own purchases. Demand increased. Prices rose. The economy entered the **recovery** stage. Recovery eventually led to **prosperity**—a time of high prices, full production, and almost no unemployment.

The Great Depression

A complete business cycle might last anywhere from two or three to five or six years. What made the **Great Depression** different was that it lasted for more than ten years. The economy declined steeply from late 1929 until the winter of 1932-33. Then it appeared to be stuck. Recovery was slow and irregular. The output of goods remained far below what it had been in 1929. Only in 1940, after the outbreak of the Second World War, did a strong recovery begin.

Throughout this long period at least 10 percent of the work force was unemployed. At the low point, early in 1933, about 25 percent of all Americans were without jobs. Americans spent $10.9 billion in food stores in 1929. But although the population increased in every year, Americans did not spend that much on food again until 1941. This was true also of money spent on furniture, clothing, automobiles, jewelry, recreation, medical care, and nearly all other items.

These cold figures tell us little about the human suffering and discouragement that the Great Depression caused. Shopkeepers who had worked for years to develop their businesses lost everything. People lost their savings in bank failures. Workers who had risen through the ranks to well-paid jobs found themselves unemployed. Those who had developed skills found that their skills were useless. Students graduating from schools and colleges could find no one willing to hire them.

Preview & Review

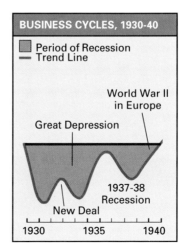

BUSINESS CYCLES, 1930-40

■ Period of Recession
— Trend Line

World War II in Europe

Great Depression

1937-38 Recession

New Deal

1930   1935   1940

LEARNING FROM GRAPHS.
What effect did the New Deal have on the Great Depression? How can you tell?

SECTION 1

PREVIEW & REVIEW RESPONSES
Understanding Issues, Events, & Ideas.
Descriptions should demonstrate an understanding of the terms used.
1. As surpluses were depleted during depressions, efficient producers would begin to increase their output. They would rehire workers, who could then begin to make purchases again. With increased demand, prices would rise and the economy would enter the recovery phase of the cycle.
2. It lasted much longer—over 10 years.
3. He asked Congress to lower taxes and increase government spending on public works. He urged farmers to form cooperatives and to decrease production, and he favored lower interest rates.
4. They marched to demand that the bonus Congress had granted World War I veterans be paid then instead of in 1945 when it was due to be paid. Hoover ordered army units to assist the police in removing the veterans. Hoover's popularity suffered because many people felt that he was unsympathetic to the plight of ordinary Americans.

Thinking Critically.
Students should support their position with sound reasoning.

The Costs of Depression 895

RESOURCES
■ You may wish to have students complete Reading 47: "The Impact of the Great Depression (1930s)" in Volume II of *Eyewitness and Others.*
◄ You may wish to have students complete Reading 42: "Sketches from the Hispanic Southwest (1920s)" in Volume II of *Eyewitnesses and Others.*

SUGGESTED CAPTION RESPONSE
It decreased because of widespread unemployment.

FOCUS/MOTIVATION:
MAKING CONNECTIONS
Student Experiences.
Ask students if they have heard their older relatives talk about the Great Depression. Encourage students to share these accounts with the class. If few students have comments to offer from relatives, try brainstorming with the class. Have students suggest anything they think relates to the Great Depression and compile a list on the chalkboard or overhead projector. You may wish to refer to the list after students have completed their study of the chapter to see which ideas were correctly included on the list and which were not on the original list. Then ask students to focus on how the depression affected individuals. Ask students to imagine how the depression would have affected children of their age. *(Answers will vary.)* Tell students that the United States had had other depressions but that this one was more severe and lasted much longer.

PRIMARY SOURCE
Description of change: excerpted.
Rationale: excerpted to focus on the ways the Great Depression affected ordinary people.

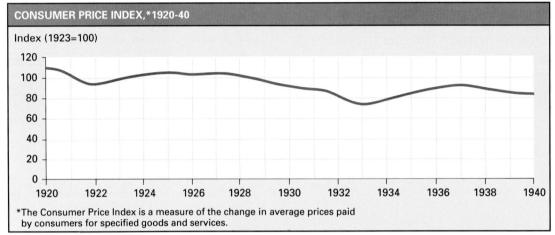

CONSUMER PRICE INDEX,* 1920-40

Index (1923=100)

*The Consumer Price Index is a measure of the change in average prices paid by consumers for specified goods and services.

Source: *Historical Statistics of the United States*

LEARNING FROM GRAPHS.
The Consumer Price Index, or CPI, is a statistic that tells economists how much a typical American can afford. What happened to the CPI during the Great Depression? Why?

The weakest and poorest suffered most. Many married women lost their jobs because employers thought they did not need to work. Unemployment was far higher among African Americans, Hispanics, and other groups than among whites. In the southwestern states thousands of Mexican-born farm laborers and their children born in the United States were gathered up by federal authorities and shipped back to Mexico when they were unable to find work. Officials excused this cruel policy by arguing that there was not enough relief money to care for them. Many Mexican-born workers who had *not* lost their jobs were also shipped back. In this case the excuse was that they were holding down jobs that United States citizens needed.

The term "depression" describes the mood of the people as well as the state of the economy. Until the middle of the 1930s there was no system of unemployment insurance and no national welfare assistance program to help the unemployed and their families. People in desperate need had no sure place they could turn to. One sufferer recalled:

❝ My first real memories come about '31. It was simply a gut issue then: eating or not eating, living or not living. My father was a coal miner, outside a small town in Illinois.
. . .
When the mine temporarily closed down in the early Thirties, my dad had to hunt for work elsewhere. He went around the state, he'd paint barns, anything. . . .[1] ❞

Great efforts were made to assist the jobless. State and city governments and private charities raised money to feed the poor and provide them with a little cash for their other needs. Special "charity drives," many led by churches and religious groups, were conducted

[1] From *Hard Times: An Oral History of the Great Depression* by Studs Terkel

RESOURCES

■ You may wish to have students complete Reading 44: "Life in the Breadlines (1930)" in Volume II of *Eyewitnesses and Others*.

SUGGESTED CAPTION RESPONSE
The onset of the Great Depression; New Deal spending created jobs.

to collect clothing for the unemployed and their families. There were **soup kitchens** and **breadlines** where hungry people could get a free ■ meal and lodging houses where the homeless could spend the night. One woman, a teenager during the Great Depression, recalled her experiences:

❝ My mother'd send us to the soup line. And we were never allowed to curse. If you happened to be one of the first ones in line, you didn't get anything but the water that was on top. So we'd ask the guy that was putting the soup into the buckets—everybody had to bring their own bucket to get the soup—he'd dip the greasy watery stuff off the top. So we'd ask him to please dip down to get some meat and potatoes from the bottom of the kettle. But he wouldn't do it. So we learned to curse.

Then we'd go across the street. One place had bread, large loaves of bread. Down the road just a little way was a big shed, and they gave milk. My sister and me would take two buckets each. And that's what we lived off for the longest time.

I can remember one time, the only thing in the house to eat was mustard. My sister and I put so much mustard on biscuits that we got sick. And we can't stand mustard till today. . . .

There was a feeling of together. . . . It's different today. People are made to feel ashamed now if they don't have anything. Back then, I'm not sure how the rich felt. I think the rich looked down on the poor as much as they do now.

Point of View

Unemployment struck every type of workplace—large and small, skilled and unskilled. One writer of the day put it in perspective.

> ❝The Ford Motor Company, in fact, serves as a good example of the devastating effect the crash had upon unemployment. In March of 1929, more than 129,000 people were on the Ford pay-roll. Two years later the number of employees had dropped to 84,000; by August of 1931 only 37,000 were employed by Ford. . . .❞
>
> From *Years of Protest*

GUIDED INSTRUCTION: COOPERATIVE LEARNING
Organize students into cooperative learning groups. Tell each group to make a diagram for the bulletin board showing the business cycle. Tell the groups to be sure to include the concepts of supply and demand, inflation and deflation, industrial output, and unemployment. Choose one of the groups to use their diagram to explain the "normal" business cycle to the class. Later, use the concepts to discuss both the downward and upward movements of the cycle and to describe what happened during the Great Depression.

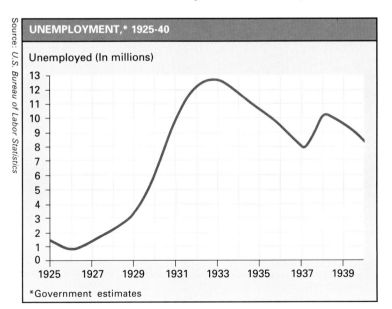

Source: U.S. Bureau of Labor Statistics

UNEMPLOYMENT,* 1925-40

Unemployed (In millions)

*Government estimates

LEARNING FROM GRAPHS.
Note the ups and downs of unemployment figures between 1925 and 1940. They are usually much more stable. What event caused them to soar in 1929–30? What helped bring them down in the mid-1930s?

PRIMARY SOURCE
Description of change: excerpted.
Rationale: excerpted to focus on the magnitude of the unemployment problem.

The Costs of Depression   897

HISTORICAL SIDELIGHTS

① People were willing to leave home to find work. In 1931, 100,000 American men applied for 6,000 skilled jobs in the Soviet Union.

SUGGESTED CAPTION RESPONSE
Most people blamed Hoover.

EXTENSION:
COMMUNITY INVOLVEMENT
Have students interview older people in either their family or community who lived through the events of 1929–1939. Before students conduct their interviews, have them develop a set of questions to ask their subjects. If possible, invite older members of the community to your school to serve as subjects for the interviews. This would give the students easy access to this important resource.

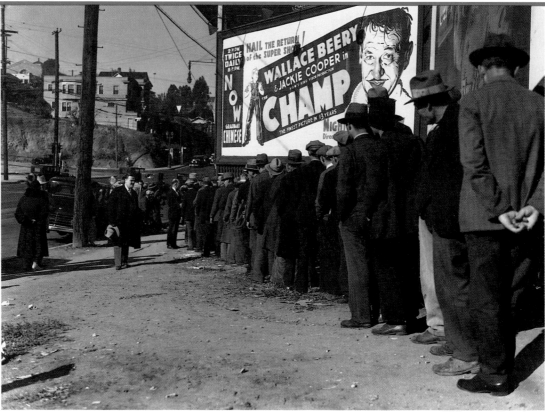

UPI/Bettmann Newsphotos

These crowds have not come to see the latest movie by the popular Wallace Beery. They stand in line in the hope that there will be bread or soup when their turn comes. "We all had an understanding that it wasn't our fault," recalled one survivor of the Great Depression, but who was to blame?

But among the people that I knew, we all had an understanding that it wasn't our fault. It was something that had happened to the system. Most people blamed Hoover, and they cursed him—it was all his fault. I'm not saying he's blameless, but I'm not saying either it was all his fault. Our system doesn't run by just one person, and it doesn't fall by just one person, either.[1] 99

Many victims of the depression received help from relatives and friends. But others stood on street corners trying to sell apples or ① pencils. Some simply held out their hands, begging for a few pennies. Some became tramps, wandering aimlessly around the country, stealing rides on railroad freight cars. Some became thieves. And some people actually starved to death.

Hoover Fights the Depression

Herbert Hoover's work during the Great World War seemed good training for dealing with the depression. He had helped the Belgians after the Germans invaded their country. He had run the American food program after 1917. As secretary of commerce during the 1920s he had won the confidence of most business leaders.

[1]From *Hard Times: An Oral History of the Great Depression* by Studs Terkel

PRIMARY SOURCE
Description of change: excerpted.
Rationale: excerpted to focus on the ways in which ordinary people reacted to the Great Depression and to charity.

Dorothea Lange, Woman of the High Plains, *Courtesy of the Dorothea Lange Collection, The City of Oakland, The Oakland Museum, 1991*

This photograph titled "Woman of the High Plains, Texas Panhandle" was taken by Dorothea Lange in 1938. It is one of the most lingering images of the depression. Note that the woman's dress probably has been made from flour sacks.

GUIDED INSTRUCTION
In order for students to see the chronology of the Great Depression as a whole, have them draw a time line spanning the years 1929–41. Student time lines should include the following: Great Stock Market Crash, election of Franklin Delano Roosevelt, creation of the Federal Deposit Insurance Corporation, creation of the Civil Works Authority, creation of the Civilian Conservation Corps, passing of the Agricultural Adjustment Act, creation of the Federal Emergency Relief Administration, passing of the Social Security Act, Roosevelt's reelection in 1936, the Recession of 1937–38, and start of World War II. You may wish to have students include other key events as they study the chapter.

Hoover also understood economics better than most politicians. When he realized that the nation had entered a serious depression, he tried to stimulate recovery quickly. He urged Congress to lower taxes so that people would have more money to spend on goods and services. He called for more government spending on **public works,** such as road construction or building dams. These measures would increase the demand for goods and put jobless people back to work, he said. Congress passed each of these measures. Unfortunately they were too limited to end the Great Depression.

Farmers in particular were hard hit by the depression. The price of most farm products fell sharply. Hoover urged farmers to form cooperatives and to raise smaller crops until prices rose. He also favored holding down interest rates so farmers and the businesses they supported could borrow money more easily. Neither bankers nor farmers were willing to follow these voluntary guidelines in the face of the crisis.

Above all, the president recognized that the American people

The Costs of Depression 899

GUIDED INSTRUCTION: COOPERATIVE LEARNING

Organize the class into cooperative learning groups. Tell each group that they will take part in a presidential press conference to discuss government responses to the depression. Choose one group to act as Hoover and his advisers. Tell the other groups that they are to work together to prepare questions to ask the president about his policies. The groups may have to use library resources to help them prepare for the press conference.

"Home Relief Station" by the artist Louis Ribak reminds us that waiting and humiliation may be a part of charity. The victims of the Dust Bowl await their turn in front of the woman who will investigate their claims. Imagine what you would say to this person when your time came.

had lost confidence in the economic system. This was part of their psychological depression. He tried to encourage them to have faith in the future. "Prosperity," he said, "is just around the corner."

But Hoover's strength as an organizer in wartime proved to be a weakness during the depression. Voluntary cooperation would not solve the nation's problems this time. During the war people knew who the enemy was and what to do to protect themselves. In the depression they could not identify any particular enemy. Therefore they did not know how they could protect themselves.

Hoover displayed still another weakness. He believed that the federal government should not increase its authority just because times were hard. If the United States took over powers that normally belonged to state and local governments, it would become a "super-state." Even when city after city proved unable to raise enough money to take care of the unemployed, Hoover opposed federal grants for relief purposes. Such aid would destroy the "real liberty" of the people, he said.

Hoover supported federal assistance to banks and big industries. These loans were sound investments, he said. The money would be used to produce goods and earn profits. Then the loans could be repaid. Lending money to a farmer to buy pig feed or more seed or a tractor was also proper, according to Hoover's theory. But he opposed giving federal aid to farmers so that they could feed their

In 1924 in response to pressure from veterans' groups, Congress had authorized Adjusted Compensation certificates, or life insurance policies, against which the former soldiers could borrow and which would be payable in cash in 1945. Each soldier's policy was based on $1.25 for each day served overseas and $1.00 for each day served in the United States. In 1936 the Senate finally agreed to pay out the urgently needed funds.

children. That would be giving them something for nothing. He believed charity was the business of state and local governments and private organizations like the Red Cross and the Salvation Army.

As the Great Depression dragged on, Hoover became more and more unpopular. People began to think that he was hardhearted. He seemed not to care about the sufferings of the poor. His critics even claimed that he was responsible for the depression.

Both charges were untrue. Hoover cared deeply about the suffering the depression was causing. He sincerely believed that his policies were the proper ones. These policies had certainly not caused the depression. After all, every industrial nation in the world had high unemployment at the time. The Great Depression affected all of Europe and most of the rest of the world.

The economies of nations that depended on agriculture were badly depressed. There was a depression in wheat-growing Australia and in beef-raising Argentina. The price of Brazilian coffee fell so low that farmers there burned the coffee beans in cookstoves. Coffee made a cheaper fuel than coal or kerosene.

Still, even if he was not responsible for the long depression, Hoover's rigid policies were not working. He was in charge of the government. Therefore people tended to blame him.

The Bonus Army

Public opinion turned further against Hoover after the **Bonus March** of the summer of 1932. Some years earlier Congress had passed a law giving veterans of the Great World War an adjusted compensation bonus. Its purpose was to make up for the low pay that soldiers had received during the war while workers at home were earning high wages. The bonus money, however, was not to be paid until 1945.

During the depression veterans began to demand that the bonus be paid at once. As you can see in this excerpt from a letter to the veteran's committee, this issue was turning public opinion and anger against Hoover and the government.

    “ Now that our income is but $15.60 a week (their are five of us My Husband Three little children and myself). My husband who is a world war Veteran and saw active service in the trenches, became desperate and applied for Compensation and was turned down and that started me thinking. . . . Oh why is it that it is allways a bunch of overley rich, selfish, dumb, ignorant money hogs that persist in being Senitors, legislatures, representatives Where would they and their possessions be if it were not for the Common Soldier, the common laborer that is compelled to work for a starvation wage, for I tell you again the hog of a Landlord gets his there is not enough left for the necessities if a man

Point of View

The editors of a collection of protest writings of the 1930s offer this introduction.

“The Great Depression, of course, did not begin with the collapse of the stock market in October 1929. For one thing, the prosperity enjoyed by many Americans in the twenties was not shared by Europeans. Europe spent the twenties first trying to restore the losses suffered as a result of World War I, and then trying to maintain the fiscal balance; it was a futile attempt . . . [This] had no more effect upon the optimism of America's leaders than did the cries of discontent which had for years been coming from rural America. America was prospering, and Europe was at peace; it was easy to ignore the signs of trouble.”

From *Years of Protest,* 1967

INDEPENDENT PRACTICE
Have students complete the
Preview & Review activity at
the beginning of the section.

CLOSURE
Tell students that while the
United States had experienced
depressions before, none
lasted so long or affected so
many. While Hoover under-
stood economics better than
most presidents, his policies
were too rigid to solve such a
serious crisis.

HOMEWORK
Ask students to write letters to
the editor of their local newspaper suggesting ways in
which local government could
help those suffering from the
depression. Read some of the
best to the class. Discuss with
the class some of the problems
associated with trying to alleviate the effects of massive
economic problems on a local
level.

PRIMARY SOURCE
Description of change: excerpted.
Rationale: excerpted to focus
on one person's resentment toward the government's apparent lack of concern.

Brown Brothers

*General Douglas MacArthur, above
left, and his aide Dwight D. Eisenhower supervise federal troops (right),
who use tear gas and bayonets in 1932
to clear the tent city set up by the
Bonus Army. (MacArthur and Eisenhower would become leading commanders in World War II.) Were the
Bonus Marchers dangerous radicals
who needed to be driven from the
capital?*

Return to the Preview & Review on
page 895.

UPI/Bettmann Newsphotos

has three or more children. . . . Oh for a few Statesmen,
oh for but one statesman, as fearless as Abraham Lincoln,
the amancipator who died for us. . . .[1]

[1] From *Down and Out in the Depression: Letters from the "Forgotten Man,"* edited
by Robert S. McElvaine

Then in July 1932 about 20,000 former soldiers marched on
Washington to demonstrate before the Capitol. When Congress refused to change the law, some of the marchers settled down on vacant
land on the edge of Washington. They put up a camp of tents and
flimsy tar-paper shacks. They announced that they would not leave
until the bonus was paid.

Hoover had opposed the bonus to begin with. Such giveaways
threatened to destroy the "self-reliance" of the people, he said. He
believed, wrongly as it turned out, that the Bonus Marchers were
being led by dangerous radicals. When trouble broke out, Hoover
ordered army units to assist police in driving out the veterans.

Troops commanded by General Douglas MacArthur went into
action. Infantrymen backed by cavalry units and five tanks swiftly
cleared the camp. No shots were fired and no one was killed. However, news film of steel-helmeted, rifle-bearing soldiers firing tear gas
grenades at ragged, unarmed war veterans shocked millions of Amer-
icans. Hoover's popularity hit rock bottom.

902   THE GREAT DEPRESSION AND THE NEW DEAL

2. ROOSEVELT COMES TO POWER

Franklin D. Roosevelt

It is safe to say that in 1932 any Democratic presidential candidate could have defeated the Republican Hoover. Somewhere between 13 and 16 million workers were unemployed. The total income of all Americans had fallen from $87 billion in 1929 to $42 billion in 1932. All the shares of the stocks listed on the New York Stock Exchange were worth only a quarter of their value before the Great Crash.

The particular Democrat who profited from this situation was ■ Franklin D. Roosevelt, the governor of New York. Roosevelt came from a wealthy family. He had graduated from Harvard College, studied law, and gone into politics. As we have seen, he had run for vice president in 1920 on the ticket with James M. Cox, who was defeated by Warren G. Harding.

The next year Roosevelt spent his usual vacation at his summer home in Campobello, Canada. One day in August 1921 he helped put out a brush fire while on an outing with his children. He returned home tired and chilled in his wet swimming suit. That night he burned with fever. Within a few days his legs were almost completely paralyzed. He had a severe case of polio. He recovered from the disease, but for the rest of his life he could walk only with the aid of metal braces and two canes. More often he was carried or used a wheelchair.

UPI/Bettmann Newsphotos

Well-wishers greet President Roosevelt at Warm Springs, Georgia. What words might you have used to describe the new president?

Preview & Review

Use these questions to guide your reading. Answer the questions after completing Section 2.
Understanding Issues, Events, & Ideas. Use the following words to trace Roosevelt's first moves to counter the depression: New Deal, relief, recovery, reform, Hundred Days, Bank Holiday, Federal Deposit Insurance Corporation, National Industrial Recovery Act, minimum wage, National Recovery Administration, Agricultural Adjustment Act, Tennessee Valley Authority, Federal Securities Act, Home Owner's Loan Corporation, Federal Emergency Relief Administration, Civil Works Authority, Civilian Conservation Corps.
1. Contrast the personalities of Herbert Hoover and Franklin Roosevelt.
2. How did the banking crisis turn out to be an advantage for the entire country?
3. What was the overall effect of the flood of laws passed during the Hundred Days?
Thinking Critically. Which do you think was the most important law passed during the Hundred Days? Why?

Roosevelt Comes to Power 903

Courtesy Vanity Fair, copyright 1934 (renewed 1962), Condé Nast Publications, Inc.

Vanity Fair, *a witty and popular magazine, offered this cover of FDR "breaking in" the rambunctious country in 1934. If the horse stands for the United States, how is Roosevelt doing?*

Roosevelt's usual high spirits sagged, but only briefly. He went on with his political career. In 1928, when Governor Alfred E. Smith of New York ran for president against Hoover, Roosevelt was chosen by the Democrats to run for governor. Hoover defeated Smith in the race for electoral votes in New York, but Roosevelt, the Democrat, was elected governor. Two years later he was reelected by a huge majority. This evidence of popular support won him the 1932 Democratic presidential nomination.

Roosevelt was almost the exact opposite of Hoover. Hoover was restrained, stiff, and by 1932, very glum. Roosevelt had a cheerful, relaxed, almost carefree personality. Indeed, in 1932 many observers thought he had more style than substance. He was no more radical than Hoover, but he was a much less rigid person. Hoover worked out careful theories and tried to apply them to the practical problems of government. Roosevelt mistrusted theories. Yet he was willing to apply any theory to any particular problem if there seemed a good chance it would work.

Roosevelt turned out to be a most popular political campaigner. He made excellent speeches. He had tremendous energy. Moreover, he was an optimist. At a time when most people were deeply depressed, his cheer encouraged and uplifted millions. The crowds that gathered when he campaigned seemed to inspire him as well. In November he defeated Hoover easily. His electoral majority was 472 to 59. The popular vote was 22.8 million to 15.8 million. The voters also gave the Democrats large majorities in both houses of Congress.

"Nothing to Fear but Fear Itself"

Roosevelt was elected in November, but he could not by law take his oath as president until March 4. Meanwhile, the economy seemed to drift downward aimlessly, like a falling leaf in a winter forest. Between December 1932 and February industrial production hit an all-time low. This, together with continuing news of bank failures, caused Americans to panic. Suddenly, in February, people all over the country began to rush fearfully to withdraw their savings from the banks. This banking panic forced even most of the soundest banks to close their doors.

The banking crisis turned out to be a great advantage for Roosevelt and indirectly for the entire country. It forced people to put politics aside and treat the depression as a great national emergency.

Inauguration Day in Washington was raw and damp. In this dark hour Roosevelt's speech came like a ray of summer sunshine. He said:

      ❝ This great nation will endure as it has endured, will revive, and will prosper.
          So, first of all, let me assert my firm belief that the only

thing we have to fear is fear itself—nameless, unreasoning, unjustified terror which paralyzes needed efforts to convert retreat into advance. . . .

Happiness lies not in the mere possession of money; it lies in the joy of achievement, in the thrill of creative effort.

We face the arduous [hard] days that lie before us in the warm courage of national unity; with the clear consciousness of seeking old and precious moral values; with the clean satisfaction that comes from the stern performance of duty by old and young alike. . . .[1]

Roosevelt spoke only generally about measures for fighting the depression. But he made his approach crystal clear. He was going to do something. "Action, and action now," was his theme. His first priority would be to put people back to work, he said.

The Hundred Days

In his inaugural address the president called upon Congress to meet in a special session on March 9 to deal with the emergency. From March 9 to June 16, when this special session ended, was 100 days. No one planned to have the session last exactly 100 days. The fact that it did dramatized how much that Congress accomplished.

In his campaign for president, Roosevelt had called for a **New Deal.** Roosevelt's New Deal had three general aims—relief, recovery, and reform. **Relief** came first and was aimed at all Americans in

[1]From *The Public Papers and Addresses, 1933* by Franklin D. Roosevelt

The Bank Panic in 1933 brought lines of New Yorkers to see if their savings or deposits were safe in the American Union Bank. Even the soundest banks had to close their doors for protection. What event of the 1980s reminded many people of the panic?

GUIDED INSTRUCTION
When discussing Hoover and Roosevelt, draw a chart on the chalkboard or an overhead projector to compare the two men. Have students help you fill in the chart by answering questions about the two men's personalities, political ideas, and strategies to end the Great Depression.

PRIMARY SOURCE
Description of change: excerpted and bracketed.
Rationale: excerpted to focus on Roosevelt's optimistic approach to fighting the depression; bracketed words added to clarify meaning.

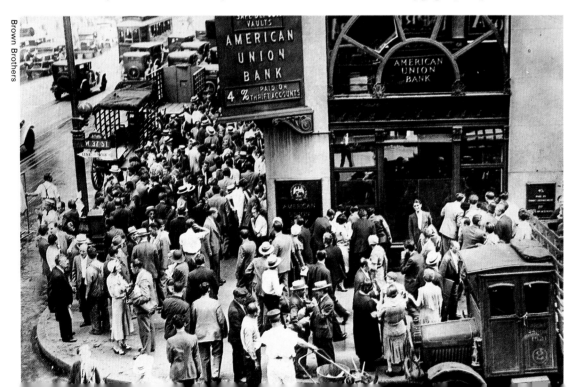

Brown Brothers

economic distress. **Recovery** would then spur the economy and get the country out of the depression. **Reform** would prevent another severe depression from happening. The flood of new laws passed during the **Hundred Days** had the effect of convincing people that old ways were indeed being tossed out, like a worn deck of cards. The country seemed to be making a fresh start.

Even before Congress met, Roosevelt declared a **Bank Holiday,** closing all the banks so that a general plan to protect the savings of the public could be developed. Congress then passed new banking laws, the most important being a measure which created the **Federal Deposit Insurance Corporation** (FDIC). The FDIC insured everyone's savings up to $5,000. Runs on banks stopped. Depositors knew that even if their bank failed, they would get their money back. Nothing did more than this measure to restore public confidence. As one of Roosevelt's advisers said:

> 66 The bank rescue of 1933 was probably the turning point of
> the Depression. When people were able to survive the
> shock of having all the banks closed, and then see the banks
> open up, with their money protected, there began to be
> confidence. Good times were coming. Most of the legisla-
> tion that came after that didn't really help the public, the
> public helped itself, after it got confidence.
> It marked the revival of hope. . . .[1] 99

But new banking laws could not create jobs or cause farm prices to rise or stimulate business activity directly. So Congress quickly passed laws to accomplish these objectives. The most important and controversial measure was the **National Industrial Recovery Act** (NIRA).

The NIRA was supposed to stimulate private business by per-mitting manufacturers to cooperate with one another without fear of violating the antitrust laws. Firms in every industry were to draw up rules, called codes of fair competition. The firms were allowed to set limits on how much each could produce in order to avoid flooding markets with goods that could not be sold. They could also fix prices to avoid cutthroat competition.

In addition the codes provided certain benefits for workers. One was the right to freely join unions. Through these unions workers could bargain collectively with their employers. **Minimum wage** rates and maximum hours of work were also guaranteed under the codes. Each industrial code had to be approved, supervised, and enforced by the government through the **National Recovery Administration** (NRA). Roosevelt selected the enthusiastic Frances Perkins as his secretary of labor. She became the first woman cabinet member and an active advocate of workers' rights.

The Granger Collection, New York

In this Vanity Fair *cover, Uncle Sam is rescued by the Blue Eagle. Why was it a hopeful symbol?*

[1] From *Hard Times: An Oral History of the Great Depression* by Studs Terkel

SUGGESTED CAPTION RESPONSES
(Top) All three were willing to cooperate to end the depression.
(Bottom) It had almost doubled.

Brown Brothers

Frances Perkins, the first woman cabinet member, greets workmen of Carnegie Steel. This is a far cry from the ugly scene of the Homestead Strike against Carnegie years earlier. How did the Great Depression bring a truce to labor, management, and government?

NRA officials made great efforts to persuade workers and employers to accept the new system. "We Do Our Part" was the slogan of the NRA. Its symbol was a picture of a Blue Eagle. Soon Blue Eagle stickers were being displayed in the windows of giant factories and small shops all over the country. This symbol was also printed on the labels of products of all kinds.

The NRA was expected to get the sluggish industrial economy moving again. Congress next dealt with the farm problem by passing the **Agricultural Adjustment Act** (AAA). During the depression farm prices had fallen even further than the prices of manufactured goods. The basic idea of the AAA was to push prices up by cutting down on the amount of crops produced.

Under this law the government rented some of the land that was normally planted in so-called basic crops, such as wheat, cotton, tobacco, and corn. No crops were planted on the land the government

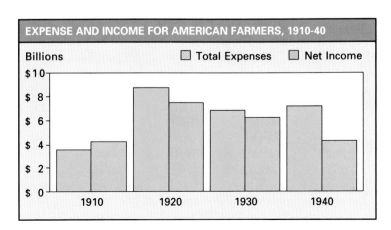

EXPENSE AND INCOME FOR AMERICAN FARMERS, 1910-40

Billings   □ Total Expenses   □ Net Income

| Billions | 1910 | 1920 | 1930 | 1940 |

LEARNING FROM GRAPHS. *The fortunes of American farmers had risen to new heights after the Great War, although expense still outdistanced income. What had happened to the difference between expense and income by 1940?*

Roosevelt Comes to Power   907

If there are WPA projects such as public buildings, murals, or dams in your area, ask students to locate them. Give them clues by showing them pictures of similar WPA projects. Have students take photographs or make drawings of the buildings or other projects as part of a local history project on the benefits of the WPA to your community. You may wish to donate the project to the local library or history museum.

Millie Wong, a ten-year-old girl in Brooklyn, received more Blue Eagles than any other individual. She wrote Washington to request ten Blue Eagles for her father, mother, and her seven sisters and brothers. She wanted to prove that all members of the Wong family were good citizens, although some were born in China and not naturalized. Her request was granted.

UPI/Bettmann Newsphotos

Senator George W. Norris of Nebraska was the "father" of the TVA, the program of flood control that brought electricity to the rural South.

rented. Farmers benefited in two ways. They got the rent money from the government, and they got higher prices for what they grew on the rest of their land because the total amount grown was smaller and therefore more valuable.

The AAA raised the money to rent the land taken out of production by what were called processing taxes. These were taxes paid by each business that processed, or prepared, the basic crops for general use—the miller who ground wheat into flour, the cotton manufacturer, and so on.

Congress also created the **Tennessee Valley Authority** (TVA) during the Hundred Days. This New Deal agency had no direct relation to the fight against the depression. Its "father" was Senator George W. Norris of Nebraska. During the 1920s, before the depression, Norris had fought efforts to get the government to sell to private interests the dam it had built at Muscle Shoals on the Tennessee River. He wanted the electricity produced at Muscle Shoals to be used as part of a broad plan to develop the resources of the entire Tennessee Valley.

Although Norris was a Republican, Roosevelt accepted his proposal. Under the TVA, Muscle Shoals was an efficient producer of electricity. The TVA had accurate information about how much electricity should cost consumers. The project therefore served as a kind of "yardstick" for measuring the fairness of prices charged by private electric power companies.

The TVA also manufactured fertilizers, built more dams for flood control, and developed a network of parks and lakes for recreation. It planted new forests and developed other conservation projects. It also provided jobs throughout the region.

Another achievement of the Hundred Days was the passage of

the **Federal Securities Act,** which regulated the way companies could issue and sell stock. Still another was the creation of the **Home Owners' Loan Corporation** (HOLC), which helped people who were unable to meet mortgage payments to hold on to their homes. Thousands of letters bombarded the president and officers of HOLC. Most showed tremendous loyalty and love for Roosevelt and begged for his help. One man wrote:

> ❝ I sincerely *hope* and *pray* you will come to my aid and help me save my home for my family, if I should loose it I don't know what I'll do as I have *no other place to go.* . . .
>
> I believe God will see us through some way but it has been the hardest thing I have had to go through, this may be His way so I'm writing to you asking and praying that you will do something to save our home.
>
> I am sure the President, if he only knew, would order that something be done, God Bless him. he is doing all he can to relieve the suffering and I am sure his name will go down in history among the other great men of our country. . . .[1] ❞

These measures brought many benefits. Still, many people became homeless. Men left their families to find work. Whole families were forced out onto the street to search for shelter.

The greatest benefits of the New Deal came from what was done about the unemployed and the poor. The poor faced problems that

[1]From *Down and Out in the Great Depression: Letters from the "Forgotten Man,"* edited by Robert S. McElvaine

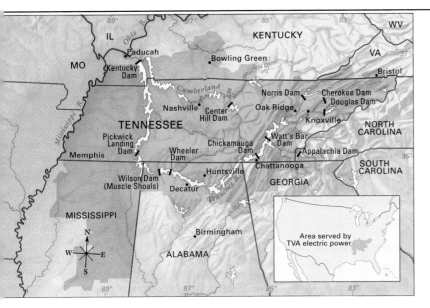

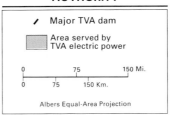

TENNESSEE VALLEY AUTHORITY

✦ Major TVA dam

▨ Area served by TVA electric power

0   75   150 Mi.

0   75   150 Km.

Albers Equal-Area Projection

LEARNING FROM MAPS. *One major aim of the Tennessee Valley Authority was flood control and river navigation. Which rivers were the heart of the TVA? The TVA stretched over vast areas in several southern states. What states were served by TVA electric power?*

RESOURCES
■ You may wish to have students review Transparency 25: "Stone City, Iowa; The Cornell Farm" in Art in American History.
◀ You may wish to have students complete Reading 49: "From Steinbeck's The Grapes of Wrath (1930s)" in Volume II of Eyewitnesses and Others.

★ You may wish to have students view Transparency 32: "Poster for The Grapes of Wrath" and complete the accompanying worksheet in Art in American History.

CHECKING UNDERSTANDING

Write the following terms on the chalkboard or an overhead projector and ask students to give the significance of each.

1. New Deal *(Roosevelt's plan of relief, recovery, and reform to end the depression)*
2. Hundred Days *(special session of Congress that passed a flood of laws to deal with the depression)*
3. Bank Holiday *(Roosevelt closed banks to restore order and to develop a plan to protect the public's savings.)*
4. Blue Eagle *(symbol of the National Recovery Administration [NRA], whose goal was to get industry moving)*
5. Federal Deposit Insurance Corporation (FDIC) *(FDIC insured savings deposits.)*
6. Agricultural Adjustment Act *(plan that took land out of production so that farm prices would rise as harvests decreased)*
7. National Industrial Recovery Act *(allowed certain industries to cooperate to set prices, etc. to eliminate cutthroat competition and stimulate business activity)*
8. Civilian Conservation Corps *(created to put unemployed men from poor families to work on conservation projects)*

THE DUST BOWL

Alexandre Hogue, *Drouth Stricken Area*, 1934, oil on canvas, Dallas Museum of Art, Dallas Art Association Purchase, 1945.6

■ Nature had seemed to smile upon the young nation in the 1830s. In the 1930s nature seemed particularly cruel. As times got harder, weather and even the land seemed to turn against the poor. Perhaps the hardest hit were the farmers of the high plains—the states from Texas and Oklahoma to South and North Dakota. This region rarely gets much rain. In the early 1930s almost none fell.

By 1934 the drought had become so bad that winds picked up powder-dry topsoil and blew it across the plains in dense, black clouds. The region came to be known as the Dust Bowl. It was impossible to grow anything on this shifting land.

◀ Broke and discouraged, many
★ Oklahoma farm families loaded

seemed almost overwhelming—no job, little food, no home. Yet many hoped and prayed that they could hold on to what they had and that better days were ahead. A woman wrote:

Phila., Pa.
November 26, 1934

Honorable Franklin D. Roosevelt
Washington, D.C.
Dear Mr. President:

I am forced to write to you because we find ourselves in *a very serious condition*. For the last three or four years we have had depression and *suffered* with my *family* and little children *severely*. . . . There has been unemployment in my house for more than three years. You can imagine that I and my family have suffered from lack of water supply in my house for more than two years. Last winter I did not have coal and the pipes burst in my house and therefore could not make heat in the house. Now winter is here again and we are suffering of cold, no water in the house, and we are facing to be forced out of the house, because I have no money to move or pay so much money as they want when after making settlement I am mother of little children, am

Silver Print, 12½ × 9⅞". Collection, The Museum of Modern Art, New York. Purchase.

into their secondhand Model T Fords and headed west toward California. There they became migrant workers, picking fruit, vegetables, cotton, and other crops. They followed the harvest in their overheated cars and spent their nights in roadside camps. Old people died alongside unfamiliar roads. Babies grew up hungry, their eyes big with suspicion.

One of the people who came to California was a young folk-

The human and physical consequences of the depression meet here. Alexandre Hogue painted "Drouth Stricken Area" with the thirsty cow, reduced to skin and bones, in the thin shadow of the windmill. The photograph of the migrant mother in California was taken in one quick ten-minute session by Dorothea Lange in 1936.

singer named Woodrow Wilson Guthrie, who arrived from Oklahoma in 1937. Californians

"needed more and more people to pick their fruits," Woody Guthrie said. "But they looked down for some reason on the people that came in there from other states to do that kind of work." The times were dangerous. "In most towns . . . it is a jailhouse offense to be unemployed," he wrote.

One of Woody Guthrie's songs put the plight of the migrant workers in this way:

> *California is a garden of Eden,*
> *A paradise to live in or see.*
> *But, believe it or not, you*
>   *won't find it so hot,*
> *If you ain't got the do-re-mi°[1]*

°"do-re-mi" is money
[1]From "Do Re Mi," words and music by Woody Guthrie. TRO © copyright 1961 and 1963 Ludlow Music Inc., New York, N.Y. Used by permission.

A tenant farmer poses with his family during the Great Depression. Why would Americans of the 1830s have welcomed such a family?

RETEACHING STRATEGY
Students with Special Needs. Pair students who are having difficulty with students who are performing well. Have each group make a chart of the New Deal programs, organizing them into the categories of relief measures, recovery measures, and reform measures. Instruct them to include a column for the specific aims of each program. After students have completed their work, discuss any differences in the charts with them. Ask students if some measures fall into more than one category.

PRIMARY SOURCE
Description of change: excerpted.
Rationale: excerpted to focus on Guthrie's view that people needed money to live in California.

Roosevelt Comes to Power 911

INDEPENDENT PRACTICE
Have students complete the Preview & Review activity at the beginning of the section.

CLOSURE
Tell students that Roosevelt's tremendous energy served him well as he tried to solve the problems of the depression. Roosevelt immediately called a special session of Congress to pass legislation aimed at providing relief, recovery, and reform.

HOMEWORK
Today homelessness is a problem that affects many people. Ask students if they know anyone who is homeless. Then discuss what they have seen on television and in newspapers about the homeless. Have each student design a program to aid the homeless. Read some of the best plans to the class. Then ask the class if there are similarities between their proposals and the New Deal programs.

PRIMARY SOURCE
Description of change: excerpted.
Rationale: excerpted to focus on the destitution that many people faced during the depression.

Brown Brothers

Civilian Conservation Corpsmen are clearing brush from scrubland in the western United States to lessen the risk of fire. Below is Harry Hopkins, a close friend of Roosevelt's, who conceived many of the attempts to remedy the Great Depression.

Culver Pictures

sick and losing my health, and we are eight people in the family, and where can I go when I don't have money because no one is working in my house. . . . Now I have *no money, no home* and *no wheres to go.* I beg of you to please help me and my family and little children for the sake of a sick mother and suffering family to give this your immediate attention so we will not be forced to move or put out on the street.

Waiting and Hoping that you will act quickly.
Thanking you very much I remain

Mrs. E.L.[1]

[1]From *Down and Out in the Great Depression: Letters from the "Forgotten Man,"* edited by Robert S. McElvaine

In response to such suffering Roosevelt rejected Hoover's ideas about what the federal government could and could not do about unemployment and poverty. Soon after Roosevelt took office, the **Federal Emergency Relief Administration** was created. This agency was headed by Harry Hopkins, a New York social worker. It distributed $500 million in federal grants among state organizations that cared for the poor. The following fall and winter another New Deal agency, the **Civil Works Authority,** also headed by Hopkins, found jobs for more than 4 million people out of work.

During the Hundred Days, Congress also created the **Civilian Conservation Corps** (CCC). This agency put unemployed young men from poor families to work on various conservation projects. CCC workers lived in camps run by the army. They cleared brush, planted trees, built small dams, and performed dozens of other useful tasks. The CCC provides a good example of how swiftly New Deal measures were put into effect. The law that created the program passed Congress on March 31, 1933. By July there were 300,000 corpsmen at work in 1,300 camps all over the country.

Return to the Preview & Review on page 903.

3. THE NEW DEAL

Why the New Deal Was Popular

The New Deal was very popular. Democrats increased their majorities in Congress in the 1934 elections. When Franklin D. Roosevelt ran for a second term in 1936, against Alfred Landon of Kansas, he won every state in the Union except Maine and Vermont. He did so despite the fact that New Deal legislation had not ended the depression. Unemployment remained extremely high. Industrial production picked up, but only very slowly.

The personality of FDR, as the newspapers came to call him, had a great deal to do with the success of the New Deal. He was an optimist. His hope for better conditions was always cheerful and encouraging, but never silly or foolish. This excerpt from a popular song of 1936 tells how the people felt about their president:

> ❝ Just hand me my old Martin°, for soon I will be
> startin'
> Back to dear old Charleston, far away.
> Since Roosevelt's been reelected, we'll not be
> neglected.
> We've got Franklin D. Roosevelt back again.
> No more breadlines we're glad to say, the donkey won
> election day,
> No more standing in the blowing, snowing rain;
> He's got things in full sway, we're all working and
> getting our pay,
> We've got Franklin D. Roosevelt back again.[1] ❞

Roosevelt had a way of reaching people that was truly remarkable. He spoke frequently on the radio. These **fireside chats** were not speeches in the usual sense. The president seemed to come right into the room with his listeners. He explained what problems lay before the nation, how he proposed to deal with them, and what people could do to help him.

Roosevelt made great use of experts. His close advisers, mostly college professors, were known as the **Brain Trust.** Yet ordinary citizens never got the idea that Roosevelt was listening to theories that were not practical and down to earth.

The president never put all the nation's eggs in one basket. This made sense to most people. The economic mess was so complicated that no single plan or project was likely to untangle it. Roosevelt's way was to experiment with many things at once. This created the impression that the best minds in the country were hard at work

°A brand of guitar
[1]From "Franklin D. Roosevelt's Back Again," in *This Singing Land*, compiled and edited by Irwin Silber

Preview & Review

Use these questions to guide your reading. Answer the questions after completing Section 3.
Understanding Issues, Events, & Ideas. Use the following words to explain the New Deal: fireside chat, Brain Trust, Rural Electrification Administration, Works Progress Administration, National Youth Administration, Second New Deal, Wagner Labor Relations Act, National Labor Relations Board, Social Security Act.
1. How did the New Deal help relieve much of the human suffering caused by the depression?
2. On what grounds did the Supreme Court rule that some New Deal measures were unconstitutional?
3. How did Roosevelt change his tactics in his battle against the depression?
Thinking Critically. Imagine that you are the owner of a large corporation in 1935. Write a letter to President Roosevelt explaining why you think that the New Deal will hurt your business. Cite specific measures in your letter.

STRATEGIES FOR SUCCESS

COMPOSING AN ESSAY

You are often asked to prepare a written report or to answer an essay question on a test. An essay is a short composition on a specific topic. It should always contain three parts: an introduction, a body of information, and a closing.

You have already learned the preliminary steps to composing an essay: Writing About History (page xxiv) and composing paragraphs (page 806). Once you have mastered that strategy, the next step is the actual writing of an essay.

How to Compose an Essay

Before learning the steps for analzying economic statistics, review Composing Paragraphs on page 806. Then to compose an essay, follow these steps.

1. **Focus on the topic.** Make sure you understand what you are to write about. The topic should be broad enough to provide enough material for an essay but not too broad to be dealt with in a short composition.
2. **Organize your ideas.** Remember that your essay should have three parts. Organize your thoughts accordingly.
3. **Compose your essay.** Clearly state your topic in the introduction. Present your evidence and supporting details in the body of the essay. Your closing should briefly sum up what you have said in the essay.

Applying the Strategy

Suppose you were given an assignment to write an essay according to the following directive:

Explain briefly what the aims and outcomes of the three parts of the New Deal were.

Your first task is to identify the topic of your essay: *the aims and outcomes of the three parts of the New Deal.* You might organize your thoughts in a manner similar to the following outline:

The New Deal
I.   Introduction
II. Three Parts of New Deal
  a. Relief
    1. Aims
    2. Outcomes
  b. Recovery
    1. Aims
    2. Outcomes
  c. Reform
    1. Aims
    2. Outcomes
III. Closing

For independent practice, see Practicing the Strategy on page 933.

Brown Brothers

President Roosevelt, originator of the "fireside chat" by radio, prepares for his message to be transmitted on all the major networks.

In Robert Caro's biography of Lyndon Johnson, Caro discusses the Texas Hill Country and its poverty during the New Deal.

"The people of the Hill Country were grateful for what the New Deal had done for them; little as had been the help they realized from its programs, it was far more help than anyone had ever given them before. But their lives were not changed by the New Deal. The Hill Country was a country in which there was unbelievably little cash.

In 1937, as in 1932, the Johnson City High School nearly missed basketball season—because the school could not afford a basketball; after several weeks of fundraising, the *News* reported that 'collections are coming in too slow on the basketball.'"

Robert A. Caro,
The Path to Power, 1982

fighting the depression. They were not winning an immediate victory. But what seemed important was that *something* was being done.

The New Deal was also popular because it made large groups of people feel that the government was genuinely trying to improve their lives. This had little to do with the depression itself. For example, workers in industries like steel and automobiles were not organized in 1933. It was not the policy of the federal government to promote unions, but the spirit of the New Deal encouraged many workers to join unions. Roosevelt certainly wanted workers to be treated more fairly and with greater respect by their employers than had been common in the past.

President Roosevelt's greatest sympathy was for farmers. New Deal farm legislation was aimed at increasing their shrunken incomes and improving the quality of rural life. The **Rural Electrification Administration,** which brought electricity to remote farm districts, is a good illustration of how the lives of farmers could be improved.

Most important, the New Deal relieved much of the human suffering caused by the depression. The Civil Works Administration, and later the **Works Progress Administration** (WPA), found useful work for millions of idle men and women. Most of the jobs were of

PRIMARY SOURCE
Description of change: excerpted.
Rationale: excerpted to focus on conditions in the Texas Hill Country during the depression.

RESOURCES
- ■ You may wish to have students view Transparency 29: *"The Sheridan Theater"* and complete the accompanying worksheet in *Art in American History*.
- ◄ You may wish to have students view Transparency 26: *"Classic Landscape"* and complete the accompanying worksheet in *Art in American History*.
- ★ You may wish to have students view Transparency 27: *"Cow's Skull: Red, White, and Blue"* and complete the accompanying worksheet in *Art in American History*.

GUIDED INSTRUCTION

Have students prepare a pictorial essay of the depression by using photographs taken by famous artists of the depression, such as Dorothea Lange, paintings by WPA artists, such as Lucienne Bloch, or their own drawings and sketches. Their presentations should include descriptions of each picture as well as background information on the artists.

Above is the work of a muralist in the Federal Arts Project. Below, many students had access to libraries for the first time under this WPA project. The advantages of such projects to society are numerous.

the pick-and-shovel type, but not all of them. Harry Hopkins insisted that the full skills of the unemployed be used whenever possible.

In the city of Boston, for example, New Deal work projects included building a subway, expanding the East Boston Airport, and improving a municipal golf course. Other Boston relief workers taught in nursery schools, cataloged books in the Boston Public Library, and read to blind people. College students employed by the **National Youth Administration** graded papers and did office chores in their schools. Singers performed in hospitals. Musicians gave concerts. Troupes of actors put on plays, including a revival of *Uncle Tom's Cabin*. Artists designed posters and painted murals on the walls of schools and libraries.

Criticism of the New Deal

The laws passed during the Hundred Days greatly increased the power of the federal government and particularly of the president. Many day-to-day decisions had to be made under these laws. The president and his appointees seemed the logical persons to make them. New Deal laws are full of such phrases as "The president is authorized . . ." and "The secretary of agriculture shall have the power to . . ." and "The Board shall have power, in the name of the United States of America, to . . ."

Some people found this trend alarming. Business leaders in particular objected to the new restrictions placed on how they conducted their affairs. The New Deal would destroy the free enterprise system, they charged. They therefore brought suits against the government in the courts, claiming that the new laws were unconstitutional.

In 1935 and 1936 the Supreme Court ruled that the National Industrial Recovery Act and the Agricultural Adjustment Act were indeed unconstitutional. The Court also declared unconstitutional some important state laws regulating economic affairs, such as a New York minimum-wage law. In the NIRA case, *Schechter v. U.S.* (1935), the Court decided unanimously that Congress had delegated too much of its law-making power to the boards that watched over industrial codes. In *U.S. v. Butler* it ruled that the AAA processing tax was not really a tax but a method of regulating farm production.

Conservatives charged that the New Deal was trying to do too much. Other critics argued that the government was not doing enough. As time passed, the excitement of the Hundred Days disappeared. Perhaps prosperity was "just around the corner," but the corner never seemed to be reached.

Courtesy of The Library of Congress

OLD RELIABLE!

Point of View

Roosevelt's biographer reminds us that the president *was* popular even when the New Deal was not.

"The decisive fact of 1938 was that most people *thought* Roosevelt had lost popular favor to a greater extent than he really had. . . . The popular attitude toward Roosevelt was marked by a deep ambivalence. On the one hand, almost everyone liked him as a person. Asked, "On the whole, do you like or dislike his personality?" eight out of ten Americans in the spring of 1938 answered "like" to only one who answered "dislike." Negroes, the poor generally, labor, the unemployed were enthusiastically for Roosevelt the person. The Southwest as a section delivered a resounding 98 percent for him, and other sections were not far behind. . . ."

From *Roosevelt: The Lion and the Fox,* James MacGregor Burns, 1956

With a wave of his wand, Roosevelt performs his trick "Old Reliable." What is this magic rabbit expected to do? Why does the cartoonist say it never fails?

EXTENSION:
COMMUNITY INVOLVEMENT
Cooperative Learning.
Organize the class into cooperative learning groups. Have each group use community resources, such as the local library, historical society, local business organizations, and labor unions, to learn more about how the New Deal affected the lives of the people in your area or town. Students should also investigate people's attitudes toward the New Deal. Which groups of people supported it? Which groups opposed it? Each group should prepare a report about what they have learned to present to the class.

PRIMARY SOURCE
Description of change: excerpted.
Rationale: excerpted to focus on attitudes toward Roosevelt.

The New Deal 917

HISTORICAL SIDELIGHTS

1 To counter Long's popularity, Roosevelt acknowledged that "it may be necessary to throw to the wolves the forty-six men who are reported to have incomes in excess of one million dollars a year. This can be accomplished through taxation."

SUGGESTED CAPTION RESPONSE

Townshend's idea for an Old-Age Revolving Pension exists today in the system of old-age insurance that the Social Security Act established.

CHECKING UNDERSTANDING

Ask students how conservatives, Senator Long, Townshend, and even some people within the Roosevelt administration criticized the New Deal. Then ask how Roosevelt responded to these criticisms. *(Conservatives, especially business leaders, believed that the government was becoming too powerful and that the restrictions placed on businesses would destroy free enterprise. Others felt that the New Deal did not go far enough. Senator Long proposed to tax away all incomes over $1 million a year and redistribute the tax money so that everyone could own a house and car. Townshend wanted Old-Age Revolving Pensions for everyone over 60 years old. Critics inside the administration wanted to spend more money. Roosevelt responded with the Second New Deal, which addressed some of these criticisms. Congress passed the Social Security Act and instituted a "soak-the-rich" income tax. Roosevelt also quit trying to please everyone, instead campaigning for support from labor, women, and other disadvantaged groups.)*

All, UPI/Bettmann Newsphotos

Three very strong critics of President Roosevelt were, from left, Huey Long of Louisiana; Father Charles Coughlin; and Dr. Francis E. Townshend. Which one of their ideas is with us to this day?

Some people who had originally supported Roosevelt now turned against him. One was Senator Huey Long of Louisiana, who ruled like a king in his home state. The "Kingfish," as he was called, had great pity for the little person. He claimed that the president had become a tool of Wall Street investors. Long wanted to tax away all incomes of more than $1 million a year. With that money, he said, everyone would be guaranteed a large enough income to own a house, a car, and everything else needed to live decently. Long's Share-Our-Wealth organization had over 4.6 million members in 1935.

Francis Townshend, a California doctor, called for granting Old-Age Revolving Pensions to every American over 60. He attracted a very large following. A Catholic priest, Father Charles E. Coughlin, spoke to millions in his weekly radio broadcasts. He criticized various New Deal programs. Eventually he made bitter personal attacks on President Roosevelt.

There were even critics within the Roosevelt administration. Some were complaining by 1935 and 1936 that the president was not fighting the depression vigorously enough. They wanted the government to spend more money in order to stimulate the economy and put more people to work.

The Second New Deal

Roosevelt responded to the criticisms of the mid-1930s by proposing more reforms. We call his new program the **Second New Deal.**

After the Supreme Court struck down the National Industrial Recovery Act, Congress passed the **Wagner Labor Relations Act** of 1935. This law again gave labor unions the right to organize and bargain collectively. It set up a **National Labor Relations Board** (NLRB) to run union elections and settle disputes. When a majority of the workers in the plant voted to join a union in an NLRB election,

Courtesy of The Library of Congress

How could Roosevelt not have been a favorite for editorial cartoonists? "New Deal Remedies" shows how Roosevelt was able to try another approach if the first failed, but it hardly meant to pay him a compliment. How many remedies on the table can you identify?

that union became the representative of all the workers in the plant, not merely of those who had voted to join it.

In 1935 Congress also passed the **Social Security Act.** This law set up a system of old-age insurance, paid for partly by workers and partly by their employers. This system paid retired people 65 years of age and over a pension. The amount of the pension was based on the number of years a worker had paid into the system. The act provided for unemployment insurance too. This supplied money for workers who had lost their jobs and were looking for new ones. Many workers, such as farmhands and maids, were not covered by the original Social Security Act. Nevertheless, the law marked a great turning point for American society.

Other laws passed in 1935 included a "soak-the-rich" income tax and an act regulating banks more strictly. Another law was aimed at breaking up combinations among electric light and gas companies.

These measures marked a change of tactics in Roosevelt's battle against the depression. In 1933 he had tried to unite all groups and classes. By 1936 he had given up on holding the support of big business and rich people. During his campaign for reelection he attacked these people, whom he called "an enemy within our gates." He and his campaign managers turned instead to the labor movement; to women voters; and to blacks, Hispanics, and other such groups for support. Their efforts were successful. As we have already noted, Roosevelt was reelected by a landslide in 1936. 🖳

Return to the Preview & Review on page 913.

Understanding Issues, Events, & Ideas.
Descriptions should demonstrate an understanding of the terms used.

1. Most African Americans voted Republican in 1932. However, in 1936, most voted for Roosevelt because they felt the government was making some effort to treat them fairly, and they were included in New Deal programs.

2. Most of the NRA industrial codes permitted employers to pay lower wages to African American workers and farm workers, especially Mexican Americans; farm policy hurt tenant farmers and sharecroppers—most of them black—since payments were made to the landowner. Social Security did not include farm laborers and household workers, which meant that it did not include millions of African Americans. CCC camps were segregated. African Americans supported the New Deal because they felt Roosevelt's intentions were good even if he was unwilling to take political risks. Roosevelt also brought African Americans, such as Clark Foreman and Mary McLeod Bethune, into government.

3. Roosevelt misjudged Congress and the public. They felt that his plan threatened the judiciary's independence.

4. Unions changed from being primarily craft unions to being industrial unions. This made it easier to organize

920

Preview & Review

Use these questions to guide your reading. Answer the questions after completing Section 4.

Understanding Issues, Events, & Ideas. Use the following words to describe some of the effects of the New Deal: Black Cabinet, Urban League, Supreme Court Reform Plan, Commodity Credit Corporation, Fair Labor Standards Act, industrial union, Congress of Industrial Organizations, welfare state, deficit spending, federal deficit.

1. What accounted for the political shift that occurred among black voters between 1932 and 1936?
2. How did many New Deal programs discriminate against blacks and Hispanics either directly or indirectly? Why did many blacks and Hispanics continue to support the New Deal?
3. Why did the Supreme Court Reform Plan produce a bitter fight?
4. How did labor unions change during the New Deal?

Thinking Critically. 1. Imagine you are a young black artist in 1934. Write a diary entry explaining why you want to move to Harlem. **2.** Do you think President Roosevelt took on too much power and responsibility during the New Deal years? Why or why not?

On his honeymoon with his wife, Marva, Joe Louis, the world heavyweight champion, strolls the streets of Harlem. Most blacks, like these onlookers, were proud rather than envious of his show of prosperity.

920

4. EFFECTS OF THE NEW DEAL

African Americans Vote Democratic

In 1936 a majority of African American voters cast their ballots for Roosevelt and other Democratic candidates. This marked one of the most significant political shifts of the 20th century. Before the New Deal most blacks had supported "the party of Lincoln." The Republicans had not done much to win or hold the loyalty of blacks since Lincoln's day. The southerners who dominated the Democratic party had usually offered blacks nothing at all.

During the 1920s African Americans lost many of the gains they had won during the Great World War when their labor had been so much in demand. The revived Ku Klux Klan was a constant source of worry. The migration of southern blacks to northern cities continued. Indeed, African Americans were the immigrants of the 1920s. They replaced the European immigrants, whose numbers had declined because of the new immigration laws.

So many African Americans moved to northern cities that they were crowded into slums, or ghettos. Harlem, in New York City,

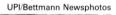
UPI/Bettmann Newsphotos

RESOURCES

■ You may wish to have students complete Reading 46: "Two Poems from Langston Hughes' *Don't You Want to Be Free?* (1937)" in Volume II of *Eyewitnesses and Others.*

National Museum of American Art/Art Resource

One of the gentlest views of home and family life during the Harlem Renaissance is evident in "The Janitor Who Paints" by Palmer Hayden.

was the best known of the black ghettos. By 1930 165,000 blacks were crowded into Harlem's run-down row houses and decaying tenements.

Like the earlier immigrants, most black newcomers were able to get only the dirtiest, most exhausting, and lowest-paid work. Most labor unions shut out black members. This kept blacks from working in industries and crafts where organized labor was strong.

Yet, as you have read, even in segregated sections like Harlem, blacks were able to improve their situation. In such places they were actually the majority. They did not have to stand aside for white people. They could vote and elect black officials. Blacks came to have considerable influence on the larger politics of the city and state. They became more self-confident and more conscious of their rights.

Black writers, musicians, actors, and journalists had found au- ■ diences in Harlem. Black doctors and lawyers and other professionals practiced and prospered too. New York City blacks had experienced the Harlem Renaissance in the 1920s. Harlem had become the black

RESPONSES *(Continued)*
the workers of a large industry such as steel.

Thinking Critically.
1. Reward thoughtful, creative answers.
2. Responses will vary. Students should support their position with sound reasoning.

FOCUS/MOTIVATION:
MAKING CONNECTIONS
Prior Knowledge.
Ask students which party most African Americans supported after the Civil War. *(Republican)* Then ask them why. *(African Americans saw the Republicans as the party of Lincoln, who had freed the slaves.)* Ask students which party has the support of most African Americans today. *(Democratic)* Then ask them if they know when this change occurred. *(Answers will vary.)* Explain that in 1932 most African Americans supported Hoover—the Republican candidate—rather than Roosevelt, but by 1936 this had completely changed. Ask: What might cause such a major change? *(Answers will vary.)* Tell them that African Americans viewed the New Deal very favorably and that the Democratic coalition put together during the New Deal consisted largely of African Americans and other minorities, liberals, labor union members, the poor and others who depended on government support, and big-city Democratic political machines.

RESORCES

■ You may wish to have students complete Reading 48: "James Agee Describes the Life of Tenant Farmers (1930s)" in Volume II of *Eyewitnesses and Others.*

GUIDED INSTRUCTION: COOPERATIVE LEARNING

Organize students into cooperative learning groups to present a program on the Harlem Renaissance. Students could play jazz recordings, read the poems of Langston Hughes, Claude McKay, Jean Toomer, and Countee Cullen and read from the stories of Zora Neale Hurston. They could display copies of the paintings of Aaron Douglas, William H. Johnson, and Palmer Hayden and pictures of the sculpture of Meta Warwick Fuller.

intellectual and cultural capital of the nation. And it remained so throughout the depression. Ambitious young blacks from other states moved there, believing Harlem was the best place to develop their talents.

However, the Great Depression took much of the glitter from this revival of confidence. It struck African Americans with cruel force, as it did Hispanic Americans. As always in hard times, these workers were "the last hired and the first fired." By 1932 more than 30 percent of all black and Hispanic workers were unemployed.

Still, most African Americans voted the Republican ticket in 1932. In Chicago, for example, Hoover got 76 percent of the black vote. In Cincinnati he got 71 percent. But in 1936 most blacks in Chicago and Cincinnati voted for Roosevelt.

Black Support of the New Deal

Today it is hard to understand why African Americans and Hispanic Americans found Roosevelt and the New Deal so attractive. Many of the most important New Deal programs did little or nothing to help them. Most of the NRA industrial codes permitted employers to pay lower wages to black and Hispanic workers than to whites. ■ New Deal farm policy badly hurt black tenant farmers and sharecroppers in the South. The AAA payments went to land *owners*. They were paid for taking tobacco land out of production. The tenants and sharecroppers who had farmed these acres lost their jobs and often their homes as well. It did nothing to help Hispanic farmers in the Southwest. Unemployed blacks and Hispanics in all parts of the country rarely got a full share of federal relief money or jobs.

The social security program did not discriminate directly against African Americans or Hispanics. However, it left out farm laborers and household workers. The millions of blacks and Hispanics who did work of this kind received no share of the new pension and unemployment benefits.

Yet African Americans and Hispanic Americans liked the New Deal. Many became enthusiastic admirers of Franklin Roosevelt. Thousands of black and Hispanic parents in the 1930s named babies after the president. The reasons for such strong feelings are best understood by keeping in mind how white society treated these groups at that time. This is another example of the need to use historical imagination. For example, the Civilian Conservation Corps camps in the South were segregated. If black youths had *not* been sent to separate camps when they joined the CCC, the program could not have functioned in the southern states. More important, the program almost certainly would not have been created by Congress. Blacks realized this. Most blacks therefore accepted the segregation of the camps as a lesser evil than being without work.

Most African Americans and Hispanic Americans thought the

main point was that they were included in New Deal programs and
that some effort to treat them fairly was being made by important
officials. Because so many of the unemployed and poor were black
or Hispanic, WPA and the federal relief programs were particularly
important to them. President Roosevelt ordered state relief officials
not to "discriminate . . . because of race or religion or politics" in
distributing government aid. This order was not always obeyed, but
Harry Hopkins and other key WPA officials tried hard to enforce it.

With the approval of Roosevelt, Harold L. Ickes, the secretary
of the interior, appointed Clark Foreman to his staff. Ickes instructed
Foreman to seek out qualified blacks and try to get them jobs in the
Interior Department and other government bureaus. Foreman also
served as a kind of watchdog, checking on cases of racial discrimination in various New Deal programs. Among distinguished African
Americans whose government service began in New Deal agencies
were Robert Weaver, who became the first head of the Department
of Housing and Urban Development in the 1960s, and William Hastie,
later a federal judge. These appointees made up what became known
as Roosevelt's **Black Cabinet.**

One of the most prominent members of the Black Cabinet was
Mary McLeod Bethune. She was the 15th child of former slaves.
Some of her brothers and sisters had been sold away from her parents
before the Civil War. Mary McLeod was fiercely independent. After
completing her education in South Carolina, she taught at several
schools for blacks in the South. In 1898 she married Albertus Bethune, also a teacher. She founded a school of her own in Florida
during the Progressive Era.

In 1936 Mary McLeod Bethune was put in charge of the Office
of Minority Affairs in the National Youth Administration. As with
male black officials, her role was broader than her title indicated.
She always had access to President Roosevelt. During the New Deal
period, she later recalled, she conferred with him privately about six
or seven times a year.

In a way their relationship points up the strengths and weaknesses of Roosevelt's way of dealing with his black supporters. His
intentions were good, but he was unwilling to take the political risk.
Once Mary Bethune asked him to act quickly on some important
matter. He refused. "Mrs. Bethune, if we must do that now, we'll
hurt our progress," he said. "We must do this thing stride by stride."

Mary McLeod Bethune worked strongly for equal rights for
African Americans and other groups. She served as president of the
National Association of Colored Women. She was a vice president
of the two most important organizations in the United States that
worked for racial equality—the NAACP and the **Urban League.** Yet
she was not offended by Roosevelt's attitude. Indeed, she admired
him enormously. Her reaction tells us a great deal about racial attitudes and the problems faced by minorities at that time.

National Portrait Gallery

*Mary McLeod Bethune shows quiet
dignity in this portrait by Betsy
Groves Reyneau. What did Roosevelt
think of Mary Bethune?*

Effects of the New Deal 923

① Roosevelt had had no opportunity to appoint a Supreme Court justice during his first term, and much of the New Deal legislation that was being overturned was done so by a 6 to 3 or 5 to 4 vote.

■ You may wish to have students complete Reading 45: "Roosevelt Defends the New Deal (1937)" in Volume II of *Eyewitnesses and Others.*

GUIDED INSTRUCTION

Ask three students to assume the roles of Mary McLeod Bethune, Eleanor Roosevelt, and Frances Perkins, three women who worked to further the rights of disadvantaged groups, workers, and women during Roosevelt's administration. Select several other students to act as journalists and advocates for disadvantaged groups, women, and workers. After they have prepared for their roles, have them hold a panel discussion for the class on the issues of disadvantaged groups', workers', and women's rights. Encourage the other class members to ask questions.

THE FIRST LADY

White House Historical Association

Eleanor Roosevelt, the first lady, had worked to improve the treatment of African Americans long before her husband became president. And no prominent white person in the United States worked harder than she during the New Deal in the struggle for racial equality. She was also a leader in women's rights organizations, a promoter of consumer protection, a friend of the working people, and a believer in the rights of young people. She constantly reminded and pleaded with her husband to remember the needs of the people who made up those groups.

As a young woman Eleanor Roosevelt attended exclusive private schools and spent holidays with her rich cousins in high society. Her uncle, President Theodore Roosevelt, gave her in marriage to her handsome distant cousin Franklin.

Eleanor had decided early to prepare herself for a life of social service. This was difficult for her. She was a shy person. She had five children to raise. She saw her husband through his crippling polio. But in the 1920s she began to timidly speak in public.

During the Great Depression Eleanor Roosevelt traveled throughout the country to find out the mood of the people. "You must be my eyes and ears," the president had told her. She seemed to be everywhere. A famous cartoon of the late 1930s showed two grime-covered coal miners looking up from their work as one said to the other, "For gosh sakes, here comes Mrs. Roosevelt."

The End of the New Deal

■
① Despite his great victory in the election of 1936, President Roosevelt feared that much of the important New Deal legislation would be declared unconstitutional by the Supreme Court. These laws had greatly increased the powers of the federal government. The more conservative justices of the Supreme Court believed, for instance, that Congress had no right under the Constitution to control the

HISTORICAL SIDELIGHTS

① Roosevelt's plan would permit the president to appoint "an additional jurist for each federal judge who, having served ten years or more, failed to retire within six months after reaching" the age of 70. If the bill had passed, Roosevelt would have been able to make six appointments to the Supreme Court.

SUGGESTED CAPTION RESPONSE
The Supreme Court Reform Plan

negotiations of workers and their employers. Nor could it force workers to contribute to an old-age pension fund without their consent.

Roosevelt was not a constitutional expert. He felt that the election had proved that the people were behind the New Deal. Necessary reforms should not be held up by technical legal questions. He therefore proposed that Congress enable him to increase the number of Supreme Court justices. He would fill these new seats with his appointees. That way he could be sure that a majority of the Court would uphold key New Deal laws. This **Supreme Court Reform Plan** ① of 1937 produced a bitter, long, drawn-out fight. Roosevelt had misjudged the attitude of Congress and the public. The plan seemed to most people to threaten the independence of the Court. Roosevelt tried hard, but Congress rejected the plan.

However, the justices who had opposed New Deal laws eventually died or resigned. Roosevelt then appointed justices favorable to his program to replace them. The Wagner Labor Relations Act,

Brown Brothers

This 1937 cartoon recalls the biblical warning "It is easier for a camel to go through the eye of a needle than for a rich man to enter the Kingdom of God." What is the political inspiration for this cartoon?

GUIDED INSTRUCTION: COOPERATIVE LEARNING
Discuss with students why Roosevelt proposed his Supreme Court Reform Plan. *(He hoped to appoint judges "friendly" to the New Deal and thereby avoid having legislation ruled unconstitutional by narrow margins.)* Then organize students into four cooperative learning groups. Ask one group to represent Constitutional experts to explain why the plan was contrary to the spirit of separation of powers, one group to represent members of the public who suffer when New Deal laws are ruled unconstitutional, one group to represent the Supreme Court to explain their feelings about such presidential meddling, and one group to represent Roosevelt and his advisers. After the groups have had time to gather evidence to support their position, have them present their views of Roosevelt's plan. After the presentations have been completed, you may wish to have the class vote on whether or not they favor the plan.

Effects of the New Deal 925

LEARNING FROM GRAPHS. *Perhaps better than any other example, the results of New Deal programs showed the effects of government spending on employment. What happened to unemployment as government spending increased? Why do you think this happened? What happened to unemployment between 1937 and 1938? Why?*

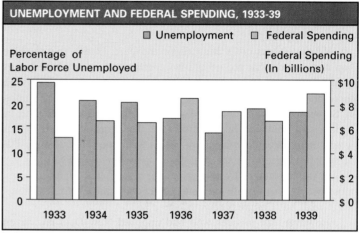

UNEMPLOYMENT AND FEDERAL SPENDING, 1933-39

☐ Unemployment   ☐ Federal Spending

Percentage of Labor Force Unemployed

Federal Spending (In billions)

Source: *Historical Statistics of the United States*

the Social Security Act, and all other New Deal laws attacked in the courts were eventually declared to be constitutional. Nevertheless, the Court fight was a serious setback for Roosevelt.

Another setback soon followed. Roosevelt had never understood modern economics. When he was running for president in 1932, he had criticized President Hoover for spending federal money recklessly and unbalancing the budget. Roosevelt had never given up the hope of cutting government expenses and eventually reducing the national debt.

During 1936 and early 1937 the economy had been gradually improving. In June 1937 Roosevelt therefore decided to cut back sharply on federal money spent for relief.

The result was to bring the recovery to a sudden stop. Business activity fell off sharply. Unemployment increased. This recession in 1937 and 1938 was deeply discouraging. Just when prosperity appeared to be *really* around the corner, things turned again for the worse. Was the Great Depression going to last forever?

Roosevelt quickly agreed to increase government spending again. Congress provided money for a big new public works program to pick up the economy. At about this time Congress also passed a new Agricultural Adjustment Act. This established the **Commodity Credit Corporation.** It provided that when prices were low, producers of wheat, cotton, and certain other crops could store their crops in government warehouses instead of selling them. The Corporation would lend them money for their crops in storage.

When prices rose, the farmers could take their crops out of storage, sell them, and pay back the loans. This new system was called the ever-normal granary. (A granary is a storehouse for grain and other farm crops.) The new system raised prices by keeping surpluses off the market. Then, in years of bad harvests, there would be reserves to prevent shortages.

Another important law passed in 1938 officially outlawed child labor. This measure was the **Fair Labor Standards Act.** It also set the length of a normal work week at 40 hours and established a national minimum wage. Many New Dealers were uneasy with this law. It contained many loopholes "protecting" particular industries such as farming and family-operated businesses from having to meet "fair standards." Still, the principles the law established were important. Eventually most of the loopholes were closed.

The Fair Labor Standards Act was the last important New Deal law. In 1939 a new world war broke out in Europe. As during the Great World War (which now became known as World War I), European purchases caused the American economy to pick up.

Significance of the New Deal

All laws passed by Congress during the New Deal and all the new agencies and boards did not end the Great Depression. Why then is the New Deal considered so important? One reason is that it produced a revolution in relations between workers and their employers.

Under the National Recovery Administration and then under the National Labor Relations Board, industrial workers formed strong national unions. The old-fashioned AFL unions had been organized along craft lines. Carpenters were in one union, plumbers in another, machinists in a third, and so on. This system made organizing the workers of a large industry, such as steel or rubber or farm machinery, very difficult. The New Deal laws encouraged workers to form new **industrial unions.** Industrial unions represented all the workers in a particular industry, regardless of their specialty. These unions joined together in a **Congress of Industrial Organizations** (CIO), which soon rivaled the AFL in importance.

Culver Pictures

John L. Lewis

There were some bitter strikes during the New Deal. In 1937 workers staged "sit-down" strikes in which they took over plants and refused to leave until their demands were met. New Deal legislation protected workers' rights and established orderly methods of settling labor-management disputes. Labor became a force that manufacturers could neither ignore nor hold back.

GUIDED INSTRUCTION
Ask students to discuss the author's statement about the New Deal and the increase in the power of the federal government that accompanied it. "Looking back, most Americans lost some freedom. . . . This seems to have been a necessary price to pay if such a complex society was to function smoothly. Still, the loss was large." (page 929) Ask students what it was that Americans lost and what they may have gained in return. *(Students will probably mention that legislation, such as the Fair Labor Standards Act, the act prohibiting child labor, and the Wagner Labor Relations Act, interfered with the freedom of businesses to deal with workers and unions. However, this same legislation prevented the exploitation of workers and helped to ensure a living wage.)* Ask students if they think the benefits outweighed the losses. *(Students should logically support their opinions.)*

Vanity Fair, Copyright © 1935, 1963 by the Condé Nast Publications, Inc.

In Jonathan Swift's famous satire
Gulliver's Travels, *Captain Lemuel*
Gulliver is staked to the ground by
tiny people called Lilliputians. The
same fate has here befallen Uncle
Sam. New Deal agencies form the
bonds, so we may assume that the art-
ist thought the 'alphabet soup' of the
New Deal had become a burden.

Labor became a force in politics too. Unions made contributions
to candidates for public office. Union leaders campaigned for candidates who supported policies favorable to organized labor. Union
lobbyists put pressure on Congress to pass pro-labor legislation.

The New Deal also created what we think of as the **welfare state.**
The popularity of New Deal relief programs and programs to create
jobs was so great that it was impossible to depend only on state and
local agencies after the depression was over. After the New Deal
nearly all people agreed that the federal government ought to do
whatever was necessary to advance and protect the general welfare.
Later Republican administrations accepted this idea as enthusiastically as the Democrats, although Ronald Reagan, once a supporter
and admirer of Roosevelt, was unrelenting in his efforts to dismantle
much of the legacy of the New Deal.

Increasing the power of the federal government meant that state
and local governments had less power. It also meant that the federal
government had more control over individuals and over private

RESOURCES
■ You may wish to have students complete one or
  more of the Chapter 25 Tests.

organizations. Looking back, most Americans lost some freedom. Federal agencies became involved in more and more aspects of life. This seems to have been a necessary price to pay if such a complex society was to function smoothly. Still, the loss was large.

The New Deal years also saw a shift in the balance of power within the federal government. Congress came to have less power as the presidency grew stronger. Ever since it created the Interstate Commerce Commission in 1887, Congress had relied on special agencies and boards to carry out and enforce complicated laws. Since the presidents appointed the members of these organizations, the White House had gained more power and influence.

Under Franklin Roosevelt this trend became an avalanche. The crisis atmosphere of the times encouraged Congress to put more responsibility on the shoulders of Roosevelt and his appointees. Dozens of new agencies, each known by its initials, such as NRA, AAA, TVA, CCC, and NLRB, made up the confusing "alphabet soup" of the New Deal.

Roosevelt's great power and remarkable personal popularity made the presidency the strongest force in the government. At the time most liberals considered this both necessary and desirable. Conservatives such as Herbert Hoover were greatly alarmed by this trend. We shall see in a later chapter that both liberals and conservatives eventually changed their attitudes.

One more change that resulted from the New Deal was not fully clear until a number of years later. Economists and political leaders learned from their experiences during the Great Depression that the economy could be stimulated by unbalancing the federal budget.

The normal reaction of people during depressions had always been to cut down on their expenses. Most ordinary citizens believed that the government should also economize in hard times.

The long depression of the 1930s demonstrated that government economizing only made things worse. When the government spent more, even more than it received in taxes, called **deficit spending,** it put money into the pockets of citizens. When people spent this money, they encouraged producers to increase output. Indirectly they were causing employers to hire more workers. This was soon fairly obvious. However, most economists and political leaders hesitated early in the New Deal era to carry the technique far enough. Roosevelt's decision to reduce spending in 1937 illustrates this point very well. Greater government spending would probably have ended the depression sooner.

After their experience with unbalanced budgets during the Second World War, most governments got over their fear of the **federal deficit** which resulted from deficit spending. Everyone learned this lesson of the Great Depression. However, as we also shall see in a later chapter, attitudes on this subject would once again change with the passage of time. ▫

Return to the Preview & Review on
■ page 920.

INDEPENDENT PRACTICE
Have students complete the Preview & Review activity at the beginning of the section.

CLOSURE
Even though the New Deal did not end the depression, it had a tremendous impact on the United States. It changed political alignments, bringing African Americans into the Democratic party. It proved to economists and politicians that government spending could stimulate the economy. Above all, it increased the importance and power of the presidency.

HOMEWORK
Have students prepare a report to present to the class on one of the following subjects: the New Deal political coalition; the role of the NAACP in the 1920s and 1930s; the Harlem Renaissance; or the long-range effects of the New Deal on the American economy.

Effects of the New Deal   929

**COOPERATIVE LEARNING:
RELATING HISTORY TO
GEOGRAPHY**

To focus on the geographic theme of *the relationships within places,* organize the class into cooperative learning groups and tell each group that they are to investigate environmental issues that affect their communities. Instruct one group to investigate air quality. This group should find out what local factors affect air quality. These should include both human activity and physical features, such as mountains, that can intensify or alleviate pollution. The second group should investigate water resources and find out how local demand affects them. Students should find out what local businesses or agricultural producers use water and how they dispose of wastewater. They might also find out whether or not the local water supply can easily meet demand or if water rationing is ever needed. The third group should investigate local land use patterns. Tell them to find out how this has changed since the 1930s and in the last 10 years. They should find out if drought is a problem in their area. If it is, they should find out what measures have been implemented to deal with the problem.

You might want to invite a speaker from a local environmental group to talk to the class about local environmental issues before the class begins working on their reports. Ask the speaker to suggest local resource people that students could contact for additional information on their group investigations.

When the groups have completed their information gath-
(Continued)

LINKING HISTORY & GEOGRAPHY

DUST FROM THE GREENHOUSE

Half a century ago huge areas of the Great Plains blew away, leaving in the wake enormous human suffering and untold damage to the land. Many geographers and scientists wonder if we are heading in that direction again.

Breadbasket of America

1. Why had the Great Plains become a great farming region?

At the beginning of the 1900s the Great Plains was a region just starting to blossom. Rain fell in abundance, and farming techniques allowed farmers to turn the fields into the "breadbasket of America." No one foresaw a coming drought even though the region had had a history of drought and dust for centuries, even before the land was plowed. Indeed, many had come to believe that the more the land was plowed, the greater would be the rainfall.

Farmers poured into the region. The soil was broken, and just as forecasted, rain fell and wheat flourished. In the Texas panhandle some 82,000 acres had been planted in wheat in 1909. Twenty years later nearly 2 million acres were lush with ripening wheat.

This seeming miracle of agriculture was made possible by the tractor. Tractors enabled farmers to cultivate more and more of the grassland. As they moved westward, they came dangerously closer to the edges of the desert region. The plow that the tractor pulled pulverized the soil into powder. This to most farmers appeared ideal. They thought the layer of dust over the top of a hard-packed base would keep the moisture in the soil from evaporating. The tragedy of this, as we look back, is that it seemed to work. So by 1930 a layer of dust covered 5 million acres of wheat land stretching from Montana and the Dakotas in the north to Texas.

The Dust Bowl

2. What caused the Dust Bowl of the 1930s?

There have been many theories about the causes of the Dust Bowl of the 1930s. Certainly drought and wind were major physical factors. But they were aided by people and their greed.

Into the 1930s the rains continued to fall and the wheat thrived. In 1931 many plains farmers harvested as much as 50 bushels an acre. Then came the day of reckoning. Once-dependable rains suddenly stopped. Drought began to spread over the land. From 1933 to 1936, 20 states set records for dryness. (Those records still stand today.) Wheat withered. The carpeting of dust that covered the landscape was no longer held in place by moisture and a dense mantle of wheat. Dry winds lifted the dust from the fields in great clouds that swept across the sky.

This dust was so dense that people couldn't see. They had to string ropes from their barns to their houses to keep from getting lost in the swirling dust. It seemed like the whole landscape was on the move. Dust seemed to infiltrate everything. It covered dishes inside closed kitchen cabinets. It had to be scooped out of bathtubs before bathing. People slept with damp cloths over their faces to keep from choking.

Lessons of the Past

3. What can we learn from the tragedy of the Dust Bowl of the 1930s?

There are many lessons to be learned from that 1930s experience if we are to prevent its recurrence in the future. In the more than 50 years since those terrible days a great deal has been learned about managing land in areas subject to drought. Today's plows dig deeply into the soil, breaking it into large clods. This keeps the topsoil from blowing away. Marginal lands are not plowed. Many farmers do not plow at all but drill their seed into soil that is still covered by the stubble of last year's crop. Some plains farmers feel their techniques will prevent another dust bowl.

Many geographers disagree. The problem in the future, they admit, may not come from either the farmers or their agricultural practices. Rather, it is more likely to come from changes in the earth's atmosphere, changes that in the 1990s are well underway. The cause of these changes is the greenhouse effect.

The greenhouse effect is the name given to the process by which natural and humanmade gases trap solar heat in the earth's atmosphere. The process works like a greenhouse. In a greenhouse the sun's rays penetrate the glass but the glass keeps the heat from escaping. The sun's rays penetrate the earth's atmosphere like they do the glass of a greenhouse and strike the

ering, they should prepare an illustrated report to present to the class.

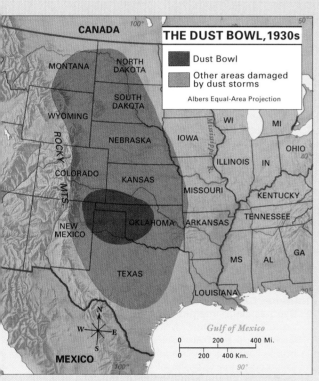

THE DUST BOWL, 1930s

■ Dust Bowl

▨ Other areas damaged by dust storms

Albers Equal-Area Projection

CANADA

MONTANA, NORTH DAKOTA, SOUTH DAKOTA, WYOMING, NEBRASKA, IOWA, WI, MI, OHIO, ILLINOIS, IN, COLORADO, KANSAS, MISSOURI, KENTUCKY, NEW MEXICO, OKLAHOMA, ARKANSAS, TENNESSEE, TEXAS, MS, AL, GA, LOUISIANA

ROCKY MTS.

Mississippi

Gulf of Mexico

MEXICO

0 200 400 Mi.
0 200 400 Km.

continues. Summers will be hotter and drier than they are today. Crops will wilt in the fields. Many areas will become unproductive. Can nothing be done? The answer is decidedly *yes,* if people are willing to pay the price.

The first and most useful step is to eliminate the production and use of chlorofluorocarbons (CFCs). CFCs are used primarily in air-conditioners and fast-food containers. In the atmosphere they trap 10,000 times as much heat as carbon dioxide. In 1990 President Bush called an international conference on CFCs. Most of the world nations agreed to totally stop the production of CFCs by the end of the 1990s. This should cut the greenhouse effect by 15 percent.

The biggest problem, however, will still be the amount of carbon dioxide pouring into the atmosphere as a byproduct of burning fossil fuels.

Unfortunately fossil fuels are comparatively cheap, and supplies are quite huge. It will be difficult and expensive to find alternatives to them. Certainly we could increase the use of solar power, hydroelectric power, and nuclear power. But these have drawbacks.

We also must stop burning the world's tropical forests to provide room for settlement and farming. Their destruction adds carbon dioxide to the atmosphere. In addition, trees naturally convert carbon dioxide into oxygen. Destroying the rain forests ruins this natural defense against the greenhouse effect.

Not all scientists and geographers agree on the extent of the greenhouse effect or the severity of its consequences. All do agree, however, that if we want to be sure to avoid the dust bowl conditions of the 1930s—which might be worldwide this time—people everywhere must awaken to the consequences of remaining ignorant of their environment.

APPLYING YOUR KNOWLEDGE
You will be organized into five groups. Each group will research and report on one of the following topics: the greenhouse effect, solar power, hydroelectric power, nuclear power, and the tropical forests. Reports should contain information on the most current research and prospects for the future. Your class will assemble the reports in a display for all the students in the school.

earth. Some of the heat is absorbed, but most is radiated back into the atmosphere. Carbon dioxide, a gas in the atmosphere given off by burning fossil fuels such as coal, oil, natural gas, and wood traps some of this heat, keeping it close to the earth's surface.

The greenhouse effect is a natural occurrence. Were it not for it, life on earth would be a nightmare of subzero temperatures. But since the Industrial Revolution there has been greatly increased use of fossil fuels, spewing more and more carbon dioxide in the atmosphere. Consequently, this atmospheric blanket is now capturing far more of the earth's radiated heat than at any time in the past. The result has been a gradual warming of the earth.

Future Effects
4. What can be done to slow or stop the greenhouse effect?

Droughts in the late 1980s showed Americans what they could expect if the warming trend

Thinking Critically

1. Students should demonstrate the use of historical imagination and show an understanding of the Bonus March and MacArthur's part in the events that followed. Reward creative, thoughtful answers.
2. Answers will vary; students should support their opinion with sound reasoning.
3. Reward imaginative, thoughtful letters that show the use of historical imagination. Students should also mention some of the facts of Bethune's life.
4. Opinions will vary; students should show an understanding of the New Deal and its importance and support their answers with sound reasoning.

REVIEW RESPONSES
Chapter Summary
Paragraphs will vary but should be evaluated on the logic of student arguments.

Reviewing Chronological Order
5, 2, 4, 3, 1

Understanding Main Ideas
1. During expansion, more goods are produced, prices rise, and more workers are hired. When output increases faster than goods are sold, surpluses accumulate, and manufacturers lay off workers. Prices fall and businesses that lose money fail. As surpluses decrease, the survivors increase output and rehire workers, who now can spend more. Demand and prices rise.
2. It created the FDIC, TVA, Federal Emergency Relief Administration, Civil Works Authority, and CCC; passed the NIRA, AAA, and a minimum wage.
3. Congress created agencies, which were known by their initials. The CCC employed young men to work on conservation projects. Under the AAA the government tried to raise farm prices by renting land, taking it out of production, and decreasing the amount produced. The WPA found work for the unemployed. While most jobs were unskilled, the WPA also funded cultural projects.
4. Before, he had tried to keep everyone's support, including business people and the rich. Now he concentrated on labor, women, and minorities for support.

932

CHAPTER 25 REVIEW

| | 1930 | THE GREAT DEPRESSION | | |

1929
Hoover becomes president
★
Stock market crash
★
Great Depression begins

1932
Bonus March
on Washington
★
Roosevelt elected president

1933
New Deal begins
★
FDIC, NIRA, NRA, AAA, TVA, CCC

Chapter Summary
Read the statements below. Choose one, and write a paragraph explaining its importance.
1. A normal business cycle has periods of recession, depression, recovery, and prosperity.
2. The Great Depression lasted longer, was steeper, and had more severe consequences than other depressions.
3. Human suffering during the depression was great. People lost their jobs and their savings. Many were hungry. In general the poor suffered most.
4. Hoover attempted to stimulate the economy, but he believed that the federal government should not provide direct relief. This attitude and his handling of the Bonus Army ruined his public image.
5. Franklin D. Roosevelt defeated Hoover and was inaugurated in the midst of a banking panic.
6. Roosevelt's New Deal was aimed at relief, recovery, and reform.
7. Roosevelt's personality and the feeling of action made the New Deal popular with most Americans, including blacks and other disadvantaged groups.
8. Some critics complained that the president had not gone far enough to end the depression more quickly. Others claimed he had gone too far.
9. The New Deal produced a revolution in employer-employee relations, created a "welfare state," and changed thinking about deficit spending.

Reviewing Chronological Order
Number your paper 1-5. Then study the time line above and place the following events in the order in which they happened by writing the first next to 1, the second next to 2, and so on.
1. Social Security Act
2. Roosevelt elected president
3. National Industrial Recovery Act
4. New Deal begins
5. Stock Market Crash

Understanding Main Ideas
1. Describe how the business cycle works.
2. What were some of the actions taken by Congress during the Hundred Days?
3. Describe these New Deal agencies or laws: Civilian Conservation Corps (CCC), Agricultural Adjustment Act (AAA), Works Progress Administration (WPA).
4. How did the Second New Deal differ from the first?
5. Give examples to show how most blacks responded to the New Deal.
6. What was the "welfare state" created in the 1930s?

Thinking Critically
1. **Synthesizing.** Imagine that you are General Douglas MacArthur writing your memoirs. Compose a brief account of your view of the Bonus March and your part in the events that followed in the summer of 1932.
2. **Analyzing.** Of the FDIC, the NRA, the AAA, the TVA, the CCC, or the WPA, which program of the New Deal do you think raised American morale the most? Why?
3. **Relating.** The year is 1938. Write a letter to the president of the NAACP nominating Mary McLeod Bethune for Woman of the Year and explaining why you think she should be chosen for this honor.
4. **Evaluating.** In your opinion, what was the most important result of the New Deal? Explain your answer and support it with sound reasoning.

Writing About History
Use your historical imagination to write a series of at least ten diary entries to describe what you see and hear during the Great Depression. Describe how your family copes with hard times. Describe people both more fortunate and less fortunate than you. What are your thoughts about President Roosevelt and the New Deal? Use the information in Chapter 25 to help you write your entries. You also may wish to interview people who lived during the Great Depression.

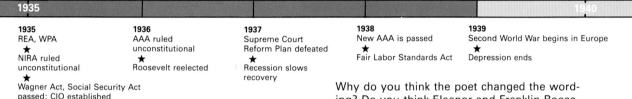

1935

1940

1935
REA, WPA
★
NIRA ruled
unconstitutional
★
Wagner Act, Social Security Act
passed; CIO established

1936
AAA ruled
unconstitutional
★
Roosevelt reelected

1937
Supreme Court
Reform Plan defeated
★
Recession slows
recovery

1938
New AAA is passed
★
Fair Labor Standards Act

1939
Second World War begins in Europe
★
Depression ends

Practicing the Strategy
Review the strategy on page 914.
Composing an Essay. Study the Chapter Summary on page 932. Choose one of the statements as your topic, then compose a short essay.

Using Primary Sources
Langston Hughes was one of the most famous writers of the Harlem Renaissance. Hughes greatly admired the work of Carl Sandburg, especially Sandburg's ability to capture the voice of the people. Hughes' "I, Too" is a response to a song millions of school children have sung: "My Country, 'tis of thee/Sweet land of liberty/Of thee I sing." As you read the following poem think about how the poet captures the voice of black Americans of the time.

I, Too

I, too, sing America.
I am the darker brother.
They send me to eat in the
kitchen
When company comes,
But I laugh,
And eat well,
And grow strong.
Tomorrow,
I'll be at the table
When company comes,
Nobody'll dare
Say to me,
"Eat in the kitchen,"
Then.
Besides,
They'll see how beautiful I am
And be ashamed—
I, too, am America.

1. To whom does the word *they* in line three refer? What do you think "the kitchen" symbolizes?
2. How does the last line differ from the first line?

Why do you think the poet changed the wording? Do you think Eleanor and Franklin Roosevelt would have agreed with the poet?
3. What prediction does the poet make? Do you think Hughes' prediction has come true? Explain your answer.

Linking History & Geography
In many ways the forces of nature were as hard on the American landscape as the economy was on the American people. Several of the programs of the New Deal were aimed at improving land use and conserving nature. To understand the impact of the New Deal on the geography of America, review President Roosevelt's first inaugural address and information on the CCC and TVA, especially the TVA map on page 909. Then answer these questions.
1. How does Roosevelt's inaugural address indicate he was concerned about the environment?
2. What did the CCC do to help conserve the nation's resources and natural environment?
3. Some critics claimed the TVA ruined rather than improved the environment. Why might they say this? Do you agree or disagree? Explain.

Enriching Your Study of History
1. **Individual Project.** Use an almanac to find unemployment figures, average income, or other economic statistics for the years 1929-39. Plot the numbers on a graph large enough to be seen by the entire class. Use the graph to illustrate how the economy changed in the 1930s.
2. **Cooperative Project.** Present-day historians sometimes record *oral history.* These are tape recorded (and sometimes video recorded) interviews that are later set down on paper. Oral history gives us the actual words of a person who recalls a period of history firsthand. Your group will prepare an oral history titled "The Great Depression: Personal Views." Group members will interview people in your community who lived through the events of 1929-39. You will then combine your interviews into a report, an audiotape, or a videotape and present it to the local library.

Chapter 25 Review 933

RESPONSES *(Continued)*
5. Most became Democrats. They felt that they were included and that officials tried to treat them fairly.
6. It was the relief and job programs and a general agreement that the federal government ought to ensure the population's welfare.

Writing About History
Encourage students to be imaginative when preparing their diary entries.

Practicing the Strategy
Students should study the appropriate section of the textbook to gather evidence and supporting details.

Using Primary Sources
1. Whites; the "kitchen" symbolizes the separation of African Americans and their relegation to an inferior position.
2. The word "sing" changes to "am." The speaker emphasizes that African Americans are part of the national "family." Many students will point out that the Roosevelts would have agreed although they were cautious about advocating equal rights.
3. African Americans will take their rightful place in society, and whites will be ashamed of the way they have treated blacks. Opinions will vary.

Linking History & Geography
1. He wanted government projects to stimulate and reorganize resource use.
2. The CCC put young men to work clearing brush, planting trees, and building dams.
3. It flooded the Tennessee River Valley; students should support their opinions.

Practicing Critical Thinking
1. Answers will vary; students should support their opinion with sound reasoning.
2. Answers will vary, but students should mention that it would tend to lessen the differences.
3. Answers will vary; reward thoughtful, imaginative questions.

REVIEW RESPONSES
Summing Up and Predicting
Paragraphs will vary but should be evaluated on the logic of student arguments.

Connecting Ideas
1. Answers will vary; students should support their opinion with sound reasoning.
2. Possible answers: Jefferson would not have approved of Roosevelt's increased presidential power; however, he might have supported New Deal programs that aided farmers. Hamilton would have recognized Roosevelt as an individual worthy of wielding power fairly; however, he would not have supported FDR's New Deal programs that aided the poor and unemployed. He probably would have approved of the programs that aided businesses, such as the National Industrial Act, which was supposed to stimulate private business by permitting manufacturers to cooperate without fear of violating antitrust laws.
3. Political cartoons should reflect understanding of the issues and candidates; campaign slogans should show understanding of each party in the election chosen.

*This source is suitable for students reading below grade level.

934

UNIT EIGHT REVIEW

Summing Up and Predicting
Read the summary of main ideas in Unit Eight below. Choose one statement, then write a paragraph predicting its outcome or future effect.
1. A variety of factors caused Europe to erupt in 1914 in the largest war in history.
2. The United States eventually declared war on the Central Powers in 1917.
3. The Treaty of Versailles reflected many of Wilson's 14 Points, including the League of Nations. But it was not the peace without victory he felt was so essential to future peace.
4. The United States rejected the Versailles Treaty and the League of Nations. American reaction to the war led to a series of actions aimed at limiting foreign influences in the United States.
5. Most Americans enjoyed the "Roaring Twenties." The automobile, jazz, sports, motion pictures, and the radio brought zest to life.
6. Despite the prevalent "get-rich-quick" attitude, problems of farmers and "sick industries" slowed the economy.
7. The Great Depression lasted longer and was steeper than other depressions, and human suffering was great, especially for the poor.
8. Roosevelt's New Deal was aimed at relief, recovery, and reform. It did not immediately end the depression, however.
9. The New Deal changed many things in American society, most importantly the role of government in business and everyday life.

Connecting Ideas
1. You know that radio became a powerful influence on American life in the 1920s. Do you think that television has less, the same, or more influence today than radio did then?
2. From what you have learned of the political ideas of Alexander Hamilton and Thomas Jefferson, how do you think each of them would have viewed President Roosevelt's use of power during the New Deal? In your answer cite some specific New Deal programs.
3. Choose any presidential election in this unit and either draw a political cartoon representing the point of view about an issue of the campaign or a candidate or create a campaign slogan for each party in that election.

Practicing Critical Thinking
1. **Analyzing.** As you have read, Oliver Wendell Holmes declared that if something said or written presents a "clear and present danger" to the war effort, the speaker or writer may be punished by law. Do you think this interpretation should also apply to peacetime crises such as the depression? Why or why not?
2. **Drawing Conclusions.** You know that during the 1920s American life was changed by the automobile. How do you think the widespread use of cars affected regional differences in the nation? Give specific examples.
3. **Synthesizing.** You are a reporter who can interview one of the following people: Herbert Hoover, Franklin Roosevelt, or Eleanor Roosevelt. Choose one, and make a list of five questions that you would ask during your interview.

Cooperative Learning
1. Your group will study the time lines at the end of each of the chapters in Unit Eight. Then you will create two time lines, one illustrating the most important domestic events in the unit and the other showing the major international events. Some group members may illustrate the time line by adding sketches or pictures. Display your time lines in the classroom.
2. Your group will create a chart to display in the classroom, showing the "alphabet soup" of the New Deal. Group members will research each agency and briefly describe its function. Others may illustrate the chart with appropriate symbols for the various agencies.
3. Your group will make a model of a battlefield on the Western Front, using clay or plaster of paris. Include trenches, barbed-wire mazes, and no man's land.

Reading in Depth
Allen, Frederick Lewis. *Only Yesterday.* New York: Harper & Row. Provides a highly readable account of life in the 1920s.

Hiebert, Roslyn and Ray Hiebert. *Franklin Delano Roosevelt, President for the People.* New York: Watts. Presents a closeup picture of the man who led America through the Great Depression.

*Horan, James David. *The Desperate Years: A Pictorial History of the Thirties.* Portland, ME: Walch. Contains a dramatic visual portrayal of the decade through photographs and paintings.

Richards, Kenneth. *Babe Ruth.* New York: Children's Press. Traces the life and career of one of baseball's greatest stars.

935

UNIT OBJECTIVES

Upon completing Unit 9, students will be able to:

1. Interpret the reactions of most Americans to the aggression of totalitarian governments during the 1930s.
2. Describe the series of events that led to America's involvement in World War II.
3. Evaluate President Truman's decision to drop the atomic bomb on Japan.
4. Discuss provisions of the Truman Doctrine and the Marshall Plan.
5. Understand the beginnings of and reasons for the Cold War and how containment and massive retaliation helped to prolong it.
6. Explain the importance of the decision in *Brown v. Board of Education.*

National Air and Space Museum, Washington

The peaceful use of atomic power came with the race for space between the Soviet Union and the United States. Here Norman Rockwell, in "Apollo 11 Space Team", shows American astronauts with eager watchers, awaiting their expeditions into the unknown heavens.

A GLOBAL AMERICA
UNIT 9

In Unit 9 you will learn about World War II and the conflict that followed, known as the Cold War. Here are some main points to keep in mind as you read the unit.

- World War II was the most savage war ever fought. Almost 40 million people died in the conflict.
- The war began with the German invasion of Poland in 1939. It ended after the United States dropped atomic bombs on Japan in 1945.
- The United States was forced into the war when Japan attacked the American naval base at Pearl Harbor.
- The Soviet Union and the United States, two victors in the war, quarreled. A "Cold War" began between them.
- In the 1950s, Dr. Martin Luther King, Jr. led a nonviolent movement to win equal rights for African Americans.

OVERVIEW

The U.S. clung to a policy of isolationism during the 1930s but was gradually drawn into another world war. The great wartime demand for American farm and industrial products ended the Great Depression. The U.S. and its allies united to defeat the Axis nations.

Following World War II the Cold War developed between the U.S. and the Soviet Union. As wartime alliances dissolved, communist and noncommunist nations became distrustful of each other.

President Eisenhower's election in 1952 ended 20 years of Democratic control of the White House. In foreign affairs Eisenhower continued Truman's containment policy, a policy that contributed to high Cold War tensions.

In 1954 the struggle for equal rights in America gained momentum with the landmark Supreme Court decision in *Brown v. Board of Education.*

John F. Kennedy was elected president in 1960 and called for Americans to look to a New Frontier.

CONNECTING WITH PAST LEARNING

Have students discuss some of the ways the U.S. tried to keep out of World War I. *(Students may mention Wilson's pleas for neutrality in thought and action, attempts to negotiate a peace, and the Sussex pledge.)* Tell them to keep this in mind as they read about U.S. efforts to keep out of World War II and the events that made this impossible.

World War II

PLANNING THE CHAPTER

TEXTBOOK	RESOURCES
1. American Neutrality	*Unit 9 Worksheets and Tests:* Chapter 26 Graphic Organizer, Directed Reading 26:1, Reteaching 26:1 *Eyewitnesses and Others, Volume 2:* Reading 57: America and the Holocaust (1940s)
2. The European War	*Unit 9 Worksheets and Tests:* Directed Reading 26:2, Reteaching 26:2
3. The Pacific War	*Unit 9 Worksheets and Tests:* Directed Reading 26:3, Reteaching 26:3, Geography 26 *Creative Strategies for Teaching American History:* Page 337 *Eyewitnesses and Others, Volume 2:* Reading 50: The Japanese Attack Pearl Harbor (1941), Reading 55: Defense Worker Rachel Wray Reminisces About Her Wartime Experiences (1940s), Reading 52: Margaret Takahashi Describes the Internment of Japanese Americans (1942), Reading 56: A Black Tank Commander's Story (1940s)
4. The Allies Regain Europe	*Unit 9 Worksheets and Tests:* Directed Reading 26:4, Reteaching 26:4
5. The Allies Win in the Pacific	*Unit 9 Worksheets and Tests:* Directed Reading 26:5, Reteaching 26:5 *Eyewitnesses and Others, Volume 2:* Reading 53: An Army Nurse at Bataan and Corregidor (1942), Reading 51: A Hawaiian American in the Pacific War (1941), Reading 54: John Hersey Records the Japanese Experience of Hiroshima (1945)
Chapter Review	*Audio Program:* Chapter 26 *Unit 9 Worksheets and Tests:* Chapter 26 Tests, Forms A and B (See also *Alternative Assessment Forms*) *Test Generator*

STRATEGIES FOR STUDENTS WITH SPECIAL NEEDS

Gifted Students.

Have interested students use resources in the school or public library to find more information on activities on the home front in the United States during World War II. Then have them prepare an oral report on their findings. Encourage students to illustrate their reports. Some students might enjoy focusing their reports on a comparison between activities on the home fronts in World War I and World War II.

Students Having Difficulty with the Chapter.

You may wish to have students listen to Chapter 26 in *The Story of America Audio Program.* Then organize the class into several cooperative learning groups. Distribute to each group an outline map of the Pacific region and of Europe and North Africa. Instruct each group to work together to show the major World War II battles that occurred in each region. Under each battle students should also note the victor and the date. Display completed maps on the bulletin board.

BOOKS FOR TEACHERS

Selig Adler, *Uncertain Giant: American Foreign Policy Between the Wars.* New York: Macmillan, 1966.

Albert R. Buchanan, *The United States and World War II.* New York: Harper & Row, 1962.

Robert Dallek, *Franklin D. Roosevelt and American Foreign Policy, 1932–1945.* New York: Oxford University Press, 1979.

Martha Hoyle, *A World in Flames: A History of World War II.* New York: Atheneum, 1970.

William E. Leuchtenburg, *Franklin D. Roosevelt and the New Deal, 1932–1940.* New York: Harper & Row, 1963.

Fletcher Pratt, *War for the World: A Chronicle of Our Fighting Forces in World War II.* New Haven: Yale University Press, 1950.

BOOKS FOR STUDENTS

Charles Ferry, *One More Time!.* Boston: Houghton Mifflin, 1985.

Charles Ferry, *Raspberry One.* Boston: Houghton Mifflin, 1983.

Jack Kuper, *Child of the Holocaust.* New York: New American Library, 1980.

Uri Orlev, *The Island on Bird Street.* Boston: Houghton Mifflin, 1983.

Ruth Minsky Sender, *The Cage.* New York: Macmillan, 1986.

Erika Tamar, *Good-bye, Glamour Girl.* New York: New American Library, 1985.

MULTIMEDIA MATERIALS

The Arsenal. Part 2 of the *America* series (film, 40 min.), Time-Life. Covers accomplishments of Franklin Roosevelt, the peacetime draft, Lend-Lease Act, Pearl Harbor, D-Day, the death of Hitler, the Manhattan Project, the atom bomb and Hiroshima, the United Nations, Korea, and Vietnam.

The Negro Soldier in the Army (film, 40 min.), Museum of Modern Art, 1944. "Army Pictorial" series directed by Frank Capra.

Victory at Sea (film, 78 min.), Films Inc. Presents events of World War II, including the bombing of London, Pearl Harbor, the Italian and French campaigns, and the war against Japan.

World War II: Homefront (filmstrip), SVE. Industry, rationing, Lend-Lease, and Selective Service.

World War II: 1942–1945 (film, 16 min.), Coronet. The United States at war in the Atlantic and the Pacific.

SUGGESTED CAPTION RESPONSE
Answers will vary. Students might point out that prejudice is grounded in ignorance.

RESOURCES
■ You may wish to have students complete the Chapter 26 Graphic Organizer as they work through this chapter.

CHAPTER OBJECTIVES
Upon completing this chapter, students will be able to:
1. Interpret how Americans reacted to the aggression of totalitarian countries during the 1930s.
2. Explain how World War II affected the election of 1940.
3. Describe the series of events that led to America's

OVERVIEW
After the experiences of World War I, Americans desired isolation despite the totalitarian aggression in Europe and Asia in the 1930s. The move away from that isolationism was slow but was complete when the Japanese bombed Pearl Harbor. The war had a great effect on the economy and on minority groups in the U.S. The Allies finally achieved success in Europe, but it took the dropping of two atomic bombs for an Allied victory over Japan.

FOCUS/MOTIVATION:
MAKING CONNECTIONS
Prior Knowledge.
Ask students to recall what the mood was in America regarding foreign involvement after World War I. *(Americans were against any foreign involvement.)* Point out that the U.S. tried to maintain a similar policy of isolationism through the 1930s, but the events that unfolded in Europe and the Far East once again drew the U.S. into a world war.

CHAPTER 26

World War II

■ O n September 1, 1939, an enormous German army of 1.7 million men invaded Poland. Two days later Poland's allies—Great Britain and France—responded to this attack by declaring war on Germany. The Second World War had begun. This great world conflict immediately affected the United States. It ended the economic depression. It forced President Roosevelt to direct nearly all of his attention to foreign affairs. And it caused the American people to look once again at their alliances in Europe and the Pacific.

Culver Pictures

"Il Duce," Benito Mussolini, and "the Führer," Adolf Hitler, ruled their countries with iron fists. Mussolini, here saluting his troops, wanted Italy to again have the greatness of ancient Rome. Hitler played on the emotions of the German people in their defeat after the Great War to forge a war machine fueled by hatred and prejudice. By 1945 both these leaders were dead, Mussolini hanged in a public square in Milan, Hitler a suicide in Berlin. Why do you think neo-Nazis and other such groups continue to express hatred for Jews and other ethnic and racial groups?

936

OBJECTIVES *(Continued)*
involvement in World War II.
4. Explain the effects World War II had on the American economy.
5. Examine the treatment of minority groups during the war.
6. Evaluate President Truman's decision to drop the atomic bomb on Japan.

HISTORICAL SIDELIGHTS
❶ Hitler became chancellor of Germany a little more than a month before Franklin Roosevelt was inaugurated president for his first term. Once in power, Hitler took the title *der Führer* (FYOOR · ur), German for "the leader."

1. AMERICAN NEUTRALITY

The Totalitarian States

The **Second World War** resulted from the efforts of three nations—Germany, Italy, and Japan—to conquer and control new territories. These nations developed what are called **totalitarian** governments. Their basic principle was that the state was everything, the individual citizen nothing. Totalitarian governments stamped out opposition. The only political party was controlled by the state. All power was in the hands of one leader, or **dictator.** The dictators allowed no criticism of their policies. They claimed absolute authority over the lives of their citizens.

Totalitarianism first developed in Italy in the 1920s. Benito Mussolini became the country's dictator. He called his political system **fascism.** The name came from the ancient Roman symbol of authority, the *fasces,* a bundle of rods tied tightly around an ax. The rods and ax represented the power of the state. Binding them closely together represented national unity. Mussolini, a swaggering, domineering leader, dreamed of controlling the entire Mediterranean region.

The Japanese system was somewhat different. The official head of the Japanese government was the emperor, Hirohito. He was considered to be a god, and he took no part in the day-to-day running of the government. In practice, however, the Japanese government was equally committed to the idea that the interests of the state were all-important.

The Japanese warlords who controlled the Japanese government in the late 1920s also dreamed of expansion and military glory. Seizing lands for raw materials for rapidly growing Japanese industries was the first step in a plan to control east Asia and the Pacific.

The Soviet Union witnessed the rise of a dictator during the 1920s too. Joseph Stalin replaced V.I. Lenin, founder of the Communist party in Russia and leader of the Communist Revolution in 1917. Stalin began a ruthless purge of all his opponents. He then openly showed his intention to spread communism throughout the world.

There were other dictators, including General Francisco Franco, who came to power in Spain in 1939 after a bloody civil war. Many Americans had watched the civil war closely, for it was the testing ground for the war machine of the European aggressors.

In Germany the National Socialists, or **Nazis,** led by Adolf Hitler, ❶ established a totalitarian government in 1933. In rousing speeches and rallies Hitler drew on the bitterness of the German people over the Versailles Treaty and the psychological effects of the postwar depression to captivate followers. Once in power he began ruthless expansion by conquest.

Hitler was a dictator who used terror and brute force to crush those Germans who opposed him. Democratic principles such as

Preview & Review

Use these questions to guide your reading. Answer the questions after completing Section 1.
Understanding Issues, Events, & Ideas. Use the following words to describe the state-controlled governments of the 1930s: Second World War, totalitarian, dictator, fascism, Nazis, concentration camp, Holocaust, genocide, pacifist, conscientious objector, merchant of death, neutrality act, quarantine, collective security.
1. How did Hitler gain support for his rise to power?
2. Why did most Americans favor a policy of isolationism?
3. What events caused Congress to pass the neutrality acts?
4. Why did Roosevelt urge a quarantine of aggressor nations by peaceful nations?

Thinking Critically. 1. Imagine that you lived in a totalitarian nation such as Germany, Italy, or Japan during the 1920s-1930s. Write a letter to an American friend, describing what your life is like in that nation. **2.** If you had been a member of Hoover's cabinet when Japan invaded China, would you have recommended the policy of nonrecognition? Why or why not?

PREVIEW & REVIEW RESPONSES
Understanding Issues, Events, & Ideas.
Descriptions should demonstrate an understanding of the terms used.
1. Hitler drew on the bitterness of the German people over the Versailles Treaty and the psychological effects of the postwar depression to gain support.
2. Americans did not want to become involved in another foreign war.
3. In 1935, 50,000 World War I veterans marched through Washington for peace, and 175,000 college students staged a one-hour strike against the war. Congress responded by passing the neutrality acts.
4. He was looking for a way to check the aggressor nations without getting involved in a shooting war.

Thinking Critically.
1. Student letters should show use of historical imagination and be based on historical fact.
2. Answers will vary, but students should support their opinions with sound judgment and reasoning.

FOCUS/MOTIVATION: MAKING CONNECTIONS
Prior Knowledge.
Ask students if they have read books or seen movies or television programs about the German concentration camps. *(Most students will probably answer that they have.)* Have students discuss what they have seen or heard regarding these concentration camps. *(Continued)*

(Students should point out such things as the millions of deaths in the gas chambers, the forced enslavement, and the horrible experiments that were carried out on humans.) Ask students to keep this in mind as they read in this section about the brutal and warped policies of Adolf Hitler.

USING HISTORICAL IMAGINATION

Show students a newsreel of either Hitler or Mussolini giving a speech before a crowd in their countries. Have students imagine that they are newspaper correspondents assigned to either Germany or Italy and are in the crowd listening to either of the dictators' speeches. Have them write newspaper articles about the speech. Tell them to include a description of the dictator, the delivery of his speech, and the crowd's reaction. You may wish to have students read their articles to the class.

GUIDED INSTRUCTION

Divide the class into two groups. Tell one group that they are isolationists and the other group that they are internationalists in 1939. Each group is to prepare a persuasive speech on their point of view, which they are going to present to Congress. Have spokespersons present their groups' speeches to the class, and then have the class vote on whether they think the U.S. should maintain the policy of isolationism or adopt the policy of internationalism.

When Berlin hosted the 1936 Olympic Games, African American Jesse Owens won four gold medals. Hitler, in a sulk, refused to award the medals as was the custom for the leader of the host nation.

freedom of speech and the press were destroyed in Germany and wherever the Nazis were victorious in the war.

Hitler believed that the Germans belonged to a special breed of humans, a "master race" that was supposed to be superior to all others. When Jesse Owens, an African American athlete from the United States, began winning gold medals in the 1936 Olympics held in Berlin, Hitler stopped attending the games. But he reserved most of his hatred for Jews, whom he considered to be morally and physically inferior. He seized Jewish property, denied Jews the right to higher education, and threw tens of thousands of Jews into horrifying 🔵 **concentration camps.**

Hitler intended to round up the millions of Jewish people in the conquered countries of Europe, force them to work in concentration camps until they dropped, and then kill them in cold blood. This was ■ the **Holocaust.** About 6 million Jews—men, women, and children alike—were murdered on Hitler's orders.

The Holocaust is an example of **genocide,** the deliberate elimination of a people, its heritage and traditions. Throughout history, madmen of one sort or other have tried to eliminate whole races of people. During the early part of the 20th century millions of Armenians were exterminated by the Turks. Many of the Armenians who escaped came to make new lives in America; many others remained behind in Armenia.

Japanese Aggression

In 1931 a Japanese army marched into Manchuria, a province in northern China. This action gave Japan control of rich coal, oil, and iron ore deposits and blocked Soviet designs on the region. Although the attack challenged the Open Door policy, President Herbert Hoover refused to take either military or economic measures against Japan. He instead announced that the United States would not recognize Japan's right to any Chinese territory seized by force.

This policy of nonrecognition had no effect on Japan. In 1932 the Japanese navy attacked the Chinese port of Shanghai. Early the following year, before Franklin D. Roosevelt took his oath of office as president, the Japanese marched into Jehol, a province in northern China.

American Isolationism

Totalitarian ideas had little appeal to Americans. Totalitarian states silenced their political opponents and stormed over the borders of weaker nations during the 1930s. This shocked and angered nearly everyone in the United States. When a totalitarian nation attacked another country, the danger of war spreading was on everyone's mind. Americans nearly always sympathized with the victims of the

HISTORICAL SIDELIGHTS

① In addition to protesting America's involvement in war, pacifists protested the sale of toy guns and toy soldiers.

Wide World Photos

invaders. But they did not want to become involved in another foreign war. Most Americans once again favored a policy of isolationism. Charles Lindbergh voiced their sentiments:

❝ No one can make us fight abroad unless we ourselves are willing to do so. . . . Over one hundred million people in this nation are opposed to entering the war. If the principles of democracy mean anything at all, that is reason enough for us to stay out. If we are forced into a war against the wishes of an overwhelming majority of our people, we will have proved democracy such a failure at home that there will be little use fighting for it abroad.[1] ❞

Also urging isolation were a large number of American **pacifists.** ① These people believed war for any cause was wrong. Throughout American history pacifists had objected to United States involvement in war. Many based their beliefs in religious teachings. Among the most notable pacifists were the Quakers. Most Quakers had refused to enter the armed forces during the Great War. War was against their religion, they said. These **conscientious objectors** had served in the medical corps in the war. The human suffering they witnessed further strengthened their belief that war was wrong.

[1] From a speech by Charles A. Lindbergh, Jr., in *The New York Times*, April 24, 1941

Never has the "civilized" world known such hatred as that of Hitler for the Jews of Eastern Europe. His deadly policy was genocide—the systematic elimination of 6 million Jews and their ancient culture. Here, Nazi soldiers drive terrified women and children from the Warsaw ghetto. Most of them will be sent to Treblinka, a death camp. Hitler's soldiers also rounded up thousands of political enemies and members of other outcast groups to be hauled off to prisons.

CHECKING UNDERSTANDING
Have students summarize military and political events that occurred in Germany, Italy, and Japan in the 1920s and 1930s. *(Germany—Adolf Hitler established a totalitarian government in 1933. He destroyed democratic principles such as freedom of speech and the press to establish control over the German people. He believed that the Germans belonged to a master race and that other people, particularly the Jews, were morally and physically inferior. He threw tens of thousands of Jews into concentration camps where most died.*

Italy—Benito Mussolini established a totalitarian dictatorship in the 1920s. His political system was called fascism. He dreamed of Italian expansion into the Mediterranean region and the Middle East. Italy took its first step toward military aggression when it invaded Ethiopia in 1935.

Japan—in the late 1920s the Japanese government was controlled by warlords who also had expansionist plans. The Japanese began seizing land for raw materials when they invaded Manchuria in 1931. In 1932 the Japanese navy attacked the Chinese port of Shanghai and in 1933 marched into Jehol in northern China. In 1937 Japan launched an all-out attack on China.)

PRIMARY SOURCE
Description of change: excerpted.
Rationale: excerpted to focus on Lindbergh's antiwar sentiments.

Pair students who are having difficulty with students who are performing well. Have the more proficient students ask the others the following questions:

1. What type of government did Hitler establish in Germany? *(a totalitarian dictatorship)*
2. How did he establish control? *(by destroying democratic principles)*
3. What did Hitler believe about the Jews and what did he do about it? *(They were morally and physically inferior. He threw tens of thousands of Jews into concentration camps where most died.)*
4. What type of government did Mussolini establish in Italy, and what did he call his political system? *(totalitarian government; fascism)*
5. What was Mussolini's first step toward military expansion? *(invasion of Ethiopia)*
6. What type of government was ruling Japan by the late 1920s? *(warlords with expansionist ideas)*
7. What acts of aggression did the Japanese perform in the 1930s? *(invaded Manchuria; attacked the Chinese port of Shanghai; marched into Jehol in northern China; launched an all-out attack on China)*

PRIMARY SOURCES
Description of change: excerpted.
Rationale: excerpted to focus on one of the ways antiwar groups were spreading their message in the 1930s.
(Point of View) Description of change: excerpted.

(continued)

Point of View

In Elsa Morante's powerful novel of World War II, a poor widow, Ida, witnesses the train that will take its Jewish occupants to the concentration and death camps.

"Perhaps ten paces from the entrance she began to hear, at some distance, a horrible humming sound, but for the moment she couldn't understand precisely where it was coming from.

The invisible voices were approaching and growing louder, . . . as if they came from an isolated and contaminated place. The sound suggested certain dins of kindergartens, hospitals, prisons; however all jumbled together. . . . At the end of the ramp on a straight, dead track, a train was standing which to Ida seemed of endless length. The voices came from inside it.

There were perhaps twenty cattle cars. . . . The cars had no windows except a tiny grilled opening up high. At each of these grilles two hands could be seen clinging, or a pair of staring eyes."
From *La Storia (History)*, 1974

The movement for disarmament and antiwar feelings were quite strong throughout the 1930s. When the ten-year naval holiday negotiated after the Great World War expired in 1932, Dorothy Dexler and the Women's International League for Peace and Disarmament doggedly insisted that Americans negotiate another. Antiwar groups spread the word in every way possible, as the following excerpt from an antiwar song shows:

> " I'll sing you a song, and it's not very long
> It's about a young man who never did wrong
> Suddenly he died one day
> The reason why no one could say
>   . . . Only one clue as to why he died
>   —A bayonet sticking in his side.[1] "

In fact, fighting the Great World War to make the world safe for democracy now seemed a terrible mistake. The totalitarian governments that arose after the war were enemies of democracy. America's allies had failed to pay back the money that the United States had lent them in their hour of desperate need. Looking back, the only Americans who appeared to have profited from the war were the manufacturers of guns and other munitions. It became popular to refer to these manufacturers as **merchants of death.**

The Neutrality Acts

Japan's attacks in China worried Roosevelt. Still, he could not ignore the strong isolationist and antiwar sentiment in the United States. On the 18th anniversary of America's entrance into the Great World War, 50,000 veterans paraded through Washington in a march for peace. A few days later some 175,000 college students across the country staged a one-hour strike against war. The government should build "schools not battleships," they claimed.

In August 1935 Congress responded by passing the first of a series of **neutrality acts.** This law prohibited the sale of weapons to either side in any war. Later neutrality acts directed the president to warn American citizens that if they traveled on the ships of warring nations, they did so at their own risk.

The idea behind the neutrality laws was to keep the country from repeating what now seemed to be the mistakes of the 1914–17 period. At that time, it will be remembered, President Wilson had insisted on American neutral rights. American ships, citizens, and goods, he stated, had the right to travel without interference on the high seas. That policy had led to the deaths of Americans in submarine attacks and eventually to America entering the war.

[1]From an antiwar song by the Almanac Singers, cited in *America in the Twentieth Century* by James T. Patterson

Roosevelt's Strategy

Soon after the passage of the first neutrality act, Italian troops invaded the African nation of Ethiopia. Roosevelt immediately applied the neutrality law. Nearly all Americans sympathized with the Ethiopians, who had done nothing to provoke Italy. Yet because the Ethiopians had few modern weapons to use against the heavily armed Italians, the neutrality act hurt them far more than their enemy.

Therefore, when Japan launched an all-out attack against China in 1937, Roosevelt refused to apply the neutrality law. Using the technicality that Japan had not formally declared war, he allowed the Chinese to buy weapons from American manufacturers.

Roosevelt was looking for a way to check the totalitarian nations without getting involved in a shooting war. In a speech in October 1937 he warned that "mere isolation or neutrality" was no protection. Peaceful nations must work together to isolate, or **quarantine,** aggressor nations. He was talking about what was called **collective security.** Safety required that democratic countries cooperate in the effort to prevent the aggressors from seizing whatever they wanted. However, Congress took no action, and Roosevelt let the matter drop.

Roosevelt's annual message to Congress in January 1939 shows how difficult the situation was becoming. Americans knew the actions of the aggressors were wrong and that they must be prepared. But officially they must remain neutral. Roosevelt said:

“ There comes a time in the affairs of men when they must prepare to defend not only their homes alone but the tenets of faith and humanity on which their churches, their governments, and their very civilizations are founded. The defense of religion, of democracy, and of good faith among nations is all the same fight. To save one we must now make up our minds to save all. . . .

The world has grown so small and weapons of attack so swift that no nation can be safe in its will for peace so long as any other single powerful nation refuses to settle its grievances at the council table.

For if any government bristling with implements of war insists on policies of force, weapons of defense give the only safety. . . .

Obviously we must proceed along practical, peaceful lines. But the mere fact that we rightly decline to intervene with arms to prevent acts of aggression does not mean that we must act as if there is no aggression at all. Words may be futile, but war is not the only means of commanding a decent respect for the opinions of mankind. . . .[1] ”

[1]From "Message of the President of the United States," January 4, 1939, *Congressional Record*, Vol. 84, Part 1

Return to the Preview & Review on page 937.

Rationale: excerpted to focus on Morante's depiction of Jews being transported to concentration camps.

INDEPENDENT PRACTICE
Have students complete the Preview & Review activity at the beginning of the section.

CLOSURE
Remind students that the rise to power of dictators in Germany and Italy, as well as the military aggressiveness of the Japanese government, began to alarm many Americans and caused the United States to move away from an isolationist policy and toward a policy of internationalism.

HOMEWORK
Have students research and prepare a report on the Holocaust. They should include pictures and statistics to support their research. You may wish to have some of the students present their reports to the class.

PRIMARY SOURCE
Description of change: excerpted.
Rationale: excerpted to focus on Roosevelt's concern over the actions of aggressor nations.

Preview & Review

Use these questions to guide your reading. Answer the questions after completing Section 2.

Understanding Issues, Events & Ideas. Use the following words to explain American attempts to help battle totalitarianism while remaining neutral: cash-and-carry policy, Dunkirk, Battle of Britain, internationalist, Four Freedoms, Lend-Lease Act, wolf pack, Battle of the Atlantic, Atlantic Charter, convoy.

1. What was Poland's fate in 1939? What had Hitler done before the invasion of Poland?
2. What was Roosevelt's destroyers-for-bases trade?
3. What promise about the war did President Roosevelt make during his campaign for a third term?
4. What were Roosevelt's Four Freedoms?
5. What was the purpose of the Atlantic Charter?

Thinking Critically. 1. Imagine that it is the fall of 1940, and you are Edward R. Murrow. Write an outline for a radio news report to broadcast from London to the United States. **2.** Construct a time line of the events that led to America's undeclared war with Germany. Start your time line with the Battle of Britain.

2. THE EUROPEAN WAR

Western Europe Falls to Hitler

After 1933 Hitler systematically violated the Versailles Treaty. His troops occupied the Rhineland and he annexed Austria. A famous American journalist had this to say about the German aggressions:

66 Write it down. On Saturday, February 12, 1938, Germany won the world war, and . . . Nazism started on the march across all of Europe east of the Rhine.

Write it down that the world revolution began in earnest—and perhaps the world war. . . .

Why does Germany want Austria? For raw materials? It has none of any importance. To add to German prosperity? Austria is a poor country with serious problems. But strategically it is the key to the whole of central Europe. Czechoslovakia is now surrounded. The wheat fields of Hungary and the oil fields of Rumania are now open. Not one of them will be able to withstand the pressure of German domination.

It is horror walking. Not that 'Germany' joins with Austria. We are not talking of 'Germany.' We see a new Crusade, under a pagan symbol, worshiping 'blood' and 'soil,' preaching the holiness of the sword and glorifying conquest. It hates the Slavs, whom it thinks to be its historic 'mission' to rule. It subjects all life to a militarized state. It persecutes men and women of Jewish blood. . . .

Today, all of Europe east of the Rhine is cut off completely from the western world. . . .[1]99

Then in the summer of 1939 Germany invaded Poland. Great Britain and France immediately declared war on Germany. The Soviet Union, which had signed a nonaggression treaty with Germany

[1]From *Let the Record Speak* by Dorothy Thompson

HISTORICAL SIDELIGHTS
● Because the German invasion of Poland moved
   so swiftly, it was called the *blitzkrieg,* German for
   lightning *(blitz)* and war *(krieg).*

SUGGESTED CAPTION RESPONSE
Ethiopia; they bordered Germany; Germany's invasion of Poland

EUROPEAN AGGRESSIONS LEADING TO WORLD WAR II

GERMAN INVASION STARTS WAR, SEPT. 1, 1939

Axis Powers

Area controlled by Axis before September 1, 1939

Azimuthal Equal-Area Projection

guaranteeing it would not interfere in German expansion, seized the
eastern part of Poland. The motorized and well-equipped German ●
army crushed its Polish opponents. In a little more than a month,
Poland was swallowed up. The Second World War, also called World
War II, had officially begun, although Japanese, Italian, and German
armies had been on the move throughout the 1930s.

In September President Roosevelt called Congress into special
session to revise the neutrality laws. After several weeks of debate
Congress agreed to allow warring nations to purchase arms and other
goods provided that they paid for them in cash and transported their
purchases in foreign ships. This **cash-and-carry policy** favored the
Allies. As in the Great World War, now called the First World War
or World War I, the British and French navies controlled the Atlantic
Ocean. German merchant ships could not reach American ports.

The Draft Lottery

As the United States moved closer to war, Congress voted to draft
men between the ages of 21 and 35 for military service. In September
1940 Congress authorized a draft to be made by a lottery.

On October 16 more than 16 million men reported to their local
draft boards to register for a possible call to military duty. Each was

LEARNING FROM MAPS. *German and Italian actions eventually
brought on World War II. Italy hoped
to claim an empire in Africa. What
country did they attack there? Why
do you think the first German aggressions were in the areas shown on the
map? Which action was the immediate cause of World War II?*

**FOCUS/MOTIVATION:
MAKING CONNECTIONS
Prior Knowledge.**
Ask students if they know
whether or not Hitler was successful in invading Great Britain. *(No, he was not.)* Point out
that, like Napoleon, Hitler was
on the verge of invading Britain
but some of his generals advised him to invade the Soviet
Union instead. Have students
look at a map of Europe and
ask them if they think Hitler
was wise in invading the Soviet
Union instead of Great Britain.
(Student answers will vary.)
Point out that Great Britain has
not been invaded since the
Norman invasion of 1066.

**RELATING HISTORY TO
GEOGRAPHY**
As students are studying the
map of Europe, ask: What geographic considerations do you
think went into Hitler's decision
to invade the Soviet Union
rather than Great Britain? *(To
invade Great Britain Hitler's
forces would have to cross the
English Channel or the North
Sea. His troops could invade
the Soviet Union across the
level plains of eastern Poland,
an easier route for an invasion
than across the waters.)* You
may wish to return to this activity after students have completed the Strategy for Success
on page 972 and have them
evaluate Hitler's decision.

1 The Western Front remained quiet for seven months following the declaration of war by Great Britain and France, which is why it became known as the "Phony War." However, this phony war ended in April 1940 when Hitler turned west and invaded Denmark and Norway.

GUIDED INSTRUCTION

Assign each student an identity as either a famous person, place, or event from World War II. Tell them not to reveal their identity to any of the other class members. Have students research and write down 10 facts about their identity. You may want to point out that these facts should not be obscure. Have the class attempt to guess the identity by having each student read a fact at a time to the class about themselves. You may wish to give points to students who guess the correct identity.

assigned a number from 1 to 8,500. Then all the numbers were placed in small capsules and dropped into a large fishbowl. On October 29 Secretary of War Henry L. Stimson, blindfolded, reached into the bowl and drew out the first capsule. It was number 158. Then others took out the rest, one by one. This determined the order in which men were called up for duty. By the end of the war 10 million men had been drafted and 6 million men and women had enlisted.

Hitler's War Machine Rolls On

Cash and carry was not enough to prevent Hitler's powerful armies
1 from crushing Poland. His war machine rolled on. In April 1940 Hitler invaded Denmark and Norway. On May 10 Nazi tanks swept into the Netherlands and Belgium. A few days later German troops broke through the French defenses at Sedan. Soon they reached the English Channel, trapping thousands of British, French, and Belgian troops at **Dunkirk.** Between May 26 and June 4 British ships managed to rescue about 340,000 soldiers from the beach at Dunkirk and carry them safely to England. But it was a crushing defeat. Swift German armored divisions rolled on through France. Before the end of June the French had surrendered. Hitler was master of most of western Europe. Only Britain and its navy stood between Hitler and victory.

Across the English Channel come boats of every shape and size in the spring of 1940. British, French, and Belgian soldiers had their backs to the channel as the Germans advanced. France was lost, but 340,000 men were saved by the courage and mettle of the British at Dunkirk.

Imperial War Museum

Nearly everyone in the United States was horrified by the thought of such a victory. Hitler was both cruel and power mad. If he conquered Great Britain, would the United States be safe from his mighty armies? Without massive American aid, Great Britain seemed in danger of being invaded and overwhelmed. German U-boats and bombers had sunk many British destroyers needed to protect Atlantic shipping and prevent a German invasion of England. In July 1940 British Prime Minister Winston Churchill appealed to President Roosevelt for help. He needed 40 or 50 American destroyers. These vessels were not being used because the United States had replaced them with more modern ships.

Roosevelt wanted to help the British. He knew that it would take time to get Congress to act. Therefore he issued an executive order turning over 50 destroyers to the British in exchange for 99-year leases on several naval and air bases in the British West Indies. This destroyers-for-bases trade was acceptable to those people who would have objected to simply giving the ships to Great Britain.

The Election of 1940

Hitler expected to crush British resistance with massive air raids and ① then invade the shattered island. The Nazi bombings brought the war uncomfortably close to the United States. In the fall of 1940 an American news commentator, Edward R. Murrow, began a series of radio broadcasts from London.

> **❝** *September 13, 1940*
> This is London at 3:30 in the morning. This has been what might be called a 'routine night'—air-raid alarm at about nine o'clock and intermittent bombing ever since. I had the impression that more high explosives and fewer incendiaries [fire bombs] have been used tonight. . . .
>
> *September 18, 1940*
> You can have little understanding of the life in London these days—the courage of the people, the flash and the roar of the guns rolling down the streets where much of the history of the English-speaking world has been made, the stench of air-raid shelters in the poor districts. These things must be experienced to be understood. . . .
>
> *September 22, 1940*
> I'm standing again tonight on a rooftop looking out over London, feeling rather large and lonesome. . . . At the moment there's an ominous silence hanging over London. But at the same time a silence that has a great deal of dignity. . . .[1] **❞**

[1]From *In Search of Light* by Edward R. Murrow

Photo Researchers

Hitler is the Grim Reaper in this political cartoon, slaughtering all who oppose his takeover of Europe by force.

Bettmann Newsphotos

Edward R. Murrow's broadcasts held Americans spellbound as they leaned closer to their radios to hear news of the war from London. He became America's most distinguished broadcaster and fighter for truth.

1 The first massive bombing of major metropolitan areas occurred during World War II. This resulted in a high rate of civilian casualties and a large amount of property destruction, including many historic buildings and cathedrals.

British Information Services

St. Paul's Cathedral, the masterpiece of famed architect Sir Christopher Wren, was so badly damaged by the nightly bombings and fires that it was not fully restored for twenty years.

The English, even school children, went about their business in spite of the deadly German bombings. In London, children learned how to use gas masks and to find the nearest shelters. In the countryside, farm children wait in a trench for the German planes to fly home once more.

John Topham/Black Star

1 The **Battle of Britain** formed the background of the presidential election of 1940. Republicans could not decide between Senator Robert A. Taft, the son of former president William Howard Taft, and Thomas E. Dewey of New York. After six ballots the convention turned to a dark horse, Wendell Willkie of Indiana. Willkie, a former Democrat, was the head of a large public utility corporation. He had led the opposition to the creation of the Tennessee Valley Authority in 1933. Willkie was a strong supporter of aid to Britain. His nomination was a victory for the Republican **internationalists** over the isolationist wing of the party, led by Senator Taft.

When the Democratic convention met in Chicago, not even Roosevelt's closest advisers knew if he would seek renomination. No president had ever run for a third term. However, Roosevelt felt he was needed because of the critical international situation. He won the nomination easily.

Roosevelt ran on his record. Willkie tried to play up the third-term issue and the failures of the New Deal to get the economy

HISTORICAL SIDELIGHTS

The Lend-Lease Act appropriated an initial sum of $7 billion for ships, planes, tanks, and anything else that the Allies needed.

moving. Late in the campaign he also accused the president of planning to involve the United States in the war. "If you reelect him," Willkie told one audience, "you may expect war in April 1941."

Roosevelt responded quickly. "I have said this before, but I shall say it again and again and again: your boys are not going to be sent into any foreign wars." In the November election Roosevelt received 449 electoral votes, Willkie only 82.

The Lend-Lease Act

Roosevelt interpreted his reelection as an endorsement of his policy of aiding Great Britain. The British were now running desperately short of money to pay for American supplies. Therefore Roosevelt proposed lending them the weapons and goods they needed to continue the struggle against Hitler. In a fireside chat he told the people that the United States "must become the great arsenal of democracy." He asked them to support increased aid to Great Britain even at the risk of becoming involved in the war.

In January 1941 Roosevelt called for support for those who were fighting in defense of what he called the **Four Freedoms**—freedom of speech and religion, freedom from want and fear. A few days later he asked Congress to pass his program for aid to Britain, the **Lend-Lease Act.** This measure gave the president authority to sell or lend war supplies, or matériel, to any nation whose defense was essential to America's security.

The Lend-Lease bill aroused fierce opposition. "Lending war equipment is a good deal like lending chewing gum," said Senator Taft. "You don't want it back." But the public was behind the president. One poll showed that 70 percent of those questioned supported aid to Britain—even at the risk of war. Congress passed the Lend-Lease Act in March.

The Battle of the Atlantic

To stop the flow of supplies to Britain, swarms of German U-boats, called **wolf packs,** ranged the Atlantic. Hitler also shifted part of his air force to attack Atlantic shipping. The **Battle of the Atlantic** was a desperate struggle. During the first half of 1941, U-boats sank ships faster than the British could build them. Roosevelt authorized the United States naval yards to repair damaged British ships, and he transferred ten Coast Guard cutters to the British navy.

In April the United States set up bases in Greenland. American naval vessels began to patrol the Atlantic. These American ships did not try to sink German submarines. Their purpose was to track the submarines and radio their location to British planes and destroyers.

On June 22, 1941, Hitler broke his 1939 nonaggression agreement with Joseph Stalin and invaded the Soviet Union. Roosevelt quickly

Point of View

In *V Was for Victory,* a scholar of the war makes these comments about Roosevelt.

"Circumstances overcame his hesitancies. When the Nazis swept across western Europe in the spring of 1940, the President, who was eager to aid the British, confronted the bankruptcy of the American armed forces. He confronted, too, the need for greater national unity at the very moment of a national political campaign. Beginning then, moving more rapidly after his re-election and the ensuing passage of the Lend-Lease Act, continuing thereafter as American involvement in the war in the Atlantic grew, he created one defense agency after another. . . ."
John Morton Blum, 1976

Frank Schershel/Life Picture Service

To cover the war in Europe—and later in the Pacific—magazines such as Life *sent artists as well as photographers. This painting shows what the camera at night might not show so well: the* Campbell, *training its searchlights on a U-boat being shelled. The U-boat was sunk, but the* Campbell *was so badly damaged that it had to be towed 800 miles to safety.*

announced that lend-lease aid would be extended to the Soviet Union. In July he ordered 4,000 Marines to Iceland. This move pushed the area under American protection farther into the Atlantic.

The Atlantic Charter

In August 1941 President Roosevelt met with Prime Minister Churchill aboard the destroyer *Augusta* at Argentia Bay in Newfoundland. There the two leaders outlined their aims for the postwar world. This **Atlantic Charter,** as it became known, is an inspiring statement of eight democratic principles. In the conclusion the president and the prime minister called for gradual disarmament:

      66 Eighth, they [the United States and Great Britain] believe that all of the nations of the world, for realistic as well as spiritual reasons, must come to the abandonment of the use of force. Since no future peace can be maintained if land, sea, or air armaments continue to be employed by nations which threaten, or may threaten, aggression outside of their frontiers, they believe, pending the establishment of a wider and permanent system of general security, that the disarmament of such nations is essential. They will likewise aid

Wide World Photos

and encourage all other practicable measures which will lighten for peace-loving peoples the crushing burden of armaments.[1]"

[1]From *The Atlàntic Charter* by Franklin D. Roosevelt and Winston S. Churchill, August 14, 1941

Franklin Roosevelt and Winston Churchill, leaders of the free world, met at sea in 1941 to plan for the postwar world and to declare the Atlantic Charter. What did they mean when they wrote, "lighten for peace-loving peoples the crushing burden of armaments"?

The Undeclared War

In September 1941 a German submarine fired a torpedo at the United States destroyer *Greer* off Iceland. The destroyer had been trailing the U-boat and relaying its position to a British plane, which had dropped four depth charges. Although the *Greer* provoked the attack, Roosevelt called the attack "piracy legally and morally." He compared Hitler to a rattlesnake. He ordered naval vessels to escort, or **convoy,** merchant ships carrying lend-lease goods across the Atlantic. And he ordered naval vessels to "shoot on sight" any German submarines they encountered.

After a submarine sank the destroyer *Reuben James* on October 30, killing over 100 sailors, Congress authorized the arming of merchant ships. All restrictions on American commerce were removed. The United States was now engaged in an undeclared war with Germany.

Return to the Preview & Review on page 942.

The European War 949

RESOURCES
■ You may wish to have students complete Reading
  50: "The Japanese Attack Pearl Harbor (1941)" in
  Volume II of *Eyewitnesses and Others.*

**PREVIEW & REVIEW
RESPONSES
Understanding Issues, Events,
& Ideas.**
Descriptions should demonstrate an understanding of the terms used.
1. Roosevelt first stopped the export of aviation gasoline and scrap iron to Japan. After Japan invaded French Indochina, he placed an oil embargo on Japan.
2. 19 warships were sunk or disabled, 3 others were damaged, 150 planes were destroyed. The U.S. declared war on Japan.
3. The demand for weapons and supplies greatly expanded American industry, which ended the Great Depression.
4. Both black and Hispanic Americans were discriminated against in the military during the war. Blacks particularly suffered because they were kept in segregated units and were often treated with disrespect. Both black and Hispanic workers continued to suffer from discrimination in industrial plants during the war. Some advances for blacks in the military were that more black officers were commissioned, and a number of blacks became pilots in the air force. Service in the military offered many Hispanic Americans their first opportunity to experience life outside their neighborhoods. Labor shortages benefited both black and Hispanic workers during the war. Thousands were able to learn new skills and earn higher wages. Hispanic American women par-

Preview & Review

Use these questions to guide your reading. Answer the questions after completing Section 3.
Understanding Issues, Events, & Ideas. Use the following words to describe the situation in America at the outbreak of World War II: Tripartite Pact, Rome-Berlin-Tokyo Axis, Pearl Harbor, National War Labor Board, withholding system, G.I. Bill of Rights, internment camp, Fair Employment Practices Committee, bracero.
1. What economic steps did Roosevelt take to check Japan?
2. What was the extent of the damage done by the Japanese attack on Pearl Harbor? How did the United States react?
3. How did the war finally bring the Great Depression to an end?
4. What problems were there for black and Hispanic Americans in the military during the war? in labor? What advances were there?
Thinking Critically. 1. Write an eyewitness account of the attack on Pearl Harbor. **2.** Imagine that you are a young Japanese American who will soon be placed in an internment camp. Explain why you think the government's reasons for this treatment are unfair.

3. THE PACIFIC WAR

Negotiations with Japan

Meanwhile Japan continued to increase its control in east Asia. In September 1940 Japanese troops had conquered part of French Indochina, now Southeast Asia. Later that month Japan, Germany, and Italy signed a mutual defense treaty, the **Tripartite Pact.** This treaty created what was called the **Rome-Berlin-Tokyo Axis.**

Roosevelt hoped to check Japanese aggression with economic weapons. In July 1940 he stopped the export of aviation gasoline and scrap iron to Japan. To prevent a total breakdown of communications with Japan, he did not cut off oil, which Japan needed most. Japan depended upon the United States for 80 percent of its oil.

In July 1941, after Hitler invaded Russia, Japanese troops moved into French Indochina (now Vietnam), obviously preparing to attack the Dutch East Indies, where there were important oil wells. Roosevelt then cut off all oil shipments to Japan.

The oil embargo stunned the Japanese. Japan had no oil supply for their rapidly growing industries. They would either have to come to terms with the United States or strike for an independent supply. Since the United States insisted that Japan withdraw from China and Indochina, Japan decided to attack the United States.

Attack on Pearl Harbor

■ The Japanese planned a surprise air attack to destroy the American fleet stationed at **Pearl Harbor** in Hawaii. They believed that by the time the United States could rebuild its Pacific forces, Japan would have further expanded its control of the Far East. Then it would be able to defeat any American counterattack. The attack date was set for Sunday, December 7.

American intelligence experts had broken Japan's diplomatic code. Decoded radio messages indicated that war was near. As early as November 22 one dispatch from Tokyo revealed that "something was going to happen" if the United States did not lift the oil embargo and stop demanding that Japanese troops leave China.

On November 27 all American commanders in the Pacific were warned to expect a "surprise aggressive move" by Japan. The Americans thought the attack was coming in southeast Asia, possibly in the Philippines. Hawaii seemed beyond the range of Japanese forces. The commanders at Pearl Harbor, Admiral Husband E. Kimmel and General Walter C. Short, took precautions only against sabotage by Japanese secret agents in Hawaii.

By the early morning hours of December 7 the Japanese naval task force was in position about 200 miles (320 kilometers) north of the Hawaiian Islands. The aircraft carriers' crews sent their planes

Wide World Photos

off with shouts of "Banzai! Banzai!"—the Japanese battle cry which means "10,000 years!" The first wave of 183 planes headed for Pearl Harbor.

The lead pilots reached their target about 7:30 on a peaceful and quiet Sunday morning in Honolulu. On the ships some sailors were still asleep. Others were getting breakfast or lounging on deck. Many were on their way to church services. Some were getting ready to go ashore for a swim at Waikiki Beach. Admiral Kimmel and General Short had a date to play a game of golf.

At 7:55 the Japanese struck. Screaming dive bombers swooped down for the kill. Explosions shattered the air. Fortunately, the American aircraft carriers were all at sea. But seven battleships were lined up on Battleship Row in the harbor. The bombers came so low over these ships that sailors could see the faces of Japanese pilots as they released their bombs.

The destruction was terrible. The worst blow came when the

Never was the United States so surprised as by the Sunday morning attack on Pearl Harbor by the Japanese. Now the U.S. had to enter the war. Apparently the attack was anticipated, but no one knew when it would come—or with what force. Read on and then report on the extent of the destruction.

RESPONSES *(Continued)*
ticularly benefited as they gained jobs in industries in the West and Southwest.

Thinking Critically
1. Student accounts should be based on events that actually took place during the attack on Pearl Harbor.
2. Student explanations should show an understanding of the the Japanese Americans' point of view on the internment camps.

FOCUS/MOTIVATION:
MAKING CONNECTIONS
Prior Knowledge.
Ask students if they can recall a time before World War II when U.S. territory was attacked by a foreign nation. *(Students should mention the British attacks on Washington D.C., New Orleans, and the Northwest Territory during the War of 1812.)* Point out to students that the Japanese attack on Pearl Harbor was the first time since the War of 1812 that there was a direct attack by a foreign nation on American territory. This created such shock and outrage among the American people that Roosevelt had the support of almost the entire country when he asked Congress for a declaration of war. Students might be interested in noting that the Japanese also attacked the Aleutian Islands of Alaska, also U.S. territory.

The Japanese attack on Pearl Harbor was one of the most well-devised plans in the history of warfare. To carry off the attack a new intelligence network was created, new torpedoes and armor-piercing shells were designed, a way of refueling planes at sea was implemented, and an elaborate training program was developed.

Point of View

On December 9, the day after the president had asked for a declaration of war, he spoke to the nation in perhaps his saddest "Fireside Chat."

"We are now in this war. We are all in it—all the way. Every single man, woman, and child is a partner in the most tremendous undertaking of our American history. We must share together the bad news and the good news, the defeats and the victories—the changing fortunes of war."

Franklin D. Roosevelt

U.S.S. *Arizona* blew apart and sank, trapping more than a thousand men inside. The Japanese planes rained bombs on every ship in the harbor. They ranged up and down the coast, attacking airfields and barracks. In less than two hours 19 warships were sunk or disabled. Three others were damaged. One hundred and fifty planes were destroyed, most of them on the ground. Then the Japanese returned to their carriers. The task force sped back to Japanese waters. The attack on Pearl Harbor was by far the worst defeat the United States navy has suffered in all its history.

Americans were shocked and angered by the attack on Pearl Harbor. President Roosevelt went before Congress on December 8 to ask that war be declared on Japan. He called December 7, 1941, "a date which will live in infamy." He had the whole country behind him. Germany and Italy, in turn, carried out the terms of their Tripartite Pact and, on December 11, declared war on the United States.

The Home Front

The United States was much better prepared to fight World War II than it had been to fight the Great World War. Long before the attack on Pearl Harbor, Roosevelt had established councils to oversee the production and distribution of war matériel. After war was declared, similar boards were given broad powers to control the distribution of raw materials to manufacturers and to stop the production of many nonessential goods. The government rationed scarce foods, such as meat, butter, and sugar, to make sure that all citizens got their fair share.

The demand for weapons and supplies finally ended the Great Depression. American industry had slowly been climbing out of the depression, helped by European war needs. Now greatly expanded production was needed. Suddenly steel, aluminum, rubber, and other raw materials needed to make weapons were in extremely short supply. There was no serious shortage of gasoline, but gas was rationed in order to discourage unnecessary travel. Gasoline rationing also saved rubber by keeping drivers from wearing out their tires.

Many manufacturers shifted their plants from the production of consumer goods to weapons. A typical example was the producer of orange juice squeezers who made bullet molds during the war. The automobile companies, of course, turned out tanks and trucks, and airplanes too. The output of airplanes increased from less than 6,000 in 1939 to 96,000 in 1944.

Hundreds of thousands of new workers were needed to produce the tools of war. Unemployment ceased to be a national problem for the first time since 1929. Men and women flocked from farms, towns, and great cities to the East Coast shipyards, to the steel plants and former automobile factories of the Midwest, and to the aircraft plants of the West.

Margaret Bourke-White/Life Magazine © Time Warner, Inc.

The famous photographer Margaret Bourke-White composed unique and striking images of the war. Note the angle she used to show these women helping to build tanks in 1943. The women enjoyed knowing they could handle this "man's work."

About 6 million women were employed during the war. Songs ■ like "Rosie the Riveter" helped persuade women to take jobs traditionally held only by men. One woman remembered her job as a riveter and the pride and confidence it brought her:

> 66 I loved working at Convair [an aircraft factory]. I loved the challenge of getting dirty and getting into the work. I did one special riveting job, hand riveting that could not be done by machine. I worked on that job for three months, ten hours a day, six days a week, and slapped three-eighths- or three-quarter-inch rivets by hand that no one else would do. I didn't have that kind of confidence as a kid growing up, because I didn't have that opportunity. Convair was the first time in my life that I had the chance to prove that I could do something, and I did.[1] 99

[1]From *The Homefront: America During World War II* by Mark Jonathan Harris, et al.

Allied intelligence was superior to the German and Japanese intelligence from the beginning of the war. For example, the British "Ultra" operation succeeded in breaking the German army's Enigma code, which helped Britain win the Battle of Britain.

MULTICULTURAL PERSPECTIVES: USING HISTORICAL IMAGINATION

Have students imagine that they are either an African American or Hispanic American and are serving in the American armed forces during World War II. They are not pleased with the discrimination they are experiencing. Have them write letters to their representative or senator describing the unfair treatment and urging him or her to pass laws that would put an end to segregation in the U.S. military.

THE TUSKEGEE AIRMEN

The role of American air force personnel was crucial to Allied victory in World War II. Among those who contributed to the defeat of the Axis powers were African Americans known as the Tuskegee Airmen. Their record of achievement during the war is particularly impressive in view of the special difficulties they faced. They had to fight not only the enemy but another tough foe as well: racial prejudice.

Since World War I, African Americans in the armed forces had been segregated from whites and given low-level work. Many military leaders and officials in the War Department thought blacks incapable of mastering highly skilled jobs. They doubted the ability of blacks to perform bravely under fire. This prejudice was widespread at the time. But African American leaders, newspapers, and organizations such as the NAACP spoke out against racial bias in the armed forces. They won supporters in Congress who pressured the military to treat blacks fairly. Gradually, African Americans were given opportunities to prove themselves.

The air force experimented with training African Americans to fly fighter planes. The first unit was the 99th Fighter Squadron. The experiment took place at a base near Tuskegee Institute in Alabama, where an airfield already existed to train civilian pilots.

To the surprise of many top air force officials, the experiment succeeded. The 99th Fighter Squadron saw combat in Africa, France, Italy, Poland, Romania, Greece, and Germany. In its more than 200 escort missions in Europe, the squadron never lost a U.S. bomber to enemy fighters. Partly because of the 99th's example, schools for bombardiers and navigators were opened to blacks in 1943.

In 1944, the 99th became part of the newly formed 332nd Fighter Group, equipped with long-range fighter-bombers. Immediately, this unit began making a record for itself, in one month downing five German planes over Munich and sinking an enemy destroyer. They proved that blacks were capable of performing highly technical jobs under stress and of showing great courage in air battle.

In March 1945, the 332nd Fighter Group was awarded the Distinguished Unit Citation (the highest unit decoration) for its 1,600-mile roundtrip air attack on Berlin. By that time the group had flown 1,578 combat missions and had destroyed 261 enemy aircraft. Group members had received 95 Distinguished Flying Crosses, a Silver Star, a Legion of Merit, 2 Soldier Medals, 14 Bronze Stars, 744 Air Medals and Clusters, and 8 Purple Hearts. On May 6, 1988, a statue of a Tuskegee airman was erected to honor the men of the unit. Today it stands at the U.S. Air Force Academy in Colorado Springs. It was sculpted by Clarence L. Shivers, a former Tuskegee airman.

Permission by Branden Publishing, Boston

HISTORICAL SIDELIGHTS

① The G.I. Bill made it possible for many veterans to go to college who otherwise may not have had the opportunity to do so. This resulted in the founding of new community and state colleges needed to meet the demand of the growing number of college enrollments.

Movies pictured the wives and sweethearts of servicemen working at these jobs while their loved ones fought against the Germans and the Japanese. It was all so new and exciting for many. One woman, who was only 18 at the time, recalled her experience as a machinist in an airplane engine plant:

" I was very unsophisticated at the time, but I was very zealous, probably overzealous. I remember some of the older guys who had been there for years used to say, 'Hey kid, don't be in such a hurry!'

But I'd get into the thing and geared up for it and I'd just keep plugging away, measuring and grinding, measuring and grinding, and they'd say, 'Hey kid, take it easy.' . . .[1]"

The wartime labor shortage cemented the gains that organized labor had made under the New Deal. A **National War Labor Board** was established in 1942 to regulate wages and prevent labor disputes.

Farmers experienced boom times. The demand for food to feed American and Allied troops was enormous. Farm income more than doubled during the war. Farmers who had suffered during the 1920s and 1930s were soon able to pay off their mortgages, improve their property, and put aside savings too.

During the war Congress adopted the **withholding system** of payroll deductions for collecting income taxes. Employers withheld a percentage of their workers' pay and sent the money directly to the treasury. The withholding system made paying taxes a little less painful. It also supplied the government with a steady flow of funds and made evading taxes almost impossible.

High taxes on personal incomes (up to 94 percent) and on the profits of corporations helped persuade Americans that no one was benefiting too much from the war while soldiers were risking their lives overseas. To boost the morale of those in uniform, Congress passed the Serviceman's Readjustment Act of 1944. This **G.I. Bill of Rights** made low-cost loans available to veterans who wished to buy houses or start new businesses. It also provided money for expenses ① such as tuition and books for those who wished to resume their education after the war.

Suspicion of Japanese Americans

World War II had great popular support. Almost no one questioned the decision to fight the Axis powers. Assured of the solid backing of the people, the Roosevelt administration adopted a relaxed attitude toward freedom of speech in wartime. There was little persecution of German Americans as had occurred during the Great World War.

The one blot on the Roosevelt record of civil liberties was the

[1]From *Americans Remember the Home Front: An Oral History* by Roy Hoopes

MULTICULTURAL PERSPECTIVES: USING HISTORICAL IMAGINATION

Have students imagine that they are Japanese Americans who lived on the West Coast at the beginning of World War II. They and their family have been moved to an internment camp in the western United States. Have them write a series of diary entries to describe their life in the camp. They should be detailed in describing their physical surroundings, how they are treated by the authorities, how they personally feel about the situation, and what they think of their government's actions. Tell them to check in their school or public library for information on this subject, which should help them write their account.

PRIMARY SOURCE

Description of change: excerpted.

Rationale: excerpted to focus on a woman's remembrances of working in an airplane plant during the war.

RESOURCES

■ You rnay wish to have students complete Reading 52: "Margaret Takahashi Describes the Internment of Japanese Americans (1942)" in Volume II of *Eyewitnesses and Others.*

CHECKING UNDERSTANDING

Have students discuss how the American economy was converted from peacetime to wartime production. *(Before the U.S. became involved in the war, Roosevelt established councils to oversee the production and distribution of war materials. After war was declared, similar boards were given broad powers to control the distribution of raw materials to manufacturers and to stop the production of many nonessential goods. There was now a great demand for weapons and supplies. Industries such as steel, aluminum, and rubber expanded to meet the need for weapons. Many industries shifted their plants from the production of consumer goods to weapons. An example is the automobile industry, which began producing tanks and trucks instead of cars. Gasoline was rationed to guard against a shortage. A National War Labor Board was established to regulate wages and prevent labor disputes. Farmers experienced boom times as they met the demand to feed American and Allied troops. Congress adopted the withholding system of payroll deductions for collecting income taxes so that the government was supplied with a steady flow of funds.)*

National Archives

Along with most Japanese Americans, these two generations of the Mochida family, tagged for evacuation from their home in Hayward, California, would be interned until the war ended—even though many were U.S. citizens. Read some of the accounts by these victims on this page and the next.

■ treatment of Japanese Americans. About 112,000 lived on the West Coast. They were forced to move to **internment camps** in barren sections of the country. The government was afraid that some were disloyal and would try to interfere with the war effort and help Japan. Others were placed in the camps for their own protection.

The white population of the American West had always been suspicious of the Chinese and Japanese who settled there. Partly this was the typical dislike of immigrants with different customs. Partly it was a matter of racial prejudice. The suspicion was greatly increased by the sneak Japanese attack on Pearl Harbor. Many people were convinced that unless everyone of Japanese origin was cleared out of the Pacific Coast region, the Japanese would soon be bombing San Francisco.

There was absolutely no evidence that the Japanese Americans were less loyal than other Americans. Most of them had been born in the United States. Immigration from Japan had been ended by the so-called Gentlemen's Agreement of 1907. Nevertheless, all were forced to sell their homes and property and leave for the camps. One woman, a college student in Seattle, Washington, at the time of her internment, described a relocation camp:

  ❝ Camp Minidoka was located in the south-central part of Idaho, north of the Snake River. It was a semidesert region. When we arrived I could see nothing but flat prairies, clumps of greasewood shrubs, and jack rabbits. And, of

RESOURCES
■ You may wish to have students complete Reading 56: "A Black Tank Commander's Story (1940s)" in Volume II of *Eyewitnesses and Others.*

course, hundreds and hundreds of barracks, to house 10,000 of us.

Our home was one room in a large army-type barracks, measuring about 20 by 25 feet [6 by 7.5 meters]. The only furnishings were an iron pot-belly stove and cots.

Our first day in camp we were given a rousing welcome by a dust storm. We felt as if we were standing in a gigantic sand-mixing machine as the gale lifted the loose earth up into the sky, hiding everything. Sand filled our mouths and nostrils and stung our faces and hands like a thousand darting needles. . . .

Idaho summer sizzled on the average of 100 degrees [43 degrees Celsius]. For the first few weeks I lay on my cot from morning to night, not daring to do more than go to the mess hall three times a day. . . .

Winter in Minidoka was as intense an experience as summer had been. . . .[1]

Another victim of the internment remembered his confusion over what was happening to him and his family.

❝ I remember the pain of being labeled a 'dirty Jap' and a 'dangerous enemy.' For me, a Los Angeles teenager of 17, it was a time when my entire value system was thrown out of kilter. If we, good Christians and loyal American citizens, could be stripped of our civil rights, it seemed that all of the values and ideals I held most dear would need to be reexamined. . . .[2]❞

After the war many Americans regretted their treatment of Japanese Americans. In 1948 Congress passed an act to help those interned to recover part of the losses. Court decisions in the 1980s further awarded retribution to the families sent to the camps.

African Americans and Hispanic Americans in Wartime

African Americans also had a difficult time during the war. About 1 ■ million enlisted or were drafted. Black servicemen were expected to risk their lives for the country. Still they were kept in segregated units and frequently treated with disrespect by both officers and enlisted men. Yet by comparison with their treatment during earlier wars, there was some improvement. More black officers were commissioned. A number of blacks became pilots in the air force.

As during the Great World War, the labor shortage benefited

[1]From *Nisei Daughter* by Monica Stone
[2]From "Point of View: A Sorry Part of Our History" by Daniel Kuzuhara, from *The Chicago Tribune*, August 26, 1981

Point of View

Roosevelt's biographer writes of the decision to intern Japanese Americans.

❝During January the climate of opinion in California turned harshly toward fear, suspicion, intolerance. Clamor arose for mass evacuation and other drastic action. The causes of the change have long been studied and defy easy explanation. Partly it was the endless Japanese advance in the Pacific, combined with a spate of false alarms . . . of attacks on the coast, stories of secret broadcasting equipment, flashing signals, strange lights and the like. . . . But the main ingredient that fired and fueled the demand for "cleaning out the Japanese" was starkly obvious. The old racism—economic, social, and pathological—toward the Japanese on the West Coast simmered a few weeks after Pearl Harbor and then burst into flames.❞

James MacGregor Burns, 1970

RETEACHING STRATEGY
Students with Special Needs. Pair students who are having difficulty with students who are performing well. Have students reread the section titled "The Home Front," and then have the more proficient students ask the others the following questions:
1. Why were industries such as steel, aluminum, and rubber expanded? *(These products were needed to produce weapons.)*
2. Give an example of an industry that shifted from the production of consumer goods to weapons. *(the automobile industry, which began producing tanks and trucks instead of cars)*
3. Why was a National War Labor Board established? *(to regulate wages and prevent labor disputes)*
4. How was the government supplied with a steady flow of funds during the war? *(Congress adopted the withholding system of payroll deductions for collecting income taxes.)*

PRIMARY SOURCES
(Top) Description of change: excerpted and bracketed. *Rationale:* excerpted to focus on a woman's description of an internment camp during the war; bracketed words added to clarify meaning.
(Bottom) Description of change: excerpted. *Rationale:* excerpted to focus on the confusion experienced by a victim of an internment camp during the war.
(Point of View) Description of change: excerpted. *Rationale:* excerpted to focus on anti-Japanese attitudes.

Riots broke out in several American cities during the war when African Americans protested against discrimination. Federal troops were called into Detroit in 1943 to restore order following the deaths of 25 African Americans and 9 whites.

INDEPENDENT PRACTICE
Have students complete the Preview & Review activity at the beginning of the section.

CLOSURE
Point out to students that the U.S. was much better prepared to fight World War II than World War I because the government began mobilizing industry long before U.S. involvement. Also, most of the American people were behind the war effort.

HOMEWORK
Have students draw World War II patriotic posters. They may be posters designed to keep up the morale of the labor force, requests for volunteers, or reminders to keep wartime secrets ("Loose lips sink ships"). For examples, direct students to posters that appear in this chapter. You may wish to display the posters around the classroom or in the hallways of the school.

Gordon Coster/Life Magazine © Time Warner, Inc.

Asa Philip Randolph was a writer and editor of the Messenger. *He had planned a march on Washington in 1941 to demand jobs for blacks in defense industries. Roosevelt persuaded him not to protest because it would disrupt the war effort. After reading further and using historical imagination, determine which man you think had the stronger argument.*

UNITED WE WIN

Return to the Preview & Review on page 950.

black workers. Thousands got a chance to learn new skills and therefore earn higher wages. Yet racial discrimination did not end. For this reason, early in 1941 a black leader, A. Philip Randolph, decided to organize a march on Washington to protest the way blacks were being treated.

President Roosevelt feared that such a march would split public opinion at a time when national unity was essential. To persuade Randolph to cancel the march, he issued an executive order prohibiting racial discrimination in defense plants. This rule was enforced by a **Fair Employment Practices Committee.** Randolph then called off the march.

This did not mean that African Americans were satisfied with their treatment after 1941. Many whites resented the concessions Roosevelt had made. There was a good deal of racial trouble in the armed services and in industrial plants throughout the war years. In 1943 it erupted in riots involving attacks on blacks in New York City and Detroit. More and more African Americans were demanding their rights as members of a democratic society. It was clear that when the war ended, demands by blacks for fair treatment were sure to increase.

The situation for Hispanic Americans was similar. Almost 400,000 of them served in the armed forces during the war. A higher percentage saw combat duty overseas than any other ethnic minority. They also received more military medals. Yet like black soldiers and sailors, Hispanic Americans suffered discrimination. On the other hand, for many it was their first chance to experience life outside their neighborhoods. When they returned home, Hispanic Americans were determined to fight for a better life.

The war brought many new opportunities for Hispanic Americans on the home front despite a vicious riot against them in Los Angeles in 1943. Hispanic American women gained jobs in many industries, especially in the West and Southwest. In July 1942 the United States and Mexico signed a treaty that allowed **braceros,** Mexican farm workers, to enter temporarily and work in the United States. Their efforts helped keep up vital food production during the war.

A Move Toward Religious Toleration

The war had an important effect on religion in America. American society moved toward religious pluralism, or the acceptance of different religions. People from all denominations found themselves supporting the war. The open hatred for Jews led by Adolf Hitler and his Nazi followers shocked all Americans. People of various faiths sang *God Bless America* as they united in the struggle to win against their common enemy. By the end of the war the various religions had grown more tolerant of each other.

4. THE ALLIES REGAIN EUROPE

The Invasion of North Africa

The nations that fought the Axis powers in World War II were known as the **Allies.** Chief among the Allies were the United States, Great Britain, France, the Soviet Union, China, Australia, and Canada. Joint planning among the Allies eventually led to an overall war strategy. Stated simply it was "Europe first, then the Far East." Allied military strategists hoped to hold the line against further Japanese advances in the Pacific. Their first major effort would be to defeat Germany. By early 1942 Hitler controlled nearly all of Europe and most of North Africa as well.

In June 1942 President Roosevelt put General Dwight D. Eisenhower in command of American troops in Europe. "Ike" was a first-rate military planner. He also got on well with all kinds of people. Managing and directing the huge and complicated Allied war machine required diplomacy as much as military talent.

Frank Scherschel/Life Picture Service

The commanders of the Allied troops in North Africa, Eisenhower of the U.S., and Montgomery of Britain—"Ike" and "Monty"—showed the stuff generals are made of by presenting a united front to their troops despite personal differences. Why is this particularly important in all team efforts?

Preview & Review

Use these questions to guide your reading. Answer the questions after completing Section 4.
Understanding Issues, Events, & Ideas. Use the following terms to describe the Allied victory in Europe: Allies, Operation Torch, Battle of Kasserine Pass, Sicily, Operation Overlord, D-Day, Normandy, Battle of the Bulge, Bastogne, Berlin, V-E Day.
1. What was the Allies' overall war strategy?
2. In what ways was Operation Overlord a massive military operation?
3. Why did Roosevelt run for a fourth term?
4. What did the Germans hope to accomplish at the Battle of the Bulge? Why were they not successful?
5. Which allied nations marched on Berlin to end the war?
Thinking Critically. 1. Why do you think the author says that Churchill was mistaken when he called Italy "the soft underbelly of Europe"? Give reasons to support your answer. **2.** Imagine that you are a member of the American Third Army. Write a letter to your family, describing your impressions of General Patton.

The Allies Regain Europe   959

Albania, Algeria, Austria, Belgium, Bulgaria, Czechoslovakia, Denmark, part of Egypt, Estonia, Finland, France, Greece, Hungary, Latvia, Lithuania, Luxembourg, Libya, Morocco, Netherlands, Norway, Poland, Romania, part of the Soviet Union, and Tunisia

RESPONSES *(Continued)*
Thinking Critically

1. Students should mention that Churchill was mistakenly suggesting that Italy would be easy to conquer. However, the German army took control of Italy, making the conquest of this nation a long and bloody process.
2. Student letters should demonstrate that they have read a biography and other additional information on General Patton.

FOCUS/MOTIVATION:
MAKING CONNECTIONS
Prior Knowledge.

Begin a class discussion by asking students what the situation in Europe in the Great War was like when American troops arrived. *(It was a stalemate. German forces had been stopped short of Paris and did not control all of Europe.)* Ask how the situation in World War II was different. *(The Germans had conquered France and controlled virtually all of Europe.)* Point out that this meant that Allied strategy had to be completely different. The Allies had to "invade" Europe, choosing a point of attack and landing enough men and equipment to drive out the Germans, who were "dug in."

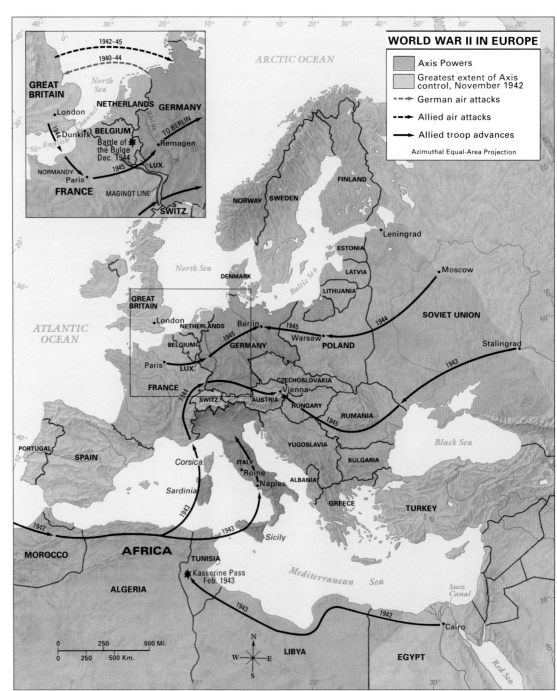

LEARNING FROM MAPS. *Allied plans called for the defeat of Germany first. German defenses were strong, but the Allies eventually won. What countries were under Axis control by November 1942?*

HISTORICAL SIDELIGHTS
① Rommel, nicknamed "the Desert Fox" during the African campaign, was later implicated in a plot to assassinate Hitler and was given the choice of a trial or death by poison. He chose poison.
② The British later defeated Rommel at El Alamein, in Egypt, keeping the Germans from vital Middle East oil supplies. Churchill saw El Alamein as a turning point in the war.

Allied leaders did not feel an invasion of Europe was possible until more troops and supplies had gathered in England. So the first major campaign that Eisenhower directed was **Operation Torch,** an attack on Morocco and Algeria in North Africa. On November 8, 1942, three separate forces, one from America, two from England, landed at three points in North Africa. About 110,000 troops, mostly American, were put ashore quickly and efficiently. There was little resistance, and Morocco and Algeria were soon in Allied control.

Then, in February 1943, the first real battle between the Americans and the Germans in North Africa took place at Kasserine Pass in Tunisia. The brilliant German general, Erwin Rommel, deployed ① his *Afrika Korps* tanks against American tanks in desert warfare. This **Battle of Kasserine Pass** ended in a standoff. But soon the ② Germans were driven out of the rest of North Africa.

The Italian Campaign

In July 1943 Eisenhower's forces invaded the Italian island of **Sicily,** the first step in an attack on what Prime Minister Churchill mistakenly called "the soft underbelly of Europe." In a little more than a month Sicily was conquered. The Italians then revolted against the dictator Mussolini and tried to surrender. Unfortunately, the German army in Italy simply took over control of the country. The Americans made a successful landing on the Italian mainland. But the conquest of Italy against fierce German resistance was a long and bloody process.

War correspondents kept Americans informed about the day-to-day events of the war, including the horrors of the battlefield. Ernie Pyle, one of the most outstanding war correspondents, spent months at the front with American troops, as did the famous photographer Margaret Bourke-White, the first woman war correspondent accredited by the U.S. army. American novelist John Steinbeck was also a war correspondent. He had this to say about the job:

66 What the correspondent really saw was dust and the nasty burst of shells, low bushes and slit trenches. He lay on his stomach, if he had any sense, and watched ants crawling among the little sticks of the sand dune. . . .

Then he saw an advance. Not straight lines of men marching into cannon fire, but little groups scuttling like crabs from bits of cover to other cover, while the deep chatter of machine guns sounded, . . .

He might have seen the splash of dirt and dust that is a shell burst, and a small Italian girl in the street with her stomach blown out, and he might have seen an American standing over a twitching body, crying. He probably saw many dead mules, lying on their sides, reduced to pulp. He saw the wreckage of houses, with torn beds hanging like shreds out of the spilled hole in a plaster wall. There were

Heinrich Hoffmann/Life Magazine © Time Warner, Inc.

"The Desert Fox," German General Erwin Rommel, effectively used his Afrika Korps to stall the Allies for months and keep them from landing on the European mainland.

RELATING HISTORY TO GEOGRAPHY
Divide the class into three groups. To reinforce the geographic themes of *location* and *movement,* have the first group prepare a map of North Africa showing the North African campaign, the second group a map of Italy showing the Italian campaign, and the third group a map of France showing the Normandy invasion and the subsequent drive to Paris and the Rhine. Students should indicate on the maps the names of the countries or territories involved, as well as the sites of important battles. They should also indicate who won the battles. Have each group choose a spokesperson to explain the military operation shown on the map. You may wish to hang the maps in the classroom.

USING HISTORICAL IMAGINATION
Have students imagine that they are German students of their age in early 1945. Tell them that U.S. bombers have been dropping bombs daily, ravaging the German countryside. In addition, fear grips the German population as the American, British, and French armies approach from the west, and the Soviet army approaches from the east. Have students write diary entries describing how they feel as their country is about to be invaded. Also, have them include a plan for what they intend to do once the Allied armies have arrived and what they intend to do when the war has finally ended.

The Allies Regain Europe   961

GUIDED INSTRUCTION
Ask what the Germans did toward the end of World War I when they realized they were losing the war. *(Students should mention that Germany asked for a truce.)* Ask students if Germany was taken over by Allied troops following its surrender. *(No, it was not.)* Point out that this was not the case at the end of World War II. American, British, French, and Soviet armies occupied Germany following its defeat. The Allies were determined to keep Germany from becoming a military power again, since they had to fight Germany in two world wars within a 30-year period. Then organize the class into cooperative learning groups. Tell students that they are delegates from one of the Allied countries who are meeting to draw up a peace treaty with Germany following the war. The peace treaty should include terms that they expect Germany and its allies to meet. You may want to remind them of the harsh terms contained in the Versailles Treaty following World War I, which made the German people bitter and paved the way for the rise of Hitler. Have each group choose a spokesperson to present their group's treaty to the class. Have the class vote on the treaty that they think is the best for all of the nations involved.

PRIMARY SOURCE
Description of change: excerpted and bracketed.
Rationale: excerpted to focus on John Steinbeck's description of what the correspondent experienced covering the war; bracketed words added to clarify meaning.

962

red carts and stalled vehicles of refugees who did not get away.

The stretcher-bearers come back from the lines, walking in off step, so that the burden will not be jounced too much, and the blood dripping from the canvas, brother and enemy in the stretchers, so long as they are hurt. And the walking wounded coming back with shattered arms and bandaged heads, the walking wounded struggling painfully to the rear.

He would have smelled the sharp cordite [gunpowder] in the air and the hot reek of blood if the going has been rough. The burning odor of dust will be in his nose and the stench of men and animals killed yesterday and the day before. . . .[1]**"**

D-Day

Now the long-awaited invasion of France, **Operation Overlord,** was about to begin. For months the United States and British air forces had been bombing industrial targets and railroad yards in Germany in preparation for the invasion. Now, on **D-Day**—June 6, 1944—4,000 landing craft and 600 warships carried 176,000 soldiers across the English Channel. They went ashore at several beaches along the coast of **Normandy,** a province in northern France. Naval guns and 11,000 planes bombarded the German defense positions. By nightfall 120,000 men were ashore. The reconquest of Europe had begun.

The Germans fought skillfully and bravely, but the Allies held the beaches. Reinforcements were brought over. In a single week 326,000 men, 50,000 tanks and trucks, and over 100,000 tons of supplies were ferried across the Channel. By the end of July more than 1 million Allied soldiers were safely landed and established on French soil.

The opening of this second front was truly the beginning of the end for the Germans. Until D-Day they had been able to concentrate their forces in eastern Europe, driving deep into the Soviet Union. Millions of Soviet soldiers and citizens died in the onslaught. Stalin became more and more frustrated as the Americans and British planned the assault. Each hesitation led to tremendous losses by Soviet forces and opened a rift among the Allies. But after D-Day the Germans had to fight on two fronts.

The Allies Enter Paris

In August, after fierce fighting, the American Third Army under General George S. Patton broke through the German defenses and raced toward Paris. Patton was a colorful and controversial general. He wore ivory-handled pistols more suitable to a cowboy than a

[1]From *Once There Was a War* by John Steinbeck

Eliot Elisofon/Life Magazine © Time Warner, Inc.

"God help me, but I love it," said General George S. Patton of war. What emotions he must have felt during Operation Overlord, shown in panorama on the facing page. In this huge military operation the Allies, on D-Day, June 6, 1944, invaded Normandy to begin their advance on Berlin.

CHECKING UNDERSTANDING
Have students summarize the role of the U.S. in the three major campaigns against the Axis powers in Europe. *(General Dwight Eisenhower was put in charge of the American troops in Europe. His first campaign was against the Germans in North Africa. The American and British forces met fierce resistance from the Germans, who were under the leadership of the brilliant General Erwin Rommel. However, the Allies were eventually able to drive the Germans out of North Africa. Eisenhower's forces invaded Sicily in 1943 and took the island within a month. However, the conquest of Italy was fierce, even though Mussolini was overthrown and the Italians attempted to surrender. The German army took control of Italy and fought desperately, making the campaign a long and bloody one. The invasion of France came on D-Day, June 6, 1944. This was a joint Allied effort involving 4,000 landing craft, 600 warships, and 176,000 men. They landed on the beaches of Normandy and fought fiercely until they established a beachhead. The Germans fought skillfully but were unable to push the invaders back. Reinforcements were brought over, and the reconquest of Europe began.)*

RETEACHING STRATEGY
Students with Special Needs.
Organize students into cooperative learning groups. Have them reread the sections titled "The Invasion of North Africa," "The Italian Campaign," and "D-Day," and have them match the following campaigns with the sentences that best describe it:

(a) North African Campaign
(b) Italian Campaign
(c) Normandy Invasion

1. This involved fierce and bloody fighting because the German army took control and fought desperately. *(b)*
2. This was General Dwight Eisenhower's first action as commander of the American troops in Europe. *(a)*
3. The American and British forces met fierce resistance from the Germans, who were under the leadership of the brilliant General Erwin Rommel. *(a)*
4. This was a joint Allied effort involving 4,000 landing craft, 600 warships, and 176,000 men. *(c)*
5. Eisenhower's forces invaded Sicily in 1943 as their first step in this effort. *(b)*
6. This occurred on June 6, 1944, when Allied troops landed on the northern coast of France and began the reconquest of Europe. *(c)*

lieutenant general. He insisted that all his soldiers, in or out of combat, wear a combat helmet and tie. He once slapped one battle-weary soldier because he thought he was a coward seeking to avoid combat. But Patton had a first-rate military mind. He was a master of tank warfare. Troops under General Patton's command moved quickly and decisively. They won victories.

Allied troops entered Paris amid great rejoicing in late August. By the end of September almost all of France was liberated. Everyone expected that the invasion of Germany would soon follow.

The Election of 1944

With victory in sight Roosevelt had to decide whether to run for a fourth term in 1944. He should not have done so because he was in very poor health. He had a bad heart, high blood pressure, and other physical ailments. Still, he was determined to bring the war to a victorious conclusion. The need for a new world organization to replace the League of Nations was also on his mind.

The president was renominated by the Democrats without opposition. Senator Harry Truman of Missouri was chosen as his running mate. The Republican candidate was Governor Thomas E. Dewey of New York. Dewey was not a particularly effective campaigner, but no one could have defeated the popular Roosevelt on the eve of victory in the war. The election was never in doubt. The popular vote was 25.6 million for Roosevelt, 22 million for Dewey. The electoral count was 432 to 99.

The Battle of the Bulge

In December 1944 the Allied armies were poised along the German border from Holland to Switzerland. On December 16, before the Allies could march, Hitler threw his last reserves—250,000 men—into a desperate counterattack. The Germans hoped to break through the Allied line and drive on to the Belgium port of Antwerp. That would split the Allied force in two.

The German attack was a total surprise. Within ten days the Germans had driven a wedge, or bulge, 50 miles (80 kilometers) deep into the Allied lines. This attack was called the **Battle of the Bulge.** American troops of the 101st Airborne Division were surrounded at the important road junction of **Bastogne.** The Germans demanded that the American commander, General Anthony C. McAuliffe, surrender his troops. "Nuts!" replied the general. Bastogne was held and the German advance stopped.

Elsewhere along the bulge every available American soldier, including platoons of black volunteers, were thrown against the German surge. For the first time white and black soldiers fought side by

① Upon the death of Roosevelt, President Truman said, "His fellow countrymen will sorely miss his fortitude and faith and courage in the time to come. The peoples of the earth who love the ways of freedom and hope will mourn for him."

Robert Capa/Magnum Photos

side, breaking the barriers of segregation that still existed in the armed services. By January the bulge had been flattened. The Allies were now ready to storm into Germany.

The Battle of the Bulge was Hitler's last attempt to break through Allied lines in Belgium. His troops succeeded in driving a wedge, or bulge, in the lines, but the Allies held.

Victory in Europe

The Battle of the Bulge shattered Hitler's hope of winning the war. The end came swiftly. In March 1945 Allied forces crossed the Rhine River into Germany. By the middle of April American, British, and French troops were within 50 miles (80 kilometers) of **Berlin,** the German capital. Russian armies were approaching the city from the east. On April 25 American and Russian troops met at the Elbe River. Five days later Adolf Hitler killed himself in his bombproof air raid shelter in Berlin. On May 8 Germany surrendered. This became known as **V-E Day,** for Victory in Europe.

American joy at the ending of the war was restrained, for President Roosevelt was dead. On April 12, while working on a speech ① at his winter home in Warm Springs, Georgia, he had died of a massive stroke. The burdens of the presidency were now upon the shoulders of Harry S Truman. 🖮

INDEPENDENT PRACTICE
Have students complete the Preview & Review activity at the beginning of the section.

CLOSURE
Point out to students that Hitler left the German people a legacy of guilt and shame. In many ways later generations of Germans still grappled with the horrors of the Hitler era, especially as the move to reunify Germany gained momentum.

HOMEWORK
Have students prepare a report on the experiences of an American soldier in Europe during or after the Normandy invasion. Their report may focus on a famous person, such as General Eisenhower, or on a common soldier. For information on this subject, tell students to look in the public library for memoirs of military personnel who fought in Europe during World War II.

Return to the Preview & Review on page 959.

The Allies Regain Europe   965

SECTION 5

PREVIEW & REVIEW RESPONSES

Understanding Issues, Events, & Ideas.

Descriptions should demonstrate an understanding of the terms used.

1. MacArthur pledged to return to the Philippines. October 1944
2. The Joint Chiefs of Staff decided on a two-pronged campaign. MacArthur was to clean out the Bismarck Islands and head for the Philippine Islands, and Nimitz was to attack the Japanese-held islands in the central Pacific and press on toward Japan.
3. They resisted stubbornly and fought desperately for every inch of ground they held.
4. Photographs of survivors of the Bataan Death March, the liberation of the concentration camps of the Holocaust, and of the barren landscapes of Hiroshima and Nagasaki brought home the horrors of war clearer than ever before.

Thinking Critically

Student conversations should show an understanding of both sides of the issue regarding the use of the atomic bomb.

PRIMARY SOURCE

Description of change: excerpted and bracketed.

Rationale: excerpted to focus on an army nurse's description of a hospital in the Philippines just before the Japanese takeover; bracketed words added to clarify meaning.

966

Preview & Review

Use these questions to guide your reading. Answer the questions after completing Section 5.

Understanding Issues, Events, & Ideas. Describe the Allied victory in the Pacific, using the following words: Philippine Islands, Battle of the Coral Sea, Battle of Midway, island-hopping, Guadalcanal, Battle of Leyte Gulf, Iwo Jima, Okinawa, kamikaze, atomic bomb, Manhattan Project, Hiroshima, Nagasaki, V-J Day.

1. What had General MacArthur pledged in 1942? When did he keep his pledge?
2. What was the American strategy in the Pacific? What was General MacArthur's role? What was Admiral Nimitz's role?
3. How did Japanese troops in the Pacific resist the American advance?
4. How did the Second World War bring home the horrors of war to people around the world?

Thinking Critically. Write a conversation between two people. One person should argue in support of the atomic bombing of Hiroshima and Nagasaki. The other person should argue against the bombing.

5. THE ALLIES WIN IN THE PACIFIC

The War in the Pacific

The war against Japan was slowly approaching its climax. The strategy, it will be recalled, was first to prevent further Japanese advances. After Pearl Harbor the Japanese had conquered the **Philippine Islands,** capturing large numbers of American troops. An army nurse described the last days before the Japanese took over:

❝ Conditions at Hospital Number 1 were not too good during the last few weeks we spent there. Patients were flooding in. We increased from 400 to 1,500 cases in two weeks time. Most of them had serious wounds, but nine out of ten patients had malaria or dysentery besides.

We were out of quinine [a drug to fight malaria]. There were hundreds of gas gangrene cases, and our supply of vaccine had run out months before. There were no more sulfa drugs. There weren't nearly enough cots, so triple-decker beds were built from bamboo, with a ladder at one end so we could climb up to take care of the patients. They had no blankets or mattresses.

There was almost no food except carabao [water buffalo]. We had all thought we couldn't eat carabao, but we did. Then came mule, which seemed worse, but we ate that too. . . .[1]❞

■ General Douglas MacArthur, the commander in the Philippines, was evacuated by submarine on the order of President Roosevelt before his troops surrendered. ''I shall return,'' he promised.

Japan, confident of victory, next prepared to invade Australia. But in the great naval **Battle of the Coral Sea** in May 1942 the Japanese fleet was badly damaged. The Japanese were forced to give up their planned invasion.

Then, in June 1942, a powerful Japanese fleet advanced toward American-owned Midway Island west of Hawaii. The plan was to force a showdown with the American Pacific fleet. But the Japanese ships never reached Midway. The Americans broke their secret codes and spy planes spotted their movements. On June 4 dive bombers from American aircraft carriers pounded the Japanese vessels. They sank four Japanese aircraft carriers and destroyed 275 Japanese planes. Again the Japanese fleet had to withdraw. This **Battle of Midway** gave the United States control of the central Pacific.

[1]From ''An Army Nurse at Bataan and Corregidor,'' as told by Annalee Jacoby in *History in the Writing* by Gordon Carroll

SUGGESTED CAPTION RESPONSE
The Japanese controlled thousands of islands in the Pacific. Capturing and maintaining control of all of these would have been too costly, both in lives and in time.

RESOURCES

■ You may wish to have students complete Reading 51: "A Hawaiian American in the Pacific War (1941)" in Volume II of *Eyewitnesses and Others.*

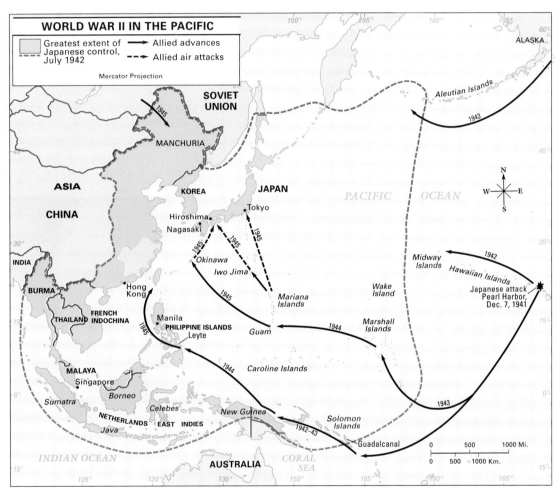

FOCUS/MOTIVATION: MAKING CONNECTIONS
Student Experiences.
Ask students to imagine what life would be like for the people who survive a nuclear bombing. *(Students should mention that life would be reduced to a daily struggle for survival. Exposed foodstuffs, water, soil, and air would all be contaminated with radiation, making even basic survival extremely difficult.)* Point out to students that since the atomic bomb was dropped on Japan, ending World War II, humans have had to live with the knowledge of the destructive capabilities of this dreadful weapon. Tell them to keep this in mind as they read this section.

The Pacific Campaign

As victory in Europe seemed assured, the Allies turned their full attention to Japan. To defeat Japan, the strategists believed, the Japanese islands must be invaded. But how to get there? The Japanese controlled thousands of small islands in the Pacific—the Bismarcks, the Carolines, the Gilberts, the Solomons, the Marshalls, and others. Capturing all these islands would be too costly, both in lives and in time.

General MacArthur, the commander of the army forces in the Pacific, was set on returning to the Philippines. He favored a sweep through the Bismarck Islands to the Philippine Sea. The Philippines could then be regained and the captive American soldiers set free.

Admiral Chester W. Nimitz, commander of the Pacific fleet,

LEARNING FROM MAPS. *After defeating the Germans, the Allies turned their full attention to the Pacific. To defeat the Japanese, the Allies had been using a tactic called "island hopping." This called for driving the Japanese from some islands while bypassing others. Why does this seem like a good strategy in the Pacific?*

The Allies Win in the Pacific   967

argued for advancing directly toward Japan itself. The military planners in Washington, the Joint Chiefs of Staff, decided on a two-pronged campaign. MacArthur was to clean out the Bismarcks and then head for the Philippines. Nimitz would attack the Japanese-held islands in the central Pacific and press on toward Japan.

From Guadalcanal to Leyte

The Allied strategy was called **island hopping.** Allied forces would seize key Japanese-held islands while bypassing others that were then isolated. First the Solomon Islands had to be captured. Early in August 1942 American troops landed on three islands of the group. Two of the islands were captured quickly. But on **Guadalcanal** Island some of the hardest fighting of the Pacific war took place. For six months the Americans struggled slowly ahead through dense jungles. The Japanese troops resisted stubbornly. They were ready to die to the last man for their country. Japanese sharpshooters tied themselves high in trees. Machine gun teams set up their weapons in caves from which retreat was impossible. Before Guadalcanal was finally reclaimed in February 1943, 20,000 Japanese were killed.

Fleet Admiral Chester W. Nimitz was made commander of the Pacific Fleet after Pearl Harbor.

As Nimitz's forces advanced, every island they attacked was defended with equal determination. The Japanese fought desperately for every inch of ground. When American marines went

LEARNING FROM TABLES. *Most people believed there would never be a war as destructive as the Great War. They were wrong. How do the statistics in this table compare with those from the Great War in the table on page 841?*

MILITARY DEATHS IN WORLD WAR II				
ALLIES			**AXIS**	
Soviet Union	7,500,000		Germany	3,500,000
China	2,200,000		Japan	1,219,000
United States	405,399		Italy*	307,448
Great Britain	329,208		Others	912,000
France	210,671			
Others	300,000			
Total	10,945,278		Total	5,938,448
		Total	16,883,726	

*Italian losses: 294,297 as member of Axis;
13,151 against Germany after Sept. 8, 1943

ashore on the island of Tarawa, they were opposed by 4,500 troops. Only 17 of these Japanese soldiers were taken prisoner. All the rest ① died in battle.

To the south MacArthur's army was carrying out its part of the plan. In October 1944 it recaptured the Philippines. In the **Battle of Leyte Gulf** the navy destroyed the last major Japanese fleet. Now the United States had complete control of Philippine waters.

Iwo Jima and Okinawa

The Allies next secured the bases needed for the invasion of Japan. The marines first fought hard to capture the tiny island of **Iwo Jima,** 750 miles (1,200 kilometers) south of Japan. The fight to capture Iwo Jima was bitter. On February 23 the victorious marines reached the top of Mount Suribachi, a volcano on the southern tip of the island.

Island-hopping forces moved determinedly across the Pacific as they closed in on Japan. Here American fighters signal the conquest of this small island by hanging an American flag between tropical palm trees.

GUIDED INSTRUCTION: USING HISTORICAL IMAGINATION
Begin a class discussion by pointing out to students that President Truman was confronted with many major decisions when he became president upon the death of Franklin Roosevelt. Ask students why Truman might have felt overwhelmed when he took over as president. *(Students should mention that the United States was fighting a world war on two fronts. Truman was suddenly responsible for decisions that would bring an end to the war, such as whether or not to use the atomic bomb. He was also responsible for decisions regarding the peace that would follow.)* Ask students if they would like to have been Truman at that time. Why or why not? *(Answers will vary.)*

The Allies Win in the Pacific   969

HISTORICAL SIDELIGHTS
① Nearly 20,000 American marines were either killed
or wounded at Iwo Jima.

**MULTICULTURAL
PERSPECTIVES: USING
HISTORICAL IMAGINATION**

Have students imagine that
they are Japanese citizens in
early August 1945. Tell them
that the American planes from
airfields on Okinawa have been
regularly bombing Japanese
cities, leaving them in ruins.
Thousands of Japanese have
died defending places like Tarawa, Iwo Jima, and Okinawa
almost to the last person. Many
of their fellow citizens are willing to defend the Japanese
mainland in the same way
should the Americans invade
it. The American president has
issued an ultimatum, warning
their country that if they do not
surrender, something horrible
is going to happen. Have students write a letter to the officials of the Japanese government either urging them to
surrender to the U.S. or to continue fighting. Remind students that they are unaware of
the existence of the atomic
bomb. Students should combine historical imagination
with historical facts and persuasive skills in preparing their
letters. You may wish to have
students read their letters to
the class.

*Driven from the Philippines early in
the war, in 1944 Douglas MacArthur
returned as he had promised. Soon the
U.S. had complete control of the Philippines and surrounding waters.*

① As they crawled toward the rim of the crater, they came under fire
from Japanese soldiers dug in on the other side of the mountain. A
fierce fight developed. To rally his men one marine picked up an iron
pipe, bound a small American flag he was carrying to it, and held it
for the men to see. Later another marine arrived with a larger flag
and pole. The victorious marines proudly planted it at the top of the
mountain. A photographer took a picture of this famous second flag
raising over Iwo Jima. That picture has become the most reproduced
image—in paintings and scupltures—of the Second World War.

Two weeks after taking Iwo Jima, American troops went ashore
on **Okinawa,** a much larger island only 350 miles (560 kilometers)
from Japan. Before the battle for Okinawa ended in June 1945, the
Japanese had suffered over 100,000 casualties, the Americans over
11,000.

The United States now had complete control of both air and sea.
From airfields throughout the Pacific, American planes bombed Japan
mercilessly. American battleships and cruisers moved in closer to
pound industrial targets with their heaviest guns. Soon every important Japanese city was a smoking ruin.

As American forces neared Japan, they were repeatedly pestered
by **kamikaze** attacks. These suicide pilots, who crashed their planes

Joe Rosenthal/Wide World Photos

into the approaching American fleet, had pledged their lives to protect Japan. They took their name from a divine wind believed to have foiled an invasion of Japan centuries before.

The Atomic Bomb

Victory was now certain. Although Japanese leaders had begun trying to arrange a surrender, progress was extremely slow. Military experts expected that Japan would have to be invaded, at tremendous cost. Japanese soldiers had demonstrated repeatedly that they would fight every battle to the last man. Some authorities believed that the United States would suffer 1 million more casualties before Japan was conquered.

This was the situation President Truman faced when he learned that American scientists had produced a new and terrible weapon—

All Americans take pride in this moment as the flag is raised on Mt. Suribachi on the island of Iwo Jima. Associated Press photographer Joe Rosenthal won a Pulitzer Prize in 1945 for this picture. It served as a model for the United States Marine Corps War Memorial in Washington, D.C.

STRATEGIES FOR SUCCESS

EVALUATING DECISIONS

Many key decisions made by world leaders have worldwide consequences, both at the time and for the future. Such decisions are debated endlessly by historians. By using historical imagination to understand the situation at the time and analyzing the consequences, it is possible to evaluate the decision. This evaluation will help you learn to make better decisions.

How to Evaluate Decisions

To evaluate decisions, follow these steps.
1. **Determine the nature of the decision to be made.** Use research and historical imagination to take into account the conditions that existed at the time the decision was made.
2. **Identify the alternatives available.** Note the possible choices the decision maker had.
3. **List the risks and benefits of each alternative.** Note the short-term and long-term effects of each choice.
4. **Weigh the costs and benefits of each alternative.** Compare the possible benefits and costs. Don't overlook possible future benefits or costs.
5. **Evaluate the decision.** Determine if, all things considered, the decision was a good one or a bad one. Remember that the long-range effects may not have been evident at the time the decision was made.

Applying the Strategy

Read the following paragraphs about Truman's decisions concerning the end of World War II.

Victory was now certain. Still, military experts expected that the cost of invading Japan would be enormous. Japanese soldiers had demonstrated repeatedly that they would fight every battle to the last man. Some authorities believed that the United States would suffer 1 million more casualties before Japan was conquered.

This was the situation President Truman faced when he learned that American scientists had produced a new and terrible weapon—the atomic bomb. . . . President Truman had to make an extremely difficult decision. Dropping an atomic bomb on a Japanese city would kill thousands of innocent civil-

ians. He also feared use of the terrible force would turn international sentiment against the United States. Yet Truman felt that he had no choice. Without the atomic bomb far more people would be killed before the war was over. He believed that the only way to convince the proud Japanese that further resistance was useless was to use this revolutionary bomb against them.

Let's evaluate Truman's decision making. What was the nature of the decision to be made? Truman had to decide how to end the war as quickly and with as few losses as possible. What were his alternatives? He could invade Japan. Or he could use the terrible new atomic bomb. What were the risks and benefits of each alternative? Invading Japan might cost 1 million more American casualties. But it followed the practices of conventional warfare. Using the atomic bomb might end the war much more quickly, sparing hundreds of thousands of lives on both sides. But unleashing the horrible destruction might turn international furor against the United States. How do the risks and benefits of each alternative compare? Truman chose to use the bomb to end the war quickly, thus avoiding a bloody invasion of Japan. The following paragraphs describe the situation further.

On August 6, 1945, in one blinding flash 75,000 people died. Another 100,000 were injured. Another atomic bomb was dropped on the city of Nagasaki. The radioactivity released by the explosions caused hundreds of persons to die horrible, lingering deaths. Later many children were born deformed because of radioactive damage suffered by their parents. Was there no way that the Japanese could have been shown the power of the bomb without using it on human beings?

On the other hand, the bomb may have saved lives— Japanese as well as American. Far more people would have died in an all-out invasion than died in the atomic blasts. There was also the hope that a demonstration of the horrors of atomic warfare would convince the entire world that such a weapon must never be used again. So far none has.

Do you think President Truman made the correct decision? Support your position.

For independent practice, see Practicing the Strategy on pages 976–77.

the **atomic bomb.** On orders from President Roosevelt, scientists had been working on the top-secret **Manhattan Project** since early 1942. Now they had produced a weapon with the explosive force of 20,000 tons of TNT. This tremendous power was released by the breaking ① of the chemical bonds that held together the atoms of uranium and plutonium, two highly radioactive elements.

President Truman had to make an extremely difficult decision. Dropping an atomic bomb on a Japanese city would kill thousands of innocent civilians. He also feared use of the terrible force would turn international sentiment against the United States. Yet Truman felt that he had no choice. Without the atomic bomb far more people might be killed before the war was over. He believed that the only way to convince the proud Japanese that further resistance was useless was to use this revolutionary bomb against them.

Bettmann Newsphotos

The mushroom cloud of nuclear destruction rose twice over wartime Japan. Such a sight recalls the address to the UN by Pope Paul VI: "Ne jamais plus la guerre": "Never again war."

CHECKING UNDERSTANDING
Have students discuss each of the following Pacific battles, and how they led to Allied victory.

Coral Sea: *(The Japanese were attempting to invade Australia. However, their fleet was badly damaged here, and they had to give up their planned invasion.)*

Midway: *(The Japanese were advancing toward American-owned Midway Island when radar detected their movements. American dive bombers pounded Japanese vessels. Japanese losses were heavy, and their fleet had to withdraw.)*

Guadalcanal: *(It was here that some of the hardest fighting in the Pacific took place. For six months the Americans struggled slowly against fierce-fighting Japanese troops, who were determined to fight to the last man. 20,000 Japanese soldiers lost their lives.)*

Leyte Gulf: *(Here the U.S. navy destroyed the last major Japanese fleet, giving the U.S. complete control of Philippine waters.)*

Iwo Jima: *(Fierce fighting developed between the American marines and Japanese soldiers who dug in on the side of a volcano. It was during this battle that a photographer took the famous picture of the marines raising the American flag.)*

Okinawa: *(This was an island located 350 miles [560 kilometers] from the Japanese mainland. After bitter fighting, the Americans overtook the island, giving them complete control over both air and sea in the Pacific.)*

① Leaflets were dropped from American planes on the city of Hiroshima warning of the impending devastation if Japan did not surrender. Tragically these leaflets were not taken seriously.

RESOURCES

■ You may wish to have students complete Reading 54: "John Hersey Records the Japanese Experience of Hiroshima (1945)" in Volume II of *Eyewitnesses and Others.*

RETEACHING STRATEGY
Students with Special Needs.
Pair students who are having difficulty with students who are performing well. Have the more proficient students help the others match the following:

(a) Coral Sea
(b) Midway
(c) Guadalcanal
(d) Leyte Gulf
(e) Iwo Jima
(f) Okinawa

1. At this battle the U.S. navy destroyed the last major Japanese fleet, giving the U.S. control of the Philippine waters. *(d)*
2. When the Americans took this island, it gave them complete control over both air and sea in the Pacific. *(f)*
3. The Japanese attempted a showdown with the American Pacific fleet and advanced toward this American-owned island in June 1942. The Japanese lost, and their fleet had to withdraw. *(b)*
4. It was during this battle that a photographer took the famous picture of the marines raising the American flag. *(e)*
5. The Japanese were attempting to invade Australia, but their fleet was badly damaged at this battle, and they had to give up their planned invasion. *(a)*
6. The Allied strategy of island-hopping landed American troops on this island in August 1942. During the fighting 20,000 Japanese soldiers died. *(c)*

INDEPENDENT PRACTICE
Have students complete the Preview & Review activity at the beginning of the section.

J.R. Eyerman/Life Picture Service

The aftermath of the bombing of Nagasaki shocked all who saw it. Is it any wonder that the Japanese surrendered when they witnessed such terrible destruction?

On August 6, 1945, an American bomber dropped the first atomic ① bomb on Hiroshima, a city of 344,000. In one blinding flash 75,000 people died. Another 100,000 were injured. John Hersey collected accounts such as the following from the survivors of the explosion.

■ ❝ Then a tremendous flash of light cut across the sky. Mr. Tanimoto has a distinct recollection that it traveled from east to west, from the city toward the hills. It seemed a sheet of sun. . . . Mr. Tanimoto took four or five steps and threw himself between two big rocks in the garden. He . . . did not see what happened. He felt a sudden pressure, and then splinters and pieces of board and fragments of tile fell on him. . . .

As Mrs. Nakamura stood watching her neighbor, everything flashed whiter than any white she had ever seen. . . .

The reflex of a mother set her in motion toward her children.
She had taken a single step . . . when something picked her
up and she seemed to fly into the next room over the raised
sleeping platform, pursued by parts of her house.

Timbers fell around her as she landed, and a shower of
tile pommelled her; everything became dark, for she was
buried. The debris did not cover her deeply. She rose and
freed herself. She heard a child cry, "Mother, help me!,"
and saw her youngest—Myeko, the five-year-old—buried
up to her breast and unable to move. As Mrs. Nakamura
started to frantically claw her way toward the baby, she
could see or hear nothing of her other children.[1]

[1]From *Hiroshima* by John Hersey

When the Japanese still hesitated to surrender, another atomic bomb
was dropped on the city of **Nagasaki.** This convinced the Japanese.
On September 2, **V-J Day** (Victory in Japan), the Japanese signed
terms of surrender. World War II was finally over.

The terrible destruction caused by the atom bombing of Hiroshima and Nagasaki has resulted in a long controversy about President Truman's decision. Even today, people disagree on whether or
not the president did the right thing. Aside from the immediate loss
of so many lives, the radioactivity—emissions harmful to humans—
released by the atomic explosions caused hundreds of people to die
horrible, lingering deaths. Later many children were born deformed
because of radioactive damage suffered by their parents. Was there
no way that the Japanese could have been shown the power of the
bomb without using it on human beings?

The bomb may have saved lives—Japanese as well as American.
Most people thought that far more Americans would have died in an
all-out invasion. There was also the hope that a demonstration of
the horrors of atomic warfare would convince the entire world that
such a weapon must never be used again. So far none has.

The final judgment on President Truman's decision lies in the
future. It depends upon what all of us and all our descendants do
with our knowledge of the atomic bomb and the dreadful consequences of atomic explosions.

The Horrors of War

The Second World War made Americans see how horrible war really
is. Photographs of survivors of the Bataan Death March in the Philippines, of the liberation of the concentration camps of the Holocaust, and of the barren landscapes of Hiroshima and Nagasaki made
the point clearer than ever before. People around the world began to
feel that the world could not survive another global war. 🖳

Point of View

A joint study by Japanese and
Americans a few months after
World War II revealed the extent
of the atomic bombing of Hiroshima.

"In the case of an atomic
bombing . . . a commu-
nity does not merely re-
ceive an impact; the com-
munity itself is destroyed.
Within 2 kilometers of
the atomic bomb's hypo-
center all life and prop-
erty were shattered,
burned, and buried under
ashes. The visible forms
of the city where people
once carried on their
daily lives vanished without a trace. The destruc-
tion was sudden and
thorough; there was vir-
tually no chance to es-
cape. . . . Citizens who
had lost no family mem-
bers in the holocaust were
as rare as stars at sunrise.
. . ."

From *The Making of
the Atomic Bomb,*
Richard Rhodes, 1986

Return to the Preview & Review on
■ page 966.

Thinking Critically
1. Student handbills should demonstrate an understanding of either the pacifists' or conscientious objectors' point of view.
2. Students should use their historical imaginations in preparing their presentation of the flag raising on Iwo Jima.

3. Student decisions should be supported by historical facts.

REVIEW RESPONSES
Chapter Summary
Paragraphs will vary but should be evaluated on the logic of student arguments.

Reviewing Chronological Order
3, 2, 1, 5, 4

Understanding Main Ideas
1. They sympathized with victims of totalitarian aggression but favored isolationism. They kept the U.S. from getting involved.
2. 1937: Roosevelt refused to apply the neutrality law; 1939: Congress agreed to a cash-and-carry policy; 1940: Congress voted on a draft for military; 1941: Lend-Lease Act passed; 1941: Congress authorized arming of U.S. merchant ships
3. Axis: Germany, Italy, Japan; Allies: U.S., Great Britain, France, Russia
4. Although still discriminated against, many were able to find jobs. Many Japanese Americans were sent to internment camps.
5. Operation Overlord and D-Day were major steps in the Allied victory in Europe, and the Coral Sea and Midway were major Allied victories which turned the tide against Japan.

Writing About History
Students should use historical imagination in preparing their letters.

Practicing the Strategy
1. In 1941, after the Japanese invaded French Indochina, Roosevelt imposed an oil embargo on Japan. Since the U.S. insisted that Japan withdraw from China and

CHAPTER 26 REVIEW

1920	1925	1930

1922
Mussolini takes power in Italy

1931
Japan seizes Manchuria

1932
Roosevelt elected president

1933
Hitler becomes dictator of Germany

Chapter Summary
Read the statements below. Choose one, and write a paragraph explaining its importance.
1. Despite the rise of totalitarian governments, most Americans believed in isolationism.
2. Hitler insisted Jews were an inferior people. He set up concentration camps for the Jews and murdered nearly 6 million of them. This genocide is called the Holocaust.
3. Roosevelt sought ways to check the aggressors without becoming involved in a shooting war.
4. Hitler's war machine invaded Poland, starting World War II.
5. Japanese bombing of Pearl Harbor brought the United States into World War II.
6. Allied efforts focused on Europe first. By early 1945 Allied armies had retaken Europe and Germany had surrendered.
7. In the Pacific the Allies then island-hopped toward Japan. Atomic bombs dropped on Japan in 1945 ended the war.
8. The horrors of World War II made many people realize that global war must now be avoided.

Reviewing Chronological Order
Number your paper 1-5. Then study the time line above and place the following events in the order in which they happened by writing the first next to 1, the second next to 2, and so on.
1. V-E Day
2. Lend-Lease Act
3. Germany invades Poland
4. V-J Day
5. Atomic bomb dropped on Hiroshima

Understanding Main Ideas
1. What was the reaction of most Americans to the aggressions of the 1930s? How were the neutrality acts part of this reaction?
2. Describe U.S. actions that showed the step-by-step movement away from the neutrality of the 1930s to open aid for the Allies by 1941.
3. By 1942 which were the major Axis and Allied countries?
4. How were minorities affected by World War II, including Japanese Americans?

5. Explain the importance of Operation Overlord and the battles of the Coral Sea and Midway.

Thinking Critically
1. **Synthesizing.** You are either a pacifist or a conscientious objector during World War II. Write a handbill explaining why you think war is wrong.
2. **Creating.** Create a poster, poem, song, or short story about the historic raising of the American flag on the island of Iwo Jima.
3. **Evaluating.** Choose either the topic of Japanese internment or the use of the atomic bomb. Discuss whether you think the correct decision was made by the United States. If you think the decision was incorrect, suggest an alternate course of action. Support your position.

Writing About History
With your classmates, use historical imagination to write letters about the war. Some of you might write letters home to your families from the front. Tell of your experiences and describe one of the U.S. generals. Other classmates might write letters to you from home telling of their work in the U.S. for the war effort. Use the information in Chapter 26 to help you write your letters.

Practicing the Strategy
Review the strategy on page 972.
Evaluating Decisions. Study the sections titled "Negotiations with Japan" and "Attack on Pearl Harbor" on pages 950–52, then answer the following questions.
1. Why did Japan attack Pearl Harbor?
2. What response did the United States make to the attack on Pearl Harbor? Do you think that the Japanese expected the United States to respond in this way? Why or why not?
3. What alternate course of action, if any, could Japan have taken? What alternate course could the U.S. have taken? If you do not think that there were alternate courses, explain why.

1935
First neutrality act

1936
Roosevelt reelected

1939
Germany
invades
Poland
★
Second
World War
begins

1940
Battle of
Britain
★
U.S.
institutes
draft
★
Roosevelt
elected to
third term

1941
Lend-Lease Act
★
Japanese attack
Pearl Harbor
★
U.S. declares
war on Japan

1942
Battles of Coral Sea,
Midway, and Guadalcanal
★
Operation Torch

1943
Italian campaign

1944
Operation Overlord
★
MacArthur returns
to Philippines
★
Roosevelt wins
fourth term

1945
Roosevelt dies, Truman takes over
★
Germany surrenders (V-E Day)
★
Hiroshima and Nagasaki
★
Japan surrenders; the war ends
(V-J Day)

---

4. Evaluate the decisions made by Japan and by the United States. Support your position.

Using Primary Sources
During World War II the American people were asked to show their loyalty to the United States. If families worked together to help the war effort, they earned a V-Home certificate, which they received from their local Defense Council and which they could place in their windows. As you read the following text of the V-Home certificate, think about how the war changed people's lives.

THIS IS A V-HOME!

We in this house are fighting. We know this war will be easy to lose and hard to win. We mean to win it. Therefore we solemnly pledge all our energies and all our resources to fight for freedom and against fascism. We serve notice to all that we are personally carrying the fight to the enemy, in these ways:

I. This home follows the instructions of its air-raid warden, in order to protect itself against attack by air.
II. This home conserves food, clothing, transportation, and health, in order to hasten an unceasing flow of war materials to our men at the front.
III. This home salvages essential materials, in order that they may be converted to immediate war uses.
IV. This home refuses to spread rumors designed to divide our nation.
V. This home buys War Savings Stamps and Bonds [stamps and bonds sold by the U.S. government to help finance the war] regularly. We are doing these things because we know we must to Win This War.

1. In what ways did the war change the everyday lives of ordinary people?

2. Do you think that the war emergency justified these changes?
3. Why do you think that it was necessary for people to conserve their health?

Linking History & Geography
The conflict that began in the 1930s erupted into the Second World War. Many nations were involved, and fighting raged throughout the world. To understand the global nature of the war and the tremendous distances involved, with your classmates prepare a world map showing the United States and the areas of North Africa, Europe, and the Pacific involved in the fighting. Then create two large maps to show the war in Europe and in the Pacific. Label the sites of the major battles and give short reports on each.

Enriching Your Study of History
1. Individual Project. On April 12, 1945, Franklin D. Roosevelt died suddenly in Warm Springs, Georgia. The new president, Harry S Truman, told reporters, "I felt like the moon, the stars, and all the planets had fallen on me." Use historical imagination to interview Truman on his first day in the White House. Discuss with him some of the major decisions he must make, such as his plans for ending the war.
2. Cooperative Project. Your group will create an oral history of one of the following: a person who fought in World War II or a person who worked on the home front. Each person in your group should prepare five questions that will lead the interview in a purposeful way. Get permission from the subject to tape the interview. Play your taped oral history for the class.

RESPONSES *(Continued)*
Indochina, Japan decided to attack the U.S.
2. The U.S. declared war. Students who answer yes should mention that the Japanese government was expecting the U.S. to retaliate but hoped that the losses inflicted at Pearl Harbor would make a U.S. victory impossible. Students who answer no should say that many Japanese believed the U.S. would not want to fight a war on two fronts — Europe and the Pacific.
3. The Japanese could have agreed to withdraw from the territories that they had seized. The U.S. could have continued sanctions against Japan without declaring war.
4. Student evaluations should be supported by sound evidence.

Using Primary Sources
1. People now had to turn their energies into helping the war effort.
2. Answers will vary.
3. So that they could continue to work toward the war effort

Linking History & Geography
You may wish to evaluate the maps and reports on their accuracy and presentation.

PRIMARY SOURCE
Description of change: excerpted.
Rationale: excerpted to focus on the way the war changed people's lives.

America in the Cold War

PLANNING THE CHAPTER

TEXTBOOK	RESOURCES
1. The United Nations	*Unit 9 Worksheets and Tests:* Chapter 27 Graphic Organizer, Directed Reading 27:1, Reteaching 27:1
2. Truman in the Cold War	*Unit 9 Worksheets and Tests:* Directed Reading 27:2, Reteaching 27:2, Geography 27A *Eyewitnesses and Others, Volume 2:* Reading 58: The Truman Doctrine and the Four Points (1947, 1949)
3. Truman Survives His Critics	*Unit 9 Worksheets and Tests:* Directed Reading 27:3, Reteaching 27:3 *Eyewitnesses and Others, Volume 2:* Reading 60: Victor Navasky Describes the Costs of "McCarthyism" (1950s)
4. The Eisenhower Legacy	*Unit 9 Worksheets and Tests:* Directed Reading 27:4, Reteaching 27:4, Geography 27B *Creative Strategies for Teaching American History:* Page 339 *Eyewitnesses and Others, Volume 2:* Reading 62: Two Views of America in the 1950s, Reading 59: President Eisenhower Intervenes at Little Rock (1957) *Art in American History:* Transparency 33: The Libraries Are Appreciated, Transparency 34: The Dugout, Transparency 35: Christina's World *Voices of America: Speeches and Documents:* Decision in *Brown v. Board of Education of Topeka* (Kansas) by Earl Warren (1954)
5. A Youthful Cold Warrior	*Unit 9 Worksheets and Tests:* Directed Reading 27:5, Reteaching 27:5, Geography 27C *Eyewitnesses and Others, Volume 2:* Reading 64: Ambassador Adlai Stevenson Confronts the Soviets over Cuba (1962) *Art in American History:* Transparency 46: Moonwalk *Voices of America: Speeches and Documents:* John F. Kennedy's Inaugural Address (1961)
Chapter Review	*Audio Program:* Chapter 27 *Unit 9 Worksheets and Tests:* Chapter 27 Tests, Forms A and B (See also *Alternative Assessment Forms*) *Test Generator*
Unit Review	*Unit 9 Worksheets and Tests:* Unit 9 Tests, Forms A and B (see also *Alternative Assessment Forms*), Unit 9 Synthesis *Test Generator*

STRATEGIES FOR STUDENTS WITH SPECIAL NEEDS

Gifted Students.

Have interested students use resources in the school or public library to find more information on the workings of the Security Council of the United Nations. Then have students prepare a mock meeting of the Big Five—the United States, the Soviet Union, France, Great Britain, and the Republic of China—of the Security Council. (Remind students that the Republic of China is the nation located on Taiwan and is not communist.) Tell students that the year is 1955 and that they are to debate a resolution condemning the Soviet Union for aggression against the nations of Eastern Europe. Have the students present the debate for the rest of the class and vote on the resolution. (Note: Students should realize that each member of the Big Five has the power to veto resolutions. Therefore, the Soviet Union would probably block the resolution even though the other four members would favor it.)

Students Having Difficulty with the Chapter.

You may wish to have students listen to Chapter 27 in *The Story of America Audio Program.* Then organize the class into several cooperative learning groups that include students who are performing well with students who are having difficulty with the chapter. Instruct each group to skim the chapter to find important events of the Cold War and construct a time line of these events. Students may choose to illustrate their time lines with drawings of the events listed. Display several of the time lines on the bulletin board.

BOOKS FOR TEACHERS

Charles C. Alexander, *Holding the Line: The Eisenhower Era, 1952–1961.* Bloomington: Indiana University Press, 1975.

James Patrick Diggins, *The Proud Decades: America in War and Peace, 1941–1960.* New York: W. W. Norton, 1988.

John L. Gaddis, *The United States and the Origins of the Cold War, 1941–1947.* New York: Columbia University Press, 1972.

James Gilbert, *Another Chance: Postwar America, 1945–1968.* Philadelphia: Temple University Press, 1981.

Eric F. Goldman, *The Crucial Decade—and After: America, 1945–1960.* New York: Alfred A. Knopf, 1961.

Norman A. Graebner, *The Age of Global Power: The United States Since 1938.* New York: Wiley, 1979.

Godfrey Hodgson, *America in Our Time: From World War II to Nixon.* Garden City, NY: Doubleday, 1976.

William E. Leuchtenburg, *A Troubled Feast: American Society Since 1945.* Boston: Little, Brown, 1979.

BOOKS FOR STUDENTS

Edward F. Dolan, Jr., and Margaret M. Scariano, *Cuba and the United States: Troubled Neighbors.* New York: Franklin Watts, 1987.

Merni Ingrassia Fitzgerald, *The Voice of America.* New York: Dodd, Mead, 1987.

Lucy P. Frisbee, *John F. Kennedy: America's Youngest President.* New York: Bobbs-Merrill, 1983.

Gerald Kurland, *The Bay of Pigs Invasion.* Charlotteville, NY: SamHar Press, 1974.

Harold Woods and Geraldine Woods, *The United Nations.* New York: Franklin Watts, 1985.

MULTIMEDIA MATERIALS

America—Edge of Abundance (film, 50 min.), Indiana. Traces America's transformation from an agricultural into an industrial society.

Atomic Age and the Challenge of Communism: 1945–1960 (filmstrip), SVE. Highlights the relationship between the United States and the Soviet Union.

The Burden of Responsibility: 1945–1953 (filmstrip), EAV. Describes the United States as world leader, victory without peace, the Cold War, the Korean War, the United Nations, and foreign aid.

The Desegregated Decade (film, 30 min.), CBSTV. Surveys the progress made from 1945 to 1955, when the NAACP launched its all-out attack on racial segregation; includes Supreme Court decisions and breakthroughs in sports and in the armed forces.

Seven Days That Shook the World (The Cuban Missile Crisis). (film, 16 min.) "Screen News Digest" series. Hearst Metrotone News, 1962.

RESOURCES

■ You may wish to have students complete the Chapter 27 Graphic Organizer as they work through this chapter.

CHAPTER OBJECTIVES
Upon completing this chapter, students will be able to:

1. Explain the goals of the United Nations.
2. Analyze the significance of the Yalta Conference and explain how the Soviet Union came to dominate much of Eastern Europe.
3. Determine why the United States did not undergo a depression following World War II.
4. State the provisions of the Twenty-second Amendment and of the Taft-Hartley Act.

OVERVIEW
After World War II the United States was preoccupied with the Cold War. On the domestic front, issues included returning industry to peacetime production and civil rights for African Americans.

FOCUS/MOTIVATION:
MAKING CONNECTIONS
Prior Knowledge.
Write the terms *foreign policy* and *domestic policy* on the chalkboard or an overhead projector. Ask students to define each. Explain that the chapter deals with both domestic and foreign policy during the years 1945-60. Then draw two lines on the chalkboard or an overhead projector, labeling one *Domestic* and the other *Foreign*. Next provide an overview of the chapter by placing major domestic and foreign policy topics on the proper time lines.

SECTION 1

PREVIEW & REVIEW RESPONSES
Understanding Issues, Events, & Ideas.
Descriptions should demonstrate an understanding of the terms used.
1. The United Nations charter was drafted at the Conference.
2. Delegates from 50 nations discussed and debated until they came to an agreement on the wording of the United Nations' charter. Then each nation ratified the charter.
3. They met to decide on the fate of Poland after the war.

Thinking Critically.
Opinions will vary; students should support their choice.

CHAPTER 27

America in the Cold War

■ The Cold War began before World War II was over. The United States and the Soviet Union, marching toward Berlin to crush Hitler's capital, already distrusted each other. Like master chess players each side played up the other's weaknesses and for the next half century they held one another in wary check. Americans criticized the Soviets for building the Berlin Wall and for violations of human rights. The Soviets challenged America to resolve its racial inequalities and to redistribute its great wealth more fairly among the people. Sympathy for communist satellite countries such as Poland, Hungary, and Czechoslovakia was strong in America. Would this Cold War rivalry erupt into a global war?

Preview & Review

Use these questions to guide your reading. Answer the questions after completing Section 1.
Understanding Issues, Events, & Ideas. Describe world politics in the late 1940s, using the following words: San Francisco Conference, United Nations, Big Three, Yalta Conference, puppet government, communist, Cold War, capitalism.
1. What was the result of the San Francisco Conference?
2. How was the United Nations created?
3. Why did the Big Three meet at Yalta in 1945?
Thinking Critically. What do you think is the most important sentence in the preamble to the United Nations Charter? Why?

1. THE UNITED NATIONS

The Search for World Peace

Any war as widespread and destructive as World War II was bound to cause difficulties and conflicts that would not disappear simply because the shooting had stopped. President Roosevelt had realized this. During the war he prepared to face postwar problems. In particular he hoped to avoid the mistakes that Woodrow Wilson had made after World War I. Wilson's policies had led to the rejection of the Versailles Treaty by the Senate.

In 1943 Congress had agreed to commit to American participation in an international peace-keeping organization. In July 1944 the United States, Great Britain, the Soviet Union, and China met to outline plans for such an organization. Then in 1945 delegates from 50 nations met in San Francisco to draft a charter for the organization to be called the United Nations.

Roosevelt succeeded in avoiding Wilson's mistake of not consulting the opposition party about the peace treaty. He made Senator Arthur Vandenberg of Michigan, who was the leading Republican on the Foreign Relations Committee, a delegate to the **San Francisco Conference** to draft the **United Nations** (UN) charter. As a result the

5. Discuss provisions of the Truman Doctrine and the Marshall Plan.
6. Give examples of the policy of containment.
7. Define McCarthyism and explain its significance.
8. Describe how containment and the threat of massive retaliation helped to prolong the Cold War.
9. Explain why the U.S. entered in the Korean War

and evaluate the war's impact on the U.S.

10. Describe the two major transportation projects begun during the Eisenhower presidency.
11. Explain the importance of *Brown v. Board of Education of Topeka*.
12. Describe the major programs of the Kennedy Administration.
13. Analyze historical interpretations.

UPI/Bettmann Newsphotos

Flanked by the flags of 50 nations, Secretary of State Edward Stettinius signs the United Nations Charter on behalf of the United States. President Truman stands to his right. With your classmates, name some of the actions taken and programs sponsored by the United Nations since its founding in 1945.

Senate approved the treaty that made the United States a member of the UN by a vote of 87 to 2.

The new international organization was created to replace the League of Nations. The United Nations did not have the power to make the United States or any other major power do anything it did not want to do. Under the UN charter the United States, Soviet Union, Great Britain, France, and China all had the right to block any UN Security Council action by their veto power.

The United Nations had wide appeal in America. Politicians, scholars, even religious figures such as evangelist Billy Graham, Rabbi Joshua Loth Liebman, and Monsignor Fulton J. Sheen, supported it. All conducted enormously popular television programs. They urged Americans to accept their place as leaders of the world community.

The United Nations Charter

The delegates in San Francisco represented three fourths of the people on the planet. Long weeks of discussion and debate were necessary for the delegates to agree on the wording of the charter. It was then ratified by the separate nations. On October 24, 1945, the world organization officially came into being.

FOCUS/MOTIVATION:
MAKING CONNECTIONS
Prior Knowledge.
Ask students what German action began World War II. *(the invasion of Poland)* Then ask what happened to Poland after the war. *(It came under control of the Soviet Union.)* Explain that while the Allies had envisioned an independent Poland after the war, Britain, the United States, and the Soviet Union negotiated a different future for Poland even before the war ended.

GUIDED INSTRUCTION
Tell students that it is the autumn of 1990. Have them research major world events and the Security Council of the United Nations. Then divide the class into 15 groups. Five of the groups should represent the following permanent members of the Security Council: the United States, China, Great Britain, France, and the Soviet Union. The other 10 groups should each represent selected countries from around the world: two from Africa, two from Latin America, three from Asia, and three from Europe. As delegates from their countries to the UN, the members of each group are to meet and come up with a problem they would like to have the UN discuss. Each group should select a spokesperson to represent its country in the Security Council. Each spokesperson is to present a problem. The members of the Security Council should then discuss the problem and vote on what action the UN should take to solve it. Nine votes must be won to take action, including the votes of all five permanent members of the council.

HISTORICAL SIDELIGHTS

● Roosevelt was as suspicious of Churchill's concern for the British colonial empire as he was about Stalin, and he saw himself as a mediator between Churchill and Stalin. In October 1944 Churchill and Stalin had agreed in Moscow to the following proportion of British-Soviet great-power interest in five Balkan nations: Yugoslavia and Hungary—50 percent each; Romania and Bulgaria—90 percent Soviet, 10 percent British; Greece, 90 percent British, 10 percent Soviet.

CHECKING UNDERSTANDING

Ask students the following questions.

1. What did Roosevelt do to avoid the mistakes that Wilson had made after World War I? *(He made a leading Republican senator a delegate to the San Francisco Conference that drafted the UN charter.)*
2. What compromise did the Big Three make about Poland? *(The Soviet Union was to add eastern Poland to its territory, and the rest of Poland was to hold an election to determine its government.)*
3. Why was the Soviet Union concerned about who governed Poland? *(The Germans had invaded the Soviet Union through Poland in 1941, and many other attackers had entered Russia from Poland.)*

PRIMARY SOURCE

Description of change: excerpted.
Rationale: excerpted to focus on the ambitious goals of the United Nations.

John Isaac, UN Photo

Olive branches—traditional symbols of peace—surround a map of the world on the United Nations flag.

The preamble to the charter is a fine statement of the hopes of the postwar world:

“ We the peoples of the United Nations, determined to save succeeding generations from the scourge of war, which twice in our lifetime has brought untold sorrow to mankind, and

To reaffirm faith in fundamental human rights, in the dignity and worth of the human person, in the equal rights of men and women and of nations large and small, and

To establish conditions under which justice and respect for the obligations arising from treaties and other sources of international law can be maintained, and

To promote social progress and better standards of life in larger freedom,

And for these ends

To practice tolerance and live together in peace with one another as good neighbors, and

To unite our strength to maintain international peace and security, and

To ensure, by the acceptance of principles and the institution of methods, that armed force shall not be used, save in the common interest, and

To employ international machinery for the promotion of the economic and social advancement of all peoples,

Have resolved to combine our efforts to accomplish these aims.[1] ”

The Yalta Conference

● President Roosevelt and Prime Minister Churchill worked closely together on military and diplomatic problems during the war. Both also consulted frequently with the Soviet dictator Joseph Stalin. The most important meeting of the **Big Three,** as they were called, took place at the Soviet seaside resort of Yalta in February 1945.

At the time of this **Yalta Conference** the war in Europe was almost over. The war had started back in 1939 when Germany had invaded Poland. The Allies had entered the war with the intention of restoring an independent Polish government. Yet by 1945 Poland had been entirely occupied by the Soviet troops who were driving the Germans out. Roosevelt and Churchill hoped to prevent the Soviet Union from keeping too much territory in Poland.

Stalin, however, was determined to prevent any government unfriendly to the Soviet Union from controlling Poland. The Germans had invaded his country from Poland in 1941. Many times in the past other enemies had crossed Poland to attack the Soviet Union.

[1]From the preamble to *The United Nations Charter*

UPI/Bettmann Newsphotos

From this meeting at Yalta on the Crimean Sea in the Soviet Union came the compromises of the Cold War. Left to right are Winston Churchill, soon to lose power in England; Franklin Roosevelt, gravely ill after twelve years as president of the United States; and the ruthless Soviet dictator Joseph Stalin. These "Big Three" worked out the plan that allowed most of Eastern Europe to remain under Soviet control. Why do you think the United States and Great Britain allowed the Soviets to dominate Eastern Europe?

The difficulty was that no freely elected Polish government was likely to be friendly to the Soviet Union. After all, the Soviet Union had joined Germany in dividing up Poland before the Great World War and again in 1939. Soviet troops had treated the Poles brutally. Thousands of Polish officers had been murdered in cold blood by the Soviets in the Katyn Forest Massacre of 1940.

After considerable discussion the Big Three worked out a compromise. The Soviet Union was to add a large part of eastern Poland to its territory. In the rest of Poland free elections were to be held. The Poles could choose whomever they wished to govern them.

The trouble was that Stalin did not keep his promise to permit free elections in the new Polish republic. Instead he set up a **puppet government,** one that he could control as completely as a puppeteer controls a puppet. This government was bitterly resented by the vast majority of the Polish people.

Probably nothing could have prevented the Soviet Union from dominating Poland. Soviet troops had already occupied the country. The Allies could have driven them out only by going to war. And war with the Soviet Union at that time was unthinkable. Rather, the Allies hoped to convince the Soviets to join them in defeating Japan, a nation the Soviets were not at war with.

② Bernard Baruch is credited with popularizing the term "Cold War." In a speech he said, "Although the war is over, we are in the midst of a cold war which is getting warmer."

SUGGESTED CAPTION RESPONSE
It ennobled their suffering, reminded them that it was for the nation and for their children.

INDEPENDENT PRACTICE
Have students complete the Preview & Review activity at the beginning of the section.

CLOSURE
Tell students that Roosevelt was careful to include the opposition party at the conference drafting the UN charter. As a result the Senate overwhelmingly approved the treaty. At Yalta, Roosevelt and Churchill reached a compromise with Stalin over the issue of Poland and opened the way for the Soviets to dominate Eastern Europe.

HOMEWORK
Ask students to imagine that they are editors working for the *Washington Post.* They are to use their historical imagination to write an editorial, draw an editorial cartoon, or create a map supporting or criticizing the agreement reached at Yalta. Make a bulletin board display of the completed editorials.

During the siege of Leningrad by the Germans and what Napoleon once called "General Winter," a woman pulls firewood across a snowy square. The poster behind her says "Death to the Murderers of Children!" Why would the Soviets choose such a subject to rally the people during the terrible siege?

Return to the Preview & Review on page 978.

① Most Americans admired and respected the Soviets in 1945, even though the Soviet Union was a **communist** society in which the government controlled the economy and was ruled by a dictator. The Soviets had defended their country bravely and had contributed their full share to the Allied destruction of the Nazi armies. Indeed, more than 7 million—perhaps as many as 20 million—Soviets died in the war, many of them civilians who starved during the two-year Siege of Leningrad by the Germans.

General Eisenhower referred at this time to the long record of "unbroken friendship" between the United States and the Soviet Union. He said, "The ordinary Russian seems to me to bear a marked similarity to what we call an 'average American.'"

② However, the seeds of what was called the **Cold War** were planted in these broken promises and suspicions. It became a standoff between western **capitalism,** in which individuals control the economy, and communism, between democracy and totalitarianism. ▣

① Truman's three heroes were Cincinnatus, who saved the Roman Republic and then retired to his farm; Cato, who preached and practiced austerity and sacrifice for the good of Rome; and George Washington, who was not tempted by power.
② In his early days in the White House, Truman felt uncomfortable with the artifacts of Roosevelt's

presidency. He had FDR's desk shipped to Roosevelt's Hyde Park home and worked instead at Hoover's old desk.

SUGGESTED CAPTION RESPONSE
War contracts were canceled and many people lost their jobs.

2. TRUMAN IN THE COLD WAR

Getting Back to "Normal"

President Roosevelt died a few weeks after returning from Yalta. Less than a month later Germany surrendered. The Soviets then declared war on Japan, keeping a promise Stalin had made to Roosevelt at Yalta. However, their contribution to the defeat of Japan was not needed because the United States ended the war by dropping the atomic bomb.

The new president, Harry S Truman, was more suspicious of Soviet motives than Roosevelt had been. He believed that the Soviets expected the United States to suffer a serious postwar economic depression. They were "planning to take advantage of our setback," he later wrote.

Truman was eager to frustrate Soviet plans by preventing a depression. But could he handle the complicated task of converting the economy from wartime to peacetime production?

Truman had grown up on a Missouri farm. He had been an artillery captain in World War I. During the 1920s he got involved in Missouri politics. He served as a local judge, and in 1934 he was elected to the United States Senate. He received the 1944 Democratic vice presidential nomination because party leaders needed a likable candidate without any enemies to replace Vice President Henry A. Wallace, whom they considered too radical.

Truman had a reputation for being honest and reasonably liberal, but he seemed a rather ordinary politician. Yet no one had ever accused him of being unwilling to accept responsibility. When he became president, he put a sign on his desk in the White House that said, "The Buck Stops Here." However, many people, including Truman himself, wondered whether he would be "big enough" to fill Franklin Roosevelt's shoes.

The depression that Truman feared never occurred. War contracts were canceled and thousands of war workers lost their jobs. However, millions of consumers had saved money during the war when there were few civilian goods to buy. The demand for all sorts of products from houses and automobiles to washing machines and nylon stockings was enormous. No automobiles had been manufactured for civilian use since 1941. Millions of people wanted to replace their worn-out cars. Returning soldiers and laid-off war workers quickly found new jobs.

Unfortunately, the huge demand for goods could not be satisfied quickly. Shortages developed. A period of confusion and bickering followed. After four years of going without and paying high taxes, people wanted to enjoy themselves. They believed that they had sacrificed enough for the common good and the national interest. Now they hoped to concentrate on their own interests. Workers

Preview & Review

Use these questions to guide your reading. Answer the questions after completing Section 2.
Understanding Issues, Events, & Ideas. Use the following words to discuss Truman's domestic programs: Fair Deal, wage and price controls, Twenty-second Amendment, Taft-Hartley Act, closed shop, "cooling-off period."

Explain Truman's foreign policy, using these words: Iron Curtain, Truman Doctrine, Marshall Plan, satellite nation, Republic of West Germany, Berlin Airlift, North Atlantic Treaty Organization, Warsaw Pact, containment policy.
1. Why didn't a postwar depression occur?
2. How did Truman respond to the Taft-Hartley Act?
3. What caused the communist parties in Europe to grow stronger?
4. What effect did the Marshall Plan have on the economy of Europe? On the politics?
5. What agreements were made by signers of the NATO treaty?
Thinking Critically. Define each word in the phrase "Iron Curtain." Then explain why you think Churchill used this phrase to describe the political division between Western and Eastern Europe.

UNEMPLOYMENT, 1945-60

Percent of Civilian
Labor Force

Source: Board of Governors of the Federal Reserve System

LEARNING FROM GRAPHS.
Why did unemployment rise between 1945 and 1950?

PREVIEW & REVIEW RESPONSES
Understanding Issues, Events, & Ideas.
Discussions and explanations should demonstrate an understanding of the terms used.
1. There had been few civilian goods available. As a result people had saved their money, and there was enormous demand for all kinds of consumer goods.
2. He vetoed it, but Congress passed it over his veto.
3. While the American economy had expanded during the war, the opposite was true in Europe. Millions of people had been killed; food, housing, and other goods were scarce and expensive. These conditions made many people look to communist parties for help.
4. It successfully stimulated economic recovery. It furthered the division of Europe into competing camps—when Czechoslovakia appeared ready to accept Marshall Plan aid, the Soviet Union supported a communist takeover. This prompted the west to strengthen its alliance.
5. They agreed on mutual defense and formed a unified military force.

Thinking Critically.
Used as an adjective, iron refers to something strong, inflexible; curtain refers to a hanging screen or barrier. Students should mention that a seemingly impenetrable barrier separated Eastern Europe from the West.

The CIO Political Action Committee sponsored this 1944 poster by Ben Shahn, an artist who portrayed important social issues.

for full employment after the war
REGISTER • VOTE
CIO POLITICAL ACTION COMMITTEE

For Full Employment After War Register Vote. Offset lithograph, 30 × 39⅞.
Collection, Museum of Modern Art, New York. Gift of CIO Political Action Committee.

PURCHASING POWER*, 1940-60

Source: *Historical Statistics of the United States*

$2.20
$2.00
$1.80
$1.60
$1.40
$1.20
$1.00
$0.80
$0.60
$0.40
$0.20
0

1940   1950   1960

*Purchasing power is computed using the average prices of specific goods and services.

LEARNING FROM GRAPHS. *Statistics on purchasing power are often a good measure of the value of money and the overall effects of inflation on consumers. For statistical purposes, 1957 was chosen as the base year. In that year the value of $1.00 was $1.00. The purchasing power of all the other years are compared to that year. How much was $1.00 worth in 1960? You may wish to find what it would buy today.*

demanded higher wages but protested angrily against increases in consumer prices. Manufacturers wanted all controls lifted and their taxes reduced.

President Truman tried to resist these demands. He proposed a group of reforms he called the **Fair Deal** to balance national and personal interests. It called for larger social security benefits, a national health insurance plan, a higher minimum wage, money for public housing, and a continuation of the Fair Employment Practices Committee. At the same time the president resisted efforts to do away with **wage and price controls**—limits the government had set during the war.

Congress refused to pass most of the laws Truman requested. Few workers or employers supported any of Truman's proposals except those that benefited them directly. The president became more and more frustrated and less and less popular.

Finally, in late 1946 nearly all wartime economic controls were removed. Prices then rose sharply. Workers responded by demanding higher wages. When they got them, their increased spending caused prices to go up again. An upward spiral of wages and prices was set in motion, one that has continued almost without interruption to the present day.

Turning Out the Democrats

By the fall of 1946 even large numbers of Democrats had decided that Truman was incompetent. "To err is Truman," became a commonly heard wisecrack. "Had enough?" Republican candidates asked during the 1946 Congressional campaign, "Vote Republican."

① In 1946 Richard Nixon and John F. Kennedy were elected to the House of Representatives. The Republicans won control of Congress in that election. As a result, Senator Fulbright of Arkansas recommended that Truman resign—like a prime minister who had lost a vote of confidence. After that, Truman always referred to Fulbright as Senator Halfbright.

② At the end of World War II the Soviets occupied Poland and its capital, Warsaw, and every capital city in Eastern Europe except Athens, Greece, and Belgrade, Yugoslavia.

SUGGESTED CAPTION RESPONSE
Truman took responsibility for decisions.

A majority of the voters in 1946 did just that. The Republican party won control of both houses of Congress for the first time since the 1920s.

This new Congress set out to reverse the trend toward liberal legislation that had begun with the election of Franklin Roosevelt. First it passed the **Twenty-second Amendment** to the Constitution, limiting future presidents to two terms. This was a slap at Roosevelt's memory. The Congress also reduced appropriations for many social welfare programs. It tried to lower the income taxes of people with large incomes, but Truman vetoed that bill.

The most controversial measure of the session was the **Taft-Hartley Act,** passed in June 1947. The Wagner Labor Relations Act of 1935 had banned unfair labor practices by employers. The new Taft-Hartley law prohibited unfair practices by unions. It outlawed the **closed shop**—the clause in many labor contracts that required job applicants to join the union before they could be hired. It also gave the president the right to get court injunctions which would force striking unions to call off their strikes for an 80-day **"cooling-off" period.** The president could only seek these injunctions when strikes threatened the national interest. Yet judges seldom refused to issue injunctions when the president asked for them. Truman vetoed the Taft-Hartley bill, but Congress repassed it over his veto.

The Truman Doctrine

Truman's domestic difficulties did not prevent him from developing a determined foreign policy. Because he was suspicious of Stalin's motives, he worried a great deal about the danger of Soviet expansion and the spread of communism.

In Europe the change from war to peace had not been easy. While the American economy had expanded during the war, in Europe the reverse was true. More than 30 million Europeans had been killed. The loss of so many potential workers was a terrible blow to the economies of every nation. More millions were homeless and hungry. Such people could not produce very effectively. In every country railroads had been wrecked, bridges blown up, factories smashed. About 25 percent of all the wealth of Great Britain was destroyed during the war. In Germany there were shortages of everything. A package of American cigarettes cost as much as a German laborer could earn in a month.

These conditions caused a rapid increase in the strength of communist parties in several Eastern European countries. Whether or not the Soviet government had anything to do with this trend, it was certainly willing to take advantage of it. Truman reasoned that once the communists got control of a government, as they had in Russia in 1917, they would do away with free elections. Then their opponents could get back into power only through revolt and bloodshed.

Senator Robert Taft was known throughout Washington as "Mr. Republican." He was the son of the 27th president of the United States and sponsor of the Taft–Hartley Act.

Harry S Truman's oil portrait was painted by Martha Kempton. Behind the president is the Capitol. What did Truman's famous sign, "The Buck Stops Here," tell visitors to the Oval Office in the White House?

UPI/Bettmann Newsphotos

White House Historical Association

RELATING HISTORY TO GEOGRAPHY
To reinforce the geographic themes of *location* and *place,* divide the class into two groups. Have students in both groups trace a map of post-World War II Europe or provide them with an outline map of the area. Ask one group to label the countries that came under the Soviet sphere of influence. Have the other group label the countries that came under the Western sphere of influence and the countries that benefited from the Marshall Plan. Have volunteers from the first group show their maps to the class and explain how the Soviets came to dominate Eastern Europe. Have volunteers from the second group explain how the Marshall Plan aided Western and Southern Europe. Display the best maps on the bulletin board or in the school library.

Truman in the Cold War   985

RESOURCES

■ You may wish to have students complete Reading 58: "The Truman Doctrine and the Four Points (1947, 1949)" in Volume II of *Eyewitnesses and Others.*

Johnny Florea/Life Magazine © Time Warner, Inc.

Robert Capa/Magnum Photos

Above are two images of postwar Germany: At left, a woman with all her belongings sits not far from the badly bombed cathedral in Cologne. At right is the Brandenburg Gate in Berlin, later closed by the famous wall built to separate East and West Germany.

It therefore seemed absolutely necessary to Truman that the spread of communism in Europe be checked. But how could this be done without starting another war? The question became urgent in early 1947. Greece seemed about to fall behind what Churchill described as the **Iron Curtain**—the striking image he used to show the political division between democratic and communist territories in western and eastern Europe. Communist guerrillas in Greece were seeking to overthrow the conservative Greek government. Great Britain had been providing aid to that government. In February 1947 the British informed President Truman that because of their own economic problems they could no longer afford to help Greece.

Truman believed that if Greece became communist, its neighbor, Turkey, might also fall under Soviet influence. He thought this would give the Soviets the confidence to move against Italy and perhaps France. He apparently believed this even though the Soviets were not supporting the Greek guerrillas. Truman was sure the communists would then seize American businesses in these countries, ruining American economic interests in Europe. The president therefore asked Congress for $400 million to aid Greece and Turkey. He said:

❝ It must be the policy of the United States to support free peoples who are resisting . . . outside pressures. . . . I believe that we must assist free peoples to work out their destinies in their own way. . . . Our help should be primarily through economic and financial aid. . . .[1] ❞

[1] From speech to Congress by Harry S Truman, March 12, 1947

PRIMARY SOURCE
Description of change: excerpted.
Rationale: excerpted to focus on Truman's plea to Congress for economic aid for Greece and Turkey.

986

986   **AMERICA IN THE COLD WAR**

STRATEGIES FOR SUCCESS

ANALYZING HISTORICAL INTERPRETATIONS

How and why did the Cold War begin? Historical interpretations of how and why it began are varied. A historical interpretation is an explanation by a historian about why an event happened as it did. One historian may emphasize a different cause or effect than another, or they may disagree completely. This difference occurs, in part, because historians bring different points of view to their interpretations. To effectively interpret historical accounts, you must analyze historical interpretations and evaluate their supporting evidence.

How to Analyze Historical Interpretations

Before learning the steps for analzying historical interpretations, review Comparing Points of View on page 855. Then to analyze historical interpretations, follow these steps.

1. **Identify the main points of the interpretation.** Determine the main points and conclusions.
2. **Determine the historian's point of view.** Identify circumstances that might have influenced the historian's interpretation. Note whether the historian was a participant or observer, or wrote a later interpretation.
3. **Assess the evidence and reasoning.** Study the information provided. Check the logic of the historian's reasoning.
4. **Compare the interpretation with other interpretations of the event.** Note similarities and differences among interpretations. If there are differences, ask yourself why such differences exist.
5. **Evaluate the interpretation.** Based on your analysis of the interpretation, assess its reliability. Accept or reject its main points.

Applying the Strategy

Read the following excerpts that offer different interpretations of how and why the Cold War began. Excerpt A is from an article written in 1947 by George Kennan, at the time Counsellor of the United States Embassy in Moscow. Excerpt B is from *The Holy Crusade: Some Myths of Origin* written in 1969 by Michael Parenti.

Excerpt A

Belief is maintained in the basic badness of capitalism, in the inevitability of its destruction, and in the obligation . . . to assist in that destruction [and in

an] antagonism between capitalism and socialism.

Basically, the antagonism remains. . . . And from it flow many of the phenomena which we find disturbing in . . . foreign policy: the secretiveness, . . . the wary suspiciousness and the basic unfriendliness.

This means that we are going to continue for a long time to find the Russians difficult to deal with.

Excerpt B

It was Harry Truman who succeeded to the Presidency before the war's end, and no reading of his opinions or actions would uphold the view that the United States was motivated by a sincere intention to extend friendly cooperation, only to be taken by surprise by Russian aggressiveness. If Truman brought anything to the White House, it was an urgency . . . "to get tough" with the Kremlin. "Unless Russia is faced with an iron fist and strong language, another war is in the making," he concluded, "The Russians would soon be put in their places" and the United States would then "take the lead in running the world in the way that the world ought to be run. . . ." What is overlooked is the probability that Truman's own belligerent, uncompromising, and ungracious approach was a major factor in actualizing [causing] the struggle and in preventing the kind of accommodation [agreement] between the United States and the Soviet Union that is just beginning to emerge today.

Note that these historians differ greatly in their interpretations. Kennan stated that the Cold War resulted from communist antagonism toward capitalism. This caused the Soviets to see Americans as the enemy. What in Kennan's background influenced his point of view? He was a high-ranking official of the United States embassy in the Soviet Union, writing in 1947 as the Cold War began. He was considered an authority on Soviet-U.S. relations.

How does Parenti's interpretation differ? He claims the Cold War started with Truman's "get-tough" policies. Parenti's point of view differs almost as much as his interpretation. He is a political analyst writing in 1969, more than 20 years after the event. What other information would help you analyze these interpretations to allow you to assess their reliability?

For independent practice, see Practicing the Strategy on pages 1024–25.

For independent practice, see Practicing the Strategy on pages 1024–25.

COOPERATIVE LEARNING: INTEGRATING STRATEGIES FOR SUCCESS

Organize students into cooperative learning groups. Ask students to reread the section on the Truman Doctrine. Then have each group analyze the author's interpretation of the Truman Doctrine. *(Garraty is a professor of history who is writing a later interpretation that is primarily political and economic. His main point is that Truman believed that the Soviets would take over other European countries if the communist guerrillas gained control of Greece and that he wanted to protect American business interests. He implies that Truman was exaggerating the Soviet threat because the Soviets were not, in fact, supporting the Greek communists.)*

PRIMARY SOURCES

(Left) Description of change: excerpted and bracketed.
Rationale: excerpted to focus on Kennan's attitudes toward American-Soviet differences; bracketed words added to clarify meaning.
(Right) Description of change: excerpted and bracketed.
Rationale: excerpted to focus on Parenti's attitude toward the origin of the Cold War; bracketed words added to clarify meaning.

This idea became known as the **Truman Doctrine.** Of course,
Truman's reference to outside pressures, namely the Soviets, was
either mistaken or a deliberate falsehood. But in the mood of the day
Congress appropriated the money and the communist threat to
Greece and Turkey was checked.

The Marshall Plan

The Truman Doctrine was popular in the United States because it
appealed to both liberals and conservatives. Liberals liked the idea
of helping the people of other countries defend their independence
and rebuild their war-torn economies. Conservatives liked the idea
of resisting communism and thus preserving the free enterprise system. Nearly everyone took pride in the great influence and prestige
that came to the United States in other parts of the world.

Critics of the Truman Doctrine argued that it was a disguised
form of imperialism. They saw it as a revived form of dollar diplomacy, similar to the old technique of encouraging American investments in nations like Nicaragua and Haiti before World War I. They
also thought that the doctrine aimed too much at attacking communism and not enough at helping people in need.

To counter these objections, George C. Marshall, whom Truman
had appointed secretary of state, proposed his **Marshall Plan** in a
speech at Harvard University in June 1947. All the nations of Europe,
including the Soviet Union, needed American help in rebuilding their
war-damaged societies, Marshall said. But they also had to help
themselves. The plan could not be imposed on the Europeans from
the outside. The United States would provide money once the European nations had developed a European recovery plan.

Marshall's offer to include the Soviet Union was a bluff, or at
least a gamble. If the Soviets had accepted it, Congress would probably not have provided the money to make the plan work. But
Marshall did not think the Soviets would accept this plan, and he
was right. They also forced the countries under its control to pull
out of the meeting. The communists had no desire to contribute to
the revival of the capitalist nations.

While the Soviet Union and the countries of eastern Europe
under its control rejected the Marshall Plan, western Europeans
adopted it eagerly. They soon created the Committee for European
Economic Cooperation (CEEC) to decide what needed to be done
and how much it would cost. Over the next few years the United
States gave CEEC about $13 billion to carry out its plans.

The Marshall Plan was a brilliant success. By 1951 the economies
of the participating nations were booming. Still, the plan had further
divided Europe into two competing systems. When Czechoslovakia
showed signs of accepting Marshall Plan aid, the local communist
party seized power with Soviet support. Democracy was destroyed.

National Portrait Gallery

*In 1953 General George C. Marshall
was awarded the Nobel Peace Prize.
How did this selection pay tribute to
the Truman Doctrine as well as the
Marshall Plan?*

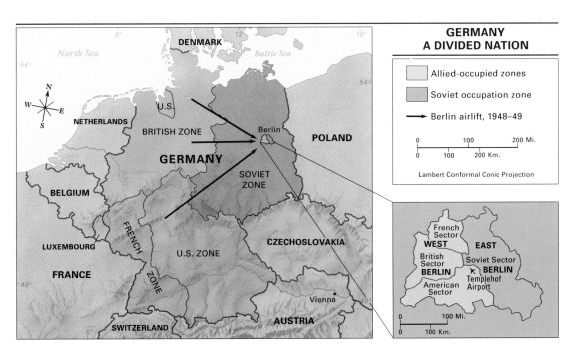

GERMANY
A DIVIDED NATION

Allied-occupied zones

Soviet occupation zone

→ Berlin airlift, 1948–49

| 0 | 100 | 200 Mi. |
| 0 | 100 | 200 Km. |

Lambert Conformal Conic Projection

French
Sector
WEST   EAST
British
Sector   Soviet Sector
BERLIN   ✈ BERLIN
Templehof
American   Airport
Sector

| 0 | 100 Mi. |
| 0 | 100 Km. |

GUIDED INSTRUCTION: COOPERATIVE LEARNING
Organize the class into three groups. Assign one group the role of West Berlin officials, one group the role of Truman and his advisers, and the third group the role of the Soviets. The Soviet group has just blockaded the roads across East Germany to Berlin. Tell each group to plan a strategy for dealing with the crisis. They should plan an immediate response, predict what the other parties to the conflict will do, and then plan their responses to these anticipated events. When each group has finished, select a spokesperson from each group to tell the class their group's strategy.

Czechoslovakia, like Poland, Hungary, and the other states of eastern Europe, fell into the Soviet orbit. The countries dominated by the Soviet Union became known as **satellite nations.**

The Berlin Airlift

After the war the victors had divided Germany into four zones. One zone was controlled by the United States, one by Great Britain, one by France, and one by the Soviet Union. Berlin, the capital city, was located in the Soviet zone. Because of Berlin's large size and importance, however, the western nations were unwilling to let the Soviets control it all. It too was divided into four zones.

In 1948 the United States, Great Britain, and France announced plans to create an independent **Republic of West Germany** from the part of Germany they controlled. This step led the Soviets to close all the roads leading across their zone to Berlin. They could not block the formation of the West German republic. But they might force the Allies to give up their zones in the capital city.

The Soviet action caused a serious crisis. If the Americans tried to ship supplies to Berlin by truck or train, they would run into a Soviet roadblock. Then they would either have to turn back or start a fight. Truman therefore decided to *fly* supplies to Berlin. Fortunately, Tempelhof Airport lay within the United States zone, in the heart of the city.

Truman's **Berlin Airlift** turned the tables on the Soviets. There was no way to block the air lanes. Now the Soviets would have to

LEARNING FROM MAPS. *The victorious Allies—the United States, Great Britain, France, and the Soviet Union—divided defeated Germany for purposes of administration. Soon after the war, however, the iron curtain clanged down across the country, separating western Germany from Soviet-dominated eastern Germany. The situation was even graver within the divided city of Berlin. West Berliners, surrounded by Soviet-controlled eastern Germany, felt seriously threatened as a result.*

CHECKING UNDERSTANDING
Ask students how the Truman administration tried to counter communist expansion. *(Truman proclaimed the Truman Doctrine, which stated that the United States would support free peoples who were trying to resist outside pressures. The Marshall Plan proposed to fund Europe's economic recovery. It was believed that economic recovery would lessen the appeal of the communist parties. The United States responded to the communist takeover of Czechoslovakia and the Berlin blockade by joining with eight Western European nations to form the North Atlantic Treaty Organization (NATO). The NATO members formed a unified military force and agreed to defend each other in case of an attack.)*

Walter Sanders/Life Picture Service

Through the clouds over Berlin a C-47 swoops down with its supplies to keep the 2 million residents of West Berlin alive. Why had the Soviets blocked all highways and railroads to Berlin?

decide whether to allow the supplies to reach West Berlin or start fighting.

The Soviets chose to do nothing. They probably believed that it would be impossible to keep the 2 million residents of West Berlin supplied with food and other necessities by air alone.

The Berlin Airlift was assigned to the United States air force. Bulky products usually shipped by river barge or freight car had to be flown in on military planes. At one point General Lucius D. Clay, who had charge of the airlift, telephoned an American air force general in Frankfurt, Germany, "Have you any planes that can carry coal?" he asked.

"We must have a bad phone connection," the air force general replied, "It sounds like you are asking if we have any planes for carrying coal."

"Yes, that's what I said—coal."

"The air force can deliver anything," the astonished general then responded. And he proved that it could indeed. Over the next 11 months American and British planes flew some 277,000 missions into Berlin. Their cargoes kept West Berliners fed and working.

In May 1949 the Soviets gave up trying to squeeze the western powers out of Berlin. They lifted the land blockade. The city, however, remained divided into Soviet and Allied zones.

Containment

The United States and its western European friends responded to the communist takeover of Czechoslovakia and the blockade of Berlin by strengthening their own alliance. In April 1949 the United States, Great Britain, France, Italy, and eight other nations signed a treaty creating the **North Atlantic Treaty Organization** (NATO). The signers agreed to defend one another in case of attack and to form a unified military force for this purpose. By the time the NATO force was organized, the Soviet Union had exploded its first atomic bomb. The American monopoly on nuclear weapons had been broken. Soon after the Soviet Union and its satellites signed the **Warsaw Pact,** pledging mutual defense as NATO members had.

Rivalry between the communist and capitalist worlds grew steadily more intense. Neither side dared risk open warfare in the atomic age. Instead they waged the Cold War. For American leaders the main objective of the Cold War was to prevent the expansion of Soviet influence in every way possible short of all-out war. In 1947 George F. Kennan, a professional diplomat who had served for many years at the American embassy in Moscow, explained how the Cold War could be won. America must build up its armed forces and be prepared to *contain* Soviet expansion wherever it was attempted.

This **containment policy,** according to Kennan, President Truman, and most other Americans, was purely defensive in purpose. The Soviets, on the other hand, felt that the containment policy,

RETEACHING STRATEGY
Students with Special Needs. Pair students who are having difficulty with students who are performing well. Have the more proficient students help the others draw pictures or create charts, graphs, or maps to illustrate the following concepts: the Fair Deal, the Taft-Hartley Act, the Truman Doctrine, and the Marshall Plan.

INDEPENDENT PRACTICE
Have students complete the Preview & Review activity at the beginning of the section.

CLOSURE
Remind students that Truman was much more suspicious of Soviet motives than Roosevelt had been. As a result his foreign policy was concerned with countering Soviet expansion.

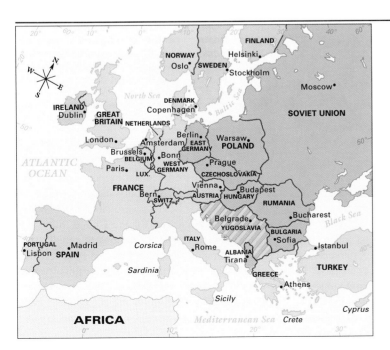

COLD WAR IN EUROPE, 1950s

- NATO members*
- Soviet Union and satellites
- Nonaligned nations
- Independent communist state

*North Atlantic Treaty Organization; other members: U.S., Canada, Iceland.

0 — 300 — 600 Mi.
0 — 300 — 600 Km.

Azimuthal Equal-Area Projection

LEARNING FROM MAPS. *Soviet refusal to leave the Eastern European countries it had liberated from Germany in World War II helped trigger the Cold War. What countries in Eastern Europe became Soviet satellites? Which have moved away from Soviet domination in recent years?*

Truman in the Cold War   991

INTERPRETING HISTORY: THE COLD WAR

Have you ever been involved in a disagreement which lasted so long that you could not remember who started it? If so, you will understand why historians have been unable to agree about who started the Cold War between the Soviet Union and the United States. It was called a "Cold War" because it was a war without direct military conflict. Yet it was bitterly contested.

The two superpowers engaged in this Cold War for more than 40 years after World War II. It began after the Yalta Conference, when the United States and the Soviet Union were still allies. It intensified in the 1950s with wars in Korea and Vietnam.

Historians agree that there was a Cold War but they have disagreed about which nation started it and why. In 1950, Thomas A. Bailey claimed in *America Faces Russia* that the Soviet Union was completely responsible. To historian William Appleman Williams, author of *American Relations* (1952), the Cold War was not a struggle between communism and democracy. Rather, it was a conflict brought about by the supposed need of American businesses for markets in other parts of the world, especially in the nations that were not industrialized.

In his 1965 book, *Atomic Diplomacy*, Gar Alperovitz insisted that the United States had started the Cold War in an effort to contain the spread of Soviet influence. Alperovitz claimed that President Truman's decision to drop the atomic bomb on Japan was part of this attempt to convince the Soviets that the United States had superior armed forces.

In the 1970s, several historians argued that the United States and the Soviet Union shared the blame. More recently, in *A Preponderance of Power* (1992), Melvyn P. Leffler attempted to explain the full significance of the Cold War, now that it is over. He argued that after the end of World War II, conditions around the world were so chaotic that American leaders felt Soviet communism was a threat to democracy everywhere. United States officials wished to stop the rise of communism in Europe and to integrate Germany and Japan into an American alliance system.

According to Leffler, some American policies like the Marshall Plan were wise. Other policies, however, were foolish, even dangerous. For example, the belief that if one developing nation went communist so would its neighbors was clearly incorrect. On balance, Leffler assigned "as much of the responsibility for the origins of the Cold War to the United States as to the Soviet Union." He reminds us, however, that a final judgment is impossible without a study of Soviet archives.

How will historians of the future explain the Cold War? Does the weakness of today's Russia indicate that American worries and fears all these years were needless? Does the ending of the conflict prove that America's foreign policy of trying to stop communism was correct? Does the Cold War's end after half a century of repeated crises mean that the atomic bomb is as much a force for peace among nations as a threat of destruction? Time will tell.

particularly the NATO force, would provoke war. Each side suspected the other of preparing all kinds of threatening schemes. In part the tensions of the Cold War were caused by poor communications between the communist and noncommunist diplomats. For this the secretive and overly suspicious Soviets were chiefly to blame.

The containment policy worked well for the United States and its allies. It enabled the western European nations to rebuild their economies and preserve their democratic political systems. It may even have helped prevent a major war. The chief difficulty with containment, from anyone's point of view, was that it tended to prolong the Cold War. A policy of negotiation and compromise might have ended it or at least avoided some of the tension and crises it produced. 🖾

Return to the Preview & Review on page 983.

3. TRUMAN SURVIVES HIS CRITICS

The Election of 1948

While the success of the Berlin Airlift was still in doubt, the 1948 presidential election campaign took place. The Democratic party was badly divided. Almost none of its leaders wanted to renominate ❶ Truman. Some supported Henry A. Wallace, who was running as the ❷ candidate of a new **Progressive party.** Wallace had been Truman's secretary of commerce. He believed that the Soviets' intentions were good—they wanted to help the countries of Eastern Europe as well as themselves—and that Truman's aggressive Cold War strategy was likely to lead to a real war. When Wallace criticized the Truman Doctrine, the president had forced him to resign. Wallace went on to attack the Marshall Plan and fight every aspect of Truman's containment policy.

Conservative southern Democrats opposed Truman because of his civil rights policy. In 1947 his **Civil Rights Committee** recommended laws protecting the right of African Americans to vote and banning segregation on railroads and buses. It also called for a federal law punishing lynching and the creation of a permanent Fair Employment Practices Committee.

Truman had urged Congress to adopt all these recommendations. He issued executive orders ending segregation in the armed forces and prohibiting job discrimination in all government agencies. After much discussion and a fruitless search for another candidate, the Democratic convention nominated Truman and made his proposals part of the party platform. Southern Democrats who were known as Dixiecrats then organized a **States' Rights party** and nominated Strom Thurmond, the governor of South Carolina, for president.

With three Democrats running, the Republican candidate, again Thomas E. Dewey, seemed sure of victory. Dewey's strategy was to avoid taking stands on controversial issues while the Democrats fought among themselves. But Truman conducted a hard-hitting campaign. In his exhausting whistle-stop tour by train he attacked the record of the "do-nothing" Republican-controlled Congress. The Republican party, he claimed, wanted to "turn the clock back" and do away with all the reforms of the New Deal era.

These tactics worked well. Organized labor supported Truman because of his veto of the Taft-Hartley Act. African Americans backed him because of his civil rights stand. Many farmers were persuaded by his argument that Congress had refused to provide adequate storage space for surplus farm products. Former New Dealers responded to his charge that the Republicans intended to repeal important New Deal laws.

Preview & Review

Use these questions to guide your reading. Answer the questions after completing Section 3.
Understanding Issues, Events, & Ideas. Use the following words to describe the Cold War atmosphere at home and abroad in the early 1950s: Progressive party, Civil Rights Committee, States' Rights party, McCarthyism, North Korea, South Korea, Inchon, Yalu River, Korean War, McCarran Internal Security Act.

1. Who were the four candidates for president in 1948? For what reasons was Truman elected?
2. What events in 1949 and 1950 prompted a widespread fear of communism among the American people?
3. What kinds of accusations did Joseph McCarthy make? Why did many Americans believe him?
4. What provoked the Korean War? How did Truman respond?

Thinking Critically. Imagine that you witnessed a speech by Truman during his whistle-stop campaign. Explain why you would or would not vote for Truman in the election of 1948.

SECTION 3

PREVIEW & REVIEW RESPONSES
Understanding Issues, Events, & Ideas.
Descriptions should demonstrate an understanding of the terms used.
1. Henry A. Wallace, Strom Thurmond, Thomas E. Dewey, and Harry S Truman; Truman's campaign persuaded farmers that Congress had not provided adequate storage for agricultural surpluses and New Dealers that Republicans would repeal New Deal laws. Labor supported him because he vetoed the Taft-Hartley Act, and African Americans supported him because of his civil rights stand.
2. The Alger Hiss trial, the conviction of several Americans for giving the Soviets secret information about atomic bombs, and the Chinese communists' defeat of Chiang Kai-shek
3. He said that he had the names of 205 policymakers in the state department who were communists; he accused General Marshall of conspiring to turn China over to the communists. While most people believed that politicians would exaggerate and mislead, they also believed that no high public official would make serious charges without some evidence.
4. The North Korean army invaded South Korea. He assumed that the Soviet Union was behind the invasion and applied the containment policy. In the name of the United Nations he

HISTORICAL SIDELIGHTS

1 Truman was the first president in the 1900s to identify himself with the struggle to end racial discrimination. Politically, his stance paid off in 1948 when he received the votes of African Americans. Still it was the closest presidential election since 1916. The popular vote was 49.5 percent for Truman, 45.1 percent for Dewey.

SUGGESTED CAPTION RESPONSE

Truman was running against two other Democrats as well as the Republican candidate, and nearly all the experts were predicting that he would lose.

RESPONSES *(Continued)*

moved U.S. troops into South Korea.

Thinking Critically.
Explanations should reflect an understanding of the campaign; reward thoughtful, creative answers.

FOCUS/MOTIVATION: MAKING CONNECTIONS

Prior Knowledge.
Ask students what the traditional attitude of Americans had been toward Europe. *(Americans traditionally had mistrusted Europeans and had avoided becoming involved in European affairs.)* Then ask them what was different about American attitudes and foreign policy after World War II. *(The United States did not return to isolationism after the war. The Truman Doctrine and the Marshall Plan showed that the United States remained involved in European affairs.)*

UPI/Bettmann Newsphotos

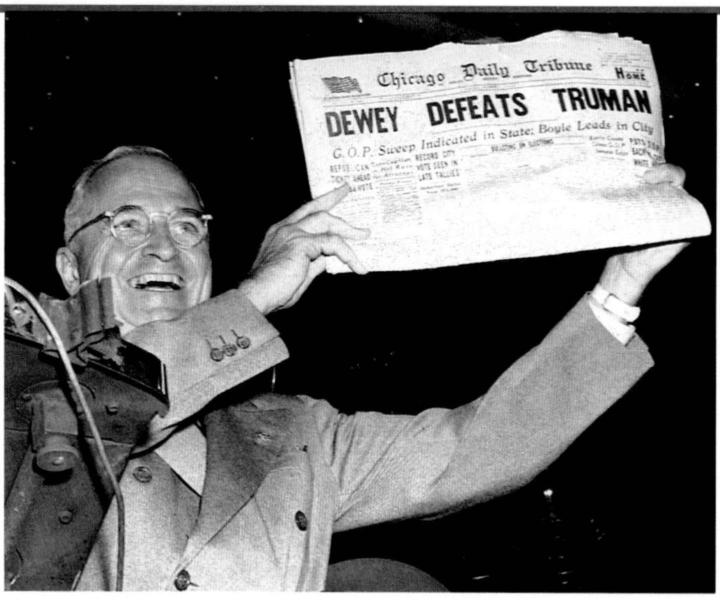

President Truman was given such a slim chance of being elected in 1948 that he took great glee when the Chicago Tribune *incorrectly proclaimed Dewey the winner. For what reasons did the newspaper's editors believe Truman had lost?*

Still, nearly all the experts continued to predict that Dewey would be elected. How could Truman win with two other candidates competing with him for Democratic votes? The editor of the *Chicago Tribune* was so sure that Dewey would win that he approved the headline "DEWEY DEFEATS TRUMAN" and went to press on election night before all the votes had been counted.

1 But the experts were wrong. Truman received over 2 million more votes than Dewey and won a solid majority in the electoral college. The States' Rights ticket won in only four southern states. Wallace's Progressive party was swamped everywhere. Truman had proved himself a clever politician. His energy, courage, and determination in fighting so hard when his cause seemed hopeless was part of the reason for his success. Another reason was that a majority of the voters wished to continue the policies of the New Deal.

The New Red Scare

Despite his remarkable victory, Truman was unable to get much of his Fair Deal program passed by Congress during his second term. More and more, the Cold War was occupying everyone's attention. A number of events in 1949 and 1950 produced widespread fear of communism similar to the Red Scare of 1919-20. One was the sensational trial of Alger Hiss, the president of the Carnegie Foundation for International Peace. Hiss had been a state department official before and during World War II. Whittaker Chambers, a former associate, charged that Hiss had been a member of the Communist party and had given him secret state department documents to pass on to the Soviets. When Hiss denied this, he was tried and found guilty of lying. He was sentenced to five years in prison.

Next came the arrest and conviction of several Americans accused of turning over secret information about the manufacture of atomic bombs to the Soviets. People panicked. Some believed that Soviet spies were hiding in every pumpkin patch and that the American government was a nest of traitors.

Then came what many called the loss of China to communism. In 1949 Chinese communists, called the Red Chinese, had defeated ① the armies of General Chiang Kai-shek. Chiang and his supporters were forced to flee to the island of Formosa (Taiwan). China, with its hundreds of millions of people, was now part of the communist world.

In the feverish atmosphere caused by the spy trials, many Americans believed that conspiracy lay behind the communists' victory in China. During the Chinese civil war state department experts had reported that the Chiang government was hopelessly corrupt and inefficient. Now these same experts were accused of being secret communists who helped cause the Chiang government's overthrow by cautioning against giving Chiang more money. The fact that their

Culver Pictures

Above, Generalissimo Chiang Kai-shek sits astride his Mongolian pony. His followers (below left) are in retreat from mainland China to the island of Formosa.

Carl Mydans/Life Magazine © Time Warner, Inc.

Point of View

When the playwright Lillian Hellman was asked to testify to the House Committee on Un-American Activities, she wrote these lines.

> "I am not willing, now or in the future, to bring bad trouble to people who, in my past association with them, were completely innocent of any talk or any action that was disloyal or subversive. I do not like subversion or disloyalty in any form and if I had ever seen any I would have considered it my duty to have reported it to the proper authorities. But to hurt innocent people I knew many years ago is, to me, inhuman and indecent and dishonorable. I cannot and will not cut my conscience to fit this year's fashions, even though I long ago came to the conclusion that I was not a political person and could have no comfortable place in any political group. . . ."
>
> From *Scoundrel Time,*
> Lillian Hellman, 1976

The "Whispering Gallery" was what some called the almost continual conferences of Senator Joseph McCarthy (left) and his lawyer Roy Cohn during the Army-McCarthy hearings. Why did people believe McCarthy at first?

reports had been accurate did not protect them. If the United States had given more military and economic aid to Chiang, the critics claimed, he could have defeated the Red Chinese forces.

The Rise of McCarthyism

Early in 1950 a Republican senator, Joseph R. McCarthy of Wisconsin, charged that the state department was riddled with traitors. He claimed to know the names of 205 communists who held policy-making posts in the department.

This accusation naturally caused a sensation. McCarthy had been almost unknown outside Wisconsin. Suddenly he was making headlines in newspapers all over the country. He quickly took advantage of his new fame by making even more astonishing charges. For example, General Marshall had for a time been a special ambassador to China. Now McCarthy accused him of being part of the conspiracy to turn that country over to the communists.

McCarthy was a total fraud. His charges were false. One of the first Americans to see through McCarthy was Edward R. Murrow, the news commentator who described the Battle of Britain. Another early critic was one of McCarthy's fellow senators, Margaret Chase Smith, who in June 1950 questioned McCarthy's tactics:

> "I think it is high time that we remembered that we have sworn to uphold and defend the Constitution. I think it is high time that we remembered that the Constitution, as amended, speaks not only of freedom of speech but also of trial by jury instead of trial by accusation. . . .

Wide World Photos

RESOURCES
- You may wish to have students complete Reading 60: "Victor Navasky Describes the Costs of 'Mc-Carthyism' (1950s)" in Volume II of *Eyewitnesses and Others*.

The American people are sick and tired of being afraid to speak their mind lest they be politically smeared as Communists or Fascists by their opponents. Freedom of speech is not what it used to be in America. It has been so abused by some that it is not exercised by others. . . .[1]"

Still, thousands of Americans assumed that no high public official would make such serious charges without evidence. Politicians often exaggerated. Sometimes they deliberately misled people. But flagrant lying was a different matter. If McCarthy announced that he had a list of 205 or 81 or even 57 communists, people thought surely there must be *some* truth in what he was saying.

In this atmosphere McCarthy did not have to prove his charges. He never showed anyone the 205 names or told anyone where he had obtained this information. The people whom he accused of being ■ "soft on communism" found their careers in government ruined. This was **McCarthyism.** When he attacked other politicians who tried to expose his lies, he was believed, not they. For a time McCarthy became one of the most powerful men in the entire United States.

The Korean War

McCarthy's rise came at a time when war broke out in Korea, a nation on the east coast of Asia. Japan had absorbed the Kingdom of Korea, a nation with a long history and a distinct and unique culture, in 1910. After World War II Korea was freed from Japanese control and divided in two. **North Korea** was supported by the Soviet Union, **South Korea** by the United States.

Efforts to reunify Korea after the war were unsuccessful. The Soviet Union blocked free elections because two thirds of the people lived in the South, which would easily control the elections. The Soviets apparently hoped for a unified Korea they could dominate as a check on the growing prestige of Communist China.

The two Korean governments exchanged serious threats. Although the United States supported South Korea, official policy considered Korea too far away to be essential to American defense. Soon South Korean leaders began mobilizing their troops. In June 1950 the North Korean army reacted to these troop movements by invading South Korea.

President Truman assumed that the Soviet Union was behind the invasion. It is possible that he was incorrect and that the North Koreans acted on their own. Truman was intent on maintaining United States prestige in the face of growing communist threats and felt he had no time to investigate the situation in detail. He decided to apply the containment policy to the situation. In the name of the

[1]From *Congressional Record*, 81st Congress, 2nd Session, June 1, 1950

EXTENSION:
COMMUNITY INVOLVEMENT
Cooperative Learning.
Organize students into cooperative learning groups. Have the groups use community resources to find out how your community was affected by the Korean War. Students should also interview veterans of the war to learn their experiences in and views of the war. When the groups have finished their research, have them report what they have learned to the class.

EXTENSION:
HOME INVOLVEMENT
Some students may have relatives who fought in the Korean War. If so, have these students do an oral history project on the role their relative played in the war. Remember that students should prepare their questions in advance. Provide them with cassette tapes that you can add to your oral history library.

PRIMARY SOURCE
Description of change: excerpted.
Rationale: excerpted to focus on Smith's opinion of McCarthy's tactics.

Above is five-star General Douglas MacArthur. At right, a helicopter picks up American marines in the harbor of Inchon.

Carl Mydans/Life Magazine © Time Warner, Inc.

Point of View

American Caesar was the title General Douglas MacArthur's biographer gave to him.

"He was a great thundering paradox of a man, noble and ignoble, arrogant and shy, the best of men and the worst of men, the most protean, most ridiculous, and most sublime. No more baffling, exasperating soldier ever wore a uniform. . . . He carried the plumage of a flamingo. . . . Yet he was also extraordinarily brave. His twenty-two medals—thirteen of them for heroism—probably exceeded those of any other figure in American history."
William Manchester,
1978

United Nations he ordered American forces stationed in Japan into Korea. General MacArthur was put in command of the campaign.

Truman did not ask Congress to declare war. Truman's power to send American troops to Korea was challenged by Robert Taft, the leading Republican in Congress. He claimed Truman had "usurped," or illegally seized, Congress' power to declare war. However, Congress took no further action. Perhaps if it had, circumstances in Vietnam 14 years later would have been different.

The North Koreans had the advantage of surprise. By September they had conquered nearly all of South Korea. Then the UN army, which consisted mainly of Americans and South Koreans, managed to check their advance. Next General MacArthur planned and executed a brilliant counterattack. He landed troops at **Inchon,** far behind

Wide World Photos

HISTORICAL SIDELIGHTS
● When Truman fired MacArthur, the White House received nearly 30,000 telegrams urging the impeachment of Truman. A Gallup Poll showed that 69 percent supported MacArthur, 29 percent Truman.

SUGGESTED CAPTION RESPONSE
Because it is bordered by the People's Republic of China and the Soviet Union—both communist countries

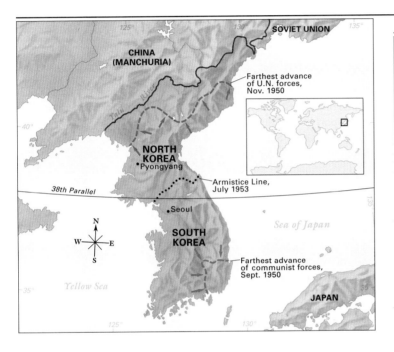

THE KOREAN WAR

---- Farthest advance
      of communist forces

---- Farthest advance
      of U.N. forces

0   100   200 Mi.
0   100   200 Km.

Lambert Conformal Conic Projection

LEARNING FROM MAPS. *The division of Korea after World War II left North Korea with most of Korea's mineral resources and heavy industry, but with scarce agricultural resources. South Korea, on the other hand, found itself with most of the country's people, commerce, farmland, and food production but almost no industrial raw materials. Since the Korean War, almost no trade between the two countries has crossed the 38th parallel. How does North Korea's relative location seem to assure that it would become communist?*

INDEPENDENT PRACTICE
Have students complete the Preview & Review activity at the beginning of the section.

CLOSURE
After World War II a new red scare influenced domestic and foreign policy. The Korean War added to the public's fear of communism and spying and thus to McCarthy's influence.

HOMEWORK
Have students create a political cartoon illustrating the new red scare or some aspect of McCarthyism.

the North Korean lines. The tide of battle turned swiftly. The North Koreans, attacked from two sides, retreated. Soon MacArthur's troops had driven the invaders out of South Korea.

However, instead of stopping at this point, MacArthur obtained permission from Truman to invade North Korea. By November his troops were approaching the **Yalu River,** the boundary between North Korea and China. This action caused the Chinese to enter the war. Striking suddenly and with tremendous force, they routed MacArthur's army, driving it back into South Korea. Finally, in the spring of 1951, the battle line was stabilized along the original border between the two Koreas.

MacArthur then requested permission to bomb China and to use anticommunist Chinese troops from Taiwan in Korea. President Truman refused to allow this expansion of the war. Still, MacArthur continued to argue for his plan. Truman was forced to remove him ● from command. The fighting in Korea continued.

The **Korean War** added to the public's worry about communist spying and therefore to the influence of Senator McCarthy. Early in the war Congress passed the **McCarran Internal Security Act.** This law required all communist organizations to register and open their financial records to the government. A special board was set up to investigate organizations that might be subversive—that is, out to overthrow the government. By 1952 Senator McCarthy was describing the Roosevelt and Truman administrations as "20 years of treason." 🖅

Return to the Preview & Review on page 993.

HISTORICAL SIDELIGHTS
① Believing that army officers should be nonpartisan, Eisenhower did not vote until he was 58 years old.

RESOURCES
■ You may wish to have students complete Reading 62: "Two Views of America in the 1950s" in Volume II of *Eyewitnesses and Others.*

PREVIEW & REVIEW RESPONSES
Understanding Issues, Events, & Ideas.
Descriptions should demonstrate an understanding of the terms used.

1. Many people thought Stevenson was too intellectual, and people wanted a change—there had not been a Republican president since Hoover. In addition, Eisenhower had the advantage of being a World War II hero and of never having been involved in politics—making it easy for Democrats to vote for him even though he ran as a Republican. He also promised to go to Korea to negotiate an end to the war there.

2. After Stalin died, Soviet leaders advocated "peaceful coexistence and competition" with the West. However, Dulles continued to use warlike language, which kept tensions high.

3. Eisenhower's policies were conservative in that he hoped to reduce government spending and favored measures to help private enterprise. His policies were liberal in that he felt that government should retain most of the 1930s social legislation, control economic growth, and stimulate the economy in hard times. His administration began two large public works projects—the St. Lawrence Seaway and the Interstate Highway System.

4. If the Supreme Court decision had not been unanimous, it would have given opponents of integration a

---

Use these questions to guide your reading. Answer the questions after completing Section 4.
Understanding Issues, Events, & Ideas. Use the following words to describe the key events of the Eisenhower years: massive retaliation, brinksmanship, Army-McCarthy Hearings, East Germany and Hungary, Vietnam, Israel, Suez Canal, Summit Meeting, U-2 Affair, St. Lawrence Seaway, Federal Highway Act, Interstate System, Warren Court, *Brown v. Board of Education of Topeka,* Little Rock, Montgomery Bus Boycott, nonviolent resistance, sit-in.

1. Why did Stevenson have little chance of defeating Eisenhower in the 1952 election?
2. Why did the Eisenhower-Dulles foreign policy tend to prolong the Cold War?
3. How was Eisenhower's domestic policy conservative? How was it liberal?
4. Why was it important that the decision of the Warren Court in *Brown v. Board of Education* be unanimous?
5. What prompted the Montgomery Bus Boycott? What was its outcome?

Thinking Critically. 1. Argue either for or against President Eisenhower's response to various world trouble spots in the 1950s. **2.** Imagine that you are one of the nine black students attending the previously all-white high school in Little Rock. Write a poem or short story describing your feelings on your first day of school.

The opponents in the 1952 presidential election, Adlai Stevenson, left, and Dwight Eisenhower, right, share a friendly handshake after the heat of the campaign.

■ 4. THE EISENHOWER LEGACY

The Election of 1952

Although the Twenty-second Amendment did not apply to him, President Truman decided not to seek reelection in 1952. Instead he gave his support at the Democratic convention to Governor Adlai Stevenson of Illinois. Stevenson was an excellent speaker, witty and thoughtful at the same time. He had the courage to attack McCarthy head-on during the campaign, something few Democrats dared do.

Yet Stevenson had little chance of being elected. Many people thought he was too intellectual. More important, a majority of the voters seemed to be ready for a change. After all, the nation had not elected a Republican president since Hoover's victory in 1928. The Republican candidate was Dwight D. Eisenhower, the outstanding hero of World War II.

Aside from his fame as a general, Eisenhower had the advantage of never having been involved in party politics. Because he did not have a long association with the Republican party, thousands of normally Democratic citizens could vote for him without feeling that they were voting for a Republican. As a matter of fact, before deciding to back Stevenson, President Truman had tried to persuade Eisenhower to run on the Democratic ticket!

In addition, Eisenhower's warm, easygoing personality appealed to millions. The campaign slogan "I like Ike" perfectly expressed the general reaction. Liberals of both parties who were worried about

Wide World Photos

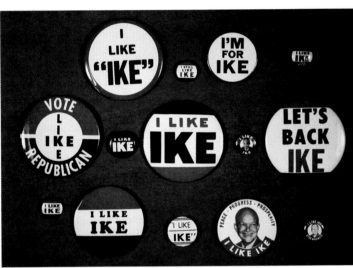
Dwight D. Eisenhower Presidential Library

Senator McCarthy voted for Eisenhower in hopes that he would be able to silence or control the senator. Further, Eisenhower announced during the campaign that if elected he would go to Korea to negotiate a settlement of the war there. Any last doubts about his victory evaporated. Eisenhower won by more than 6 million votes.

When asked how he felt after being so badly beaten, Stevenson said that he felt like a small boy who had stubbed his toe—too grown-up to cry but too hurt to laugh. These were the same words used to concede defeat in 1858 by another candidate from Illinois, Abraham Lincoln.

Eisenhower's Foreign Policy

President Eisenhower made no basic changes in the containment policy. But he was under great pressure from conservative Republicans to reduce government spending. He and his secretary of state, John Foster Dulles, developed a strategy called **massive retaliation.** In simple terms, massive retaliation meant threatening to respond to Soviet aggression anywhere in the world by dropping nuclear bombs on Moscow and other Soviet cities. It meant being willing to go "to the brink" of all-out war to contain communism. This policy came to be known as **brinksmanship.**

Atom bombs were replacing "what used to be called conventional weapons," Dulles said. There was no need, he argued, to spend huge amounts on tanks, battleships, and other expensive "military hardware."

Dulles' policy was pure bluff. By 1953 both the Soviets and the United States had made hydrogen bombs hundreds of times more deadly than the bomb that destroyed Hiroshima. Neither Dulles nor

Carl Mydans/Life Magazine © Time Warner, Inc.

John Foster Dulles

Eisenhower ever seriously considered dropping a nuclear bomb on anyone. It would have been suicidal to do so because a nuclear strike would almost surely have caused the world to erupt in nuclear war.

The warlike language Dulles used tended to keep Cold War tensions high at a time when the Soviets were taking a less aggressive position. Joseph Stalin died in 1953. The new Soviet leaders claimed to favor "peaceful coexistence and competition" with the western nations. This gave them an advantage in the worldwide competition to influence public opinion, for Dulles seemed unable to back off from his policy of brinksmanship.

The Eisenhower-Dulles foreign policy also increased Senator McCarthy's influence in the United States because it focused attention on the danger of a clash with the communist powers. The popular President Eisenhower detested McCarthy and his tactics, but he was unwilling to criticize the senator openly.

Eisenhower stiffened the already harsh loyalty program that Truman had set up to clean out possible communist sympathizers in the government. Employees found to be "security risks" were to be fired even if they had not actually done anything wrong. For example, persons who had been convicted of crimes in the past might be classified as security risks. The idea was that communist agents might threaten to expose such people's pasts unless they turned over secret information. Under this program about 3,000 employees were fired.

Joseph Welch, seated at left, represented the Army in the Army-McCarthy hearings. After a vicious smear of a young aide of Welch's by McCarthy, millions of television viewers heard Welch exclaim, "Have you no decency left, sir?" How was McCarthy's spell broken?

Robert Phillips/Black Star

① Eisenhower let it be known that he might use atomic weapons to break the stalemate in the Korean peace talks. In July 1953 an armistice was signed at Panmunjon. It provided for a demilitarized zone between North and South Korea. No peace treaty was ever signed, but Eisenhower had fulfilled his campaign promise to end the fighting.

GUIDED INSTRUCTION: COOPERATIVE LEARNING
Select three students to play the parts of Eisenhower, Dulles, and Khrushchev. They are to prepare for a press conference at the close of the Geneva Summit Meeting in July 1955. Organize the rest of the class into cooperative learning groups, each one of which will represent a newspaper or network news organization. They should prepare to interview the summit participants. After students have prepared for their roles, conduct the press conference.

An even larger number resigned. Yet almost none of these people had actually done anything disloyal.

McCarthy finally went too far. Early in 1954 one of his assistants was drafted into the army. McCarthy tried unsuccessfully to get him excused from service. Out of spite he then announced an investigation of "subversive activities" in the army. These **Army-McCarthy Hearings** were televised. They destroyed McCarthy's prestige completely. Day after day the emptiness of his charges and his snarling cruelty and insensitivity were seen by millions of viewers. The people he attacked were aware that they were being watched and judged by this enormous audience. They *had* to fight back. When they fought and survived, McCarthy's spell was broken.

The hearings produced no specific political or legal results. Later, in August 1954, the Senate voted to investigate McCarthy's behavior. In December the Senate voted to censure him. By a vote of 67 to 22 the Senate resolved "that the conduct of the Senator from Wisconsin, Mr. McCarthy, is contrary to senatorial traditions and is hereby condemned." McCarthy's power to do harm was gone. He remained in the Senate until his death in 1957, ignored if not forgotten.

Eisenhower and the Cold War

During his campaign Eisenhower had promised to go to Korea. Soon after his victory, and before becoming president, he flew to Korea to meet with U.S. commanders to discuss strategy. Eisenhower and ① Dulles decided on a "peace or else" policy. Early in 1953 the U.S. increased air attacks on North Korea while hinting to the Chinese that if peace talks did not start soon they would send bombers across the Chinese border—perhaps carrying nuclear weapons. Finally in July 1953 a truce was signed. Although peace talks have continued, no final treaty has ever been signed. Armies continued to face each other across a narrow demilitarized zone near the 38th parallel. The United States has refused to remove its soldiers until a final settlement has been reached. United States soldiers still guard the border.

Elsewhere President Eisenhower avoided military solutions to international problems. Dulles had spoken of "liberating" the people of eastern Europe who had been forced to accept communist governments after World War II. There were revolts against these governments in **East Germany** in 1953 and in **Hungary** in 1956. But Eisenhower did not intervene.

When the French, who had colonized Southeast Asia in the 1860s, were being driven out of **Vietnam** by local communists in 1954, Eisenhower rejected the suggestion that the air force bomb communist positions. Instead the United States supported the division of Vietnam into a northern, procommunist section and a southern, pro-Western government. This United States position was contrary to the Geneva Accords signed in 1954 by the French and the leaders of

GUIDED INSTRUCTION
Discuss with students what they have seen on television or read in newspapers about the Arab-Israeli conflict. Then organize the class into two groups. Tell one group that they are Israelis, and tell the other group that they are Palestinians. Each group may need to use library and community resources to find out more about their group's position on the current conflict between the Israelis and the Palestinians. After students have prepared, tell each group to write a plan proposing an equitable settlement to the conflict. Ask volunteers to read the plans, and then discuss them with the class.

John Sadovy/Life Magazine © Time Warner, Inc.

A young Hungarian freedom fighter stands guard in Budapest. Behind him are burned-out Soviet tanks and anti-tank guns. But what sad lesson did supporters of a free Hungary learn in 1956? How many years did it take to win true freedom?

rival Vietnamese groups. That agreement called for a unified and independent Vietnam by 1956.

Another example of Eisenhower's restraint occurred in 1956 in the Middle East. In 1948 the state of **Israel**, which had formerly been the British mandate, or colony, of Palestine, declared its independence. Many Jews who had escaped Hitler's Holocaust flocked to Israel after the war to start a new life. So did thousands of Jews from all over the world, many of them former residents of the United States.

However, the Arab nations surrounding Israel took up arms to prevent what they considered an invasion of their territory. A series of wars resulted. Although outnumbered, the Israelis overcame the Arabs. Nearly 1 million Arabs who had lived in the area when it was Palestine fled to neighboring regions. They then conducted raids and terrorist attacks on Israel, determined to recover their homeland and drive the Jews from the Middle East.

A crisis erupted in 1956 when Egypt stepped up its raids against Israel and seized control of the **Suez Canal,** which was an international waterway. Israel fought back, joined by Great Britain and France, who wanted to reopen the canal.

Eisenhower faced a serious dilemma. The United States had supported the independence of Israel from the start. Most Americans felt that the Jews were entitled to a country of their own after their terrible suffering during World War II. In addition, Great Britain and France were also allies of the United States. But Eisenhower objected to their using force to regain the canal. He demanded that the invaders pull back. So did the Soviets, who threatened all-out war. As a result the allies withdrew, and Egypt kept control of the Suez Canal.

By 1954 Nikita Khrushchev had become the head of the Soviet government. Khrushchev was a difficult person to understand. At one moment he was full of talk about peace, at the next he was threatening to use nuclear bombs. One historian described Khrushchev as a mixture of Santa Claus and a "wild, angry Russian bear."

Eisenhower and the heads of the British and French governments met with Khrushchev in Geneva, Switzerland, in July 1955. They accomplished little at this Geneva **Summit Meeting,** or gathering of world leaders, but their discussions were friendly. Experts spoke hopefully of a possible end of the Cold War. Yet, little more than a year later, Khrushchev threatened to bomb Great Britain and France if they did not pull back from their war with Egypt over the Suez Canal.

Soviet scientists then shocked the world on October 4, 1957, when they sent into orbit around the earth a small satellite called *Sputnik.* (Sputnik is the Russian word for "traveling companion.") In November they launched a larger satellite, *Sputnik II,* which carried a dog. These amazing feats shattered American self-confidence and provided a great propaganda boost for the Soviet Union and communism. Soon "rocket fever" swept the United States. After repeated embarrassing failures the Americans hurled a grapefruit-sized satellite into space in January 1958. The United States and the Soviet Union were now in the space race.

The success of *Sputnik* sent shock waves through American society. Americans felt they led the world in science and technology. Now many people blamed the educational system for falling behind the Soviets in the space race. Courses in science and mathematics were added to school and college curriculums, and valuable scholarships were awarded to promising students in these fields. America was determined to "catch up."

Perhaps the most serious Cold War test of Eisenhower was the **U-2 Affair.** In 1960 the Soviets scored a second propaganda victory over the United States when they shot down an American U-2 "spy plane" which was illegally taking photographs high over Soviet territory. President Eisenhower at first denied that the plane had been on a spying mission. Later, when Premier Khrushchev revealed that the pilot had survived the plane crash, the president was forced to admit the truth about the U-2 mission.

GUIDED INSTRUCTION: COOPERATIVE LEARNING
Organize students into cooperative learning groups. Ask each group to imagine that they have been asked to serve on a national commission to prepare recommendations for a nationwide response to *Sputnik.* When the groups have completed their work, select a student from each group to present their group's recommendations to the class.

ART IN HISTORY:
COMMUNITY INVOLVEMENT
Organize the class into four groups and assign them the 1950s, 1960s, 1970s, and 1980s. Tell the groups that they are to research the art, music, and popular culture of their decade and present a report to the class. Suggest to the students that they ask their parents and other relatives if they have memorabilia from the decade that they are researching. If so, perhaps the relatives would allow the students to bring items in to show the class. After all the groups have made their presentations, discuss with them the changes that have occurred in popular culture since the 1950s.

MINIMUM HOURLY WAGE RATES 1950-91	
Year	Minimum Hourly Wage Rate
1950	$0.75
1955	$0.75
1960	$1.00
1965	$1.25
1970	$1.60
1975	$2.10
1980	$3.10
1985	$3.35
1990	$3.80
1991	$4.25

Source: Statistical Abstract of the United States, 1989

LEARNING FROM TABLES. *The minimum hourly wage rate, set by the government after studying statistics on inflation, purchasing power, and other economic indicators, influences the wages of both hourly and salaried employees. What might explain the unusually large increase in the rate between 1975 and 1980?*

Eisenhower's Domestic Policies

President Eisenhower stood halfway between the conservative domestic policies of the Republicans of the 1920s and the liberal policies of the New Deal. He was eager to reduce government spending. He favored measures designed to help private enterprise. He hoped to turn over many federal programs to the individual states.

Yet Eisenhower was unwilling to do away with most of the social welfare legislation of the 1930s. He agreed that it was the government's job to try to regulate economic growth and stimulate the economy during hard times.

While Eisenhower was president, 11 million more workers were brought into the social security and unemployment system. The minimum wage was raised. A start was made in providing public housing for low-income families. Eisenhower also established the new cabinet-level Department of Health, Education, and Welfare. The first head of this important department was Oveta Culp Hobby, the former director of the Women's Army Corps.

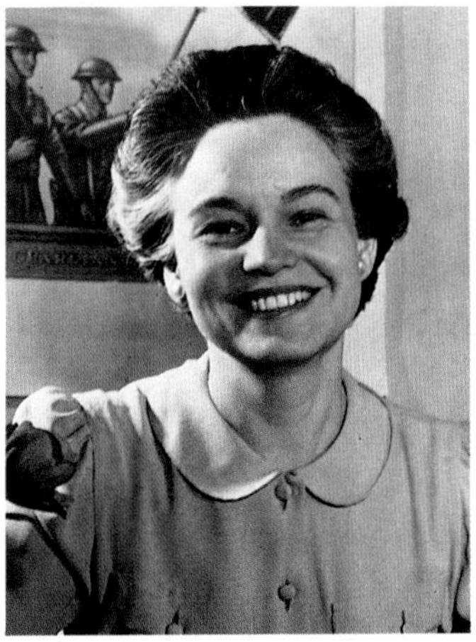

Although Eisenhower genuinely wished to hold federal spending to a minimum, he approved two very large new projects. One was the construction of the

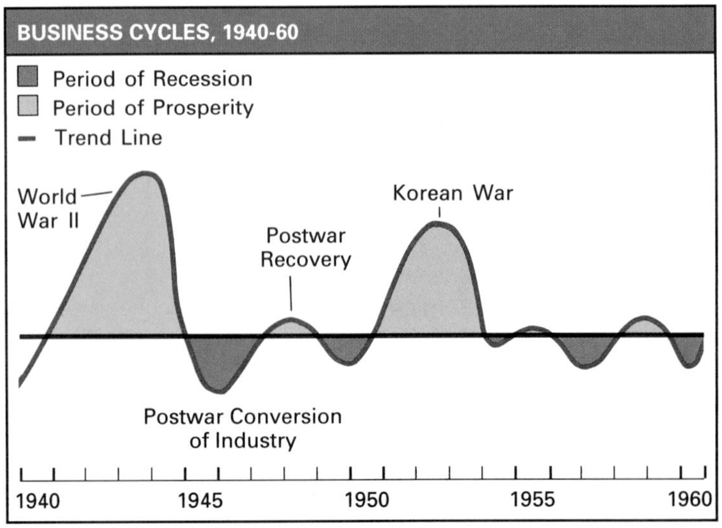

Myron Davis/Life Magazine © Time Warner, Inc.

Oveta Culp Hobby

LEARNING FROM GRAPHS. *As you can see from the graph, the business cycle entered strong periods of prosperity during World War II and the Korean War. What economic problem troubled both Truman and Eisenhower, and had a negative effect on the business cycle as well?*

BUSINESS CYCLES, 1940-60
- Period of Recession
- Period of Prosperity
- Trend Line

World War II
Postwar Recovery
Korean War
Postwar Conversion of Industry

1940   1945   1950   1955   1960

HISTORICAL SIDELIGHTS

① The lawyer who presented the case to the Court was Thurgood Marshall, who later became the first African American Supreme Court Justice.

SUGGESTED CAPTION RESPONSE

Eisenhower sent soldiers to help integrate Little Rock schools.

RESOURCES

■ You may wish to have students view Transparency 34: *"The Dugout"* and complete the accompanying worksheet in *Art in American History.*

◄ You may wish to have students view Transparency 35: *"Christina's World"* and complete the accompanying worksheet in *Art in American History.*

St. Lawrence Seaway, which deepened the channel of the St. Lawrence River so that ocean-going ships could sail directly into the Great Lakes. The other was the **Federal Highway Act** of 1956. This measure authorized the construction of an enormous network of superhighways, the **Interstate System.** Eisenhower considered both these projects necessary for defense in case of war. Yet it was also Eisenhower who in his Farewell Address warned against the rising power of the "military-industrial complex." By this he meant the economic power and prestige of defense industries that had developed during World War II and had grown during the Cold War.

While Eisenhower was president, the last of the 50 states were added to the Union. Alaska became a state in January 1959 and Hawaii was admitted in August of the same year.

School Desegregation

In 1956 Eisenhower again defeated Adlai Stevenson for president. His margin was even larger than in 1952. Clearly a majority of the voters approved of his middle-of-the-road philosophy.

Yet Eisenhower's most important action during his first term produced radical social changes. Eisenhower himself strongly disapproved of some of these changes. No better modern example exists of how difficult it is to understand the historical significance of events until long after they have occurred.

The action in question was Eisenhower's appointment of Governor Earl Warren of California as Chief Justice of the United States in 1953. Warren had served three terms as governor. He had also run for vice president in 1948 on the ticket with Thomas E. Dewey.

Although Warren had never been a judge before, he quickly became the most important member of the Supreme Court. Under his leadership the Court became a solid unit, at least where civil rights cases were concerned.

In 1954 this **Warren Court** made one of the most important decisions in the history of the Supreme Court. It decided in the case known as **Brown v. Board of Education of Topeka** (Kansas) that it was unconstitutional for states to maintain separate schools for black and white children. This case overturned the "separate but equal" doctrine established in *Plessy v. Ferguson* in 1896. The decision said:

66 Today, education is perhaps the most important function of state and local governments. Compulsory school attendance laws and the great expenditures for education both demonstrate our recognition of the importance of education in a democratic society. It is required in the performance of our most basic public responsibilities, even the armed forces. It is the very foundation of good citizenship. Today, it is a principle instrument in awakening the child to cultural values, in preparing him for later professional training, and

Yousuf Karsh/Woodfin Camp

Chief Justice Earl Warren, who had been the Republican governor of California, was appointed by President Eisenhower. But the Warren Court's growing liberalism and strong stance against segregation scattered the American landscape with "Impeach Earl Warren" signs. Eisenhower was not as strongly criticized when he enforced the Court's decision to integrate schools in Brown v. Board of Education. *Explain how the president proved to be a defender of the Constitution in this action.*

GUIDED INSTRUCTION

Many students are probably unaware of the segregated conditions that existed in the United States until a few years ago. Ask students to look for illustrations from history books or old texts that are examples of the so-called "separate but equal" conditions prevalent in the United States before *Brown v. Board of Education of Topeka.* Have them bring in the pictures they find and show them to the class. They may also wish to interview family or community members about their memories of separate schools and other aspects of segregation. Then discuss with students their reactions to the pictures and the effects of segregation on those who suffer discrimination.

THE STARS AND STRIPES

The American flag of fifty stars and thirteen stripes has gone through many changes. The early colonies had a variety of flags depicting patriotic themes, such as one showing Benjamin Franklin's advice: "Join, or Die." Others showed rattlesnakes with the warning "Don't tread on me." By the 1750s many of the flags were using 13 alternating stripes, usually red and white, to symbolize the 13 colonies.

As conflicts with England drew the colonies closer together, the desire for a colonial flag grew. The 1775 Continental Colors was the first national flag. It had 13 alternating red and white stripes (7 red, 6 white) and the British flag in the upper left. After the Declaration of Independence, the Continental Congress acted to remove the British flag from the American flag. In 1777 Congress resolved that "the Flag of the united states be 13 stripes alternate red and white, and the Union be 13 stars white on a blue field representing a new constellation." This was the original American flag.

No one knows for sure who designed this flag, or who made the first one. Soon after it was adopted, Congressman Francis Hopkinson of Pennsylvania said he was its designer. In 1870 William J. Canby claimed that his grandmother, Betsy Ross, a Philadelphia seamstress and flag maker, had designed and sewn the first flag. Historians are unable to support either claim.

The stripes were probably taken from the most popular patriotic flag of the Revolution, the flag of the Sons of Liberty. On it the stripes represented the 13

America's strong young navy showed a rattlesnake ensign in 1775. Its warning seems perfectly clear.

This early flag of the revolutionary period, with twelve stars in a wreath and one in the center, was first adopted by the famed Third Maryland Regiment and flown by them at the Battle of Cowpens, South Carolina, in 1781.

"Beautiful as a flower to those who love it, terrible as a meteor to those who hate it." This unique "Great Flower" flag was made in 1861.

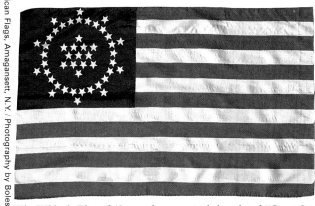

This ensign has 38 stars displayed in a "double-wreath" pattern, 13 in the inner ring and the balance for states joining the Union until 1877.

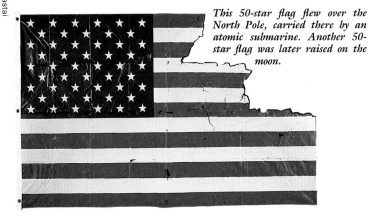

The Whipple Flag of 48 stars has a central six-pointed "Great Star" for the 13 colonies and was designed by Wayne Whipple.

This 50-star flag flew over the North Pole, carried there by an atomic submarine. Another 50-star flag was later raised on the moon.

original colonies. This part of the flag's design has changed little over the years. The first flags after independence added stripes as well as stars for new states. The flag of 1795, for example, had 15 of each. But the flag of 1818 went back to 13 stripes, the standard for all flags afterward.

The stars in the first design stood for the states. The Continental Congress in 1777 stated there should be 13 of them. But it did not indicate how they should be arranged. The most common arrangement of the time was alternating rows of three stars, two, three, two, and three. Another flag had twelve stars in a circle around the 13th star. And still another had all thirteen stars in a circle. In 1818 Congress ordered that a new star be added on the July 4th after a state joined the Union. It still did not say how the stars should be arranged. So many arrangements were seen until 1912. Since then presidential orders have fixed the positions of the stars as new ones are added.

The Continental Congress also never stated why red, white, and blue were chosen for the flag's colors. But later when designing the nation's seal—also red, white, and blue—they listed the following meanings: *red* for courage and hardiness, *white* for purity and innocence, *blue* for justice, vigilance, and perseverance.

The flag is saluted by the Pledge of Allegiance:

"I pledge allegiance to the flag of the United States of America and to the Republic for which it stands, one Nation under God, indivisible, with liberty and justice for all."

① When the South proposed to set up private white schools, the Nobel Prize-winning author William Faulkner, himself a Mississippian, said that schools in Mississippi were already among the worst in the nation and that two identical school systems wouldn't be good for anyone.

■ You may wish to have students complete Reading 59: "President Eisenhower Intervenes at Little Rock (1957)" in Volume II of *Eyewitnesses and Others.*

EXTENSION:
COMMUNITY INVOLVEMENT
Multicultural Perspectives.
Have students interview an African American or other adult who remembers the civil rights movement of the 1950s and 1960s. Students should research the subject in their local or school library before conducting the interview so that their questions are relevant and meaningful. They should ask interviewees if they were directly involved in the movement and, if they were, to describe the part they played in it. They may also want to ask interviewees to give their impressions of events, such as the Montgomery boycott. Have students record their interview and play it for the class.

GUIDED INSTRUCTION
Have students clip or photocopy articles about racial equality from newspapers and magazines. Discuss the clippings and collect them in a class scrapbook on the continuing struggle for equal rights. Emphasize that the case of *Brown v. Board of Education of Topeka* set in motion the widespread movement for equal rights that continues to this day.

PRIMARY SOURCE
Description of change: excerpted and bracketed.
Rationale: excerpted to focus on what the Supreme Court said about school segregation in its ruling in the case of *Brown v. Board of Education of Topeka;* bracketed words added to clarify meaning.

in helping him adjust normally to his environment. In these days, it is doubtful that any child may reasonably be expected to succeed in life if he is denied the opportunity of an education. Such an opportunity, where the state has undertaken to provide it, is a right which must be made available to all on equal terms.

We come then to the question presented: Does segregation of children in public schools solely on the basis of race, even though the facilities and other 'tangible' factors may be equal, deprive the children of the minority group of equal educational opportunities? We believe it does. . . .

We conclude that in the field of public education the doctrine [idea or principle] of 'separate but equal' has no place. Separate educational facilities are inherently [by nature] unequal. . . .[1]**99**

The Court ruled that a separate education was by its very nature an unequal education. This would be true even if the conditions in the separate schools were identical. Segregation, in other words, suggests that the people kept out are inferior. As Chief Justice Warren wrote, segregation had harmful effects on all children, white as well as black.

In 1954 all the southern states had separate school systems for whites and blacks. Many northern schools were also segregated in fact if not by law. Putting the *Brown v. Board of Education of Topeka* decision into effect was bound to be time consuming and difficult. Therefore, a year later the Court announced that the states must go ahead "with all deliberate speed." This actually meant that they could change slowly. Still, they must begin to change promptly and move steadily toward single, racially integrated school systems.

The *Brown* decision was a unanimous one. This was extremely important. If even one of the nine justices had written a dissenting opinion arguing against the ruling, opponents of desegregation could have used his reasoning to justify resisting the law.

① Even in the face of a unanimous Court, many southern whites were unwilling to accept school integration, no matter how slowly carried out. There was talk of "massive resistance." This was not mere bluff as in the case of Dulles' "massive retaliation." In 1957 the school board of **Little Rock,** Arkansas, following a court order to integrate schools, voted to admit nine black students to a high school for whites. Governor Orville Faubus called out the Arkansas National Guard to prevent the children from entering the school.

President Eisenhower was not personally opposed to school integration. He believed, however, that it was "just plain *nuts*" to
■ force white parents to send their children to integrated schools be-

[1]From *Brown v. Board of Education of Topeka,* Supreme Court of the United States, 347 U.S. 483, 1954

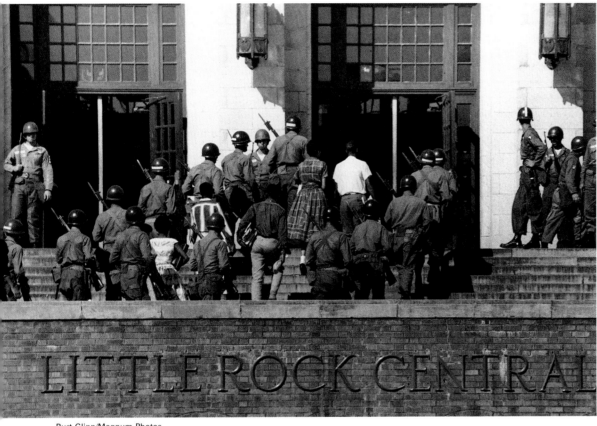

Burt Glinn/Magnum Photos

cause of the problems such a move would cause. But Faubus' act was a direct challenge to federal authority. The president promptly sent 1,000 soldiers to Little Rock. With this force behind them, the black children were admitted to the school. The president of the Arkansas chapter of the NAACP described the day:

> ‟ At 9:22 A.M. the nine Negro pupils marched solemnly through the doors of Central High School, surrounded by twenty-two soldiers. An army helicopter circled overhead. Around the massive brick schoolhouse 350 paratroopers stood grimly at attention. Scores of reporters, photographers, and TV cameramen made a mad dash for telephones, typewriters, and TV studios. Within minutes a world that had been holding its breath learned that the nine pupils, protected by the might of the United States military, had finally entered the 'never-never land.'
>
> When classes ended that afternoon, the troops escorted the pupils to my home. . . .
>
> I asked if they had a rough day. Not especially, they said.

President Eisenhower ordered U.S. troops to escort nine black students into Central High School in Little Rock, Arkansas. Why had they been denied admission to the school? What effect did photographs such as this one have on the American public in the late 1950s?

The Eisenhower Legacy   1011

Point of View

In *Parting the Waters* the Montgomery Bus Boycott is seen in
two perspectives.

" Only the rarest and odd-
est of people saw histor-
ical possibilities in the bus
boycott. Of the few peo-
ple who bothered to write
the *Advertiser* at first,
most were women who
saw it as a justifiable demand for simple decent
treatment. One woman
correspondent did specu-
late that there must be a
Communist hand behind
such strife, but the great
mass of segregationists
did not bother to address
the issue. . . . As for the
boycotters themselves, the
religious fervor they went
to bed with at night al-
ways congealed by the
next morning into cold
practicality, as they faced
rainstorms, mechanical
breakdowns, stranded rel-
atives, and complicated
relays in getting from
home to job without
being late or getting
fired. . . . "

Taylor Branch, 1988

'Then why the long faces?' I wanted to know.

'Well,' Ernest [Green] spoke up, 'you don't expect us to
be jumping for joy, do you?'

Someone said, 'But, Ernest, we *are* in Central. . . .'

'Sure we're in Central,' Ernest shot back, somewhat im-
patiently. 'But how did we get in? We got in, finally, because
we were protected by paratroops. Some victory!' he said
sarcastically.

'Are you sorry,' someone asked him, 'that the President
sent the troops?'

'No,' said Ernest. 'I'm only sorry it had to be that
way.'[1] "

Photographs and motion pictures showed the nine black youngsters being taunted by crowds of angry adults or walking beside army
paratroopers in battle dress. These scenes had a powerful impact on
millions of people, southerners as well as northerners.

The Struggle for Equal Rights

African Americans had been fighting for their rights long before
Brown v. Board of Education. After the Supreme Court declared

[1]From *The Long Shadow of Little Rock* by Daisy Bates

UPI/Bettmann Newsphotos

Rosa Parks sits at the front *of a Montgomery, Alabama, bus one year after
she refused to give up her seat to a
white man. What emotions do you
suppose she felt when this picture was
taken?*

school segregation unconstitutional, African Americans began to speak out even more vigorously against all forms of racial discrimination. In December 1955, Rosa Parks, a black woman in Montgomery, Alabama, was arrested because she refused to give up her seat on a city bus to a white man. Her arrest led the blacks of Montgomery to refuse to ride the buses until the rule requiring blacks to sit in the rear was changed. This boycott was a heavy financial loss for the city's bus system.

The **Montgomery Bus Boycott** lasted for nearly a year. It ended with a victory for the African Americans. The Supreme Court ruled that the Alabama segregation laws were unconstitutional. It was in leading the strike that a young African American clergyman, Martin Luther King, Jr., first became well known. When asked why Rosa Parks had refused to move, he explained how she and many African Americans felt:

> 66 No one can understand the action of Mrs. Parks unless he realizes that eventually the cup of endurance runs over, and the human personality cries out, 'I can take it no longer.' Mrs. Park's refusal to move back was her intrepid affirmation [brave statement] that she had had enough. It was an individual expression of a timeless longing for human dignity and freedom. . . .[1] 99

[1]From *Stride Toward Freedom* by Martin Luther King, Jr.

Throughout the long contest he advised blacks to avoid violence no matter how badly provoked by whites.

King believed in **nonviolent resistance,** what he called nonviolent direct action, for basically religious reasons. He argued that love was a more effective weapon than hate or force. There were also practical reasons for nonviolence. African Americans were a minority in the United States. To obtain fair treatment, they needed the help of white moderates. They were more likely to get that help by appeals to reason and decency than by force.

By the end of Eisenhower's second term real progress had been made. School desegregation was moving ahead slowly. Other forms of segregation were being ended. In 1960, African Americans began an attempt to desegregate lunch counters and similar facilities by staging **sit-ins.** A group would enter a place that served only whites, sit down quietly, and refuse to leave. They were either served or arrested. In either case their actions attracted wide attention and strengthened the drive for fair treatment. By 1960, new organizations such as the Southern Christian Leadership Conference, founded by Reverend King, and the Student Nonviolent Coordinating Committee (SNCC) had sprung up to organize and direct the campaign for equal rights. 🖳

Wide World Photos

"Say I was a drum major for justice," said the Reverend Martin Luther King, Jr., seen here marching in Montgomery in 1956. What philosophy did he preach and practice?

Return to the Preview & Review on page 1000.

INDEPENDENT PRACTICE
Have students complete the Preview & Review activity at the beginning of the section.

CLOSURE
Tell students that while foreign policy continued to be concerned with the Cold War during the Eisenhower years, important domestic changes occurred. The Supreme Court declared school segregation unconstitutional and the Montgomery Bus Boycott renewed the African American campaign for equal rights.

HOMEWORK
Ask students to write a newspaper feature article on one of the Cold War crises such as the revolts in East Germany or Hungary, Vietnam, the Suez Canal, or the U-2 Affair. Read some of the best ones to the class and use the articles to make a bulletin board display.

PRIMARY SOURCE
Description of change: excerpted and bracketed.
Rationale: excerpted to focus on Martin Luther King, Jr.'s, analysis of the reasons behind Rosa Park's refusal to move to the back of the bus; bracketed words added to clarify meaning.

① Kennedy's father, Joseph P. Kennedy, had made a fortune importing liquor "for medicinal purposes" into the United States in the last months of Prohibition. Roosevelt appointed the elder Kennedy as ambassador to Great Britain, but the two later came to dislike one another. As a young Congressman, John F. Kennedy attacked Roosevelt's Soviet policies, and he angered Eleanor Roosevelt by not standing up to McCarthyism.

② Eisenhower did not help Nixon's campaign. When asked by the press what major decisions Nixon had participated in during his administration, Eisenhower replied, "If you give me a week, I might think of one."

PREVIEW & REVIEW RESPONSES
Understanding Issues, Events, & Ideas.
Discussions should demonstrate an understanding of the terms used.

1. Nixon's strengths were cleverness, intelligence, and hard work. His weaknesses were his association with McCarthy, his reckless charges against others, and his obsession with winning at the expense of fair play. Kennedy's advantages were his youth, intelligence, shrewdness, and wealth and his status as a war hero. He could appeal to both liberals and conservatives. His primary disadvantage was his Catholicism.

2. He had criticized the Eisenhower administration for supporting undemocratic governments in Latin America solely because they were anticommunist. Therefore he hesitated to support the overthrow of a government solely because it was procommunist. Kennedy's prestige plummeted.

3. Khrushchev took advantage of the Bay of Pigs Affair to build the Berlin Wall without consulting the Allies. This was viewed as testing Kennedy's willingness to stand up to the Soviet Union.

4. The Soviets built missile bases on Cuba, which the Soviets claimed were only for defensive purposes. Kennedy knew this was untrue because of the evidence in photographs that U-2 planes had taken of the installations. Kennedy demanded that the Soviets re-

Preview & Review

Use these questions to guide your reading. Answer the questions after completing Section 5.
Understanding Issues, Events, & Ideas. Use the following words to discuss the Kennedy years: New Frontier, Cuba, Central Intelligence Agency, Bay of Pigs, Peace Corps, Alliance for Progress, Berlin Wall, Cuban Missile Crisis, "hot line," Camelot.

1. What were Nixon's strengths and weaknesses as a candidate for president in 1960? What were Kennedy's strengths and weaknesses?

2. Why did President Kennedy hesitate to allow the CIA to carry out its invasion of Cuba? What happened to his prestige after the invasion failed?

3. Why did Khrushchev build the Berlin Wall?

4. What provoked the Cuban Missile Crisis? What was Kennedy's response? What was Khrushchev's response?

Thinking Critically. 1. Nixon and Kennedy were the first presidential candidates to hold a televised debate. Suppose you were a member of the studio audience. List five topics that you would have liked to hear the candidates debate. **2.** Imagine that you had been able to interview President Kennedy. What three questions would you have wanted to ask him?

5. A YOUTHFUL COLD WARRIOR

The Election of 1960

In 1960 the Republicans nominated Richard M. Nixon for president. Nixon was Eisenhower's vice president. Before that he had been a congressman and a senator from California.

In Congress Nixon had been a leading communist-hunter. Long before most people took the charges against Alger Hiss seriously, Nixon was convinced of Hiss' guilt. He worked closely with Senator McCarthy in his search for traitors in the government. He was almost as reckless in his charges as McCarthy. While running for vice president in 1952, for example, Nixon claimed that Adlai Stevenson was "soft on communism."

Nixon was a clever politician, but victory was more important to him than fair play. He was an intelligent and hard-working legislator. He sympathized with the civil rights movement, and he had strongly supported President Truman's foreign policy. While vice president he had toned down his talk about traitors in the government. He tried to act more like a statesman. This "new Nixon" persuaded Eisenhower and other Republican leaders to back him for president.

Still, many people did not trust Nixon. Nixon tried hard to explain his controversial reputation. "I believe in battle," he said. "It's always been there, wherever I go." He wrote that his life had been a series of crises. In each one, he claimed, he had triumphed by being "cool and calm" and working hard. But he may have appeared quarrelsome along the way, he admitted.

The Democratic candidate for president in 1960 was Senator ① John F. Kennedy of Massachusetts. Kennedy was young, handsome, intelligent, and rich. He was a war hero, seriously injured in a rescue mission in the Pacific. He was a Pulitzer prize-winning author and a shrewd politician. And he was an excellent campaigner. Kennedy appealed to liberals because he seemed imaginative and forward looking. Many conservatives supported him too because his policies were moderate.

Kennedy's major handicap was his Catholic religion. Al Smith's crushing defeat by Herbert Hoover in 1928 suggested that the anti-Catholic prejudices of voters in normally Democratic states might be difficult to overcome.

During the campaign Kennedy argued that Eisenhower had been too cautious and conservative. The economy was not growing rapidly enough. The nation needed new ideas. He called his program the **New Frontier.** He would open up new fields for development by being ② imaginative and vigorous. Nixon, on the other hand, defended Eisenhower's record and promised to follow the same lines. In the election the popular vote was extremely close. Kennedy won by only

UPI/Bettmann Newsphotos

100,000 votes out of a total of more than 68 million. But in the electoral vote his margin was 303 to 219.

In his inaugural address on January 20, 1961, the president stirred the nation with these words:

❝ We observe today not a victory of party but a celebration of freedom—symbolizing an end as well as a beginning—signifying renewal as well as change. For I have sworn before you and Almighty God the same solemn oath our forebears prescribed nearly a century and three quarters ago.

The world is different now. For man holds in his mortal hands the power to abolish all forms of human poverty and all forms of human life. And yet the same revolutionary beliefs for which our forebears fought are still at issue around the globe—the belief that the rights of man come not from the generosity of the state but from the hand of God.

We dare not forget that we are the heirs of that first revolution. Let the word go forth from this time and place, to friend and foe alike, that the torch has been passed to a new generation of Americans—born in this century, tempered by war, disciplined by a hard and bitter peace, proud of our ancient heritage—and unwilling to witness or permit the slow undoing of those human rights to which this nation has always been committed, and to which we are committed today at home and around the world.

① *Crowds press forward to see John F. Kennedy during his campaign for president in 1960. Both Kennedy and his opponent, Richard Nixon, traveled widely between Labor Day, when campaigns traditionally began, and election day. Kennedy's presidential portrait below is by Aaron Shikler.*

Copyright by the White House Historical Association; photograph by the National Geographic Society

A Youthful Cold Warrior   1015

> Let every nation know, whether it wishes us well or ill,
> that we shall pay any price, bear any burden, meet any
> hardship, support any friend, oppose any foe to assure the
> survival and success of liberty. . . .
>
> And so, my fellow Americans: Ask not what your country
> can do for you—ask what you can do for your country. . . .
>
> With good conscience our only sure reward, with history
> the final judge of our deeds, let us go forth to lead the land
> we love, asking His blessing and His help, but knowing that
> here on earth God's work must truly be our own.[1] **99**

Close listeners could hear behind such golden rhetoric the old
challenges of the Cold War hurled down by this young leader.

The Bay of Pigs

President Kennedy had stressed domestic economic issues in the
1960 campaign. But shortly after he took office, foreign problems
began to occupy most of his time. During President Eisenhower's
second term there had been a revolution in **Cuba** led by Fidel Castro.
Castro set up a communist-type government on this island just 90
miles (144 kilometers) off the tip of Florida. Americans had invested
heavily in Cuba, and Castro now claimed that property for Cuba.
The Eisenhower administration had cut off trade with Cuba. Castro
took an increasingly unfriendly attitude toward the United States and
established close ties with the Soviet Union.

Meanwhile, the **Central Intelligence Agency** (CIA), a government
bureau created in 1947, began to train a small army of Cuban refugees. The plan was to have this force invade Cuba from Central
America in order to overthrow Castro. Of course this was done in
complete secrecy.

When Kennedy learned of the plan, he hesitated to allow the
CIA to put it into effect. He had criticized Eisenhower for supporting
conservative governments in Latin America only because they were
anticommunist. Should he now encourage the overthrow of a government only because it was procommunist?

Kennedy decided to go ahead with the CIA scheme. But he
altered the plan. He encouraged the Cuban patriots to invade the
island, but he withheld American air cover for them. On April 17,
1961, the Cuban force was put ashore in southern Cuba, at a place
known as the **Bay of Pigs.** The invaders hoped to be joined by other
Cubans. Instead they met only Castro's army. All were captured or
killed.

The Bay of Pigs dealt a terrible blow to the prestige of the United
States and to Kennedy in particular. Was the youthful new president

Andrew St. George/Magnum Photos

*Fidel Castro, the communist leader of
Cuba, is surrounded by flags of his
country as he speaks in Havana.
What is the connection between Castro and President Kennedy?*

[1]From *Public Papers of the Presidents of the United States: John F. Kennedy,* 1961

1016

GUIDED INSTRUCTION
Ask interested students to study the history of the U.S. space program. These students could research and prepare a chart for the bulletin board to show information on manned space flights. These should include dates, names of missions, names of astronauts, and the results of the missions. Students could illustrate the chart with pictures of mission highlights.

P. Meyer/Black Star

A Peace Corps volunteer in Ecuador tries making friends with a child, who appears curious about the American.

a reckless adventurer? Could he stand up to his clever communist opponents? Citizens who had voted for Kennedy because they did not trust Nixon were especially shocked by the mission's secrecy. Everyone was shocked by its failure.

The disaster in Cuba all but hid the fact that Kennedy was eager to develop good relations with Latin American countries and to help them improve the lives of their poor. In early 1961 he created the **Peace Corps,** an organization that sent volunteers to help the people of needy countries. It earned tremendous worldwide goodwill for the U.S. as it still does today. Kennedy also proposed what he called an **Alliance for Progress** to provide economic aid for Latin American countries.

The Berlin Wall

The Soviets had taken advantage of Eisenhower and the United States with the publicity of the U-2 Affair. They had pointed their finger at the United States, claiming it was the aggressor, not the Soviet Union. Now Khrushchev decided to take advantage of the Bay of Pigs Affair and test Kennedy's will to resist Soviet pressure.

Without consulting the western authorities in Berlin, Khrushchev suddenly had a wall built across the city, sealing the Soviet zone off from the three western zones. This **Berlin Wall** was actually a sign of communist weakness. Thousands of people from East Germany had fled to the West by way of Berlin since the end of World War II. They went in search of greater personal freedom and the higher wages they could earn there.

The wall reduced this flow to a trickle. But it also reminded the world that large numbers of people in the eastern European countries were captives of communism.

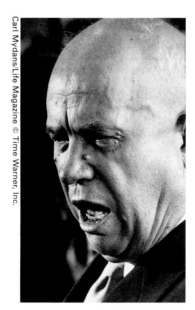

Carl Mydans/Life Magazine © Time Warner, Inc.

The powerful Soviet premier Nikita Khrushchev is shown here at the time of the U-2 Affair. Who could believe that with trembling lip he would soon leave his condolences at the U.S. Embassy upon the death of President Kennedy?

Flip Schulke/Black Star

President John F. Kennedy watches Air Force fighter planes in 1962.

The Cuban Missile Crisis

The United States let the Berlin Wall stand. Khrushchev then apparently decided to test Kennedy still further. The Soviets began to build bases in Cuba from which rocket-powered missiles could be fired. When Kennedy inquired about the purpose of these weapons, the Soviets assured him that only defensive, antiaircraft missiles were being installed.

This was a bald-faced lie, and Kennedy knew it. American U-2 planes had secretly photographed the new installations. The Soviets were preparing longer-range offensive missile bases from which they could fire nuclear warheads at American targets.

Now came the most dangerous moment in the long Cold War. If the United States destroyed the missile bases, a third world war might result. If the Americans did nothing, they risked destruction.

On October 22, 1962, Kennedy appeared on television to tell the public about the **Cuban Missile Crisis.** He demanded that the Soviets remove all their offensive weapons from Cuba and close down the new missile bases. The United States navy would stop and search all ships approaching Cuba to make sure that no more weapons were brought in. If atomic missiles were fired from Cuba, the United States would launch an all-out attack on the Soviet Union.

For three days the world held its breath. Then Khrushchev agreed to remove the missiles. Kennedy won a great personal victory. More important, the possibility of a nuclear war between the United States and the Soviet Union seemed less likely. Both sides had finally come to the brink that John Foster Dulles had foreseen but never actually faced in the 1950s. Both sides had stepped back rather than risk the destruction of the whole world. The United States pledged never to invade Cuba and to remove some missile bases in Turkey, pledges it kept.

Following the Cuban Missile Crisis, a **"hot line"** telephone connection was set up between Washington and Moscow. In any future crisis American and Soviet leaders could talk to each other directly. In the summer of 1963 the two nations took a small first step toward disarmament. They agreed to stop testing nuclear weapons above ground, where the explosions would release dangerous radioactivity into the atmosphere.

Triumph and Tragedy

His success in dealing with the missile crisis made Kennedy seem sure of being reelected in 1964. After years of wartime austerity and the modest styles of the Trumans and the Eisenhowers, Americans were captivated by the style of the new administration. French chefs now prepared their specialties at White House dinners for dazzling people from the arts and sciences who mingled with world leaders, listening to musicians such as the great cellist Pablo Casals. This side of the Kennedy administration later came to be known as **Camelot,** a reference to the mythical Court of King Arthur. In his travels to France with his wife Jacqueline and to Berlin, Kennedy proved what a popular international figure he had become. But at their summit meeting in Vienna in 1961 Kennedy had his ears boxed by the wily Khrushchev who treated the president like a young boy who still had much to learn about international politics. Determined to regain his forceful image, Kennedy prepared more carefully for the international stage. In divided Berlin he electrified the huge crowd:

    ❝ All free men, wherever they may live, are citizens of Berlin. And therefore, as a free man, I take pride in the words *'Ich bin ein Berliner'* ['I am a Berliner']. **❞**

Before his famous speech in Berlin, President Kennedy gazed into the world enslaved by communism beyond the Berlin Wall.

John Dominus/Life Magazine © Time Warner, Inc.

RESOURCES

■ You may wish to have students view Transparency 47: "Moonwalk" and complete the accompanying worksheet in *Art in American History*.

CHECKING UNDERSTANDING

Ask students what Cold War crises Kennedy faced and how he responded to them. *(The Bay of Pigs: Kennedy hesitated then decided to go ahead with the CIA's plan, but he withheld the air cover. The invasion was a disaster, damaging the country's and the president's prestige. Khrushchev felt that this was an advantageous time to put up the Berlin Wall. The Berlin Wall: Kennedy went to Berlin and made a stirring speech but did nothing about the wall. The Cuban Missile Crisis: This was perhaps the most serious crisis of the Cold War. When Kennedy demanded an explanation for the new Soviet missile base in Cuba, the Soviets lied about its purpose. Kennedy responded by demanding that the Soviets remove the missiles and said that the United States navy would search all incoming Soviet ships for weapons cargos. He threatened massive retaliation against the Soviet Union if the Cuban missiles were ever launched. Khrushchev agreed to remove the missiles, and the United States agreed to remove some of its bases in Turkey and to never invade Cuba. This crisis had some positive results. A "hot line" between Washington and Moscow was established, and the two nations stopped above-ground testing of nuclear weapons.)*

PRIMARY SOURCES

(Top) Description of change: excerpted.
Rationale: excerpted to focus on Kennedy's plea to Congress to fund the space program.
(Bottom) Description of change: excerpted.
Rationale: excerpted to focus on Armstrong's words just as he set foot on the moon.

Nevertheless, Kennedy was not able to get Congress to enact much of his domestic program into law. For example, in 1963 he supported a large tax cut. Reducing taxes would stimulate the economy, he claimed. If people paid lower taxes, they would have more money left to spend on goods. Their purchases would cause producers to increase output. More workers would be hired. Unemployment would go down. Personal and business incomes would rise.

In the long run, the president argued, the lower tax rates would actually produce more income for the government. But conservative members of Congress in both parties objected to lowering taxes while the government's budget remained in the red.

Kennedy also introduced a strong civil rights bill in 1963. His proposal outlawed racial discrimination in all places serving the public, such as hotels, restaurants, and theaters. Like the tax reduction, it failed to pass Congress.

Kennedy tried repeatedly to inspire the stubborn Congress. In a typical Cold War challenge, the president told Congress on May 25, 1961:

   ❝ I believe that this nation should commit itself to achieving the goal, before this decade is out, of landing a man on the moon and returning him safely to earth.**❞**

Congress agreed to fund this venture and two presidents later, in July 1969—six months before Kennedy's deadline—American ingenuity prevailed. Apollo 11 with its crew of three astronauts—Neil Armstrong, Edwin "Buzz" Aldrin, and Michael Collins—settled into orbit around the moon. While Collins remained in the command module, Armstrong and Aldrin landed on the moon in an area known as the Sea of Tranquillity. Millions watching on TV saw them step from the lunar lander and heard Armstrong say:

   ❝ That's one small step for a man, one giant leap for mankind.**❞**

To try to smooth local political matters before the election of 1964, the president and his wife visited Texas in November of 1963. On November 22, 1963, while riding through Dallas in an open car, President Kennedy was shot dead. The deed was done so quickly that onlookers scarcely saw the president slump into his wife's lap. The governor of Texas, riding in the front of the car, was wounded. Vice President Johnson, two cars behind in the motorcade, was safe. He was sworn in as president two hours later on *Air Force 1* as it carried the slain president's body home for burial in Arlington National Cemetery. Millions saw the orderly transfer of power on television, as well as the stately funeral procession of world heads of state led by the president's widow Jacqueline.

The man accused of assassinating the president was Lee Harvey Oswald, a mysterious figure who, it turned out, had at one time lived

Fred Ward/Black Star

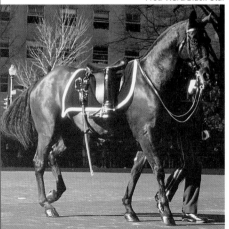

The riderless horse, boots reversed in the stirrups, symbolizes a leader's death in President Kennedy's funeral procession.

RESURCES

■ You may wish to have students complete one or more of the Chapter 27 Tests.

In its way, this photograph is as important as Columbus' journal describing the first sighting of the Americas. To report "Man Walks on Moon," The New York Times had to make special headline type large enough for the biggest story of the 20th century. Neil Armstrong took this picture of Edwin Aldrin, his fellow walker on the moon. Note Armstrong's reflection in Aldrin's face mask.

RETEACHING STRATEGY
Students with Special Needs.
Pair students who are having difficulty with students who are performing well. Have the pairs work together to make a time line of the Kennedy administration.

INDEPENDENT PRACTICE
Have students complete the Preview & Review activity at the beginning of the section.

CLOSURE
Tell students that Kennedy continued American Cold War policies. Domestically his New Frontier program was progressive, and he had a unique gift for inspiring his fellow citizens.

HOMEWORK
Ask students to imagine that they were in Berlin at the time the wall was erected and again when the wall began to come down. Then ask them to write a letter to a friend describing the two events and how they reacted. Read some of the best ones to the class.

in the Soviet Union. Before Oswald could be properly questioned, *he* was murdered while being transferred from one jail to another. This amazing incident caused many people to believe that Oswald had been killed to keep him from confessing that he was acting with a group of enemies of the president. There have been many investigations of the assassination and many theories put forth to explain it. But none have ever been proved.

Return to the Preview & Review on
■ page 1014.

To reinforce the geographic
theme of *location,* give students outline maps of the
world. Instruct them to locate
and label the American colonies in the Pacific and Caribbean. Then have them create a
chart of statistics about these
territories. Have them include:
location (latitude and longitude
coordinates), size, and how acquired. (Students may wish to
add other information.)

LINKING HISTORY & GEOGRAPHY

POLITICAL GEOGRAPHY: UNCLE SAM'S ISLANDS

Political geographers have long been interested in the connections between mother countries and their colonies, especially their locations and the movements between them. The aftermath of World War II and the accompanying tide of independence movements all but ended colonialism. Yet, surprisingly, the United States found itself in possession of an "empire."

An American Empire

1. How did the United States find itself in control of an "empire"?

Few Americans actually like the idea of colonies. After all, our nation once held that status, and we fought a war over 200 years ago to end it. Military conquest and strategic needs have created an American Empire that is a collection of island colonies.

Most American islands have their own governments and fly their own flags. But they are not independent countries. They use American currency, but are not actually part of the United States. They have no direct say in the decisions made for them by Congress. So, while the U.S. has never officially labeled its possessions as colonies, they are precisely that politically.

The total population of Uncle Sam's islands is just a little under four million persons. The total amount of land they occupy is a modest 4,000 square miles [10,360 square kilometers], less than the area of our third-smallest state, Connecticut. These islands stretch from the Pacific to the Caribbean.

Colonial Status and Benefits?

2. What advantages does colonial status provide for islanders?

The five largest American island colonies—Puerto Rico, the Virgin Islands, Samoa, the Northern Marianas, and Guam—are democracies in the sense that they all have locally elected governors and legislators. But they are definitely not independent, self-governing political entities. To varying degrees each possession answers to some branch of the federal government in Washington, D.C., and each is subject to American laws. Although considered citizens of the United States, islanders cannot vote in presidential elections. They elect as their representative in Washington one *non-voting* delegate to the United States House of Representatives.

The United States does not collect federal income taxes from the residents of its possessions. Instead, it allows the local governments of the islands to claim these monies. In addition, islanders do enjoy the opportunity to travel, live, and work in the states. More than 2 million Puerto Ricans have moved to the mainland, especially to New York, although many return to Puerto Rico when they retire. Some 85,000 Samoans, more than twice the population of American Samoa itself, now reside in Hawaii, California, and the state of Washington.

American Islands in the Caribbean

3. What islands in the Caribbean does America control?

Puerto Rico is both the largest and most populous of Uncle Sam's islands. Its people are American citizens, and they are generally proud of it. Many would like to see Puerto Rico become the 51st state. A small but vocal minority would rather see it become an independent nation.

Puerto Rico enjoys a key economic benefit in its relationship with the U.S. Tax laws give American companies exemptions from United States taxes on business done in Puerto Rico. These laws also allow the profits earned in Puerto Rico to go back to mainland offices without incurring taxes. Such laws are powerful incentives for American companies to build plants in Puerto Rico and to employ large numbers of Puerto Rican workers.

In 1917, during World War I, the United States bought some of Puerto Rico's neighboring islands, the Virgin Islands, from Denmark. The purpose of the purchase was to protect the Panama Canal from possible German submarine attack. The American Virgin Islands consist of 50 small islands and three larger ones—St. Thomas, St. Croix, and St. John.

Although poor in many natural resources, the American Virgin Islands are all rich in natural beauty and climate. Virgin Islanders have made the most of these. Each year nearly two million tourists visit the islands. The money they spend equals half the islands' total income.

The Pacific Possessions

4. Why do these islands welcome their present colonial status?

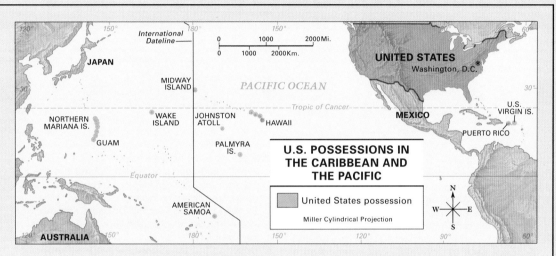

Far to the west, in the South Pacific Ocean, is American Samoa. Its 38,000 people have been generally satisfied with how the American government has administered the island. Although many Samoans have left the island, they keep close ties to home. They send money home to supplement local incomes, most of which are earned from U.S. businesses. And even though the average income earned by American Samoans is less than that of Puerto Ricans or Virgin Islanders, it is three and one-half times that of residents of independent Western Samoa just 80 miles away. This is a powerful incentive to retain its current colonial status.

Guam is the most populous and largest American possession in the Pacific. Most Guamanians are proud to be Americans. Yet they are not entirely happy with the present relationship. In particular Guam would like the opportunity to operate more like Puerto Rico in encouraging American businesses to open in Guam.

Guam is an important military base. Much of its income is from military spending. But tourism is growing. Half a million tourists a year now visit the island, most of them from Japan. Meeting the needs of this booming industry is spurring development on Guam, which seems headed for a more secure economic future.

Few Americans have even heard of the Northern Mariana Islands. After being liberated from the Japanese in World War II, many of the islands in the Pacific were turned over to the United States. Most of these territories have since voted for independence. The Northern Marianas, a group of 16 islands, on the other hand, feel they benefit from their status. The United States department of the interior is responsible to the United Nations for the islands' finances, communications, education, public health, agriculture, and legal problems. The islands receive about $33 million dollars a year for development. And they, like Guam, are attracting large numbers of Japanese tourists. Their sun-drenched beaches are just 1,400 miles (2,240 kilometers) south of Tokyo.

Beyond these larger possessions, the American empire consists of a handful of sparsely populated dots in the Pacific, most of which are important as military bases. Wake Island is a base for the air force. The Midway Islands and Kingman Reef are naval bases. Johnston Atoll is property controlled by the Defense Nuclear Agency, and Palmyra, about 1,000 miles (1,600 kilometers) south of Hawaii, is privately owned. Thus, in the 1990s, the United States is actually one of the few nations in the world retaining colonies. Interestingly, our "colonies" seem unlikely to want this to change in the near future!

APPLYING YOUR KNOWLEDGE
Your class will work in groups to report on U.S. possessions. Each group's report will include maps, pictures, and information on the people, geography, and economy of the possession. Display the reports in the school library.

Thinking Critically

1. Answers will vary; students should support their choices with sound reasoning.
2. It did not apply to him because the amendment specifically excludes the president serving at the time the amendment was proposed and adopted.
3. Students should mention the significance of the meeting for deciding the fate of postwar Europe.

The Big Three agreed on the division of Poland with a portion becoming part of the Soviet Union and the remainder choosing its type of government in free elections.

REVIEW RESPONSES
Chapter Summary
Paragraphs will vary but should be evaluated on the logic of student arguments.

Reviewing Chronological Order
1, 2, 4, 5, 3

Understanding Main Ideas
1. The Soviet Union would annex a major part of eastern Poland, the rest of the Polish people would freely determine their form of government. However, Stalin set up a puppet Polish government that he could control.
2. Both the Truman Doctrine and the Marshall Plan provided economic aid to European countries. Postwar hardships and inflation had strengthened the appeal of the communist parties. By financing economic recovery the United States hoped to end communism's appeal.
3. The Democratic convention nominated Truman, but few party leaders supported him. Some supported Wallace who became the new Progressive party candidate. He had been Truman's secretary of commerce and was highly critical of Truman's containment policy. When Truman's civil rights policy became part of the Democratic platform, Conservative Southern Democrats, or Dixiecrats, formed the States' Rights party and nominated Strom Thurmond.
4. He assumed that the Soviets were behind the attack and, applying the containment policy, he ordered U.S.

CHAPTER 27 REVIEW

1945		1950			
1945 World War II ends ★ United Nations is formed	**1947** Truman Doctrine ★ Taft-Hartley Act **1948** Marshall Plan enacted ★ Berlin Airlift begins ★ Truman elected president	**1949** NATO is formed ★ Communists control China	**1950** McCarran Internal Security Act ★ Korean War begins **1951** Twenty-second Amendment	**1952** Eisenhower elected president **1953** Department of Health, Education, and Welfare created ★ Truce halts the Korean War	**1954** *Brown v. Board of Education* ★ Communists attack in Vietnam **1955** Montgomery Bus Boycott

Chapter Summary
Read the statements below. Choose one, and write a paragraph explaining its importance.
1. After World War II the search for world peace led to the establishment of the United Nations, with the United States as a leading member.
2. President Truman concentrated on getting America back to "normal," and established a program called the Fair Deal. Congress, however, refused to pass most of the legislation.
3. Despite the help of the Marshall Plan to war-ravaged countries, communists gained power in Europe and China, leading the United States to adopt a policy of containment and involvement in the Korean War. It also led to McCarthyism at home.
4. The Cold War between capitalism and communism caused widespread tension.
5. President Eisenhower's foreign policy threatened massive retaliation based on brinksmanship, but avoided direct conflict.
6. Eisenhower's domestic policies were moderate, sometimes liberal, sometimes conservative. He supported the Constitution after *Brown v. Board of Education of Topeka* and sent troops to enforce school integration in Little Rock.
7. John Kennedy's victory in 1960 brought the nation to a New Frontier. He was more assertive toward the communists than either Truman or Eisenhower. Kennedy's leadership, however, was cut short by an assassin's bullet.

Reviewing Chronological Order
Number your paper 1-5. Then study the time line above and place the following events in the order in which they happened by writing the first next to 1, the second next to 2, and so on.
1. Berlin Airlift
2. Korean War erupts
3. Cuban Missile Crisis
4. Fighting in Vietnam erupts
5. Kennedy elected president

Understanding Main Ideas
1. What major decision about Poland did the Big Three make at Yalta? How did the Soviet Union come to dominate Poland?
2. Explain how the Truman Doctrine and the Marshall Plan were intended to stop the spread of communism.
3. Describe the three-way split in the Democratic party in the election of 1948.
4. Why did President Truman order U.S. troops into Korea? Why did he remove General MacArthur from command?
5. Explain the case of *Brown v. Board of Education*. What did the Supreme Court direct in its unanimous decision?

Thinking Critically
1. **Resolving Issues.** Imagine that you are a delegate to the United Nations when it is first created. What three world problems would you most like to see resolved?
2. **Analyzing.** President Truman was not affected by the Twenty-second Amendment. Read the amendment and explain why the amendment did not apply to him.
3. **Synthesizing.** You are a magazine reporter who has been assigned to cover the meeting at Yalta in 1945. Write an article describing the meeting and explaining its historical significance.

Writing About History
Use historical imagination to write a thank you letter from a Berliner for the airlift of 1948-49. Use the information in Chapter 27 and other accounts of the airlift to help you write your letter.

Practicing the Strategy
Review the strategy on page 987.
Analyzing Historical Interpretations. Read the following passage by historian John Lewis Gaddis on the origins of the Cold War. Then answer the questions that follow.

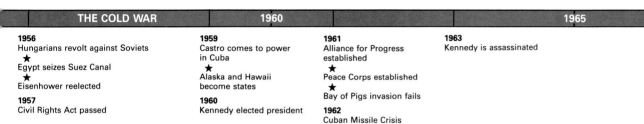

1956
Hungarians revolt against Soviets
★
Egypt seizes Suez Canal
★
Eisenhower reelected
1957
Civil Rights Act passed

1959
Castro comes to power in Cuba
★
Alaska and Hawaii become states
1960
Kennedy elected president

1961
Alliance for Progress established
★
Peace Corps established
★
Bay of Pigs invasion fails
1962
Cuban Missile Crisis

1963
Kennedy is assassinated

Historians have debated at length the question of who caused the Cold War.... Too often they view that event only as a series of actions by one side and reactions by the other.... officials in Washington and Moscow brought to the task of policy making a variety of fixed ideas, shaped by personality, ideology, political pressures, even ignorance and irrationality, all of which influenced their behavior.... it becomes clear that neither side can take complete responsibility for the Cold War.

1. Do you agree with Gaddis' reasoning that brings him to the conclusion that neither side was completely responsible for the Cold War? Why or why not?
2. Would you say that Gaddis' analysis was biased? Why or why not?

Using Primary Sources
The following excerpt is from an interview with Diane Nash, who led the movement to desegregate lunch counters in Nashville's department stores. The interview was published in *Eyes on the Prize: America's Civil Rights Years, 1954–1965*. As you read the excerpt, think about how the civil rights movement accomplished social change.

I think it's really important that young people today understand that the movement of the sixties was really a people's movement. The media and history seem to record it as Martin Luther King's movement, but young people should realize that it was people just like them, their age, that formulated goals and strategies, and actually developed the movement. When they look around now, and see things that need to be changed, they should say: "What can I do?"

1. How does Diane Nash offer encouragement to young people today?
2. What do you see that needs to be changed? How could you help to make that change?
3. The civil rights movement used nonviolent direct action. Why do you think the movement chose this strategy?

Linking History & Geography
Geographers often study the earth by dividing it into regions that share similar features, including similar political goals. During the Cold War in Europe, three separate regions developed—NATO members, communist nations of the Warsaw Pact, and neutral nations. Study the map on page 991 and similar maps in reference atlases. Then on an outline map of Europe show the members of NATO and the Warsaw Pact. You may also wish to create a map that illustrates the European Community, the Council for Mutual Economic Assistance, and the European Free Trade Association.

Enriching Your Study of History
1. **Individual Project**. Complete one of the following projects: Listen to recordings of the Army-McCarthy Hearings of 1954 and prepare a class report; prepare a report on the life of Martin Luther King, Jr., and his long struggle for equal rights; prepare a large version of the map on page 991 to show Europe during the Cold War. Use the map to illustrate a series of written reports on major events of the Cold War. Topics should include the Marshall Plan, containment, Churchill's Iron Curtain speech, the Berlin Airlift, uprisings in East Germany and Hungary, the establishment of NATO and of the Warsaw Pact, the brinksmanship of John Foster Dulles, and the 1955 Geneva Summit Conference.
2. **Cooperative Project**. Your class will use library periodicals and reference books to find out how meetings of the Security Council of the United Nations are conducted. Some of your class will represent the members of the council and discuss a matter of current world interest. Try to bring the matter to some resolution. The permanent council members are: the United States, China, Great Britain, France, and the U.S.S.R. Other members of your class will represent African and Asian countries, Eastern Europe, Latin America, and Western Europe.

Practicing Critical Thinking
1. Answers will vary; students should use sound reasoning to support their answer.
2. Answers will vary, but students should logically support their answer.
3. Answers will vary; students should use sound reasoning in supporting their view.

REVIEW RESPONSES
Summing Up and Predicting
Paragraphs will vary but should be evaluated on the logic of student arguments.

Connecting Ideas
1. Answers will vary; students should support their choice with sound reasoning.
2. The governor of Arkansas called out the Arkansas National Guard to prevent the implementation of the Supreme Court's decision. Since this was a direct challenge to federal authority, Eisenhower sent a force of 1,000 soldiers in to ensure that the court order was obeyed. The soldiers escorted the African American children into school. Pictures of these scenes had a powerful influence on public opinion. Section 1 of the Fourteenth Amendment to the Constitution states that "no state shall make or enforce any law which shall abridge the privileges or immunities of citizens of the United States; nor shall any State . . . deny to any person within its jurisdiction the equal protection of the laws."

* These sources are suitable for students reading below grade level.

1026

UNIT NINE REVIEW

Summing Up and Predicting
Read the summary of the main ideas in Unit Nine below. Choose one statement, then write a paragraph predicting its outcome or future effect.
1. Most Americans believed in isolationism after the Great World War.
2. Totalitarian governments in Italy, Japan, and Germany began aggressive actions in both Europe and Asia. President Roosevelt sought ways to check them without becoming involved in a shooting war.
3. Hitler's war machine invaded Poland, touching off World War II. Japanese bombing of Pearl Harbor brought the U.S. into the war.
4. The Allies first defeated Hitler in Europe. They then turned their full attention on the Japanese. Atomic bombs dropped on Hiroshima and Nagasaki ended the war.
5. The horrors and inhumanity of the Second World War made people realize that war must now be avoided at all costs.
6. After World War II the search for world peace led to the establishment of the United Nations, with the United States as a leading member.
7. At home after the war, American presidents—Truman and Eisenhower—concentrated on getting America back to "normal."
8. Meanwhile communists gained power in Europe and China, leading to a Cold War between capitalism and communism.
9. John Kennedy's victory in 1960 brought the nation to a New Frontier. Kennedy's leadership, however, was cut short by an assassin's bullet.

Connecting Ideas
1. If you could have been a member of the White House staff during the Roosevelt, Truman, Eisenhower, or Kennedy administrations, which would you have chosen to work for? Why?
2. Describe the incident at Little Rock High School in constitutional terms. Explain the conflict between state and federal powers. How was the conflict resolved? Cite the part of the Constitution that explains how conflicts of this nature should be solved.

Practicing Critical Thinking
1. **Predicting.** What do you think might have happened if Germany had developed the atomic bomb before the United States?
2. **Analyzing.** One of the arguments for the intern-

ment of Japanese Americans was that the constitutional rights of citizens are suspended during wartime. Do you think that the constitutional rights of all citizens should be suspended during wartime? Why or why not?
3. **Evaluating.** The Cuban Missile Crisis brought the United States to the brink of war with the Soviet Union. Do you agree with Kennedy's decision to stand tough? Support your view.

Cooperative Learning
1. Your group will prepare a multimedia presentation on one of the following: the *Brown* decision and school desegregation, Martin Luther King, Jr.'s, struggle for equal rights, the assassination of John Kennedy, or the fears and reactions in America during the height of the Cold War. Reports should include pictures and recordings when possible.
2. On April 12, 1945, President Franklin Roosevelt died suddenly. The new president, Harry Truman, told reporters, "I felt like the moon, the stars, and all the planets had fallen on me." One member of your group will play the part of Truman, and the rest of your group will act as reporters. Stage a press conference for the class. The reporters will interview President Truman on his first day in office. Reporters should ask the president about some of the major decisions he will have to make.

Reading in Depth
Barker, Elisabeth. *The Cold War.* New York: Putnam. Contains a description of the beginnings of tensions between the United States and the Soviet Union.
*Frank, Anne. *Diary of a Young Girl.* Garden City, NY: Doubleday. Provides a vivid account of a Jewish girl and her family as they hide from the Nazis.
Hichiya, M. *Hiroshima Diary.* Chapel Hill, NC: University of North Carolina Press. Presents eyewitness accounts of the devastation caused by the atomic bomb.
Litz, Richard. *Many Kinds of Courage: An Oral History of World War II.* New York: Putnam. Contains interviews with the men and women who took part in the Second World War.
*Savage, Katherine. *The Story of the United Nations.* Portland, ME: Walck. Provides accounts of the international movement for peace and the beginnings of the UN.

UNIT OBJECTIVES
Upon completing Unit 10, students will be able to:
1. Identify programs of the Great Society.
2. Evaluate the progress made by women, American Indians, and African Americans between the end of World War II and the present.
3. Trace America's involvement in Vietnam.

4. Describe the events related to the Watergate cover-up that led to President Nixon's resignation.
5. Discuss U.S. policies during the Ford and Carter administrations.
6. Analyze problems Americans had to face in the 1970s and 1980s.

Larry Downing/Woodfin Camp

Mikhail Gorbachev and Ronald Reagan meet in one of their several summits.

MODERN AMERICA UNIT 10

I n Unit 10 you will learn about the Vietnam War, the Watergate Affair, and the Reagan-Bush Era. Here are some main points to keep in mind as you read the unit.

- Medicare and the Voting Rights Act were among the successes of President Johnson's Great Society program.
- As the United States grew more involved in the Vietnam conflict, millions of Americans began to oppose the war.
- 1968 was a tragic year in American history. Martin Luther King, Jr., and Robert Kennedy both were assassinated.
- President Nixon had many successes in foreign policy, such as improving relations with China and the Soviet Union.
- Nixon's involvement in the coverup of the Watergate burglary forced him to resign the presidency.
- President Reagan in the 1980s moved the nation in a more conservative direction.
- The Soviet Union collapsed in the early 1990s. Russia and Ukraine were the two most important successor nations.

OVERVIEW
Lyndon Johnson initiated a number of domestic reforms in a program known as the Great Society. Major scientific developments, dramatic changes in population trends, and economic prosperity made a dramatic impact upon American society by the mid-1960s. Women, American Indians, and African Americans continued to organize efforts to gain equal rights. The optimistic mood of the 1950s and early 1960s changed with the escalation of the Vietnam War. Trust in the government was eroded when the Watergate scandal was revealed to the American public. The continuing problems of urban decay, pollution, and dwindling energy reserves were issues presidents Ford, Carter, and Reagan attempted to solve with varying degrees of success. As the final decade of the century began, it appeared that the Cold War was ending and America was entering a new era of world peace.

CONNECTING WITH PAST LEARNING
Ask students if they think that society is changing at an increasingly faster rate. *(Most will probably say that it is.)* Then ask them if their parents ever talk about changes in society since they were younger and what kind of changes they mention. Tell students that, in general, social conditions have improved since World War II but that there have been setbacks in some areas. Ask students for examples. *(increased drug use, rising crime rate, and the increase in the number of homeless men and women)*

The Great Society

PLANNING THE CHAPTER

TEXTBOOK	RESOURCES
1. The Johnson Presidency	**Unit 10 Worksheets and Tests:** Chapter 28 Graphic Organizer, Directed Reading 28:1, Reteaching 28:1 **Eyewitnesses and Others, Volume 2:** Reading 67: President Johnson Defines the Great Society (1964) **The Constitution: Past, Present, and Future:** Case 12: *Gideon v. Wainwright*; Case 13: *Miranda v. Arizona*
2. A Prosperous America	**Unit 10 Worksheets and Tests:** Directed Reading 28:2, Reteaching 28:2 **Art in American History:** Transparency 37: Eve of St. John, Transparency 38: The Family, Transparency 39: Return of the Prodigal Son **Eyewitnesses and Others, Volume 2:** Reading 62: Two Views of America in the 1950s
3. A Society of Many Members	**Unit 10 Worksheets and Tests:** Directed Reading 28:3, Reteaching 28:3, Geography 28A and 28B
4. Movements for Equal Rights	**Unit 10 Worksheets and Tests:** Directed Reading 28:4, Reteaching 28:4 **Creative Strategies for Teaching American History:** Page 345 **Eyewitnesses and Others, Volume 2:** Reading 61: Betty Friedan Discusses the Feminine Mystique (1950s), Reading 63: A Declaration of Indian Purpose (1961), Reading 73: N. Scott Momaday Describes the Indian Vision (1970s), Reading 66: The Reverend Martin Luther King, Jr., Preaches Nonviolence from the Birmingham Jail (1963) **The Constitution: Past, Present, and Future:** Case 11: *Loving v. Virginia* **Voices of America: Speeches and Documents:** "I Have a Dream" Speech by the Reverend Martin Luther King, Jr. (1963)
Chapter Review	**Audio Program:** Chapter 28 **Unit 10 Worksheets and Tests:** Chapter 28 Tests, Forms A and B (See also *Alternative Assessment Forms*) **Test Generator**

STRATEGIES FOR STUDENTS WITH SPECIAL NEEDS

Gifted Students.
Have interested students use resources in the school or public library to find more information on one of the programs of the Great Society. Then have them work in groups to prepare a television news account of the program. During their presentation students should plan to interview people who favor the legislation as well as those who oppose it. Have students present their news account for the rest of the class. After the presentation has been made, allow other members of the class to ask questions about the Great Society program that was profiled.

Students Having Difficulty with the Chapter.
You may wish to have students listen to Chapter 28 in *The Story of America Audio Program.* Then pair students who are having difficulty with students who are performing well. Instruct each pair to study the illustrations in the chapter. Have the more proficient students ask the others to describe what they think is going on in each illustration. If the illustration depicts people, ask the students to describe what they believe the people are feeling and thinking at the exact moment shown. After the pairs have completed the assignment, discuss the illustrations with the entire class.

BOOKS FOR TEACHERS
Robert Caro, *The Years of Lyndon Johnson: The Path to Power.* New York: Knopf, 1982.

James Gilbert, *Another Chance: Postwar America, 1945–1968.* Philadelphia: Temple University Press, 1981.

William E. Leuchtenburg, *In the Shadow of FDR: From Harry Truman to Ronald Reagan.* Ithaca, N.Y.: Cornell University Press, 1983.

John E. Schwarz, *America's Hidden Success: A Reassessment of Twenty Years of Public Policy.* New York: W. W. Norton, 1983.

BOOKS FOR STUDENTS
David A. Adler, *Martin Luther King, Jr.: Free at Last.* New York: Holiday House, 1986.

Harold Coy, *Chicano Roots Go Deep.* New York: Dodd, 1975.

Arlene Hirschfelder, *Happily May I Walk: American Indians and Alaska Today.* New York: Scribner's, 1986.

Milton Meltzer, *Betty Friedan: A Voice for Women's Rights.* New York: Viking, 1985.

Brenda Wilkinson, *Not Separate, Not Equal.* New York: Harper & Row, 1987.

MULTIMEDIA MATERIALS
American Foreign Policy (software), SSSS. Sections applicable to this chapter.

An American Tragedy: The Death of President Kennedy (film, 21 min.), Hearst. A survey of Kennedy's life; includes a speech he gave to students.

Equality in America (filmstrip), SSSS. Asks students to examine their own attitudes toward equality in America.

I Can Hear It Now—the Sixties (record), EDRECS. Presents the sounds of events in the 1960s: the assassination of President Kennedy; the first moon landing; riots in Watts, Newark, and Detroit; and the work of Martin Luther King, Jr.

The War on Poverty (filmstrip), EAV. Discusses major trends, events, and issues concerning Johnson's war on poverty.

CHAPTER OBJECTIVES
Upon completing this chapter, students will be able to:

1. Identify major programs of the Great Society.
2. Explain why the United States was called the Affluent Society.
3. Identify major scientific achievements of the 1950s.
4. Discuss factors that have led many Americans to move to the Sun Belt.
5. Analyze the effects of the growth of the suburbs.

OVERVIEW
During the presidency of Lyndon Johnson domestic programs known as the Great Society were initiated. Major trends that began at the end of World War II and that included increasing affluence, scientific advances, and major population shifts became more visible in American society by the mid 1960s. The equal rights struggle for women, native Americans, and African Americans took on even more of a focus as new organizations were founded to implement their goals.

FOCUS/MOTIVATION:
MAKING CONNECTIONS
Student Experiences.
Ask students to name the man who is probably the most famous African American leader today. *(Jesse Jackson)* Ask them how he came into national prominence in recent years. *(He ran for president in the 1984 and 1988 elections.)* Tell students that Reverend Jackson's public career began in the 1960s when he worked with Dr. Martin Luther King, Jr., in the civil rights movement. Point out to students that this chapter discusses how the civil rights movement gathered momentum in the early and mid 1960s under the leadership of Dr. King and that women and American Indians also struggled for equal rights during this period.

PRIMARY SOURCE
Description of change: excerpted.
Rationale: excerpted to focus on Johnson's speech urging Congress to pass the Civil Rights Act.

CHAPTER 28

The Great Society

Point of View

Lyndon Johnson's first address to Congress as president.

  ❝ No memorial oration or eulogy could more eloquently honor President Kennedy's memory than the earliest possible passage of the civil rights bill for which he fought so long. We have talked enough in this country about equal rights. We have talked for one hundred years or more. It is time now to write the next chapter—and to write it in the books of law.

  I urge you again, as I did in 1957 and again in 1960, to enact a civil rights law so that we can move forward to eliminate from this nation every trace of discrimination and oppression that is based upon race or color. . . . ❞
      Lyndon Johnson, 1963

■ Once again an assassin's bullet claimed an American president when John F. Kennedy was shot in 1963. And again the transfer of power to the vice president, clearly outlined in the Constitution, was orderly as Lyndon Baines Johnson succeeded to the presidency.

    Perhaps no man has come to the presidency with greater qualifications than Johnson. He had served President Kennedy faithfully. Now he would be an active president. No one knew Washington more intimately. He decided to try to get President Kennedy's legislation passed by Congress as a memorial. He would build a Great Society to improve the lives of all people, but especially the poor and the powerless. And Lyndon Johnson, a Son of the South, would preside over the passage of the Civil Rights Act. The Johnson presidency reminded some people of the early days of Johnson's hero Franklin Delano Roosevelt. Could Johnson truly build a great society where others had failed?

Wide World Photos

Lyndon B. Johnson takes the oath from Judge Sarah T. Hughes, Lady Bird and Jacqueline Kennedy at his side.

SUGGESTED CAPTION RESPONSE
Opinions will vary.

1. THE JOHNSON PRESIDENCY

A Whirlwind of Energy

Before becoming vice president Johnson served for many years in the House and Senate. A lifelong Democrat, he worshipped Franklin Roosevelt and admired Harry Truman. Yet as majority leader of the Senate he had worked with President Eisenhower, a Republican, on most legislative matters. His years in Washington taught him much about government and how to get things done.

In personality and style Johnson resembled Andrew Jackson more than any other president. He was both warmhearted and hot-tempered. And like Jackson, he was energetic. He seemed to be everywhere—inspecting offices, signing bills, greeting tourists, settling disputes.

Johnson's first goal as president was to make sure there was no disruption in leadership. He was also determined to get Kennedy's program adopted by Congress. This would honor Kennedy's memory and establish Johnson's own reputation. Here Johnson's long service in Congress was an enormous advantage. He bullied, wheedled, and bargained. He had a way of brushing aside or smothering other people's objections and doubts. He would call in a hesitating lawmaker, rise intimidatingly to his full height of nearly six and a half feet, grab him by the lapels of his suitcoat, and say, "Come, let us reason together." More often than not the legislator would do what Johnson wanted, moved by a combination of awe and fear.

Wide World Photos

Preview & Review

Use these questions to guide your reading. Answer the questions after completing Section 1.
Understanding Issues, Events, & Ideas. Use the following words to describe the economic and social programs proposed by Lyndon Johnson: Civil Rights Act, Economic Opportunity Act, Head Start, Job Corps, VISTA, Great Society, Medicare, Immigration Act of 1965, Housing Act, Highway Safety Act, Voting Rights Act.
1. Why was Lyndon Johnson considered highly qualified for the presidency?
2. For what reasons was Johnson determined to get President Kennedy's programs adopted by Congress?
3. What was contained in the Civil Rights Act of 1964?
4. What were some Great Society measures passed by Congress?
Thinking Critically. 1. Imagine that you are an American citizen who has benefited from one of the Great Society programs. Write a letter to a friend in which you describe how this program has improved your life. **2.** If you had been a voter in 1964 would you have supported Johnson or Goldwater for president? Explain your answer.

With a stroke of his pen Lyndon Johnson, a Son of the South, signs into law the Civil Rights Act of 1964. Johnson was such a forceful personality that Washington still debates whether the act passed as a memorial to President Kennedy or because of Johnson's sheer willpower. Which do you think?

PREVIEW & REVIEW RESPONSES
Understanding Issues, Events, & Ideas.
Descriptions should demonstrate an understanding of the terms used.
1. He served as vice president, served in the House and Senate, and had been Senate majority leader.
2. He wanted to honor Kennedy's memory and establish his own reputation.
3. It prohibited racial discrimination in public facilities and made it easier and safer for southern blacks to register and vote.
4. Medicare, Immigration Act of 1965, Housing Act, Highway Safety Act, Voting Rights Act

Thinking Critically.
1. Student letters should demonstrate an understanding of the Great Society programs.
2. Students should support their answers with sound reasoning and logic.

FOCUS/MOTIVATION:
MAKING CONNECTIONS
Prior Knowledge.
Begin a class discussion by asking students to name some of the programs that were part of the New Deal. *(Students may mention the Civilian Conservation Corps as an example.)* Point out to students that under the programs initiated by President Johnson the federal government again played an active role in improving social conditions in America, such as fighting poverty.

HISTORICAL SIDELIGHTS

● The Office of Equal Opportunity's anti-poverty program received funding of $1.5 billion from Congress. In addition, Congress voted funding of $1 billion to aid the economy of 11 depressed states in Appalachia.

RESOURCES

■ You may wish to have students complete Reading 67: "President Johnson Defines the Great Society (1964)" in Volume II of *Eyewitnesses and Others.*

GUIDED INSTRUCTION: COOPERATIVE LEARNING

Divide the class into three groups. Assign each group one of the following topics: civil rights, poverty, or education. Tell them that these were three of the major areas of concern facing Lyndon Johnson when he became president. Have each group draw up a proposal that lists specific ways of solving problems related to their topic. Have each group select a spokesperson to present their proposal to the class. Allow time for class discussion following each presentation.

CHECKING UNDERSTANDING

Have students review the following programs and acts that were passed by Congress at Lyndon Johnson's urging.

1. Head Start program *(It gave extra help to children at risk even before they were old enough to go to school.)*
2. Job Corps *(Its purpose was to train school dropouts and set up adult education programs.)*
3. VISTA *(It was like the Peace Corps except the participants worked within the U.S.)*
4. Medicare *(It provided health insurance for people over 65.)*
5. Immigration Act of 1965 *(It abolished the system of favoring immigrants from nations of northern and Western Europe.)*
6. Housing Act *(It helped pay the rent of poor people.)*

A volunteer for VISTA—Johnson's domestic program to parallel the Peace Corps—consoles a child at school.

As a result of Johnson's hard work, Congress passed in 1964 a bill reducing taxes by over $10 billion and a **Civil Rights Act** prohibiting racial discrimination in restaurants, theaters, hotels, hospitals, and public facilities of all sorts. This Civil Rights Act also made it easier and safer for southern blacks to register and vote.

● Congress also passed the **Economic Opportunity Act** of 1964 at Johnson's urging. This law sought to help poor people improve their ability to earn money. It attacked the problem at every level. It set up the **Head Start** program to give extra help to children at risk even before they were old enough to go to school. There was a **Job Corps** to train school dropouts as well as an adult education program. The law also founded **VISTA,** a domestic parallel to the overseas Peace Corps.

Johnson wanted to leave his own legacy as well. He tended to dislike the "Harvard intellectuals" left over from the Kennedy presidency and was particularly suspicious of Robert Kennedy, the attorney general and former president's brother. He gradually replaced most of them with people he trusted.

The Great Society

■ Lyndon Johnson easily won the Democratic nomination for president in 1964. Although there had been great popular support for choosing Robert Kennedy for vice president, Johnson chose Hubert Humphrey, a liberal senator from Minnesota. His Republican opponent was Senator Barry Goldwater of Arizona. Even people who disliked Goldwater's ideas tended to like him personally. He was sincere and frank, not the kind of politician who adjusts positions to the mood and the prejudices of the voters. Goldwater was extremely conservative. He spoke critically of such basic policies as the social security system. He favored selling all the facilities of the Tennessee Valley

RESOURCES
- ■ You may wish to have students complete Case 12: *"Gideon v. Wainwright"* in *THE CONSTITUTION: Past, Present, and Future.*
- ◄ You may wish to have students complete Case 13: *"Miranda v. Arizona"* in *THE CONSTITUTION: Past, Present, and Future.*

SUGGESTED CAPTION RESPONSE
Goldwater was a conservative who favored fewer government programs. He also favored direct attacks on the spread of communism. Johnson believed that the government should fund social programs. He was not as ready as Goldwater to commit American forces to stopping the spread of communism.

Authority to private companies. He wanted to cut back or eliminate many other long-established functions of the federal government. ■

In his acceptance speech at the Republican National Convention, Goldwater frightened many of his listeners when he said:

❝ Extremism in the defense of liberty is no vice. And . . . moderation in the pursuit of justice is no virtue. ❞

Most voters found Goldwater's ideas *too* extreme. Johnson defeated him easily. The Democrats increased their majorities in Congress as well.

Johnson then proposed what he called the **Great Society** program. With typical energy he sent Congress 63 messages calling for legislation in a single year. He stated his vision of the Great Society:

❝ The Great Society is a place where every child can find knowledge to enrich his mind and to enlarge his talents. It is a place where leisure is a welcome chance to build and reflect, not a feared cause of boredom and restlessness. It is a place where the city of man serves not only the needs of the body and the demands of commerce but the desire for beauty and the hunger for community.

It is a place where man can renew contact with nature. It is a place which honors creation for its own sake and for what it adds to the understanding of the race. It is a place where men are more concerned with the quality of their goals than the quantity of their goods.

But most of all, the Great Society is not a safe harbor, a resting place, a final objective, a finished work. It is a challenge constantly renewed, beckoning us toward a destiny where the meaning of our lives matches the marvelous products of our labor.[1] ❞

[1]From *History of U.S. Political Parties* by Arthur M. Schlesinger

Congress approved nearly everything Johnson asked for. It cre- ◄ ated **Medicare,** providing health insurance for people over 65. It supplied huge grants to improve elementary and secondary education. The **Immigration Act of 1965** abolished the system of favoring immigrants from the nations of northern and western Europe. Future admission to the United States was to be based on the skills and abilities of the newcomers, regardless of nationality.

There was also a **Housing Act** to help pay the rent of poor people and a **Highway Safety Act.** Another civil rights measure, the **Voting Rights Act,** was passed. This law appointed new federal officials called registrars in districts where local white officials were refusing to allow African Americans to register to vote. These federal officials made sure there were no problems or irregularities in voter registration in those districts. Within a year and a half a million southerners were added to the voter lists. 🖻

Paul Slade/Globe Photos

Senator Barry Goldwater became the chief spokesman for the conservative wing of the Republican party. In the early 1960s his firm stand against communism earned him national prominence. His widely read 1960 book The Conscience of a Conservative *was a statement of his views on American foreign policy and the use of force against communism. How did Goldwater's ideas differ from Johnson's?*

Return to the Preview & Review on page 1029.

RETEACHING STRATEGY
Students with Special Needs.
Pair students who are having difficulty with students who are performing well. Have students create a poster advertising one of the following programs:
1. Head Start program
2. Job Corps
3. VISTA
4. Medicare
5. Housing Act

You may wish to have students create a small poster for each of the programs listed.

INDEPENDENT PRACTICE
Have students complete the Preview & Review activity at the beginning of the section.

CLOSURE
Point out to students that many of the programs of the Great Society continued the tradition of government involvement begun by the New Deal. Like the New Deal programs, many were dismantled by subsequent presidents. Others, such as Medicare, are still in existence.

HOMEWORK
In the early 1980s Congress, at Reagan's urging, began to dismantle many programs of Roosevelt's New Deal and Johnson's Great Society. Have students choose one of these programs and prepare a rationale for continuing funding for it.

PRIMARY SOURCES
(Top) Description of change: excerpted.
Rationale: excerpted to focus on Goldwater's views on extremism.
(Bottom) Description of change: excerpted.
Rationale: excerpted to focus on Lyndon Johnson's vision of the Great Society.

PREVIEW & REVIEW RESPONSES
Understanding Issues, Events, & Ideas.
Explanations should demonstrate an understanding of the terms used.
1. The standard of living was high; a prosperous society with an abundance of wealth
2. Victory in World War II, the unprecedented period of economic prosperity, and scientific and technological advances contributed to America's optimism.
3. Nuclear power was used to make and distribute electricity.
4. New products included synthetic textiles, transistors, computers, and antibiotics.

Thinking Critically.
Student answers will vary but should be supported by sound reasoning and logic.

Preview & Review

Use the questions to guide your reading. Answer the questions after completing Section 2.
Understanding Issues, Events, & Ideas. Explain America's progress in the 1950s and 1960s, using the following words: standard of living, Affluent Society, factors of production, AFL-CIO, nuclear energy, synthetic textile, transistor, antibiotic, polio vaccine, white-collar worker, blue-collar worker, television, computer, fiscal policy, monetary policy.
1. What was the standard of living in America by the mid-1960s? What is meant by the Affluent Society?
2. What were some of the reasons that Americans were so optimistic after World War II?
3. What peacetime use of nuclear energy began in the 1950s?
4. What were some products developed after World War II?
Thinking Critically. Americans were optimistic about the future of their society in the 1950s and 1960s. Do you think that Americans in the 1990s still have this feeling of optimism about their country's future? Give reasons to support your answer.

2. A PROSPEROUS AMERICA

The Affluent Society

■ The 1950s had seemed settled and comfortable. Americans were enjoying the great prosperity that had developed after World War II. Yet some who looked forward, like folksinger Bob Dylan, warned, "A hard rain's gonna fall." The Cold War and the space race had placed new and greater demands on American science, technology, and education. Not all Americans shared equally in the nation's prosperity, and the rising protests of African Americans and others against discrimination and poverty called for government action.

The election of the vigorous and energetic John F. Kennedy in 1960 had signaled that the nation was ready to take up the challenges of change. Kennedy had promised a bold new course for the nation. Lyndon Johnson's first actions as president showed he planned to follow a similar course.

In the mid-1960s the United States seemed to be entering a new Golden Age. Looking back over the 20 years since the end of World War II, most observers were struck by the tremendous advances that had been made. The **standard of living** of the nation as a whole—the measure of the necessities, comforts, and luxuries available—had never been so high. The percentage of poor people had fallen sharply and would probably be further reduced by President Johnson's Great Society program. The worst tensions of the Cold War with the Soviet Union seemed over. Science and technology had produced many new marvels and promised still further advances. America was the most productive country in the world. The question now, wrote the economist John Kenneth Galbraith in 1958, was how to use the abundant wealth created by this **Affluent Society.**

The dominant mood of the 1950s and early 1960s was one of optimism. This does not mean that everyone was satisfied with the state of American society. On the contrary, optimism made many people dissatisfied. They felt that society had serious weaknesses, especially the unequal distribution of wealth. But because they were optimistic, they believed that these weaknesses could be eliminated.

This hopeful, forward-looking mood had many roots. Victory in World War II was certainly one of the most important. Millions of soldiers and sailors came home confirmed optimists, if only because they had survived amid the death and destruction of battle. They and other millions who had not actually fought in the war found that victory strengthened their belief that the American way of life was superior to all others. The contrast between the United States and war-torn Europe further strengthened this belief, as did the dependence on American aid of both the Allies and the defeated Germans and Japanese.

RESOURCES
■ You may wish to have students complete Reading 62: "Two Views of America in the 1950s" in Volume II of *Eyewitnesses and Others*.

So optimistic were the times that some people believed the Great Society would eliminate poverty from America altogether. The resources to do so existed.

■ *Although it may look like a foreclosure and bankruptcy auction of the 1980s, this 1950s family displays every item purchased with the new easy credit available in the Affluent Society.*

The Growing Economy

The unprecedented period of prosperity the United States had created by 1960 was built on what economists call "an economy of abundance." This meant that American businesses were able to produce more goods and services than Americans could consume. In the late 1950s a group of distinguished economists described the growing economy:

> ❝ America today has the strongest, most productive economic system in human history. . . . The United States, with little more than 6 percent of the world's population and less than 7 percent of the land area, now produces well over one third of the world's goods and services and turns out nearly half of the world's factory-produced goods. ❞

There were many reasons for America's remarkable prosperity. The United States had the key **factors of production**—the resources used to produce goods and services. The nation enjoyed abundant natural resources, an excellent transportation network, and a large and skilled labor force. In addition, businesses and industries became more highly organized and efficiently managed. More effective methods of distribution overcame problems of getting products to customers. Advertising created new ways to convince Americans they needed more and better goods and services. And American capitalism

FOCUS/MOTIVATION: MAKING CONNECTIONS
Student Experiences.
Ask students how many hours of television they watch during an average day. *(Most students will probably answer anywhere from two to six.)* Have them answer the following with a show of hands: How many watch situation comedies? How many watch dramas? How many watch movies? How many watch music video programs? How many watch the news? How many watch sports? How many watch documentaries? Ask by a show of hands how many students watch each category a majority of the time. After each question ask those who raised their hand why they chose that type of program and how they think they benefited from it. Point out to students that much of the time Americans watch television to be entertained rather than informed. Ask them why they think this is so. *(Answers will vary.)*

Point of View

In *Henderson the Rain King,* a Nobel Prize-winning novelist wrote of the desire for more.

> ❝ There was a disturbance in my heart, a voice that spoke there and said, *I want, I want, I want!* It happened every afternoon and when I tried to suppress it it got even stronger. . . . It never said a thing except *I want, I want, I want!* ❞
>
> *Saul Bellow, 1958*

PRIMARY SOURCES
Description of change: excerpted.
Rationale: excerpted to focus on a group of economists' description of the growing U.S. economy in the 1950s.
(Point of View) Description of change: excerpted.
Rationale: excerpted to focus on the character's materialism.

The American Federation of Labor merged with the Congress of Industrial Organizations in 1955. What do you think the illustration on the seal is meant to symbolize?

Walter Sanders/Life Magazine © Time Warner, Inc.

The latest in 1950s clock-radios did more than wake you up. It also could turn on the electric coffeepot in the morning.

and the new prosperity rewarded both individual effort and teamwork.

The steadily improving relations between labor and management also helped spur economic growth. Naturally the labor force grew in size as the population increased. The two major branches of the labor movement—the American Federation of Labor (AFL) and the Congress of Industrial Organizations (CIO)—united to form the **AFL-CIO,** with George Meany, head of the AFL Plumbers Union, as president. The new union had 16 million members. American workers were convinced unions would protect their rights, and management showed a willingness in many instances to negotiate. Politicians eagerly sought union backing.

The Wonders of Science

🔵 New scientific and technological advances caused America's economy to boom. Increasingly efficient and complex power-driven machinery became common in almost every business and industry. Farms, mines, offices, even homes benefited. New goods and services poured out of American factories and businesses in ever-increasing quantities.

Scientific advances caused American farm production to soar. Fertilizers and insecticides and other applications of science to agriculture as well as advances in farm management provided Americans with the abundant and varied diet that made them among the best-fed people in the world. The United States exported huge amounts of farm products each year.

Many industries experienced explosive growth. The aircraft industry became a multibillion-dollar industry. Thousands of men and women were employed in plants producing huge new jets. Thousands more were employed by airlines as pilots, ticket agents, maintenance workers, and flight attendants. The electronics industry expanded in similar fashion. It had been spurred by the need during World War II for radio transmitters, radar, and other military equipment. After the war it continued to grow. The production of radios, phonographs, and countless new appliances for homes and offices made electronics one of the fastest-growing American businesses. Then in the 1950s the industry skyrocketed with the popularity of television and demand for television sets.

The products of the new technology that these discoveries made possible added to the general optimism. One of the most exciting was **nuclear energy.** The same laws of physics that had led to the atom bomb could be used to produce controlled nuclear reactions instead of violent explosions. The enormous energy released by these reactions could be converted into electricity. Some experts predicted that energy would soon be almost as plentiful as water and air. What

1034

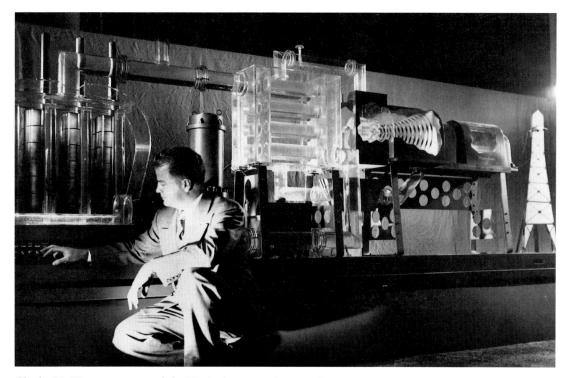

Charles H. Weaver, manager of the Westinghouse atomic power division, explains a station's workings.

this would mean in more wealth and leisure for everyone was easy to imagine. The United States had launched the nuclear-powered submarine *Nautilus* in 1954. By 1956 nuclear power plants could make and distribute electricity, and they began to do so in the United States in 1957. Few people then understood the problems that the nuclear age could bring.

Dozens of products and techniques that made life more comfortable and interesting were introduced in the years after World War II. Television and jet airliners and home air conditioners changed the way people used their spare time and where they lived and worked. New products included such **synthetic textiles** as Orlon and Dacron, water-based latex paint, small portable radios, and even smaller hearing aids. These radio, hearing aids, and a host of other devices used tiny **transistors** instead of bulky vacuum tubes.

Medical advances contributed to the general optimism. Penicillin, first used in military hospitals during World War II, became available to everyone. Along with other new **antibiotics,** penicillin practically eliminated many infectious diseases as major causes of death. The discovery by Dr. Jonas Salk of a **polio vaccine** virtually eliminated infantile paralysis, a particularly frightening crippler of children and some adults, like Franklin D. Roosevelt.

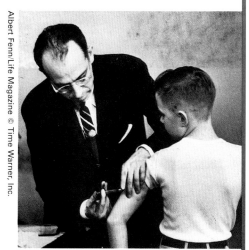

Dr. Jonas Salk gives 10-year-old Randy Bazilausakas his first innoculation of polio vaccine. How was the vaccine a godsend?

Albert Fenn/Life Magazine © Time Warner, Inc.

LEARNING FROM TABLES. *As you can see from the table, both the number and the percentage of women in the labor force have increased greatly over the last 100 years. What are some of the reasons for this increase? During what decade was the increase the greatest? Why do you think the increase was largest at that time?*

WOMEN IN THE LABOR FORCE, 1890-1990		
Year	Number of Women Employed Outside the Home	Percentage of the Total Labor Force
1890	3,600,000	16.8
1900	5,000,000	17.0
1910	7,700,000	19.5
1920	8,300,000	20.0
1930	10,600,000	20.4
1940	13,800,000	27.1
1950	18,300,000	29.6
1960	23,200,000	33.4
1970	32,500,000	38.1
1980	45,400,000	42.4
1990	53,479,000	45.4

Source: *U.S. Bureau of Labor Statistics*

A Changing Labor Force

The labor force that created the products of this period of American prosperity was significantly different from the American labor force before World War II. Many more women were now employed outside the home. In 1940 about 25 percent of the employees were women. By 1960 the percentage had risen to about 35 percent.

This rapid rise, the largest ever to that point, was the result of several developments. The demand for workers on the home front during World War II had helped break down prejudices against women, and it allowed women to show they could handle the same tasks as men in many jobs. Even more importantly, the rapidly growing economy created many more and new jobs. Most did not require sheer muscle. Because labor-saving devices had freed many women from household chores, they filled a large portion of these new jobs.

There was also a striking increase in the number of white-collar workers. In 1956 **white-collar workers**—teachers, doctors, lawyers, sales persons, secretaries, clerks, and others who worked in offices—for the first time outnumbered **blue-collar workers**—those who worked in factories or did other types of manual labor. Many of these workers held jobs in government. By 1960 nearly one of every seven workers was employed by the federal, state, or local government.

The Impact of Television and Computers

Even before World War II inventors had developed a way to transmit pictures similar to the way sound is transmitted by radio. As you know, this technique was called **television.** Only in the late 1940s, however, did manufacturers first offer reliable television sets—appliances to receive television signals—at prices that many people could afford. The demand for television sets proved to be tremendous. Throughout the 1950s television sets were sold at a rate of about 7 million a year. By 1960 nearly every family in America had at least one set. Television was one modern advance that even the poorest people seemed able to afford.

Television combined the virtues of radio and motion pictures. Techniques for broadcasting realistic sound combined with the newest visual techniques from the movies to make television an instant hit. Sports events such as baseball and football games were popular from the start. So were musical programs, comedy hours, and serial dramatic shows. Serials were known as soap operas because many of them were sponsored by manufacturers of soap and similar household products. News programs kept viewers informed and used pictures and maps to illustrate their reports. For the first time people could watch images of the news of the day.

Television soon became a force that influenced public opinion and events as well as one that reported them. For example, televised hearings exposed Senator McCarthy for the bully he was. Many observers believed that John F. Kennedy won the 1960 presidential election because he made a better impression before the TV camera than Richard Nixon. It was even suggested that if Nixon had used better makeup, the election might have gone to him. This was almost certainly an exaggeration. Still, the fact that people could think it was so shows how important television had become. And, as we shall see in the next chapter, when live television began bringing into American homes the war in Southeast Asia and inner cities torn with riots and looting, ordinary people were shocked to see this dark side of America.

The power of television and its almost hypnotic effect on viewers quickly became apparent. Critics warned of the potential hazards of watching what they called "the one-eyed monster." They claimed people would read less, even socialize less, as they locked themselves

TELEVISIONS IN AMERICA		
Year	Number of Households with Televisions	Percentage of American Homes with Televisions
1945	5,000	Less than 0.1
1950	3,880,000	9.0
1955	30,700,000	64.5
1960	45,750,000	87.1
1970	59,550,000	95.2

Source: *Bureau of the Census*

LEARNING FROM TABLES. *Americans soon fell in love with television. In which five-year period did television "come of age"?*

Ed Clark/Life Magazine © Time Warner, Inc.

The Thomas Knox family of Cornelius, North Carolina, watches with delight "The Ed Sullivan Show"—a popular program that brought vaudeville to television. Here Elvis Presley and the Beatles were introduced to the American television-viewing public. Why did the Chairman of the FCC call television "a vast wasteland"?

in with their "TV dinners" to watch "the tube." The head of the Federal Communications Commission (FCC) challenged broadcasters in these early days to improve the quality of television. Would his review be much different today?

❝ I am the Chairman of the FCC. I am also a television viewer and the husband and father of other television viewers. I have seen a great many television programs that have seemed to me eminently worthwhile. When television is good, nothing—not the theater, not magazines or newspapers—nothing is better.

But when television is bad, nothing is worse. I invite you to sit down in front of your television set when your station goes on the air and stay there without a book, magazine, newspaper, profit-and-loss sheet or rating book to distract you—and keep your eyes glued to that set until the station signs off. I can assure you that you will observe a vast wasteland.

You will see a procession of game shows, violence, audience participation shows, formula comedies about totally unbelievable families, blood and thunder, mayhem, violence, sadism, murder, Western badmen, Western good men, private eyes, gangsters, more violence, and cartoons. And most of all boredom. True, you will find a few things you will enjoy. But they will be very, very few. . . .❞[1]

[1]From *Equal Time: The Private Broadcaster and the Public Interest* by Newton N. Minnow, edited by Lawrence Laurent

Perhaps equal to the impact on American life of the television was that of the electronic **computer.** People began to refer to the computer revolution. The first computers were huge, cumbersome, and slow. But advances in computer technology were startlingly rapid, and by 1960 there were 5,000 computers in use in the United States. In a fraction of a second these computers performed tremendously complex calculations. By the 1960s they could perform nearly 360,000 additions or subtractions or 180,000 multiplications in one second. Laboratories used them to analyze complex technical information. Computers took over many of the mental and manual tasks once performed by men and women. They measured, counted, filed, and stored information—usually more efficiently than humans. Banks and businesses used them for bookkeeping and billing. The government used them to collect statistics and to check income tax returns. And there were many other business uses for these fantastic machines. The flights into space would have been unthinkable before the computer came of age.

Eventually the United States would become a computerized society. Schools, businesses, laboratories, hospitals, banks, government offices, hundreds of other organizations, even private homes would come to rely on computers.

Advances in computer technology also led to developments such as robots which seemed straight out of science fiction. Robots—machines that perform the tasks usually done by humans—became commonplace in some factories. These industrial robots worked on assembly lines run by computers. Scientists and engineers have worked to develop robots for every setting in which humans work—even the home. In 1983 one science writer foresaw the development of household robots that seemed somewhat humanlike.

      “ Times change fast, especially on the technological landscape. . . . The development of the microcomputer [a very small computer] bolstered [supported] the belief that intelligent machines, able to work and act as well as ponder, could be built.

      Today they are with us. . . . The Japanese are calling it a “robolution,” a revolution that extends from factory spot welders to devices that slice sushi [cold rice cakes usually topped with raw fish] for overworked chefs to piano-playing home robots (available, with many other talents and a price tag of $42,000, from a leading Tokyo department store).

      Robotics is breeding a new generation of machines that we may soon meet as pets. . . . BOB, short for Brain On Board . . . scuttles across the room, relying on ultrasonic detectors to avoid walls. When it senses a warm body with infrared detectors, it stops, swaying ever so slightly. BOB does get disoriented, a feature that makes it slightly human.

CHECKING UNDERSTANDING
Have students discuss the reasons for America's prosperity in the 1950s and 1960s. *(The standard of living was high. The economy grew because America had abundant natural resources. Improving relations between labor and management also helped to spur the economy. Science and technology had produced marvels, such as fertilizers, insecticides, nuclear power for electricity, synthetic textiles, transistors, and computers.)*

A bop on the head and it speaks—20 words with a mild robot accent.[1] ”

Household robots have not yet become common. But who knows what the future holds?

Of course, the wonders of science are the result of human effort and creativity. As one robotics engineer told the science writer of the *Smithsonian* article:

“ BOB is cute, a delightful gimmick, but even among those robotics engineers working on more serious problems, there is a singular awe and admiration of the human organism. . . . 'The only ones who really appreciate how smart people are, are those who try to do some of these things [get them to perform human tasks] with a robot.'[2] ”

[1]From "Robots are playing new roles as they take a hand in our affairs" by Jeanne McDermott in *Smithsonian*, November 1983
[2]*Ibid.*

J. R. Eyerman/Life Magazine © Time Warner, Inc.

This photograph shows one consequence of the computer revolution. A single operator in the foreground does the work of the 31 clerks in the background. Why did computers make many people apprehensive?

Fine-tuning the Economy

In another important advance economists seemed to have figured out a way to prevent depressions. When business activity began to slow down, they said, the government should stimulate it. There were two ways to do this. One, called **fiscal policy,** involved the federal budget. The government must increase spending and lower taxes. Its spending would increase the demand for goods and services through direct purchases by the government and through increased buying by businesses and individuals who received government money. Lower taxes would leave consumers with more money to buy goods.

The other method for preventing economic recessions or depressions involved **monetary policy.** It called for having the Federal Reserve Board lower interest rates. Then businesses and consumers could borrow money more easily in order to expand business output and increase consumer consumption.

If the economy began to grow too rapidly, causing prices to rise, fiscal and monetary policies could be reversed. If that happened, economists said, the government should reduce its expenditures, increase taxes, and raise interest rates. Economists claimed that it was possible to "fine-tune" the economy by shifting these policies back and forth. A steady rate of economic growth would follow.

For the most part in the 1950s and 1960s these methods worked. The Federal Reserve Board and government economic analysts kept an eye on indicators of business activity such as the rate of inflation, unemployment, and the prime rate—the rate of interest banks charged on loans to their best customers. They then worked to coordinate fiscal and monetary policies to keep the economy growing steadily. 🖂

The popular cartoonist Oliphant takes a dimmer view than the Federal Reserve Board of efforts to fine-tune the economy. Is this cartoon critical of fiscal policy or monetary policy?

Return to the Preview & Review on page 1032.

A Prosperous America   1041

PREVIEW & REVIEW RESPONSES
Understanding Issues, Events, & Ideas.
Explanations should demonstrate an understanding of the terms used.

1. Many people, particularly the retired, were drawn there by the warm climate. Home air conditioners became available in the 1950s, making the hot southern summers more bearable.
2. Relatively cheap, comfortable homes with many conveniences became available to the middle class. Shopping centers with supermarkets, department stores, movie theaters, and small shops sprang up. Because they lost most of their tax revenues, city finances were strained when the middle class, businesses, and manufacturing moved to the suburbs.
3. The suburbs had the tax revenues to build attractive schools, with money for extras such as art and athletic programs. They were also able to pay their teachers better than cities could. The city schools suffered because tax revenues decreased.
4. There was easier access to a college education following World War II. Many young people, whose parents had not had the opportunity, were attending college.
5. Vacations, golfing, bowling, boating, spectator sports, and television watching were some of the ways Americans used their leisure time.

Use these questions to guide your reading. Answer the questions after completing Section 3.
Understanding Issues, Events, & Ideas. Use the following words to explain the direction of American society in the 1950s and 1960s: Sun Belt, National Aeronautics and Space Administration, suburb, development, shopping center, public housing project, shopping mall, Elementary and Secondary Education Act.

1. What were some of the reasons for the shift in population to the Sun Belt?
2. What changes did the shift to the suburbs bring in housing and shopping? How did this shift put a strain on the finances of city governments?
3. Why did suburban schools benefit from the education boom? Why did city schools suffer?
4. What caused college enrollments to jump between 1946 and 1960?
5. What were some of the ways that Americans used their leisure time in the 1950s and 1960s?

Thinking Critically. Imagine that you are living in a major U.S. city in the early 1960s. Your city is suffering from urban decay and you are very concerned about this situation. Write a letter to the mayor and city council suggesting ways to keep middle class families and businesses from moving to the suburbs.

3. A SOCIETY OF MANY MEMBERS

The Population Explosion

One result of prosperity and public optimism was a rapid increase in the population of the United States. During the Great Depression many people had been too poor to marry and have children. During the war millions of men were overseas. Between 1929 and 1946 the population rose quite slowly, from about 122 million to about 145 million. This was a rate of a little more than 1 million people a year.

In 1946 the depression was over and soldiers had returned home from the war. In that year the population increased by nearly 3 million. The new trend continued for about 20 years. By the end of 1965 the population of the United States had reached 195 million.

The Sun Belt

After World War II the entire population distribution of the United States shifted. The American population had been moving westward since the first colonists arrived. But the shift in the 1950s and 1960s was as dramatic as that of the westward movement 100 years before. The territories of Alaska and Hawaii were admitted to statehood in 1959. This was a sign of their population growth and economic development. All the western states grew rapidly during these years. There was a similar population shift to the South. Florida and other southern states soon had population growth rates that rivaled those of western states.

The South and Southwest came to be called the **Sun Belt** because so many people were being drawn there by the warm climate. Retired people in particular moved to Florida and the Southwest to avoid the harsh northern winters. Home air conditioners, which became available in the 1950s, made the hot southern summers more bearable. By the late 1960s nearly 20 million homes were air conditioned.

There were other reasons for the migration to the West and South. Many firms in the aircraft and electronics industries tended to locate in these regions where lower taxes and living costs meant reduced production costs. Thousands of young families followed, attracted by the high wages and pleasant working conditions in specially designed and newly built offices and factories these industries provided. The new federal highway network made it possible for people to move long distances easily.

The federal government encouraged the shift by establishing huge new facilities in the Sun Belt. The best known were the John F. Kennedy rocket-launching base at Cape Canaveral in Florida and the headquarters of NASA—the **National Aeronautics and Space Administration** in Houston, Texas.

South and West; Home air conditioners made warmer summers more bearable, and aircraft and electronics industries tended to locate in these regions, luring young families with high wages and pleasant working conditions.

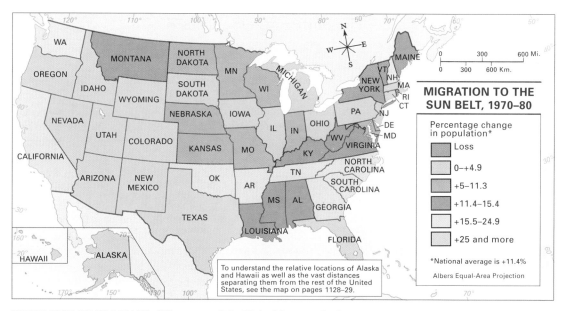

MIGRATION TO THE SUN BELT, 1970–80

Percentage change in population*

- Loss
- 0–+4.9
- +5–11.3
- +11.4–15.4
- +15.5–24.9
- +25 and more

*National average is +11.4%

Albers Equal-Area Projection

To understand the relative locations of Alaska and Hawaii as well as the vast distances separating them from the rest of the United States, see the map on pages 1128–29.

LEARNING FROM MAPS. *What parts of the United States gained population during the 1970s? Why?*

Below is a colorful view of a blast-off from Cape Canaveral.

NASA

Point of View

From the book *Cities on a Hill* comes this observation:

> **In a sense, the residents of Sun City Center and their peers across the United States are living on a frontier. Not a geographical frontier but a chronological one. Old age is nothing new, of course, but for an entire generation to reach old age with its membership almost intact is something new. . . . In seventeenth-century France, for example, a quarter of all human beings died before the age of one, another quarter died before the age of twenty . . .**
>
> Frances Fitzgerald, 1986

RESPONSES *(Continued)*
Thinking Critically.
Student letters should demonstrate an understanding of the problems facing U.S. cities in the 1960s.

FOCUS/MOTIVATION:
MAKING CONNECTIONS
Prior Knowledge.
Ask students where their families do most of their shopping. *(Unless their community is in an isolated rural area, most students will probably name major franchised stores.)* Ask them where these stores are located. *(Students will probably say malls or shopping centers.)* Point out to students that it is only since the end of World War II that malls and shopping centers have been built and that before that time people shopped in stores that were mostly located in downtown areas of towns and cities.

PRIMARY SOURCE
Description of change: excerpted.
Rationale: excerpted to focus on Americans living longer.

Jumping rope and counting-out songs will be found wherever there are children. The game below is in Levittown, one of the first planned suburbs in the United States. On the opposite page children play in front of their Chicago housing project. How might the lives of the schoolchildren in each of these groups differ?

The Shift to the Suburbs

A second major change in the nation's population distribution came when people in every part of the United States began moving from cities to their surrounding **suburbs.** These suburbanites, as they were called, were looking for the space, fresh air, privacy, and contact with nature that country life provided. Still they needed to remain near the cities where most of them worked. They also wanted to take advantage of the excitement, conveniences, and cultural opportunities of city life.

Young, recently married couples with small children were particularly attracted to the suburbs. Builders responded to their demand for homes by constructing huge **developments.** Levittown, New York, which became a suburb in itself on Long Island, was the best known of these developments. Its comfortable, relatively cheap tract houses stretched row upon row with a sameness that later came to disturb many Americans. But at the time nearly all purchasers were delighted with the houses. Most had three bedrooms and an extra bathroom. Dishwashers, washing machines, and dryers were already installed. Between 1950 and 1960 nearly a million new homes and apartments were built each year. The construction of schools, hospitals, roads, and offices accompanied this housing boom.

In and around the developments **shopping centers** sprang up, complete with supermarkets, department store branches, movie theaters, and dozens of small shops. The shopping centers were surrounded by acres of paved parking lots, for suburbanites traveled everywhere by automobile. Almost any product that local residents might want could be purchased in these shopping centers. Bulldozers busily cleared an estimated 3,000 acres (1,200 hectares) of land a day for these developments.

Joe Schershel/Life Magazine © Time Warner, Inc.

① Not only were most African Americans unable to afford homes in the suburbs, but many developments were closed to them. For example, William Levitt refused to allow African Americans to purchase homes in Levittown because he feared that if African Americans moved in, whites would move out. It was not until 1960, following a lawsuit charging that discrimination in the sale of homes bought with federally assisted mortgages was unconstitutional, that Levittown was opened to African Americans.

Fritz Goro/Life Magazine © Time Warner, Inc.

Few poor people lived in the new suburbs. The poor could not afford even the smallest tract homes. There were almost no apartment houses or other places to rent. In other words, suburbs were mostly for members of the middle class—office workers, shopkeepers, teachers and other government employees—and well-paid blue-collar wage earners such as carpenters, electricians, and automobile assembly-line workers.

The government tried to improve the living conditions of poor people in the cities by putting up large **public housing projects.** These nonprofit apartments were rented at relatively low rates. Usually the rents were based on the income of the tenants.

The problem was that when the percentage of poor people in the cities increased, more and more middle-class people moved out to the suburbs. This seriously strained the finances of city governments because when the well-to-do left, income from taxes collected by cities fell off. Sales tax receipts dwindled as less and less money was spent on goods and services in cities, and property tax collections sagged as residents vacated more expensive city housing. Because cities had less money, public housing projects were largely neglected and soon become unsafe places to live and raise children.

Many manufacturers shifted to the suburbs to find room to expand and because property taxes were lower. This shift caused many of their employees to become suburbanites. Stores built suburban branches—**shopping malls**—and followed their customers to the suburbs. Each of these moves from the city to the suburbs also meant decreased city tax revenues.

Since many of the poor who remained in the cities were non-whites, a new kind of segregation developed. The worst effects of ① this segregation were not felt until after 1965. Until then well-meaning people had high hopes that President Johnson's Great Society programs would solve this problem along with others.

GUIDED INSTRUCTION: COOPERATIVE LEARNING
After students have read the section titled "The Shift to the Suburbs," organize the class into cooperative learning groups. Have each group prepare a chart entitled *Positive and Negative Effects of the Growth of the Suburbs.* Have them list aspects of the shift as either positive or negative to their locale. After students have completed their charts, lead a class discussion on whether or not the shift to the suburbs has affected their community and if so whether it has been a positive or negative effect.

RELATING HISTORY TO GEOGRAPHY
To reinforce the five basic themes of geography—*location, place, relationships within places, movement,* and *regions*—have students discuss aspects of the shift to the suburbs that illustrate each theme. If they completed a chart on the positive and negative effects of suburbanization, you may wish to use that to help students categorize aspects under the themes.

In 1940 the average American had an eighth-grade education. In addition, one in six college-age people attended college, and one in twelve graduated. However, by 1960 these figures had changed dramatically. The average American had a high school education, 50 percent of college-age people attended college, and more than 20 percent graduated.

Have students research and then prepare reports on the growth of their community in the 1950s and 1960s. They should include the following in their reports: the age of the community in the 1950s and 1960s; how much the population increased; what new communities were built; how shopping and transportation networks changed; how land use changed; and what, if any, aid the community received from the federal government. Students may find information on this subject by checking with the planning and zoning department, looking in old editions of the local newspaper, checking in the public library, talking to members of the community who are old enough to remember that period, or consulting the local historical society. It is especially effective to use aerial photographs and maps of the area to illustrate these changes. These are usually available from the planning and zoning department or another government agency.

Jan Branneis/Life Magazine © Time Warner, Inc.

Graduates celebrate commencement at the University of California at Berkeley in 1962. There is no sign here of the protest movements that would temporarily shut down this university in the 1970s.

The Education Boom

With so many children being born after the war, thousands of new schools had to be built. Most schools in the suburbs were low, light, and airy brick buildings. In addition to ordinary classrooms, space was provided for teaching arts and crafts and for sports activities. Teachers' salaries rose, for the increased enrollments created a teacher shortage.

As wealthy and middle-class residents moved out of cities, schools there suffered when the tax revenues that supported them declined. The **Elementary and Secondary Education Act** of 1965 supplied large amounts of federal money to improve these schools.

Changes in higher education were even more dramatic in the affluent society of the 1950s. College enrollments jumped from 1.6 million in 1946 to 3.5 million in 1960. Clearly, many young people, whose parents had not had the opportunity, were going to college. Making a college education available to so many more people had important economic and social effects. There was a close relationship between the amount of education people got and the kinds of lives they led when their training was completed.

In business and in many other fields people with intelligence, imagination, and energy often succeeded brilliantly with little formal schooling. Education helped, but it was not essential. College training, however, was required for entry into the professions such as

STRATEGIES FOR SUCCESS

USING THE CENSUS

April 1, 1990 marked the bicentennial of the first census of the population of the United States, taken in 1790. In that year 17 U.S. marshals and 200 assistants went door-to-door to count the number of people in the brand-new American nation. The Constitution, ratified in 1788, called for a census within three years of the first Congress and every tenth year thereafter. The 1990 Census was the 21st such survey.

The most important reason for taking a census then (and now) was to ensure that citizens were fully represented in the federal government. Under the one person, one vote principle, states must redraw their Congressional election districts to reflect population shifts. (By law the number of representatives is set at 435.)

The census provides a wealth of other information about the American people. The 1990 census included questions about race and ethnic backgrounds, the disabled population, income and medical costs, energy use, housing, and much more. All the information is closely studied by various groups, especially those who work in various local, state, and federal government agencies.

The census contains an amazingly rich resource about trends in American society. Using the census data will give you a picture of the nation's people and insights into changes the nation and its people are undergoing.

How to Use the Census

To use the census, follow these steps.
1. **Select a topic.** Because the information collected by the census is almost overwhelming, it is necessary to focus on a specific body of information.
2. **Study the census data.** Check all the data about your topic. Remember that information may be provided in a variety of forms—in narrative descriptions, on maps, charts and tables, and on graphs.
3. **Note the trends.** Study the changes reflected by the data.
4. **Use the census information.** Draw conclusions and form hypotheses based on census figures. Remember that the statistics portray American society.

Applying the Strategy

Study the table of census data below. It illustrates information for the years 1970 and 1980 in three categories: land area, population, and population density. By how much did the urban population increase between 1970 and 1980? As you can see, it increased by over 17 million people. By how much did the rural population increase between 1970 and 1980? It increased by over 5 million. What is one conclusion you can draw from the data in this table?

For independent practice, see Practicing the Strategy on page 1059.

For independent practice, see Practicing the Strategy on page 1059.

CHANGES IN URBAN AND RURAL POPULATION DENSITIES, 1970-80

	1970			1980		
	Land Area (sq. mi.)	Population (in millions)	Density (per sq. mi.)	Land Area (sq. mi.)	Population (in millions)	Density (per sq. mi.)
Total	3,540,023	203,212	57	3,539,289	226,546	64
Urban	54,103	149,325	2,760	73,930	167,051	2,260
Rural	3,485,920	53,887	15	3,465,360	59,495	17

BASEBALL LEAVES BROOKLYN

Tears rolled down the cheeks of young boys and old men alike the day the decision was announced—the Dodgers were leaving Brooklyn. The team led by Jackie Robinson and Duke Snider was moving west. The fabled and successful franchise—five National League championships and one World Series crown in the 1950s—was moving to Los Angeles in 1958. And to add to the shock of New Yorkers their Giants were heading for San Francisco that same year. Why were these teams leaving their loyal fans?

Teams had moved throughout baseball's history. Usually a team moved when attendance sagged sharply. New cities meant more fans—baseball's life blood. But before World War II these moves were limited to the East Coast and the Middle West. Most western cities were not as large and the West Coast was just too far away. It would take too long for opposing teams to travel there to play.

But the same changes that swept the rest of American society after the war affected baseball. Large numbers of people were moving to booming cities in the West and the Sun Belt, creating huge markets for sports franchises. Technology was producing rapid modes of transportation that pulled the widespread parts of the country more closely together. With the coming of television baseball entered the homes of millions of viewers who quickly became fans. Soon television revenues became a major source of income for a team. Suddenly the West Coast didn't seem so far away—or such a bad investment for team owners.

The Boston Braves had moved to Milwaukee in 1953 and the Philadelphia Athletics to Kansas City in 1955. (Both would move again—the Braves to Atlanta and the Athletics to Oakland—in search of fans and dollars.) But the Dodgers and Giants took the biggest step, moving across the continent to bring baseball to California and the West. Soon major league baseball had spread to all the corners of the nation—and the continent. Teams now play in Seattle in Washington, Denver in Colorado and Miami in Florida, even Montreal and Toronto in Canada.

Other sports have followed baseball's lead. Major league sports teams now represent San

Los Angeles Dodgers on parade

Wide World Photo

medicine, law, and teaching. Easier access to a college education after World War II opened the professions to a much broader section of the population than ever before.

Leisure Time

Advances in technology created an unexpected benefit for many workers: shorter workweeks. Between 1940 and 1960 the average workweek decreased from 44 to 40 hours. In some of the skilled trades it actually dropped to 35 hours. At the same time the average paid vacation increased from one to two weeks.

Americans began to look for ways to spend their increased free time and money. Millions bought new cars—nearly 50 million during the 1950s. By 1960 nearly 75 percent of all American families owned at least one car, and more than 15 percent owned two or more.

Antonio, Salt Lake City, San Diego, Portland, and Phoenix.

Technology has continued to influence baseball. In 1965 the Houston baseball team—then called the Colt .45's—moved into the engineering masterpiece of its day, an indoor stadium called the Astrodome. Baseball and football teams now play in huge indoor arenas in such places as Minneapolis, New Orleans, and Seattle. Several other teams, along with many college and university teams, play on the artificial surface created to replace the grass that simply would not grow under the Astrodome's roof. Most of those same college teams now use aluminum bats, which have replaced breakable wood bats on every level below the highest minor and major leagues.

Baseball, all America's traditional game, is part of American culture. As such it reflects many of the changes that influence society—the shifting populations, technological advances, and social changes.

Dan Uhrbrock/Life Magazine © Time Warner, Inc.

The Astrodome with its artificial turf

These families climbed into their cars and headed for vacations at the beach, the mountains, or the country. More and better roads were needed to handle the growing traffic. The Highway Act in 1956 provided funding for the construction of 42,500 miles (68,400 kilometers) of new superhighways. State and local funds paid for thousands of miles of roads and streets. Motels, fast-food restaurants, and service stations soon lined these roads and highways.

Hundreds of golf courses and bowling alleys were built and were soon crowded. People bought boats of all descriptions. These soon appeared on lakes and harbors throughout the country. Attendance at spectator sports grew tremendously as well. Baseball and football teams built new stadiums to hold the crowds that numbered in the tens of thousands.

At home families gathered around their wonderful new television sets. By 1960 the television was turned on for at least 5 hours a day

Point of View

From *God's Country and Mine:*

❝Whoever wants to know the heart and mind of America had better learn baseball, the rules and realities of the game—and do it by watching first some high school or small-town teams.❞

Jacques Barzun, 1954

SUGGESTED CAPTION RESPONSES
(Top) 5 months; Answers will vary, but students may suggest that it has broken down regional and cultural barriers because most people are able to travel long distances.
(Bottom) If people did not learn to protect their environment, nature would not be able to renew itself as it does every spring.

INDEPENDENT PRACTICE
Have students complete the Preview & Review activity at the beginning of the section.

CLOSURE
Point out to students that Americans have always been on the move. In the 1950s and 1960s they moved in large numbers to the suburbs, and many retired people were attracted to the Sun Belt because they wanted to avoid harsh winters. Ask students why young families were attracted to the Sun Belt as well. *(Many firms in the aircraft and electronics industries located in the Sun Belt. Young people were attracted by the high wages and pleasant working conditions these industries provided.)*

HOMEWORK
Have students prepare a report describing the benefits public schools received from the Elementary and Secondary School Act of 1965. Have them include a list of programs that are still funded by guidelines set down in this Act.

PRIMARY SOURCES
(Top) Description of change: excerpted.
Rationale: excerpted to focus on the magnitude of health problems caused by industrial chemicals.
(Bottom) Description of change: excerpted.
Rationale: excerpted to focus on Carson's list of dangerous chemicals.

LEARNING FROM TABLES. *As you can see from the table, the changing technology of travel has made the United States "smaller." Now you can travel coast to coast in a few hours. How long did it take by covered wagon? What changes do you think more rapid transportation has brought to America?*

TRANSCONTINENTAL TRAVEL*	
Vehicle	Time It Took To Make Journey
Covered wagon	5 months
Steamship through Panama Canal	30 days
Overland stagecoach	23 days
Railroad, 1875	7 days
Railroad, 1900	4 days
Railroad, 1945	2.5 days
Airplane, propeller	7.5 hours
Airplane, jet	4 hours
*From east coast to west coast	

Alfred Eisenstaedt/Life Magazine © Time Warner, Inc.

Rachel Carson wrote so movingly of the natural environment that not all her readers realized at first that she was warning America to change its ways before the environment deteriorated and cities decayed. Explain the title Silent Spring.

Return to the Preview & Review on page 1042.

in the average home. But television did not claim all of Americans' new leisure time. Sales of magazines, books, records, and audio tapes climbed steadily in the 1950s and early 1960s.

The New Generation

A major concern of many Americans in the midst of all these changes was the direction being taken by the young men and women reaching adulthood in the 1950s and early 1960s. Their goals appeared to be having plenty of money, a good job, a house in the suburbs, and comfortable retirement. Critics accused them of a lack of concern about politics and the issues confronting the United States and the world.

Critics even went so far as to claim that this tendency to avoid controversy and to conform was not confined to young people. They said that all age groups, men and women alike, seemed to share the same attitude of conformity. Among other critics, John Kenneth Galbraith and Rachel Carson warned Americans that they were neglecting the poor, causing the environment to deteriorate, and permitting cites to decay. In *Silent Spring*, Carson said,

“ As the tide of chemicals born of the Industrial Age has arisen to engulf our environment, a drastic change has come about in the nature of the most serious health problems.[1]”

She challenged people to protect the earth from the hazards

“ created by radiation in all its forms, born of the never-ending stream of chemicals of which pesticides are a part, chemicals now pervading the world in which we live, acting upon us directly and indirectly, separately and collectively.[2]”

[1]From *Silent Spring* by Rachel Carson
[2]*Ibid.*

It is a challenge Americans still face.

4. MOVEMENTS FOR EQUAL RIGHTS

Women Seek Equal Rights

Women in the 1960s continued their long struggle for equal rights. The 1964 Civil Rights Act had banned discrimination on the basis of sex as well as race. Still, women's organizations pressed for a Constitutional amendment that would guarantee their equality under law.

Tens of thousands of women from relatively poor families had always had to work. Middle-class women, however, had tended to work in the home after marriage. In the 1950s more and more of these women took jobs outside the home. They discovered that in nearly every field the wages and salaries paid to women were lower than those earned by men doing the same work. Moreover, the best jobs were rarely open to women. It was much harder for women to gain admission to law schools and medical colleges. In the business world women were rarely promoted to important positions, especially to those where they might be issuing orders to men.

Most male employers justified their practice by claiming that women usually worked only while waiting to be married. There was no use in promoting women, they said, because most would soon leave in order to marry and raise a family. When it was pointed out that more and more married women were working away from home, employers shifted their argument. They claimed that it was all right to pay married women less than men because married women did not have to support a family on their own!

Women naturally resented being discriminated against in the job market. When their numbers increased in the 1950s and 1960s, their resentment burst forth in the **Women's Liberation Movement.** The movement first attracted widespread public attention with the publication in 1963 of *The Feminine Mystique* by Betty Friedan. By "feminine mystique" Friedan meant the image of women society holds and the specific attributes of femininity.

Friedan had become interested in the problems of well-educated ■ women after she made a study of graduates of Smith College, one of the nation's leading women's colleges. She discovered that a large percentage of these women were unhappy. Why, she wondered, were so many intelligent women so dissatisfied with their lives?

The answer, Friedan concluded, was that women felt held back ① by family responsibilities. They did not see themselves as individuals. In her own mind the typical woman was "Mrs. Jones" or "Billy Jones' mother." Not even her name could she call her own.

Most women thought that they *ought* to be completely satisfied with their roles as wives and mothers, Friedan wrote. Were not popular magazines like the *Ladies' Home Journal* full of articles describing the satisfactions of raising a large family?

Preview & Review

Use these questions to guide your reading. Answer the questions after completing Section 4.
Understanding Issues, Events, & Ideas. Discuss the movements for equal rights that took place in the 1960s, using the following words: Women's Liberation Movement, consciousness-raising, National Organization for Women, Red Power, Indian Rights Act, American Indian Movement, Wounded Knee, poverty line, nonviolent direct action, Birmingham, March on Washington.
1. What did Betty Friedan discover in her survey of women?
2. What were some of the goals of the National Organization for Women?
3. How did the Indian Rights Act of 1968 cause problems for tribal governments?
4. What did Dr. Martin Luther King, Jr., hope to accomplish by his policy of nonviolent direct action?
5. How did Dr. King share in the optimism that was typical of the early 1960s?

Thinking Critically. 1. Imagine that you are one of the founders of the National Organization for Women or the American Indian Movement. Write a list of goals which you would like to see the organization carry out in order to help the people for whom it was founded. 2. Write an eyewitness account of the March on Washington. Include a description of how you felt hearing Dr. King's speech as well as the reaction of the crowd to his famous words.

PREVIEW & REVIEW RESPONSES
Understanding Issues, Events, & Ideas.
Discussions should demonstrate an understanding of the terms used.
1. She discovered that a large percentage of college-educated women were unhappy and full of feelings of inadequacy.
2. They wanted to end legal restrictions on women and see that women got equal employment opportunities in all fields.
3. It weakened tribal government because powerful chiefs, who did not respect the needs and opinions of their tribe members, were being challenged by this law.
4. He was attempting to achieve racial equality by using "Love, not hate or force" as the means for changing people's minds.
5. He once said, "The believer in nonviolence has deep faith in the future." He believed sincerely that the nation was making progress toward the goals he was seeking.

Thinking Critically.
1. Students who choose the National Organization for Women may mention government-supported day-care centers. Students who choose the American Indian movement may mention monetary settlement for tribal lands previously taken by the U.S. government.
2. Students should rely on historical imagination as well as historical facts when preparing their accounts.

RESOURCES
■ You may wish to have students review Transparency 36: *"Prairie Fire"* in *Art in American History.*

Among the marchers for women's rights are Bella Abzug, in hat, and Betty Friedan, far right.

Steve Northrup/Time Magazine © Time Warner, Inc.

Point of View

In *The Feminine Mystique* we read:

> ❝ Who knows what women can be when they are finally free to become themselves? Who knows what women's intelli-gence will contribute when it can be nourished without denying love? . . . The time is at hand when the voices of the feminine mystique can no longer drown out the inner voice that is driving women on to become complete.❞
>
> Betty Friedan, 1963

Many women who read *The Feminine Mystique* experienced what has come to be called **consciousness-raising.** They became aware that their personal doubts and dissatisfactions were shared by others.

Betty Friedan was not a radical. She did not argue that caring for a family was a bad thing. While she was writing her book, she was also bringing up three children of her own. But she insisted that the way to have a satisfying life was the same for women as for men: they must find some sort of "creative work."

In 1966 Friedan helped found the **National Organization for Women** (NOW). Its purpose was to end legal restrictions on women and see that they got equal employment opportunities in all fields. The government should provide day-care centers and other assis-tance for working women with small children, NOW officials argued. What would come of all this we shall see in a later chapter.

The American Indian Movement

Other American groups also struggled for equal rights, among them
■ American Indians. During the New Deal period the federal govern-ment had given up the effort begun with the Dawes Act of 1887 to force Indians to copy white ways and adopt white values.

Instead, the Indian Reorganization Act of 1934 encouraged the revival of tribal life. Indians should choose their own leaders and run their own affairs, supporters of the new policy believed. Many In-dians did so.

Indian schools began to teach Indian languages and history. Ancient arts and crafts were relearned and developed. A National Indian Youth Council, founded in 1961, pressed for the return of Indian lands in many parts of the nation. Some Indians coined the term **Red Power** to rally supporters.

RESOURCES

■ You may wish to have students complete Reading 63: "A Declaration of Indian Purpose (1961)" in Volume II of *Eyewitnesses and Others.*

◀ You may wish to have students complete Reading 73: "N. Scott Momaday Describes the Indian Vision (1970s)" in Volume II of *Eyewitnesses and Others.*

In 1968 Congress passed the **Indian Rights Act.** This law was intended to protect Indians against discrimination and mistreatment. But it had the unintended effect of weakening the governments the tribes had set up under the Indian Reorganization Act. These were often dominated by powerful chiefs who did not respect the needs and opinions of other tribe members. Many Indians used the new law to have these chiefs removed.

In 1972 a new organization, the **American Indian Movement** ■ (AIM) began to use more radical tactics. The most dramatic of AIM's actions occurred in 1973 at the town of **Wounded Knee**, South Dakota. AIM leaders chose to publicize their demands at Wounded Knee because white soldiers had massacred Indian women and children there in 1890. The Indians held the town for weeks before laying down their arms. ◀

The Struggle Continues

African Americans did not receive their fair share of the new affluence. As late as 1960 about half were still either poor or barely keeping their heads above the so-called **poverty line.** But in 1965 the economic condition of the average black seemed to be improving. More opportunities were opening up. The new AFL-CIO labor federation had promised "to encourage all workers without regard for color" to join their organization. Although some unions shut out black workers, the leaders of the AFL-CIO spoke out strongly against this practice. The United Automobile Workers and a number of other big unions achieved excellent records in promoting harmony between black and white workers. Perhaps even more promising, Jackie Robinson became the first black player in major league baseball. This quickly opened opportunities for blacks in many sports.

Jim Cartier/Photo Researchers

Seminole children in Big Cypress, Florida, work with their teacher at the Ahfachkee School. Note that they are learning their native American language as well as English.

MULTICULTURAL PERSPECTIVES: GUIDED INSTRUCTION

Divide the class into groups of two. Tell each group that they are to create a fictional interview of one of the following: a woman who is helping to organize NOW in 1966; an Indian who is part of the Red Power Movement in 1972; or an African American who has marched with Dr. Martin Luther King, Jr., in either Birmingham or Washington in 1963. Have students look in the school or public library for additional information on the movement, so that they may add authentic facts to their interview. Tell students that one student is to be the interviewer while the other is to be the interviewee. Some samples for questions the interviewer may ask are: What made you decide to join the movement? What rights does your group feel are being denied to them? How does your group plan to see that your grievances are met? Have each pair present their interview for the class. You may wish to videotape some of the better interviews and show them to other classes.

Point of View

In his famous *Letter from a Birmingham Jail,* Dr. King described the impact of segregation on children.

> **❝ You suddenly find your tongue twisted and your speech stammering as you seek to explain to your six-year-old daughter why she can't go to the public amusement park that has just been advertised on television, and see tears welling up in her little eyes when she is told that Funtown is closed to colored children. . . .❞**
> **Martin Luther King, Jr., 1963**

"Injustice anywhere is a threat to justice everywhere," said Martin Luther King, Jr., who was killed by an assassin. Try to listen to King's famous speeches on records or tapes.

Martin Luther King, Jr.

The greatest leadership for blacks was provided by a Baptist minister, the Reverend Martin Luther King, Jr. After his success in leading the Montgomery bus boycott, King became a national figure. Everywhere he preached the idea of **nonviolent direct action,** as the best way to achieve racial equality. "Nonviolent resistance is not a method for cowards," he said. One must "accept blows from the opponent without striking back." Love, not hate or force, was the way to change people's minds.

The movement also used songs to tell its aim and hopes—songs of protest, adaptations of spirituals, and newly composed songs.

C. Ray Moore/Black Star

These expressed what King felt was fundamental to the movement's success: determination. The unofficial theme song of the movement was "We Shall Overcome," which was adapted from a version of an old spiritual by the staff at the Highland Folk School in Tennessee. It was sung everywhere the movement went. Here are the first three verses:

> ❝ We shall overcome, we shall overcome,
> We shall overcome someday.
> Oh, deep in my heart, I do believe,
> We shall overcome someday.
>
> We are not afraid, we are not afraid,
> We are not afraid today.
> Oh, deep in my heart, I do believe,
> We shall overcome someday.
>
> We are not alone, we are not alone,
> We are not alone today.

RESOURCES

■ You may wish to have students complete Reading 66: "The Reverend Martin Luther King, Jr., Preaches Nonviolence from the Birmingham Jail (1963)" in Volume II of *Eyewitnesses and Others.*

◄ You may wish to have students complete Case 11: *"Loving v. Virginia"* in *THE CONSTITUTION: Past, Present, and Future.*

Charles Moore/Black Star

Oh, deep in my heart, I do believe,
We are not alone today.[1] **99**

Protesters in Birmingham, Alabama, were assailed by firemen with powerful hoses.

In April 1963 King led a campaign against segregation in ■ **Birmingham,** Alabama. The police turned fierce dogs on the peaceful demonstrators and drove them from the streets with jets of water from powerful fire hoses. King was thrown into jail. Yet this incident proved the value of King's approach. Millions of Americans who saw reports of the events on television were impressed by the demonstrators' courage and outraged by the brutality of the police. They reacted strongly on the behalf of the blacks, writing letters to the editors of their local newspapers and even joining protest marches.

Later in 1963, 200,000 people gathered in Washington to demonstrate peacefully in favor of President Kennedy's civil rights legislation. During the proceedings King made his famous "I Have a Dream" speech. He dreamed of a time, he told the huge audience who had come to this **March on Washington,** when all white and black ◄ Americans could live together in peace and harmony. The printed page can scarcely do justice to the moving and powerful speech King delivered. But part of it is reproduced on the following pages:

[1]New words and music arrangement by Zilphia Horton, Frank Hamilton, Guy Carawan, and Pete Seeger. TRO Copyright © 1960 and 1963 by Ludlow Music, Inc.

PRIMARY SOURCE
Description of change: excerpted.
Rationale: excerpted to focus on the purpose of the civil rights movement.

Fred Ward/Black Star

The crowd of more than 200,000 that assembled around the reflecting pool in Washington, D.C., marched to support President Kennedy's civil rights legislation. The speech Dr. King delivered that day seemed particularly inspired.

❝ Five score years ago, a great American, in whose symbolic shadow we stand today, signed the Emancipation Proclamation. This momentous decree came as a great beacon light of hope for millions of Negro slaves who had been seared in the flames of withering injustice. It came as a joyous daybreak to end the long night of their captivity.

But one hundred years later the Negro is still not free. One hundred years later, the life of the Negro is still badly crippled by the manacles of segregation and the chains of discrimination. One hundred years later, the Negro lives on a lonely island of poverty in the midst of a vast ocean of material prosperity. One hundred years later, the Negro is still languishing in the corners of American society and finds himself an exile in his own land. So we have come here today to dramatize a shameful condition. . . .

I say to you today, my friends, even though we face the difficulties of today and tomorrow, I still have a dream. It is a dream deeply rooted in the American dream. I have a

dream that one day this nation will rise up and live out the
true meaning of its creed: 'We hold these truths to be self-
evident, that all men are created equal. . . .'

I have a dream that one day on the red hills of Georgia,
the sons of former slaves and the sons of former slaveown-
ers will be able to sit down together at the table of brotherhood.

I have a dream that one day, even the State of Mississippi,
a state sweltering with the heat of oppression, will be transformed into an oasis of freedom and justice. . . .

I have a dream that one day, down in Alabama, with its
vicious racists . . . little black boys and black girls will be
able to join hands with little white boys and white girls as
sisters and brothers.

I have a dream today!

I have a dream that one day every valley shall be exalted,
every hill and mountain shall be made low, the rough places
will be made plain and the crooked places will be made
straight and the glory of the Lord shall be revealed and all
flesh shall see it together.

This is our hope. This is the faith that I go back to the
South with. With this faith we will be able to hew out of
the mountain of despair a stone of hope. With this faith we
will be able to transform the jangling discords of our nation
into a beautiful symphony of brotherhood. With this faith
we will be able to work together, to pray together, to struggle together, to go to jail together, to stand up for freedom
together, knowing that we will be free one day. . . .

From every mountainside, let freedom ring. And when
we let freedom ring, when we let it ring from every village
and every hamlet, from every state and every city, we will
be able to speed up that day when all of God's children,
black men and white men, Jews and Gentiles, Protestants
and Catholics, will be able to join hands and sing in the
words of the old Negro spiritual: 'Free at last! Free at last!
Thank God almighty, we are free at last!'[1] **99**

[1]From Martin Luther King, Jr.'s "I Have a Dream" speech. Copyright © 1963 by
Martin Luther King, Jr. Reprinted by permission of Joan Daves.

King was an exceptional person, but his optimism was typical
of the times. "The believer in nonviolence has deep faith in the
future," he once said.

No one knew better than Martin Luther King, Jr., that American
society was far from perfect. Yet he believed sincerely that the nation
was making progress toward the goals that he was seeking. Millions
of other Americans, black and white alike, faced the future in the
mid-1960s as hopefully as he did. 🖪

■ Return to the Preview & Review on
page 1051.

1. Answers will vary. Students who say the effect has been positive may mention that television programming has kept the American public entertained and informed. Students who say that the effect has been negative may mention that programming often lacks intellectual value because people can watch television for hours without hav-

ing to think. They may also mention the harmful effects of television, particularly when the programming is violent. Students may suggest more programs with educational value as a way of improving television programming.
2. Students may include problems such as segregation of public facilities, the need to enforce the desegregation of public schools, and unequal op-

---

Chapter Summary
Paragraphs will vary but should be evaluated on the logic of student arguments.

Reviewing Chronological Order
4, 3, 5, 2, 1

Understanding Main Ideas
1. It had a high standard of living and an abundance of wealth.
2. Insecticides, nuclear energy, computers, and antibiotics
3. Monetary policy: the Federal Reserve Board lowers interest rates so that businesses and consumers can borrow money to expand business and increase consumer consumption. Fiscal policy: the government increases spending, which increases the demand for goods and services through direct government purchases, and lowers taxes, which leaves consumers with spending money. If the economy grew too fast, fiscal and monetary policies could be reversed.
4. The good effects were comfortable homes, convenient shopping centers, and well-built schools. The bad effects were that cities lost tax revenues, causing urban decay, and most of the poor in the cities were nonwhites, leading to a new kind of segregation.
5. Because of the civil rights movement, African Americans were making progress by the mid-1960s. Women made headway when the Women's Liberation Movement began in the early 1960s. Indian rights began

1058

CHAPTER 28 REVIEW

| 1955 | | | 1960 | AFFLUENT AMERICA | |

1957
Nuclear power plants begin to generate electricity

1958
The Affluent Society published

1963
March on Washington and "I Have a Dream" speech
★
The Feminine Mystique published
★
Kennedy assassinated; Johnson becomes president

1964
Civil Rights Act
★
Johnson elected president

Chapter Summary
Read the statements below. Choose one, and write a paragraph explaining its importance.
1. Lyndon Johnson used forceful personality and his experience in government to accomplish many of his goals as president.
2. As a result of Johnson's hard work, Congress passed the laws which enacted his domestic program called the Great Society.
3. The unprecedented period of prosperity in the 1950s and early 1960s led to a mood of optimism in the United States.
4. There was a difference in the labor force following World War II as the percentage of women and the number of white collar workers increased greatly.
5. Television and the computer had a significant impact on American life in the 1950s and 1960s.
6. A dramatic shift in population occurred following World War II when many Americans moved to the Sun Belt and from the cities to the outlying suburbs.
7. The Women's Liberation Movement gained momentum following the publication of *The Feminine Mystique* in 1963.
8. Red Power became a rallying point for Indian Rights activists in the 1960s.
9. Dr. Martin Luther King, Jr., gained support for the civil rights movement in the early 1960s by a campaign in Birmingham and the March on Washington.

Reviewing Chronological Order
Number your paper 1–5. Then study the time line above and place the following events in the order in which they happened by writing the first next to 1, the second next to 2, and so on.
1. American Indian Movement founded
2. National Organization for Women founded
3. Johnson elected president
4. March on Washington
5. Elementary and Secondary Education Act passed

Understanding Main Ideas
1. Explain why the United States was called the Affluent Society in the mid-1960s.
2. What were some wonders of science that were developed after World War II?
3. Explain the difference between monetary policy and fiscal policy. Tell how economists planned to use each to prevent future depressions.
4. What were the good and bad effects of the growth of the suburbs following World War II?
5. Describe the efforts of African Americans, women, and Indians in the 20 years following World War II to secure equal rights.

Thinking Critically
1. **Evaluating.** Television began to greatly influence public opinion in the United States in the 1950s, and it continues to do so today. Discuss whether you think television has had a positive or negative effect on society. If you think its effect has been negative, suggest several ways that the television industry could improve its programming.
2. **Problem Solving.** Imagine that you are an African American in 1963 and have just participated in the March on Washington. You heard Dr. King's "I Have a Dream" speech which has greatly inspired you. Make a list of some of the problems faced by African Americans in the early 1960s and suggestions for how these problems may be solved.
3. **Comparing Ideas.** A major concern of many adult Americans in the 1950s and early 1960s was the direction taken by many young people who were becoming adults during this period. Their goals appeared to be having plenty of money, a good job, a house in the suburbs, and comfortable retirement. They were accused of

portunities in jobs and housing. Solutions may include pressuring legislators to pass and enforce desegregation laws and using peaceful demonstrations and boycotts to pressure individuals into abiding by these laws.

3. Answers will vary, but students should present well thought-out arguments and examples to support their answers.

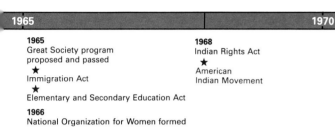

1965
Great Society program
proposed and passed
★
Immigration Act
★
Elementary and Secondary Education Act

1966
National Organization for Women formed

1968
Indian Rights Act
★
American
Indian Movement

1973
Wounded Knee

conforming and lacking in concern for the poor and the environment. Would you say that this description could be used to describe America's youth today? Why or why not?

Writing About History
America's Affluent Society is discussed in this chapter. Write a newspaper editorial in which you outline how America's abundant wealth and resources can be put to better use so that all of its people benefit from them. Conclude your editorial by mentioning which of America's riches you most appreciate and how they have benefited you and your family.

Practicing the Strategy
Review the strategy on page 1047.
Using the Census. Study the census data on page 1047 and answer these questions.
1. Did the total of square miles increase or decrease in urban areas between 1970 and 1980?
2. Did urban density increase or decrease from 1970 to 1980?
3. What conclusion can you draw from the information you found regarding square miles and density?

Using Primary Sources
In 1963 during an attempted nonviolent campaign against segregation in Birmingham, Alabama, Dr. Martin Luther King, Jr., was arrested. He drew severe criticism from local white clergymen, who accused Dr. King of being an outside agitator. They claimed his demonstrations ignited violence by forcing a confrontation between demonstrators and police. In answer to these accusations Dr. King wrote his now famous "Letter from a Birmingham Jail" while imprisoned in that city. As you read the following excerpt from Dr. King's letter, think about the wisdom of his words and the impact they had on those who continued using nonviolent methods in their campaign for civil rights.

In your statement you assert that our actions, even though peaceful, must be condemned because they precipitate [cause] violence. But is this a logical assertion [statement]? Isn't this like condemning a robbed man because his possession of money precipitated the evil act of robbery? . . . We must come to see that, as the federal courts have consistently affirmed, it is wrong to urge an individual to cease his efforts to gain his basic constitutional rights because the quest may precipitate violence. Society must protect the robbed and punish the robber.

1. Who do you think Dr. King is referring to when he uses the term "robber?"
2. What is it that Dr. King implies is being stolen by the robber?
3. Do you agree or disagree with Dr. King that it is wrong to tell people not to seek their constitutional rights because it "may precipitate violence?" Explain your answer.

Linking History & Geography
People moved from rural to urban areas in ever-increasing numbers in the decades following World War II. To better understand the dramatic impact of this population shift, study the map on page 1043. Then with your classmates prepare a map of the United States showing the major urban areas in 1940 and in 1980. You may need to refer to an historical atlas, the *Statistical Abstract of the United States*, or other reference books for the years 1940 and 1980 to complete your maps.

Enriching Your Study of History
1. **Individual Project.** Prepare an oral report on one of the following changes or trends that occurred in the 1950s and 1960s: advances in science and technology; population growth and shifts; higher standard of living. Tell how these changes affected American life in the 1950s and 1960s.
2. **Cooperative Project.** Your group will make a collage that illustrates leisure time activities enjoyed by Americans today. Each of you should contribute to the collage by bringing in as many pictures from magazines and newspapers as you can find on the subject or subjects chosen by your group.

RESPONSES *(Continued)*
to be recognized in 1961 with the founding of the Indian Youth Council. The Indian Rights Act of 1968 was an attempt by the government to protect Indians against discrimination, but it resulted in weakening tribal government.

Writing About History
Encourage students to be imaginative when preparing their editorials.

Practicing the Strategy
1. Increased
2. Decreased
3. As the population increased in urban areas, cities extended their boundaries.

Using Primary Sources
1. He is referring to segregationists.
2. People's civil rights
3. Student answers will vary but should show sound reasoning and logic.

Linking History & Geography
Student maps should indicate that adequate time was spent on research and preparation.

PRIMARY SOURCE
Description of change: excerpted and bracketed.
Rationale: excerpted to focus on Dr. King's defense of passive resistance; bracketed words added to clarify meaning.

The Vietnam Era

PLANNING THE CHAPTER

TEXTBOOK	RESOURCES
1. War in Vietnam	**Unit 10 Worksheets and Tests:** Chapter 29 Graphic Organizer, Directed Reading 29:1, Reteaching 29:1, Geography Worksheet 29 **Eyewitnesses and Others, Volume 2:** Reading 70: An African American GI in Vietnam (1969–1970), Reading 69: Senator Fulbright and President Johnson Debate the Vietnam War (1966, 1968) **The Historian (Investigative Software):** The United States in Vietnam
2. A Year of Tragedy	**Unit 10 Worksheets and Tests:** Directed Reading 29:2, Reteaching 29:2 **Eyewitnesses and Others, Volume 2:** Reading 65: James Meredith Cracks Ole Miss (1962) **Art in American History:** Transparency 49: Dream 2: King and the Sisterhood
3. Nixon as President	**Unit 10 Worksheets and Tests:** Directed Reading 29:3, Reteaching 29 **Art in American History:** Transparency 45: Vietnam Veterans Memorial **The Constitution: Past, Present, and Future:** Case 14: *Tinker v. Des Moines Independent Community School District*
4. The Watergate Affair	**Unit 10 Worksheets and Tests:** Directed Reading 29:4, Reteaching 29:4 **Creative Strategies for Teaching American History:** Page 351 **The Constitution: Past, Present, and Future:** Case 15: United States v. Nixon **Eyewitnesses and Others, Volume 2:** Reading 72: Elizabeth Drew Recounts the Vote to Impeach President Nixon (1973)
Chapter Review	**Audio Program:** Chapter 29 **Unit 10 Worksheets and Tests:** Chapter 29 Tests, Forms A and B (See also *Alternative Assessment Forms*) **Test Generator**

STRATEGIES FOR STUDENTS WITH SPECIAL NEEDS

Gifted Students.

Have interested students prepare research reports on the antiwar movement during the Vietnam War. Encourage students to interview both Vietnam veterans and antiwar activists and to include the results of these interviews in their final reports. Inform students that the results of these interviews are examples of oral history.

Students Having Difficulty with the Chapter.

You may wish to have students listen to Chapter 29 in *The Story of America Audio Program.* Then organize the class into cooperative learning groups. Instruct each group to skim the chapter to make a list of important dates to include on a time line. After the groups have placed the dates on their time lines, instruct them to draw pictures illustrating major events on the time lines. When all groups have completed their time lines, have spokespersons from each group explain their time lines and illustrations to the rest of the class.

BOOKS FOR TEACHERS

Ronald Berman, *America in the Sixties: An Intellectual History.* New York: Harper & Row, 1970.

Joseph R. Conlin, *The Troubles: A Jaundiced Glance Back at the Movement of the 1960s.* New York: Watts, 1982.

John Kenneth Galbraith, *The Affluent Society.* Boston: Houghton Mifflin, 1958.

Sheilah M. Rothman, *Woman's Proper Place: A History of Changing Ideas and Practices, 1870 to the Present.* New York: Basic Books, 1978.

Charles E. Silberman, *Crisis in Black and White.* New York: Random House, 1964.

Arthur M. Schlesinger, Jr., *The Bitter Heritage: Vietnam and American Democracy, 1941-1966.* Boston: Houghton Mifflin, 1967.

James L. Sundquist, *Politics and Policy: The Eisenhower, Kennedy, and Johnson Years.* Washington, D.C.: Brookings Institution, 1968.

BOOKS FOR STUDENTS

Jacqueline L. Harris, *Martin Luther King, Jr.* New York: Franklin Watts, 1983.

Don Lawson, *An Album of the Vietnam War.* New York: Franklin Watts, 1986.

Timothy S. Lowry, *And Brave Men, Too.* New York: Crown, 1985.

Margot, C. J. Mabie, *Vietnam: There and Here.* Austin: Holt, Rinehart and Winston, 1985.

Elaine Pascoe, *Racial Prejudice.* New York: Franklin Watts, 1985.

MULTIMEDIA MATERIALS

Anti-War Protest (film, 15 min.), Mert Koplin. Juxtaposes speeches opposing United States entry into World War II with speeches from the anti-Vietnam War campaign.

Immigration: Maintaining the Open Door (software), SSSS. Students decide how to deal with refugees who are trying to immigrate to the United States.

The 1960s: A Decade of Hope (filmstrip), GA. Commentary by experts shows the pervasive effects of the Vietnam War on all aspects of American life; how the 1960s have influenced American culture.

Nixon: Checkers to Watergate (film, 20 min.), PFP. Surveys President Nixon's rise and fall.

The Vietnam Commitment: Where Historians Disagree (filmstrip), SSSS. Highlights of the controversy surrounding the American presence in Vietnam.

RESOURCES

■ You may wish to have students complete the Chapter 29 Graphic Organizer as they work through this chapter.
◄ You may wish to have students complete "The United States in Vietnam" in *The Historian.*

SUGGESTED CAPTION RESPONSE

By helicopter; the jungle vegetation was too dense and the terrain too rugged to move troops by land transport.

CHAPTER OBJECTIVES

Upon completing this chapter, students will be able to:

OVERVIEW

The escalating American involvement in Vietnam increasingly divided American society. Nixon tried to deescalate the war with his Vietnamization plan. Finally a treaty ending American involvement was signed in 1973. Nixon also established relations with Red China and détente with the Soviet Union. Nixon's successes were, in the end, overshadowed by the Watergate Affair and his resignation.

FOCUS/MOTIVATION:
MAKING CONNECTIONS
Prior Knowledge.

Obtain one or two pictorial history books of the 1960s and early 1970s. Look for several photographs to dramatize the events that the students will read about (for example; the fighting in Vietnam; protests against the war; the assassinations of Martin Luther King, Jr., and Robert Kennedy; President Nixon's visits to China and the Soviet Union; and the Watergate Affair and cover-up). Set up a display, make copies, or use an opaque projector to show several photos to the class while giving your own personal remembrances of these events.

CHAPTER 29

The Vietnam Era

■ In August 1964 President Johnson announced that North Vietnam-
◄ ese gunboats had attacked the American destroyer *Maddox* in the Gulf of Tonkin, off the coast of Southeast Asia. He called upon Congress to approve and support in advance "the determination of the president, as commander in chief, to take all necessary measures to repel any armed attack against the forces of the United States." Congress voted for this resolution almost unanimously. As we shall soon see, this is another example of how an event that seems unimportant at the time can have far-reaching and unexpected historical significance. What consequences would commitment to the war in Vietnam have for America and its people?

Larry Burrows/Collection

American troops land at Da Nang to pit their sophisticated weaponry against the tunnels and jungle hideouts of the Viet Cong. What vehicle did the United States commonly use to move troops during the war? This picture give you a hint. After reading about the war in this section, explain why this vehicle was used.

1. Trace America's growing involvement in the Vietnam War.
2. Identify the groups that made up the opposing sides in the Vietnam War.
3. Give reasons why 1968 was called a year of tragedy.
4. Explain President Nixon's plan of Vietnamization.

5. Discuss President Nixon's foreign and domestic policies.
6. Explain the Watergate Affair.
7. Describe the events related to the Watergate cover-up that led President Nixon to resign.
8. Draw conclusions from written information.

1. WAR IN VIETNAM

The Domino Theory

In the summer of 1964 the former French colony of Vietnam was torn by war. Vietnam had been divided into two countries in 1954. Communist North Vietnam was supplying aid to pro-communist South Vietnamese guerrillas, who were known as the **Viet Cong.** The Viet Cong had been seeking to overthrow the government of South Vietnam, which was pro-American. They controlled large parts of the country, especially the rural regions.

While Dwight Eisenhower was president, a small number of American military advisers had been sent to South Vietnam to help train the South Vietnamese army. The United States also gave South Vietnam large sums of money for military supplies and economic aid. President Kennedy continued this policy.

The president of South Vietnam, Ngo Dinh Diem, was incompetent and unpopular. Many of the men around him were openly corrupt. Shortly before President Kennedy was assassinated, a group of Vietnamese army officers overthrew the Diem government and killed Diem. Unfortunately, they proved no better than he at defeating the Viet Cong.

President Johnson did not change American policy toward Vietnam until the Gulf of Tonkin affair. Even then, he was mainly interested in *appearing* to be more aggressive. His Republican opponent in the 1964 presidential election, Senator Barry Goldwater, demanded that the United States make a bigger effort to ''check communism'' in Vietnam. Johnson hoped that the **Tonkin Gulf Resolution,** which gave him broad war powers, would convince the voters that he was pursuing that objective vigorously. But he made a special point of not getting *too* involved in Vietnam. He insisted that he ''would never send American boys to do the fighting that Asian boys should do themselves.''

After winning the election, however, Johnson decided to step up American military activity in Vietnam. This would restore morale to the South Vietnamese. President Eisenhower had warned of a ''falling domino'' effect if communist expansion were allowed to go unchallenged. He had said in 1954:

> ❝ You have a row of dominoes set up, you knock over the first one, and . . . the last one . . . will go over very quickly.❞

According to this **domino theory,** if South Vietnam were controlled by the communists, its neighbors, Laos and Cambodia, would also become communist. Then all Southeast Asia, and perhaps even India with its hundreds of millions of people, would follow.

Preview & Review

Use these questions to guide your reading. Answer the questions after completing Section 1.
Understanding Issues, Events, & Ideas. Use the following words to describe American involvement in Vietnam: Viet Cong, Gulf of Tonkin Resolution, domino theory, escalation, doves, hawks, Saigon, Tet offensive.
1. How did Johnson respond to communist expansion in Southeast Asia after the Tonkin Gulf Resolution?
2. How was Johnson's Vietnam policy different from the policies of Eisenhower and Kennedy?
3. Why did President Johnson and his advisers believe they were acting with restraint in Vietnam?
4. What effect did the Tet offensive have on Americans?
Thinking Critically. 1. Why do you think Congress passed the Tonkin Gulf Resolution so easily? 2. What do you think the American officer meant when he said that ''we had to destroy it in order to save it?'' Imagine that you are Vietnamese. How would you react to such a remark?

FOCUS/MOTIVATION: MAKING CONNECTIONS
Prior Knowledge.
Set up a row of dominoes so that they are close enough that each will hit the next as it falls. Ask students what they think will happen to the row of dominoes when the first one is pushed over. *(They all topple.)* Have a student push over the first domino. Then ask them if they have ever heard the domino theory applied to American foreign policy. *(Students may be familiar with the domino theory as applied to Vietnam and Southeast Asia.)* Explain that the demonstration illustrates the idea behind the domino theory of U.S. foreign policy. The first domino was a communist country that influenced the next to "fall" to communism and so on. People were afraid that if South Vietnam fell to the communists, the rest of Southeast Asia would also become communist.

PRIMARY SOURCES
Description of change: excerpted.
Rationale: excerpted to focus on Johnson's resolve to fight in Vietnam.
(Point of View) Description of change: excerpted.
Rationale: excerpted to focus on one couple's reaction to the news that their son has been killed in action.

Point of View

A priest and an army sergeant come to tell Gene and Peg Mullen that their son has been killed in Vietnam.

> "Gene looked beyond Father Shimon to the sergeant and asked again, "Is my boy *dead?*"
>
> "Let's go into the house, Gene," Father Shimon said. "I want to talk to you there."
>
> "No!" Gene said, not moving. "I want to *know!* Tell me, *is my boy dead?*"
>
> "I can't tell you here," Father Shimon said, his hand fluttering up toward Gene's shoulder. "Come into the house with us please?"
>
> Gene spun away before the priest's pale fingers could touch him.
>
> Peg Mullen heard the back door open, heard Gene rushing up the stairs into the kitchen, heard him shouting, "It's Mikey! It's Mikey!" his voice half a scream. . . ."
>
> From *Friendly Fire,*
> C.D.B. Bryan, 1976

Recent events in Korea and the Cuban Missile Crisis seemed to show that the way to check communist expansion was by firmness and force. President Johnson, urged on by a military with unprecedented power and prestige, felt he could not waver. He said:

> "We could tuck our tails between our legs and run for cover. That would just whet the enemy's appetite for greater aggression and more territory, and solve nothing."

The assumption behind this reasoning was that the fighting in South Vietnam was between local Vietnamese patriots and "outside" communists. If the outsiders were allowed to conquer the country, the argument ran, they would be encouraged to press farther. In reality the struggle in South Vietnam was a civil war between supporters of the government and the Viet Cong. "Outside" communists from China and the Soviet Union were supplying the Viet Cong with weapons and advice, just as the United States was helping the anti-communist government of South Vietnam. The communist government of North Vietnam was deeply involved too. Its objective was to unite the two Vietnams under a communist regime.

America Escalates the War

In February 1965 Johnson made a fateful decision. After Diem's assassination in late 1963, the Viet Cong had gained control of more and more South Vietnamese villages. The war now became a test of the president's will. "I will not be the President who saw Southeast Asia go the way China went," he said, referring to the communist takeover in China in 1949. He ordered the air force to bomb selected targets in North Vietnam. In March he sent two battalions of marines to Vietnam. Their job was to protect the air base from which the bombers were operating. Soon more troops had to be sent in to reinforce the marines!

A few months later the American forces in Vietnam were given permission to seek out and attack Viet Cong units. Still, many restrictions on how American troops could fight the war remained. Nonetheless, more troops were shipped to Vietnam. By the end of 1965 there were 185,000 American fighting men in the country.

This steady **escalation,** or increase, in American military strength and involvement in Vietnam went on for three years. Each increase brought more North Vietnamese into the conflict in support of the Viet Cong. By 1968 more than half a million Americans were fighting in Vietnam. Yet Congress never officially declared war. Johnson instead waged war by the authority of the Tonkin Gulf Resolution, which had seemed to have little historical significance when it was passed by Congress in 1964.

The president and his advisers thought they were acting with great restraint. The enormous difference in size and wealth between

SUGGESTED CAPTION RESPONSE
Like Korea, Vietnam is a mountainous peninsula that
has a long S-shaped seacoast on the east and is
bordered by China—a communist country—on the
north. The North Vietnamese were sending supplies
down the Ho Chi Minh trail that went through
Cambodia.

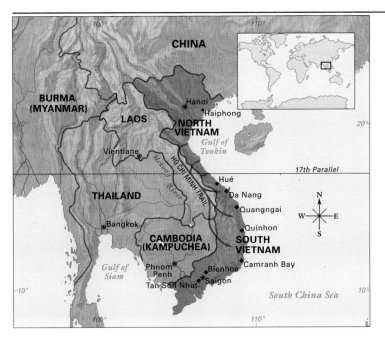

THE WAR IN VIETNAM

→ Ho Chi Minh Trail

◆ U.S. base

| 0 | | 200 | | 400 Mi. |

| 0 | 200 | 400 Km. |

Mercator Projection

LEARNING FROM MAPS. *Compare this map to the one of Korea on page 999. Note that the geography of Vietnam is similar to that of Korea. Describe how the geography of the two is similar. After reading about President Nixon's decision to extend U.S. bombing into Cambodia, study this map. What was the geographic reasoning behind Nixon's decision?*

RELATING HISTORY TO GEOGRAPHY
To reinforce the geographic theme of *location,* have students trace a map of Southeast Asia. Have them label the following: North Vietnam, South Vietnam, Cambodia, Thailand, Laos, China, 17th parallel, the Mekong River, Hanoi, Haiphong, Hue, Da Nang, and Saigon. They should use their map to trace the course of the Vietnam War.

GUIDED INSTRUCTION: COOPERATIVE LEARNING
Organize the class into cooperative learning groups. Make sure that students understand the widespread belief in the domino theory and the fear this caused. Then have students conduct group research and prepare a position statement detailing whether their group supports or opposes American involvement in the Vietnam War. Have each group select a spokesperson to present the group's statement to the class. After all of the statements have been heard, discuss the issue of American involvement.

USING HISTORICAL IMAGINATION
Have students imagine that they are President Johnson and must decide whether to commit more American troops to the war in Vietnam or to begin withdrawing troops. Have them write a short speech explaining what decision they have made and why. Have some of the students read their speeches to the class.

PRIMARY SOURCE
Description of change: excerpted and bracketed.
Rationale: excerpted to focus on reactions to a sniper attack; bracketed words added to clarify meaning.

the United States and North Vietnam lulled them into believing that the United States could win the war whenever it chose. How, asked the advisers, could a tiny country like North Vietnam successfully resist the United States? They wanted to risk the lives of as few Americans as possible. When each escalation proved to be not enough, they hoped just one more increase would do the job.

But North Vietnam was successful because the war in Vietnam was like no other war Americans had fought. Much of it was guerrilla warfare. The enemy, the Viet Cong, wore no uniforms and fought by ambush and by night. By day they blended with the rest of the population. Much of the war was fought in dense jungles and rugged mountains where tanks, even jeeps, were almost useless. Small squads of American soldiers slowly worked their way through vegetation so thick they could see only a few feet in any direction. The enemy could be hiding anywhere. Snipers would pick off one or two men and then disappear. One soldier recalled an attack in the jungle:

66 Men all around me were screaming. The fire [shooting] was now a continuous roar. We were even being fired at by our own guys. No one knew where the fire was coming from, and so the men were shooting everywhere. Some were in shock and were blazing away at everything they saw or imagined they saw. . . .[1]99

[1]From "Death in the Ia Drang Valley" by Jack Smith in the *Saturday Evening Post,* January 28, 1967

HISTORICAL SIDELIGHTS

Teach-ins began on college campuses to debate American involvement in Vietnam, and they helped to intensify opposition to the war.

SUGGESTED CAPTION RESPONSE

Most students will suggest that it does.

RESOURCES

■ You may wish to have students complete Reading 70: "An African American GI in Vietnam (1969-1970)" in Volume II of *Eyewitnesses and Others.*

GUIDED INSTRUCTION

Organize a class discussion on the escalation of American involvement in the Vietnam War. Center the discussion around these questions: (1) Why did the war escalate? (2) How did increased American involvement affect the economy? and (3) What happened to the economy once the United States pulled out of Vietnam?

Larry Burrows/Life Magazine © Time Warner, Inc.

The United States became mired in a land war in Southeast Asia, just as the French had before them. Critics sharply opposed the war. Much of the antiwar sentiment focused on American soldiers. Later came a time of reconciliation. Many efforts today are directed at helping Vietnam veterans reestablish their place in American society. Do you think the government has this responsibility after a war?

Mines and booby traps—hidden explosive devices—made movement through the countryside terrifying. Added to these difficulties were the limits placed on American troops. Often, they could not fire until fired upon, could not pursue the enemy in many places, could not bomb certain areas. And while American forces struggled in Vietnam, large numbers of people at home turned against the war, focusing much of their opposition on the soldiers fighting the war under the orders of others.

Time passed without victory. Large numbers of Americans began thinking that the war was a terrible mistake. Some claimed that keeping in power the government of South Vietnam, which was weak and very unpopular with the South Vietnamese people, was not worth the cost in American lives and money. Others argued that it was wrong for Americans to be killing people in a small country that was quite literally on the other side of the world.

The fighting in Vietnam was savage. Both sides showed a capacity for cruelty. Prisoners were sometimes tortured and killed. Hundreds of civilians died in air raids. Peaceful villages were burned to the ground to root out Viet Cong sympathizers. Local South Vietnamese officials were murdered by Viet Cong terrorists.

Americans who wanted to stop the war were called **doves,** after the traditional bird of peace. Those who insisted that the war must be fought until it was won were known as **hawks.** For a long time the hawks were in the majority. National pride and hatred of communism made many hawks believe that it would be cowardly and shameful for the United States to pull out of South Vietnam.

RESORCES
■ You may wish to have students complete Reading 69: "Senator Fulbright and President Johnson Debate the Vietnam War (1966, 1968)" in Volume II of *Eyewitnesses and Others*.

Both sides grew more vocal as escalation proceeded. President ■ Johnson expressed the determination of the United States government to see victory in Vietnam. Early in 1965 he said:

> " Tonight Americans and Asians are dying for a world where each people may choose its own path to change.
>
> Why must we take this painful road?
>
> Why must this nation endanger its ease, and its interest, and its power for the sake of a people so far away?
>
> We fight this war because we must fight if we are to live in a world where every country can shape its own destiny [fate]. And only in such a world will our own freedom be secure. . . .
>
> Why are we in South Vietnam?
>
> We are there because we have a promise to keep. Since 1954 every American president has offered support to the people of South Vietnam. We have helped to build, and we have helped to defend. Thus over many years have we made a national pledge to help South Vietnam defend its independence.
>
> And I intend to keep that promise.
>
> To dishonor that pledge, to abandon this small and brave nation to its enemies, and to the terror that must follow, would be an unforgivable wrong. . . .[1] "

Equally determined opponents spoke out against American involvement in the war. One opponent, Senator J. William Fulbright of Arkansas, chairman of the Senate Foreign Relations Committee, said:

> " We [the United States] are in a war to 'defend freedom' in South Vietnam. . . .
>
> One wonders how much the American commitment to Vietnamese freedom is also a commitment to American pride—the two seem to have become part of the same package. When we talk about the freedom of South Vietnam, we may be thinking about how our pride would be injured if we settled for less than we set out to achieve. We may be thinking about our reputation as a great power, fearing that a compromise settlement would shame us before the world, marking us as a second-rate people with failing courage and determination.
>
> Such fears are senseless. They are unworthy of the richest, most powerful, most productive, and best educated people in the world. . . .[2] "

[1] From "Peace Without Conquest," a speech by Lyndon B. Johnson on April 7, 1965
[2] From *The Arrogance of Power* by J. William Fulbright

PRIMARY SOURCES
(Top) Description of change: excerpted and bracketed.
Rationale: excerpted to focus on Johnson's reasons for American involvement in Vietnam; bracketed word added to clarify meaning.
(Bottom) Description of change: excerpted and bracketed.
Rationale: excerpted to focus on Fulbright's reasons for opposing American involvement in Vietnam; bracketed words added to clarify meaning.

STRATEGIES FOR SUCCESS

DRAWING CONCLUSIONS

One of the most important ways to use the information you read and study is as a basis to draw conclusions. A conclusion is a reasoned judgment arrived at by studying evidence. Historians draw conclusions based on evidence from primary and secondary sources, maps, charts and graphs, the census, and many other sources.

How to Draw Conclusions

To draw conclusions, follow these steps.
1. **Study the evidence carefully.** Note all trends and other relationships.
2. **Read "between the lines."** Make inferences by using your reasoning abilities to look for implied or suggested meanings. (But be sure to treat all inferences with caution. Use them carefully to support or refute the solid evidence you collect.
3. **Continually test your conclusions and revise if necessary.** Collect additional evidence. Refine your conclusion to fit the additional information. The more supporting facts you have, the more likely the conclusion you have drawn is correct.
4. **Use your conclusions.** Apply the conclusions you draw to the topic you are studying to help you understand the topic.

Applying the Skill

Read the following excerpt. It contains conclusions by a historian. See if you can identify one of the conclusions.

President Johnson did not change American policy toward Vietnam until the Gulf of Tonkin Affair. Even then he was mainly interested in appearing to be more aggressive. His Republican opponent in the 1964 presidential election, Senator Barry Goldwater, demanded that the United States make a bigger effort to "check communism" in Vietnam. Johnson hoped that the Tonkin Gulf Resolution would convince the voters that he was pursuing that objective vigorously. But he made a special point of not getting too involved in Vietnam. He insisted that he "would never send American boys to do the fighting that Asian boys should do themselves."

The most obvious conclusion stated by the historian in the excerpt is that President Johnson only wanted to appear more aggressive. The historian has reached this conclusion based on his research into this situation. Now read the following except and draw at least two conclusions based on your reading.

After winning the election, however, Johnson decided to step up American military activity in Vietnam. . . . In February 1965 Johnson made a fateful decision. He ordered the air force to bomb selected targets in North Vietnam. In March he sent two battalions of marines to Vietnam. Their job was to protect the air base from which the bombers were operating. Soon more troops had to be sent in to reinforce the marines!

A few months later the American forces in Vietnam were given permission to seek out and attack Viet Cong units. More troops were shipped to Vietnam. By the end of 1965 there were 185,000 American fighting men in the country.

This steady escalation, or increase, in American military strength in Vietnam went on for three years. Each increase brought more North Vietnamese into the conflict in support of the Viet Cong. By 1968 more than half a million Americans were fighting in Vietnam. Yet Congress never officially declared war. Johnson instead waged war by the authority of the Tonkin Gulf Resolution, which had seemed to have little historical significance when it was passed by Congress in 1964.

The president and his advisers thought they were acting with great restraint. The enormous difference in size and wealth between the United States and North Vietnam lulled them into believing that the United States could win the war whenever it chose. How, asked the advisers, could a tiny country like North Vietnam successfully resist the United States? They wanted to risk the lives of as few Americans as possible. When each escalation proved to be not enough, they hoped just one more increase would do the job.

What conclusions can you draw from this information? You might conclude that Johnson took his election victory as a sign that the American people supported escalated American involvement in Vietnam. Another conclusion you might draw is that Johnson's advisers did not portray an accurate picture of what it would take to win the war. What are some other conclusions you can draw from this excerpt?

For independent practice, see Practicing the Strategy on page 1086.

Charles Gatewood/Magnum Photos

In New York's Washington Square Park, protesters of the war light candles in a moratorium. What does the word moratorium *mean?*

Point of View

The author of *A Bright Shining Lie* brings a historical perspective to the Tet offensive.

"Yet to turn the war decisively in [the Viet Cong's] favor they had to achieve a masterstroke that would have the will-breaking effect on the Americans that Dien Bien Phu had had on the French. The masterstroke was Tet, 1968. . . . In cities and towns all across South Vietnam, tens of thousands of Communist troops were launching . . . a 'panorama of attacks.' . . . The goal was to collapse the Saigon regime with these military blows. . . . Ho Chi Minh and his confederates hoped to knock the prop out from under the American war, force the United States to open negotiations under disadvantageous conditions, and begin the process of wedging the Americans out of their country. . . ."
Neil Sheehan, 1988

Return to the Preview & Review on page 1061.

Early in 1968 the American commander in Vietnam, General William C. Westmoreland, announced that victory was near. Soon the Viet Cong would be crushed. But on January 30, the Vietnamese New Year's Day (*Tet*), the Viet Cong suddenly attacked cities all over South Vietnam. They even briefly gained control of parts of **Saigon,** the capital. They held a number of important cities for weeks.

The American and South Vietnamese troops fought back, as one historian has put it, "with the fury of a blinded giant." Eventually they regained control of the cities. In doing so, however, they destroyed even more of Vietnam. In a remark that soon became famous, an American officer justified the smashing of the town of Ben Tre. "We had to destroy it in order to save it," he said.

The American counterattack crushed the **Tet offensive.** Viet Cong and North Vietnamese losses were enormous. Still, the American public was profoundly shocked at the strength shown by the communists after so many years of war. The tide of opinion turned against the war. When General Westmoreland asked for another 200,000 men, President Johnson turned him down.

RETEACHING STRATEGY
Students with Special Needs.
Pair students who are having difficulty with students who are performing well. Ask the more proficient students to help the others make a time line of American involvement from the Tonkin Gulf Resolution to Westmoreland's request for more troops.

INDEPENDENT PRACTICE
Have students complete the Preview & Review activity at the beginning of the section.

CLOSURE
Remind students that the United States had been continuously involved in Vietnam since the Eisenhower administration (1950s). Under Johnson American involvement in the war began to escalate; by 1968, 500,000 Americans were fighting there. But every time the United States stepped up its involvement, so did the North Vietnamese. At home more and more Americans began to oppose the war.

HOMEWORK
Have students write a newspaper editorial favoring or opposing U.S. involvement in Vietnam. Use completed editorials to create an editorial page for the bulletin board.

PRIMARY SOURCE
Description of change: excerpted and bracketed.
Rationale: excerpted to focus on the Tet offensive; bracketed words added to clarify meaning.

RESOURCES
■ You may wish to have students complete Reading 65: "James Meredith Cracks Ole Miss (1962)" in Volume II of *Eyewitnesses and Others.*
◄ You may wish to have students view Transparency 49: "Dream 2: King and the Sisterhood" and complete the accompanying worksheet in *Art in American History.*

SUGGESTED CAPTION RESPONSE
The Tet offensive caused the tide of opinion to turn against the war and made people more sympathetic to McCarthy's position.

SECTION 2

PREVIEW & REVIEW RESPONSES
Understanding Issues, Events, & Ideas.
1. He did not seek reelection.
2. Riots broke out in 125 cities in 28 states.
3. Antiwar protesters, many of whom supported McCarthy, gathered in Chicago to demonstrate at the convention. Mayor Daley, a Humphrey supporter, packed the area with police. The demonstrators taunted the police, who reacted by attacking and arresting the demonstrators.
4. Nixon was such a sore loser when he was defeated in the 1962 California governor's race that no one expected him to ever be president. However, Nixon worked tirelessly for the Republican party. Many local Republican officials and delegates to the 1968 Republican convention came to feel that he deserved another chance.
5. Spiro Agnew's tough stands against crime, African American activists, and all kinds of protesters made the Nixon-Agnew ticket acceptable to people who might otherwise have voted for George Wallace, who was running as an independent.

Thinking Critically.
1. Students should support their position with sound reasoning.
2. Students should support their answers with sound reasoning.

PRIMARY SOURCE
Description of change: excerpted.
Rationale: excerpted to focus on King's vision of the future.

Preview & Review

Use these questions to guide your reading. Answer the questions after completing Section 2.
1. How did Lyndon Johnson acknowledge that his Vietnam policy had failed?
2. How did many Americans react to the assassination of Martin Luther King, Jr.?
3. What caused the riots at the 1968 Democratic convention?
4. Why did many Americans think Nixon would never be president? How did he get another chance in 1968?
5. Why was the selection of Agnew as Nixon's running mate a key to the 1968 election?

Thinking Critically. 1. Imagine you are a delegate to the Democratic National Convention in 1968. Write an article for your local newspaper explaining who you are supporting and why. 2. Imagine that Martin Luther King, Jr., and Robert Kennedy had not been assassinated in 1968. How might this have changed events in the years after 1968?

Senator Eugene McCarthy in his Children's Crusade—so called because his supporters were young and had yet to vote for president—was the first candidate to challenge President Johnson. How did the Tet offensive make McCarthy's candidacy a serious challenge?

2. A YEAR OF TRAGEDY

1968 Shocks Americans

In March 1968 President Johnson acknowledged that his Vietnam policy had failed. He had been planning to run for a second full term in 1968. Senator Eugene McCarthy of Minnesota had announced that he would oppose Johnson for the Democratic nomination. McCarthy was a leading dove. Before the Tet offensive no one gave him any chance of defeating Johnson.

After Tet, however, the situation changed. McCarthy almost defeated Johnson in the New Hampshire presidential primary. Then Robert F. Kennedy, brother of the slain president, declared that he too was a candidate. Faced with a difficult fight that would probably divide the country still further, Johnson announced that he would not seek reelection.

On April 4, less than a week after Johnson's withdrawal, came another shock. Martin Luther King, Jr., was murdered in Memphis, Tennessee, where he had gone to support a strike of garbage collectors. King had foreseen the price he might have to pay for his leadership. In a speech delivered in Memphis just before his assassination he observed:

66 Well, I don't know what will happen now. We've got some difficult days ahead. But it really doesn't matter with me now, because I've been to the mountaintop. And I don't mind. Like anybody, I would like to live a long life. Longevity has its place. But I'm not concerned about that now. I just want to do God's will. And He's allowed me to go up to the mountain, and I've looked over, and I've seen the promised land. I may not get there with you. But I want you to know tonight, that we as a people will get to the promised land. And so I'm happy tonight. I'm not worried about anything. I'm not fearing any man. Mine eyes have seen the glory of the coming of the Lord.[1] 99

King's murder caused an explosion of anger in black communities all over the country. Riots broke out in 125 cities in 28 states. Whole sections of Washington were aflame in the shadow of the Capitol.

Robert Kennedy was among those who tried to calm the waters. In an impromptu speech in an Indiana ghetto, he announced King's assassination with these words:

66 Martin Luther King dedicated his life to love and to justice for his fellow human beings, and he died because of that effort.

[1]From *Bearing the Cross* by David J. Garrow

Declan Haun/Black Star

Flip Schulke/Black Star

In this difficult day, in this difficult time for the United
States, it is perhaps well to ask what kind of a nation we
are and what direction we want to move in. For those of
you who are black—considering the evidence there evi-
dently is that there were white people who were responsible—you can be filled with bitterness, with hatred, and a
desire for revenge. We can move in great polarization—
black people amongst black, white people amongst white,
filled with hatred toward one another.

Or we can make an effort, as Martin Luther King did, to
understand and to comprehend, and to replace that violence, that stain of bloodshed that has spread across our
land, with an effort to understand with compassion and
love. . . .

What we need in the United States is not division; what
we need in the United States is not hatred; what we need
in the United States is not violence or lawlessness, but love
and wisdom, and compassion toward one another, and a
feeling of justice towards those who still suffer within our
country, whether they be white or they be black. . . .

*Martin Luther King, Jr., received a
traditional African American funeral procession. In the photograph
above left, his mourners march
through the streets of Atlanta behind
a wagon drawn by mules. How was
this a reminder of King's heritage?
King's widow, Coretta Scott King,
and his daughter Yolanda are pictured above at his funeral service.*

A Year of Tragedy   1069

GUIDED INSTRUCTION

The year 1968 could be called a year of tragedy. Two popular American leaders, Martin Luther King, Jr., and Robert Kennedy, were assassinated. So that students have a better understanding of the issues and concerns that these two men championed, organize the class into two groups, with one group preparing an illustrated presentation about Dr. King and the other preparing one about Robert Kennedy. They should collect pictures and research the beliefs and events in the life of the man they are studying. Have each group select a spokesperson to make their group's presentation to the class.

RELATING HISTORY TO GEOGRAPHY

On a map of the United States, have students outline and label all of the states. By using reference works such as an atlas and almanac, have them gather statistics on the presidential election of 1968. They should create a map of the election results by color coding the states according to winner and writing in the popular and electoral totals for each state. They should then draw two pie graphs next to the map showing the total percentage of electoral and popular votes for each candidate.

PRIMARY SOURCE

Description of change: excerpted.
Rationale: excerpted to focus on Kennedy's plea to overcome violence with compassion and understanding.

B. Glinn/Magnum Photos

Robert Kennedy became nearly as popular as his presidential brother when he campaigned for the Democratic nomination in 1968. What chance had he of winning the nomination?

We've had difficult times in the past. We will have difficult times in the future. It is not the end of violence; it is not the end of lawlessness; it is not the end of disorder.

But the vast majority of white people and the vast majority of black people in this country want to live together, want to improve the quality of our life, and want justice for all human beings who abide in our land.

Let us dedicate ourselves to what the Greeks wrote so many years ago: to tame the savageness of man and to make gentle the life of this world.

Let us dedicate ourselves to that, and say a prayer for our country and for our people.[1] ""

In June Robert Kennedy himself was assassinated by an Arab immigrant who objected to the support the United States was giving the country of Israel. Kennedy had just won the California presidential primary. He had seemed likely to win the nomination at the Democratic national convention in Chicago. After his death, Vice President Hubert H. Humphrey became the favorite.

Humphrey loyally supported Johnson's policy in Vietnam. (If

[1]From *Robert Kennedy and His Times* by Arthur M. Schlesinger, Jr.

he had not, Johnson would not have supported him for president.) When the convention met, large numbers of antiwar protesters, many of whom favored Senator McCarthy for president, flocked to Chicago to demonstrate. Mayor Richard Daley, a Humphrey supporter, packed the area around the convention hall with city police.

Radicals among the demonstrators insulted and taunted the police. They called them "pigs" and other vulgar names. The police responded by rushing into the crowd, clubs swinging. Millions of television viewers who had tuned in to watch the convention debates saw instead helmeted policemen repeatedly hitting the demonstrators with their nightsticks and herding them dazed and bloody into police wagons.

Not many people at the time realized that the protests in Chicago were a continuation of the antiwar and free-speech movements spreading across the land. At the University of California, students burned draft cards, and at Columbia University they took over many campus buildings.

The Election of 1968

Humphrey won the Democratic nomination easily. But thousands of Democrats blamed him, quite unfairly, for the police riot in Chicago. Most of these same Democrats resented his support of the war in Vietnam.

This split in the Democratic party helped the Republican candidate, Richard M. Nixon, the former vice president whom Kennedy had defeated in 1960. Few had expected Nixon to get a second chance to run for president. In 1962 he had run unsuccessfully for governor of California. At the time he seemed a sore loser, blaming reporters for his defeat.

However, Nixon had worked hard for the Republican party during the Kennedy and Johnson administrations. Hundreds of local Republican officials felt that he deserved a second chance for the presidency. When the 1968 Republican convention met, he had a majority of the delegates in his camp and was easily nominated.

Governor George C. Wallace of Alabama, an outspoken foe of racial integration, also ran for president in 1968 on an independent ticket. For this reason, Nixon chose Spiro T. Agnew of Maryland as his running mate. Agnew had taken a tough stand against black activists, urban crime, and protesters of all kinds. He was not well known nationally, but his record on several issues made him acceptable to many voters who might otherwise have supported Wallace.

In the three-way contest for president, Nixon won. He got only about 43 percent of the popular vote, less than 1 percent more than Humphrey. But he received a solid majority (56 percent) of the electoral vote. 🖃

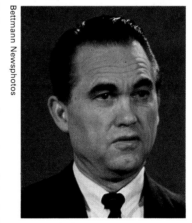

Fred Ward/Black Star

Bettmann Newsphotos

Dennis Brack/Black Star

From top: 1968 presidential candidates Hubert Humphrey, George Wallace, and Richard Nixon.

Return to the Preview & Review on page 1068.

A Year of Tragedy 1071

CHECKING UNDERSTANDING
Ask students to explain why 1968 can be called a year of tragedy. *(Tet led many people to reevaluate U.S policy in Vietnam. Martin Luther King, Jr., and Robert Kennedy were assassinated. Riots broke out in many cities after King's assassination. The Democratic convention in Chicago was the sight of violent clashes between antiwar demonstrators and police.)*

RETEACHING STRATEGY
Students with Special Needs.
Pair students who are having difficulty with students who are performing well. Ask the more proficient students to help the others make a chart showing why 1968 was a year of tragedy. Students should list the events on the left side and write a paragraph telling how the event affected the country on the right side. Have the limited English proficient students illustrate their charts rather than write paragraphs.

INDEPENDENT PRACTICE
Have students complete the Preview & Review activity at the beginning of the section.

CLOSURE
Tell students that the turbulent year of 1968 saw reversals in Vietnam, the assassinations of Martin Luther King, Jr., and Robert Kennedy, riots in the cities, and violent demonstrations at the Democratic convention.

HOMEWORK
Ask students to write an obituary for their local newspaper for either Martin Luther King, Jr., or Robert Kennedy.

1071

SECTION 3

PREVIEW & REVIEW RESPONSES
Understanding Issues, Events, & Ideas.
Descriptions should demonstrate an understanding of the terms used.

1. Johnson had refused to choose between guns and butter. Government spending for weapons and supplies for the Vietnam War was infusing huge sums into the economy without increasing the supply of consumer goods or raising taxes. As a result prices rose sharply. Nixon tried to check inflation by reducing government spending and raising interest rates. Instead of slowing, inflation continued to rise and unemployment also went up. Then Nixon ordered a wage-and-price freeze while a board was set up to regulate wage and price increases. This did not stop inflation, but it did slow it.

2. Nixon expanded the war to Cambodia because the North Vietnamese were using that country as a sanctuary from which to attack South Vietnam. The policy led to a revitalization the antiwar movement.

3. Nixon made trips to China and to the Soviet Union. These trips increased his popularity with Americans.

4. His diplomatic missions and efforts to wind down the Vietnam War increased his popularity, and there was no opposition in the Republican party to his nomination for a second term. The Democrats, however, were deeply divided. McGovern, the antiwar candidate, won

1072

Preview & Review

Use these questions to guide your reading. Answer the questions after completing Section 3.
Understanding Issues, Events, & Ideas. Use the following words to discuss key events during Nixon's first term in office: wage-and-price freeze, antiwar movement, Vietnamization, Cambodia, Ho Chi Minh Trail, Kent State and Jackson State, Strategic Arms Limitation Treaty, détente, Hanoi, Six Days' War, Arab Oil Crisis, shuttle diplomacy.

1. What was a major cause of the inflation that President Nixon set out to check? How did he attempt to check it?
2. Why did Nixon order American troops into Cambodia? What was the response in the United States to this move?
3. What diplomatic moves did President Nixon make in 1972? What effect did they have on the American people?
4. What were some reasons that Nixon was reelected by such an overwhelming majority?
5. What were the terms of the first Vietnam War peace agreement negotiated by Henry Kissinger? What reasons were given for its failure?

Thinking Critically. 1. Why do you think the United States, with its far greater wealth and technology was unable to win the war in Vietnam? What other lessons do you think Americans can learn from the Vietnam War? **2.** Why might it have been easier for Nixon to visit China and initiate regular diplomatic relations than it would have been for Eisenhower or Kennedy?

---

3. NIXON AS PRESIDENT

Nixon and the Economy

The new president favored moderation. He sought to please middle-income voters and persons who were neither radicals nor reactionaries. (Politically, radicals favor extreme change; reactionaries resist change or want to return to old-fashioned ways, an extreme change in itself.) These moderates and middle-income people were worried about high taxes and rising prices. Inflation in particular seemed the most alarming economic issue of the times. President Nixon set out to end it.

President Johnson was partly responsible for the inflation. Each time he ordered an escalation of the war in Vietnam, the government had to spend billions of additional dollars on weapons and other supplies. Government purchases put huge sums of money into the economy, but the economy was not producing more consumer goods. So people had money but a limited supply of goods to spend the money on. The prices of goods rose sharply. In addition, Johnson had not asked Congress to increase taxes to pay for the war, partly because he feared that his domestic programs would be cut back if he did so. (He also wished to avoid the congressional debate on the war that asking for a tax hike would cause.) A popular expression of the day was, "He refused to choose between guns and butter," or between spending money on the war and on domestic programs. As a result, the federal budget was badly unbalanced.

Nixon used fiscal and monetary policies to check inflation. He ① reduced government spending and persuaded the Federal Reserve Board to raise interest rates to discourage borrowing. The economy slowed down. These policies caused unemployment to go up. Plants cut back production, and people were laid off as consumer buying dropped off. But for some reason prices continued to go up too. Economists were as puzzled by the trend as the president. Throughout 1969 and 1970 the trend continued.

Finally, in August 1971, Nixon took a drastic step. He suddenly ordered a **wage-and-price freeze.** During a 90-day period, he set up new government boards to supervise wages and prices. Then he announced guidelines that placed maximum limits on future increases in wages and prices. This program did not stop inflation, but it did slow it down.

Nixon and the War

Nixon also sought a middle-of-the-road solution to the war in Vietnam. He was unwilling to give up the American goal of keeping the communists from conquering South Vietnam. Yet every report of

SUGGESTED CAPTION RESPONSE
American military involvement in South Vietnam had escalated because the South Vietnamese had been unable to defeat the communists, and there had been no improvement in South Vietnamese capabilities.

RESOURCES
■ You may wish to have students complete Case 14: *"Tinker v. Des Moines Independent Community School District"* in *THE CONSTITUTION: Past, Present, and Future.*

This Vietnamese army nurse attends a fallen soldier as American fighters look on. The picture was taken during the Vietnamization of the war. Why was there doubt from the start about this policy?

Robert Ellison/Black Star

new American casualties in Vietnam increased the strength of the ■ American **antiwar movement**—the organized effort to stop the war. Nixon's problem was how to reduce the casualties without losing the war in Vietnam.

He decided to shift the burden of fighting the Viet Cong and North Vietnamese to the South Vietnamese army. Gradually, as that army grew stronger, American troops could be withdrawn. This was called the **Vietnamization** of the war.

Whether Vietnamization would work was doubtful from the start. After all, the escalation of the American effort in Vietnam had

The Vietnam War split families and divided the United States along lines of race, class, and age. Looking back at that time, one commentator noted that those who could afford a college education were protected by student deferments, while the poor and minorities bore the brunt of the war. "Those who went, the kids who couldn't avoid the draft or the patriots who wanted to fight, came home talking about gooks and slopes, which added to the image of a racist war."

Point of View

The Port Huron Statement launched the movement of students who made up the New Left in the 1960s.

"We are people of this generation, bred in at least modest comfort, housed now in universities, looking uncomfortably at the world we inherit."
Tom Hayden, 1962

been necessary because the South Vietnamese had not been able to defeat the communists on their own. At best, Vietnamization would take a long time. The first reduction of American strength amounted to only 25,000 out of an army of more than 540,000.

As time passed, however, Nixon was able to reduce the size of the American force in Vietnam considerably. By the spring of 1970 it was down to 430,000. Nixon proudly announced that he intended to pull out another 150,000 men within a year.

Instead, only a few days later, on April 30, the president suddenly announced an expansion of the war. He was sending American troops into **Cambodia,** the nation on the western border of Vietnam. The reason for this invasion, Nixon said, was that the North Vietnamese were using Cambodia as a sanctuary, or safe base of operations, from which to launch attacks on South Vietnam. The Americans were going to destroy these bases.

For years, the North Vietnamese had been moving soldiers and supplies into South Vietnam along the **Ho Chi Minh Trail** in Cambodia and Laos. (Ho Chi Minh had been the president of North Vietnam.) The Americans had responded by bombing the trail. Since Cambodia was a neutral country, this bombing was done secretly. And like so much in this frustrating war, the bombings were in vain. No large bases were ever found in Cambodia.

Nixon's public announcement of the invasion of Cambodia set off a new storm of protest in the United States. In November 1969 250,000 people had staged a protest demonstration in Washington against the war. But the antiwar movement had become less vigorous as Nixon reduced the number of American soldiers in Vietnam. It now suddenly revived. If Vietnamization was a success, why was it necessary to send Americans into Cambodia?

College students in particular reacted angrily to news of the invasion. Throughout the spring of 1970 there were demonstrations on campuses all over the country. Much property was destroyed. The worst trouble occurred at **Kent State** University in Ohio. Rioting there led the governor of Ohio to send National Guard troops to the campus to preserve order. After several days of troubles in May, an overly tense guard unit opened fire on protesting students. Four students were killed and nearly a dozen more were wounded. Some of the victims had merely been walking across the campus on their way to classes when the guardsmen began shooting.

Several days later two students were shot down by Mississippi state police at **Jackson State.** The killings at Kent State and Jackson State caused still more student protests. Some colleges were forced to close down for the remainder of the school year. Parents were shaken by the spectacle of their children under fire. They had thought such things could never happen in the United States.

The Cambodian invasion did not lead immediately to much heavy fighting. Nixon depended increasingly on air attacks on North

John Paul Filo

Americans were deeply shocked by this picture taken in 1970 at Kent State University. There, National Guardsmen opened fire on students during a campus protest. What announcement by President Nixon prompted this demonstration?

Vietnam to weaken the communists. Soon the American troops in Cambodia were ordered back into South Vietnam. Nixon continued the troop withdrawals. By the end of 1972, fewer than 100,000 Americans were fighting the war, and the number was declining steadily.

Nixon Visits China and the Soviet Union

As American soldiers withdrew from Vietnam, President Nixon tried to end the war by diplomacy. His chief foreign policy adviser, Henry Kissinger, entered into secret discussions with North Vietnamese leaders in Paris. In February 1972, Nixon himself made a dramatic 1 trip to China, a nation that supported North Vietnam.

The United States had never officially recognized the communists as the legal rulers of China. At the time of the 1949 civil war that brought the communists to power in China, Nixon had been a leader of the group in Congress that opposed recognizing the new government. Like Senator Joseph McCarthy, Nixon had blamed the state department for the loss of China to the communists. Over the years he had opposed having any dealings with the "Red Chinese."

Now Nixon reversed himself completely. He no longer saw the need for containment. Instead he hoped to establish a balance of power. "It will be a safer world and a better world if we have a

GUIDED INSTRUCTION

In 1973 Richard Nixon ended a long period of icy relations between the United States and China that extended back to the communist victory over Chiang Kai-shek's Nationalists in 1949. Have students give Nixon's motives for changing American policy (*to establish a balance of power, to woo China away from the Soviet Union, to reestablish friendly relations that had been traditional since the days of the Open Door Policy, to have China on America's side as America tried to get out of the Vietnam War, to develop trade*)

John Dominis/Life Picture Service

In Beijing, President and Mrs. Nixon were greeted by Mao Tse-tung, communist leader of China. This was one of two historic visits made by the Nixons. What was the other?

strong, healthy United States, Europe, Soviet Union, China, Japan— each balancing the other, not playing one against the other, an even balance," he said in 1971. America's withdrawal from Vietnam— where it had been involved since the Eisenhower administration in the early 1950s—also helped open the way.

His visit to China was his boldest step towards a balance of power, and it was a great success. The Chinese leaders greeted him warmly. He agreed to support the admission of Red China to the United Nations in place of Taiwan, which had represented China since 1949. Important trade agreements were worked out. It was clear that the two nations would soon establish regular diplomatic relations.

A few months later Nixon made another important diplomatic move. This time he went to the Soviet Union. Again he was given an extremely friendly welcome. This happened despite the fact that the Soviet Union, like China, was supporting the North Vietnamese in the war. Out of this visit came the first **Strategic Arms Limitation Treaty** (SALT). This treaty placed limits on the use of nuclear weapons by the two powers. The two powers seemed to be entering a period of **détente,** or reduction of tensions between them.

The Election of 1972

President Nixon rose in popularity after his successful diplomatic visits and his sincere efforts to wind down the war in Vietnam. The

Republicans nominated him for a second term without opposition. The Democrats, however, had no obvious leader in 1972. Hubert Humphrey hoped to face Nixon again. Senator Edmund Muskie of Maine had many supporters. But the nomination went to Senator George McGovern of South Dakota, who had campaigned hard in the primaries on an antiwar platform.

McGovern's campaign was bungled from the start. His running mate, Senator Thomas Eagleton of Missouri, was discovered to have been hospitalized in the past for psychiatric treatment. At first McGovern announced that he would stand behind Eagleton "one thousand percent." Then he changed his mind. He asked Eagleton to withdraw. Sargent Shriver, a brother-in-law of John F. Kennedy, was chosen instead. This incident made McGovern seem both indecisive and unfaithful to a loyal supporter.

Bettmann Newsphotos

Shortly before the election, Nixon's negotiator, Henry Kissinger, announced that he had reached an agreement with North Vietnamese leaders. "Peace is at hand," he said. As a result, Nixon won an overwhelming victory on election day. He won more than 60 percent of the popular vote and carried every state but Massachusetts.

America Leaves Vietnam

After Kissinger's "peace is at hand" announcement, Nixon stopped the bombing of North Vietnam. The agreement Kissinger had negotiated called for a cease-fire, joint North and South Vietnamese administration of the country, and free elections. Then the last of the

---

Point of View

In *White House Years* Secretary of State Henry Kissinger describes the banquet hall where the leaders of China and the U.S. met.

66The banquets in the capital took place in the gigantic Great Hall of the People that commemorates the Communist takeover. . . . [It] faces the vermilion walls of the Forbidden City across Tien An Men Square. . . . The banquet protocol throughout my visits was unvarying. One reached the banquet hall by a grand staricase that rose steeply through various levels to seemingly distant heights. No visitor with a heart condition could possibly make it to the top alive. . . .**99**
Henry Kissinger, 1979

Henry Kissinger, left, Nixon's tireless national security adviser and later secretary of state, announced "Peace is at hand" shortly before Nixon stood for reelection in 1972. What happened instead?

GUIDED INSTRUCTION

Have students prepare a time line showing the growing involvement of the United States in the Vietnam conflict. Have them make the time line in class on the chalkboard or a large piece of butcher paper. Begin with the Tonkin Gulf Resolution of 1964 and end with the evacuation of the American embassy in Saigon in 1975. On the time line, show events that occurred in the United States that made the period of American involvement even more turbulent. *(antiwar protests, election campaigns, assassinations, etc.)*

ART IN HISTORY: COOPERATIVE LEARNING

Organize students into cooperative learning groups. Tell each group to prepare a visual display of war memorials to present to the class. After students have presented their displays to the class, tell them that when the winning design for the Vietnam Veterans Memorial was shown to the public, many people strongly disapproved of the choice. Ask students why they think some people disliked the proposed memorial. *(It is not the conventional monument portraying noble soldiers or glorifying war.)* Tell students that once people actually saw the memorial and the responses it evoked, attitudes changed.

PRIMARY SOURCE

Description of change: excerpted.
Rationale: excerpted to focus on veterans' views of the main lesson of Vietnam.

American troops would go home and the American prisoners of war held by the North Vietnamese would be released.

After the presidential election this agreement fell through. According to the Americans, the Vietnamese communists backed away from terms they had accepted earlier. But perhaps the main reason the talks ended was the refusal of South Vietnamese president Thieu to cooperate because his government objected to parts of the agreement. President Nixon then resumed the air strikes.

This time the president sent B-52 bombers, the largest in the air force, to strike at **Hanoi,** the capital of North Vietnam. These were far heavier attacks than any launched on Germany in World War II.

Nixon halted the bombing in December; peace negotiations resumed in Paris. Finally, in January 1973, an agreement was signed. So far as the United States was concerned, the war was over. But American policy had been a failure. The United States had lost the war. By the time the last Americans were airlifted out of Saigon (which was later renamed Ho Chi Minh City) the war had cost more than $100 billion and the lives of more than 58,175 Americans and a much larger number of Vietnamese. No one then anticipated how great would be the adjustment for the returning veterans, many of whom were deeply shocked by the war. There were few parades for them, few joyous public celebrations. Some Americans saw them as the symbol of all that was wrong with the war. Yet had they not been drafted and sent to that war by the American government, just as soldiers had been sent to previous wars? The veterans deeply resented the treatment they received.

What did the Vietnam War teach us? One of the most important lessons of the war in Vietnam was the effect a truly divided nation has on the war effort and the people fighting it. Antiwar sentiments focused first on government leaders and then on the soldiers themselves. Perhaps just as important is the lesson learned from fighting a war without going ''all out.'' As one article on the war said:

> 66 Viet Nam veterans argue passionately that Americans must never again be sent to die in a war that 'the politicians will not let them win.' And by win they clearly mean something like a World War II-style triumph ending in unconditional surrender.[1] 99

The aftermath of the Vietnam War brought another point to light. It proved the domino theory was wrong. The communist victory in Vietnam did not lead to the long-feared communist control of East and Southeast Asia. The countries of the region, such as Vietnam and Cambodia (also called Kampuchea), began fighting among themselves. The dominoes, instead of falling one after the other against Western democracy, seemed to crash angrily into each other.

[1]From *Time* magazine, April 15, 1985

THE VIETNAM VETERANS MEMORIAL

Etched in the polished black granite are 58,175 names. They are the names of the Americans who died in the Vietnam War. The names are listed in order of death, showing the war as a series of personal sacrifices and giving each person a special place in history.

To most Americans, the Vietnam Veterans Memorial is a symbol of long-overdue public recognition of the Americans who fought in the controversial war. The nation's commitment to this war had never been as intense as it had been to previous wars that involved American troops. In fact, public opinion about America's involvement in the war was sharply divided. Even many of those who fought in Vietnam came to question why they were there and how the war was being fought.

In other times war-weary veterans were greeted by cheering crowds and parades. Vietnam veterans returned instead to indifference, and sometimes hostility. Many buried their memories of the war and kept silent. Some had a difficult time readjusting to life after the stress of combat and their reception at home. Others returned successfully to civilian life. Gradually Vietnam veterans organized and began to insist on public recognition of their war efforts.

In July 1980, Congress selected a site for a Vietnam memorial in the Constitutional Gardens near the Lincoln Memorial in Washington, D.C. The memorial's design would be chosen through a national competition open to all American citizens 18 years of age or older. The only criterion set by the committee was that the memo-rial must display the names of the Americans who had died in the war.

In May 1981 a jury of eight internationally famous artists, designers, and architects announced their unanimous first choice from the 1,421 entries. The winning entry had been submitted by Maya Ying Lin of Athens, Ohio. At the time she was a 21-year-old student at Yale University. In March 1982 ground was broken and construction began. The memorial was dedicated on November 13, 1982.

Maya Lin's design creates a park within a park—a quiet and peaceful place. The mirrorlike surfaces of the polished black granite reflect the surroundings—trees, flowers, and the faces of the people who search the memorial for names. The memorial's walls point to the Lincoln Memorial and the Washington Monument.

Flowers, pictures, and other mementos cover the ground at the base of the walls. They are remembrances brought by parents, friends, and loved ones. But the most striking feature of the memorial is the list of names. As Lin had planned, the names became the memorial. They are the ultimate honor to those who died in America's most controversial war. 🔵

Christopher Morris/Black Star

INDEPENDENT PRACTICE

Have students complete the Preview & Review activity at the beginning of the section.

CLOSURE

Tell students that Nixon tried to steer a middle-of-the-road course with the economy and in the way he conducted the Vietnam War. Although he did pull troops out of Vietnam, he expanded the war into Cambodia and intensified the bombing of North Vietnam. However, Nixon did have diplomatic successes. In 1973 a peace treaty ended the war for the United States. He made successful trips to China and the Soviet Union, and his secretary of state helped negotiate a cease-fire between Israel and Egypt.

HOMEWORK

Tell students to imagine that the peace treaty ending U.S. participation in the Vietnam War has just been announced. They are to write an article for their local newspaper, detailing the effects that the war has had on the United States and what changes peace will bring.

Source: World Book Encyclopedia

THE COSTS OF AMERICA'S WARS		
War	Military Deaths	Financial Costs
Revolutionary	25,324*	$101,100,000
War of 1812	2,260	$90,000,000
Mexican	13,283	$71,400,000
Civil	529,332	$5,183,000,000
Spanish-American	2,446	$283,200,000
The Great War	126,000	$18,676,000,000
World War II	405,399	$263,259,000,000
Korean	54,246	$67,386,000,000
Vietnam	58,132*	$150,000,000,000
Persian Gulf	268	$31,500,000,000
*Estimated		

LEARNING FROM TABLES. *This table contains the number of military deaths and financial costs of each of America's wars. In which war did the most Americans die? Why? Why do you think the expenditures for World War II and the Vietnam War were so high?*

Middle Eastern Diplomacy

Vietnam was not the only trouble spot to attract America's attention. The Arab states of the Middle East continued to present perplexing problems, mostly because they remained opposed to the very existence of Israel. In 1967 Israel had won a smashing victory over Egypt in the **Six Days' War.** A precarious peace, broken by Arab raids and Israeli reprisals, had held until October 6, 1973. On that day, Yom Kippur, the Jewish holy day of atonement, Egypt and Syria again attacked Israel. While the war raged, the Arab-controlled Organization of Petroleum Exporting Countries (OPEC) banned all oil shipments to the United States in retaliation for its support of Israel. The Netherlands, Portugal, and South Africa also suffered the oil embargo.

The impact surprised many Americans. Petroleum products, most notably gasoline, were rationed. Long lines of cars waited at gas pumps all over America.

This **Arab Oil Crisis** caused Americans to realize that an extended ban would threaten the American economy and life-style. They had known petroleum was a limited and nonrenewable resource since the automobile boom of the 1920s. They had learned to conserve petroleum during the emergency of World War II. Now they began to conserve petroleum in their everyday lives. People were encouraged to use carpools or mass transit. Gasoline prices were raised, in part to discourage extra driving. Schools and public buildings closed on the coldest or hottest days to conserve the electricity or oil needed to heat or cool the building.

Nixon realized that America's two Middle Eastern interests—Israel and oil—created a complex situation. He sent his master negotiator, Henry Kissinger, into action. Kissinger visited the Middle East nearly every month. His **shuttle diplomacy,** so-called because of his frequent diplomatic trips, brought Egypt and Israel to a cease-fire. He kept the region from erupting into the flames of war and reestablished the flow of Middle Eastern oil to the United States. 🖻

Return to the Preview & Review on page 1072.

1080   THE VIETNAM ERA

4. THE WATERGATE AFFAIR

Nixon's Power Begins to Crumble

The ending of the war and his landslide victory in the 1972 election made Richard Nixon seem one of the most powerful of American presidents. He used his power to cut back sharply on various New Deal and Great Society programs designed to help poor people, blacks, and other disadvantaged groups. He hoped the cut in government spending would slow inflation. He also announced that it was time to crack down hard on crime. He criticized what he called the "permissiveness" of many Americans.

Yet, at the very moment of his great election success, Nixon's power began to crumble. The cause was the **Watergate Affair,** one of the strangest episodes in the entire story of America.

On the night of June 17, 1972, shortly before the presidential nominating conventions, five burglars were arrested in the headquarters of the Democratic National Committee in Washington, D.C. The headquarters were located in the Watergate, a modern office building and apartment house complex on the Potomac River.

The burglars had large sums of money in new $100 bills in their wallets when they were arrested. They were carrying two expensive cameras, 40 rolls of film, and a number of tiny listening devices, or "bugs." They had obviously intended to copy Democratic party records and attach the bugs to the office telephones.

Suspicion naturally fell on the Republican party. One of the men arrested was James W. McCord, a former CIA employee who was working for Nixon's campaign organization, the Committee for the Reelection of the President (CREEP). Soon it was discovered that two other campaign officials had been involved in the break-in. Other CREEP techniques came to light. CREEP workers had joined the campaign of Senator Muskie in 1972 and disrupted it by spreading damaging and false rumors to the press and mixing up schedules so that Muskie and his supporters missed several important appearances and appointments.

Both Nixon's campaign manager, former Attorney General John Mitchell, and the president himself denied that anyone on the White House staff had anything to do with Watergate. Nixon's press secretary described it as a "third-rate burglary." Vice President Spiro Agnew suggested that the Democrats might have staged the affair to throw suspicion on the Republican party. Most people accepted the president's denial. The Watergate Affair had no effect on the election.

The Cover-up

Early in 1973 the Watergate burglars were put on trial in Washington. Most of them pleaded guilty. This meant that they could not be

Preview & Review

Use these questions to guide your reading. Answer the questions after completing Section 4.
Understanding Issues, Events, & Ideas. Use the following words to explain Nixon's fall from power: Watergate Affair, executive privilege, Saturday Night Massacre, Twenty-fifth Amendment, articles of impeachment.
1. What three articles of impeachment were passed by the House Judiciary Committee against Nixon?
2. How was the Supreme Court involved in the case against Nixon?
3. Why were the transcripts of the White House tapes unable to prove the president's claim of innocence?
4. In your opinion, should the president be allowed to resign to avoid impeachment? Explain your view.

Thinking Critically. Do you think that President Ford should have offered Nixon a pardon? Why or why not?

PREVIEW & REVIEW RESPONSES
Understanding Issues, Events, & Ideas.
Explanations should demonstrate an understanding of the terms used.
1. The three charges against Nixon were obstructing justice, misusing presidental power, and refusing to turn over evidence to the committee.
2. The Supreme Court ruled that Nixon must turn over the tapes to Jaworski.
3. Rather than proving him innocent, the tapes proved that Nixon had not only known about but had ordered the cover-up from the beginning.
4. Answers will vary; students should support their opinions with sound reasoning.

Thinking Critically.
Answers will vary; students should support their opinions with sound reasoning.

Gjon Mili/Life Magazine © Time Warner, Inc.

All of Washington sought passes to the Watergate hearings held to determine whether or not the president of the United States should be impeached. Here John Dean, the president's lawyer, is sworn in.

questioned about the case. But one of them, James McCord, told the trial judge, John Sirica, that a number of important Republican officials had been involved in planning the burglary.

McCord's charges were found to be true. The Justice Department renewed its efforts to locate the people behind the break-in. One by one, important members of the Nixon administration admitted that they had known about the incident. The head of the FBI confessed that he had destroyed documents related to the affair. Clearly there had been a cover-up of evidence, which is a crime—obstruction (blocking) of justice. The Senate began an investigation.

John Dean, the president's lawyer, provided particularly damaging evidence to investigators. The president fired Dean, whom he considered a traitor. Nixon's two closest aides, H. R. Haldeman and John Ehrlichman, were forced to resign. Still, Nixon insisted that they were loyal public servants who had done nothing wrong.

As the Senate investigation proceeded, witnesses brought out more and more details about Watergate and other illegal activities connected with Nixon's campaign for reelection. Evidence suggested that many large corporations had made secret contributions to the campaign fund. Such gifts were illegal. John Dean testified that the president had helped plan the cover-up from the beginning. When he had gone on television to deny that anyone in the White House was involved, the president had lied, Dean said.

Dean's testimony was extremely important because it so directly involved the president. He appeared to be telling the truth. When details of his testimony could be checked against other sources, they proved to be correct. But Nixon denied the charges. It seemed to be his word against Dean's.

Then another witness revealed to the startled investigators that Nixon had been secretly recording all the conversations that had taken place in his office. These tape recordings would show whether or not Dean had told the truth! At once the Senate investigators demanded that the president allow them to listen to these and other White House tapes that might reveal important information.

Nixon refused to allow anyone to listen to the tapes. He claimed what he called **executive privilege**—the right to keep information secret when it related to presidential business.

More and more people came to the conclusion that Nixon was lying. Charges that he had cheated on his income taxes while president by claiming large illegal deductions further turned public opinion against him. Yet how could the full truth be discovered while people Nixon had appointed ran the Justice Department? To end the criticism, Nixon agreed to the appointment of a distinguished law professor, Archibald Cox, as a special prosecutor for the Justice Department to take charge of the case. Cox was promised a free hand and told to pursue the truth wherever the facts led him.

Professor Cox also demanded that the White House tapes be turned over to his investigators for study. Again Nixon refused. A federal judge then ordered him to give Cox the tapes. Instead of doing so, Nixon ordered Attorney General Elliot L. Richardson, head of the Justice Department, to fire Cox!

Richardson resigned rather than carry out this order. So did the assistant attorney general. But Nixon persisted and finally a third member of the Justice Department, Robert G. Bork, discharged Cox. These events occurred on the evening of Saturday, October 20, 1973. The affair was called the **Saturday Night Massacre.**

Nixon's entire administration seemed riddled with scandal. Only ten days before the Saturday Night Massacre, Vice President Spiro Agnew admitted that he had been cheating on his income taxes. He resigned from office. Actually, the official record of his case revealed that he had also accepted $200,000 in bribes while serving as a public official in Maryland. To avoid the national shame of having a vice president in prison, government lawyers had allowed him to admit guilt by pleading nolo contendere (no contest) to the charge of income tax evasion. Agnew was fined and placed on probation.

The **Twenty-fifth Amendment** of the Constitution, ratified in 1967, includes a provision that when the vice presidency falls vacant, the president shall appoint a new vice president. Nixon chose Congressman Gerald R. Ford of Michigan. The appointment was approved by Congress and Ford became vice president.

Nixon Falls from Power

The Saturday Night Massacre led many people to demand that Nixon be impeached. (*Impeachment* is the legal process of charging a high

GUIDED INSTRUCTION
Organize a class debate on the following resolution about Watergate.
   RESOLVED: President Nixon should have been impeached for his role in Watergate.
   Have students consider how Watergate led to the downfall of President Nixon—the first resignation of a president in American history. Ask: Should Nixon have been *impeached*? Should Ford have granted Nixon a *pardon*? At the close of the debate, poll students on their positions.

GUIDED INSTRUCTION
Organize the class into small groups. Have them research the Watergate Affair at their school or public library and prepare a Watergate chronology. Their chronology may be in the form of a time line, chart, or list. Tell them to use newspaper and magazine accounts of the events from the break-in to the resignation of Richard Nixon. Have a spokesperson from each group present their group's chronology to the class.

CHECKING UNDERSTANDING

Ask students to identify the person referred to in each statement.

1. "I was the special prosecutor until I demanded that Nixon give me the White House tapes." *(Archibald Cox)*
2. "I refused the president's order to fire the special prosecutor." *(Attorney General Elliot Richardson)*
3. "I became president when Nixon resigned." *(Gerald Ford)*
4. "I fired the special prosecutor." *(Robert Bork)*
5. "I became the special prosecutor after Nixon ordered my predecessor fired." *(Leon Jaworski)*
6. "I was the president's lawyer and testified against him." *(John Dean)*
7. "I was the first president to resign." *(Richard Nixon)*

RETEACHING STRATEGY

Students with Special Needs. Pair students who are having difficulty with students who are performing well. Ask the more proficient students to help the others create a matching test about the participants and their roles in the Watergate Affair. When the pairs of students have completed their work, tell them to exchange quizzes. After they have finished the matching exercise, they should exchange quizzes again and check the answers for accuracy.

PRIMARY SOURCE

Description of change: excerpted and bracketed.
Rationale: excerpted to focus on the major changes agains Nixon; bracketed words added to clarify meaning.

Point of View

The House Judiciary Committee left little doubt how they felt about Nixon's behavior during the Watergate investigation.

Article I

"... Richard M. Nixon, has prevented, obstructed, and impeded the administration of justice. ...

Article II

... Richard M. Nixon ... has repeatedly engaged in conduct violating the constitutional rights of citizens, ... contravening [blocking] the laws of governing agencies. ...

Article III

... Richard M. Nixon ... has failed without lawful cause or excuse to produce papers and things, as directed by duly authorized subpoenas [writs commanding a person to turn over evidence or to testify]. ...

Wherefore, Richard M. Nixon, by such conduct, warrants impeachment and trial, and removal from office."

From *Articles of Impeachment,* July 30, 1974

official with wrongdoing.) To quiet those demanding his impeachment, Nixon promised to cooperate with Cox's successor as Watergate prosecutor, Texas lawyer Leon Jaworski. Nevertheless, the Judiciary Committee of the House of Representatives began an investigation to see if there were grounds for impeaching Nixon.

While the Judiciary Committee studied the evidence of Nixon's involvement, prosecutor Jaworski proceeded against the others involved in CREEP's illegal activities. One after another, men who had been involved in Nixon's campaign for reelection were charged and convicted of crimes. Some had lied under oath, others had obstructed justice, and one had raised money for the campaign in an unlawful manner.

Late in April 1974 Nixon released edited transcripts of some of his taped conversations. These, he said, would prove his innocence. However, important parts of conversations were left out in these printed versions. At many places the typescripts contained blanks because, Nixon claimed, the tapes had not recorded what was said clearly enough to be understood. Still he refused to let others check on the editing by listening to the tapes.

Both what the transcripts revealed and what they left out led to increased demands that the president allow investigators to listen to the key tapes themselves. Nixon still refused. He would not turn them over to either the House Judiciary Committee or to special prosecutor Jaworski.

Jaworski therefore asked the Supreme Court to order the president to give him the tapes of 64 specific conversations known to have taken place in the White House. While the Court considered the matter, the Judiciary Committee decided to allow its sessions to be broadcast and televised. In July 1974 the committee passed three **articles of impeachment,** or charges against the president. One accused Nixon of obstructing justice. Another accused him of misusing the powers of the presidency. The third concerned his refusal to let the committee listen to the tapes.

Under the Constitution, the Judiciary Committee's report would be submitted to the full House of Representatives. If the report was accepted, the House would then impeach Nixon by presenting the articles of impeachment to the Senate. The Senate would act as a court hearing the charges. If two thirds of the senators voted in favor of any of the three articles, Nixon would be removed from office.

While the Judiciary Committee was still debating, the Supreme Court ruled that Nixon must turn the tapes over to prosecutor Jaworski. Nixon hesitated. If he defied the Court's order, it was difficult to see how it could be enforced. But Nixon's advisers convinced him that if he refused to obey the court order, the Senate was certain to remove him from office. At last he gave up the tapes.

The tapes proved conclusively that Nixon had known about and even ordered the Watergate cover-up from the start. Only one day

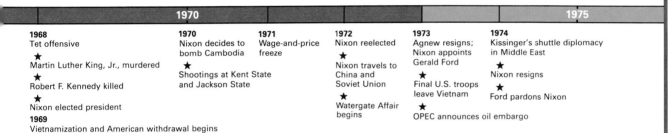

1968
Tet offensive
★
Martin Luther King, Jr., murdered
★
Robert F. Kennedy killed
★
Nixon elected president
1969
Vietnamization and American withdrawal begins

1970
Nixon decides to bomb Cambodia
★
Shootings at Kent State and Jackson State

1971
Wage-and-price freeze

1972
Nixon reelected
★
Nixon travels to China and Soviet Union
★
Watergate Affair begins

1973
Agnew resigns; Nixon appoints Gerald Ford
★
Final U.S. troops leave Vietnam
★
OPEC announces oil embargo

1974
Kissinger's shuttle diplomacy in Middle East
★
Nixon resigns
★
Ford pardons Nixon

Using Primary Sources

While many people the world over applauded the new détente between the United States and the Soviet Union, others cautioned Americans to beware of Soviet tricks. One was famous Soviet writer Aleksandr Solzhenitsyn, who had spent many years in detention and labor camps for writings that were critical of Stalin and later Soviet leaders. Finally in 1974 he was forced to leave the Soviet Union and live in exile. As you read the excerpt from a 1975 speech by Solzhenitsyn, consider his warning in light of more recent events in the Soviet Union.

America—in me and among my friends and among people who think the way I do over there [in the Soviet Union], among all ordinary Soviet citizens—brings forth a mixture of admiration and compassion. You're a country of the future; a young country; a country of still unused possibilities; a country of tremendous geographical distances; a country of tremendous spirit; a country of generosity. But these qualities—strength and generosity—usually make a person and even a whole country trusting. This already has done you a disservice several times.

I would like to call upon America to be more careful with its trust and prevent those people who are falsely using the struggle for peace and social justice to lead you down a false road. They are trying to weaken you. They are trying to disarm your strong and magnificent country.

1. According to Solzhenitsyn, what makes Americans particularly trusting?
2. Do you agree with Solzhenitsyn that being trusting has done America a disservice several times? Give examples to support your answer?
3. What do you think Solzhenitsyn is warning Americans against?

Linking History & Geography

The Middle East has been an area of concern for the United States since World War II. To better understand its relative location and the countries of the region, create two maps. On an outline map of the world, label the Mediterranean Sea, the Nile River, Egypt, Israel, and the Middle East. Then draw or use an outline map of the Middle East to label all the countries, their capitals, major bodies of water, and the Suez Canal.

Enriching Your Study of History

1. **Individual Project.** Create a map of the Vietnam War. Your map should show the two Vietnams and the surrounding countries, major cities and towns, battle sites, and physical features. Display your map on the bulletin board or use it to illustrate a discussion of the war.
2. **Cooperative Project.** As an oral history project, have members of your group ask family members to describe their reactions to major events of the late 1960s and early 1970s. Topics should include the Vietnam War and the antiwar movement; the assassinations of Martin Luther King, Jr., and Robert Kennedy in 1968; the Chicago riot between antiwar demonstrators and police; the opening of China by President Nixon; and the Watergate Affair and Nixon's resignation. Compile the responses into a group report, either written or on tape. Combine members' reports into a single commentary on the late 1960s and early 1970s.

Modern Times

PLANNING THE CHAPTER

TEXTBOOK	RESOURCES
1. The Ford Presidency	**Unit 10 Worksheets and Tests** Chapter 30 Graphic Organizer, Directed Reading 30:1, Reteaching 30:1 **Art in American History** Transparency 43: East Building of the National Gallery of Art
2. America's Changing Face	**Unit 10 Worksheet and Tests** Directed Reading 30:2, Reteaching 30:2, Geography 30A **Eyewitnesses and Others, Volume 2** Reading 68: Stokely Carmichael Explains "Black Power" (1966), Reading 71: Mario Suarez Describes El Hoyo, the Tucson Barrio (1960s), Reading 76: The Man with the Guitar (1980s), Feature: Corridos: Songs of Exodus, Reading 77: Francisco Jiménez Describes the Circuit (1980s), Reading 75: Lois Banner Evaluates the Gains of the Women's Movement (1980s) **Art in American History** Transparency 41: *El Amigo de Chepo*, Transparency 47: *Tamalada* **The Constitution: Past, Present, and Future** Case 17: *Plyler v. Doe;* Case 16: *Regents of the University of California v. Bakke,* Case 18: *Roberts v. United States Jaycees*
3. Three American Challenges	**Unit 10 Worksheets and Tests** Directed Reading 30:3, Reteaching 30, Geography 30B **American History Map Transparencies** Transparency 9: Urban Growth in the United States, 1775–1980 **Art in American History** Transparency 40: *Walk, Don't Walk,* Transparency 42: *Ansonia,* Transparency 48: *High Wall* **The Constitution: Past, Present, and Future** Case 7: *Everson v. Board of Education* and *Aguilar v. Felton,* Case 19: *Central Hudson Gas & Electric Corporation v. Public Service Commission*
4. The Democrats Take a Turn	**Unit 10 Worksheets and Tests** Directed Reading 30:4, Reteaching 30:4 **Creative Strategies for Teaching American History** Page 357 **The Constitution: Past, Present, and Future** Case 8: *Reynolds v. United States* and *Wisconsin v. Yoder*

5. The Republicans Triumphant	***Unit 10 Worksheets and Tests*** Directed Reading 30:5, Reteaching 30:5 ***Eyewitnesses and Others, Volume 2*** Reading 74: President Reagan Delivers His First Inaugural Address (1981), Reading 78: Presidential Candidates Bush and Dukakis Debate the Issues (1988) ***The Constitution: Past, Present, and Future*** Case 20: *Hazelwood School District v. Kuhlmeier* ***American History Map Transparencies*** Transparency 10: U.S. Exports and Imports
6. Toward a New Century	***Unit 10 Worksheets and Tests*** Directed Reading 30:6, Reteaching 30:6
Chapter Review	***Audio Program*** Chapter 30 ***Unit 10 Worksheets and Tests*** Chapter 30 Tests, Forms A and B (See also *Alternative Assessment Forms*) ***Test Generator***
Unit Review	***Unit 10 Worksheets and Tests*** Unit 10 Tests, Forms A and B (See also *Alternative Assessment Forms*), Unit 10 Synthesis ***Test Generator***
End-of-Book Review	***Unit 10 Worksheets and Tests*** End-of-Book Tests, Forms A and B ***Test Generator***

STRATEGIES FOR STUDENTS WITH SPECIAL NEEDS

Gifted Students.

Have interested students do more research in the school or public library about the 1976 presidential election and prepare a mock presidential debate between Jimmy Carter and Gerald Ford to present to the class.

Students Having Difficulty with the Chapter.

You may wish to have students listen to Chapter 30 in *The Story of America Audio Program*. Then organize the class into five cooperative learning groups. Assign each group one of the sections in Chapter 30, and have the more proficient students in each group help the others skim through the headings and major points in their assigned section. Then have each group prepare a series of drawings showing three or four of the major concepts presented in their section.

BOOKS FOR TEACHERS

Rosalynn Carter, *First Lady From Plains*. Boston: Houghton Mifflin, 1984.

Melvyn Dubofsky and Athan Theoharis, *Imperial Democracy: The United States Since 1945*. 2d ed. Englewood Cliffs, N.J.: Prentice-Hall, 1988.

Diane Ravitch, *The Troubled Crusade: American Education 1945–1980*. New York: Basic Books, 1983.

Donald Regan, *For the Record*. Orlando: Harcourt Brace Jovanovich, 1988.

BOOKS FOR STUDENTS

Dorothy Chaplik, *Up with Hope: A Biography of Jesse Jackson*. Minneapolis: Dillon Press, 1986.

Carol Gorman, *America's Farm Crisis*. New York: Franklin Watts, 1987.

David Olmos, *National Defense Spending: How Much Is Enough?*. New York: Franklin Watts, 1984.

Margaret Flesher Ribaroff, *Mexico and the United States Today: Issues Between Neighbors*. New York: Franklin Watts, 1985.

MULTIMEDIA MATERIALS

American Foreign Policy (software), SSSS. Offers enrichment activities designed to help students understand foreign policy decisions. Last section applicable to this chapter.

The American Indian Speaks (film, 23 min.), EBEC. American Indians seek equal opportunities and the right to their own cultural identity.

Portrait of a Minority: Spanish-Speaking Americans (filmstrip), SSSS. Traces the history of Spanish-speaking Americans and their present-day problems and goals.

RESOURCES
■ You may wish to have students complete the Chapter 30 Graphic Organizer as they work through this chapter.
CHAPTER OBJECTIVES:
Upon completing this chapter, students will be able to:
1. Explain President Ford's attempts to end stagfla-

tion.
2. Outline the reasons that led Congress to pass the Equal Rights Amendment (ERA) and state the arguments of supporters and opponents of ERA.
3. Identify the countries from which large numbers of immigrants have come to the United States since 1965.
4. Explain the ways in which Hispanic Americans,

OVERVIEW

In the 1970s and 1980s, Presidents Ford, Carter, Reagan, and Bush attempted to solve economic problems, contend with the problems caused by increasing immigration from Asian and Spanish-speaking countries, and deal with the continuing struggle of various groups to gain equal rights and a greater share of the wealth of America. At the same time, urban decay, pollution, and questions about the future of energy resources plagued the nation.

FOCUS/MOTIVATION:
MAKING CONNECTIONS
Prior Knowledge.

To introduce this chapter, draw a time line on the chalkboard for the years 1970 through the present. Then have the students practice their skills of skimming and scanning. Have them scan for dates and tell why each date in the book is given. Locate the dates on the time line and write a word or phrase noting each event. *Briefly* discuss the events. When you have finished, you will have provided a visual overview that will help students structure their reading of the chapter. You may wish to close the activity by asking students which events on the time line continue to be in the news.

CHAPTER 30

Modern Times

■ A ll the recent presidents of the United States have had to grapple with extremely complex domestic problems. How will the famous American melting pot accommodate all the newcomers to the United States? How can the crisis in America's cities be resolved if decaying housing and conditions bred by poverty drive working-class and middle-class residents out into the suburbs? How can America cope with pollution—smog, oil spills, acid rain—and preserve its fragile environments? How will Americans cope with growing energy needs? What is the future of nuclear energy? How can the treatment of women in the workplace be made equal to that of men? And, finally, with the pace of world affairs quickened by the collapse of the Soviet Union, the liberation of Eastern Europe, the reunification of Germany, and the end of the Cold War, what will be the future role of the United States in the world community?

Cross/Miami Herald/Black Star

Flags fly in this celebration of citizenship in Miami. Cuban immigrants swear to uphold the Constitution. Even though they are relative newcomers, Cubans have contributed greatly to the nation's culture and prosperity.

African Americans, American Indians, and women worked to win more rights.
5. Analyze major problems Americans had to confront in the 1970s and 1980s.
6. Discuss the reasons for the decline of President Carter's popularity.
7. Discuss Ronald Reagan's accomplishments as president.

8. Analyze the issues in and results of the presidential election of 1988.
9. Explain the momentous changes that occurred in the Soviet Union and Europe between 1988 and 1990.
10. Explain the causes and results of the Persian Gulf War.
11. Analyze the 1992 presidential election, including H. Ross Perot's role in the campaign.

1. THE FORD PRESIDENCY

A Different Style

Before he became president, Gerald Ford was known as an honest, hardworking politician. Nearly everyone in Congress liked him. He got along easily with people. But he had never been noted for vision or originality. When he became president, he announced that he would work closely with Congress. Because both Ford and his vice president, Nelson Rockefeller, had been appointed rather than elected by the people, Ford's style seemed the proper one to adopt.

Dennis Brack Black Star

Economic Slowdown

Ford's biggest problem was the economy. By 1974, business activity had slowed down. Unemployment was increasing and the inflation rate was rising. Democrats wanted to increase government spending in order to speed recovery. Most Republicans, however, feared the economic slump less than they feared inflation. Even when the economy was slowing down, prices had continued to rise. Republicans predicted that more government spending would push prices still higher.

Preview & Review

Use these questions to guide your reading. Answer the questions after completing Section 1.
Understanding Issues, Events, & Ideas. Use the following words to describe important events that occurred during the presidency of Gerald Ford: stagflation, Bicentennial, Operation Sail.
1. Why did President Ford's style seem a proper one for him to adopt when he assumed the presidency?
2. What were some of the bills passed by the Democratic-controlled Congress during Ford's administration? How did President Ford react to them?
3. What helped to end the economic stagflation that occurred in the mid-1970s?
4. In what ways did the tall ships symbolize pride and hope?
Thinking Critically. Imagine that you are present at one of the following events on July 4, 1976: the swearing in ceremony in Miami Beach; the president's speech in either Valley Forge or at Independence Hall; the celebration at the Mall in Washington, D.C.; Operation Sail in New York Harbor; a ceremony in your community or anywhere in the U.S. Write a brief eyewitness account of what you see going on around you. Include a description of your participation, and how you feel as an American on this day.

PREVIEW & REVIEW RESPONSES
Understanding Issues, Events, & Ideas.
Descriptions should demonstrate an understanding of the terms used.
1. Ford announced that he would work closely with Congress and that there would be an openness about his presidency. Since he was appointed rather than elected, this seemed a proper style to adopt.
2. Congress passed bills to help the poor and to create new jobs. He vetoed all of them.
3. Ford reluctantly signed a bill reducing taxes, which helped to end the recession.
4. The tall ships had endured, just as the U.S. had endured, in a time of enormous change. They were old but still strong, sound, and very beautiful. They had a quiet dignity in contrast to the noise around them. They stood for the value of tradition, for past achievements, and for history.

Thinking Critically.
Encourage students to use historical imagination in preparing their accounts of America's Bicentennial celebration.

Cartoon by S.C. Rawls, reprinted by permission of N.E.A., Inc.

Gerald Ford was a popular president. Much was made of his days as a college football player. Hence the cartoon, "Bad Tackle, Jer," showing the override of Ford's veto of spending bills by Congress.

RESOURCES

■ You may wish to have students view Transparency 44: "East Building of the National Gallery of Art, Washington, D.C." and complete the accompanying worksheet in *Art in American History*.

SUGGESTED CAPTION RESPONSES

(Top) The cycles have been shorter and the level of economic growth has decreased; there have been no large public projects or wars to stimulate the economy.

(Bottom) In 1975 Ford signed a bill reducing taxes and putting more money into circulation.

**FOCUS/MOTIVATION:
MAKING CONNECTIONS
Student Experiences.**

Ask students if they have ever noted an increase in the price of products that they buy and to name those products. Point out that the rise in prices of goods and services is called inflation. Ask: What causes inflation? *(An increase in the cost of materials or in production costs that is passed along to the consumer)* Why do people want to avoid inflation? *(A rise in prices means that people cannot afford to buy as many goods and services.)* Tell students to keep this in mind as they study this section.

**GUIDED INSTRUCTION:
COOPERATIVE LEARNING**

Organize the class into several cooperative learning groups. Tell each group that they are congressional leaders during the presidency of Gerald Ford. The nation is suffering from stagflation, and people are losing faith in the government's ability to solve economic problems. Instruct each group to formulate a plan to combat stagflation and restore people's faith in the government. Have spokespersons for each group present their plan to the rest of the class.

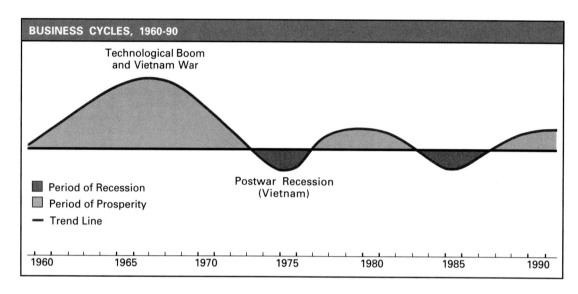

LEARNING FROM GRAPHS.
How would you describe the rise and fall of the business cycle since 1975? What factors might account for such behavior?

Charles Gatewood/Magnum Photos

Hopes for a rollback in the costs of food during the stagflation of the Ford administration were dashed by presidential vetoes. How was the recession finally ended?

In the 1974 congressional elections, voters, still stung by Watergate, expressed their dislike of scandals by voting many Republicans out of office. As a result, the Democrats increased their majorities in both houses of Congress. When the new Congress met, it passed bills designed to help poor people and to create new jobs. Measures providing for construction of public housing, aid to education, and health care were sent to President Ford. He vetoed all of them. Spending more money, he argued, would lead to greater inflation. In most cases the Democrats were not able to get the two-thirds majorities needed to override the president's vetoes.

The recession continued. Economists began to describe the country as passing through a period of **stagflation**—a word coined by combining "*stag*nation," which means not developing or advancing, and "*inflation*." Finally, in the spring of 1975, Ford reluctantly signed a bill reducing taxes, a step he had avoided for fear it would fuel greater inflation. The cut put more money in circulation and helped to end the downturn. By early 1976 the recession was over.

■ The Bicentennial

American spirits were lifted by the recession's end. In 1976 the United States also celebrated its **Bicentennial,** the 200th anniversary of the signing of the Declaration of Independence. The celebration was carried out in grand style. Communities all over the country organized and carried out hundreds of special programs.

In Miami Beach, Florida, 7,000 immigrants were sworn in as citizens of the United States in a mass ceremony at Convention Hall. A man in Oro Grande, California, unfurled a giant American flag measuring 102 by 67 feet (about 30 by 20 meters). There was a balloon

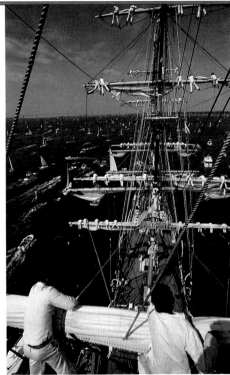

Kenneth Garrett/Woodfin Camp

A burst of fireworks over New York Harbor and the Statue of Liberty salute the nation's Bicentennial in 1976. At right, crew members secure the rigging of a tall ship as it enters the Hudson River. What did the tall ships symbolize?

race to celebrate the occasion in San Antonio, Texas, and a cherry-pie eating contest in Traverse City, Michigan. In other cities and towns there were parades, fireworks, and reenactments of Revolutionary War battles.

President Ford spoke at Valley Forge, where Washington's army had spent the hard winter of 1777–78, and at Independence Hall in Philadelphia, where the Declaration had been signed.

The highlight of the Bicentennial was **Operation Sail,** a majestic procession of gaily decorated ships in New York harbor. No fewer than 16 great, high-masted sailing ships from different nations participated. Millions of people lined the New York waterfront and crowded the windows of skyscrapers to watch these "tall ships" and the hundreds of other craft that accompanied them.

Somehow the tall ships became a symbol of pride and hope. They had come to New York from all over the world, sent by nations with close ties to the United States as well as those with not-so-close ties to help celebrate the anniversary. This was a recognition of the importance of the United States and even more of what America had meant over the centuries to the people of other nations.

And the tall ships had endured, just as the United States had endured, through a time of enormous change. They were old but still strong, sound, and very beautiful. Although dwarfed by the great Verrazano Bridge across the harbor entrance and by the skyscrapers of Manhattan, they seemed to tower over their surroundings. They had a quiet dignity in contrast to the noise and bustle of the tugs, ferries, and other craft that swarmed about them. They stood for the value of tradition, for past achievements, for history. Better than any military parade or other display of modern power, they reflected the strength of the American people. 🖳

Return to the Preview & Review on page 1089.

CHECKING UNDERSTANDING
Ask: What was the major economic problem that plagued the Ford administration? *(stagflation)* What is stagflation? *(A combination of poor economic growth—stagnation—and rising prices—inflation)*

RETEACHING STRATEGY
Students with Special Needs.
Pair students who are having difficulty with students who are performing well. Have each pair devise a definition for stagflation. *(a period of economic stagnation coupled with inflation)* Groups may wish to design a chart, graph, or picture to illustrate their definitions.

INDEPENDENT PRACTICE
Have students complete the Preview & Review activity at the beginning of the section.

CLOSURE
Point out that an economic slowdown plagued the Ford administration. Nevertheless, the nation celebrated the Bicentennial with festivities throughout the nation.

HOMEWORK
Have students imagine that they are George Washington and that they have been transported to the United States to witness the Bicentennial celebrations. Ask them to write a short diary entry detailing Washington's impressions of the nation in 1976.

The Ford Presidency   1091

SECTION 2

PREVIEW & REVIEW RESPONSES

Understanding Issues, Events, & Ideas.
Descriptions should demonstrate an understanding of the terms used.

1. Most of the immigrants who came to this country from Korea and Vietnam did so to escape the political situation in their countries.
2. Cesar Chavez formed the NFWA to improve wages and the poor conditions in migrant camps.
3. Most were very poor, came from rural backgrounds, could not speak English, and had few skills needed to get good-paying jobs.
4. They continued to emphasize peaceful means of achieving civil rights and warned that violence only leads to more violence. They encouraged blacks to work within the political and economic systems.
5. Reservation life deteriorated and Indians were forced to rely on welfare. This led to high rates of alcoholism and suicide, and many dropped out of school.
6. Their status improved financially as thousands of women entered the work force, many of them buying or starting their own businesses.

Thinking Critically.
Encourage students to research the great *huelga* and to use facts as well as historical imagination to prepare their editorials.

1092

Cambodian refugees leave Phnom Pehn in their 1975 exodus after the city fell to the Khmer Rouge. Some of these refugees eventually reached the United States, setting out on boats that were not seaworthy. Report on the "boat people" who reached America.

Preview & Review

Use these questions to guide your reading. Answer the questions after completing Section 2.

Understanding Issues, Events, & Ideas. Use the following words to describe immigration and social changes in American society from the 1960s to the 1990s: National Farm Workers Association, barrios, Black Power, Equal Rights Amendment.

1. For what reasons did immigrants come from Korea and Vietnam after 1965?
2. By whom and why was the NFWA formed?
3. How were the Puerto Rican immigrants similar to the European immigrants before World War I?
4. How did older African American leaders respond to the race riots of the 1960s?
5. What were some of the problems faced by Indians on reservations in the 1980s?
6. How did the status of women improve in the 1970s and '80s?

Thinking Critically. Imagine that you are a member of the United Farm Workers during the great *huelga* against the California grape growers. Write a newspaper editorial explaining why you are striking, what you hope to achieve by the strike, and why you support Cesar Chavez as your leader.

2. AMERICA'S CHANGING FACE

Immigration and Social Change

■The composition of the population of America at the time of the Bicentennial was changing rapidly because of the passage of the Immigration Act of 1965. Europeans no longer accounted for the majority of new immigrants. In their place were people from Mexico, the Caribbean, Central and South America, and Asia. Under the old regulations, the entire continent of Asia was allowed only 20,000 immigrants to America in a 40-year period. In the single year 1973, almost 120,000 Asians entered this country.

The tensions left over from the Korean War and the stern policies of the South Korean government led thousands of South Koreans to migrate to the United States. Most of them settled in California and Hawaii, but considerable numbers came to New York and other eastern cities. Still larger numbers of Filipinos moved to the United States. When the islands became independent after World War II, immigration slowed to a trickle. After the 1965 immigration act, it soared again. Many Filipino immigrants were skilled workers and professional people dissatisfied with prospects in their homeland.

After the Vietnam War, large numbers of South Vietnamese who had worked with the Americans during the war came to the United States to escape persecution by the victorious communists. The United States government helped these refugees settle in this country.

The growth of the Asian American population has been dramatic. Although Asian Americans currently make up only about 3 percent of the population, experts expect their numbers to approach 10 million by the year 2000, about ten times as many as in 1970. Why are people attracted to the United States? Studs Turkel, who has interviewed hundreds of recent immigrants, observed:

RESOURCES
- You may wish to have students complete Reading 76: "The Man with the Guitar (1980s)" in Volume II of *Eyewitnesses and Others.*
- You may wish to have students view Transparency 41: "*El Amigo de Chepo*" and complete the accompanying worksheet in *Art in American History.*

★ You may wish to have students view Transparency 47: "*Tamalada*" and complete the accompanying worksheet in *Art in American History.*

❝ New immigrants are trying all over again to integrate themselves into the system. They have the same hunger. . . .

The Vietnamese boat people [who fled Vietnam after the communist takeover in 1975] express it as well as anyone. They don't know if they're gonna land, if the boat's gonna sink. They don't know what's gonna happen to 'em, but they've a hunch they might make it to the U.S. as the 'freedom place.'

There is the plain hard fact of hunger. In order to eat, a person will endure tremendous hardship.[1] ❞

Mexican Americans Increase Their Numbers

During the 1980s, the Hispanic population of the United States grew by 40 percent, more than four times as fast as the rest of the population. Census experts estimate that by the year 2025, Hispanic Americans may constitute as much as 20 percent of the nation's population.

By far the largest group among the new immigrants has come from Mexico. When the United States entered World War II, the demand for labor in the Southwest soared. The United States and Mexico signed an agreement allowing Mexicans to work temporarily in this country. These workers were called *braceros*, a name that comes from the Spanish word for "arm." Between 1942 and 1964, almost 5 million *braceros* came to the United States under the program. They came north to harvest crops, and most of them returned to Mexico when the harvest season ended. But each year, many stayed rather than return to Mexico.

Many of the Mexicans who settled found the United States a true land of opportunity. Some obtained farms of their own. Others found good jobs in manufacturing. Their success caused thousands of other Mexicans to want to come to the United States. After the 1965 immigration law put a limit on the number of newcomers from the Western Hemisphere, many Mexicans entered the United States illegally.

Throughout the postwar years, Mexican-born workers harvested most of the crops grown in the Southwest. Cesar Chavez emerged as their leader. Chavez had grown up in the migrant camps of California. He founded the **National Farm Workers Association** (NFWA), a labor union.

The NFWA worked hard to improve wages and the poor conditions in migrant camps. Most workers received less than half the minimum wage, which at the time (1965) was $1 per hour. Their camps were usually no more than rough cabins, often without running water. To attract attention to these problems, Chavez called for a great *huelga*, or strike, against the California grape growers.

The strikers won a great deal of public sympathy. Chavez's

[1]From *American Dreams: Lost and Found* by Studs Terkel

Nina Barnett

Proudly displaying his drawing of the flag of his country, this Chinese American boy celebrates democracy with his parents. Below is Cesar Chavez, whose fasts for the National Farm Workers drew worldwide attention.

Paul Fusco/Magnum Photos

FOCUS/MOTIVATION: MAKING CONNECTIONS Prior Knowledge.
Discuss with students U.S. immigration policies since World War I. How did the policy differ after World War I from policy in the 1800s? *(The United States limited the number of immigrants according to nation of origin.)* Under postwar policy, what peoples used to form the greatest number of immigrants? *(Europeans)* What peoples do so now? *(Asians, Hispanics)* What caused this change? *(The Immigration Act of 1965)* What problems do immigrants encounter? *(They must adapt to a new and different culture.)* Point out that all immigrants, from the first settlers to the most recent, have faced these problems. Ask students why the United States continues to be a beacon of hope for the world.

GUIDED INSTRUCTION: COOPERATIVE LEARNING
Organize the class into cooperative learning groups. Assign each group one of these subjects: African Americans, women, Asian Americans, Hispanic Americans, or Native Americans. If you have students in the class from other ethnic or cultural groups, you may wish to assign them to groups representing their ethnic or racial background. Each group is to prepare a collage showing its subjects participating in American society. You may wish to hang these collages around the classroom.

PRIMARY SOURCE
Description of change: excerpted and bracketed.
Rationale: excerpted to focus on attitudes toward Asian Americans; bracketed words added to clarify meaning.

RESOURCES

■ You may wish to have students complete Case 17: *"Plyer v. Doe"* in THE CONSTITUTION: *Past, Present, and Future.*

▶ You may wish to have students complete the Feature: "Corridos: Songs of Exodus" in Volume II of *Eyewitnesses and Others.*

★ You may wish to have students complete Reading 77: "Francisco Jiménez Describes the Circuit (1980s)" in Volume II of *Eyewitnesses and Others.*

GUIDED INSTRUCTION: MULTICULTURAL PERSPECTIVES

Tell students that while Cesar Chavez worked with white society at large—liberals, union and political leaders—other Chicanos supported a Hispanic version of Black Power: *La Raza.* They rejected traditional white values and wanted their own political organizations, the teaching of Spanish in public schools, and Chicano studies in colleges. Chicanos would maintain their cultural identity within the majority, mainstream culture. This is called **pluralism.** Some Native Americans and African Americans also favored pluralism. Organize a class discussion on how pluralism might affect American society. Ask: Would it benefit the United States or further polarize the various groups within the country? How would it work for and against racial, ethnic, and disadvantaged groups?

PRIMARY SOURCE

Description of change: excerpted.

Rationale: excerpted to focus on Gonzales' attempt to make all Chicanos aware of their common history and culture.

1094

The plentitude of food on your family's kitchen table comes in part from these Mexican-born harvesters called **braceros.** *When this photo was taken, many Mexicans had to cross the border illegally to find work until a public amnesty program was approved by Congress.*

Michael Rougier/Life Picture Services

personal dedication was almost as important in winning support as was the public's realization of the plight of the poorly paid workers. Eventually the grape growers recognized the union and settled the strike. Chavez inspired migrant workers with a sense of their own worth. "We . . . stood tall outside the vineyards where we had stooped for years," the grape pickers stated proudly.

Yo Soy Joaquín	I am Joaquín
. . . Y en todos los terrenos fértiles	And in all the fertile farmlands,
los llanos átidos,	the barren plains,
los pueblos moñtaneros	the mountain villages,
cuidades ahumadas	smoke-smeared cities
empezamos a AVANZAR.	we start to MOVE.
La Raza!	La Raza!
Mejicano!	Mejicano!
Español!	Espanol!
Latino!	Latino!
Hispano!	Hispano!
Chicano!	Chicano!
o lo que me llame yo,	or whatever I call myself,
yo parezco lo mismo,	I look the same
yo siento lo mismo	I feel the same
yo lloro	I cry
y	and
canto lo mismo	sing the same
Yo soy el bulto de mi gente y	I am the masses of my people and
yo renuncio ser absorbida.	I refuse to be absorbed.
Yo soy Joaquín	I am Joaquín
Las desigualdades son grandes	The odds are great
pero mi espíritu es firme	but my spirit is strong,
mi fé impenetrable	my faith unbreakable
mi sangre pura.	my blood is pure.
Soy príncipe Azteca y Cristo cristiano	I am Aztec Prince and Christian Christ
YO PERDURARE!	I SHALL ENDURE!
YO PERDURARE!	I WILL ENDURE![1]

Other Hispanic Newcomers

Another major group of Hispanic immigrants came from Puerto Rico. Because Puerto Rico was a commonwealth of the United States, Puerto Ricans were already American citizens. Immigration laws did not apply to them. Hundreds of thousands of Puerto Ricans settled in New York City, which soon had a larger Puerto Rican population than San Juan, the capital of Puerto Rico.

In many ways the Puerto Ricans were like the European immigrants of the years before World War I. Most of them were poor farm laborers unaccustomed to city life. Few could speak English. In New York they were crowded into **barrios,** or Hispanic neighborhoods, in neglected pockets of the city.

Yet many Puerto Ricans did very well for themselves. Herman

[1]From "I am Joaquín" by Corky Gonzales

SUGGESTED CAPTION RESPONSE
Answers will vary, but students should provide credible reasons for their responses.

SUGGESTED CAPTION RESPONSE
Puerto Rican Americans and Mexican Americans experience the highest rates of poverty among Hispanics. Cubans and Central and South Americans more closely match the characteristics of non-Hispanic Americans.

Badillo came to New York from Puerto Rico in the early 1940s, when he was eleven. He worked washing dishes and setting up pins in a bowling alley. Later he earned a college degree and a law degree. In 1970 he was elected to Congress.

Since 1960, more than 2 million people from other Latin American nations have immigrated to the United States. After the Cuban revolutionary leader Fidel Castro made an alliance with the Soviet Union, many Cubans were admitted to the United States under laws that allowed refugees from communist countries to come. About half of them settled in southern Florida. For the next 20 years, Castro made it almost impossible for Cubans to leave their country. In 1980, however, he changed his mind. When he did, more than 100,000 Cubans flocked to the United States. Even more Hispanic people have immigrated from Central and South America.

As the graph on this page shows, Hispanic Americans have not shared equally in America's wealth. The average Hispanic American has fewer years of schooling, and the average Hispanic family has a lower-than-average income. Yet great variations exist within the Hispanic American population. Cuban Americans have reached levels close to non-Hispanic Americans in average years of schooling and average family income. Puerto Rican Americans, on the other hand, have a poverty rate that is nearly four times that of non-Hispanics.

Jason Laure/Photo Researchers

This smiling girl is a marcher in New York City's Puerto Rican Day Parade. She is holding the flag of Puerto Rico. Do you think Puerto Rico should become the 51st state? Explain.

Source: *Current Population Reports, Series p-20, No. 416, 1987*

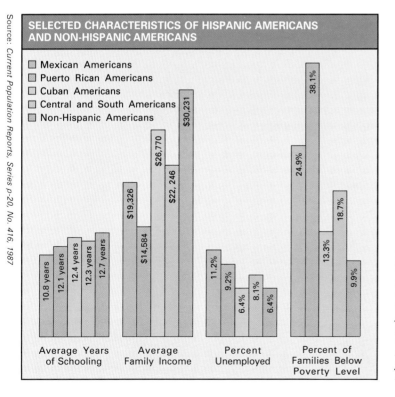

SELECTED CHARACTERISTICS OF HISPANIC AMERICANS AND NON-HISPANIC AMERICANS

- ☐ Mexican Americans
- ☐ Puerto Rican Americans
- ☐ Cuban Americans
- ☐ Central and South Americans
- ☐ Non-Hispanic Americans

Average Years of Schooling: 10.8 years, 12.1 years, 12.4 years, 12.3 years, 12.7 years

Average Family Income: $19,326, $14,584, $26,770, $22,246, $30,231

Percent Unemployed: 11.2%, 9.2%, 6.4%, 8.1%, 6.4%

Percent of Families Below Poverty Level: 24.9%, 38.1%, 13.3%, 18.7%, 9.9%

GUIDED INSTRUCTION: MULTICULTURAL PERSPECTIVES
If you have any students in your class who are recent immigrants from Asia or Latin America, and if you think that it would be appropriate, you may wish to have them tell the class why their families left their homeland and what their experiences as immigrants have been.

GUIDED INSTRUCTION: COOPERATIVE LEARNING
Organize students into cooperative learning groups. Have each group write a short biography of an imaginary immigrant who arrived in the United States in the 1980s from either Southeast Asia or Latin America. Students should discuss why their character left his or her homeland, the difficulties their character faces, and the positive experiences that he or she might have. Encourage students to illustrate their biographies.

LEARNING FROM GRAPHS.
The label Hispanic American *encompasses people from many different backgrounds. This graph shows certain characteristics of the largest groups of Hispanic Americans. Compare the data on the graph. Then state a comparison of the four Hispanic American groups. How do these groups compare to non-Hispanic Americans?*

SUGGESTED CAPTION RESPONSE
Between 1959 and 1980 the percentage of African Americans living below the poverty line steadily decreased. It increased between 1980 and 1990. The trends for white Americans were the same except that between 1985 and 1990 the number of white Americans living below the poverty line decreased.

RESOURCES
■ You may wish to have students complete Reading 68: "Stokely Carmichael Explains 'Black Power' (1966)" in Volume II of *Eyewitnesses and Others*.

EXTENSION:
COMMUNITY INVOLVEMENT
Invite a speaker from the NAACP, Urban League, or another organization that works to advance the interests of African Americans to speak to the class. Have them discuss the programs their organization sponsors to improve the life chances of African Americans.

PRIMARY SOURCE
Description of change: excerpted.
Rationale: excerpted to focus on Naipaul's assessment of the South today.

PRIMARY SOURCE
Description of change: excerpted.
Rationale: excerpted to focus on Malcolm X's beliefs on what direction the civil rights movement should take.

Point of View

V. S. Naipaul, who grew up in Trinidad, observed this about the American South today.

66"Nearly sixteen millions of hands will aid you in pulling the load upward, or they will pull against you the load downward. We shall constitute one-third and more of the ignorance and crime of the South, or one-third of its intelligence and progress; we shall contribute one-third to business and industrial prosperity of the South; or we shall prove a veritable body of death, stagnating, depressing . . . the body politic?

The words read like special pleading. They come from the speech Booker T. Washington made in Atlanta in 1895, when he was only thirty-nine: a famous speech that . . . calmed white people down and offered hope to black people at a time of near hopelessness. . . . Those words now read like prophecy.99
From *A Turn in the South,* 1989

LEARNING FROM GRAPHS. *This graph shows the number of white Americans and African Americans below the poverty level. What trend do you note for African Americans? Is the trend the same for white Americans? Explain any differences you find.*

African Americans Continue the Struggle

Increased awareness of past injustices made African Americans even more determined to gain respect and equal treatment. In the 1960s, Martin Luther King, Jr.'s policy of persuasion and nonviolent direct action no longer satisfied some black activists. Leaders such as Stokely Carmichael advocated what they called **Black Power**, a more radical approach to the struggle for equal rights that advocated the use of force when necessary. King's movement had taken the first steps, but it seemed obvious to Carmichael and others that white people "cannot understand the black experience."

Other blacks, such as Malcolm X, went even further. Some joined the Black Muslims, who believed in separating themselves entirely from white society. Malcolm X, broke with the Black Muslims in 1964 and called for "a working unity among all peoples, black as well as white." But before he could embark on this new direction, he was murdered in 1965, apparently as a result of his break with the Black Muslims. Malcolm X and Carmichael both spoke of action for African Americans. In a speech Malcolm X put it this way:

66 Whether you like it, or I like it, or they like it, or not, you will see that there is a generation of black people becoming mature to the point where they feel that they have no more business in being asked to take a peaceful approach than anybody else takes, unless everybody's going to take a peaceful approach. . . .
You get freedom by letting your enemy know that you'll do anything to get your freedom. . . . When you stay radical long enough . . . you'll get your freedom.[1]99

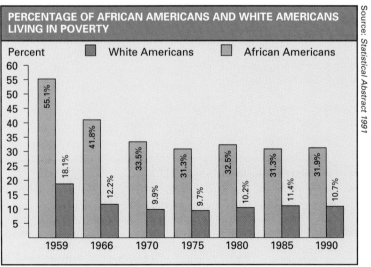

PERCENTAGE OF AFRICAN AMERICANS AND WHITE AMERICANS LIVING IN POVERTY

Source: *Statistical Abstract 1991*

Percent   ■ White Americans   ■ African Americans

Year	White Americans	African Americans
1959	55.1%	18.1%
1966	41.8%	12.2%
1970	33.5%	9.9%
1975	31.3%	9.7%
1980	32.5%	10.2%
1985	31.3%	11.4%
1990	31.9%	10.7%

[1]From *Malcolm X Speaks*, edited by George Breitman

RESOURCES

■ You may wish to have students complete Case 16: "Regents of the University of California v. Bakke" in THE CONSTITUTION: Past, Present, and Future.

SUGGESTED CAPTION RESPONSE

$29,454; $21,848; Answers will vary, but students might suggest that the differences are a result of many years of discrimination.

SUGGESTED CAPTION RESPONSE

That schools should have more ethnic representation and influence

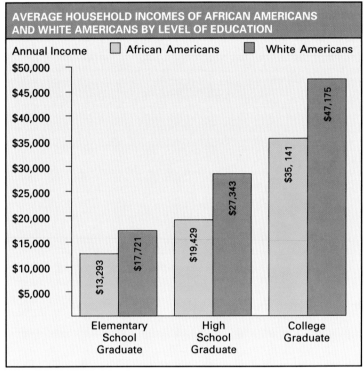

AVERAGE HOUSEHOLD INCOMES OF AFRICAN AMERICANS AND WHITE AMERICANS BY LEVEL OF EDUCATION

Annual Income — African Americans — White Americans

Elementary School Graduate: $13,293; $17,721
High School Graduate: $19,429; $27,343
College Graduate: $35,141; $47,175

Source: Bureau of the Census

LEARNING FROM GRAPHS. *Years of schooling completed has a dramatic effect on income, as this graph shows. How much more on average does a white college graduate make than a white American who only completed elementary school? What is the difference for African Americans in the same categories? Why do you think this is true?*

The frustration of African Americans was demonstrated by marchers and picketers in the 1960s. Study the sign carried by the young mother below. What are her complaints?

Eli Reed/Magnum Photos

This call to action appealed to many young African Americans. They met white aggression and violence with their own. Between 1965 and 1967, riots scorched cities such as Los Angeles, Chicago, Tampa, Detroit, and Newark. Many people, including African Americans, thought the riots and violence had gone too far. Older leaders continued to emphasize peaceful means. They warned that violence only leads to more violence. They were sure that black pride and working within the political and economic systems would pay off in the long run.

To many American blacks, their African heritage was a source of pride. They preferred to be known as African Americans. An increasing number of schools and colleges offered courses in African history and culture. Voter-participation drives resulted in an upswing in the number of African American elected officials. By the early 1990s there were approximately 450 blacks elected to state and national legislatures, up from a mere 182 in 1970.

Problems for Native Americans

Like African Americans, native Americans continued to search for ways to revive their culture. But the violence of the confrontation at Wounded Knee in 1973 drained some of the public's sympathy for the American Indian movement.

America's Changing Face   1097

RESOURCES
■ You may wish to have students complete Reading 75: "Lois Banner Evaluates the Gains of the Women's Movement (1980s)" in Volume II of *Eyewitnesses and Others*.

ART IN HISTORY
Ask interested students to make collages showing women working at traditionally male occupations (and vice versa). Make a classroom display of the completed collages.

GUIDED INSTRUCTION: COOPERATIVE LEARNING
Organize the class into cooperative learning groups to plan a debate on the ERA. Have the groups research the history of the ERA and the arguments used both for and against it. After the groups have completed their research, have them hold a debate on the necessity for an equal rights amendment.

EXTENSION: COMMUNITY INVOLVEMENT
If possible, have interested students interview a woman who remembers the struggle to adopt the Nineteenth Amendment giving women the right to vote, or a spokesperson of the local chapter of NOW.

PRIMARY SOURCE
Description of change: excerpted.
Rationale: excerpted to focus on a young American Indian's views on leaving the reservation.

1098

Ernest Haas/Magnum Photos

This young Crow in beaded tribal headdress helps us recall the past. Yet what does the speaker quoted on this page say about the past of native Americans?

In the late 1970s, courts began to award millions of dollars in damages to tribes who sued the government over broken treaties. These rulings provided some small sense of justice. But by the 1980s, Indians on reservations faced several disastrous problems. Life on many reservations had deteriorated. Unable to recapture past ways of life, many Indians were forced to rely on government welfare and help from religious and charitable groups. The demoralizing effects of this situation led to alcoholism and suicide at far higher rates than the national average, especially for Indian teenagers. Many Indians dropped out of school and left their reservations. One Hopi girl described the feelings of many young native Americans:

66 We would like to leave the reservation. We wouldn't mind seeing how Indians live in cities. A lot of Hopis say you stop being a Hopi when you go into a city and live in big buildings and forget about our land, and our hills, and the sky over us. Maybe. I don't know. The Indian can't just sit and think of his past. My mother says it's a pity; our people were happy here for so long. Now, a lot of us want to leave.[1] 99

For Indians who were not on reservations, life was somewhat better. Many became successful professionals and leaders in their communities. But most still felt the loss of their culture. In schools and in the job market, they continued to face discrimination.

Women Fight for Equality

"I am woman, hear me roar," went a popular song of the 1970s. The roar continues to grow louder. Census reports predict that by the year 2000, women will outnumber men in the United States by 6 million. Women continue to fight to maintain the gains they have made in the political arena, in business, and on the domestic front ■ since World War II.

After much debate, Congress passed an Equal Rights Amendment (ERA) to the Constitution in 1972 and sent it on to the states for ratification. The ERA provided that "equality of rights under the law shall not be denied or abridged by the United States or any state on account of sex." The proposed amendment was controversial. Opponents believed it was unnecessary because, they said, women were protected against discrimination by laws that already existed. They also claimed that the ERA would eliminate existing laws that provided special benefits to female workers. Supporters of the ERA said that it would simply make equality for women legal. The ERA did not receive the approval from the needed three-fourths of the state legislatures and consequently failed to become part of the Constitution.

[1]From *Eskimos, Chicanos, Indians: Volume IV of Children in Crisis* by Robert Coles

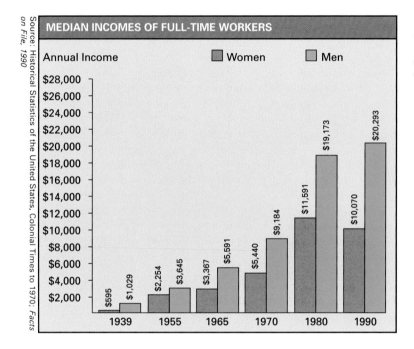

Source: Historical Statistics of the United States, Colonial Times to 1970; Facts on File, 1990

MEDIAN INCOMES OF FULL-TIME WORKERS

Annual Income — Women — Men

LEARNING FROM GRAPHS.
Although women have begun to claim more higher-paying jobs than ever before, a gap between the average salary for women and men still exists. What was that gap in 1990? How would you explain the difference?

More and more people became concerned about the inequality ■ of women in American society. As a result, administrations from the 1970s onward have increasingly recognized the contributions of women and appointed many to top positions in the federal government. Yet by 1991, women held only two seats in the Senate and 27 in the House of Representatives. Democrat Geraldine Ferraro's campaign for the vice presidency in 1984, though unsuccessful, was a first: a woman as a candidate on a major party ticket.

From the 1970s through the early 1990s, women entered the American workforce by the millions. "Equal pay for equal work" was a feminist slogan of the 1970s. Today, that ideal is still far from realized, although women who work outside the home make up more than 45 percent of the total workforce. In 1989, statistics showed that on the average, an American woman earned only about 68 percent of a man's income. This figure had risen only 6 percentage points since 1955. This "disparity gap" also includes representation in various fields of work. Minority women, for example, disproportionately hold poor-paying part-time jobs. These inequalities indicate that the trend continues: low status and low pay go hand in hand with female-dominated occupations.

In recent decades, social critics have also noted the "glass ceiling" felt by many women who could advance only to a certain level in business or government. The top positions seemed reserved exclusively for men. Perhaps partly as a reaction to this situation, many women bought or started their own businesses in the 1970s and

GUIDED INSTRUCTION
Tell students that two factors can be used to predict which women will live their adult lives in poverty. Ask students if they can figure out what they are. *(Responses will vary; most will probably mention being born into a poor family.)* Tell students that women who complete high school and who do not have an illegitimate child before they graduate generally avoid poverty. This is true for 97% of European American women and 87% of African American women. Ask students why they think this is. *(Students should mention that the more education a person has, the more qualified for a well-paying job he or she is likely to be and that having children before graduating increases the probability that the mother will never finish. Families headed by women are disadvantaged because women earn less than men and affordable child care is usually unavailable.)*

CHECKING UNDERSTANDING
To reinforce the geographic theme of *place*, distribute to the class outline maps of the world. Then have students locate South Korea, the Philippines, Vietnam, Mexico, Cuba, Central and South America, and Puerto Rico on the maps. Point out that most of the immigrants to the United States since 1965 have come from these locations.

RETEACHING STRATEGY
Students with Special Needs.
Pair students who are having difficulty with students who are performing well. Have the more proficient students read the following quotations to the others who are to identify the speaker's native land.

1. "I came to America to escape the communist regime of Fidel Castro." *(Cuba)*
2. "Since my country is a commonwealth of the U.S., immigration quotas do not apply." *(Puerto Rico)*
3. "When my country won its independence from the U. S. after World War II, immigration slowed." *(the Philippines)*
4. "Cesar Chavez represented many workers who had come from my country to help on the farms of the Southwest." *(Mexico)*
5. "After my country was conquered by communists from the north, I came to the U.S." *(Vietnam)*

INDEPENDENT PRACTICE
Have students complete the Preview & Review activity at the beginning of the section.

CLOSURE
Point out that since 1965, people from Asia and the Americas have made up a majority of newcomers to the U. S. At the same time, ethnic and racial groups and women have worked to win more rights.

HOMEWORK
Have students imagine that they are recent immigrants. Have them write a letter to friends in their country of origin describing their first days in an American school. Encourage students to include both positive and negative impressions.

In 1991, Clarence Thomas (top right) replaced Justice Thurgood Marshall after controversial confirmation hearings. The other justices of the Supreme Court are, left to right, (back row): David Souter, Antonin Scalia, Anthony Kennedy; (front row) John Paul Stevens, Byron White, Chief Justice William Rehnquist, Harry Blackmun, and Sandra Day O'Connor, the first female justice.

Return to the Preview & Review on page 1091.

1980s—5.4 million by 1987. In fact, the Small Business Administration has predicted that by the year 2000, half the businesses in the United States will be owned by women.

With more mothers working, child-care issues moved into the national spotlight. Providing more resources, public and private, for early childhood programs, including child care, is regarded by supporters of women's rights as one of the major goals for the 1990s. Census data from the mid 1980s showed that a large number of working mothers used some kind of day care. But by 1987, only 18 states had created new child-care programs and increased the number of children served since 1981. Demographics indicate that the number of children will increase dramatically because the post-World War II baby boomers are having more children than the generation preceding them. A sharp increase in the employment of mothers will likely produce a demand for more high-quality, affordable child care.

In 1991, a relatively new women's issue received national attention: sexual harassment in the workplace. The subject arose during the confirmation hearings by the Senate Judiciary Committee of Clarence Thomas, an African American judge nominated to the Supreme Court by President George Bush. Professor Anita Hill of the University of Oklahoma charged Thomas with having sexually harassed her earlier when she had worked for him. When Thomas was cleared of all allegations and given a seat on the country's highest court, many women were angered. Sexual harassment became an important issue for women. 🖭

RESOURCES
■ You may wish to have students view Transparency 9: "Urban Growth in the United States, 1775–1980" and complete the accompanying worksheet in *American History Map Transparencies.*
◀ You may wish to have students view Transparency 40: *"Walk, Don't Walk"* and complete the accompanying worksheet in *Art in American History.*

3. THREE AMERICAN CHALLENGES

Crisis in America's Cities

■ By the 1970s, about three-quarters of the American people were living in cities and their surrounding suburbs. As these metropolitan areas expanded, they began to meet one another to form super metropolitan areas. One such **megalopolis** (Greek for "great city") stretched from Portland, Maine, through Boston, New York City, Philadelphia, Baltimore, and Washington, D.C., to Richmond, Virginia. It became known as BosWash. Another, ChiPitt, reaches from Chicago to Pittsburgh. A third, SanSan, extended from San Francisco
◀ to San Diego along the California coast. The central areas, or **inner cities**, of these regions wasted away as well-to-do and middle-class residents moved to the suburbs. Poor city dwellers, many of them African Americans, Puerto Ricans, and Mexican Americans, remained behind.

A vicious cycle of decay resulted from this population shift. When the people with money to spend began to leave an area, retail stores and other businesses followed. This meant that there were fewer jobs for inner-city residents. It meant also that city tax collections fell off.

"East Side, West Side, All Around the Town." Songs sung in what seemed more innocent times would today mask the urban decay and blight that has spread through whole areas of America's cities.

Michael Weisbrot/Black Star

SECTION 3

PREVIEW & REVIEW RESPONSES
Understanding Issues, Events, & Ideas.
Explanations should demonstrate an understanding of the terms used.
1. Cities and their surrounding suburbs expand to such an extent that they begin to meet other metropolitan areas and form supercities.
2. When residents with money to spend began to leave, stores and other businesses followed. There were then fewer jobs for inner-city residents, and tax revenues decreased.
3. The number of homeless people grew when many mental patients were deinstitutionalized without having anywhere else to go.
4. By the late 1960s pollution was at a critical level. It became necessary for the government to monitor pollution and seek ways to eliminate it; therefore, the EPA was established.
5. A serious accident at a nuclear power plant at Three Mile Island, Pennsylvania, in 1979 and an even more serious one at Chernobyl in the Soviet Union in 1986 made many people question the safety of nuclear power plants and led to a cut-back in construction.
Thinking Critically.
1. Student plans should be well thoughtout and practical. 2. Encourage students to research possible solutions to pollution problems and to use facts in their letters.

**FOCUS/MOTIVATION:
MAKING CONNECTIONS
Student Experiences.**
Ask students whether they have seen television news programs or read newspaper articles about problems in American cities today. Point out that almost every day there are programs and articles about these problems. Then organize the class into two groups. Have the first group determine the greatest problems facing large cities in America today. *(loss of businesses, people moving to suburbs, shrinking tax revenues and a resulting decline in services, high crime, decay, overcrowding, racial problems, poverty, unemployment)* Have the second group discuss the positive side of cities today. *(cultural and ethnic diversity, centers of commerce, culture, and government)* Tell students that suburbs—as they get older—develop some of the same problems as the older cities. Discuss how cities and suburbs are solving some of these problems. Ask: What is being done in your community? (You may wish to have students contact the mayor's office, the city planner, or county administrator for information for this discussion.) What kinds of similar problems do rural areas face? *(poverty, inadequate schools, and lack of social services)*

PRIMARY SOURCE
Description of change: excerpted.
Rationale: excerpted to focus on Jackson's attitudes toward the environment.

Point of View

The Reverend Jesse Jackson presented this view of environmental concern.

"The question is not, 'will we start treating our environment better?' The question is, 'will we start treating ourselves better by not contaminating the environment that we live in and are part of?'

This is, at its very heart, a spiritual question. Ultimately we must decide how much respect and love we have for other human beings....

The environment is, in the final analysis, a political question. That means we must organize across and against lines of race, class, gender, nation and geography in order to save the earth.... If we can take down the Berlin Wall, we can take down the wall that prevents us from seeing what must be done to leave our children a livable world."
Greenpeace, 1990

Public services then declined. If the city governments raised tax rates to make up for the loss, more middle-income citizens moved away. Higher property taxes also made it difficult for landlords to make a profit. In their efforts to do so, they skimped on maintaining their buildings. Heating systems broke down in winter. Roofs leaked. Corridors were dark and littered with refuse. Buildings soon deteriorated beyond repair, and what had been decent neighborhoods became slums. As the population of the inner cities fell, whole neighborhoods were abandoned.

This decline made life harder for the people who had to remain in the inner cities. Many of these were discriminated against because of their race or color. Poverty and dreadful living conditions commonly resulted in the breakup of inner-city families. Bitterly discouraged, some people sought escape in alcohol and various illegal drugs. Those who became drug addicts were even more desperate. Because they were without work, many addicts resorted to robbery and mugging to get money to support their habits.

■ Because the city governments had less money, the schools began to suffer too. Classes were overcrowded. Teachers were underpaid. Supplies were inadequate. Equipment broke down. Faced with such conditions, many students lost interest in school. They learned few skills and had little hope of getting decent jobs when they completed their schooling. They were called "dropouts" because they left school (dropped out) before receiving their diplomas.

Unable to find jobs because they were poorly trained or not trained at all, many of these dropouts hung idly around, causing trouble. Hopeless and resentful, some of them turned to crime. For example, many of the children of drug addicts were badly neglected or even abused. Many young people were left to roam the streets unsupervised. Others turned to drug dealing, where they could make considerable sums of money—at the risk of going to prison or losing their lives. Some also turned to violent crime.

One of the worst examples of this **urban decay** was the section of New York City called the South Bronx. Many of the buildings in the South Bronx became fire-blackened, empty shells. Such places were sometimes the scene of violence and rioting. In Los Angeles in 1991, Rodney King, a black motorist, was arrested for speeding after a hectic chase by several white policemen. When they caught up with King, the angry officers beat him mercilessly. Unknown to the policemen, a bystander recorded the scene with a video camera. The pictures of the brutal beating were soon played repeatedly on television and printed in newspapers all over the country. The policemen were charged with assault, but, to the surprise of many, an all-white jury found them not guilty.

The jury's decision caused a terrible outburst of violence in inner-city Los Angeles. Rioters put buildings to the torch, looted shops, and beat innocent passersby. The violence was inexcusable but understandable. It reminded the white majority that despite desegregation and equal rights legislation, much remained to be done before true equality and justice for all could be achieved.

Another example of urban decay in the 1980s was the astonishing increase in the number of homeless people. These people wound up living on the streets and in parks with only shopping bags to hold their meager belongings. Visitors to America were shocked. The problem was compounded when many nonviolent mental patients were "deinstitutionalized," that is, released from mental hospitals on the theory that they would be better off "free" and supplied with shelter and medication locally. But no one seemed able to devise a system that would allow the homeless to retain their dignity and human rights while receiving the assistance that many of them needed.

Riots in Los Angeles' predominately African American neighborhoods followed the outcome of the Rodney King case. Millions of dollars worth of property went up in smoke amid angry violence, destruction, and looting.

EXTENSION:
COMMUNITY INVOLVEMENT
Have students contact local officials or social service agencies to find information on what services are offered to help homeless people in the community. Encourage students to ask whether the programs use volunteers and to volunteer their time if they so desire. Have students invite one of the officials or social service representatives to address the class and explain what problems the homeless encounter and create, what services are offered to homeless people.

RESOURCES
■ You may wish to have students view Transparency 48: *"High Wall"* and complete the accompanying worksheet in *Art in American History.*

GUIDED INSTRUCTION
Tell the class that they are all members of the urban planning board of a large American city. In the past several years, most of the middle- and upper-income residents have moved to the suburbs. In addition, the decay in the inner city has reached a crisis stage. The board must now meet to devise a plan to rejuvenate the inner city and ensure that city services can be maintained and improved. Part of the plan should include suggestions for attracting new businesses and residents into the city. Explain that board members realize that such a plan might take several years to become effective, but the purpose of today's meeting is to decide what can be done in the next year to begin restoring vitality to the inner city. Write students' suggestions on the chalkboard or an overhead projector. Discuss them with the entire class. After discussing several suggestions, work with the students to decide which course of action to take. You may wish to invite members of the city or county council to attend the discussion.

Ken Biggs/After Image

Werner Wolff/Black Star

Los Angeles, "The City of Angels," lies smothered in the smog created in part by the movement of traffic along the freeways. But environmentalists with activities such as Earth Day, below, have fought for 20 years to awaken the consciences of polluters.

Coping with Pollution

Beginning in the 1960s, the crowding of people and manufacturing into metropolitan areas caused serious **pollution**—substances that harm the environment. Millions of automobiles, buses, and trucks poured harmful exhaust fumes into the air. The furnaces of factories and utility companies released clouds of smoke and cinders. Denver, Colorado, the "mile-high city" once famous for its pure air, was veiled in haze. At certain times in Los Angeles, polluting substances called **smog** (a term coined by combining the words *smoke* and *fog*) made venturing outside actually dangerous. Some people with heart trouble, allergies, or lung diseases began wearing gas masks outdoors to protect themselves! Air-borne wastes from American factories were carried by winds to Canada, where they fell back to earth as **acid rain**, or rain that contains a high concentration of industrial chemicals and falls as pollution. Acid rain caused much damage to forests, lakes, and human beings. Also, accidents involving offshore oil wells or huge oil tankers released tons of thick, black crude oil into the oceans. The oil smothered birds and fish and covered miles of beaches with tar and grease.

Chemicals used to kill insects and to fertilize the soil proved harmful too. Scientists claimed that the gases used in spray cans caused damage in the upper atmosphere by weakening the ozone layer that protects the earth from dangerous radiation from the sun. According to weather experts, increased burning of coal, oil, and other fuels in homes, factories, and automobiles was raising the amount of carbon dioxide in the atmosphere. This was causing a **greenhouse effect**: The increased amount of carbon dioxide was preventing heat from escaping into space, thereby raising the average ■temperature on Earth.

In 1970, Congress established an **Environmental Protection Agency** (EPA) to monitor pollution and seek ways to eliminate it. But the EPA's efforts were seldom successful. The cost of cleanup was high, and auto makers and other manufacturers often resisted obeying EPA directives.

Coping with Energy Shortages

The soaring price of oil in the 1970s forced Americans to cut back ① on their consumption of petroleum products. They turned down the ■ thermostats in their homes during winter, for example, and bought smaller automobiles to replace the "gas guzzlers" they had previously favored. Eventually, conservation and the discovery of new oil fields in non-OPEC nations caused the price to fall considerably—but not nearly as low as it had been in 1973.

Meanwhile, the search for other sources of energy went on. One source, **nuclear energy**, was already producing large amounts of electricity. Nuclear plants make electricity by splitting atoms of uranium, the same element used in atomic bombs. But instead of exploding, in nuclear plants the uranium is split under controlled conditions in reactors. The process results in enormous amounts of heat. The heat turns water into steam, just as the heat of coal or oil fires does in conventional power plants. The steam turns the turbines that create electricity.

Nuclear power plants are efficient, but if an accident caused the uranium to "overheat," it might explode, releasing deadly radioactive particles over large areas. In 1979, an accident at the **Three Mile Island** nuclear plant in Pennsylvania did great damage to the plant and caused a near panic in surrounding communities. In 1986, the explosion of a Soviet plant at **Chernobyl**, near Kiev, spewed huge amounts of radiation into the air. Its effect was felt over thousands of miles. After Chernobyl, plans to construct more nuclear power plants in the United States ground to a halt. 🖳

Return to the Preview & Review on page 1101.

This pair of photos shows a nuclear power plant from cooling tower to the central core. Explain briefly how nuclear energy is produced.

Chris Harris/Gamma-Liaison

Mike Maple/Woodfin Camp

SECTION 4

PREVIEW & REVIEW RESPONSES
Understanding Issues, Events, & Ideas.
Descriptions should demonstrate an understanding of the terms used.
1. Carter's strategy was to picture himself as an "outsider" who had no connection with the corruption and scandal that seemed to surround Washington in the Watergate era.
2. The support he received from Mexican Americans and African Americans
3. He ruffled the feathers of members of Congress. He often displayed a kind of petulance and spoke to Americans about things they could not feel or understand. African Americans complained that he did not appoint enough blacks to posts in his administration.
4. He brought Israel's premier and Egypt's president together to negotiate an agreement to work for peace, known as the Camp David Accords.

Thinking Critically.
1. Student answers will vary but should be based on sound reasoning and judgment.
2. Encourage students to view videotapes of Jimmy Carter during his presidency before preparing their reports.

PRIMARY SOURCE
Description of change: excerpted.
Rationale: excerpted to focus on Carter's goal to reestablish Americans' pride in their government.

Preview & Review

Use these questions to guide your reading. Answer the questions after completing Section 4.
Understanding Issues, Events, & Ideas. Use the following words to describe Jimmy Carter's election to the presidency and his term in office: Twenty-Sixth Amendment, Camp David Accords.
1. What was Carter's strategy in his campaign against Ford for the presidency in 1976?
2. What was a major factor in Carter's victory at the polls?
3. How did Carter manage to alienate himself from Congress and the American people? Why were many African Americans dissatisfied with Carter?
4. In what way did Carter help to bring peace to the Middle East?
Thinking Critically. 1. If you had been a voter in 1976 would you have supported Ford or Carter for president? Explain your answer.
2. Imagine that you are a newspaper reporter and have just interviewed President Carter. Write an account of your impressions of him, including a description of some of his characteristics, such as his mannerisms and style.

4. THE DEMOCRATS TAKE A TURN

The Election of 1976

In the mid 1970s, the United States was beginning to face those three challenges. As a result of the Watergate affair, many Americans lost faith in their country's leadership. The Democrats nominated James Earl Carter, Jr., for president. Jimmy Carter, as he preferred to be known, had been a little-known governor of Georgia, peanut farmer, and businessman. At the Republican nominating convention, President Ford won a narrow victory over Ronald Reagan, a former Hollywood actor who had served two terms as governor of California.

During the campaign, Carter's strategy was to present himself as an outsider, one who had no connection with the corruption and scandal that surrounded Washington in the Watergate era. He ■ stressed his sincerity, his honesty, and his deep religious faith. He would run the federal government efficiently, he said, and he would balance the budget. In one campaign speech, he voiced the concerns of many Americans and his vision of the nation:

> “Can our government in Washington, which we love, be decent? Is it possible for it to be honest and truthful and fair and idealistic, compassionate, filled with love? Is it possible for our government to be what the American people are, or what we would like to be? Can it once again be a source of pride instead of apology and shame and embarrassment?
>
> A lot of people think the answer is no. I think the answer is yes. . . . We still have a system of government that's the best on earth. The vision that was ours 200 years ago is still there. Our Constitution still says the same thing. Equality, equity, fairness, decency, are still aspects of our government. Freedom, liberty, individualism, are still integral aspects of our government. We have a nation of which we ought to be proud. . . .
>
> We ought to be searching for a way to make our nation more decent and more fair.[1]”

By comparison, President Ford emphasized his political experience. He compared his more than 25 years in national politics to Carter's brief stint at the state level. Neither candidate presented imaginative solutions to the nation's problems, and people took little interest in the campaign. Barely half of the eligible voters went to the polls. Actually, this was part of a continuing trend. But it was worrisome that relatively few of the people aged 18 to 20 bothered to cast ballots. They had only recently been given the right to vote by the **Twenty-Sixth Amendment**, ratified in 1971.

[1]From *A Government as Good as Its People* by Jimmy Carter

The election was close. Carter won in the electoral college by 297 votes to 240. He carried the northern industrial states and the South. A major reason for his victory was the support he received from Mexican Americans, particularly in south Texas, and from African Americans. Almost 95 out of every 100 African American voters cast their ballots for Carter.

The election of Carter, who publicly affirmed his religious convictions, also represented a change that had developed in American society since World War II. He symbolized the reawakening of an American religious spirit, especially among conservative Protestants. Despite radical movements and unprecedented scientific breakthroughs, the tide of popular religion had continued to rise. Many people—including political candidates and even Catholic priests—described experiences something like a traditionally Protestant "rebirth."

These "born again" Americans spread the experience, publicly and privately. Some born-again Protestant ministers made effective use of radio and television to attract converts and raise money. The Reverend Jimmy Swaggart, for example, was said to have more than 2 million followers. (In the 1980s, however, some of the most popular of these preachers would be convicted of misusing money they had collected. Others would be exposed for committing scandalous personal behavior. By 1990, the movement would experience a decline.)

Carter at Home

In office Carter stressed an informal style. He tried to make himself more available to ordinary people than most recent presidents. Instead of riding to the White House in a limousine after his inauguration, he and his wife and small daughter walked down Pennsylvania Avenue at the end of the inaugural parade, waving and smiling to the crowd. He appeared on television wearing a cardigan sweater instead of a suit coat. He had a "call in" program in which he answered questions phoned in by citizens.

As time passed, however, Carter often displayed a kind of peevishness—he seemed almost arrogant and acted in a haughty manner, especially in dealing with Congress. And though he was a good orator, he often spoke to the people about things they could not feel or understand. Carter claimed there was "a growing *malaise* of the American spirit." By this French word he meant a vague uneasiness, a discomfort that would be difficult to treat. This pessimism could hardly console troubled Americans who were hoping that the economy would improve and that foreign tensions would ease. Carter also stressed that with citizenship came certain obligations, such as obeying the law and striving for the common good. How bright the future would be depended in large part on how actively each American worked toward creating a just and prosperous society.

The Carters appear at one of the inaugural balls celebrating the return of the Democrats to the White House. Report to your classmates on the most recent evaluations of the Carter presidency. Predict for whom the woman registering to vote below cast her ballot: Carter or Ford?

① By 1978 the Carter presidency left people uninspired. The *Washington Post* wrote: "He did not promise to excite us or entertain us or even 'lead' us in the public fashion of a Franklin D. Roosevelt, John F. Kennedy or Lyndon B. Johnson. He promised only to manage our affairs sensibly and with a degree of charity."

② Leonard Silk wrote in *The New York Times* that "Jimmy Carter will be remembered as the first Democrat who reoriented the party away from its fixation with the New Deal."

SUGGESTED CAPTION RESPONSE
They signed the Camp David Accords, an agreement to work for peace.

RETEACHING STRATEGY
Students with Special Needs.
Pair students who are having difficulty with students who are performing well. Have the more proficient students read the following list to the others who should indicate whether each item was a strength or weakness of Jimmy Carter's presidency.
1. Poor relations with Congress *(weakness)*
2. Informal style *(strength)*
3. Pictured himself as an "outsider" *(strength)*
4. Spoke to the American people about things they could not understand *(weakness)*

INDEPENDENT PRACTICE
Have students complete the Preview & Review activity at the beginning of the section.

CLOSURE
Point out that although Jimmy Carter won the election of 1976 by stressing that he was an "outsider" in Washington, critics soon claimed that this hurt his effectiveness as president.

HOMEWORK
Have students imagine that they are delegates to the 1976 Democratic convention. Ask them to write a letter home giving their impressions of Jimmy Carter.

PRIMARY SOURCE
Description of change: excerpted.
Rationale: excerpted to focus on Carter's commitment to human rights.

D. B. Owen/Black Star

The triumph of the Carter presidency was bringing together the leaders of two ancient rivals: Egypt, represented by Anwar Sadat, and Israel, represented by Menachem Begin. What agreement did they reach at Camp David before this handshake?

① As the months passed, critics began to claim that Carter was a poor leader. His economic policies were not achieving results, and his civil rights measures were not strong enough. Within his own party some Democrats insisted that to stimulate the economy and reduce unemployment, Carter should urge Congress to increase government spending.

② Instead, the president attempted to slow inflation by cutting government spending. He set out with zeal to protect the environment, the workplace, the consumer, and the nation's highways. But each new regulation brought protests from businesses, which feared losing profits if they complied with the new laws. Carter named three women to his cabinet, and more women, African Americans, and Hispanics received federal jobs and judgeships than ever before. Some African Americans complained bitterly, however, that President Carter had not appointed enough of their members to posts in his administration.

Carter and Foreign Relations

Although Carter's intentions were good, his inexperience in foreign relations caused problems. He bravely set the tone for his foreign policy in his inaugural address:

66 Because we are free we can never be indifferent to the fate of freedom elsewhere. . . . Our commitment to human rights must be absolute.[1] 99

[1]From his inaugural speech by Jimmy Carter, January 20, 1977

Securing these rights for people in other countries, however, proved difficult. Pressure for human rights weakened American ties with anticommunist nations such as Iran and Nicaragua and undermined their autocratic governments, which regularly violated the human rights of their citizens. For the same reasons, it threatened detente with the Soviets. Then Carter's firm stand against the Soviet invasion of Afghanistan in 1979 sent detente into a tailspin and led the president to withdraw the important Strategic Arms Limitation Treaty (SALT II) that had just been negotiated with the Soviets.

Yet President Carter did win much praise for his efforts to bring peace to the troubled Middle East. He invited Israel's premier, Menachem Begin, and Egypt's president, Anwar Sadat, to Camp David, the presidential retreat outside Washington. With Carter's help, Begin and Sadat hammered out an agreement known as the **Camp David Accords**. Israel withdrew from all captured Egyptian territory, and Egypt extended formal recognition to Israel. As a result of their efforts toward ending the Arab–Israeli conflict, Begin and Sadat shared the 1978 Nobel Peace Prize.

Return to the Preview & Review on page 1106.

Bettmann Newsphotos

Even his sharpest critics concede that Ronald Reagan, shown here with his wife, Nancy, was a very popular president.

5. THE REPUBLICANS TRIUMPHANT

The Election of 1980

The energy crisis of the 1970s aggravated the problem of inflation. The skyrocketing price of gasoline, heating oil, and everything made from petroleum helped push the **inflation rate** to about 13 percent by 1979. With prices rising much more rapidly than wages, inflation became the main issue in the 1980 presidential election.

President Carter won the Democratic nomination after a hard campaign against Senator Edward M. Kennedy, a younger brother of President John F. Kennedy. During the primaries, Carter faced an international crisis that had broken out in November 1979. A mob in Teheran, the capital of Iran, had broken into the American embassy and held as hostages the Americans in the building. The leaders demanded that the United States turn over to the Iranian government the former shah, or king, of Iran, who had been deposed a year earlier and who was receiving treatment for cancer in the United States.

The United States refused to return the shah, and a stalemate resulted. For months, the Iranians held more than 50 Americans prisoner in the embassy in Teheran. In desperation, President Carter in April 1980 ordered a team of marine commandos flown into Iran by helicopter to rescue the hostages. The mission had to be called back after several of the helicopters developed mechanical problems. Then, eight commandos died when two helicopters collided during a refueling stop in the desert. The Iranians shocked the world with a ghoulish display of the dead.

The effort earned Carter a mixture of blame, because it failed, and praise for having at least tried to free the hostages, but they remained in captivity. This was a severe blow to Carter and to the prestige of the United States.

Preview & Review

Use these questions to guide your reading. Answer the questions after completing Section 5.
Understanding Issues, Events, & Ideas. Use the following words to describe the presidential elections of 1980 and 1984, as well as the Reagan years: inflation rate, supply-side economics, Sandinistas, Income Tax Act of 1986, Contras, Boland Amendment, *glasnost, perestroika,* strategic defense initiative.

1. What international crisis helped cause the defeat of Jimmy Carter in the 1980 presidential election?
2. What is supply-side economics?
3. Why did Reagan send aid to the El Salvador government and anti-government Nicaraguans?
4. What was a major difference in policy between Reagan and Mondale?
5. What were some of the alarming changes occurring in American society at the end of the 1980s?

Thinking Critically. Imagine that you are a member of Congress in the early 1980s. Write a press statement in which you either defend or attack Reagan's policy of sending military and economic aid to the Contras in Nicaragua.

The hostages held in Iran, shown above upon their arrival on free soil, were given a boisterous ticker tape parade a few days later in New York (below).

The Republicans nominated Ronald Reagan, who had lost the nomination four years earlier by only a narrow margin. In the election, Reagan won a sweeping victory, 43.9 million popular votes to 35.5 million for Carter. A third party candidate, John Anderson, received 5.7 million popular votes. Reagan's majority in the electoral college was even more stunning: 489 to Carter's 49. The Republican party also made large gains in seats in both houses of Congress.

On January 20, 1981, Reagan took the oath of office as president. At a luncheon immediately afterward, he announced that the hostages in Iran had been freed.

After leaving office, Jimmy Carter devoted himself to world peace and to sheltering the poor and homeless. Eventually, many of his former critics would see him in a new light. Yet he seemed unequal to many of the challenges during his term as president.

Reagan as President

A committed conservative, President Reagan believed that the federal government had grown too big and was involved in too many aspects of everyday life. "It is my intention to curb the size and influence of the Federal establishment," he announced in his inaugural address. He hoped that by 1988, many major federal programs would have been taken over by the states. He called his plan "The New Federalism."

Reagan was determined to increase the amount of money spent on defense but to cut back on other government spending. He also wished to reduce taxes. He argued that the budget could be balanced despite the lower taxes. He said it would work this way: Americans would invest the money they saved on taxes in new business enterprises, which in turn would cause the economy to boom. More jobs would be created, and profits would increase. With more people working and businesses earning more money, tax revenues would go up, even though tax rates were lower. This theory was known as **supply-side economics**, also called "trickle-down economics" by its opponents.

Reagan proved to be an extremely skillful politician. By midsummer 1981, the Reagan budget and bills reducing the federal income tax by 25 percent over three years had been enacted into law.

Despite Reagan's economic policies, the nation's economic problems persisted, and a serious recession developed. Business activity lagged. Unemployment rose to more than 10 percent, and interest rates remained high. With tax revenues down and the government spending billions on defense, the deficit rose to nearly $200 billion in 1983.

The recession did have one good result: The inflation rate tumbled from more than 12 percent to less than 4 percent by early 1984.

came when his first marriage broke up, his career seemed on the decline, and, most important, when he took on the job of introducing the General Electric Theater and toured the country for the company, which was noted for its conservative stands.

With that, business began to pick up. Thousands of idle workers ① found new jobs.

But the huge budget deficit remained. Some advisers urged Reagan to reduce it by cutting military spending. He refused to do so because he believed that the Soviet Union was out to dominate the globe. He said that it was "the focus of evil in the modern world." The president wanted the Soviets to know that the United States was stronger than they were and would resist aggression. Then the Soviets would restrain themselves, he said.

This policy caused Reagan to take a strong stand against possible Soviet "penetration" of Central America. Some years earlier, rebels in Nicaragua known as **Sandinistas** had overthrown the country's reactionary dictator. The Sandinistas had set up a government that was friendly to the Soviet Union. They were also supporting rebel forces in the neighboring nation of El Salvador. Reagan provided advisers and military and economic aid to the government of El Salvador and ordered the CIA to organize antigovernment Nicaraguans who were seeking to defeat the Sandinistas.

The Election of 1984

Reagan's Central American policy was controversial, but he remained popular. In 1984 the Republican convention unanimously nominated him for a second term as president. For the first time, an African American—the Reverend Jesse Jackson—waged a serious campaign for the Democratic nomination. He attracted wide support by denouncing Reagan's economic policies as harmful to the poor. But the nomination went to Walter Mondale, who had been Carter's vice president.

Mondale electrified the country by selecting a woman, Representative Geraldine Ferraro of New York, as his running mate. He also announced that if elected he would ask Congress to raise taxes in order to reduce the budget deficit. This was a direct challenge to President Reagan, who had sworn not to increase taxes under any circumstances.

The election resulted in a landslide for Reagan. He won nearly 60 percent of the popular vote and carried the electoral college by 525 to 13. African Americans were one of the few traditionally loyal Democratic groups to support Mondale. The Democratic tactic of nominating a woman for vice president was a failure. Far more women voted for Reagan than for Mondale.

The Reagan "Revolution"

In his second term, President Reagan continued attempts to cut back government spending on social welfare projects and to lower taxes still further. The **Income Tax Act** of 1986 relieved 6 million low-income

Griffiths/Magnum Photos

The Mondale/Ferraro ticket failed to capture the imagination of most American voters. In spite of Geraldine Ferraro's presence on the Democratic ticket, for whom did most women vote?

① Reagan had a knack for escaping criticism of his political actions. In response to Reagan's ability to deflect criticism and accusations, Democratic Congresswoman Pat Schroeder of Colorado named him "the Teflon president."

Cynthia Johnson/Time Picture Syndication

Cynthia Johnson/Time Picture Syndication

Top: marchers for Women's Equal Rights come to Washington. Above is Norma McCorvey, who used the name "Jane Roe" to protect her identity in the case of Roe v. Wade.

people from paying income taxes and lowered the maximum rate for anyone else to 28 percent. The taxes paid by corporations also were reduced.

The president also pursued his policy of appointing and promoting as many conservatives as possible in public office. When Chief Justice Warren Burger resigned from the Supreme Court in 1986, Reagan nominated Associate Justice William Rehnquist, an extremely conservative justice, to the top post. Rehnquist's position was filled by Antonin Scalia, another conservative. The next year, when another justice retired, Reagan named Robert Bork, a judge so extremely conservative that the Senate refused to confirm him. It did confirm Reagan's next choice, however, the more moderate conservative Anthony Kennedy.

The composition of the high court was especially important to those on both sides of the issue of abortion. "Right to life" advocates argued that all life is sacred, and that only in the most extreme cases should an unborn child be aborted. They were challenged by the pro-choice movement, which claimed that a woman had the constitutional right to control her own body, and thus to end an unwanted pregnancy during the early stages, if she chose to do so. The Court was drawn into the argument by the 1973 landmark case, *Roe v. Wade*, which ruled that a woman's constitutional right to privacy included the right to have an abortion during the first three months of pregnancy. Later Supreme Court decisions, however, authorized the states to limit the circumstances under which abortions might be performed. (The pro-choice versus pro-life debate continued heatedly, well into the 1990s.)

① President Reagan's success in having many of his programs adopted was the result partly of his personal popularity. His appointments of federal office holders were also moving the government in

STRATEGIES FOR SUCCESS

EXPRESSING A POINT OF VIEW

You may often be called upon to express and defend your point of view on a topic—in class discussions, essay tests, research papers, or debates. At such times you need to clearly state your positions and provide support.

How to Express a Point of View

To express a point of view, follow these guidelines.

1. **Research the issue.** Make sure you know what you are talking about. Find out what the opposing points of view are.
2. **Decide on your position.** Study the evidence and evaluate the situation. Decide how you stand on the issue. Begin to collect support for your position.
3. **State your position simply and clearly.** Prepare an introduction that identifies the issue and states your position in simple and clear terms.
4. **Support your position.** When writing your point of view, develop additional paragraphs that provide support for your position. End with a concluding paragraph briefly restating your position and reasoning.

Applying the Skill

Today the issue of gun control raises a controversy in many parts of the United States. The basic question is: To what degree should the government regulate and limit the sale and ownership of guns? Those who are against gun control point for their defense to a portion of the Second Amendment which guarantees a "right of the people to keep and bear arms." However, those who favor gun control cite the rise in violent, gun-related crimes to support their call for legislation regulating the sale and ownership of guns, particularly handguns and semi-automatic weapons. State your point of view on gun control. Be sure to support your position.

For independent practice, see Practicing the Strategy on page 1125.

The Granger Collection, New York

INTEGRATING STRATEGIES FOR SUCCESS

Organize the class into cooperative learning groups. Distribute to each group an editorial page from a recent local newspaper. Have the groups choose one of the editorials and describe the author's point of view and explain how he or she supports this point of view. Have spokespersons for each group describe their conclusions to the rest of the class.

GUIDED INSTRUCTION

Discuss voter turnout in recent elections by telling students that some research suggests that low voter turnout may simply signify that people are generally satisfied and feel no need to vote. Other people theorize that low turnout means that voters feel that candidates' views are too similar or that candidates do not address real issues. Choosing between candidates becomes either too difficult or unnecessary. Ask the class why they think so few eligible voters—especially young voters—exercise their right to vote in the United States.

RESOURCES
■ You may wish to have students complete Case 20: *"Hazelwood School District v. Kuhlmeier "*in *THE CONSTITUTION: Past, Present, and Future.*
◀ You may wish to have students view Transparency 10: *"United States Exports and Imports "*and complete the accompanying worksheet in *American History Map Transparencies.*

John Chiaisson/Gamma–Liaison

Realization that mothers could pass the deadly AIDS virus to their unborn children came slowly. The children who contracted the disease were sometimes abandoned. Mother Hale, pictured above, cares for such children. The disease has no cure nor vaccine. Your families, schools, and churches can help you understand how the AIDS virus is spread.

the conservative direction that he favored. But at the same time, serious social problems were changing the face of America. Despite efforts to get tough with criminals, crime rates were rising. Illegal, habit-forming drugs flooded the country. "Crack," a particularly habit-forming type of cocaine, became especially troublesome because it was relatively cheap, widely available, and potentially lethal.

Equally, if not more, disturbing was the sudden appearance of a deadly new disease, acquired immunodeficiency syndrome, or AIDS. AIDS was caused by a virus that prevents the body from fighting off pneumonia and other diseases. Because there was no known cure for AIDS, almost everyone who contracted it eventually died.

Although the economy was booming in the late 1980s, few people were sharing in the wealth being produced. Many of the rich were getting richer, but many of the poor were getting poorer. Many Americans became victims of technological unemployment. That is, computers and automated machinery were replacing human workers at the lower end of the wage scale.

Reagan's policy of eliminating government restrictions on business resulted in a great deal of healthy competition. But competition hurt inefficient producers, who were swallowed up by the more successful. Ending government regulation also encouraged recklessness. Savings banks and savings-and-loan associations (S&Ls) in particular, freed from strict control, sometimes invested in extremely risky ventures. Additionally, when falling oil prices caused a severe depression in Texas and other oil-producing states, many companies were unable to repay their loans. Area banks and S&Ls went "belly up" by the dozens.

Another problem resulted from the flood of imports from Japan and other Asian countries such as South Korea and Taiwan. The imports were eagerly sought by American consumers, but American businesses that competed with the imports suffered.

The Iran Contra Scandal

In two foreign areas, Reagan pursued policies that made his last years in office unhappy. One involved the Central American nation of Nicaragua. In 1981 Reagan persuaded Congress to provide weapons and other supplies to the **Contras** (counter-revolutionaries), who were seeking to overthrow the pro-communist Sandinistas. But the Contra revolt made little progress. In 1984, fearing that continued military assistance might lead to "another Vietnam," Congress passed the **Boland Amendment**, which banned such aid in the future.

Meanwhile, a savage war had broken out in the Middle East between Iran and Iraq. Like most Americans, President Reagan had no love for the Iranians because of their anti-American policies and the 1979 attack on the American embassy in Teheran. Additionally, a number of Americans had been held captive for years at secret

John Ficara/Woodfin Camp

locations in Lebanon by radicals supported by Iran. Reagan was eager to obtain their release. In 1986, despite his stated opposition to bargaining with hostage takers, he authorized the secret sale of American arms to Iran, expecting that Iran would arrange the release of the hostages in exchange.

The man who managed this Iranian arms deal was Oliver North, a marine colonel assigned to the White House. After Congress' ban on aid to the Contras, North had been given the job by administration officials of persuading foreign countries and well-to-do individuals to contribute money to the Contras' cause. North, with the knowledge of his immediate superiors, used the profits of the arms sale to Iran ($12 million) to supply the Contras in Nicaragua. This, of course, was against the law. When the secret sales became known in late 1986, during a series of hearings by a Senate investigating committee, North and Reagan's national security adviser were forced from office. Most Americans disapproved of the Iran-Contra deal and did not believe that President Reagan was telling the truth when he denied knowing anything about it. In any case, his final term was ending.

The End of an Era

The most important event that occurred abroad during Reagan's second term was the dramatic change in the Soviet Union after Mikhail Gorbachev became the Soviet leader in March 1985. Because of the problems undermining the Soviet economic system, a failure that also affected the Soviet satellite nations in Eastern Europe, Gorbachev decided to impose some drastic reforms. First he encouraged the Soviet people to discuss public issues and even to criticize government actions (the policy called *glasnost*). He then tried

The Iran-Contra hearings began with the swearing in of Colonel Oliver North, whose performance impressed many television watchers but not the members of the committee. Name another of the Washington hearings you've read about in The Story of America *that attracted wide interest.*

The Republicans Triumphant   1115

Point of View

The magazine *Vanity Fair* published this profile of Mikhail Gorbachev after the collapse of the communist governments in Russia's eastern satellites.

"The eyes. Everyone is struck by the gleam that blazes behind his dark eyes. Presidents, Sovietologists, resident C.I.A. psychologists, Wall Street deal makers—all come away talking about some strange chemical reaction, as if with the intensity of his belief Mikhail Gorbachev had burned his image of a new world onto their own retinas and they will never be the same.

'His eyes convey an intensity that is slightly abnormal,' muses a senior analyst . . . 'It's as though his temperature is a little higher than normal, and he's running a little faster than anybody else.'"
Gail Sheehy, 1990

Return to the Preview & Review on page 1109.

Arm in arm in the Kremlin are Ronald Reagan, Raisa Gorbachev, Mikhail Gorbachev, and Nancy Reagan.

to stimulate the Soviet economy by encouraging individual enterprise. This was called *perestroika*.

At first Reagan was suspicious of these new Soviet policies. He urged Congress to appropriate large sums to build a **strategic defense initiative** (referred to by the press as "Star Wars"), a complicated and expensive computerized system of nuclear-armed missiles designed to destroy incoming missiles while they were still in outer space. Such a system would only be needed in case of a Soviet attack. But by 1986 it was clear that Gorbachev was really interested in reducing international tensions. Disastrously small harvests had forced the Soviets to sign trade agreements with many nations, including the United States. Other breakdowns in the Soviet economic system followed soon after. Gorbachev announced that the Soviet Union wanted to be readmitted to the world community, on which it had turned its back at the outbreak of the Cold War.

At a summit meeting in 1987, Reagan and Gorbachev finally signed a treaty eliminating medium-range nuclear missiles, a major step toward reducing the danger of nuclear war. People all over the world cheered the efforts of the two world leaders.

Bill Fitzpatrick/The White House

RESOURCES
- You may wish to have students complete Reading 78: "Presidential Candidates Bush and Dukakis Debate the Issues (1988)" in Volume II of *Eyewitnesses and Others*.

Bettmann Newsphotos

6. TOWARD A NEW CENTURY

The Election of 1988

Reagan was a very popular president. He was, as his show-business friends would say, "a tough act to follow." To succeed him, the Republicans chose the logical candidate, Reagan's vice president, George Bush. There were so many lesser-known candidates battling for the Democratic nomination that some political writers referred to them as "the Seven Dwarfs." Eventually, the field shrank to two: the Reverend Jesse Jackson and Governor Michael Dukakis of Massachusetts. Jackson, who ran another exciting campaign, attracted more white support than he had in 1984. But Dukakis had a solid majority of the delegates at the convention and was nominated on the first ballot. Dukakis presented himself as the efficient governor of a prosperous state. At the start, he seemed the likely winner, as Bush appeared overshadowed by Reagan.

But the race did not turn out as expected. Bush attacked Dukakis ■ at every turn, while Dukakis was slow to respond in defense of himself. Neither candidate aroused much popular enthusiasm. But Bush's campaign made skillful use of television advertising to depict Dukakis as irresponsible and frighteningly liberal. Although President Reagan threw very little support behind his vice president, by election day it was clear that most of the voters preferred Bush. He won easily, carrying the electoral college by 426 to 112.

Preview & Review

Use these questions to guide your reading. Answer the questions after completing Section 6.
Understanding Issues, Events, & Ideas. Use the following word in describing an important event that occurred during the Bush presidency: apartheid.
1. How was Bush able to beat Dukakis, even though Dukakis was favored to win at the beginning of the race?
2. What were the important world political events viewed as positive by the Bush administration?
3. Why were some Americans unhappy with the results of the war in the Persian Gulf?
4. What factors contributed to President Bush's defeat in the 1992 election?

Thinking Critically. Imagine that you are a newspaper columnist. Write a column for the day after the 1992 election, analyzing the ups and downs of the campaign and giving what you think are the reasons for the election results.

Steve Liss/Time Picture Syndication

Rivals for the Democratic nomination in a friendly moment, above, are the Reverend Jesse Jackson and Michael Dukakis. Both had a formidable opponent in George Bush, who promised to continue much of the Reagan legacy. The Bush inaugural and the grandeur of the Capitol are pictured at top.

Eric Bouvet/Gamma-Liaison

The people, not their leaders, decided the Wall separating West and East Germany must come tumbling down. The celebration at the reconciliation of East and West drew millions to the Brandenburg Gate in Berlin.

Diana Walker/Time Picture Syndication

George Bush and Mikhail Gorbachev met in Malta in 1989, just before the communist bloc of eastern countries began to tumble.

Into the 1990s

Bush's presidency began well. Encouraged by Gorbachev's policies, the satellite countries of Eastern Europe—Poland, East Germany, Czechoslovakia, Hungary, Romania, and Bulgaria—turned out their communist leaders. Even republics within the Soviet Union, such as Lithuania and Georgia, demanded independence. Meanwhile, the Berlin Wall was torn down by East and West Germans, who were eager to reunite their country. Then the central committee of the Soviet Union itself, under Gorbachev's prodding, called for a popular election of a president and announced that the communist party would no longer be the only legal political party. Other political parties would be encouraged. The committee made these changes in hopes of reversing the economic collapse that threatened the nation and in hopes of preventing revolts that such a collapse might cause.

In February 1990, the ruling Sandinistas were defeated in democratic elections in Nicaragua. Violeta Barrios de Chamorro became president. In Africa, after the United States and many other nations had applied economic sanctions, South Africa moved to ease its policy of **apartheid**—separation of the races.

These heartening developments were not repeated elsewhere. In China, after taking part in peaceful demonstrations in Tiananmen Square in Beijing calling for democracy, dozens of students were mowed down by tanks and government troops, untold numbers of others were imprisoned, and all criticism of the communist authorities was ruthlessly suppressed.

EXTENSION:
COMMUNITY INVOLVEMENT
Ask students if any of their friends or relatives participated in the Persian Gulf War. If so, invite one or more of these persons to speak to the class about their experiences in the Persian Gulf. If not, invite a representative from the local media (television, radio, or newspaper) to speak about the impact of the war on your community and what the media's responsibilities were in reporting the war and its impact.

In Central America, drug dealers often controlled the leaders of their countries through force and violence, making the war on drugs difficult to wage. Panama was ruled by a notorious leader with drug-dealer connections, Manuel Noriega. After Noriega was indicted in the United States for drug dealing, Bush mounted a successful invasion of the country to capture him. Unfortunately, some American soldiers and many innocent Panamanians were killed during the fighting. Noriega was captured, brought to the United States, tried, and convicted. Other Latin American nations were alarmed by Bush's use of military force in the area. Nevertheless, Bush remained popular in the United States.

Above left: American soldiers prepare for "Operation Desert Storm" in Saudi Arabia. Above, Colin Powell, chairman of the U.S. Joint Chiefs of Staff, appears at a press conference with General Norman Schwarzkopf, commander of the mostly American United Nations forces in the Persian Gulf War. Below is Iraq's Saddam Hussein, whose invasion of Kuwait triggered the war.

The War in the Persian Gulf

President Bush's popularity further increased when he acted decisively after President Saddam Hussein of Iraq invaded and occupied Kuwait, Iraq's tiny oil-rich neighbor. This gross act of aggression led the United Nations to impose a total ban on trade with Iraq. At the invitation of Saudi Arabia, which Saddam also threatened to attack, the United States and several other U.N. member nations sent troops and warships to the area. When Saddam refused to withdraw his troops from Kuwait, the United Nations authorized the use of forces to drive them out.

In January 1991, the mostly American UN force, commanded by General Norman Schwarzkopf of the United States Army, was unleashed. For one month, planes bombed Iraqi targets. Finally, when Saddam still refused to pull out of Kuwait, hundreds of thousands of U.N. ground troops swept into Kuwait and Iraq. In three days Kuwait was liberated, Iraq's army was smashed, and many

Rising unemployment and slow economic growth hurt retail sales during the Bush administration. To stay in business, some merchants were forced to cut prices drastically in order to sell goods.

AP/Wide World Photos

Boris Yeltsin had to confront the terrible economic problems in Russia after the fall of communism. Many people in western countries feared he might fail and be overthrown by the Russian military.

thousands of Iraqi soldiers were killed. Saddam then agreed to United Nations terms, which included paying Kuwait for damages.

President Bush expected that Saddam's opponents in Iraq would force him from office, and Bush urged them to do so. However, the overwhelming defeat of Saddam's forces did not lead to his overthrow. Saddam used what was left of his army to crush his Iraqi opponents, and he refused to carry out many of the terms of the peace agreement. Bush's critics in the United States began to complain that he should have captured Baghdad, the Iraqi capital, and arrested Saddam just as he had arrested Noriega.

Bush had predicted that the American economy would boom after the Gulf War. Instead, growth slowed almost to a stop. Unemployment rose to more than 7 percent in 1992. As a result of the economic problems, Bush's standing in opinion polls began to fall.

At the same time, the world situation seemed less encouraging. In August 1991, hard-line communists in the Soviet Union tried to seize power by arresting Gorbachev. Their coup failed and they were imprisoned. The Soviet Union was then dissolved, replaced by a loose federation of republics.

During this period, Boris Yeltsin was the leader of Russia, the largest of the republics. He courageously defied the hard-liners during the coup and emerged as the most powerful leader in the federation. With the end of the Soviet Union, Gorbachev went into retirement.

The Election of 1992

The overwhelming American victory in the Gulf War of January and February 1991 had increased President Bush's already high standing in public opinion polls. Because his reelection seemed almost certain, many prominent Democrats were discouraged from seeking their party's presidential nomination. The best organized of the Democrats who did enter the primaries was Governor Bill Clinton of Arkansas. Although charged with misrepresenting facts about how he had avoided being drafted during the Vietnam War, Clinton won most of the primaries and was nominated at the convention on the first ballot.

Despite resentment from many conservative Republicans over President Bush's breaking his campaign promise "No new taxes," he won solid victories in the Republican primaries. For a time, an independent candidate, H. Ross Perot, a billionaire businessman from Texas, entered the race as an independent. Perot was ready, he said, to spend $100 million of his own money on his campaign. While he attacked Bush's handling of the economy and other domestic issues, his main argument was that the Democrats and Republicans alike were out of touch with "the people."

Perot was strong in Texas and the Southwest, a traditionally Republican region, so he seemed a greater threat to Bush than to

John Swart/Wide World Photos, Inc.

The three-way campaign for the presidency made 1992 an exciting election year. Above left are Democrats Al Gore and Bill Clinton, victors in the race for vice president and president, respectively. Above, George Bush and Dan Quayle accept the Republican party's nomination for their reelection. H. Ross Perot, below, delivers some homespun wit at a press conference during his campaign.

© 1992 Ben Van Hook/Black Star

Return to the Preview & Review on page 1117.

Clinton. He lost many supporters, however, when he withdrew from the race, then reentered it only eleven weeks later. At the Republican convention, President Bush and Vice President Quayle were nominated without opposition.

In the campaign, Clinton accused Bush of failing to deal effectively with the lingering economic recession. He promised to create jobs, to encourage private investment, and to improve the nation's education and health insurance systems. Bush played down the seriousness of the recession and national debt, and he emphasized the need for "family values."

Most polls showed Bill Clinton well ahead as the fall campaign progressed, even after Ross Perot reentered the race in October. Late in the campaign, President Bush, worried by his consistently poor standing in the opinion polls, launched personal attacks on his opponent, charging that Clinton was untrustworthy and lacked experience in world affairs.

On election day, however, Clinton won an easy victory. The popular vote was more than 43 million for Clinton, 38 million for Bush, and 19 million for Perot. Because of Perot's large vote, nearly 20 percent of the total, Clinton did not gain a majority. On election night, however, his electoral college victory was substantial, 370 to Bush's 168. Perot did not win the electoral votes of any state.

Experts agreed that a political turning point had been reached. Clinton and his running mate, Senator Albert Gore of Tennessee, represented a new, younger generation of political leaders—energetic, optimistic, and ambitious. With the Democrats controlling both branches of the new Congress, Clinton was determined to make good on his campaign promises to put an end to the recession and reduce the national debt. Whether he would succeed remained to be seen. Meanwhile, we draw the curtain on our story of America.

tion's economic problems." *(George Bush)*

3 "I have no intention of leaving Kuwait." *(Saddam Hussein)*

4 "When campaigning for president, I promised to create jobs, to encourage private investment, and to improve the nation's education and health insurance systems." *(Bill Clinton)*

5 "When the Soviet Union was dissolved, I was leader of Russia." *(Boris Yeltsin)*

INDEPENDENT PRACTICE
Have students complete the Preview & Review activity at the beginning of the section.

CLOSURE
Point out that after winning the Persian Gulf War in 1991, George Bush was very popular with the Amerian people. Yet only a year later, partly because of slow economic growth, he was defeated in his bid for reelection.

HOMEWORK
Have students research and prepare a report on some major issue or achievement of the Clinton administration.

LINKING HISTORY & GEOGRAPHY

FATAL ERROR: OIL ON WATER

Prince William Sound is an emerald jewel, one of Alaska's scenic wonders. It is a bay with 1,000 miles of shoreline. Its waters teem with fish. It is the playground of hundreds of thousands of sea otters, seals, sea lions, and whales. Sea birds and bald eagles nest along its rocky shores. Surrounding the sound are snow-capped peaks and enormous glaciers that send icebergs floating off into the crystal-clear water. This is how it had been for centuries. Then, a little after midnight, on March 24, 1989, a fatal error was made.

The Disaster Begins

1. What caused the *Exxon Valdez* to snag on the rocks in the sound?

Late Thursday night, March 23, the *Exxon Valdez,* a supertanker as long as three football fields, left the port of Valdez filled with crude oil. There was nothing unusual about the impending voyage. Since 1977 some 8,700 loaded tankers had made the trip out of Valdez with virtually no incidents. Visibility was 10 miles or more and the seas were calm that night. All electrical and mechanical systems aboard the ship were working perfectly.

The captain radioed the Coast Guard for permission to cross from the outbound lane to the inbound lane to avoid some small icebergs. It was a routine request. The Coast Guard gave permission. Within 10 minutes the huge ship had swung into the inbound lane. But instead of following the lane to the southwest, it headed due south. Fifteen minutes later it had completely crossed the inbound lane and had sailed into waters closed to oil tankers.

Half an hour later the *Exxon Valdez* passed close to Busby Island, far outside the well-established and clearly marked tanker lanes. Suddenly the unlicensed third mate commanding the ship realized that an error had been made. He frantically gave orders to turn sharply to the west to reenter the traffic lanes. Meanwhile, the captain was asleep in his cabin.

But the mate's orders came too late. At four minutes after midnight the *Exxon Valdez* scraped the rocks of Bligh Reef. The enormous tanker crunched to a halt, balanced on a pinnacle of rock. From its ripped hull 10.1 million gallons of thick crude oil gushed into the pristine waters of Prince William Sound.

The Disaster Grows

2. Why did emergency plans fail?

In 1973, when Congress approved the Alaska pipeline, all of the oil companies involved made solemn promises in writing to do everything possible to protect Alaska's fragile environment. Yet on that tragic night, Alyeska Pipeline Service Company had no emergency crew on hand and little equipment ready for use. It did virtually nothing for three days. During those first few critical days the sound's waters were flat calm, there was almost no wind, and it was unseasonably warm and sunny. Conditions for clean-up were ideal. The spill spread to cover only a five-square mile area, and it was entirely manageable.

Then, 66 hours after the accident, rapidly rising winds and seas sent the main mass of oil racing southwestward. It surged forward at more than a mile per hour, churning the sound into a foamy mixture of oil and water.

By the second week the oil had sunk to depths of more than 90 feet, making the water hazardous even for bottom-feeding marine life. It had spread across more than 3,000 square miles of water. In the cold water, the surface of the spill had weathered into a heavy, tar-like substance. Under this coating was a 6- to 18-inch layer of oil with the consistency of peanut butter. The annual spring migration of salmon and herring was on a collision course with black, oily death.

Fourteen days after the ship hit the reef just 630,000 gallons out of 10.1 million gallons of oil had been picked up. The western beaches along the sound were covered with oozing, stinking tar. The poisoned bodies of otters and seabirds lay matted and almost unrecognizable in the gooey mess. Five weeks after the accident the spill covered an area the size of Massachusetts.

The Disaster's Effects

3. What human and environmental toll did the spill take?

The sound's fishing industry had been among Alaska's most productive. It had yielded about $100,000,000 annually. Now it was ruined.

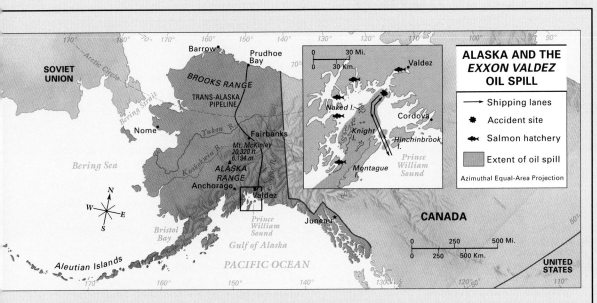

ALASKA AND THE EXXON VALDEZ OIL SPILL

→ Shipping lanes
✳ Accident site
🐟 Salmon hatchery
▨ Extent of oil spill

Azimuthal Equal-Area Projection

Despair tore at the hearts of the residents of tiny fishing villages. Their way of life was disappearing before their eyes. Not only were millions of fish dying, but there was danger that toxins in the oil might become embedded in the still-living fish, making them unfit to eat. The public would fear eating fish, shrimp, or crab from the sound. They knew it would be years before they could rebuild their industry, if ever.

Lessons to be Learned

4. What lessons can we learn from this disaster? One of things that makes the situation difficult to analyze is that the issues are so loaded with emotion. Oil spills and dying animals make a powerful case against current methods of transporting dangerous materials.

But it should be remembered that for 12 years oil had flowed safely through the pipeline and had been safely transported out of Prince William Sound. Also for 12 years the oil industry had assured the public that through technological feats it could handle any emergency.

For 12 years few people worried. A large number of Alaskans make their living from the oil industry. The state's economy rests comfortably on the money received in taxes from the oil industry. Many schools, symphonies, and museums were handsomely financed by donations from large oil companies. Oil was good for Alaska!

Perhaps the most valuable long-term lesson to be learned is that alertness, when untested for too long, deteriorates into complacency. Human failing is the thing to attack, not oil exploration or oil transportation. The world needs oil.

History shows clearly that the oil-shipping industry is basically safe. There have been amazingly few spills considering the enormous volume of oil that has been transported around the world. But the industry seemed so safe that responsible people forgot that they are still required to run it properly. Environmental protection demands constant vigilance. Powerful incentives must keep that protection on task. Human errors must be made harder to repeat and too expensive and too dangerous to be tolerated.

APPLYING YOUR KNOWLEDGE

Your class will study environmental concerns in your local community. Each group will select or will be assigned a concern to research. The group will then create a display or presentation that informs others about the concern. Donate your display to the local library or perform your presentation for the city or county council.

Thinking Critically
1. Answers will vary, but students should use sound judgment and logic in choosing and explaining why they chose a particular action.
2. Student essays should demonstrate that they have given much thought to the way a sense of American history can help Americans meet important challenges today.

3. Answers will vary, but students should present well thought-out arguments and examples to support their answers.

REVIEW RESPONSES
Chapter Summary
Paragraphs will vary but should be evaluated on the logic of student arguments.

Reviewing Chronological Order
5, 1, 3, 4, 2

Understanding Main Ideas
1. He believed that spending more money would lead to inflation. He reluctantly signed a bill reducing taxes.
2. The committee worked hard to attract public attention to their cause, and the personal dedication of their leader, César Chávez, won public support.
3. Gone were "whites only" signs and segregated schools; more African Americans attended college and medical schools, were elected to office, and owned businesses.
4. He successfully persuaded Congress to enact into law his budget and bills reducing the federal income tax. The deficit rose to nearly $200 billion.
5. The nations of Eastern Europe staged some form of democratic elections; the Soviet Union allowed the election of a president and announced that communism would no longer be the only political ideology allowed there; the Middle East harbored a hotbed of terrorists intent on keeping the world off balance; Latin American drug dealers often used violence to influence their governments' leaders; South Africa moved to ease its policy of apartheid.

1124

CHAPTER 30 REVIEW

1970					
	1971 Twenty-Sixth Amendment ratified	**1973** *Roe v. Wade*	**1974** Nixon resigns; Ford becomes president	**1976** U.S. Bicentennial ★ Carter elected president	**1979** Three Mile Island ★ Hostages seized in Iran

Chapter Summary
Read the statements below. Choose one, and write a paragraph explaining its importance.
1. In 1976 people throughout the United States celebrated the nation's Bicentennial.
2. Jimmy Carter brought the leaders of Egypt and Israel together to sign the Camp David Accords.
3. During the 1970s and 1980s Americans had to cope with the problems of urban decay, pollution, and energy shortages.
4. Many of the immigrants of the 1970s came from Asia and Latin America.
5. Many modern blacks were eager to recover their lost heritage and preferred to be known as African Americans.
6. The problem of searching for ways to revive their lost culture continued to plague many American Indians in the 1980s.
7. In 1972 Congress passed the Equal Rights Amendment, but it was not ratified by the states.
8. President Reagan proved to be a determined leader and a skillful politician.
9. In the 1990s, America faced difficult problems with difficult solutions, such as a rising crime rate, drug abuse, and the devastating AIDS virus.
10. Under George Bush, American forces helped liberate Kuwait from Iraqi occupation.

Reviewing Chronological Order
Number your paper 1–5. Then study the time line above and place the following events in the order in which they happened by writing the first next to 1, the second next to 2, and so on.
1. Sandra Day O'Connor becomes first woman on the Supreme Court
2. Eastern European countries begin to allow free elections
3. Iran Contra deal becomes known
4. George Bush becomes the forty-first president of the United States
5. Twenty-Sixth Amendment ratified

Understanding Main Ideas
1. Why did President Ford veto spending projects approved by Congress in the mid-1970s? What action did he later take to end stagflation?
2. Why do you think the United Farm Workers won public sympathy in their strike against California grape growers?
3. In what ways did the civil rights movement transform the United States?
4. What economic actions did Reagan take after his 1980 election? What happened as a result of the decrease in tax revenues and the increase in government spending on defense?
5. What were the cause and the outcome of the Persian Gulf War?

Thinking Critically
1. **Hypothesizing.** Throughout *The Story of America* you have been encouraged to use your historical imagination. You have also been asked to think about historical significance. Two good examples of historical significance are the Monroe Doctrine and the Tonkin Gulf Resolution. Neither seemed particularly important when first announced. Yet 35 presidents have based Latin American policy on the Monroe Doctrine. And Lyndon Johnson waged war in Vietnam under the Tonkin Gulf Resolution. What government actions in recent years do you think might have historical significance? Explain.
2. **Analyzing.** Prepare a brief essay in which you describe what you think is the most important challenge facing America today. Include a paragraph in which you tell how you think our sense of American history can help us meet the challenge.
3. **Evaluating Ideas.** If you were a member of Congress would you have voted for the Reagan budget? The Income Tax Act of 1986? The Boland Amendment? Why or why not?

Writing About History
Imagine that it is the year 2040. Write a letter to your grandchildren describing what it was like

The Reagan Presidency					

1980   **MODERN TIMES**   **1990**

1980
Reagan elected President

1981
Hostages in Iran freed
★
Sandra Day O'Connor becomes first woman Supreme Court Justice

1984
Reagan reelected as president

1985
Gorbachev becomes Soviet leader

1986
Iran-Contra deal becomes known

1988
Bush elected president

1989
Berlin Wall comes down; democratic movements in Eastern Europe

1992
Clinton elected president

growing up in the 1980s and 1990s in America. Include descriptions of your family life, school, leisure-time activities, and styles in clothes and music. It might be interesting to save your letter and read it in the year 2040.

Strategies for Success
Review the strategy on page 1113.
Expressing a Point of View. Reread the section titled "Women Fight for Equality" on page 1098. Then write an essay in which you answer the following questions.
1. What is your position on the Equal Rights Amendment?
2. Why do you take that position?
3. How would American society have changed if the ERA had been ratified? What were the effects of its being rejected?

Using Primary Sources
Like his hero, Dr. Martin Luther King, Jr., African American leader Reverend Jesse Jackson also has a dream for a better America. The following is an excerpt from Jackson's autobiography, *Straight from the Heart*, in which he implores young people to dream.

I am more convinced than ever that we can win. We'll vault up the rough side of the mountain—we can win. But I just want the youth of America to do me one favor. Exercise the right to dream. You must face reality—that which is. But then dream of the reality that ought to be, that must be. Live beyond the pain of reality with the dream of a bright tomorrow. Use hope and imagination as weapons of survival and progress. Use love to motivate you and obligate you to serve the human family. . . .

Young people, dream a new value system. . . . Dreams of authentic leaders who will mold public opinion against a headwind, not just ride the tailwinds of opinion polls. Dream of a world where we measure character by how much we share and care, not by how much we take and consume. Preach and dream. Our time has come.

We must measure character by how we treat the least of these, by who feeds the most hungry people, by who educates the most uneducated people, by who cares and loves the most, by who fights for the needy and seeks to save the greedy. We must dream and choose the laws of sacrifice, which lead to greatness, and not the laws of convenience, which lead to collapse.

1. What does Reverend Jackson mean when he says, "We'll vault up the rough side of the mountain?"
2. Do you agree with Reverend Jackson that we need "a new value system?" Explain.
3. Do you find Reverend Jackson's words inspirational? Why or why not?

Linking History & Geography
As the American population continued its shift to urban areas, major metropolitan regions expanded to the point where they met one another. To comprehend the size and to identify the location of these supercities, with your classmates prepare a map of a megalopolis mentioned in this chapter. On your map you should label the most important city or cities, suburbs, and transportation links. You may need to use an atlas or gazetteer to prepare your map. Discuss with your classmates the impact that these supercities have had on America.

Enriching Your Study of History
1. **Individual Project**. Prepare a classroom display to show various forms of energy in use today, and those proposed for tomorrow. Prepare an oral report to go along with the display in which you describe the strengths and weaknesses of each.
2. **Cooperative Project**. Your group will make a collage on the theme that America is a country of many peoples and special interest groups. Each group member should participate in preparing the collage by bringing in as many pictures from magazines and newspapers as he or she can find on this subject.

Chapter 30 Review   1125

Writing About History
Encourage students to be creative and imaginative when preparing their letters to their grandchildren in the year 2040.

Practicing the Strategy
1. Student positions should be stated in simple and clear terms.
2. Students should support their positions with statements that show that they have researched the subject, and that they have used sound reasoning and judgement in arriving at this position.
3. Answers will vary but should be presented logically.

Using Primary Sources
1. We will overcome the worst obstacles to achieve our goal.
2. Answers will vary, but students should support their position.
3. Answers will vary, but most students will probably say that they do find the words inspirational.

Linking History & Geography
Student maps should indicate that adequate time was spent on research and preparation.

PRIMARY SOURCE
Description of change: excerpted.
Rationale: excerpted to focus on Reverend Jackson's call to the youth of America to dream.

Practicing Critical Thinking

1. Student answers will vary. Many voters felt that his ideas were too extreme.
2. Answers will vary, but students may suggest that it would have been extremely difficult and embarrassing for Americans to see their president on trial.
3. Student answers will vary. Students may mention that Carter could have been tougher in dealing with the militant Iranians. Other students may mention that there was really nothing more he could have done.

REVIEW RESPONSES
Summing Up and Predicting
Paragraphs will vary but should be evaluated on the logic of student arguments.

Connecting Ideas
1. Answers will vary, but students should support their position with sound facts. Students may mention how computers are now used in everyday life for such things as banking transactions, and that most new cars have computerized components.
2. Answers will vary, but students may mention that many 18- to 20-year-olds do not as yet feel a part of the system. Students may mention campaigns by the major political parties to educate young people before their 18th birthday about the importance of exercising their right to vote.

*These sources are suitable for students reading below grade level.

UNIT TEN REVIEW

Summing Up and Predicting
Read the summary of the main ideas in Unit Ten below. Choose one statement, then write a paragraph predicting its outcome or future effect.
1. Among the successes of the Great Society were Medicare and the Voting Rights Act.
2. By the 1960s the United States was called the Affluent Society because no nation in the world had ever been so productive.
3. Movements for equal rights by women, Indians, and African Americans continued.
4. The belief in the domino theory led to U.S. involvement in South Vietnam.
5. The year 1968 was a tragedy because of the Tet offensive in Vietnam, the assassinations of Dr. Martin Luther King, Jr., and Robert Kennedy, and the riots at the Democratic convention in Chicago.
6. The Watergate cover-up led to the resignation of President Nixon.
7. Presidents Ford, Carter, Reagan, and Bush struggled with the economy.
8. By the early 1990s the Cold War ended after the Soviet Union collapsed.
9. American forces helped liberate Kuwait from its Iraqi conquerors in a short war in 1991.

Connecting Ideas
1. The author says that by 1960 the impact of computers was beginning to be felt in the United States. He said that "Eventually the United States would become a computerized society." Do you think the author was correct in his prediction and that we have become a "computerized society?" What are some of the ways that we rely on computers?
2. The Twenty-Sixth Amendment to the Constitution, which lowered the voting age to 18, was ratified in 1971. However, in every national election since ratification the voter turnout for 18- to 20-year-olds has been relatively low. How would you account for this? What can be done to encourage 18- to 20-year-olds to vote?

Practicing Critical Thinking
1. **Analyzing.** In his acceptance speech as Republican presidential candidate in 1964 Barry Goldwater said, "Extremism in the defense of liberty is no vice. And . . . moderation in the pursuit of justice is no virtue." Do you agree or disagree with Goldwater? Why do you think many voters were frightened by this statement?
2. **Predicting.** What do you think might have happened if President Nixon had not resigned and had been put on trial by the Senate?
3. **Evaluating.** During the hostage crisis in Iran in 1979-80 President Carter, acting out of desperation, sent a team of marine commandos to Iran in an attempt to rescue the hostages. Tragically the plan failed. Do you agree with the way that President Carter handled the crisis? How might he have handled it differently?

Exploring History Together
1. Your group will prepare a pictorial essay of either a major event that occurred or a policy that was enacted in the United States from 1964 to the present. Your group will prepare an oral report to go along with the essay and choose a member of the group to present the report.
2. Working in two groups, your class will research and then prepare a debate on a current controversial topic. A speaker from each side should be chosen to present the case. After the speakers have finished, each side should present a rebuttal or final argument defending their side's point of view. Present your debate before a civic or community group.

Reading in Depth
Greene, Laura. *Computer Pioneers.* New York: Franklin Watts/First Books. Presents an account of men and women of the electronic age.

Harlan, Judith. *American Indians Today: Issues and Conflicts.* New York: Franklin Watts/Impact Books. Focuses on the problems of Native Americans today.

*Lasky, Kathryn. *Home Free.* Soquel, Ca.: Four Winds Press. Contains the story of a fifteen-year-old boy and his valiant effort to protect endangered bald eagles whose home is being threatened by a developer.

*Thomas, Joyce Carol. *Water Girl.* New York: Avon Books/Flare Books. Provides an account of an African American teenage girl who unwittingly comes across a piece of her own history.

Woods, Geraldine, and Harold Woods. *The Right to Bear Arms.* New York: Franklin Watts. Provides a better understanding of the debate over gun control.

REFERENCE
SECTION

The Reference Section contains a variety of features designed to enhance your understanding of the story of America. The atlas includes a world map and several United States maps that illustrate absolute and relative locations and other geographic themes. The section of graphs and charts presents statistical profiles of major social and economic changes in American society. The glossary lists boldfaced words and their definitions. The index provides page references for the topics discussed in *The Story of America*. Source citations for the Points of View identify the work from which each excerpt was taken. Acknowledgments list the title and publisher of the primary sources used in *The Story of America*.

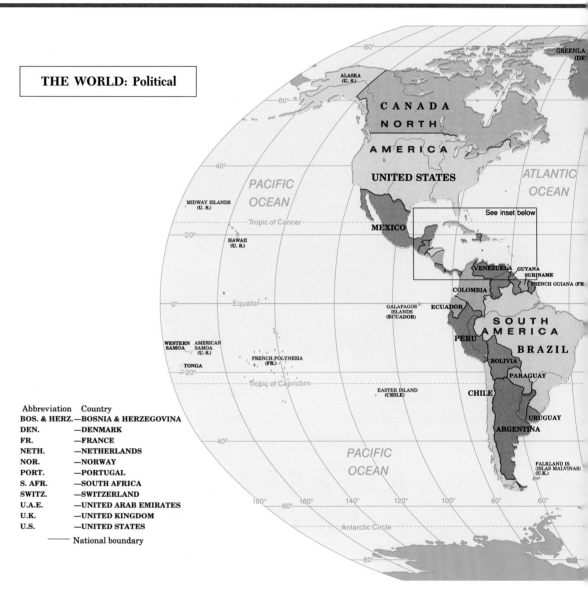

THE WORLD: Political

PACIFIC OCEAN

ATLANTIC OCEAN

GREENLAND (DE

ALASKA (U. S.)

CANADA

NORTH

AMERICA

UNITED STATES

MIDWAY ISLANDS (U. S.)

MEXICO

See inset below

Tropic of Cancer

HAWAII (U. S.)

VENEZUELA GUYANA
SURINAME
FRENCH GUIANA (FR.)

COLOMBIA

GALAPAGOS ISLANDS (ECUADOR)

ECUADOR

Equator

SOUTH

AMERICA

PERU

BRAZIL

WESTERN SAMOA

AMERICAN SAMOA (U. S.)

FRENCH POLYNESIA (FR.)

BOLIVIA

TONGA

PARAGUAY

EASTER ISLAND (CHILE)

CHILE

URUGUAY

ARGENTINA

PACIFIC OCEAN

FALKLAND IS. (ISLAS MALVINAS) (U.K.)

Tropic of Capricorn

Antarctic Circle

Abbreviation	Country
BOS. & HERZ.	—BOSNIA & HERZEGOVINA
DEN.	—DENMARK
FR.	—FRANCE
NETH.	—NETHERLANDS
NOR.	—NORWAY
PORT.	—PORTUGAL
S. AFR.	—SOUTH AFRICA
SWITZ.	—SWITZERLAND
U.A.E.	—UNITED ARAB EMIRATES
U.K.	—UNITED KINGDOM
U.S.	—UNITED STATES

—— National boundary

Central America and West Indies

Gulf of Mexico

FLORIDA (U.S.)

BAHAMAS

Tropic of Cancer

CUBA

ATLANTIC OCEAN

MEXICO

HAITI

DOMINICAN REPUBLIC

VIRGIN ISLANDS (U.S., U.K.)

BELIZE

JAMAICA

PUERTO RICO (U.S.)

ANTIGUA & BARBUDA

ST. KITTS & NEVIS

GUADELOUPE (FR.)

GUATEMALA

Caribbean

N

DOMINICA

HONDURAS

Sea

ST. LUCIA

MARTINIQUE (FR.)

EL SALVADOR

NETHERLANDS ANTILLES (NETH.)

ST. VINCENT AND THE GRENADINES

BARBADOS

NICARAGUA

PACIFIC OCEAN

GRENADA

COSTA RICA

TRINIDAD & TOBAGO

PANAMA

VENEZUELA

0 200 400 Miles

0 200 400 Kilometers

COLOMBIA

GUYANA

MERCATOR PROJECTION

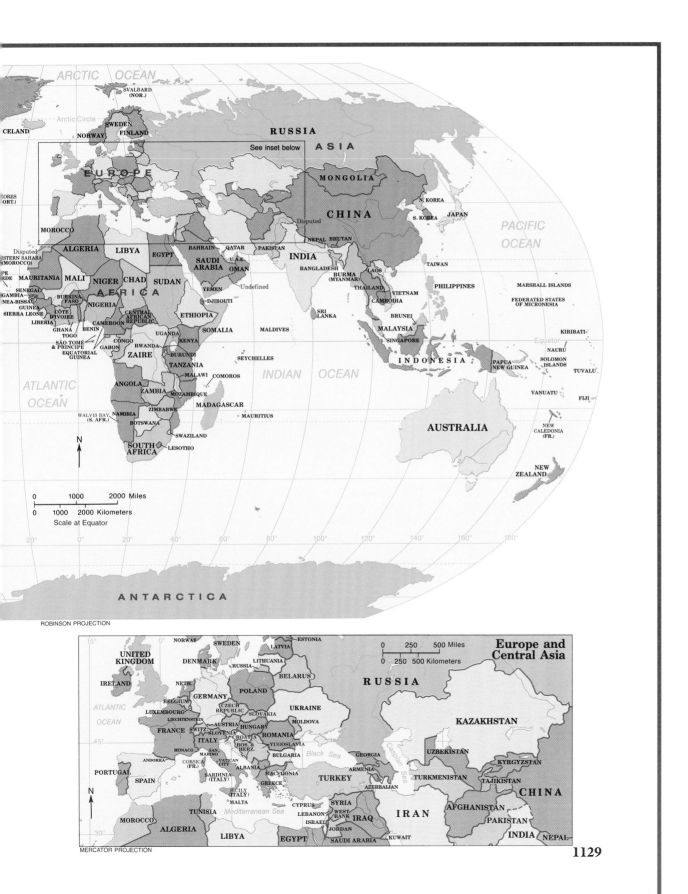

ARCTIC OCEAN

SVALBARD
(NOR.)

CELAND

Arctic Circle

SWEDEN

NORWAY   FINLAND

RUSSIA

ASIA

See inset below

EUROPE

MONGOLIA

N. KOREA

JAPAN

CORES
ORT.)

CHINA

S. KOREA

PACIFIC

OCEAN

MOROCCO

Disputed

Disputed
ESTERN SAHARA
(MOROCCO)

ALGERIA   LIBYA   EGYPT

BAHRAIN   QATAR   PAKISTAN

SAUDI
ARABIA   U.A.E.
OMAN

NEPAL BHUTAN

INDIA

TAIWAN

PE
RDE   MAURITANIA   MALI   NIGER   CHAD   SUDAN
GAMBIA-   SENEGAL   BURKINA   AFRICA
NEA-BISSAU   GUINEA   FASO   NIGERIA
SIERRA LEONE   CÔTE
D'IVOIRE   CENTRAL
AFRICAN
REPUBLIC   ETHIOPIA
LIBERIA   CAMEROON
GHANA   BENIN   UGANDA   KENYA
TOGO
SÃO TOMÉ
& PRINCIPE   CONGO   RWANDA
EQUATORIAL   GABON   BURUNDI
GUINEA   ZAIRE   TANZANIA

YEMEN

BANGLADESH

BURMA
(MYANMAR)
LAOS
THAILAND   VIETNAM
CAMBODIA

PHILIPPINES

MARSHALL ISLANDS

FEDERATED STATES
OF MICRONESIA

Undefined

DJIBOUTI

SRI
LANKA

SOMALIA   MALDIVES

BRUNEI
MALAYSIA
SINGAPORE

KIRIBATI

Equator

NAURU

SEYCHELLES

INDONESIA   PAPUA
NEW GUINEA
SOLOMON
ISLANDS

TUVALU

INDIAN   OCEAN

MALAWI   COMOROS

ANGOLA   ZAMBIA
MOZAMBIQUE

VANUATU

FIJI

ATLANTIC
OCEAN

NAMIBIA
ZIMBABWE   MADAGASCAR

NEW
CALEDONIA
(FR.)

WALVIS BAY
(S. AFR.)   BOTSWANA

MAURITIUS

AUSTRALIA

N

SWAZILAND

SOUTH
AFRICA   LESOTHO

NEW
ZEALAND

0   1000   2000 Miles

0   1000   2000 Kilometers

Scale at Equator

20°   0°   20°   40°   60°   80°   100°   120°   140°   160°   180°

ANTARCTICA

ROBINSON PROJECTION

NORWAY   SWEDEN   ESTONIA

5°   LATVIA

UNITED
KINGDOM   DENMARK   LITHUANIA
RUSSIA   BELARUS

0   250   500 Miles

0   250   500 Kilometers

Europe and
Central Asia

IRELAND   NETH.
GERMANY   POLAND

RUSSIA

BELGIUM
LUXEMBOURG   CZECH
REPUBLIC   UKRAINE

ATLANTIC   LIECHTENSTEIN   SLOVAKIA
OCEAN   FRANCE   SWITZ.   AUSTRIA   HUNGARY   MOLDOVA
SLOVENIA
45°   ITALY   CROATIA   ROMANIA

KAZAKHSTAN

MONACO   SAN
MARINO   BOS. &
HERZ.   YUGOSLAVIA

ANDORRA   CORSICA
(FR.)   VATICAN
CITY   BULGARIA   Black Sea   GEORGIA   UZBEKISTAN
SARDINIA   ALBANIA
PORTUGAL   (ITALY)   MACEDONIA   ARMENIA   KYRGYZSTAN
SPAIN   GREECE   TURKEY   Caspian Sea   TURKMENISTAN   TAJIKISTAN

SICILY
(ITALY)   AZERBAIJAN   CHINA

N   MALTA   CYPRUS   SYRIA

TUNISIA   Mediterranean Sea   LEBANON   WEST
BANK   IRAQ   IRAN   AFGHANISTAN

MOROCCO   ISRAEL   PAKISTAN

30°   JORDAN   INDIA   NEPAL

ALGERIA   LIBYA   EGYPT   SAUDI ARABIA   KUWAIT

MERCATOR PROJECTION

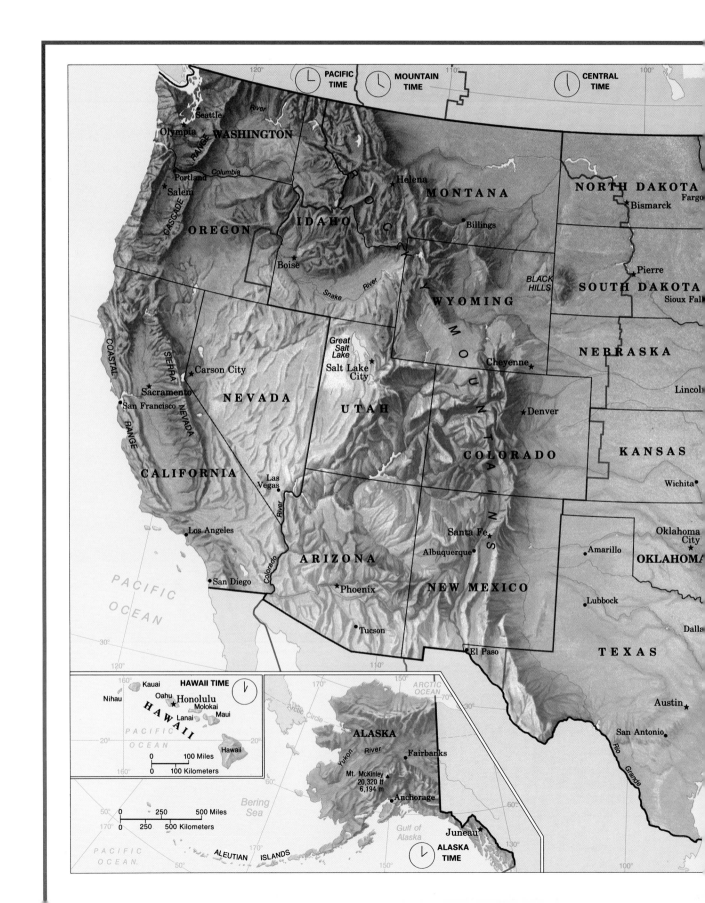

EASTERN
TIME

UNITED STATES: PHYSICAL

⊛ National capital
★ State capital
• Other city
— National boundary
— State boundary

Standard time zones are indicated by clocks. (When it is 2 P.M. in western Alaska, it is 6 P.M. along the eastern coast of the United States.)

Albers Equal-Area Projection

N

| 0 | 250 | 500 Miles |

| 0 | 250 | 500 Kilometers |

1131

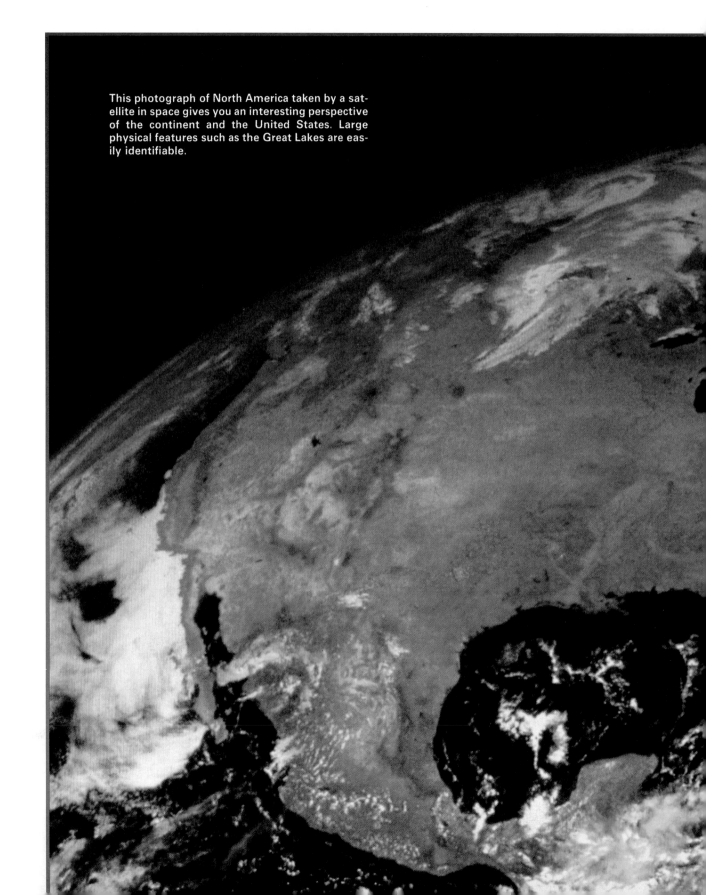

This photograph of North America taken by a satellite in space gives you an interesting perspective of the continent and the United States. Large physical features such as the Great Lakes are easily identifiable.

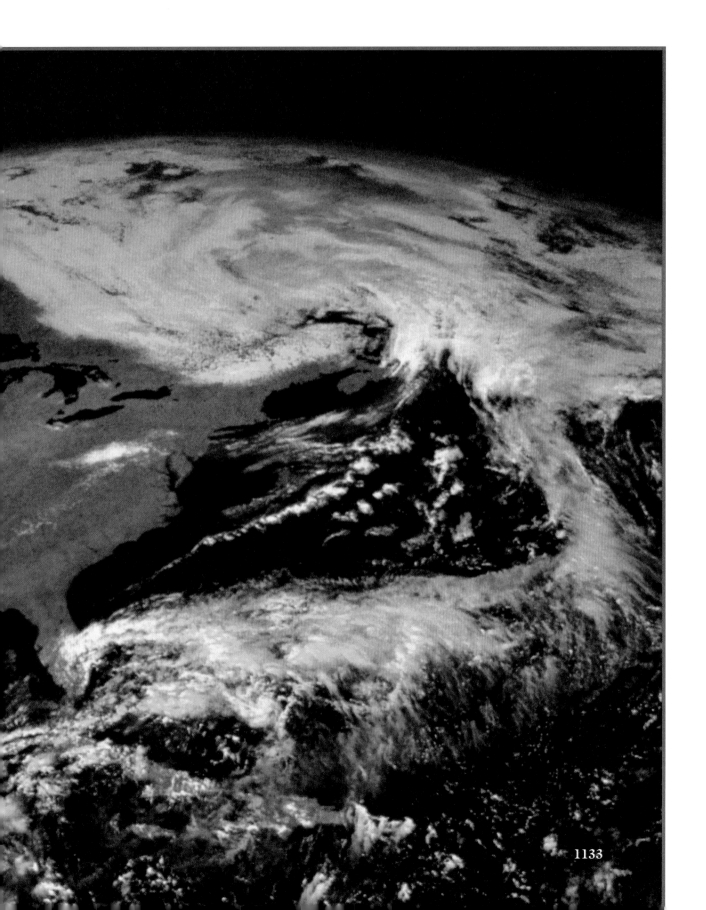

1133

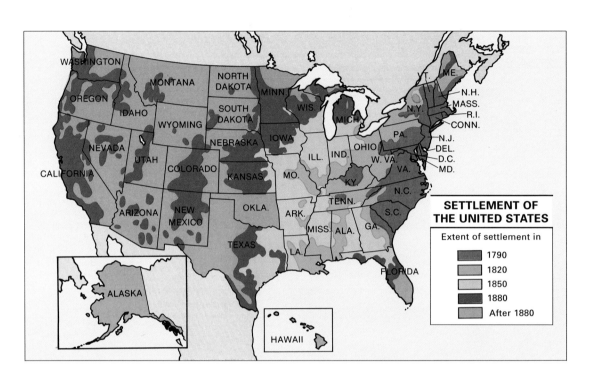

SETTLEMENT OF THE UNITED STATES

Extent of settlement in
- 1790
- 1820
- 1850
- 1880
- After 1880

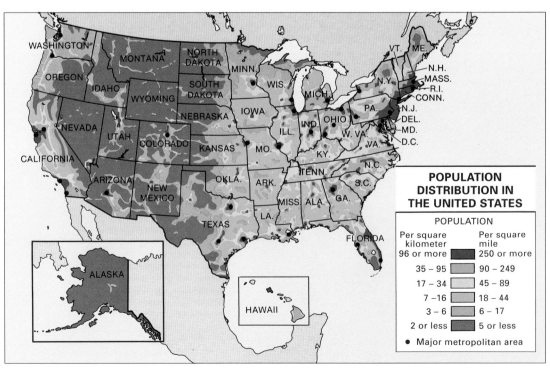

POPULATION DISTRIBUTION IN THE UNITED STATES

POPULATION

Per square kilometer	Per square mile
96 or more	250 or more
35 – 95	90 – 249
17 – 34	45 – 89
7 – 16	18 – 44
3 – 6	6 – 17
2 or less	5 or less

● Major metropolitan area

FACTS ABOUT THE STATES

State	Year of Statehood	1990 Population	Reps. in Congress	Area (Sq. mi.)	Population Density (Sq. mi.)	Capital	Largest City
Alabama	1819	4,040,587	7	51,705	79.6	Montgomery	Birmingham
Alaska	1959	550,043	1	591,004	1.0	Juneau	Anchorage
Arizona	1912	3,665,228	6	114,000	32.3	Phoenix	Phoenix
Arkansas	1836	2,350,725	4	53,187	45.1	Little Rock	Little Rock
California	1850	29,760,021	52	158,706	190.8	Sacramento	Los Angeles
Colorado	1876	3,294,394	6	104,091	31.8	Denver	Denver
Connecticut	1788	3,287,116	6	5,018	678.4	Hartford	Bridgeport
Delaware	1787	666,168	1	2,045	340.8	Dover	Wilmington
District of Columbia	—	606,900	—	69	9,882.8	—	Washington
Florida	1845	12,937,926	23	58,664	239.6	Tallahassee	Jacksonville
Georgia	1788	6,478,216	11	58,910	111.9	Atlanta	Atlanta
Hawaii	1959	1,108,229	2	6,471	172.5	Honolulu	Honolulu
Idaho	1890	1,006,749	2	83,564	12.2	Boise	Boise
Illinois	1818	11,430,602	20	56,345	205.6	Springfield	Chicago
Indiana	1816	5,544,159	10	36,185	154.6	Indianapolis	Indianapolis
Iowa	1846	2,776,755	5	56,275	49.7	Des Moines	Des Moines
Kansas	1861	2,477,574	4	82,277	30.3	Topeka	Wichita
Kentucky	1792	3,685,296	6	40,410	92.8	Frankfort	Louisville
Louisiana	1812	4,219,973	7	47,752	96.9	Baton Rouge	New Orleans
Maine	1820	1,227,928	2	33,265	39.8	Augusta	Portland
Maryland	1788	4,781,468	8	10,460	489.2	Annapolis	Baltimore
Massachusetts	1788	6,016,425	10	8,284	767.6	Boston	Boston
Michigan	1837	9,295,297	16	58,527	163.6	Lansing	Detroit
Minnesota	1858	4,375,099	8	84,402	55.0	St. Paul	Minneapolis
Mississippi	1817	2,573,216	5	47,689	54.9	Jackson	Jackson
Missouri	1821	5,117,073	9	69,697	74.3	Jefferson City	Kansas City
Montana	1889	799,065	1	147,046	5.5	Helena	Billings
Nebraska	1867	1,578,385	3	77,355	20.5	Lincoln	Omaha
Nevada	1864	1,201,833	2	110,561	10.9	Carson City	Las Vegas
New Hampshire	1788	1,109,252	2	9,279	123.7	Concord	Manchester
New Jersey	1787	7,730,188	13	7,787	1,042.0	Trenton	Newark
New Mexico	1912	1,515,069	3	121,593	12.5	Santa Fe	Albuquerque
New York	1788	17,990,455	31	49,108	381.0	Albany	New York City
North Carolina	1789	6,628,637	12	52,669	136.1	Raleigh	Charlotte
North Dakota	1889	638,800	1	70,702	9.3	Bismarck	Fargo
Ohio	1803	10,847,115	19	41,330	264.9	Columbus	Columbus
Oklahoma	1907	3,145,585	6	69,956	45.8	Oklahoma City	Oklahoma City
Oregon	1859	2,842,321	5	97,073	29.6	Salem	Portland
Pennsylvania	1787	11,881,643	21	45,308	265.1	Harrisburg	Philadelphia
Rhode Island	1790	1,003,464	2	1,212	960.3	Providence	Providence
South Carolina	1788	3,486,703	6	31,113	115.8	Columbia	Columbia
South Dakota	1889	696,004	1	77,116	9.2	Pierre	Sioux Falls
Tennessee	1796	4,877,185	9	42,144	118.3	Nashville	Memphis
Texas	1845	16,986,510	30	266,807	64.9	Austin	Houston
Utah	1896	1,722,850	3	84,899	21.0	Salt Lake City	Salt Lake City
Vermont	1791	562,758	1	9,614	60.8	Montpelier	Burlington
Virginia	1788	6,187,358	11	40,767	156.3	Richmond	Virginia Beach
Washington	1889	4,866,692	9	68,139	73.1	Olympia	Seattle
West Virginia	1863	1,793,477	3	24,232	74.5	Charleston	Charleston
Wisconsin	1848	4,891,769	9	56,153	90.1	Madison	Milwaukee
Wyoming	1890	453,588	1	97,809	4.7	Cheyenne	Cheyenne

PRESENTS OF THE UNITED STATES

PRESIDENTS OF THE UNITED STATES

No.	Name	Born–Died	Years in Office	Political Party	Home State	Vice President
1	George Washington	1732–1799	1789–97	None	Va.	John Adams
2	John Adams	1735–1826	1797–1801	Federalist	Mass.	Thomas Jefferson
3	Thomas Jefferson	1743–1826	1801–09	Republican*	Va.	Aaron Burr
						George Clinton
4	James Madison	1751–1836	1809–17	Republican	Va.	George Clinton
						Elbridge Gerry
5	James Monroe	1758–1831	1817–25	Republican	Va.	Daniel D. Tompkins
6	John Quincy Adams	1767–1848	1825–29	Republican	Mass.	John C. Calhoun
7	Andrew Jackson	1767–1845	1829–37	Democratic	Tenn.	John C. Calhoun
						Martin Van Buren
8	Martin Van Buren	1782–1862	1837–41	Democratic	N.Y.	Richard M. Johnson
9	William Henry Harrison	1773–1841	1841	Whig	Ohio	John Tyler
10	John Tyler	1790–1862	1841–45	Whig	Va.	
11	James K. Polk	1795–1849	1845–49	Democratic	Tenn.	George M. Dallas
12	Zachary Taylor	1784–1850	1849–50	Whig	La.	Millard Fillmore
13	Millard Fillmore	1800–1874	1850–53	Whig	N.Y.	
14	Franklin Pierce	1804–1869	1853–57	Democratic	N.H.	William R. King
15	James Buchanan	1791–1868	1857–61	Democratic	Pa.	John C. Breckenridge
16	Abraham Lincoln	1809–1865	1861–65	Republican	Ill.	Hannibal Hamlin
						Andrew Johnson
17	Andrew Johnson	1808–1875	1865–69	Republican	Tenn.	
18	Ulysses S. Grant	1822–1885	1869–77	Republican	Ill.	Schuyler Colfax
						Henry Wilson
19	Rutherford B. Hayes	1822–1893	1877–81	Republican	Ohio	William A. Wheeler
20	James A. Garfield	1831–1881	1881	Republican	Ohio	Chester A. Arthur
21	Chester A. Arthur	1830–1886	1881–85	Republican	N.Y.	
22	Grover Cleveland	1837–1908	1885–89	Democratic	N.Y.	Thomas A. Hendricks
23	Benjamin Harrison	1833–1901	1889–93	Republican	Ind.	Levi P. Morton
24	Grover Cleveland		1893–97	Democratic	N.Y.	Adlai E. Stevenson
25	William McKinley	1843–1901	1897–1901	Republican	Ohio	Garrett A. Hobart
						Theodore Roosevelt
26	Theodore Roosevelt	1858–1919	1901–09	Republican	N.Y.	
						Charles W. Fairbanks
27	William Howard Taft	1857–1930	1909–13	Republican	Ohio	James S. Sherman
28	Woodrow Wilson	1856–1924	1913–21	Democratic	N.J.	Thomas R. Marshall
29	Warren G. Harding	1865–1923	1921–23	Republican	Ohio	Calvin Coolidge
30	Calvin Coolidge	1872–1933	1923–29	Republican	Mass.	
						Charles G. Dawes
31	Herbert Hoover	1874–1964	1929–33	Republican	Calif.	Charles Curtis
32	Franklin D. Roosevelt	1882–1945	1933–45	Democratic	N.Y.	John Nance Garner
						Henry Wallace
						Harry S Truman
33	Harry S Truman	1884–1972	1945–53	Democratic	Mo.	
						Alben W. Barkley
34	Dwight D. Eisenhower	1890–1969	1953–61	Republican	Kans.	Richard M. Nixon
35	John F. Kennedy	1917–1963	1961–63	Democratic	Mass.	Lyndon B. Johnson
36	Lyndon B. Johnson	1908–1973	1963–69	Democratic	Texas	
						Hubert H. Humphrey
37	Richard M. Nixon	1913–	1969–74	Republican	Calif.	Spiro T. Agnew
						Gerald R. Ford
38	Gerald R. Ford	1913–	1974–77	Republican	Mich.	Nelson A. Rockefeller
39	Jimmy Carter	1924–	1977–81	Democratic	Ga.	Walter F. Mondale
40	Ronald Reagan	1911–	1981–89	Republican	Calif.	George H.W. Bush
41	George H.W. Bush	1924–	1989–1993	Republican	Texas	J. Danforth Quayle
42	Bill Clinton	1946–	1993–	Democratic	Ark.	Albert Gore, Jr.

*The Republican party of the third through sixth presidents is not the party of Abraham Lincoln, which was founded in 1854.

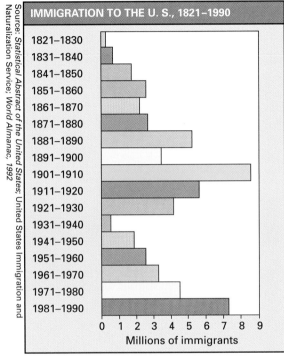

Source: Statistical Abstract of the United States; United States Immigration and Naturalization Service; World Almanac, 1992

IMMIGRATION TO THE U. S., 1821–1990

1821–1830	
1831–1840	
1841–1850	
1851–1860	
1861–1870	
1871–1880	
1881–1890	
1891–1900	
1901–1910	
1911–1920	
1921–1930	
1931–1940	
1941–1950	
1951–1960	
1961–1970	
1971–1980	
1981–1990	

Millions of immigrants

As the graphs on this page indicate, the United States has a rich and varied racial and cultural heritage. This rich heritage is due in large part to immigration. Prior to World War II the majority of immigrants to the United States came from Europe. The Immigration Act of 1965, however, made it easier for non-Europeans to enter the United States. As a result, people from Central and South America, the Caribbean, and Asia now make up the majority of new immigrants.

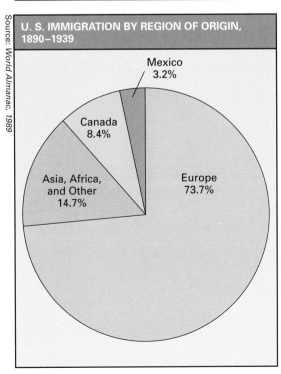

Source: World Almanac, 1989

U. S. IMMIGRATION BY REGION OF ORIGIN, 1890–1939

Mexico 3.2%
Canada 8.4%
Asia, Africa, and Other 14.7%
Europe 73.7%

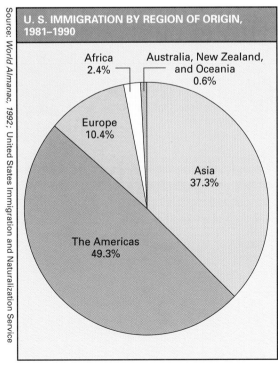

Source: World Almanac, 1992; United States Immigration and Naturalization Service

U. S. IMMIGRATION BY REGION OF ORIGIN, 1981–1990

Africa 2.4%
Australia, New Zealand, and Oceania 0.6%
Europe 10.4%
Asia 37.3%
The Americas 49.3%

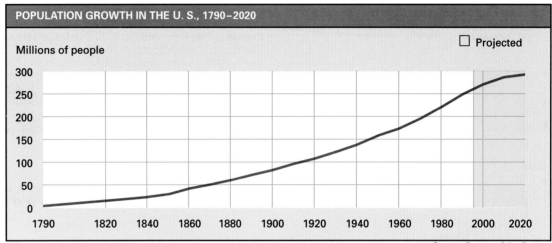

POPULATION GROWTH IN THE U. S., 1790–2020

Millions of people

☐ Projected

Source: Bureau of the Census

Technology also has helped shape American society. The graphs on this page illustrate some of the social consequences of new technologies. Advances in medicine and public sanitation, for instance, have increased the number of years most people live. As a result, the population of the United States has grown. More efficient farming methods have reduced the number of farmers needed to produce food for the American people. This decrease in the demand for farm labor has meant that more workers have been available to fill the jobs created by industrialization. Because these jobs tend to be located in or near cities, the population of the United States has become increasingly urban.

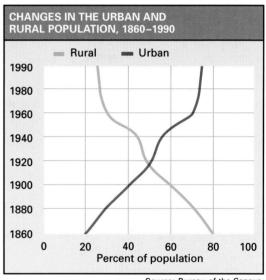

CHANGES IN THE URBAN AND RURAL POPULATION, 1860–1990

Rural   Urban

Percent of population

Source: Bureau of the Census

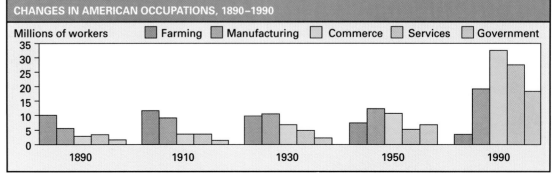

CHANGES IN AMERICAN OCCUPATIONS, 1890–1990

Millions of workers   ■ Farming ■ Manufacturing ☐ Commerce ■ Services ☐ Government

Source: U.S. Dept. of Agriculture; *Monthly Labor Review*

Over its history the United States has enjoyed strong economic growth. Not everyone in society, however, has shared equally in this prosperity. This is evident when one examines the graphs on family income and unemployment on this page. On average, white Americans have enjoyed the highest family incomes and the lowest rates of unemployment.

Social Security and other government programs have made the retirement years more secure for most older Americans. As the graph on the over-65 population indicates, however, the number of elderly is expected to increase over the next few decades. This increase will place new pressures on the government to develop ways to meet the needs of older Americans.

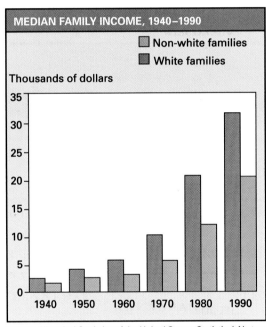

MEDIAN FAMILY INCOME, 1940–1990

Non-white families
White families

Source: *Historical Statistics of the United States; Statistical Abstract of the United States, 1988*; Bureau of the Census, 1990

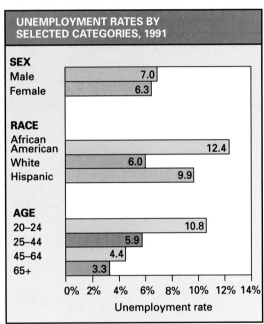

UNEMPLOYMENT RATES BY SELECTED CATEGORIES, 1991

SEX
Male — 7.0
Female — 6.3

RACE
African American — 12.4
White — 6.0
Hispanic — 9.9

AGE
20–24 — 10.8
25–44 — 5.9
45–64 — 4.4
65+ — 3.3

Unemployment rate

Source: U.S. Bureau of Labor Statistics

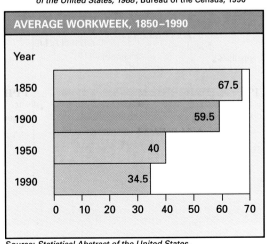

AVERAGE WORKWEEK, 1850–1990

Year
1850 — 67.5
1900 — 59.5
1950 — 40
1990 — 34.5

Source: *Statistical Abstract of the United States, 1989*; U.S. Bureau of Labor Statistics

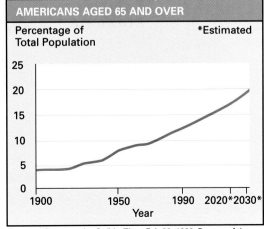

AMERICANS AGED 65 AND OVER

Percentage of Total Population   *Estimated

Year

Source: "Grays on the Go" in *Time*, Feb.22, 1988; Bureau of the Census, 1990

Statistical Profiles 1139

The federal government must have enough money to finance its programs and activities. The money the government collects for this purpose is called receipts. Most government receipts are in the form of taxes. The money the government spends is referred to as outlays. As can be seen from the graph at the top left, in recent decades the federal government has spent more than it has taken in. This shortfall is called a budget deficit. When the federal government experiences a budget deficit, it must borrow money to finance its spending. This borrowed money is called the national debt. As the graph on the top right shows, paying the interest on the national debt is a major outlay for the federal government.

In recent years, the United States also has experienced a trade deficit. A trade deficit occurs when a nation imports more than it exports. The graph at the bottom of the page shows the relationship between United States import and export values since 1950. The inset traces the rise and fall of United States tariffs.

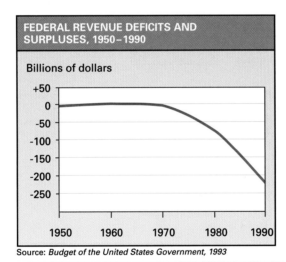

FEDERAL REVENUE DEFICITS AND SURPLUSES, 1950–1990

Billions of dollars

Source: *Budget of the United States Government, 1993*

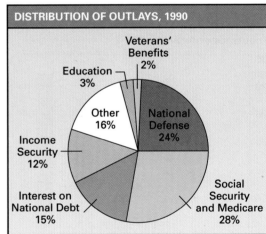

DISTRIBUTION OF OUTLAYS, 1990

Source: *Statistical Abstract of the United States, 1991*

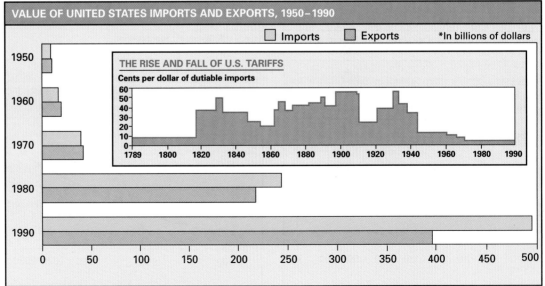

VALUE OF UNITED STATES IMPORTS AND EXPORTS, 1950–1990

☐ Imports   ☐ Exports   *In billions of dollars

THE RISE AND FALL OF U.S. TARIFFS

Cents per dollar of dutiable imports

Source: *Statistical Abstract of the United States, 1991*

All societies must face the fact that the resources needed to produce goods and services are limited. Thus each society must decide how best to use its limited resources. A society makes this decision by answering three basic economic questions: (1) What goods and services should be produced? (2) How should these goods and services be produced? (3) For whom should these goods and services be produced?

In the United States these three questions are answered in a free-market environment. By free market, we mean that people are free to produce, sell, and buy whatever they wish and to work for whomever they want. What goods and services are actually produced, however, is determined by the forces of supply and demand. Producers supply those goods and services that are demanded by consumers.

Over time, changes in technology and in the types of goods and services available from other markets around the world have altered the nature of business and industry.

MAJOR ADVANCES IN AMERICAN BUSINESS AND INDUSTRY

	1607–1783	1783–1850	1850–1900	1900–1920	1920–Present
Power	Human muscles Animals' muscles Wind and water power	Steam power	Electric power Internal combustion engines		Atomic energy Geothermal energy
Manufacturing Materials	Copper, bronze, iron Wood Clay Plant and animal fibers	Large-scale production of iron	Large-scale production of steel Development of combustion fuels: coal, oil, gas	Large-scale production of light metals and alloys Development of plastics and synthetics	Large-scale production of plastics and synthetics
Factory Methods	Handforges and tools Hand-powered equipment	Machinery powered by water and steam Interchangeable parts	Mass production, with centralized assembly of interchangeable parts	Conveyor-belt assembly line	Automation Computer-operated machinery
Agriculture	Wooden plows Spades and hoes Axes and other hand tools	Iron and steel plows Cotton gin Mowing, threshing, and haying machines	McCormick reaper Barbed-wire fencing	Scientific agriculture	Large-scale mechanized agriculture Corporation farms
Transportation	Horses Animal-drawn vehicles Sailing vessels	Canals Clipper ships Development of railroads and steamships	Large-scale steam-ship and railroad lines City trolleys, elevated trains	Automobiles, trucks, and buses Develoment of propeller-driven aircraft	Space exploration Monorail trains Supersonic airplanes
Communication	Hand-operated printing presses Newspapers	Mechanized printing pressess Telegraph Mass-circulation books and magazines	Transatlantic cable Telephones Phonographs Typewriters Cameras	Motion pictures Radios	Television Transistors Computers Compact discs Lasers Satellite transmissions FAX machines
Merchandising and Business Organization	Small shops Peddlers	Individual and family-owned factories and mills General stores	Chain stores Mail-order houses Growth of corporations Trusts	National advertising Holding companies	Shopping malls Conglomerate corporations Multinational corporations

OUR LIVING HERITAGE

One of the best ways to use your historical imagination is by visiting the sites of important events or the homes of famous people. The places listed here are but a few of the many historic sites in the United States. For more information about sites in your community or state, write your county or state historical society.

Many of the sites listed below are under the care of the federal government. These national historic locales are abbreviated **NMP** for military parks, **NHP** for historic parks, **NHL** for landmark, **NHB** for battlefields, **NHS** for sites, and **NM** for national monuments. Page references are included to help you review the importance of the sites described in this book. For further information write the appropriate regional office of the National Park Service.

Western Region, 450 Golden Gate Avenue, San Francisco, CA 94102; **Midwest Region,** 1709 Jackson, Omaha, NB 68102; **North Atlantic Region,** 15 State Street, Boston, MA 02109; **National Capital Region,** 1100 Ohio Drive, SW, Washington, DC 20242; **Southeast Region,** 75 Spring Street, SW, Atlanta, GA 30303; **Rocky Mountain Region,** 655 Parfet Street, PO Box 25287, Denver, CO 80225; **Southwest Region,** PO Box 728, Santa Fe, NM 87501; **Pacific Northwest Region,** Westin Building, Room 1920, Seattle, WA 98121; **Alaska Area,** 540 West 5th Avenue, Room 202, Anchorage, AK 95501.

ALABAMA

Horseshoe Bend NMP north of Dadeville is the site of Andrew Jackson's victory over the Creek nation in 1814. The visitor center has exhibits of Creek culture and frontier life. **307**

Tuskegee Institute NHS in Tuskegee is the site of the pioneer school founded for blacks in 1881 by Booker T. Washington. **617**

Alabama Space and Rocket Center in Huntsville features exhibits including simulated travel to the moon and tours of the Marshall Space Flight Center. **1005**

The First White House of the Confederacy and the **Alabama State Capitol** in Montgomery commemorate the role of Jefferson Davis as president of the Confederacy. **544**

ALASKA

Alaskaland-Pioneer Park in Fairbanks is a 40-acre park recreating a gold rush town and an Indian village. **The University of Alaska Museum** in Fairbanks has displays on Eskimo culture as well as on Russian and gold rush history of the state.

Sitka NHP north of Sitka is a memorial to the Tlingit Indians. The visitor center also has exhibits on life during the time Russia owned Alaska. **740**

ARIZONA

Tombstone NHS preserves this silver rush town of the 1880s. Visitors can see exhibits of the town's history at Schieffelin Hall and the Wells Fargo Museum and tour the underground silver mines.

The Heard Museum of Anthropology and Primitive Art in Phoenix displays arts and crafts of southwestern Indians and Mexicans. It has exhibits on South American cultures and Spanish colonial days.

Casa Grande Ruins in Casa Grande, **Montezuma Castle** east of Prescott, and the **Navajo National Monument** east of Kaibab all have ruins of prehistoric Indian cultures.

ARKANSAS

Arkansas Territorial Restoration in downtown Little Rock is one of the nation's finest, consisting of 13 buildings dating from the 1820s and 1830s.

Ozark Folk Center at Mountain Valley is an 80-acre living museum that features arts, crafts, music, and Ozarks lore.

Fort Smith NHS features Indian and pioneer artifacts in the commissary building, all that remains of a fort that was famous as a gateway to the West.

CALIFORNIA

Hearst San Simeon State Historic Park south of Monterey contains the castle built by publishing tycoon William Randolph Hearst and designed by Julia Morgan. **753**

Marshall Gold Discovery State Historic Site at Coloma, near Sacramento, is where the Gold Rush began in 1848. Attractions include Sutter's Mill, Marshall's cabin, a museum, and the Wah Hop store, which explains the role of the Chinese in the Gold Rush. **432**

Sutter's Fort NHL in Sacramento is a recontruction of that early settlement. The **State Indian Museum** is also located in Sacramento. **431**

Santa Barbara Mission NHL at Santa Barbara is one of the 21 missions founded by Father Junípero Serra. It has a fine collection of original mission treasures. **426**

Bodie NHL near Bridgeport is a ghost town of 170 buildings, reminders of its Gold Rush days. **432**

Fort Ross NHL near Jenner is a restoration of a Russian fort used by seal and otter hunters on the Pacific. **376**

COLORADO

Central City is the site of Colorado's first important gold discovery in 1859. **Cripple Creek, Telluride,** and **Georgetown** are other restored mining towns. **639**

Mesa Verde National Park near Cortez contains hundreds of dwellings inhabited by Indians between 400 and 1300 A.D. **6**

Bent's Old Fort NHS near La Junta preserves a fort and trading post on the Santa Fe Trail. **430**

CONNECTICUT

Old New-Gate Prison in East Granby was originally a copper mine opened in 1707. It was used during the

Revolutionary War to house prisoners of war. Attractions include the prison yard with its scaffold, a museum, and tours of the restored mine and dungeons.

Mystic Seaport and Museum is one of the oldest shipbuilding and whaling ports in the U.S. The seaport preserves the atmosphere of a mid-19th century New England maritime village. At berth is the *Charles W. Morgan*, the last of the 19th-century wooden whaleships.

DELAWARE

Henry Francis du Pont Winterthur Museum in Winterthur contains almost 200 period rooms and displays devoted to American furniture and decorative arts.

The Delaware State Museum in Dover has exhibits on state history, the plantation home of Revolutionary War leader John Dickinson, and the Octagonal School House, a restored school house built in 1836.

Fort Christina NHL in Wilmington marks the landing place of Swedish colonists in 1638. **63**

DISTRICT OF COLUMBIA

The White House, home of every president but Washington, has tours of its splendid public rooms. **270**

The Smithsonian Institution includes the National Air and Space Museum, showing the history of aviation and space travel, the National Collection of Fine Arts; the National Portrait Gallery, from which many portraits in this book were obtained; and the National Museum of History and Technology.

The Library of Congress began with the purchase of Thomas Jefferson's library. On display are Jefferson's rough draft of the Declaration of Independence and Lincoln's drafts of the Gettysburg Address.

The National Archives displays the original Declaration of Independence, the Constitution, and the Bill of Rights.

The U.S. Capitol, seat of Congress, features murals of historic events and statues of presidents and other famous Americans. **270**

Vietnam Veterans Memorial NM in the Congressional Gardens features a black granite wall with the names of those Americans who died in the Vietnam War. **1079**

The Supreme Court Building, seat of the Supreme Court, features murals of the chief justices and other exhibits detailing Court history. **273**

FLORIDA

Cape Canaveral Air Force Station and **John F. Kennedy Space Center,** both near Titusville, are the launching sites of the U.S. manned space flights and the space shuttle. There are tours of the Moon Launch Pad, Vehicle Assembly Building, Mission Control Center, and the Air Force Museum. **1043**

St. Augustine NHL reflects the Spanish heritage of the oldest city in the U.S. The city has many restored buildings and ships. **117**

GEORGIA

New Echota in Calhoun is a restoration of the Cherokee capital. It explains the Cherokees' efforts to establish a republican form of government. **393**

Fort Benning in Columbus has exhibits of U.S. history from the Revolutionary War to the present.

Andersonville NHS preserves this infamous Civil War prison camp.

HAWAII

Pu'uhonua o Honaunau (City of Refuge) NHP features exhibits on life in Hawaii before outsiders arrived in the 1700s.

U.S.S. *Arizona* NM at Pearl Harbor on Oahu is the site of the Japanese bombardment on December 7, 1941. **950**

IDAHO

Massacre Rocks State Park west of American Falls marks an 1862 ambush on a wagon train on the Oregon Trail.

Nez Perce NHP near Spaulding contains 23 historic sites showing the tribe's history and culture. **634**

Fort Hall NHL north of Pocatello is a reconstruction of a fort that was important in the westward migration.

ILLINOIS

Nauvoo Restoration was a Fox Indian village until the Mormons arrived in 1839. **427**

Among Chicago's great museums are the **Chicago Historical Society,** which recreates the Great Chicago Fire, and the **Art Institute,** with its splendid American art.

The Ulysses S. Grant Home is in Galena, once the wealthiest city in Illinois. **580**

Springfield has memorials to Abraham Lincoln including the **Lincoln Home** and the **Old State Capitol** NHL where Lincoln served in the state legislature. Nearby is **New Salem State Park,** a reconstruction of the town as Lincoln knew it in the 1830s. **531**

INDIANA

Lincoln Boyhood National Memorial south of Lincoln City and **Lincoln Pioneer Village** in Rockport preserve the childhood residences of Abraham Lincoln. **377**

The Benjamin Harrison Home NHL in Indianapolis features many of the original furnishings in the home of the 23rd president. **712**

Vincennes, the oldest town in Indiana, has many historic sites, including George Rogers Clark NHP and Grouseland, the home of William Henry Harrison. **173**

The Tippecanoe County Historical Museum in Lafayette has relics of the Battle of Tippecanoe. **299**

IOWA

Herbert Hoover NHS in West Branch features the two-room cottage where the 31st president was born and his presidential library. **889**

The Living History Farm near Des Moines is a working pioneer farm with an 1870 mansion.

Amana Village NHL west of Iowa City gives a view of life in this ideal community founded in the 19th century. **490**

KANSAS

Dodge City, founded in 1872, features Boot Hill; Old Fort Dodge Jail, which houses a museum; and a replica of Old Front Street. **647**

Pawnee Indian Village in Belleville features Pawnee earth lodges from the early 1800s and a museum. **623**

Dwight D. Eisenhower Home in Abilene is the boyhood home of the 34th president and site of his library. **1001**

The John Brown Memorial Park and **John Brown Cabin** in Osawatomie commemorate the abolitionist in Kansas. **522**

KENTUCKY

Cumberland Gap NHP south of Middlesboro marks this pathway to the West first blazed by Daniel Boone. The park includes parts of Boone's Wilderness Road and Hensley Settlement, a reconstructed mountain community. **349**

The Appalachian Museum in Berea features a smoke-house, blacksmith shop, and a country store.

Ashland NHL, a reconstruction of Henry Clay's mansion, is in Lexington. His law office may also be visited. **379**

LOUISIANA

New Orleans Jazz Museum traces the history of jazz and honors jazz greats like Louis Armstrong. **870**

The Vieux Carre Historic District in New Orleans preserves the flavor of the city when it was Spanish and French. Among landmarks are the Cabildo and Jackson Square, where the U.S. flag was first raised over Louisiana Territory. **277**

Chalmette NHP near New Orleans marks the site of the Battle of New Orleans. **310**

MAINE

Shaker Village near Poland is maintained as a living museum of life in this religious community. **490**

Boothbay Railway Museum, the **Grand Banks Schooner Museum,** and the **Boothbay Regional Museum** are all in Boothbay.

The Old Conway House Complex in Camden is an 18th-century farmhouse and restored community.

The Bath Maritime Museum honors the state's ties to the sea. Several grand mansions also stand in Bath.

Roosevelt Campobello International Park on Campobello Island features the summer home of Franklin and Eleanor Roosevelt. **903**

MARYLAND

The U.S. Frigate *Constellation* NHL, the nation's oldest warship, is in Baltimore. **Mount Clare Station** is the nation's first railroad station and the **Baltimore & Ohio Transportation Museum** has a collection of antique railroad engines and cars. **The Peale Museum** NHL features paintings by the Peales, several of which appear in this book. **302**

Fort McHenry NM in Baltimore is the site where Francis Scott Key composed "The Star-Spangled Banner" during the War of 1812. **310**

Antietam National Battlefield near Sharpsburg marks the site of a decisive but costly battle of the Civil War. **568**

MASSACHUSETTS

Lexington Green NHL commemorates the Battle of Lexington and Concord. Nearby are the Buckman Tavern, where the Minute Men gathered before battle, Hancock-Clarke House, where Sam Adams and John Hancock stayed, and Monroe Tavern, headquarters of the British troops. **143**

Freedom Trail in Boston takes visitors past many historic sites, including Faneuil Hall, Paul Revere's House, Old North Church, and the Old State House. At the Boston Naval Shipyard is the U.S.S. *Constitution*. **302**

Among the numerous restored, recreated, or preserved historic towns are **Old Deerfield** (117), **Hancock, Shaker Village** near Pittsfield (490), **Plymouth Plantation** at Plymouth (53), **Quincy** with the Adams NHS (256), **Salem,** and **Old Sturbridge Village.**

Lowell NHP features seven mills, a canal, and the 19th-century buildings of a factory town. **339**

MICHIGAN

Greenfield Village in Dearborn is a recreated American community of the early 19th century. The Henry Ford Museum includes exhibits on American arts and crafts.

The International Afro-American Museum in Detroit tells the history of blacks in America. Also in Detroit are the **Historical Museum** and **Fort Wayne Military Museum.**

Mackinaw Island NHL features many historic buildings, including one of the oldest existing forts in the U.S.

The Gerald R. Ford Museum in Grand Rapids has presidential papers. **1089**

MINNESOTA

Winona is an old steamboat town which features an 1898 Mississippi riverboat at the **Steamboat Museum,** the **Bunnell House,** a pioneer home, and a country museum.

Old Mendota, the oldest permanent settlement in the state, has historic buildings that recall the days when Mendota was a trading post village.

Fort Snelling State Park NHL has been restored near Minneapolis and St. Paul. **The Gibbs Farm Museum** in St. Paul features the farm's original equipment.

MISSISSIPPI

Natchez features many historical sites, including a number of ante-bellum mansion, reflecting its steamboat days. Attractions include Connelly's Tavern, Stanton Hall, and Longwood.

Beauvoir near Biloxi was the home of Jefferson Davis after the Civil War. **544**

Vicksburg National Military Park features extensive remains of breastworks and gun emplacements. **579**

Old Natchez Trace Museum is near Tupelo. The trace was a road used by people who floated their goods down the Mississippi.

MISSOURI

The Trail of Tears State Park near Cape Giradeau contains part of the trail taken by the Cherokees in 1838. **394**

Among the many sites in St. Louis is the sweeping arch of the **Jefferson National Expansion Memorial.** Within the park, site of the original French village, is the **Old Courthouse,** where the Dred Scott case was heard. **527**

Harry S Truman Memorial Library, with its presidential memorabilia, is in Independence. **985**

Sainte Genevieve, the oldest permanent settlement in Missouri, has many buildings in the French style.

MONTANA

Custer Battlefield NM on the Crow reservation marks the site where Sioux and Cheyenne defeated Custer. **632**

Fort Benton Museum features dioramas recalling the days when the site was a stopping point for the Lewis and Clark Expedition and later a trading post. **281**

Virginia City, home of Montana's 1863 gold strike, has restored buildings and museums.

The Grand-Kohrs Ranch NHS near Deer Lodge recaptures life on a large 19th-century cattle ranch. **643**

The C. M. Russell Gallery in Helena holds a good collection of Russell's work, which appears frequently in this book; dioramas; and a recreated 1880 street scene.

NEBRASKA

Buffalo Bill Ranch State Historic Park near North Platte was the ranch of Buffalo Bill Cody. **635**

Brownville, a steamboat town founded in 1854, features a museum with exhibits on pioneer life.

The Stuhr Museum of the Prairie Pioneer in Grand Island recreates a prairie town of the 19th century.

The Bryan House NHL in Lincoln was the home of William Jennings Bryan. **726**

NEVADA

The Nevada State Museum in Carson City features Indian and pioneer history and an underground mine tour.

Virginia City NHL near Carson City is the mining boom town that made fortunes. **639**

NEW HAMPSHIRE

Old Fort No. 4 in Claremont, a replica of a 1744 fort, has exhibits and demonstrations of early means of defense.

The Historic Information Center in Portsmouth, housed in a grand 1784 mansion, can provide information on many buildings of historic interest including the **Strawberry Banks** restoration.

NEW JERSEY

Waterloo Village near Morristown has been restored as a pre-Revolutionary village. **Morristown** NHP was winter headquarters for Washington. The park includes the Ford Mansion, where the Washingtons stayed, Fort Nonsense, and Jockey Hollow. **164**

Edison NHS in West Orange is a complex of buildings in which Thomas A. Edison worked. **667**

Monmouth Battlefield NHL near Freehold is the site of Washington's battle in 1778 that boosted American morale. **170**

NEW YORK

Among the many museums in New York City is **Castle Clinton** NM, a restored fort built to protect New York City during the War of 1812. **The Statue of Liberty** NM, off the tip of Manhattan, features the American Museum of Immigration. **685**

Richmondtown Restoration on Staten Island is a group of 40 buildings that show the evolution of the American village.

The Black History Museum in Hempstead traces the history of American blacks from colonial times. Also on Long Island are **Old Bethpage Village** restoration and **Sagamore Hill** NHS, home of the Theodore Roosevelt family. **798**

The Vanderbilt Mansion NHS and the **Franklin D. Roosevelt Home** and presidential library are in Hyde Park. **903**

Washington's Headquarters NHL at Newburgh is the site where the Washingtons lived in 1782–83. Also at Newburgh are the **Knox Headquarters** and the **Windsor Cantonment,** a military village planned by General von Steuben. **164**

Saratoga NHP near Stillwater marks the site where General Burgoyne surrendered his British army. **167**

West Point NHL is the site chosen by Washington for the U.S. Military Academy. **173**

NEW MEXICO

The Indian Pueblo Cultural Center in Albuquerque explains the Pueblo culture through demonstrations and tours. **6**

Los Alamos Scientific Laboratory has exhibits at Bradbury Science Hall on the uses and applications of nuclear energy. **1106**

The Taos Pueblo NHL, two large five-story pueblos that are still inhabited, and the **Mission of St. Francis of Assisi,** built in the early 1700s, are both near Toas.

Impressive Indian village remains are at **Aztec Ruins** NM near Farmington, **Gila Cliff Dwellings** NM, **Chaco Canyon** NM, and **Bandelier** NM.

NORTH CAROLINA

Oconaluftee Indian Village near Cherokee is a replica of an 18th-century Cherokee village with a museum. **394**

Wright Brothers NM south of Kitty Hawk is the site of the first successful flight in 1903. **873**

Fort Raleigh NHS on Roanoke Island is a reconstruction of the Lost Colony of Roanoke. **43**

Guilford Court House NMP near Greensboro is the site of the Revolutionary War battle that sent Cornwallis in retreat to the coast. **171**

NORTH DAKOTA
Fort Abercrombie State Historic Site near Wahpeton contains reconstructed blockhouses, a stockade, and a museum.
Bonanzaville, U.S.A. near Fargo is a recreated village in the Red River Valley, where gigantic farms flourished. **653**
Frontier Museum and Pioneer Village near Williston has two museums and a reconstructed village.
Fort Mandan State Historic Site near Washburn is a reconstruction of the fort where the Lewis and Clark Expedition spent the winter of 1804–05. **281**

OKLAHOMA
Cherokee National Capitol NHL in Tahlequah was the site of the capital city of the Cherokee Nation. **394**
Indian City U.S.A. near Anadarko is a reconstruction of villages of the Plains Indians.
The National Cowboy Hall of Fame and Western Heritage Center outside Oklahoma City has exhibits on the Old West, including a sod house and an Indian village. **623**

OHIO
Mound City Group NM near Chillicothe is an excavation of a cultural center of the prehistoric Hopewell Indians. **8**
Harriet Beecher Stowe House in Cincinnati is a museum dedicated to the author of *Uncle Tom's Cabin*. **512**
Au Glaize Village near Defiance, **Geauga County Historical Society Century Village** at Burton, **Hale Farm** and **Western Reserve Village** at Bath and **Zoar Village** at Zoar are all 19th-century villages.
Fort Recovery is a state memorial near Fort Recovery and includes a partially restored fort and museum with exhibits on the Indian Wars of the 1790s.

OREGON
Fort Clatsop National Memorial near Astoria is a replica of the fort erected by Lewis and Clark in 1805. **280**
Collier Memorial State Park near Klamath Falls has a logging museum and pioneer village.
Jacksonville Historic District is a restored 1880s gold rush town.

PENNSYLVANIA
In Philadelphia a visitor center provides maps and information about **Independence** NHP, which includes the Liberty Bell, Independence Hall, Congress Hall, and buildings dating from 1732 to 1834. **180**
Gettysburg NMP is the site of a major battle of the Civil War fought in 1863. Here Lincoln later delivered his famous address. **574**
Valley Forge NHP is the place where the American army spent the hard winter of 1777–78. **169**
Fort Duquesne and **Fort Pitt** are landmark sites on the Ohio River. **119**

PUERTO RICO
San Juan NHS contains the Spanish fortresses Castillo El Morro and Castillo San Cristobal, the San Juan Gate, and La Fortaleza, the governor's palace built in 1530.

RHODE ISLAND
Old Slater Mill in Pawtucket consists of restored buildings of the 1793 mill built for early mass production. **335**
Bowen's Wharf of Newport has been restored to show houses and public buildings dating from 1675 to 1820.
Mount Zion Black Museum in Newport exhibits black history and culture in a pre-Civil War church.

SOUTH CAROLINA
In or near Charleston are the sites of **Old Charles Towne,** a restoration of the state's first permanent settlement (66), **Fort Sumter** NM (548), and the **Old Slave Mart Museum.** This beautiful city preserves many gracious homes.
Historic Camden is a restoration of the town the British burnt during the Revolutionary War. **171**
King's Mountain NMP near Spartansburg is the 4,000-acre site of the decisive American victory in 1780. **171**
The Calhoun House (also known as Fort Hill) on the campus of Clemson University in Clemson is the plantation house of John and Floride Calhoun. **374**
Lexington County Homestead Museum, near Columbia, honors Swiss-German settlers.

SOUTH DAKOTA
Wounded Knee Battlefield NHL near Hot Springs is a museum and mass grave commemorating the last important battle between Plains Indians and U.S. army soldiers. **637**
Prairie Village at Madison is a reconstructed late 19th-century town.
Deadwood near Rapid City preserves buildings of a mining town of the Old West. **641**

TENNESSEE
The American Museum of Atomic Energy in Oak Ridge has tours explaining atomic energy and its uses. **1106**
Cades Cove near Gatlinburg is a living museum of pioneer homesteads along an 11-mile stretch of road.
The Hermitage NHL near Nashville is the beautiful home of Andrew and Rachel Jackson, kept as it was when Jackson died in 1845. **382**
Shiloh NMP, the Civil War site, is near Savannah. **578**

TEXAS
The rich historical heritage of San Antonio includes the **Alamo** NHL; **La Villita,** a restoration of San Antonio's earliest community, and the **Spanish Governor's Palace. The San Antonio Mission** NHP includes four of the finest missions in the United States. **406**
Square House Carson County Historical Museum near Amarillo is an 1893 ranch with displays on life in the West. **643**

The **NASA Lyndon B. Johnson Space Center** in Houston has a visitor center and self-guiding tours. **1042**

The **Sam Houston Memorial Museum** in Huntsville has exhibits on Texas Pioneers and the Texas Revolution. **408**

The **Lyndon B. Johnson Presidential Library** in Austin has a replica of the Oval Office and excellent displays. **1029**

UTAH

Pioneer Museum near Provo has a fine collection of regional pioneer artifacts and a pioneer village.

The **Golden Spike** NHS at Promontory marks the spot where the last spike was driven to lay tracks for the first transcontinental railroad. **628**

Salt Lake City Temple Square NHL commemorates achievements of the Mormons. **The Utah Pioneer Village** recreates their pioneer life. **426**

VERMONT

The **President Coolidge Homestead** near White River Junction is the home where Coolidge was sworn in as president. A museum exhibits 19th-century tools. **884**

The **Outdoor Shelburne Museum** at Shelburne includes 18th- and 19th-century houses and a 1903 side-wheel steamboat.

VIRGINIA

Williamsburg NHL, with its over 100 restored buildings in the colonial capital, is a living demonstration of colonial life. **72**

Colonial NHP includes Jamestown Island, site of the Jamestown Colony, and Yorktown, the site where Cornwallis surrendered to Washington in 1781. **47**

Mount Vernon is the lovely home of George and Martha Washington. **236**

Monticello near Charlottesville is the elegant and functional home designed by Thomas Jefferson. **266**

The **Appomattox Court House** NHP at Appomattox was the scene of Lee's surrender to Grant in 1865. **584**

Manassas National Battlefield Park commemorates the Civil War battles of Bull Run and Richmond. **556**

WASHINGTON

The **U.S.S.** *Missouri* in the Naval Shipyard at Bremerton was the scene of the Japanese surrender in 1945. **975**

The **Whitman Mansion** NHS near Walla Walla depicts missionary activity in the West. **412**

The **Willis Carey Historical Museum** near Wenatchee features a typical 19th-century community and many Indian artifacts.

Point Defiance Park at Tacoma holds a replica of the first fort built by the Hudson Bay Company on the Pacific Coast, an old logging camp, and a pioneer home.

WEST VIRGINIA

Lewisburg near White Sulphur Springs features a restoration of the colonial town.

Harpers Ferry NHP preserves the town as it was at the time of John Brown's raid in 1859. **532**

Fort New Salem at Salem is a reconstruction of a settlement founded in 1792.

WISCONSIN

Historic Galloway House and Village in Fond du Lac is a replica of an 1890 village, including a 30-room Victorian mansion.

Stonefield at Cassfield includes a 19th-century frontier village, the home of a gentleman farmer, and a museum.

La Follette Home NHL in Maple Bluff was the home of Robert and Belle Case La Follette. **790**

WYOMING

Fort Laramie NHS near Torrington was an important stop for travelers on the Oregon Trail. **626**

South Pass City near Lander offers a museum and restoration of this gold rush town.

The **Oregon Trail Ruts** NHL near Guernsey shows the ruts made by wagons on the Oregon Trail, some six feet deep. **413**

Glossary

This glossary contains the words you need to understand as you study American history. After each word there is a brief definition or explanation of the meaning of the word as it is used in *The Story of America*. The page number(s) refer to the page(s) on which the word first appears in the textbook.

Phonetic Respelling and Pronunciation Guide

Many of the key terms in this textbook have been respelled to help you pronounce them. The following Phonetic Respelling and Pronunciation Guide offers the simplest form of usage, and for this Glossary is adapted from *Webster's Ninth New Collegiate Dictionary, Webster's New Geographical Dictionary,* and *Webster's New Biographical Dictionary.* The letter combinations used in the respellings are explained below.

MARK	AS IN	RESPELLING	EXAMPLE
a	alphabet	a	*AL·fuh·bet
ā	Asia	ay	AY·zhuh
ä	cart, top	ah	KAHRT, TAHP
e	let, ten	e	LET, TEN
ē	even, leaf	ee	EE· vuhn, LEEF
i	it, tip, British	i	IT, TIP, BRIT·ish
ī	site, buy, Ohio	y	SYT, BY, oh·HY·oh
	iris	eye	EYE ·ris
k	card	k	KARD
ō	over, rainbow	oh	oh·vuhr, RAYN·boh
ù	book, wood	ooh	BOOHK, WOOHD
ò	all, orchid	aw	AWL, AWR·kid
òi	foil, coin	oy	FOYL, KOYN
aù	out	ow	OWT
ə	cup, butter	uh	KUHP, BUHT·uhr
ü	rule, food	oo	ROOL, FOOD
yü	few	yoo	FYOO
zh	vision	zh	VIZH·uhn

*A syllable printed in small capital letters receives heavier emphasis than the other syllable(s) in a word.

A

ABC Powers The countries of Argentina, Brazil, and Chile. **820**

Abilene (AB·uh·leen) Kansas meeting place for Western cattle ranchers and Eastern buyers. **643**

abolitionist (ab·uh·LISH·uh·nists) Person who wanted to end slavery in the U.S. **465**

abominable Hateful or offensive. **385**

absolute monarch Ruler who has complete control. **742**

accommodation Going along with the desires of others. **617**

account Description of facts, conditions, or events. **27**

accountability Responsibility or having to answer for something. **827**

acid rain Rain containing a high concentration of industrial chemicals that falls as pollution. **1104**

ace Pilot in the Great War who shot down five or more enemy airplanes. **840**

adobe (uh·DOH·bee) Building material made of sun-baked brick plastered with mud. **6**

adventure school School for girls that focused on the arts and handicrafts. **485**

advice and consent Senate approval required by the Constitution for major presidential appointments or treaties. **224**

advocate One who supports or defends a cause. **906**

Affluent (AF·loo·unt) **Society** Economist's term to describe the wealthy America of post-World War II. **1032**

AFL-CIO. Organization of labor unions formed when the American Federation of Labor and the Congress of Industrial Organizations merged in 1955. **1034**

aftermath Period immediately following a devastating event such as a war. **1078**

Age of Realism Literary and artistic movement characterized by works that portrayed life and people as they really were. **706**

Age of Reform Period in America between about 1830 and 1850 of social concern and improvement. **476**

Agricultural Adjustment Act (AAA) New Deal legislation passed in 1933 that aided farmers by paying them subsidies for land taken out of production. This reduced the crop surplus and helped raise prices for farm goods. **907**

air pollution Exhaust fumes and other pollutants that harm the earth's atmosphere. **828**

Alamo (AL·uh·mo) San Antonio fort where 187 Texans died fighting for independence. **410**

Alaskan Purchase Land deal by which the United States acquired Alaska from Russia for $7.2 million in 1867. **740**

Albany Plan of Union First plan for uniting the colonies drafted by Benjamin Franklin in 1754. **100**

Alien and Sedition (si·DISH·uhn) **Acts** Four 1798 laws aimed at foreigners and others in the U.S. who were supposedly undermining the government by helping France. **261**

Alliance for Progress President Kennedy's program to provide economic assistance for Latin American countries. **1017**

alliance Agreement made between nations to support each other, especially in times of attack. **817**

Allies (AL·eyez) Nations which fought together in World War I, including the U.S., Great Britain, Italy, and Russia; and those that fought together in World War II, including the U.S., Great Britain, France, and the Soviet Union. **817**

almshouse Home for poor people. **499**

alphabet soup Term referring to the many New Deal agencies that were known by their initials. **929**

Amana (uh·MAN·uh) **community** Shaker settlement founded by Christian Metz in early 1800s. **490**

ambush Trap or surprise attack. **631**

amendment. Change or addition to a bill or law such as to the Constitution. **237**

America Name given to the lands discovered in New World—later North, Central, and South America; after explorer Amerigo Vespucci. **27**

American Colonization Society Group that offered to help former slaves resettle in Africa. **449**

American expansionism Belief that North and South America and the islands of the Pacific should be under the control of the U.S. **738**

American Expeditionary (ek·spuh·DISH·uh·ner·ee) **Force** U.S. military forces that fought in Europe during the Great War. **833**

American Federation of Labor (AFL) National labor union of skilled workers founded in 1886. **681**

American Indian Movement (AIM) Organization founded in 1968 to work for fairer treatment of Native Americans. **1053**

American System Plan developed by Henry Clay in early 1800s for sectional cooperation on legislation. **379**

***Amistad* mutiny** Shipboard revolt by African slaves who were then jailed in America but finally freed when the Supreme Court declared their mutiny legal. **526**

amnesty (AM·nuhs·tee). Official pardon for crimes committed against the government. **593**

Amnesty Act of 1872 Law that reversed the decision to bar former Confederate officials and soldiers from holding public office. **611**

anarchist (AN·uhr·kuhst). One who opposes all government. **767**

anguished (AN·gwisht) Distressed or full of sorrow. **497**

annexation (an·ek·SAY·shuhn) Addition of territory to a country. **405**

anthropologist (an·thruh·PAHL·uh·juhst) Scientist who studies the physical, social, and cultural development of people. **9**

antibiotic (ant·ih·by·OHT·ik) Substance such as penicillin which is produced to kill disease-carrying organisms. **306**

anticipating Looking forward to or expecting. **1035**

Antifederalist Person who supported

strong state governments and opposed ratification of the U.S. constitution. **226**

anti-imperialist Person opposed to imperialism or owning colonies. **762**

antitrust movement Organized effort to regulate business practices that restrained free trade. **676**

antiwar movement Campaign in the United States to end war, especially the Vietnam War. **1073**

Apache (uh·PAACH·ee) Plains Indian tribe that lived in Texas and New Mexico. **623**

apartheid (uh·PAR·teyt) South African policy of separation of the races. **1118**

apocalyptic Forecasting disaster; prophetic. **935**

Appeal to the Colored Citizens of the World Essay by David Walker urging African Americans to fight for freedom. **471**

appellate (uh·PEL·uht) **court** Lower federal appeals court. **224**

Appomattox (ap·uh·MAT·uhks) **Court House** Virginia town where Lee surrendered to Grant ending the Civil War. **584**

appropriate (ah·PRO·pre·ayt) Set money aside for a specific use. **741**

appropriations Funds designated for a specific purpose or program. **985**

Arab Oil Crisis Shortage of petroleum products in the United States in 1973 created by an Arab-controlled OPEC ban on the shipment of oil to countries that supported Israel. **1080**

Arapaho (uh·RAP·uh·ho) Indian tribe that occupied the central region of the Great Plains. **623**

arbitration (ahr·buh·TRAY·shun) Hearing on and settlement of a dispute between two parties by a neutral third party. **745**

arbitration treaties Agreements between nations to try and settle their differences and avoid war. **818**

arch Chief or principal (as in arch-rival). **513**

archaeologist (ahr·kee·AHL·uh·juhst) Scientist who studies history and culture by examining the remains of early human cultures. **9**

archipelago (ahr·kuh·PEL·uh·go) Group of islands. **741**

ardent Very strong. **237**

armistice Truce or agreement between countries to stop fighting. **844**

Army-McCarthy Hearings Senator Joseph McCarthy's investigation of subversive activities in the army. **1003**

Army of Northern Virginia Confederate army commanded by Robert E. Lee. **559**

Army of the Potomac Union army near Washington, D.C., during the Civil War. **557**

arsenal Storehouse of weapons. **195**

Articles of Confederation Agreement under which the thirteen original colonies established a government of states in 1781. **185**

article of impeachment Charge of wrongdoing against the president or other government official. **1084**

artifact (AHRT·i·fakt) Objects made by humans, such as jewelry, tools, or weapons. **9**

assassination (uh·sas·uhn·AY·shuhn) Murder of a public figure. **592**

assay. Test or analyze for content. **639**

assembly Lawmaking body elected by the people. **110**

asset Advantage or helpful resource. **730**

assimilate To absorb into the culture tradition. **686**

astrolabe (AS·truh·layb) Instrument used to measure a ship's latitude or distance from the equator. **19**

Atlanta Major southern city in Georgia that was captured and burned to the ground by General Sherman (1864). **582**

Atlanta Compromise Proposal by Booker T. Washington that blacks and whites both honor the separate-but-equal principle. **617**

Atlantic Charter Agreement between Great Britain and the U.S. to work for a world free of war, signed by Roosevelt and Churchill on August 14, 1941. **948**

atomic bomb Powerful explosive used by the United States to destroy two Japanese cities during World War II. **971**

atonement Being forgiven or reconciled for past sins. **1080**

atrocious (uh·TROH·shus) Horrifying or disgusting. **518**

attainment Accomplishment of a goal. **1097**

attorney general Chief law officer of the nation and legal advisor to the president. **235**

austerity Simple and unadorned. **1019**

autocratic Ruled by a government with absolute authority over all aspects of life. **1109**

Aztecs (AZ·teks) Power Indian rulers of Central Mexico at the time of the Spanish invasion in 1519. **29**

B

Bacon's Rebellion Revolt of Virginia colonists led by Nathaniel Bacon in 1676 which resulted in the killing of Indians, the burning of Jamestown, and the removal of the governor. **105**

balance of power Equal military and economic strength among nations. **817**

Bank Holiday Order by Franklin Roosevelt closing all banks for several days in 1933 while a program to protect the savings of the public was developed. **906**

bank note Paper money supported by gold or silver. **242**

Bank of the United States Central banking system created by Congress in 1791 to support American industries. **242**

bankrupt Out of funds or unable to pay debts. **389**

Barbary pirate Seaman from the North African states who in the early 1800s helped seize and rob ships traveling on the Mediterranean Sea. **275**

barnstorming Traveling from place to place, especially through rural areas, making brief stops. **874**

barrio Hispanic neighborhood in a city. **1094**

base metal Non-precious metal that lies under a coating of gold or silver. **683**

Bastogne (ba·STOHN) French town where Allied forces held back a German advance during World War II. **964**

Battle of Antietam (an·TEET·uhm) (1862) Bloody Civil War clash that caused Confederate troops to withdraw from Maryland. **568**

Battle of Britain Germany's attempt to break Britain spirit and destroy its air force by massive bombings in 1940. **946**

Battle of Buena Vista (bway·nuh·VEE·stuh) American victory by General Taylor in 1847 in Northern Mexico. **420**

Battle of Bunker Hill (1775) First major battle of the Revolutionary War; British suffered heavy losses in defeating patriots. **149**

Battle of Chancellorsville (CHAN·suh·luhrz·vil) Brilliant 1863 Confederate victory in which Stonewall Jackson was killed. **574**

Battle of Cold Harbor Last major victory for Lee and third clash against Union forces led by Grant (1864). **581**

Battle of Cowpens Defeat in 1781 of British in South Carolina. **171**

Battle of Fallen Timbers Decisive fight in 1794 in the Northwest Territory in which Wayne defeated Indians led by Blue Jacket. **248**

Battle of Fredericksburg Victory in 1862 by Confederate forces under Lee that left 12,000 Union soldiers dead. **573**

Battle of Gettysburg Defeat in 1863 of Lee's invasion of the North. **575**

Battle of Horseshoe Bend Defeat of Creek Indians by Andrew Jackson in 1814. **307**

Battle of Kasserine (kas·uh·REEN) **Pass** Tank warfare in 1943 between Americans and Germans in North Africa in World War II. **961**

Battle of Leyte (LAYT·ee) **Gulf** World War II fight in 1944 in the Pacific in which the U.S. navy defeated the Japanese. **968**

Battle of Long Island Revolutionary War conflict in which British General Howe defeated Washington's forces (1776). **164**

Battle of Midway Naval defeat of the Japanese that gave the U.S. control of the central Pacific during World War II (1942). **966**

Battle of Monmouth Court House British defeat by George Washington in 1778. **170**

Battle of New Orleans Major fight won by Jackson after the War of 1812 was officially over (1815). **312**

Battle of Princeton (1776) Revolutionary War battle in which Washington defeated two British regiments. **165**

Battle of Put-in-Bay Perry's defeat of the British navy on Lake Erie in 1813. **305**

Battle of Saratoga Important 1778 American victory in Revolutionary War after which France recognized American independence. **168**

Battle of Seven Pines Civil War clash in which Confederate Commander Johnston was wounded and succeeded by Robert E. Lee. **559**

Battle of Shiloh Costly 1862 Union victory in Mississippi. **579**

Battle of the Argonne Forest Site of 1918 Great War fight in which American forces drove back German troops. **844**

Battle of the Atlantic. Naval war waged between German submarines and the British navy and air force from 1941 to 1943. **947**

Battle of the Bulge. Major German counterattack in 1944 that created a bulge in the Allied line of advance in Europe during World War II. **964**

Battle of the Coral Sea. World War II naval contest in which heavy damage to the Japanese fleet stopped Japan's planned invasion of Australia (1942). **966**

Battle of the Little Big Horn Fight between U.S. Calvary led by Custer and Sioux led by Sitting Bull in which Custer and his men were all killed (1876). **632**

Battle of the Marne. Great War conflict in which French and British troops stopped German advance toward Paris (1914). **822**

Battle of the Thames (TEMZ) Fight in which Harrison won back the Great Lakes region from the British and Tecumseh was killed (1813). **306**

Battle of the Wilderness Clash of Lee's and Grant's forces in the forests southwest of Washington, D.C., resulting in heavy losses on both sides (1864). **581**

Battle of Tippecanoe Fight with the Indians in 1811 that made William Henry Harrison a hero. **299**

Battle of Trenton (1776) Revolutionary War victory during which George Washington defeated Hessian mercenaries. **165**

Bay of Pigs. Site in Cuba of a failed invasion by exiles trained by the U.S. (1961). **1016**

Bear Flag Revolt Defeat of Mexican forces in California by American settlers in 1847. **420**

Beecher's Bibles Name given to guns bought with money raised by abolitionist minister Henry Ward Beecher of New York and sent to antislavery forces in Kansas in the 1850s. **519**

Berlin Capital of Germany that was divided into East and West Berlin after World War II. **965**

Berlin airlift Rescue mission during the Cold War in which the U.S. flew supplies to West Berlin after the Soviets blocked roads. **990**

Berlin Wall Wall built in 1961 to close off communist-controlled East Berlin from West Berlin. **1017**

besieged Under attack or surrounded by the enemy. **547**

Bessemer (BES·uh·muhr) **converter** Invention by Henry Bessemer that made the mass production of steel possible. **661**

bias (BY·us) Prejudice. **267**

Bicentennial Nationwide celebration in 1976 of the 200th anniversary of the Declaration of Independence. **1090**

"big business" Term applied to large

companies with political and social influence. **783**

Big Four Leaders of the Versailles Peace Conference after the Great War; British Prime Minister Lloyd George, French premier Clemenceau, Italian prime minister Orlando, and President Wilson. **848**

Big Red Scare Widespread fear of a communist takeover that swept the U.S. after World War I. **861**

Big Three During World War II, British Prime Minister Churchill, U.S. President Roosevelt, and Soviet dictator Stalin. **980**

Bill of Rights Name given to the first ten amendments to the Constitution. **182**

Birmingham Alabama site of 1963 protest led by Reverend Martin Luther King, Jr., in which local police used dogs and fire hoses against demonstrators. **1055**

Black Cabinet African Americans appointed to government jobs under Roosevelt's New Deal. **923**

Black Codes Regulations passed by southern governments after Reconstruction to restrict the rights of African Americans. **594**

"black gold" Another name for oil. **664**

Black Power Movement in the 1960s by African Americans that supported the use of force and political and economic power in the struggle for equal rights. **1096**

"Black Republican" Name given to the post-Civil War governments in the South. **602**

Black Tuesday Day the stock market crashed, October 29, 1929. **891**

blacklist List of workers in unions who were denied employment. **682**

Bladensburg Village in Maryland taken by the British in 1814 just before their march on Washington. **308**

Bland-Allison Act Law that authorized the purchase and coinage of from $2 to $4 million worth of silver each month (1878). **719**

"Bleeding Kansas" Name given in eastern newspaper accounts to the fighting in Kansas in the 1850s between proslavery and antislavery forces. **522**

blockade runner Small, fast ship used during the Civil War. **563**

blot Bad mark on one's reputation or record. **955**

blue-collar worker Generally an industrial worker or one whose job involves manual labor. **1036**

board of directors Group that makes the decisions for a corporation. **661**

Boland Amendment Law passed in 1984 that prohibited U.S. aid to foreign revolutionary groups. **1116**

bolstered Supported or reinforced. **581**

bonanza (buh-NAN-zuh). Rich deposit of ore. **639**

Bonus March March of Great War veterans on Washington in July 1932 to protest the government's decision to not pay early their compensation for their low pay as soldiers in the war. **901**

boom Period of thriving business activity. **392**

boom town Town that grows suddenly near a gold or silver strike. **641**

boot hill Cemetery for cowboys who "died with their boots on." **647**

bootlegger Person who produces, sells, or transports liquor illegally, especially during Prohibition. **866**

border state State such as Maryland, West Virginia, Kentucky, Delaware, and Missouri that held slaves but did not leave the Union during the Civil War. **536**

borer Tool used to make holes. **334**

borough Administrative district in which a city is divided. **1096**

boss Leader of political machine. **699**

Boston Massacre Incident between British soldiers and Americans in 1770 Boston in which several Americans were killed. **131**

Boston Tea Party Protest in 1773 against British tax on tea during which colonists dumped three shiploads of tea into Boston harbor. **141**

bound Under legal or moral obligation; required. **15**

Boxer Rebellion Uprising in 1900 in China during which foreign property was destroyed and foreign missionaries and business people were held captive. **769**

boycott (BOY-kaht) Refusal to buy certain goods or services as a protest. **128**

Bozeman Trail Route across the Great Plains marked by John M. Bozeman. **630**

bracero (brah-SER-oh) Mexican farm laborer allowed to enter the United States temporarily to do seasonal work. **958**

Brain Trust Advisers of Franklin Roosevelt who were mostly college professors. **913**

brand Mark burned on an animal's hide with a hot iron to show ownership. **645**

Brandeis (BRAN-dys) **brief** Argument presented by Louis D. Brandeis before the Supreme Court that long work hours injured the health of women and children; research for the brief was done by Florence Kelley and Josephine Goldmark. **795**

bread-and-butter issue Concern of labor such as higher wages, shorter hours, and better working conditions. **681**

breadbasket of America Name for the wheat-growing region of the Great Plains. **653**

breadline People waiting to be given free food during the Great Depression. **897**

breadwinner Primary wage earner in a family. **480**

breechcloth Clothing worn by American Indian braves that hung from the waist. **625**

brief Outline of a lawyer's argument or case. **795**

brink Edge. **804**

brinksmanship Policy under President Eisenhower promoted by Secretary of State Dulles to risk all-out war to contain communism. **1001**

bristle Stiffen to show anger or defiance. **614**

British Being of Great Britain, which in colonial days was England, Scotland, Wales, or Ireland. **86**

Brooklyn Bridge Span between Brooklyn and Manhattan that, at the time of its completion in 1883, was the longest bridge in the world. **693**

Brown v. Board of Education of Topeka Landmark 1954 Supreme Court decision that schools must be integrated, overturning "separate but equal" ruling of *Plessy v. Ferguson*. **849**

bugler (BYOO-gler) Person who sounds signals with a bugle or trumpet. **414**

Bull Moose party Nickname for the Progressive party when Theodore Roosevelt ran for president in 1912. **800**

Bull Run Site in Virginia of first battle between Union and Confederate armies, a Confederate victory (1861). **557**

bungled Mishandled. **799**

business cycle Economic trends that move through periods of prosperity and recession. **894**

bust Complete failure or disappointment. **630**

busybody Nosy person who interferes in someone else's business. **500**

C

cabinet Officials who head government agencies and are appointed by and advise the president. **235**

cable car Trolley car pulled up a steep hill by a moving cable. **692**

The Calhouns of South Carolina Wealthy southern family headed by plantation owner and statesman John C. Calhoun. **374**

Cambodia (kam-BOH-dee-uh) Country bordering Vietnam where American troops were sent in 1970 causing widespread protest in the U.S; also called Kampuchea (kam-poo-CHEE-uh). **1073**

Camelot (CAM-uh-laht) Legendary site of King Arthur's court which was noted for its faith in human goodness; often applied to the years of the Kennedy administration. **1019**

Camp David Accords Peace agreement between Israel's Premier Begin and Egypt's President Sadat initiated by President Carter in 1979. **1109**

Canal Zone Strip of land leased to the U.S. by Panama that extends five miles on each side of the Panama Canal. **771**

canal Waterway dug (especially in the 1800s) for transportation, to link rivers and lakes, and for irrigation. **351**

capitalism Economic system in which individuals own and control the factors of production and government intervention is limited. **982**

captor Person who takes someone prisoner. **636**

carbon-14 dating Process used to determine the age of an ancient object by measuring its radioactive content. **9**

Carpetbagger Northerner who went to the South after the Civil War to profit financially from confused and unsettled conditions. **602**

cash-and-carry policy Plan that allowed the United States to sell weapons to warring nations that paid cash and transported the goods in foreign ships. **943**

cash crop Product raised to be sold rather than consumed on the farm. **90**

cattle baron Wealthy and powerful cattle rancher. **644**

cattle kingdom Grasslands of the High Plains that stretched from Texas to Canada and from the Rockies to eastern Kansas used to graze hundreds of thousands of cattle. **643**

cattle town Western town where cattle were bought and sold. **643**

censure (SEN-shur) Officially condemn or disapprove of. **1003**

Central Intelligence Agency (CIA) U.S. organization created in 1947 to gather and analyze political, economic, and military information about other countries. **1016**

Central Powers Germany, Austria, and later Hungary, Turkey, and Bulgaria during the Great War. **817**

Cerro Gordo (ser-uh-GAWRD-oh) Mexican town where Americans won an important battle in 1847 in the War with Mexico. **420**

chain store Store with a number of outlets in different areas. **888**

Challenger U.S. space shuttle that exploded after takeoff in 1986. **869**

championed Defended or upheld. **462**

charter Official government document granting special rights and privileges to a person or company. **42**

Château-Thierry (sha-TOH-ty-ree) French town where American and French forces stopped the German advance in the Great War (1917). **840**

Chattanooga (chat-uh-NOO-guh) Important railway center in Tennessee around which several Civil War battles were fought. **580**

chauvinist (SHOW-vuh-nuhst) Person who has an attitude of superiority toward the opposite sex. **163**

checks and balances. System in which the three branches of government have powers to limit the other branches so that no branch will become too powerful. **224**

Chernobyl (chuhr-NOH-buhl) Soviet nuclear power plant that exploded in 1986 and released massive amounts of radiation over a widespread area. **1105**

Cherokee (CHER-uh-kee) Nation Large group of Indian tribes united under Cherokee law. **395**

Cheyenne (shy-AN) Indian tribe of the Central Great Plains. **623**

Chicago Illinois city that is a major railway and meatpacking center. **643**

Children's Aid Society Group founded to help homeless children by relocating them to farm families and lodging houses. **500**

Chilean Crisis Tension in 1891–92 between Chile and the U.S.

started by a fight in Valparaiso between U.S. sailors and Chileans. **744**

Chinese Exclusion Act Law passed in 1882 that barred Chinese laborers from entering the United States for 10 years. **689**

Chisholm Trail One main route over which Texans drove cattle to market. **643**

Chivington Massacre Slaughter of Cheyenne that provoked Indian attacks on settlers; also called the Sand Creek Massacre. **630**

cholera (KOL·er·uh) Deadly intestinal disease. **347**

church school Early American school taught by the minister and his wife. **484**

Circular Letter Plea issued by the Massachusetts legislature to other colonial assemblies that all colonists act together to resist taxation without representation. **130**

circumnavigate (suhr·kuhm·NAV·uh·gayt) To sail completely around the world. **29**

citizenship Legal membership in a country or state; a citizen is granted rights by the country or state and in return has certain duties and obligations, such as obeying the law. **1109**

civic Of or relating to citizens and citizenship. **600**

Civil Rights Act of 1866 Law that made African Americans citizens of the United States. **595**

Civil Rights Act of 1875 Law that prohibited segregation of public places. **614**

Civil Rights Act of 1964 Law that made it easier and safer for southern African Americans to vote and that prohibited racial discrimination in public facilities. **853**

Civil Rights Cases Lawsuits concerning the constitutional rights of black Americans. **614**

Civil Rights Committee Group appointed by Truman in 1947 to recommend laws to protect the rights of African Americans. **993**

Civil Rights Movement Campaign in the 1960s to achieve equality for Black Americans. **856**

Civil Service Commission Agency established in 1883 to design and administer examinations for certain government positions. **705**

civil service reform Effort to improve government service by adopting an employment system based on skill and merit rather than on politics. **704**

Civil War (1861–1865) Conflict between the northern (Union) and southern (Confederacy) states over the issues of slavery and states' rights. **548**

Civil War Amendments Three constitutional amendments (13th, 14th and 15th) guaranteeing civil rights to African Americans. **600**

Civil Works Authority New Deal agency created in 1934 to help the unemployed find jobs. **912**

Civilian Conservation Corps (CCC) New Deal agency that put some 3 million young men to work on conservation and rural improvement projects. **912**

clan Social or family group. **5**

Clayton Antitrust Act Law that prohibited a person from serving as a director in more than one corporation and which exempted labor unions from antitrust laws (1914). **804**

Clayton-Bulwer Treaty Agreement in 1850 between Great Britain and America that neither would take exclusive control of a canal between the Atlantic and Pacific oceans. **770**

clipper ship Sailing ship of the 19th century built for speed. **432**

close state State neither strongly Republican or strongly Democratic where either party might win a national election. **698**

closed shop Business that hires only members of a labor union. **985**

clout Influence or power. **686**

Coercive (ko·UHR·siv) **Acts** Series of laws passed by the British to punish the colonists for the Boston Tea Party; also called Intolerable Acts. **142**

Cold War Tensions between the U.S. and Russia after World War II. **982**

collective bargaining Right of a labor union to bargain for all workers employed by a business. **682**

collective security World security guaranteed by an agreement among all nations to join in action against a nation that attacks any one of them. **941**

Columbian Exchange Exchange of material things and ideas between Europe and America. **36**

Comanche (kuh·MAN·chee) Plains Indians of Texas and New Mexico. **623**

commandos Small force of soldiers who specialize in raids in enemy territory. **532**

commenced Began. **133**

Commercial Revolution Economic expansion in Europe that occurred from 1450 to the 1700s. **18**

commissioned Awarded a military rank and the authority that goes with it. **958**

commission Committee formed for a specific purpose and with specific powers to act. **101**

Committee of Correspondence Group formed by radicals in colonies to spread the protest of British rule. **143**

Commodity Credit Corporation Organization created in 1938 that paid farmers money for surplus crops kept in storage, resulting in higher prices because there were fewer crops on the market. **926**

commodities (kuh·MAH·duht·ees) Goods. **831**

common man Ordinary American rather than a representative of the rich and wealthy. **383**

commonwealth Territory in which there is self-government. **58**

communications revolution More rapid, long-distance communication made possible by the inventions of the telegraph and telephone. **665**

communist Economic system in which the government owns or controls almost all the means of production. **982**

Communist Revolution Rebellion in 1917 in Russia in which the communist party took control. **838**

compass Instrument used to tell direction. **19**

compelled Forced or driven. **86**

compensated Given payment to make up for a loss or shortage. **569**

component Part or ingredient. **893**

Compromise of 1850 Resolution that temporarily settled disputes between the North and South over slavery issues. **443**

Compromise of 1877 Concessions made by Republicans and Democrats that settled disputed election of 1876 by which Hayes became president. **612**

compulsive Having the power to compel or force. **197**

computer (kohm·PYOO·ter) Electronic machine that can store, retrieve, and process information rapidly. **1039**

Comstock (KAHM·stahk) **Lode** Extremely rich silver deposit in Nevada. **639**

conceive To think of. **86**

concentration System of separating and thereby controlling the Indian tribes of the Great Plains by placing them on reservations. **626**

concentration camp Nazi prison were prisoners of war, especially the Jews, are held. **938**

concept Thought or idea. **59**

concession Something given in a compromise. **223**

conclusively Without a doubt. **1084**

Concord One of two Massachusetts towns (along with Lexington) where the first battles of the Revolutionary War were fought (1775). **144**

Conestoga (kahn·uh·STOH·guh) **wagon** Sturdy covered wagon used by many of the pioneers who moved westward. **374**

confederacy Alliance of independent states. **544**

Confederate States of America Association of 11 independent southern states formed after their secession from the Union in 1860–61. **544**

confederation Union of groups for a common cause. **9**

conferring Giving or bestowing

upon; as in an honor or award. **1111**

conform To go along with the majority or to behave according to rules or standards set by society. **1050**

Congress Legislative, or lawmaking, branch of government made up of the House of Representatives and the Senate. **220**

Congress of Industrial Organizations (CIO) National labor union formed in 1935 to organize all the workers in mass production industries. **927**

conquest Something that has been taken over or conquered. **2**

conquistador (kawn·KEES·tuh·dawr) Spanish soldier who helped conquer Mexico and Peru. **31**

Conscience Whigs. Northern members of the Whig party who were against slavery (see **Cotton Whigs**). **523**

conscientious Behaving according to what is right or honest. **234**

conscientious objector. One who refuses to serve in the military because of moral or religious beliefs. **939**

consciousness-raising Increasing awareness, usually about a social or political issue. **1052**

conscript To draft people by law to serve as soldiers. **565**

conservation Protection or preservation from waste or loss, such as natural resources. **798**

conservative Tending to go by established methods; slow to change. **182**

consolidated Joined together into one or under one system. **781**

constitution Written plan of government that includes its laws and principles. **182**

Constitutional Convention Meeting of 12 states (all but Rhode Island) in Philadelphia in 1787 to draft the U.S. Constitution. **197**

Constitutional Unionist Party Political party formed in 1860 that ignored the slavery issue in hopes of preserving the Union. **536**

consumption Using up of, as of goods or services. **560**

containment policy U.S. strategy in the 1950s aimed at limiting the spread of communism. **991**

contempt Disrespect or scorn. **119**

contend Struggle or compete. **273**

continental divide Ridge of the Rocky Mountains that separates rivers flowing generally east from those flowing generally west. **281**

Continental dollars Paper money printed by Congress after the Revolutionary War to pay its debts. **196**

contraband (KAWN·truh·band) Slave who crossed Union lines during the Civil War. **565**

contrary Opposite or not in agreement with. **465**

Contras (KAWN·truhs) Nicaraguan counter-revolutionaries who received aid from the U.S. in their effort to overthrow the ruling Sandinista government. **1114**

cooperatives Farms or other enterprises owned and operated jointly by members who share in the benefits. **899**

covenant Formal and binding agreement. **849**

Convention of 1800 Treaty that prevented war between France and the United States in 1799. **269**

convoy Fleet of ships that is accompanied or escorted by a protective force. **286**

"cooling-off" period Time that a union could be forced to delay a strike if that strike threatens national interest. **985**

co-op (KOH·ahp). Group formed through the Farmers' Alliance in order to sell crops and to purchase goods at better prices for members. **720**

Copperhead Northerner who opposed the Civil War. **561**

corporation Business owned by stockholders and run by a board of directors. **661**

Corps of Discovery Group chosen by Lewis and Clark to help them explore the Louisiana Territory. **280**

cotton boll (bol) Seed pod of a cotton plant that grows into a fibrous ball. **450**

cotton diplomacy Belief that England

and France would support the Confederacy to insure their supply of cotton. **564**

cotton gin Machine invented by Eli Whitney in 1793 that separated cotton fibers from the seeds. **451**

"Cotton Is King" Southern slogan which meant that cotton, and therefore slavery, was essential to the region. **463**

county court Local government in the southern colonies. **110**

court Official gathering to rule on legality of an action. **182**

Coxey's Army Band of unemployed workers who, led by Jacob Coxey, marched on Washington to protest the plight of the unemployed (1894). **724**

cradle Tool used to cut grain. **561**

Creek War Indian attacks in 1813 in Alabama in which more than 400 settlers were killed. **306**

Crime of 1873 Name given by farmers and miners to the law that discontinued the mining of silver. **718**

crop-lien (KRAWP·leen) **system** Agreement in which supplies were lent to a farmer by merchants or landowners in exchange for portions of the crops. **608**

Cross of Gold speech William Jennings Bryan's stirring appeal for the free coinage of silver that got him the Populist Party's nomination for president (1896). **728**

crucial (KREW·shuhl) Extremely important. **184**

Crusade One of a series of religious wars between 1100 and 1300 undertaken by the Christians in Europe to regain the Holy Land from the Moslems. **16**

Cuba Island with a communist government about 90 miles south of Florida. **1016**

Cuban Missile Crisis Tense confrontation in 1962 between the U.S. and the Soviet Union over the building of Soviet missile bases in Cuba. **1018**

culminated Reached the end or resulted in. **363**

culture Special characteristics of the people who make up a society, such as their language, govern-ment, how they make a living, family relationships, and how they educate their children. **4**

Cumberland Road First road built linking East and West from Maryland to Illinois; also called the National Road. **350**

cumbersome Hard to handle because of weight or bulk. **152**

curriculum Courses offered by a school. **450**

cutbacks Reductions or decreases. **889**

D

D-Day Beginning of the Allied invasion of France on June 6, 1944, to drive out Hitler's occupying armies. **963**

dadaism Art movement of the 1920s that was a protest against traditional artistic values. **871**

dame schools Urban school in early America taught by women. **484**

dark horse Political candidate who unexpectedly wins a party's nomination. **405**

Dawes Severalty (SEV·uh·ruhl·tee) **Act** Law that divided reservations into quarter sections of land owned by individual Indian families (1887). **638**

deadlock Standstill created when opposing sides are unable to break a tie. **885**

Declaration of Independence Document adopted by the Second Continental Congress in 1776 that declared American independence from Great Britain and listed the reasons for this action. **157**

Declaratory (di·KLAR·uh·tawr·ee) **Act** Law passed in 1766 by the British parliament that declared the American colonies subject to British law. **128**

deep-seated Firmly established or hard to remove. **85**

Deerfield English settlement in Massachusetts destroyed by the French during Queen Anne's War. **117**

defame To speak badly of or ruin a reputation. **261**

deficit (DEF·uh·suht) **spending** Paying out more public funds than are raised in taxes. **834**

deflation (de·FLAY·shun) Decline in prices caused by a decrease in money supply or spending. **703**

deliberate Slow and careful in acting. **546**

demand Amount of a product or service that the public is ready and able to buy. **875**

demilitarized Not controlled or used by the military. **1003**

Democrat Member of the political party begun in the early 1800s that supported strong states' rights and government made up of many classes of people. **382**

Democratic-Republican Member of one of the first two political parties; its members favored policies of Jefferson such as restricting the powers of federal government over the states. **255**

democracy Form of government in which power is vested in the people and exercised by them through a system of free elections. **79, 162**

demoralizing Weakening the spirit. **1100**

denounced Stated disapproval of or condemned. **503**

department of state Government bureau that advises the president on foreign relations. **234**

department store Large store selling a variety of goods arranged in different sections. **669**

depressed Period of low economic activity. **895**

depression Period of severe decline in business activity, usually marked by high levels of unemployment. **191**

descendant Offspring. **9**

desist Stop or cease to act. **804**

destined Intended or determined beforehand. **404**

destiny Something to which a person or group is destined; a predetermined course. **819**

détente (day·TAHNT) Reduction of or tensions between two countries, particularly the United States and the Soviet Union. **1076**

Glossary   1157

deteriorate (dee·TIHR·ee·ohr·ayt) To grow worse or decline in quality or condition. **1050**

detonated. Set off or caused to explode. **843**

development Generally a suburban neighbrhood in which a number of similar houses have been built. **1044**

dickering Bargaining to reach an agreement or compromise. **316**

dictator (DIK·tayt·uhr) Ruler with absolute power. **269**

dignified Calm, reserved, or noble. **237**

diplomacy Art of handling negotiations between nations. **827**

direct primary Preliminary election within the parties to choose candidates to run for public office. **791**

disallow Refuse permission. **110**

disarmament (dis·AHRM·uh·ment) Reduction or limitation in the number of weapons of war. **859**

disrepair In need of repair. **890**

dissent Judge's statement of disagreement with the opinion or decision of the majority. **616**

distinct Clearly different or distinguishable. **4**

distortion Twisting or stretching of the true facts. **367**

district court Lower federal trial court in each specified U.S. region. **224**

District of Columbia Federal area designated as the permanent capital of the United States. **255**

diversified (duh·VUHR·suh·fyd) **economy** Type of economy that depends on both manufacturing and agriculture. **330**

divide and conquer Military strategy to weaken an opponent by scattering its forces. **626**

division of labor Separation of the manufacturing steps into specialized tasks to speed and increase production. **663**

doctrine Statement of principles, system of beliefs, or government policy. **97**

doctrine of nullification (nuhl·uh·fuh·KAY·shun) Theory put forth in 1798 that because the United States Constitution limited power of the federal government over the states, a state had the right to refuse to accept a national law it disagreed with. **268**

Dodge City Kansas cattle town famous as a rowdy entertainment center for cowboys. **647**

dogfight Battle between fighter planes, usually at close range. **840**

doggedly In a stubborn, persistent manner. **940**

dollar diplomacy U.S. policy in the early 1900s of investing money in Latin American countries in hopes that more stable governments would result. **777**

domineering Controlling or ruling with arrogance or tyranny. **937**

dominate Control or rule over. **2**

Dominion of New England Territory created by King James II of England in 1686 in an attempt to unify the British colonies. **111**

domino theory Idea that if a country fell to communism, the countries on its borders would also fall; key principle of U.S. foreign policy from the 1950s to the 1970s. **1061**

Dorchester Heights Site near Boston of General Washington's first victory against the British in the Revolutionary War. **155**

dormant Not actively growing but protected from the environment (as in the life cycle of plants.) **2**

dove Person opposed to war. **1064**

"Drake's Folly" Nickname for the first oil well, drilled by E. L. Drake of Titusville, Pennsylvania (1859). **664**

Dred Scott v. Sandford Supreme Court ruling in 1857 that Scott, a former slave who sued for his freedom, was still a slave despite living in a free state for a time. **527**

dredged. Widened or made deeper by removing dirt. **772**

drought Long period of dry weather that stunts crop growth. **651**

drudgery Dull and tiresome work. **596**

dry farming Technique used to raise crops in areas with little rainfall. **651**

dry states States that adopted prohibition. **866**

dumbfounded Surprised to the point of being speechless. **278**

Dunkirk. French town where German troops forced a major evacuation of Allied forces during World War II. **944**

duty Tariff or tax placed on foreign goods brought into the country. **124**

dwindled Grew less and less. **1045**

dynamic Energetic, forceful or powerful. **97**

E

East Germany Country under communist control created when Germany was divided between Allied powers after World War II. **1003**

East India Company British company; given assistance in selling tea in the colonies by the parliament in 1773, leading to the Boston Tea Party. **138**

Eastern Front Combat zone in Eastern Europe during the Great War. **822**

Economic Opportunity Act Law passed in 1964 that attacked poverty in the U.S. through programs such as Head Start, the Job Corps and VISTA. **1030**

economy System of producing, distributing, and consuming goods or services. **35**

egalitarian Marked by the belief in equal social and political rights for all people. **385**

Eighteenth Amendment Constitutional change that prohibited the manufacture and sale of alcoholic beverages (1919). **866**

El Caney (el·kuh·NAY) Site of major 1898 battle in Cuba during Spanish-American War. **756**

elaborate Complicated or very detailed. **7**

elastic clause "Necessary and proper" clause of the Constitution often used to expand the powers of Congress. **243**

elderly People approaching old age. **888**

elector Person selected in a state to cast an electoral vote for president. **223**

electric light Invention by Edison that makes light by passing electricity through a fine wire housed in a bulb. **667**

electric trolley System of streetcars propelled along tracks by electric currents from overhead wires. **692**

electrified Excited or thrilled. **1019**

Elementary and Secondary Education Act Law passed in 1965 that provided federal money to support school programs in low-income areas. **1046**

eligible Meeting the requirements or being qualified. **698**

elite (uh·LEET) Small privileged group. **505**

Elk Hills Government-owned oil reserve in California. **884**

emancipate To free. **569**

emancipation (i·man·suh·PAY·shun) Freedom. **466**

Emancipation Proclamation Decree issued by Abraham Lincoln in 1863 freeing slaves in the South. **570**

Embargo Act Law passed in 1807 prohibiting all exports from the U.S. in response to the impressment of American sailors by the British. **288**

embodied Represented. **199**

Emergency Quota Act Law passed in 1921 limiting by nationality the number of United States immigrants. **865**

empresario Mexican word to describe businessmen who brought settlers into Texas. **408**

enclosure movement Period when British landowners fenced in their fields and began raising sheep. **44**

endeavor Effort or attempt to accomplish something. **449**

endorsement Public statement of approval. **947**

enlightened Informed. **222**

Enlightenment Intellectual movement in the 1750s characterized by a belief in the power of human reason and marked by many scientific discoveries and inventions. **98**

enterprise Project or undertaking. **48**

entrepreneur (ahn·truh·pruh·NUHR) Person who develops a business. **670**

enumerated (i·NOOH·muh·rayt·uhd) **articles** Goods produced in the American colonies that could be sold only within the British empire. **114**

environment Everything in people's surroundings that affects them in any way; nature. **6**

Environmental Protection Agency (EPA) Department established in 1970 to monitor pollution and seek ways to reduce it. **1098**

Equal Rights Amendment Failed Constitutional amendment proposed in 1972 to provide that equal rights for women. **1101**

"Era of Good Feelings" Period from 1817 to 1821 when the country was prosperous and at peace under President Monroe. **364**

Erie Canal New York waterway completed in 1825 that connected the Hudson River to Lake Erie. **351**

escalation Increase in military involvement. **1062**

escapades Wild adventures. **41**

Espionage Act Law passed in 1917 that made it a crime to help enemy countries or to interfere with military recruitment. **837**

ethical Behaving according to what is considered moral or right. **238**

ethics Code of morals of a particular society, religion, or group. **708**

ethnic neighborhood City community made up of immigrants from the same country. **686**

even-handed Fair or just. **253**

ever-normal granary System of storing grain in government granaries rather than selling it to help regulate prices and keep surpluses off the market. **926**

evolution Theory that all living species and animals developed from simpler lifeforms. **867**

excavate To uncover objects underground by digging. **280**

excerpts Selected or quoted sections of a book or other source. **117**

executive Person or branch of the government responsible for enforcing or carrying out the laws. **182**

executive privilege Right to keep information about presidential matters secret. **1083**

exempted Released or freed from duty. **565**

expatriate Person who leaves his or her native country permanently. **877**

expeditionary force Name given to American troops sent to foreign countries. **754**

exploit (EK·sploit) Heroic and daring act. **303**

exploitation Unfair use of another person or situation for one's own advantage. **738**

extorted Took by force. **142**

extremist Person who holds radical ideas or supports radical measures. **245**

F

faction Group within a group that has its own goals. **535**

factors of production Resource used to produce goods and services. **1033**

Fair Deal President Truman's proposals to extend New Deal programs. **984**

Fair Employment Practices Committee Commission created in 1941 to prevent job discrimination against racial and ethnic groups and women. **958**

Fair Labor Standards Act. Act that outlawed child labor and set a 40-hour work week (1938). **927**

far-flung Widely spread or distributed. **108**

Farm bloc Group of U.S. representatives from heavily agricultural states organized to support the interests of farmers (1921). **889**

Farmers Alliance Social organization that became a political force to represent farm interests. **720**

fascism (FASH·iz·uhm) Political movement that stresses nation and race; begun in Italy in 1919 under Mussolini. **937**

fateful Having important consequences. **1062**

favorable balance of trade Situation in which a country exports more than it imports, or sells more than it buys. **112**

federal deficit Shortage in federal income. **929**

Federal Deposit Insurance Corporation (FDIC) Federal agency created to protect savings deposits in banks. **906**

Federal Emergency Relief Administration Department created in 1933 to distribute money to agencies that helped the poor. **912**

Federal Highway Act Law passed in 1956 that provided federal funding for construction of interstate highways. **1007**

Federal Reserve Act Law passed in 1913 that created a national banking system of 12 Federal Reserve Banks. **804**

Federal Reserve Board Government agency that oversees the operation of the Federal Reserve System. **804**

Federal Securities Act Law passed in 1933 that regulated the way companies issue and sell stock. **908**

Federal Trade Commission Agency-created in 1914 to help eliminate unfair business practices and to enforce antitrust laws. **804**

federalism Sharing of power by the national and state governments. **198**

Federalist Papers Series of newspaper articles written in 1787-88 that explained and defended the U.S. Constitution. **228**

Federalists One of the first two political parties; its members supported a strong central government and a powerful executive branch. **226**

feudal system Structure of society in medieval Europe in which peasants were bound to a lord who, in turn, owed service or payments to a higher ruler. **15**

Fifteenth Amendment Constitutional amendment that guarantees all citizens the right to vote. **600**

Fifty-Niner Nickname given to a prospector who went to Colorado in 1859 in search of gold. **630**

figurehead Leader in name only, wih little or no power. **222**

filament Fine, threadlike wire that glows when heated by electric current. **667**

fireside chat Informal presidential speech given by Franklin Roosevelt in the 1930s. **913**

First Amendment Constitutional amendment that guarantees freedom of speech, religion, and the press, and the right to assemble peacefully. **266**

First Continental Congress. Meeting of colonial delegates in 1774 at which the colonies demanded repeal of the Intolerable Acts. **143**

fiscal (FIS·kuhl) **policy** Means of stimulating the economy through government spending and taxation. **1041**

Five Nations League of Iroquois tribes that inhabited the eastern woodlands of the Northern United States. **9**

Five-Power Naval Treaty Agreement in 1922 between the U.S., Great Britain, Japan, France, and Italy to a ten-year ban on the construction of warships. **859**

five themes of geography Basic concepts—location, place, relationships within places, movement, and region—considered by many geographers as key to the understanding of geography. **860**

fixed cost Regular expense involved in running a business. **673**

flagrant Obviously wrong. **997**

flagship Ship that carries the commander of a fleet. **752**

flank Right or left edge of an army. **171**

flappers Young women whose bold actions and dress expressed a new spirit of freedom after World War I. **871**

fleet Swift. **622**

fluently With an easy command of the language. **246**

folk tale Story that has been passed down from generation to generation. **9**

foothold Secure position that can be used as a base for further advance. **519**

forge Furnace or shop where iron products are made. **114**

forged Formed or shaped, usually with great effort. **593**

Fort Donelson Confederate fort n Tennessee taken in 1862 by Grant sson after his capture of Fort Henry. **578**

Fort Henry Confederate fort in Tennessee captured by Grant in 1862. **578**

Fort McHenry Fort in Baltimore harbor where Americans stopped a British attack in 1814; this battle was the inspiration for "The Star-Spangled Banner." **310**

Fort Pitt French Fort Duquesne captured and renamed by the British during the French and Indian War. **121**

Fort Sumter Federal fort in Charleston, South Carolina, harbor where an attack by southern forces began the Civil War. **543**

Forty-Niner Nickname given to a prospector who went to California in 1849 in search of gold. **432**

Four Freedoms Freedom of speech and religion, freedom from want and fear, mentioned in 1941 Franklin Roosevelt speech. **947**

Fourteen Points Peace program outlined by President Wilson in 1918. **845**

Fourteenth Amendment Constitutional amendment that made African Americans citizens of their states as well as of the U.S., guaranteed their civil rights, and gave them equal protection of the laws. **597**

Fourth of July American Independence Day celebrating the anniversary of the signing of the Declaration of Independence. **157**

framer Author of a document. **254**

franchise (FRAN·chyz) Right to do business granted by the government. **699**

frayed Ragged or torn. **273**

free coinage Act of turning all available silver into coins. **720**

free enterprise Economic system in which there is limited government control over business practices. **677**

free soiler Person opposed to slavery who could go to Kansas and vote to keep slaves out. **519**

Free-Soil party Political party founded in 1848 by northern Democrats who were opposed to popular sovereignty. **437**

free state State that did not allow slavery. **436**

freedmen Former slaves. **594**

Freedmen's Bureau Organization run by the army to care for protect southern blacks after the Civil War. **595**

freeman Person who has all the political and civil rights of citizebship in a city, state, or nation. **58**

Freeport Doctrine Stephen Douglas' statement that the people have the ultimate power to decide if slavery should or should not exist in a location. **531**

French Revolution Rebellion beginning in 1789 of the poor French lower classes against the monarchy that resulted in the establishment of a Republic. **244**

frenzy State of wild excitement. **980**

frigate American warship of the early 1800s. **302**

frontier Edge of a settled region. **79**

Fulton's Folly Name skeptics gave the *Clermont*, Fulton's first steamboat. **354**

functional illiteracy Not being able to read or write well enough to hold a job or function in a complex society. **891**

Fundamental Orders First written form of government in America; drafted by representatives of the first settlements along the Connecticut River. **58**

fundamentalism. Conservative religious beliefs. **867**

fur trade Early American industry involving the sale of hides and furs to Europe. **92**

G

Gadsden Purchase Land along the southern borders of New Mexico and Arizona purchased from Mexico in 1853 to allow construction of the Southern Pacific Railroad. **515**

galleon Heavy sailing ship used as a commercial vessel or a warship in the 15th to 18th centuries. **41**

generalization Broad statement based on loosely associated facts. **5**

genocide Deliberate and planned destruction of a race or cultural group. **938**

Gentlemen's Agreement Deal in 1907 in which Japan promised not to allow laborers to come to the United States. **805**

geography Study of the the physical and cultural features of the earth. **22**

Gettysburg Address Speech containing a classic expression of American democratic ideals delivered by President Lincoln in 1863. **575**

ghetto Section of a city where members of racial or ethnic groups live because of economic or social pressures. **862**

ghost town Abandoned mining town. **435**

ghoulish (GOOL·ish) Horrible or disgusting. **1110**

G.I. Bill of Rights Program under established in 1944 which enabled veterans to obtain low-cost loans to buy homes or start businesses. **955**

Gilded Age Period between 1865 and 1900 that was marked by growth in industry and the availability of consumer goods but also by business corruption, greed and materialism. **683**

glasnost (GLAS·nohst) Spirit of openness and freedom in the Soviet Union begun under Gorbachev. **1115**

Glorious Revolution English uprising in 1688 in which the Catholic king James II was replaced by the Protestant monarchs William and Mary. **111**

Gold Rush Surge of 80,000 miners to California to look for gold in 1848. **432**

gold standard Monetary system that used only gold to mint coins and to back bank notes. **723**

Golden Age of Sports Period during the 1920s when the radio, increased leisure time and money, and public relations efforts caused spectator sports to become very popular. **873**

Golden Rule Principle of conduct that states,"Do unto others as you would have them do unto you" followed by reform mayor Samuel M. Jones. **789**

Goliad Texas town where 350 Texans were killed by Mexican troops in 1836. **410**

government bond Interest-bearing certificate sold by the government to raise revenue. **241**

governor Chief executive of an English colony or American state. **109**

grandfather clause Law which eliminated literacy tests and poll taxes for persons who had voted before 1867 and their descendants. This meant only white men qualified to vote. **613**

graphic Showing realistic or lifelike detail. **709**

grappled Grab hold of. **273**

"Great American Desert" Nickname given to the Great Plains by early explorers. **623**

Great Awakening Time in the 1740s of widespread religious fervor; a force for toleration in the colonies. **95**

Great Compromise Agreement made at the Constitutional Convention in 1787 to create a House of Representatives elected by the people on the basis of population and a Senate elected by the state legislatures, two members from each state. **220**

Great Depression Economic crisis from 1929 to 1940. **895**

Great Plains Geographic region that extends from western Texas north to the Dakotas and into Canada and west to the foothilss of the Rockies. **623**

Great Society Social and economic programs of President Lyndon Johnson. **1031**

Great Stock Market Crash Disastrous fall in the stock prices in 1929 that signaled the end of the prosperity of the 1920s. **891**

Great War Name given to World War I, which broke out in Europe in 1914. **809**

greenback Paper money which was not exchangeable for gold or silver coins. **702**

greenhouse effect Warming of the earth's surface caused by air pollution in the earth's atmosphere. **1104**

Guadalcanal (gwahd·uhl·ka·NAL) Pacific island that was the scene of heavy fighting during World War II. **968**

Guam (GWAHM) Pacific island that became U.S. territory after the Spanish-American War. **761**

guano (GWAHN·oh) Manure of sea birds or bats used as fertilizer. **369**

guerrilla (guh·RIL·uh) Fighter who commits sabotage or surprise attacks. **522**

guerrilla warfare Fighting by ambush and surprise raids, often behind enemy lines. **747**

Guilford Court House Site in South Carolina of an American victory in 1781. **171**

gunboat diplomacy Name for the policy of the Roosevelt Corollary, which said the U.S. would make a show of force to prevent European interference in events in the Western Hemisphere. **777**

H

haggled Argued about terms or price. **745**

hail Relentless showering. **312**

Hanoi (ha·NOY) Capital of North Vietnam. **1078**

haphazard Without any plan or order. **690**

hard-hitting Forceful. **785**

hard money Gold or silver coins, or paper money that could be exchanged for gold or silver. **193**

Harlem Globetrotters Traveling team of African American basketball players famous for its skill and fancy ball-handling. **874**

Harlem Renaissance (ren·uh·SAHNS) Period during the 1920s when New York City's Harlem became an intellectual and cultural capital for African Americans. **872**

Harpers Ferry Site of a government arsenal raided in 1859 by John Brown and his commandos. **532**

Hartford Convention Meeting of New England states in 1814 to discuss separation from the Union. **313**

havoc Great damage or ruin. **755**

Hawaiian Islands Group of islands in the Pacific Ocean that the United States annexed in the 1890s. **741**

hawk Person who supports war. **1064**

Hay-Bunau-Varilla Treaty Agreement with Panama granting the U.S. a 10-mile canal zone through Panama (1903). **772**

Haymarket bombing Incident during an 1886 Chicago strike in which a bomb exploded, turning public opinion against unions. **681**

Hay-Pauncefote (PAHNS·fooht) **Treaty** Agreement in 1901 between Great Britain and the U.S. giving the U.S. sole right to build and control a canal between the Atlantic and Pacific oceans. **770**

headright Agreement by colonists to pay their way or that of others to Virginia in exchange for 50 acres of land for each "head" transported from England. **50**

Head Start Program created in 1964 to give disadvantaged children a better start in school and life. **1030**

heartened Encouraged. **525**

heavy-handed Harsh. **64**

Hepburn Act Law giving the Interstate Commerce Commission the power to inspect the business records of railroad companies and to regulate rail rates (1906). **797**

heralded Proclaimed or announced with enthusiasm. **330**

hereafter Life after death. **19**

Highway Safety Act Law passed in 1966 that established safety standards for vehicles and roadways. **1031**

Hindenburg Line Line of trenches on the Western Front from which German forces launched attacks in the Great War. **844**

Hiroshima (hir·uh·SHEE·muh) Japanese city that was site of the first atomic bombing by the U.S. in August 1945. **974**

Hispaniola (his·puhn·YOH·la) First island settled by Columbus and his crew in 1492; today the site of the Dominican Republic and Haiti. **25**

historical imagination Ability to look at past events objectively by recognizing what people knew and did not know at a particular time. **3**

historical significance Importance of an event to other events. **325**

Ho Chi Minh (HO·CHEE·MIN) **Trail** Path running from North Vietnam through Cambodia and Laos to South Vietnam that was used by the North Vietnamese as a supply trail during the Vietnam War. **1074**

Holocaust (HO·luh·kawst) Hitler's program to exterminate the Jews. **938**

Holy Land Palestine; important to Christians as the birthplace of Jesus and site of biblical events. **16**

Home Owners' Loan Corporation (HOLC) Organization created in 1933 to help people meet house payments by refinancing home mortgages at lower rates. **908**

home schools Educational system in which children are taught at home by parents or other relatives. **484**

Homestead Act Law passed in 1862 that granted free public land to farmers who agreed to cultivate the land for a given period of time. **535**

Homestead Strike Violent 1892 AFL strike in Homestead, Pennsylvania, during which steel workers and Pinkerton detectives were killed. **682**

hotbed Fertile starting place. **1120**

"hot-line" Direct emergency telephone line set up in 1963 between Moscow and Washington, D.C., to reduce the risk of accidental war. **1019**

House of Burgesses First elected

government body in America, in Virginia in 1619. **50**

house of refuge Place built to house delinquent and homeless children and separate them from adult criminals. **500**

House of Representatives House of Congress in which states are represented according to their population. **220**

Housing Act Law passed in 1961 that helped poor people pay their rent. **1031**

Hull House Chicago settlement house founded in 1889 by social worker Jane Addams which became a model for others throughout the country. **691**

human right Privilege belonging to all human beings. **238**

Hundred Days First part of Franklin Roosevelt's first term during which Congress passed many New Deal programs. **906**

Hungary Eastern European nation in which a revolt against communist control took place in 1956 and the 1980s. **1003**

I

Ice Age Period when icecaps and glaciers covered large parts of the earth's surface. **2**

ideal community. Settlement established far from other communities in which residents could live as they wished. **490**

ideology Opinions or theories that make up a social or political program. **1120**

ill-advised Unwise or without sound advice. **129**

immigrant Person who comes to another country to live. **343**

Immigration Act of 1965 Law that changed admission quotas to the U.S. based on nationality. **1031**

immoral Wicked or morally wrong. **440**

immunity Resistance to a disease. **35**

impartial Not favoring one side. **746**

impartiality Fairness or objectivity. **819**

impeachment Formal charge of wrongdoing brought against a official of the federal government. **225, 598**

imperialism Practice of establishing and controlling colonies. **762, 817**

imposed Established or applied by authority. **837**

impressment Practice used by the British in the early 1800s of forcing sailors of British ancestry to serve in the British navy. **287**

impromptu Without preparation. **1068**

improvised Composed, invented, or arranged on the spur of the moment. **871**

inadmissable Not allowed. **470**

Incas (ING·kuhs) Highly civilized nation of people who lived in the mountains of Peru at the time of the Spanish invasion. **34**

Inchon (IN·chawn) Korean port from which American forces launched a successful attack against the North Korean army during the Korean War. **998**

income tax Tax upon a person's earnings. **804**

Income Tax Act Law passed in 1986 that lowered income taxes, especially for the poor. **1111**

inconclusively Done without settling anything or reaching a definite result. **294**

indentured servant Laborer who signed a contract agreeing to work for a period of time without wages in return for passage to America. **50**

Independent Treasury System System in the 1840s where debts to government were paid in gold and silver and stored in vaults. **400**

Indian Rights Act (1968) Law passed to protect the rights of American Indians. **1053**

Indies Islands off the east coast of Asia. **18**

indifference Lack of interest. **163**

indigo (IN·dug·goh) Plant that produces a dark blue dye used in manufacturing cloth. **91**

indirect tax Tax on imports that were collected from shippers and paid by consumers in the form of higher prices. **130**

Industrial Revolution Change in production methods in the early 1800s from human to machine power. **335**

Industrial Workers of the World (IWW) A radical organization of laborers who wanted to put industry under the control of the workers. **837**

industrial technology Tools and machines used to produce goods. **333**

industrial unions Organization of all the laborers involved in a particular industry. **927**

inequity Lack of fairness or objectivity. **1100**

infamy Extreme disgrace or dishonor. **952**

infant mortality rate Annual number of children under one year of age that die for every 1,000 that live. **886**

infested Overrun or swarming with. **47**

inflamed Intensely excited or angered. **749**

inflation Rise in price levels resulting from an increase in the amount of money or a decrease in the amount of goods available for sale. **193**

inflation rate Amount of inflation or the degree to which inflation affects the economy. **1110**

inflationary (in-FLAY·shuh·ner·ee) **spiral** Continuous rise in prices that occurs when the higher cost of one product or service causes the prices of other goods and services to rise. **392**

inhumanity The quality or state of being cruel or brutal. **458**

initiative (in·ISH·uht·iv) Procedure allowing voters to propose a law to the legislature. **791**

injunction Court order that prohibits an individual or group from carrying out a given action. **985**

inner city Usually an older, run-down and densely populated central section of a city. **1101**

insight Clear understanding of the inner or true nature of something. **504**

installation Military camp, fort or base. **1018**

interchangeable (in·tuhr·CHAYN·juh·buhl) **parts** Production advance involving parts that can be substituted one for the other; an essential process for mass production. **334**

interlocking Connected so that each part is dependent on another to operate. **673**

internal improvements Parts of the transportation network such as roads and canals built at public expense. **380**

Internationalism A policy of cooperation among nations. **859**

internationalists Those who support political and economic involvement with other nations. **946**

internment (in·TUHRN·muhnt) **camps** Enclosed compounds in a barren section of the U.S. where Japanese-Americans were held during World War II. **956**

interstate commerce Business transactions between residents or companies in different states. **676**

Interstate Commerce Act Law passed in 1887 to regulate railroad freight rates and business practices and which set up a commission to oversee railroad affairs. **676**

Interstate System Network of superhighways begun in 1956 under President Eisenhower. **1007**

intimately In a very personal or familiar way. **1028**

Intolerable Acts Name colonists gave to the Coercive Acts passed by the British government in 1774 to punish the colonists for the Boston Tea Party. **142**

Iran Country in the Middle East where 53 Americans were held hostage during the Carter administration and which fought a long war with Iraq. **866**

Iron Curtain The term Winston Churchill used to describe the barrier of censorship and secrecy between communist countries and the rest of the western world. **986**

ironmaster Manufacturer of iron. **663**

Irreconcilables Group of senators who refused to approve the WWI Versailles Peace Treaty under any condition. **853**

Islam Muslim religion founded by the prophet Mohammed. **16**

island hopping Military strategy used in World War II where important consecutive islands were seized and used as bases. **968**

isolationism A national policy of maintaining a nation's interests without being involved in alliances with other countries. **859**

isthmus Narrow strip of land connecting two larger segments of land. **28, 770**

isolationism (eye·suh·LAY·shuh·niz·uhm) Policy that stresses freedom from foreign alliances and national self-sufficiency. **737**

Israel Country in the Middle East formed in 1948 for Jews. **1016**

Iwo Jima (EEH·woh·JEE·muh). Small Pacific island captured by the Americans in World War II after heavy fighting with the Japanese. **968**

J

Jackson State Mississippi university where two students were killed in 1970 by state police during a protest of the Vietnam War. **1074**

Jacksonian Follower of Andrew Jackson who believed in the rights and abilities of typical Americans or the common man. **384**

Jamestown First successful English colony in America. **47**

Jay's Treaty Treaty in which the British agreed to withdraw troops from western ports and give shipping and trading concessions to the United States. **250**

Jazz Music created by African American musicians in New Orleans in the late 1800s that became popular during the 1920s. **870**

Jazz Age Nickname for the 1920s. **871**

Jim Crow law Any law that promoted segregation. **614**

Job Corps A Great Society program to train poor, unskilled workers. **1030**

joint-stock company Group of investors formed to outfit colonial expeditions in the early 1600s. **44**

jokester Comedian or one who cracks jokes. **194**

junta (HOON·tah) In this case, committee established in the U.S. by Cuban revolutionaries to gather support in the late 1890s. **749**

justice of the peace Chief official of county courts in the South. **110**

juvenile delinquency Problem of children and teens breaking the law. **499**

K

kamikaze (kom·i·KAH·zee) Japanese pilots who committed suicide with honor by crashing their planes into enemy targets. **971**

Kansas-Nebraska Bill Law that allowed the question of slavery in the Nebraska Territory to be decided by popular sovereignty and which created the Kansas and Nebraska territories. **516**

keelboat Shallow covered riverboat that is towed, poled or rowed. **281**

Kent State Northern Ohio university where four students were killed in 1970 during a riot protesting the Vietnam War. **1074**

Kentucky and Virginia Resolutions Statements written in 1798 by Jefferson and Madison to question the power of the federal government over the states **267**

kickbacks Illegal practice of receiving back part of the money paid for a job. **699**

King George's War Third conflict between the French and English in America from 1744 to 1748. **117**

King William's War (1689–97) First in a succession of colonial conflicts between the English and French. **116**

kingpin Leader in a group or undertaking. **76**

King's Mountain Site of Tory defeat in South Carolina (1780). **171**

Knights of Labor Union of skilled and unskilled workers founded in 1869. **680**

Know-Nothings Name given to members of the Native American party during the 1850s. **523**

Korean War War in 1950-52 between North and South Korea in which South Korea was supported by U.N. troops, mainly from the U.S. **999**

Ku Klux Klan (koo·kluhks·KLAN) Secret organization which terrorized African Americans. **610**

L

Lancasterian (lan·KAS·tree·ahn) **system** Educational system where teachers taught older pupils who then taught younger students. **489**

Land Ordinance of 1785 Law that setup a method for surveying and selling western territories by townships. **189**

Land Ordinance of 1787 Plan for governing the lands in the Northwest Territory as they grew to statehood (also Northwest Ordinance). **189**

lathe (LAYTH) Machine that shapes wood by holding and turning it against a cutting tool. **334**

Latin America Countries in Central and South America settled by Spain and Portugal. **323**

Law of Prior Appropriation Law that states that rights of water use belong to the person who first uses the water, as long as it is for beneficial purposes such as farming. **430**

Law of Riparian Rights Law that states that all property owners along whose land borders a river or stream have equal right to the water; they may not increase or decrease its flow or change its quality. **429**

League of Nations International organization established in 1920 to seek world peace; dissolved in 1946 when many of the League's functions were taken over by the United Nations. **846**

Lecompton Constitution Proposed Kansas state constitution that would have allowed slavery. **528**

legacy (LEG·uh·see) Something left or handed down by a predecessor. **1030**

legal right Privilege given to people by law. **238**

legislature Elected body given the responsibility of making laws. **110**

Lend-Lease Act Law passed in 1941 that allowed for the sale or lease of war supplies to any country whose defense was important to the security of the United States. **947**

Lexington One of two Massachusetts towns (along with Concord) where the first battles of the American Revolution were fought. **144**

liberal Openminded and supportive of individual freedom. **929**

Liberia (ly·BIR·ee·ah) Country on West Coast of Africa where some formers slaves settled. **449**

lien (leen) Claim on property as security for a debt. **608**

life chance Possibility for a person to share in the in the opportunities and benefits society has to offer. **878**

likening Comparing or pointing out as similar. **727**

limited liability One advantage of corporations; investors risk only the amount of money they have invested. **661**

The Lincolns of Indiana Rugged pioneer family in which President Abraham Lincoln was raised. **377**

Line of Demarcation (dee·mahr·KAY·shahn) Agreement in 1493 that dividing the Atlantic Ocean gave claim to all lands west of the line to Spain and all lands east to Portugal. **25**

literacy test Proof of a person's ability to read and write as a requirement for voting. **613**

Little Rock Arkansas capital where U.S. soldiers were sent in 1957 to escort black students to a high school for whites to achieve court-ordered segregation. **1010**

livelihood Means of support. **328**

lobbyist Person representing a special interest group who tries to influence legislators. **791**

lockout Refusal by an employer to allow employees to come to work unless they agree to his terms. **682**

lock Canal chamber where ships are raised and lowered from one water level to another. **772**

lode Deposit of mineral ore. **639**

Lodge Reservations A series of changes to the WWI Versailles Peace Treaty supported by Senator Henry Cabot Lodge. **853**

The Lodges of Boston Wealthy Boston family who began a political dynasty in the 1800s. **372**

Log Cabin Campaign Whig strategy to win votes for William Henry Harrison based on his reputation as a rugged man of the people. **400**

long drive. Two-month journey that brought cattle from Texas to the railroads. **643**

Long Night Period of racial segregation after the Civil War. **613**

loophole Omission or unclear statement in a document such as a law or contract through which the intent of the document can be evaded or negated. **927**

Lost Generation American writers whose works expressed the disillusionment felt after World War I. **828**

lot One's fate in life. **336**

lottery Process of drawing lots to choose or decide something. **943**

Louisiana Purchase Acquisition from France made by the United States in 1803 of all the land between the Mississippi River and the Rocky Mountains for $15 million. **278**

Lowell system Method of employing young women to operate power looms first used in 1813 to recruit laborers for factories in Lowell, Massachusetts. **339**

Loyalist American during the Revolution who remained loyal to the king of England; also called a Tory. **155**

lush Growing thick and rich. **643**

Lusitania British passenger ship sunk by German U-boats in May 1915 during the Great War; 128 Americans were among the more than 1,200 people who died. **826**

M

machine gun Automatic weapon that fire a rapid, continuous stream of bullets. **840**

Macon's Bill Number Two (1810) Law that removed restrictions on trade with France and Britain and promised American support to either nation that stopped attacks on American ships. **291**

Maine Free state created through the Missouri Compromise of 1820 to keep a balance of slave and free states in Congress. **437**

mainland Continent or main body of a continent. **543**

mainstay Chief means of support. **7**

malice (MAHL·us) Hatred toward or the desire to hurt others. **593**

mandate Wishes of the people expressed to a candidate as an authorization to follow campaign proposals; also a territory or colony under the management of the League of Nations. **712**

Manhattan Project Code name for the top-secret plan to develop the atom bomb. **973**

manifest destiny Belief popular in the 1840s that the obvious future role of the U.S. was to extend its boundaries to the ocean. **412**

Manila (mah·NIL·ah) **Bay** Site in the Philippines of Commodore Dewey's victory over the Spanish fleet in the first battle of the Spanish-American War (1898). **752**

manor Land and village ruled over by a feudal lord. **15**

Marbury v. Madison Legal case that established the power of the Supreme Court to declare an act of Congress unconstitutional. **273**

March on Washington (1963) Huge civil rights demonstration in Washington, D.C., during which Martin Luther King delivered his famous "I Have a Dream" speech. **1055**

market Economic term for the buying and selling of goods and services. **875**

marl Crumbly soil of sand and clay rich in calcium carbonate and used as fertilizer. **369**

Marshall Plan United States program for the economic recovery of Europe after World War II. **988**

Mason-Dixon line Boundary between Maryland and Pennsylvania, traditional line separating North and South. **101**

masonry Stone or brickwork. **65**

mass production Manufacture, usually by machinery, of goods in large quantities. **333**

Massachusetts Bay Company American colony established by the Puritans in 1630. **58**

massive retaliation (ri·tal·ee·AY·shun) U.S. policy under Eisenhower that threatened to respond to Soviet aggression with nuclear weapons. **1001**

materialistic Caring more about money and material things than spiritual things. **867**

matériel (mah·TEER·ee·el) Equipment and supplies used by a military force. **831**

matrilineal Descendants or kinship traced down through the mother's side. **5**

Mayflower Compact Document drawn up by the Pilgrims in 1620 that provided a legal basis for self-government. **53**

McCarran Internal Security Act 1950 law that required Communists to register with the government and made it illegal for communists to work for the government. **999**

McCarthyism Use of American suspicion of communists in the 1950s by Senator Joseph McCarthy to gain power by presenting charges of communist infiltration in the State Department. **997**

McKinley Tariff Act in 1890 that lifted the tariff on raw sugar imports causing Hawaii's sugar industry to suffer. **742**

meager Small amount; scanty. **65**

mechanical reaper Machine invented by Cyrus McCormick to harvest wheat. **560**

mediate (MEE·dee·ayt) To be the impartial party that helps settle a dispute between two parties in disagreement. **820**

Medicare A Great Society program that provided health insurance for people over 65. **1031**

megalopolis Continuous heavily-populated urban area connecting a number of cities. **1101**

melting pot Idea that immigrants of various racial and cultural backgrounds eventually become adapted to American ways. **805**

mercantilism Economic policy in which a country tries to maintain a favorable balance of trade by producing goods and services for export and limiting imports in every way possible.

mercenary (MUHRS·uhn·er·ee) Soldier hired to fight for money. **165**

merchant adventurer English merchant in the early 1600s who backed exploration and colonization. **44**

merchants of death Nickname given to companies that profited from the manufacture of weapons used during WWI. **940**

merit system Policy adopted by the U.S. Civil Service to make government appointments and promotions on the basis of ability rather than politics. **704**

Mesabi (muh·SAH·bee) **Range** Region in Minnesota where rich deposits of iron ore were found in the 1890s. **662**

Mexican Revolution Rebellion beginning in 1910 which ended the dictatorship of Porfirio Diaz and led to a constitutional government begun in 1917. **820**

Mexico City Capital of Mexico where Mexican forces surrendered to Americans in 1847. **420**

middleman Trader who buys products from one person and sells them at higher prices to a merchant or directly to the consumer. **20**

Middle Passage Slaves' voyage across the Atlantic. **88**

Midway Islands Islands northwest of Hawaii occupied by the United States navy in 1867; site of an important U.S. naval victory in World War II. **738**

midwife Woman who assists in childbirth. **336**

mild reservationist Republican senator who could accept the WWI Treaty of Versailles with only a few minor changes. **853**

militant Aggressive or ready to fight. **482**

military dictatorship Control of a country by the leaders of the military. **820**

military-industrial complex Phrase used by Eisenhower to describe the special interest groups representing the military and defense industries that had risen to unprecedented power during and after World War II. **1007**

mindful Being aware or bearing in mind. **239**

minimum wage Least pay a worker can receive by law. **795**

mining camps Village formed by miners working a strike. **434**

Minute Men Revolutionary War civilian-soldiers who were trained to fight on short notice. **144**

mission Task for which a person feels called or destined. **33**

Missouri Compromise Act passed in 1820 which allowed Missouri to become a slave state and Maine a free state and attempted to settle the question of slavery's spread by allowing slavery only in territories south of 36 30°N **437**

Model A Ford car that made after the Model T that introduced different colors and body styles. **880**

Model T First mass-produced car that made automobile transportation affordable for many Americans; introduced by Henry Ford in 1908. **880**

moderate Person who avoids extreme political views. **593**

moderation State of being reasonable and temperate. **1072**

monetary (MAHN·uh·ter·ee) **policy** Plan that dictates the coinage, printing and circulation of money; also method of stimulating business activity by lowering interest rates on loans to business owners and consumers. **702**

monopoly (muh·NAHP·uh·lee) Exclusive control of a product or service that results in fixed prices and elimination of competition. **139, 673**

Monroe Doctrine Important statement of foreign policy that said the United States would not tolerate European interference in the Western Hemisphere. **324**

Montgomery Bus Boycott 1955 protest by African Americans against Montgomery Alabama's segregation of city buses. **1013**

monumental Enormous and long-lasting. **814**

Mormon Trail Route to Utah used by Mormon pioneers. **429**

Mormons Religious group begun in the 1920s Society by Joseph Smith. **427**

Moslems Followers of the Islamic faith. **16**

motivated Supplied the reason or desire for acting. **670**

Mound Builders Prehistoric American Indians who buried their dead in elaborate earthen mounds. **8**

moving assembly line Method of mass production used by Henry Ford in which each worker or team performed only one simple task as the product moved past. **880**

muckraker (MUHK·rayk·uhr) Author who exposed corruption in the early 1900s. **785**

multinational Corporation that has branches in a number of countries. **876**

municipal socialism Plan which transferred private ownership of streetcar lines and gas and electric companies to city governments. **792**

mutual (MYOO·choo·ahl). Shared in common. **539**

N

Nagasaki (nah·gah·SAH·kee) Japanese city, site of the second atomic bombing by the U.S. in 1945 which ended the war. **974**

National Aeronautics (ar·oh·NAH·tiks) **and Space Administration (NASA)** Government agency responsible for space research programs. **1042**

National Association for the Advancement of Colored People (NAACP) Civil rights organization formed in 1909. **808**

National Farm Workers Association Labor union of Mexican-born farm workers founded by migrant leader Cesar Chavez. **1093**

national government Level of government with jurisdiction over all people and all other levels of government. **197**

National Grange (GRAYNJ) Farmers' organization that became politically active during the 1870s. **715**

National Industrial Recovery Act (NIRA) New Deal law that allowed industry to set fair codes of competition, guaranteed the right of workers to join unions, and set minimum wage rates. **906**

national judiciary Highest level courts in a country. **220**

National Labor Relations Board (NLRB) Board created by the Wagner Labor Relations Act to settle union disputes and guarantee fair union elections. **918**

National Organization for Women (NOW) Association founded by Betty Freidan in 1966 to promote equal opportunities for women. **1052**

National Origins Act. (1924) Law that severely restricted immigration from certain countries to the United States **865**

National Recovery Administration (NRA) Government body organized to supervise the industrial codes created under the National Industrial Recovery Act in 1933. **906**

National Road First road built linking East and West from Maryland to Illinois; also called the Cumberland Road. **350**

National Trades' Union Organization formed in 1834 by groups of skilled workers to promote better wages and working conditions. **503**

National War Labor Board Board created during World War II to stabilize wages and settle labor disputes. **955**

National Youth Administration New Deal agency that helped people between 16 and 25 years of age find employment. **916**

nationalism Patriotic feelings for one's country. **197**

Native American Party Political organization formed by native-born Americans to oppose immigration and immigrants. **523**

native sons Political candidate from a key state who is nominated in hopes of carrying that state in a national election. **698**

nativist Former whig who favored strict immigration controls. **343**

natural rights Privilege of all people defined by what is instinctively felt to be moral or good. **238**

Nauvoo (naw·VOO) City in Illinois settled by Mormons in the 1800s. **427**

naval stores Product produced from the pine forests of the South, such as pitch used to make ships watertight. **91**

navigation Science of charting the position or course of a ship, aircraft, or similar vehicle. **22**

Navigation Acts British laws that were a key aspect of mercantile policy and that restricted the production of goods by American colonies and forbade trade with countries other than England between 1651 and 1733. **113**

Nazis (NAHT·seez) Members of the National Socialists party that controlled Germany from 1933 to 1945 under the dictatorship of Adolf Hitler. **937**

necessary and proper clause Section of the Constitution often used to expand the powers of Congress; also called the "elastic clause." **243**

Negro Fort Florida fort controlled by runaway slaves that was destroyed by American troops in 1816. **314**

Negro Hill Site of rich gold deposit discovered by two African-Americans. **435**

neutrality Policy of avoiding permanent ties with other nations. **253**

neutrality acts Laws passed in the 1930s to prevent United States involvement in another war. **940**

New Deal Franklin Roosevelt's program to revive the country from the Great Depression. **905**

New England Name given in the early 1600s to the northeasternmost colonies; still used as a label for that section of the United States. **57**

New Freedom Woodrow Wilson's progressive program proposed in 1912. **802**

New Frontier John F. Kennedy's social and economic programs of the early 1960s. **1014**

New Immigration Wave of immigration between 1880 and the 1920s that brought millions of people from Eastern and Southern Europe to America. **683**

New Jersey Plan Design for Congress presented by William Peterson during 1787 Constitution Convention that favored a one-state, one-vote system. **220**

New Nationalism Theodore Roosevelt's progressive platform in 1912. **800**

New Netherland Name given to the colony in the Hudson River area claimed and settled by the Dutch. **63**

New Spain Areas in North and Central America, and the Caribbean claimed and settled by the Spanish. **65**

New Sweden Colony along the Delaware River founded by Swedish settlers. **64**

New World Name given in the early 1500s by explorer Amerigo Vespucci to the lands in Central and South America. **27**

Nez Perce (NEZ·PUHRS) Indian tribe routed out of Western Idaho and eventually moved to reservations in Oklahoma. **634**

Niagara (ny·AG·ruh) **Movement.** Effort begun in 1905 by prominent African American leaders to fight racial segregation. **807**

nickelodeon Early movie houses where admission was five cents. **875**

Nineteenth Amendment Constitutional amendment in 1920 that gave women the right to vote. **858**

no man's land Devastated area between the trenches on the Western Front during the Great War. **1016**

nominal Very small or insignificant. **484**

nominating convention Meeting of party members to choose presidential and vice presidential candidates. **384**

Non-Intercourse Act Law passed in 1809 permitting trade with all countries except Britain and France. **291**

nonviolent direct action Method proposed by Martin Luther King for protesting without violence against discrimination. **1054**

nonviolent resistance Showing opposition or resistance to something without the use of violence. **1013**

normal school Teacher training school. **489**

Normandy Northern French province that was the site of the D-Day invasion during World War II. **963**

North Atlantic Treaty Organization (NATO) Agreement made in 1949 to stand firm against Soviet military threats, made between the U.S., Great Britain, France, and eight other nations. **991**

North Korea Korea north of the 38th parallel and under Soviet control since World War II. **997**

Northern Securities Case Antitrust lawsuit in which the Supreme Court dissolved the combination of three major railroads. **796**

Northwest Ordinance Plan of government for the lands in the Northwest Territory: also Land Ordinance of 1787. **189**

Northwest passage Shipping route from the Atlantic to the East Indies through North America. **44**

nuclear energy Energy released by controlled nuclear reactions; developed in the twentieth century as an alternative energy source to fossil fuels. **1034**

Nueces (nooh·AY·suhs) **River** Texas River Mexicans claimed was the boundary between Mexico and Texas. **418**

Nullification (nuhl·uh·fuh·KAY·shuhn) **Crisis** Episode in 1832 in which South Carolina nullified, or refused to follow, a tariff law causing the government to threaten force if the law was not followed. **387**

nullify (NUHL·uh·fy) To cancel the legal force of a law. **267**

O

oil refining Removing the impurities from crude oil. **664**

Okinawa (ohk·i·NAH·wa) Japanese island captured by American forces in World War II after heavy losses on both sides. **970**

"Old Ironsides" Nickname for the American warship *Constitution* used in the War of 1812. **303**

Olive Branch Petition Plea sent in 1775 to King George III requesting protection of the American colonies from the British Parliament. **151**

one person, one vote Principle of electing legislators from districts with populations of approximately the same size. **104**

Oneida (oh·NYD·uh) **community** Ideal settlement in New York. **490**

onslaught An especially fierce attack. **962**

Open Door An 1899 U.S. policy that assured all nations equal trade rights with China. **860**

Open Door Note Note sent in 1889 by John Hay requesting nations to accept the Open Door Policy in China. **768**

open-minded Willing to listen to new ideas. **73**

open range Government-owned grazing land used by ranchers to feed their herds. **643**

Operation Overlord British and American invasion of France that began the Allied conquest of Europe during World War II. **963**

Operation Sail Procession of decorated ships in New York Harbor in honor of the American Bicentennial. **1091**

Operation Torch Allied occupation of French North Africa led by Eisenhower during World War II. **961**

oppressed Burdened or kept down by a harsh and unjust authority. **407**

optimist One who always sees the bright side or expects the best to happen. **913**

oratory The art of fine public speaking. **634**

ordeal Severe trial or painful experience. **28**

ordinance Public act or law. **387**

ordinance of nullification Legal proposal made by John C. Calhoun that described an orderly way for a state to cancel a federal law it believed unconstitutional. **387**

Oregon Trail Route followed by pioneers to the Northwest. **414**

Organization of Petroleum Exporting Countries (OPEC) Oil cartel founded in 1960 to control oil prices that included Venezuela, Saudi Arabia, Iran, Kuwait, and Iraq. **863**

orrery Mechanical model that illustrates the movement of the sun and planets. **100**

Ostend (ahs·TEND) **Manifesto** Secret proposal that stated that the United States would be justified to take Cuba from Spain by force if Spain refused to sell it; news of the manifesto outraged northerners, who saw it as an attempt by southerners to gain more territory. **518**

outpost Pioneer settlement on the frontier. **306**

outraged Shocked and angered by a serious or terrible offense. **511**

overemphasis Too much stress on or attention to. **785**

overhead Fixed costs. **673**

override Constitutional power of Congress to overrule a presidential veto by a two-thirds vote. **225**

overseer Person who supervises other workers. **374**

P

Pacific Ocean Largest ocean; west of North and South America; first European sighting by Balboa in 1513 and named by Magellan in 1520. **28**

Pacific Railway Act Law passed in 1862 authorizing construction of a railroad from Nebraska to the Pacific Coast. **627**

pacifist Person who is against violence and war. **939**

Palmer raids Raids on radical groups ordered by Attorney General A.Mitchell Palmer during the Big Red Scare. **861**

Pan American Conference (1899) Meeting with representatives of Latin American countries sponsored by the U.S. with the hopes of bringing the nations of the Western Hemisphere closer together. **744**

"Pancho" Villa (PAHN·choh·VEE·yah) Mexican bandit and revolutionary who helped overthrow the Diaz dictatorship but failed to win the presidency for himself. **820**

Panic of 1837 Economic collapse caused by reckless lending and too much paper money in circulation. **392**

parallel Counterpart or something that is similar in nearly every way. **1030**

paraphrased Put into one's own words something that has been stated or written before. **783**

parcel Section or plot of land. **644**

Parliament Law-making body of England. **109**

partnership Business organization of two or more people who share the profits and losses. **661**

Pasha Title of rank or honor in Turkey and North Africa. **275**

passive resistance Method of demonstrating nonviolent opposition to a policy or program considered unjust. **856**

patriot During the American Revolution, a person who favored independence for the American colonies. **144**

patronage Awarding of government positions to political supporters by office holders. **705**

patroon Landholder who controlled a huge estate in colonial Dutch New York and New Jersey. **64**

Pawnee (paw·NEE) Indian tribe that occupied western Nebraska. **623**

Peace Corps Program established by President Kennedy that sent trained American volunteers to needy countries. **1017**

peace movement Efforts made by organized groups to promote peace among nations. **818**

Peace of Ghent Treaty signed in 1814 that ended the War of 1812. **313**

Peace of Paris Agreement in 1783 between Great Britain and the United States that ended the Revolutionary War. **188**

peace without victory Topic of a speech by President Wilson calling for the Allies and Central Powers to end the war. **829**

Pearl Harbor Port in the Hawaiian Islands where the American Pacific fleet was destroyed in a Japanese surprise attack in 1941. **950**

peculiar institution Name some gave to slaveholding. **86**

Pendleton Act (1883) Law which created a Civil Service Commission to administer exams for applicants seeking government jobs. **705**

People's party Third party formed in 1892 that represented the interests of farmers and labor unions; also called the Populist Party. **721**

peppered Fired shots at repeatedly. **145**

perestroika (per·uh·STROY·kuh) Plan to improve and broaden the Soviet economy initiated by Mikhail Gorbachev. **1116**

Perkins Institution School for the blind founded in 1830s by Samuel Gridley Howe. **498**

perplexing Complicated or puzzling. **1080**

persistent Continuing steadily despite interference. **2**

pervading Spreading throughout. **1050**

"pet bank" State banks chosen by President Jackson to receive deposits or funds removed from the Bank of the United States in 1833. **391**

Petersburg Town in Virginia where Grant's army kept up a nine-month attack against Lee's army. (1865). **581**

petulance Show of irritableness or rudeness in speech and behavior. **1108**

Philippine Islands Group of islands in the South Pacific that became a battleground for Japanese and U.S. forces during World War II. **966**

phonograph Machine that reproduced sound from tracings made on a cylinder or disk. **667**

picaroons (pik·ah·ROONS) French merchant ships that seized cargo from American merchant ships in the 1790s. **257**

piety Devotion to religious duties. **56**

Pilgrims Community of people who settled in Massachusetts in the 1620s to practice their religion freely; also called Separatists. **53**

Pinckney's Treaty Agreement between Spain and the United States that gave Americans shipping access to the Mississippi and recognized Florida boundary line set by Americans. **251**

Pinkerton Armed guard who worked as an agent for the Pinkerton Detective Agency. **682**

pious Having or showing religious devotion. **70**

Plains Indian Member of an Indian tribe that lived on the grasslands between the Rocky Mountains and the Mississippi River. **7**

Plattsburg New York city where Americans defeated the British during the War of 1812. **306**

Plessy v. Ferguson. Supreme Court case concerning civil rights that legalized the "separate-but-equal" rule. **615**

plodded Walked slowly and heavily. **351**

plunder Rob or take by force. **622**

Plymouth Site in Massachusetts where the Pilgrims first landed in America in 1620. **55**

pockmarked Covered with pits or indentations as in the scars left by smallpox. **823**

poison gas A chemical weapon first used by the Germans during World War I. **838**

polio vaccine (vak·SEEN) An inoculation developed by Dr. Jonas Salk which protected people from the polio virus. **1035**

political equity Principle that all citizens have the right to vote regardless of wealth. **79**

political machines Big city organization run by bosses who won elections by controlling poor and immigrant voters. **698**

poll tax Fee charged for voting. **613**

pollution Harmful substances that affect the quality of the environment. **1104**

polygamy (puh·LIG·uh·mee) Practice of having more than one wife or husband. **427**

pommel Rounded knob at the top of a saddle. **647**

pomp Showy or grand display. **273**

Pontiac's Rebellion Indian uprising in 1763 led by Chief Pontiac. **123**

pool Agreement between businesses to charge the same rates and share available markets. **673**

popular sovereignty (SAHV·uh·ruhn·tee) System that allowed settlers in each territory to decide whether or not they would have slavery. **437**

popular vote Vote of the people. **384**

Populist party Third party formed in 1892 that represented the interests of farmers and labor unions; also called People's party. **721**

Port Hudson Mississippi River stronghold in Louisiana captured by Union forces in 1862 to split the Confederacy in two. **580**

postwar reaction Response to the horrors of the Great War felt by many young people; characterized by xenophobia, disillusionment, and a return to fundamental values. **860**

Pottawatomie (paht·uh·WAHT·uh·mee) **Massacre** Murder of five people at Pottawatomie Creek, Kansas, by John Brown and his followers in revenge for pro-slavery attack on Lawrence, Kansas (1856). **522**

potent Strong or powerful in effect. **1116**

poverty line Level of income below which one is classified as poor according to the federal government. **1053**

Preamble Introduction to the Constitution that explains its purpose. **197**

precedent Guide for later action. **234**

president Elected head of the executive branch of government. **220**

presidio Fort in which Spanish soldiers were stationed. **406**

pressing Calling for immediate attention; urgent. **123**

prestige High standing or reputation based on achievement or character. **76**

prevail Triumph or succeed. **98**

price system Economic system where the cost of items determines the amounts and types of goods produced. **875**

primary elections Process for selecting candidates to run for public office. **791**

privateer (pry·vuh·TIR) U.S. merchant ship or crew who flew the French flag and attacked unarmed British ships in the early 1800s. **246**

Privy (PRIV·ee) **Council** Advisers to the King of England who set policies for governing the American colonies. **109**

Proclamation of 1763 Decision by the British to close to colonial settlers the area west of the Appalachians. **123**

productivity Amount of goods or services a worker produces. **876**

profoundly Deeply or intensely. **222**

Progressive Movement Period in the early 1900s marked by social reforms and a general feeling of hope and optimism. **781**

Progressive party Third party formed to support Roosevelt in his 1912 bid for the presidency; and party formed in 1948 to support Wallace's bid for presidency against Truman. **800**

progressives People who sought to improve life American society. **781**

prohibition Act of forbidding the manufacture, transportation, and sale of alcoholic beverages. **500**

Promontory Utah city where the Union Pacific and Central Pacific Railroads met to complete the first American transcontinental railroad. **628**

propaganda Information or ideas spread in order to gain public support for a cause or to damage an opposing cause. **836**

proprietary (pruh·PRY·uh·ter·ee) **colony** Colony granted by the British crown to an individual owner who had all the governing rights. **60**

prospective Likely to be or become. **478**

prospector One who searched for gold or silver. **432**

prosperity Economic term for a time of high production and low unemployment. **895**

protective tariff Tax on imports to increase their cost, helping American manufacturers compete with foreign producers. **330**

Protestant Reformation Religious movement in the 16th century aimed at reforming the Catholic church and resulting in the formation of several Protestant religions. **53**

provided Made the condition or established. **185**

proviso Special clause in any document that introduces a condition. **438**

public housing project Housing development for low-income families that is made affordable by public funds. **1045**

public school Free school funded by taxes and open to all children. **74**

public servant Government official. **183**

public works Roads, railways, bridges and other structures that are built for public use at public cost. **899**

Puebla (poo·EB·luh) Site of an important American victory in 1847 in the Mexican War. **420**

pueblo (poo·EB·loh) Indian village of the Southwestern U.S.; from the Spanish word for town. **6**

Puerto Rico (pohrt·uh·REE·koh) Island east of Cuba and southeast of Florida ceded to the United States after the Spanish-American War; now a self-governing commonwealth of the U.S. **756**

Pullman Strike Major railway work stoppage in 1894 begun by workers of the Pullman Palace Car Company that resulted in a violent clash with federal troops. **725**

puppet government Government whose actions are dictated or controlled by another nation. **981**

Pure Food and Drug Act Law passed in 1906 that provided for the inspection of food and drugs and the supervision of slaughterhouses. **797**

purge To get rid of someone or something undesirable such as a political opponent. **937**

Puritans English Protestants who wished to purify the Church of England and who came to America in the early 1600s for religious freedom. **58**

putting-out system Method of production in which workers wove cloth on looms in their own homes from thread "put out" by the manufacturer. **336**

Q

quadruplex (kwah·DROO·plehx) **telegraph** Edison's first major invention, a machine that could send four messages over one wire at the same time. **667**

Quaker Member of a Pacifist religious sect which came to America seeking religious freedom. **67**

quarantine (KWAHR·un·teen) Policy of isolating aggressor nations in the 1930s. **941**

quartered Housed or sheltered. **130**

Quebec (kwi·BEK) First permanent French settlement in North America founded in 1608. **62**

Queen Anne's War French and English conflict after which England gained control of Nova

Scotia, Newfoundland and the Hudson Bay (1702–1713). **117**

R

radiated Shone brightly as if sending out rays from a center. **95**

radical Person who favors sudden or extreme changes. **53**

railroad baron Person who made a fortune through railroads, often by using illegal or unfair methods. **660**

ramrod Marked by rigidity or stiffness. **383**

ranchero (ran·CHER·oh) Mexican landholder who owned a *rancho*. **405**

rancho (RAN·cho) Vast estate with cattle grazing lands owned by a Mexican citizen. **405**

range right Claim in dry areas to the water of a stream which allowed control of the lands around it. **643**

range war Battle in the 1880s between sheep and cattle ranchers for control of grasslands. **648**

rangy (RAYN·gee) Tall and long-limbed. **643**

rank-and-file Enlisted men or common soldiers as distinguished from the officers. **557**

ratify To approve. **186**

ratifying convention Meeting held in a state for the purpose of approving the Constitution. **226**

ravaged Violently destroyed. **594**

reactionary Person who wants to oppose political or social change. **255**

rebate (REE·bayt) Illegal kickback, or money returned, to preferred shippers by the railroads in the 1870s. **673**

recall Process of removing an official from office by public vote. **791**

reckoning Figuring or calculating. **302**

reclusive Withdrawn from society. **497**

reconcentrado (ree·kawn·sen·TRAH·doh) Concentration camp in Cuba in the 1890s. **749**

Reconstruction Process after the Civil War, of bringing the southern states back into the Union. **595**

Reconstruction Act Four-part measure passed in 1867 that ordered a military occupation of the South and ordered Southerners to give African Americans constitutional rights. **598**

recovery Part of the New Deal plan aimed at boosting the economy. **906**

Red Power Term used by American Indians in the '60s to rally support for the Indian rights movement. **1053**

Red Stick Confederacy Alliance of all Indian tribes east of the Mississippi formed by Tecumseh to resist white expansion. **298**

referendum (ref·uh·REN·duhm) Legal procedure by which the people can revoke a law passed by the legislature. **791**

refined Polished and well-mannered. **30**

reform Part of the New Deal plan aimed at preventing another depression. **906**

regime (ruh·ZHEEM) Form of government. **1062**

regulatory (REG·yuh·luh·tohr·ee) **agency** Government group that supervise business operations. **676**

relatively Somewhat or to a relative extent. **15**

relentless Unwilling to be less harsh or to show pity. **663**

relief Aim of Roosevelt's New Deal to relieve the poverty of many Americans following the Depression. **905**

reminiscent Suggestive of or tending to remind one of. **1120**

Removal Act Law passed in 1830 that provided money to help Indian tribes move west. **396**

reparations (rep·ah·RAY·shunz) Money given by defeated nations as payment for wrongs, damages, or injuries suffered by other nations during a war. **848**

repeal To reject or revoke a law. **268**

repel To drive back. **1060**

Republic of California Name that Californians gave to their country after declaring independence from Mexico. **420**

Republic of Panama Nation formed in 1903 after Panamanians revolted, with U.S. support, against the Republic of Columbia. **771**

Republic of Texas Country formed after Texans declared independence from Mexico in 1836. **410**

Republic of West Germany. Nation formed by combining the zones of Germany controlled by Britain, France and the U.S. after World War II. **989**

Republican Type of government in which power is held by representatives elected by the people. **190**

Republican party Political party formed in 1854 by Northern Whigs and Democrats who opposed slavery. **523**

rescind. To cancel. **130**

reservations Limiting conditions or specific objections. **856**

restrained Quiet or controlled in behavior and manner. **464**

restraint of trade Interference with the free flow of goods or with fair competition. **796**

restraint A control that prevents extreme behavior or activity. **224**

retribution Reward or compensation for good done; can also mean punishment for evil done. **957**

revitalization The giving of new life or restoring energy to. **872**

revived Brought back to life or renewed. **313**

Revolutionary War War for American independence fought by the American colonies against Great Britain (1775-83); also called the War for American Independence. **147**

rhetoric Eloquent but insincere speech. **1016**

Rhode Island system Labor force of children who operated spinning machines in Rhode Island mills. **337**

riddled Pierced with many holes as in rapid gunfire. **823**

rift Split or a drawing apart. **962**

rigging The ropes used to work the sails on a ship. **303**

right of deposit Right to load and unload cargo, especially at New Orleans in the early 1800s. **250**

right of way Strip of land granted by the government to railroad companies laying down tracks. **627**

rigorous Harsh or severe. **50**

Rio Grande (ree·oh·GRAND·ee) "Great River" that forms the border between Texas and Mexico. **418**

Roanoke (ROH·uh·nohk) Island off the coast of North Carolina where two English settlements failed. **43**

Romantic Age Movement in art and literature in the 19th century marked by an interest in nature and an emphasis on natural feelings, emotions and imagination over logic. **495**

Rome-Berlin-Tokyo Axis Alliance formed by Italy, Germany and Japan during World War II. **950**

Roosevelt Corollary Policy that extended the Monroe Doctrine and said that the United States had the right to force countries in the Western Hemisphere to pay their debts in order to prevent European interference. **776**

Rosa Parks Black woman arrested in Alabama in 1955 because she refused to give up her seat on a bus to a white man. **1013**

rotation in office Replacing of government jobholders with other members of the political party in power. **385**

Rough Rider Member of Theodore Roosevelt's regiment sent to Cuba during the Spanish-American War. **754**

round-up Bringing together cattle scattered over the open range. **645**

rubble Broken pieces of masonry or rock; usually associated with the destruction of houses or buildings. **606**

runaway inflation Uncontrollable rise in prices due to a high circulation of paper money. **718**

Rural Electrification Administration New Deal agency that helped bring electricity to remote areas. **915**

Rush-Bagot Agreement Agreement between Great Britain and the United States not to allow naval forces on the Great Lakes. **314**

S

saga Traditional Scandinavian story form that tells about legendary figures and events. **14**

Saigon (sy·GON) Capital of South Vietnam. **1067**

St. Lawrence Seaway Waterway created by deepening the St. Lawrence River from the Atlantic Ocean to the Great Lakes. **1007**

Saint-Mihiel salient (san·mee·YEL SAYL·yahnt). Point on the Western Front where U.S. forces defeated the Germans in WWI. **844**

Salt Lake City City in Utah where the Mormons settled and prospered. **428**

San Francisco Conference The meeting held in 1945 to draft the United Nations Charter. **979**

San Jacinto (san·juh·SINT·oh) Texas town where 1836 defeat of Santa Anna's forces led to Texan independence from Mexico. **410**

San Juan (san·WAHN) **Hill** Site in Cuba of a key victory by Roosevelt's Rough Riders during Spanish-American War (1898). **756**

San Salvador (san·SAL·vuh·dawr) Island where in 1492 Christopher Columbus first landed in the Americas. **24**

sanction Penalty for violating a treaty. **849**

Sandinistas (san·duh·NEES·tuhs) Rebels in Nicaragua who set up a government friendly to the Soviets. **1111**

Santiago (sant·ee·AHG·oh) Cuban seaport captured by American forces during Spanish-American War. **755**

satirize Ridicule or make fun of. **497**

satellite nation Country that is politically or economically controlled by a larger, stronger country. **989**

Saturday Night Massacre The resignations and discharge, in one evening, of top officials in the Justice Department who refused to aid President Nixon in the Watergate cover-up. **1083**

Savannah Georgia city captured by Sherman during Civil War (1863). **583**

scalawag (SKAL·i·wag) Southern white in the Republican party during Reconstruction. **602**

scavenger (SKAV·en·juhr) Animal or organism that feeds on garbage. **347**

Schenectady (skuh·NEK·tuhd·ee) New York town attacked by French and Indians at the start of King Williams' War in 1689. **116**

sea dog Nickname given to English sea captains in the 16th century. **41**

Sea Island cotton Type of Cotton that grew well only on the Sea Islands along the coasts of Georgia and South Carolina. **450**

seaboard Part of the country by the sea. **342**

seaports Harbor town whose economy depends upon the sea. **80**

secede (si·SEED) To withdraw from, as a state leaving the union. **440**

secession (si·SESH·uhn) Withdrawal from an association or group. **278**

Second Bank of the United States National Bank founded in 1816. **388**

Second Battle of Bull Run Confederate victory in Northern Virginia in 1862 that preceded Lee's invasion of Maryland. **568**

Second Continental Congress Meeting of colonial delegates in 1776 at which the Declaration of Independence was written and approved. **150**

Second Great Awakening. Period of religious revival in the 1820s. **494**

Second New Deal New program of reforms introduced by President Roosevelt in 1935 after many of his original New Deal reforms were declared unconstitutional. **918**

Second Open Door Note Second half of U.S. Open Door policy which declared opposition to foreign occupation of China. **769**

Second World War Conflict provoked in 1939 by Germany's invasion of Poland which caused

England and France to declare war on Germany; the United States became involved after the bombing of Pearl Harbor. **937**

sectional conflict Disagreements between the Northeast, South and West over government policies. **371**

secular Pertaining to worldly matters or things not religious or sacred. **818**

secure In this case, to get or obtain. **450**

security Something given as a promise or guarantee of payment. **242**

Sedition Act Law passed in 1918 that made it illegal to oppose the government and its policies. **837**

seepage Pool of oil that has oozed up from the ground. **664**

seethed Boiled with anger. **521**

segregation Separation of people on the basis of racial, religious, or social differences. **511**

Selective Service Act Law passed in 1917 that provided for the draft of men into military service for World War I. **833**

self-determination Principle that all people should be able to decide for themselves which nation they belong to. **846**

self-sufficient Able to take care of oneself. **19**

semiarid Partially dry or getting only light rainfall. **429**

Senate House of Congress in which each state is represented by two senators. **220**

Seneca (SEN·i·kuh) **Falls Declaration** Statement issued by delegates to the 1840 women's rights convention that demanded that women be given the same rights and privileges as men. **483**

separate-but-equal Argument which supported the legality of segregation when races were separated in supposedly equal public schools. **616**

separatist Person who withdrew or separated from the Church of England; also called a Pilgrim. **53**

serf Peasant who under the feudal system was bound to work a master's land. **15**

serial (SIHR·ee·uhl) Story told or TV show shown in continuing parts or sequences. **1037**

servitude Slavery. **613**

settlement house Community center in an urban neighborhood. **690**

Seven Days Before Richmond Series of 1862 Civil War battles during which McClellan's Union forces failed to take Richmond, the Confederate capital. **559**

Seven Years' War European conflict from 1756 to 1763 between England, France and their allies; called the French and Indian War in America. **121**

Seventeenth Amendment Constitutional amendment that provided for the election of senators by popular vote. **791**

"Seward's Folly" Nickname Americans gave the purchase of Alaska in 1867 by Secretary of State William Seward. **741**

shady Not honest or trustworthy. **257**

Shaker Member of a religious group founded in England in 1747 that established several communities in America. **490**

shaman Religious leader in an American Indian tribe who used magic or rituals to heal sickness or control events. **393**

sharecropping System in which landowners provided laborers with the supplies needed for farming in exchange for a portion of their crops. **606**

Shays' Rebellion Uprising in 1787 in Massachusetts protesting high state taxes. **195**

Sherman Antitrust Act Law enacted in 1890 to prevent monopolies by banning trusts and other business combinations that restricted competition. **676**

Sherman Silver Purchase Act Law passed in 1890 that increased the amount of silver bought to 4.5 million ounces a month. **719**

ship of the line During the War of 1812 a British ship armed with 70 or more cannons. **302**

shirker One who avoids his or her duties. **165**

shopping center Stores, restaurants and other businesses grouped together and sharing one parking lot. **1044**

shopping mall Large enclosed building that houses a number of stores, restaurants and other service establishments. **1045**

shrewd Cunning or clever. **44**

shuttle diplomacy Negotiations between two nations carried out by a diplomat who travels back and forth between the two countries; used most often to describe Henry Kissinger's role in seeking peace in the Middle East in the 1970s. **863**

Sicily (SIH·suh·lee) Italian island in the Mediterranean taken by Allied prior to the occupation of Italy during World War II. **961**

sick industry Business such as coal and textiles which did not prosper during the 1920s. **888**

sidled Moved sideways in a sly manner. **641**

Siege of Vicksburg Union attack led by General Grant in 1863 on a key port in the Mississippi River. **580**

Sioux (SOO) Plains Indians who occupied the Dakotas; also called the Dakota. **623**

sit-in Form of protest where a group sits down in a public place and refuses to leave. **1013**

sitting on the fence Political term for not taking a strong stand on a political issue. **701**

Six Days' War Conflict in 1967 between Egypt and Israel quickly won by Israel. **1080**

Sixteenth Amendment Constitutional amendment that gave Congress the power to levy an income tax. **804**

skimped Spent too little money. **1104**

skyscraper Very tall building. **668**

slapstick Crude type of comedy in which the humor depends on horseplay or rough physical activity. **876**

slave state State that permitted slavery. **436**

slave Person who is owned and forced to work for others either by capture, purchase or birth. **86**

sluggish Slow in movement or growth as in a sluggish economy. **907**

smelt To melt away impurities in ore to obtain metal. **662**

smog "Smoke" plus "fog" produced by smoke and chemical fumes. **1104**

sniper Sharpshooter who harasses the enemy by shooting at individuals from a hidden position. **145**

Social Security Act Law passed in 1935 that created a system to provide old-age insurance and unemployment compensation. **919**

socialists Person who believes in public ownership and operation of all means of production and distribution of goods. **792**

society Group of people who live and work together and share similar values and patterns of behavior. **4**

sod house Home made of chunks of grassy soil built by the pioneers of the Great Plains. **650**

soldier of fortune Professional fighter who is willing to fight for any country or group that will pay him. **47**

Solid South Term applied to the southern states who as a group supported the Democratic party after the Civil War. **697**

somber Gloomy or depressing. **1085**

Sons of Liberty Patriot groups who fought against British authority in the American colonies. **128**

soup kitchen Places where food was served to the needy during the Great Depression. **897**

South Korea Korea south of the 38th parallel and backed by U.S. support since World War II. **997**

southern hospitality Term for the friendly welcome given strangers by southerners. **75**

southern regionalism Loyalty to the South, its way of life, and its values. **539**

Spanish-American War (1898) War between Spain and the United States over Cuban independence. **752**

Spanish Armada Large Spanish war fleet defeated by the British in 1588. **42**

Spanish influenza Disease that killed 20 million people worldwide in 1918. **844**

spar Pole used to support the sails of a ship. **80**

special interest group Organization that seeks to influence the government to support its own specific cause. **252**

specialization (spesh·luh·ZAY·shun) Concentration on the manufacture of a particular product; division of labor in which each person does one specific part of the whole process. **369**

speculator Person who invests money where there is a considerable risk but also the possibility of large profits. **241**

spheres of influence Area controlled in large part by a more powerful country, such as parts of China in the 19th century that were influenced by various European nations. **768**

spinning jenny Mechanical spinning wheel invented by James Hargreaves in 1765. **335**

spite Petty ill will or hatred. **422**

spoils of office Term for the dividing up of political rewards by the party that wins. **385**

spoils system Practice by an elected party of rewarding party supporters with appointments to government offices. **385**

Spotsylvania Court House Site of a bloody 1864 Civil War clash between Grant and Lee. **581**

squatters Person who clears and settles a tract of land that he or she does not own. **79**

squeamish Easily shocked or overly sensitive. **221**

stagflation Word coined by combining parts of "*stag*nation" and "in*flation*" which means inflation that is not improving. **1090**

stake a claim To declare ownership of an area by marking it with wooden stakes; especially during the Gold Rush. **434**

stalemate (STAYL·mayt) Deadlock in which neither opposing side can act effectively. **823**

Stamp Act British law that placed a tax on all printed matter in the colonies. **127**

standard of living Average quantity and quality of goods, services, and comforts available in a society. **1032**

Standard Oil Company Business founded in 1870 and built into a monopoly by John D. Rockefeller. **674**

standoff Tie or draw in a contest. **982**

starving time Period of severe hunger in Jamestown that lasted from 1609 to 1611. **48**

states' rights Doctrine that holds that the states not the federal government have the ultimate power. **268**

States' Rights party Political party formed by Southern Democrats (Dixiecrats) in 1948. **993**

Statue of Liberty Statue of the Goddess of Liberty in New York Harbor that was given to the United States by France. **685**

status Position or standing. **470**

steam engine Motor driven by steam patented by James Watt in 1769. **369**

steel plow Farming tool manufactured by James Oliver in 1868 that helped make farming of the hard, dry soil of the Great Plains possible and profitable. **653**

stemmed Stopped or checked a flow. **523**

stint Period of time spent at a particular activity. **1107**

stock certificate Document that shows ownership of stock in a corporation. **661**

stockholder Person who buys shares in a corporation. **661**

Stone Age Early period of human cultural development when stone was used to make tools and weapons. **5**

stovepipe hat Tall silk hat worn during the 1800s. **546**

straggling Wandering from the direct course or from the main group. **724**

strait Narrow water passage connecting two larger bodies of water. **28**

Strait of Magellan Water passage between the Atlantic and Pacific Oceans at the tip of South America. **28**

straitlaced Morally strict or prudish. **69**

Strategic (struh·TEE·jik) **Arms Limitation Treaty** (SALT) Agreement between the U.S. and the Soviet Union to limit nuclear weapons. **1076**

strategic defense initiative ("Star Wars") Complex, computerized anti-missile system that president Reagan urged Congress to support with large sums of money. **1116**

strategy Military plan made to gain an advantage over the enemy. **542**

strife Struggle or conflict. **876**

strike Refusal of employees to work until their demands for better wages or working conditions are met; sudden discovery of gold or silver. **680**

strong reservationist Republican senator who would not support the Treaty of Versailles unless it underwent major changes. **853**

stronghold In this case an area dominated by a particular group such as a political party. **364**

subordinate Under the control of another. **128**

subsidy (SUB·suh·dee) Financial aid provided by the government for programs that benefit the public. **889**

substantial Of a large size or amount. **79**

suburb Residential area located outside a city. **882**

suburbanite One who lives in a suburb. **1044**

subversive Having the intention to undermine or overthrow a government by secretly working from within. **999**

Suez Canal International waterway in the Middle East seized by Egypt in 1956. British, French, and Israeli troops unsuccessfully attempted to end Egyptian control. **1004**

Sugar Act. Law passed in 1764 which taxed the colonists' imports of sugar, wine, and coffee. **124**

summit meeting Conference between the heads of governments to settle political issues. **1005**

Sun Belt Warm weather states in the South and Southwest where population is increasing. **1042**

sunshine patriot Term used by Thomas Paine to describe an American who supported independence only when things were going well. **165**

superstate Government or state having complete power over other subordinate states. **900**

supply Quantity of products and services offered for sale at a certain time or at one price. **875**

supply-side economics Policy followed by President Reagan that lowered tax rates in order to increase spending, which would thereby increase tax revenues. **1110**

Supreme Court Highest U.S. court of appeals, composed of nine justices. **220**

Supreme Court Reform Plan President Roosevelt's unsuccessful plan to add New Deal supporters to the Supreme Court. **925**

suspension bridge Roadway held up by chains or cables anchored on either sides. **668**

Sussex pledge Promise made by the Germans during WWI not to sink passenger or merchant ships. **827**

Sutter's Fort Fortified town built by John Sutter on California's American River in 1839. **413**

swashbuckler Swaggering, boasting soldier. **47**

sweatshop Factory in which workers toil in bad working conditions for low pay. **679**

synthetic Artificial substance or material. **888**

synthetic textile Cloth made from artificial substances. **1035**

T

Taft-Hartley Act Law passed in 1947 to regulate labor union activities and outlaw unfair practices by labor unions as well as employers. **985**

Tammany (TAM·uh·nee) **Hall** Political machine run by New York City Democrats. **698**

Tanks Heavily armed vehicles that move on metal belts first used during WWI. **838**

Tariff of Abominations Act of 1828 that placed a high tariff on imports and was bitterly opposed by Southern states. **385**

tariff question Disagreement between northeastern and southern states in 1830s over tariffs on foreign imports. **385**

tariff Tax on imports; in some countries also placed on exports. **130**

taskmaster A stern boss. **169**

taunted Teased or pestered. **131**

taxation without representation Argument by colonists that they were taxed by the British without being represented in Parliament. **125**

Tea Act Laws passed on 1773 that gave the East India Company exclusive rights to sell tea directly to American retailers. **138**

Teapot Dome Rich government oil reserve in Wyoming that was the subject of a scandal involving the illegal leasing of federal lands during President Harding's administration. **884**

telegraph Machine invented by Morse in the 1840s that transmitted messages through electronic signals sent over wire. **665**

telephone Instrument invented by Bell in 1876 that sends speech over distances by turning sound into electrical current. **665**

television Process of transmitting pictures by radio or wire. **1037**

Teller Amendment Resolution adopted on the eve of the Spanish-American War stating that the United States would not take control of Cuba. **752**

temperance (TEM·puh·ruhns) Movement to restrict the drinking of alcoholic beverages. **500**

tenement (TEN·uh·muhnt) Building in which several families live crowded together, often in unsafe and unsanitary conditions. **348**

tenet Principle or belief outlined in a doctrine or held in common by an organization or group. **539**

Tennessee Valley Authority (TVA) Federal agency established in 1933 to develop the water-power resources of Tennessee River valley. **908**

Tenure (TEN·yuhr) **of Office Act** Law passed in 1867 that prohibited the president from removing appointed officials with the consent of Congress. **598**

territory Area of land under the jurisdiction of the United States government but not yet a state. **190**

Tet offensive Major attack in 1968 on South Vietnamese cities by the North Vietnamese. **1067**

Texas longhorn Type of cattle with low, wide horns that once grazed freely in Texas. **643**

Thanksgiving Day American holiday tradition begun when the Pilgrims gave thanks for the help of the Indians and their first harvest in America. **56**

theory An abstract idea or hypothetical set of facts, principles or circumstances. **606**

third party Political group organized to compete against the two major political parties, usually in a national election. **712**

Thirteenth Amendment Constitutional amendment that abolished slavery. **594**

three-dimensional Having depth or being described in well-rounded completeness, as the characters in a book. **706**

Three-Fifths Compromise Agreement made by the writers of the Constitution to include three fifths of slaves in counting a state's population. **221**

Three Mile Island Nuclear power plant near Harrisburg, Pennsylvania that was the site of an accident in 1979. **1105**

Three R's Fundamental subjects of early American schools—reading, writing, and 'rithmetic. **489**

ticket List of candidates nominated by a political party. **387**

tidewater Name given southern coastal areas where rivers were affected by the ocean tides. **91**

tinkerer One who works on something in an unskilled, clumsy or experimental manner. **667**

Toleration Act Maryland law passed in 1649 that granted freedom of religion to all Christians. **61**

Tom Thumb First steam-driven locomotive, built by Peter Cooper in 1830. **355**

Tonkin Gulf Resolution Authority granted by Congress to Lyndon Johnson in 1964 to approve and support in advance ''the determination of the President, as Commander in Chief, to take all necessary measures to repel any armed attack against the forces of the U.S.'' **1060**

Tory Colonist who remained loyal to England during the Revolutionary War. **155**

total abstinence (AB·stuh·nuhns) Drinking no alcohol. **500**

total war Strategy of war such as that used in the Civil War that calls for the destruction of resources of the enemy's civilian population as well as the army. **583**

totalitarian (toh·tal·uh·TER·ee·uhn) Type of government in which the state has absolute control over all citizens and no opposition to the government is allowed. **937**

tourism Traveling or sightseeing for pleasure. **881**

Townshend Acts (TOWN·zuhnd) Tariff of 1767 that taxed things in everyday use that were not produced by Americans. **130**

tow path Track along the bank of a canal used by men or animals in towing boats. **351**

town common Park-like square in the center of a New England village where the church, meeting house and school were located. **74**

town meeting Gathering of townspeople to act upon town business; early form of government, especially in New England. **110**

township Section of land equalling 36 square miles. **189**

trade deficit Economic situation in which the value of a country's imports is greater than the value of its exports. **877**

Trail of Tears Name expressing the sadness and hardships of the forced removal of Cherokee Indians from Georgia in 1838. **394**

transcendentalism (trans·en·DENT·uhl·is·uhm) Philosophy promoted by a group of New England idealists that people could rise above reason by having faith in themselves. **492**

transcontinental railroad Railway that extends across North America from coast to coast. **628**

Transcontinental Treaty Agreement in 1818 between the U.S. and Spain that extended America's southern boundaries to the Pacific Coast. **311**

transfer payment Money distributed through government programs that provide financial aid to individuals in need. **878**

transistor Miniature electronic device used to control and increase an electronic current. **1035**

Transportation Revolution Advances during the mid-1800s in the speed and ease of transportation systems which joined people in the West with those in the East. **357**

travesty Mockery or grossly inferior imitation. **865**

tread To walk or step. **234**

treasury Department of the government that manages the nation's finances. **234**

treaty of alliance Agreement among countries of support in case of attack. **168**

Treaty of Dancing Rabbit Creek Treaty of 1830 under which Choctaw Indians agreed to move West of the Mississippi. **397**

Treaty of Greenville Agreement in 1795 in which Indians turned over the Southern half of Ohio to American settlers. **250**

Treaty of Guadalupe Hidalgo (GWAHD·uhl·OOP·ay·hi·DALL·goh)

Agreement that ended the Mexican war and arranged the sale of vast territories to the United States. **422**

trench warfare Fighting during World War I that took place in trenches that ran across northern France from the sea to Switzerland. **823**

trend General direction or line of development especially with social change. **502**

Triangle Fire. New York factory fire that killed 140 women and prompted the passing of factory inspection laws. **793**

triangular trade Name given to the profitable trade between the northern colonies, the West Indies, and England although trade did not always flow in a simple triangular fashion. **93**

tribute In this case, any forced payment of money. **276**

Tripartite Pact Mutual defense treaty signed by Germany, Italy and Japan during World War II. **950**

Truman Doctrine U.S. policy to give financial and military aid to nations so they could resist communist rule. **988**

trust Group of corporations formed by a legal agreement and organized especially for the purpose of reducing competition. **674**

trust buster Person who wants to dissolve an established trust. **796**

trustee Person who is entrusted with the management of another person's property. **69**

turbine Rotary engine driven by a pressure of steam, water, or air against the vanes of a wheel; often used to generate electricity. **1106**

turbulent Causing disorder, violence or disturbance. **28**

turnover Shift or change in a company's personnel. **713**

turnpike Road on which tolls are collected. **349**

Tuskegee (tuhs·KEE·gee) **Institute** School for African Americans located in Alabama and founded by Booker T. Washington in 1881. **617**

Twelfth Amendment Constitutional amendment that clarified the electoral process by separating votes for the president and vice president. **271**

Twenty-fifth Amendment Constitutional amendment that said if the president is removed from office the vice president shall become president and that a vacancy in the vice president's office shall be filled by a presidential appointment. **1083**

Twenty-first Amendment Constitutional amendment that ended prohibition by repealing the Eighteenth Amendment. **867**

Twenty-second Amendment Constitutional amendment that said no one could hold the office of president for more than two terms. **985**

Twenty-sixth Amendment Constitutional amendment that gave 18- to 20-year-olds the right to vote. **1106**

two-party system Political system with two major parties of similar strength; in the U.S. these are now the Democratic and Republican parties. **254**

tyranny (TIR·uh·nee) Oppressive and unjust government. **156**

U

U-boats German submarines or "undersea ships" used during World War II. **824**

ultimate Final goal or the maximum point possible. **181**

ultimatum (uhl·tuh·MAYT·uhm) Final offer or demand. **752**

unassuming Not forward or arrogant; modest. **420**

unconditionally Absolutely, without any reservations or restrictions. **974**

unconstitutional Not in keeping with or supported by the laws of the Constitution. **194**

Underground Railroad System by which escaping slaves were secretly helped to reach Canada. **472**

undermine Weaken or hurt by unfair means. **608**

Underwood Tariff Act passed in 1913 that created an income tax and reduced tariffs on imports where American goods controlled the market. **804**

United Farm Workers Organizing Committee Labor union for migrant farm workers formed when the National Farm Workers Association and an organization of Filipino-born laborers merged. **1094**

United Nations International organization of nations formed in 1945 to promote world peace; replaced the League of Nations. **979**

United States of America Country formed by the 13 British colonies in North America who declared independence from Great Britain in 1776. **155**

unprecedented Never been done before. **1033**

unrelenting Determined or persistent. **928**

upheaval Sudden, violent change or disturbance in affairs. **820**

upland cotton Variety of cotton that withstands cold temperatures, making it hardy enough to grow almost anywhere in the southern states. **451**

uppity Arrogant or acting superior. **611**

urban center Area with a population of at least 2,500 persons. **347**

urban decay Decline in prosperity or ruining of a city area caused by a population shift to the suburbs. **1102**

urban frontier Western cities that developed on the edge of settled areas and were used as outposts and depots from which settlers spread. **346**

Urban League Organization founded in 1910 to work for equal rights for African Americans. **923**

usurped Seized power or authority illegally or by force. **998**

U-2 Affair Incident in 1960 when an American spy plane was shot down during a mission over the Soviet Union. **1005**

V

V-E Day Allied victory in World War II when Germany surrendered to the Allies on May 8, 1945. **965**

V-J Day Allied victory in the South Pacific in World War II when Japan surrendered to the U.S. on August 14, 1945. **974**

vagrant Tramp or beggar who wanders from place to place.**154**

vain Thinking too highly of oneself; conceited. **270**

Valley Forge General Washington's winter camp in Pennsylvania where in 1777 the Continental army lost thousands of men to harsh weather and desertion. **169**

vaquero (vah·KAH·roh). Spanish cowhand; they invented almost all the tools of the cowhand's trade. **645**

Venezuela Boundary Dispute Disagreement between Great Britain and Venezuela over boundary between British Guiana and Venezuela that was settled by United States arbitration in 1899. **746**

Veracruz (ver·uh·KROOZ) Mexican seaport captured by Americans in 1847 in War with Mexico. **420**

Verdun French city and site of one of the longest World War I battles. **840**

verge Brink or edge. **522**

Versailles (vuhr·SY) **Peace Treaty** Agreement ending World War I that placed the blame for the war on Germany; also created the League of Nations. **849**

veto Presidential power to reject bills passed by Congress. **225**

viceroy Spanish colonial ruler appointed by the King. **65**

Viet Cong South Vietnamese guerrilla soldiers who are procommunist. **1061**

Vietnam Southeast Asian country where United States and South Vietnam forces fought a war against the communist North Vietnamese. **1003**

Vietnamization Policy of building up the South Vietnamese army so that American troops could be withdrawn. **1073**

vigilance committee Group of volunteers organized to keep watch over a town. **642**

vigilante Volunteer crime fighter; member of a vigilance committee. **642**

Viking. Scandinavian sailor who traveled the seas between the 8th and 10th centuries. **14**

Vincennes (vin·SENZ) Site in the present-day Indiana of 1778 Revolutionary War battle where Clark's forces defeated the British, securing the Northwest in 1778. **173**

Vinland Name for North America used in ancient Viking sagas. **14**

Virginia City Famous Nevada mining boom town. **641**

Virginia Plan Proposal presented at the Constitutional Convention that recommended a government with three separate branches and representation based on population. **220**

virtue Quality of goodness. **400**

void Law no longer in force. **527**

volley Firing of many shots at once. **145**

Volstead Act Law passed in 1919 that declared beverages containing one-half of one percent of alcohol intoxicating. **866**

Volunteers in Service to America (VISTA). Organization similar to the overseas Peace Corps but operating on a domestic level. **1030**

voter participation rate Percentage of eligible voters who vote. **1108**

Voting Rights Act Law passed in 1965 that greatly increased the number of African American voters by putting an end to literacy tests and other practices used to keep African Americans from registering. **1031**

vulcanization Heat and chemical process for hardening rubber. **369**

W

wadding Soft padding material; in colonial days used in packing a bullet in a rifle barrel. **152**

wage and price controls Economic controls set by the government during World War II. **984**

wage and price freeze Controls imposed for 90 days by President Nixon in 1971 to regulate the economy. **1072**

Wagner Labor Relations Act Law passed in 1955 that gave labor unions the right to organize and bargain collectively. **918**

wake Track or path left by a moving ship in the water. **324**

war department Bureau of government in charge of military affairs. **234**

war hawk People from the West and South who favored the War of 1812 against England. **295**

War Industries Board Group that reorganized American industry to support the war effort during WWI. **831**

War of 1812 Conflict from 1812 to 1814 between the U.S. and Great Britain over Indian agitation and freedom of the seas. **301**

warlords Military leaders who controlled the government of an area or country. **937**

Warren Court Supreme court that passed important civil rights legislation under the liberal leadership of Chief Justice Warren from 1953 to 1968. **1007**

Warsaw Pact Twenty-year mutual defense agreement signed in response to NATO by most of the communist nations of Eastern Europe. **991**

wary Cautious or carefully suspicious. **978**

Washita (WAHSH·uh·taw) Site in present-day Oklahoma where Arapaho and Cheyenne were defeated by U.S. army in 1868. **630**

water-frame Spinning machine invented in 1768 by Richard Arkwright; one of the first inventions of the Industrial Revolution because it used a power source other than human or animal muscle. **335**

Watergate Affair Government scandal that began in 1972 and led to the resignation of President Nixon in 1974. **1081**

watershed Important turning point in history. **593**

welfare state Situation in which the government assumes a large measure of responsibility for the social well-being of the people. **801**

well-meaning Having good intentions. **1045**

wended Went or proceeded on one's way. **542**

Western Front WWI combat zone between the Allied states of Belgium, France and Italy and the Central Powers of Germany and Austria-Hungary. **822**

wheedled Coaxed or flattered to get something. **1029**

whet Sharpen or stimulate. **1062**

Whig American who believed in patriotic resistance to King George III; member of a major political party of the 1830s and 1840s. **155**

whirlwind Fast or rushed. **744**

whistle-stop Brief, personal appearance by a political candidate in the course of a tour. **993**

white-collar worker Generally a professional whose job does not involve manual labor. **1036**

wildcatter Name given to oil prospectors in the 1860s. **664**

Willamette Valley Fertile area in Oregon where missionaries began a settlement in the 1830s. **412**

Wilmot Proviso (pruh·VY·zoh) Failed proposal presented in 1846 to prohibit slavery in any land gained from Mexico. **438**

Wisconsin Idea Program of progressive reforms by Robert M. La Follette of Wisconsin in the early 1900s. **790**

withholding system System of paying income taxes where the employer withholds part of an employee's wages to be paid to the government. **955**

Wobblies Nickname for members of the Industrial Workers of the World. **837**

wolf packs Groups of German U-boats that attacked convoys in the Atlantic during WWII. **947**

Women's Liberation Movement Campaign of political action and demonstrations begun in the late 1960s aimed at attaining equal rights for women. **1051**

Women's Rights Convention Meeting in Seneca Falls, New York, in 1840 to seek equal rights for women. **482**

Works Progress Administration (WPA) New Deal agency that found useful work for millions of unemployed persons. **915**

world market International demand for goods and services. **608**

Wounded Knee Site in South Dakota where Sioux Indian families were massacred by United States troops in 1891; also site of 1973 Indian protest. **638**

X

XYZ Affair Scandal in the 1790s in which the French sought bribes from American diplomats. **92**

xenophobia Fear of foreigners or strangers. **865**

Y

Yalta Conference Meeting in 1945 at Yalta in the Crimea between Churchill, Stalin and Roosevelt to plan the defeat and occupation of Germany and German-occupied territories. **980**

Yalu (YOL·oo) **River** River that marks the border between China and North Korea.**999**

Yankee ingenuity (in·juh·NOO·uht·ee) Nickname for American knack for solving difficult problems in clever ways. **92**

yellow journalism Writing style of newspapers that played up the Spanish-American war as well as crime and scandal during the 1890s. **753**

yellow-dog contract Agreement signed by an employee that the employee will not join a union. **682**

Yorktown Battle site in Virginia where in 1871 British general Cornwallis surrendered to George Washington ending the Revolutionary War. **173**

Z

zest Keen enjoyment. **706**

Zimmermann Note Document which showed that Germany was trying to make an alliance with Mexico in 1917 and which prompted the U.S. to declare war on Germany. **830**

Index

Page numbers in *italics* that have a *p* written before them refer to pictures or photographs; *c,* to charts, graphs, tables, or diagrams; and *m,* to maps.

A

AAA. *See* Agricultural Adjustment Act

ABC Powers, 820

Abilene, Kans., 643

abolitionism, 465-67, 470-73, 477, 480, 482, 512, 519, 526, 527, 532, 535

abortion, 1114

absolute monarch, 742

accommodation, 617

acid rain, 1104

ACLU. *See* American Civil Liberties Union

Adams, Abigail, 162-63, 215, 237, *p237*

Adams, John: Boston Massacre and, 133; Declaration of Independence and, 157; election of 1796, 256-57; 1800, 269-71; presidency of, *p256,* 257, 259-61, 266, 268-69, 273, 275, 286; at Second Continental Congress, 150; Treaty of Paris and, 187, *p188;* as vice president, 231; view on conquering the West, 412

Adams, John Quincy: *p399; Amistad* mutiny and, 526; manifest destiny and, 318; presidency of, 380-81, *p380;* as presidential candidate, 379, 382-83; during Revolutionary War, 316; as secretary of state, 316-17, 323-24, 379; and Transcontinental Treaty, 316-17

Adams, Samuel, *p130,* 131, 133, 135, 140, 141, 144, 150, 197, 227

Addams, Jane, 690, *p690,* 762

adding machine, 668

adobe, 6

Adventists, 494

adventure schools, 485

advertising, 669, 876, *887*

advice and consent, 224

Affluent Society, 1032-33

Afghanistan, 1108, *m1128-29*

AFL. *See* American Federation of Labor (AFL)

Africa, *p81-84, m81,* 86, 87-88, 176, 449, 470-71, 822, 849, 862, 941, 959, 961, 1120

African Americans: abolitionists, 470-73, *p471-73;* in Civil War, 570-71, *p571;* after Civil War, 594-98, 601-04, 606-17; cowhands, 646; current status of, 1096-1097, *c1098, p1099, c1100;* Democratic party and, 920, 922, 1107, 1111; Depression of 1893 and, 723; discrimination against, 449-50, 511, 613-16, 805, 807, 833-34, 861-65, 922, 993, 1013, 1030, 1053-55, 1096-1097; draft riots during Civil War and, 572; education of, 449, 450, 601-02, 616, 617, *p617,* 807, 1007, 1010-12, *c1097;* employment of, 958; equality for, 807-08, 862-64, 872, 923, 924, 958, 993, 1007, 1010-13, 1025, 1030, 1031, 1053-57, *p1054-56,* 1096-97, *p1097;* as farmers, 717; free African Americans before Civil War, 449-50, 566-67; Gold Rush and, 435, *p435;* in government, 270, 602-04, *p604,* 923; Great Depression and, 896, 922; after the Great War, 860, 861-65; during the Great War, 833-34; Harlem Renaissance and, 872; heritage of, *p81-84, m81;* income of, *c1096, c1100;* inventors, 668; in labor unions, 680; Lewis and Clark expedition and, 281; literature of, 872, 933; lynching of, 617, 808-09, 862; migration to northern cities, 862, 920-21; in the military, 163, 570-71, *571,* 833-34, *p863,* 957-58, 964-65; music of, 870-71, *p870, p871;* New Deal and, 922-23; during 1920s, 920-22; population of, *c463;* during Progressive Era, 787, 805, 807-09, *p807, p808;* race riots and, 860, 862, 1068, 1097; during Reconstruction, 602-12, *p602, p604, p607, p609, p610,* 619; Republican party and, 698, 920, 922; during Revolutionary War, 163; in Spanish-American War, 756; in sports, 874, 938, *p938;* in the Twenties, 870-72, *p870, p871;* voting rights of, 214, 613; in War of 1812, 306; on Woodrow Wilson, 828; during World War II, 957-58, *p958. See also* Africa; National Association for the Advancement of Colored People; slavery

African National Congress, 862

Afrika Korps, 961

Age of Discovery, 20-26, *p20, p22, p23, m24, p26,* 36

Age of Realism, 706-11, *p710-11*

Age of Reason, 98-99

Age of Reform, 476-94, 498-05

Agee, W. H. R., 614

Agnew, Spiro T., 1071, 1081, 1083

Agricultural Adjustment Act (AAA), 907-908, 917, 922, 926

agriculture. *See* farming and farmers

agriculture, department of, 703

Aguinaldo, Emilio, 762, *p762,* 767

AIDS (Acquired Immune Deficiency Syndrome), 1114

AIM. *See* American Indian Movement (AIM)

airplanes, 840, *p840,* 873, 952, 954, 1034, *c1050*

Alabama, 188, 306, 307, 365, 393, 395, 452, *m649, m655, m715,* 1013, *m1130-31*

Alamo, 410, *p410, m411,* 417

Alaska, 7, *m649, m655, m715,* 737, 740-41, *m740,* 799, 1007, 1042, 1122-23, *m1123, m1130-31*

Alaska pipeline, 1122-23, *m1123*

Alaskan Purchase, 740-41, *m740*

Albany, N.Y., *p476*

Albany Congress, 184

Albany Plan of Union, 100,101, 184

alcohol, prohibition of, 500-02, *p501,* 866-67, *p866*

Alcott, Bronson, 491-92, *p492*

Alcott, Louisa May, 492

Aldrin, Edwin "Buzz", 1020

Alexander, E. P., 573

Alger, Horatio, Jr., 670-71

Algonquin (ship), 830

Algonquin Indians, *m10*

Alien and Sedition Acts, 261, 267, 268, 269, 273

Allan, John, 495

Allen, Ethan, 147

Alliance for Progress, 1017

alliances, 817

Allies: in Great War, 817-18, *m841, c841;* in World War II, 959

Allison, William B., 718-19

almshouse, 499

Alperovitz, Gar, 992

Altgeld, John Peter, 725, *p728*

Amalgamated Association of Iron and Steel Workers, 682

Amana community, 490-91

Amazon River, 176

ambush, 631

amendments: Bill of Rights, 210-12, 237-38, *c239,* 266-67; Equal Rights Amendment, 1101-02; procedures for amending Constitution, 209, 239; text of, 211-18; 1st, 266-67; 12th, 206, 271; 13th, 594; 14th, 597, 598, 611, 614, 794-95; 15th, 600; 16th, 802; 17th, 791-92; 18th, 866; 19th, 858; 20th, 202; 21st, 867; 22nd, 985; 25th, 1083; 26th, 1106

America (naming of), 27

American Anti-Imperialist League, 764

American Anti-Slavery Society, 466

American Civil Liberties Union (ACLU), 865, 868

American Colonization Society, 449

American Expeditionary Force (AEF), 833, 840

American Federation of Labor (AFL), 681-82, 833, 927, 1034

American Fur Company, 412

American Indian Movement (AIM), 1053

American Indians. *See* Indians

American Protective Association, 686

American Railway Union, 724

American Red Cross Society, 574

American Revolution, 124-75; interpreting causes of, 132. *See also* Revolutionary War

American Samoa, 1022, *m1023*

American System, 379-80

American Telephone and Telegraph Company, 666

American Temperance Union, 501

Amistad **mutiny,** 525, 526

amnesty, after Civil War, 593

Amnesty Act of 1872, 611

Amory, Thomas, 94

Anaconda, 640, p640

anarchists, 767, 860, 865

Anasazi Indians, *p6,* 9

Anderson, John, 1110

Anderson, Robert, 543, 547

Andes Mountains, 176, *m325*

André, John, 173

Andros, Sir Edmund, 111-12

Anglican Church, 53

animals, 37, *p43,* 280, 283, *p283,* 623, 624-25, 1122-23. *See also* cattle; horses; sheep; ranches and ranching

annexation, 405

Anthony, Susan B., 483

anthropology, 9

antibiotics, 1035

anti-imperialists, 762-64

Antietam, Battle of, 568-69, *p569, m570*

Antifederalists, 226-29, 231

antitrust movement, 674-77, 802

antiwar movement, 939-40, 1071, 1073, 1074, *p1075,* 1078

Apache Indians, 407, 623

Apalachicola River, 314

apartheid, 1118

Apollo 11, 1020

Appalachian Mountains, *m10,*101, 120, 123, 186, *m186, m274, m296,* 317, *m349, m351, m356,* 586, 810, *m811, m1130-31*

appellate courts, 224

Appleby, John, 653

Appomattox Court House, *m582,* 584-85, *p585*

Arab oil crisis, 1080

Arab states, 1004-05, 1080

Arapaho Indians, *m10,* 358, 623, 630

arbitration treaties, 818

archaeology, 9

archipelago, 741

architecture, 871

Argentina, *m325,* 820, *m1128-29*

Argonne Forest, Battle of the, *m841,* 844

Arizona, *m444,* 629, *m636, m644,* 639, 640, *m649, m655, m715,* 820, 836, *m1130-31*

Arizona, U.S.S., 952

Arkansas, 452, *m517, m649, m655, m715, m1130-31*

Arkansas River, 285, *m624*

Arkwright, Richard, 335, *p335*

Armenians: genocide by Turks in World War I, 938

armistice, 844

Armstrong, Louis "Satchmo," 870

Armstrong, Neil, 1020

army: African Americans in, 163, 570-71, *p571,* 833-34, *p863,* 957-58, 964-65; in Civil War, 549-57, *p553, p555,* 559, 565, 572; draft for, 565, 572, 833, 943-44; in the Great War, 817, 822-24, 840, 842-44; Hispanic Americans in, 836, 958; in Revolutionary War, 152-55, *p152, p153;* in Spanish-American War, 753-55; in World War II, 936, 959, 961-65; in Korean War, 998-99, *p998,* 1003; in Vietnam War, 1060-67, *p1060, p1064,* 1072-74, *p1073,* 1077-80, *c1080*

Army-McCarthy Hearings, *p1002,* 1003

Army of Northern Virginia, 559

Army of the Potomac, 557

Arnold, Benedict, 168, 170, 173, 187, 191

art, 415, 709-11, *p710-11;* Ashcan School, *p782;* during 1920s, 871; Realism in, 709-11, p710-11. *See also* captions for information about specific art

Arthur, Chester A., 705, *p705*

Articles of Confederation, 185-87, 196, 197, 199, *c199,* 200, 210, 222

Asia. *See* names of specific countries

Connell, Evan S., 632
Conot, Robert, 668
conquistadors, 31, 33-34, p33
conscientious objectors, 939
consciousness-raising, 1052
conservation, 798-99
conservatism, of early state constitutions, 182-83
Constellation, U.S.S., 286
Constitution, Confederate, 543-44
Constitution, U.S.: amendments of, 202, 206, 209, 211-18, 237-38, c239, 266-67, 271, 594, 597, 598, 600, 611, 614, 791-92, 794-95, 802, 858, 866, 867, 985, 1083, 1106; branches of government in, 220, 222-24; checks and balances and, 224-25, c225; federalism and, 197-99, c198, c199; Great Compromise and, 220; Preamble of, 197, 199, 201; ratification of, 210, 226-229, c227, 231; historical interpretations of reasons for writing, 219; secession and, 538-39; signing of, p196, 221; slavery and, 220-22; text of, 200-18; women and, 222
Constitution, U.S.S., 286, 302, p302, 303, 305
Constitutional Convention, 196-99, p197, 200, 220-25
Constitutional Unionist party, 536-37
constitutions, state, 182-83, 184, 190, 209
containment policy, 991-92
Continental Congress: First, 143, 184; Second, 150-51, p150, 157, 184
continental divide, 281-82
Continental dollars, 192-93
contrabands, 565
Contras, in Nicaragua, 1114-15
Convention of 1800, 269
convoys, 949
Coolidge, Calvin, 861, 884-89, p885
Coolidge, Grace Goodhue, p885
Cooper, James Fenimore, 330, 367-68, p367, 377
Cooper, Peter, 355, p703
Cooper, Sir Anthony Ashley, 66
copper, 640, 654
Copperheads, 561-62, p561
Coral Sea, Battle of, 966
corn production, 378
Cornwallis, Charles, 171-75, p175, 187, 191
Coronado, Francisco, 34

corporations, 661, 781-83, 802
Corps of Discovery, 280-81, p283
corrupt bargain, 381
Cortés, Hernan, 29-31, 33, 35
cotton, 372-73, 450-55, p450, m457, c457, 463, 564, p607, p609
cotton boll, 450, p450
cotton diplomacy, 564
cotton gin, 451-52, p452
"Cotton is King," 463
cotton mills, 332
Coughlin, Charles E., 918, p918
Council of New England, 57-58
county courts, 110
courts: federal, 208, 224, 273; Jefferson's presidency and, 273; reform and, 795; state, 182
Covey, James, 526
cowhands, 645-47, p645, p647
Cowpens, Battle of, 171, m171
Cox, Archibald, 1083
Cox, James M., 858, p858, 903
Coxey, Jacob, p723, 724
Coxey's Army, 723-24
Craft, Ellen, 512
Craft, Samuel, 163
Craft, William, 512
Crane, Stephen, 708-09, p709
Crawford, William H., 379, 380
Crazy Horse, Chief, 632
Creek Indians, m10, 306, 314, 396
Creek War, m301, 306-07
Creel, George, 836
CREEP. *See* Committee for the Reelection of the President (CREEP)
crime, 866-67, 1114
Crime of 1873, 718
Crockett, Davy, 410
Croker, Richard, p699
crop-lien system, 608-09
Cross of Gold speech, 727-28, p727
Crusades, 16-17, p17
Cuba: communism in, 1016-17; Cuban Missile Crisis, 1018-19; dollar diplomacy and, 777; immigrants from, 1095; Ostend Manifesto and, 518; revolution in, 747-50, p748, 751, 753; as Spanish colony, 747; Spanish-American War in, 753-56, m756, 761, 762; sugar production in, 742; U.S. interest in, 323-24, 518, 541
Cuban Americans, p1088, 1095, c1095
Cuban Missile Crisis, 1018-19
Cuffe, Paul, 470-71

Cullen, Countee, 872
cultural landscape, 358
culture, 4
Cumberland Road, m349, 350
Currier, Nathaniel, 415
Custer, George Armstrong, 632, p632, 633
Custis, Martha Dandridge, 76, p76. *See also* Dandridge, Martha; Washington, Martha
Czechoslovakia, 849, 988-89, 991, m991, m960, m989, 1118, m1128-29
Czolgosz, Leon, 767

D

D-Day, 962, p963
Da Gama, Vasco, 22
dadaism, 871
Dakota Territory, 623, 630, 631, 632, m636, m644, 651, 653
Dale, Thomas, 49, 50
Daley, Richard, 1071
Dalrymple, Oliver, 653
Daly, Marcus, 640
dame schools, 484
dance, 871
Dandridge, Martha, 73. *See also* Custis, Martha Dandridge; Washington, Martha
Dare, Ellinor, 43
Dare, Virginia, 43
dark horse candidate, 405
Darrow, Clarence, 837, 869
Darwin, Charles, 37, 738-39, 783, 868
Davis, Jefferson, 544-46, p544, p545, 547, 574, 582
Davis, John W., 885-86
Dawes, William, 144
Dawes Severalty Act, 638-39, 1052
Dayton, Ohio, 690
De La Warr, Lord, 48
De León, Juan Ponce, 33
De Tocqueville, Alexis, 355, p478, 499, 504-05
Dean, John, 1082-83
Debs, Eugene V., 725, 802, 838
Decatur, Stephen, 275, p275, p276
decisions, evaluation of, 972
Declaration of Independence, 157-63, 174, 184, 222, 465, 482-83, 531
Declaratory Act, 128-29
Deerfield, Mass., p116, 117

m818; casualties and costs of, *p841*, 844, 848, *c1080;* Eastern Front of, 822, *m822;* end of, 844, 846; European boundaries after, 846, *m847*, 849; postwar reaction in U.S., 852-65; propaganda during, 836; protest during, 836-38; time line of, *c850-51;* U.S. activities at home during, 831-38, *p832-33, 835;* U.S. entry into, 830, 851; U.S. involvement in, 840, 842-44; U.S. neutrality at beginning of, 818-19; Versailles Peace Conference, 846, 848-49, *p848;* war on the Atlantic, 824-27, *m825, p825;* weapons used during, 826-27, 838, *p839*, 840; Western Front of, 822-24, 840, *m841*, 842-44; Wilson's peace plans, 829-30, 845-46, 848

Greece, *m943, m960,* 986, *m991, m1128-29*

Greek Americans, 683

Greeley, Andrew M., 343-44

Greeley, Horace, 633

Green Mountain Boys, 147

Greenback party, 712

greenbacks, 702-03

Greene, Nathanael, 171

greenhouse effect, 930-31, 1104

Greenville, Fort, 248

Grenville, George, *p109*, 124, 127, 128

Grimké, Angelina, 466, *p466*, 482

Grimké, Sarah, 466, *p466*, 482

Guadalcanal, Battle of, 968, *m967*

Guam, 761, *m767*, 1022, 1023, *m1023*

guerrillas, 522

Guilford Court House, Battle of, 172

Guinn v. U.S., 613

Guiteau, Charles, 705

Gulf of Mexico, 176, 177, *m177, m1130-31*

Gulf Stream, 177

gun control, 1113

gunboat diplomacy, 777

Gutenberg, Johann, 19

Guthrie, Woody, 911

H

habeas corpus, right of, 562

Haldeman, H. R., 1082, 1085

Hale, Sara Josepha, 480

Hallidie, Andrew S., 692

Hamilton, Alexander: Bank of the United States and, 204, 242-43, 256, 273, 388; at Constitutional Convention, 196; death of, 279, *p279;* disagreements with Jefferson and, 255-56; Federalist Papers and, 228-29; Federalists and, 255; national debt and, 240-41, 252, 273; as secretary of treasury, 235, *p235*, 236, *p240;* support for war, 261, 269; view of Adams, 257, 269-70; view of government, 784; view of Senate, 224

Hampton, Wade, 611

Hancock, John, 144, 150, 227

Hancock, Winfield Scott, 712

Handy, W. C., 870, *p870*

Hanna, Marcus, 729

Hanoi, *m1063,* 1078

hard money, 193, 388, 702

Harding, Warren G., 858, 859-60, 884, *p885*, 903

Hargreave, James, *p334,* 335

Harkins, George M., 397

Harlan, John Marshall, 616, *p616*

Harlem, 920-22

Harlem Globetrotters, 874

Harlem Renaissance, 872, *p872*, 921-22

Harmar, Joseph, 247

Harpers Ferry, Va., 532-35, *p534*

Harriman, E. H., 796, *p797*

Harris, Joel Chandler, 706

Harrison, Benjamin, 712, *p712, p713*, 743, 744

Harrison, William Henry, 297, 298, *p298*, 299, *p299*, 305-06, 400-01, 404

Harte, Bret, 641

Hartford Convention, 313

Hastie, William, 923

Hawaii, 741-43, *m649, m655, m715, m742, p743, p757-60*, 762, *m767*, 779, 950-52, *p951*, 1042, 1092, *m1130-31*

hawks, 1064

Hawthorne, Nathaniel, 495-96, *p496*, 706

Hay, John, 762, 768, 771

Hay-Bunau-Varilla Treaty, 772

Hay-Pauncefote Treaty, 770

Hayden, Tom, 1074

Hayes, Rutherford B.,611-12, *p611*, 698, 704-05

Haymarket bombing, 681

Haywood, William D., 837

Head Start, 1030

headright, 50

health, education and welfare department, 1006

Hearst, George, 640

Hearst, William Randolph, 750, 753

Hellman, Lillian, 996

Hemingway, Ernest, 877-78, *p877*

Henry, Fort, *m577*, 578

Henry, Patrick, 150-51, 173

Henry the Navigator (Prince), 22, *p22*

Henry VII (king of England), 23, 40, 62

Henry VIII (king of England), 53

Hepburn Act, 797

heritage, cultural: portfolios of: American Indian, *p10-14;* Hispanic, *p81-84;* Pacific, *p757-60;* West African, *p81-84*

Hernandez, Joseph, 400

Hessians, 165

Hicks, Edward, 101, *p102*

Hidalgo y Costilla, Miguel, 323, 407

Hill, Anita, 1100

Hill, James J., 660, 796, *p797*

Hillsborough, Lord, 130, 133

Hindenburg Line, *m841,* 844

Hirohito (Emperor), 937

Hiroshima, 974, *m967*

Hispanic Americans: in Civil War, 571; culture of, 407-09, 423-26, 717-18; current status of, 1093-95, *p1093, p1094, p1095, c1095;* Depression of 1893 and, 723; discrimination against, 1093-94; elected officials, 400, 836; farmers, 717; Great Depression and, 896, 922; heritage of, 319, *p319-22*, 1093-95; New Deal and, 922-23; during World War II, 958. *See also* Mexican Americans; Cuban Americans

Hispaniola, 25

Hiss, Alger, 994, 1014

historical significance, 325

Hitler, Adolf, *p936*, 937-38, 942, 944-45, 947, 949, 959, 965

Ho Chi Minh, 1074

Ho Chi Minh City, 1078

Ho Chi Minh Trail, *m1063,* 1074

Hoar, George F., 762

Hobart, Garret A., 767

Hobby, Oveta Culp, 1006, *p1006*

Hodgdon, Mary, 339

Hodgdon, Sarah, 339-40

103; drawing conclusions, 1066; editorial cartoons, 775; election results, 716; essay composition, 914; evaluation of decisions, 972; facts versus opinions, 258; graph of business cycles, 605; graphs, 78, 605; latitude and longitude, 46; maps, 32, 46, 146, 274, 356, 517, 649; paragraph composition, 806; photographs, 399; physical maps, 274; points of view, 855; sequence, 481; special-purpose maps, 356; statistical charts, 558; statistics, 457, 558; study plan, 230; synthesizing information, 296; tables, 688; time lines, 21; tracing of movements on maps, 146; using SQ3R, 230; expressing point of view, 1113

street cars, 693
strikes, 680-82, 724-25, *p725*, 798, 802, 837, 860-61, *p861*, 927, 985. *See also* unions
Strong, Josiah, 738-39
strong reservationists, 853
Student Nonviolent Coordinating Committee (SNCC), 1013
Students Against Drunk Driving (S.A.D.D.), 501
study skills. *See* strategies for success
Stuyvesant, Peter, 64
submarines, 824-27, 829-30, 947-48, *p948*, 949, 1035
subsidies, 888
suburbs, 882, *p882*, 1044-45, *p1044*
Suez Canal crisis, 1004-05
suffrage. *See* voting rights
sugar, *p90*, *m91*, 93, 114, 124-27, *p125*, 741-42
Sugar Act, 124-27, 130
sugar cane, 372
Sullivan, Anne, 498, *p498*
summit meeting, 1005
Sumner, Charles, 521
Sumter, Fort, 543, 547-48, *p548*, 550, *m577*
Sumter, Thomas, 171
Sun Belt, 1042, *p1043*, *m1043*
Sunday, Billy, 869
supply-side economics, 1110
supremacy clause, 209
Supreme Court: on abortion, 1112; *Amistad* mutiny and, 525, 526; Bank of the United States and, 388, 391; black peonage ruling,

608; *Brown v. Board of Education of Topeka* decision, 1007, 1010-12; business rulings, 677, 715, 796; civil rights, 1007, 1010, 1013; congressional law as unconstitutional, 527; in Constitution, 220, 224; Dred Scott case decision, 525, 526, 527; freedom of speech, 838; grandfather clause ruling, 613; Indian claims and, 394, 395; Jefferson's presidency and, 273; New Deal and, 917, 918, 924-25, *p925;* and power of federal government, 204; Reagan appointments to, 1112, 1113-14; responsibilities of, 224, 273; separate-but-equal argument of, 614-16; Watergate Affair and, 1084; female justice, 1100; women's employment, 795

Supreme Court Reform Plan, 925
survival of the fittest theory, 672, 738-39, 783
suspension bridges, 668
Sussex (ship), 827
Sussex pledge, 827
Sutter, John A., 413, 431
Sutter's Fort, 413, *p413*, 419-20, 431
Sutter's Mill, 431-32, *p431*
Swamp Fox. *See* Marion, Francis
Sweden: *m63*, 64, *m818*, *m847*, *m943*, *m960*, *m991*, *m1128-29*
Swedish West India Company, 64
swimming, 874
Swing, A. J., *p189*
synthesizing of information, 296
synthetics, 887, 1035

T

tables, reading of, 688, *c1137-40*
Taensa Indians, *p62*
Taft, Robert A., 946, 998
Taft, William Howard, 698, 776-77, 799, *p799*, 800, 802, 818, 946
Taft-Hartley Act, 985, 993
Taiwan (Formosa), 995, 999, 1114, *m1128-29*
Talleyrand, Charles de, 259-60, 269, 277-78
Tammany Hall, 698-99, *p699*, *p700*
Tampa, Fla., 1099
Taney, Roger B., 526, 527
tanks, 838, *p839*
Tappan, Arthur, 466
Tappan, Benjamin, 466

Tarbell, Ida, 785, *p785*, 786-87
Tariff Act (1789), 240
Tariff of Abominations, 385-87
Tariff of 1816, 331, 332
tariffs, 130, 192, 198, 240, 330-31, *c331*, 380, 385-87, 502, 535-36, 701-02, 714, 742, 799, 802, 886, *c1140*
taxation without representation, 125-26
taxes and taxation, 124-31, 133, 138-40, 143, 192-93, 198, 203, 252, 886, 919, 955, 1020, 1110, 1111-12
Taylor, Zachary, 418, *p418*, 420, 437, *p437*, 443
Tea Act, 138-40
Teapot Dome reserve, 884
technology. *See* science and technology
Tecumseh, 297-99, *p297*, 305, 306
telegraph, 665, 667
telephone, 665-66, *p665*, 887
television, 1003, 1020, 1034, 1036-38, *c1037*, *p1038*, 1050, 1107
Teller, Henry M., 752
Teller Amendment, 752
temperance, 500
temperance movement, 500-02, 866-67
Temple, Lewis, 449
tenements, 348, 690-92, 787-88, *p788*, 793
Tennessee, 252, 614, *m649*, *m655*, *m715*, *m1130-31*
Tennessee Valley Authority (TVA), 908, *m909*, 946, 1030-31
tennis, 874
Tenskwatawa (the Prophet), *p298*, 299
Tenure of Office Act, 598-99
territories, U.S., 190, 436-43, *c737*, 1022-23, *m1023*
terrorism, 817, 861
Tet offensive, 1067
Texas: *m444*, *m624*, *m649*, *m655*, *m715*, *m1130-31;* agriculture in, 452, 720; annexation by treaty, 405, 417; cattle kingdom in, 643-48, *m644;* exploration of, 34, 285; Indians in, 623; Lone Star flag of, *p417;* Mexican Americans in, 405-08, 423-24, 820, 836; as Mexican possession, 405, 408-09; as Mexican province, 316; and Mexican War, 418-22, *m422;* oil industry in, 883, 1114; and railroads, 643-44,

nial wars, 119, *p119*, 120; as hero to French, 244; inauguration of, 207, *p222*, 230, 231, *p231*; interest in farming, 100; plans for District of Columbia, 270, *p272*; presidency of, 207, 222, 234-37, *p235*, *p236*, 242-43, 246-48, 250-53, *p253*, 263, 272, 275, 388, 737; in Revolutionary War, 154-55, *p154*, 164-70, *p169*, 174-75, *p175*, 196; at Second Continental Congress, 151; as slaveholder, 163; view on Indians, 398

Washington, Martha, *p151*, 163, 236-37, *p236*

Washington Disarmament Conference, 859-60

Washita, Battle of, 630, *m636*

water rights, 429-31, 643-45

water-frame, 335

Watergate Affair, 1081-85

watershed (of history), 593

Watt, James, 353

Wayne, Anthony, 248, *p248*, 251, *p251*, 280

weapons: atomic bombs, 971-75, *p973*, 991, 992, 1001-02; of Civil War, 555-56; of the Great War, 826-27, 838, *p839*, 840; gun control, 1113; manufacturers of, 940; nuclear weapons, 1019; Plains Indians, 625; production of, 330, 333-34; in Revolutionary War, 152-53, *p152*, 154; right to own, 211, 237; Star Wars (Strategic Defense Initiative), 1116; in World War II, 954

Weatherford, William. *See* Red Eagle

Weaver, James Baird, 722, *p722*

Weaver, Robert, 923

Webster, Daniel, *p439*, 440, 441-43

Webster, Noah, 485, *p485*

Weedon, John, 194

Weismuller, Johnny, 874

Weld, Theodore Dwight, 461, 466-67, 512

welfare state, 801, 928

Wellington, Duke of, 308

Wells, Ida B., 808-09

West: changing geographic location of, 810-11; Civil War in, 577-80, *m577*, *p579*, *p580*; effect on democracy of, 374-75, 633; in early 19th century, 374-78, *p375, p378*; geography of, 444-45, *m444*; im-

ages of, 810; and Japanese Americans during World War II, 956-57; manifest destiny, 412-13; Mexican American communities in, 717-18; Oregon Trail, 413-14, 416-17; paintings of, *p62*; Revolutionary War in, 173, *m173*; settlement of, 633; water rights in, 429-31; water routes to, *m430*; women in, 377. *See also* frontier; names of specific states

West Germany, 989, *m991, m1128-29*

West Indies, *p90, 92-94, m94*, 114, 191, 250, 286, 287

Western Trail, 643, *m644*

Western Union Telegraph Company, 665, 666

Westmoreland, William C., 1067

westward expansion, 317-18, *p363, m1134*

Wetatonmi, 636-37

Weyler, Valeriano, 749, 753

whaling, 449

Wheatley, Phillis, 154

Whig party, 400-01, 404-05, 437, 516, 523, 524

Whigs, in Revolutionary War, 155, 163

Whiskey Rebellion, 252, *p253*

Whistler, James A. McNeill, 711, *p711*

White, John, 43, *p43*

white-collar workers, 1036

Whitefield, George, 95-96, *p95, 493*

Whitman, Marcus, 413, 414

Whitman, Narcissa Prentice, 413

Whitman, Walt, 496-97, *p497*, 592, 659, 709

Whitney, Eli, 333-34, 368, 451-52, *p451, 663*

Whittier, John Greenleaf, 495, 706

wildcatters, 664

Wilderness, Battle of, 581, *m582*

Willamette River, 413

Willamette Valley, 412-13, *m444*

Willard, Emma Hunt, 478

William and Mary (king and queen of England), 111-12, *p111*

Williams, Euphemia, 512

Williams, Roger, 59-60, *p59*

Williams, William A., 992

Williamson, Joel, 604

Willkie, Wendell, 946-47

Wills, Helen, 874, *p874*

Wilmot, David, 438, 516

Wilmot Proviso, 438, 516

Wilson, Woodrow: arbitration treaties and, 818; domestic activities during Great War of, 831-32, 836, 838; in election of 1916, 828-29, *p828*; foreign policy of, 819; Fourteen Points of, 845-46; and the Great War, 830, 840, 845-46, 851; illness of, 854, *p854*, 856; League of Nations and, 849, 852-56; Mexican Revolution and, 820-21; neutrality and, 819, 940; Versailles Peace Conference and, 846, 848-49, *p848*; Versailles Peace Treaty and, 852-56, *p856*, 978

Winnemucca, Sarah, 638

Winslow, Edward, 71

Winthrop, John, 58, *p58*

Wisconsin, *m186*, 190, *m190, m649, m655, m715*, 790-91, *m1130-31*

Wisconsin Idea, 790-91

withholding system, for income taxes, 955

Wobblies, 837

Wolcott, Oliver, 334

wolf packs (submarines), 947

Wolfe, James, 121, *p122*, 147, 149

women: as abolitionists, 471-72, 477, 480, 482; child-rearing and, 75, 480; during Civil War, 567, 574; in colonial America, 56, 60, 75-76, *p75, p76, 79, p80*; education of, 239, 337, 477-78, *p 478*, 485; employment of, 669, 670, 795, 834-35, *p835*, 952-53, *p953*, 955, 958, 1036, *c1036*, 1051, *c1099*; Equal Rights Amendment and, 1098; equal rights and, 1051-52, 1098-99; factories and, 336-37, 339-41, 952-53, *p953*; in federal government, 906, 1099; during Great Depression, 896; during the Great War, 834-35, *p835*; income of, *c1101*; in Jacksonian America, 477-79, *p477*; in labor unions, 680; in Mexico, 408; in politics, 1111; in professions, 479-80, *p479, p480*; during Revolutionary War, 162-63; in Roaring Twenties, 871; and sexual harrassment, 1100; voting rights for, 214, 791, *p792, p857, m857*, 858; in the West, 377; westward journeys of, 414, 416-17; women-owned businesses, 1099-1100; on Woodrow Wilson, 828; during World War II, 952-53,

Acknowledgments

For permission to reprint copyrighted material, grateful acknowledgment is made to the following sources:

American Federation of Labor and Congress of Industrial Organizations: Adapted from "America, We Beg You to Interfere" by Aleksandr I. Solzhenitsyn in the *AFL-CIO American Federationist,* July 1975. Copyright © 1975 by AFL-CIO.

Anchor Books, an imprint of Doubleday, a division of Bantam, Doubleday, Dell Publishing Group, Inc: From "The Immigrant Experience" from *The Ordeal of Assimilation: A Documentary History of the White Working Class,* edited by Stanley Feldstein and Lawrence Costello. Copyright © 1974 by Stanley Feldstein and Lawrence Costello.

Atheneum Publishers, an imprint of Macmillan, Inc.: From "The Vast Wasteland" from *Equal Time: The Private Broadcaster and The Public Interest* by Newton N. Minow, edited by Lawrence Laurent. Copyright © 1964 by Newton N. Minow.

Atlantic Monthly Press: From "A New Hopi Girl" from *Eskimos, Chicanos, Indians: Volume IV of Children of Crisis* by Robert Coles, M.D. Copyright © 1977 by Robert Coles.

Beacon Press: Adapted from *The Broken Spears, The Aztec Account of the Conquest of Mexico,* edited by Miguel Leon-Portilla. Copyright © 1962 by Beacon Press.

Laura Benet: "Fifth Avenue and Grand Street" by Mary Carolyn Davies.

Columbia University Press: From "Conclusion" from *The United States and the Origins of the Cold War, 1941–1947* by John Lewis Gaddis. Copyright © 1972 by Columbia University Press.

Crisis Publishing Company, Inc.: From "The Task for the Future—A Program for 1919" by the NAACP. Copyright 1919 by Crisis Publishing Company, Inc.

The Dial Press/James Wade, an imprint of Bantam, Doubleday, Dell Publishing Group, Inc: From "The Man Upstairs" from *Dulles: A Biography of Eleanor, Allen, and John Foster Dulles and Their Family Network* by Leonard Mosley. Copyright © 1978 by Leonard Mosley.

Fortress Press, a division of Augsburg Fortress Publishers: From *Straight from the Heart* by Reverend Jesse L. Jackson, edited by Roger D. Hatch and Frank E. Watkins. Copyright © 1987 by Jesse L. Jackson.

Rodolfo Gonzáles: From *I Am Joaquín/Yo Soy Joaquín: An Epic Poem* by Rodolfo Gonzáles. Copyright © 1967 by Rodolfo Gonzáles.

Greenpeace: From "Jesse Jackson" from "How We Can Save It" from *Greenpeace,* vol. 15, no. 1, January/February 1990. Copyright © 1990 by Greenpeace.

Greenwood Press: From "God's Country and Mine" by Jacques Barzun.

Harcourt Brace Jovanovich, Inc.: From "War Lords and Vassals" from *V was for Victory: Politics and American Culture During World War II* by John Morton Blum. Copyright © 1976 by John Morton Blum. From *The Constitution: Foundation of Our Freedom* by Warren E. Burger. Copyright © 1990 by Warren E. Burger; additional material copyright © 1990 by Harcourt Brace Jovanovich, Inc. From "Defeat: The Endless Battlefields" from *Roosevelt: The Soldier of Freedom* by James MacGregor Burns. Copyright © 1970 by James MacGregor Burns. From "The East Side" from *World of Our Fathers: The Journey of the East European Jews to America and the Life They Found and Made* by Irving Howe. Copyright © 1976 by Irving Howe. From "Apple of Knowledge" from *Autobiography of Values* by Charles A. Lindbergh. Copyright © 1978 by Harcourt Brace Jovanovich, Inc. and Anne Morrow Lindbergh. From "Using Leisure" from "Inventions Re-Making Leisure" from *Middletown: A Study in Contemporary American Culture* by Robert S. Lynd and Helen Merrel Lynd. Copyright 1929 by Harcourt Brace Jovanovich, Inc.; copyright renewed © 1957 by Robert S. and Helen M. Lynd. From two songs by the left-wing, antiwar Almanac Singers, 1940–41 from "Nonintervention to War 1929–1941" from *America in the Twentieth Century: A History,* Second Edition by James T. Patterson. Copyright © 1976, 1983 by Harcourt Brace Jovanovich, Inc. "Chicago" from *Chicago Poems* by Carl Sandburg. Copyright 1916 by Holt, Rinehart and Winston, Inc.; copyright renewed 1944 by Carl Sandburg. "Song for a Youth Temperance Group" from *A History of the American People, Volume One: To 1877* by Stephan Thernstrom. Copyright © 1984 by Harcourt Brace Jovanovich, Inc.

Harper & Row, Publishers, Inc.: From *O America: When You and I Were Young* by Luigi Barzini. Copyright © 1977 by Luigi Barzini. From *The Day Lincoln was Shot* by Jim Bishop. Copyright © 1955 by Jim Bishop. From *In the Days of McKinley* by Margaret Leech. Copyright © 1959 by Margaret Leech Pulitzer. From *Andrew Jackson and the Course of American Empire, 1767–1821* by Robert V. Remini. Copyright © 1977 by Robert V. Remini. From "Toward the Sunset" from *Giants in the Earth* by O. E. Rölvaag. Copyright 1927 and copyright renewed © 1955 by Harper & Row, Publishers, Inc.

Harvard University Press and the Trustees of Amherst College: "This is my letter to the world" from *The Poems of Emily Dickinson,* edited by Thomas H. Johnson: The Belknap Press of Harvard University Press. Copyright 1951, © 1955, 1979, 1983 by the President and Fellows of Harvard University.

Louise Levitas Henriksen: From "How I Found America" from *Hungry Hearts* by Anzia Yezierska. Copyright 1920 by Anzia Yezierska; copyright © 1948 by Louise L. Henriksen.

Hill and Wang, Inc., a division of Farrar, Straus & Giroux: From *How the Other Half Lives: Studies Among the Tenements of New York* by Jacob Riis. Copyright © 1957 by Hill and Wang.

Houghton Mifflin Company: From "The Shimerdas" from *My Ántonia* by Willa Cather. Copyright 1918 and copyright renewed 1946 by Willa Sibert Cather; copyright 1926 by Willa Sibert Cather and copyright renewed 1954 by Edith Lewis; copyright 1949 by Houghton Mifflin Co. and copyright renewed © 1977 by Bertha Handlan. From "Write It Down" from *Let the Record Speak* by Dorothy Thompson. Copyright 1939 by Dorothy Thompson Lewis.

V. Annette Grant: Adapted from "Johnny Reb and Billy Yank" by Alexander Hunter from *The Blue and the Gray: The Story of the Civil War as Told by Participants,* Volume I, edited by Henry Steele Commager. Copyright 1950 by Henry Steele Commager.

Alfred A. Knopf, Inc.: From "Reaping" from *The Years of Lyndon Johnson: The Path to Power* by Robert A. Caro. Copyright © 1982 by Robert A. Caro, Inc. "I, Too" from *Selected Poems of Langston Hughes.* Copyright 1926, 1948 by Alfred A. Knopf, Inc.; renewed 1954 by Langston Hughes. "Merry-

Go-Round'' from *Selected Poems of Langston Hughes*. Copyright 1942 by Langston Hughes; copyright renewed © 1970 by Arna Bontemps and George Houston Bass. From *History: A Novel* by Elsa Morante, translated from Italian by William Weaver. Translation copyright © 1977 by Alfred A. Knopf, Inc. From "September 13, 1940," "September 18, 1940," and "September 22, 1940" from *This Is London* by Edward R. Murrow. Copyright 1941 by Edward R. Murrow, copyright © 1967 by the Estate of Edward R. Murrow. Originally published in *This Is London*. From " 'I Am the Sire de Coucy': The Dynasty'' from *A Distant Mirror: The Calamitous 14th Century* by Barbara W. Tuchman. Copyright © 1978 by Barbara W. Tuchman.

Lerner Publications: "Farewell to thee" from *The Irish in America* by James E. Johnson. Copyright © 1967 by Lerner Publications.

Little, Brown and Company: From *The Longhorns* by J. Frank Dobie. Copyright 1941 by Little, Brown and Company. From *White House Years* by Henry Kissinger. Copyright © 1979 by Henry Kissinger. From "Reville" from *American Caesar: Douglas MacArthur 1880–1964* by William Manchester. Copyright © 1978 by William Manchester.

Little, Brown and Company in association with The Atlantic Monthly Press: From "A New Hopi Girl" from *Eskimos, Chicanos, Indians: Volume IV of Children of Crisis* by Robert Coles, M.D. Copyright © 1977 by Robert Coles. From "Henry's Wedding and a Most Curious Tea Party" from *Nisei Daughter* by Monica Sone. Copyright 1953 by Monica Sone.

Ludlow Music, Inc.: From "Do Re Mi," words and music by Woody Guthrie. TRO, Copyright © 1961 (renewed) and 1963 by Ludlow Music, Inc. New York, NY. From "We Shall Overcome," new words and music arrangement by Zilphia Horton, Frank Hamilton, Guy Carawan, and Pete Seeger. TRO, Copyright © 1960 (renewed) and 1963 by Ludlow Music, Inc., New York, NY.

Macmillan Publishing Company: From "Two Motherlands" by José Martí from *The Yellow Canary Whose Eye Is So Black*, edited and translated by Cheli Durán. Copyright © 1977 by Cheli Durán Ryan. From "Afterward" from *The Guns of August* by Barbara W. Tuchman. Copyright © 1962 by Barbara W. Tuchman.

David McKay Co., Inc. From *The Long Shadow of Little Rock: A Memoir* by Daisy Bates. Copyright © 1962 by Daisy Bates.

Music Sales Corporation: From "Franklin D. Roosevelt's Back Again" from *This Singing Land*, compiled and edited by Irwin Silber. Copyright © 1965 by AMSCO Music Publishing.

The New York Times Company: From "The Text of Colonel Lindbergh's Address at Rally of the America First Committee Here" from *The New York Times*, April 24, 1941. Copyright 1941 by The New York Times Company. From "Aviators Save Him From Frenzied Mob of 100,000" by Edwin L. James from *The New York Times*. May 22, 1927. Copyright 1927 by The New York Times Company.

North Point Press: From *Son of the Morning Star* by Evan S. Connell. Copyright © 1984 by Evan S. Connell.

October House, Inc.: Excerpt from "Homage to the Express of the Blues" by Robert Hayden from *Robert Hayden: Selected Poems*. Copyright © 1966 by Robert Hayden.

Oxford University Press, Inc.: From "Schoolhouses and Scholars" from *The Culture Factory: Boston Public Schools, 1789–1860* by Stanley K. Schultz, pp. 69–92. Copyright © 1973 by Oxford University Press, Inc.

Pantheon Books, a division of Random House, Inc: From *Hard Times: An Oral History of the Great Depression* by Studs Terkel. Copyright © 1970 by Studs Terkel. From "The Stream" by Leonel I. Castillo from *American Dreams: Lost and Found* by Studs Terkel. Copyright © 1980 by Studs Terkel.

Pathfinder Press: From "To Mississippi Youth" from *Malcolm X Speaks:*

Selected Speeches and Statements, edited by George Breitman. Copyright © 1965 by Merit Publishers.

Putnam Publishers, Inc.: From "The League of Nations" from *American Problems; A Selection of Speeches and Prophecies* by William E. Borah, edited by Horace Green. Copyright 1924 by Duffield & Company. From *The Home Front: America During World War II* by Mark Jonathan Harris, et al. Copyright © 1984 by The Putnam Publishing Group.

Ramparts Magazine, Inc.: From "The Organizer's Tale" by César Chávez from *Ramparts,* vol. 5, no. 2, July 1966. Copyright © 1966 by Ramparts Magazine.

Random House, Inc.: From *Washington Journal: The Events of 1973–1974* by Elizabeth Drew. Copyright © 1974, 1975 by Elizabeth Drew. From *The Arrogance of Power* by J. William Fulbright. Copyright © by J. William Fulbright. From *A Bright Shining Lie: John Paul Vann and America in Vietnam* by Neil Sheehan. Copyright © 1988 by Neil Sheehan.

Marian Reiner for Joan Daves: From "I Have a Dream" by Martin Luther King, Jr. Copyright © 1963 by Martin Luther King, Jr. From *Stride Toward Freedom: The Montgomery Story* by Martin Luther King, Jr. Copyright © 1958 by Martin Luther King, Jr. From "Letter From Birmingham Jail" by Martin Luther King, Jr. Copyright © 1963, 1964 by Martin Luther King, Jr.

Saturday Evening Post Company: From "I Saw Lee Surrender" by Seth M. Flint from *The Saturday Evening Post,* July/August 1976, vol. 248, no. 5. Copyright © 1976 by The Saturday Evening Post Company. From "Death in the Ia Drang Valley" by Jack P. Smith from *The Saturday Evening Post,* January 28, 1967, 240th year, no. 2. Copyright © 1967 by The Curtis Publishing Company.

Charles Scribner's Sons, an imprint of Macmillan Publishing Company: From *The Great Gatsby* by F. Scott Fitzgerald. Copyright 1925 by Charles Scribner's Sons; copyright renewed 1953 by Frances Scott Fitzgerald Lanahan. From *A Farewell to Arms* by Ernest Hemingway. Copyright 1929 by Charles Scribner's Sons; copyright renewed © 1957 by Ernest Hemingway.

Simon & Schuster, Inc.: From "The Montgomery Bus Boycott" from *Parting the Waters* by Taylor Branch. Copyright © 1989 by Taylor Branch. From "I Intend to Win" from "Toward the Nomination/1975–1976" from *A Government as Good as Its People* by Jimmy Carter. Copyright © 1977 by The Carter Foundation for Governmental Affairs, Inc. From "Sun City—1983" from *Cities on a Hill* by Frances Fitzgerald. Copyright © 1981, 1983, 1986 by Frances Fitzgerald. From *The Making of the Atomic Bomb* by Richard Rhodes. Copyright © 1986 by Richard Rhodes.

Smithsonian Institution: From "Robots are Taking a Hand in Our Affaris" by Jeanne McDermott from *Smithsonian,* November 1983. Copyright © 1983 by Smithsonian Institution.

State Historical Society of Wisconsin: Adapted from "Documents: The Letters of Eldon J. Canright" from "Some War-Time Letters" from *The Wisconsin Magazine of History,* vol. V, 1921–1922. Copyright 1921 by The State Historical Society of Wisconsin.

Summit Books, a division of Simon & Schuster, Inc.: From *The Fords: An American Epic* by Peter Collier and David Horowitz. Copyright © 1987 by Peter Collier and David Horowitz.

Texas Folklore Society: From "Shelling Corn by Moonlight" by Jovita González from *Tone the Bell Easy,* edited by J. Frank Dobie. Copyright 1932 by Texas Folklore Society. Published by Southern Methodist University Press.

Time, Inc.: From "Lessons from a Lost War" from *Time,* April 15, 1985. Copyright © 1985 by Time, Inc. From "Hospital Number 1, As Told to Annalee Jacoby" from *History in the Writing* by the Foreign Correspondents of Time, Life & Fortune, selected and edited by Gordon Carroll. Copyright 1945 by Time, Inc. Adapted from *Memoirs: Volume One, Year of Decisions* by Harry S Truman. Copyright © 1955 by Time, Inc. From "For President Kennedy: An Epilogue" by Theodore H. White from *Life,* vol. 55, no. 23. December 6, 1963. Copyright © 1963 by Time, Inc.

University of Nebraska Press: From *Black Elk Speaks: Being the Life Story of a Holy Man of the Oglala Sioux,* as told through John G. Neihardt (Flaming Rainbow). Copyright 1932, 1959, 1972 by John G. Neihardt; copyright © 1961 by the John G. Neihardt Trust; copyright © 1979 by the University of Nebraska Press.

The University of North Carolina Press: Adapted from *Down & Out in the Great Depression: Letters from the "Forgotten Man",* edited by Robert S. McElvaine. Copyright © 1983 by The University of North Carolina Press.

University of Oklahoma Press: From *The Mining Frontier: Contemporary Accounts from the American West in the Nineteenth Century,* collected and edited by Marvin Lewis. Copyright © 1967 by the University of Oklahoma Press.

University Press of New England: "The First Modern War" from *America Goes to War* by Bruce Catton. Copyright © 1958 by William B. Catton.

Viking Penguin Inc., a division of Penguin Books USA: "American Bores Common, Ex Div." from *Christopher Columbus and Other Patriotic Verses* by Franklin P. Adams. Copyright 1931 by Franklin P. Adams. From *Henderson The Rain King* by Saul Bellow. Copyright © 1958, 1959 by Saul Bellow. From "Italy" from *Once There Was a War* by John Steinbeck. Copyright © 1943, 1958, by John Steinbeck, From *Eyes on the Prize: America's Civil Right Years, 1954–1965* by Juan Williams, with the Eyes on the Prize Production Team. Copyright © 1987 by Blackside, Inc.

A.P. Watt Limited: From *The Outline of History: Being a Plain History of Life and Mankind* by H. G. Wells. Copyright 1920, 1931, 1940 by H. G. Wells; copyright 1949 by Doubleday & Company, Inc.

Wylie, Aitken & Stone, Inc.: From "The Truce with Irrationality—I" from *A Turn in the South* by V. S. Naipaul. Copyright © 1989 by V. S. Naipaul.

Picture Credits

vania Academy of The Fine Arts, Philadelphia. Gift of Mrs. Sarah Harrison. **CHAPTER THREE** Page: 75, John Greenwood, *Abigail Gerrish with her grand-mother, Abigail (Flint) Holloway Gerrish''*, c. 1750. Courtesy of The Essex Institute of Art, Salem, MA; 76, Washington/Custis/Lee Collection, Washington and Lee University, Lexington, VA; 79, W.J. Bennett (after George Harvey), *Spring #2: Burning Fallen Trees in a Girdled Clearing.* Copyright Yale University Art Gallery, The Mabel Brady Garvan Collection; 80, Winthrop Chandler, *Mrs. Samuel Chandler* c. 1780. National Gallery of Art, Washington. Gift of Edgar William and Bernice Chrysler Garbisch; 84(tr), Abby Aldrich Rockefeller Folk Art Center. The Colonial Williamsburg Foundation; 84(bl), Abby Aldrich Rockefeller Folk Art Center. The Colonial Williamsburg Foundation; 84(br), Romare Howard Bearden, SHE-BA, 1970. Collage on composition board. Wadsworth Atheneum, Hartford. The Ella Gallup Sumner and Mary Catlin Sumner Collection; 85, Thomas Coram, *View of Mulberry Plantation* oil on paper, 10.17.6 cm. The Gibbes Museum of Art, Carolina Art Association; 88, National Maritime Museum, Greenwich, London; 90, Courtesy of the John Carter Brown Library at Brown University; 96, Courtesy of the New-York Historical Society, NYC; 99(l), Harvard University Portrait Collection, Cambridge, Massachusetts. Bequest of Dr. J.C. Warren, 1856; 104, Anonymous, *Quaker Meeting* British, 4th quarter, 18th century or 1st qtr 19th century. Oil on canvas, 25 1/4 x 30in. Courtesy, Museum of Fine Arts, Boston. Bequest of Maxim Karolik. **CHAPTER FOUR** Page: 120, Washington/Custis/Lee Collection, Washington and Lee University, Lexington, VA; 122, Benjamin West, *The Death of General Wolfe.* The National Gallery of Canada, Ottawa; 130(t), John Singleton Copley, American, 1738-1815, *Samuel Adams.* Oil on canvas, 50 x 40 1/4 in. Deposited by the City of Boston. Courtesy, Museum of Fine Arts, Boston; 130(b), John Singleton Copley, American, 1738-1815, *Paul Revere.* Oil on canvas, 35 x 28 1/2 in. Gift of Joseph W., William B. and Edward H.R. Revere. Courtesy, Museum of Fine Arts, Boston.

UNIT TWO—CHAPTER FIVE Page: 148, *Attack on Bunker's Hill, with the Burning of Charles Town,* 1783 or later, National Gallery of Art, Washington; Gift of Edgar William and Bernice Chrysler Garbisch; 151(b), Courtesy, The Henry Francis du Pont Winterthur Museum; 152, Anne S. K. Brown Military Collection, Courtesy of the John Hay Library at Brown University; 153, Howard Pyle, *The Battle of Bunker Hill.* Oil on Canvas. Acc#2025. Delaware Art Museum, Wilmington; 154(r),Picture Collection, The Branch Libraries, The New York Public Library; 156, The National Portrait Gallery, Smithsonian Institution. (L/NPB.2.80); 158, John Trumbull, *The Declaration of Independence.* Copyright, Yale University Art Gallery; 165, John Trumbull, *The Death of General Mercer at the Battle of Princeton.* Yale Univeristy Art Gallery; 173, The National Portrait Gallery, Smithsonian Institution. **CHAPTER SIX** Page: 181, William Birch, *The Arch Street Ferry,* The City of Philadelphia. Rare Book Department, Free Library of Philadelphia/Photo by Joan Broderick; 188, Courtesy, The Henry Francis du Pont Winterthur Museum; 192, Courtesy of the John Carter Brown Library at Brown University; 220, Mrs. B.S. Church, *Portrait of William Paterson* (1745-1806), oil on canvas, 36 1/8 x 26 1/8 in. The Art Museum, Princeton University **CHAPTER SEVEN** Page: 240, Photo by Bradley Smith/Laurie Platt Winfrey,Inc./The Historical Society of Pennsylania; 244, Cliche des Musees Nationaux—Paris; 248, Courtesy, The Henry Francis du Pont Winterthur Museum; 256, John Singleton Copley, American, 1738-1815, *John Adams.* Oil on canvas, 20 x 13 1/2 in. Seth Kettell Sweetser Residuary Fund; Courtesy, Museum of Fine Arts, Boston

UNIT THREE—CHAPTER EIGHT Page: 265, Jules Tavernier, *Indian Village.* From The Collection of The Gilcrease Museum, Tulsa; 267(b), Gilbert Stuart, *James Madison.* Bowdoin College. Museum of Art, Brunswick, Maine; 269(t), Copyrighted by the White House Historical Association. Photograph(s) by the National Geographic Society; 269(b), John Vanderlyn, *Aaron Burr,* 1802. Oil on canvas, 22 1/4 x 16 1/2. Courtesy of The New-York Historical Society, N.Y.C.; 270, Picture Collection, The Branch Libraries, The New York Public Library; 276(t), W.A. Martin, *Decatur at Tripoli.* Courtesy, United States Naval Academy Museum; 282, From The Collection of The Gilcrease Museum, Tulsa; 283(t), Courtesy, Amon Carter Museum, Fort Worth; 288, Thomas Jefferson Memorial Foundation, Monticello. Charlottesville, VA. **CHAPTER NINE** Page: 294, Alfred Jacob Miller, *Shoshone Encampment at Green River Rendezvous.* From The Collection of The Gilcrease Museum, Tulsa; 297, Field Museum of Natural History; 298(t), The National Portrait Gallery, Smithsonian Institution (NPG.75.27); 298(b), George Catlin, *The Open Door, Known as the Prophet, Brother of Tecumseh* (1830). The National Museum of American Art, Smithsonian Institution; 304, The National Archives Trust Fund Board; 305, William Powell, *Battle of Lake Erie.* United States Capitol Historical Society. Photograph(s) by the National Geographic Society; 308(t), Anne S.K. Brown Military Collection, Courtesy of the John Hay Library at Brown University; 308(b), Bass Otis, *Mrs. James Madison* ca. 1817. Oil on canvas, 29 x 24. Courtesy of The New-York Historical Society, N.Y.C.; 310, Collection of the Maryland Historical Society, Baltimore; 311(tr), National Museum of American History, Smithsonian Institution; 312, Hyecinth Laclotte, *Defeat of the British Army (Battle of New Orleans).* Yale University Art Gallery, The Mabel Brady Garvan Collection; 316, John Singleton Copley, American 1738-1815, *John Quincy Adams.* Oil on canvas, 30 x 25 in. Bequest of Mrs. Charles Francis Adams. Courtesy, Museum of Fine Arts Boston; 318, Thomas Birch, *Conestoga Wagon on a Pennsylvania Pike in 1814.* Shelburne Museum, Shelburne, Vermont; 319(l), Diego Rodriquez de Silva y Velazquez, *Las Meninas,* Giruadon/Art Resource, N.Y.; 319(r), Frenando Botero, *Princess Margarita after Velazquez.* Courtesy of Christie's of New York; 321(t), MAS, Barcelona, Spain; 321(br), Artist Unknown, *Atahualpa.* From The Collection of The Gilcrease Museum, Tulsa; 322(tl), Amelia Pelaez del Casal, *Fishes.* 1943. Collection, The Museum of Modern Art,

New York; 323, Museum of Modern Art of Latin American, Organization of American States; 324(t), The National Portrait Gallery, Smithsonian Institution. 324(b), Copyrighted by the White House Historical Association; Photograph(s) by the National Geographic Society. **CHAPTER TEN** Page: 332, Artist Unknown, *The Yankee Pedlar,* 1830. Oil on canvas, 24 x 31 inches. Collection IBM Corporation, Armonk, New York; 333, William Giles Munson, *The Eli Whitney Gun Factory.* Yale University Art Gallery. The Mabel Brady Garven Collection; 342, *Barfoot for Darton: Progress of Cotton #6, Spinning.* Yale University Art Gallery. Mabel Brady Garvan Collection; 346, Francis Guy, *Tontine Coffee House.* Oil on canvas, 42 1/4 x 64 1/4. Courtesy of The New-York Historical Society, N.Y.C.; 350, George Tattersail, English, 1817-1849, *Highways and Byeways of the Forest.* Sketch in brown & white wash on gray paper, 8 1/2 x 11 3/4 in. M.& M. Karolik Collection of American Watercolors & Drawings. Courtesy, Museum of Fine Arts, Boston; 352, Print Collection, Miriam & Ira D. Wallach Division of Art, Prints and Photographs. The New York Public Library. Astor, Lenox and Tilden Foundations; 363, Albert Bierstadt, *The Oregon Trail.* The Butler Institute of American Art, Youngstown, Ohio.

UNIT FOUR—CHAPTER ELEVEN Page: 365, John Lewis Krimmel, *Fourth of July in Centre Square.* Courtesy of The Pennsylvania Academy of The Fine Arts, Philadelphia. Pennsylvania Academy purchase (from the Estate of Paul Beck,Jr.); 367, John W. Jarvis, *James Fenimore Cooper.* Yale University Art Gallery. Gift of Edward S. Harkness; 373, Joshua Tucker, *South East View of Greenville, South Carolina.* Abby Aldrich Rockefeller Folk Art Center. The Colonial Williamsburg Foundation; 374(t), The National Portrait Gallery, Smithsonian Institution (NPG 65.58); 375, Thomas Coke Ruckle, *Fairview Inn or Three Mile House on Old Frederick Road,* 1829 (?). Watercolor on paper. Collection of the Maryland Historical Society, Baltimore; 376, Oriana Day, *Mission San Gabriel Arcangel.* The Fine Arts Museums of San Francisco, Gift of Eleanor Martin; 378, Karl Bodmer, *Settler's Farm in Indiana.* Joslyn Art Museum, Omaha, Nebraska; 380, The National Portrait Gallery, Smithsonian Institution (NPG.70.12); 382, Thomas Sully, *Andrew Jackson,* 1845. National Gallery of Art, Washington, Andrew W. Mellon Collection; 397, John M. Stanley, *International Indian Council,* 1843. National Museum of American Art, Smithsonian Institution, Gift of the Misses Henry, 1908.; 399(br), The National Portrait Gallery, Smithsonian Institution. **CHAPTER TWELVE** Page: 404, The National Portrait Gallery, Smithsonian Institution (NPG.70.23); 411, San Jacinto Museum of History Association; 413, 419, Picture Collection, The Branch Libraries, The New York Public Library; 421, Anne S.K. Brown Military Collection, Courtesy of the John Hay Library at Brown University; 425, Julio Michaud, *Hacendado y Su Mayordomo.* From The Collection of The Gilcrease Museum, Tulsa; 427., C.C.A. Christensen, *Handcart Pioneers.* ©1989 by The Church of Jesus Christ of Latter-Day Saints. Reprinted by Permission; 428, Christian Inger, *View of Great Salt Lake City,* lithograph, 1867. Courtesy, Amon Carter Museum, Fort Worth; 432(t), Olaf C. Seltzer, *Prospector.* From the Collection of The Gilcrease Museum, Tulsa; 432(b), Frank Vining Smith, *Flying Cloud.* From the Marine Art Collection of The Seamen's Bank for Savings; 433, Charles C. Nahl & Frederick August Wenderoth, *Miners In The Sierras,* 1851-1852. National Museum of American Art, Smithsonian Institution, Gift of The Fred Heilbron Collection; 434, Charles Christian Nahl, American, 1818-1878, *Sunday Morning In The Mines,* 1872. Oil on canvas Crocker Collection, Crocker Art Museum.; 436, The Philbrook Museum of Art, Tulsa, Oklahoma; 437, 441, 443, The National Portrait Gallery, Smithsonian Institution; 447, Texas State Archives. **CHAPTER THIRTEEN** Page: 450, Picture Collection, The Branch Libraries, The New York Public Library; 451, Samuel F.B. Morse, *Eli Whitney.* Yale University Art Gallery. Gift of George Hoadley, B.A. 1801.; 460, E. Crowe *Slave Auction at Richmond.* Private Collection. Photograph courtesy of Kennedy Galleries, Inc. New York; 473, The National Portrait Gallery, Smithsonian Institution (NPG.74.45). **CHAPTER FOURTEEN** Page: 477, Jerome B. Thompson, American, 1814-1886, *A "Pic Nick," in the Woods of New England.* Oil on canvas 41 x 62 in. Gift of Maxim Karolik for the Karolik Collection of American Paintings, 1815-1865. Courtesy, Museum of Fine Arts, Boston; 478, Anonymous, *Girls Evening School,* American. Pencil and watercolor, 13 1/2 x 18 1/8 in. Gift of Maxim Karolik for the M. & M. Karolik Collection of American Drawings and Watercolors, 1800-1875. Courtesy, Museum of Fine Arts, Boston; 483(b), The National Portrait Gallery, Smithsonian Institution (NPG.74.72); 485, The National Portrait Gallery, Smithsonian Institution (NPG.67.31); 488, The National Portrait Gallery, Smithsonian Institution; 492(r), The National Portrait Gallery, Smithsonian Institution (NPG.72.119); 492(c), The National Portrait Gallery, Smithsonian Institution (NPG.78.6); 496(t), Charles Osgood, *Nathaniel Hawthorn,* 1840. Oil on canvas. Courtesy of The Essex Institute, Salem, MA; 496(b), Berkshire Athenaeum, Herman Melville Memorial Room; 500, Thomas LeClear, *Buffalo Newsboy,* 1953. Oil on canvas, 24 x 20''. Albright-Knox Art Gallery Buffalo, New York. Charlotte A. Watson Fund, 1942.

UNIT FIVE—CHAPTER FIFTEEN Page: 509, *Gettysburg Cyclorama,* Photography by Henry Groskinsky. Gettysburg National Military Park, United States Department of the Interior; 511(t), Eastman Johnson, *A Ride for Liberty—The Fugitive Slaves,* 1862. The Brooklyn Museum, Gift of Miss Gwendolyn O.L. Conkling; 511(b), Picture Collection, The Branch Libraries, The New York Public Library; 512, The National Portrait Gallery, Smithsonian Institution (NPG.68.1); 516, The National Portrait Gallery, Smithsonian Institution (NPG.65.49); 519, The National Portrait Gallery, Smithsonian Institution (NPG 76.68); 522, F.O.C.Darley, *Border Ruffians Invading Kansas.* Yale University Art Gallery. The Mabel Brady Garvan Collection; 524(t), The National Portrait Gallery, Smithsonian Institution. Transfer from The National Gallery of Art. Gift of Andrew W. Mellon, 1942 (NPG.65.48); 524(b), The National

Portrait Gallery, Smithsonian Institution (NPG 72.17); 526, Nathaniel Jocelyn *Cinque,* 1839. Oil on canvas, 30 1/4 x 25 1/2. New Haven Colony Historical Society; 530, The National Portrait Gallery, Smithsonian Institution (NPG77.163); 534, Thomas Hovenden, *The Last Moments of John Brown.* Copyright Hovenden 1884. The Metropolitan Museum of Art, Gift of Mr. and Mrs. Carl Stoeckel, 1897 (97.5); 536, Thomas Cole, *Home in the Woods.* Reynolda House, Museum of American Art. Winston-Salem, North Carolina. **CHAPTER SIXTEEN** Page: 542, E.B. & E.C. Kellogg, *The Eagle's Nest.* The Connecticut Historical Society; 544, John Robertson, *Jefferson Davis* (portrait 1863). Photography by Katherine Wetzel. The Museum of the Confederacy, Richmond, Virginia; 548, Picture Collection, The Branch Libraries, The New York Public Library; 549, *Richmond, From the Hill above the Water-works,* Colored Aquatint, Stokes Collection -1833-E-58. Miriam and Ira D. Wallach Division of Art, Prints and Photographs. Astor, Lennos & Tilden Foundatons. The New York Public Library; 553, Picture Collection, The Branch Libraries, The New York Public Library; 555, Winslow Homer, *Young Soldier.* Oil, gouache, graphite on canvas, 36 x 18.2 cm. Gift of Charles Savage Homer. Courtesy of the Cooper Hewitt Museum, Smithsonian Institution/ Art Resource, NY. Photo by Scott Hyde; 563, Conrad Wise Chapman, *Quaker Battery.* Photography by Katherine Wetzel. The Museum of the Confederacy, Richmond, Virginia; 571(r), The National Portrait Gallery, Smithsonian Institution (NPG 76.101); 578, The National Portrait Gallery, Smithsonian Institution. Gift of Mrs. Harry Newton Blue, 1966 (NPG76.8); 579, William Heysham Overend, *An August Morning with Farragut: the Battle of Mobile Bay, August 5, 1864,* 1883. Wadsworth Atheneum, Hartford. Giftof Citizens of Hartford by Subscription; 581, Charles Hoffbauer, *Summer.* Photographer, Richard Cheek. Collections of the Virginia Historical Society; 583(b), The Brady Collection, The National Archives Trust Fund Board; 585, Louis M.D. Guillaume, *Surrender of General Lee to General Grant.* Photography by Russ Finley. Appomattox Court House National Historical Park. **CHAPTER SEVENTEEN** Page: 600, The National Portrait Gallery, Smithsonian Institution, Transfer from the National Museum of American Art. Gift of Mrs. Ulysses S. Grant, Jr.; 601, Richard Norris Brooke, *A Pastoral Visit,* In the Collection of The Corcoran Gallery of Art, Museum Purchase, Gallery fund; 602, Rufus and S. Willard Saxton Papers, Manuscripts and Archives, Yale University Library; 604, Robert B. Elliott, *The Shackle Broken by the Genius of Freedom (detail),* 1874. Lithograph, published by E. Sachs & Co., Baltimore. Chicago Historical Society; 607(t), Winslow Homer, *Cotton Pickers,* 1876, oil on canvas. The Los Angeles County Museum of Art, Acquisition made possible through Museum Trustees: Robert Anderson, R. Stanton Avery, B. Gerald Cantor, Edward W. Carter, Justin Dart, Charles E. Ducommun, Mrs. Daniel Frost, Julian Ganz, Jr., Dr. Armand Hammer, Harry Lenart, Dr. Franklin D. Murphy, Mrs. Joan Palevs, Richrd E. Sherwood. Maynard J. Toll and Hal B. Wallis; 610, Picture Collection, The Branch Libraries, The New York Public Library; 611(t), The National Portrait Gallery, Smithsonian Institution. (NPG 76.1); 615, Edward Lamson Henry, *Kept In,* 1888. New York State Historical Association, Cooperstown; 621, William Hahn, *Sacramento Railroad Station,* 1874. The Fine Arts Museums of San Francisco, Gift of the M.H. de Young Endowment Fund.

UNIT SIX—CHAPTER EIGHTEEN Page: 622, Albert Bierstadt, *The Last of the Buffalo,* 1889. In The Corcoran Gallery of Art, Gift of Mrs. Albert Bierstadt, 1909; 626, Alfred Jaboc Miller, *Fort Laramie.* Beinecke Rare Book and Manuscript Library, Yale University; 627, Joseph Becker, *Snow Sheds on the Central Pacific Railroad in the Sierra Nevada Mountains.* From The Collection of The Gilcrease Museum, Tulsa; 630, Henry H. Cross, *Red Cloud and His Granddaughter, Burning Heart.* From The Collection of The Gilcrease Museum, Tulsa; 632, Henry H. Cross, *General George A. Custer.* From The Collection of The Gilcrease Museum, Tulsa; 633, Henry H. Cross, *Sitting Bull.* From The Collection of The Gilcrease Museum, Tulsa; 634, The National Portrait Gallery, Smithsonian Institution (NG68.19); 645, Charles Marion Russell, *Jerked Down.* From The Collection of The Gilcrease Museum, Tulsa; 647, Montana Historical Society, Helena. **CHAPTER NINETEEN** Page: 666, J.J. Fogerty, *Broadway and Maiden Lane,* 1880. Lithograph, colored. Courtesy of The New-York Historical Society, N.Y.C.; 667, U.S. Department of the Interior, National Park Service, Edison National Historic Site; 681(t), Robert Koehler, *The Strike,* 1886. Private Collection, Lee Baxandall. Laurie Pratt Winfrey, Inc.; 681(b), The George Meany Memorial Archives. Official Archives of the Americn Federation of Labor and Congress of Industrial Organizations. **CHAPTER TWENTY** Page: 703, Courtesy of the Cooper-Hewitt Museum, Smithsonian Institution; 705(t), 705(b), Copyrighted by the White House Historical Association. Photograph(s) by the National Geographic Society; 709(tr), George Arents Research Library for Special Collections. Syracuse University Library; 710(b), Winslow Homer, *The Croquet Game.* © The Art Institute of Chicago. All Rights Reserved; 711(r), Mary Cassatt *The Bath,* 1891-92. Oil on canvas, 39 1/2 x 26 in. Robert A. Waller Fund, 1910.2. © 1989 The Art Institute of Chicago. All Rights Reserved; 712(r), The National Portrait Gallery, Smithsonian Institution; 729, Copyrighted by the White House Historical Association. Photograph(s) by the National Geographic Society; 731, Frederick Childe Hassam, American, 1859-1935, *Boston Common at Twilight.* Oil on canvas, 42x60". Gift of Miss Maude E. Appleton. Courtesy, Museum of Fine Art, Boston. **CHAPTER TWENTY-ONE** Page: 742, The Bernice P. Bishop Museum, The Liliuokalani Trust; 754, Courtesy Frederic Remington Art Museum, Ogdensburg, New York; 758-759 (tr), Fernand Bourges/Life Picture Service; 768, Hubert Vos, *Portrait of H.I.M. The Empress Dowager of China, Tz'u-Hsi,* 1905-1906, oil on canvas. The Fogg Art Museum, Cambridge, MA. Bequest of Grenville L. Winthrop (1943.162); 776, Copyrighted by the White House Historical Association. Photograph(s) by the National Geographic Society; **CHAPTER TWENTY-TWO** Page: 780, William Glackens, *The Drive, Central Park,* 1905. Oil on Canvas. Purchase from the J.H. Wade Fund, 39.524. The Cleveland Museum of

Art; 782, John Sloan, *Women's Work,* c. 1911. Oil on Canvas. Gift of Amelia Elizabeth White, 64.160. The Cleveland Museum of Art; 791, The National Portrait Gallery (detail), Smithsonian Institution. Transfer from the National Museum of American History, Gift of the National American Woman Suffrage Association through Mrs. Carrie Chapman Catt, 1939 (NPG 71.31); 799, Copyrighted by the White House Historical Association. Photograph(s) by the National Geographic Society; 801, Picture Collection, The Branch Libraries, The New York Public Library; 802, National Portrait Gallery (detail), Smithsonian Institution. Transfer from the National Museum of American Art. Gift of the City of New York through the National Art Committee, 1923 (NPG 65.42); 808, The National Portrait Gallery, Smithsonian Institution; 815, John Steuart Curry, *Tornado over Kansas,* 1929. Courtesy of the Muskegon Museum of Art, Muskegon, Michigan.

UNIT EIGHT—CHAPTER TWENTY-THREE Page: 821(b), Diego Rivera, *Agrarian Leader Zapata,* 1931. Fresco, 7' 9 3/4: x 6' 2". Collection, The Museum of Modern Art, New York. Abby Aldrich Rockefeller Fund; 833(t), 835, 842, The National Archives Trust Fund Board; 845, Childe Hassam, *Allies Day, May 1917,* 1917. National Gallery of Art, Washington. Gift of Ethelyn McKinney in memory of her brother, Glenn Ford McKinn. **CHAPTER TWENTY-FOUR** Page: 853, The National Portrait Gallery, Smithsonian Institution; 864, Grant Wood, *Daughters of Revolution.* Cincinnati Art Museum, The Edwin and Virginia Irwin Memorial. © Estate of Grant Wood/VAGA New York 1990.; 865, Ben Shahn, *The Passion of Sacco and Vanzetti.* 1931-32. Tempera on Canvas. 84 1/2 x 48 inches. Collection of Whitney Museum of American Art. Gift of Mr. & Mrs. Milton Lowenthal in memory of Julian Force. (#49.22); 866, Thomas Hart Benton, *The Bootleggers,* 1927. Reynolda House, Museum of Amerian Art. Winston-Salem, North Carolina; 867, John Steuart Curry, *Baptism in Kansas,* (1928). Oil on Canvas, 40 x 50 inches. Collection of Whitney Museum of American Art. Gift of Gertrude Vanderbilt Whitney. #31.159; 871, Romare Bearden, *Jazz.* Photo by E. Irving Blomstrann. From the collection of the New Britain Museum of American Art, Connecticut. Friends Purchase Fund; 872, Photography by Edward Weston (C) 1981, Arizona Board of Regents. Center for Creative Photography/ National Portrait Gallery, Smithsonian Institution (NPG 77.264);877(b), Pablo Picasso (1881-1973), *Gertrude Stein,* 1906. Oil on canvas, 39 1/8 x 32 in. The Metropolitan Museum of Art, New York: Bequest of Gertrude Stein, 1946; 885(tl), The National Portrait Gallery, Smithsonian Institution (NPG66.21); 885(tr), The National Portrait Gallery, Smithsonian Institution (NPG65.13); 885(b), Copyrighted by the White House Historical Association. Photograph(s) by the National Geographic Society. **CHAPTER TWENTY-FIVE** Page: 894, Paul Starrett Sample, *Unemployment,* 1931. Oil on canvas, 36 x 40 1/4 inches. National Academy of Design, New York City; 899, Dorothea Lange, *Woman of the High Plains.* Courtesy of the Dorothea Lange Collection. © The City of Oakland, The Oakland Museum, 1992; 900, Louis Ribak, *Home Relief Station,* (1935-36). Oil on canvas, 28 x 36 inches. Collection of Whitney Museum of American Art. #36.148; 910, Alexander Hogue, *Drought Stricken Area.* The Dallas Museum of Art, DMA 1945.6; 911(t), Dorothea Lange, *Migrant Mother,* 1936. Silver Print 12 1/2 x 9 7.8 in. Collection, The Museum of Modern Art, New York. Purchase; 921, Palmer Hayden, *The Janitor Who Paints,* 1937. National Museum of American Art, Smithsonian Institution, Gift of The Harmon Foundation; 923, The National Portrait Gallery, Smithsonian Institution (NPG 67-78); 924, Copyrighted by the White House Historical Association; Photograph(s) by the National Geographic Society.

UNIT NINE—CHAPTER TWENTY-SIX Page: 935, National Air and Space Museum, Washington, D.C./Printed by permisson of the Estate of Norman Rockwell. Copyright © 1969 Estate of Norman Rockwell; 944, Charles Cundall, *The Withdrawal From Dunkirk, June 1940.* The Imperial War Museum, London; 945(t), AKG/Photo Researchers, Inc.; 948, Anton Otto Fischer, *Campbell.* Photograph by Frank Scherschel. Life Picture Service; 956, The National Archives Trust Fund Board; 959, Frank Scherschel/Life Magazine © Time Inc.; 969, Associated Press/Wide World Photos. **CHAPTER TWENTY-SEVEN** Page: 984, *For Full Employment after the War Register—Vote,* 1944. Offset lithograph, 30 x 39 7/8 inches. Collection, The Museum of Modern Art, New York. Gift of the CIO Political Action Committee; 985(b), Copyrighted by the White House Historical Association. Photograph(s) by the National Geographic Society; 988, The National Portrait Gallery, Smithsonian Institution. Transfer from the National Museum of American Art. Gift of the International Business Machines Corporation to the Smithsonian Institution, 1962 (NPG 66.64); 995, 1001, Carl Mydans/Life Magazine © Time Inc.; 1004, John Sadovy/Life Magazine © Time Inc.; 1008(t,c,b), 1009 (t,c,b), Flags from Mastai Collection of Antique American Flags, Amagansett, New York/Photography by Boleslaw Mastai. From *The Stars and The Stripes—The American Flag as Art and As History, From the Birth of The Republic to The Present* by Boleslaw and Marie Louise d'Otrange Mastai (Alfred Knopf), New York, 1973; 1015(b), Copyrighted by the White House Historical Association. Photography(s) by the National Geographic Society.

UNIT TEN—CHAPTER TWENTY-EIGHT Page: 1030, © Bruce Roberts/Photo Researchers, Inc.; 1046, Jon Brenneis/ Life Magazine © Time Inc.; 1053, © Jim Cartier/Photo Researchers, Inc. **CHAPTER TWENTY-NINE** Page: 1070, Burt Glinn/Magnum Photos; 1073, Paul Stephanus/R. Ellison/Black Star; 1082, Gjon Mili/Life Magazine © Time Inc. **CHAPTER THIRTY** Page: 1089(b), Cartoon by S.C. Rawls, Palm Beach Post, 1974. Reprinted by Permission of NEA, Inc.

REFERENCE SECTION Page: 1127, 1132, Science Photo Library/Photo Researchers, Inc.